PRIVACY LAW:
CASES AND MATERIALS

By

Richard C. Turkington
Villanova University School of Law

Anita L. Allen
University of Pennsylvania Law School

AMERICAN CASEBOOK SERIES®

WEST GROUP

ST. PAUL, MINN., 1999

American Casebook Series, and the West Group symbol
are registered trademarks used herein under license.

COPYRIGHT © 1999 By WEST GROUP
     610 Opperman Drive
     P.O. Box 64526
     St. Paul, MN 55164–0526
     1–800–328–9352

ISBN 0–314–23863–8

 TEXT IS PRINTED ON 10% POST
CONSUMER RECYCLED PAPER

Preface

During the past three decades in the United States, privacy has emerged as a preeminent and sometimes controversial value. Lawmakers and the general public increasingly judge policies based, in part, on their implications for harming or enhancing personal privacy. Privacy law has mushroomed in response to developments in technology and journalism that challenge traditional expectations of privacy in the name of efficiency, health and safety, law enforcement, consumer preferences, property rights and morality. These trends have made privacy law an essential subject for inclusion in curricula of law schools, business schools, medical schools, schools of government, public policy and public health.

RICHARD C. TURKINGTON
ANITA L. ALLEN

*

Acknowledgments

The structure of this book was initially developed twenty years ago for a three-credit course on Privacy Law at Villanova University School of Law. I continue to be indebted to my colleagues for having the flexibility to allow me to experiment with an elective course that attempts to deal with the law of privacy in a comprehensive way. It has been my pleasure and good fortune to have Anita L. Allen as a co-author of this book. Any student of privacy knows of the importance of Professor Allen's scholarship to philosophical and legal discourse on privacy. The book has benefitted much from Professor Allen's contributions.

To my former Dean Steven P. Frankino, and my current Dean, Mark Sargent, I express gratitude for the unqualified institutional support for this project. I thank my colleagues Anne Poulin, James Maule, and Hank Perritt for their suggestions on a variety of subjects. I greatly appreciate the support of William James, the librarian at Villanova University School of Law, the library staff, and especially Margaret Coyne for diligent efforts in providing all aspects of library and computer services to me. I also appreciate the assistance of Mary Cornaby, Director of Academic Computing, and Yolanda Jones, Assistant Director for Computer Services. I owe a special debt of gratitude to my administrative assistant, Terri LaVerghetta. I thank my research assistants at Villanova. Finally, I thank the many lawyers who, having learned privacy law initially by studying from this book, continue to demonstrate the usefulness of this approach to teaching privacy law by their work, support, and comments.

I dedicate this book to my wife, Tricia, and to my daughters, Tracey and Clare. Their love and support make all of this possible.

RICHARD C. TURKINGTON

Villanova, PA 19085

*

v

Acknowledgments

I have taught privacy law for fifteen years, most recently at the University of Pennsylvania School of Law. About ten years ago I began working with Professor Richard Turkington, who shares my enthusiasm for a complex body of law that reflects the needs, passions and antagonisms of American society. It has been my pleasure to work with Professor Richard Turkington on this casebook. Professor Turkington's intellectual role in shaping the framework of this book remains central. I am pleased to have contributed to this casebook a revised and updated version of Chapter VII, "Privacy, Autonomy and Intimacy," materials on the meaning, value and history of privacy in Chapter 1; and notes and background materials on medical and genetic privacy in Chapter II.

I would like to thank my former research assistants at Georgetown University Law Center. I dedicate this book to my family, Paul, Adam and Ophelia Castellitto, and to the inspiring memories of Carrye M. Allen and Adam J. Castellitto.

ANITA L. ALLEN

Haverford, PA 19041

*

Summary of Contents

*

Table of Contents

_____

*

Table of Cases

The principal cases are in bold type. Cases cited or discussed in the text are roman type. References are to pages. Cases cited in principal cases and within other quoted materials are not included.

PRIVACY LAW:

CASES AND MATERIALS

*

Chapter One

INTRODUCTION

A. PRIVACY LAW

This book was originally conceived as a response to a paradox. Although the volume of privacy law was huge and growing, the law schools were offering few privacy law courses and no books were available to teach in a comprehensive privacy course.

There were reasons other than the absence of effective teaching materials that explain why most law schools' curricula neglected this important area of law. Many law teachers were simply unfamiliar with the new privacy law and compartmentalized it as a subset of traditional courses in the curriculum.

Some law teachers mistakenly viewed privacy law as a branch of the common law of torts. This was undoubtedly because of the prominence and influence of Louis Brandeis and William Prosser, both of whom focused on tort privacy law. Other branches of privacy law were compartmentalized as subsets of traditional legal subjects. Electronic surveillance, for example, was thought of and taught as a minor part of fourth amendment search and seizure law in criminal procedure courses. Reproductive, sexual and family privacy was deemed a subset of first and fourteenth amendment jurisprudence, family law, or health law.

As a result, important areas of privacy law fell through the cracks in the curriculum. Students were not exposed to state and federal statutes that regulate electronic surveillance of conversations, and unauthorized accessing of e-mail and voice mail by employers and others in the private sector; statutory, common law and constitutional law regulating testing of government and private employees for drug and alcohol abuse was not taught in a systematic way because the tests were not for criminal law purposes or much affected by the common law of torts. Data and computer privacy law, mostly found in federal and state statutes that focus on certain public and private records, did not fit narrow views of privacy law and were not systematically studied. Torts that protect privacy, such as breach of confidence and wrongful dismissal, were probably not taught; but if they were, their role in privacy law was not examined.

1

To some extent, privacy fell victim to the ascendancy of feminist legal theory, critical legal studies and critical race theory in the academy. Much of privacy law jurisprudence is based upon notions of individual autonomy and personhood—based on rights and norms that come from the liberal tradition. The distinction between the public and the private is central to much of privacy law. The emphasis in post-modern grounded courses on the critique of the liberal tradition and especially the concept of the public and private sphere has deflected attention in the academy away from this important area of developing law.

The significance and pervasiveness of privacy law is increasingly well recognized. In the casebook, we have selected representative examples of legislation, court decisions, and agency regulations that are the basis of claims brought on behalf of those who assert rights of privacy against governmental officials, business entities, and private individuals. These claims arise in a variety of contexts. In our view, privacy law shares the characteristic of other areas of law that are basic staples of a law school curriculum. Privacy law, like Environmental Law, Administrative Law, and Local Government Law involves a broad range of legal institutions.

The book is not organized around traditional legal categories such as torts or constitutional law. The materials focus on the legal theories, principles, doctrines, enactments, rules or policies that are employed when legal claims are asserted against government, individuals or other entities for invasion of privacy in some form. Thus in the informational privacy chapter, there is an examination of a broad range of areas of law and legal theories, including torts, constitutional law, contracts and estates, as well as numerous statutes and agency regulations at the state and federal level that provide some legal protection for privacy.

The central structure of the book is reflected in the six major chapters that follow the introductory chapter. The primary benefit of the broad structure of this book is that a foundation is developed for investigating the similarities and differences in the various branches of the law of privacy that are rapidly developing in our legal system. General structures are essential to practical understandings of complex phenomena. As rapid as the growth of privacy law has been, it has lagged considerably behind both technological and political forces that threaten privacy.

We have opted for a broad approach to teaching privacy because in our view it provides the most useful method to prepare students with the tools and understandings they will need to analyze the prospect for successful prosecution, defense and evaluation of privacy claims.

1. ORIGINS OF PRIVACY IN THE HISTORY OF IDEAS AND SOCIAL VALUES

Formal legal protection for privacy is largely a phenomenon of the United States' legal system over the last century. However, the intellectual foundations upon which formal recognition of a legal right to privacy was built are of ancient origin. Precedent for recognition of privacy as an important value is found in the centuries-old social practices and norms of Western societies. What follows is a brief sketch of some of this heritage.

a. The Public and Private Realm

One of the most venerated and important tenets of political philosophy since the time of the Greeks has been the dichotomy between the private and public realms. From the age of Socrates and Aristotle to the present day, discussions of human nature and the appropriate role of the government and the individual have utilized the notion of a boundary that marks what is private and what is public. Though controversial within contemporary social, political, and legal theory, the distinction between the public and private persists.

MILTON R. KONVITZ, PRIVACY AND THE LAW: A PHILOSOPHICAL PRELUDE

31 Law & Contemp. Probs. 272, 272–76 (1966).

Almost the first page of the Bible introduces us to the feeling of shame as a violation of privacy. After Adam and Eve had eaten the fruit of the tree of knowledge, "the eyes of both were opened, and they knew that they were naked; and they sewed fig leaves together and made themselves aprons." Thus, mythically, we have been taught that our very knowledge of good and evil—our moral nature, our nature as men—is somehow, by divine ordinance, linked with a sense and a realm of privacy. When, after the Flood, Noah became drunk, he "lay uncovered in his tent," and Ham violated his father's privacy by looking upon his father's nakedness and by telling his brothers about it. His brothers took a garment, "laid it upon their shoulders, and walked backward and covered the nakedness of their father. Their faces were turned away, and they did not see their father's nakedness."

. . .

Once a civilization has made a distinction between the "outer" and the "inner" man, between the life of the soul and the life of the body, between the spiritual and the material, between the sacred and the profane, between the realm of God and the realm of Caesar, between church and state, between rights inherent and inalienable and rights that are in the power of government to give and take away, between public and private, between society and solitude, it becomes impossible to avoid the idea of privacy by whatever name it may be called—the idea of a "private space in which man may become and remain 'himself.' " Western Man's interest in our subject is thus accounted for.

In the history of this profound but discrete idea it is doubtful if anyone can be said to have played a greater role than Socrates—the Socrates of the *Apology*, the *Crito*, and the *Phaedo*; the philosopher who discovered or invented the soul; the philosopher who, at the end of the

Phaedrus, prayed that the gods would give him beauty in the inward soul and let "the outward and inward man be as one." The most dramatic expression of the identification of the real self with the soul is in Plato's report of the last few moments before Socrates drank the cup of hemlock. Crito ventured to ask Socrates: "And in what way shall we bury you?" The question amused Socrates. To bury him, he answered, Crito would first need to catch him. "Crito," he said,

> fancies that I am the other Socrates whom he will soon see, a dead body—and he asks, How shall he bury me? . . . I would not have him . . . say at the burial, Thus we lay out Socrates, or, Thus we follow him to the grave or bury him. . . . Be of good cheer then, my dear Crito, and say that you are burying my body only, and do with that whatever is usual, and what you think best.

Several centuries later it was not difficult for the Stoic philosophers to mark off, even more sharply than had been done by Socrates, the real self from the man who occupied public space. The first chapter of the *Discourses* of Epictetus is entitled "Of the things which are under our control and not under our control." The basic distinction, argued Epictetus, is between "the knowledge of what is mine, and what is not mine." The inner man, and his dispositions and thoughts, are "what is mine"; it is these "which are under our control." Epictetus wrote:

> "Tell your secrets." I say not a word; for this is under my control. "But I will fetter you." What is that you say, man? fetter me? My leg you will fetter, but my moral purpose not even Zeus himself has power to overcome. "I will throw you into prison." My paltry body, rather! "I will behead you." Well, when did I ever tell you that mine was the only neck that could not be severed?

"Tell your secrets!" was precisely the command that the prosecution, acting for Henry VIII, made of Thomas More, whose stance was strictly in line with that of Socrates and Epictetus. Three questions were put to him:

> 1. Whether he could obey the King as Supreme Head [of the Church]?
>
> He can make no answer.
>
> 2. Whether he will acknowledge the King's marriage with Queen Anne to be lawful, and that with Lady Catherine invalid?
>
> Never spoke against it, "nor thereunto can make no answer."
>
> 3. Where it was objected to him by the said statute he, as one of the King's subjects, is bound to answer the said question and recognize the King as Supreme Head, like all other subjects.

He can make no answer.

"For this my silence," More told the court, "neither your law nor any law in the world is able justly and rightly to punish me."

Socrates told the Athenian jury that they could not justly and rightly convict him *for what he had said*, and Thomas More told the court that they could not justly and rightly convict him *for his silence.* Silence may be a public act, and speech may be a private act; yet both may relate to the inner man, who is outside the jurisdiction of the state. Yet reasonable men may differ as to whether a refusal to salute the flag or a speech from a soap box shall be respected as a private act or punished as a public act.

To mark off the limits of the public and the private realms is an activity that began with man himself and is one that will never end; for it is an activity that touches the very nature of man.... For our purpose, the figure of speech used by Locke to describe this process may be helpful; for in his description of the phenomenon of transcendence Locke saw and projected the distinction between public and private, which, despite disguises, can be detected in the rationale of privacy.

In the state of nature, Locke wrote, the earth and all the fruit produced by nature belong to mankind in common. "The fruit or venison which nourishes the wild Indian ... must be his, and so his—*i.e.*, a part of him—that another can no longer have any right to it before it can do him any good for the support of his life." "[E]very man has a 'property' in his own 'person.' This nobody has any right to but himself." But a man is more than his skin and bones. A man works with his body and his hands. He thus transcends his skin. His very sweat, as he works, reaches out beyond his skin. By labor, man extends "his own person." That with which he mixes his labor becomes a part of his person. Since a man has "a property in his own person," that with which he mixes his labor becomes "his property." But if "property" is that which pertains to a man's "own person," then the term encompasses his life and liberty as well as that with which his sweat has mixed. What is important here, in the context of our discussion, is Locke's view of each man being and making his "own person," so that all that he becomes and all that he makes are part of "his own person."

Perhaps no thinker carried the logic of this view further than did Ralph Waldo Emerson.... Almost as if he were recalling Locke's *Second Treatise of Civil Government*, Emerson wrote:

> Each creature puts forth from itself its own condition and sphere, as the slug sweats out its slimy house on the pear-leaf, and the woolly aphides on the apple perspire their own bed, and the fish its shell.

Once man's power of self-transcendence is posited, it becomes impossible to confine the self within marked-off limits and to say positively, "*This* is the self, *this* is a man's 'own person,' and the rest is not self."

The transcendent character of man cries out against any attempt to fence him in. Locke was satisfied to let the matter go after saying that a man's life, liberty, and estate are his "property" because they pertain to his very own person; Emerson was not satisfied until he made all a man's actions, and even all the events in his life, his *sub-persons*.

JURGEN HABERMAS, THE STRUCTURAL TRANSFORMATION OF THE PUBLIC SPHERE

3–4 (1962).

We are dealing here with categories of Greek origin transmitted to us bearing a Roman stamp. In the fully developed Greek city-state the sphere of the *polis*, which was common (*koine*) to the free citizens, was strictly separated from the sphere of the *oikos*; in the sphere of the *oikos*, each individual is in his own realm (*idia*).... The political order, as is well known, rested on a patrimonial slave economy. The citizens were thus set free from productive labor; it was, however, their private autonomy as masters of households on which their participation in public life depended. The private sphere was attached to the house.... Movable wealth and control over labor power were no more substitutes for being the master of a household and of a family than, conversely, poverty and a lack of slaves would in themselves prevent admission to the *polis*.... Status in the *polis* was therefore based upon status as the unlimited master of an *oikos*. The reproduction of life, the labor of the slaves, and the service of the women went on under the aegis of the master's domination; birth and death took place in its shadow; and the realm of necessity and transitoriness remained immersed in the obscurity of the private sphere. In contrast to it stood, in Greek self-interpretation, the public sphere was a realm of freedom and permanence.... Just as the wants of life and the procurement of its necessities were shamefully hidden inside the *oikos*, so the *polis* provided an open field for honorable distinction: citizens indeed interacted as equals with equals (*homoioi*), but each did his best to excel (*aristoiein*). The virtues, whose catalogue was codified by Aristotle, were the ones whose test lies in the public sphere and there alone receive recognition.

b. *The Special Value of Privacy in the Home*

The distinction between "the public" and "the private" made today has much—though not everything—in common with the ancient Greek and Roman conceptions. One important commonality is that the home or household is presumed to be the center of the appropriately private sphere. A second equally important commonality is that the biological family is deemed to have its seat in the private domain. Privacy in the home often is expressed as a positive value throughout the history of the western world in social practices, literature, religion and the legal tradition.

NELSON LASSON, THE HISTORY AND DEVELOPMENT OF THE FOURTH AMENDMENT TO THE UNITED STATES CONSTITUTION

13–15 (1970).

The peculiar immunity that the law has thrown around the dwelling house of man, pithily expressed in the maxim, "a man's house is his castle," was not an invention of English jurisprudence. Even in ancient times there were evidences of that same concept in custom and law, partly as a result of the natural desire for privacy, partly an outgrowth, in all probability, of the emphasis placed by the ancients upon the home as a place of hospitality, shelter, and protection. Biblical literature affords a number of illustrative instances of a relatively strong respect for the dwelling as a place which was not subject to arbitrary visitation, even on the part of official authority. In the story concerning Achan, Joshua did not send his messengers to search for and seize the prohibited articles in Achan's tent, even after his detection, until the latter had first confessed both his deed and the place where the articles were concealed.[1] . . .

Where the point does arise incidentally in certain civil cases, a right not to be disturbed in the occupation of the home seems everywhere to be upheld. One old leading commentator broadly states as a principle of ancient law that no one could enter the house of another without express permission. By Biblical law a creditor is forbidden to enter his debtor's house to get security for his debt but must wait outside for the bringing forth of the pledge. Even a bailiff of the court is enjoined from entering for that purpose. And the high regard that the law had for the home is reflected in the protection with which it sought to surround it by punishing housebreaking at night with the death penalty.[2]

In Roman history and law there are also instances of the prevalence of similar ideas. According to the primitive view, the house was not only an asylum but was under the special protection of the household gods, who dwelt and were worshipped there. If even an enemy reached the fireplace of the house, we read that he was sure of protection. Cicero expressed the general feeling in this matter when he said in one of his orations: "What is more inviolable, what better defended by religion

---

1. Joshua 7: 10–26. Earlier in the same book we find that when the king of Jericho received information of the presence of the spies in the dwelling of Rachab, he did not thereupon dispatch a searching party to that place, but sent a message ordering Rachab to produce them. This gave her the opportunity to conceal the spies and throw their pursuers off the track. *Ibid.* 2: 1–7. Note also the apparent hesitation of the crowd, even in a community of the enlightenment of Sodom, in front of the house of Lot and the demand, before any attempt was made to force an entry, that he bring out the strangers he had sheltered. Genesis 19: 4–11.

2. W. W. Davies, *Codes of Hammurabi and Moses* (Cincinnati 1915), p. 33. Article 21 of the Code of Hammurabi, a contemporary of Abraham, provides: "If a man makes a breach into a house, one shall kill him in front of the breach, and bury him in it." Cf. Exodus 22: 2, 3. The code may also be found in A. Kocourek and J. H. Wingmore, *Sources of Ancient and Primitive Law* (Boston, 1915), pp. 395 ff.

than the house of a citizen.... This place of refuge is so sacred to all men, that to be dragged from thence is unlawful."[3]

c. Critique of the Traditional View

Commentators are increasingly challenging prior assumptions about the values assigned to the public and private aspects of life, and the privacy of the home under the traditional view that is captured in the writings by Konvitz, Habermas and Lasson. Many believe that it is no longer possible to sustain a cogent distinction between "public" and 'private." Critics say that this distinction and the notion of the special value of the privacy of the home have contributed to the abnegation of collective responsibility for the common good and the subordination of women. The readings in this section develop the critique of privacy in detail and conclude with an effort by C. Keith Boone to respond to some of the criticisms.

HANNAH ARENDT, THE HUMAN CONDITION

38–78 (1958).

THE RISE OF THE SOCIAL

The emergence of society ... from the shadowy interior of the household into the light of the public sphere, has not only blurred the old borderline between private and political, it has also changed almost beyond recognition the meaning of the two terms and their significance for the life of the individual and the citizen. Not only would we not agree with the Greeks that a life spent in the privacy of "one's own" (*idion*), outside the world of the common, is "idiotic" by definition, or with the Romans to whom privacy offered but a temporary refuge from the business of the *res publica*; we call private today a sphere of intimacy whose beginnings we may be able to trace back to late Roman ... antiquity, but whose peculiar manifoldness and variety were certainly unknown to any period prior to the modern age.

This is not merely a matter of shifted emphasis. In ancient feeling the privative trait of privacy, indicated in the word itself, was all-important; it meant literally a state of being deprived of something, and even of the highest and most human of man's capacities. A man who lived only a private life, who like the slave was not permitted to enter the public realm, or like the barbarian had chosen not to establish such a

---

3. Professor Radin states that many of the safeguards against oppression found in our present-day bills of rights were maintained in Roman law as general principles and embodied in maxims which were frequently cited. "The famous maxim 'every man's house is his castle' cited by Coke, 5 Rep. 92, and generally regarded as a peculiarly English privilege, comes directly from the Roman law. *Nemo de domo sua extrahi debet*" [editor's note, literally this means, "no one ought to be driven out of his house".] But as has been indicated above, it would seem that the concept far antedates that body of law.

Professor Radin goes on to say that the criminal system of England and all other modern states, until the 19th century, were far more rigid and less humane than the Roman system adopted by the Corpus Juris. Max Radin, *Roman Law* (St. Paul, 1927), pp. 475–476.

realm, was not fully human. We no longer think primarily of deprivation when we use the word "privacy," and this is partly due to the enormous enrichment of the private sphere through modern individualism. . . .

. . .

THE PUBLIC REALM: THE COMMON

The term "public" signifies two closely interrelated but not altogether identical phenomena:

It means, first, that everything that appears in public can be seen and heard by everybody and has the widest publicity. . . .

. . .

Second, the term "public" signifies the world itself, in so far as it is common to all of us and distinguished from our privately owned place in it. This world, however, is not identical with the earth or with nature, as the limited space for the movement of men and the general condition of organic life. It is related, rather, to the human artifact, the fabrication of human hands, as well as to affairs which go on among those who inhabit the man-made world together. . . .

. . .

. . . To live an entirely private life means above all to be deprived of things essential to a truly human life: to be deprived of the reality that comes from being seen and heard by others, to be deprived of an "objective" relationship with them that comes from being related to and separated from them through the intermediary of a common world of things, to be deprived of the possibility of achieving something more permanent than life itself. The privation of privacy lies in the absence of others; as far as they are concerned, private man does not appear, and therefore it is as though he did not exist. Whatever he does remains without significance and consequence to others, and what matters to him is without interest to other people.

. . .

[Yet the private realm is not all privative.] In order to understand the danger to human existence from the elimination of the private realm, it may be best to consider those non-privative traits of privacy which are older than, and independent of, the discovery of intimacy. The difference between what we have in common and what we own privately is first that our private possessions, which we use and consume daily, are much more urgently needed than any part of the common world; without property, as Locke pointed out, "the common is of no use." The same necessity that, from the standpoint of the public realm, shows only its negative aspect as a deprivation of freedom possesses a driving force whose urgency is unmatched by the so-called higher desires and aspirations of man; not only will it always be the first among man's needs and worries, it will also prevent the apathy and disappearance of initiative which so obviously threatens all overly wealthy communities. Necessity and life are so intimately related and connected that life itself is threatened where necessity is altogether eliminated. For the elimination of necessity, far from resulting automatically in the establishment of freedom, only blurs the distinguishing line between freedom and necessity. (Modern discussions of freedom, where freedom is never understood as an objective state of human existence but either presents an unsolvable problem of subjectivity, of an entirely undetermined or determined will, or develops out of necessity, all point to the fact that the objective, tangible difference between being free and being forced by necessity is no longer perceived.)

The second outstanding non-privative characteristic of privacy is that the four walls of one's private property offer the only reliable hiding place from the common public world, not only from everything that goes on in it but also from its very publicity, from being seen and being heard. A life spent entirely in public, in the presence of others, becomes, as we would say, shallow. While it retains its visibility, it loses the quality of rising into sight from some darker ground which must remain hidden if it is not to lose its depth in a very real, non-subjective sense. The only efficient way to guarantee the darkness of what needs to be hidden against the light of publicity is private property, a privately owned place to hide in.

. . .

The distinction between the private and public realms, seen from the viewpoint of privacy rather than of the body politic, equals the distinction between things that should be shown and things that should be hidden. Only the modern age, in its rebellion against society, has discovered how rich and manifold the realm of the hidden can be under the conditions of intimacy; but it is striking that from the beginning of history to our own time it has always been the bodily part of human existence that needed to be hidden in privacy, all things connected with the necessity of the life process itself, which prior to the modern age comprehended all activities serving the subsistence of the individual and the survival of the species. Hidden away were the laborers who "with their bodies minister to the [bodily] needs of life," and the women who with their bodies guarantee the physical survival of the species. Women and slaves belonged to the same category and were hidden away not only because they were somebody else's property but because their life was "laborious," devoted to bodily functions. In the beginning of the modern age, when "free" labor had lost its hiding place in the privacy of the household, the laborers were hidden away and segregated from the community like criminals behind high walls and under constant supervision. The fact that the modern age emancipated the working classes and the women at nearly the same historical moment must certainly be counted among the characteristics of an age which no longer believes that bodily functions and material concerns should be hidden. It is all the more symptomatic of the nature of these phenomena that the few remnants of strict privacy even in our own civilization relate to "necessities" in the original sense of being necessitated by having a body.

HOWARD B. RADEST, THE PUBLIC AND THE PRIVATE: AN AMERICAN FAIRY TALE

89 Ethics 280, 280–88 (1979).

. . . [We] need to take a look at the belief that there is an intelligible distinction between the "public" and the "private."

We use these words in various ways. For example, we speak of a public and a private sector when debating issues of allocation. Or, we hear that someone has left business or the academy for public service. We defend a "right" to privacy. These usages are by no means identical and grow more ambiguous in practice.

We can still distinguish "official" from "unofficial" acts and "governmental" from "non-governmental" institutions. The former term of each pair seems to name the public domain while the unofficial and nongovernmental by contrast are private. Yet, as John Dewey [observed] . . . , "The distinction between private and public is not equivalent to the distinction between individual and social. . . . There is therefore no necessary connection between the private character of an act and its nonsocial or antisocial character. The public, moreover, cannot be identified with the socially useful. . . .".

   . . .

Liberal democratic states ordinarily take the private to be a synonym for the "personal," and the public to be a synonym for the "communal." . . .

In liberal theory, the individual enters a "contract" which thereby generates both a public and a private domain. . . . The individual is a rational, self-interested voluntarist. . . . Whatever may have been its roots, however, the liberal idea of individuality comes to be defined by statute and judicial decision. One or another form of positivism has demythologized the notions of the "state of nature" and of "natural law."

   . . .

Standard criteria for differentiating public from private institutions, then, are blurred. Thus, a once convenient and explicit index of privacy, private sources of financial support, is less and less significant, with growing amounts of tax support and tax credit appearing in all institutional budgets. Research funds, educational grants, capital supports, and specialized federal and state programs are larger and larger fractions. Another index of privacy was the right of policy control. But this too, as we well know, is eroded by due process requirements, licensing provisions, standard achievement measurements, standard cost benefits ratios, and the like.

   . . .

The defenses of intimacy must be found elsewhere than in [a] safe private domain.

DUNCAN KENNEDY, THE STAGES OF THE DECLINE OF THE PUBLIC/PRIVATE DISTINCTION

130 U. Pa. L. Rev. 1349, 1349–57 (1982).

Success for a legal distinction has two facets. First, it must be possible to make the distinction: people must feel that it is intuitively sensible to divide something between its poles, and that the division will come out pretty much the same way regardless of who is doing it. Second, the distinction must make a difference: a distinction without a difference is a failure even if it is possible for everyone to agree every time on how to make it. Making a difference means that it seems plain that situations should be treated differently depending on which category of the distinction they fall into.

The history of legal thought since the turn of the century is the history of the decline of a particular set of distinctions—those that, taken together, constitute the liberal way of thinking about the social world. I suggest that there is an invariant sequence of six stages in a distinction's passage from robust good health to utter decrepitude. I will use the public/private distinction to illustrate each stage. [The six stages are: 1. Hard Cases With Large Stakes. 2. The Development of Intermediate Terms. 3. Collapse. 4. Continuumization. 5. Stereotypification. 6. Loopification.] . . .

6. LOOPIFICATION

Loopification is the most interesting (to me) of all the stages. . . .

In the case of the public/private distinction, loopification occurs when one realizes that the private sector includes both the market and the family. We often conceive the family in terms very much like those we apply to the state, and treat the family as a domain "affected with a public interest" to the very extent that it is intensely private. Likewise, we tend to understand the transactions of individual consumers, investors, tenants, and clients as more private than those of large or small businesses, but at the same time conceive of these individual transactions as more, rather than less, amenable to public regulation. . . .

One ends up where one began because of all the ways in which we think of the family and the political community as close together rather than far apart. First, there are many analogies between them. They are both "units of government," rather than markets though some law and economics types have recently argued for seeing them otherwise). Within them, actors play roles—occupy offices or statuses—which are fiduciary. There are lots of duties and lots of discretion, but neither the duty nor the discretion is like that of market actors. In the family and in the state, we tend to feel that overarching ideals ought to inform every decision, while we conceive the market actor as "free to do whatever she wants so long as she obeys the ground rules."

Second, political philosophy refers constantly to the ideals of the family, and philosophers of the family refer constantly to political ideals.

The interpenetration of the two realms of discourse is so thorough that we might better speak of a single political/familial rhetoric. We use the market concept of consent or voluntariness only in a qualified, metaphorical, or "implied" sense in state and family. We temper the notion that you get what you paid for with natural law, natural light, immemorial custom, organic communitarian norms, divine wills, and so forth.

Third, the blurring of institutional lines between the state and the family is more obvious than blurring along the market/family or market/state boundaries. It has been common forever to speak of the public functions of the family in producing and socializing "the next generation." Using this and other rationales, the state attempts to determine the content of and then enforce performance of familial roles, both of parents and children. Modern statutory schemes authorize social welfare agencies backed by courts to intervene on no more precise grounds than the "best interests of the child" or the child's "need for supervision." It often seems that the legislator sees parents as a mere adjunct or subagency of the state.

Finally and paradoxically, when people are speaking and thinking of the economy, or "world of work," as the "public sphere," they tend to lump politics, religion and sexuality together as an opposed sphere, into which an employer (for example) has no business intruding. In this perspective, what life in the state has in common with life in the family is that both are quintessentially private.

Following out these lines of similarity and difference, one simply loses one's ability to take the public/private distinction seriously as a description, as an explanation, or as a justification of anything.

CHARLOTTE PERKINS GILMAN, WOMEN AND ECONOMICS

255, 258–260 (1898).

Of all popular paradoxes, none is more nakedly absurd than to hear us prate of privacy in a place where we cheerfully admit to our table-talk and to our door service—yes, and to the making of our beds and to the handling of our clothing—a complete stranger. . . .

. . . The progressive individuation of human beings requires a personal home, one room at least for each person. . . . [F]or the vast majority of the population no such provision is possible. To women, especially, a private room is a luxury of the rich alone. . . . The home is the one place on earth where no one of the component individuals can have any privacy. A family is a crude aggregate of persons of different ages, sizes, sexes, and temperaments, held together by sex-ties and economic necessity. . . .

At present any tendency to withdraw and live one's own life on any plane of separate interest or industry is naturally resented, or at least regretted, by the other members of the family. This affects women more than men, because men live very little in the family and very much in the world.... [T]he women and children live in the home—because they must. For a woman to wish to spend time elsewhere is considered wrong, and children have no choice.... Yet the home times bind us with a gentle dragging hold that few can resist. Those who do resist, and who insist upon living their individual lives, find that this costs them loneliness and privation; and they lose so much in daily comfort and affection that others are deterred from following them.

CATHARINE A. MACKINNON, FEMINISM UNMODIFIED: DISCOURSES ON LIFE AND LAW

96–102 (1987).

The idea of privacy, if regarded as the outer edge of the limitations on government, embodies, I think, a tension between the preclusion of public exposure or governmental intrusion, on the one hand, and autonomy in the sense of protecting personal self-action on the other. This is a tension, not just two facets of one whole right. In the liberal state this tension is resolved by demarking the threshold of the state at its permissible extent of penetration into a domain that is considered free by definition: the private sphere. It is by this move that the state secures to individuals what has been termed "an inviolable personality" by ensuring what has been called "autonomy or control over the intimacies of personal identity." The state does this by centering its self-restraint on body and home, especially bedroom. By staying out of marriage and the family, prominently meaning sexuality—that is to say, heterosexuality—from contraception through pornography to the abortion decision, the law of privacy proposes to guarantee individual bodily integrity, personal exercise of moral intelligence, and freedom of intimacy. But if one asks whether *women's* rights to these values have been guaranteed, it appears that the law of privacy works to translate traditional social values into the rhetoric of individual rights as a means of subordinating those rights to specific social imperatives.

. . .

In the context of a sexual critique of gender inequality, abortion promises to women sex with men on the same reproductive terms as men have sex with women. So long as women do not control access to our sexuality, abortion facilitates women's heterosexual availability. In other words, under conditions of gender inequality, sexual liberation in this sense does not free women; it frees male sexual aggression. The availability of abortion removes the one remaining legitimized reason that women have had for refusing sex besides the headache. As Andrea Dworkin put it, analyzing male ideology on abortion, "Getting laid was at stake." . . .

Privacy doctrine is an ideal vehicle for this process. The liberal ideal of the private—and privacy as an ideal has been formulated in liberal terms—holds that, so long as the public does not interfere, autonomous individuals interact freely and equally. Conceptually, the private is hermetic. It *means* that which is inaccessible to, unaccountable to, unconstructed by anything beyond itself. By definition, it is not part of or conditioned by anything systematic or outside of it. It is personal, intimate, autonomous, particular, individual, the original source and final outpost of the self, gender neutral. It is, in short, defined by everything that feminism reveals women have never been allowed to be or to have, and everything that women have been equated with and defined in terms of *men's* ability to have. To complain in public of inequality within it contradicts the liberal definition of the private. In this view, no act of the state contributes to—hence should properly participate in—shaping the internal alignments of the private or distributing its internal forces. Its inviolability by the state, framed as an individual right, presupposes that the private is not already an arm of the state. In this scheme, intimacy is implicitly thought to guarantee symmetry of power. Injuries arise in violating the private sphere, not within and by and because of it.

In private, consent tends to be presumed. It is true that a showing of coercion voids this presumption. But the problem is getting anything private to be perceived as coercive. Why one would allow force in private—the "why doesn't she leave" question asked of battered women—is a question given its urgency by the social meaning of the private as a sphere of choice. But for women the measure of the intimacy has been the measure of the oppression. This is why feminism has had to explode the private. This is why feminism has seen the personal as the political. The private is the public for those for whom the personal is the political. In this sense, there is no private, either normatively or empirically. Feminism confronts the fact that women have no privacy to lose or to guarantee. We are not inviolable. Our sexuality is not only violable, it is—hence, we are—seen *in* and *as* our violation. To confront the fact that we have no privacy is to confront the intimate degradation of women as the public order.

In this light, a right to privacy looks like an injury got up as a gift. Freedom from public intervention coexists uneasily with any right that requires social preconditions to be meaningfully delivered. For example, if inequality is socially pervasive and enforced, equality will require intervention, not abdication, to be meaningful. But the right to privacy is not thought to require social change. It is not even thought to require any social preconditions, other than nonintervention by the public. . . .

. . .

When the law of privacy restricts intrusions into intimacy, it bars change in control over that intimacy. The existing distribution of power and resources within the private sphere will be precisely what the law of privacy exists to protect. It is probably no coincidence that the very things feminism regards as central to the subjection of women—the very place, the body; the very relations, heterosexual; the very activities, intercourse and reproduction; and the very feelings, intimate—form the core of what is covered by privacy doctrine. From this perspective, the legal concept of privacy can and has shielded the place of battery, marital rape, and women's exploited labor; has preserved the central institutions whereby women are deprived of identity, autonomy, control and self-definition; and has protected the primary activity through which male supremacy is expressed and enforced. Just as pornography is legally protected as individual freedom of expression—without questioning whose freedom and whose expression and at whose expense—abstract privacy protects abstract autonomy, without inquiring into whose freedom of action is being sanctioned at whose expense.

To fail to recognize the meaning of the private in the ideology and reality of women's subordination by seeking protection behind a right *to* that privacy is to cut women off from collective verification and state support in the same act. I think this has a lot to do with why we can't organize women on the abortion issue. When women are segregated in private, separated from each other, one at a time, a right to that privacy isolates us at once from each other and from public recourse. This right to privacy is a right of men "to be let alone" to oppress women one at a time. It embodies and reflects the private sphere's existing definition of womanhood. This is an instance of liberalism called feminism, liberalism applied to women as if we *are* persons, gender neutral. It reinforces the division between public and private that is *not* gender neutral. It is at once an ideological division that lies about women's shared experience and that mystifies the unity among the spheres of women's violation. It is a very material division that keeps the private beyond public redress and depoliticizes women's subjection within it. It keeps some men out of the bedrooms of other men.

C. KEITH BOONE, PRIVACY AND COMMUNITY
9 Social Theory and Practice 1, 6–24 (1983).

CONFLICT IN ACTUAL SOCIETIES

One way of stating the case against privacy is to contend that privacy and community are antagonistic in actual societies, even if they are not conceptually so.... There seems to be some exterior validity to this claim, inasmuch as the state of privacy seems to isolate the individual from society, and insofar as the right to privacy legitimates that isolation. But a closer look at actual societies demonstrates a different principle; whether or not privacy and community are antagonistic depends on the *kind* of society in question. Consider two kinds of societies lying at opposite poles of the political spectrum, as in the cases of a statist totalitarian society and a liberal democracy. Essential to the development of the totalitarian society is the full expansion of the public into the private sphere, such that no society may properly be termed totalitarian until it has "simply liquidated the whole sphere of privacy." The reason privacy must be eliminated is that totalitarian control hinges on the atomization of society into fully individualized units that recognize only one plane of existence—the relationship between the state and the individual. If the only truth of politics is the truth of the state, then it must be the case that "autonomous units are denied privacy, traditional confidential relationships are destroyed, surveillance systems and informers are widely installed, and thorough dossiers are compiled on millions of citizens." Communal relations suffer unbearable strains toward disintegration, and former community bonds generated by geography, ethnic identity, religion, and the like deteriorate.... Spontaneous, natural forms of community are squeezed out by the pressures of enforced community, that is, by the larger "community" of the state.

... Privacy in this sense constitutes a great barrier against the atomization of society and the destruction of real community. If, however, the community of the state is thought to qualify as a real community, then the critics of privacy must be even more distressed, for the kind of community wherein privacy and community are most purely antithetical turns out to be a totalitarian community.

By contrast, consider a liberal democratic system committed to long-standing political concepts of equal liberty, individual rights and freedoms, and an open, nonrepressive democratic process. Far from conflicting with the goals of such a society, privacy is in principle quite supportive of them. Linked as it is to the moral and material well-being of individuals, liberal social philosophy emphasizes the importance of nourishing individuality and liberty in its citizenry. On the one hand, privacy is associated with individuality because it provides critical opportunities for reaping the fruits of individuality—creativity, query, experiment, initiative, distinctiveness. On the other hand, it is linked to liberty because it protects freedoms in areas most important to the development of selfhood—intimacy, anonymity, solitude, and reserve. Privacy seems vital to a democratic society in several specific ways as well. For example, it underwrites the freedom to vote, to hold political discussions, and to associate freely away from the glare of the public eye and without fear of reprisal. Also, it is likely that a sense of privacy fortifies the right to secret jury deliberations as well as the right not to have to reveal such personal information as religious affiliation or political preferences.

Finally, privacy contributes to the protection of group associations, from family to larger social organizations, that compete for the individual's loyalties. Such groups are integral to the development of nonpolitical centers of value that serve a number of vital democratic functions: they testify to the richness and variety of human allegiances other than the political; they serve as resource centers for the derivation of normative social and political goals; they help define the parameters of the legitimate exercise of power. Thus privacy fortifies modern democracy's prophylactic intention of preventing the total politicization of a person's life—a prospect that is characteristic of political religions and totalitarian ideologies, but repugnant to the democratic ideal. To the extent that privacy is a condition for the cultivation of individuality and liberty, it is a friend to community—at least to the kind of community that treasures these ideals as major foci of its identity. It is apparent, then, that within the normative framework of a liberal democracy, it is the suppression of privacy, not its invigoration, that is antagonistic to community.

Conflict with Welfare and Equality

But many critics do not dispute this conclusion. In fact, they rush to confirm it in what is perhaps the most commonly expressed suspicion of the legitimation of privacy, particularly as a fundamental right: it is *too* friendly to a liberal society. They argue that a strong right to privacy has the trademark of a libertarian shift in social philosophy that enhances individual freedoms at the expense of social goals embodying fairness and benevolence. American critics cite with displeasure assertions of a "right to be let alone" or expressions of the nostrum that "a man's home is his castle." They often view such claims as a blind for social irresponsibility, and they're particularly worried that past and future gains in equality and social welfare are threatened by the libertarian impulse. Some construe the right to privacy as a ruse by the "haves" of American society to prevent the "have-nots" from participating in the enjoyment of a certain level of social goods. Viewing privacy as a class weapon, they hold that it is simply one more privilege invented by the bourgeoisie for the bourgeoisie, one more freedom that turns away from the communal good in behalf of individual interests. At stake in these allegations is a particular normative conception of the societal good that places welfare and equality at or close to the center of its political philosophy. Those treasuring these goals reason that increased liberties create zones of immunity that are difficult or impossible to penetrate in behalf of the common good. A right to privacy is suspect because it ensures that such zones will, like the heads of Hydra, rapidly multiply.

It is important to evaluate this argument in view of the sheer moral weight it carries, and in view of the increasing modern concern for equality and social welfare. What, for example, are the implications of a right to privacy for turning away blacks from membership in a "private club," or women from high-level jobs in "privately-owned" businesses? What are the implications of fashioning a strong right to privacy in the absence of any explicit right to sustenance or welfare? In sum, in what sense does a right to privacy contribute to the development of a libertarian or quasi-libertarian society that many of us would judge to be morally offensive?

. . .

[I]t is critical to note that the kinds of liberties that typically stand in the way of equality and social welfare have little or nothing to do with the generally negative liberties of privacy. Among these the most prominent are property rights, including the freedom from trespass, the right to free enterprise, and the freedom to hire employees or admit students under solely meritocratic or utilitarian standards. These *public* freedoms are the ones that hold the greatest potential for conflicting with the nonlibertarian social goals of a liberal democracy in the American variety, and certainly with those of a social democracy. But even in a social democracy there is not a great deal of room for truly private concerns to conflict with the public welfare. What one does in one's bedroom, to whom one chooses to disclose personal information, or what one thinks about or writes about in the solitude of the study usually are matters having no direct relevance to social welfare or equality. By contrast, how one may hire, educate, manipulate tax shelters, or exploit migrant workers may have a devastating effect on such goals....

On the other hand ... there may be times when actual claims to privacy may conflict with these ideals. This is particularly true if the meaning of privacy can reasonably be expanded to comprehend groups as well as individuals....

... In that case, some sort of balancing would be necessary. Such balancing would not necessarily be dysfunctional to a vigorous pursuit of privacy, for we can affirm privacy while agreeing wholeheartedly that the "functions of privacy in liberal systems do not require that it be an absolute right."

. . .

Privacy and Individualism

Underlying many critiques of privacy is the peculiarly modern anxiety that the empowerment of privacy is just one more wheel bolted onto the juggernaut of individualism. It is said that our age is the era of the loss of community, notable by the preoccupation of the contemporary thought with "personal alienation and cultural disintegration." ...

Attaching the pursuit of privacy rights to the modern canonization of individualism, critics reason that privacy, beneath its benevolent exterior, is a threat to building and maintaining community. They argue that it embodies an anachronism, a vision of the discrete and autonomous person in an era that must judge such a view as life-threatening. They aver further that any sort of right to privacy that anchors such an attitude in legal rules and principles ends up sanctioning social and political irresponsibility. In short, it undermines participation in the *res publica*, corrodes the sense of communal responsibility, and underwrites social negligence at a time when the "key word is not privacy but responsibility."

. . .

But while it is natural to think of privacy as compatible with and even enhanced by the spirit of independence, it need not be the case that they be viewed as inherently correlative social phenomena. The fact that privacy is prized in cultures that have no discernible history of individualism amply demonstrates the point. Moreover, evidence that privacy was valued prior to strong modern English and American affirmations of individualism suggests caution against a too analytical association of the two. Can we ever believe that the human desire for moments of solitude, the protection of sexual and familial intimacy, or the modesty associated with bodily functions were introduced only with the advance of individualism? Did Socrates not often enjoy the reprieve of privacy? Did not Antony and Cleopatra treasure the emotional latitude afforded by privacy?

... [P]rivacy cannot be fully accounted for by reference to a strong sense of independence from the community. In some cultures, privacy is a totally communal concept, both created and strictly enforced by society, allowing little or no latitude for the individual to prefer *more* privacy than his fellows. And as a condition *sui generis*, it alone permits the pursuit of certain goals that are quintessentially communal.... [T]he *growth* of individuality has heightened the demand for privacy.... [But] compatibility with the individualistic spirit does not necessarily mean that the claim to privacy is being driven by purely or even dominantly individualistic impulse. Rather, it may be driven by an impulse that is social in essence, the product of what socialization into a society with particular values would entail. In all societies, socially "objective" norms that confront the individual as facts are typically internalized by that person, and subsequently externalized as a form of social behavior. In a particular society, assuming that "the community in question has certain moral convictions about privacy as a moral good" for itself and its members, privacy is a deeply social phenomenon and in that sense a function of community.

. . .

What we saw was true about privacy and community on the conceptual level is true about individuality and community in actual societies: whether or not they reflect a zero infrastructure depends on the kind of society in question. For example, a liberal democracy is most accurately pictured by sociological theory that views the individual and the community as moments in a reciprocal process wherein each contributes to the vitality of the other. The liberal society promotes individuality as a fountain of initiative, enterprise, freedom of thought and expression, responsibility—at the same time that it is sensitive to the need for limits that function to preserve the society. To some extent all noncoerced societies strive for this structural mutuality of function that achieves a harmony of interests beneath a sea of day-to-day disharmonies. In that sense individuality and community are not always weights on the opposite ends of a seesaw, but may be complementary modes in a larger unitary process.

. . .

From this perspective, the view that privacy endangers community is exceedingly strange. If a community is, in the broad Platonic definition, a "having-in-common" (*koinonia*), it is hard to see how not holding *everything* in common threatens those goods.... Always retaining the imprint of the community upon them, individuals who seek privacy remove themselves out of society's sight, but not out of its mind.

It may be that some critics who set privacy and community at odds mistake privacy for privatization, the former a temporary relief from participation in community, and the latter a process through which one becomes increasingly cut off from the life of the community.... Complete privatization heralds the epiphany of mass man, the atomized individual whose absorption into private life paves the road for abduction into the totalitarian scheme....

... Privatized individuals or social misfits may use the protections of privacy as a shield against the world, but such deviations do not detract from the legitimacy of the sphere itself. Moreover, there may be other explanations for the alleged lack of contemporary public concern that have nothing to do with the protection of the private sphere. For example, it may be that people retreat from participation in public affairs because the magnitude and bureaucratic impenetrability of the political process make meaningful participation seem remote. The size and impersonality of urban societies, as well as the humane movement of the modern state into the role of caretaker of social welfare, may generate passivity. The sense of manageability, importance of individual action, and return on one's social investments that may have characterized smaller communities of bygone eras are hard to come by in today's Brobdignagnian cities and suburbs. As I will argue later in this paper, the currents of a lost sense of community in modern industrialized societies run much deeper than can be adequately probed in an analysis of privacy.

. . .

There are two prominent ways in which privacy could become too strong a legal doctrine and contradict the limitations in the definition I have elaborated. One way is that the right become so powerful that it not be vulnerable to the judicial balancing process wherein other weighty rights and principles are set against it. Such a development is not likely, as is indicated by a number of cases in which the appeal to privacy has been overridden, some involving bodily privacy, privacy of personal information, and even sexual intimacy. The second possibility is more likely, namely, the gross expansion of the private sphere such that it would gratuitously encompass public rights that are already guaranteed in the 1st, 4th, and 5th amendments. True, there is no instant formula for clearly marking the fuzzy boundaries of what we call the "private," but there are sound theoretical and practical reasons for not conflating privacy with established public freedoms that are frequently associated with it.... What the Court has found in those hazy penumbras of some constitutional amendments has sometimes to do with privacy, but other times merely with personal autonomy, personal sovereignty, or what the Court calls "personal liberty." In actual cases, personal autonomy may or may not involve a state of privacy. The Court has muddied its own waters by implying that the right to privacy embraces all cases of personal autonomy. There is still some question as to what extent *Roe v. Wade* actually involved privacy, and to what extent it was wise or necessary for the Court to invoke privacy discourse beyond the reliable discourse of "personal liberty." Even the *Griswold* Court's intention to circumscribe areas "fundamentally affecting a person" may have extended the parameters of the truly private too far. It is true that in most accounts the protection of privacy has something to do with inviolate personhood; but everything that is either personal or fundamental, or both, is not necessarily private, as we have seen. The Court's tendency to confuse privacy with everything related to procreative liberty is disturbing because it casts the net of privacy too widely, dilutes the concept, and lends credence to current criticisms of endorsing a right to privacy.

. . .

The inescapable conclusion from a comparison of total and nontotal communities is that privacy is a premier *condition* for personhood. In order fully to appreciate what this means, one need only imagine a society in which the instruments for total surveillance have been perfected such that people's thoughts as well as their actions are transparent to others. In this kind of society it is evident that people could no longer have their *own* thoughts, their *own* sentiments, their *own* inner lives. The distinction between self and other would become blurred as one's alienated identity merged into the great river of totalitarian group identity. True, one might still sense pain and pleasure as one's *own* in such circumstances; but this potential is not evidence of a sense of selfhood, as can be inferred from the fact that even animals can experience it. The capacity to have one's own thoughts and one's own life, and to *call* them one's own, seems essential for selfhood, and this is precisely what is threatened in a totalitarian society. Since the capacity for selfhood is a principle condition for personhood, in the absence of minimal privacy, personhood is inconceivable because selfhood is inconceivable. Correspondingly, in the absence of adequate privacy, the development of personhood, and hence personal autonomy, is threatened. Thus it becomes quite clear why—as the unanimous opinion of authorities on totalitarianism indicates—totalitarian societies must destroy the private sphere.

2. ORIGINS OF THE LEGAL RIGHT OF PRIVACY

Explicit recognition of rights to privacy in our legal system did not occur before the latter part of the nineteenth century. Privacy was protected prior to that time by legal norms which did not explicitly refer to privacy, such as the first amendment rights of freedom of speech, of the press and of association. The third amendment right to not have troops quartered in one's home, the fourth amendment right to be free from unreasonable searches and seizures and the fifth amendment right against self-incrimination are constitutional norms which also protected privacy. There were also examples of implicit protection for privacy in the common law of nuisance, trespass and in the restriction on private eavesdropping. For an account of the extent to which American law provided some protection for privacy during the century following the adoption of the Constitution and Bill of Rights, see the prominent book by Alan Westin, *Privacy and Freedom*, 330–38 (1967). For a discussion of privacy before American independence see David H. Flaherty, *Privacy in Colonial New England* (1972).

Privacy as a legal concept has perplexed scholars and judges since talk about privacy first appeared in court opinions and scholarly writings. The earliest discussion of privacy in an appellate court opinion occurred in 1881. The Michigan Supreme Court granted tort relief to a woman because the defendant had observed her during childbirth without her consent in *DeMay v. Roberts*, 46 Mich. 160, 9 N.W. 146 (1881). In sustaining a tort judgment Justice Marston, speaking for a unanimous court, stated:

> The plaintiff had a legal right to the privacy of her apartment at such a time, and the law secures to her this right by requiring others to observe it, and to abstain from its violation.

46 Mich. at 165–66, 9 N.W. at 149.

A year earlier, Judge Thomas Cooley included the "right to be let alone" as a class of tort rights in his initial legal treatise on torts. In 1873, Sir James Fitzjames Stephen published the first explicit philosophical exposition on privacy in, J.F. Stephen, *Liberty, Equality, Fraternity* (1st. ed. 1873).

Notwithstanding these judicial and academic precedents, the official line on the evolution of the legal right of privacy, repeated in so many cases and legal publications that it has become an academic cliche, treats privacy rights as having been conceived by Samuel Warren and Louis Brandeis in an article published in the Harvard Law Review in 1890. At first courts did not rush to embrace Warren and Brandeis' call for explicit legal recognition of the right of privacy. Judicial response was tentative. Twelve years after the article the New York Court of Appeals refused to recognize that legal protection for privacy was part of the common law of New York in *Roberson v. Rochester Folding Box Co.*, 171 N.Y. 538, 64 N.E. 442 (1902). The New York Legislature responded to *Roberson* by creating a limited statutory privacy right. Merely fifteen years after the publication of the article, however, Judge Reid, writing for the Georgia Supreme Court, declared the right of privacy to be part of Georgia law in *Pavesich v. New England Life Ins. Co.*, 122 Ga. 190, 50 S.E. 68 (1905). *Pavesich* is a classic example of the evolution of a common law right and natural law jurisprudence.

3. CONSOLIDATION OF THE TORT AND CONSTITUTIONAL RIGHT TO PRIVACY

By 1939, when the final volume of the First Restatement of Torts was published, explicit tort protection for privacy was included. This occurred but two years after Professor Bohlen concluded that the campaign for recognition of the right of privacy so auspiciously inaugurated by Warren and Brandeis had "almost completely failed." Francis H. Bohlen, *Fifty Years of Torts*, 50 Harv. L. Rev. 725, 731 (1937). Professor Feinberg, writing in the Columbia Law Review a decade after Bohlen, could point to nine jurisdictions which had recognized a common law right of privacy from 1937 to 1948. Feinberg, *Recent Developments in the Law of Privacy*, 48 Colum. L. Rev. 713 (1948). In 1960, Dean Prosser authored one of the most influential articles on the torts aspect of privacy in the twentieth century. William L. Prosser, *Privacy*, 48 Calif. L. Rev. 383 (1960). He identified over three hundred appellate court cases involving privacy in our legal system.

The considerable body of common law precedent Prosser identified in 1960 clearly demonstrated that the common law right of privacy was firmly entrenched. However, at that time the constitutional right of privacy was expressly recognized by the Supreme Court only as a part of the general fourth amendment right against unreasonable government searches and seizures and the fifth amendment right against government compelled self-incrimination. In 1965, the Supreme Court for the first time established a general constitutional right of privacy independent of the fourth and fifth amendments in *Griswold v. Connecticut*, 381 U.S. 479 (1965).

As of this writing all of the states have now recognized some form of common law protection for privacy. Formal recognition of privacy in torts and constitutional law over the seventy-five year period from the Warren and Brandeis article to *Griswold v. Connecticut* has occurred amidst simultaneous and continual expressions of doubt about the wisdom and efficacy of a legal right of privacy. The controversy continues today despite an unmistakable trend towards proliferation of privacy rights in our legal system.

4. EXPANSION, CRITICISM AND CONFUSION

Although recent judicial decisions have retarded the development of privacy rights in some areas, as a general matter privacy is a legal right that is in the process of growth. Over the last fifty years the allure of privacy has been more than courts and legislatures have been able to resist. The Supreme Court has found that the constitutional right to privacy protects against illegal searches of persons and homes; government coercion of incriminating statements; governmental wiretapping; noise pollution; and government interference with the personal decision to use contraceptives or to have an abortion. Use of privacy to protect the decision to use contraceptives and to have an abortion, as controversial as it has become, has not impeded new uses by judges to protect the right to die naturally and the right to engage in certain sexual intimacies with consenting adults.

Common law judges have found that the tort right of privacy includes protection against commercial exploitation of name or likeness, damage to reputation, private spying, and emotional distress, as well as against government activities that are also protected under the constitutional right of privacy. State and federal legislatures have enacted privacy statutes to protect the confidentiality of information in the possession of government agencies, businesses and individuals. Significant state legislation has also been directed at both government and private spying.

With this rapid proliferation of privacy rights in our legal system it is not surprising to find considerable confusion and disagreement over what privacy means. It is likewise not surprising to find bitter denials that sufficient justification exists for new privacy rights.

Those who complain about new privacy rights, do, of course, have plenty of good reasons for their concerns. Desks are locked, bedroom doors and drawers are closed because we want privacy, and privacy in these situations means we want to limit acquaintance with information about us. On the other hand, the decision to have an abortion or to use contraceptives seems on the face of the matter to be far removed from this clear sense of informational privacy. Indeed, the more one thinks about it, the more the right sought to be protected seems to be a right to decide fundamental matters for oneself even if the government or others decide to the contrary, rather than a right to protect information.

The quantity of confusion as well as the quality of criticism concerning privacy as a ground for protecting interests (beyond limiting access to information) strongly suggests that judges and scholars have not satisfactorily connected up the cluster of interests which enjoy common law, statutory and constitutional protection under the right of privacy. The connection problem is a recurring theme through much of the dialogue of this book.

Sources of Confusion About the Legal Concept of Privacy

Confusion about the legal concept of privacy is the result of several factors. A primary source of confusion is the fact that "privacy" is employed by lay persons, lawyers, and judges in a variety of circumstances, and in these circumstances, the term has different meanings. Sometimes "privacy" concerns relate to the acquisition or disclosure of information, sometimes to physical seclusion, sometimes to ownership or control, and sometimes to personal decisionmaking. In short, privacy has informational, physical, proprietary and decisional meanings. Because "privacy" has different uses, senses or meanings, attempts to develop a unitary definition or theory of privacy will invariably be over or underinclusive. "Privacy" can denote a neutral condition or state of affairs, a desired condition or state of affairs, a psychological state, a claim, a legal right, a legal interest, and a moral argument.

Some of the disparate uses of privacy are illustrated by the following ordinary situations in which the term "privacy" is employed:

1. A and B are conversing in A's office. C enters the room and says to A, "Excuse me, could I speak to you for a moment?" B responds, looking at A and C, "do you want privacy?"

2. A learns that her father has been listening to her conversations over the extension phone at the family home, and says, "Dad, that is not right; it is an invasion of my privacy."

3. A owns two and one-half acres of property which is surrounded by two hundred and fifty acres of property owned by B which was undeveloped when A purchased his property. B

builds two hundred and twenty single, detached homes on the property. A comments, "Since B developed his property, I don't have as much privacy."

4. A is studying for her law exams in her favorite spot in her apartment. The phone rings. It is B who is selling storm windows. A hangs up. Twenty minutes later the phone rings again. This time it is C who wants to know whether the check for the monthly phone bill has been mailed. A says, "It is in the mail." Thirty minutes later, the phone rings again. This time it is D who is working her way through college selling magazines. A says, "Not interested," and hangs up the phone. Ten minutes later, the phone rings again. This time it is E, a fellow student who asks A how studying is going. A says, "Terrible, I can't get any privacy; the phone has been ringing off the hook all night."

5. A and B have been married for four years. Both are lawyers. C and D are A's parents and are having dinner at A and B's home. For the umpteenth time, C says to B, "when are you two going to start a family?" A, in frustration, says, "Father, that is a private matter. It is none of your business."

6. A is employed by B. A requires B, who operates heavy machinery, to submit to random drug and alcohol testing. B begrudingly complies, but complains to friends that "every part of my body and everything I put in it should be private".

Privacy as a Condition of Life or State of Affairs

Several commentators have observed that one of the characteristic uses of privacy is to denote a condition of life or state of affairs. *See* Anita L. Allen, *Uneasy Access: Privacy for Women in a Free Society*, 13–15 (1988); Ruth Gavison, *Privacy and the Limits of Law,* 89 Yale L.J. 421, 425–40 (1980); Richard C. Turkington, *Legacy of the Warren and Brandeis Article: The Emerging Unencumbered Constitutional Right to Informational Privacy*, 10 N. Ill. Univ. L. Rev. 479, 509–10 (1990). Some commentators have rejected the notion that privacy is a condition or state of affairs. *See* Robert C. Post, *The Social Foundations of Privacy: Community and Self in the Common Law Tort*, 77 Calif. L. Rev. 957, 969 (1989).

Consider some of the implications of the view that one of the characteristic uses of privacy is to describe a condition of life or state of affairs. Conditions in life either exist or they do not. Conditions in life also may improve, worsen, change or remain the same; they may be lost or regained. If privacy is a condition or state of affairs, it is correct to say that someone has lost privacy (a condition) but has not been deprived of the legal right of privacy. This would be the case, for example, if a police officer, acting with probable cause and pursuant to a valid search warrant, enters someone's home and searches the home thoroughly. Under these circumstances that person has lost the condition of privacy but no violation of that person's state or federal constitutional right to privacy has occurred. There has been a loss of the condition of privacy because the police officer has gained access to personal and perhaps intimate information about that individual without that individual's consent. However, no legal right to privacy has been violated; the government is excused under these circumstances because the search was made pursuant to a properly authorized warrant. In the material that follows, we think that it is helpful to consider the instances when privacy is employed to describe a state of affairs or condition of life and when it is employed to indicate that a personal right has or has not been violated. Failure to distinguish between the sense of privacy as a condition of life and the sense of privacy as a right is a source of confusion in the dialogue about privacy. The fact that privacy is a condition of life has additional implications. The condition of privacy impedes access to us as persons. The condition of privacy is central to our sense of security. If there is a loss of the condition of privacy, we often very clearly sense that loss. Privacy is an essential aspect of life in our society, and people learn about and develop a sense of privacy at a very early age. We think it is both correct and useful to speak of the socially developed sense of privacy as a persons' moral or intuitive sense of privacy. This sense of privacy is a source of political and social pressure to recognize and protect privacy in law. In addition, the moral or intuitive sense of privacy is a basis for natural law justification for the creation and elaboration of legal rights of privacy in judicial opinions.

5. THE VALUE OF PRIVACY

(1) A pervasive viewpoint is that many forms of privacy merit protection. Numerous legal and moral philosophers have undertaken to explain the value of one or more forms of privacy, by virtue of which protection is warranted. See, e.g., Edward Bloustein, *Privacy as an Aspect of Human Dignity: An Answer to Dean Prosser,* 39 N.Y.U.L. Rev. 34 (1967); Joel Feinberg, *Autonomy, Sovereignty and Privacy: Moral Ideals in the Constitution,* 58 Notre Dame Law Review 445–490 (1983);) Charles Fried, *An Anatomy of Values* (1970); James Rachels, *Why Privacy is Important,* 4 Philosophy and Public Affairs 323–33 (1975); Judith Thomson, *The Right to Privacy,* 4 Philosophy and Public Affairs 295–314 (1975). See generally, Anita L. Allen, *Uneasy Access,* 35–52 (1988); Ferdinand Schoeman, *Privacy and Social Freedom* (1992); Id., *Philosophical Dimensions of Privacy: An Anthology* (1984), Julie Inness, *Privacy, Intimacy, and Isolation* (1992); Patricia, Boling, *Privacy and the Politics of Intimate Life* (1996); Judith W. DeCew, *In Pursuit of Privacy: Law, Ethics and the Rise of Technology* 1997). For social science assessments of the value of privacy see, e.g., Carl Schneider, *Shame, Exposure and Privacy* (1977); Barrington Moore, *Privacy: Studies in Social and Cultural History* (1984), Amitai Etzioni, *The Limits of Privacy* (1999).

(2) A few theorists depict "privacy" as denoting a basic human good, whose value is intrinsic. However, most theorists describe "privacy" as denoting conditions of life that are valued as a good or evil depending upon whether they satisfy the extrinsic demands of, for

example, moral respect for persons, worthwhile intimate relationships or economic utility. The idea that moral respect for persons demands broad protection for privacy appears in many of the most influential accounts of the value of privacy. These accounts maintain that opportunities for physical, informational decisional, and/or proprietary privacy promote two things. They promote, first, ideals of human personhood, consisting of rational, self-determining, morally autonomous individuals. Second they promote ideals of human relationships, consisting of intimate association, complementing appropriately confidential and anonymous ties.

Theories that base privacy's value on the importance of promoting individual personhood and relationships presuppose highly individualistic understandings of human flourishing. Yet communitarian and care-based understandings of human flourishing also entail privacy protection. Men and women are embedded in social worlds replete with responsibilities for self and others. Without privacy for purposes of rest, reflection, experimentation and independent action, individuals would be less fit for meeting their responsibilities as citizens and caretakers. A degree of privacy may be needed to facilitate the flourishing of self-determining, autonomous individuals; but a degree of privacy also seems necessary to facilitate the flourishing of responsible members of families and wider communities. Legal rules of privacy can be viewed as shared understandings of the privacy needed to create and preserve social civility.

Normative accounts of decisional privacy—less so informational, physical and proprietary privacy—commonly stress political values. Some political accounts of the value of decisional privacy emphasize the importance within a liberal democracy of self-determination and individual autonomy respecting reproduction, sex and health care. Others stress the importance of a limited and neutral government. Collective toleration of a wide range of popular and unpopular choices empowers individuals, thereby keeping in check potentially totalitarian government and tyrannical majorities.

6. RIGHT TO PRIVACY AS A DEFEASIBLE LEGAL CLAIM

Privacy as a legal right is part of the bundle of rights which enjoy a preferred status in the hierarchy of rights in our legal system. If government or individual activities benefit the public generally they may still be illegal if the activities encroach on privacy. Privacy rights require the government to at least have a good reason for encroaching on privacy. In many instances individual privacy rights override or in Ronald Dworkin's imagery "trump" that which would generally benefit the citizenry. However, privacy rights, like other legal rights, are not absolute. In the litigation process, privacy interests collide with other important individual and governmental interests. In the trade-off that must inevitably occur, privacy is sometimes the loser. Claims of a legal right to privacy share the characteristics of defeasibility that claims of other similar rights possess. The rights consist of prima facie claims of injury and the absence of excusing conditions or defenses. When an individual, business entity or the government, directly or indirectly, adversely affects a person's interest in limiting acquaintance with personal affairs, autonomy or mental repose, that person has a claim of violation of privacy rights which, if properly presented, will acquire the status of at least a prima facie claim. Whether that individual's claim of legal privacy rights will be successful in achieving a specific remedy through court or administrative action depends on the availability of excusing circumstances or defenses to the party whose action encroached upon the legally protected privacy interest. The most important defenses or excusing conditions in privacy litigation are: (1) consent, and (2) overriding private or public interest. Consent is a defense that permeates all privacy law and, if available, invariably results in the determination that no responsibility attaches for the individual or government action. Private and public interests are also frequently asserted as a general defense to various claims of invasion of privacy. Discrete defenses such as newsworthiness and the first amendment privilege of the press play an important role in limiting the liability of media defendants against claims of invasion of privacy. The scope of these defenses and excusing conditions as well as others are explored throughout this book. For an account of the defeasible character of legal concepts, see, H.L.A. Hart, *Assumption of Responsibility and Rights*, Proceedings of the Aristotelian Society, New Series, XLIX (1949).

B. THE WARREN AND BRANDEIS ARTICLE

WARREN & BRANDEIS, THE RIGHT TO PRIVACY

4 Harv. L. Rev. 193, 193–220 (1890).

That the individual shall have full protection in person and in property is a principle as old as the common law; but it has been found necessary from time to time to define anew the exact nature and extent of such protection. Political, social, and economic changes entail the recognition of new rights, and the common law, in its eternal youth, grows to meet the demands of the society. Thus, in very early times, the law gave a remedy only for physical interference with life and property, for trespasses *vi et armis*. Then the "right to life" served only to protect the subject from battery in its various forms; liberty meant freedom from actual restraint; and the right to property secured to the individual his lands and his cattle. Later, there came a recognition of man's spiritual nature, of his feelings and his intellect. Gradually the scope of these legal rights broadened; and now the right to life has come to mean the right to enjoy life,—the right to be let alone; the right to liberty secures the exercise of extensive civil privileges; and the term "property" has grown to comprise every form of possession—intangible, as well as tangible.

Thus, with the recognition of the legal value of sensations, the protection against actual bodily injury was extended to prohibit mere attempts to do such injury; that is, the putting another in fear of such injury. From the action of battery grew that of assault. Much later there came a qualified protection of the individual against offensive noises and odors, against dust and smoke, and excessive vibration. The law of nuisance was developed. So regard for human emotions soon extended the scope of personal immunity beyond the body of the individual. His reputation, the standing among his fellow-men, was considered, and the law of slander and libel arose. Man's family relations became a part of the legal conception of his life, and the alienation of a wife's affection was held remediable. Occasionally the law halted,—as in its refusal to recognize the intrusion by seduction upon the honor of the family. But even here the demands of society were met. A mean fiction, the action *per quod scruitium amisit,* was resorted to, and by allowing damages for injury to the parents' feelings, an adequate remedy was ordinarily afforded. Similar to the expansion of the right to life was the growth of the legal conception of property. From corporeal property arose the incorporeal rights issuing out of it; and then there opened the wide realm of intangible property, in the products and processes of the mind, as works of literature and art, goodwill, trade secrets, and trademarks.

This development of the law was inevitable. The intense intellectual and emotional life, and the heightening of sensations which came with the advance of civilization, made it clear to men that only part of the pain, pleasure, and profit of life lay in physical things. Thoughts, emotions, and sensations demanded legal recognition, and the beautiful capacity for growth which characterizes the common law enabled the judges to afford the requisite protection, without the interposition of the legislature.

Recent inventions and business methods call attention to the next step which must be taken for the protection of the person, and for securing to the individual what Judge Cooley calls the right "to be let alone." Instantaneous photographs and newspaper enterprise have invaded the sacred precincts of private and domestic life; and numerous mechanical devices threaten to make good the prediction that "what is whispered in the closet shall be proclaimed from the house-tops." For years there has been a feeling that the law must afford some remedy for the unauthorized circulation of portraits of private persons; and the evil of the invasion of privacy by the newspapers, long keenly felt, has been but recently discussed by an able writer.

The alleged facts of a somewhat notorious case brought before an inferior tribunal in New York a few months ago, directly involved the consideration of the right of circulating portraits; and the question whether our law will recognize and protect the right to privacy in this and in other respects must soon come before our courts for consideration. Of the desirability—indeed of the necessity—of some such protection, there can, it is believed, be no doubt. The press is overstepping in every direction the obvious bounds of propriety and of decency. Gossip is no longer the resource of the idle and of the vicious, but has become a trade, which is pursued with industry as well as effrontery. To satisfy a prurient taste the details of sexual relations are spread broadcast in the columns of the daily papers. To occupy the indolent, column upon column is filled with idle gossip, which can only be procured by intrusion upon the domestic circle. The intensity and complexity of life, attendant upon advancing civilization, have rendered necessary some retreat from the world, and man, under the refining influence of culture, has become more sensitive to publicity, so that solitude and privacy have become more essential to the individual; but modern enterprise and invention have, through invasions upon his privacy, subjected him to mental pain and distress, far greater than could be inflicted by mere bodily injury. Nor is the harm wrought by such invasions confined to the suffering of those who may be made the subjects of journalistic or other enterprise. In this, as in other branches of commerce, the supply creates the demand. Each crop of unseemly gossip, thus harvested, becomes the seed of more, and, in direct proportion to its circulation, results in lowering of social standards and of morality. Even gossip apparently harmless, when widely and persistently circulated, is potent for evil. It both belittles and perverts. It belittles by inverting the relative importance of things, thus dwarfing the thoughts and aspirations of a people. When personal gossip attains the dignity of print, and crowds the space available for matters of real interest to the community, what wonder that the ignorant and thoughtless mistake its relative importance. Easy of comprehension, appealing to that weak side of human nature which is never wholly cast down by the misfortunes and frailties of our neighbors, no one can be surprised that it usurps the place of interest in brains capable of other things. Triviality destroys at once robustness of thought and delicacy of feeling. No enthusiasm can flourish, no generous impulse can survive under its blighting influence.

It is our purpose to consider whether the existing law affords a principle which can properly be invoked to protect the privacy of the individual; and, if it does, what the nature and extent of such protection is.

. . .

It is not however necessary, in order to sustain the view that the common law recognizes and upholds a principle applicable to cases of invasion of privacy, to invoke the analogy, which is but superficial, to injuries sustained, either by an attack upon reputation or by what the civilians called a violation of honor; for the legal doctrines relating to infractions of what is ordinarily termed the common-law right to intellectual and artistic property are, it is believed, but instances and applications of a general right to privacy, which properly understood afford a remedy for the evils under consideration.

The common law secures to each individual the right of determining, ordinarily, to what extent his thoughts, sentiments, and emotions shall be communicated to others.[2] Under our system of government, he

2. "It is certain every man has a right to keep his own sentiments, if he pleases. He has certainly a right to judge whether he will make them public, or commit them only to the sight of his friends." Yates, J., in Millar v. Taylor, 4 Burr. 2303, 2379 (1769).

can never be compelled to express them (except upon the witness-stand); and even if he has chosen to give them expression, he generally retains the power to fix the limits of the publicity which shall be given them. The existence of this right does not depend upon the particular method of expression adopted. It is immaterial whether it be by word, or by signs, in painting, by sculpture, or in music. Neither does the existence of the right depend upon the nature or value of the thought or emotion, nor upon the excellence of the means of expression. The same protection is accorded to a casual letter or an entry in a diary and to the most valuable poem or essay, to a botch or daub and to a masterpiece. In every such case the individual is entitled to decide whether that which is his shall be given to the public. No other has the right to publish his productions in any form, without his consent. This right is wholly independent of the material on which, or the means by which, the thought, sentiment, or emotion is expressed. It may exist independently of any corporeal being, as in words spoken, a song sung, a drama acted. Or if expressed on any material, as a poem in writing, the author may have parted with the paper, without forfeiting any propriety right in the composition itself. The right is lost only when the author himself communicates his production to the public,—in other words, publishes it. It is entirely independent of the copyright laws, and their extension into the domain of art. The aim of those statutes is to secure to the author, composer, or artist the entire profits arising from the publication; but the common-law protection enables him to control absolutely the act of publication, and in the exercise of his own discretion, to decide whether there shall be any publication at all. The statutory right is of no value, unless there is a publication; the common-right law is lost as soon as there is a publication.

What is the nature, the basis, of this right to prevent the publication of manuscripts or works of art? It is stated to be the enforcement of a right to property; and no difficulty arises in accepting this view, so long as we only have to deal with the reproduction of literary and artistic compositions. They certainly possess many of the attributes of ordinary property: they are transferable; they have a value; and publication or reproduction is a use by which that value is realized. But where the value of the production is found not in the right to take the profits arising from publication, but in the peace of mind or the relief afforded by the ability to prevent any publication at all, it is difficult to regard the right as one of property, in the common acceptation of that term. A man records in a letter to his son, or in his diary, that he did not dine with his wife on a certain day. No one into whose hands those papers fall could publish them to the world, even if possession of the documents had been obtained rightfully; and the prohibition would not be confined to the publication of a copy of the letter itself, or of the diary entry; the restraint extends also to a publication of the contents. What is the thing which is protected? Surely, not the intellectual act of recording the fact that the husband did not dine with his wife, but that fact itself. It is not the intellectual product, but the domestic occurrence. A man writes a dozen letters to different people. No person would be permitted to publish a list of the letters written. If the letters or contents of the diary were protected as literary compositions, the scope of the protection afforded should be the same secured to a published writing under the copyright law. But the copyright law would not prevent an enumeration of the letters, or the publication of some of the facts contained therein. The copyright of a series of paintings or etchings would prevent a reproduction of the paintings as pictures; but it would not prevent a publication of a list or even a description of them. Yet in the famous case of Prince Albert v. Strange, the court held that the common-law rule prohibited not merely the reproduction of the etchings which the plaintiff and Queen Victoria had made for their own pleasure, but also "the publishing (at least by printing or writing), though not by copy or resemblance, a description of them, whether more or less limited or summary, whether in the form of a catalogue or otherwise." Likewise, an unpublished collection of news possessing no element of a literary nature is protected from piracy.

That this protection cannot rest upon the right to literary or artistic property in any exact sense, appears the more clearly when the subject-matter for which protection is invoked is not even in the form of intellectual property, but has the attributes of ordinary tangible property. Suppose a man has a collection of gems or curiosities which he keeps private: it would hardly be contended that any person could publish a catalogue of them, and yet the articles enumerated are certainly not intellectual property in the legal sense, any more than a collection of stoves or of chairs.

. . .

Although the courts have asserted that they have rested their decisions on the narrow grounds of protection to property, yet there are recognitions of a more liberal doctrine. Thus in the case of Prince Albert v. Strange, already referred to, the opinions of both the Vice–Chancellor and of the Lord Chancellor, on appeal, show a more or less clearly defined perception of a principle broader than those which were mainly discussed, and on which they both placed their chief reliance. Vice–Chancellor Knight Bruce referred to publishing of a man that he had "written to particular persons or on particular subjects" as an instance of possibly injurious disclosures as to private matters, that the courts would in a proper case prevent; yet it is difficult to perceive how, in such a case, any right of property, in the narrow sense, would be drawn in question, or why, if such a publication would be restrained when it threatened to expose the victim not merely to sarcasm, but to ruin, it should not equally be enjoined, if it threatened to embitter his life. To deprive a man of the potential profits to be realized by publishing a catalogue of his gems cannot per se be wrong to him. The possibility of future profits is not a right of property which the law ordinarily recognizes; it must, therefore, be an infraction of other rights which constitutes the wrongful act, and that infraction is equally wrongful, whether its results are to forestall the profits that the individual himself might secure by giving the matter a publicity obnoxious to him, or to gain an advantage at the expense of his mental pain and suffering. If the fiction of property in a narrow sense must be preserved, it is still true that the end accomplished by the gossip-monger is attained by the use of that which is another's, the facts relating to his private life, which he has seen fit to keep private. Lord Cottenham stated that a man "is entitled to be protected in the exclusive use and enjoyment of that which is exclusively his," and cited with approval the opinion of Lord Eldon, as reported in a manuscript note of the case of Wyatt v. Wilson, in 1820, respecting an engraving of George the Third during his illness, to the effect that "if one of the late king's physicians had kept a diary of what he heard and saw, the court would not, in the king's lifetime, have permitted him to print and publish it;" and Lord Cottenham declared, in respect to the acts of the defendants in the case before him, that "privacy is the right invaded." But if privacy is once recognized as a right entitled to legal protection, the interposition of the courts cannot depend on the particular nature of the injuries resulting.

These considerations lead to the conclusion that the protection afforded to thoughts, sentiments, and emotions, expressed through the medium of writing or of the arts, so far as it consists in preventing publication, is merely an instance of the enforcement of the more general right of the individual to be let alone. It is like the right not to be assaulted or beaten, the right not to be imprisoned, the right not to be maliciously prosecuted, the right not to be defamed. In each of these rights, as indeed in all other rights recognized by the law, there inheres the quality of being owned or possessed—and (as that is the distinguishing attribute of property) there may be some propriety in speaking of those rights as property. But, obviously, they bear little resemblance to what is ordinarily comprehended under that term. The principle which protects personal writings and all other personal productions, not against theft and physical appropriation, but against publication in any form, is in reality not the principle of private property, but that of an inviolate personality.

If we are correct in this conclusion, the existing law affords a principle which may be invoked to protect the privacy of the individual from invasion either by the too enterprising press, the photographer, or the possessor of any other modern device for recording or reproducing scenes or sounds. For the protection afforded is not confined by the authorities to those cases where any particular medium or form of expression has been adopted, nor to products of the intellect. The same protection is afforded to emotions and sensations expressed in a musical composition or other work of art such as literary composition; and words spoken, a pantomime acted, a sonata performed, is no less entitled to protection than if each had been reduced to writing. The circumstance that a thought or emotion has been recorded in a permanent form renders its identification easier, and hence may be important from point of view of evidence, but it has no significance as a matter of substantive right. If, then, the decisions indicate a general right to privacy for thoughts, emotions, and sensations, these should receive the same protection, whether expressed in writing, or in conduct, in conversation, in attitudes, or in facial expression.

. . .

After the decisions denying the distinction attempted to be made between those literary productions which it was intended to publish and those which it was not, all considerations of the amount of labor involved, the degree of deliberation, the value of the product, and the intention of the publishing must be abandoned, and no basis is discerned upon which the right to restrain publication and reproduction of such so-called literary and artistic works can be rested, except the right to privacy, as a part of the more general right to the immunity of the person,—the right to one's personality. It should be stated that, in some instances where protection has been afforded against wrongful publication, the jurisdiction has been asserted, not on the ground of property, or at least not wholly on that ground, but upon the ground of an alleged breach of an implied contract or of a trust or confidence.

Thus, in Abernethy v. Hutchinson, 3 L. J. Ch. 209 (1825), where the plaintiff, a distinguished surgeon, sought to restrain the publication in the "Lancet" of unpublished lectures which he had delivered at St. Batholomew's Hospital in London, Lord Eldon doubted whether there could be property in lectures which had not been reduced to writing, but granted the injunction on the grounds of breach of confidence, holding "that when persons were admitted as pupils or otherwise, to hear these lectures, although they were orally delivered, and although the parties might go to the extent, if they were able to do so, of putting down the whole by means of short-hand, yet they could do that only for the purposes of their own information, and could not publish, for profit, that which they had not obtained the right of selling."

In Prince Albert v. Strange, I McN. & G. 25 (1849), Lord Cottenham, on appeal, while recognizing a right of property in the etchings which of itself would justify the issuance of the injunction, stated, after discussing the evidence, that he was bound to assume that the possession of the etchings by the defendant had "its foundation in a breach of trust, confidence, or contract," and that upon such ground also the plaintiff's title to the injunction was fully sustained.

In Tuck v. Priester, 19 Q.B.D. 639 (1887), the plaintiffs were owners of a picture, and employed the defendant to make a certain number of copies. He did so, and made also a number of copies for himself, and offered them for sale in England at a lower price. Subsequently, the plaintiffs registered their copyright in the picture, and then brought suit for an injunction and damages. The Lords Justices differed as to the application of the copyright acts to the case, but held unanimously that independently of those acts, the plaintiffs were entitled to an injunction and damages for breach of contract.

In Pollard v. Photographic Co., 40 Ch. Div. 345 (1888), a photographer who had taken a lady's photograph under ordinary circumstances was restrained from exhibiting it, and also from selling copies of it, on the ground that it was a breach of an implied term in the contract, and also that it was a breach of confidence. . . .

This process of implying a term in a contract, or of implying a trust (particularly when the contract is written, and where there is no established usage or custom), is nothing more nor less than a judicial declaration that public morality, private justice, and general convenience demand the recognition of such a rule, and that the publication under similar circumstances would be considered an intolerable abuse. So long as these circumstances happen to present a contract upon which such a term can be engrafted by the judicial mind, or to supply relations upon which a trust or confidence can be erected, there may be no objection to working out the desired protection through the doctrines of contract or of trust. But the court can hardly stop there. The narrower doctrine may have satisfied the demands of society at a time when abuse to be guarded against could rarely have arisen without violating a contract or a special confidence; but now that modern devices afford abundant opportunities for the perpetration of such wrongs without any participation by the injured party, and protection granted by the law must be placed upon a broader foundation. While, for instance, the state of the photographic art was such that one's picture could seldom be taken without his consciously "sitting" for the purpose, the law of contract or of trust might afford the prudent man sufficient safeguards against the improper circulation of his portrait; but since the latest advances in photographic art have rendered it possible to take pictures surreptitiously, the doctrines of the contract and of trust are inadequate to support the required protection, and the law of tort must be resorted to. The right of property in its widest sense, including all possession, including all rights and privileges, and hence embracing the right to an inviolate personality, affords alone that broad basis upon which the protection which the individual demands can be rested.

Thus, the courts, in searching for some principle upon which the publication of private letters could be enjoined, naturally came upon the ideas of a breach of confidence, and of an implied contract; but it required little consideration to discern that this doctrine could not afford all the protection required, since it would not support the court in granting a remedy against a stranger; and so the theory of property in the contents of letters was adopted. Indeed, it is difficult to conceive on what theory of the law the casual recipient of a letter, who proceeds to publish it, is guilty of a breach of contract, express or implied, or of any breach of trust, in the ordinary acceptation of that term. Suppose a letter has been addressed to him without his solicitation. He opens it, and reads. Surely, he has not made any contract; he has not accepted any trust. He cannot, by opening and reading the letter, have come under any obligation save what the law declares; and however expressed, that obligation is simply to observe the legal right of the sender, whatever it may be, and whether it be called his property in the contents of the letter, or his right to privacy.

. . .

We must therefore conclude that rights, so protected, whatever their exact nature, are not rights arising from contract or from special trust, but are rights as against the world; and, as above stated, the principle which has been applied to protect these rights is in reality not the principle of private property, unless that word be used in an extended and unusual sense. The principle which protects the personal writings and any other productions of the intellect or of the emotions, is the right to privacy, and the law has no new principle to formulate when it extends this protection to personal appearance, sayings, acts, and to personal relation, domestic or otherwise.[1]

If the invasion of privacy constitutes a legal *injuria*, the elements for demanding redress exist, since already the value of mental suffering, caused by an act wrongful in itself, is recognized as a basis for compensation.

The right of one who has remained a private individual, to prevent his public portraiture, presents the simplest case for such extension; the right to protect one's self from pen portraiture, from a discussion by the press of one's private affairs, would be a more important and far reaching one. If casual and unimportant statements in a letter, if handiwork, however inartistic and valueless, if possessions of all sorts are protected not only against reproduction, but against description and enumeration, how much more should the acts and sayings of a man in his social and domestic relations be guarded from ruthless publicity? If you may not reproduce a woman's face photographically without her consent, how much less should be tolerated the reproduction of her face,

---

1. The application of an existing principle to a new state of facts is not judicial legislation. To call it such is to assert that the existing body of law consists practically of the statutes and decided cases, and to deny that the principles (of which these cases are ordinarily said to be evidence) exist at all. It is not the application of an existing principle, but the introduction of a new principle, which is properly termed judicial legislation.

But even the fact that a certain decision would involve judicial legislation should not be taken as conclusive against the propriety of making it. This power has been constantly exercised by our judges, when applying to a new subject principles of private justice, moral fitness, and public convenience. Indeed, the elasticity of our law, its adaptability to new conditions, the capacity for growth, which has been able to meet the wants of an ever changing society and to apply immediate relief for every recognized wrong, have been its greatest boast.

I cannot understand how any person who has considered the subject can suppose that society could possibly have gone on if judges had not legislated, or that there is any danger whatever in allowing them that power which they have in fact exercised, to make up for the negligence or the incapacity of the avowed legislator. That part of the law of every country which was made by judges has been far better made than that part which consists of statutes enacted by the legislature.

I Austin's Jurisprudence, p. 224.

The cases referred to above show that the common law has for a century and a half protected privacy in certain cases, and to grant the further protection now suggested would be merely another application of an existing rule.

her form, and her actions, by graphic descriptions colored to suit a gross and depraved imagination?

[The authors then discuss various defenses to the tort. Their discussions of publication of matters in the public interest, privileged communications, and oral publications are reprinted in the sections of the materials which deal with those specific defenses.] . . . .

It would doubtless be desirable that the privacy of the individual should receive the added protection of the criminal law, but for this, legislation would be required. Perhaps it would be deemed proper to bring the criminal liability for such publication within narrower limits; but that the community has an interest in preventing such invasions of privacy, sufficiently strong to justify the introduction of such a remedy, cannot be doubted. Still, the protection of society must come mainly through a recognition of the rights of the individual. Each man is responsible for his own acts and omissions only. If he condones what he reprobates, with a weapon at hand equal to his defence [sic], he is responsible for the results. If he resists, public opinion will rally to his support. Has he then such a weapon? It is believed that the common law provides him with one, forged in the slow fire of the centuries, and to-day fitly tempered to his hand. The common law has always recognized a man's house as his castle, impregnable, often, even to its own officers engaged in the execution of its commands. Shall the courts thus close the front entrance to constituted authority, and open wide the back door to idle or prurient curiosity?

1. NOTE ON THE ARTICLE

a. The Article's Philosophical Linkage to Natural Law

It is likely that the Warren and Brandeis article has had as much impact on the development of law as any single publication in legal periodicals. It is certainly one of the most commented upon and cited publications in the history of our legal system. A more influential piece of scholarship is difficult to imagine. The article has acquired a special place in the fantasies of those who toil in the dusty basements of law libraries or sit bleary-eyed in front of a computer screen researching and writing with the hope that their efforts will produce insights which will dramatically shape legal history. The official theory of the legal right of privacy as expressed in numerous publications springs the right *eo instanti* from the pen of Warren and Brandeis in 1890. This view underplays the significance of the ground swell of moral rights to which the authors were sensitive and for which the article provides a legal collector. As Professor Wellington has noted:

> [The article] is an extraordinary essay by many tests, especially for its attempt to fashion a legal principle from changes in moral perception.

... Apart from pace, that article does model better than anything in the literature the emergence of a common law principle.

Harry H. Wellington, *Common Law Rules and Constitutional Double
Standards: Some Notes on Adjudication*, 83 Yale L.J. 221, 249–51 (1973).

Privacy is a value that is reflected in everyday ordinary life and in
the language that we use to blame others and defend ourselves against
claims of moral responsibility for wrongs. Warren and Brandeis recognized that it was time for the legal system to expressly recognize and
protect privacy rights which had long been valued in the moral and
social relations. They suggested that the core principle at stake in
privacy cases was the principle of "inviolate personality." Wellington's
view is that Warren and Brandeis drew this core principle from conventional morality. As such, the argument for recognition of a right to
privacy was ultimately grounded on natural law philosophy. But it was
natural law in the general and contemporary sense, where morality that
develops from social interaction and everyday moral discourse is an
appropriate source for common law rights.

The jurisprudential tradition of the article may also be traced to
natural law views of a more classic kind. Warren and Brandeis twice
cited an article by E.L. Godkin in *Scribner's Magazine* which considered
"the right to decide how much knowledge ... of [an individual's] own
private ... affairs ... the public at large shall have" to be a natural
right. E.L. Godkin, *The Rights of the Citizen, IV.—To His Own Reputation*, 8 Scribner's Magazine 58, 65 (July 1890). Professor Barron contends that the views expressed by Godkin laid the conceptual foundation
for the Warren and Brandeis article. *See* James H. Barron, *Warren &
Brandeis, The Right To Privacy, 4 Harv. L. Rev. 193 (1890): Demystifying a Landmark Citation*, 13 Suffolk Univ. L. Rev. 875, 876 (1979). The
natural law foundation for the right to privacy advocated in the article
was fully affirmed by the first high court to recognize the right to
privacy as part of a state's common law. Endorsing the reasoning of the
article, the Georgia Supreme Court concluded that the "right of privacy
has its foundation in the instincts of nature ... and ... is therefore
derived from natural law." *Pavesich v. New England Life Ins. Co.*, 122
Ga. 190, 194, 50 S.E. 68, 69–70 (1905).

b. *Contemporary Commentary on the Right to Privacy*

The virtual nonexistence of attention in legal literature to the
subject of privacy and the absence of privacy as an explicit ground for
relief in case law prior to 1890 is one of the reasons that the historic
birth of the right of privacy is traced to the Warren and Brandeis article.
However, Warren and Brandeis' commentary on the concept of privacy
was not unprecedented. In the latter half of the nineteenth century,
privacy had been the subject of commentary by several philosophers,
jurists and writers.

(1) James Fitzjames Stephen

Professor Gerety has pointed out that an Englishman, Sir James Fitzjames Stephen, was the first modern philosopher to discuss the concept of privacy explicitly, seventeen years prior to the Warren and Brandeis article in a work that largely responded to the philosophy of John Stuart Mill. *See* Tom Gerety, *Redefining Privacy*, 12 Harv. C.R.- C.L. L. Rev. 232 (1977). The core of Mill's philosophy was a right against unwarranted government interference, founded on the principle of utility. The branch of the constitutional right of privacy developed in the contraception and abortion line of cases amounts to a right against governmental interference with intimate decision-making. It is clear in retrospect that much of Mill's views on personal liberty in his famous book, *On Liberty*, constituted de facto advocacy of privacy rights.

Consider part of the brief comments by Stephen:

> To define the province of privacy distinctly is impossible, but it can be described in general terms. All the more intimate and delicate relations of life are of such a nature that to submit them to unsympathetic observation, or to observation which is sympathetic in the wrong way, inflicts great pain and may inflict lasting moral injury. Privacy may be violated not only by the intrusion of a stranger, but by compelling or persuading a person to direct too much attention to his own feelings and to attach too much importance to their analysis. The common usage of language affords a practical test which is almost perfect upon this subject. Conduct which can be described as indecent is always in one way or another a violation of privacy.

J.F. Stephen, *Liberty, Equality and Fraternity*, 160 (1873).

Do Stephen's views on privacy parallel those of Warren and Brandeis? Consider Stephen's definition of privacy as conduct which can be described as indecent. Is his definition at all useful? In the article, Warren and Brandeis employ the term "invasion of privacy" numerous times. They use the term without explication. Is this because they viewed its meaning as plain to the reader? Was its meaning clear to you as you read the article? One may look at the Warren and Brandeis article as incorporating the sense of privacy that the reader has developed from ordinary life situations and everyday discourse. This intuitive sense of privacy and of moral responsibility for invasions of privacy is tied closely to notions of decency and conventional morality. Similarly, Stephen identifies privacy with notions of decency in English society of the nineteenth century, as reflected in ordinary language and conventional morality.

(2) The Godkin Connection

In July of 1890, E.L. Godkin, the editor of *The Nation*, wrote an article in *Scribner's Magazine* that argued for recognition of a right to privacy. Godkin's article was cited without comment twice in the Warren and Brandeis article. Writing in 1905, Professor Adams was the first of several scholars to suggest that Warren and Brandeis were influenced by the ideas expressed by Godkin. Elbridge L. Adams, *The Right to Privacy, and its Relation to the Law of Libel*, 39 Am. L. Rev. 37 (1905). Professor James H. Barron concluded that Godkin "laid much of the foundation for the argument advanced in 'The Right to Privacy,' " James H. Barron, *Warren and Brandeis, The Right to Privacy, 4 Harv. L. Rev. 193 (1890): Demystifying a Landmark Citation*, 13 Suffolk U.L. Rev. 875, 887 (1979).

Consider excerpts from Godkin:

> The right to decide how much knowledge of [a man's] personal thought and feeling, and how much knowledge, therefore, of his tastes, and habits, of his own private doings and affairs, and those of his family living under his roof, the public at large shall have, is as much one of his natural rights as his right to decide how he shall eat and drink, what he shall wear, and in what manner he shall pass his leisure hours.

> ... Personal dignity is the fine flower of civilization, and the more of it there is in a community, the better off the community is.... But without privacy its cultivation or preservation is hardly possible....

> The chief enemy of privacy in modern life is that interest in other people and their affairs known as curiosity, which in the days before newspapers created personal gossip....

> In all this the advent of the newspapers, or rather of a particular class of newspapers has made a great change. It has converted curiosity into what economists call an effectual demand, and gossip into a marketable commodity.

E. L. Godkin, *The Rights Of The Citizen, IV.—To His Own Reputation*, 8 Scribner's Magazine 58, 65–66 (July 1890).

Godkin's view of the need for privacy to preserve personal dignity under the conditions of modern life is echoed in Warren and Brandeis' claim that privacy is essential to provide us with a retreat from the increasing complexity and intensity of life "attendant upon advancing civilization." Warren and Brandeis certainly viewed the influence of newspapers on the public with a disapproval which was more than a match for Godkin's distaste for the marketing of gossip by the print media. But Brandeis specifically denied that Godkin's writing had been the source for the article. Brandeis wrote in a letter to Warren of his recollection that "it was not Godkin's article but a specific suggestion of yours, as well as your deep seated abhorrence of the invasions of social privacy, which led to our taking up the inquiry." Letter from Louis D. Brandeis to Samuel D. Warren (April 8, 1905), reprinted in I Letters of Louis D. Brandeis (1870–1907): Urban Reformer 302–03 (M. Urofsky & D. Levy eds. 1971).

c. *Legal Precedent*

The most significant legal precedent prior to the publication of the article was a Michigan Supreme Court Case which has gone largely unnoticed in discussion of the subject of privacy. *DeMay v. Roberts*, 46 Mich. 160, 9 N.W. 146 (1881), involved a tort action against a person that had observed the plaintiff during childbirth without her consent. In sustaining a tort judgment for the plaintiff Justice Marston, speaking for a unanimous court, stated:

> The plaintiff had a legal right to the privacy of her apartment at such a time, and the law secures to her this right by requiring others to observe it, and to abstain from its violation.

Id. at 165–66, 9 N.W. at 149.

Blackstone's commentaries on the common law describe eavesdropping as a common law nuisance. Additionally, gossiping about one's neighbor could result in an indictment for public nuisance at common law if one was found to be a "common scold," a legal condition apparently limited in those prehistoric times to members of the female sex. *See* W. Blackstone, 4 *Commentaries on the Laws of England* 168 (9th ed. 1783).

THE DANCER IN TIGHTS CASE: MANOLA v. STEVENS AND MEYERS

Early in the article, Warren and Brandeis refer to a New York trial court decision in which an *ex parte* injunction was issued on behalf of an actress against the distribution of a photograph of her that was surreptitiously taken while she performed a role on a broadway stage, wearing tights. Warren and Brandeis cite the newspaper account of the unreported case in three editions of the *New York Times* on June, 15, 18 and 21st of 1890. The *Times* reports that the photograph was taken of Marion Manola without her consent by a photographer hired by the management of the Opera Company that she was performing for. The actress was reported to have "thrown her mantle over her face and ran off the stage" after the flash from the camera caused her to realize her picture had been taken. The report in the *Times* also stated that Manola alleged that she had refused to be photographed in tights because of her "modesty," *New York Times*, p.2, col. 2, June 15, 1890. Recall that the article characterizes the case as involving "the right of circulating portraits" and treated it as an example of legal protection for the right to privacy. For a more thorough account of the actress and the circumstances that precipitated the lawsuit, *see* Dorothy Glancy, *Privacy and the Other Miss M*, 10 N. Ill. L. Rev. 401 (1990).

d. *Historical and Societal Conditions*

Law mirrors the society that creates it. What forces and conditions in society were reflected in the call for recognition of the right to privacy in 1890?

(1) Shils' Thesis: Did Urbanization and Industrialization Bring Greater Demand for Privacy?

The last half of the nineteenth century was a period of dramatic change in America. Two features of this change were the massive influx of immigrants and the industrialization of society, with the resultant movement of the population from rural to urban centers. Between 1840 and 1890 the population in urban areas jumped from 1,845,000 to 22,000,000 and the percentage of the population living in urban areas rose from 11 to 35. Donald R. Pember, *Privacy and the Press*, 7 (1972). The sociologist Edward Shils argued that living in urban America brought greater needs and demands for privacy. Rural America provided individuals with physical privacy, but in the closed rural society everybody knew what everybody else was doing and there were fewer other kinds of informational privacy. Physical privacy was lost in urban centers, but lives were more private. Shils argued that many urban dwellers were more indifferent to the personal business of their neighbors than their rural counterparts. Once they experienced the condition of being let alone, urban dwellers came to desire and demand that privacy be respected and protected. At the same time, the greater population density of the urban areas and the close proximity in which people were required to live placed increased strains on physical privacy. *See* Shils, *Privacy: Its Constitution and Vicissitudes*, 31 Law & Contemp. Probs. 281 (1966).

(2) Pember's Thesis—Additional Factors: Growth of the Popular Press, Increased Literacy, Influence of Affluent and Socially Conscious Upper Class

Professor Don R. Pember, author of the important book *Privacy and the Press* (1972), suggests that additional important conditions in society also shaped the initial development of the right to privacy. These included the growth of the press, free public education and the emergence of a wealthy social class whose activities were of considerable interest to urban dwellers. The 1890s was a decade of excesses, as reflected by the enormous growth of the print media in the period immediately preceding the publication of the Warren and Brandeis article. Between 1880 and 1890 the number of weekly newspapers grew from 7,811 to 13,559; the circulation of daily newspapers expanded from 2,607,000 in 1870 to 8,387,000 in 1890. With this growth came increased revenues and competition for readers. Advertising revenues in the print media went from 39 million dollars in 1880 to 71 million dollars in 1890. Pember, *supra*, at 10–11. This expansion was possible because of increased literacy in the general population as a result of the establishment of free, compulsory public education in the country. Technological advances prompted by the increasing revenues from publications allowed for mass production, more attractive packaging and regional and national distribution of newspapers. The competition for this wider audience expanded newspaper coverage to include local news and social events. The national habit of looking to the print media for daily accounts of local and national life began in this period.

(3) Copple's Thesis: Frontier Values of Individualism as an Impetus for Privacy Law Development

Was the development of the legal right to privacy influenced by values of individualism that were spawned by settlement of America's frontier? In 1893 a young historian named Frederick Jackson Turner announced that the period of the American frontier was over. Turner further claimed that the experience of settling the frontier had significantly influenced the uniqueness of the American culture. Robert F. Copple, writing in the American Journal of Jurisprudence nearly a century later, built from Turner's frontier thesis and argued that there was a connection between the "frontier experience" and the development of privacy law. Copple's interesting article suggests that the assertion of claims of privacy rights in courts was a consequence of the collision between the previously noted dynamic developments in our society at the end of the nineteenth century and "frontier-shaped individualism."

Copple examines the evolution of privacy tort law in all of the states and demonstrates a pattern of the spread of litigation of common law privacy claims and enactments of statutory protection for privacy that followed the geographical pattern of settlement that had been described by Turner:

> The geographical spread of privacy actions and statutory enactments, like the advancement of the frontier line, began on the East Coast, progressed through the Midwest, jumped to and reformed on the West Coast, and then encompassed the Great Plains, the Mountain States, and the Southwest. This pattern of development, from east to west and back to the middle, corresponds with the progression of the frontier line and the closing of the frontier as described by Turner.

Robert Copple, *Privacy and the Frontier Thesis: An American Intersection of Self and Society*, 34 American Journal of Jurisprudence 87, 104 (1989).

Copple maintains that the gradual closing of the western frontier symbolized a loss of opportunities for independent, secluded lifestyles. Assuming Shils and Copple are correct, industrial urbanization and the disappearance of the western frontier dealt individual privacy a simultaneous double blow.

Copple does not view the Frontier Thesis as inconsistent with the "Patrician Class" theory of development of privacy law.

> Whether founded in a threat to frontier individualism or high society sensitivities, this alternative view of the development of privacy law is not inconsistent with the thesis presented in this article. In an established Old World society, such upper class concerns would have been protected by customs that directed class interaction. In America, however, these class-based customs had been eroded to the point where particular groups of citizens began to think of themselves as privileged or special, there was no customary system to provide them with the protection they perceived they were entitled to by their new found rank or position. As a result, they turned to the rule of law and the formation of a new legal right.

Copple, *supra*, at 97 n. 38.

(4) The Dawn of the Age of Electronic Surveillance

Instantaneous photographs and newspaper enterprise have invaded the sacred precincts of private and domestic life; and numerous mechanical devices threaten to make good the prediction that "what is whispered in the closet shall be proclaimed from the house-tops."

Warren and Brandeis, *Privacy*, 4 Harv. L. Rev. 193, 195 (1890).

Did the technological developments of the latter half of the nineteenth century provide added force to Warren and Brandeis' call for formal recognition of a right to privacy? The capacity for "instantaneous photographs" that is referred to in the quotation from the article was the by-product of dry-plate technology that had been perfected by Kodak in the 1880s. This technology made it possible for candid snapshots to be taken of people and events where earlier technology had required the subject to sit for several minutes. In his seminal book, *Privacy and Freedom* (1967), Alan Westin reports that a 1902 article in the New York Times complained of the "wanton invasion of privacy" to public figures caused by "kodakers lying in wait." Westin, *supra*, at 338. Other technological advances during the period immediately before and after the publication of the article were of such significance that Westin viewed their introduction as altering "the balance between personal expression and third-party surveillance that had prevailed since antiquity." These included the telephone, microphone and digital recorder. The capacity to tap telephone lines was simultaneous with the invention of the telephone itself. The capacity to eavesdrop and record telephone conversations was technically feasible by the 1890s. Prior to these inventions conversational privacy could only be invaded by the physical presence of someone listening with the human ear. Invasions of privacy of written information required physical access of a letter or written record. Westin concludes that American law did not effectively respond to the threats to privacy produced by this "First Era of Technological Challenges" [to privacy] until the late 1950s. Westin, *supra,* at 339.

e.   The Detractors

The Warren and Brandeis article has had its detractors. Criticism of the article has focused on the virulence of the authors' attack upon the press and on the practical limitations on pursuing a legal remedy for invasion of privacy for public disclosures when the litigation itself will generate further publicity of the sensitive information.

(1) Warren and Brandeis and the Press

What motivated Warren and Brandeis to write the article? Was the article a reflection of the anger and annoyance of the authors regarding invasions of privacy caused to the Warren family by highly offensive disclosure of the details of their social affairs? In 1979 Professor Barron wrote an article in which he concluded that *The Right to Privacy* "deserved historical value" but that it "had only a limited impact on the substantive development of 'public disclosure' privacy law." Barron, *supra,* at 922. Barron challenged the generally prevailing view of scholars that the article was a direct response to the excesses and unfairness of the Boston press' reporting on the social affairs of the Warren family. Dean Prosser had been largely responsible for this view. In describing the context for the writing of the article in his influential essay of 1960, Prosser traced the genesis of the piece as follows:

> The matter came to a head when the newspapers had a field day on the occasion of the wedding of a daughter, and Mr. Warren became annoyed. It was an annoyance for which the press, the advertisers and the entertainment industry of America were to pay dearly over the next seventy years.

William L. Prosser, *Privacy,* 48 Calif. L. Rev. 383 (1960).

Barron demonstrates the inaccuracy of this account by showing that Warren's oldest daughter could have been no more than seven years old when the article was written. According to Barron there was a report of the wedding of Warren's cousin in the "Table Gossip" section of the Boston Globe on June 8, 1890. But the content of that column consisted primarily of the names in the wedding party and praise for the attractiveness of the celebration. The Warrens were mentioned for hosting a wedding breakfast for the bride at their home. A day earlier, the Saturday Evening Gazette had reported on the wedding breakfast in more detail, but with the possible exception of mentioning that no bridesmaids were present the account of the breakfast was positive and, as Barron observed, did not contain the highly personal and embarrassing details that might cause the "annoyance" Prosser described.

(2) "Yellow Journalism" in Nineteenth Century Boston

Barron then examined whether there was a basis for the general attack on the press in the article. (Recall the authors' complaint about the press "in every direction overstepping the obvious bounds of propriety and decency.") In his study of the newspapers of the period, Barron built on research that Don R. Pember had begun in his 1972 book *Privacy and the Press.*

Pember's analysis of four of the eight daily newspapers in Boston in 1890 revealed some instances of sensationalism and bad taste. But in Pember's judgment "[t]he examination failed to uncover, however, any instances in which the press was 'overstepping in every direction the obvious bounds of propriety and decency.' . . . These were the charges made by Warren and Brandeis," and the facts did not support Warren and Brandeis' allegations of the deleterious effects of the Boston press on its readers. Pember, *supra,* at 40. Pember concluded that Warren and Brandeis' description of the Boston press was less than accurate.

Professor Barron took up the question by examining the available copies of the Boston *Saturday Evening Gazette,* a newspaper that had allegedly been the source of particular annoyance to Warren and Brandeis. He concluded that the paper "does not seem to have been, from an objective viewpoint, so lacking in taste that its coverage should have provoked such a violent attack." Barron, *supra*, at 902. He did not find the claim that the article was a consequence of excesses of the press and "yellow journalism" to be supported by the historical evidence.

(3) The Article Viewed as a Reflection of the Patrician Class of the Authors

Several scholars have viewed the article as a reflection of the social class of the authors. Warren was born into a prominent, wealthy family and Brandeis was a member of the patrician class by virtue of his academic achievements and success in law practice. Professor Westin concludes that the "Godkin and Warren Essays were essentially a protest by spokesmen for patrician values against the rise of the political and cultural values of 'mass society.' " A. Westin, *Privacy and Freedom*, 348 (1967). Pember offered a similar view. "The Warren–Brandeis proposal was essentially a rich man's plea to the press to stop its gossiping and snooping. . . ." Pember, supra, at 23. Professor Barron also contends that the origin of the article to a great extent is traceable to "the hypersensitivity of the patrician lawyer-merchant [Warren] and the verbal facility and ideological ambivalence of his friend and former law partner." Barron, supra, at 907. Anita L. Allen and Erin Mack further conclude that the proposal for a privacy right grounded on human spirituality reflected the "ideology of culture" that once played a major role in the elite of intellectual life of the American Northeast.

The ideology of "culture" stood over and in opposition to the supposed crass effects of commerce and industry on the human spirit. E.L. Godkin was a noted advocate of the standard of culture. Anita L. Allen and Erin Mack, *How Privacy Got Its Gender*, 10 N. Ill. L. Rev. 441, 456 (1990).

(4) The Feminist Critique

Anita Allen and Erin Mack launched the first feminist critique of the Warren and Brandeis article. The authors describe the article as "deeply conventional and conservative when it came to gender," Anita L. Allen and Erin Mack, *How Privacy Got Its Gender*, 10 N. Ill. L. Rev. 441, 446 (1990). They suggest that the rhetorical force of the Warren and Brandeis article significantly stems from a skillful exploitation of nineteenth-century attitudes about women as "creatures of special modesty" with roles properly limited to the home.

Allen and Mack focus on the early sections of the article in which Warren and Brandeis recount the "inevitable" development of the common law from the narrow conception of non-interference with body and property to the non-interference with a *man's* "family relations":

> To argue that the law had already begun to make progress
> in the direction of recognizing . . . offenses to our spiritual

natures, [Warren and Brandeis] cited a line of cases in which parents and husbands were held to have had rights of recovery against male seducers. Their recognition of an historical "regard for human emotions" was based on cases in which remedies were granted for the alienation of a wife's affections and for wounded feelings, such as shame and dishonor, caused by a daughter's seduction. In addition, they relied upon Godkin's *Scribner's* essay, in which he vehemently argued for greater appreciation of a man's reputation, with scant mention of women except as targets of social opprobrium for their misdeeds.

Allen and Mack, *supra,* at 458. Allen and Mack also view the article's reliance upon *Manola v. Stevens & Meyers* as an illustration of the proper judicial response to invasive uses of photography. In this 1890 case, a New York court granted an injunction restraining the publication of an unauthorized photograph of an actress performing in tights. According to Allen and Mack:

> ... The photographic assault on Manola's modesty was [presumed to be] a paradigm ... of privacy invasion.... Warren and Brandeis cited *Manola* as a clear example of judicial protection of the inviolate personality and delicate feelings injured by unwanted publicity.... If courts must ascribe privacy rights to a stage actress, then clearly they must ascribe them to ordinary men and women who live discreetly at home.

Allen and Mack, *supra,* at 459–60.

By 1890 a new conception of the role of women was emerging in the United States. Indeed, 1890 was the year of the New Woman and the Gibson Girl. Against this background of burgeoning female independence, Allen and Mack compare the Warren and Brandeis article to the work of a noted feminist of the period. Charlotte Perkins Gilman published *Women and Economics* from Boston in 1898. Observing that "Gilman may not have read *The Right to Privacy,*" Allen and Mack maintain that she nonetheless "devoted a chapter of her book to exploding myths the Warren and Brandeis article enshrined." Allen and Mack, *supra,* at 466.

The central "myth" that Gilman took on was the premise that, absent the interference of strangers, the family home is a place of privacy and repose. Allen and Mack suggest that, steeped in the perspectives of genteel patriarchy, Warren and Brandeis overlooked the differential impact social roles can have on the attainment of personal privacy. By contrast, Gilman argued in detail that typical domestic lifestyles impair the individual privacy of family members. Home life especially impairs the privacy—and personality development—of women who serve in traditional female caretaking roles. As a precondition for meaningful privacy at home, Gilman called for fundamental changes in the organization of home life, including reallocation of responsibilities for food preparation and child-care.

(5) Further Criticism of the Article: Publicity in Pursuit of the Remedy

The Warren and Brandeis article has been criticized not only because of the possible ulterior motives of the authors for attacking the Boston press but also because the authors supported a damages remedy for invasions of privacy. Critics point out that one whose privacy has been violated may be reluctant to incur further invasions of privacy by instituting legal action.

In an article for *The Nation*, E.L. Godkin concluded that the realities of pursuing a remedy at law, with the attendant public exposure, created insurmountable practical obstacles to developing a legal right to privacy. "[T]he man who feels outraged by publicity will, in order to stop or punish it ... have to go through a process which will result in an exposure of his private affairs tenfold greater than that originally made by the offending article." E.L. Godkin, *The Right to Privacy*, 51 The Nation 496 (Dec. 25, 1890). Barron also noted the inherent difficulty of the damages remedy proposed by Warren and Brandeis, commenting that the possible reluctance of potential plaintiffs to take legal action for invasions of privacy could cause the remedy to lose its effectiveness. As a result, Barron concluded, "the protected right becomes more vulnerable to further infringements by the press." Barron, *supra*, at 882.

An additional expression of this concern comes from Professor Harry Kalven. In an article written in 1966, he asserts that "privacy will recruit claimants inversely to the magnitude of the offense to privacy involved" because the fear of additional exposure will prevent all but those with an interest in vindicating their genteel sensibilities and in exploiting the tort process from coming forward. Kalven characterized the privacy tort advocated by Warren and Brandeis as "petty." He suggested that the article had an impact on the law primarily because it gave "social status" to the tort of privacy, *see* Kalven, *Privacy in Tort Law—Were Warren and Brandeis Wrong?*, 31 Law & Contemp. Probs. 326, 328, 338 (1966).

f. *Human Dignity and Respect for Persons*

A THEORY OF PRIVACY RIGHTS

Warren and Brandeis focus a good deal of space in the article on the excesses of the press and the loss of the condition of privacy that is caused by the publication of information and images in the press about someone. As previously noted, Dean Prosser irreverently suggested that the article was prompted by a gossip column in a Boston paper that detailed a social affair of the Warrens in Boston. William L. Prosser, *Privacy*, 48 Cal. L. Rev. 383 (1960). The article contains a level of discussion which suggests that, notwithstanding the observations of Prosser, Pember, Westin and others, the authors considered that much more was at stake than abuses of the press with resulting anxiety and embarrassment to the high society of Boston.

This discussion contains a theoretical perspective that provides the basis for an approach to privacy that permeates opinions and scholarly writings both in law and in other disciplines. The core theoretical concepts and assumptions that are employed in the article view privacy as a condition and right that is essentially tied to human dignity, the principle of equal respect for persons, and the notion of personhood itself.

These views were expressed as part of the thesis that privacy is part of a more general right. The more general right was said to be the "right to immunity of person," the "right to be let alone," and the "right to one's own personality." The authors also suggested in a related observation that the core principle at stake in privacy cases was the principle of "inviolate personality." Warren and Brandeis thus viewed the essence of privacy to be a compendium of values. These values can be summarized as "personal autonomy," "personality," and "personhood." The notions contained in the article were more fully refined in a very important article by Dean Bloustein in 1964. Dean Bloustein argues that the recognition of the right of privacy in legal writings and judicial opinions reflects a concern by writers and courts for protecting human dignity. Edward J. Bloustein, *Privacy as an Aspect of Human Dignity: An Answer to Dean Prosser*, 39 N.Y.U. L. Rev. 962 (1964).

The E.T. Hypothetical: On Privacy and Personhood

The above theoretical perspectives can be illustrated by the following hypothetical. Suppose that an extraterrestrial (E.T.) lands on earth near one of the accredited AALS law schools. E.T. wanders into the law school and runs across Student A. E.T. and Student A begin a casual conversation. Student B approaches them. E.T. points to B and says to A, "That is an interesting bag of skin and bones." Student A responds, "But that is more than a bag of skin and bones, that is a person." E.T.: "What is the difference between a bag of skin and bones and a person?" Student A: "A person has a name, an identity, a personality, and certain basic rights as against the government and other individuals." E.T.: "What are those rights?" Student A: "The most central of these are the right to decide fundamental matters for yourself, the right to a minimum amount of respect from the government and other individuals and the right to privacy. When these rights are provided to someone, then we say that individual has human dignity. Sometimes we generalize about these things by referring to the right of privacy and indicating that personhood cannot exist without that right."

Joel Feinberg, the moral philosopher, has also commented upon the essential relationship between rights, human dignity and respect for persons:

> Having rights enable us to "stand up like men," to look others
> in the eye, and to feel in some fundamental way the equal of

anyone. To think of oneself as the holder of rights is not to be unduly but properly proud, to have that minimal self-respect that is necessary to be worthy of the love and esteem of others. Indeed, respect for persons (this is an intriguing idea) may simply be respect for their rights, so that one cannot be the one without the other; and what is called "human dignity" may simply be the recognizable capacity to assert claims.

Joel Feinberg, *The Nature and Value of Rights*, 4 J. Value Inquiry 243, 252 (Winter 1970).

An influential voice in explicitly connecting up the right to privacy and respect for persons' principles has been that of the philosopher Stanley Benn. Benn contends that the essence of the wrong that occurs through invasions of privacy from unlicensed observations of someone is lack of respect for the subject as a person. *See* Stanley I. Benn, *Privacy, Freedom and Respect for Persons*. For a useful evaluation of the evolution of the theoretical exposition of the human dignity personhood model of privacy, see the introductory essay by Professor Schoeman in *Philosophical Dimensions of Privacy: An Anthology* (F. Schoeman, ed. 1984). The judicial decisions and legislative enactments that rely on or are based upon a variation of this view of the core of privacy permeate the materials that follow. Other important theoretical models for the right to privacy have been sponsored by commentators. Kim Lane Scheppele has forcefully presented the case for a contractarian theory of privacy, *see* Kim L. Scheppele, *Legal Secrets* (1988). Richard A. Posner has developed an economic theory of privacy, *see* Richard Posner, *The Right of Privacy*, 12 Ga. L. Rev. 393 (1978). These theories and others will be examined in later sections of these materials.

C. COOLEY, A TREATISE ON THE LAW OF TORTS

29 (1st ed. 1880)

Personal Immunity. The right to one's person may be said to be a right of complete immunity: to be let alone. The corresponding duty is, not to inflict an injury, and not, within such proximity as might render it successful, to attempt the infliction of an injury. In this particular the duty goes beyond what is required in most cases; for usually an unexecuted purpose or an unsuccessful attempt is not noticed. But the attempt to commit a battery involves many elements of injury not always present in breaches of duty; it involves usually an insult, a putting in fear, a sudden call upon energies for prompt and effectual resistance. There is very likely a shock to the nerves, and the peace and quiet of the individual is disturbed for a period of greater or less duration. There is consequently abundant reason in support of the rule of law which makes the assault a legal wrong, even though no battery takes place. Indeed, in this case the law goes still further and makes the attempted blow a criminal offense also.

D. REJECTION OF A COMMON LAW TORT RIGHT OF PRIVACY— APPROPRIATION TORT

ROBERSON v. ROCHESTER FOLDING BOX CO.

171 N.Y. 538, 64 N.E. 442 (1902).

PARKER, C.J. . . .

[The complaint alleged that the Franklin Mills company, one of the defendants, had posted 25,000 advertisements for its flour bearing a photograph of the plaintiff (which had been obtained without her consent) and accompanied by the caption "Flour of the Family" and the name and address of the company. The plaintiff alleged that her likeness had been recognized by many friends and others, and that the resulting humiliation had caused her a severe nervous shock, forcing her to seek medical attention. The plaintiff sought to enjoin the defendant from further use of her likeness and claimed $15,000 in damages. The defendant appeals from a decision by the appellate court affirming an interlocutory judgment in favor of the plaintiff and overruling demurrers to the complaint.]

. . .

There is no precedent for such an action to be found in the decisions of this court. . . . Mention of such a right [of privacy] is not to be found in Blackstone, Kent, or any other of the great commentators upon the law; nor, so far as the learning of counsel or the courts in this case have been able to discover, does its existence seem to have been asserted prior to about the year 1890, when it was presented with attractiveness, and no inconsiderable ability, in the Harvard Law Review (volume 4, p.193) in an article entitled "Rights of a Citizen to His Reputation." . . . If such a principle be incorporated into the body of the law through the instrumentality of a court of equity, the attempts to logically apply the principle will necessarily result not only in a vast amount of litigation, but in litigation bordering upon the absurd, for the right of privacy, once established as a legal doctrine, cannot be confined to the restraint of the publication of a likeness, but must necessarily embrace as well the publication of a word picture, a comment upon one's looks, conduct, domestic relations or habits. And, were the right of privacy once legally asserted, it would necessarily be held to include the same things if spoken instead of printed, for one, as well as the other, invades the right to be absolutely let alone. An insult would certainly be in violation of such a right, and with many persons would more seriously wound the feelings than would the publication of their picture. . . .

The legislative body could very well interfere and arbitrarily provide that no one should be permitted for his own selfish purpose to use the picture or the name of another for advertising purposes without his consent. In such event no embarrassment would result to the general body of the law, for the rule would be applicable only to cases provided for by the statute. The courts, however, being without authority to legislate, are required to decide cases upon principle, and so are necessarily embarrassed by precedents created by an extreme, and therefore unjustifiable, application of an old principle.... [W]hile justice in a given case may be worked out by a decision of the court according to the notions of right which govern the individual judge or body of judges comprising the court, the mischief which will finally result may be almost incalculable under our system, which makes a decision in one case a precedent for decisions in all future cases which are akin to it in the essential facts. So, in a case like the one before us, which is concededly new to this court, it is important that the court should have in mind the effect upon future litigation and upon the development of the law which would necessarily result from a step so far outside of the beaten paths of both common law and equity, assuming—what I shall attempt to show in a moment—that the right of privacy, as a legal doctrine enforceable in equity, has not, down to this time, been established by decisions. The history of the phrase "right of privacy" in this country seems to have begun in 1890, in a clever article in the Harvard Law Review,—already referred to,—in which a number of English cases were analyzed, and, reasoning by analogy, the conclusion was reached that, notwithstanding the unanimity of the courts in resting their decisions upon property rights in cases where publication is prevented by injunction, in reality such prevention was due to the necessity of affording protection to thoughts and sentiments expressed through the medium of writing, printing, and the arts, which is like the right not to be assaulted or beaten; in other words, that the principle actually involved, though not always appreciated, was that of an inviolate personality, not that of private property....

　.　.　.

... An examination of the authorities leads us to the conclusion that the so-called "right of privacy" has not as yet found an abiding place in our jurisprudence, and, as we view it, the doctrine cannot now be incorporated without doing violence to settled principles of law by which the profession and the public have long been guided....

GRAY, J. (DISSENTING)

　.　.　.

... In the social evolution, with the march of the arts and sciences and in the resultant effects upon organized society, it is quite intelligible that new conditions must arise in personal relations, which the rules of the common law, cast in the rigid mold of an earlier social status, were not designed to meet. It would be a reproach to equitable jurisprudence if equity were powerless to extend the application of the principles of common law or of natural justice in remedying a wrong, which, in the progress of civilization, has been made possible as the result of new social or commercial conditions.... Instantaneous photography is a modern invention, and affords the means of securing a portraiture of an individual's face and form in invitum their owner. While, so far forth as it merely does that, although a species of aggression, I concede it to be an irremediable and irrepressible feature of the social evolution. But if it is to be permitted that the portraiture may be put to commercial or other uses for gain by the publication of prints therefrom, then an act of invasion of the individual's privacy results, possibly more formidable and more painful in its consequences than an actual bodily assault might be.... [I]n the existing state of society new conditions affecting the relations of persons demand the broader extension of those legal principles which underlie the immunity of one's person from attack....

Note on the Jurisprudence of Roberson: Legal Positivism

The *Roberson* court was the first high state appellate court to be faced with whether to recognize a common law right to privacy after the publication of the Warren and Brandeis article. Justice Parker's majority opinion embodies a view of law and the role of the judiciary in a democracy that is quite restrictive: legal positivism. Positivism has a long tradition in legal philosophy that is often traced as a fully developed theory to the British philosopher John Austin and his *Lectures on Jurisprudence*, initially published as *The Providence of Jurisprudence Determined*, in 1832. Austin was indebted to Jeremy Bentham and to Thomas Hobbes. For an introduction to the evolution of legal positivism, *see* George C. Christie and Patrick H. Martin, *Jurisprudence Text and Readings on the Philosophy of Law* (1995). In its most pristine form "legal positivism" views "law" as consisting solely of an objectively determined body of enactments, principles, doctrines and rules which are fixed in advance of litigation. The sources of positive law include, cases, statutes, administrative rulings and constitutions. "Positive" law, as contrasted with moral or social rules and principles, is promulgated by judges or public officials who have the authority to make law. The authority to make law is itself derived from identifiable positive sources. The positivist may understand the role of judges very narrowly, i.e., judges select the applicable rule from the network of known public rules and deduce the result in a particular case. Legal positivists say it is inappropriate for judges to go beyond preexisting rules, principles or enactments in deciding a case. Judges who do so are engaging in judicial legislation which may be undesirable in a democracy. For an influential, sophisticated view of legal positivism, *see* H.L.A. Hart, *The Concept of Law* (1961).

Two of the central features of "legal positivism" are the view that rules must have a certain pedigree before they may appropriately be called "law" and a skepticism over the ability of courts to determine values on a basis other than the judges' own preferences. These features link the positivistic tradition of interpreting the common law that is reflected in Justice Parker's opinion in *Roberson*, to a tradition of constitutional interpretation that is reflected in many of the cases in these materials that involve assertions of rights to privacy under state and federal constitutions. The positivistic tradition in constitutional law is expressed in a contemporary theory of the appropriate approach to constitutional interpretation that is called "interpretivism." The interpretivist theory holds that it is inappropriate for a judge to go beyond the language, structure or values of the framers in constitutional cases. *See generally* Raoul Berger, *Government by the Judiciary*, 363–372 (1972); John Hart Ely, *Democracy and Distrust I* (1980). Justice Black espouses a classically "positivistic" or "interpretivistic" view of law and the role of the court in *Griswold v. Connecticut, infra. See, e.g.*, Frank Michelman, *Law's Republic*, 90 Yale L.J. 1 (1987) (commenting on the positivistic nature of Justice White's opinion in *Bowers v. Hardwick*), *infra*; and S. Wasserstrom and L. Seidman, *The Fourth Amendment as Constitutional Theory*, 77 Geo. L.J. 19 (1988) (commenting on the positivistic underpinnings of the Court's concept of "reasonable expectation of privacy" in fourth amendment cases), examined *infra*. Much of the focus of the interpretivist complaint is on a tradition of constitutional interpretation where the Supreme Court declares values (rights) to be fundamental where no explicit reference to the right is found in the text of the constitution. See the discussion on the Abortion Decision, *infra*, Chapter VII.

The New York State Legislature responded to *Roberson* by enacting a statutory cause of action for invasion of privacy in 1903. Sections 50 and 51 of the New York Civil Rights Act, the current privacy statute, are discussed in considerable detail, *infra*, Chapter VI.

E. RECOGNITION OF THE COMMON LAW RIGHT OF PRIVACY; THE APPROPRIATION TORT

PAVESICH v. NEW ENGLAND LIFE INS. CO.

122 Ga. 190, 50 S.E. 68 (1905).

COBB, J. . . .

[The defendant placed an advertisement in an Atlanta newspaper with a photograph of the plaintiff, and a caption reading "In my healthy and productive period of life I bought insurance in the New England Mutual Life Insurance Co., of Boston, Mass., and to-day my family is protected and I am drawing an annual dividend on my paid-up policies." The picture was obtained without the plaintiff's consent, and the plaintiff had never had a life-insurance policy with the defendant. The complaint contained one count of libel and one of invasion of privacy, and claimed $25,000 in damages. The court sustained a general demurrer, and the plaintiff excepted.]

Error from City Court of Atlanta; H.M. Reid, Judge. . . .

. . .

The individual surrenders to society many rights and privileges which he would be free to exercise in a state of nature, in exchange for the benefits which he receives as a member of society. But he is not presumed to surrender all those rights, and the public has no more right, without his consent, to invade the domain of those rights which it is necessarily to be presumed he has reserved, than he has to violate the valid regulations of the organized government under which he lives. The right of privacy has its foundation in the instincts of nature. It is recognized intuitively, consciousness being the witness that can be called to establish its existence. Any person whose intellect is in a normal condition recognizes at once that as to each individual member of society there are matters private, and there are matters public so far as the individual is concerned. Each individual as instinctively resents any encroachment by the public upon his rights which are of a private nature as he does the withdrawal of those of his rights which are of a public nature. A right of privacy in matters purely private is therefore derived from natural law. . . .

. . . All will admit that the individual who desires to live a life of seclusion cannot be compelled, against his consent, to exhibit his person in any public place, unless such exhibition is demanded by the law of the land. He may be required to come from his place of seclusion to perform public duties—to serve as a juror and to testify as a witness, and the like; but, when the public duty is once performed, if he exercises his liberty to go again into seclusion, no one can deny him the right. One who desires to live a life of partial seclusion has a right to choose the times, places, and manner in which and at which he will submit himself to the public gaze. Subject to the limitation above referred to, the body of a person cannot be put on exhibition at any time or at any place without his consent. The right of one to exhibit himself to the public at all proper times, in all proper places, and in a proper manner is embraced within the right of personal liberty. The right to withdraw from the public gaze at such times as a person may see fit, when his presence in public is not demanded by any rule of law, is also embraced within the right of personal liberty. Publicity in one instance, and privacy in the other, are each guaranteed. If personal liberty embraces the right of publicity, it no less embraces the correlative right of privacy, and this is no new idea in Georgia law. . . .

[The court then referred to instances under English, Roman and Constitutional law where the right to be let alone had been legally protected, and reasoned that the commercial use of a portrait was analogous to these instances. The court referred to the common law protection of individuals from excessive noise, eavesdroppers and common scolds, the Roman law prohibition against nonconsensual entry of the home, and the fourth amendment prohibition against unreasonable searches and seizures.]

It therefore follows from what has been said that a violation of the right of privacy is a direct invasion of a legal right of the individual. It is a tort, and it is not necessary that special damages should have accrued from its violation in order to entitle the aggrieved party to recover. Civ. Code 1895, section 3807. In an action for an invasion of such right the damages to be recovered are those for which the law authorizes a recovery in torts of that character, and, if the law authorizes a recovery of dangers for wounded feelings in other torts of a similar nature, such damages would be recoverable in an action for a violation of this right. . . .

. . .

As we have already said, cases may arise where it is difficult to determine on which side of the line of demarkation [sic] which separates the right of privacy from the well-established rights of others they are to be found; but we have little difficulty in arriving at the conclusion that the present case is one in which it has been established that the right of privacy has been invaded, and invaded by one who cannot claim exemption under the constitutional guaranties of freedom of speech and of the press. The form and features of the plaintiff are his own. The defendant insurance company and its agent had no more authority to display them in public for the purpose of advertising the business in which they were engaged than they would have had to compel the plaintiff to place himself upon exhibition for this purpose. The latter procedure would have been unauthorized and unjustifiable, as every one will admit, and the former was equally an invasion of the rights of his person. . . .

What we have ruled cannot be in any sense construed as an abridgment of the liberty of speech and of the press as guarantied [sic] in the Constitution. Whether the reproduction of a likeness of another which is free from caricature can in any sense be declared to be an exercise of the right to publish one's sentiments, certain it is that one who merely for advertising purposes, and from mercenary motives, publishes the likeness of another without his consent, cannot be said, in so doing, to have exercised the right to publish his sentiments.

Note on the Jurisprudence of Pavesich: Natural Law

Justice Cobb's opinion in the instant case, which was supported by all of the members of the Georgia high court, is a striking example of natural law philosophy providing a basis for expanding rights at common law. Natural law is a view of law which recognizes ideals of morality and justice as a central source of law. Under this view it is appropriate for a judge to look beyond positive rules and principles to notions of morality in society in order to decide cases. *See generally* George Christie and Patrick H. Martin, *Jurisprudence: Text and Readings on the Philosophy of Law* (1995). The idea that rights emanate from human nature is perhaps the core notion of natural law philosophy. But the basic tenet of natural law theory is that nature, God or reason sets the standard for human conduct and the law. Natural law theories provide that communities may judge the justice or injustice of their laws by appeal to recognizably objective, moral or social standards. St. Augustine, a fourth century North African Christian philosopher, provided natural law with its famous slogan that "an unjust law is no law at all," however, the roots of natural law philosophy extend into classical Greek thought. *See* Lloyd L. Weinreb, *Natural Law and Justice* (1987). Contemporary secular exponents of natural law provide that principles of natural law known to human reason require that legal authority be exercised in accordance with the rule of law and with respect for natural human rights.

The influential natural law philosophy of John Locke was secular in its origin. From a pregovernmental state of nature, government and laws evolved from a social compact between individuals and the state. Locke, *Second Treatise on Civil Government* (1690). Contemporary natural law writers focus on morality as it develops from social interaction and everyday moral discourse. This conventional morality is a source of the moral principles of contemporary natural law. For examples of the range of modern natural law philosophy, *see* David A. J. Richards, *The Moral Criticism of Law* (1977); Ronald Dworkin, *Taking Rights Seriously* (1977); Ronald Dworkin, *Natural Law Revisited*, 34 U. Fla. L. Rev. 165 (1982); John Finnis, *Natural Law and Natural Rights* (1980); Michael Perry, *The Constitution, the Courts and Human Rights* (1982); Harry H. Wellington, *Common Law Rules and Constitutional Double Standards: Some Notes on Adjudication*, 83 Yale L. J. 221 (1973). As the materials that follow demonstrate, much of the evolution of legal privacy rights is justified on a natural law basis.

F. CONSOLIDATION OF THE TORT RIGHT OF PRIVACY

WILLIAM L. PROSSER, PRIVACY

48 Calif. L. Rev. 383, 388–89 (1960).

In the year 1890 Mrs. Samuel D. Warren, a young matron of Boston, which is a large city in Massachusetts, held at her home a series of social entertainments on an elaborate scale. She was the daughter of Senator Bayard of Delaware, and her husband was a wealthy young paper manufacturer, who only the year before had given up the practice of law to devote himself to an inherited business. Socially, Mrs. Warren was among the èlite [sic]; and the newspapers of Boston, and in particular the *Saturday Evening Gazette*, which specialized in "blue blood" items, covered her parties in highly personal and embarrassing detail. It was the era of "yellow journalism," when the press had begun to resort to excesses in the way of prying that have become more or less commonplace today; and Boston was perhaps, of all of the cities in the country, the one in which a lady and a gentleman kept their names and their personal affairs out of the papers. The matter came to a head when the newspapers had a field day on the occasion of the wedding of a daughter, and Mr. Warren became annoyed. It was an annoyance for which the press, the advertisers and the entertainment industry of America were to pay dearly over the next seventy years.

Mr. Warren turned to his recent law partner, Louis D. Brandeis, who was destined not to be unknown to history. The result was a noted article, *The Right to Privacy*, in the *Harvard Law Review*, upon which the two men collaborated. It has come to be regarded as the outstanding example of the influence of legal periodicals upon the American law. In the Harvard Law School Class of 1877 the two authors had stood respectively second and first, and both of them were gifted with scholarship, imagination, and ability. Internal evidences of style, and the probabilities of the situation, suggest that the writing, and perhaps most of the research, was done by Brandeis; but it was undoubtedly a joint effort, to which both men contributed their ideas.

. . .

. . . At the present time the right of privacy, in one form or another, is declared to exist by the overwhelming majority of the American courts. . . .

At the time of writing the right of privacy stands rejected only by a 1909 decision in Rhode Island, and by more recent ones in Nebraska, Texas, and Wisconsin, which have said that any change in the old common law must be for the legislature, and which have not gone without criticism.

In nearly every jurisdiction the first decisions were understandably preoccupied with the question whether the right of privacy existed at all, and gave little or no consideration to what it would amount to if it did. It is only in recent years, and largely through the legal writers, that there has been any attempt to inquire what interests are we protecting, and against what conduct. Today, with something over three hundred cases in the books, the holes in the jigsaw puzzle have been largely filled in, and some rather definite conclusions are possible.

What has emerged from the decisions is no simple matter. It is not one tort, but a complex of four. The law of privacy comprises four distinct kinds of invasion of four different interests of the plaintiff, which are tied together by the common name, but otherwise have almost nothing in common except that each represents an interference with the right of the plaintiff, in the phrase coined by Judge Cooley, "to be let alone." Without any attempt to exact definition, these four torts may be described as follows:

1. Intrusion upon the plaintiff's seclusion or solitude, or into his private affairs.

2. Public disclosure of embarrassing private facts about the plaintiff.

3. Publicity which places the plaintiff in a false light in the public eye.

4. Appropriation, for the defendant's advantage, of the plaintiff's name or likeness.

It should be obvious at once that these four types of invasion may be subject, in some respects at least, to different rules; and that when what is said as to any one of them is carried over to another, it may not be at all applicable, and confusion may follow.

Note on the Prosser Article

The disparate tort theory and the four part interest analysis that Dean Prosser developed to explain the appellate court decisions recognizing privacy rights was incorporated into the Second Restatement of Torts. The Prosser article and the Restatement have had a significant influence on the tort right to privacy.

The four privacy torts concepts reflected by section 652, summarized on the following page, are sometimes referred to with the short-hand expressions: The Intrusion Tort (section 652B); The Appropriation Tort (section 652C); The Private Facts Tort (section 652D); and The False Light Tort (section 652E). The Restatement is generally embraced by courts as an initial premise in analysis of tort privacy claims. However, as the materials that follow indicate, many jurisdictions depart from the Restatement position on some issues and other issues are not addressed by the Restatement.

DEAN BLOUSTEIN'S HUMAN DIGNITY THESIS

In 1964, Edward Bloustein argued persuasively against Prosser's disparate tort theory of privacy in *Privacy as an Aspect of Human Dignity: An Answer to Dean Prosser*, 39 N.Y.U.L. Rev. 962 (1964). Bloustein's position is that tort, constitutional and statutory protection for informational privacy reflect a unified concept, namely, protection for individual liberty to do as we will and from the affront to human dignity that occurs when individuals and the government invade our privacy. Bloustein, as noted in the introductory materials, is a major theorist in the personhood human dignity school. The centerpiece of his position is that emotional distress is not the core injury incurred when privacy rights are violated. He supports this view by (1) pointing to the distinctions between the legal requirements of the intentional infliction of emotional distress tort and the privacy torts, and (2) showing in fourth amendment cases that the gist of the injury is deprivation of liberty of the person and privacy, not emotional equanimity. According to Bloustein the emotional distress one feels when the condition of privacy is lost is the *consequence* of the affront to dignity that has occurred. Emotional distress is the measure of one's damages, but affront to human dignity is the basis of one's legal injury.

G. RESTATEMENT DEFINITIONS OF COMMON LAW PRIVACY ACTIONS

PRIVACY

Chapter 28A

INVASION OF PRIVACY

Restatement (Second) of Torts Sections 652B, C, D, E

1. Section 652B. Intrusion upon Seclusion.

One who intentionally intrudes, physically or otherwise, upon the solitude or seclusion of another or his private affairs or concerns, is subject to liability to the other for invasion of his privacy, if the intrusion would be highly offensive to a reasonable person.

2. Section 652C. Appropriation of Name or Likeness.

One who appropriates to his own use or benefit the name or likeness of another is subject to liability to the other for invasion of his privacy.

3.   Section 652D. Publicity Given to Private Life.

One who gives publicity to a matter concerning the private life of another is subject to liability to the other for invasion of his privacy, if the matter publicized is of a kind that

>   (a) would be highly offensive to a reasonable person, and

>   (b) is not of legitimate concern to the public.

4.   Section 652E. Publicity Placing Person in False Light.

One who gives publicity to a matter concerning another that places the other before the public in a false light is subject to liability to the other for invasion of his privacy, if

>   (a) the false light in which the other was placed would be highly offensive to a reasonable person, and

>   (b) the actor had knowledge or acted in reckless disregard as to the falsity of the publicized matter and the false light in which the other would be placed.

H.   DISCOVERY OF A CONSTITUTIONAL RIGHT OF PRIVACY

GRISWOLD v. CONNECTICUT

381 U.S. 479 (1965)

MR. JUSTICE DOUGLAS delivered the opinion of the Court. . . .

[Enforcement of the Connecticut birth control statute led to the conviction in a "test case" of the executive and medical directors of the Planned Parenthood League of Connecticut, Estelle Griswold and Dr. C. Lee Buxton. Convicted as accessories for giving married persons information, instruction and medical advice concerning the means of preventing conception, each was fined $100. Appellants alleged at trial that the statute as applied violated the Fourteenth Amendment.]

We think that appellants have standing to raise the constitutional rights of the married people with whom they had a professional relationship. . . . The rights of husband and wife, pressed here, are likely to be diluted or adversely affected unless those rights are considered in a suit involving those who have this kind of confidential relation to them.

Coming to the merits, we are met with a wide range of questions that implicate the Due Process Clause of the Fourteenth Amendment. Overtones of some arguments suggest that Lochner v. New York, 198 U.S. 45, should be our guide. . . . We do not sit as a super-legislature to determine the wisdom, need, and propriety of laws that touch economic problems, business affairs, or social conditions. This law, however, operates directly on an intimate relation of husband and wife and their physician's role in one aspect of that relation.

The association of people is not mentioned in the Constitution nor in the Bill of Rights. The right to educate a child in a school of the parent's choice—whether public or private or parochial—is also not mentioned. Nor is the right to study any particular subject or any foreign language. Yet the First Amendment has been construed to include certain of those rights.

By Pierce v. Society of Sisters, 268 U.S. 510, the right to educate one's children as one chooses is made applicable to the States by the force of the First and Fourteenth Amendments. By Meyer v. Nebraska, 262 U.S. 390, the same dignity is given the right to study the German language in a private school. In other words, the State may not, consistently with the spirit of the First Amendment, contract the spectrum of available knowledge. The right of freedom of speech and press includes not only the right to utter or to print, but the right to distribute, the right to receive, the right to read . . . and freedom of inquiry, freedom of thought, and freedom to teach. . . .

In NAACP v. Alabama, 357 U.S. 449, 462, we protected the "freedom to associate and privacy in one's associations," noting that freedom of association was a peripheral First Amendment right. . . . In like context, we have protected forms of "association" that . . . pertain to the social, legal, and economic benefit of the members. NAACP v. Button, 371 U.S. 415, 430–431.

The foregoing cases suggest that specific guarantees in the Bill of Rights have penumbras, formed by emanations from those guarantees that help give them life and substance. See Poe v. Ullman, 367 U.S. 497, 516–522 (dissenting opinion). Various guarantees create zones of privacy. The right of association contained in the penumbra of the First Amendment is one, as we have seen. The Third Amendment in its prohibition against the quartering of soldiers "in any house" in time of peace without the consent of the owner is another facet of privacy. The Fourth Amendment explicitly affirms the "right of the people to be secure in their persons, houses, papers, and effects, against unreasonable searches and seizures." The Fifth Amendment in its Self–Incrimination Clause enables the citizen to create a zone of privacy which government may not force him to surrender to his detriment. The Ninth Amendment provides: "The enumeration in the Constitution, of certain rights, shall not be construed to deny or disparage others retained by the people." . . .

We have had many controversies over these penumbral rights of "privacy and repose." See, e.g., Breard v. Alexandria, 341 U.S. 622, 626, 644; Public Utilities Comm'n v. Pollak, 343 U.S. 451; Monroe v. Pape, 365 U.S. 167; Lanza v. New York, 370 U.S. 139; Frank v. Maryland, 359 U.S. 360; Skinner v. Oklahoma, 316 U.S. 535, 541. These cases bear witness that the right of privacy which presses for recognition here is a legitimate one.

The present case, then, concerns a relationship lying within the zone of privacy created by several fundamental constitutional guarantees. And it concerns a law which, in forbidding the *use* of contraceptives rather than regulating their manufacture or sale, seeks to achieve its goals by means having a maximum destructive impact upon that relationship. Such a law cannot stand in light of the familiar principle, so often applied by this Court, that a "governmental purpose to control or prevent activities constitutionally subject to state regulation may not be achieved by means which sweep unnecessarily broadly and thereby invade the area of protected freedoms." ... Would we allow the police to search the sacred precincts of marital bedrooms for telltale signs of the use of contraceptives? The very idea is repulsive to the notions of privacy surrounding the marriage relationship.

We deal with a right of privacy older than the Bill of Rights—older than our political parties, older than our school system. Marriage is a coming together for better or for worse, hopefully enduring, and intimate to the degree of being sacred. It is an association that promotes a way of life, not causes; a harmony in living, not political faiths; a bilateral loyalty, not commercial or social projects. Yet it is an association for as noble a purpose as any involved in our prior decisions. Reversed.

MR. JUSTICE GOLDBERG, whom the CHIEF JUSTICE and MR. JUSTICE BRENNAN join, concurring.

.   .   .

The language and history of the Ninth Amendment reveal that the Framers of the Constitution believed that there are additional fundamental rights, protected from governmental infringement, which exist alongside those fundamental rights specifically mentioned in the first eight constitutional amendments.

The Ninth Amendment reads, "The enumeration in the Constitution, of certain rights, shall not be construed to deny or disparage others retained by the people." The Amendment is almost entirely the work of James Madison. It was introduced in Congress by him and passed the House and Senate with little or no debate and virtually no change in language. It was proffered to quiet expressed fears that a bill of specifically enumerated rights ... could not be sufficiently broad to cover all essential rights and that the specific mention of certain rights would be interpreted as a denial that others were protected....

While this Court has had little occasion to interpret the Ninth Amendment ... "[i]t cannot be presumed that any clause in the constitution is intended to be without effect." Marbury v. Madison, 1 Cranch 137, 174....

In determining which rights are fundamental, judges are not left at large to decide cases in light of their personal and private notions. Rather, they must look to the "traditions and [collective] conscience of our people" to determine whether a principle is "so rooted [there] ... as to be ranked as fundamental." Snyder v. Massachusetts, 291 U.S. 97,

105. The inquiry is whether a right involved "is of such a character that it cannot be denied without violating those 'fundamental principles of liberty and justice which lie at the base of all our civil and political institutions'...." Powell v. Alabama, 287 U.S. 45, 67....

I agree fully with the Court that, applying these tests, the right of privacy is a fundamental personal right....

The Connecticut statutes here involved deal with a particularly important and sensitive area of privacy—that of the marital relation and the marital home.... Although the Constitution does not speak in so many words of the right of privacy in marriage, I cannot believe that it offers these fundamental rights no protection....

Finally ... the Court's holding today ... in no way interferes with a State's proper regulation of sexual promiscuity or misconduct. [quoting Harlan's dissent in Poe v. Ullman at 553, observing that, unlike marriage, "adultery, homosexuality and the like are sexual intimacies which the state forbids."]

In sum, I believe the right of privacy in the marital relation is fundamental and basic—a personal right "retained by the people" within the meaning of the Ninth Amendment.... I agree with the Court that petitioners' convictions must therefore be reversed.

MR. JUSTICE HARLAN, concurring in the judgment.

I fully agree with the judgment of reversal, but find myself unable to join the Court's opinion....

In my view, the proper constitutional inquiry in this case is whether this Connecticut statute infringes the Due Process Clause of the Fourteenth Amendment because the enactment violates basic values "implicit in the concept of ordered liberty." Palko v. Connecticut, 302 U.S. 319, 325. For reasons stated at length in my dissenting opinion in Poe v. Ullman, I believe that it does.

MR. JUSTICE WHITE, concurring in the judgment. In my view this Connecticut law as applied to married couples deprives them of "liberty" without due process of law, as that concept is used in the Fourteenth Amendment.

MR. JUSTICE BLACK, with whom MR. JUSTICE STEWART joins, dissenting.

... I get nowhere in this case by talk about a constitutional "right of privacy" as an emanation from one or more constitutional provisions. I like my privacy as well as the next one, but I am nevertheless compelled to admit that government has a right to invade it unless prohibited by some specific constitutional provision....

... Surely it has to be admitted that no provision of the Constitution specifically gives such blanket power to courts to exercise such a supervisory veto over the wisdom and value of legislative policies and to

hold unconstitutional those laws which they believe unwise or dangerous.... While I completely subscribe to the holding of Marbury v.
Madison, 1 Cranch 137, and subsequent cases, that our Court has
constitutional power to strike down statutes, state or federal, that violate
commands of the Federal Constitution, I do not believe that we are
granted power by the Due Process Clause or any other constitutional
provision or provisions to measure constitutionality by our belief that
legislation is arbitrary, capricious or unreasonable, or accomplishes no
justifiable purpose, or is offensive to our own notions of "civilized
standards of conduct." Such an appraisal of the wisdom of legislation is
an attribute of the power to make laws, not of the power to interpret
them.

I realize that many good and able men have eloquently spoken and
written, sometimes in rhapsodical strains, about the duty of this Court
to keep the Constitution in tune with the times. The idea is that the
Constitution must be changed from time to time and that this Court is
charged with a duty to make those changes. For myself, I must with all
deference reject that philosophy. The Constitution makers knew the
need for change and provided for it. Amendments suggested by the
people's elected representatives can be submitted to the people or their
selected agents for ratification.... I cannot rely on the Due Process
Clause or the Ninth Amendment or any mysterious and uncertain
natural law concept as a reason for striking down this state law.

Mr. Justice Stewart, whom Mr. Justice Black joins, dissenting.

... We are not asked in this case to say whether we think this law is
unwise, or even asinine. We are asked to hold that it violates the United
States Constitution. And that I cannot do.

... It is the essence of judicial duty to subordinate our own personal
views, our own ideas of what legislation is wise and what is not. If, as I
should surely hope, the law before us does not reflect the standards of
the people of Connecticut, [they] can freely exercise their true Ninth and
Tenth Amendment rights to persuade their elected representatives to
repeal it. That is the constitutional way to take this law off the
books....

Note

Griswold v. Connecticut is the first decision squarely holding that the
Constitution protects a right of privacy independent of the fourth amendment. Since *Griswold* numerous Supreme Court cases, including the abortion decision in *Roe v. Wade*, 410 U.S. 113 (1973), have extended the right of
privacy first established in *Griswold*. The case law is sufficiently extensive to
view this line of cases as a separate branch of the legal right of privacy
(privacy and autonomy) which is treated exhaustively in Chapter VII of these
materials.

I. CONSOLIDATION OF THE CONSTITUTIONAL RIGHT TO PRIVACY

WHALEN v. ROE

429 U.S. 589 (1977).

MR. JUSTICE STEVENS delivered the opinion of the Court.

[In 1972 the New York Legislature enacted a statute which classifies potentially harmful drugs and provides that prescriptions for the most dangerous legitimate drugs (Schedule II) be prepared on an official form. One copy of the form, which identifies the prescribing physician, dispensing pharmacy, drug and dosage, and patient's name, address and age, must be filed with a central registry at the state Health Department. The Health Department logs the forms, records the data on magnetic tapes for processing by a computer, and then stores the forms in a room which is surrounded by a locked wire fence and protected by an alarm system. The computer tapes are kept in a locked cabinet, and the computer is run "off-line" when the tapes are run, so that no terminal outside the computer room can read or record any information on the tapes. Public disclosure of the identity of patients is expressly prohibited by the statute, except when disclosure is made: (1) to another person employed by the Department; (2) pursuant to judicial subpoena or court order; (3) to a government agency authorized to regulate a person who is authorized by the statute to deal in controlled substances; or (4) to the central registry at the Department.

A few days before the statute became effective, this litigation was commenced by a group of patients regularly receiving prescriptions for Schedule II drugs, by prescribing doctors, and by two associations of physicians. The plaintiffs offered evidence tending to prove that people in need of Schedule II drugs may decline such treatment because of a fear that the misuse of the computerized data could cause them to be stigmatized as "drug addicts." The District Court enjoined enforcement of the provisions of the statute dealing with the reporting of patients' names and addresses, holding that the doctor-patient relationship is a zone of privacy accorded constitutional protection and that the identification provisions invaded that zone. The case came before the Supreme Court on direct appeal under a procedure used under the Three Judge Court Act, which was repealed in 1976. See Pub. L. No. 94–381, 90 Stat. 1119, section 3.]

The constitutional question presented is whether the State of New York may record, in a centralized computer file, the names and addresses of all persons who have obtained, pursuant to a doctor's prescription, certain drugs for which there is both a lawful and an unlawful market. . . .

The New York statute challenged in this case represents a considered attempt to deal with such a problem. It is manifestly the product of an orderly and rational legislative decision. It was recommended by a specially appointed commission which held extensive hearings on the proposed legislation, and drew on experience with similar programs in other States. There surely was nothing unreasonable in the assumption that the patient-identification requirement might aid in the enforcement of laws designed to minimize the misuse of dangerous drugs. For the requirement could reasonably be expected to have a deterrent effect on potential violators as well as to aid in the detection or investigation of specific instances of apparent abuse. At the very least, it would seem clear that the State's vital interest in controlling the distribution of dangerous drugs would support a decision to experiment with new techniques for control. For if an experiment fails—if in this case experience teaches that the patient-identification requirement results in the foolish expenditure of funds to acquire a mountain of useless information—the legislative process remains available to terminate the unwise experiment. It follows that the legislature's enactment of the patient-identification requirement was a reasonable exercise of New York's broad police powers. . . .

Appellees contend that the statute invades a constitutionally protected "zone of privacy." The cases sometimes characterized as protecting "privacy" have in fact involved at least two different kinds of interests. One is the individual interest in avoiding disclosure of personal matters, and another is the interest in independence in making certain kinds of important decisions. Appellees argue that both of these interests are impaired by this statute. The mere existence in readily available form of the information about patients' use of Schedule II drugs creates a genuine concern that the information will become publicly known and that it will adversely affect their reputations. This concern makes some patients reluctant to use, and some doctors reluctant to prescribe, such drugs even when their use is medically indicated. It follows, they argue, that the making of decisions about matters vital to the care of their health is inevitably affected by the statute. Thus, the statute threatens to impair both their interest in the nondisclosure of private information and also their interest in making important decisions independently.

We are persuaded, however, that the New York program does not, on its face, pose a sufficiently grievous threat to either interest to establish a constitutional violation.

Public disclosure of patient information can come about in three ways. Health department employees may violate the statute by failing, either deliberately or negligently, to maintain proper security. A patient or a doctor may be accused of a violation and the stored data may be offered in evidence in a judicial proceeding. Or, thirdly, a doctor, a pharmacist, or the patient may voluntarily reveal information on a prescription form.

The third possibility existed under the prior law and is entirely unrelated to the existence of the computerized data bank. Neither of the other two possibilities provides a proper ground for attacking the statute as invalid on its face. There is no support in the record, or in the experience of the two States that New York has emulated, for an assumption that the security provisions of the statute will be administered improperly. And the remote possibility that judicial supervision of the evidentiary use of particular items of stored information will provide inadequate protection against unwarranted disclosures is surely not a sufficient reason for invalidating the entire patient-identification program.

Even without public disclosure, it is, of course, true that private information must be disclosed to the authorized employees of the New York Department of Health. Such disclosures, however, are not significantly different from those that were required under the prior law. Nor are they meaningfully distinguishable from a host of other unpleasant invasions of privacy that are associated with many facets of health care. Unquestionably, some individuals' concern for their own privacy may lead them to avoid or to postpone needed medical attention. Nevertheless, disclosures of private medical information to doctors, to hospital personnel, to insurance companies, and to public health agencies are often an essential part of modern medical practice even when the disclosure may reflect unfavorably on the character of the patient. Requiring such disclosures to representatives of the State having responsibility for the health of the community, does not automatically amount to an impermissible invasion of privacy.

Appellees also argue, however, that even if unwarranted disclosures do not actually occur, the knowledge that the information is readily available in a computerized file creates a genuine concern that causes some persons to decline needed medication. The record supports the conclusion that some use of Schedule II drugs has been discouraged by that concern; it also is clear, however, that about 100,000 prescriptions for such drugs were being filled each month prior to the entry of the District Court's injunction. Clearly, therefore, the statute did not deprive the public of access to the drugs.

Nor can it be said that any individual has been deprived of the right to decide independently, with the advice of his physician, to acquire and to use needed medication. Although the State no doubt could prohibit entirely the use of particular Schedule II drugs, it has not done so. This case is therefore unlike those in which the Court held that a total prohibition of certain conduct was an impermissible deprivation of liberty. Nor does the State require access to these drugs to be conditioned on the consent of any State official or other third party. Within dosage limits which appellees do not challenge, the decision to prescribe, or to use, is left entirely to the physician and the patient.

We hold that neither the immediate nor the threatened impact of the patient-identification requirements in the New York State Controlled Substances Act of 1972 on either the reputation or the independence of patients for whom Schedule II drugs are medically indicated is sufficient to constitute an invasion of any right or liberty protected by the Fourteenth Amendment. . . .

A final word about issues we have not decided. We are not unaware of the threat to privacy implicit in the accumulation of vast amounts of personal information in computerized data banks or other massive government files. The collection of taxes, the distribution of welfare and social security benefits, the supervision of public health, the direction of our Armed Forces, and the enforcement of the criminal laws all require the orderly preservation of great quantities of information, much of which is personal in character and potentially embarrassing or harmful if disclosed. The right to collect and use such data for public purposes is typically accompanied by a concomitant statutory or regulatory duty to avoid unwarranted disclosures. Recognizing that in some circumstances that duty arguably has its roots in the Constitution, nevertheless New York's statutory scheme, and its implementing administrative procedures, evidence a proper concern with, and protection of, the individual's interest in privacy. We therefore need not, and do not, decide any question which might be presented by the unwarranted disclosure of accumulated private data—whether intentional or unintentional—or by a system that did not contain comparable security provisions. We simply hold that this record does not establish an invasion of any right or liberty protected by the Fourteenth Amendment.

Reversed.

MR. JUSTICE BRENNAN, concurring.

I write only to express my understanding of the opinion of the Court, which I join.

The New York statute under attack requires doctors to disclose to the State information about prescriptions for certain drugs with a high potential for abuse, and provides for the storage of that information in a central computer file. The Court recognizes that an individual's "interest in avoiding disclosure of personal matters" is an aspect of the right of privacy, but holds that in this case, any such interest has not been seriously enough invaded by the State to require a showing that its program was indispensable to the State's effort to control drug abuse. The information disclosed by the physician under this program is made available only to a small number of public health officials with a legitimate interest in the information. As the record makes clear, New York has long required doctors to make this information available to its officials on request, and that practice is not challenged here. Such limited reporting requirements in the medical field are familiar, and are not generally regarded as an invasion of privacy. Broad dissemination by state officials of such information, however, would clearly implicate constitutionally protected privacy rights, and would presumably be justified only by compelling state interests. See, e.g., Roe v. Wade.

What is more troubling about this scheme, however, is the central computer storage of the data thus collected. Obviously, as the State argues, collection and storage of data by the State that is in itself legitimate is not rendered unconstitutional simply because new technology makes the State's operations more efficient. However, as the example of the Fourth Amendment shows, the Constitution puts limits not only on the type of information the State may gather, but also on the means it may use to gather it. The central storage and easy accessibility of computerized data vastly increase the potential for abuse of that information, and I am not prepared to say that future developments will not demonstrate the necessity of some curb on such technology. In this case, as the Court's opinion makes clear, the State's carefully designed program includes numerous safeguards intended to forestall the danger of indiscriminate disclosure. Given this serious and, so far as the record shows, successful effort to prevent abuse and limit access to the personal information at issue, I cannot say that the statute's provisions for computer storage, on their face, amount to a deprivation of constitutionally protected privacy interests, any more than the more traditional reporting provisions. . . .

Mr. Justice Stewart, concurring.

In Katz v. United States, the Court made clear that although the Constitution affords protection against certain kinds of government intrusions into personal and private matters, there is no "general constitutional 'right to privacy.' . . . [T]he protection of a person's *general* right to privacy—his right to be let alone by other people—is, like the protection of his property and of his very life, left largely to the law of the individual States."

Mr. Justice Brennan's concurring opinion states that "(b)road dissemination by state officials of [the information collected by New York State] . . . would clearly implicate constitutionally protected privacy rights. . . ."

The only possible support in his opinion for this statement is its earlier reference to two footnotes in the Court's opinion.

The footnotes, however, cite to only two Court opinions, and those two cases do not support the proposition advanced by Mr. Justice Brennan.

The first case referred to [is] Griswold v. Connecticut. . . . Whatever the *ratio decidendi* of *Griswold*, it does not recognize a general interest in freedom from disclosure of private information.

The other case referred to, [is] Stanley v. Georgia. . . . Although *Stanley* makes some reference to privacy rights, the holding there was simply that the *First* Amendment—as made applicable to the States by the Fourteenth—protects a person's right to read what he chooses in circumstances where that choice poses no threat to the sensibilities or welfare of others.

Upon the understanding that nothing the Court says today is contrary to the above views, I join its opinion and judgment.

Note on Whalen v. Roe: Consolidation of the Constitutional Right to Privacy

Whalen is the first case in which the Supreme Court squarely faced the question of whether the constitutional right to privacy encompasses the collection, storage and dissemination of information in government data banks. The majority opinion written by Justice Stevens assumes as a basis of its holding that constitutional privacy rights are implicated in the acquiring, storage and dissemination of information by state agencies. Only Justice Stewart in concurrence rejects this interpretation of the case, but his view seems at odds with the clear import of the general text of Justice Stevens's opinion. *Whalen* is also the first Supreme Court decision in which the Court acknowledged that the constitutional right of privacy consists of two branches, informational privacy and privacy-autonomy. In a passage of considerable significance, Justice Stevens states:

> Appellees contend that the statute invades a constitutionally protected "zone of privacy." The cases sometimes characterized as protecting "privacy" have in fact involved at least two different kinds of interests. One is the individual interest in avoiding disclosure of personal matters, and another is the interest in independence in making certain kinds of important decisions.

429 U.S. at 598–99.

Whalen is also important because it is an example of judicial recognition that constitutional protection for limiting government access to personal confidential or intimate information about individuals is not confined to unreasonable searches and seizures in violation of the fourth amendment.

The Supreme Court held that constitutional protection of informational privacy is not limited to fourth amendment governmental activities in *Nixon v. Administrator of General Services*, 433 U.S. 425 (1977). In that case the Court rejected the former president's challenge to the Presidential Recordings and Materials Preservation Act of 1974. A majority of the Court, however, assumed in sustaining the statute that the former president had a constitutionally protectable privacy interest in avoiding disclosure of personal matters in respect to some of the taped conversations and papers covered by the Act. However, the Court found the governmental interest promoted by the statute to override the privacy interest. The supposition by the Court in *Whalen* and *Nixon* that in appropriate circumstances the acquiring and dissemination of information about a person implicates a constitutional right to privacy that is independent of the fourth amendment is explored in a later section of these materials. *See generally* Richard C. Turkington, *Legacy of the Warren and Brandeis Article: The Emerging Unencumbered Constitutional Right To Informational Privacy*, 10 N. Ill. U.L. Rev. 479 (1990).

J. THE FEDERAL STATUTORY DEVELOPMENT

In a relatively short period of time from 1968 to 1978, Congress enacted six statutes that began an era of protecting informational privacy through legislation that regulates the acquiring, storage and dissemination of certain kinds of information. The first of these, the Omnibus Crime Control and Safe Street Act of 1968, U.S.C.A. §§ 2510–2520 (West Supp. 1970), initially regulated the use of electronic devices to eavesdrop on conversations. The Fair Credit Reporting Act, 15 U.S.C.A. § 1681–81t (1970), provides some privacy protection for information in credit reports. The Family Educational Rights and Privacy Act of 1974, 20 U.S.C.A. §§ 1232g(a)–1232g(g) (1983 & Supp. IV 1986), provides some rights to parents and students for information in school records. The privacy of information in criminal justice record systems is a subject of the Crime Control Act of 1973, 42 U.S.C.A. § 3789g (1982 and Supp. III 1985). Information in the computerized records of the federal government and in the banking records of financial institutions were the subjects of the 1974 Privacy Act, 5 U.S.C.A. § 552a(a)–552a(g) (West 1977 and Supp. 1988), and the Right to Financial Privacy Act of 1978, 12 U.S.C.A. § 3401 (1982 and Supp. III 1985). The Right to Privacy Protection Act of 1980, 42 U.S.C.A. § 2000aa (1998) establishes standards for law enforcement agencies to access records and other information in the possession of newspapers or the media.

The Electronic Funds Transfer Act of 1980, 15 U.S.C.A. § 1693–1693r(1988) provides notice for routine third party disclosure of personal records made by an automated transfer of money. In 1986 Congress enacted The Electronic Communications Privacy Act (ECPA) as an amendment to Title III of the Omnibus Crime Control and Safe Streets Act of 1968. The ECPA was enacted to update federal privacy protection in view of the changes in telecommunications spawned by computer and digital technologies. ECPA is codified in 18 U.S.C.A. §§ 2510–2522, 2701–2711; 3121–3127 (1994). Video rental and purchase records are provided security in the Video Privacy Protection Act, 18 U.S.C.A. § 2710 (1994). The Employee Polygraph Protection Act, 29 U.S.C.A. §§ 20001–2009 (1988) limits private sector employers from using polygraph examinations of prospective employees. The Computer Matching and Privacy Protection Act of 1988 (CMA), 5 U.S.C.A. § 552a(1988) establishes procedures for monitoring of computer matching practices of federal agencies. The 1994 Drivers Privacy Protection Act, 18 U.S.C.A. §§ 2721–2725 (1994) (Effective 1997) restricts state department of motor vehicle agencies from certain disclosures and use of personal information in motor vehicle records. The Telecommunications Act of 1996, 47 U.S.C.A. § 222 (West. Supp. 1997) limits disclosure by telecommunication carriers of customer proprietary information. The statutory privacy development continues today at both the state and federal levels and has been expanded into additional areas such as the use of polygraph examinations. This development is more fully examined in later chapters of this book.

K. DEFINITIONS OF PRIVACY

. . . "Conduct which can be described as indecent is always in one way or another a violation of privacy." J.F. Stephen, *Liberty, Equality, Fraternity*, 160 (1967; 1st ed. 1873).

... "[T]he right to live one's life in seclusion, without being subjected to unwarranted and undesirable publicity. In short, it is the right to be let alone." *Melvin v. Reid*, 112 Cal.App. 285, 289, 297 P. 91, 92 (1931).

"A person who unreasonably and seriously interferes with another's interest in not having his affairs known to others or his likeness exhibited to the public is liable to the other." Restatement (First) of Torts section 867 (1939).

... "[T]he right of a person to be free from unwarranted publicity, ... [or] ... the unwarranted appropriation or exploitation of one's personality, the publicizing of one's private affairs with which the public has no legitimate concern, or the wrongful intrusion into one's private activities, in such manner as to outrage or cause mental suffering, shame, or humiliation to a person of ordinary sensibilities." 41 Am. Jur. *Privacy* section 2 (1942).

... "[P]rivacy exists where the persons whose actions engender or become the objects of information retain possession of that information, and any flow outward of that information from the persons to whom it refers (and who share it where more than one person is involved) occurs on the initiative of its possessors." Edward Shils, *Privacy: Its Constitution and Vicissitudes*, 31 Law & Contemp. Probs. 281, 282 (1966).

... "[T]he condition of human life in which acquaintance with a person or with affairs of his life which are personal to him is limited." Hyman Gross, *The Concept of Privacy*, 42 N.Y.U. L. Rev. 34, 36 (1967).

... "[C]laim of individuals, groups or institutions to determine for themselves when, how, and to what extent information about them is communicated to others." Alan Westin, *Privacy and Freedom*, 7 (1967).

... "That area of a man's life which, in any given circumstance, a reasonable man with an understanding of the legitimate needs of the community would think it wrong to invade." *Privacy and the Law, A Report by the British Section of International Comm'n of Justice*, 19 (1970).

... "[C]ontrol we have over information about ourselves." Charles Fried, *An Anatomy of Values*, 140 (1970).

... "Privacy is the exclusive access of a person (or other legal entity) to a realm of his own." Ernest van den Haag, *On Privacy*, Nomos XIII *Privacy* 149 (1971).

... "Control over who can sense us." Richard B. Parker, *A Definition of Privacy*, 27 Rut. L. Rev. 275, 281 (1974).

... "Privacy is a social ritual by means of which an individual's moral title to his own existence is conferred. Privacy is an essential part of the complex social practice by means of which the social group recognizes—and communicates to the individual—that his existence is his own." Jeffrey H. Reiman, *Privacy, Intimacy and Personhood*, 8 Philosophy and Public Affairs 26 (1976).

... "[A]utonomy or control over the intimacies of personal identity." Tom Gerety, *Redefining Privacy*, 12 Harv. C.R.-C.L. L. Rev. 233, 236 (1977).

... "[P]rivacy is a limitation of others' access to an individual.... [A] person enjoys *perfect* privacy when he is completely inaccessible to others.... In perfect privacy no one has information about X, no one pays attention to X, and no one has physical access to X." Ruth Gavison, *Privacy and the Limits of Law*, 89 Yale L.J. 421, 429 (1980).

... "[Privacy] is the condition of being protected from unwanted access by others—either physical access, personal information or attention." Sissela Bok, *Secrets*, 10 (1982).

... "[P]rivacy denotes a degree of inaccessibility of persons, their mental states, and information about them to the senses and surveillance of others." Anita L. Allen, *Uneasy Access: Privacy for Women in a Free Society*, 34 (1988).

Chapter Two

INFORMATIONAL PRIVACY

A. INTRODUCTION

This chapter investigates the legal protection afforded individuals when governmental officials, business entities or private individuals invade their privacy by acquiring or disseminating information about their personal affairs. "Informational privacy" is a shorthand expression that will be used throughout these materials to identify that factual condition in life that embodies concern about limiting acquaintance with personal affairs. Informational privacy is probably the sense of privacy that is of concern most often in ordinary life. Basic social practices of locking file cabinets and desks, wearing clothes, utilizing window blinds and closing bedroom doors reflect our everyday concern about informational privacy. Maintaining informational privacy may require limiting access to persons as well as to sources of facts about them.

Individuals have a legal right to informational privacy if the legal system would protect them against loss of the condition of informational privacy that is caused by the actions of governmental officials, business entities or private persons. The legal protection against loss of informational privacy might take the form of a damage award, injunction or declaratory judgment. A broad range of legal theories are utilized to vindicate the right to informational privacy. Informational privacy rights may be asserted under federal or state constitutions, federal and state legislation or agency regulations or on the basis of the common law of torts. A comprehensive investigation of all of the facets of protection in our legal system for informational privacy is beyond the scope of these materials. Representative areas of the right to informational privacy are included.

There is some disagreement amongst commentators as to whether informational privacy adequately reflects the privacy concern in a number of cases where information about a person is acquired without that person's consent. This perspective contends the emphasis on informational privacy leaves other important dimensions of privacy, such as physical, decisional and proprietary privacy, in the shadows of analysis. Physical privacy concerns are about access to persons and personal space that is reflected in actions such as unauthorized physical contact, remote surveillance, population screening or the testing of adults. Emphasis on informational privacy may also mask the linkage or clustering of values that is involved in areas of privacy law. Privacy and first amendment values, for example, are linked in fourth amendment cases and cases interpreting electronic eavesdropping statutes and freedom of information and privacy acts. We integrate the proposition that informational privacy is underinclusive as an explanation of privacy values and concerns in some of the contexts where privacy claims are raised in this chapter through discussions in the text and the notes.

B. CONSTITUTIONAL PROTECTION FOR INFORMATIONAL PRIVACY

1. THE FOURTH AMENDMENT

In the first section of this chapter, the right to informational privacy that is protected in the fourth amendment proscriptions against unreasonable "searches and seizures" of persons is examined. This will require an examination of some cases that are typically studied in criminal procedure courses. We have selected these cases because of the important role they play in the evolution of the constitutional right to informational privacy. The text and historical origins of the amendment clearly demonstrate that it protects not just privacy but a cluster of linked values including property and freedom of the press. The amendment grants the right of people to be "secure in their persons, houses, papers and effects against unreasonable searches and seizures." The amendment was a response to the use of general search warrants and writs of assistance by the English Crown to suppress printed material and to seize smuggled goods. *See generally* N. Lasson, *The History and Development of the Fourth Amendment to the United States Constitution*, 42–50 (1970). The focus here is on the role of the fourth amendment in protecting privacy. Search and seizure cases are an appropriate place to begin examination of the constitutional right to informational privacy for several reasons: there is over a century of explicit recognition by the Supreme Court that a core reason for constitutional limitations on governmental searches is to protect privacy; the principles and concepts that have evolved in fourth amendment cases to protect privacy have been transported by legislatures and courts to many other areas of privacy law.

Beyond that, many of the important questions about the appropriate bounds of government use of modern technology that poses serious threats of loss of informational privacy have been presented to courts as questions of whether the use of that technology is a "search" of a person that is "reasonable." One example of this is the jurisprudence that has evolved in fourth amendment cases where the government has utilized electronic technology to acquire the content of conversations between two or more persons.

2. DOES ELECTRONIC SURVEILLANCE OF A CONVERSATION BY THE GOVERNMENT CONSTITUTE A "FOURTH AMENDMENT SEARCH" OF THE CONVERSING PARTIES?

Privacy rights in constitutional law began initially with Supreme Court interpretations of the fourth amendment right against unreasonable searches and seizures of the home and papers and the fifth amendment right against self-incrimination. Since the fourth and fifth amendments did not become applicable to the states until the selective incorporation cases of the Warren Court in the 1960's, privacy cases under these amendments until that time all involved constitutional challenges to federal law. The early cases tied privacy to individual interests in physical exclusiveness in respect to a dwelling or property interests in a tangible seized item. In *Ex parte Jackson*, 96 U.S. 727 (1877) the Supreme Court held that a sealed letter entrusted in the mail is subject to fourth amendment warrant requirements. Some nine years later the Court in *Boyd v. United States*, 116 U.S. 616 (1886) held that governmental-compelled production of a person's private papers violated the fourth and fifth amendments. Justice Bradley relied extensively on Lord Camden's discussion in *Entick v. Carrington and Three Other King's Messengers*, 19 Howell's State Trials, 1029 (1762) where the seizure of private books and papers under a general search warrant was found to be actionable in trespass for damages. Although Lord Camden had emphasized the importance of protecting security of property, it was clear that Justice Bradley had broader notions of the scope of fourth and fifth amendment limitations on government:

> The principles laid down in this opinion [*Entick*] affect the very essence of constitutional liberty and security. They reach farther than the concrete form of the case then before the court, with its adventitious circumstances; they apply to all invasions on the part of the government and its employees [sic] of the sanctity of a man's home and the *privacies of life*. (Emphasis added) It is not the breaking of his doors, and the rummaging of his drawers, that constitutes the essence of the offence; but it is the invasion of his indefeasible right of personal security, personal liberty and private property, where the right has never been forfeited by his conviction of some public offence,—it is the invasion of this sacred right which underlies and constitutes the essence of Lord Camden's judgment. Breaking into a house and opening boxes and drawers are circumstances of aggravation; but any forcible and compulsory extortion of a man's own testimony or of his private papers to be used as evidence to convict him of crime or to forfeit his goods, is within the condemnation of that judgment. In this regard the Fourth and Fifth Amendments run almost into each other.

116 U.S. at 630.

Jackson and *Boyd* were on their facts limited to private papers which are specifically referred to in the language of the fourth amendment. They involve a kind of government trespass on private property. Yet, as Justice Bradley's quote suggests, the Court might have been inclined to break fourth amendment privacy away from the limited notion of protection of property interests against government trespass to a more general protection against governmental invasions of privacy. This backdrop set the stage for the Court to decide a question of growing importance in twentieth century America, namely, does the constitutional right of privacy protect individuals against electronic surveillance by the government? The electronic surveillance of telephone conversations by a wiretap presented the Court with a pure informational privacy case. The individual injury could no longer be cabined within the physical trespass to property concept of search. Property was not being seized by the government in the home or dwelling or on the person. Conversations were overheard and personal information about the individual was acquired by the government and the conversers did not in fact want the information to be disclosed to the uninvited ear of the government listener.

Olmstead v. United States, 277 U.S. 438 (1928), gave Justice Brandeis the occasion to expound his view of privacy as a Supreme Court Justice. Brandeis, who as a young attorney had coauthored an article viewed as spawning the legal right of privacy, seized this opportunity to write an important dissent.

A majority of the Court in *Olmstead* held that conversations over the telephone were not within fourth amendment protection. Chief Justice Taft, the author of the five member majority opinion, relied primarily on the physical trespass notion. In rejecting the fourth amendment claim he concluded, "The Amendment does not forbid what was done here. There was no searching. There was no seizure. The evidence was secured by the use of the sense of hearing and that only. There was no entry of the houses or offices of the defendants." 277 U.S. at 464.

Justice Brandeis dissented, along with Justices Holmes, Stone and Butler. Justice Brandeis:

When the Fourth and Fifth Amendments were adopted, "the form that evil had theretofore taken," had been necessarily simple. Force and violence were then the only means known to man by which a Government could directly effect self-incrimination. It could compel the individual to testify—a compulsion effected, if need be, by torture. It could secure possession of his papers and other articles incident to his private life—a seizure effected, if need be, by breaking and entry. Protection against such invasion of "the sanctities of a man's home and the privacies of life" was provided in the Fourth and Fifth Amendments by specific language. *Boyd v. United States*, 116 U.S. 616, 630. But "time works changes, brings into existence new conditions and purposes." Subtler and more far-reaching means of invading privacy have become available to the Government. Discovery and invention have made it possible for the Government, by means far more effective than stretching upon the rack, to obtain disclosure in court of what is whispered in the closet.

Moreover, "in the application of a constitution, our contemplation cannot be only of what has been but of what may be." The progress of science in furnishing the Government with means of espionage is not likely to stop with wire-tapping. Ways may some day be developed by which the Government, without removing papers from secret drawers can reproduce them in court, and by which it will be enabled to expose to a jury the most intimate occurrences of the home. Advances in the psychic and related sciences may bring means of exploring unexpressed beliefs, thoughts and emotions. "That places the liberty of every man in the hands of every petty officer" was said by James Otis of much lesser intrusions than these. To Lord Camden, a far slighter intrusion seemed "subversive of all the comforts of society." Can it be that the Constitution affords no protection against such invasion of individual security?

. . .

In *Ex parte Jackson*, 96 U.S. 727 (1877), it was held that a sealed letter entrusted to the mail is protected by the Amendments. The mail is a public service furnished by the Government. The telephone is a public service furnished by its authority. There is, in essence, no difference between the sealed letter and the private telephone message. As Judge Rudkin said below: "True the one is visible, the other invisible; the one is tangible, the other intangible; the one is sealed and the other unsealed, but these are distinctions without a difference." The evil incident to invasion of the privacy of the telephone is far greater than that involved in tampering with the mails. Whenever a telephone line is tapped, the privacy of the persons at both ends of the line is invaded and all conversations between them upon any subject, and although proper, confidential and privileged, may be overheard. Moreover, the tapping of one man's telephone line involves the tapping of the telephone of every other person whom he may call or who may call him. As a means of espionage, writs of assistance and general warrants are but puny instruments of tyranny and oppression when compared with wire-tapping.

. . .

The protection guaranteed by the Amendments is much broader in scope. The makers of our Constitution undertook to secure conditions favorable to the pursuit of happiness. They recognized the significance of man's spiritual nature, of his feelings and of his intellect. They knew that only a part of the pain, pleasure and satisfactions of life are to be found in material things. They sought to protect Americans in their beliefs, their thoughts, their emotions and their sensations. They conferred, as against the Government, the right to be let alone—the most comprehensive of rights and the right most valued by civilized men. To protect that right, every unjustifiable intrusion by the Government upon the privacy of the individual, whatever the means employed, must be deemed a violation of the Fourth Amendment. And the use, as evidence in a criminal proceeding, of facts ascertained by such intrusion must be deemed a violation of the Fifth.

Applying to the Fourth and Fifth Amendments the established rule of construction, the defendants' objections to the evidence obtained by wire-tapping must, in my opinion, be sustained. It is, of course, immaterial where the physical connection with the telephone wires leading into the defendants' premises was made. And it is also immaterial that the intrusion was in aid of law enforcement. Experience should teach us to be most on our guard to protect liberty when the Government's purposes are beneficent. Men born to freedom are naturally alert to repel invasion of their liberty by evil-minded rulers. The greatest dangers to liberty lurk in insidious encroachment by men of zeal, well-meaning but without understanding.

277 U.S. at 473–479.

Note: Informational Privacy Rights in Tort and Constitutional Law

Does the Brandeis dissent provide a link between informational privacy rights in tort and constitutional law? Federal constitutional rights are rights that individuals have against the government; the federal constitution generally does not grant rights to persons that are wronged by non-governmental entities such as private persons or businesses. Tort rights are rights that individuals generally have against private persons and business entities. This distinguishing feature of constitutional and common law tort rights has led some commentators to conclude that there is no significant link between the right to informational privacy in constitutional law and torts, *see* J. Thomas McCarthy, *The Rights of Publicity and Privacy*, sec. 5.7 (B), 5–59 (Release 13, 3/95) (1989). Other commentators have found a linkage in Brandeis' dissent in *Olmstead*. Brandeis, as co-author of the 1890 Harvard Law Review article, had argued for recognition of a tort right to privacy for the publication of private facts. Brandeis did not cite the Harvard Law Review article in the *Olmstead* dissent. However, as noted by Edward J. Bloustein, several passages from the article were included almost verbatim in the *Olmstead* dissent. Bloustein concluded that "the underlying conceptual scheme of the article and dissent is identical." He found that the "parallelism" between the article and the dissenting opinion suggested that Brandeis believed that the principle of inviolate personality was intended to be protected under the Fourth Amendment, *see* Edward J. Bloustein, *Privacy as an Aspect of*

Human Dignity: An Answer to Dean Prosser, 39 N.Y.U.L. Rev. 962, 976–77 (1964).

Building on this point, Richard Turkington suggests that:

> [t]he connection ... between informational privacy rights in constitutional law and torts is in the nature of the injury and not in the character of the actor that causes the injury. It is the loss of the condition of privacy and the intellectual tradition that is the foundation of the privacy rights that links informational privacy rights in tort and constitutional law.

Richard C. Turkington, *Legacy of the Warren and Brandeis Article: The Emerging Unencumbered Constitutional Right to Informational Privacy,* 10 N. Ill. L. Rev. 479, 490–91 (1990).

See, also, discussion in *Hill v. NAACP,* 865 P.2d 633 (Cal.1994), *infra,* where the California Supreme Court interprets the right of privacy under the California Constitution to apply to invasions of privacy in the private sector. In interpreting the state constitution, the *Hill* court sought to "draw upon the one hundred years of legal experience surrounding the term 'privacy' ". *Id.* p. 649.

On the question of the connection between tort and constitutional protection for informational privacy, compare the elaboration of doctrine by courts in fourth amendment governmental surveillance of conversation cases with privacy intrusion tort cases involving surveillance of conversations by private parties in [Chapter Five]. Consider the extent to which the fourth amendment "expectation of privacy principle" has been grafted onto the privacy intrusion torts. *See, e.g.,* discussion following *Nader v. General Motors, infra.*

Note: Privacy and the Fifth Amendment
Right Against Self–incrimination

The fourth amendment right against unreasonable searches and seizures and the fifth amendment right against self-incrimination were linked historically. In *Boyd v. United States, supra,* Justice Bradley, speaking for the Court that had found that the seizure of Boyd's private papers violated both amendments, noted that "the fourth and fifth amendments run almost into each other." 116 U.S. 616 at 630. *See also* Alan Westin, *Privacy and Freedom,* 330, 333 (1967). Recent Supreme Court decisions have limited the fifth amendment right against self-incrimination to evidence that is testimonial in nature. See *Schmerber v. California,* 384 U.S. 757, 765 (1966), where the Court held that the use of a blood sample did not implicate self-incrimination rights because the evidence was not testimonial. Does the restriction of the right against self-incrimination to compelled disclosure of information of a testimonial nature eviscerate any significant role for the fifth amendment in protecting privacy? For a thoughtful examination of this and other questions about the relationship between privacy and self-incrimination, see Robert S. Gerstein, Privacy and Self–Incrimination, in *Philosophical Dimensions of Privacy: An Anthology,* 245 (F. Schoeman ed., 1984).

ALAN F. WESTIN, SCIENCE, PRIVACY, AND FREEDOM: ISSUES AND PROPOSALS FOR THE 1970'S

66 Colum. L. Rev. 1003, 1006–09 (1966).

Listening to private speech is probably the most important type of physical surveillance, and it is here that the greatest advances in technology have been made. The most complete audio surveillance is obtained by making the subject a walking transmitter. This is accomplished by building subminiature radio transmitters into his clothing or personal effects in much the same way that signal tags are planted. One such unit places a microphone in one button of a person's suit; a subminiature transmitter in a second button; and the battery source in a third and uses conductive wire that matches the thread of seams and decoration as the unit's antenna. Such installations can be made in a matter of minutes if access can be obtained to a person's clothing through, for example, his dry cleaner or a public check room.

Since wiring a person's effects may pose problems and since the site of conversation is often known in advance, wiring the premises is the most frequently used method of eavesdropping. Microphones the size of a sugar cube are presently available at less than $10 each. Once secreted in objects within a room these miniaturized microphones can be attached to the electrical, telephone, or intercom systems, or wired directly by electrically conductive paint to the investigator's location. One microphone and transmitter unit has been built into a light bulb; it starts automatically when the light is turned on in a room and goes off when the light is extinguished. The microphones can also be supplied with their own power source, such as an FM transmitter unit commercially sold in a 1 to 2 cubic inch size and in smaller sizes for government security work. The range of such eavesdropping broadcasts to the investigator's listening and recording equipment is 1 to 3 blocks in cities and several miles in less dense locations. Various methods are available to activate the listening devices by remote control and they can even be started by the alteration which occurs in a room's electronic balance when someone enters. One tiny device—consisting of a microwave cavity containing a thin diaphragm and microwave antenna—can be used where it is dangerous to have a power source in the room under surveillance, as where periodic electronic sweeps are made to detect transmitting signals. The device is inert until a microwave beam sent into the room from outside (such beams penetrate solid walls with no difficulty) activates it to transmit conversations to an outside receiver. This device was used by the Soviets in a hollowed-out crevice in the wooden Great Seal hanging in the American Ambassador's office in Moscow.

When entry to the room is not possible, speech can be monitored by contact microphones placed on walls, "spike" microphones inserted into the air space between walls, or through the vibrations carried along pipes, vents and ducts leading from the room. Directional microphones of the "shotgun mike" and parabolic mike types sold in retail outlets make it possible to listen from distances of several hundred feet to conversations held in rooms with open windows or on porches and balconies; such eavesdropping from building to building across a city street is quite simple. The high-frequency sounds produced on the outside of windows and thin walls by speech in the room can be obtained even without contact microphones by means of ultrasonic waves sent onto the surface and reflected back to the sending apparatus, the wave being modulated by the speech vibrations. In addition, windowpanes can be coated with a transparent radar-reflecting coating which allows sensitive radar equipment to monitor from considerable distances the vibrations caused by conversations. Modern office and government buildings, with great glass surfaces, make ideal targets for such new sound surveillance technology.

Though any of the techniques just mentioned will transmit one end of any telephone conversation held in the room under surveillance, investigators often want to hear both sides of a telephone call; this requires a telephone tap. New technology has supplemented the direct connection and induction coil tap of earlier decades and has produced far more sophisticated induction devices than were previously available. For example, miniaturized devices are now available that fit within the telephone handset itself, and portable induction coils attached to miniaturized recorders make it possible for a person to sit in waiting rooms and lobbies outside business, law, and government offices and record all the calls going on inside. This can often be done even from the street outside a ground floor office or residence, from hotel rooms adjoining those of the subject, and at distances of 10 to 20 feet from a telephone booth.

Vital information passing over new data-communication systems has also become a target of new surveillance technology. A growing volume of business and governmental data is being transmitted from point to point by teletype machines, data-phone systems (which use telephone company equipment), and computers. Surveillance devices are available to intercept teletype signals and feed them into the investigator's teletype printer; the same can be done with data-phone transmissions that are not transmitted in scrambled form. Computer tapping is also possible through direct connections to a parallel computer or, if fairly close contact can be achieved, by radio tapping of the electrical signals produced by the print-out mechanism. . . .

Prospects for physical surveillance technology in the coming decade indicate that the problem of insulating private conduct will be further intensified. Increased miniaturization and the solution of existing power source problems will make possible smaller and smaller signal tags and room microphones. TV "eyes" the size of buttons may be perfected, operating by microwave transmission rather than cables. Existing "voiceprint" identification systems may be linked to computers to make possible computer monitoring of thousands of telephone lines and tapes to single out conversations by previously identified persons or by anyone mentioning certain word patterns (such as "Communist China" or "Lyndon Johnson").

II B. Privacy and Individual Life

Precise knowledge of the varying content of the word "privacy" is essential to a full understanding of the roles played by that concept in society. Privacy in the sense of being "let alone" actually encompasses four different psychological and physical relations between an individual and those around him. These are the states of solitude, intimacy, anonymity, and reserve.

1.   The Four States of Privacy. The first state of privacy is solitude; here the individual is separated from the group and freed from observation by other persons. He may still be subjected to jarring physical stimuli such as noise, odors, and vibrations. His peace of mind may continue to be disturbed by physical sensations of heat, cold, itching, and pain. He may believe that he is being observed by God or some supernatural force, or fear that some authority is secretly watching him. Finally, in solitude he will be especially subject to that familiar dialogue with the mind or conscience. But despite all of these physical or psychological intrusions, solitude is the most complete state of privacy that individuals can achieve.

In the second state of privacy, intimacy, the individual is acting as part of a small unit that claims and is allowed to exercise corporate seclusion so that it may achieve that special close, relaxed, and frank relationship between two or more individuals which the word intimacy conveys in popular speech. Typical units of intimacy are husband and wife, the family, a friendship circle, or a work clique. Whether close contact brings relaxed relations or abrasive hostility depends on the personal interaction of the members, but without intimacy, a basic need for human contact would not be met. The third state of privacy, anonymity, occurs when the individual is in public places or doing public things but still seeks, and finds, freedom from identification and surveillance. He may be riding a subway, attending a ball game, or walking the streets. He is among people and knows that he is being observed. But, unless he is a well-known celebrity, he does not expect to be personally identified and held to the full rules of behavior and role that would operate if he were known to those observing him. In this state, the individual is able to merge into the "situational landscape." Knowledge or fear that one is under systematic observation in public places destroys the sense of relaxation and freedom that men seek in open spaces and public arenas.

Anonymous relations give rise to what Simmel called the "phenomenon of the stranger," the person who "often received the most surprising openness—confidences which sometimes have the character of a confessional and which would be carefully withheld from a more closely related person." In this aspect of anonymity, the individual can express himself freely because he knows the stranger will not continue in his life and that, although he may give an objective response to the questions put to him, he is able to exert no authority or restraint over the individual.

Still another kind of anonymity is the anonymous expression of views. Here the individual wants to present some idea publicly to the community or to a segment of it but does not want everyone to identify him at once as the author—especially not the authorities, who may have to take action if they "know"" who said this. The core of each of these types of anonymous action is the desire of individuals for times of "public privacy."

Reserve, the fourth and most subtle state of privacy, occurs when the individual's need to limit communication about himself is protected by the willing discretion of those surrounding him. Most of our lives are spent not in solitude or anonymity but in situations of intimacy and group settings where we are known to others. Yet communication of self to others is always incomplete, even in the most intimate relations, and is always based on the need to hold back some parts of one's self as either too personal and sacred or too shameful and profane to express in the particular situation. This gives rise to what Simmel called "reciprocal reserve and indifference," the relation that creates "mental distance" to protect the personality. This creation of mental distance—a variant of the concept of "social distance"—takes place in every sort of relationship under rules of social etiquette; it expresses the individual's choice to withhold or disclose information—the choice that is the dynamic aspect of privacy in daily, interpersonal relations. Simmel identified this tension within the individual as being between "self-revelation and self-restraint" and, within society, between "trespass and discretion." The manner in which individuals claim reserve and the extent to which it is respected or disregarded by others is at the heart of securing meaningful privacy in the crowded, organization-dominated settings of modern industrial society and urban life. . . .

a. Personal autonomy. In democratic societies, there is a fundamental belief in the uniqueness of the individual, his basic dignity and worth as a human being, and in the need to maintain social processes that safeguard his sacred individuality. Psychologists and sociologists have linked the development and maintenance of this sense of individuality to the human need for autonomy—the desire to avoid being manipulated or dominated wholly by others.

One of the accepted ways of representing the individual's need for an ultimate core of autonomy, as expressed by theorists like Simmel, Park, Lewin and Goffman, has been to describe the individual's relations with others in terms of a series of "zones" or "regions" of privacy leading to a "core self." This core self is pictured as an inner circle surrounded by a series of larger concentric circles. The inner circle shelters the individual's "ultimate secrets"—those hopes, fears, and prayers that are beyond sharing with anyone unless the individual comes under such stress that he must pour out these ultimate secrets to secure emotional relief. Under normal circumstances no one is admitted to this sanctuary of the personality. The next circle outward contains "intimate secrets," those that can be willingly shared with close relations, confessors, or strangers who pass by and cannot injure. The next circle is open to members of the individual's friendship group. The series continues until it reaches the outer circles of casual conversation and physical expression that are open to all observers.

The most serious threat to the individual's autonomy is that someone will penetrate the inner zone and learn his ultimate secrets, either by physical or psychological means. This deliberate penetration of the individual's protective shell, his psychological armor, would leave him naked to ridicule and shame and put him under the control of those who know his secrets. Autonomy is also threatened by those who penetrate the core self because they do not recognize the importance of ultimate privacy or think that the casual and uninvited help they may be doing an individual compensates for the violation.

Each person is aware of the gap between what he wants to be and what he actually is, between what the world sees of him and what he knows to be his much more complex reality. In addition, there are aspects of himself that the individual does not fully understand but is slowly exploring and shaping as he develops. Every individual lives behind a mask in this manner; indeed, the first meaning of the word "person" etymologically was "mask," indicating both the conscious and expressive presentation of the self to a social audience. If this mask is torn off and the individual's real self bared to a world in which everyone else still wears his mask and believes in masked performances, the individual can be seared by the hot light of selective, forced exposure. The numerous instances of suicides and nervous breakdowns resulting from such exposures by government investigation, press stories, and even published research constantly remind a free society that only grave social need can ever justify destruction of the privacy which guards the individual's ultimate autonomy.

The autonomy that privacy protects is also vital to the development of individuality and consciousness of individual choice in life. Leontine Young has noted that "without privacy there is no individuality. There are only types. Who can know what he thinks and feels if he never has the opportunity to be alone with his thoughts and feelings?" This development of individuality is particularly important in democratic societies, since qualities of independent thought, diversity of views, and nonconformity are considered desirable traits for individuals. Such independence requires time for sheltered experimentation and testing of ideas, for preparation and practice in thought and conduct without fear of ridicule or penalty, and for the opportunity to alter opinions before making them public. The individual's sense that it is he who decides when to "go public" is a crucial aspect of his feeling of autonomy. Without such time for incubation and growth, through privacy, many ideas and positions would be launched into the world with dangerous prematurity. As Robert MacIver has said, "Everything that grows first of all does so in the darkness before it sends its shoots out into the light."

Summing up the importance of privacy for political liberty, Clinton Rossiter has also stressed the feature of autonomy:

> *Privacy* is a special kind of independence, which can be understood as an attempt to secure autonomy in at least a few personal and spiritual concerns, if necessary in defiance of all the pressures of modern society.... [I]t seeks to erect an unbreachable wall of dignity and reserve against the entire world. The free man is the private man, the man who still keeps some of his thoughts and judgments entirely to himself, who feels no over-riding compulsion to share everything of value with others, not even with those he loves and trusts.

3.   THE COURT JUNKS THE TRESPASS DOCTRINE

Alan Westin proved to be prophetic in his description of the future technology that would be available for invading privacy through electronic surveillance. Some of the technology that he alluded to—miniature cameras, electronic mail and microwave transmission of information—will be examined further in later chapters. The seriousness of the threat to privacy that electronic surveillance presents was recognized by Justice Brandeis in his dissent in *Olmstead* and is further expanded upon by Professor Westin. Constitutional protection for serious invasions of informational privacy through electronic surveillance had not occurred at the time the Westin article was published. Then in 1967 the Supreme Court decided two cases that launched the modern era of informational privacy rights in our legal system.

BERGER v. NEW YORK

388 U.S. 41 (1967).

In *Berger v. New York*, 388 U.S. 41 (1967), the Supreme Court found sections of New York's eavesdrop statute unconstitutional under the fourth amendment. The New York statute authorized the issuance of an eavesdrop order if there was "reasonable ground to believe" that evidence of a crime "may be obtained." The Court held that the probable cause requirement of the fourth amendment applied to the electronic surveillance in the case but did not decide whether the "reasonable ground" language was constitutionally sufficient because the statute was found to violate the constitution on other grounds—the "particularization" requirement of the fourth amendment. Constitutional deficiencies were found in the failure to require (1) description of the communications, conversations or discussions that were to be seized, (2) the length of the authorized surveillance and the failure to require a separate showing of probable cause for extensions of the order. Justice Clark responding to the argument that the importance of electronic eavesdropping to law enforcement required less rigorous application of the constitution said:

> [W]e cannot forgive the requirements of the Fourth Amendment in the name of law enforcement. This is no formality that

we require today but a fundamental rule that has long been recognized as basic to the privacy of every home in America.

388 U.S. at 62–63.

In a concurring opinion, Justice Douglas said:

A discreet selective wiretap or electronic "bugging" is of course not rummaging around, collecting everything in the particular time and space zone. But even though it is limited in time, it is the greatest of all invasions of privacy. It places a government agent in the bedroom, in the business conference, in the social hour, in the lawyer's office—everywhere and anywhere a "bug" can be placed.

If a statute were to authorize placing a policeman in every home or office where it was shown that there was probable cause to believe that evidence of crime would be obtained, there is little doubt that it would be struck down as a bald invasion of privacy, far worse than the general warrants prohibited by the Fourth Amendment. I can see no difference between such a statute and one authorizing electronic surveillance, which, in effect, places an invisible policeman in the home. If anything, the latter is more offensive because the homeowner is completely unaware of the invasion of privacy.

The traditional wiretap or electronic eavesdropping device constitutes a dragnet, sweeping in all conversations within its scope—without regard to the participants or the nature of the conversations. It intrudes upon the privacy of those not even suspected of crime and intercepts the most intimate of conversations.

389 U.S. at 64–65.

Note

Congress enacted federal legislation regulating electronic surveillance shortly after *Berger* was decided (Title III of the Omnibus Crime Control and Safe Streets Act of 1968). This statute is reproduced in Chapter Eight and is extensively examined in Chapter Three.

The probable cause and particularity provisions of Title III are found in Sections 2518(1)(b)(i), (ii), (iii) and Sections 2518(4)(b), (c) of Title III.

a.   *Search Defined by the Expectation of Privacy Principle*

KATZ v. UNITED STATES
389 U.S. 347 (1967).

MR. JUSTICE STEWART delivered the opinion of the Court.

[Katz was convicted under an eight-count indictment charging him with transmitting wagering information by telephone between states in violation of a federal statute. At trial, evidence was admitted of petitioner's telephone conversations overheard by an electronic listening and recording device attached to the outside of a public telephone booth by FBI agents. The Court of Appeals affirmed the conviction, rejecting the argument that the recordings were obtained in violation of the fourth amendment. Certiorari was granted to consider whether the electronic surveillance constituted a search.]

The petitioner has phrased those questions as follows:

A.   Whether a public telephone booth is a constitutionally protected area so that evidence obtained by attaching an electronic listening recording device to the top of such a booth is obtained in violation of the right to privacy of the user of the booth.

B.   Whether physical penetration of a constitutionally protected area is necessary before a search and seizure can be said to be violative of the Fourth Amendment to the United States Constitution.

We decline to adopt this formulation of the issues. In the first place, the correct solution of Fourth Amendment problems is not necessarily promoted by incantation of the phrase "constitutionally protected area." Secondly, the Fourth Amendment cannot be translated into a general constitutional "right to privacy." That Amendment protects individual privacy against certain kinds of governmental intrusion, but its protections go further, and often have nothing to do with privacy at all. Other provisions of the Constitution protect personal privacy from other forms of governmental invasion. But the protection of a person's *general* right to privacy—his right to be let alone by other people—is, like the protection of his property and of his very life, left largely to the law of the individual States.

. . .

The Government stresses the fact that the telephone booth from which the petitioner made his calls was constructed partly of glass, so that he was as visible after he entered it as he would have been if he had remained outside. But what he sought to exclude when he entered the booth was not the intruding eye—it was the uninvited ear. He did not shed his right to do so simply because he made his calls from a place where he might be seen. No less than an individual in a business office, in a friend's apartment, or in a taxicab, a person in a telephone booth may rely upon the protection of the Fourth Amendment. One who occupies it, shuts the door behind him, and pays the toll that permits him to place a call is surely entitled to assume that the words he utters into the mouthpiece will not be broadcast to the world. To read the Constitution more narrowly is to ignore the vital role that the public telephone has come to play in private communication.

The Government contends, however, that the activities of its agents in this case should not be tested by Fourth Amendment requirements, for the surveillance technique they employed involved no physical penetration of the telephone booth from which the petitioner placed his calls. It is true that the absence of such penetration was at one time thought to foreclose further Fourth Amendment inquiry, Olmstead v. United States, 277 U.S. 438, 457, 464, 467 (1928); Goldman v. United States, 316 U.S. 129, 134–136 (1942), for that Amendment was thought to limit only searches and seizures of tangible property....

We conclude that the underpinnings of *Olmstead* and *Goldman* have been so eroded by our subsequent decisions that the "trespass" doctrine there enunciated can no longer be regarded as controlling. The Government's activities in electronically listening to and recording the petitioner's words violated the privacy upon which he justifiably relied while using the telephone booth and thus constituted a "search and seizure" within the meaning of the Fourth Amendment. The fact that the electronic device employed to achieve that end did not happen to penetrate the wall of the booth can have no constitutional significance.

The question remaining for decision, then, is whether the search and seizure conducted in this case complied with constitutional standards. In that regard, the Government's position is that its agents acted in an entirely defensible manner: they did not begin their electronic surveillance until investigation of the petitioner's activities had established a strong probability that he was using the telephone in question to transmit gambling information to persons in other States, in violation of federal law. Moreover, the surveillance was limited, both in scope and in duration, to the specific purpose of establishing the contents of the petitioner's unlawful telephonic communications. The agents confined their surveillance to the brief periods during which he used the telephone booth, and they took great care to overhear only the conversations of the petitioner himself.

Accepting this account of the Government's actions as accurate, it is clear that this surveillance was so narrowly circumscribed that a duly authorized magistrate, properly notified of the need for such investigation, specifically informed of the basis on which it was to proceed, and clearly apprised of the precise intrusion it would entail, could constitutionally have authorized, with appropriate safeguards, the very limited search and seizure that the Government asserts in fact took place....

... It is apparent that the agents in this case acted with restraint. Yet the inescapable fact is that this restraint was imposed by the agents themselves, not by a judicial officer. They were not required, before commencing the search, to present their estimate of probable cause for detached scrutiny by a neutral magistrate. They were not compelled, during the conduct of the search itself, to observe precise limits established in advance by a specific court order. Nor were they directed, after the search had been completed, to notify the authorizing magistrate in detail of all that had been seized. In the absence of such safeguards, this Court has never sustained a search upon the sole ground that officers reasonably expected to find evidence of a particular crime and voluntarily confined their activities to the least intrusive means consistent with that end. . . .

. . .

. . . The government agents here ignored "the procedure of antecedent justification . . . that is central to the Fourth Amendment," a procedure that we hold to be a constitutional precondition of the kind of electronic surveillance involved in this case. Because the surveillance here failed to meet that condition, and because it led to the petitioner's conviction, the judgment must be reversed. . . .

(MR. JUSTICE BLACK, dissenting.)

If I could agree with the Court that eavesdropping carried on by electronic means (equivalent to wiretapping) constitutes a "search" or "seizure," I would be happy to join the Court's opinion. . . .

My basic objection is twofold: (1) I do not believe that the words of the Amendment will bear the meaning given them by today's decision, and (2) I do not believe that it is the proper role of this Court to rewrite the Amendment in order "to bring it into harmony with the times" and thus reach a result that many people believe to be desirable.

While I realize that an argument based on the meaning of words lacks the scope, and no doubt the appeal, of broad policy discussions and philosophical discourses on such nebulous subjects as privacy, for me the language of the Amendment is the crucial place to look in constructing a written document such as our Constitution. . . .

. . . A conversation overheard by eavesdropping, whether by plain snooping or wiretapping, is not tangible and, under the normally accepted meanings of the words, can neither be searched nor seized. In addition the language of the second clause indicates that the Amendment refers not only to something tangible so it can be seized but to something already in existence so it can be described. Yet the Court's interpretation would have the Amendment apply to overhearing future conversations which by their very nature are nonexistent until they take place. How can one "describe" a future conversation, and, if one cannot, how can a magistrate issue a warrant to eavesdrop one in the future? . . .

Tapping telephone wires, of course, was an unknown possibility at the time the Fourth Amendment was adopted. But eavesdropping (and wiretapping is nothing more than eavesdropping by telephone) was, as even the majority opinion in *Berger*, supra, recognized, "an ancient practice which at common law was condemned as a nuisance. 4 Blackstone, Commentaries 168. . . . " There can be no doubt that the Framers were aware of this practice, and if they had desired to outlaw or restrict the use of evidence obtained by eavesdropping, I believe that they would have used the appropriate language to do so in the Fourth Amendment. . . .

Since I see no way in which the words of the Fourth Amendment can be construed to apply to eavesdropping, that closes the matter for me. In interpreting the Bill of Rights, I willingly go as far as a liberal construction of the language takes me, but I simply cannot in good conscience give a meaning to words which they have never before been thought to have and which they certainly do not have in common ordinary usage. I will not distort the words of the Amendment in order to "keep the Constitution up to date" or "to bring it into harmony with the times." It was never meant that this Court have such power, which in effect would make us a continuously functioning constitutional convention.

(1) *From Olmstead to Berger and Katz*

(A) INTRODUCTION

From *Olmstead* to *Katz*, a period of almost forty years, constitutional protection for informational privacy was primarily confined to the fourth amendment. The threshold question in determining whether there was a search or seizure within the meaning of the fourth amendment was whether the government had physically intruded into or trespassed upon a constitutionally protected area. Core areas which were clearly within this sphere of fourth amendment protection included those places which were explicitly referred to in the amendment, i.e., "persons, houses, papers, and effects." In addition, protection was extended to those areas which were closely analogous to the core places in the text of the amendment. Apartments, hotel rooms, garages, business offices, stores, and warehouses were found to be protected areas. In 1925, in *Carroll v. United States*, 267 U.S. 132 (1925), the Supreme Court initially extended the fourth amendment notion of protected areas to motor vehicles. Professor LaFave, the leading expert on the fourth amendment, characterizes the motor vehicle cases as an interpretation of "effects" in the fourth amendment. *See* LaFave, *Search and Seizure*, § 2.19, at 381 (3d ed. 1996). Several fourth amendment privacy "bugging" cases were decided by the Court during the thirty-nine year period from *Olmstead* to *Berger* and *Katz*. In *Goldman v. United States*, 316 U.S. 129 (1942), the Court found that the use of a detectaphone placed against an office wall in order to hear private conversations in the office next door did not violate the fourth amendment because there was no physical trespass in connection with the interception. On the grounds that "no trespass was committed," the Court found that an electronically recorded conversation in a laundry did not violate the fourth amendment in *On Lee v. United States*, 343 U.S. 747 (1952). The trespass limitation on fourth amendment protection began to be eroded somewhat in *Silverman v. United States*, 365 U.S. 505 (1961), where the Court found a violation of the fourth amendment when eavesdropping was accomplished by the use of a foot long spike with a microphone attached which was inserted under a baseboard into a party wall until it made contact with a heating device that ran through an entire house. On the trespass question the Court held that its decision did "not turn upon the technicality of a trespass upon a party wall as a matter of local law.

It is based upon the reality of an actual intrusion into a constitutionally protected area." 365 U.S. at 512.

The intrusion trespass into a protected place doctrine was the basis upon which a majority of the Court in *Olmstead* declined to give fourth amendment protection to conversational privacy when there was government wiretapping of a telephone. In *Berger* and *Katz*, the Court extended the fourth amendment protection to electronic surveillance of conversations by a wiretap, and to transmission monitoring. In so doing, the Court necessarily rejected the *Olmstead* reasoning. Justice Stewart, writing for the majority in *Katz*, explicitly rejected petitioners' attempt to characterize the central legal issue as whether the public telephone booth that Katz was in was a constitutionally protected area. Justice Stewart responded, "[i]n the first place, the correct solution of Fourth Amendment problems is not necessarily promoted by incantation of the phrase 'constitutionally protected area.' " 389 U.S. at 350. For conversational privacy cases, the majority in *Katz* utilized an expectation of privacy test rather than a constitutionally protected area test. The majority concluded that Katz had a justified expectation of privacy in his telephone conversation. Justice Harlan, in a concurring opinion, concluded that Katz had a "reasonable expectation" of privacy in the conversation occurring in the public telephone booth.

(B) JUSTICE HARLAN'S CONCURRING OPINION IN KATZ

In his concurring opinion in *Katz*, Justice Harlan articulated a two-fold requirement for the threshold fourth amendment determination of whether the governmental action constitutes a search. These requirements were, first, that a person have exhibited an actual (subjective) expectation of privacy and, second, that the expectation be one that society is prepared to recognize as "reasonable." The cases in this section demonstrate how dominant Harlan's two-fold test has become in the fourth amendment area.

Harlan's discussion of the "subjective" requirement in *Katz* would suggest that a "subjective" expectation of privacy is a sine qua non for a legitimate expectation of privacy and a fourth amendment search. Yet such a view would result in both absurd and horrendous results for privacy rights. For example, if someone receives a call from a police officer at his or her home and is informed that the officer is going to be at the home and search the house in thirty minutes, the subject of the call would not have a subjective expectation of privacy in respect to that search. Yet it is absolutely clear that in this situation the non-consensual entry into the home or apartment by the police officer would constitute a search. The proposition that a subjective expectation of privacy is a necessary condition before there can be a search is critically flawed.

Justice Harlan apparently recognized this conceptual problem with his language on subjective expectancy in *Katz* in his dissent in *United States v. White, infra,* where he stated that:

The analysis must ... transcend the search for subjective expectations.... Our expectations ... are in large part reflections of law that translate into rules the customs and values of the past and present.

401 U.S. at 786.

Consider the example given by Harlan in *Katz* of the absence of "subjective expectancy," i.e., where the individual has in fact exposed objects, statements or activities to "plain view" of outsiders. Suppose the absence of a minimum requirement of subjectivity for purpose of fourth amendment rights was limited to the kind of situation referred to by Harlan in *Katz*. Then only when someone consents to the presence of someone else and chooses to expose objects or statements to the plain view of that person would he or she have no subjective expectation of privacy in respect to these objects or statements for purposes of the fourth amendment. However, in situations like the above hypothetical where an individual has notice of impending government intrusions, fourth amendment rights would not be defeated on the grounds of absence of a subjective expectation of privacy because, in such instances, the individual has not consented to the intrusion nor voluntarily exposed the objects and information in the home to the officer (outsider).

The Court recognized the difficulties noted above with the "subjective" expectation requirement in 1979 in *Smith v. Maryland*, 442 U.S. 735, 740 n. 5 (1979):

... [I]f the Government were suddenly to announce on nationwide television that all homes henceforth would be subject to warrantless entry, individuals thereafter might not in fact entertain any actual expectation of privacy regarding their homes, papers, and effects.... In such circumstances, where an individual's subjective expectations had been "conditioned" by influences alien to well-recognized Fourth Amendment freedoms, those subjective expectations obviously could play no meaningful role in ascertaining what the scope of the Fourth Amendment protection was. In determining whether a "legitimate expectation of privacy" existed in such cases, a normative inquiry would be proper.

(2) Katz as an Embodiment of the Historic–Rights Oriented Obstacle Course–Perspective of a "Reasonable Search."

The fourth amendment states:

The right of the people to be secure in their persons, houses, papers and effects against unreasonable searches and seizures, shall not be violated, and no Warrants shall issue, but upon probable cause supported by Oath or affirmation and particularly describing the place to be searched, and the persons or things to be seized.

One of the evils that the fourth amendment was clearly intended to reach was invasions of the privacy of the home pursuant to "general search warrants." Such warrants authorized a search of a home for evidence of crime without the government having to produce evidence that illegal activities or evidence of a crime were in the house to be searched. General search warrants were also tied historically to the licensing of the press system in England.

The general authority to search for publications that had not been licensed was recognized for three centuries in England and the abuse of search powers was a vehicle for suppressing seditious and heretical books or printed matter. The fourth amendment presupposes that the power to search is always subject to abuse:

> The Fourth Amendment was not a construct based on abstract considerations of political theory, but was drafted by the framers for the express purpose of providing enforceable safeguards against a recurrence of highhanded search measures which Americans, as well as the people of England, had recently experienced. These abuses, which in the American colonies took place largely in the fifteen years before the American Revolution and which extended over a much longer period of time in England, had done violence to the ancient maxim that "A man's house is his castle."

Jacob W. Landynski, *Search and Seizure and the Supreme Court* 20 (1966).

The assumption that abuse of the authority to invade privacy through a governmental search will occur is not based upon the notion that governmental officials will invariably be evil or corrupt. As Justice Brandeis noted:

> Experience should teach us to be most on our guard to protect liberty when the Government's purposes are beneficent. Men born to freedom are naturally alert to repel invasion of their liberty by evil-minded rulers. The greatest dangers to liberty lurk in insidious encroachment by men of zeal, well-meaning but without understanding.

Olmstead v. United States, 277 U.S. at 479 (dissenting opinion).

These historic rights-oriented, anti-authoritarian values are reflected in the three major limitations the fourth amendment imposes on the government's power to search: (1) requiring that the government justify the search by demonstrating probable cause, (2) requiring intervention by an impartial tribunal prior to the search to test the justification for the search (the warrant requirements) and (3) requiring that the search be limited in its scope (the particularization requirement). The exclusionary rule is a judicially created restriction on the use of evidence that is acquired when the search has not conformed to the requirements of the fourth amendment. As such it is a derivative restriction on governmental searches. In a core search and seizure case these proscriptions contained in the fourth amendment and the exclusionary rule are anti-utilitarian in the sense that the rights granted to persons are obstacles to efficient enforcement of the criminal law. Suppose the following:

> A bank has been robbed. The police arrive within minutes of the commission of the crime. They cordon off an area forming a one mile circle around the bank. Within that area are fifteen houses, and fifty apartments. It is certain that the bank robbers and their loot are located within the area. Statistical evidence demonstrates that if bank robbers are not caught within a few hours of committing the crime the chances of apprehending them are very slim. The responsible governmental official presents these facts to a court and argues that the most efficient and only realistic way to capture the criminals is for the court to issue a warrant to search all the houses and apartments in the encircled area.

It is certain that a search of a house or apartment under the authority of such a warrant would be unconstitutional because the probable cause requirement is not satisfied. This requirement imposes a duty on the government to produce evidence that would lead a reasonable person to believe that evidence of the bank robbery would be found in the particular house or apartment that is to be searched.

In this case the probable cause requirement protects the right to privacy in the home of all persons except for those who the government can demonstrate to a court are likely to have engaged in illegal activities. The probable cause requirement is rights oriented in that it grants primacy to the rights of privacy of citizens generally over the interest in efficient crime control. Although the government has demonstrated that a collective benefit to society, the apprehension of a criminal, will be furthered by the general search warrant, the right to privacy of persons generally "trumps" this common good.

The trumping metaphor is that of Professor Dworkin in his influential work, *Taking Rights Seriously*, 22–28 (1978). Ronald Dworkin has developed a concept of rights which provides in part that "a successful claim of right, in the strong sense I described has this consequence. If someone has a right to something then it is wrong for the government to deny it to him even though it would be in the general interest to do so." Dworkin, *supra*, at 269. Do the probable cause and warrant requirements bring the right to informational privacy as reflected in search cases into Professor Dworkin's notion of rights? *Compare* S. Wasserstrom & L. Seidman, *The Fourth Amendment as Constitutional Theory*, 77 Geo. L.J. 19, 61–62 (1988). The authors argue that the fourth amendment does not "establish a right to privacy that trumps competing policy concerns" because it does not provide an "absolute shield" against invasions of privacy. Wasserstrom & Seidman, *supra* at 61.

THE WARRANT REQUIREMENT

By no longer restricting searches to physical intrusions into protected places *Katz* expanded constitutional protection for informational privacy beyond earlier precedent to electronic surveillance of conversations generally. The fourth amendment deficiency in *Katz* was not the absence of probable cause but the failure of the government to procure a search warrant. The warrant requirement mandates that there be judicial intervention before there be an invasion of privacy through a governmental search. The warrant requirement, like the probable cause requirement, is rights oriented and an obstacle to maximum efficiency in criminal law enforcement and crime control. In *Katz* relevant evidence of criminal activity was excluded from a criminal prosecution because the government had not submitted its version of probable cause to be tested before a detached judicial officer. *Katz* not only expanded the scope of the fourth amendment but also extended the rights oriented obstacle course perspective of historic fourth amendment jurisprudence to the employment by the government of the contemporary technology of electronic surveillance.

4. THE "REASONABLE EXPECTATION OF PRIVACY" TEST IN OPERATION

The "reasonable expectation of privacy" principle emerged from *Katz* as the general test for determining whether government action constitutes a fourth amendment search. Does the Court in *Katz* provide sufficient elaboration about the expectation of privacy concept to guide courts in fourth amendment cases beyond the facts of the case? In an important article published in 1974, Anthony G. Amsterdam described *Katz* as marking a "watershed in fourth amendment jurisprudence . . . [that had] rapidly become the basis of a new formula of fourth amendment coverage." Anthony Amsterdam, *Perspectives on the Fourth Amendment*, 58 Minn. L. Rev. 349, 382–83. However, Professor Amsterdam is critical of the "reasonable expectation of privacy" formula that emerged from *Katz*. One of the points he makes is that to view *Katz* as standing for a formula—the reasonable expectation test—ignores the essence of the decision. That was to expand the fourth amendment by rejecting the view that the concept of "search" was limited by any formula (e.g. the protected area principle). Amsterdam, supra, at 385. In the cases that follow consider the question raised by Professor Amsterdam's observation: has employment of the "reasonable" or "legitimate expectation of privacy test" in cases following Katz replaced one "talismanic solution" for fourth amendment problems with another?

a. "Search" Limited by the "Legitimacy" of the Privacy Expectations of "One Contemplating Illegal Activities"

Legitimate Expectations of Privacy: Assumption of the Risk

The period from *Olmstead* to *Katz* included a number of cases where the introduction of testimony by a government agent about conversations between the agent and charged defendant was challenged as a violation of the fourth amendment. The central thrust of these challenges was that the consent of the defendant to the presence of the informer at the defendant's home and to the conversation with the informer was vitiated because of the misrepresentations of the informer as to his status as a government agent. During that pre-*Katz* trespass era, a majority of the Court rejected this view, taking the position that the fourth amendment does not protect a "wrongdoer's misplaced belief that a person to whom he voluntarily confides his wrongdoing will not reveal it," *Hoffa v. United States*, 385 U.S. 293, 302 (1966). *Hoffa* did not involve the use of a concealed tape recorder by the informer. *Lopez v. United States*, 373 U.S. 427 (1963), did involve the use of such a device, and earlier in *On Lee v. United States*, 343 U.S. 747 (1952), the Court had rejected the contention that the transmission of defendant's conversation by a device concealed on an informer's person constituted a trespass and fourth amendment search. One of the questions that was raised by the rejection of the trespass concept of search by the *Katz* court was whether *Hoffa, Lopez, On Lee*, and other similar decisions of the pre-*Katz* era continued to be good fourth amendment law under the new fourth amendment expectation of privacy era launched by *Katz*.

(1) One Party Consent, Misplaced Trust

UNITED STATES v. WHITE
401 U.S. 745 (1971)

Mr. Justice White announced the judgement of the Court in an opinion in which The Chief Justice, Mr. Justice Stewart, and Mr. Justice Blackmun join. . . .

[White was convicted of various illegal transactions in violation of two federal narcotic statutes. The trial court overruled objections to the testimony of governmental agents who related certain conversations which had occurred between White and a government informant. The agents overheard the conversations by the use of a radio transmitter concealed on the informant. On four occasions conversations were overheard by an agent concealed in the informant's house and by a second agent outside the house using radio equipment. Four other conversations—one in White's home, one in a restaurant, and two in the informant's car—were overheard by the use of radio equipment. The jury returned a guilty verdict and White appealed. The Court of Appeals reversed, interpreting *Katz* and the fourth amendment to forbid the introduction of the agent's testimony in the circumstances of this case.]

The Court of Appeals understood *Katz* to render inadmissible against White the agents' testimony concerning conversations that Jackson broadcast to them. We cannot agree. *Katz* involved no revelation to the Government by a party to conversations with the defendant nor did the Court indicate in any way that a defendant has a justifiable and constitutionally protected expectation that a person with whom he is conversing will not then or later reveal the conversation to the police.

. . . .

Concededly a police agent who conceals his police connections may write down for official use his conversations with a defendant and testify concerning them, without a warrant authorizing his encounters with the defendant and without otherwise violating the latter's Fourth Amendment rights. Hoffa v. United States, 385 U.S. 293, 300–303 (1966). For constitutional purposes, no different result is required if the agent instead of immediately reporting and transcribing his conversations with defendant, either (1) simultaneously records them with electronic equipment which he is carrying on his person, Lopez; (2) or carries radio equipment which simultaneously transmits the conversations either to recording equipment located elsewhere or to other agents monitoring the transmitting frequency. On Lee v. United States. If the conduct and revelations of an agent operating without electronic equipment do not invade the defendant's constitutionally justifiable expectations of privacy, neither does a simultaneous recording of the same conversations made by the agent or by others from transmissions received from the agent to whom the defendant is talking and whose trustworthiness the defendant necessarily risks.

Our problem is not what the privacy expectations of particular defendants in particular situations may be or the extent to which they may in fact have relied on the discretion of their companions. Very probably, individual defendants neither know nor suspect that their colleagues have gone or will go to the police or are carrying recorders or transmitters. Otherwise, conversation would cease and our problem with these encounters would be nonexistent or far different from those now before us. Our problem, in terms of the principles announced in *Katz*, is what expectations of privacy are constitutionally "justifiable"—what expectations the Fourth Amendment will protect in the absence of a warrant. So far, the law permits the frustration of actual expectations of privacy by permitting authorities to use the testimony of those associates who for one reason or another have determined to turn to the police, as well as by authorizing the use of informants. . . .

Inescapably, one contemplating illegal activities must realize and risk that his companions may be reporting to the police. If he sufficiently doubts their trustworthiness, the association will very probably end or never materialize. But if he has no doubts, or allays them, or risks what doubt he has, the risk is his. In terms of what his course will be, what he will or will not do or say, we are unpersuaded that he would distinguish between probable informers on the one hand and probable informers with transmitters on the other. Given the possibility or probability that one of his colleagues is cooperating with the police, it is only speculation to assert that the defendant's utterances would be substantially different or his sense of security any less if he also thought it possible that the suspected colleague is wired for sound. . . .

Nor should we be too ready to erect constitutional barriers to relevant and probative evidence which is also accurate and reliable. An electronic recording will many times produce a more reliable rendition of what a defendant has said than will the unaided memory of a police agent. It may also be that with the recording in existence it is less likely that the informant will change his mind, less chance that threat or injury will suppress unfavorable evidence and less chance that cross-examination will confound the testimony. Considerations like these obviously do not favor the defendant, but we are not prepared to hold that a defendant who has no constitutional right to exclude the informer's unaided testimony nevertheless has a Fourth Amendment privilege against a more accurate version of the events in question.

. . .

The judgement of the Court of Appeals is reversed.

Mr. Justice Brennan, concurring in the result. (omitted)

Mr. Justice Douglas, dissenting.

The issue in this case is clouded and concealed by the very discussion of it in legalistic terms. What the ancients knew as "eaves-dropping," we now call "electronic surveillance"; but to equate the two is to treat man's first gunpowder on the same level as the nuclear bomb. Electronic surveillance is the greatest leveler of human privacy ever known. How most forms of it can be held "reasonable" within the meaning of the Fourth Amendment is a mystery. To be sure, the Constitution and Bill of Rights are not to be read as covering only the technology known in the 18th century. Otherwise its concept of "commerce" would be hopeless when it comes to the management of modern affairs. At the same time the concepts of privacy which the Founders enshrined in the Fourth Amendment vanish completely when we slavishly allow an all-powerful government, proclaiming law and order, efficiency, and other benign purposes, to penetrate all the walls and doors which men need to shield them from the pressures of a turbulent life around them and give them the health and strength to carry on.

. . .

The threads of thought running through our recent decisions are that these extensive intrusions into privacy made by electronic surveillance make self-restraint by law enforcement officials an inadequate protection, that the requirement of warrants under the Fourth Amendment is essential to a free society.

Monitoring, if prevalent, certainly kills free discourse and spontaneous utterances. Free discourse—a First Amendment value—may be frivolous or serious, humble or defiant, reactionary or revolutionary, profane or in good taste; but it is not free if there is surveillance. Free discourse liberates the spirit, though it may produce only froth. The individual must keep some facts concerning his thoughts within a small zone of people. At the same time he must be free to pour out his woes or inspirations or dreams to others. He remains the sole judge as to what

must be said and what must remain unspoken. This is the essence of the
idea of privacy implicit in the First and Fifth Amendment as well as in
the Fourth.

. . .

... I can imagine nothing that has a more chilling effect on people
speaking their minds and expressing their views on important matters.
The advocates of that regime should spend some time in totalitarian
countries and learn first-hand the kind of regime they are creating here.

Mr. Justice Harlan, dissenting.

. . .

The plurality opinion seeks to erase the crucial distinction between
the facts before us and these holdings by the following reasoning: if A
can relay verbally what is revealed to him by B (as in Hoffa), or record
and later divulge it (as in Lopez), what difference does it make if A
conspires with another to betray B by contemporaneously transmitting
to the other all that is said? The contention is, in essence, an argument
that the distinction between third-party monitoring and other undercover techniques is one of form and not substance. The force of the
contention depends on the evaluation of two separable but intertwined
assumptions: first, that there is no greater invasion of privacy in the
third-party situation, and, second, that uncontrolled consensual surveillance in an electronic age is a tolerable technique of law enforcement,
given the values and goals of our political system.

The first of these assumptions takes as a point of departure the so-
called "risk analysis" approach of *Lopez*, and to a lesser extent *On Lee*,
or the expectations approach of *Katz*. While these formulations represent
an advance over the unsophisticated trespass analysis of the common
law, they too have their limitations and can, ultimately, lead to the
substitution of words for analysis. The analysis must, in my view,
transcend the search for subjective expectations or legal attribution of
assumptions of risk. Our expectations, and the risks we assume, are in
large part reflections of laws that translate into rules the customs and
values of the past and present.

Since it is the task of the law to form and project, as well as mirror
and reflect, we should not, as judges, merely recite the expectations and
risks without examining the desirability of saddling them upon society.
The critical question, therefore, is whether under our system of government, as reflected in the Constitution, we should impose on our citizens
the risks of electronic listener or observer without at least the protection
of a warrant requirement.

This question must, in my view, be answered by assessing the
nature of a particular practice and the likely extent of its impact on the
individual's sense of security balanced against the utility of the conduct
as a technique of law enforcement. For those more extensive intrusions
that significantly jeopardize the sense of security which is the paramount
concern of Fourth Amendment liberties, I am of the view that more than

self-restraint by law enforcement officials is required and at the least warrants should be necessary.

The impact of the practice of third-party bugging, must, I think, be considered such as to undermine that confidence and sense of security in dealing with one another that is characteristic of individual relationships between citizens in a free society. It goes beyond the impact on privacy occasioned by the ordinary type of "informer" investigation upheld in *Lewis* and *Hoffa*. The argument of the plurality opinion, to the effect that it is irrelevant whether secrets are revealed by the mere tattletale or transistor, ignores the differences occasioned by third-party monitoring and recording which insures full and accurate disclosure of all that is said, free of the possibility of error and oversight that inheres in human reporting.

Authority is hardly required to support the proposition that words would be measured a good deal more carefully and communication inhibited if one suspected his conversations were being transmitted and transcribed. Were third-party bugging a prevalent practice, it might well smother that spontaneity—reflected in frivolous, impetuous, sacrilegious, and defiant discourse—that liberates daily life. Much off-hand exchange is easily forgotten and one may count on the obscurity of his remarks, protected by the very fact of a limited audience, and the likelihood that the listener will either overlook or forget what is said, as well as the listener's inability to reformulate a conversation without having to contend with a documented record.[24] All these values are sacrificed by a rule of law that permits official monitoring of private discourse limited only by the need to locate a willing assistant.

. . .

Finally, it is too easy to forget—and, hence, too often forgotten—that the issue here is whether to interpose a search warrant procedure between law enforcement agencies engaging in electronic eavesdropping and the public generally. By casting its "risk analysis" solely in terms of the expectations and risks that "wrongdoers" or "one contemplating illegal activities" ought to bear, the plurality opinion, I think, misses the

---

24. From the same standpoint it may also be thought that electronic recording by an informer of a face-to-face conversation with a criminal suspect, as in *Lopez*, should be differentiated from third-party monitoring, as in *On Lee* and the case before us, in that the latter assures revelation to the Government by obviating the possibility that the informer may be tempted to renege in his undertaking to pass on to the Government all that he has learned. While the continuing vitality of *Lopez* is not drawn directly into question by this case, candor compels me to acknowledge that the views expressed in this opinion may impinge upon that part of the reasoning in *Lopez* which suggested that a suspect has no right to anticipate unreliable testimony. I am now persuaded that such an approach misconceives the basic issue, focusing, as it does, on the interests of a particular individual rather than evaluating the impact of a practice on the sense of security that is the concern of the Fourth Amendment's protection of privacy. Distinctions do, however, exist between *Lopez*, where a known Government agent uses a recording device, and this case which involves third-party overhearing. However, unlikely that the participant recorder will not play his tapes, the fact of the matter is that in a third-party situation the intrusion is instantaneous. Moreover, differences in the prior relationship between the investigator and the suspect may provide a focus for future distinctions.

mark entirely. *On Lee* does not simply mandate that criminals must daily run the risk of unknown eavesdroppers prying into their private affairs; it subjects each and every law-abiding member of society to that risk. The very purpose of interposing the Fourth Amendment warrant requirement is to redistribute the privacy risks throughout society in a way that produces the results the plurality opinion ascribes to the *On Lee* rule. Abolition of *On Lee* would not end electronic eavesdropping. It would prevent public officials from engaging in that practice unless they first had probable cause to suspect an individual of involvement in illegal activities and had tested their version of the facts before a detached judicial officer. The interest *On Lee* fails to protect is the expectation of the ordinary citizen, who has never engaged in illegal conduct in his life, that he may carry on his private discourse freely, openly, and spontaneously without measuring his every word against the connotations it might carry when instantaneously heard by others unknown to him and unfamiliar with his situation or analyzed in a cold, formal record played days, months, or years after the conversation. Interposition of a warrant requirement is designed not to shield "wrongdoers," but to secure a measure of privacy and a sense of personal security throughout our society.

The Fourth Amendment does, of course, leave room for the employment of modern technology in criminal law enforcement, but in the stream of current developments in Fourth Amendment law I think it must be held that third-party electronic monitoring, subject only to the self-restraint of law enforcement officials, has no place in our society.

. . .

I find in neither the ABA study nor Title III any justification for ignoring the identifiable difference—albeit an elusive one in the present state of knowledge—between the impact on privacy of single-party informer bugging and third-party bugging, which in my opinion justifies drawing the constitutional line at this juncture between the two as regards the necessity for obtaining a warrant. Recognition of this difference is, at the very least, necessary to preserve the openness which is at the very core of our traditions and is secure only in a society that tolerates official invasion of privacy simply in circumscribed situations.

The Fourth Amendment protects these traditions, and places limitations on the means and circumstances by which the Government may collect information about its citizens by intruding into their personal lives. The spirit of the principle is captured by the oft-quoted language of Boyd v. United States.

> The principles laid down in this opinion [speaking of Entick v. Carrington, 19 How.St.Tr. 1029 (1765)] affect the very essence of constitutional liberty and security. They reach farther than the concrete form of the case then before the court, with its Adventitious circumstances; they apply to all invasions on the part of the government and its employees of the sanctity of a man's home and the privacies of life. It is not the breaking of

his doors, and the rummaging of his drawers, that constitutes the essence of the offence; but it is the invasion of his indefeasible right of personal security. . . .

What this means is that the burden of guarding privacy in a free society should not be on its citizens; it is the Government that must justify its need to electronically eavesdrop.

(A) EXTENSION OF THE WHITE PRINCIPLE TO NONCONSENSUAL DISCLOSURES OF TELEPHONE NUMBERS AND BANK RECORDS

The principle emanating from *White* that a person has no constitutionally protected expectation of privacy in information that has been voluntarily disclosed to someone who consents to sharing it with the government, was extended to bank records in *United States v. Miller*, 425 U.S. 435 (1976), discussed further in a later section of Chapter II.

In *Smith v. Maryland*, 442 U.S. 735 (1979), five members of the Supreme Court, in an opinion written by Justice Blackmun, held that a governmental recording of numbers dialed from a person's telephone by use of a pen register was not a search, and thus there was no violation of the person's constitutional right to privacy when this occurred. Applying the legitimate expectation of privacy principle, Justice Blackmun concluded that it was "doubtful" that the petitioner or persons in general entertain an actual expectation of privacy in the numbers they dial. In addition, even if the petitioner did harbor a subjective expectation that the phone numbers would remain private such an expectation was not "reasonable." Relying upon *United States v. Miller*, 425 U.S. 435 (1976), the Court equated the bank customer to the public utility customer. Both have exposed the information and, therefore, assume the risk that the company will reveal the information to the government. Justices Brennan and Marshall dissented. The majority's analysis of whether an expectation of privacy regarding telephone numbers was reasonable was wrong-headed in two regards, according to the dissenters. First, no choice to disclose the information in any meaningful sense is involved because there is no realistic alternative to use of the phone system in conversing long distance. Second, risk analysis should not be dispositive in assessing the reasonableness of privacy expectation for fourth amendment purposes. If awareness of the risk were dispositive, announcing the monitoring of phone conversations in advance would then vitiate fourth amendment claims since the user of the phone would be put on notice.

(B) SEPARATION OF THE TRANSACTIONAL DATA FROM THE CONVERSATION

One of the most significant aspects of *Smith v. Maryland* is that the data that underlies the contractual transaction that is essential for conversing over the telephone is separated from the conversation and not given constitutional protection. The conversation is protected but the underlying data is not. It was the transactional data itself that was the sole basis of the claim of privacy protection for financial records in *United States v. Miller* and *Smith v. Maryland*. Do *Miller* and *Smith* stand for the proposition that there is no reasonable expectation of privacy in all transactional data? Is the key to understanding the significance of *Smith* and *Miller* the consensual disclosure of the transactional data by the recipient of the data? If so, then would the correct legal principle of these cases be that a person has no constitutionally protected privacy interest in transactional data that is voluntarily disclosed to the government by the recipient of the data? Compare the Supreme Court of New Jersey's analysis of the constitutional protection for transactional data provided to the telephone company in *State v Hunt*, infra .

(c) Second Class Status for Communication Attributes

Is the Supreme Court's failure to understand the significance of not providing constitutional protection for transactional data based upon a lack of familiarity about digital technology? In an important article Susan Freiwald suggests that the Supreme Court's segregation of communication content and underlying transactional data displays a lack of understanding about the foundation features of digital technology that produces inadequate protections for important privacy interests. See, *Uncertain Privacy: Communication Attributes After the Digital Telephony Act*, 69 Ca. L.Rev. 949 (1996). Freiwald introduces the concept of "communication attributes" to distinguish between all of the characteristics about a communication that can be learned about it, other than its content. Freiwald considers "communication attributes" as a shorthand expression about all noncontent aspects of a communication. She defines "communication attributes" as: "[A]ttributes [that] include the existence, duration and subject matter of the communication, the identities of the parties to it, their physical locations and their electronic addresses." Id. at 952.

Freiwald contends that technological changes since *Smith v. Maryland* have greatly increased the role of the telephone and computer in the daily activities of citizens and dramatically enhanced the amount of communication attribute data that is generated about individuals. Developments in caller identification technology and in forms of computer networking such as the Internet are examples of post *Smith* developments cited by Freiwald. The concept of "communication attributes data" is more precise and inclusive than than "transactional data." The placement of communication attributes information at a low tier of legal protection that is illustrated by *Smith v. Maryland* and *United States v. Miller* is the norm in recent legislation. See, discussion of various legislative measures involving electronic communications and data processing in Chapters Three and Four.

(d) Whose Privacy is at Risk in Fourth Amendment Cases? Justice Harlan's "Risk" Analysis in United States v. White

United States v. White, *supra*, *United States v. Miller*, *infra*, and *Smith v. Maryland*, *supra*, taken together, stand for the general proposition that a person who voluntarily exposes information to someone who shares the information with the government has no legitimate expectation of privacy in respect to that information for purposes of whether there has been a "search or seizure" within the meaning of the fourth amendment.

The notion that exposure of the information results in no legitimate expectation of privacy has played a major role in the constriction of constitutionally based informational privacy rights by the Burger and Rehnquist Courts. As the materials that follow indicate, some state courts have not found this idea appealing in interpreting state constitutional provisions. *Commonwealth v. Sell*, *infra* p. 128, a Pennsylvania Supreme Court case, goes to the extreme of suggesting that the "expectation of privacy" test is not part of search and seizure law in Pennsylvania.

Is part of the difficulty with the expectation of privacy test as employed by the Supreme Court that conclusions in particular cases are counter-intuitive? Is it the case that many ordinary reasonable folks expect a degree of privacy in bank records and telephone numbers? Would it be surprising to learn that the sense of justice of many bank and telephone customers was pricked upon learning that the bank could constitutionally turn over all of the information in its records to a government agent without implicating the Constitution? The testimony of the bank officials and customers in *Burrows*, *infra* p. 134, the California state supreme court case that extends constitutional protection to bank records, provides some empirical support for the proposition that bank customers expect financial institutions to protect the privacy of information disclosed to them by not making such information available to persons who are not involved in the contemplated commercial transaction. Perhaps the judicial decision that the legitimate expectation of privacy test is not satisfied in a particular case is simply a conclusion that the crime control interest outweighs the privacy interest. However, the bald assertion that no legitimate expectation of privacy exists does not provide any elaboration as to why crime control interests ought to outweigh privacy interests in a particular situation.

Justice Harlan went through some intellectual soul searching about the expectancy test after he authored the test in his concurring opinion in *Katz*. His refinement of the subjective feature of that test has already been noted. In his dissent in *United States v. White*, *supra* pp. 98–104, Justice Harlan suggested that the risk and expectation concepts as utilized by the Court had led to the substitution of "words for analysis." 401 U.S. at 786. He argued that the threshold determination in a fourth amendment case should involve a weighing of the impact of the government practice on the individual's sense of security (privacy) and the utility of the practice as a law enforcement technique. In applying this analysis to participatory monitoring, Harlan concluded that the impact of the practice of third party bugging on personal security and privacy was so considerable that a search of White's conversation had occurred when his conversations were transmitted without his consent.

Justice Harlan then considered the implications of the majority decision in *White* in terms of a different kind of risk analysis under the fourth amendment. He suggested that the probable cause and warrant requirements of the fourth amendment were intended to distribute the risk of loss of privacy in our society. By requiring that there be probable cause and the issuance of a warrant by an impartial magistrate before the government can encroach upon privacy in a serious way the fourth amendment places the risk of loss of privacy on those who are involved in illegal activity. The effect of *White* and its assumption of the risk notion is to immunize one party consent participant monitoring from the probable cause and warrant requirements of the fourth amendment. Thus, the risk of loss of privacy is redistributed so that the risk is upon law abiding citizens and not those who have likely engaged in illegal activity. Justice Harlan concluded that this redistribution of the risk is intolerable in our constitutional system.

Review footnote 24 in Justice Harlan's dissenting opinion in *United States v. White, supra* p. 98. Do you find the distinction he makes in fourth amendment cases between the tape recording and the transmission of a conversation to be valid?

(E) CRITICAL REACTION TO THE BURGER AND REHNQUIST COURTS' EMPLOYMENT OF THE LEGITIMATE EXPECTATION OF PRIVACY TEST

The first case in which a majority of the Court utilized the "legitimate expectation" of privacy language was *United States v. Miller, infra.* Does the linguistic change from "reasonable" to "legitimate" expectation of privacy reflect in an obscure way the Burger and Rehnquist Courts' focus on crime control interests to the exclusion of privacy interests in many of its decisions interpreting the fourth amendment? Consider Professor Tracey Maclin's observation:

> The United States Supreme Court is constructing fourth amendment jurisprudence from the perspective of the government official or police officer engaged in intrusive activity, rather than from the perspective of the individual who is the subject of government intrusion. This approach to fourth amendment doctrine marks a significant change from the approach utilized in *Katz v. United States*, and diminishes the scope of fourth amendment protection.

Tracey Maclin, *Constructing Fourth Amendment Principles From the Government Perspective: Whose Amendment Is It, Anyway?*, 28 Am. Crim. L. Rev. 669 (1988).

Is Professor Maclin's suggestion that there has been a shift in emphasis in fourth amendment cases from a privacy-focused concept of search under the *Berger-Katz* analysis, to a crime control evaluation of "search" under *Miller, White* and *Smith*, supported by the following recent Supreme Court decisions?

See Hudson v. Palmer, 468 U.S. 517 (1984) (prisoners have no legitimate expectation of privacy as to the jail cells in respect to any matter in the cell); *Illinois v. Andreas*, 463 U.S. 765 (1983) (once package is lawfully inspected by customs agents, the consignee has no reasonable expectation of privacy in respect to subsequent physical opening of package at police station); *United States v. Place*, 462 U.S. 696 (1983) (police dog "sniffing" of luggage at airport not a "search"); *California v. Ciraolo*, 476 U.S. 207 (1986) (homeowner has no legitimate expectation of privacy in information in backyard that is observed by aerial observation from police helicopter flying in navigable airspace); *California v. Greenwwood* 486 U.S. 35 (1988) (homeowner has no reasonable expectation of privacy in trash placed at curbside outside residence).

In many instances, from the perspective of protecting the condition of privacy against government encroachment, employment of the expectation of privacy concept by the Court results in no accountability under the Constitution for some clear encroachments on privacy. As Justice Harlan has noted, "It is too easy to forget—and hence too often forgotten—" that the issue before the court in determining whether there has been a search is whether the Constitution imposes a search warrant procedure between governmental agencies and the public generally.

Professor Maclin is just one of a large number of critics of the Supreme Court's fourth amendment jurisprudence. Professor LaFave, a leading commentator on the fourth amendment, concludes that "it is almost as if a majority of the Court was hell-bent to seize any available opportunity to define more expansively the constitutional authority of law enforcement officials." Wayne LaFave, *Fourth Amendment Vagaries (Of Improbable Cause, Imperceptible Plain View, Notorious Privacy, and Balancing Askew)*, 74 J. Crim. L. & Criminology 1171, 1222 (1983). For a summary of the growing body of critical commentary that spans the spectrum of political views, *see* Wasserstrom and Seidman, *The Fourth Amendment as Constitutional Theory*, 77 Geo. L.J. 19 (1988). These authors suggest that much of the Court's deference to law enforcement in fourth amendment cases may be explained as a reflection of the positivist tradition in constitutional interpretation. Wasserstrom & Seidman, *id.* at 69. The positivist tradition is discussed in the notes following the *Roberson* decision, *supra* pp. 54–55; Justice Black's dissent in *Katz* is an example of a positivistic interpretation of the fourth amendment concept of search. See also John F. Decker, *Revolution to the Right, Criminal Procedure Jurisprudence during the Burger–Rehnquist Court Era* (Garland 1992). Professor Decker views *Miller, White, Smith* and the cases noted above as examples of the Rehnquist–Burger Courts' use of a "public exposure" concept to shrink privacy protection under the fourth amendment. Id. at 37.

State v. Hunt, infra, Burrows v. Superior Court of San Bernardino County, infra, Commonwealth v. Blood, infra, and *Commonwealth v. Sell, infra,* are part of a growing line of state court precedents which reject the Supreme Court's perspective in fourth amendment cases. These decisions endorse an approach to the fourth amendment which takes the view that where the condition of privacy is encroached upon by the government in a direct and substantial way, a "search" has occurred. This expansive approach to the concept of "search" shifts the burden to the state to demonstrate sufficient justification in furthering crime control interests to warrant the encroachment on privacy. This shift occurs, of course, by triggering the probable cause and warrant requirements. This mode of fourth amendment analysis is consistent with a risk theory that works quite differently from the risk theory of *White, Miller,* and *Smith.* These decisions reflect Justice Harlan's assessment of the risks to law abiding citizens of allowing governmental invasions of privacy without imposition of the safeguards of the fourth amendment.

COMMONWEALTH v. BLOOD

507 N.E.2d 1029 (Mass.1987).

Liacos, J.

[The Massachusetts Eavesdropping Statute contains a one party consent exception for law enforcement investigations. A police informant, Charles Hudson, consented to wear a concealed transmitter and act as one of the conspirators enabling him to tape record several incriminating conversations, each occurring in a private home. The recorded conversations led to charges and to guilty verdicts of conspiracy to break and enter a building with an intent to commit a felony and conspiracy to commit larceny. A pretrial motion to suppress the recorded conversations on the grounds that they were unlawfully obtained, was made by the defendants. The trial court denied the motion, and the defendant appealed.]

Article 14 of the Massachusetts Declaration of Rights provides: "Every subject has a right to be secure from all unreasonable searches, and seizures, of his person, his houses, his papers, and all his possessions. All warrants, therefore, are contrary to this right, if the cause or foundation of them be not previously supported by oath or affirmation; and if the order in the warrant to a civil officer, to make search in suspected places, or to arrest one or more suspected persons, or to seize their property, be not accompanied with a special designation of the persons or objects of search, arrest, or seizure: and no warrant ought to be issued but in cases, and with the formalities prescribed by the laws."

At issue in this appeal is the sufficiency, in light of art. 14, of that portion of the statutory design which renders admissible the evidentiary fruits of warrantless electronic surveillance of organized crime where police have obtained the consent of at least one, but not each, party to a conversation.

. . . We conclude, in the circumstances of this case, that this statutory exemption does not meet the mandate of art. 14. . . . The defendants concede that warrantless surveillance with "one party consent" has been held to lie beyond the protective reach of the Fourth Amendment to the United States Constitution. (citing United States v. White) . . . The Supreme Court's reasoning in White, *supra*, has been rejected by numerous commentators and judges . . . We have often recognized that art. 14 of the Declaration of Rights does, or may, afford more substantive protection to individuals than that which prevails under the Constitution of the United States. When we confront the question whether police activities amount to a search or seizure within the meaning of art. 14, we ask "whether the defendants' expectation of privacy [in the circumstances] is one which society could recognize as reasonable. The privacy interests protected under art. 14 (and the Fourth Amendment) exist when it is shown "that a person [has] exhibited an actual (subjective) expectation of privacy," and when that "expectation [is] one that society is prepared to recognize as 'reasonable.'" Since the conversations at issue took place in private homes, and there is no evidence to suggest that the participants intended the contents to become more widely known, we conclude that the participants exhibited a subjective expectation of privacy.

We consider whether society at large would think it reasonable for the defendants to expect that, in normal course, conversations held in private homes will not be broadcast and recorded surreptitiously. At common law "[i]t is certain every man has a right to keep his own sentiments, if he pleases. He has certainly a right to judge whether he will make them public, or commit them only to the sight of his friends." The Legislature also has recognized the reasonableness, within limits, of every person's claim to control the flow of personal information. This recognition is found, not only in the Fair Information Practices Act and in the statutory right to privacy, but also in those other provisions of which outlaw electronic eavesdropping by ordinary citizens without the consent of all parties to a conversation. Thus, it has long been thought reasonable to expect that what is supposedly said only to friends or close associates will not become generally, indiscriminately known or "etched in stone" without the speaker's consent.

. . . But it is not just the right to a silent, solitary autonomy which is threatened by electronic surveillance: It is the right to bring thoughts and emotions forth from the self in company with others doing likewise, the right to be known to others and to know them, and thus to be whole as a free member of a free society. The instruments of electronic eavesdropping are peculiarly adapted to search our thoughts and emotions. Thus, these devices are peculiarly valuable to those charged with policing crimes, such as the crime of conspiracy at issue here. Indeed, the modern art of eavesdropping may be invaluable in the multitude of situations where specific intent must be proved. But, because the peculiar virtues of these techniques are ones which threaten the privacy of our most cherished possessions, our thoughts and emotions, these techniques are peculiarly intrusive upon that sense of personal security which art. 14 commands us to protect.

Therefore, in circumstances not disclosing any speaker's intent to cast words beyond a narrow compass of known listeners, we conclude that it is objectively reasonable to expect that conversational interchange in a private home will not be invaded surreptitiously by warrantless electronic transmission or recording. The remaining question is whether "one party consent" so alters the balance as to obviate the need for a warrant requirement. It does not. Such consent only affords the State a person willing to transport the invisible instruments of eavesdropping into "earshot."[11]

The vice of the consent exception is that it institutionalizes the historic danger that art. 14 was adopted to guard against (the Court discusses the historical concerns of the colonialists over general search warrants and writs of assistance). In like manner, the consent exception puts the conversational liberty of every person in the hands of any officer lucky enough to find a consenting informant. What was intolerable in 1780 remains so today.

In counterpoint to these considerations, however, the Commonwealth relies primarily on three arguments. None is persuasive. The first of these arguments asserts, . . . that because "the person subject to the warrantless interception is a 'wrongdoer,' [he] should be made to bear the risk of betrayal." This argument proceeds from a pernicious assumption, that anyone subjected to surveillance by police is, because of that fact, necessarily a "wrongdoer." It is the purpose of the warrant requirement in art. 14 to subject police suspicions to the scrutiny of "a neutral and detached magistrate instead of [leaving them to be] judged by the officer engaged in the often competitive enterprise of ferreting out crime. Little would be left "of anyone's justifiable reliance on privacy . . . if everyone must realize that he will be free from warrantless electronic intrusion only so long as someone in the government does not suspect him of improper conduct or wrong thinking.

. . . The White plurality underestimated this risk because it perceived no distinction of constitutional moment between the common

---

11. If there is logic underlying the notion that one party consent obviates the need for judicial supervision, it is logic reminiscent of a bygone era in constitutional jurisprudence. As a practical matter, that surveillance which escapes the statutory warrant requirement by way of the consent exception is eavesdropping accomplished by an undercover agent or informer. Since such a person, if he is admitted as a "party" to a conversation, is likely to be a licensee or invitee in the place where it occurs, such eavesdropping is unlikely to involve trespassory acts of intrusion on property rights. Such acts would not have been of Fourth Amendment significance in the first half of the Twentieth Century, because at that time it was "insisted only that the electronic device not be planted by an unlawful physical invasion of a constitutionally protected area. In the years since however . . . the nontrespassory nature of surveillance done with one party consent is no longer relevant; nor do we perceive any relevance which survives.

gossip and the "wired" informant. For us, however, a distinction lies in the disparity between that sense of security which is felt among trusted friends and the feelings of hostility encountered among competitors or combatants. The sense of security is essential to liberty of thought, speech, and association.

We think it a constitutional imperative to recognize that "the differences between talking to a person enswathed in electronic equipment and one who is not are very real, and they cannot be reduced to insignificance by verbal legerdemain. All of us discuss topics and use expressions with one person that we would not undertake with another and that we would never broadcast to a crowd. Few of us would ever speak freely if we knew that all our words were being captured by machines for later release before an unknown and potentially hostile audience. No one talks to a recorder as he talks to a person."[13]

We conclude that it is unreasonably intrusive to impose the risk of electronic surveillance on every act of speaking aloud to another person. We cannot conclude that, in the absence of a warrant, the consent of less than all the partakers of a conversation is sufficient to waive any participant's rights pursuant to art. 14 not to be recorded.[16] Each conversation whose recorded contents was admitted at trial had unfolded in a person's home, in circumstances not even remotely suggestive of any speaker's intent to be heard beyond the circle of known listeners. As to each of those conversations, we hold that its warrantless electronic search by surreptitious transmission and its electronic seizure by surreptitious recording were in violation of art. 14. We further conclude that this case involves circumstances in which art. 14 requires exclusion of evidence.

DISSENT: NOLAN, J. (dissenting, with whom LYNCH, J., joins).

. . . [The one party consent exception] represents an inescapable legislative judgment that members of organized crime who converse about a designated offense do not have a reasonable expectation of privacy in that conversation. This is a sound judgment.

---

13. To gauge the likely impact of unfettered surveillance on the individual's sense of security, and to appreciate the absurdity of the White rationale, one need only imagine the kind of person who does think it reasonable that his every word is overheard and seized for use against him. "He easily becomes suspicious and distrustful. He finds it difficult to confide in others, and if he does confide . . . he expects to be betrayed. . . . [H]e is a person with lifelong tendencies toward secretiveness, seclusiveness, and solitary rumination, although these may be concealed behind a brittle facade of superficial social give and take. . . . [To him, people] are unpredictable as well as untrustworthy; they must be watched." 1 N. Cameron, Paranoid Conditions and Paranoia, American Handbook of Psychiatry 512–513 (1959) (describing the paranoid personality disorder). The world of the White thesis is a topsy-turvy one in which the paranoid's delusory watchfulness is the stance held "reasonable."

16. We are mindful that the showing which police must make to obtain warrants passing constitutional muster is extensive. Conformance with such requirements may be viewed as inconvenient for police, especially when compared with the ease of "wiring" an informant. In many ways, however, it is the ease of participant monitoring which renders it a threat to the citizens of a free society.

Yet somehow, in a way that strains credulity, the court manages to evade society's judgment. Since art. 14 protects people, not places, the location of the conversation is constitutionally immaterial. It is the conversation that is being searched and not the home. These defendants are not passive victims of governmental intrusions into their zones of privacy. Rather, by taking Hudson into their confidence the defendants effectively extended their zones of privacy to include him. There is no constitutional principle that prohibits Hudson from disclosing confidential information to the police. Moreover, even if a person's home is where he has the most reasonable expectation of privacy, that expectation of privacy is no longer reasonable when the home becomes a site for planning criminal activity. But more importantly, the Eavesdropping Statute informs this court that society does not recognize that expectation as reasonable. It is also incredible for the court to maintain that it is "objectively reasonable" that these defendants did not expect their conversation to be electronically recorded.

... Of course, I also assumed that a determination of society's reasonable expectations is merely a descriptive endeavor and not infused with whatever normative content judges think such expectations should possess.

Even assuming that the defendants had a reasonable expectation of privacy in these circumstances, the question is whether the police conduct was "unreasonable." ... I am unable to comprehend how "free speech and privacy values are unduly threatened by the risk that when one [member of an organized criminal conspiracy] speaks to a known [member of the same conspiracy] he may be recording the conversation."

This statute represents a modern response to a modern problem. The framers of the Massachusetts Declaration of Rights did not foresee the development of electronic surveillance just as they could not imagine the formation of highly organized and disciplined criminal groups. They did, however, intend that art. 14 and other provisions provide the framework in which the republican ideals of liberty and order could flourish. But the court demands a liberal interpretation of art. 14 so that modern privacy rights are protected, while it insists upon a narrow reading when the needs of modern law enforcement are considered. In the guise of protecting privacy, it only protects those who are its greatest threat. I dissent.

Note: State Court Developments: Post Blood

The use of informers who are wired for sound either with a tape recorder or transmitter is referred to as participant monitoring (or consent surveillance). Participant monitoring is one of the most basic investigative techniques of law enforcement agencies. The use of a transmitter by the informer and the contemporaneous recording of the conversations by the officer that receives the transmission is preferable to a tape recorder that is on the body of the informer. With the transmitter the conversation is more easily admitted into evidence if the informer is unable to testify. The incriminating statement of the defendant is admissible under the admission exception to the hearsay rule in both cases. But the tape of the conversation that is transmitted is easier to authenticate.

Only a few state courts have agreed with the reasoning of *Blood* and interpreted their state constitution to require a warrant before the government may engage in participant monitoring in the home. Pennsylvania and Vermont are in accord, see, *Commonwealth v. Brion*, 539 Pa. 256, 652 A.2d 287 (1994); *State v. Brooks*, 157 Vt. 490, 601 A.2d 963 (1991). In *State of Alaska v. Glass*, 583 P.2d 872 (Alaska 1978), the Supreme Court found that participant monitoring in the home violated an explicit privacy provision of the state constitution ("The right of the people to privacy is recognized and shall not be infringed ..." Ala. Const. Art. I, § 22). The Supreme Court of Alaska has extended *Glass* to conversations outside of the home, see, *State v. Thornton*, 583 P.2d 886 (Alaska 1978). In Pennsylvania, Massachusetts and Vermont the requirement of a warrant for participant monitoring has been limited to the home, see, *Commonwealth v. Rodriguez*, 519 Pa. 415, 548 A.2d 1211 (1988); *Commonwealth v. Pratt*, 407 Mass. 647, 555 N.E.2d 559 (1990); *State v. Blow*, 157 Vt. 513, 602 A.2d 552 (1991). In a state that requires a warrant before participant monitoring is allowed in the home, must the warrant that is issued contain a particularized description of the premises where the conversation is to occur?

The Montana Supreme Court interpreted the state constitution to require a warrant in *State v. Brackman*, 178 Mont. 105, 582 P.2d 1216 (1978), but later reversed that decision in *State v. Brown*, 232 Mont. 1, 755 P.2d 1364 (1988). The Louisiana high court initially decided to require a warrant for participant monitoring but, on rehearing the court reversed the initial opinion. *See, State v. Reeves*, 427 So.2d 403 (La.1982). The decision by the Florida Supreme Court in *State v. Sarmiento*, 397 So.2d 643 (Fla.1981), to require a warrant for participation monitoring was superseded by a constitutional amendment. The 1982 amendment to the Florida Constitution (Art I, § 12) contains a proscription against unreasonable searches and seizures but also states, that, "This right shall be construed in conformity with the fourth amendment to the United States Constitution as interpreted by the United States Supreme Court."

Some courts have been more generous in expanding privacy rights under state constitutions for pen registers than they have for participant monitoring. New Jersey requires a warrant for pen registers but not for consent surveillance. Pennsylvania requires a warrant for pen registers in all instances but only requires a warrant for consent surveillance if it occurs in the home. What is your explanation for a court giving greater privacy protection for pen registers than for consent surveillance? Are the privacy and crime control interests different when pen registers are used then when government engages in participant monitoring? For review of state courts' response to *White*, see, Dubis, *The Consensual Electronic Surveillance Experiment: State Courts React to United States v. White*, 47 Vand. L. Rev. 857 (1994).

(2) State Constitutional Protection for Telephone Records After Smith v. Maryland

STATE v. HUNT

91 N.J. 338, 450 A.2d 952 (1982).

SCHREIBER, J. . . .

[Defendants Hunt and Pirillo were indicted for various gambling and bookmaking activities in violation of three New Jersey statutes. Defendants pled guilty pursuant to a plea bargain after moving unsuccessfully to suppress evidence of allegedly unlawful searches and seizures by police. The Appellate Division summarily affirmed defendants' convictions on appeal. Defendants' joint petition for certification was granted to review the constitutionality of the warrantless search and seizure of defendants' telephone toll billing records.

In 1977, pursuant to a court order, police intercepted three conversations between Hunt and one Robert Notaro, who was engaged in an illegal sports bookmaking enterprise and observed Hunt and Pirillo meeting with Notaro to discuss gambling. A reliable informant had advised police that Pirillo was a bookmaker. In 1978 another informant advised police that Hunt was running a gambling business over two telephone numbers listed in Hunt's name. A state detective then obtained records of Hunt's home toll billing records for a two month period from the telephone company, without a court order. The records revealed frequent calls to Sports Phone Service, which provides up-to-the-minute results of sporting events. Subsequently, information gathered by tapping Hunt's phone and searching his apartment clearly established bookmaking activity.]

The defendants moved to suppress the following evidence: (1) Hunt's toll billing records; (2) the data obtained from the pen registers; (3) the information obtained from the wire interceptions of the Hunt and Pirillo telephones between October 14 and October 23; and (4) the evidence uncovered during the search of the Hunt and Pirillo premises.

As indicated at the outset, our concern is with the toll billing records. The key questions are whether an individual has a protectible interest in those records under the Fourth Amendment to the federal Constitution or Article I, par. 7 of the New Jersey Constitution. Both constitutional provisions acknowledge the "right of the people to be secure in their persons, houses, papers, and effects, against unreasonable searches and seizures." The historical roots of the Fourth Amendment centered about protection from unwarranted intrusions into the home. This privacy interest in the home and place of business has continued unabated throughout our judicial history. Indeed, as the telephone has taken its place in the home and at business, the privacy interest has expanded to include telephone conversations.

The United States Supreme Court has protected a telephone conversation from governmental eavesdropping by an electronic recording device. Katz v. United States. That Court has also indicated that it will not protect information or material beyond the conversation itself. We surmise as much because of its decision in Smith v. Maryland. . . .

The Court then summarized the two questions central to Justice Blackmun's majority opinion in Smith v. Maryland, *supra*.

The expectation of privacy in a pen register, both subjectively and objectively, is substantially similar to that in toll billing records. The difference between toll billing records, which reflect long distance completed calls, and the pen register, which identifies all local and long distance numbers dialed, whether completed or not, does not have any impact upon Justice Blackmun's analysis. His rationale places the toll billing record into the pen register mold. This conclusion is borne out by the federal courts that have passed on this question and have concluded that toll billing records are not entitled to Fourth Amendment protection.

Our inquiry does not end at this point, for we must consider the application of the search and seizure safeguard in the New Jersey Constitution. This Court has seen fit to hold that the search and seizure provisions in the federal and New Jersey Constitutions are not always coterminous, despite the congruity of the language. Though notions of federalism may seem to justify this difference, enforcement of criminal laws in federal and state courts, sometimes involving the identical episodes, encourages application of uniform rules governing search and seizure. Divergent interpretations are unsatisfactory from the public perspective, particularly where the historical roots and purposes of the federal and state provisions are the same.

Sound policy reasons, however, may justify a departure. New Jersey has had an established policy of providing the utmost protection for telephonic communications. Long before the Supreme Court's opinion in Katz v. United States, the New Jersey Legislature had in a 1930 statute made it a misdemeanor to tap a telephone line. . . .

In addition to the legislative restrictions on wiretaps, our case law has adopted a policy of protecting the privacy of telephonic communications. . . .

In this case we are persuaded that the equities so strongly favor protection of a person's privacy interest that we should apply our own standard rather than defer to the federal provision. We do so in the spirit announced in a recent comment, "The Interpretation of State Constitutional Rights," 95 Harv.L.Rev. 1324, 1367 (1982):

> In our federal system, state constitutions have a significant role to play as protectors of individual rights and liberties. This role derives its character from the freedom of state courts to move beyond the protections provided by federal doctrine and from the distinctive character of state courts and state constitutions. But the state constitutional role is also shaped by the emergence of the federal Bill of Rights in recent decades as the

primary constitutional shield against intrusions by all levels of government. The present function of state constitutions is as a second line of defense for those rights protected by the federal Constitution and as an independent source of supplemental rights unrecognized by federal law.

Technological developments have enlarged our conception of what constitutes the home. The telephone has become an essential instrument in carrying on our personal affairs. It has become part and parcel of the home. When a telephone call is made, it is as if two people are having a private conversation in the sanctity of their living room. It is generally understood to consist of a conversation between two persons, no third person being privy to it in the absence of consent. It is well settled that telephone conversations carried on by people in their homes or offices are fully protected from governmental intrusions. Katz v. United States.

Not all telephone conversations enjoy the same privacy. If one party makes the conversation available to others, such as through the use of a speaker phone or by permitting someone else to hear, as was done on occasion in this case when the informant permitted the detective to listen to the conversation, the privacy interest does not remain the same. However, when neither party permits any interference with the call and only the telephone company in the course of its operations is privy to any information, the question remains whether the company's participation destroys the sanctity of the call, which comprises data as to both who was contacted and what message was conveyed, so as to permit unauthorized governmental intrusion.

The telephone caller is "entitled to assume that the words he utters into the mouthpiece will not be broadcast to the world." Katz. Similarly, he is entitled to assume that the numbers he dials in the privacy of his home will be recorded solely for the telephone company's business purposes. From the viewpoint of the customer, all the information which he furnishes with respect to a particular call is private. The numbers dialed are private. The call is made from a person's home or office, locations entitled to protection under the Fourth Amendment and Article I, par. 7 of the New Jersey Constitution.

. . .

It is unrealistic to say that the cloak of privacy has been shed because the telephone company and some of its employees are aware of this information. Telephone calls cannot be made except through the telephone company's property and without payment to it for the service. This disclosure has been necessitated because of the nature of the instrumentality, but more significantly the disclosure has been made for a limited business purpose and not for release to other persons for other reasons. The toll billing records privacy is a part of the privacy package.

. . .

The decision we adopt herein should be applied only to all billing records processed after today. It will cause a sharp break in the practice of the police authorities, announces a new rule, and changes prior law. Moreover, we are satisfied that retroactivity would have a considerable adverse impact on the administration of justice. The Attorney General has advised us that there have been a significant number of telephone toll record acquisitions in criminal investigations and that the investigative technique of obtaining telephone billing records, like pen registers, has been employed generally in the initial stages of investigations. There are hundreds of pending cases, with innumerable defendants, involving these records. Under these circumstances and since we are concerned with the exclusionary rule, retroactivity is not appropriate.

The Court then denied defendants' motion to suppress the information obtained subsequent to the toll billing records as inadmissible fruits of the poisonous tree. The Court held that the wrongfully acquired telephone records had no bearing on the court orders providing for the justified issuance of the wire intercepts or search warrants and the evidence obtained was properly seized.

    . . .

The judgments are affirmed.

Pashman, J., concurring. (omitted)

Handler, J., concurring.

I agree with the result reached by the majority in this case and its decision to utilize the State Constitution to vindicate a right seemingly neglected by the federal Constitution. I write separately to expose the reasoning that I find implicit in our decision and to explain more fully the judicial principles which I believe underlie the salutary resort to state constitutions as a fountainhead of individual rights.

    . . .

There is surely no impropriety in state courts building an independent body of state constitutional law. . . .

Nevertheless, our national judicial history and traditions closely wed federal and state constitutional doctrine. It is not entirely realistic, sound or historically accurate to regard the separation between the federal and state systems as a schism. The states are not always free to act independently under their own constitutions. State constitutions may be used to supplement or expand federally guaranteed constitutional rights. However, they may never be used to undermine or circumscribe them. . . .

. . . [S]tate courts should be sensitive to developments in federal law. Federal precedent in areas addressed by similar provisions in our state constitutions can be meaningful and instructive. . . . The opinions of the Supreme Court, while not controlling on state courts construing their own constitutions, are nevertheless important guides on the subjects which they squarely address.

It is therefore appropriate, in my estimation, to identify and explain standards or criteria for determining when to invoke our State Constitution as an independent source for protecting individual rights. There are several considerations that are relevant and important in making that determination.

(1) Textual Language—A state constitution's language may itself provide a basis for reaching a result different from that which could be obtained under federal law. Textual language can be relevant in either of two contexts. First, distinctive provisions of our State charter may recognize rights not identified in the federal Constitution....

Second, the phrasing of a particular provision in our charter may be so significantly different from the language used to address the same subject in the federal Constitution that we can feel free to interpret our provision on an independent basis....

. . .

(2) Legislative History—Whether or not the textual language of a given provision is different from that found in the federal Constitution, legislative history may reveal an intention that will support reading the provision independently of federal law....

(3) Preexisting State Law—Previously established bodies of state law may also suggest distinctive state constitutional rights. State law is often responsive to concerns long before they are addressed by constitutional claims. Such preexisting law can help to define the scope of the constitutional right later established. (citing Howard, State Courts and Constitutional Rights in the Day of the Burger Court, 62 Va. L. Rev. 873, 1416–1418 (1976)).

(4) Structural Differences—Differences in structure between the federal and state constitutions might also provide a basis for rejecting the constraints of federal doctrine at the state level. The United States Constitution is a grant of enumerated powers to the federal government. Our State Constitution, on the other hand, serves only to limit the sovereign power which inheres directly in the people and indirectly in their elected representatives. Hence, the explicit affirmation of fundamental rights in our Constitution can be seen as a guarantee of those rights and not as a restriction upon them.

(5) Matters of Particular State Interest or Local Concern—A state constitution may also be employed to address matters of peculiar state interest or local concern. When particular questions are local in character and do not appear to require a uniform national policy, they are ripe for decision under state law.... Moreover, some matters are uniquely appropriate for independent state action. For example, in Alston [88 N.J. 211, 440 A.2d 1311 (1981)], we adopted a rule of standing to challenge searches and seizures that is broader than the federal standard. We felt free to do so because that question implicated the management of our own court system, which is of peculiarly local concern. It also reflected a strong state policy in favor of access to our courts and liberalized standing to vindicate legal claims.

(6) State Traditions—A state's history and traditions may also provide a basis for the independent application of its constitution. Thus, in *Schmid* [84 N.J. 535, 423 A.2d 615 (1980)], we emphasized New Jersey's strong tradition of protecting individual expressional and associational rights in holding that the New Jersey Constitution provided greater protections for the right to free speech than those found in the federal Constitution....

(7) Public Attitudes—Distinctive attitudes of a state's citizenry may also furnish grounds to expand constitutional rights under state charters. While we have never cited this criterion in our decisions, courts in other jurisdictions have pointed to public attitudes as a relevant factor in their deliberations.

Note

Additional state courts that have interpreted state constitutions' provisions prohibiting unreasonable searches and seizures to reach call tracing devices include: Colorado, *People v. Sporleder*, 666 P.2d 135 (Colo.1983); Hawaii, *State v. Rothman*, 779 P.2d 1 (Haw.1989); Idaho, *State v. Thompson*, 760 P.2d 1162 (Idaho 1988); Pennsylvania, *Commonwealth v. Melilli*, 361 Pa.Super. 429, 522 A.2d 1107 (1987).

See also Comment on Privacy, *Pen Registers and State Constitutions: The Colorado Supreme Court Rejects Smith v. Maryland*, 15 U. Tul. L. Rev. 1467 (1984).

Note: The Importance of Toll–Call Records to Law Enforcement

How important is accessibility of toll records to law enforcement? Consider portions of the statement of Donald E. Campbell, Assistant United States Attorney in the District of Columbia, that were quoted in the majority opinion in *Reporters Comm. v. American Tel. & Tel.*, 593 F.2d 1030 (D.C.Cir. 1978).

> The continued access to [toll] records, without advance notice to subscribers, is absolutely necessary for law enforcement to successfully investigate and prosecute certain criminal activity.

> Subscriber and toll information without advance notice to subscribers is critical in any major narcotic, gambling, fencing, loan-sharking or corruption matter or any other major ongoing conspiratorial or other criminal activity. The upper echelons of the criminal community go to great extremes to insulate themselves from detection by law enforcement. However, these upper echelon individuals must communicate with those individuals on the "street" who are doing their "bidding," and who are visible to law enforcement. For example, an individual is identified in the D.C. area as a major drug trafficker, and drugs are purchased from this individual by an undercover officer. If law enforcement has conducted a detailed and careful investigation, there will be a telephone on which this trafficker has contacted his out-of-town supplier, because no conspiracy can be carried forward without communication between the conspirators. Experience has shown that a telephone is usually used by one of the parties to the conspiracy to communicate to the principal

receiver of a large shipment of drugs, the time, place and means of arrival of the shipment. Therefore, the drug trafficker is not arrested at this time and a careful review of toll records is made. This may permit law enforcement to identify an individual in another part of the country who is known to law enforcement in that area to be involved in drugs....

In every case where law enforcement considers the use of a wire interception, toll records are not only one of the critical factors in establishing probable cause, but are probably the most revealing factor as to how successful a wire intercept will be. If advance notice is given to the subscriber that law enforcement is interested in his toll records, the effectiveness of wire intercepts will be greatly reduced. Advance notice to subscribers will only serve to frustrate law enforcement in its effort to immobilize the upper echelons of the criminal community and result in more concentration on the lesser figures.

593 F.2d 1030, n. 7 1037.

Note: The Threat of Unrestricted Access to Toll Records to Privacy and First Amendment Rights

In *Reporters Comm. v. American Tel. & Tel.*, 593 F.2d 1030 (D.C.Cir. 1978), the court rejected claims by newspaper publishers, individual journalists and a press organization that government access to toll records violated their first and fourth amendment rights. On the first amendment issue the court rejected the requested relief—prior notice to journalists—on the basis that the plaintiffs had not satisfied the evidentiary requirements for injunctive relief.

Judge Skelly Wright dissented on the first amendment question and would require judicial scrutiny of subpoenas requesting toll records of journalists. Judge Wright cited examples of governmental abuse from the record in the case that demonstrated to him the need for prior judicial scrutiny of government requests in toll records in order to protect the crucial first amendment interests:

On at least five, and allegedly six, occasions the toll billing records of appellants were provided to the Government in accordance with this general practice. During the summer of 1971, for example, after the printing of portions of the Pentagon Papers in publications with which Richard Dudman and Knight Newspapers were affiliated, the Chesapeake & Potomac Telephone Company (C & P) provided agents of the Federal Bureau of Investigation (FBI) involved in the Daniel Ellsberg–Pentagon Papers Investigation with the long distance records for telephones listed to Dudman and Knight Newspapers. That same summer the FBI, acting on a White House request that it learn the sources of a column by Jack Anderson about an official of the Agency for International Development who had "crashed" a party for Vice President Agnew which, in the words of a State Department cable quoted by Anderson, "culminated in his getting sloshed," secured from C & P toll records for telephones listed to Anderson and three of his employees. A final example worthy of note occurred in early 1974 and involved David Rosenbaum of the New York Times. A taxpayer complained to the Internal Revenue Service (IRS) that Rosenbaum knew about an investigation of the taxpayer being conducted by the IRS, and that Rosenbaum had suggested to the taxpayer that the investigation was being suppressed for political reasons. Although the IRS knew the identity of the agent likely to be Rosenbaum's source, it nonetheless requested and received from C & P the toll billing records, not only for Mr. Rosenbaum's telephone, but for all the telephones of the entire staff of the Washington Bureau of the New York Times for a six-month period.[7]

In none of these or the other admitted cases of Government requests for appellants' phone records was the Government agency involved required to establish probable cause for its request or to secure any form of judicial approval. Nor did the telephone companies in any way challenge the Government's authority to obtain the requested information. And neither the Government nor the telephone companies made any effort in any of these cases to notify the reporter or newspaper whose records were being sought of the request. As a result, at no time was the validity or constitutionality of the Government requests subject to any form of judicial scrutiny.

593 F.2d at 1080–81.

Note: Expanded Protection for Privacy Under State Constitutions

State v. Hunt is a classic example of expanded protection of constitutional informational privacy rights through judicial interpretation of the constitution of a state. In our federal system it is clear that states may act independently and interpret their own constitutions in a more expansive way than the United States Supreme Court interprets the United States Constitution, even when the case before the state court involves a state constitutional provision that is identical in language to a clause in the United States Constitution. This is because the supremacy clause of the federal constitution imposes a floor, but not a ceiling, on a state court's interpretation of individual rights. It is an increasingly important feature of our federal system that states may develop their own distinctive tradition of individual rights against state government. During the Warren Court era when the Supreme Court was extending due process and equal protection rights under the federal constitution, the independent expansion of rights by state courts was seldom invoked, and little noticed when it was.

During the last two decades, the Burger and Rehnquist Courts have put an end to, or at least retarded the extension of due process and equal

7. The six-month period chosen was unrelated to the investigation itself; rather, it was based on the IRS inspector's understanding "that they only maintained records for a six-month period of time. . . . [H]ad the phone company had more than just the six-month period of time involved, I would have obtained all of the records."

As soon as the New York Times learned of this matter and communicated its concern to IRS Commissioner Alexander, the Commissioner immediately ordered all records returned to the telephone company.

protection rights previously undertaken by the Warren Court, especially in the areas of criminal procedure. This has prompted a revitalized practice of expansively interpreting individual rights under state constitutions. This development, initially coined "new federalism" is now an established aspect of our legal system. *See generally*, Donald E. Wilkes, Jr., *The New Federalism in Criminal Procedure: State Court Evasion of the Burger Court*, 62 Ky. L.J. 421 (1974); Project Report, *Toward an Activist Role for State Bill of Rights*, 8 Harv. Civ. Rights—Civ. Lib. L. Rev. 271 (1973). Justice Brennan has encouraged the movement to enhance informational privacy rights under state constitutions in both judicial opinions and scholarly writings. *See* Brennan, *State Constitutions and the Protection of Individual Rights,* 90 Harv. L. Rev. 489 (1977). This phenomenon has been commented upon extensively. Two important publications on the subject are: *Symposium: The Emergence of State Constitutional Law*, 63 Tex. L. Rev. 959 (1985) and *Developments in the Law, The Interpretation of State Constitutional Rights*, 95 Harv. L. Rev. 1324 (1982).

Although there is no doubt that state courts have the authority in our legal system to diverge from federal precedent in interpreting state constitutional provisions, even when the text of the state constitution is identical in wording, there has been considerable controversy as to whether it is desirable for state courts to do so. The arguments for and against state court activism in this area are often linked to the debate over the appropriate role of the judiciary in interpreting the constitution generally. Recall the discussion of the philosophy of law utilized by the high state courts in *Roberson* and *Pavesich* earlier in the materials. The dichotomy between "positivistic" and "natural law" approaches to interpreting the common law are paralleled by the two schools of philosophy that are often invoked in debates over the appropriate approach to constitutional interpretation—interpretivism and noninterpretivism. Interpretivist judges view themselves as limited by the language, structure and intent of the framers in constitutional cases. *See generally* Raoul Berger, *Government by the Judiciary* 363–72 (1972); John Hart Ely, *Democracy and Distrust I* (1980). Noninterpretivist judges consider it appropriate to consider other sources—such as long standing traditions of morality in deciding whether the constitution is violated by state law. *See generally* Michael J. Perry, *The Constitution, The Courts and Human Rights* (1982); Justice Harlan dissenting opinion in *Poe v. Ullman*, 367 U.S. 497 (1961).

(A) EXPANDED INTERPRETATION OF STATE CONSTITUTIONAL PROVISIONS EQUIVALENT TO THOSE IN THE FEDERAL CONSTITUTION

In cases like *State v. Hunt*, *supra*, and *Commonwealth v. Sell*, *infra*, state courts were interpreting state constitutional provisions that tracked the language of the fourth amendment. Yet the courts found that the proscription against "unreasonable searches and seizures," under the state constitution had different meaning than what the Supreme Court had found similar language to mean under the fourth amendment. Arguments calling for lockstep interpretation of state constitutions with federal precedent focus on cases where the language in the constitutions is identical. Inconsistent interpretation of identical language is at odds with the philosophical assumptions of interpretivism. Interpretivists presuppose that similar language in constitutional texts has similar meaning; language in constitutional text is an expression of the intent or values of the framers.

(B) Justice Handler's "Criteria" for Principled Expansion of Rights

Are extended and inconsistent interpretations of similar textual provisions by state courts unprincipled? Are cases like *State v. Hunt*, unprincipled, result-oriented cases that reflect biases of some state judges against what they perceive to be the anti-rights pro-government view of the Supreme Court?

Justice Handler's thoughtful concurrence in *Hunt* is one of the fullest elaborations of the range of principled justifications that a court might invoke to support an independent and more expansive interpretation of language in a state constitution that is equivalent to language in the federal constitution. Does Justice Handler suggest that state courts adopt a presumption in favor of federal precedent when equivalent constitutional texts are involved? Which of the seven criteria advanced by Justice Handler support the Court's independent interpretation of New Jersey's proscription against unreasonable searches and seizures?

Justice Handler suggests that decisions like *Hunt* "supplement" and "expand" but do not "undermine" or "circumscribe" federally guaranteed rights. Do you agree? In arguing for expanded rights under state constitutional provisions that are equivalent to their federal counterparts, the "criteria" summarized in Justice Handler's opinion constitute the basic range of arguments that should be considered.

(C) Explicit Right-to-Privacy Clauses

The strongest case in support of state court activism in invalidating government invasions of privacy is made when the state constitutional text specifically provides for protection for privacy. Several of the concerns that are raised about state courts going off on their own in rights elaboration have no bearing on judicial interpretation of state constitutional provisions expressly referring to privacy. Interpretivists should have no general complaint. State constitutional language reflects the distinct values and intentions of the framers under the state constitution. From a noninterpretivist perspective, these provisions should be viewed as representing expressions of political morality that are distinctive features of the history and traditions of the state in respect to privacy. It is well settled that in our legal systems, states may express their own political morality of privacy rights against the government as long as it is no less generous than that developed under the federal constitution. Where the political morality is expressed in specific and unique textual language, judicial recognition of greater privacy rights is a reflection of the independence and autonomy of the states in our federal system and not a rejection of the call for deference to traditions of political morality developed under the federal constitution. Several state courts' decisions that have extended privacy protection have been in states with specific state constitutional provisions. At least ten state constitutions contain explicit right-to-privacy clauses.

They include: California, Cal. Const., art. I, sec. 1 ("All people ... have inalienable rights. Among these are enjoying and defending life and liberty, acquiring, possessing, and protecting property, and pursuing and obtaining safety, happiness, and privacy."); Florida, Fla. Const., art. I, sec. 23 ("Every natural person has the right to be let alone and free from governmental intrusion into his private life except as otherwise provided herein."); Louisiana, La. Const., art. I, sec. 5 ("Every person shall be secure in his person, property, communications, houses, papers and effects against ... invasions of privacy."); Alaska, Alaska Const., art. I, sec. 22 ("The right of the people to privacy is recognized and shall not be infringed."); Arizona, Ariz. Const., art. II, sec. 8 ("No person shall be disturbed in his private affairs, or his home invaded, without authority of law."); Hawaii, Hawaii Const., art. I, secs. 6–7 ("The right of the people to privacy is recognized and shall not be infringed without the showing of a compelling state interest.... The right of the people to be secure in their persons, houses, papers and effects against unreasonable searches, seizures and invasions of privacy shall not be violated.... "); Illinois, Ill. Const., art. I, sec. 6 ("The people shall have the right to be secure in their persons, houses, papers and other possessions against unreasonable searches, seizures, invasions of privacy or interceptions of communications by eavesdropping devices or other means.... No warrant shall issue without probable cause, supported by affidavit particularly describing the place to be secured and the persons or things to be seized."); Montana, Mont. Const., art. II, sec. 10 ("The right of individual privacy is essential to the well-being of a free society and shall not be infringed without the showing of a compelling state interest."); South Carolina, S.C. Const., art. I, sec. 10 ("The right of the people to be secure in their persons, houses, papers, and effects against unreasonable searches and seizures and unreasonable invasions of privacy shall not be violated, and no warrants shall issue but upon probable cause, supported by oath or affirmation, and particularly describing the place to be searched, the person or thing to be seized, and the information to be obtained."); and Washington, Wash. Const., art. I, sec. 7 ("No person shall be disturbed in his private affairs, or his home invaded, without authority of law.").

Cases that have expanded privacy rights under state constitutions in protecting personal autonomy are examined in Chapter 7, *infra*.

What price might be paid if state courts' decisions expanding rights were perceived as expedient political reactions to Burger and Rehnquist Court decisions? Justice Handler suggests a heavy price: the "erosion or dilution of constitutional doctrine." *Hunt*, 450 A.2d at 963. Consider this observation in footnote 1 of his opinion:

This, in a sense, has occurred in California, labeled "the birthplace of th[e] new judicial independence" by one commentator. Note, *State Constitutional Guarantees as Adequate State Ground: Supreme Court Review and Problems of Federalism*, 13 Am. Crim. L. Rev. 737, 740 (1976). The voters of that state recently passed a referendum requiring state courts to give the same meaning to provisions of the California Constitution as is given to parallel provisions in the U.S. Constitution. See, Proposition 8 (adopted June 8, 1982). The referendum may effect the ability of the California courts to give their own charter independent force.

(D) THE NEED FOR STATE COURTS TO CLEARLY INDICATE THAT THE STATE CONSTITUTION IS AN INDEPENDENT BASIS FOR PROTECTING AGAINST INVASIONS OF PRIVACY

Erroneous interpretations of the federal constitution are subject to review by the United States Supreme Court. This normally occurs when the state court has erroneously upheld a state law that has been challenged under the United States Constitution. The Supreme Court may also review state court invalidation of a state law based upon an erroneous interpretation of the federal constitution. However, if a state court's invalidation of state legislation is based on the state constitution, the Supreme Court will not review the decision. *See generally* Stewart G. Pollock, *Adequate and Independent State Grounds as a Means of Balancing the Relationship Between State and Federal Courts*, 63 Tex. L. Rev. 977, 980 (1985) (tracing proposition that Supreme Court will not review decisions with independent and adequate state grounds to *Murdock v. Memphis*, 87 U.S. 590 (1875)).

Until recently, it probably was sufficient if there was any reference to the state constitution in the state court decision. *See, e.g., In re Estate of Cavill*, 329 A.2d 503, 505 n. 7 (Pa.1974) (invalidating Pennsylvania's mortmain statute almost exclusively on basis of fourteenth amendment of United States Constitution, with reference to state proscription against special legislation in footnote). However, *Michigan v. Long*, 463 U.S. 1032 (1983), strongly suggests that a closer evaluation of the state court basis will occur. The majority opinion in *Long*, written by Justice O'Connor, adopts a presumption that the state court decision is based upon the federal constitution where state and federal grounds are intertwined, and requires a plain statement that the state ground was relied upon. *Id.* at 1040–41; *cf. Oregon v. Hass*, 420 U.S. 714 (1975) (state decision rested on federal grounds as neither state constitutional grounds nor state law was cited as basis for decision). Note that *Michigan v. Long* was a case involving equivalent state and federal constitutional provisions—proscriptions against "unreasonable searches and seizures." Would the requirement of *Long* that the state court opinion contain a plain statement of reliance upon the state constitution be different in cases where an explicit right-to-privacy clause was involved?

b. Standing

Note: The Personal Standing Rule in Informational Privacy Cases

In informational privacy cases in tort and constitutional law, courts have generally adopted a personal standing rule and limited standing to sue or challenge the government action to those persons whose privacy has been invaded. The leading case establishing a personal standing rule in cases challenging electronic surveillance by the government under the constitution is *Alderman v. United States*, 394 U.S. 165 (1969). Justice White, speaking for seven members of the Court said:

> "We adhere to those cases and to the general rule that Fourth Amendment rights are personal rights which, like some other constitutional rights, may not be vicariously asserted.... There is no necessity to exclude evidence against one defendant in order to preserve the rights of another. No rights of the victim of an illegal search are at stake when the evidence is offered against some other party. The victim can, and very probably will, object for himself when and if it becomes important for him to do so."

Id. at 174.

In a case involving electronic surveillance of conversations, according to the personal standing rule of *Alderman*, both the individual who owns or possesses the premises where the electronic surveillance occurred and the person whose conversation is overheard have standing to challenge the constitutionality of the surveillance and exclude evidence that is unconstitutionally seized. Suppose public officials are suspicious that A, B, C and D are involved in criminal activity but do not have sufficient evidence to get a court order authorizing interception of conversations on either of the suspects phone. Without a court order A's phone is tapped. B is talking to D on A's phone. In the conversation, C is implicated in criminal acclivity. Under the *Alderman* rule, A, B and D would have standing. But C would not have standing to exclude the introduction of the taped conversations in a criminal proceeding even though the taping violated the Fourth Amendment and Title I. Does the *Alderman* standing rule create an incentive for law enforcement officials to eavesdrop on conversations in violation of law?

The personal standing rule is sometimes expressed in the proposition that there is no relational right to privacy. Courts generally hold that parents cannot assert the common law privacy rights of their children, *see e.g., Nelson v. Maine Times*, 373 A.2d 1221 (Me.1977) (citing Restatement (Second), Torts Secs. 652 (A)—(C)); and that corporations cannot assert privacy rights of their employees, *see e.g., N.O.C., Inc. v. Schaefer*, 197 N.J.Super. 249, 484 A.2d 729 (1984). But compare the granting of standing to the parents of a deceased rape victim to assert her common law tort privacy right against the media for publishing her name in *Cox v. Cohn, infra* p. 476. ("the appellee's complaint properly stated a cause of action, whether it was denominated 'relational' or not," *Cox Broadcasting Corp. v.*

Cohn, 231 Ga. 60, 64, 200 S.E.2d 127, 131 (1973)). The Georgia Supreme Court decision in *Cox* was later reversed on first amendment grounds by the United States Supreme Court, and is discussed later in this book. The standing rule of the Georgia Supreme Court is a matter of state law and was not addressed by the Supreme Court. Compare the personal standing rule in informational privacy cases with the broader rule of *jus tertii* standing that is employed in privacy cases protecting personal autonomy, *see* discussion in Chapter VII, *infra*.

Note: Beyond Alderman: The Vicarious Standing Rule—The Automatic Standing Rule

Louisiana has applied a broader standing rule for excluding evidence procured in violation of search and seizure provision of the state constitution, *see, State v. Culotta*, 343 So.2d 977 (La.1976). Pertinent portions of the constitutional provision state: "Any person adversely affected by a search or seizure conducted in violation of this section shall have standing to raise its legality in the appropriate court." La. Const. Art. I Section 5. In *People v. Martin*, 45 Cal.2d 755, 290 P.2d 855 (1955), the California Supreme Court adopted a broad standing rule, and held that evidence is excluded if acquired in violation of the state or federal prohibition against unreasonable search and seizures even though the privacy rights of the party who seeks exclusion were not violated. The *Martin* rule is sometimes referred to as the "vicarious standing" rule and its continued vitality in California was reaffirmed after *Alderman* in *Kaplan v. Superior Court of Orange County*, 6 Cal.3d 150, 491 P.2d 1, 98 Cal.Rptr. 649 (1971). The *Martin* standing rule is not constitutionally based as is the Louisiana rule. New Jersey adopts an "automatic standing" rule in prosecutions for possessory crimes, *see State v. Alston*, 88 N.J. 211, 440 A.2d 1311 (1981).

COMMONWEALTH v. SELL
504 Pa. 46, 470 A.2d 457 (1983).

Before ROBERTS, C.J., and NIX, LARSEN, FLAHERTY, MCDERMOTT, HUTCHINSON, and ZAPPALA, JJ.

OPINION OF THE COURT

NIX, JUSTICE. . . .

[Sell, a partner in an amusement arcade business, was charged with receiving stolen property and criminal conspiracy after firearms were recovered during a search warrant executed at the arcade. The firearms were located in an area to which all employees had access. The Court of Common Pleas granted Sell "automatic standing" to assert the illegality of the search and granted Sell's motion to suppress the evidence on the basis that the warrant was defective. The Superior Court disagreed and held that Sell did not have standing to contest the admissibility of the evidence because the concept of "automatic" standing had been overruled and Sell was unable to establish "actual" standing. The Pennsylvania Supreme Court granted review to decide whether a defendant accused of a possessory crime will continue to have "automatic standing" under the Pennsylvania Constitution.

The court first indicated that the case raised an issue of the standing rule under the Pennsylvania constitutional proscription against unreasonable searches and seizures. The court then reviewed the history of the federal personal standing rule that had culminated in recent Supreme Court cases that required the defendant to have a possessory interest in the items seized or the property searched in order to raise fourth amendment challenges to evidence. The personal standing rule created a dilemma in possessory crimes because, under the formulation of standing in the "trespass doctrine," a defendant "was obligated to testify as to his ownership or possession ... risking the possibility of subsequent use of such admission by the prosecution.... " The tension between the fourth and fifth amendments in possessory cases resulted in the Supreme Court initially adopting an automatic standing rule in possession cases in Jones v. United States, 362 U.S. 257 (1960). That feature of *Jones* was initially eroded in Rakas v. Illinois, 439 U.S. 128 (1978), where the Court found a passenger in an automobile had no legitimate expectation of privacy in the space in the vehicle because he had no possessory interest in the vehicle. The *Rakas* court also said that only individuals who have personally been searched have standing to suppress evidence from an illegal search. Following *Rakas*, the automatic standing rule of *Jones* was overruled by the Supreme Court in United States v. Salvucci, 448 U.S. 83 (1980).

In construing the state constitutional proscription against unreasonable search and seizure, the court noted that this provision had existed since 1776, some fifteen years before the fourth amendment was adopted. It then summarized cases where the state supreme court had adopted a more expansive view of "search" under the state search and seizure provision. One of the cases was Commonwealth v. DeJohn, where the Pennsylvania Supreme Court held that seizure of bank records by the government was a "search" of the customer.

Justice Nix, speaking for all but two members of the court summarized the Pennsylvania approach as follows:]

We decline to undermine the clear language of Article I, section 8 by making the Fourth Amendment's amorphous "legitimate expectation of privacy" standard a part of our state guarantee against unreasonable searches and seizures. We do so ... because we believe the United States Supreme Court's current use of the "legitimate expectation of privacy" concept needlessly detracts from the critical element of unreasonable governmental intrusion.

Article I, section 8 of the Pennsylvania Constitution, as consistently interpreted by this Court, mandates greater recognition of the need for protection from illegal governmental conduct offensive to the right of privacy....

Moreover, we have held that personal possessions remain constitutionally protected under Article I, section 8 until their owner meaningfully abdicates his control, ownership or possessory interest therein. We remain convinced that ownership or possession of the seized property is adequate to entitle the owner or possessor thereof to invoke the constitutional protection of Article I, section 8 by way of a motion to suppress its use as evidence.

Since we regard ownership or possession of the seized property as sufficient to confer standing to challenge a search and seizure under Article I, section 8, it necessarily follows that a person charged with a possessory offense must be accorded "automatic standing" adopted by this Court....

. . .

Accordingly, the Order of the Superior Court is reversed and the case is remanded to the Superior Court.

c.   The Legitimate Expectations Test in Other Contexts

UNITED STATES v. MILLER
425 U.S. 435 (1976).

MR. JUSTICE POWELL delivered the opinion of the Court....

[Miller was convicted of possessory crimes involving an unregistered whiskey still and conspiracy to defraud the United States of tax revenue on whiskey produced. Miller's pre-trial motion to suppress copies of his bank records and checks obtained by allegedly defective subpoenae duces tecum served on two banks where Miller maintained accounts was denied by the District Court. The subpoenae were issued on the basis of evidence found in a truck occupied by two of Miller's alleged co-conspirators and whiskey making equipment found in a warehouse rented to Miller. Without notifying Miller, the banks produced all records available on microfilm of relevant accounts and copies of deposit slips and checks for agents of the Treasury Department in lieu of appearing in person before the grand jury. The Court of Appeals reversed on the ground that bank records maintained pursuant to the Bank Secrecy Act obtained by a defective subpoena violate a depositor's fourth amendment rights.]

... We find that there was no intrusion into any area in which respondent had a protected Fourth Amendment interest and that the District Court therefore correctly denied respondent's motion to suppress....

The Court of Appeals, as noted above, assumed that respondent had the necessary Fourth Amendment interest, pointing to the language in Boyd v. United States, which describes that Amendment's protection against the "compulsory production of a man's private papers."

On their face, the documents subpoenaed here are not respondent's "private papers." Unlike the claimant in *Boyd*, respondent can assert neither ownership nor possession. Instead, these are the business records of the banks.... "Banks are ... not ... neutrals in transactions involving negotiable instruments, but parties to the instruments with a substantial stake in their continued availability and acceptance." The records of respondent's accounts, like "all of the records [which are required to be kept pursuant to the Bank Secrecy Act,] pertain to transactions to which the bank was itself a party."

Respondent argues, however, that the Bank Secrecy Act introduces a factor that makes the subpoena in this case the functional equivalent of a search and seizure of the depositor's "private papers." We have held, in California Bankers Assn. v. Shultz, 416 U.S. 21, 24 (1974), that the mere maintenance of records pursuant to the requirements of the Act "invade[s] no Fourth Amendment right of any depositor." But respondent contends that the combination of the recordkeeping requirements of the Act and the issuance of a subpoena to obtain those records permits the Government to circumvent the requirements of the Fourth Amendment by allowing it to obtain a depositor's private records without complying with the legal requirements that would be applicable had it proceeded against him directly. Therefore, we must address the question whether the compulsion embodied in the Bank Secrecy Act as exercised in this case creates a Fourth Amendment interest in the depositor where none existed before. This question was expressly reserved in *California Bankers Assn.*

Respondent urges that he has a Fourth Amendment interest in the records kept by the banks because they are merely copies of personal records that were made available to the banks for a limited purpose and in which he has a reasonable expectation of privacy. He relies on this Court's statement in Katz v. United States, 389 U.S. 347, 353 (1967), quoting Warden v. Hayden, 387 U.S. 294, 304 (1967), that "we have . . . departed from the narrow view" that " 'property interests control the right of the Government to search and seize,' " and that a "search and seizure" become unreasonable when the Government's activities violate "the privacy upon which [a person] justifiably relie[s]." But in Katz the Court also stressed that "[w]hat a person knowingly exposes to the public . . . is not a subject of Fourth Amendment protection." 389 U.S., at 351. We must examine the nature of the particular documents sought to be protected in order to determine whether there is a legitimate "expectation of privacy" concerning their contents. CF. Couch v. United States, 409 U.S. 322, 335 (1973).

Even if we direct our attention to the original checks and deposit slips, rather than to the microfilm copies actually viewed and obtained by means of the subpoena, we perceive no legitimate "expectation of privacy" in their contents. The checks are not confidential communications but negotiable instruments to be used in commercial transactions. All of the documents obtained, including financial statements and deposit slips, contain only information voluntarily conveyed to the banks and exposed to their employees in the ordinary course of business. The lack of any legitimate expectation of privacy concerning the information kept in bank records was assumed by Congress in enacting the Bank Secrecy Act, the expressed purpose of which is to require records to be maintained because they "have a high degree of usefulness in criminal, tax, and regulatory investigations and proceedings." 12 U.S.C. Section 1829b(a)(1).

The depositor takes the risk, in revealing his affairs to another, that the information will be conveyed by that person to the Government. United States v. White. This Court has held repeatedly that the Fourth Amendment does not prohibit the obtaining of information revealed to a third party and conveyed by him to Government authorities, even if the information is revealed on the assumption that it will be used only for a limited purpose and the confidence placed in the third party will not be betrayed. Hoffa v. United States, Lopez v. United States. . . .

Since no Fourth Amendment interests of the depositor are implicated here, this case is governed by the general rule that the issuance of a subpoena to a third party to obtain the records of that party does not violate the rights of a defendant, even if a criminal prosecution is contemplated at the time the subpoena is issued. . . .

Many banks traditionally kept permanent records of their depositors' accounts, although not all banks did so and the practice was declining in recent years. By requiring that such records be kept by all banks, the Bank Secrecy Act is not a novel means designed to circumvent established Fourth Amendment rights. It is merely an attempt to facilitate the use of a proper and long-standing law enforcement technique by insuring that records are available when they are needed.

We hold that the District Court correctly denied respondent's motion to suppress, since he possessed no Fourth Amendment interest that could be vindicated by a challenge to the subpoenas.

.   .   .

MR. JUSTICE BRENNAN, dissenting.

. . . In Burrows v. Superior Court, 13 Cal. 3d 238, 529 P.2d 590 (1974), the question was whether bank statements or copies thereof relating to an accused's bank accounts obtained by the sheriff and prosecutor without benefit of legal process, but with the consent of the bank, were acquired as a result of an illegal search and seizure. The California Supreme Court held that the accused had a reasonable expectation of privacy in his bank statements and records, that the voluntary relinquishment of such records by the bank at the request of the sheriff and prosecutor did not constitute a valid consent by the accused, and that the acquisition by the officers of the records therefore was the result of an illegal search and seizure. In my view the same conclusion, for the reasons stated by the California Supreme Court, is compelled in this case under the practically identical phrasing of the Fourth Amendment. . . .

.   .   .

I would therefore affirm the judgment of the Court of Appeals. I add only that *Burrows* strikingly illustrates the emerging trend among high state courts of relying upon state constitutional protections of individual liberties[4]—protections pervading counterpart provisions of the United States Constitution, but increasingly being ignored by decisions of this Court. . . .

MR. JUSTICE MARSHALL, dissenting.

In California Bankers Assn. v. Shultz, 416 U.S. 21 (1974), the Court upheld the constitutionality of the recordkeeping requirement of the Bank Secrecy Act. 12 U.S.C. Section 1829b(d). I dissented, finding the required maintenance of bank customers' records to be a seizure within the meaning of the Fourth Amendment and unlawful in the absence of a warrant and probable cause. While the Court in *California Bankers Assn.* did not then purport to decide whether a customer could later challenge the bank's delivery of his records to the Government pursuant to subpoena, I warned:

> [I]t is ironic that although the majority deems the bank customers' Fourth Amendment claims premature, it also intimates that once the bank has made copies of a customer's checks, the customer no longer has standing to invoke his Fourth Amendment rights when a demand is made on the bank by the Government for the records. . . . By accepting the Government's bifurcated approach to the recordkeeping requirement and the acquisition of records, the majority engages in a hollow charade whereby Fourth Amendment claims are to be labeled premature until such time as they can be deemed too late.

416 U.S. at 97.

Today, not surprisingly, the Court finds respondent's claims to be made too late. Since the Court in *California Bankers Assn.* held that a bank, in complying with the requirement that it keep copies of the checks written by its customers, "neither searches nor seizes records in which depositor has a Fourth Amendment right," there is nothing new in today's holding that respondent has no protected Fourth Amendment interest in such records. *A fortiori*, he does not have standing to contest the Government's subpoena to the bank. Alderman v. United States.

---

4. . . . In the past, it might have been safe for counsel to raise only federal constitutional issues in state courts, but the risks of not raising state-law questions are increasingly substantial, as revealed by a colloquy during argument in Michigan v. Mosley:

> QUESTION: Why can't you argue all of this as being contrary to the law and the Constitution of the State of Michigan?

> MR. ZIEMBA: I can because we have the same provision in the Michigan Constitution of 1963 as we have in the Fifth Amendment of the Federal Constitution, certainly.

> QUESTION: Well, you argued the whole thing before.

> MR. ZIEMBA: In the Court of Appeals?

> QUESTION: Yes.

> MR. ZIEMBA: I really did not touch upon—I predicated my entire argument on the Federal Constitution, I must admit that. I did not mention the equivalent provision of the Michigan Constitution of 1963, although I could have. And I may assure this Court that at every opportunity in the future, I shall.

> [Laughter.]

> QUESTION: But you hope you don't have that opportunity in this case.

> MR. ZIEMBA: That's right.

I wash my hands of today's extended redundancy by the Court. Because the recordkeeping requirements of the Act order the seizure of customers' bank records without a warrant and probable cause, I believe the Act is unconstitutional and that respondent has standing to raise that claim. Since the Act is unconstitutional, the Government cannot rely on records kept pursuant to it in prosecuting bank customers. The Government relied on such records in this case and, because of that, I would affirm the Court of Appeals' reversal of respondent's conviction. I respectfully dissent.

Note

In *California Bankers Association v. Shultz,* 416 U.S. 21 (1974), the Supreme Court in a divided opinion upheld provisions in the Bank Secrecy Act of 1970 requiring financial institutions to make records of the identities of their customers, microfilm certain checks drawn on them and report certain domestic and foreign currency transactions. The record-keeping requirements were held to be a reasonable exercise of the commerce power as against the bank's fifth amendment due process arguments; claims of depositors based upon future subpoena of bank information were found not to be ripe, as were similar privacy and association objections to the record-keeping requirements.

d. State Constitutional Protection for Informational Privacy: Does the Katz Expectation of Privacy Principle Apply to Bank Records?

BURROWS v. SUPERIOR COURT OF SAN BERNARDINO COUNTY

13 Cal.3d 238, 529 P.2d 590 (1974).

MOSK, JUSTICE.

[Burrows is an attorney suspected of having misappropriated the funds of a client. Pursuant to a warrant authorizing the search of his office, the police searched Burrows' office and automobile. A detective then contacted several banks where Burrows maintained accounts, and without a warrant obtained copies of Burrows' financial statements from at least one bank. Burrows was charged with grand theft and his motion to suppress the evidence obtained from his office, automobile, and the bank was denied. The Supreme Court issued a writ of mandate directing the court to suppress the evidence.]

Initially, we discuss the most significant and novel issue in this case: whether the police violated petitioner's rights under the California Constitution, article I, section 13,[5] in obtaining, without benefit of legal process, copies of statements from a bank in which he maintained an account. We have held, consonant with Katz v. United States, that, in

---

5. Article I, section 13, of the California Constitution provides, in part: "The right of the people to be secure in their persons, houses, papers, and effects against unreasonable seizures and searches may not be violated. . . . "

determining whether an illegal search has occurred under the provisions of our Constitution, the appropriate test is whether a person has exhibited a reasonable expectation of privacy and, if so, whether that expectation has been violated by unreasonable governmental intrusion.

It cannot be gainsaid that the customer of a bank expects that the documents, such as checks, which he transmits to the bank in the course of his business operations, will remain private, and that such an expectation is reasonable. The prosecution concedes as much, although it asserts that this expectation is not constitutionally cognizable. Representatives of several banks testified at the suppression hearing that information in their possession regarding a customer's account is deemed by them to be confidential.

In the present case, although the record establishes that copies of petitioner's bank statements rather than of his checks were provided to the officer, the distinction is not significant with relation to petitioner's expectation of privacy. That the bank alters the form in which it records the information transmitted to it by the depositor to show the receipt and disbursement of money on a bank statement does not diminish the depositor's anticipation of privacy in the matters which he confides to the bank. A bank customer's reasonable expectation is that, absent compulsion by legal process, the matters he reveals to the bank will be utilized by the bank only for internal banking purposes. Thus, we hold petitioner had a reasonable expectation that the bank would maintain the confidentiality of those papers which originated with him in check form and of the bank statements into which a record of those same checks had been transformed pursuant to internal bank practice.

. . .

The People assert that no illegal search and seizure occurred here because the bank voluntarily provided the statements to the police, and the bank rather than the police conducted the search of its records for papers relating to petitioner's accounts. If, as we conclude above, petitioner has a reasonable expectation of privacy in the bank statements, the voluntary relinquishment of such records by the bank at the request of the police does not constitute a valid consent by this petitioner....

. . . [T]he fact that the bank voluntarily acceded to a police officer's request to deliver papers regarding petitioner's account cannot serve to validate the governmental conduct. It is not the right of privacy of the bank but of the petitioner which is at issue, and thus it would be untenable to conclude that the bank, a neutral entity with no significant interest in the matter, may validly consent to an invasion of its depositor's rights. However, if the bank is not neutral, as for example where it is itself a victim of the defendant's suspected wrongdoing, the depositor's right of privacy will not prevail.

. . .

We hold that any bank statements or copies thereof obtained by the sheriff and prosecutor without the benefit of legal process were acquired as the result of an illegal search and seizure (Cal. Const., art. I, section 13), and that the trial court should have granted the motion to suppress such documents.

Since we have concluded that petitioner's motion to suppress should have been granted on the basis of the provisions of the California Constitution, it is not necessary to consider his rights under the Fourth Amendment to the United States Constitution....

. . .

The underlying dilemma in this and related cases is that the bank, a detached and disinterested entity, relinquished the records voluntarily. But that circumstance should not be crucial. For all practical purposes, the disclosure by individuals or business firms of their financial affairs to a bank is not entirely volitional, since it is impossible to participate in the economic life of contemporary society without maintaining a bank account. In the course of such dealings, a depositor reveals many aspects of his personal affairs, opinions, habits and associations. Indeed, the totality of bank records provides a virtual current biography. While we are concerned in the present case only with bank statements, the logical extension of the contention that the bank's ownership of records permits free access to them by any police officer extended far beyond such statements to checks, savings, bonds, loan applications, loan guarantees, and all papers which the customer has supplied to the bank to facilitate the conduct of his financial affairs upon the reasonable assumption that the information would remain confidential. To permit a police officer access to these records merely upon his request, without any judicial control as to relevancy or other traditional requirements of legal process, and to allow the evidence to be used in any subsequent criminal prosecution against a defendant, opens the door to a vast and unlimited range of very real abuses of police power.

WRIGHT, C. J., and McCOMB, TOBRINER, SULLIVAN, CLARK and BURKE, JJ., concur.

Note: State Constitutional Protection for
Credit Card and Telephone Records

Burrows is an example of a state court applying the reasonable expectation of privacy principle to extend the reach of the state constitution to invasions of privacy by the government that were not before the court in *Katz*. Notice that while the *Burrows* court invokes *Katz* as the source of the expectation of privacy principle, it is careful to indicate that the decision was based upon state constitutional law. The significance of clearly indicating that the state constitution is the basis for a decision in cases like *Burrows* is explored in a latter section of this chapter. As it turns out, the United States Supreme Court concluded that bank customers do not have a reasonable expectation of privacy in bank records for purposes of the fourth amendment in *United States v. Miller, supra.* p. 130. Do you find the reasoning of the United States Supreme Court or the California Supreme Court most persuasive?

Colorado and Pennsylvania have followed the lead of the *Burrows* Court and have found that bank depositors have a reasonable expectation of privacy in respect to bank records and that such records are protected by the right of privacy under their respective state constitutions. *See Charnes v. DiGiacomo*, 200 Colo. 94, 612 P.2d 1117 (1980); *Commonwealth v. DeJohn*, 486 Pa. 32, 403 A.2d 1283 (1979).

The *Burrows* decision has been extended to credit cards and telephone records in California. *See People v. Blair*, 25 Cal.3d 640, 602 P.2d 738, 159 Cal.Rptr. 818 (1979); *People v. Mejia*, 95 Cal.App.3d 828, 157 Cal.Rptr. 233 (1979).

(1) Common Law Informational Privacy Rights in Bank Records

SUBURBAN TRUST COMPANY v. WALLER

44 Md.App. 335, 408 A.2d 758 (1979)

Court of Special Appeals of Maryland.

Argued before GILBERT, C.J., and MELVIN and WEANT, JJ.

GILBERT, CHIEF JUDGE. . . .

Street and Smith[1] would have probably entitled this case as "The Bank That Talked Too Much." The matter presents us with a novel question of the existence and scope of a bank's duty of confidentiality concerning the affairs of its depositors.[2]

The appellee, Maurice Waller deposited $800 in his account at the Suburban Trust Company (Bank). Because of the actions of a security official, Waller was arrested on a charge of robbery with a dangerous and deadly weapon. The facts surrounding the deposit led a jury in the Circuit Court of Montgomery County to withdraw, in the form of a verdict in favor of Waller, $50,000 from the Bank's coffers and transfer it to Waller's treasury. Understandably upset by the judgment entered on the jury's verdict, the Bank has appealed in an effort to divest itself of what it apparently sees as an unjust liability.

THE FACTS.

Waller, in February 1976, opened an account at the Bank's Langley Park branch. About a month later, March 16, 1976, he attempted to have an income tax refund check cashed there, but that attempt was rebuffed because the balance in his account was insufficient to "cover" the check. He, along with Marvin Turner, a fellow employee of Waller who also wanted a check cashed, went to the United States Treasury Department

---

1. Former publishers of so-called "pulp magazines." "Pulps," descendants of dime novels, originated in 1896 when Frank Munsey changed his *Argosy* to an all fiction magazine and printed it on a rough wood pulp paper to save money. The subjects of the publications fell into four main categories: adventure, love, detective, and western stories. Street and Smith were successful publishers of pulps, pioneering the latter three categories with *Love Story*, *Detective Story*, and *Western Story*. In the middle of

the 1940's, however, rising production costs caused Street and Smith to abandon pulps as unprofitable. Peterson, *Magazines in the Twentieth Century*, 283–86 (1958).

2. "Banks," Jim Oigan used to say, "are like people. Some are big, some are small; some are secretive, others tell all." [Jim Oigan is the authority cited for propositions in a number of opinions written by Chief Judge Gilbert. He describes Jim Oigan as "a mythical character in a child's fantasy."]

in the District of Columbia. The checks were cashed, and Waller and his companion returned to the Bank, where Waller made a deposit of $800. Simultaneously, Turner deposited an identical amount in a new account. The money was in fifty and one hundred dollar bills, and the serial numbers printed thereon were sequential.

The employee[3] who handled Waller's deposit was a teller-trainee. Believing the transaction involving large sequentially numbered bills to be of an unusual nature, he called the matter to the attention of Mrs. Bane, who, together with her duties at her own teller station, was charged with supervising the trainees' work. Mrs. Bane, in turn, notified the assistant manager, James Jones, who contacted the security department. Jones spoke to William Brandt, an assistant security officer for the Bank. Brandt was asked if the serial numbers on the bills were on any of the "warning lists that the Bank receives periodically." The security officer told Jones that he would check out the matter. Pending information from Brandt, Assistant Manager Jones instructed Mrs. Bane to withhold the bills from circulation.

Brandt first contacted the Federal Bureau of Investigation in order to ascertain whether the serial numbers had appeared on that agency's "N.C.I. register." The reply, we infer, was in the negative. Brandt, seemingly unsatisfied with stopping at that point, began to call the local law enforcement agencies. When he contacted the Montgomery County Police Department, he spoke to Corporal Howell. The police officer testified[5] that Brandt asked him if there had been any large cash robberies recently. Howell replied that in a recent "residential robbery" $3,000 in fifty and one hundred dollars bills had been taken. He then read the description of the suspects to Brandt, who replied that they were "similar to two individuals who had come in the Suburban Trust Bank, the branch at Langley Park." Brandt then disclosed to Howell Waller's name, address, description, and employment, as well as the information concerning his deposit of that morning. Subsequently, the Bank's surveillance photographs were also made available to the police.[6]

Howell turned over the information that had been furnished by Brandt to Detective Ingels, who was the person who obtained Waller's photographs from Brandt. The pictures were shown to the victim of the residential robbery, one Brody, who tentatively identified Waller as one of the perpetrators of the crime. The police then acquired a different photograph from Waller's employer. Brody then positively identified Waller as one of the robbers. Waller was arrested and criminally processed. Ultimately, the victim retracted the identification, and the charges against Waller were dropped.

---

3. Unfortunately, as it turned out for the Bank, this was not the same teller who had handled Waller on his first visit to the Bank.

5. Brandt testified that he remembered little or nothing of his conversation with Corporal Howell. As a result, the testimony of the officer on what transpired was uncontradicted.

6. This was the last contact, until this suit, that the Bank had with the matter.

He then filed suit alleging that the bank had (1) invaded his privacy and (2) breached an implied condition of their contract, i.e., the obligation of confidentiality.[7] The case proceeded to trial, where, at the close of Waller's evidence, the trial judge directed a verdict against him on the count for invasion of privacy and on the matter of punitive damages.[8] Following the presentation of the Bank's defense, the court directed a verdict in favor of Waller on the issue of liability, leaving the assessment of damages to the jury.

. . .

The Law.

At common law, the relationship of a bank to its customer was not considered to be fiduciary in nature, but rather as that of a debtor and his creditor. . . .

Modern society virtually demands that one maintain a bank account of some sort. "In a sense a person is defined by the checks he writes. By examining them . . . [one] get[s] to know his doctors, lawyers, creditors, political allies, social connections, religious affiliation, educational interests, the papers and magazines he reads, and so on *ad infinitum.*" California Bankers Association v. Shultz, (Douglas, J. dissenting). The message of Mr. Justice Douglas in *Shultz* is clear: If it is true that a man is known by the company he keeps, then his soul is almost laid bare to the examiner of his checking account. More recently, these revelations have been recorded and preserved under compulsion of law. The court cites the federal Right to Financial Privacy Act of 1978. Patently, the vital information placed within the bank's control presents potential sources of use as well as abuse.[11]

Courts have recognized the special considerations inherent in the bank-depositor relationship implicitly warrants to maintain, in strict confidence, information regarding its depositor's affairs.

The seminal case with respect to a bank's obligation of "strict confidence" appears to be Tournier v. National Provincial and Union Bank of England, 1 K.B. 461 (1923). . . .

. . .

The decisions of appellate courts in this country are generally in accord with *Tournier*. The Supreme Court of Idaho, in Peterson v. Idaho

---

7. Waller's original declaration alleged only an invasion of privacy, but was later amended to add the *ex contractu* claim.

8. Waller did not cross-appeal, and we, therefore, express no opinion as to the propriety of the trial judge's rulings with respect to the directed verdicts on invasion of privacy and punitive damages.

11. We observe that this potential for dissemination of the privileged information is increased where all employees of the bank are not *fully* informed as to bank

policy on confidentiality. Brandt testified that he received no formal training in such matters, although he understood that "no account information" was to be disclosed. In the instant case, Brandt felt that the disclosure of account information was justified by the unusual nature of Waller's transaction. It appears to us that "bank policy" thus would be determined largely by Brandt's discretion as to what was or was not an unusual transaction.

First National Bank, 83 Idaho 578, 588, 367 P.2d 284, 290 (1961), opined:

> It is inconceivable that a bank would at any time consider itself at liberty to disclose the intimate details of its depositors' accounts. Inviolate secrecy is one of the inherent and fundamental precepts of the relationship of the bank and its customers or depositors. This high ethical standard is recognized by the defendant bank in the instant case, as outlined in the manager's deposition.
>
> It is implicit in the contract of the bank with its customer or depositor that no information may be disclosed by the bank or its employees concerning the customer's or depositor's account. . . .
>
>   . . . .

The appellant readily concedes that it was under such a duty, but attempts to execute a "Green Bay sweep" around its obligation. Specifically, the Bank avers that the duty imposed upon it by the contract is qualified in nature. The Bank posits that it was required only "under reasonable circumstance" not to disclose "unnecessarily, promiscuously, or maliciously . . . such information," and that "as a matter of law it acted reasonably under the circumstances." We have an entirely different view.

Although the courts, without exception, have implied a warranty of confidentiality, they have diverged in their outlook as to the circumstances under which the bank is released from its obligation. Lord Justice Atkins, in Tournier, classified the qualification of the contractual duty of secrecy under four headings:

> (a) Where disclosure is under compulsion by law; (b) where there is a duty to the public to disclose; (c) where the interests of the bank require disclosure; (d) where the disclosure is made by the express or implied consent of the customer.

1 K.B. at 473.

. . . Notwithstanding what is written in 10 Am.Jur.2d Banks Section 332, the American cases generally are more restrictive with respect to the exceptions from the obligation of confidentiality. . . .

The Idaho Court, in *Peterson*, stated that "no information may be disclosed . . . unless authorized by law or by the customer or depositor. . . . " 83 Idaho at 588, 367 P.2d at 290.

Justice Mosk, speaking for the California Supreme Court in Burrows v. Superior Court of San Bernardino County, said that "[a] bank customer's reasonable expectation is that, *absent compulsion by legal process*, the matters he reveals to the bank will be utilized by the bank only for internal banking purposes."[15] (Emphasis supplied.)

---

15. While the California court took this position where the bank was a "neutral" party, Justice Mosk would have permitted the bank a broader latitude of disclosure where it was placed in an adversarial position *vis-a-vis* the depositor.

We specifically reject ... the *Tournier* fourfold classification of qualifications to the implied contractual obligation of confidentiality owed by a bank to its depositors.... We so do because we believe that *Tournier* confers upon a bank entirely too much discretion. Were we to follow *Tournier*, we would permit a bank to decide what is or is not in the public interest to disclose, and what is or is not in the best interest of the bank to disclose. That vast area of discretion, it seems to us, transmogrifies confidentiality to the point that it bears little, if any, resemblance to its original meaning. Moreover, *Tournier* ... appear[s] to be a potential source of numerous law suits in order to establish the fixed perimeters of the bank's discretion....

We think that a bank depositor in this State has right to expect that the bank will, to the extent permitted by law, treat as confidential, all information regarding his account and any transaction relating thereto. Accordingly, we hold that, absent compulsion by law, a bank may not make any disclosures concerning a depositor's account without the express or implied consent of the depositor. Our conclusion is buttressed by the action taken by the General Assembly in enacting Laws 1976, ch. 252.

Apparently disturbed by what it believed to be the trend, out of all scotch and notch,[17] among banks and other fiduciary institutions to furnish information without compulsion to governmental agencies, the Legislature in its preamble to Laws 1976, ch. 252 said:

(a) The General Assembly of Maryland finds and declares that:

(1) procedures and policies governing the relationship between fiduciary institutions and government agencies have in some cases developed without due regard to the constitutional rights of customers of those institutions; and

(2) the confidential relationships between fiduciary institutions and their customers must be preserved and protected.

(b) It is the purpose of this Act to protect and preserve the confidential relationship between fiduciary institutions and their customers and to promote commerce by prescribing policies and procedures applicable to the disclosure of customer records by fiduciary institutions.

By the enactment of Laws 1976, ch. 252, the people of Maryland, through their duly elected representatives, made explicit what had theretofore been implicit—banks may not, absent legal compulsion or express or implied authorization from the depositor concerned, reveal

---

17. The expression comes from the child's game of hopscotch. It means "beyond all bounds" and refers to the bound-ary lines (scotches) and corners (notches) used in the game. Morris, Dictionary of Word and Phrase Origins 425 (1977).

any information to anyone, including police and other government agencies, about the depositor's dealings with the bank. . . .

The purpose of the Act having been made crystal clear, the Legislature then declared:

A fiduciary institution may not disclose to any person, except to the customer or his duly authorized agent, any financial records relating to that customer of that fiduciary institution unless:

(a) The customer has authorized disclosure to the person; or

(b) The financial records are disclosed in response to a lawful subpoena, summons, warrant or court order which meets the requirements of Section 226(a).[1]

Laws 1976, ch. 252, Section 1; Md.Ann.Code art. 11, Section 225.

. . .

II

The Bank next asserts that the trial judge erred in failing to find as a matter of law that Brandt's actions were not the proximate cause of Waller's damages. His injuries, the Bank avers, were occasioned by the arrest following the police department's independent investigation. That investigation, the Bank says, was a superseding cause of the alleged harm to Waller.

. . .

An intervening causative factor, in order to be a superseding cause must "alone, without . . . [the defendant's] negligence contributing thereto in the slightest degree, . . . [produce] the injury." State v. Hecht Co., 169 A. 311 (1933).

The evidence adduced at trial of the instant case disclosed that the report by Brandt caused the police to focus their investigation upon Waller. Detective Ingel's testimony established that the information divulged by the Bank through Brandt was listed in the probable cause section of the application for an arrest warrant for Waller. Additionally, the photographs supplied by the Bank were those from which Brody, the residential robbery victim, made his initial identification of Waller as one of the culprits involved.

---

1. Lest there be any doubt that it meant to tighten bank security so as to protect the people of this State from unauthorized disclosures of the financial records of individual customers by bank officers or employees, the General Assembly imposed stringent conditions as to the issuance of the court order and the procedures that must be followed after the order is obtained and before it is effective. Md.Ann.Code. art. 11, Section 226(a) provides:

A fiduciary institution shall disclose financial records under section 225 of this article pursuant to a lawful subpoena, summons, warrant or court order only if the subpoena, summons, warrant or court order is served upon the customer and upon the fiduciary institution; however, the court for good cause may waive service of the subpoena, summons, warrant or court order upon the customer.

We think the evidence was such that reasoning minds could conclude only that the Bank's action was the proximate cause of Waller's damages.

III

The appellant makes one final sortie against the judgment of the circuit court. The Bank asseverates that the evidence adduced at trial was insufficient to permit the issue of damage to Waller's reputation to go to the jury.

To obtain compensatory damages in this State, they must be proven with reasonable certainty and may not be based on speculation or conjecture.

The record in the case now before us discloses no evidence that Waller's reputation was damaged. He suggests that the damage is established by inference from the fact that his neighbors and family saw him being arrested. To draw that inference, we would have to engage in the very sort of speculation that is prohibited by the decisions of the Court of Appeals.

We think that the trial judge erred in submitting the issue to the jury, and we must, therefore, reverse the judgment, but only as to damages. All is not lost for Waller because he lives to fight another day. When the case is retired on the question of damages, Waller is, of course, free to produce such witnesses as he may in order to support his claim.

Note: The Common Law Breach of Fiduciary Theory for Recovery of Tort Damages for Unauthorized Disclosure of Information in Bank Records

Suburban Trust is the initial exposure in these materials to a common law theory that plays an important role in providing legal protection for invasions of privacy by individuals and business entities. This theory proceeds from the initial judicial characterization of certain information-sharing relationships as "fiduciary" in nature. This characterization triggers common law duties of non-disclosure on the recipient of the information. Although the information is shared as part of a contract between the parties, the duty of non-disclosure is imposed by the common law and not by the express terms of the agreement. The breach of fiduciary theory is a hybrid that incorporates features of contracts, torts and the law of trusts. A contractual relationship is necessary but not sufficient to trigger the fiduciary duty. From the law of trusts, the concept of fiduciary obligation that is at the core of the trustee-beneficiary relationship is applied to analogous relationships like bank-depositor and physician-client. Damages reflect the underlying informational privacy interest that is at stake and are governed by principles of tort, and not contract law. Damages recoverable under the breach of fiduciary theory are for the emotional distress, physical injury and lost wages that are caused by the unauthorized disclosure of information.

The core of a fiduciary relationship is that the parties expect the relationship to be a repository of confidence and trust. Consider the definition of a fiduciary relationship by the Illinois Supreme Court in *Niland v. Kennedy*: "[W]here there is a special confidence reposed in one who in equity and good conscience is bound to act in good faith and with due regard to the interests of the one reposing the confidence." 316 Ill. 253, 258, 147 N.E. 117, 119 (1925). What reasons does the court in *Suburban Trust* give for treating the bank-depositor relationship as a fiduciary one? On the basis of *Suburban Trust* and the definition of the *Niland* court above, would the relationship that is entered into between an innkeeper and guest be such that disclosure of information that is supplied to the innkeeper as a condition of renting the room be actionable? What about disclosure of information about an employee by an employer when the information was supplied to the employer in the application for employment?

As Chief Judge Gilbert notes in *Suburban Trust*, the English common law initially viewed the relationship between a bank and its depositors as a debtor-creditor relationship that was essentially contractual in nature. The imposition of fiduciary obligations of non-disclosure on a bank initially occurred in England in *Tournier v. Nat'l Provincial and Union Bank of England*, 1 K.B. 461 (1923). The English rule, as set forth in *Tournier*, and as summarized in *Suburban Trust*, lists four exceptions to the duty of secrecy that is imposed upon banks by virtue of their fiduciary relationship with depositors. These are: (1) disclosure under compulsion by law; (2) when the bank is under a legal duty to disclose to the public; (3) where disclosure furthers the interests of the bank; and, (4) where the customer has expressly or impliedly consented to the disclosure. Some jurisdictions have followed this approach and not allowed a cause of action against the bank where disclosure was to governmental officials who were investigating the depositor for possible violations of law. Disclosure is excused under the second exception because financial institutions are viewed as having a legal duty to disclose such information. *See Indiana Nat'l Bank v. Chapman*, 482 N.E.2d 474 (Ind.App.1985) (disclosure of financial condition of customer's account to police officer investigating theft of customer's automobile not actionable); *O'Coin v. Woonsocket Institution Trust Co.*, 535 A.2d 1263 (R.I.1988) (disclosure of financial information to employee of Auditor General's office investigating alleged embezzlement by customer's spouse not actionable).

Under the stricter view of the duty of secrecy imposed upon financial institutions that is the law of Maryland after *Suburban Trust*, disclosure is justified only in two circumstances: (1) under compulsion by law and (2) when there is express or implied authorization by the bank customer. Under this stricter view, courts interpreting *Suburban Trust* have upheld disclosures by a bank pursuant to subpoenas by government agencies. *See In re Special Investigation No. 242*, 53 Md.App. 360, 452 A.2d 1319 (1982).

The strict view of the duty of secrecy that is embodied in *Suburban Trust* has been adopted by statute in some states. *See, e.g.*, Oklahoma Financial Privacy Act, 6 O.S. sec. 2202 et. seq. (1981). The Oklahoma statute prohibits the release by any financial institution of any information to a government authority unless there is written consent of the customer for the specific record pursuant to section 2204 of the Act.

In response to *United States v. Miller, supra*, Congress enacted the Right to Financial Privacy Act of 1978, 12 U.S.C.A. § 3401 et seq. (West 1990). What impact would the Privacy Act have on a case identical to *Suburban Trust* if that case arose after the Act was enacted? In states like

Oklahoma that have enacted state financial privacy acts do the procedures for subpoenas of financial records under the state or federal statute control?

The breach of fiduciary theory will be explored further *infra*, where application of the theory to disclosure of information acquired in a physician-patient relationship will be examined.

The plaintiff in *Suburban Trust*, also sued the bank for invasion of privacy under the common law of torts. No appeal was taken by the plaintiff for dismissal of this claim. In *Peterson v. Idaho First Nat'l Bank*, 83 Idaho 578, 367 P.2d 284 (1961), the Supreme Court of Oregon rejected an invasion of privacy claim in tort that was brought against the bank by a customer for the unauthorized disclosure of financial information to the employer of the customer. The privacy tort—public disclosure of private facts—requires that the information be disseminated to the public generally and the *Peterson* court found that the limited disclosure did not satisfy the "publicity" requirement of the tort. (A cause of action on behalf of the customer was recognized by the court on the breach of implied duty theory that was later more fully developed in *Suburban Trust*.) *Peterson* is a leading case on the unavailability of the public disclosure tort in circumstances where there is limited disclosure of the sensitive information. The publicity requirement of the public disclosure tort leaves the breach of confidentiality tort theory of cases like *Suburban Trust* and *Peterson* the most significant legal vehicle for protecting privacy in cases where the invasion of privacy occurs through limited disclosure. A fuller elaboration of the breach of confidentiality theory and its relationship to the common law tort of privacy is considered in a later section of these materials, *infra*, Chapter V.

C. CONSTITUTIONAL RIGHT OF INFORMATIONAL PRIVACY GENERALLY

THE RIGHT AND THE REMEDY: FEDERAL CIVIL RIGHTS ACTION

Section 1983 Civil Action for Deprivation of Rights (42 U.S.C.A. § 1983)

Every person who, under color of any statute, ordinance, regulation, custom, or usage, of any State or Territory or the District of Columbia, subjects, or causes to be subjected, any citizen of the United States or other person within the jurisdiction thereof to the deprivation of any rights, privileges, or immunities secured by the Constitution and laws, shall be liable to the party injured in an action at law, suit in equity, or other proper proceeding for redress, except that in any action brought against a judicial officer for an act or omission taken in such officer's judicial capacity, injunctive relief shall not be granted unless a declaratory decree was violated or declaratory relief was unavailable. For the purposes of this section, any Act of Congress applicable exclusively to the District of Columbia shall be considered to be a statute of the District of Columbia.

YORK v. STORY

324 F.2d 450 (9th Cir.1963).

HAMLEY, CIRCUIT JUDGE.

This action was brought by Angelynn York against three officers of the Police Department of the City of Chino, California, to recover damages for taking and distributing photographs of her in the nude. District court jurisdiction was asserted under 28 U.S.C. Section 1343(3) and (4) (1958), it being alleged that the claim arises under Rev.Stat. Section 1979 (1875), 42 U.S.C. Section 1983 (1958). The action was dismissed on motion. Plaintiff appeals.

We first state the allegations of the amended complaint. In October, 1958, appellant went to the police department of Chino for the purpose of filing charges in connection with an assault upon her. Appellee Ron Story, an officer of that police department, then acting under color of his authority as such, advised appellant that it was necessary to take photographs of her. Story then took appellant to a room in the police station, locked the door, and directed her to undress, which she did. Story then directed appellant to assume various indecent positions, and photographed her in those positions. These photographs were not made for any lawful or legitimate purpose.

Appellant objected to undressing. She stated to Story that there was no need to take photographs of her in the nude, or in the positions she was directed to take, because the bruises would not show in any photograph. A policewoman was present at the police station but was not requested to be present in the room where the pictures were taken, and was not present. No person except appellant and Story was present in the room when the pictures were taken.

Later that month, Story advised appellant that the pictures did not come out and that he had destroyed them. Instead, Story circulated these photographs among the personnel of the Chino police department. In April, 1960, two other officers of that police department, appellee Louis Moreno and defendant Henry Grote, acting under color of their authority as such, and using police photographic equipment located at the police station made additional prints of the photographs taken by Story. Moreno and Grote then circulated these prints among the personnel of the Chino police department. Appellant did not learn of the described actions of Story, Moreno, and Grote in distributing these photographs until December, 1960.

. . .

The only question before us, therefore, is whether the district court erred in holding that the amended complaint did not state a claim under [42 U.S.C. Sec. 1983].

A complaint states a claim under section [1983] if the facts alleged show that the defendant: (1) while acting under color of state or local authority, (2) subjected the plaintiff, or caused the plaintiff to be subjected, to the deprivation of any rights, privileges or immunities secured to the plaintiff by the Constitution and laws of the United States.

. . .

The district court's determination that this pleading does not state a claim under section [1983] rests solely upon the ground that, under the allegations of the amended complaint, appellant had not been deprived of any federally-protected right.

Contending that the district court erred in this regard, appellant advances alternative arguments, as follows: (1) under the facts alleged there was an unreasonable search within the meaning of the Fourth Amendment and since the guarantee against unreasonable searches and seizures contained in the Fourth Amendment has been made applicable to the states by reason of the Due Process Clause of the Fourteenth Amendment, she was protected from such a search at the hands of city police officers; (2) the Fourth Amendment is premised upon a basic right of privacy, made available to appellant as against city police officers by reason of the Due Process Clause of the Fourteenth Amendment, which right was violated without regard to whether such violation constituted an unreasonable search in the Fourth Amendment sense; and (3) the alleged acts of appellees constituted such an invasion of appellant's privacy as to amount to a deprivation of liberty, without due process of law, as guaranteed to her by the Due Process Clause of the Fourteenth Amendment.

The alleged act of Story in taking photographs of appellant in the nude, if proved, may or may not constitute an unreasonable search in the Fourth Amendment sense. But if we should hold that it does, this would not dispose of the whole case for the alleged subsequent acts of Story and Moreno in distributing prints of these photographs, of which appellant also complains, could hardly be characterized as unreasonable searches.

It is therefore necessary, in any event, to reach appellant's second or third argument, or both, relating to invasions of privacy. Accordingly, we turn at once to appellant's third contention—that all of these acts constituted such invasions of her privacy as to amount to deprivations of liberty without due process of law, guaranteed to her by the Due Process Clause of the Fourteenth Amendment.

. . .

We cannot conceive of a more basic subject of privacy than the naked body. The desire to shield one's unclothed figure from view of strangers, and particularly strangers of the opposite sex, is impelled by elementary self-respect and personal dignity. A search of one's home has been established to be an invasion of one's privacy against intrusion by the police, which, if "unreasonable," is arbitrary and therefore banned under the Fourth Amendment. We do not see how it can be argued that the searching of one's home deprives him of privacy, but the photographing of one's nude body, and the distribution of such photographs to strangers does not.

Nor can we imagine a more arbitrary police intrusion upon the security of that privacy than for a male police officer to unnecessarily photograph the nude body of a female citizen who has made complaint of an assault upon her, over her protest that the photographs would show no injuries, and at a time when a female police officer could have been, but was not, called in for this purpose, and to distribute those photographs to other personnel of the police department despite the fact that such distribution of the photographs could not have aided in apprehending the person who perpetuated the assault.*

But granting all of that, must it still be held that the particular intrusions here alleged are not secured against by the Due Process Clause of the Fourteenth Amendment because they are not expressly proscribed in the Bill of Rights?

We think not. In the field of civil rights litigation the cases are not infrequent in which law enforcement action not banned in terms by any provision of the Bill of Rights has been made the subject of a successful claim.

. . .

The fact that this is the first such case to reach a court of appeals indicates that civil rights actions of this kind are not likely to swamp the federal courts. But, in any event, . . . if giving effect to the Congressional intent manifested in section [1983] will "open the flood gates," the remedy, if one is needed, is not for this court, but for Congress, to prescribe. It is no legitimate concern of ours whether a decision, correct under present law, will add to the work load of the courts.

Appellees assert that appellant has a civil remedy in the courts of California. But it is immaterial, insofar as the right to pursue remedies under the Civil Rights Act is concerned, that state remedies may also be available.

We therefore conclude that, under the allegations of the amended complaint, appellant has laid a foundation for proving, if she can, not only that appellees were acting under color of local authority at the times in question, but that such acts constituted an arbitrary intrusion upon the security of her privacy, as guaranteed to her by the Due Process Clause of the Fourteenth Amendment. It was therefore error to dismiss the action on the ground that the amended complaint did not state a claim upon which relief can be granted.

* [Editor's Note: In footnote 6 of the opinion, the court quotes from the appellees' brief:

The taking of photographs was not an invasion of privacy but only an attempt to preserve evidence which Appellees, as police officers, are authorized to do and which was done with the implied consent and cooperation of the Appellant. . . . Since the photographs were lawfully obtained, it was not improper for authorized personnel to review or discuss them.

324 F.2d 450, 454 n. 6 (1963).]

The judgment is reversed and the cause is remanded for further proceedings.

MacBRIDE, DISTRICT JUDGE.

I respectfully dissent. I believe that the facts alleged are insufficient to establish a violation of appellant's constitutional rights and, therefore, that they do not state a claim under the Civil Rights Act, 42 U.S.C. Section 1983.

In a case involving facts such as those alleged here, the right to privacy is not, and should not be held to be, a constitutional right.

In the first place, the allegations do not establish an unreasonable search and seizure. The Fourth Amendment prohibits unreasonable searches and seizures. Recent Supreme Court cases have established that the Fourth Amendment's prohibition applies to the states through the Fourteenth Amendment. But these cases did not create a broad, new constitutional right to privacy; they merely made the existing right to privacy which is implicit in the Fourth Amendment's prohibition applicable to the states. This prohibition applies primarily to searches for evidence to be used in a criminal prosecution against the person searched. When an unreasonable invasion of privacy in the home is involved, it may also apply to a search which is unrelated to a criminal prosecution.

Since the facts alleged here involve neither criminal proceedings against the appellant nor an invasion of privacy in the home, I cannot hold that they* come within the constitutional prohibition against searches and seizures.

Moreover, I cannot agree that, apart from any question of unreasonable search and seizure, the allegations show such an invasion of appellant's privacy as to amount to a deprivation of liberty without due process. In a particular set of facts, there may be a constitutional right to privacy. Here, however, the allegations show only that appellant suffered great and unjustified mental suffering, not that any of her basic constitutional rights were prejudiced; and the mere fact that appellant was a complaining witness and the alleged acts of appellees were, to some extent, connected with their official duties as policemen does not, I feel, require a different conclusion.

. . .

When an invasion of privacy is part of, or incident to, an unreasonable search and seizure, it rises to constitutional importance, and when the victim of police misconduct is a prisoner or a person accused or suspected of crime, his right to freedom from such misconduct deserves constitutional protection. But in a case involving facts such as those alleged here, there is no more than a private wrong; and the person aggrieved should be left to his civil remedies in the State Courts.

. . .

For the reasons stated, I would affirm the judgment below.

1. IS THERE A CONSTITUTIONAL RIGHT TO INFORMATION-AL PRIVACY THAT IS INDEPENDENT OF THE FOURTH AMENDMENT?

(a) *York v. Story* recognized a cause of action under the constitution for the publication of the pictures of York by the police. Did this publication constitute a fourth amendment "search"? Is there a constitutional informational privacy right, and, if so, where is its textual base in the constitution? Does *Whalen v. Roe, supra,* provide a basis for answering these questions?

(b) Although the Supreme Court has never squarely held that governmental disclosure of highly personal or intimate information violates a right to informational privacy that is independent of the fourth amendment, dicta in several cases has suggested that a right to informational privacy exists as part of "liberty" under the fifth and fourteenth amendments. *See Nixon v. Administrator of Gen. Servs.,* 433 U.S. 425 (1977) (weighing President's expectation of privacy in personal correspondence against public interest in disclosure), *aff'g* 429 U.S. 976 (1976); *Whalen v. Roe,* 429 U.S. 589 (1977) (discussing constitutionality of collection of patient identification data for persons using prescription medications).

For over a decade, the constitutional rights analysis of *York* was not followed by other federal courts. The Ninth Circuit initially refused to extend *York* beyond its facts. *See Baker v. Howard,* 419 F.2d 376 (9th Cir.1969). Since *Nixon v. Administrator of General Services* and *Whalen,* a significant number of federal and state appellate courts have embraced the notion that encroachments on informational privacy by government action that does not constitute a search may violate a constitutional right to privacy under either the state or federal constitutions. The right is recognized as to both the acquisition and dissemination of information by the government. Most of the federal courts that have considered the issue have recognized the informational privacy right. See, *United States v. Westinghouse Electrical Corp.,* 638 F.2d 570, 570–580 (3d Cir. 1980); *Plante v. Gonzalez,* 575 F.2d 1119, 1132, 1134 (5th Cir. 1978), cert. denied, 439 U.S. 1129 (1979) (describing the rights as a "right to confidentiality"); *Barry v. City of New York* 712 F.2d 1554, 1559 (2d Cir. 1983); *Hawaii Psychiatric Society Dist. Branch v. Ariyoshi,* 481 F.Supp. 1028, 1043 (D. Hawaii 1979); *McKenna v. Fargo,* 451 F.Supp. 1335, 1381 (D.N.J. 1978). The theory has been expressly rejected by the Sixth Circuit in *J.P. v. DeSanti* 653 F.2d 1080, 1090 (6th Cir. 1981) The District of Columbia Circuit has rejected the freestanding informational privacy right in dicta. *See, A.M. Fed. Of Govt. Employees v. Dept. of Housing,* 118 F.3d 786, 791 (D.C. Cir. 1997).

The court decisions in California and Alaska have grounded the right on textual provisions in their state constitutions that explicitly refer to privacy. *See Falcon v. Alaska Pub. Offices Comm'n,* 570 P.2d 469 (Alaska 1977); *People v. Stritzinger,* 34 Cal.3d 505, 194 Cal.Rptr. 431, 668 P.2d 738 (1983). For the most part, state and federal courts have found the informational privacy right to be part of those important rights that are implicit in the concept of "liberty" under both federal and state constitutions and that government action that encroaches upon informational privacy is subject to the substantive limitations of the due process clauses of the fifth and fourteenth amendments. For a general collection of the cases recognizing this independent or free standing informational privacy right and an accounting of this development, *see* Richard Turkington, *Legacy of the Warren and Brandeis Article: The Emerging Unencumbered Constitutional Right to Informational Privacy*, 10 N. Ill. U.L. Rev. 479, 493–510 (1990); Note, *The Constitutional Protection of Informational Privacy*, 71 B.U.L. Rev. 133, 145–50 (1991) (Francis S. Chlapowski).

Most of the cases have involved the government compelling disclosure of personal or intimate information about someone. The theory has been recognized in many cases where courts have compelled disclosure of health care information through subpoena of health records or the threat of contempt to health professionals who refuse to testify about health care information that is relevant to civil and criminal proceedings. The effect of recognizing the patient's or client's constitutional right to privacy in health information in these instances is to create a constitutionally based evidentiary or testimonial privilege. A leading case is *Rasmussen v. South Florida Blood Service, infra.*

The scope of the independent constitutional right to informational privacy is generally determined by a flexible balancing of interest test to determine whether the encroachment on informational privacy by the government is justified. The analysis of the Third Circuit in *United States v. Westinghouse*, 638 F.2d 570 (3d Cir. 1980), has been influential in cases involving compelled disclosure of health care information. In *Westinghouse*, the court described five factors that are to be considered in determining the appropriate constitutional balance between personal privacy and the governmental interest in disclosure: (1) the type of health record requested and the type of health care information it does or may contain; (2) the potential for harm in any subsequent nonconsensual disclosure of the information; (3) the injury from disclosure to the relationship in which the record was generated; (4) the adequacy of safeguards to prevent unauthorized disclosure; and, (5) the degree of need for access. *Id.* at 578.

In performing their legitimate functions and obligations, governmental officials need to have access to certain information about individuals. A great deal of information must be acquired and disseminated in order for the government to work the way it is supposed to in a democracy. Any concept of a right to limit the acquisition and disclosure of information by the government must take into account the central role of information acquisition and dissemination activities in our constitutional system. It is an understanding of this that has contributed to the care with which the judiciary has dealt with informational privacy rights claims. The courts have rejected invitations to construe the Constitution as embodying a type of national privacy act that generally restricts disclosure of information by federal, state and local governmental activities. In the majority of cases where the independent informational privacy right is litigated the government prevails by justifying the acquisition or disclosure under the ad hoc balancing of interest test.

The subject of constitutional limitations on governmental disclosures of personal information has been comprehensively explored recently in an important article written by Seth F. Kreimer. One of Kreimer's arguments is that in certain cases the ad hoc balancing approach is the preferable method for determining the appropriate accommodation between privacy and government disclosure under the constitution. Promiscuous disclosure of intimate information by the government is one of the cases where Professor Kreimer contends that ad hoc balancing is "inescapable" and appropriate. Such disclosure:

> constitutes a powerful governmental sanction that assaults the dignity and undermines the independence of the population.... Still, the nature of the impact on the individual is likely to differ incrementally depending on the precise data in question, and the importance of legitimate interests in disclosure varies contextually. If we are to limit dissemination, there is no alternative to comparing the actual harm done with the level of governmental justification.

Seth F. Kreimer, *Sunlight, Secrets, and Scarlet Letters: The Tension Between Privacy and Disclosure in Constitutional Law*, 140 U. Pa. L. Rev. 1, 145 (1991).

If plaintiffs who litigate constitutionally based informational privacy claims in government dissemination cases lose more times than they win under the ad hoc balancing approach, what protection does this approach provide for privacy? Professor Kreimer finds the benefit to privacy comes in providing the individual with the right to raise the privacy claim before a court:

> Even if privacy claims predictably lose in most cases after litigation, the shadow of the claim remains. Officials who take seriously the rights enunciated by the courts, (or pressure groups who can invoke those rights), will take into account the citizen's interests in privacy when constructing government operating procedures. When confronting a government demand for information under a balancing regime, a citizen retains the negotiating ability to raise a privacy claim, and ultimately to go to court. A claim that is too weak to prevail may be sufficient to induce a pre-litigation dialogue, resulting in more protection than the government was initially inclined to grant.

Kreimer, *supra*, at 147.

Note: Governmental Disclosure of HIV–Related Information

The currently accepted basic medical facts about the transmission of HIV are summarized in a later section of these materials. See *infra* p. 204. Several government commissions have concluded that persons infected with the AIDS virus or suffer from the full-blown disease have been subjected to intolerance, ostracism, discrimination and violence. These are basic and fundamentally important social facts about AIDS. The Report of The Presidential Commission on the Human Immunodeficiency Virus Epidemic noted that "(a)t virtually every Commission hearing, witnesses have attested to discrimination's occurrence and its serious repercussions for both the individual who experiences it and for this nation's effort to control the epidemic." *See* Presidential Commission On The Human Immunodeficiency Virus Epidemic 119 (1988); *see also* Nat'l Gay & Lesbian Task Force, Anti–Gay Violence, Victimization & Defamation in 1986 (attributing part of the increase in reported incidents of violence against gays to the AIDS epidemic).

Would the unauthorized disclosure of HIV–Related information by the government violate the subject's constitutional right to information privacy? *See Woods v. White*, 689 F.Supp. 874 (W.D.Wis.1988) (holding that constitutional right to privacy extended to the fact that a prison inmate had tested positive for HIV where allegedly disclosed by prison medical personnel to nonmedical staff and other inmates), *aff'd without opinion*, 899 F.2d 17 (7th Cir.1990); *Doe v. Borough of Barrington*, 729 F.Supp. 376 (D.N.J.1990) (holding a resident's constitutional right to privacy was violated when an agent of the borough published the fact that the resident was infected with HIV).

Given the extent to which the government discloses information about persons in the course of its everyday operations, the right to informational privacy that is the basis of *York v. Story*, *Woods v. White* and *Doe v. Borough of Barrington* would need to be limited to disclosures of information that seriously implicate privacy. Consider the information that was the basis of the constitutional claims in these cases. Are there shared characteristics of the information which give rise to special privacy concerns if there is disclosure of the information? The independent right to informational privacy enjoys a universal feature of constitutional rights: it is not absolute and must be weighed against countervailing governmental interests. In *Woods*, the court found it unnecessary to engage in this balancing of interests because the state made no claim that an important interest was furthered by disclosure. Under what circumstances would the interest in preventing harm to others by reducing the risk of transmission of HIV be furthered by disclosure in a prison setting? *Woods* was a Section 1983 action. Is a qualified immunity available to officials sued in *Woods* under Section 1983? Were the officials performing discretionary functions? *See Woods v. White*, *supra*.

Compare *Doe v. Borough of Barrington* and *Woods* with *Doe v. SEPTA*, 72 F.3d 1133 (3rd Cir. 1995). In *Doe v. SEPTA*, the Third Circuit recognized that a SEPTA employee had a constitutional right to privacy in personal drug prescription records. But applying the balancing test, the court found that Doe's right had not been violated by inadvertant discovery of Doe's HIV status during SEPTA's review of utilization reports by its prescription drug carrier. The Third Circuit distinguished *Doe v. Borough of Barrington* on the basis that SEPTA, as a self-insurer, had a legitimate interest in reviewing prescription information to monitor the cost of the insurance plan, the disclosure was limited to those with a need to know and SEPTA had established adequate procedures to insure against a recurrence of the unecessary disclosure that occurred in the case.

Note: Paul v. Davis: The Government Defamation Case

In *Paul v. Davis*, 424 U.S. 693 (1976), a closely divided court held that publication of a false and defamatory statement about Paul by the Louisville police department did not deprive him of a liberty interest that was protected under the fourteenth amendment. Paul had been referred to in a flyer as an "active shoplifter" although he had been acquitted of the crime. Justice Rehnquist, writing for a bare majority of the Court, characterized Paul's major argument as a "classic claim for defamation actionable in courts of virtually every state." *Id.* at 697. Concluding that violation of state law by a government agent did not by itself implicate federal rights protected under the fourteenth amendment, the majority rejected Paul's procedural due process argument. The majority also rejected Paul's argument that the publication violated Paul's constitutional right to privacy because none of the Court's substantive privacy decisions had held that the publication of "a record of an official act such as an arrest" violated the Constitution. *Id.* at 713.

To what extent does *Paul v. Davis* undercut the holding of *Doe v. Borough of Barrington* and *Woods v. White*? Only one federal circuit court has rejected the independent informational privacy right theory on the basis that the Court implicitly repudiated it in *Paul v. Davis. See J.P. v. DeSanti*, 653 F.2d 1080 (6th Cir.1981). Other federal circuit and district courts have not adopted the reasoning of the Sixth Circuit in *DeSanti. See, for example, Crain v. Krehbiel,* 443 F.Supp. 202 (N.D.Cal.1977); *Fadjo v. Coon*, 633 F.2d 1172 (5th Cir.1981), and other cases discussed supra. The decisions that have dealt with informational privacy claims based upon government acquisition of information have not considered *Paul v. Davis* to be pertinent to this type of governmental invasions of privacy. But why is *Paul v. Davis* not controlling precedent in cases like *Doe v. Borough of Barrington* where the claim is that government dissemination of information violates the subject's constitutional right to privacy? Suppose Paul's arrest record was a public record under Kentucky law. Would the fact that the defamation in *Paul v. Davis* consisted of a statement that falsely embellished information that had appeared in a public record limit the scope of the Court's holding on the right to privacy? See Comment, A Constitutional Right to Avoid Disclosure of Personal Matter: Perfecting Privacy Analysis in J.P. DeSanti, 653 F.2d 1080 (6th Cir.1981), 71 Geo. L.J. 219 (1982), for a general critique of *DeSanti* that focuses on this feature of *Paul v. Davis*, and especially footnote 33 that explains how under Kentucky law Paul's arrest record was a public record.

Note on the Constitutional Tort Remedy: Section 1983 of the Federal Civil Rights Act (42 U.S.C.A. § 1983)

In a case like *York v. Story*, the plaintiff had the option of suing in state court under the common law privacy tort of intrusion in respect to the taking of the pictures and the public disclosure tort for the dissemination of the pictures. False imprisonment, false arrest, assault and battery claims might have been brought as well. Instead, the plaintiff chose to proceed directly in federal district court under section 1983 of Title 42 of the United States Code. The predecessor to section 1983 was section 1979 (1875). At the time *York* was decided the statute appeared in Title 42 as § 1983. But Title 42 had not been enacted into positive law. So the court referenced both § 1979 and § 1983. Section 1983 was enacted by Congress under the authority granted to it in section 5 of the fourteenth amendment.

As fourteenth amendment legislation, section 1983 requires that there be state action before the statute may be invoked. This requirement is encompassed in the language, "under color of any state law." As an enforcement vehicle for fourteenth amendment rights, the statute is exclusively remedial, and does not, itself, create substantive rights. *See Chapman v. Houston Welfare Rights Organization*, 441 U.S. 600, 617 (1979).

By providing for damage and injunctive relief, actions brought under the statute are appropriately referred to as constitutional tort actions. Section 1983 is available to vindicate both informational privacy rights and privacy-autonomy rights when those rights involve violations of the fourteenth amendment.

In recent years, the statute has become an extremely important vehicle for enforcing fourteenth amendment rights in general, and constitutional privacy rights in particular. In 1998, for example, there were 38,819 civil rights cases brought in federal courts. The majority of these were section 1983 actions. In addition, 24,606 civil rights actions were filed by prisoners. The majority of these cases were also initiated under section 1983. See Administrative Office of the U.S. Courts. Statistical Tables for the Federal Judiciary, for the twelve month period ending Dec. 31, 1998. Washington, D.C.: GPO, 1998.

In *Howlett v. Rose*, 496 U.S. 356, 371 (1990), the Supreme Court held that under the Supremacy Clause of the United States Constitution state courts are required to hear section 1983 cases in the absence of a valid excuse. The Court rejected as a valid excuse the argument by the Florida state courts that dismissal was warranted in the 1983 action because the state sovereign immunity rule provided blanket immunity to state government entities. Section 1983 actions are commonly brought in state court.

The following material sketches the major issues that would be involved in section 1983 actions brought to vindicate constitutional privacy rights violations under the fourteenth amendment. A thorough examination of section 1983 would itself be sufficient for a separate course. Here, the objective is to deal with some of the basic questions that would arise in constitutional tort actions brought to remedy governmental encroachment on privacy.

2. JURISDICTION BASIS: NO AMOUNT IN CONTROVERSY REQUIREMENT

Although section 1983 creates a cause of action for fourteenth amendment violations, it is not a source of jurisdiction for federal courts. Until recently, the jurisdictional statutes that needed to be invoked in a section 1983 action were sections 1331 and 1343 (3) of Title 28 of the United States Code. Section 1331 grants jurisdiction for federal questions arising under the constitution and 1343 (3) exempts section 1983 actions from the amount in controversy requirements that historically had applied in some federal question federal cases. *See Lynch v. Household Finance Corp.*, 405 U.S. 538 (1972). The amount in controversy requirement has now been eliminated in federal question cases under section 1331. Jurisdiction will be satisfied in section 1983 cases simply by invoking section 1331.

3. EXHAUSTION OF STATE REMEDIES UNDER § 1983

York v. Story, follows the general rule in section 1983 cases that plaintiffs need not exhaust state remedies as a condition for suing in federal court under the statute. The leading case is *Monroe v. Pape*, 365 U.S. 167 (1961), where the Supreme Court held that a Chicago family who had been subject to a warrantless unreasonable search of their home by thirteen Chicago police officers were not required to exhaust state judicial or administrative remedies before suing in federal court under section 1983. Thus, under the statute, as a result of the no exhaustion rule, plaintiffs may bypass the state court system and take their constitutional claim directly into federal court after suffering constitutional injury. Under some circumstances, the plaintiffs may bring an action for declaratory relief under section 1983, before the constitutional injury occurs. Declaratory relief is largely discretionary, and when it is sought for imminent fourteenth amendment violations the federal declaratory judgment statutes, sections 2201 and 2202 of Title 28, must be included in the jurisdiction paragraph of the section 1983 complaint.

The absence of an exhaustion requirement in section 1983 suits means that in some instances a person with a privacy claim has the choice of a state or federal forum to adjudicate his rights. Although the Supreme Court over the last two decades has rendered several decisions that restrict access to federal courts in section 1983 actions, the no exhaustion rule of *Monroe* is still viable. *See Carter v. Stanton*, 405 U.S. 669 (1972) (per curiam); *Patsy v. Board of Regents*, 457 U.S. 496 (1982). *Compare Eisen v. Eastman*, 421 F.2d 560 (2d Cir.1969), *aff'd*, 400 U.S. 841 (1970); 4 K. Davis, Administrative Law Treatise Section 26.14 at 476–77 (1983). See, also, Jeffrey M. Shaman & Richard C. Turkington, *Huffman v. Pursue Ltd.: The Federal Courthouse Door Closes Further*, 56 B.U.L. Rev. 907, 919–922 (1976).

Contrast the section 1983 exhaustion of administrative remedies rule with the approach under the federal statutes protecting privacy, such as the 1974 Privacy Act and the Freedom of Information Act (FOIA), discussed *infra* pp. 338–349, 363–397. These statutes require exhaustion of administrative remedies before a suit in federal court for violation of the statutes may be prosecuted.

4. THE UNDER "COLOR OF STATE LAW" OR "STATE ACTION" REQUIREMENT OF SECTION 1983

As the language of section 1983 indicates, there must be a demonstration that fourteenth amendment rights were denied to the plaintiff "under color of state law." The under color of state law requirement of section 1983 is viewed by the Supreme Court as synonymous with "state" under the fourteenth amendment. Indeed, some of the most important Supreme Court state action cases were litigated under section 1983. *See, e.g., Burton v. Wilmington Parking Authority*, 365 U.S. 715 (1961); *Lugar v. Edmondson Oil Co.*, 457 U.S. 922 (1982). If the allegations in *Monroe* were that the police officers had searched the plaintiff's house without legal authority to do so, then what was the basis upon which the court concluded they were the "state" (acting under color of state law)? It is clear after *Monroe* that police officers are the state when they are on duty, but what if an off duty police officer arrests someone? Would a police officer who is moonlighting as a security guard for a fast food chain or a large retail business be "acting under color of state law" for purposes of section 1983? *See Bethel v. Jendoco Constr. Corp.*, 570 F.2d 1168 (3d Cir.1978); *compare Bonsignore v. New York*, 683 F.2d 635 (2d Cir.1982); *Stengel v. Belcher*, 522 F.2d 438 (6th Cir.1975), *cert. granted*, 425 U.S. 910, *cert. dismissed*, 429 U.S. 118 (1976).

5. THE GOVERNMENTAL IMMUNITY DEFENSE UNDER SECTION 1983

Section 1983 is silent on many issues that are necessarily part of the civil action for damages under the statute. One important set of questions involves the extent to which the state, local government agencies, and governmental officials are granted immunity in a damage action. The holding in *Monroe* that the city of Chicago was not a "person" under the statute and was thus immune in the damage action under section 1983 was overruled by the Supreme Court in *Monell v. Department of Social Services*, 436 U.S. 658 (1978). The *Monell* court held that municipalities and counties were subject to liability in section 1983 actions provided that the constitutional injury sued upon was causally traceable to "a policy statement, ordinance, regulation, or decision adopted by that body's offices," or to a local governmental custom. 436 U.S. at 676.

The effect of *Monell* is to allow damage actions against local governmental agencies where constitutional injuries flow from express governmental policies or acquiesced-to custom, but to deny recovery for damages under a respondeat superior theory in section 1983 actions.

Although *Monell* abrogated the governmental immunity defense in respect to local governmental agencies, states or state agencies are not "persons" within the statute and are immune from liability. *See Quern v. Jordan*, 440 U.S. 332 (1979); *Will v. Michigan Dep't of State Police*, 491 U.S. 58 (1989).

The same result is achieved when the eleventh amendment is raised as a ban of section 1983 claims brought against the state for retroactive damages. *See Edelman v. Jordan*, 415 U.S. 651 (1974); *Quern v. Jordan*, 440 U.S. 332 (1979).

6. OFFICIAL IMMUNITY UNDER SECTION 1983

Even if the government entity is immune under *Monroe* and *Monell*, the governmental official that directly caused the constitutional injury may still be liable. Thus, in section 1983 actions, suits are generally initiated against governmental officials. When such individuals raise an immunity defense, it should be described as the "official immunity defense" and be distinguished from the governmental immunity defense discussed supra. In *Pierson v. Ray*, 386 U.S. 547 (1967), the Supreme Court held that judges are absolutely immune from damage liability under section 1983 and that police officers were liable for damages in actions for violations of the fourth amendment only on a showing that they had not acted in good faith and with probable cause. As *Pierson* indicates, some officials such as judges enjoy absolute immunity for damages under the statute. Other officials, such as police officers enjoy a qualified immunity—no liability for damages if the official demonstrates good faith and probable cause.

Other officials granted absolute immunity are: legislators in their legislative functions, *e.g., Eastland v. United States Servicemen's Fund*, 421 U.S. 491 (1975); judges, in their judicial function, *see, e.g., Stump v. Sparkman*, 435 U.S. 349 (1978); prosecutors and similar officials, *see, e.g., Butz v. Economou*, 438 U.S. 478 (1978); the President of the United States, *see, e.g., Nixon v. Fitzgerald*, 457 U.S. 731 (1982).

Other executive officials generally, like police officers, only get a qualified immunity in damage actions. This is the case for presidential aides, *e.g., Harlow v. Fitzgerald*, 457 U.S. 800 (1982); a state governor and his aides, *see, e.g., Scheuer v. Rhodes*, 416 U.S. 232 (1974).

7. DAMAGES UNDER SECTION 1983

The elements and prerequisites for damages that are essential for recovery in section 1983 actions have proven to be a troublesome area for courts. As a general matter, where the constitutional injury is analogous to a redressable injury in the state common law where the section 1983 action is brought the state tort damage rule will apply unless the state law is inconsistent with the purposes of the statute. *See Basista v. Weir*, 340 F.2d 74 (3d Cir.1965). Section 1988 of Title 42 of the United States Code authorizes courts to borrow state law rules when to do so is consistent with section 1983.

However, where there is no analogous state tort damage rule, the federal common law as defined by the Supreme Court is to apply. The leading Supreme Court case on section 1983 damages is *Carey v. Piphus*, 435 U.S. 247 (1978). In *Piphus*, a procedural due process case, the court held that under the federal common law of damages presumed damages were not recoverable. However, where the interests involved in the fourteenth amendment case are analogous to interests protected by the state common law of torts, Justice Powell in *Piphus* strongly suggested that the common law tort rules of damages would apply directly to the section 1983 action. In section 1983 actions for violations of information privacy interests, either under the fourth amendment or where there has been a violation of the free standing right to informational privacy, the general common law damage requirements that have developed under the public disclosure and privacy intrusion torts would therefore likely apply. As discussed in sections dealing with these torts, the plaintiff would at least have to introduce credible evidence of emotional distress to recover compensatory damages. *See, e.g., Caperci v. Huntoon*, 397 F.2d 799 (1st Cir.1968), *cert. denied*, 393 U.S. 940 (1968); *Monroe v. Darr*, 221 Kan. 281, 559 P.2d 322 (1977), discussed *infra*.

8. PUNITIVE DAMAGES UNDER SECTION 1983

In *City of Newport v. Fact Concerts, Inc.*, 453 U.S. 247 (1981), the Supreme Court held that punitive damages are not recoverable against a municipality under section 1983. However, in *Smith v. Wade*, 461 U.S. 30 (1983), the Supreme Court opinion written by Justice Brennan held that punitive damages were available in a section 1983 action against individuals upon a demonstration that he or she acted with reckless disregard for the rights or safety of others. For purposes of section 1983 the Court adopted the general common law standard that is applied to privacy tort claims, i.e. "reckless disregard." Justice Rehnquist dissented in an opinion that was joined in by Chief Justice Burger and Justice Powell. They contended that a higher standard for punitive damages under section 1983 was required, i.e., malicious intent, and questioned whether punitive damages ought to be available under section 1983. Justice O'Connor agreed that malicious intent was the appropriate standard but on other grounds.

9. STATUTE OF LIMITATIONS

In *Wilson v. Garcia*, 471 U.S. 261 (1985), the Court held that the appropriate statute of limitations in a section 1983 action was the state statute of limitations for personal injury cases. In *Owens v. Okure*, 488 U.S. 235 (1989), a section 1983 action was brought against police officers for unlawful arrest and the use of excessive force in violation of the fourth amendment. New York law contained a one year statute of limitations for specified intentional torts and a three year residual statute of limitations for personal injury actions not dealt with by a specific provision. The Court held that where there were more than one statute of limitations that might be applicable, the general or residual personal injury statute was to be applied.

10. ATTORNEYS' FEES

Section 1988 of Title 42 authorizes a court to allow the prevailing party to recovery attorneys fees in a section 1983 action. Although the statute says that the awarding of fees shall be at the discretion of the court, fees are awarded as a matter of right to the plaintiff who prevails in section 1983 actions. Fees are to be based upon the number of hours "reasonably expended on the litigation multiplied by a reasonable hourly rate." *Hensley v. Eckerhart*, 461 U.S. 424, 433 (1983). In *Osterneck v. Ernst & Whinney*, 489 U.S. 169 (1989), the Court held that a contingency fee agreement did not place a ceiling on the fees that could be awarded under section 1988. The availability of attorneys' fees have proven to be a powerful incentive to prosecute constitutional tort actions where violations of the constitution causes intangible injuries as in first amendment, procedural due process cases or privacy cases.

11. VIOLATION OF CONSTITUTIONAL PRIVACY RIGHTS BY FEDERAL OFFICIALS

Section 1983 specifically applies to individuals acting under color of state law and not to federal officials and federal government action. However, in *Bivens v. Six Unknown Named Agents of Federal Bureau of Narcotics*, 403 U.S. 388 (1971), the Supreme Court held that a cause of action for damages is available against federal officials for violating the plaintiff's fourth amendment constitutional privacy rights. The *Bivens* court found that federal courts had the inherent power to grant a damage remedy for violations of the constitution by federal officials. The *Bivens* cause of action theory of damage relief tracks section 1983 in respect to the enforcement issues discussed in this note. *See generally, Butz v. Economou*, 438 U.S. 478 (1978).

D. NON–LAW ENFORCEMENT SEARCHES: THE "SPECIAL GOVERNMENTAL NEEDS BALANCING TEST"

In the late 1960's the Court departed from long standing traditions in fourth amendment cases and found some governmental searches reasonable even though the searches were executed without probable cause or judicial intervention through the issuance of a warrant. In certain cases the Court adopted a balancing of interest test to determine whether the search was justified without the historic requirements of probable cause and judicial intervention (a search warrant). The pivotal event is *Terry v. Ohio*, 392 U.S. 1 (1968), where the Court held that a limited search (stop and frisk) would be reasonable within the fourth amendment even though the officer did not have probable cause to believe the individual had committed a crime. A majority of the Court in *Terry* reasoned that a stop and frisk was a minor intrusion which constituted reasonable prophylactic action to protect the police against physical harm. Given the limited invasion of personal security and the "reasonable suspicion" by the police officer that Terry was "armed and dangerous," a limited search for weapons was constitutional.

Terry is one of the judicial decisions in our legal system where the generalized factual pattern seems to compel a pragmatic solution and purports to be a limited exception to a longstanding tradition. Yet the shift in perspective and conceptual analysis that underlies the pragmatic result facilitates a dramatic change in the direction and approach of the law. *Terry* broke from a tradition which had been uninterrupted since the fourth amendment became part of our Constitution, holding for the first time that a search of a person was reasonable without probable cause to believe the subject of the search had committed a crime. The shift in perspective that underlay that linguistic shift from "probable cause" to "reasonable suspicion" was from a rights oriented anti-utilitarian approach to a straight forward utilitarian approach of weighing the relative costs (to privacy) and benefits (to crime control). The cost benefit approach to the reasonableness of fourth amendment searches had been utilized a year before *Terry* to carve out a further exception to the probable cause requirement in administrative searches of businesses to determine health and safety code violations in *Camara v. Municipal Court*, 387 U.S. 523 (1967) and *See v. City of Seattle*, 387 U.S. 541 (1967). *Camara* and *See* required judicial intervention and warrants for searches of businesses but found such searches reasonable without "probable cause" or "reasonable suspicion." Again, cost benefit balancing was the approach. The limited expectation of privacy in highly regulated industries (cost) was weighed with the benefit to efficient enforcement of health and safety codes by random inspection of industries with a history of health and safety problems.

This utilitarian weighing of interest perspective has become the controlling view of the Supreme Court in cases where the justification for governmental searches of persons is to further interests other than enforcement of the criminal law.

1. SCHOOL SEARCHES: STUDENTS' CONSTITUTIONAL RIGHT TO INFORMATIONAL PRIVACY

The initial case where the Court clearly indicated that different and less demanding fourth amendment standards applied to government searches that were not for the purposes of enforcing criminal laws was *New Jersey v. T.L.O.*, 469 U.S. 325 (1985). In *T.L.O.*, the Court upheld the constitutionality of a warrantless search of a fourteen year old high school freshman by an assistant vice principal where there was reasonable suspicion that the student had violated the school policy against smoking cigarettes on school premises. The Court found that high school students had fourth amendment rights that were implicated by searches conducted by school authorities and that T.L.O. had a legitimate expectation of privacy in a closed purse or other bag carried on her person. A majority of the Court concluded that the probable cause and warrant requirements were incompatible with the non-law enforcement (special) purpose of the search—preserve order on school premises. In determining that the reasonable suspicion satisfied the fourth amendment requirements the Court balanced the school's interest in preserving order with the student's privacy interest.

2. THE SPECIAL GOVERNMENTAL NEEDS BALANCING TEST APPLIED TO PRIVACY IN THE WORKPLACE

Although *T.L.O.* involved a search of a student for non-law enforcement purposes, the analytical framework developed in the case has been applied to other contexts where the government has invaded privacy to further interests other than enforcement of the criminal law. The core idea of *T.L.O.* and other similar cases is that suspension of the traditional fourth amendment restrictions on governmental searches is justified because the "special needs" of the government beyond the need for law enforcement make the probable cause and warrant requirements impractical. The "special needs" exception to the warrant and probable cause requirements was initially applied to invasions of the privacy of governmental employees in *O'Connor v. Ortega*, 480 U.S. 709 (1987). *Ortega* involved the search of a state employed psychiatrist's desk and file cabinets when he was on a compelled administrative leave because of suspicions of improprieties in his management of a residency program. Because Ortega had occupied the office for seventeen years and kept personal and intimate information in his desk, a unanimous Court concluded that he had a reasonable expectation of privacy in his desk and file cabinets and that the federal government actions constituted a search under the Fourth Amendment.

The Court did not decide whether the search in the case was reasonable because of the inadequacy of the record on that question. However, a majority of the Court clearly indicated that the special needs test of *T.L.O.* applied to searches of governmental employees and that the search of a governmental employee would be reasonable if it was for a work-related purpose and was not excessively intrusive. The four dissenters in *Ortega* rejected the application of the special needs test to the search and would have applied the probable cause and warrant requirements to the case.

Note: Drug Testing, Breathalyzers, Testing for HIV

Bodily fluids and tissues are a biological library about a person. From these a great variety of information may be discovered. Employers in the governmental and private sector commonly adopt testing requirements for their employees to determine whether they have recently or are currently using illegal drugs. Tests for alcohol and drug use are also performed when employees are involved in accidents in the work place. Similar efforts are under way to test employees for the Human Immunodeficiency Virus (HIV), the agent that causes AIDS. Blood is used to test for HIV and drug consumption and alcohol use; urine is procured to test for use of cocaine, marijuana and other illegal drugs. When the government extracts bodily fluids of employees for testing without the employees' consent, does a "search" occur? The extraction of blood by law enforcement officials to determine alcohol content was found to be a search by the Supreme Court in *Schmerber v. California*, 384 U.S. 757 (1966).

In its initial examination of the fourth amendment implications of governmental compelled testing of employees, the Supreme Court rejected the argument that extraction of urine or breath implicated expectations of privacy that were of less constitutional significance than the extraction of blood:

> Unlike the blood-testing procedure at issue in *Schmerber*, the procedures prescribed by the FRA regulations for collecting and

testing urine samples do not entail a surgical intrusion into the body. It is not disputed, however, that chemical analysis of urine, like that of blood, can reveal a host of private medical facts about an employee, including whether he or she is epileptic, pregnant, or diabetic. Nor can it be disputed that the process of collecting the sample to be tested, which may in some cases involve visual or aural monitoring of the act of urination, itself implicates privacy interests. As the Court of Appeals for the Fifth Circuit has stated:

> There are few activities in our society more personal or private than the passing of urine. Most people describe it by euphemisms if they talk about it at all. It is a function traditionally performed without public observations; indeed, its performance in public is generally prohibited by law as well as social custom.

As to compelled breathalyzers, the Court noted that such a test, "generally requires the production of alveolar or "deep lung" breath for chemical analysis ... and ... should also be deemed a search...." *Skinner v. Railway Labor Executives' Ass'n.*, 489 U.S. 602, 616–17 (1989).

NATIONAL TREASURY EMPLOYEES v. VON RAAB
489 U.S. 656 (1989).

JUSTICE KENNEDY delivered the opinion of the Court.

[The United States Custom Service implemented a drug-screening program which required urinalysis tests of Service employees seeking a transfer or a promotion to positions having a direct involvement in drug interdiction or which required the incumbent to carry firearms or to handle "classified" material. The program requires that the applicant be notified that his selection is contingent upon successful completion of drug screening and it sets forth the procedures for collection and analysis of the requisite samples. These procedures are designed to ensure against substitution of a specimen and to limit the intrusion into employee privacy. The procedures did not require visual observation of urination; the employee could provide the specimen in the privacy of a stall and the urine sample was collected by a monitor of the same sex. The test was limited to specified drugs and the test results could not be turned over to any other agency, including criminal prosecutors, without the employee's written consent. Only positive tests resulted in disclosure of medical information and then the disclosure was to a licensed physician Medical Review Officer. The plaintiffs, a federal employees' union and one of its officials, filed suit on behalf of service employees seeking covered positions, alleging that the drug-testing program violated the Fourth Amendment. The district court agreed and enjoined the program. The court of appeals vacated the injunction. The Supreme Court affirmed in part, vacated in part, and remanded.]

We granted certiorari to decide whether it violates the Fourth Amendment for the United States Customs Service to require a urinalysis test from employees who seek transfer or promotion to certain positions.

. . .

While we have often emphasized, and reiterate today, that a search must be supported, as a general matter, by a warrant issued upon probable cause, . . . our [decisions reaffirm] the longstanding principle that neither a warrant nor probable cause, nor, indeed, any measure of individualized suspicion, is an indispensable component of reasonableness in every circumstance. [O]ur cases establish that where a Fourth Amendment intrusion serves special governmental needs, beyond the normal need for law enforcement, it is necessary to balance the individual's privacy expectations against the Government's interests to determine whether it is impractical to require a warrant or some level of individualized suspicion in the particular context. It is clear that the Customs Service's drug-testing program is not designed to serve the ordinary needs of law enforcement. Test results may not be used in a criminal prosecution of the employee without the employee's consent. The purposes of the program are to deter drug use among those eligible for promotion to sensitive positions within the Service and to prevent the promotion of drug users to those positions. These substantial interests . . . present a special need that may justify departure from the ordinary warrant and probable-cause requirements . . .

Even where it is reasonable to dispense with the warrant requirement in the particular circumstances, a search ordinarily must be based on probable cause. Our cases teach, however, that the probable-cause standard " 'is peculiarly related to criminal investigations.' " In particular, the traditional probable-cause standard may be unhelpful in analyzing the reasonableness of routine administrative functions, especially where the Government seeks to prevent the development of hazardous conditions or to detect violations that rarely generate articulable grounds for searching any particular place or person. . . . We think the Government's need to conduct the suspicionless searches required by the Customs program outweighs the privacy interests of employees engaged directly in drug interdiction, and of those who otherwise are required to carry firearms.

The Customs Service is our Nation's first line of defense against one of the greatest problems affecting the health and welfare of our population. We have adverted before to "the veritable national crisis in law enforcement caused by smuggling of illicit narcotics." Our cases also reflect the traffickers' seemingly inexhaustible repertoire of deceptive practices and elaborate schemes for importing narcotics,. . The record in this case confirms that, through the adroit selection of source locations, smuggling routes, and increasingly elaborate methods of concealment, drug traffickers have managed to bring into this country increasingly large quantities of illegal drugs.

The record also indicates, and it is well known, that drug smugglers do not hesitate to use violence to protect their lucrative trade and avoid apprehension.

Many of the Service's employees are often exposed to this criminal element and to the controlled substances it seeks to smuggle into the country … The physical safety of these employees may be threatened, and many may be tempted not only by bribes from the traffickers with whom they deal, but also by their own access to vast sources of valuable contraband seized and controlled by the Service. The Commissioner indicated below that "Customs [o]fficers have been shot, stabbed, run over, dragged by automobiles, and assaulted with blunt objects while performing their duties." At least nine officers have died in the line of duty since 1974. He also noted that Customs officers have been the targets of bribery by drug smugglers on numerous occasions, and several have been removed from the Service for accepting bribes and for other integrity violations. . . .

It is readily apparent that the Government has a compelling interest in ensuring that front-line interdiction personnel are physically fit, and have unimpeachable integrity and judgment … The public interest demands effective measures to bar drug users from positions directly involving the interdiction of illegal drugs.

The public interest likewise demands effective measures to prevent the promotion of drug users to positions that require the incumbent to carry a firearm, even if the incumbent is not engaged directly in the interdiction of drugs. Customs employees who may use deadly force plainly "discharge duties fraught with such risks of injury to others that even a momentary lapse of attention can have disastrous consequences." We agree with the Government that the public should not bear the risk that employees who may suffer from impaired perception and judgment will be promoted to positions where they may need to employ deadly force. Indeed, ensuring against the creation of this dangerous risk will itself further Fourth Amendment values, as the use of deadly force may violate the Fourth Amendment in certain circumstances. . . .

Against these valid public interests we must weigh the interference with individual liberty that results from requiring these classes of employees to undergo a urine test. The interference with individual privacy that results from the collection of a urine sample for subsequent chemical analysis could be substantial in some circumstances. We have recognized, however, that the "operational realities of the workplace" may render entirely reasonable certain work-related intrusions by supervisors and co-workers that might be viewed as unreasonable in other contexts … While these operational realities will rarely affect an employee's expectations of privacy with respect to searches of his person, or of personal effects that the employee may bring to the workplace, it is plain that certain forms of public employment may diminish privacy expectations even with respect to such personal searches. Employees of the United States Mint, for example, should expect to be subject to certain routine personal searches when they leave the workplace every day. Similarly, those who join our military or intelligence services may not only be required to give what in other contexts might be viewed as extraordinary assurances of trustworthiness and probity, but also may expect intrusive inquiries into their physical fitness for those special positions.

We think Customs employees who are directly involved in the interdiction of illegal drugs or who are required to carry firearms in the line of duty likewise have a diminished expectation of privacy in respect to the intrusions occasioned by a urine test. Unlike most private citizens or government employees in general, employees involved in drug interdiction reasonably should expect effective inquiry into their fitness and probity. Much the same is true of employees who are required to carry firearms. Because successful performance of their duties depends uniquely on their judgment and dexterity, these employees cannot reasonably expect to keep from the Service personal information that bears directly on their fitness ... While reasonable tests designed to elicit this information doubtless infringe some privacy expectations, we do not believe these expectations outweigh the Government's compelling interests in safety and in the integrity of our borders.

Petitioners ... contend that the Service's drug-testing program is unreasonable in two particulars. First, petitioners argue that the program is unjustified because it is not based on a belief that testing will reveal any drug use by covered employees. In pressing this argument, petitioners point out that the Service's testing scheme was not implemented in response to any perceived drug problem among Customs employees, and that the program actually has not led to the discovery of a significant number of drug users. .Counsel for petitioners informed us at oral argument that no more than 5 employees out of 3,600 have tested positive for drugs. Second, petitioners contend that the Service's scheme is not a "sufficiently productive mechanism to justify [its] intrusion upon Fourth Amendment interests," ... because illegal drug users can avoid detection with ease by temporary abstinence or by surreptitious adulteration of their urine specimens. These contentions are unpersuasive.

Petitioners' first contention evinces an unduly narrow view of the context in which the Service's testing program was implemented. Petitioners do not dispute, nor can there be doubt, that drug abuse is one of the most serious problems confronting our society today. There is little reason to believe that American workplaces are immune from this pervasive social problem ... See also Masino v. United States, 589 F.2d 1048, 1050, 218 Ct.Cl. 531 (1978) (describing marijuana use by two Customs inspectors). Detecting drug impairment on the part of employees can be a difficult task, especially where, as here, it is not feasible to subject employees and their work product to the kind of day-to-day scrutiny that is the norm in more traditional office environments. Indeed, the almost unique mission of the Service gives the Government a compelling interest in ensuring that many of these covered employees do not use drugs even off duty, for such use creates risks of bribery and blackmail against which the Government is entitled to guard. In light of the extraordinary safety and national security hazards that would attend the promotion of drug users to positions that require the carrying of firearms or the interdiction of controlled substances, the Service's policy of deterring drug users from seeking such promotions cannot be deemed unreasonable.

The mere circumstance that all but a few of the employees tested are entirely innocent of wrongdoing does not impugn the program's validity. The same is likely to be true of householders who are required to submit to suspicionless housing code inspections, . . . and of motorists who are stopped at the checkpoints . . . The Service's program is designed to prevent the promotion of drug users to sensitive positions as much as it is designed to detect those employees who use drugs. Where, as here, the possible harm against which the Government seeks to guard is substantial, the need to prevent its occurrence furnishes an ample justification for reasonable searches calculated to advance the Government's goal.

We think petitioners' second argument—that the Service's testing program is ineffective because employees may attempt to deceive the test by a brief abstention before the test date, or by adulterating their urine specimens—overstates the case. As the Court of Appeals noted, addicts may be unable to abstain even for a limited period of time, or may be unaware of the "fade-away effect" of certain drugs. More importantly, the avoidance techniques suggested by petitioners are fraught with uncertainty and risks for those employees who venture to attempt them. A particular employee's pattern of elimination for a given drug cannot be predicted with perfect accuracy, and, in any event, this information is not likely to be known or available to the employee. Petitioners' own expert indicated below that the time it takes for particular drugs to become undetectable in urine can vary widely depending on the individual, and may extend for as long as 22 days. (noting Court of Appeals' reliance on certain academic literature that indicates that the testing of urine can discover drug use " 'for . . . weeks after the ingestion of the drug' "). Thus, contrary to petitioners' suggestion, no employee reasonably can expect to deceive the test by the simple expedient of abstaining after the test date is assigned. Nor can he expect attempts at adulteration to succeed, in view of the precautions taken by the sample collector to ensure the integrity of the sample. In all the circumstances, we are persuaded that the program bears a close and substantial relation to the Service's goal of deterring drug users from seeking promotion to sensitive positions.[2]

2. Indeed, petitioners' objection is based on those features of the Service's program—the provision of advance notice and the failure of the sample collector to observe directly the act of urination—that contribute significantly to diminish the program's intrusion on privacy. See supra, at 1394, n. 2. Thus, under petitioners' view, "the testing program would be more likely to be constitutional if it were more pervasive and more invasive of privacy." 816 F.2d, at 180.

In sum, we believe the Government has demonstrated that its compelling interests in safeguarding our borders and the public safety outweigh the privacy expectations of employees who seek to be promoted to positions that directly involve the interdiction of illegal drugs or that require the incumbent to carry a firearm. We hold that the testing of these employees is reasonable under the Fourth Amendment.

We are unable, on the present record, to assess the reasonableness of the Government's testing program insofar as it covers employees who are required "to handle classified material." We readily agree that the Government has a compelling interest in protecting truly sensitive information from those who, "under compulsion of circumstances or for other reasons, . . . might compromise [such] information." . . . We also agree that employees who seek promotions to positions where they would handle sensitive information can be required to submit to a urine test under the Service's screening program, especially if the positions covered under this category require background investigations, medical examinations, or other intrusions that may be expected to diminish their expectations of privacy in respect of a urinalysis test. . . .

It is not clear, however, whether the category defined by the Service's testing directive encompasses only those Customs employees likely to gain access to sensitive information. [W]e think it is appropriate to remand the case to the Court of Appeals for such proceedings as may be necessary to clarify the scope of this category of employees subject to testing. Upon remand the Court of Appeals should examine the criteria used by the Service in determining what materials are classified and in deciding whom to test under this rubric. In assessing the reasonableness of requiring tests of these employees, the court should also consider pertinent information bearing upon the employees' privacy expectations, as well as the supervision to which these employees are already subject.

. . .

JUSTICE MARSHALL, with whom JUSTICE BRENNAN joins, dissenting.

. . . Here, as in Skinner, the Court's abandonment of the Fourth Amendment's express requirement that searches of the person rest on probable cause is unprincipled and unjustifiable. But even if I believed that balancing analysis was appropriate under the Fourth Amendment, I would still dissent from today's judgment for the reasons stated by Justice SCALIA in his dissenting opinion,

. . .

JUSTICE SCALIA, with whom JUSTICE STEVENS joins, dissenting.

The issue in this case is not whether Customs Service employees can constitutionally be denied promotion, or even dismissed, for a single instance of unlawful drug use, at home or at work. They assuredly can. The issue here is what steps can constitutionally be taken to detect such drug use. The Government asserts it can demand that employees perform "an excretory function traditionally shielded by great privacy," while "a monitor of the same sex . . . remains close at hand to listen for the normal sounds," and that the excretion thus produced be turned over to the Government for chemical analysis. The Court agrees that this constitutes a search for purposes of the Fourth Amendment—and I think it obvious that it is a type of search particularly destructive of privacy and offensive to personal dignity.

Until today this Court had upheld a bodily search separate from arrest and without individualized suspicion of wrongdoing only with respect to prison inmates, relying upon the uniquely dangerous nature of that environment . . . Today, in Skinner, we allow a less intrusive bodily search of railroad employees involved in train accidents. I joined the Court's opinion there because the demonstrated frequency of drug and alcohol use by the targeted class of employees, and the demonstrated connection between such use and grave harm, rendered the search a reasonable means of protecting society. I decline to join the Court's opinion in the present case because neither frequency of use nor connection to harm is demonstrated or even likely. In my view the Customs Service rules are a kind of immolation of privacy and human dignity in symbolic opposition to drug use.

The Fourth Amendment protects the "right of the people to be secure in their persons, houses, papers, and effects, against unreasonable searches and seizures." While there are some absolutes in Fourth Amendment law, as soon as those have been left behind and the question comes down to whether a particular search has been "reasonable," the answer depends largely upon the social necessity that prompts the search. . . .

The Court's opinion in the present case, however, will be searched in vain for real evidence of a real problem that will be solved by urine testing of Customs Service employees. Instead, there are assurances that "[t]he Customs Service is our Nation's first line of defense against one of the greatest problems affecting the health and welfare of our population," that "[m]any of the Service's employees are often exposed to [drug smugglers] and to the controlled substances [they seek] to smuggle into the country," that "Customs officers have been the targets of bribery by drug smugglers on numerous occasions, and several have been removed from the Service for accepting bribes and other integrity violations," ibid.; that "the Government has a compelling interest in ensuring that front-line interdiction personnel are physically fit, and have unimpeachable integrity and judgment," ante, at——; that the "national interest in self-protection could be irreparably damaged if those charged with safeguarding it were, because of their own drug use, unsympathetic to their mission of interdicting narcotics," and that "the public should not bear the risk that employees who may suffer from impaired perception and judgment will be promoted to positions where they may need to employ deadly force," To paraphrase Churchill, all this contains much that is obviously true, and much that is relevant; unfortunately, what is obviously true is not relevant, and what is relevant is not obviously true. The only pertinent points, it seems to me, are supported by nothing but speculation, and not very plausible speculation at that. It is not apparent to me that a Customs Service employee who uses drugs is significantly more likely to be bribed by a drug smuggler, any more than a Customs Service employee who wears diamonds is significantly more likely to be bribed by a diamond smuggler—unless, perhaps, the addiction to drugs is so severe, and requires so much money to maintain, that it would be detectable even without benefit of a urine test. Nor is it apparent to me that Customs officers who use drugs will be appreciably less "sympathetic" to their drug-interdiction mission, any more than police officers who exceed the speed limit in their private cars are appreciably less sympathetic to their mission of enforcing the traffic laws. (The only difference is that the Customs officer's individual efforts, if they are irreplaceable, can theoretically affect the availability of his own drug supply—a prospect so remote as to be an absurd basis of motivation.) Nor, finally, is it apparent to me that urine tests will be even marginally more effective in preventing gun-carrying agents from risking "impaired perception and judgment" than is their current knowledge that, if impaired, they may be shot dead in unequal combat with unimpaired smugglers—unless, again, their addiction is so severe that no urine test is needed for detection.

What is absent in the Government's justifications—notably absent, revealingly absent, and as far as I am concerned dispositively absent—is the recitation of even a single instance in which any of the speculated horribles actually occurred: an instance, that is, in which the cause of bribe-taking, or of poor aim, or of unsympathetic law enforcement, or of compromise of classified information, was drug use. Although the Court points out that several employees have in the past been removed from the Service for accepting bribes and other integrity violations, and that at least nine officers have died in the line of duty since 1974, ante, at 1392, there is no indication whatever that these incidents were related to drug use by Service employees. Perhaps concrete evidence of the severity of a problem is unnecessary when it is so well known that courts can almost take judicial notice of it; but that is surely not the case here. The Commissioner of Customs himself has stated that he "believe[s] that Customs is largely drug-free," that "[t]he extent of illegal drug use by Customs employees was not the reason for establishing this program," and that he "hope[s] and expect[s] to receive reports of very few positive findings through drug screening." The test results have fulfilled those hopes and expectations. According to the Service's counsel, out of 3,600 employees tested, no more than 5 tested positive for drugs.

The Court's response to this lack of evidence is that "[t]here is little reason to believe that American workplaces are immune from [the] pervasive social problem" of drug abuse. Perhaps such a generalization would suffice if the workplace at issue could produce such catastrophic social harm that no risk whatever is tolerable—the secured areas of a nuclear power plant, for example, ... But if such a generalization suffices to justify demeaning bodily searches, without particularized suspicion, to guard against the bribing or blackmailing of a law enforcement agent, or the careless use of a firearm, then the Fourth Amendment has become frail protection indeed . . .

Today's decision would be wrong, but at least of more limited effect, if its approval of drug testing were confined to that category of employees assigned specifically to drug interdiction duties. Relatively few public employees fit that description. But in extending approval of drug testing to that category consisting of employees who carry firearms, the Court exposes vast numbers of public employees to this needless indignity. Logically, of course, if those who carry guns can be treated in this fashion, so can all others whose work, if performed under the influence of drugs, may endanger others—automobile drivers, operators of other potentially dangerous equipment, construction workers, school crossing guards. A similarly broad scope attaches to the Court's approval of drug testing for those with access to "sensitive information." . . . [T]here is no reason why this super-protection against harms arising from drug use must be limited to public employees; a law requiring similar testing of private citizens who use dangerous instruments such as guns or cars, or who have access to classified information, would also be constitutional.

There is only one apparent basis that sets the testing at issue here apart from all these other situations—but it is not a basis upon which the Court is willing to rely. I do not believe for a minute that the driving force behind these drug-testing rules was any of the feeble justifications put forward by counsel here and accepted by the Court. . . . What better way to show that the Government is serious about its "war on drugs" than to subject its employees on the front line of that war to this invasion of their privacy and affront to their dignity? To be sure, there is only a slight chance that it will prevent some serious public harm resulting from Service employee drug use, but it will show to the world that the Service is "clean," and—most important of all—will demonstrate the determination of the Government to eliminate this scourge of our society! I think it obvious that this justification is unacceptable; that the impairment of individual liberties cannot be the means of making a point; that symbolism, even symbolism for so worthy a cause as the abolition of unlawful drugs, cannot validate an otherwise unreasonable search. . . .

Those who lose because of the lack of understanding that begot the present exercise in symbolism are not just the Customs Service employees, whose dignity is thus offended, but all of us—who suffer a coarsening of our national manners that ultimately give the Fourth Amendment its content, and who become subject to the administration of federal officials whose respect for our privacy can hardly be greater than the small respect they have been taught to have for their own.

Note: Skinner v. Railway Labor Executives' Association

In *Skinner v. Railway Labor Executives' Ass'n.*, 489 U.S. 602 (1989), a companion case to *Von Raab*, seven members of the Court, speaking through Justice Kennedy, found the testing of railroad employees to be reasonable. The Court held that the governmental interest in insuring the safety of the traveling public by maintaining a work force in safety sensitive positions that were not impaired because of the influence of drugs or alcohol presents "special needs" that justified departure from the traditional warrant and probable cause requirements. The burden of imposing a duty to obtain a warrant on the railroad would frustrate the objective of the search because the delay necessary to procure a search might result in the destruction of valuable evidence. In addition, the Court also found that the specificity of the testing regulations, the standardized nature of the tests, and the limited discretion vested in those that administered the test left little benefit to be derived from judicial intervention. The invasion of privacy from the testing was minimal in this context because employees of an industry that has been regulated pervasively to ensure public safety had diminished expectations of privacy. In contrast the government benefit in protecting the public was compelling because railroad employees in safety sensitive positions can cause great harm before any signs of impairment become noticeable to supervisors or to others. The record before the Court in *Skinner* established that there had been numerous accidents that were directly traceable to railroad employee impairment.

a. The Government as a Teacher: Setting an Example With a Morally Cleansed Workforce

One of the objectives of the testing of governmental employees may be symbolic: teaching the public by example that the government has cleansed its workforce of drug users and is committed to eliminating drug abuse from the society. If so, should this be a sufficient basis for justification of drug testing? Consider Justice Scalia's reflection on this question in dissent in *Von Raab*.

> I think it is obvious that this justification is unacceptable; that the impairment of individual liberties cannot be the means of making a point; that symbolism, even symbolism for so worthy a cause as the abolition of unlawful drugs, cannot validate an otherwise unreasonable search.

489 U.S. at 687.

Justice Ginsburg speaking for eight members of the Court in *Chandler v. Miller* (the political candidate drug testing case) discussed below said that the fourth amendment shields society against state action that "diminishes personal privacy for a symbol's sake" and cited Justice Brandeis in dissent in *Olmstead*, "Our Government is the potent omnipresent teacher. For good or for ill, it teaches the whole people by its example."

Questions

(1) Under what circumstances would a governmental search of an employee or student for non-law enforcement purposes not satisfy the special needs exception to the warrant and probable cause requirements?

(2) Is it constitutional to require mandatory or random testing for drugs and alcohol use of any governmental employees whose job descriptions are

such that if their judgment were impaired by drugs or alcohol a risk of harm to members of the public would be created?

(3) Is it constitutional to require mandatory or random testing for drug or alcohol abuse of all governmental personnel employed in the law enforcement system?

(4) What is the significance of the remand in *Von Raab* (to determine whether the testing applied only to employees with access to sensitive information)? Does the remand indicate that the Court is going to require a demonstration of a connection or nexus between the employees' job activities and the government's interest in preserving national security?

Note: The Student–Athlete Drug Testing Case

The "special needs" balancing of interest approach of *T.L.O.* and *Von Raab* was utilized by the Court to uphold the random urinalysis drug testing of student athletes in *Vernonia School Dist. v. Acton*, 515 U.S. 646 (1995). Applying the two part privacy analysis developed in *T.L.O.* and *Von Raab*, Justice Scalia, speaking for the majority, concluded that student athletes had diminished expectations of privacy and the drug testing procedure was minimally intrusive. Students generally have diminished expectations of privacy with respect to medical procedures because of the general requirements of physical examinations, vaccinations, and screening for vision and skin disorders. The Court found the method of acquiring the urine sample to be minimally intrusive because the conditions were "nearly identical to those typically encountered in public restrooms" (males remain fully clothed and are only observed from behind and females produce samples in an enclosed stall, with a female monitor standing outside listening only for sounds of tampering). The scope of the search and disclosure, only for drugs—not for medical conditions like pregnancy or epilepsy and disclosure not authorized for law enforcement authorities or disciplinary functions—was also found to be minimally intrusive. The Court rejected the argument that only testing athletes for which there was a reasonable suspicion of drug use was a less onerous and more efficient method to control drug use partially on the basis that a "reasonable suspicion" regime carried a "badge of shame" because it was more accusatory.

On the governmental interest side the Court found the school had important interests in deterring drug use by school children and in protecting the safety of athletes that were furthered by requiring testing of a group of "role models" like student athletes.

Justice O'Connor's dissent, joined in by Justices Stevens and Souter, contended that Supreme Court precedent justified at best only individualized suspicion (reasonable suspicion) searches of school students. Exceptions carved out in fourth amendment searches for suspicionless searches (as in *T.L.O.* and *Von Raab*) were limited to instances where the government had demonstrated that "suspicion-based" regimes would be ineffectual:

> [T]he individualized suspicion requirement has a legal pedigree as old as the Fourth Amendment itself, and it may not be easily cast aside in the name of policy concerns. It may only be forsaken, the cases in the personal search context had established, if a suspicion-based regime would likely be ineffectual. But having misconstrued

the fundamental role of individualized suspicion requirement in Fourth Amendment analysis, the Court never seriously engages the practicality of such a requirement in the instant case. And that failure is crucial because nowhere is it less clear that an individualized suspicion requirement would be ineffectual than in the school context. In most schools, the entire pool of potential search targets—students—is under constant supervision by teachers and administrators and coaches, be it in classrooms, hallways, or locker rooms, *Id.* at 2403

Justice O'Connor noted that most of the instances cited in the record to justify random searches consisted of instances where there was evidence to determine that there was reasonable suspicion of in-school drug use that would have justified the search under the *T.L.O.* decision, discussed, *supra.*

Random drug testing of urine samples of students in grades seven through twelve was upheld against fourth amendment challenges by the Eight Circuit in *Miller v. Wilkes*, 1999 WL 173632 (8th Cir.(Ark.)). Under the testing policy each student and the student's custodial parent or guardian must sign consent forms for random urinalysis. Failure to sign the forms or for the student to submit to the test resulted in the student being barred from participating in any school activity. The Eight Circuit took judicial notice of the fact that drug and alcohol abuse in public schools is a serious social problem (there was no evidence in the record of any drug or alcohol problem in the school). Relying on the majority in *Von Raab* and *Vernonia* the court concluded that the school district's substantial interest in preventing possible harm to the school from drug and alcohol abuse outweighed the student's diminished privacy interest.

Is *Wilkes* a warranted extension of *Vernonia*? Would the rational of *Wilkes* sustain the constitutionality of a policy that required consent to random urinalysis as a condition for acceptance to a public school?

Note: Suspicionless Drug Tests: Closely Guarded or Loose General Exceptions?

The disagreement amongst the Justices in *Vernonia* is about the scope of the exception under the fourth amendment for suspicionless searches. Is the exception as suggested by the dissenters narrow, so that the government would have the burden of demonstrating that the governmental interest could not be substantially furthered by a probable cause or reasonable suspicion regime? Consider the factual record and arguments that were accepted by the Court as sufficient to justify the suspicionless searches in *Von Raab*. Facts about drug use in society generally were sufficient for the government to demonstrate a drug problem in the workplace and to establish a "special need" to balance away the requirements of probable cause, judicial intervention and reasonable suspicion. How strong was the evidence and how compelling were the government arguments that suspicionless drug testing (as compared to a reasonable suspicion regime) would reduce drug use in the workplace?

The trend of the Supreme Court upholding suspicionless drug testing was placed on hold in *Chandler v. Miller*, 520 U.S. 305 (1997). Eight members of the Court found that a Georgia law that required candidates for some offices to produce negative urinalysis drug tests as a condition for nomination or office violated the fourth amendment. Justice Ginsburg speaking for the Court characterized *Skinner*, *Von Raab*, and *Vernonia*, as part of a "closely guarded" class of exceptions to the "main rule" requiring individualized suspicion of wrongdoing in fourth amendment cases. The Court found that Georgia had not demonstrated the "concrete danger" required to depart from the Fourth Amendments "main rule." Georgia had contended that drug use was incompatible with holding high state office because drug use raises questions about an official's judgment and integrity and jeopardizes the official's ability to discharge official duties. Posed claims of drug hazards were described by the Court as hypotheticals for "Georgia's polity." It was not enough for the government to justify mandatory drug testing as symbolic of a state's commitment to enforcement of the drug laws. The Court concluded that only where there is a substantial risk to public safety might suspicionless searches be reasonable.

The Court acknowledged that the government in *Von Raab* had not demonstrated drug use amongst Custom Service employees. But characterized *Van Raab* as involving the "unique context" of governmental employees who are "routinely exposed to the vast network of organized crime that is inextricably tied to illegal drug use."

Justice Rehnquist, the sole dissenter, contended that the search came within the rule of *Skinner* and *Von Raab* and that the majority had distorted these precedents to reach a desired result in the case.

The Court in *Chandler* focuses on the threshold question under the special needs test: has the government demonstrated a special need to suspend the requirement of individualized suspicion. Assume that the Court in *Chandler* is tightening up this threshold requirement for establishing "special need" by requiring a demonstration of a real risk to public safety by drug use in the workplace. What practical significance would the requirement have on the constitutional authority of governmental employers to require suspicionless urinalysis drug testing?

Note: The Governmental Action Issue in Testing of Employees

Informational privacy rights under the federal and state constitutions like other individual constitutional rights limit what the state and federal government can do but do not determine the legality of actions by private individuals or business entities. This feature of our constitutional system is generally reflected in the requirement that a party asserting a constitutional right demonstrate that there is a nexus between the state or federal government and the asserted constitutional injury. Whether there is a sufficient connection between the government and the individual's injury for the constitutional requirement of state or federal action to be satisfied is a complicated question that is fully explored in constitutional law courses. For our purpose it is sufficient to recognize that the right to informational privacy that is embodied in the fourth amendment proscriptions against unreasonable searches does not apply to the drug testing of employees in the private sector. The legality of testing of employees in the private sector will depend upon the extent to which such testing violates common law or statutory rights to privacy, a subject explored in a later section of this chapter.

There was no significant issue as to whether the testing was government action in *Von Raab* because in that case the testing was required by the Transportation Department and Customs Service, both agencies of the federal government. Since the testing at issue in *Skinner* applied to employees of private corporations—railroads—a significant question of whether there was government action sufficient to implicate the fourth amendment was presented to the Court. Subpart C of the transportation regulations required drug testing of railroad employees following a "major accident." Since a railroad that tested pursuant to this section did so under the compulsion of the sovereignty of the federal government, such tests were found to be clearly imbued with federal action and controlled by the fourth amendment. Subpart D of the regulations authorized railroads to test employees under other circumstances but the testing was permissible and not mandatory. However, the court found that tests administered under this part of the regulations were sufficiently encouraged, endorsed or participated in by the federal government to implicate the fourth amendment. Some of the indicia of federal action were the preemptive effect of the regulations on state law, the prohibition on employers contracting away the authority to test, and the fact that the regulations granted the Federal Railway Administration the right to receive certain of the biological samples and test results that were procured pursuant to Subpart D.

Note: The California Constitutional Right to Privacy

In the section above the constitutionality of compulsory drug testing of governmental employees was examined. As noted then, for the constitutional right to informational privacy to be implicated the test must be compelled or sufficiently endorsed by the state or federal government for the government action requirement to be satisfied. There is at least one exception to this general proposition. The California Constitution applies to private action. In *Porten v. University of San Francisco*, 64 Cal.App.3d 825, 134 Cal.Rptr. 839 (1976), the court held that a cause of action had been stated under the California Constitution for the disclosure of the plaintiff's grades by the University of San Francisco, a private institution, to the Scholarship and Loan Commission, a state agency. Section I of the California Constitution provides:

> All people are by nature free and independent and have inalienable rights. Among these are enjoying and defending life and liberty, acquiring, possessing, and protecting property, and pursuing and obtaining safety, happiness, and privacy.

The specific reference to privacy in the California Constitution was a central reason given by the court for extending the constitution to private action.

The right of privacy in the California constitution was applied to the drug testing program of a private corporation in *Wilkinson v. Times Mirror Corp.*, 215 Cal.App.3d 1034, 264 Cal.Rptr. 194 (1989). Matthew Bender, the law publishing company enacted a drug testing policy for job applicants that was challenged as violating the prospective employee's state constitutional right to privacy. The testing procedure applied only to employees who had passed initial screening procedures and had received a "conditional" offer of employment. The offer was conditioned on the employee successfully completing a medical examination which included a medical history, certain diagnostic tests, and a test for drugs and alcohol. Applicants who accepted the conditional offer were sent to an independent lab for the medical examination. The urine sample was taken without personal observation. Employees were rated on a scale from 1 to 5, but no medical information was provided to the employer. rather, the employer was given only the numerical rating assigned to each prospective employee. A "5" indicated that the employee was not recommended for employment, "due to medical reasons or in accordance with employer's policy on alcohol or drugs." Thus a positive rating of "5" might indicate a medical problem other than testing positive for drug or alcohol abuse.

In *Wilkinson v. Times Mirror Corp.* the court of appeals upheld the constitutionality of Matthew Bender's testing procedure. The court found that the United States Supreme Court's decisions in *Skinner* and *Von Raab, supra,* were sufficiently analogous to be of guidance, even though they were fourth amendment search and seizure cases. The court concluded that the employee's right to privacy was not violated in this case because of the limited "intrusiveness of the collection process, and the procedural safeguards which restrict access to test results." *Id.* at 1051, 264 Cal. rptr. at 205–206. The court was careful to limit its holding to the specific testing procedure employed by Matthew Bender.

b. *Hill v. NCAA*

The Supreme Court of California extended the state constitutional privacy right to the private sector for the first time in *Hill v. NCAA,* 865 P.2d 633 (Cal.1994). In *Hill* the Court upheld the constitutionality of the NCAA's policy of random testing of selected athletes competing in postseason championships. As a condition of participating in NCAA sponsored competition the policy requires athletes to consent to being tested before, during, or after any NCAA championship. A selected athlete must provide a urinalysis sample after receiving written notice. The sample is taken at a collection station in the presence of a same sex official monitor, identified, documented and subject to a strict chain of custody during testing. Jennifer Hill and Barry McKeever, Stanford University athletes, successfully argued that the policy violated the California Constitution and won an injunction against enforcement of the policy against them.

In granting the injunction the courts found that the NCAA drug testing program did not survive strict scrutiny under the compelling state interest test. The lower courts relied heavily on findings that the NCAA drug testing program invaded the student's privacy by: (1) requiring that they disclose health information about medication and physical and medical conditions; (2) requiring that they urinate in the presence of a person; and (3) provide urine samples that revealed the presence of chemicals and other substances in their bodies. There also was a finding that college athletes did not use drugs more frequently than the general student population.

In reversal Chief Justice Lucas, writing for a majority of the Court, rejected strict scrutiny as the appropriate test under the California Constitution for invasions of privacy in the privacy sector noting that in cases in the private sector there is no "state" interest. Instead, the Court adopted a balancing of interest test. The test requires the plaintiff to demonstrate a reasonable expectation in a legally protected privacy interest that has been seriously invaded by the defendant. Once this is established, the defendant has to demonstrate that the invasion of privacy is justified by a competing interest. Applying this test the Court found that student athletes had a reasonable expectation of privacy in freedom from observation during urination and in the health information acquired from the test. As athletes the expectation was diminished for the same reasons as advanced in *Vernonia, supra,* and in addition because the athlete gets advance notice and consents to the test. The court found the NCAA's requirement of direct observation of urination to be unique and sufficiently intrusive to warrant examining the competing interest in testing. The NCAA's interest in maintaining the integrity of athletic competition and the health and safety of student athletes was sufficiently justifiable to sustain the constitutionality of the testing regime. The court concluded that the findings of the lower court did not invalidate the drug testing program under the less demanding balancing of interest test. The majority also found that the NCAA's evidence that urine samples could be altered or substituted justified the direct observation policy of the NCAA.

Justice Kennard agreed with the majority as to a lesser test for privacy invasions for nongovernmental entitles but would have remanded the case and given the plaintiffs an opportunity to establish a violation of the constitutional right to privacy under the balancing test. Justice George concurred but because he thought the compelling interest test had been satisfied by the NCAA. Justice Mosk issued a vigorous dissent where he rejected the application of a lesser test in private sector testing cases and would find the NCAA testing regime unconstitutional under a compelling interest test.

Compare, *Luedtke v. Nabors, Alaska Drilling, Inc.,* 768 P.2d 1123 (Alaska 1989), where the Supreme Court of Alaska refused to extend the Alaskan Constitution to compulsory drug testing of employees by a private corporation even though Article I Section 22 of the Alaska Constitution reads:

> Right of Privacy. The Right of the people to privacy is recognized and shall not be infringed. The legislature shall implement this section.

Questions

The common law public disclosure and privacy intrusion torts are examined in Chapter Five. On the facts of *Porten* would the student be able to prevail under the public disclosure privacy tort? Would the employees in *Luedtke* be able to prevail under the privacy intrusion tort for the compulsory drug testing? See the above cases for the answers given to these questions by two courts. Read the discussion of *Ruth Shulman v. Group W. Productions*, 955 P.2d 469 (Cal.1998), infra p. 438–39, in conjunction with this note.

DRUG TESTING IN THE PRIVATE SECTOR

BORSE v. PIECE GOODS SHOP, INC.

963 F.2d 611 (3d Cir. 1992).

BECKER, CIRCUIT JUDGE

Sarah Borse brought suit against her former employer, Piece Goods Shop, for dismissing her when she refused to sign a consent form to submit to urinalysis screening and purse searches when on it's premises (conducted by her employer at the workplace pursuant to its drug and alcohol policy). The district court dismissed her complaint for failure to state a claim on which relief could be granted. Borse appealed on the question of whether an at-will employee who is discharged for refusing to consent to urinalysis screening for drug use and to searches of her personal property states a claim for wrongful discharge under Pennsylvania law.

Because we predict that, under certain circumstances, discharging a private-sector, at-will employee for refusal to consent to drug testing and to personal property searches may violate the public policy embodied in the Pennsylvania cases recognizing a cause of action for tortious invasion of privacy, and because the allegations of Borse's complaint are not sufficient for us to determine whether the facts of this case support such a claim, we will vacate the district court's order and remand with directions to grant leave to amend.

. . . Ordinarily, Pennsylvania law does not provide a common-law cause of action for the wrongful discharge of an at-will employee. Rather, an employer "may discharge an employee with or without cause, at pleasure, unless restrained by some contract . . . Courts construing Pennsylvania law have interpreted this language as implicitly recognizing that a cause of action for wrongful discharge exists in appropriate circumstances . . . (where to do so would violate public policy). The public policy violated must be clear and specific before the court will uphold the cause of action.

. . . Borse primarily relies upon the First and Fourth Amendments to the United States Constitution and the right to privacy included in the Pennsylvania Constitution. [T]he court concluded that the federal or state constitution could not be the source of a public policy exception in a wrongful dismissal action unless there was government action]. Although we have rejected Borse's reliance upon constitutional provisions as evidence of a public policy allegedly violated by the Piece Goods Shop's drug and alcohol program, our review of Pennsylvania law reveals other evidence of a public policy that may, under certain circumstances, give rise to a wrongful discharge action related to urinalysis or to personal property searches. Specifically, we refer to the Pennsylvania common law regarding tortious invasion of privacy. Pennsylvania recognizes a cause of action for tortious "intrusion upon seclusion." ...

We can envision at least two ways in which an employer's urinalysis program might intrude upon an employee's seclusion. First, the particular manner in which the program is conducted might constitute an intrusion upon seclusion as defined by Pennsylvania law. The process of collecting the urine sample to be tested clearly implicates "expectations of privacy that society has long recognized as reasonable," ... In addition, many urinalysis programs monitor the collection of the urine specimen to ensure that the employee does not adulterate it or substitute a sample from another person. Monitoring collection of the urine sample appears to fall within the definition of an intrusion upon seclusion because it involves the use of one's senses to oversee the private activities of another ... If the method used to collect the urine sample fails to give due regard to the employees' privacy.

Second, urinalysis "can reveal a host of private medical facts about an employee, including whether she is epileptic, pregnant or diabetic. A reasonable person might well conclude that submitting urine samples to tests designed to ascertain these types of information constitutes a substantial and highly offensive intrusion upon seclusion.

The same principles apply to an employer's search of an employee's personal property. If the search is not conducted in a discreet manner or if it is done in such a way as to reveal personal matters unrelated to the workplace, the search might well constitute a tortious invasion of the employee's privacy.... It may be granted that there are areas of an employee's life in which his employer has no legitimate interest. An intrusion into one of these areas by virtue of the employer's power of discharge might plausibly give rise to a cause of action, particularly where some recognized facet of public policy is threatened ...

In view of the foregoing analysis, we predict that the Pennsylvania Supreme Court would apply a balancing test to determine whether the Shop's drug and alcohol program (consisting of urinalysis and personal property searches) invaded Borse's privacy. The test we believe that Pennsylvania would adopt balances the employee's privacy interest against the employer's interest in maintaining a drug-free workplace in order to determine whether a reasonable person would find the employer's program highly offensive.[3]

---

3. We recognize that other jurisdictions have considered individualized suspicion and concern for safety as factors to be considered in striking the balance, see, for example, Twigg, 406 SE2d at 55 (allowing urinalysis based on individualized suspicion or when employee's job implicates safety concerns). We do not doubt that, in an appropriate case, Pennsylvania would include these factors in the balance, but we do not believe that the Pennsylvania Supreme Court would require private employers to limit urinalysis programs or personal property searches to employees suspected of drug use or to those performing safety-sensitive jobs. n20

In sum, based on our prediction of Pennsylvania law, we hold that dismissing an employee who refused to consent to urinalysis testing and to personal property searches would violate public policy if the testing tortiously invaded the employee's privacy.

Note: The Wrongful Dismissal Tort

A number of legal theories have been invoked by employees in an attempt to challenge the legality of mandatory urinalysis testing. Courts have been most receptive to the wrongful dismissal theory that is the basis of the decision in *Borse*. However, the balancing of interest concept that is the core of this theory does not generally prohibit mandatory testing as a condition for continued employment. The employer's interest in a drug free workforce is generally sufficient to justify mandatory testing as long as the circumstances under which the urine sample is collected and the storage and use of the test results do not excessively intrude upon employee privacy. Other courts disagree with the *Borse* notion of the balancing of interest outcome in wrongful dismissal cases. The Supreme court of West Virginia assigned a greater value to the privacy interest and limits a private employer's right to mandatory testing to those employees whose job involves "public safety or safety of others" and to those employees that the employer has a "reasonable good faith objective suspicion" is a drug user. See, *Twigg v. Hercules Corp.*, 406 S.E. 2d 52 (W. Va. 1990). In New Jersey the Supreme Court allowed for random urinalysis tests but limited mandatory non consensual testing to jobs that posed a threat to co-workers, the workplace or public at large if the employee was impaired, *Hennessey v. Coastal Eagle Point Oil Co.*, 609 A.2d 11, 23 (N.J. 1992).

The New Jersey Supreme Court in *Hennessey* set down guidelines for appropriate notice and testing procedures:

> Measures include a testing procedure that allows as much privacy and dignity as possible, and notice, close in time to the beginning of a testing program but sufficient to provide adequate advance warning, that announces the program, details the methods for selecting employees to be tested, warns employees of the lingering effect of certain drugs in the system, explains how the sample will be analyzed, and notifies employees of the consequences of testing positive or refusing to take the test. Furthermore, employers may conduct only those tests necessary to determine the presence of drugs in the urine, and are under an obligation not to disclose information obtained as a result of testing.

Note: The Privacy Intrusion Tort

In Chapter V the common law privacy intrusion tort is examined. The right to informational privacy that is encompassed in the privacy intrusion tort provides legal protection against individuals or business entities that acquire personal or intimate information about someone. Does the testing of employees for drugs, alcohol, and HIV by the extraction and examination of blood or urine constitute an intrusion into their "solitude, seclusion or private affairs" for purposes of the privacy intrusion tort? Given the widespread business practice of such testing, it is surprising that there are only a few decisions dealing with this question. All of the appellate courts have rejected the argument that compulsory drug testing by a private employer constitutes a violation of the privacy intrusion tort. When the testing has occurred as part of a physical examination in which there has been consent to extract blood, but no specific consent to test for drug or alcohol use, the Supreme Court of Alaska has held that the testing was not an "offensive method" of intrusion within the requirements of the tort. Because consent for the extraction of the blood had been given, the further testing was not "unreasonable." In addition, the court found that the objective of that testing was to protect the public safety and was itself "reasonable." *See Luedtke v. Nabors Alaska Drilling, Inc.*, 768 P.2d 1123 (Alaska 1989). The court rejected the privacy claims of employees who refused to be tested on the view that since they were not tested there was no intrusion into their private affairs.

In *Jennings v. Minco Technology Labs, Inc.*, 765 S.W.2d 497 (Tex.Ct. App.1989), the court upheld a testing program for employees and awarded the employer $45,000 for attorneys' fees. The program authorized the random testing of employees who gave their consent for the test. An employee who did not consent could be terminated from employment for refusing to be tested. Texas is an "at-will" employment state that had previously recognized an employee's right to sue under a wrongful discharge action when the individual had been discharged for refusing to perform an illegal act. The plaintiff in *Jennings* argued that this exception to the employer's discretion to terminate an employee "at will" should be extended to threats to terminate employment for failure to be tested because the testing constituted an intrusion into her private affairs in violation of her common law tort right to privacy. The court rejected this claim, and concluded that the threatened test did not constitute an unlawful invasion of any employee's privacy interest because the test was "consensual." The employee was given a choice to be tested or terminated. If the choice was to be tested, the test was consensual and a justifiable invasion of privacy under the common law. *Id*. at 502.

Why have courts been more receptive to wrongful dismissal claims against drug testing regimes than privacy intrusion claims? Is it because the privacy intrusion tort challenges the legality of drug testing as a condition for applying for employment while the wrongful dismissal tort only comes into play with someone whose employment is terminated?

c. *State Statutory Regulation of Drug Testing in The Private Sector*

In addition to state the common law remedies discussed above the legality of drug testing in the private sector may turn on the rights negotiated for union employees in a collective bargaining agreement or rights created in state legislation. One interesting example of statutory regulation is found in Massachusetts. The statutory right to privacy provides that, "A person shall have a right against unreasonable, substantial or serious interference with his privacy ...", General Laws c.214, sec. IB (1992 ed.) Two "at-will" employees challenged the drug testing requirements of Motorola Communications and a subsidiary, Codex Corporation, under the privacy statute. One employee, James

Webster, was employed as an account executive; the other employee, Michael P. Joyce, was employed as a principle technical editor.

The Massachusetts high court applying the balancing test developed under the statute found that the mandatory testing of Webster did not violate the statutory right to privacy but the testing of Joyce did. A general interest in protecting the safety of employees and in providing a drug-free environment was not a sufficient interest to justify the privacy intrusion from urinalysis. But an interest in protecting the employees' safety and the safety of others was. Webster's job included driving a company-owned vehicle 20,000 to 25, 000 miles a year and implicated these safety interests. Joyce's job as a technical editor did not sufficiently implicate safety interest to justify mandatory testing. Although some of the products were sold to airline industries, the FAA, Defense Department and the White House the nexus between the text that Joyce was editing and national security or public safety was found to be attenuated. See, Webster v. Motorola, 637 N.E.2d 203 (Mass. 1994).

Note: Polygraph Testing and the Right of Privacy

Does involuntary polygraph examination of public and private employees violate their right to privacy? Recall Warren and Brandeis:

> The common law secures to each individual the right of determining, ordinarily, to what extent his *thoughts*, sentiments, and emotions shall be communicated to others.

Warren and Brandeis, *The Right to Privacy*, 4 Harv. L. Rev. 193, 198 (1890)(emphasis added).

Does an involuntary polygraph constitute an invasion of privacy because it requires communication of "thoughts"? Justice Broussard encapsulates the California Supreme Court's position as follows:

> If there is a quintessential zone of human privacy it is the mind. Our ability to exclude others from our mental processes is intrinsic to the human personality. . . .

> A polygraph examination is specifically designed to overcome this privacy by compelling communication of "thoughts, sentiments and emotions" which the examinee may have chosen not to communicate.

Long Beach City Employees Ass'n v. City of Long Beach, 41 Cal.3d 937, 940, 719 P.2d 660, 663 (1986).

This passage suggests that the court considers lie detectors more intrusive than other methods used by employers to acquire information about individuals. Applications for employment in the public and private sector typically require prospective employees to disclose information as a condition of employment. Central to the claim that polygraph examinations seriously invade personal privacy is that the standard polygraph test is far more intrusive than the questions that are asked of prospective employees on an application form or in a personal interview.

Consider the procedures and context of a standard polygraph test. Initially, the subject is seated in a reception area and provided literature that depicts the lie detector as a reliable indicator of the credibility of the subject. Preliminary evaluations of the subject's attitude—whether she is hostile or cooperative toward the examination—are made; the results are a factor in the ultimate determination of credibility. Prior to the actual examination, the administrator of the polygraph does a "pretest interview." The object is to determine whether the subject has emotional or psychological factors which would adversely affect the reliability of the test. Typical questions in the pretest interview would be: "Any history of heart trouble or epilepsy? Ever been treated by or consulted a psychiatrist for any reason? Ever been arrested for any reason? Did you ever experiment with any types of drugs—reds, whites, LSD caps, heroin or cocaine? Have you ever smoked marijuana in your life? When was the last time?"

After the pretest interview, the subject is seated in a chair and a number of instruments are attached to her body. These include a blood pressure cuff wrapped around the arm, a pneumograph tube tied to the chest, and electrodes attached to the hands. A continuous graphic recording begins with the hooking up of these instruments. The questioning then begins. The objective of the questions is to develop a record of the physiological response of the subject to her answers when she has lied. In order to do this, "control" questions must initially be asked to elicit a lie from the subject. The physiological response to the lie is then used as a basis for comparing the subject's answer to other questions. Typically, questions about illegal or immoral conduct that most have engaged in will be asked (have you ever stolen anything?). A control question is ideally one about misconduct that is similar to the incident or conduct that is the subject of the investigation by the polygraph. The California Supreme Court, citing various authorities, concludes that the polygraph test is more intrusive than a written examination or verbal interrogative for three basic reasons: (1) the test merely records general emotional arousal and since it cannot distinguish between anxiety, indignation or guilt, repressed beliefs, guilt feelings and fantasized events may actually be discovered by a polygraph; (2) the pretext and control question—when it involves embarrassing questions—may cause the subject to be reluctant or refuse to answer questions because of a fear of appearing dishonest; and (3) even when an employee chooses not to answer a question on a personal matter, her physiological response is recorded. Thus, the polygraph is more intrusive because it continuously records the physiological functions of the subject. Unlike in the case of questionnaires or verbal interrogation, the subject cannot control disclosure by not answering a question or by remaining silent: information is still revealed about the subject. See Meyer, *Do Lie Detectors Lie?*, Science '82, June 1982 at 24, 26; Donald H.J. Herman III, *Privacy, The Prospective Employee, and Employment Testing: The Need to Restrict Polygraph and Personality Testing*, 47 Wash. L. Rev. 73, 84–85 (1971); Comment, *Regulation of Polygraph Testing in the Employment Context: Suggested Statutory Control on Test Use and Examiner Competence*, 15 U.C. Davis L. Rev. 113, 118, n.21 (1981); Susan Gardner, *Wiretapping the Mind: A Call to Regulate Truth Verification in Employment*, 21 San Diego L. Rev. 295, 305 (1984).

In *Long Beach City Employees Association v. City of Long Beach*, 41 Cal.3d 937, 719 P.2d 660 (1986), the California Supreme Court invalidated the compulsory polygraph testing of selected public employees. In 1972, via referendum, California voters amended the constitution to include protection for the right of privacy. The wording of Article I, Section I of the California Constitution was changed slightly, again by constitutional amendment, in 1974. Article I, Section I now reads:

> All people are by nature free and independent and have inalienable rights. Among these are enjoying and defending life and liberty, acquiring, possessing, and protecting property, and pursuing and obtaining safety, happiness, and *privacy*. (emphasis added).

The process of referendum in California includes arguments that are presented to the voters in support of constitutional amendments. Ballot arguments in support of the amendment regarding privacy included:

> The right of privacy is the right to be left alone. It is a fundamental and compelling interest. It protects our homes, our families, our thoughts, our emotions, our expressions, our personalities, our freedom of communication and our freedom to associate with the people we choose.... [T]his right should be abridged only when there is a compelling public need....

Construing the use of polygraph testing in light of the language of the California Constitution and the ballot arguments, the court found that polygraph examinations constituted a significant invasion of privacy. However, because the legislative scheme exempted certain groups of employees, the court invalidated the legislation under the equal protection clause. The legislation excluded private employees from mandatory polygraph testing and, within the government, also excluded public safety officers. Since the legislation infringed on the right to privacy of some employees but not others, it was an invidious discrimination subject to strict judicial scrutiny. Under this standard the state was required to demonstrate that the distinctions in the legislation furthered a compelling state interest. Interests asserted by the state in support of the polygraph testing requirements were (1) the interest in an honest and impartial government and (2) the interest in maintenance of the real and apparent integrity of the public service. The court acknowledged that public employees did hold a special position of trust that distinguished them from private employees. However, the court found that there were less intrusive alternative means for protecting these interests. These alternatives were not fully explored by the court except to suggest that the normal investigative techniques invoked after suspicion of improper conduct would be as effective and be less intrusive into privacy. It also found the exception for public safety officers to be greatly under and over inclusive. This was because the definition included employees who were not involved in critical services and also excluded employees who were.

Chief Justice Byrd concurred in the result but contended that the court should have addressed the broader question: did mandatory polygraph testing violate the right to privacy under the California Constitution? The Chief Justice's the courts in California had considered the results of polygraph examinations to be too unreliable to be admitted in court or administrative proceedings. Therefore, given the significant invasion of privacy that occurs from the use of such tests, and the unreliability of the test, other investigative methods would generally be as effective and less detrimental to the interest in privacy.

The Texas Supreme Court directly addressed the issue of the right to privacy shortly after *Long Beach* was decided, and held that mandatory polygraph tests of employees of the state department of health violated the implied right to privacy guaranteed under the Texas Constitution. In *State Employees Union v. Department of Mental Health*, 746 S.W.2d 203 (Tex. 1987), the court agreed with the trial court's conclusion that in view of its unreliability, the polygraph test did not constitute a reasonable means for identifying "miscreant" employees within the meaning of the compelling state interest test. The court indicated that mandatory tests might be constitutional in respect to employees directly involved with public safety, such as policemen and firemen.

Compare *Long Beach* and *State Employees Union* with *Anderson v. City of Philadelphia*, 845 F.2d 1216 (3d Cir.1988). In *Anderson*, the Third Circuit upheld a Pennsylvania statute that restricted the use of polygraph tests as a pre-employment screening device for employers, with a few specific exceptions including one for public law enforcement agencies. The exception was challenged on procedural and substantive due process and equal protection grounds by unsuccessful applicants for employment as police officers or correctional officers who had failed the required polygraph examination. The Third Circuit held that the rational basis test was the appropriate standard of review in the case because the claim of unconstitutionality in the denial of public employment did not involve a fundamental right or a suspect classification. In such cases the party challenging the legislation has the burden of demonstrating that requiring the test constitutes such a "lack [of] rationality" that it amounts to a denial of equal protection. 845 F.2d at 1223. Under this deferential standard of review the fact that the evidence was mixed regarding the effectiveness of the test as an employment screening device was not enough to invalidate the statute.

d. The Employee Polygraph Protection Act

In 1988, Congress passed The Employee Polygraph Protection Act for the purpose of regulating the use by private employers of the polygraph and other mechanical and electronic truth verification devices. 29 U.S.C.A. §§ 2001–2009 (1988). The Act prohibits employers from expressly or impliedly requiring that existing or prospective employees submit to polygraph examinations in order to obtain or continue employment. Section 2002(1)-(2). The Act further prohibits discrimination or discipline against any present or prospective employee who refuses to take a polygraph test. Section 2002(3)(A).

The Secretary of Labor has the authority to enforce the Act's provisions, Section 2003, issue compliance rules and regulations to employers, Section 2004, and require employers to post notice of employees' rights under the Act.

The Act provides a civil remedy for damages not in excess of $10,000. Section 2005. The Act also allows the Secretary of Labor to enjoin employer practices that are inconsistent with the provisions of the Act. Section 2005(b).

The Act contains a number of exemptions in Section 2006. It does not apply to federal, state, or local government employees. Section 2006(a). The Act does not cover any experts or consultants under contract with the Department of Defense, nor those of the Department of Energy who work on atomic energy matters, nor does it apply to certain classes of individuals whose duties affect national security or who are contractors with the FBI.

The Act allows private employers to require employees to submit to polygraph tests in connection with ongoing investigations into criminal acts that have resulted in economic loss to the employer in situations wherein the employee had access to the property in question, and the employer has a reasonable suspicion that the employee was involved in the matter being investigated and after the employer has issued a written statement that details the specific incidents requiring the testing of specific employees. Section 2006(d)(2)-(4). Employers engaged in security services may test prospective employees, Section 2006(e)(1), as may employers engaged in the sale, storage, distribution, or manufacturing of controlled substances, Section 2006(f)(1).

Finally, the Act outlines the procedures to be followed prior to and during the permissible testing of employees. These procedures require that the employee be given notice of the condition under which the test will be given, the questions that will be asked, the location, time, and place of the test, and the maximum duration of the test. Section 2007(b).

The Employee Polygraph Protection Act is included in Chapter VIII of these materials, *infra*.

E. CONVERSATIONAL PRIVACY: ASSOCIATIONAL PRIVACY

1. NATIONAL SECURITY

UNITED STATES v. UNITED STATES DISTRICT COURT

407 U.S. 297 (1972)

Mr. Justice Powell delivered the opinion of the Court.

[Three defendants were charged in the United States District Court for the Eastern District of Michigan with conspiracy to destroy government property in violation of 18 U.S.C.A. § 371. One defendant, Plamondon, was charged with bombing the Central Intelligence Agency in Michigan. Defendants moved during pretrial proceedings to compel disclosure of electronic surveillance information gathered by the government and for a hearing to determine if this information "tainted" evidence on which the indictment was based or evidence to be used at trial. The government filed an affidavit in response which acknowledged that its agents had overheard conversations involving Plamondon by the use of wiretaps which the Attorney General had approved. The government asserted that although the surveillance was conducted without judicial approval, it was lawful as a reasonable exercise of the President's power through the Attorney General to protect national security. The District Court granted the motion compelling disclosure of the overheard conversations and held that the surveillance violated the fourth amendment. The Court of Appeals affirmed.]

It is important at the outset to emphasize the limited nature of the question before the Court. This case raises no constitutional challenge to electronic surveillance as specifically authorized by Title III of the Omnibus Crime Control and Safe Streets Act of 1968. Nor is there any question or doubt as to the necessity of obtaining a warrant in the surveillance of crimes unrelated to the national security interest. Katz v. United States, Berger v. New York. Further, the instant case requires no judgment on the scope of the President's surveillance power with respect to the activities of foreign powers, within or without this country. The Attorney General's affidavit in this case states that the surveillances were "deemed necessary to protect the nation from attempts of *domestic organizations* to attack and subvert the existing structure of the Government" (emphasis supplied). There is no evidence of any involvement, directly or indirectly, of a foreign power.

Our present inquiry, though important, is therefore a narrow one. It addresses a question left open by *Katz*:

> "Whether safeguards other than prior authorization by a magistrate would satisfy the Fourth Amendment in a situation involving the national security...."

The determination of this question requires the essential Fourth Amendment inquiry into the "reasonableness" of the search and seizure in question, and the way in which that "reasonableness" derives content and meaning through reference to the warrant clause.

.   .   .

It has been said that "[t]he most basic function of any government is to provide for the security of the individual and of his property." And unless Government safeguards its own capacity to function and to preserve the security of its people, society itself could become so disordered that all rights and liberties would be endangered. As Chief Justice Hughes reminded us in Cox v. New Hampshire, 312 U.S. 569, 574 (1941):

Civil liberties, as guaranteed by the Constitution, imply the existence of an organized society maintaining public order without which liberty itself would be lost in the excesses of unrestrained abuses.

But a recognition of these elementary truths does not make the employment by Government of electronic surveillance a welcome development—even when employed with restraint and under judicial supervision. There is, understandably, a deep-seated uneasiness and apprehension that this capability will be used to intrude upon cherished privacy of law-abiding citizens.[13] We look to the Bill of Rights to safeguard this privacy. Though physical entry of the home is the chief evil against which the wording of the Fourth Amendment is directed, its broader spirit now shields private speech from unreasonable surveillance. Our decision in *Katz* refused to lock the Fourth Amendment into instances of actual physical trespass. Rather, the Amendment governs "not only the seizure of tangible items, but extends as well to the recording of oral statements ... without any 'technical trespass under ... local property law.' " That decision implicitly recognized that the broad and unsuspected governmental incursions into conversational privacy which electronic surveillance entails[14] necessitate the application of Fourth Amendment safeguards.

National security cases, moreover, often reflect a convergence of First and Fourth Amendment values not present in cases of "ordinary" crime. Though the investigative duty of the executive may be stronger in such cases, so also is there greater jeopardy to constitutionally protected speech. "Historically the struggle for freedom of speech and press in England was bound up with the issue of the scope of the search and seizure power." History abundantly documents the tendency of Government—however benevolent and benign its motives—to view with suspicion those who most fervently dispute its policies. Fourth Amendment protections become the more necessary when the targets of official surveillance may be those suspected of unorthodoxy in their political beliefs.... The price of lawful public dissent must not be a dread of subjection to an unchecked surveillance power. Nor must the fear of unauthorized official eavesdropping deter vigorous citizen dissent and discussion of Government action in private conversation. For private

13. Professor Alan Westin has written on the likely course of future conflict between the value of privacy and the "new technology" of law enforcement. Much of the book details techniques of physical and electronic surveillance and such possible threats to personal privacy as psychological and personality testing and electronic information storage and retrieval. Not all of the contemporary threats to privacy emanate directly from the pressures of crime control. Privacy and Freedom (1967).

14. Though the total number of intercepts authorized by state and federal judges pursuant to Tit. III of the 1968 Omnibus Crime Control and Safe Streets Act was 597 in 1970, each surveillance may involve interception of hundreds of different conversations. The average intercept in 1970 involved 44 people and 655 conversations, of which 295 or 45% were incriminating. 117 Cong. Rec. 14052.

dissent, no less than open public discourse, is essential to our free society.

. . .

Over two centuries ago, Lord Mansfield held that common-law principles prohibited warrants that ordered the arrest of unnamed individuals who the *officer* might conclude were guilty of seditious libel. "It is not fit," said Mansfield, "that the receiving or judging of the information should be left to the discretion of the officer. The magistrate ought to judge; and should give certain directions to the officer." Leach v. Three of the King's Messengers, 19 How. St. Tr. 1001, 1027 (1765).

Lord Mansfield's formulation touches the very heart of the Fourth Amendment directive: that, where practical, a governmental search and seizure should represent both the efforts of the officer to gather evidence of wrongful acts and the judgment of the magistrate that the collected evidence is sufficient to justify invasion of a citizen's private premises or conversation. Inherent in the concept of a warrant is its issuance by a "neutral and detached magistrate." The further requirement of "probable cause" instructs the magistrate that baseless searches shall not proceed.

. . .

... The independent check upon executive discretion is not satisfied, as the Government argues, by "extremely limited" post-surveillance judicial review.[19] Indeed, post-surveillance review would never reach the surveillances which failed to result in prosecutions. Prior review by a neutral and detached magistrate is the time-tested means of effectuating Fourth Amendment rights.

It is true that there have been exceptions to the warrant requirement. But those exceptions are few in number and carefully delineated, *Katz*; in general, they serve the legitimate needs of law enforcement officers to protect their own well-being and preserve evidence from destruction. Even while carving out those exceptions, the Court has reaffirmed the principle that the "police must, whenever practicable, obtain advance judicial approval of searches and seizures through the warrant procedure."

. . .

Thus, we conclude that the Government's concerns do not justify departure in this case from the customary Fourth Amendment requirement of judicial approval prior to initiation of a search or surveillance. Although some added burden will be imposed upon the Attorney General, this inconvenience is justified in a free society to protect constitution-

---

19. The Government argues that domestic security wiretaps should be upheld by courts in post-surveillance review "[u]nless it appears that the Attorney General's determination that the proposed surveillance relates to a national security matter is arbitrary and capricious, *i.e.*, that it consti- tutes a clear abuse of the broad discretion that the Attorney General has to obtain all information that will be helpful to the President in protecting the Government ..." against the various unlawful acts in Section 2511(3). Brief for United States 22.

al values. Nor do we think the Government's domestic surveillance powers will be impaired to any significant degree. A prior warrant establishes presumptive validity of the surveillance and will minimize the burden of justification in post-surveillance judicial review. By no means of least importance will be the reassurance of the public generally that indiscriminate wiretapping and bugging of law-abiding citizens cannot occur.

We emphasize, before concluding this opinion, the scope of our decision. As stated at the outset, this case involves only the domestic aspects of national security. We have not addressed, and express no opinion as to, the issues which may be involved with respect to activities of foreign powers or their agents.[20] Nor does our decision rest on the language of Section 2511(3) or any other section of Title III of the Omnibus Crime Control and Safe Streets Act of 1968. That Act does not attempt to define or delineate the powers of the President to meet domestic threats to the national security.

. . .

As the surveillance of Plamondon's conversations was unlawful, because conducted without prior judicial approval, the courts below correctly held that Alderman v. United States is controlling and that it requires disclosure to the accused of his own impermissibly intercepted conversations. As stated in *Alderman*, "the trial court can and should, where appropriate, place a defendant and his counsel under enforceable orders against unwarranted disclosure of the materials which they may be entitled to inspect."[21]

The judgment of the Court of Appeals is hereby *Affirmed*.

. . .

MR. JUSTICE DOUGLAS, concurring.

. . .

We are told that one national security wiretap lasted for 14 months and monitored over 900 conversations. Senator Edward Kennedy found recently that "warrantless devices accounted for an average of 78 to 209 days of listening per device, as compared with a 13–day per device average of those devices installed under court order."[3] He concluded that

20. See n. 8, *supra*. For the view that warrantless surveillance, though impermissible in domestic security cases, may be constitutional where foreign powers are involved, see *United States v. Smith*, 321 F. Supp. 424, 425–426 (C.D.Cal.1971); and American Bar Association Project on Standards for Criminal Justice, Electronic Surveillance 120, 121 (Approved Draft 1971, and Feb. 1971 Supp. 11). See also *United States v. Clay*, 430 F.2d 165 (C.A.5 1970).

21. We think it unnecessary at this time and on the facts of this case to consider the arguments advanced by the Government for

a re-examination of the basis and scope of the Court's decision in *Alderman*.

3. Letter from Senator Edward Kennedy to Members of the Sub-committee on Administrative Procedure and Practice of the Senate Judiciary Committee, Dec. 17, 1971, p. 2. Senator Kennedy included in his letter a chart comparing court-ordered and department-ordered wiretapping and bugging by federal agencies. This chart is reproduced in the Appendix to this opinion. For a statistical breakdown by duration, location, and implementing agency of the 1,042 wiretap orders issued in 1971 by state

the Government's revelations posed "the frightening possibility that the conversations of untold thousands of citizens of this country are being monitored on secret devices which no judge has authorized and which may remain in operation for months and perhaps years at a time."[4] Even the most innocent and random caller who uses or telephones into a tapped line can become a flagged number in the Government's data bank.

. . .

The Warrant Clause has stood as a barrier against intrusions by officialdom into the privacies of life. But if that barrier were lowered now to permit suspected subversives' most intimate conversations to be pillaged then why could not their abodes or mail be secretly searched by the same authority? To defeat so terrifying a claim of inherent power we need only stand by the enduring values served by the Fourth Amendment. As we stated last Term in Coolidge v. New Hampshire: "In times of unrest, whether caused by crime or racial conflict or fear of internal subversion, this basic law and the values that it represents may appear unrealistic or 'extravagant' to some. But the values were those of the authors of our fundamental constitutional concepts. In times not altogether unlike our own they won . . . a right of personal security against arbitrary intrusions. . . . If times have changed, reducing everyman's scope to do so as he pleases in an urban and industrial world, the changes have made the values served by the Fourth Amendment more, not less, important." We have as much or more to fear from the erosion of our sense of privacy and independence by the omnipresent electronic ear of the Government as we do from the likelihood that fomenters of domestic upheaval will modify our form of governing.[14]

Note: The Foreign Intelligence Surveillance Act of 1978 (FISA)

The questions raised by the *District Court* case about the constitutionality of the President's power to employ electronic surveillance to gather information for national security were addressed by Congress in the Foreign Intelligence Surveillance Act of 1978 (FISA). This statute creates special courts consisting of federal district and circuit court judges designated by the Chief Justice to review applications for electronic surveillance under FISA and to decide appeals from denial of applications. FISA generally provides for

and federal judges, see Administrative Office of the United States Courts, Report on Applications for Orders Authorizing or Approving the Interception of Wire or Oral Communications for 1971; The Washington Post, May 14, 1972, p. A30, col. 1 (final ed.).

4. Kennedy, *supra*, n. 3, at 2. See also H. Schwartz, *A Report on the Costs and Benefits of Electronic Surveillance* (American Civil Liberties Union 1971); Schwartz, *The Legitimation of Electronic Eavesdropping: The Politics of "Law and Order,"* 67 Mich. L. Rev. 455 (1969).

14. I continue in my belief that it would be extremely difficult to write a search warrant specifically naming the particular conversations to be seized and therefore any such attempt would amount to a general warrant, the very abuse condemned by the Fourth Amendment. As I said, dissenting in *Osborn v. United States*, 385 U.S. 323, 353: "Such devices lay down a dragnet which indiscriminately sweeps in all conversations within its scope, without regard to the nature of the conversations, or the participants. A warrant authorizing such devices is no different from the general warrants the Fourth Amendment was intended to prohibit."

surveillance pursuant to a warrant based upon probable cause that the object of the surveillance is intelligence information of a foreign power. One party consent surveillance is exempt from FISA. An examination of the complex issues and provisions that are involved with applications for foreign intelligence surveillance under FISA is not undertaken in this book. For general commentary, *see* J. Carr, *The Law of Electronic Surveillance*, sections 9.1–9.11 (1991).

Note: Privacy and First Amendment Values

Historically, privacy and first amendment values have been intertwined. Perhaps the best example of this is demonstrated by the circumstances that gave birth to the fourth amendment. The proscription against unreasonable searches and seizures is the legacy of centuries of the use of general search warrants and writs of assistance by the Crown to suppress printed material and to seize smuggled goods. The history of this conflict between the press and the use of general search warrants by the Crown to enforce laws that prohibited seditious libel and that required a license for printed publications during the 16th, 17th and 18th centuries is chronicled in Fredrick Seaton Siebert, *Freedom of the Press in England, 1476–1776: The Rise and Decline of Government Control*, 83, 85–86, 97 (University Microfilms International 1952); *see also,* Nelson Lasson, *The History and Development of the Fourth Amendment to The United States Constitution*, 42–50 (1970).

An often quoted statement from Justice Douglas links not only the first, fourth, and fifth amendments but ties values reflected in these amendments to the role of the Constitution and individual rights in protecting human dignity. "These three amendments are indeed closely related, safeguarding not only privacy and protection against self-incrimination, but 'conscience and human dignity and freedom of expression as well.'" *Frank v. Maryland*, 359 U.S. 360, 376 (1959) (Douglas, J., dissenting). The court on numerous occasions has recognized the historical interdependence between the rights that are protected in the first, fourth, and fifth amendments, *e.g., Marcus v. Search Warrant*, 367 U.S. 717, 724–29 (1961); *Boyd v. United States*, 116 U.S. 616 (1886); *Stanford v. Texas*, 379 U.S. 476, 482–486 (1965).

Two of the most significant historical landmarks in the battle between liberty of the press and privacy and the authority of the government to search without restrictions are *Wilkes v. Wood*, 19 How. St. Tr. 1153 (1763) and *Entick v. Carrington*, 19 How. St. Tr. 1029 (1765). John Wilkes was the anonymous publisher of the *North Britain*; John Entick was the author of *The Monitor* or *British Freeholder*. Both Wilkes and Entick were awarded damages against the government for the invasions of privacy and seizures of property that occurred through the issuance of general search warrants. In Entick's case the King's messenger, pursuant to the warrant, ransacked Entick's home for several hours and carried away large quantities of books and papers.

Lord Camden's opinion in *Entick* invalidating the warrant was recognized very early by the Supreme Court to be the foundation of rights protected by the fourth amendment.

As every American statesman, during our revolutionary informative period as a nation, was undoubtedly familiar with this monument of English freedom, and considered it as the true and ultimate expression of constitutional law, it may be confidently asserted that its propositions were in the minds of those who framed the Fourth Amendment to the Constitution. . . .

Boyd v. United States, 116 U.S. at 626–27.

The balance of this Note examines further examples in the twentieth century of Supreme Court decisions that recognize in one form or another the extent to which the Constitution views privacy and first amendment values as interdependent.

A couple of things are meant by speaking of privacy and first amendment values as "linked" or "interdependent." One is that the two depend upon one another in the sense that one can't exist without the other. Secondly, the values are linked under constitutional theory in the sense that a government action that affects one may be viewed with special concern because of the linkage that value has with the other. Perhaps the classic example of the interdependence and linkage of privacy and first amendment values is *NAACP v. Alabama,* 357 U.S. 449 (1958). In *NAACP v. Alabama,* the state of Alabama subpoenaed records of the NAACP. The request was made as part of litigation in which the state sought an injunction against the NAACP from conducting business in Alabama because they had allegedly failed to conform to requirements of foreign corporations that were "doing business" in the state. The NAACP complied with the subpoena except that it refused to disclose its membership list, arguing that compelled disclosure of that information violated the privacy and associational rights of the organization and its members. Justice Harlan, speaking for a unanimous court, held that the compelled disclosure violated the right of association that was protected under the first amendment. He found that associational rights were violated even though the governmental action was directed at disclosing information and not punishing individuals for their association:

> It is hardly a novel perception that compelled disclosure of affiliation with groups engaged in advocacy may constitute as effective a restraint on freedom of association as the forms of governmental action in the cases above were thought likely to produce upon the particular constitutional rights there involved. This Court has recognized the vital relationship between freedom to associate and privacy in one's associations. . . . Inviolability of privacy in group association may in many circumstances be indispensable to preservation of freedom of association, particularly where a group espouses dissident beliefs.

357 U.S. at 462.

Consider the role that *NAACP v. Alabama* plays in the arguments of Justice Douglas and Justice Harlan in support of recognition of an implied right to privacy under the Federal Constitution. See Justice Douglas' opinion in *Griswold v. Connecticut, supra,* and Justice Harlan's dissenting opinion in *Poe v. Ullman, infra.*

2. GOVERNMENT SURVEILLANCE OF DISSIDENT GROUPS

Over the last several decades, a number of decisions of the Supreme Court have involved surveillance by the government that took the form of shadowing specified individuals in public places and of acquiring information about individuals from others. Earlier in this chapter, governmental surveillance of individuals by the acquiring of their telephone toll records by the FBI were examined. *See* discussion of *Reporters Comm. for Freedom of the Press v. American Tel. & Tel., supra* pp. 120–121. Resolution of the precise issue in that case was driven by precedent which did not extend constitutional protection to telephone numbers because the subscriber had voluntarily disclosed such information to the telephone company and had no legitimate expectation of privacy in respect to that information. Constitutional challenges to other forms of governmental surveillance have similarly been unsuccessful. *See* discussion of *Smith v. Maryland, supra* p. 104.

Laird v. Tatum, 408 U.S. 1 (1972), arose out of the utilization of a massive data-gathering system by the Army in response to the riots that occurred in many urban areas in the summer of 1967 and following the assassination of Dr. Martin Luther King in the spring of 1968. One of the areas that was dramatically affected by civil disorders was Detroit, Michigan. President Johnson ordered federal troops to quell the disorders of that city. The data-gathering system that resulted from the 1967 experience of the Army essentially involved information about "public activities" that had some potential for civil disorder. The collected information was disseminated to Army intelligence headquarters and to other Army posts around the country. It was stored in a computer data bank that was under the control of the Army. The information collection activities included: (1) information acquired from the news media and publications in general circulation; (2) information acquired by Army intelligence agents attending public meetings and submitting field reports describing in detail the identity of speakers, numbers of persons in attendance, and other information; (3) information garnered from law enforcement agencies.

Individuals subject to the Army surveillance initiated a class action in which they sought declaratory and injunctive relief on the theory that the "surveillance of lawful and peaceful civilian political activity" inhibited and "chilled" the expression and associations in violation of the First Amendment. 408 U.S. at 2.

Then Chief Justice Burger, in an opinion supported by four other members of the Court, concluded that the allegations of governmental surveillance did not contain sufficient claims of first amendment injury to constitute a "case" or "controversy" within the meaning of Article III of the Federal Constitution. Allegations of "subjective chill" on speech and association activities did not satisfy the constitutional requirements that the parties claim "specific present objective harm or threat of specific future harm" in order for first amendment issues to properly be before the Court. 408 U.S. at 13–14. The effect of *Tatum* is to immunize governmental surveillance that takes the form of photographing and data gathering at public meetings from first amendment challenges. These activities without more create only a "subjective chill" and are legally unobjectionable. The "more" that is required to satisfy the requirement of specific objective present or future harm is that the government action be regulatory, proscriptive or compulsory in nature. *See, e.g., Baird v. State Bar of Arizona*, 401 U.S. 1, 7 (1971) (denial of admission to the bar for refusing to answer questions regarding organizational associations).

BEYOND "SUBJECTIVE CHILL": *PHILADELPHIA YEARLY MEETING OF THE RELIGIOUS SOCIETY OF FRIENDS V. TATE*

When does a governmental surveillance system become so intrusive that it creates an "objective" chill on first amendment and privacy associations rights? In *Philadelphia Yearly Meeting of the Religious Society of Friends v. Tate*, 519 F.2d 1335 (3d Cir.1975), the court found that some of the claims of surveillance by the Philadelphia Police Department of the activities of individuals and groups were more than allegations of "subjective chill" within the meaning of *Laird*. The plaintiffs in *Tate* alleged that the Police Department through its Political Disobedience Unit had compiled 18,000 files on numerous individuals and groups and that these files contained information about the subjects' political views and associations and personal lives and habits. The files were kept separate from other police records and it was alleged that there were no safeguards to insure the confidentiality of information in the files and that the information was available to government agencies, private employers, and private political organizations. The complaint also claimed that agents of the police department disclosed information in the files to the electronic media. The activities of photographing and data gathering at public meetings and disclosure of information to law enforcement agencies were found by the court to not raise issues of illegality. A different view was taken on the allegations of the lack of safeguards and dissemination of the information to the media. The availability to non-police groups of information gathered by the government of a citizen's political view and personal life constituted immediate threatened injury to the plaintiffs by chilling their "rights of freedom of speech and associational privacy." Similarly, allegations of disclosure on national television of the contents of the files, in "the absence of a lawful purpose" were adequate to raise justiciable issues of invasion of associational privacy and speech rights.

See also Alliance to End Repression v. Chicago, 627 F.Supp. 1044 (N.D.Ill.1985) (holding dissemination of false information gathered on lawful speech activities of plaintiffs violated First Amendment-distinguishing *Laird v. Tatum*). *Compare Gordon v. Warren Consol. Bd. of Educ.*, 706 F.2d 778 (6th Cir.1983) (holding allegation of placement of undercover policemen in classrooms to investigate drug trafficking only constituted a claim of "subjective chill" and was not justiciable).

Does the view of a majority of the Court in *Laird v. Tatum* adequately account for the impact of governmental surveillance of the legal activities of citizens on associational privacy and speech rights? The four dissenters in the case—Justices Brennan, Marshall, Douglas and Stewart—concluded that the majority opinion failed to recognize the danger such surveillance posed to these rights.

JUSTICE DOUGLAS' dissent quoted from a statement by Alexander Solzhenitsyn:

> A kind of forbidden, contaminated zone has been created around my family, and to this day, there are people in Ryazan [where Solzhenitsyn used to live] who were dismissed from their jobs for having visited my house a few years ago. A corresponding member of the Academy of Sciences, T. Timofeyev, who is director of a Moscow institute, became so scared when he found out that a mathematician working under him was my wife that he dismissed her with unseemly haste, although this was just after she had given birth and contrary to all laws....

> It happens that an informant [for his new book on the history of prerevolutionary Russia] may meet with me. We work an hour or two and as soon as he leaves my house, he will be closely followed, as if he were a state criminal, and they will investigate his background, and then go on to find out who this man meets, and then, in turn, who that [next] person is meeting.

> Of course they cannot do this with everyone. The state security people have their schedule, and their own profound reasoning. On some days, there is no surveillance at all, or only superficial surveillance. On other days, they hang around, for example when Heinrich Boll came to see me [he is a German writer who recently visited Moscow]. They will put a car in front of each of the two approaches [to the courtyard of the apartment house where he stays in Moscow] with three men in each car—and they don't work only one shift. Then off they go after my visitors, or they trail people who leave on foot.

> And if you consider that they listen around the clock to telephone conversations and conversations in my home, they analyze recording tapes and all correspondence, and then collect all these data in some vast premises—and these people are not underlings—you cannot but be amazed that so many idlers in the prime of life and strength, who could be better occupied with productive work for the benefit of the fatherland, are busy with my friends and me, and keep inventing enemies.

408 U.S. at 37–38 (Douglas, J., dissenting) (quoting Washington Post, Apr. 3, 1972).

For an exhaustive account of surveillance in the twentieth century in the United States of various individuals and groups that were viewed as subversive, see, Frank J. Donner, *The Age of Surveillance* (1980).

a. Dataveillance

In Chapter IV, the unprecedented capacity to develop data profiles of individuals through the use of digital technology and linked computer databases is examined. Government surveillance through the maintenance of records of individuals is a central feature of totalitarian governments. A number of important books have been devoted to examining the role of computer technology in governmental surveillance, see, *Computers, Surveillance & Privacy,* (David Lyon & Elia Zureik, eds 1996); David H. Flaherty, *Protecting Privacy in Surveillance Societies* (1989); David Burnham, *The Rise of the Computer State* (1983). Roger Clarke developed the concepts of a "digital persona" and "dataveillance" to illuminate the new capacities for surveillance that digital technology provides to both government and private entities. Clarke provides the following working definition for the digital persona, "the digital persona is a model of an individual's public personality based on data and maintained by transactions, and intended for use as a proxy for the individual." Dataveillance is, "the systematic use of personal data systems in the investigation or monitoring of the actions or communications of one or more persons." Roger Clarke, "The Digital Persona and Its Application to Data Surveillance," 10 Information Society (2) 77–92 (1994)

F. HEALTH PRIVACY

PRIVACY AND HEALTH CARE: AN OVERVIEW ADAPTED FROM A. ALLEN, "PRIVACY IN HEALTH CARE"

Encyclopedia of Bioethics 2064–2073(1995), 1999 adapted.

Privacy considerations have a major role in the assessment of health care practices, policies and law. Commentators ascribe health-related privacy interests to individuals, families, and institutions, and criticize public and private sector failures to protect those interests.

BODILY PRIVACY AND INTEGRITY

Complete privacy is inconsistent with the demands of modern health care. The modern delivery of health services presupposes that patients and medical professionals mutually accept nudity, touching and observation as unavoidable aspects of examination, treatment, surgery and hospitalization. Typical patients willingly sacrifice the desire for bodily concealment and seclusion for a chance at better health. Yet, patients often expect their physicians, nurses, hospital staff and other caretakers to assiduously guard against unnecessary bodily exposure. The special examination gowns and pajamas provided hospital patients respond to the expectation of privacy, as well as the need for warmth.

Hospital patients—and their lawyers—have sometimes characterized unauthorized medical treatments as invasions of privacy, along with the bedside presence of inessential medical attendants, spectators or cameras. The desire for physical privacy may lead patients who have a choice to chose single over shared hospital rooms. Because for many Americans bodily exposure to persons of the opposite sex is a more significant loss of privacy than same-sex exposures, the desire for physical privacy has led some patients to prefer physicians of their own sex. Norms of quietude surrounding hospitals reflects the sentiment that patients have heightened physical and psychological needs for solitude and peace of mind.

INFORMATIONAL PRIVACY

Informational privacy concerns in the health care setting have traditionally focussed on the confidentiality of the physician/patient relationship and on limiting access to medical and insurance records. The willingness of patients to speak openly about physical and mental health concerns depends, in part, upon expectations of confidentiality. The administrative demands of managed care interject decisionmakers other than doctor and patient in the context of care at a cost to privacy. Proposals for governmentally or institutionally mandated testing, reporting and identification raise other informational privacy concerns.

Managed care, the AIDS epidemic, and the Human Genome Project have spawned numerous proposals for federal regulations governing health information. For example, Senators Jeffords and Dodd introduced into the 106th Congress, 1st Session, S.578, the "Health Care Personal Information Nondisclosure (PIN)Act of 1999," aimed at ensuring "confidentiality with respect to medical records and health care-related information."

On September 11, 1997, the Department of Health and Human Services filed an "urgent" report recommending national medical information privacy legislation. See *Recommendations of the Secretary of Health and Human Services, pursuant to section 264 of the Health Insurance Portability and Accountability Act of 1996*, submitted to the Committee on Labor and Human Resources and the Committee on Finance of the Senate and the Committee on Commerce and the Committee on Ways and Means of the House of Representatives. The report calls for a "basic national standard of confidentiality," governed by a respect for personal boundaries, data security, consumer control, accountability, and public responsibility. Id. at 7–8. According to this report:

> Every day our private health care information is being collected, shared, analyzed and stored with few legal safeguards. There was a time when our health care privacy was protected by our family doctors–who kept hand-written records about us sealed away in big file cabinets. Today, revolutions in our health care delivery system mean that we have to place our trust in entire networks of insurers and health care professionals. The comput-

er revolution means that our family secrets travel quickly from doctors to hospitals to insurance companies–and cannot be protected by simply locking up the office doors each night. And, revolutions in biology mean that a whole new world of genetic tests have the potential to help either prevent or reveal our most personal secrets.

Id. at 4. The report stressed the increasing interstate character of health care information, the increasing use of computers, and the limited nature of existing protections under state law, and a scattering of federal law:

> Today the legal control of health information is, in general, a matter of state law. Limited Federal law covers specialized classes of information such as information about substance-abuse patients and information gathered in some Federally funded programs. The Privacy Act provides some procedures and protections for records, including health records, held by Federal agencies. All States have legal controls on the use and disclosure of health information, including a few comprehensive acts similar in broad outline to he Federal legislation we recommend here. Two States have enacted the *Uniform Health–Care Information Act* recommended by the National Conference of Commissioners on Uniform State Laws in 1985. Many State laws protect special classes of health information about HIV infection and AIDS patients and about mental health patients, for example. Some State case law imposes confidentiality duties. These State laws vary greatly in scope and strength, ad the situation has been described as "a morass of erratic law, both statutory and judicial, defining the confidentiality of health information."

Id. at 4–5.

Two Georgetown University Law Center researchers, Lawrence O. Gostin and James G. Hodge have argued that improved state legislation is also a worthy goal, quite apart from the goal of improved national laws. They have therefore begun to develop what they call a *Model State Public Health Privacy Act*. According to the February 18, 1999 draft, the purpose of the Act is to develop a model state law "addressing privacy and security issues arising from the acquisition, use, disclosure, and storage" of identifiable by public health agencies at the state and local levels.

Health records maintained by government, hospitals and insurers have been open to qualified health researchers engaged in scientific research. Health research is useful for advancing knowledge of health markets, public health, health services, basic science, and health technology. Health research, like health care, raises informational privacy concerns, particularly when it comes to the use of personally identifiable data about health and genetics, and insecure computer networks. Some research does not require sensitive information about research subjects; however researchers often cite scientific rationales for access to information about the ethnicity, race, and identity of research subjects. A recent Government Accounting Office report argues that researchers need access to health records, but notes that responsible medical research requires meaningful privacy oversight. In May 1997, the Department of Health and Human Services' Office of the Assistant Secretary for Planning and Evaluation published a report by William W. Lowrance, *Privacy and Health Research*. The Lowrance report concluded that "Health Research, compared with all of the other potential avenues for intrusion, hardly threatens privacy." Id. at v. Still, although "many effective protections are in place," the "possibilities for harm always exist." Id. Lowrance calls for "[e]mphasis on the need for uniform criteria and standards that will foster the international flow of health data."

Privacy requires appropriate forms of secrecy, sometimes defined as intentional concealment of fact; and confidentiality, defined as selective disclosure of fact to authorized persons. In institutional settings security requires mechanisms capable of limiting access to information, such as locked file cabinets, computer passwords and encryption. In addition to security, concern about the privacy of information overlaps with concerns about what are sometimes called "fair information" practices. These include maintaining accurate information in confidence. The accuracy of information contained in health, insurance, adoption, and gene research records potentially bears on the quality of health care, and therefore holds special importance.

HEALTH-CARE DECISIONMAKING

Decisional privacy concerns in the health context relate to responsibility for important decisions about treatment, non-treatment, and the allocation of scarce medical resources. Legal and ethical disagreements about who has the "right to decide" or the "right to choose" sometimes have turned collaborating patients, physicians, nurses, hospitals, families, researchers, and lawmakers into competitors and litigants.

In the United States, conceptions of decisional privacy have come to dominate discussions of government regulation of abortion, and the treatment of patients who are severely disabled, terminally ill, or in a persistent vegetative state. In the context of surrogate parenting, privacy for infertile couples has meant the freedom to make legally enforceable agreements to procreate with the assistance of third parties. Gay men and lesbians invoke the ideal of privacy in their quest for the freedom to engage in consensual adult sexual relationships and marriage, free from the fear of criminal prosecution and legally sanctioned discrimination. Parents sometimes invoke "family privacy" to mean the freedom of heads of households to decide how those for whom they are responsible will be reared, educated, and medically assisted. Invocations to respect privacy accompany defenses of autonomous decision-making respecting heterosexual sex, contraception, midwifery, women's prenatal conduct, use of experimental medical remedies, psychotropic drug therapy, refusal and withdrawal of medical treatment, physician-assisted suicide, organ sales and transplants and hunger striking.

PATIENT'S PRIVACY RIGHTS

The oldest American legal case decided by reference to rights of privacy, *DeMay v. Roberts* (1881), supra, Chapter I, vindicated interests in physical privacy and modesty. A Michigan husband and wife successfully sued a physician who permitted an "unprofessional young, unmarried man" to enter their home and help deliver their baby. A century later a married couple in Maine brought *Knight v. Penobscot Bay Medical Center* (1980), infra, Chapter V, a similar, though unsuccessful, lawsuit claiming that a hospital violated their privacy by permitting a layperson, the spouse of a nurse, to observe delivery of their child through a glass partition from a distance of twelve feet.

All patients generally may share the obstetrical patient's sense that adequate privacy is lacking in hospitals where well-intentioned medical, administrative, and support staff move freely in and out of (even nominally "private") in-patient wards. The feeling that one's privacy has been invaded may be especially acute in busy, crowded public hospitals serving low-income patients, or in any hospital where groups of several physicians, interns, and medical students simultaneously conduct physical examinations and discussions at one's beside. Some men and women report feeling their privacy invaded by having to share a room in an intensive care unit with a person of the opposite sex. The law is unclear about the extent to which medical resources or the general written consent to treatment patients give upon admission to hospitals eliminates legitimate expectations of physical and informational privacy. Specific waivers of legal privacy claims may give patients clear notice of the privacy losses associated with treatment in teaching and research hospitals, but arguably do not eliminate hospitals' ethical obligations to respect privacy to the extent possible.

Moral outrage over the discovery that health care providers have recorded, filmed, or photographed a patient for scholarly or research purposes sometimes, though infrequently, results in litigation. Respect for privacy would appear to dictate obtaining prior consent to the publication of graphic images of a person, particularly if the person is identifiable in an image or is named in connection with its publication.

The legal importance of obtaining prior informed consent was underscored by the holding of the California court in the highly publicized case, *Moore v. Regents of the University of California*, 793 P.2d 479 (1990). John Moore brought a multi-million dollar lawsuit when he discovered that University of California medical researchers who treated him for hairy-cell leukemia had failed to disclose that "certain blood products and blood components were of great value in a number of commercial and scientific efforts." Moore's right to privacy claims were based on the notion that exploitation of his blood for commercial purposes was a highly offensive appropriation of a person's name, likeness, or identity compensable as an invasion of privacy under state tort law. The court threw out Moore's privacy claims on the ground that the researchers did not appropriate Moore's likeness or identity in a sense recognized by law. Although Moore lost his privacy battle, the court held he could validly assert claims of breach of fiduciary duty and lack of informed consent. According to the California court, a patient has a right to know the medical purpose of treatment and the treating physicians personal economic stake; otherwise treatment is battery, presumably no better than sterilizing a fertile woman or performing a Caesarian section on a cancer patient without her consent.

Courts have approached abortion and "the right to die" as patient privacy issues. Opponents of laws prohibiting abortions say that state and federal regulations should not prevent women from acting on their own decisions about whether to terminate pregnancy through medical abortion. On the other hand, it is also argued on privacy grounds that women should not be forced or counseled to abort for any reason, including where they are seropositive for the virus that causes AIDS. Privacy signifies freedom to choose the circumstances of death for oneself, a family member, or an intimate friend. It means the absence of criminal laws and bureaucratic procedures that constrain the choice to accelerate the death of a person who is terminally ill or to refuse artificial nutrition and hydration to preserve life in a person in persistent vegetative state. The right to privacy may also prove to be the ethical refuge of supporters of physician-assisted suicide.

The privacy implications of non-voluntary and routine AIDS testing of obstetrical patients, surgical patients and newborns have been of great interest to public authorities and private health care providers for two reasons. First, nonconsensual testing is a prima facie denial of decisional privacy or autonomy. Some individuals prefer not to be tested and forced to confront the specter of terminal illness. And while this precise concern has never applied to newborns, newborn testing can reveal the HIV status of birth mothers. Second, where the confidentiality of an HIV or AIDS-infected person is breached by medical or insurance providers, far-ranging implications for private lives and employment can follow due to prejudice and discrimination. In this context, policy analysts often assert that the individual interest in privacy is outweighed by societal interests, including the societal interest in controlling the spread of deadly disease through inappropriate handling of contaminated blood and other tissues. But societal interests do not always outweigh individual privacy rights.

The federal courts have upheld the mandatory AIDS testing policies of the United States military and the nation's prisons. However, in *Glover v. Eastern Nebraska Community Office of Retardation*, infra, (1989), a federal court struck down a state requirement that all persons working closely with mentally retarded clients disclose their HIV and hepatitis B status, and undergo periodic HIV and hepatitis B blood testing. Against the argument that persons working in highly regulated state agencies have lower expectations of privacy, the court stressed that constitutional values do not permit mandatory testing where the risk of disease transmission is extremely low. A similar weighing of the costs of testing against its benefits in view of the low risk of transmission may explain government reluctance to mandate AIDS testing for all dentists, physicians and other health care providers who come in close contact with patients.

1. MEDICAL FACTS ABOUT AIDS

AIDS: LAW AND SOCIETY, REPORT OF THE PENNSYL-VANIA BAR ASSOCIATION TASK FORCE ON AC-QUIRED IMMUNE DEFICIENCY SYNDROME

4–13 (1989) (updated 1999).

I. THE DISEASE

The disease called AIDS (acquired immune deficiency syndrome) results from infection with a virus called HIV (human immunodeficiency virus). When an individual is first infected, an acute phase of infection may occur. This infection may be accompanied by fever, malaise and swollen glands, or it may be asymptomatic (without symptoms). This acute phase usually occurs shortly after exposure (two to six weeks), and one of the responses of the body to infection is to make antibodies (blood proteins) against the virus. Production of antibody may be delayed up to six months to one year following infection and in rare cases for much longer (two to five years). The presence of anti-HIV antibodies is what is routinely measured in licensed diagnostic tests. However, these tests do not diagnose the disease AIDS; they only determine if a person has been infected with HIV. There are also commercially available tests to measure the amount of virus in the blood. During early stages of infection, virus may be present while antibody is not. In other words, individuals may be infectious before they demonstrate symptomatic AIDS and before they are antibody positive.

Following the acute phase, the virus continues to persist in the body. During this latent period the infected individuals may again be infectious to others but remain relatively asymptomatic themselves. HIV infection is a precursor of AIDS. The disease AIDS is only diagnosed when the HIV-infected individual shows signs of immune suppression and evidences onset of certain unusual infections and cancers. AIDS-related dementia frequently occurs if the virus infects cells that travel to the central nervous system.

HIV was first isolated in 1983, and it has been extensively studied. It is a ribonucleic acid (RNA) containing virus of the retrovirus group. The virus infects certain types of white blood cells and possibly other cells from the body. Virus binds to a cell surface molecule called the "CD4 receptor." We now know that other molecules on the cell surface act as "co-receptors" and help to facilitate virus binding and entry. These are called CXCR4 and CCR5. In the past, the virus has also been called "human T-lymphotropic virus (HTLV)-III," "lymphadenopathy-associated virus (LAV)," or "AIDS-associated retrovirus (ARV)." The virus physically consists of a core, containing the genetic material (the RNA) plus virus protein, and a lipid (fat-containing) envelope that contains additional virus proteins. During infection of cells with this virus, the RNA can be copied into another form of genetic material called deoxyribonucleic acid (DNA). This DNA form of the virus (the provirus) can sit inside the infected cell for a long time in a relatively inactive state. Activation of the provirus results in new synthesis of RNA and virus proteins and in production of new virus. Even asymptomatic, HIV + persons may make substantial virus in their lymph nodes.

The total process of virus replication is complex and involves many steps, some of which are biochemically unique. We now know that the virus contains several genes for virus structural and regulatory proteins. Some regulatory proteins are involved in increasing virus reproduction while others are involved in decreasing virus reproduction. In addition, synthesis of the virus genetic material can be increased or decreased by external factors, for example, protein products of other viruses. The replication of HIV therefore is a highly complex process.

The treatment of HIV has undergone dramatic change as a result of new therapeutic agents that have become available to interfere with the virus replication. Initially the drug azidothymidine (AZT) was used to block virus replication in culture and in infected patients. This drug is in a class of drugs called "nucleoside analogue inhibitors" and targets the "reverse transcriptase" of the virus, a protein required for virus genome replication. The drug was first given to symptomatic AIDS patients and then was subsequently shown to be beneficial when given to asymptomatic HIV positive persons and also effective in preventing the transmission of virus to children born to HIV infected mothers if taken during pregnancy. Recommendations were formulated to give AZT early in infection and during pregnancy. AZT resistant virus mutants soon appeared however and were the source of some relapses and public health concern.

Within the last several years, two additional classes of drugs have been developed; one class of these is called "protease inhibitors" and targets the HIV protease, a protein required to cleave and assemble the protein building blocks of the virus and the other class is called "non-nucleoside=analogue reverse transcriptase inhibitors" and again targets the reverse transcriptase but by a chemical mechanism distinct from that of AZT. Each of the three classes of agents, the protease inhibitors, the non-nucleoside-analogue inhibitors of reverse transcriptase and the nucleoside analogue inhibitors of reverse transcriptase, can inhibit virus replication, and effectively lower the amount of HIV in the body, as measured by the amount of detectable virus. Resistant mutants to each of these compounds have been derived experimentally and they have also been seen in patients. However, the risk of developing a single mutant virus strain that could resist all three compounds is very low, much lower than the risk of developing resistance against only one of them. This fact has led to the advent of "triple combination therapy" where HIV positive persons are administered drug combinations containing one of each drug class. Effective and dramatic lowering of HIV virus burden and concomitant restoration of immune function has been demonstrated in many patients. Some patients have reverted to the status of virus being undetectable in their blood and/or lymph nodes. However, samples of many patients on triple therapy still contain detectable virus and the possibility exists that cessation of therapy will allow virus recurrence. It is therefore important that the therapy be maintained. This breakthrough has increased length and quality of life for many patients but the risk of resistant mutants occurring in patients and/or being transmitted to others remain.

Combination triple therapy still is generally unavailable to infected individuals in developing countries due to the poor health care infrastructure and to the expense of these agents. World Health Organization officials and policymakers at the National Institutes of Health, recognize that the development and use of female controlled topical microbicides and condoms still remain as the major approaches to stop the epidemic in these parts of the world.

HIV has been found in blood, semen, vaginal fluids, breast milk, saliva, tears, urine, and cerebrospinal fluid. However, documented transmission has occurred only with blood, semen, vaginal fluids and breast milk. The amount of virus in the other fluids is very low.

HIV is a devastating virus inside the body. It is a relatively fragile virus outside of the body. It can live and replicate only inside the body cells. Its potency decreases greatly on drying, and it can be readily and completely inactivated by a number of commonly-used disinfectants including soaps, detergents, alcohol, and a 1:10 dilution of household bleach. It can be inactivated by heat and by normal laundering of clothes and cleaning of dishes. Dry cleaning also will destroy the virus.

Scientists are also trying to develop vaccines that will block HIV infection. An effective vaccine would cause the vaccinated person to make antibodies that bind to the virus proteins on the virus surface. These antibodies then would physically prevent attachment of the virus to the target cell (in the case of HIV, mainly white blood cells of the T4 helper class). The result would be prevention of initial penetration of the virus into the cells.

Some major stumbling blocks have been noted in HIV vaccine development. First, the protein surface of HIV continually changes, which means that it will be difficult to develop an effective vaccine. The changing protein surface results from the rapid mutation rate of the virus genetic material. Scientists are looking for common regions on the surface proteins of different HIV strains which might be used for vaccine development. Virus surface proteins bound to their receptors have been recently used as starting material to produce immunity to many strains. This needs to be confirmed. Second, HIV is frequently transmitted from one individual to another in the form of intracellular virus or as provirus DNA. These forms of virus are not accessible to antibody attack. Third, there is not a good animal model for HIV infection. Limited vaccine studies are being carried out in chimpanzees. However, vaccine trials in primates are severely hampered by reluctance to use these higher animals for such studies, by shortage of animals, and by lack of money. Recent advances that enable transfer of human white blood cells to mice may assist vaccine efforts. Limited Vaccine Trials in humans are about to begin.

The major point that needs to be emphasized is that the cause of AIDS and the methods of transmission are no longer medical mysteries. In addition to the scientific data, much is known about the disease because of epidemiologic data.

II. EPIDEMIOLOGY

A. *Introduction*

Epidemiologists study the distribution of diseases as they occur in a population. The fundamental assumption upon which the entire field of epidemiology is based is that diseases do not occur by chance, and they are not randomly distributed in the population. Because diseases are not randomly distributed, their distribution must tell how and why the disease process occurred.

Epidemiologists began the study of AIDS in 1981. The first step was to create a case definition of this new phenomenon. There were no laboratory tests available to determine who had and who did not have the disease. The original Centers for Disease Control (CDC) United States Public Health Service (USPHS) case definition of AIDS stated that in order to be counted as a case, the patient has to have an unusual infection (10 infections listed) or an unusual cancer (Kaposi sarcoma or primary lymphoma of the brain and be under 60 years of age), and be otherwise normal. This definition is called a surveillance definition, and it was developed for one purpose—to trace the spread of this disease in the population, and it has served that purpose well. The original definition was modified in 1985 and again in 1987 [Centers for Disease Control. Revision of the CDC surveillance case definition for acquired immunodeficiency syndrome. MMWR 1987;36 (supply no. 1S):[1S–15S].

The most recent expansion of the AIDS surveillance case definition occurred in 1993 (1993 Revised Classification System for HIV Infection and Expanded Surveillance Case Definition for AIDS Among Adolescents and Adults, MMWR: 12/18/92, Vol. 41, NO. RR-17).

The second step was to develop a standardized questionnaire so that the information collected on each case was uniform. The questions asked in every state were identical. The final step was to make the symptomatic disease AIDS reportable to local and state health departments and through them to the CDC.

In June, 1997, the Council of State and Territorial Epidemiologist (CSTE) decided to also add HIV infection in adults (13 years of age) to the list of nationally notifiable diseases. This decision was because the improved health status of many HIV+ individuals (as a result of combination drug therapy) causes them to not be included as AIDS cases under the surveillance case definition. Thus, reporting of only AIDS cases would underestimate the size and direction of the epidemic.

Much of what is known about the epidemiologic characteristics of this disease has been determined by the CDC analysis of the nationally reported cases. This analysis uses three epidemiologic variables—time, person and place—to develop national recommendations for case management and control.

B. Epidemiologic Variables: Time, Person, Place

1. Time.

Although the medical community became aware of the outbreak in the summer of 1981, medical records indicate that cases of AIDS probably began to occur in this country around 1978. There are now confirmed AIDS cases in humans as early as 1959. Since the epidemic was first recognized, there has been a dramatic increase in the total number of cases. The CDC now reports over 580,000 confirmed cases of AIDS. (CDC HIV/AIDS Surveillance AIDS cases reported through December 31, 1996) The first 30,000 cases were reported between December 1987 and July 1989. Because of: (a) under diagnosis and under reporting of AIDS cases, (b) delayed reports and (c) the restrictive CDC AIDS surveillance case definition, reported cases underestimate the true number of severe HIV infections that have occurred since 1981.

AIDS has already become in some areas of the country, and will shortly become nationwide, a major cause of morbidity and mortality (sickness and death) in children and young adults. In fact, in the United States AIDS ranked 1st among causes of death from notifiable diseases in 1997.

2. Person

a. Case Distribution

The person variable is used to determine who is most likely to become infected, and to determine how the disease is transmitted. The U.S. epidemic is evolving. Originally, most infections were in homosexual men and intravenous drug users. Now heterosexual transmission is the most rapidly increasing subset of U.S. AIDS cases while the epidemic in some other subpopulations is leveling off. This is especially true for women under 25 years of age, a group that represented more than 1/2 the AIDS cases in 1996. While there has been a four-fold rise in the number of cases in women over the last 5 years, there has only been a two-fold rise in the number of cases in men.

Sexually transmitted disease (STD) co-factors play an effect in HIV transmission. In young women, African American women have a disproportionately high level of STDs and have the most striking recent increase in AIDS. An increasing proportion of all AIDS cases and cases among young women are in the southeastern United States. In 1996, new AIDS cases increased by 19% among heterosexual African American men, 12% among heterosexual African American women, 13% among Hispanic men and 5% among Hispanic women. The incidence of new infections in older homosexual men is declining but in young men who have sex with men the rate of new infections continues to climb. Of all AIDS cases increased by 19% among heterosexual African American men, 12% among heterosexual African American women, 13% among Hispanic men and 5% among Hispanic women. The incidence of new infections in older homosexual men is declining but in young men who have sex with men the rate of new infections continues to climb. Of all AIDS cases reported in the U.S. between 1981 and 1997, the vast majority occurred in persons between the ages of 25 and 50, 44% of women and 45% of men being between 30 and 39 years of age at diagnosis. Adolescent populations engaging in unprotected intercourse, with increased STD burdens or using illegal drugs remain at increased risk.

Nationally, in 1997, 33% of AIDS cases occurred in non-Hispanic whites, 45% in blacks and 21 in Hispanics. The racial distribution of pediatric cases (<13 years of age) was 62% in blacks, 23% in Hispanics and 13% in non-Hispanic whites. AIDS remains disproportional in the African–American and Hispanic communities.

AIDS remains a major cause of mortality in the U.S. Through 1997, of 633,000 reported adult/adolescent cases, there have been 385,968 deaths. In children, of 8,086 reported cases, there have been 4,724 deaths.

The modes of transmission of HIV can be determined by looking at who has gotten AIDS and who has not gotten AIDS. Gay/bisexual men, and IV drug users, and women who have sex with infected men are the three adult groups that are well recognized as being at risk for developing AIDS. Studies have shown that the risk behavior appears to be related to sexual activity (especially unprotected sex, multiple partners and anal intercourse) and/or to the sharing of needles in IV drug use. A small proportion of the cases have occurred in hemophiliacs who have received contaminated blood-clotting factors, and in individuals receiving contaminated blood components as transfusions. Routine blood screening has dramatically reduced the risk in this population.

b. Modes of Transmission Ruled Out by Who Does Not Have AIDS

It is important to note that the two groups that have not been significantly affected by the disease are health care workers and household contacts of confirmed AIDS cases. The CDC estimates that the risk of contracting HIV from an AIDS patient following a contaminated needle stick is less than one percent. In April 1988, the CDC reported 15 documented cases of HIV infection in health care workers infected by exposure to contaminated blood or to virus concentrate. Nine people inadvertently stuck a needle in their hand after drawing blood from an AIDS patient, one got cut with a sharp object contaminated with a concentrated virus solution, and the remaining five got infected blood on non-intact skin or mucous membrane (Centers for Disease Control. Update: Acquired immunodeficiency syndrome and human immunodeficiency virus infection among health care workers. MMWR 1988;37:229–234, 239. See Appendix E.) There will undoubtedly be more health care workers infected in the same way but the risk is low. There are no reported instances of AIDS/HIV transmission through normal, casual (i.e., non-sexual) contact, even when the individuals live in the same household. See, Fischl, Dickinson, Scott, et al., Evaluation of Heterosexual Partners, Children, and Household Contacts of Adults With Aids, 257 J. A.M.A. 640 (1987); Friedland, Saltzman, Rogers, et al., Lack of Transmission of HTLV–III/LAV Infection to Household Contacts of Patients With Aids or AIDS–Related Complex With Oral Candidiasis, 314 New Eng. J. Med. 344 (1986).

e. Modes of Transmission

There are only three known modes of transmission of HIV. The first is through intimate homosexual and heterosexual contact. There are no known sexually-transmitted diseases unique to the homosexual population. Whatever occurs in the gay community can also occur in the heterosexual community. The second mode of transmission is by percutaneous exposure to contaminated blood, which means that contaminated blood entered the body through breaks in the skin as in IV drug use, transfusions, or in infected health care workers. The third method is from mother to child in utero or at the time of delivery.

The following statements about how the disease cannot be transmitted are also significant. HIV is not an airborne virus; a person cannot be infected simply by being in the same room or breathing the same air as someone who is infected. It is not transmitted by toilet seats, touching, saliva, tears, or insects. Eating food prepared by an infected individual cannot transmit infection. If such modes of transmission played any significant role in this disease process, secondary spread to the general population, to health care workers and certainly to household contacts would have been seen by now. HIV is a communicable virus, but it is one of low communicability.

*The Medical Facts About Aids and its update were prepared by Robert G. Sharrar, M.D., M.Sc. and Mary K. Howett, Ph.D. Doctor Sharrar was Director of the Division of Disease Control in Philadelphia and is now working in the private sector. Dr. Howett is a Professor of Molecular Biology and Immunology at the Pennsylvania State University College of Medicine. Her research efforts focus on microbicides as an agency to kill sexually transmitted viruses, including HIV.

a. Testing Employees For HIV in the Private Sector

There is an even greater paucity of appellate court decisions dealing with the question of whether the testing of an employee for HIV constitutes an invasion of the employee's common law right to privacy. As of this writing, we have found only one such appellate court opinion, Doe v. Dyer–Goode, 389 Pa.Super. 151, 566 A.2d 889 (1989), appeal denied, 588 A.2d 509 (Pa. 1990). Doe alleged that he had agreed to the extraction of blood for a pre-marital test and that the physician had tested for HIV without his consent. In addition, Doe alleged that the physician had initially notified Doe that he had tested positive, but that subsequent tests were negative. The appellate court dismissed John Doe's cause of action for negligence, informed consent battery, intentional infliction of emotional distress and for the privacy intrusion tort. In holding that no cause of action for violation of the privacy intrusion tort was stated on these facts, the court concluded that since:

> ... John Doe relinquished his blood sample to the doctor, this sample was no longer held in "private seclusion" by Mr. Doe. Thus the fact that an unauthorized test was performed on this sample cannot establish a claim for invasion of privacy.

Id. at 155, 566 A.2d at 891.

Is *Doe v. Dyer–Goode* reconcilable with Glover v. Eastern Neb. Community Office of Retardation, supra.

Doe v. Dyer–Goode was overruled by comprehensive legislation in Pennsylvania that prohibits the surreptitious testing of a patient with HIV. The Confidentiality of HIV–Related Information Act (Act 148) is included in the statutory appendix in Chapter VIII.

Note: Mandatory Testing of Health Care Professionals and Patients

The revelation that five patients were likely to have been infected by their dentist prompted proposals for mandatory testing of health care professionals and patients. The medical facts about the disease and testing for HIV are described in these materials on pages 204–210, supra. Would mandatory testing of health care professionals and patients significantly reduce transmission of the virus by removing infected health care professionals from the health care delivery system?

Consider the following argument against mandatory testing by Mary K. Howett, Professor of Microbiology and Immunology at Penn State College of Medicine. She considers both cost and inefficiency to support her argument. Using the state of Pennsylvania as an example, she estimates that the cost of mandatory testing and pre-and post-test counseling of all 443,000 health care workers in Pennsylvania would be about $13.8 million if tested only once a year. This amount is a significant proportion of the total federal and state funds annually spent on AIDS prevention in Pennsylvania.

To demonstrate the inefficiency of mandatory testing to timely remove infected health care workers from the health care delivery system, she explains HIV testing and results. There is a window of time where an individual may be infectious to others yet test negative in standard tests because seroconversion has not yet occurred. This window can extend from a few weeks to two years. While a two year window is unusual, a six month period is common.

This point is essential to understanding the efficacy of mandatory testing: Professor Howett continues:

> Points concerning the validity of the test can be simply illustrated if one sets up a hypothetical case where testing occurs annually on January 1 for health care workers. A prospective

analysis of the pool of individuals who test negative will reveal that they are composed of:

    1.   truly negative (non-infected) persons,

    2.   falsely negative, HIV infected individuals who were infected anywhere from three weeks to six months prior to the test but who had not yet seroconverted.

The infectious potential of these workers over the course of one year can be analyzed. Everyone in group 2 is potentially infectious and will remain infectious for the entire year prior to the next test. They will continue their professional activities during that time. In group 1, several outcomes will occur. The large majority of group 1 will remain truly non-infected. Individuals who become infected shortly following their annual negative result will be capable of transmitting virus for a large portion of the following year prior to their next test. Half of the infections in group 1 will occur between January 1 and June 30, since there is not a seasonal risk of transmission. These individuals will all become infectious shortly after their HIV infection and, for the most part, will be seropositive by the following annual test. Most of this subset will be infectious and delivering health care for at least six months prior to their positive test result. The subset of group 1 individuals that becomes infected between July 1 and December 31 will also become infectious shortly after HIV infection and therefore the amount of time that they are infectious will be proportional to the date they became infected. On an average, half of these individuals will become seropositive by the testing date, and the other half will remain seronegative. The half that becomes seropositive will be delivering health care while infectious for an average length of three months. The half that remains seronegative will be infectious for an average of three months and for the entire next following year. The bottom line of this analysis is that about seventy five percent of infected health care workers will continue to deliver health care for about one year prior to the detection of their infection. Given these suppositions, the value of mandatory annual testing is extremely minimal and will only serve as false security. It is far better to have responsible health care workers submit to voluntary, confidential testing at the time when they determine a significant exposure has occurred. [Most patients who are sources of significant exposure will also submit to voluntary, confidential testing and if they refuse, it is possible for medical personnel to request a court order for their testing.]

The quoted text is part of an article published in the *American Journal of Ethics & Medicine*, 1 (1991): 13-18.

Note: Testing of Governmental Employees for HIV

The disease called AIDS (acquired immune deficiency syndrome) results from infection with a virus called HIV (human immunodeficiency virus). Two popular tests have been developed to detect the presence of the antibody to HIV—the Enzyme Linked Immunosorbent Assent (ELISA) and the Western Blot (WB). If both tests are administered properly there is 99 percent certainty that those who test positive for the presence of the antibody have been infected with HIV. However, production of the antibody may be delayed up to six months to one year and in rare cases much longer (two to five years).

Consider the epidemiological features and medical facts of the disease that are described in the report of the Pennsylvania Bar Association Task Force on AIDS, supra. These views reflect the current consensus in the scientific community on modes of transmission of HIV. Suppose that an agency of state X adopts a policy for the mandatory testing for HIV of the state employees in the Community Office of Retardation who are employed in positions that involve direct extensive contact with clients (mentally retarded persons). The asserted purpose for testing is to protect clients from infection from HIV through contact with employees. There have been numerous cases of mentally retarded persons scratching and biting such employees. However, there is no documented case of transmission of HIV to a client from an infected employee.

Would the drawing of blood to test for HIV be constitutional?

On virtually identical facts, the Eighth Circuit Court of Appeals found that the testing of employees violated their fourth amendment rights, Glover v. Eastern Neb. Com. Office of Retardation, 867 F.2d 461 (8th Cir.1989). The Glover court relied primarily on O'Connor v. Ortega, supra, and concluded that given the medical facts of transmission of HIV, the search was not "reasonable" at its inception. Glover was decided before the Supreme Court decisions in *Skinner* and *Von Raab*. Would the testing be constitutional on the basis of these decisions?

Compare *Glover* with, *Dunn v. White*, 880 F.2d 1188 (10 Cir.1989) (nonconsensual HIV testing of prisoners does not violate fourth amendment); *Anonymous Fireman v. City of Willoughby*, 779 F.Supp. 402 (N.D.Ohio 1991) (nonconsensual HIV testing of firefighters or paramedics does not violate the fourth amendment); *Kruger v. Erickson*, 875 F.Supp. 583 (D.Minn.1995) (taking blood sample for construction of a DNA database of sexual offenders does not violate fourth or eighth amendments); *Matter of Juveniles A,B,C,D,E*, 847 P.2d 455 (Wash. 1993) (testing of juvenile offenders does not violate fourth amendment).

Glover was distinguished in *Leckelt v. Board of Comm'rs of Hospital*, 909 F.2d 820 (5th Cir.1990) where the court upheld mandatory disclosure to the plaintiff's employer of HIV test. The Fifth Circuit Court of Appeals concluded that the disclosure policy was narrower than the policy in *Glover* because it was applied to an employee strongly suspected of being HIV positive who had a position (nurse) that provided a greater opportunity for HIV transmission than the government employees tested under the policy found unconstitutional in *Glover*.

Would state laws requiring the testing for HIV of the patients of all health professionals whose skin had been punctured by a needle that contained the patients' blood be constitutional? Would a state law requiring the testing for HIV of all persons arrested for rape or sexual abuse be constitutional? Would state mandated testing of all newborns be constitutional? Such tests would disclose the HIV/AIDS status of the newborns gestational mother. Are there additional medical and social facts that you would need to know before the constitutionality of testing in these three instances could be fully evaluated? See Amitai Etzioni, *The Limits of Privacy* 19–42 (1999), Professor Etzioni argue that privacy concerns should not block newborn testing.

The legality of the testing of employees in the private sector for HIV is examined in this chapter supra p. 210.

b. *Genetic Privacy*

(a) *Human Genome Initiative*. The Human Genome Initiative is a billion-dollar commitment to decode the human genes. The Initiative has accelerated efforts in the United States to map the location of genes along the chromosomes and to decode the complex sequence of hereditary instructions for which genes are responsible. Officials at the National Institutes of Health's National Center for Human Genome Research predict that scientists will complete the sequencing of the human genome early in the first decade of the 21st century.

The Human Genome Initiative has spawned a new ethical, social, and legal concept: genetic privacy. See generally, A. Allen, *Genetic Privacy: Emerging Concepts and Values*, in Mark Rothstein, ed. *Genetic Secrets: Privacy, Confidentiality and the New Genetic Technology* (1997) 31–59.

(b) *Genetic Information*. Alan F. Westin defined genetic privacy by reference to what he called the "core concept of privacy," namely, "the claim of an individual to determine what information about himself or herself should be known by others." See A. Westin, *Privacy and Genetic Information,* in Mark S. Frankel and Albert H. Teich, eds., The Genetic Frontier: Ethics, Law, and Policy (Washington, D.C.: American Association for the Advancement of Science, 1994), 53–76, at 53. Indeed, "genetic privacy" often denotes informational privacy, including the confidentiality, anonymity or secrecy of the data that result from genetic testing and screening, sampling and research. Substantial limits on third-party access to confidential, anonymous or secret genetic information are requirements of respect for informational privacy. However, family members and prospective family members may possess moral rights to undisclosed personal genetic data that patients and the professionals who serve them could legitimately withhold from other third-parties. See Suter, *Whose Genes are These Anyway? Familial Conflicts over Access to Genetic Information*, 91 Mich. L. Rev. 1854–1908 (1993). See Allen, *Genetic Privacy*, supra at 41–46, discussing unique issues of confidentiality, secrecy and anonymity raised by genetics.

(c) *Bodily Integrity, Autonomy and Identity*. Genetic privacy concerns extend beyond the domain of informational privacy, to concerns about physical, decisional and proprietary privacy. Physical privacy concerns include issues relating to genetic testing, screening or treatment without voluntary and informed consent. In the absence of consent, these practices constitute unwanted physical contact, compromising interests in bodily integrity and security. Some concerns about genetic privacy relate to autonomous decision making by individuals, couples or families. A degree of choice with regard to genetic counseling, testing, screening or procreation, are requirements of respect for decisional privacy. Proprietary privacy concerns encompass issues raised by the appropriation of individuals' possessory and economic interests in their genes and other putative repositories of personality, such as human tissue, cells, and cell lines. See Lori Andrews, *My Body, My Property*, 16 Hastings Center Rep. 728 (1986); Barrad, *Genetic Information and Property Theory*, 87 N.W.U. L. Rev. 1037–1086 (1993). Cf. Eisenberg, *Patenting the Human Genome*, 39 Emory L.J. 721 (1990).

(d) *Legislative Responses*. In the wake of genetic privacy losses comes the potential for social stigma, discrimination in employment, barriers to health insurance, government interference, and other problems. Just a few years after the Human Genome Initiative began, a model Genetic Privacy Act appeared. See George J. Annas, Leonard H. Glantz and Patricia A. Roche, *Drafting the Genetic Privacy Act: Policy and Practical Considerations*, 23 Journal of Law, Medicine and Ethics 360–66 (1995). State lawmakers have introduced genetic privacy legislation. See Neil A. Holtzman, *The Attempt to Pass the Genetic Privacy Act in Maryland*, 23 Journal of Law, Medicine and Ethics 367–70(1995). Members of the United States Senate and House of Representatives have introduced several genetic privacy bills into Congress, including the Genetic Privacy and Nondiscrimination Act of 1995 and a Human Genome Privacy Act.

(e) *Proprietary Genetic Privacy and the Common Law*. According to legal doctrine, to appropriate a person's name or likeness is a way of invading his or her privacy. See Restatement (Second) Torts, Chapter 28A, Section 652 B, C, D, and E. Section 652 B states that "One who appropriates to his own use or benefit the name or likeness of another is subject for liability for invasion of his privacy." Privacy, it appears, has something to do with controlling one's own identity. Leading 19th century defenses of moral and legal rights of privacy by E. L. Godkin, supra p. 40, and Warren and Brandeis, supra p. 29, equated the protection of privacy with protecting "inviolate personality" and humankind's supposed "spiritual" nature. These understandings forged links between privacy norms and the human essence that have yet to be entirely broken. The genetic privacy controversies prove the point.

Do our genes constitute our identities? See Brock, *The Human Genome Project and Human Identity*, 29 Hous. L. Rev. 1–16 (1992); Kaye, *Are We the Sum of Our Genes ?* 16 Wilson Q. 77–84 (1992). A "proprietary" variant of genetic privacy is suggested by the idea that the human DNA is a repository of valuable human personality. Proprietary genetic privacy is further suggested by the related notion that human DNA is owned by the persons from whom it is taken, as a species of private property.

If DNA is the human essence—that is, the thing that makes individuals special and perhaps unique—it arguably ought to belong to the individual from whom it was ultimately derived. If DNA "belongs" to individual sources, it might belong to them exclusively and inalienably. Or, DNA could qualify as alienable property that others can acquire lawfully through voluntary private transactions, or wrongfully through nonconsensual appropriation. Linking human essence with DNA invests DNA with importance. Yet if human essence is equated with genotype, low self-esteem and self-stigma might easily result from learning about genetic mutations.

Despite its apparent dangers, the idea that genetic materials are valuable repositories of human personality has enjoyed wide appeal, both as literal and as a metaphorical truth. Annas trades on the "repository of personality" idea when he likens our DNA molecules to future diaries. See George J. Annas, *Privacy Rules for DNA Databanks: Protecting Coded Future Diaries,* Journal of the American Medical Association 270 (1993): 2346–50, 2346. The oxymoronic "future diary" metaphor has the potential for confusion. People do not record their phenotypes in their diaries; they record their reflections and interpretations of lived experiences. Keeping a diary is a voluntary, even artistic social practice. A process of creative selection decides what goes in and what does not. We are personally responsible for what goes into diaries, present or future. We may choose not to include narratives of health in our diaries. Exercise and good nutrition can improve health, but our probable medical futures are not self-initiated. They are not necessarily narratives we will choose to author. For these reasons our genes are inaptly likened to coded passages of a future diary. See Allen, Genetic Privacy, at 49–51.

Discussions of rights respecting stored tissue samples and information gleaned from families with genetic disorders frequently raise proprietary privacy issues. The proposed Genetic Privacy and Nondiscrimination Act of 1995 would have created rights of confidentiality, but without assigning ownership of genetic information or DNA samples to anyone. The proposed Genetic Privacy Act expressly places ownership of DNA in the person from whom samples are derived. There are at least two reasons to invest ownership in DNA to the sample source. One is to protect consumer expectations. A second reason is to advertise limits on exploitative appropriation. Placing genetic information in the public domain—as everyone's property and no one's exclusive property—could avoid the need to confront limits on the sale of cells, cell lines, tissues and fetuses. See Allen, *Genetic Privacy,* at 49–51.

The proprietary privacy concept has not had much of a legal life in cases specifically relating to the appropriation of genes of other bodily endowments. University of California research physicians removed John Moore's diseased spleen. He later learned that they stood to make a profit from products manufactured from a line of cells manufactured from his organ tissue. Because campus researchers made use of Moore's excised tissue without his prior knowledge or consent, he brought a highly publicized civil suit alleging that the University was liable to him for torts including treatment without informed consent, conversion, and invasion of privacy. See *Moore v. Regents of the University of California*, 793 P.2d 479 (Cal. Supr. Ct. 1990). The court rejected Moore's property and invasion of privacy claims. However, the idea that commercial appropriation of a person's cells harms their property and privacy interests persists. See Allen, *Genetic Privacy* at 49–51.

(f) Genetic testing and tissue storage may raise Fourth Amendment privacy issues, where the government requires information for a DNA databank or other purposes. See *Mayfield v. Dalton*, 109 F.3d 1423 (9th Cir.1997), below.

MAYFIELD v. DALTON

109 F.3d 1423 (9th Cir.1997).

SCHROEDER, CIRCUIT JUDGE:

The plaintiffs-appellants in this case, John C. Mayfield and Joseph Vlacovsky, filed this action when they were on active duty in the Marine Corps. They challenged the constitutionality of a Department of Defense program to collect and store blood and tissue samples from all members of the armed forces for future DNA analysis (the "repository"). Mayfield and Vlacovsky argued that the compulsory taking of specimens without proper safeguards to maintain the privacy of the donor was a violation of the Fourth Amendment prohibition against unreasonable searches and seizures. Mayfield v. Dalton, 901 F. Supp. 300, 303 (D.Hawai'i 1995). In addition, they feared that information obtained from the repository samples, regarding the donors' propensities for hereditary diseases and genetic disorders, might be used to discriminate against applicants for jobs, insurance or benefit programs. Id. at 304.

Refusing to comply with the program, Mayfield and Vlacovsky turned to the district court. They sought to represent a class of " 'all military personnel serving on active duty in the United States Navy and/or the United States Marine Corps who have been or may be compelled to provide blood and/or other tissue samples for DNA identification or testing procedures under currently applicable Navy and/or Marine Corps policies, practices and/or regulations.' " Id. at 305. The district court granted summary judgment in favor of the government and denied class certification. Id. at 302.

On the merits, the district court first held that the DNA repository did not violate any constitutional rights because the taking of specimens without the service members' consent did not constitute an unreasonable seizure in violation of the Fourth Amendment. Id. at 304. The court also stressed that the repository was instituted for the purpose of assisting in the identification of soldiers' remains, a purpose that plaintiffs-appellants did not challenge, and that other potential, more nefarious, uses were too speculative to be justiciable. Id. The district court also held that Mayfield and Vlacovsky could not adequately represent all members of the class and therefore denied them class certification. Id. at 305–306.

The district court's decision came down on September 8, 1995. In the intervening period between its decision and oral argument before this court, Mayfield and Vlacovsky have been honorably separated from active duty without ever having given any blood or tissue samples. The government suggests their claims may thus be moot. Mayfield and Vlacovsky counter that separation from active duty means that they are still contractually obligated to remain in the Marine Corps Reserves, and may thus be required to return to active duty in an emergency situation. Therefore, they argue, their case is not moot.

We agree with the government that Mayfield and Vlacovsky's challenge is moot because they are no longer subject to the DNA collection program, and face only a remote possibility that they may ever be subject to the repository policies they seek to challenge.

Moreover, in the intervening time between the district court judgment and oral argument before this court, the military changed the repository in ways that appear to respond to some of plaintiffs-appellants' main concerns. As of April 1996, for example, the maximum length of time that the specimens will now be retained has been shortened from the originally challenged duration of 75 years to 50 years. In addition, upon the request of the donor, the military will now destroy individual specimen samples following the conclusion of the service member's military obligation. See April 2, 1996 Memorandum from the Assistant Secretary of Defense for Health Affairs. . . . The changes made, which materially alter many aspects of the policy that Mayfield and Vlacovsky challenged in the district court, fortify our conclusion that the likelihood that these plaintiffs-appellants will ever be subject to the policy they challenged in the district court is too remote to make their suit justiciable.

Note: The Mayfield Case

After the Mayfield case was heard in the District Court, concerns about privacy and discrimination led the Department of Defense ("DoD") to amend its specimen collection and DNA analysis requirements. The 1996 amended regulations provide as follows:

> 1. Routine destruction schedule. The period of retention of specimen samples in the repository, established as 75 years . . . shall be reduced to 50 years.

> 2. Individual specimen sample destruction. Individual specimen samples will be destroyed upon the request of the donor following the conclusion of the donor's complete military service obligation or other applicable relationship to DoD. Upon receipt of such requests, the samples shall be destroyed within 180 days, and notification of the destruction sent to the donor.

> 3. Permissible uses. Authority to permit the use of any specimen sample in the repository for any purpose other than remains identification is further clarified. Reference (b) limited use of speci-

men samples to remains identification (exclusive of internal, quality assurance purposes), but did not prohibit the possibility of use under other circumstances in "extraordinary cases" when "no reasonable alternative means of obtaining a specimen for DNA profile analysis is available" and when the request is approved by the [Assistant Secretary of Defense Health Affairs]. To date, no nonconsensual exception request has been approved. This policy refinement limits "extraordinary cases" to cases in which a use other than remains identification is compelled by other applicable law. Consequently, permissible uses of specimen samples are limited to the following purposes:

a.   identification of human remains;

b.   internal quality assurance activities to validate processes for collection, maintenance and analysis of samples;

c.   a purpose for which the donor of the sample (or surviving next-of-kin) provides consent; or

d.   as compelled by other applicable law in a case in which all of the following conditions are present:

(1) the responsible DoD official has received a proper judicial order or judicial authorization;

(2) the specimen sample is needed for the investigation or prosecution of a crime punishable by one year or more of confinement;

(3) no reasonable alternative means for obtaining a specimen for DNA profile analysis is available; and

(4) the use is approved by the [Assistant Secretary of Defense, Health Affairs] after consultation with the DoD General Counsel.

Should these policies alleviate all reasonable concerns service members and their families might have about genetic privacy?

c.   *Genetic Testing, Privacy, and Discrimination*

Current Developments

As the preceding materials suggest, there are several features of genetic information that raise privacy and discrimination issues that are not implicated by the acquisition and disclosure of other kinds of medical information. These include: (1) an analysis of DNA provides information not only about an individual but also about the individual's parents, siblings and children. Genetic testing implicates both personal and family privacy; (2) because of the stability of DNA, a sample may be tested for generations after it has been acquired and with each new test, additional personal information may be discovered about the subject and the subject's biological family; (3) information about genes is perceived by the public as saying something about the essence of an individual. A person with a marker for a disease or for the potential for disease, may be perceived as in some way "defective." Genetic information presents a greater potential for stigmatization than many other kinds of healthcare information. Recent developments in the Human Genome Initiative and discrimination laws are summarized in the statement of Francis S. Collins, Director of the National Human Genome Research Institute.

CONGRESSIONAL TASK FORCE ON HEALTH RECORDS AND GENETIC PRIVACY PREVENTING GENETIC DISCRIMINATION IN HEALTH INSURANCE

July 22, 1997.

DEPARTMENT OF HEALTH AND HUMAN SERVICES
National Institutes of Health
Statement of Francis S. Collins, M.D., Ph.D.
Director
National Human Genome Research Institute

Briefly, the products of the HGP include genetic maps with closely spaced molecular markers throughout the human genome, physical maps consisting of sets of contiguous, cloned DNA spanning the entirety of each human chromosome, computer methods for easy data storage, retrieval, and manipulation, and ultimately, the complete nucleotide sequence of the human genome. Its first goal, creating a detailed genetic map for the human genome, has already been accomplished. The second goal, a comprehensive physical map of the human genome, is over 98 percent completed—well ahead of the 1998 anticipated date of completion. The Project thus far has been successful in meeting or exceeding the goals outlined in its original plan.

These accomplishments have set the stage for the project's ultimate goal, sequencing all the DNA in the human genome by 2005.

With the prospect of completing the human DNA sequence early in the next century, we are eager to begin the translation and interpretation of this information. The HGP is producing detailed information about the chemical structure and organization of human DNA—the order (sequence) of its three billion bases and the location of the approximately 80,000 genes it contains. However, the structural information that will result from the Project is only the beginning of biological interpretation. We will still face the challenge of understanding what the "instructions" encoded in human DNA mean; in other words, how the genes actually function.

The impact on the future of biology of knowing the order of all 3 billion human DNA bases has been compared to Mendeleev's establishment of the Periodic Table of the Elements in the 19th century and the advances in chemistry that followed. The complete set of human genes—the biologic periodic table—will make it possible to begin to understand how they function and interact. Rapidly evolving technologies, comparable to those used in the semi-conductor industry, will allow scientists to build detectors that trace hundreds or thousands of these gene signatures in a single experiment. Scientists will use the powerful new tools to reveal the secrets of disease susceptibility, create broad new opportunities for preventive medicine, and provide unprecedented information about the origin and migration of human populations.

Already as a result of the Human Genome Project technologies, new genes that are associated with diseases are discovered almost weekly. A recent example is the precise identification, by scientists at the NHGRI, of a gene abnormality that causes some cases of Parkinson's disease. Parkinson's disease, a common progressive neurological disorder that results from loss of nerve cells in a region of the brain that controls movement, afflicts about 500,000 people in the United States alone, with about 50,000 new cases reported every year. The gene, identified by NHGRI researchers, spells out instructions for a protein called alpha synuclein. Because the normal gene plays a role in the function of nerve cells, the finding gives researchers a powerful new tool for understanding cellular abnormalities in Parkinson's disease and demonstrates a connection between Parkinson's disease research and research into other neurological disorders, such as Alzheimer's disease. Until this discovery, most experts believed that Parkinson's disease was probably due to unknown factors present in the environment. The identity of this gene may ultimately help us prevent or delay the cell death that is responsible for some forms of degenerative brain disease.

Once a disease gene, such as Parkinson's disease gene, is identified it is often only a matter of months before a diagnostic test can be made available. Genetic tests can identify DNA alterations in people who have already developed a disease, in healthy persons who may be at risk of developing a genetic disorder later in life, or in people who are at risk of having a child with an inherited disorder. In some instances the development of accurate diagnostic technologies can be potentially life-saving. Genetic tests for glaucoma, colon cancer, inherited kidney cancer, and other disorders are already helping to identify high-risk individuals before they become ill, allowing potential life-saving interventions. Today, genetic tests are available primarily in academic medical centers for some 450 disorders, most of which are rare. But over the next decade, genetic testing will become ever more commonplace throughout the health care system, and will be applied to increasingly common disorders.

As our technology grows in genetic testing, more information will be made available to concerned individuals about their potential for developing certain conditions. While potentially providing enormous benefit by allowing individualized programs of preventive medicine, the increased availability of genetic information raises concerns about who will have access to this potentially powerful information. Each of us has an estimated 5 to 30 serious misspellings or alterations in our DNA; thus, we could all be targets for discrimination based on our genes. Of particular concern is the fear of losing jobs or health insurance because of a genetic predisposition to a particular disease. For example, a woman who carries a genetic alteration associated with breast cancer, and who has close relatives with the disease, has an increased risk of developing breast and ovarian cancer. Knowledge of this genetic status can enable women in high-risk families, together with their health care providers, to better tailor surveillance and prevention strategies. However, because of a concern that she or her children may not be able to obtain or change health insurance coverage in the future, a woman currently in this situation may avoid or delay genetic testing.

These are real concerns for too many Americans. In a recent survey of people in families with genetic disorders, 22 percent indicated they, or a member of their family, had been refused health insurance on the basis of their genetic information. The overwhelming majority of those surveyed felt that health insurers should not have access to genetic information. A 1995 Harris poll of the general public found a similar level of concern. Over 85 percent of those surveyed indicated they were very concerned or somewhat concerned that insurers or employers might have access to and use genetic information.

Discrimination in health insurance, and the fear of potential discrimination, threaten both society's ability to use new genetic technologies to improve human health and the ability to conduct the very research we need to understand, treat, and prevent genetic disease.

To unravel the basis of complex disorders, scientists must analyze the DNA of many hundreds of people for each disease they study. Thus valid research on complex disorders will require the participation of large numbers of volunteers. But a pall of mistrust hangs over research programs because study volunteers are concerned that their genetic information will be used by insurers to discriminate against them. For example, in genetic testing studies at the NIH, nearly one third of eligible people offered a test for breast cancer risk decline to take it. The overwhelming majority of those who refuse cite concerns about health insurance discrimination and loss of privacy as the reason.

Today, 19 states have enacted laws to restrict the use of genetic information in health insurance. Since January of this year, at least 31 states have introduced legislation to prohibit genetic discrimination in insurance, which is a positive indication of the level of concern about this important issue. Despite the initiatives of various states to pass legislation aimed at protecting individuals from being denied health insurance based on their genetic status, we have at best a patchwork of privacy and anti-discrimination proposals. In addition, state laws do not provide protection for the approximately 125 million Americans who obtain their health insurance coverage through private sector, employer sponsored, self-funded plans, because the federal Employee Retirement Income Security Act (ERISA) exempts the administration of these plans from state oversight. Therefore, the state legislative approach does not provide a comprehensive solution to genetic discrimination in health insurance.

In 1996, Congress enacted a law, called the Health Insurance Portability and Accountability Act (HIPAA), which took a significant step toward expanding access to health insurance. But HIPAA doesn't go far enough. Americans are still largely unprotected by federal law against insurance rate hikes based on genetic information and against unauthorized people or institutions having access to the genetic information contained in their medical records. HIPAA includes genetic information among the factors that may not be used to deny or limit insurance coverage for members of a group plan. Further, HIPAA explicitly excludes genetic information from being considered a preexisting condition in the absence of a diagnosis of the condition related to such information. The law specifically uses the broad, inclusive definition of genetic information recommended by the NAPBC–ELSI Working Group. Finally, HIPAA prohibits insurers from charging one individual a higher premium than any other "similarly situated" individual in the group.

These steps towards preventing discrimination based on genetics are significant, but HIPAA left several serious gaps that can now be closed by Administration-supported legislation. First, the protections in HIPAA do not extend to the individual health insurance market. Thus, individuals seeking coverage outside of the group market may still be denied access to coverage and may be charged exorbitant premiums based on genetic information. While only approximately 5 percent of Americans obtain health insurance outside the group market today, many of us will, at some point in our lifetime, purchase individual health insurance coverage. Because genetic information persists for a lifetime and may be transmitted through generations, people who are now in group plans are concerned about whether information about their genes may, at some point later in their life, disallow them from being able to purchase health insurance outside of the group market.

Second, while HIPAA prohibits insurers from treating individuals within a group differently from one another, it leaves open the possibility that all individuals within a group could be charged a higher premium based on the genetic information of one or more members of the group.

Finally, HIPAA does nothing to limit an insurer's access to or release of genetic information. No federal law prohibits an insurer from demanding access to genetic information contained in medical records or family history or requiring that an individual submit to a genetic test. In fact, an insurer can demand that an individual undergo genetic testing as a condition of coverage. Further, there are no restrictions on an insurers' release of genetic information to others. For example, at present, an insurer may release genetic information, and other health-related information, to the Medical Information Bureau which makes information available to other insurers who can then use it to discriminate. Because genetic information is personal, powerful, and potentially predictive, it can be used to stigmatize and discriminate against people. Genetic information must be private.

d. *Medical Records Privacy Law*

Currently there is no comprehensive federal legislation regulating the privacy and confidentiality of health records. Health records privacy law consists of a patchwork of state and federal laws that leaves large segments of health records with little legal protection. This state of affairs is summarized in recent commentary:

> Legal assures of confidentiality and privacy depend largely on the medical treatment that is the subject of the health record and where that health record is found. A caste system of records protection characterizes confidentiality law. Health records that are viewed as containing especially intimate and highly personal information enjoy strong privacy protections. The paradigms here are drug and alcohol and mental health treatment records and HIV status records. These records are regulated by legislation providing remedies for breaches of confidentiality and evidentiary privileges restricting their migration into public court records. General health records that are housed in federal or state government agencies, although of lower caste, are also provided some legal assurances of confidentiality. Such records are protected by privacy acts, by privacy and medical records exemptions in freedom of information and privacy acts,and by some fair information practices acts. They also enjoy a degree of constitutional protection.

> General health records that are located in the private sector receive the lowest legal assurances of confidentiality. General releases that authorize the recipient to disclose further health information for any legal reason are the norm in insurance and third-party payers contracts. These blanket releases license redisclosure and secondary use of information and result in loss of privacy and confidentiality for much health information.

Richard C. Turkington, *Medical Records Confidentiality Law, Scientific Research, and Data Collection in the Information Age,* 24 Jour. of Law, Medicine & Ethics, 113, 119 (1997).

For a general discussion of the array of laws that touch on confidentiality and health records see, Gostin, *Health Information Privacy,* 80 Cornell Law Review, 480 (1995) and Turkington, *Legal Protection for the Confidentiality of Health Care Information in Pennsylvania: Patient and Client Access; Testimonial Privilege; Damage Recovery for Unauthorized Extra–Legal Disclosure,* 31 Villanova law Review, 259 (1987). See, also, Paul M. Schwartz, *The Protection of Privacy in Health Care Reform,* 48 Vand. L. Rev. 295 (1995) for a general discussion of privacy and data process issues in health reform.

Health Records in the Private Sector

Access to health records in the private sector is determined by the contracts among patients, providers, and payers. These contractual arrangements permit disclosure between and within health care systems and payer organizations. With corporate management of health delivery services through health maintenance organizations becoming more prevalent, there has been a significant increase in the number of persons permitted to access health information.

The black hole of confidentiality for private sector health records is the legal sanctioning of general releases or blanket consents for the disclosure of health information. The general release form pervades the health care industry and provides for release of information to others not directly involved in the provider-patient relationship.

The general release form has fueled a huge growth industry in the collection and sale of health data by commercial medical data clearinghouses, which provide information to large consortiums of clients. It is well documented that health information provided to insurance companies under general release forms is forwarded to the Medical Information Bureau (MIB). MIB was formed in 1902 by fifteen insurance companies. In 1990, about 700 insurance companies belonged to MIB. MIB keys approximately three million health records annually into its data bank and has information on 15 million Americans. Secondary use of data acquired through general releases is the basis of marketing lists used in the sale of health-related products. Much medical data in health data base organizations (HDOs) are also available because of the general practice of blanket releases. Turkington, "Medical Records Confidentiality Law, Scientific Research, and Data Collection in the Information Age" supra at 115.

For a description of the Medical Information Bureau's health information gathering practices and the information practices of similarly structured organizations such as the Physician Computer Network and PSC Health Systems, see, *Office of Technology Assessment, Protecting Privacy in Computerized Medical Information* (Washington, D.C.: U.S. Government Printing Office, OTA–TCT—576, Sept. 1993). The Office of Technology Assessment report describes PSC as a managed prescription drug care company that "looks at 120 million" prescriptions annually, Id. at 34. See also generally, M.S. Donaldson and K.N. Lohr, eds., *Institute of Medicine, Health Data in the Information Age: Use, Disclosure, and Privacy* (Washington, D.C.: National Academy Press, (1994) at 50, 52, 151–52.

Note on HIPPA and Federal Legislative proposals

The health payment system is currently going through dramatic restructuring with the emergence of HMO's and the increased involvement of state and federal governments in payment for healthcare. Cost containment has become a priority of national policy. Health records are increasingly computerized. Lawrence Gostin, a leading commentator on privacy and health records, and others, argue that the creation of a national computerized system of health records would save the health delivery system billions of dollars and improve the quality of health services. Gostin suggests that this computerized health record system is well in place and has "an aura of inevitability." Gostin, *supra*, p. 480. All of this has created an urgency to enact national legislation that will regulate access to personal health information. There is broad based support for national legislation. An important step toward this goal was the enactment of Title II of the Health Insurance Portability and Accountability Act (HIPAA). HIPPA sets a timetable for enacting federal law on medical data privacy—by February, 2000. See 42 U.S.C.A. § 1320d to d–8 (West. Supp.1998). (This timetable could be rescinded by Congress.) Numerous proposals for federal legislation are currently before Congress. For a general review of the privacy and confidentiality issues raised by some of these proposals, see, Turkington, *supra*, p. 122; see, also, Comment, *Enacting a Health Information Confidentiality Law: Can Congress Beat the Deadline?*, 77 U.C.L.Rev. 283 (1998).

Laws Prohibiting Blanket Consent

In the absence of legislation or regulations restricting their use, blanket consent forms for disclosure of health information are legal. Yet the valid consensual waiver of important rights require that the waiver be knowingly and voluntarily made. For medical procedures the rule is that patients be fully informed and consent voluntarily given. Do blanket consent forms for disclosure of health information involve even the most rudimentary features of informed consent? Are these, as Paul Schwartz suggests, a form of "uninformed consent," Schwartz, supra, p. 311. By regulation or statute release of certain health records must be in writing and limited to specific purposes. Redisclosure is prohibited unless there is written consent. This is the law for sensitive health records that receive greater confidentiality and privacy protection than general health records. Core examples are drug and alcohol treatment, HIV status and mental health records. For an illustration of a statutory restriction on nonconsensual secondary use, review the written consent requirements for release of HIV status information in the Pennsylvania Confidentiality of HIV–Related Information Act, *infra*, Chapter 8, p. 881.

Should written consent be required for the release of health records to third party payors or to government oversight agencies that are investigating fraud or reviewing health care practices for the purpose of cost containment? Should the written consent of patients be required for the release of health records for research? These issues are addressed in the various legislative proposals currently before Congress on national medical privacy legislation. For a review of how proposals differ on these and other issues, see, Turkington, *supra*, at p. 122 and comment, *supra* at p. 318. Compare the strong policy against nonconsensual secondary disclosure of health records contained in the EU Data Privacy Directive, discussed, *infra*, Chapter 4 at p. 325.

Judicial Direction Under Discovery Rules

Parties have rights of access to each other's evidence during discovery in a lawsuit. Under rules of discovery the holder of a medical record may seek a protective order to prevent discovery. Under discovery rules judges have discretion to grant orders to protect someone from "annoyance, embarrassment, oppression or undue burden....)" See, for example, Fed. R. Civ. P. 26(c). Courts have exercised this discretion to maintain the confidentiality of health records.

In exercising discretion courts are required to balance privacy and discovery interests. Clear abuses of discretion are subject to reversal on appeal. See, for example, *Farnsworth v. Procter Gamble Co., Andrews v. Ely Lilly & Co.* 97 F.R.D. 494 (N.D. Ill. 1983), *vacated by* 740 F.2d 556 (7th Cir.1984). In *Ely Lilly, Dr. Arthur Herbst,* the leading researcher on diethystilbestrol (DES) successfully quashed subpoena requesting access to virtually every record in the registry maintained by Dr. Herbst on genital tract cancer. Access was sought under discovery rules in a personal injury DES case. The court applied a balancing of interest test under discovery rules and denied access to the health information in the registry. In favoring confidentiality in the balance the court emphasized the importance of credible promises of confidentiality and the damage to ongoing epidemiological research from premature disclosure of information. The court also rejected the defendant's offer to settle for redacted records because the risk of reidentifying the subjects, given the other personal information in the record would remain. However, on appeal, the motion to quash was vacated. See *Deitchman v. E.R. Squibb & Sons, Inc.,* 740 F.2d 556 (7th Cir.1984). The Seventh Circuit held that Squibb was entitled to discovery of some data and remanded the case to the district court to fashion an order that more appropriately balanced the privacy and discovery interests.

The freestanding constitutional right to informational privacy discussed, supra, has also been a source for protecting medical records from compelled judicial disclosure. See *Rasmussen v. South Florida Blood Service* and discussion in notes infra, Chapter V. at p. 497. The common law breach of confidentiality tort also provides a remedy against unauthorized disclosure of information in medical records in some circumstances. See *Hammonds v. Aetna Casualty & Surety Company* and discussion in notes infra, Chapter V. at p. 499.

Chapter Three

FEDERAL AND STATE STATUTORY PROTECTION FOR CONVERSATIONAL PRIVACY AND E–MAIL PRIVACY

A. INTRODUCTION

Section 605 of the Federal Communications Act

Justice Taft noted in *Olmstead* that while government wiretaps were not within the fourth amendment, the privacy of telephone conversations could be protected through direct legislation. Congress obliged in 1934 by enacting the Federal Communications Act. Section 605 of the Act was Congress' initial legislation dealing with electronic surveillance of conversations.

The pertinent part of § 605 reads:

> No person not being authorized by the sender shall intercept any communication and divulge or publish the existence, contents, substance, purport, effect or meaning of such intercepted communication to any person, ... and no person having received such intercepted communication or having become acquainted with the contents, substance, purport, effect, or meaning of the same or any part thereof, knowing that such information was so obtained, shall divulge or publish the existence, contents, substance, purport, effect or meaning of the same or any part thereof, or use the same or any information therein contained for his own benefit or for the benefit of another not entitled thereto....

Federal Communications Act, 1934, ch. 652, Section 605, 48 Stat. 1103 (1934) amended by 47 U.S.C.A. § 605 (1968).

Coverage of section 605 was limited. The statute was not intended to preempt state law and, therefore, evidence procured by an electronic surveillance that did not conform to the standards in section 605 could be admitted in state criminal prosecutions. *See*, J. Carr, *The Law of*

Electronic Surveillance, section 2.4(a) at 2–15 (Release #20, 3/97). Initially the Justice Department and Federal Bureau of Investigation interpreted section 605 03 to prohibit only wiretaps which were "divulged." *See, e.g.*, Herbert Brownell, Jr., *The Public Security and Wire Tapping*, 39 Cornell L. Q. 195, 197–99 (1954); John F. Decker and Joel Handler, *Electronic Surveillance: Standards, Restrictions, and Remedies*, 12 Cal. W.L. Rev. 60, 163 (1975). The Supreme Court severely restricted the application of section 605 beyond telephone wiretapping by imposing a trespass element on other forms of electronic eavesdropping. In *Goldman v. United States*, 316 U.S. 129 (1942), a dictaphone placed against an outer wall was held not to be an interception within section 605 with respect to conversations overheard in a business office. The absence of a physical trespass or invasion of the home of a person under surveillance produced a similar result in *On Lee v. United States*, 343 U.S. 747 (1952), where a conversation had been recorded by an acquaintance of the defendant who was "wired for sound." The physical trespass intrusion notion of section 605 produced anomalous results where the application of the statute turned on specious factual distinction. *See, e.g.*, *Silverman v. United States*, 365 U.S. 505 (1961) (section 605 application to foot-long spike microphone); *Clinton v. Virginia*, 377 U.S. 158 (1964) (listening device tacked in wall of adjoining apartment).

B. TITLE III OF THE OMNIBUS CRIME CONTROL AND SAFE STREETS ACT OF 1968

18 U.S.C.A. §§ 2510–2520 (1970).

1. INTRODUCTION

In response to the limited protection provided within § 605, the emergence of constitutional requirements from *Berger* and *Katz*, and a growing concern over organized crime, Lyndon Johnson's democratically controlled Congress produced the first comprehensive federal statute regulating virtually all forms of electronic surveillance of conversations in 1968.

Title III of the Omnibus Crime Control and Safe Streets Act of 1968 nationalized the law of federal, state and private electronic surveillance of conversations. *See generally* Jeremiah Courtney, *Electronic Eavesdropping, Wiretapping and Your Right to Privacy*, 26 Fed. Comm. B.J. 1 (1973); James G. Carr, *The Law of Electronic Surveillance* (1994).

The regulation of electronic surveillance of conversations under Title III represents an accommodation of crime control interests and privacy which is premised on the view that electronic surveillance by the government is essential to effective enforcement of the criminal law. Title III opts to protect the privacy of citizens by dictating the circumstances and manner in which the government may eavesdrop on conversations, rather than by severely limiting or restricting the government's ability to engage in the conduct.

a. The 1986 Amendments: The Electronic Communications Privacy Act (The ECPA)

As originally written, Title III was directed at the existing technology for electronic surveillance of conversations. This consisted primarily of wiretaps and small recorders or transmitters placed on a person, a phone or in the place where the conversation occurred. Surveillance of conversations by use of the telephone was dealt with by the concept of "wire communication," the essential meaning of which was a communication transferred in whole or in part over wires provided by a telephone company (or other licensed common carrier). Face to face conversations were regulated through the concept of "oral communication."

Title III was enacted in 1968 to deal with the then current state of communications of conversations over wire (by telephone) and face to face. The technology of communications has changed dramatically in the years since Title III was enacted. By 1986 many communications were transmitted by means other than the telephone or face to face conversations and by systems owned and managed by entities that were not licensed common carriers. Today most conversations are transmitted digitally and not by analog. Many conversations are transmitted by radio signals through cellular phone systems or cordless phones; many companies have private phone systems which they tie into the systems of common carriers. Paging devices facilitate communication and electronic mail and facsimile machines are used to communicate information electronically.

In 1986 Congress responded to the technological advances in electronic surveillance that had developed since 1968 and amended Title III by enacting the Electronic Communications Privacy Act of 1986 (the ECPA). The response to the new technology is embodied in the addition of the concept of "electronic communication" to the statute. This addition brings the surveillance of digitally transmitted conversations, electronic mail, cellular phones and pen registers within the regulatory reach of the statute. As amended by ECPA, the federal electronic eavesdropping statute is divided into three titles. Title I amends the original 1968 legislation (previously referred to as Title III) and regulates interceptions of wire, oral or electronic communications. As amended, Title I is codified in 18 U.S.C.A. §§ 2510–2522. Title II regulates the acquisition of stored wire and electronic communications and transactional records and is codified in 18 U.S.C.A. §§ 2701–2711 (1994). Title III regulates the use of pen registers and trap and trace devices and is codified in 18 U.S.C.A. §§ 3121–3127 (1994). The full text of the legislation as amended by the ECPA is contained in Chapter VIII of this book. The discussion in this chapter is designed to introduce the reader to the basic structure and concepts of Title I and Title II. The regulation of pen registers and trap and trace devices in Title III will be discussed briefly at the end of the chapter.

Terminology After ECPA

Title III of the 1968 Omnibus Crime Control and Safe Streets Act was often referred to as The Federal Wiretap Act or Title III. The ECPA amendments to the Wiretap Act now divide the Act into Title I, II, and III. The former Title III is now Title 1 of the ECPA. In this book we will refer to the current Federal Wiretap Act by the short title of the ECPA and the three titles as "Title I, II or III of the ECPA." Cases and commentary prior to the ECPA will, of course use Title III as the short title of The Federal Wiretap Act prior to 1986 when the ECPA was enacted.

[*Editors note*. Some courts still refer to the federal statute as Title III; other courts refer to Title I as the Wiretap Act and Title II as the Stored Communications Act.]

b.   *General Analysis in Title I Cases*

(Interception of a Wire, Oral or Electronic Communication)

A general four step analysis should be utilized in analyzing Title I cases. First there must be a determination as to whether there was an "interception" of a "wire, oral or electronic communication" within the meaning of section 2510 ("a 2510 interception"). Title I does not apply to the case unless this has occurred. Section 2511 generally prohibits such interceptions subject to the specific exceptions in that section ("2511 exceptions"). Therefore, if a section 2510 interception has occurred the second step in examining a Title I violation is to determine whether one of the section 2511 exceptions applies to the case. If there is a section 2510 interception and no section 2511 exception applies to the case, the interception is in violation of Title I unless it is authorized by a court order that satisfies the requirements of section 2518 (2518 court order). Section 2518 establishes the necessary procedure for obtaining a court approved interception and sets forth the appropriate contents of an application for a court ordered electronic surveillance. Section 2518 also imposes restrictions on the scope and duration of the surveillance. If the non-exempt interception occurred pursuant to a court order, the third step in determining a Title I violation is to examine whether the requirements of section 2518 have been met. If there has been a violation of Title I the fourth step is to consider the applicability of a criminal sanction, civil remedy or right to exclude the contents of the illegal interception in court proceedings under sections 2511, 2515 and 2520.

c.   *Permissible Electronic Surveillance Without a Court Order*

Electronic surveillance of conversations without a court order is allowable under Title I. Exceptions to the requirement of a court order under Title I basically occur in three ways. First, the electronic surveillance may not be of a "wire, oral, or electronic communication" within the meaning of (1) and (2) of section 2510; second, the surveillance may not constitute an "interception" within the meaning of section 2510(4); third, the electronic surveillance may come within one of the specified exceptions found in section 2511, or within the limited exception found in section 2518(7) applicable to emergencies, providing a warrant is issued within 48 hours.

d. The Concept of "Wire Communication"

One of the core notions in Title I is "wire communication." The concept is intended to apply to conversations which are transmitted in whole or part over telephone wires. As with other provisions of the Statute, the changes in communication technology that have taken place since 1968 required some retooling of the definition of "wire communication" in the 1986 Amendments to the statute.

The current definition of "wire communication" under section 2510(1) follows; the bracketed language indicates language that was in the earlier version of the statute but was omitted from the 1986 version. The italicized terms are those that were added in the ECPA.

Section 2510. Definitions

As used in this chapter—

(1) "wire communication" means any [communication] *aural transfer* made in whole or in part through the use of facilities for the transmission of communications by the aid of wire, cable, or other like connection between the point of origin and the point of reception (*including the use of such connection in a switching station*) furnished or operated by any person engaged [as a common carrier] in providing or operating such facilities for the transmission of interstate or foreign communications *or communications affecting interstate or foreign commerce and such term includes any electronic storage of such communication.*

Notice that "aural transfer" has been substituted for the term "communication." This change was intended to extend the scope of wire communications beyond transmission of voice signals by traditional telephone services to systems that convert the voice signal from analog to digital form for purposes of transmission. "Aural transfer" is defined as "a transfer containing the human voice at any point between and including the point of origin and the point of reception." *As long as the communication includes the human voice at some point from origin to reception and is transferred by the aid of wire, cable or other like connector at some point from origin to reception, it is a "wire communication" under Section 2510(1).*

The 1986 Amendments removed the limitation contained in the original legislation that restricted wire communications to conversations transmitted by facilities furnished by common carriers. The common carrier limitation exempted communications transmitted by in-house telephone systems from statutory restrictions on the interception of "wire communications." This would include as core cases department store intercom systems, *e.g., United States v. Christman*, 375 F.Supp. 1354, 1355 (N.D.Cal.1974), and phones in the visiting area of a jail. Of course, even if there is an in-house phone system, conversations involving telephone calls from outside common carrier systems into the business or the in-house system were viewed as "wire communications." *See Campiti v. Walonis*, 453 F.Supp. 819 (D.Mass.1978), *aff'd*, 611 F.2d 387 (1st Cir.1979). Communications over purely in-house telephone systems could come within the statutory protection but were analyzed as "oral communications" and needed to satisfy the legitimate expectation of privacy test.

The elimination of the common carrier requirement reflected Congress' recognition of the proliferation of private network and intra-company communication systems since 1968. Such systems, common today, come within the protection of Title I providing that communications that are part of the system affect interstate commerce. The cases exempting in-house systems prior to the 1986 Amendments no longer have precedential value under Title I.

Voice Mail

The electronic storage of a wire communication is treated as a wire communication under section 2510 (1). Electronic storage is defined as (A) "any temporary intermediate storage of a wire or electronic communication incidental to the electronic transmission thereof; and (B) any storage of such communication by an electronic communication service for the purpose of back up protection of such communications." 18 USCA § 2510(1). Saved voice mail messages would constitute the electronic storage of a wire communication and would be protected to the same extent that the wire communication is. Compare the different treatment of the storage of electronic communications in *Steve Jackson Games*, 36 F.3d 457 (5th Cir.1994) *infra*.

e. *The Concept of "Oral Communication" Under Title I*

Title I also protects conversations which are not communicated via telephone. Such conversations are dealt with by the concept of "oral communication" as defined in section 2510(2). Face to face conversations are "oral communications." Note that in respect to oral communications, Title I in its plain language incorporates the reasonable expectation concept of *Katz v. United States*, 389 U.S. 347 (1967), and the two-pronged expectations test that was enunciated in Justice Harlan's concurring opinion.

The two-prong test of Title I protection for oral communication requires: (1) that the person challenging the surveillance must exhibit an expectation that his or her utterances are not subject to interception, and (2) that the person must also be justified in respect to the subjective expectation of privacy that, in fact, was present. If either of these two requirements is not satisfied in a particular instance, then the oral utterance is not protected under Title I. For that matter, in view of *Katz* and *White*, the conversation also is not protected under the constitution against warrantless surveillance. Clear examples of failure to satisfy the first part of the expectation test in section 2510(2) include (1) a person who speaks to a public audience; (2) a person who has been informed that a room is bugged and still converses; (3) situations where a person expresses evidence of awareness that his or her conversation is being monitored or overheard. *See, e.g., United States v. Tijerina*, 412 F.2d 661 (10th Cir.), *cert. denied*, 396 U.S. 990 (1969); *United States v. Hoffa*, 436 F.2d 1243 (7th Cir.1970), *cert. denied*, 400 U.S. 1000 (1971). The electronic surveillance of utterances spoken into a telephone by one party to a telephone conversation are not interceptions of "wire communications" because they are not conversations that are overheard or heard by tapping into the telephone wire. *See United States v. McLeod*, 493 F.2d 1186, 1188 (7th Cir.1974). The surveillance in *Katz* then would be analyzed under Title I as an "oral communication."

f. The Concept of Electronic Communication

The 1986 Amendments added the concept of "electronic communication" to Title I. Section 2510 (12) reads:

> (12) "electronic communication" means any transfer of signs, signals, writing, images, sounds, data or intelligence of any nature transmitted in whole or in part by a wire, radio, electromagnetic, photoelectronic or photooptical system that affects interstate or foreign commerce, but does not include—
>
> (A) any wire or oral communication;
>
> (B) any communication made through a tone-only paging device; or
>
> (C) any communication from a tracking device (as defined in section 3117 of this title).

Note that wire and oral communications are excluded from the definition of "electronic communication." If wire or oral communications are excluded, electronic communication then involve the electronic transfer of signs, writings, images, sounds, data or intelligence of any nature *other than the human voice.*

Although the definitions of wire, oral and electronic communications are mutually exclusive of each other, as made clear in the legislative history, more than one type of communication may be involved with current communication technology:

> It is important to recognize that a transaction may consist, in part, of both electronic communications and wire or oral communications, as those terms are defined in section 2510 as amended by the Electronic Communications Privacy Act. Accordingly, different aspects of the same communication might be characterized differently. For example, the transmission of data over the telephone is an electronic communication. If the parties use the line to speak to one another between data transmis-

sions, those communications would be wire communications. At the same time, for a person overhearing one end of the telephone conversation by listening in on the oral utterance of one of the parties, those utterances are oral communications.

H.R. Rep. No. 647, 99th Cong., 2d Sess. 35 (1986)

g. The Concept of "Interception" Under Title I

For Title I to be applicable there must be "interception" of the communication. A Title I Interception is defined by paragraph 4 of section 2510. This section states:

> (4) "intercept" means the aural or other acquisition of the contents of any wire, electronic or oral communication through the use of any electronic, mechanical, or other device.

The 1986 Amendments added "or other" to the definition of "intercept." The legislative history of the 1986 Amendments makes it clear that the addition of "or other" to the definition was intended to make it clear that the legislation reaches interceptions of non-voice portions of a wire communication such as the digitalized portion of a communication. The addition of "or other" appears also to have eliminated an issue that had arisen under the pre-ECPA definition, which limited interception to the "aural" acquisition of contents of wire or oral communications.

The explicit requirement of "aural" acquisition of the contents provided support for the argument that recording of a conversation which is not simultaneously heard by a human monitor is not an interception because there is no "aural" acquisition of the contents of the communication. The majority of courts that had confronted this argument rejected it. *See United States v. Turk*, 526 F.2d 654 (5th Cir.1976). These courts noted the absence of an explicit reference in the exception section of Title I (section 2511) to recorded but non-monitored conversations and invoked the overall purpose of the statute. In addition, James Carr, a leading textbook author on the ECPA, has argued that the problem can be avoided by utilization of a constructive possession doctrine which would consider the person who taped the conversation as in possession of the recorder and therefore constructively intercepting the conversation. There is some authority holding that recorded, but not simultaneously heard surveillance does not fall within the coverage of the ECPA. *See United States v. Bynum*, 360 F.Supp. 400 (S.D.N.Y.), *aff'd*, 485 F.2d 490 (2d Cir.1973), *vacated*, 417 U.S. 903 (1974). These decisions seem to be manifestly incorrect.

A related problem involved the situation in which a party to the conversation recorded the conversation by an electronic device attached to his phone. Some courts viewed this type of surveillance as an "aural acquisition" of the conversation. *See, e.g., United States v. Turk*, 526 F.2d 654 (5th Cir.1976); *Meredith v. Gavin*, 446 F.2d 794 (8th Cir.1971). Other decisions took a contrary view and characterized the recorder as a "mere accessory designed to preserve the contents of the communication." *See, e.g., United States v. Harpel*, 493 F.2d 346, 350 (10th

Cir.1974). If such activities are viewed as interceptions of wire communications, then liability would attach under the ECPA if the participant recorder acted with the intent to commit a criminal act within the meaning of the consent exception under Section 2511(2)(d). The Fifth Circuit represented the better view on this question. If the Tenth Circuit's approach is adopted then no violation of the ECPA would occur even if the recording was for the purpose of committing a crime because the threshold requirements of Title I would not be satisfied.

By extending the concept of interception from "aural" acquisitions to "aural or other" acquisitions, Title I now clearly treats the non-monitored recording of a conversation as an interception. Any ambiguity as to whether the recording of a conversation by an electronic device attached to one party's phone is an interception has been removed by the addition of "or other" to the definition of interception.

h.   Cordless Phones: The Pre–1986 Caselaw

Cordless phones provide phone subscribers with the convenience of conversing by telephone with portable phone sets. Conversations are transmitted from the portable hand set unit to the base unit by FM signals in the same way that radio signals are transmitted. The FM signal is non-directional and reaches out in all directions simultaneously. The signal will penetrate material such as the concrete or wood that is normally used to construct walls in commercial or residential buildings. The FM signal utilized by the mobile and base units may be the same or similar to the frequency used by commercial FM radio stations. A person playing a standard FM radio may pick up the radio transmission of any portion of a conversation which occurs between two cordless phone handsets, between a cordless handset and the base unit, or between the base unit and a cordless handset.

Is a conversation over a cordless phone that is listened to and or recorded by someone who was operating an FM radio within the protection of the ECPA? Most of the courts that dealt with this question prior to 1986 found that the statute did not reach the radio transmitted portion of a conversation involving a cordless phone. In a prosecution for cocaine possession in *State v. Howard*, 235 Kan. 236, 679 P.2d 197 (1984), the Supreme Court of Kansas refused to exclude evidence of conversations that were recorded by a neighbor of the defendant after the neighbor had heard the conversations over his AM/FM radio. Since the recording did not constitute the interception of a "wire or oral" communication, there was no violation of the statute. Although the Statute defined "wire communications" as those transmitted in "whole or part" over wires, the Kansas court held that the recording in *Howard* was not an interception of a "wire" communication under the statute. The court followed the rule that a statute should not be "given a literal construction, if such construction is contrary to the legislative intent and leads to *absurd conclusions.*" *Id.* at 205 (quoting *United States v. Bryan*, 339 U.S. 323 (1950)). The court concluded that the statutory purpose of protecting privacy was not significantly implicated by cordless phone use because the user had no "reasonable expectation of privacy" in the publicly transmitted portion of a radio transmitted communication. Furthermore, the court was reluctant to extend the criminal and civil sanctions of the statute to the inadvertent act of picking up a conversation through the normal operation of an AM/FM radio. Other high state courts adopted a similar construction. *See Dorsey v. State*, 402 So.2d 1178 (Fla.1981); *State v. Delaurier*, 488 A.2d 688 (R.I.1985).

The leading case applying the plain construction rule of statutory construction to extend the Federal Wiretap Act to the radio portion of a conversation over a cordless phone is *United States v. Hall*, 488 F.2d 193 (9th Cir.1973). However, the *Hall* court limited its construction to cordless phone conversations that included a land-line telephone. Conversations transmitted solely between cordless phones were not wire or oral communications under the statute.

i. Cellular Phones and Cordless Phones Under the ECPA and the 1994 Digital Telephony Act

The 1986 Amendments to the statute contained a cordless phone exclusion. The definitions of wire or electronic communications specifically excluded "the radio portion of a cordless telephone communication that is transmitted between the cordless telephone and the base unit."

Consider a telephone call from A to B. A places the call from a wall phone in A's house to B's home. The wall phone in B's den rings and the call is transmitted by signal to the cordless telephone that B is holding in her backyard. The portion of A's conversation with B is picked up by an (FM) radio receiver that is in a police officer's automobile that is parked on the street over one hundred feet from B's house. Has there been an interception of a "wire or oral or electronic communication" within the meaning of the Statute?

Cellular phones use the radio technology of cordless phones but also utilize the wire system to extend telephone services to automobiles, a briefcase and in some instances to rural areas that are not currently covered by traditional telephone wire systems. Title I reaches cellular phone systems through the concept of "switching stations" that was added to the definition of "wire communication" in section 2510(1). This addition is intended to extend the reach of the ECPA to cellular systems as defined in 47 C.F.R. Section 22.2. The Eighth Circuit has confirmed this view of the ECPA and held that cellular phone communications are protected but that the radio portion of a conversation over a cordless phone is not. *See Tyler v. Berodt*, 877 F.2d 705 (8th Cir.1989), *cert. denied*, 493 U.S. 1022 (1990). The disparate treatment of cordless and cellular phones in the statute has been criticized as inconsistent. *See* Comment, *The Electronic Communication and Privacy Act: Discriminatory Treatment for Similar Technology, Cutting the Cord of Privacy*, 23 J. Marshall L. Rev. 661 (1990).

The 1994 Digital Telephony Act amended the ECPA to remove the exception for cordless telephones. Older generations of cordless phones do not have scrambling or other technologies that make it difficult to intercept the conversation, see, Basil W. Mangano, Note, *The Communications Assistance for Law Enforcement Act and Protection of Cordless Telephone Communications: The Use of Technology as a Guide to Privacy*, 44 Clev. St. L. Rev. 99, 119 (1996). No distinction between older and newer cordless phones was recognized in the legislative history of the 1994 amendments to the ECPA, nor has it been recognized by courts, see, for example, *Spetalieri v. Kavanaugh*, 36 F.Supp.2d 92 (N.D.N.Y. 1998) (holding the ECPA applies to all cordless telephones).

Without scrambling technology a cordless phone conversation can be intercepted by a scanner. Scanners are commonly purchased to monitor police and fire department activities. Picking up a telephone conversation by use of a scanner is an interception of a wire communication under Title I of the ECPA that may trigger criminal or civil responsibility. Is this too harsh a rule? Does the requirement that interceptions be intentional to constitute a violation of the ECPA protect innocent and acceptable uses of scanners?

(1) The Argument Against Extending the Statute to Cellular Phones: From the Perspective of the "Scanner" Industry

The inclusion of cellular phone systems within the scope of the ECPA was controversial. Consider the following excerpts from the written testimony of Richard Brown, a representative of Regency Electronics, Inc. ("Regency"), a major manufacturer of radio band scanners which are capable of intercepting communications from cellular systems. He submitted testimony before the subcommittee of the House of Representatives that was holding hearings on the Electronic Communications Act of 1986. Brown noted that ten million scanners were currently in use throughout the country.

> Cellular radio licensees and users have had absolutely no legitimate expectation of privacy for cellular radio communication. Cellular licensees were aware that cellular radio conversations were not secure when they received their licenses from the FCC. Cellular radio telephone communications are transmitted via the RF spectrum and in that regard are no different than any other omni-directional communication transmitted over the radio spectrum. Cellular telephone licensees have never had any reason to believe that such communication would be secured by the FCC's Regulations or by Congressional legislation. It is submitted that any user expectancy of privacy could have only come from misleading promotions.

> The expectation of privacy in the use of wireline telephone technology is comparable to the public's right to expect privacy in the delivery of mail and Regency supports this right. It has developed as a fundamental right in the American way of life. But if a wireline telephone conversation is akin to mailing a letter, then a cellular conversation is akin to mailing a postcard.

There is no expectation of privacy. The fabric of American society is not grounded in the expectation of privacy for car telephone conversation or indeed for a wide variety of radio conversations. Just as a mail carrier is not engaging in a criminal act when reading a third party postcard, neither should a consumer be liable for listening to the postcard of the telephone industry: the cellular radio telephone conversation. If the postcard sender wishes security, he is responsible to take his own precautions—likewise with the cellular radio telephone user. . . .

There is no compelling evidence which would justify singling out cellular telephone communications as entitled to Congressional mandated security when all other spectrum users are responsible for securing their own communications. For example, cordless telephones, which act like mini-cellular systems, have been on the market for many years and have never been subjected to any expectation of privacy. Like cordless telephone users, cellular telephone users have no expectation of privacy and to the extent that the American public has been informed otherwise, it appears that requiring public disclosure is a more appropriate manner to protect the public interest. . . .

In its *Second Report and Order*, released June 5, 1985, looking to new interim provisions for cordless telephones, the FCC proposed a labeling requirement whereby the consumer would be informed of the security features possessed by the cordless telephone he/she plans to purchase. The proposed requirement calls for the box or other package in which the cordless telephone is marketed to carry a statement in a prominent location which reads as follows:

> *CAUTION* The base unit in this cordless telephone may respond to the nearby units or radio noise resulting in telephone calls being dialed through this unit without your knowledge and possibly calls being misbilled. In order to protect against such occurrences, this cordless telephone is provided with the following features:

> . . .

The potential for interception of cellular radio communication in all of the above instances is enormous.

For example:

1.   A cellular telephone subscriber places a call to the office of a business associate. the receptionist tells him that his business associate, tom, is in his car which is equipped with a radio and that they will "patch" the cellular telephone call through. Tom's company has a two-way radio system licensed in one of the private radio services and is authorized to interconnect with the telephone network. FCC regulations mandate that

other parties sharing tom's radio channel must monitor before transmitting so as to not cause interference to an ongoing transmission. Any portion of the cellular telephone communication is subject to interception by any other two-way radio licensee who is monitoring tom's two-way frequency before beginning a transmission.

2. A consumer owns an older television set with continuous UHF tuning. In other words, the consumer can tune to the cellular band with her television set. While searching for a channel she receives a cellular conversation. A friend who was also present thinks this is most interesting and later tells others about it. word eventually gets to an individual who reports the consumer to the authorities. The consumer's only comfort is that there are at least several million other citizens who have the same potentiality of intercepting a cellular communication.

3. A typical American family is in the kitchen having dinner. Mom is tuning in some easy listening music at the high end of the am band. Mom comes across a voice conversation and recognizes the voice as the next door neighbor with whom the family is not on very good terms. Apparently the neighbor has a cordless telephone which operates within the range of an am radio. The next day the family's ten year old, who is on better terms with the neighbor's ten year old son, spills the beans about overhearing the conversation. The family has all but forgotten about the incident when it is served a subpoena. Here again, there are millions of citizens who will become at risk if the proposed legislation is not clarified.

j. *Video Surveillance*

The telescreen received and transmitted simultaneously. Any sound that Winston made, above the level of a very low whisper, would be picked up by it; moreover, so long as he remained within the field of vision which the metal plaque commanded, he would be seen as well as heard. There was of course no way of knowing whether you were being watched at any given moment.

—from *1984*, by George Orwell

The evolution of reliable miniature video cameras has prompted prosecutors to utilize surreptitious video surveillance as an investigatory tool. Video surveillance in places that have traditionally been the subject of legal protection of privacy, such as a residence or office, raises the spectra of the "telescreens" that were used by "Big Brother" to watch the population in George Orwell's 1949 classic, the futuristic novel *1984*. Does the comprehensiveness of the invasion of privacy that occurs through government surveillance by use of a hidden camera make surreptitious video surveillance in private places per se unreasonable under the fourth amendment?

In *United States v. Torres*, 751 F.2d 875 (7th Cir.1984), the leading case, the court rejected the view that surreptitious video surveillance by the government was absolutely prohibited by the fourth amendment. In *Torres*, a federal court had authorized the FBI to make surreptitious entries into an apartment to install electronic "bugs" and television cameras in every room. The government had demonstrated that there was probable cause to believe the apartment was a safe house for the Fuerzas Armadas de Liberacion Nacional Puertorriquena (FALN). The FALN was known by the FBI to be a secret organization of separatists that had used violent tactics including bombing in their efforts to win independence for Puerto Rico. After the television surveillance of the apartment revealed persons assembling bombs, a search warrant was granted for the audio and video surveillance of a second apartment.

Judge Richard Posner, speaking for the Seventh Circuit, applied a cost/benefit analysis in concluding that surreptitious video surveillance was not prohibited under the Constitution.

> We do not think the Fourth Amendment prevents the government from coping with the menace of this organization by installing and operating secret television cameras in the organization's safe houses. The benefits to the public safety are great, and the costs to personal privacy are modest. A safe house is not a home. No one lives in these apartments, amidst the bombs and other paraphernalia of terrorism. They are places dedicated exclusively to illicit business; and though the Fourth Amendment protects business premises as well as homes, the invasion of privacy caused by secretly televising the interior of business premises is less than that caused by secretly televising the interior of a home, while the social benefit of the invasion is greater when the organization under investigation runs a bomb factory than it would be if it ran a chop shop or a numbers parlor. There is no right to be let alone while assembling bombs in safe houses.

751 F.2d at 883.

A major argument against the reasonableness of the search in *Torres* was that the warrant authorizing the video surveillance did not satisfy the particularization requirements of the fourth amendment. Judge Posner held that since the warrant satisfied the requirements in section 2518 of the statute, and since those requirements related to the constitutional requirements of particularity, the fourth amendment was satisfied.

Judge Posner's approach in *Torres* has been followed by all the circuits that have considered the question of video surveillance. See *United States v. Falls*, 34 F.3d 674 (8th Cir.1994); *United States v. Mesa–Rincon*, 911 F.2d 1433 (10th Cir.1990); *United States v. Koyomejian*, 970 F.2d 536 (9th Cir.1992), cert. denied, 506 U.S. 1005 (1992); *United States v. Cuevas–Sanchez*, 821 F.2d 248 (5th Cir.1987); *United States v. Biasucci*, 786 F.2d 504 (2d Cir.1986), cert. denied, 479 U.S. 827 (1986). *Torres* was extended to court-authorized interceptions of Telex communications in *United States v. Gregg*, 629 F.Supp. 958 (W.D.Mo.1986), *aff'd*, 829 F.2d 1430 (8th Cir.1987).

Does the cost/benefit analysis of *Torres* suggest that authorization for video surveillance and the application of the particularization and minimization requirements depend upon the seriousness of the crime under investigation and the place of the surveillance? Courts have rejected this view and have not limited court authorized video surveillance to the type of criminal activities investigated in *Torres*. See *United States v. Williams,* 124 F.3d 411, 417 (3d Cir.1997) (stating that video surveillance may be available for all crimes for which wiretapping and bugging is authorized under Title I. Courts have taken a similar view on the Title I reasonableness test that is adopted in video surveillance cases. See *Williams, Id.* at 417, (holding that case law in general Title I cases determined the government's burden in video surveillance cases). So the government is only required to demonstrate that, "normal investigative techniques ... reasonably appear to be unlikely to succeed if tried. *Id.* at 18.

k. *Video Surveillance Under Title I*

Although Judge Posner adopted the particularization requirements of section 2518 of the statute as the standard for determining the constitutionality of video surveillance under the fourth amendment in *Torres*, he did not find that Title I applied to video surveillance by the government. The judicial authority to issue a warrant for such surveillance was found in the federal common law. All of the courts that considered this question prior to 1986 concurred, and construed silent television surveillance as being outside the definition of "aural" acquisition of a wire or oral communication under the statute.

Review the definition of "electronic communication," *supra*. Does Title I now reach surreptitious video surveillance by the government or by individuals? The legislative history suggests that the answer is negative:

> Although this bill does not address questions of the application of [the statutory] standards to video surveillance and only deals with the interception of closed circuit television communications to a limited extent, closed circuit television communications do provide another example of the importance of, and the inter-relationship between, the definitions contained in this legislation. If a person or entity transmits a closed circuit television picture of the meeting using wires, microwaves, or another method of transmission, the transmission itself would be an electronic communication. Interception of the picture at any point without either consent or court order would be a violation of the statute. By contrast, if law enforcement officials were to install their own cameras and create their own closed circuit television picture of the meeting, the capturing of the video

images would not be an interception under the statute because their would be no interception of the contents of an electronic communication. Intercepting the audio portion of the meeting would be an interception of an oral communication and the statute would apply to that portion.

If video surveillance is exempt from the ECPA, what other legal protection for invasions of privacy through video surveillance are available?

Most of the courts that have considered the question have found that the addition of the concept of "electronic communications" in the 1986 Amendments did not extend the statute to surreptitious video surveillance by the government. See *United States v. Mesa–Rincon*, 911 F.2d 1433, 1437 (10th Cir.1990). However, such surveillance is viewed as a fourth amendment search that requires judicial intervention (court order) and probable cause. In addition, the particularization and minimization requirements of Title I have been adopted as the appropriate fourth amendment standard for the reasonableness of video surveillance. The five requirements that emerge from these cases are: (1) probable cause in respect to the person and the criminal offense; (2) particular description in the court order of the place and things that are to be viewed; (3) minimization of the recording activities not related to the crime under investigation; (4) that normal investigative techniques have failed in the sense that they are unlikely to be successful or appear to be too dangerous; (5) that the period of the surveillance be limited to that time necessary to achieve the objective of the search or no longer than thirty days. *Id.*

If the surveillance is with equipment that has both video and audio capabilities, does Title I apply to the audio portion of the video tape? Is the conversation a "wire" or "oral" communication? What is the intercepting device? For one court's answer, see *People v. Teicher*, 52 N.Y.2d 638, 422 N.E.2d 506, 439 N.Y.S.2d 846 (1981). Suppose the police initiate a sting operation and a police officer or informer consents to the surreptitious videotaping of drug use or the offer of a bribe in the police officer or informant's hotel room or home. What issues are raised under Title I? Under the fourth amendment?

For a case raising some of these issues in a bizarre factual setting, see *Commonwealth v. Kean*, 382 Pa.Super. 587, 556 A.2d 374 (1989), *appeal denied*, 525 Pa. 596, 575 A.2d 563 (1990). In *Kean*, the defendants, married and nearly sixty years of age, were prosecuted for sexual activities with two neighbor boys under the age of sixteen. The boys had surreptitiously videotaped (without sound) the sexual intercourse with the wife while the husband observed in the bedroom of the defendants. The video was later given to the police by the mother of one of the juveniles, and subsequently viewed by the police. The police did not obtain a search warrant at any time. The defendants moved to suppress the videotape on the grounds that the taping and subsequent playing of the tape by the police violated the federal and state constitutional proscriptions against unreasonable searches and seizures. What result?

AN ECONOMIC THEORY OF PRIVACY,
RICHARD A. POSNER

Regulation, 19–26 (May/June 1978).

I shall first attempt to develop a simple economic theory of privacy. I shall then argue from this theory that, while personal privacy seems today to be valued more highly than organizational privacy (if one may judge by current legislative trends), a reverse ordering would be more consistent with the economics of the problem.

THEORY

People invariably possess information, including the contents of communications and facts about themselves, that they will incur costs to conceal. Sometimes such information is of value to other people—that is, other people will incur costs to discover it. Thus we have two economic goods, "privacy" and "prying." We could regard them as pure consumption goods, the way turnips or beer are normally regarded in economic analysis, and we would then speak of a "taste" for privacy or for prying. But this would bring the economic analysis to a grinding halt because tastes are unanalyzable from an economic standpoint. An alternative is to regard privacy and prying as intermediate rather than final goods—instrumental rather than final values. Under this approach, people are assumed not to desire or value privacy or prying in themselves but to use these goods as inputs into the production of income or some other broad measure of utility or welfare. This is the approach that I take here; the reader will have to decide whether it captures enough of the relevant reality to be enlightening.

NOT SO IDLE CURIOSITY

Now the demand for private information (viewed, as it is here, as an intermediate good) is readily understandable where the existence of an actual or potential relationship, business or personal, creates opportunities for gain by the demander. These opportunities obviously exist in the case of information sought by the tax collector, fiancé, partner, creditor, competitor, and so on. Less obviously, much of the casual prying (a term not used here with any pejorative connotation) into the private lives of friends and colleagues that is so common a feature of social life is, I believe, motivated—to a greater extent than we usually think—by rational considerations of self-interest. Prying enables one to form a more accurate picture of a friend or colleague, and the knowledge gained is useful in one's social or professional dealings with that friend or colleague. For example, one wants to know in choosing a friend whether he will be discreet or indiscreet, selfish or generous. These qualities are not necessarily apparent on initial acquaintance. Even a pure altruist needs to know the (approximate) wealth of any prospective beneficiary of his altruism in order to be able to gauge the value of a gift or transfer to him.

The other side of the coin is that social dealings, like business dealings, present opportunities for exploitation through misrepresentation. Psychologists and sociologists have pointed out that even in everyday life people try to manipulate other people's opinion of them, using misrepresentation. The strongest defenders of privacy usually define the individual's right to privacy as the right to control the flow of information about him. A seldom-remarked corollary to a right to misrepresent one's character is that others have legitimate interest in unmasking the misrepresentation.

. . .

Who Owns Secrets?

The fact that disclosure of personal information is resisted by (is costly to) the person to whom the information pertains, yet is valuable to others, may seem to argue for giving people property rights in information about themselves and letting them sell those rights freely. The process of voluntary exchange would then ensure that the information was put to its most valuable use. The attractiveness of this solution depends, however, on (1) the nature and source of the information and (2) transaction costs.

The strongest case for property rights in secrets is presented where such rights are necessary in order to encourage investment in the production of socially valuable information. This is the rationale for giving legal protection to the variety of commercial ideas, plans, and information encompassed by the term "trade secret." It also explains why the "shrewd bargainer" is not required to tell the other party to the bargain his true opinion of the values involved. A shrewd bargainer is, in part, one who invests resources in obtaining information about the true values of things. Were he forced to share this information with potential sellers, he would get no return on his investment and the process—basic to a market economy—by which goods are transferred through voluntary exchange into successively more valuable uses would be impaired. This is true even though the lack of candor in the bargaining process deprives it of some of its "voluntary" character.

At some point nondisclosure becomes fraud. One consideration relevant to deciding whether the line has been crossed is whether the information sought to be concealed by one of the transacting parties is a product of significant investment. If not, the social costs of nondisclosure are reduced. This may be decisive, for example, on the question whether the owner of a house should be required to disclose latent (nonobvious) defects to a purchaser. The ownership and maintenance of a house are costly and productive activities. But since knowledge of the house's defects is acquired by the owner costlessly (or nearly so), forcing him to disclose these defects will not reduce his incentive to invest in discovering them.

As examples of cases where transaction-cost considerations argue against assigning a property right to the possessor of a secret, consider (1) whether the Bureau of Census should be required to buy information from the firms or households that it interviews and (2) whether a magazine should be allowed to sell its subscriber list to another magazine without obtaining the subscribers' consent. Requiring the Bureau of the Census to pay (that is, assigning the property right in the information sought to the interviewee) would yield a skewed sample: the poor would be overrepresented, unless the bureau used a differentiated price schedule based on the different costs of disclosure (and hence prices for cooperating) to the people sampled. In the magazine case, the costs of obtaining subscriber approval would be high relative to the value of the list. If, therefore, we are confident that these lists are generally worth more to the purchasers than being shielded from possible unwanted solicitations is worth to the subscribers, we should assign the property right to the magazine, and this is what the law does.

The decision to assign the property right away from the individual is further supported, in both the census and subscription-list cases, by the fact that the costs of disclosure to the individual are low. They are low in the census case because the government takes precautions against disclosure of the information collected to creditors, tax collectors, or others who might have transactions with the individual in which they could use the information to gain an advantage over him. They are low in the subscription-list case because the information about the subscribers that is disclosed to the list purchaser is trivial and cannot be used to impose substantial costs on them.

Even though the type of private information discussed thus far is not in general discreditable to the individual to whom it pertains, we have seen that there may still be strong reasons for assigning the property right away from that individual. Much of the demand for privacy, however, concerns discreditable information—often information concerning past or present criminal activity or moral conduct at variance with a person's professed moral standards—and often the motive for concealment is, as suggested earlier, to mislead others. People also wish to conceal private information that, while not strictly discreditable, would if revealed correct misapprehensions that the individual is trying to exploit—as when a worker conceals a serious health problem from his employer or a prospective husband conceals his sterility from his fiancée. It is not clear why society in these cases should assign the property right in information to the individual to whom it pertains; and under the common law, generally it does not. A separate question, taken up a little later, is whether the decision to assign the property right away from the possessor of guilty secrets implies that any and all methods of uncovering those secrets should be permitted.

An analogy to the world of commerce may clarify why people should not—on economic grounds in any event—have a right to conceal material facts about themselves. We think it wrong (and inefficient) that a seller in hawking his wares should be permitted to make false or incomplete representations as to their quality. But people "sell" themselves as well as their goods. A person professes high standards of behavior in order to induce others to engage in social or business dealings with him from which he derives an advantage, but at the same time conceals some of the facts that the people with whom he deals need in order to form an accurate picture of his character. There are practical reasons for not imposing a general legal duty of full and frank disclosure of one's material personal shortcomings—a duty not to be a hypocrite. But each of us should be allowed to protect ourselves from disadvantageous transactions by ferreting out concealed facts about other individuals that are material to their implicit or explicit self-representations.

It is no answer that, in Brandeis's phrase, people have "the right to be let alone." Few people want to be let alone. They want to manipulate the world around them by selective disclosure of facts about themselves. Why should others be asked to take their self-serving claims at face value and prevented from obtaining the information necessary to verify or disprove these claims?

Some private information that people desire to conceal is not discreditable. In our culture, for example, most people do not like to be seen naked, quite apart from any discreditable fact that such observation might reveal. Since this reticence, unlike concealment of discreditable information, is not a source of social costs and since transaction costs are low, there is an economic case for assigning the property right in this area of private information to the individual; and this is what the common law does. I do not think, however, that many people have a general reticence that makes them wish to conceal nondiscrediting personal information. Anyone who has sat next to a stranger on an airplane or a ski lift knows the delight that some people take in talking about themselves to complete strangers. Reticence appears when one is speaking to people—friends, family, acquaintances, business associates—who might use information about him to gain an advantage in business or social transactions with him. Reticence is generally a means rather than an end.

The reluctance of many people to reveal their income is sometimes offered as an example of a desire for privacy that cannot be explained in purely instrumental terms. But I suggest that people conceal an unexpectedly low income because being thought to have a high income has value in credit markets and elsewhere, and they conceal an unexpectedly high income in order to (1) avoid the attention of tax collectors, kidnappers, and thieves, (2) fend off solicitations from charities and family members, and (3) preserve a reputation of generosity that would be shattered if the precise fraction of their income that was being given away were known. Points (1) and (2) may explain anonymous gifts to charity.

Prying, Eavesdropping, and Formality

To the extent that personal information is concealed in order to mislead, the case for giving it legal protection is, I have argued, weak. Protection would simply increase transaction costs, much as if we permitted fraud in the sale of goods. However, it is also necessary to consider the means by which personal information is obtained. Prying by means of casual interrogation of acquaintances of the object of the prying must be distinguished from eavesdropping (electronically or otherwise) on a person's conversations. A in conversation with B disparages C. If C has a right to hear this conversation, A, in choosing the words he uses to B, will have to consider the possible reactions of C. Conversation will be more costly because of the external effects and this will result in less— and less effective—communication. After people adjust to this new world of public conversation, even the Cs of the world will cease to derive much benefit in the way of greater information from conversational publicity: people will be more guarded in their speech. The principal effect of publicity will be to make conversation more formal and communication less effective rather than to increase the knowledge of interested third parties.

Stated differently, the costs of defamatory utterances and hence the cost-justified level of expenditures on avoiding defamation are greater the more publicity given the utterance. If every conversation were public, the time and other resources devoted to ensuring that one's speech was free from false or unintended slanders would rise. The additional costs are avoided by the simple and inexpensive expedient of permitting conversations to be private.

It is relevant to observe that language becomes less formal as society evolves. The languages of primitive people are more elaborate, more ceremonious, and more courteous than that of twentieth-century Americans. One reason may be that primitive people have little privacy. There are relatively few private conversations because third parties are normally present and the effects of the conversation on them must be taken into account. Even today, one observes that people speak more formally the greater the number of people present. The rise of privacy has facilitated private conversation and thereby enabled us to economize on communication—to speak with a brevity and informality apparently rare among primitive peoples. This valuable economy of communication would be undermined by allowing eavesdropping.

In some cases, to be sure, communication is not related to socially productive activity. Communication among criminal conspirators is an example. In these cases—where limited eavesdropping is indeed permitted—the effect of eavesdropping in reducing communication is not an objection to, but an advantage of, the eavesdropping.

The analysis here can readily be extended to efforts to obtain people's notes, letters, and other private papers; communication would be inhibited by such efforts. A more complex question is presented by photographic surveillance—for example, of the interior of a person's home. Privacy enables a person to dress and otherwise disport himself in his home without regard to the effect on third parties. This economizing property would be lost if the interior of the home were in the public domain. People dress not merely because of the effect on others but also because of the reticence, noted earlier, concerning nudity and other sensitive states. This is another reason for giving people a privacy right with regard to the places in which these sensitive states occur.

ENDS AND MEANS

The two main strands of my argument—relating to personal facts and to communications, respectively—can be joined by remarking the difference in this context between ends and means. With regard to ends, there is a prima facie case for assigning the property right in a secret that is a by-product of socially productive activity to the individual if its compelled disclosure would impair the incentives to engage in that activity; but there is a prima facie case for assigning the property right away from the individual if secrecy would reduce the social product by misleading others. However, the fact that under this analysis most facts about people belong in the public domain does not imply that intrusion on private communications should generally be permitted, given the effects of such intrusions on the costs of legitimate communications.

Admittedly, the suggested dichotomy between facts and communications is too stark. If you are allowed to interrogate my acquaintances about my income, I may take steps to conceal it that are analogous to the increased formality of conversation that would ensue from abolition of the right to conversational privacy, and the costs of these steps are a social loss. The difference is one of degree. Because eavesdropping and related modes of intrusive surveillance are such effective ways of eliciting private information and are at the same time relatively easy to thwart, we can expect that evasive maneuvers, costly in the aggregate, would be undertaken if conversational privacy were compromised. It is more difficult to imagine people taking effective measures against casual prying. An individual is unlikely to alter his income or style of living drastically in order to better conceal his income or private information from casual or journalistic inquiry. (Howard Hughes was a notable exception to this generalization.)

We have now sketched the essential elements of an economically based legal right of privacy: (1) Trade and business secrets by which businessmen exploit their superior knowledge or skills would be protected. (The same principle would be applied to the personal level and would thus, for example, entitle the social host or hostess to conceal the recipe of a successful dinner.) (2) Facts about people would generally not be protected. My ill health, evil temper, even my income would not be facts over which I had property rights, though I might be able to prevent their discovery by methods unduly intrusive under the third category. (3) Eavesdropping and other forms of intrusive surveillance would be limited (so far as possible) to the discovery of illegal activities.

APPLICATION

To what extent is the economic theory developed above reflected in public policy? To answer this question, it is necessary to distinguish sharply between common law and statutory responses to the privacy question.

THE COMMON LAW

The term common law refers to the body of legal principles evolved by English and American appellate judges in the decision of private suits over a period of hundreds of years. I believe, and have argued in greater detail elsewhere, that the common law of privacy is strongly stamped by the economics principles (though nowhere explicitly recognized by the judges) developed in this article. That law contains the precise elements that an economically based right of privacy would include. Trade secrets and commercial privacy generally are well protected. It has been said by one court: "almost any knowledge or information used in the conduct of one's business may be held by its possessor secret." In another well-known case, aerial photography of a competitor's plant under construction was held to be unlawful, and the court used the term "commercial privacy" to describe the interest it was protecting.

An analogy in the personal area is the common law principle that a person's name or photograph may not be used in advertising without his consent. The effect is to create a property right which ensures that a person's name or likeness (O.J. Simpson's, for example) will be allocated to the advertising use in which it is most valuable. Yet, consistent with the economics of the problem, individuals have in general no right in common law to conceal discrediting information about themselves. But, again consistent with the economics of the problem, they do have a right to prevent eavesdropping, photographic surveillance of the interior of a home, the ransacking of private records to discover information about an individual, and similarly intrusive methods of penetrating the wall of privacy that people build about themselves. The distinction is illustrated by Ralph Nader's famous suit against General Motors. The court affirmed General Motors' right to have Nader followed about, to question his acquaintances, and, in short, to ferret out personal information about Nader that the company might have used to undermine his public credibility. Yet I would expect a court to enjoin any attempt through such methods to find out what Nader was about to say on some subject in order to be able to plagiarize his ideas.

When, however, we compare the implications of the economic analysis not with the common law relating to privacy but with recent legislation in the privacy area, we are conscious not of broad concordance but of jarring incongruity. As noted, from the economic standpoint, private business information should in general be accorded greater legal protection than personal information. Secrecy is an important method of appropriating social benefits to the entrepreneur who creates them, while in private life it is more likely simply to conceal legitimately discrediting or deceiving facts. Communications within organizations whether public or private, should receive the same protection as communications among individuals, for in either case the effect of publicity would be to encumber and retard communication.

THE TREND IN LEGISLATION

But in fact the legislative trend is toward giving individuals more and more privacy protection with respect to facts and communications, and business firms and other organizations (including government agencies, universities, and hospitals) less and less. The Freedom of Information Act, sunshine laws opening the deliberations of administrative agencies to the public and the erosion of effective sanctions against breach of government confidences have greatly reduced the privacy of communications within the government. Similar forces are at work in private institutions such as business firms and private universities (note, for example, the Buckley Amendment and the opening of faculty meetings to student observers). Increasingly, moreover, the facts about an individual—arrest record, health, credit-worthiness, marital status, sexual proclivities—are secured from involuntary disclosure, while the facts about business corporations are thrust into public view by the expansive disclosure requirements of the federal securities laws (to the point where some firms are "going private" in order to secure greater confidentiality for their plans and operations), the civil rights laws, "line of business" reporting, and other regulations. A related trend is the erosion of the privacy of government officials through increasingly stringent ethical standards requiring disclosure of income.

The trend toward elevating personal and downgrading organizational privacy is mysterious to the economist (as are other recent trends in public regulation). To repeat, the economic case for privacy of communications seems unrelated to the nature of the communicator, whether a private individual or the employee of a university, corporation, or government agency, while so far as facts about people or organizations are concerned, the case for protecting business privacy is stronger, in general, than that for protecting individual privacy.

. . .

Conclusion

Discussions of the privacy question have contained a high degree of cant, sloganeering, emotion, and loose thinking. A fresh perspective on the question is offered by economic analysis, and by a close examination of the common law principles that have evolved under the influence (perhaps unconsciously) of economic perceptions. In the perspective offered by economics and by the common law, the recent legislative emphasis on favoring individual and denigrating corporate and organizational privacy stands revealed as still another example of perverse government regulation of social and economic life.

Note on Posner's Economic Theory of Privacy

Posner's economic theory presumes that privacy is not something that is desired for its own sake. Privacy is valued as a means to produce income or some other benefit. He invites the reader to decide whether his economic theory of privacy "captures enough of the relevant reality to be enlightening." Consider the "relevant reality" to be the law of informational privacy as reflected in the court decisions, legislation and agency regulations that are presented in these materials. Posner suggests that the economic model of informational privacy would not assign the property claim of discrediting personal information to the subject of the information. Under this view a person has no significant privacy claims in respect to discrediting information about them. Does this contention fit the law of informational privacy? Posner claims that the common law does not generally protect privacy in respect to discrediting information. Do you agree? Does the statutory protection for privacy that is emphasized in the chapter on computers and privacy (Chapter IV) fit Posner's view of diminished legal protection for discrediting information?

(1) Electronic Surveillance and Posner's Economic Theory

Posner argues for a right to privacy in conversations even though discrediting information may be communicated. This is because there is a benefit to protecting the privacy of conversations—privacy is an incentive to produce information through one person talking to another. Posner's argument relies heavily upon a distinction between "facts" and "communications." A party has a primary claim to relevant discrediting "facts" about a person but not to "communications" that include relevant discrediting facts about that person. This is because electronic surveillance is the primary means of acquiring information that is part of the communications of a person and the cost of inhibiting the activity of communication by electronic surveillance would be excessive. The general practice of electronic surveillance would make communications public and therefore place undue costs on legitimate conversations and effective communications. One of the consequences of Posner's view is to take much of the personal information that is contained in records out of privacy protection since the acquiring of information from records does not involve electronic surveillance of conversations. Are you persuaded by Posner's claim that the means for acquiring facts about a person which are in the possession of others—such as informal questioning of associates—do not impose excessive social costs? Is Posner's distinction between "facts" and "communications" useful? If A tells B that "A makes $300,000 a year," is the $300,000 salary a "fact" about A? Is a statement that A's salary is $300,000 less of a "fact" about A because B tells C?

Consider Judge Posner's analysis of the reasonableness of a search in *Torres* and compare it with his analysis of the right to conversational privacy in the excerpt from his article. Is the analysis in *Torres* an example of Posner's economic theory of privacy at work? Does Posner view the fourth amendment as implicitly incorporating an economic theory of the right to privacy? Is such a view warranted? If Posner is interpreting the fourth amendment from the vantage point of his economic theory of privacy, is it incumbent on him to say so?

The economic theory that is propounded by Judge Posner is the subject of significant commentary, some of which is critical. See Posner, *Utilitarianism, Economics & Legal Theory*, 8 J. of Legal Studies, 103 (1979); Posner, *The Right of Privacy*, 12 Ga. L. Rev., 393–554 (1978).

(2) Contractarian Theories of the Right of Privacy

Secrets are a familiar feature of social life. The rules of social etiquette and ethics regulate secrecy, prescribing when it is wrongful to keep information to oneself and when it is wrongful to tell what one knows.

The law also regulates secrecy. Like etiquette and ethics, the law sanctions wrongful concealment and disclosure to deter certain harms, protect certain confidential relations, and preserve certain forms of intimacy and dignity. The evidentiary privileges, the statutes governing sealed criminal and adoption records, in camera judicial proceedings, privacy exemptions to freedom of information laws, executive privileges, criminal surveillance and covert domestic surveillance are examples of lawful secrecy. In addition, the common law of privacy, trade secrets and fraud establish legal ground rules for keeping and telling secrets.

It is not always clear how courts justify common law liability for keeping or failing to keep information secret. To make sense of the cases, several scholars have attempted to identify implicit general norms in the jurisprudence of laws governing privacy-as-secrecy.

In *The Economics of Justice* (1981) and related articles, Judge Richard Posner argued that the underlying rationale of the common law of secrecy is an economic one: courts decide the cases in ways that respect efficient economic actors' rational demands for concealment and disclosure. Professor Kim Lane Scheppele's *Legal Secrets* (1988) challenged the economic account from a social contractarian perspective, influenced by John Rawls' A Theory of Justice (1971). She maintained that, although law and economics may successfully explain individual cases, it does not provide an adequate account of the central features of the law of privacy and secrecy.

Based on her analysis of a diverse range of cases, Scheppele attempted to show that law and economics cannot explain why (a) individuals are typically allowed to withhold information only if it is not relevant to others' interest; (b) the law typically encourages minimal disclosure of personal information; and (c) the law of trade secrets primarily penalizes breaches of confidence. Professor Scheppele's alternative to the efficiency principle is an equality principle illuminable through Rawlsian social contract theory.

Rawls identified justice as the fairness that comes about when individuals are only subject to those public constraints that they could agree to as rational, self-interested individuals behind a "veil of ignorance" about their own status or resources. Rawls maintained that such hypothetical individuals would choose egalitarian principles mandating for all, first, the most extensive liberty possible consistent with like liberty for others; and, second, permitting only arbitrary inequalities that benefit the least advantaged members of society.

In the spirit of Rawlsian equality, Scheppele concluded that courts decide secrecy cases in ways "that ensure that actors have equal access to information when that information would be used strategically to influence another person." Scheppele at 258. The law does not require all and only the disclosures that efficiency would require, she claimed; instead it characteristically requires those that reciprocal respect for others as equals would require. The common law of fraud, for example, penalizes failure to disclose if the other party to a transaction did not have the same probability of locating strategic information with the same level of effort. Likewise, the privacy torts grant "special attention to the spread of information beyond the bounds necessary to ensure that social actors have equal access to relevant and necessary information." Scheppele at 258.

Do the cases covered thus far in these materials seem to bear out Scheppele's theory? Posner's? How likely is it that one principle—whether an efficiency principle or an equality principle—can account for the holdings of all of the intentional concealment and disclosure cases?

In *Toleration and the Constitution* (1986), David A.J. Richards sets out a comprehensive contractarian theory of a constitutional privacy right. Despite Richards' and Scheppele's efforts to locate the normative basis of privacy rights in the social contract ideal, it should be observed that the early European social contract theorists, including Thomas Hobbes and John Locke, did not expressly identify a "right of privacy" as among those parties to the social contract would seek to secure.

l. *Pen Registers, Billing Records and Other Call Tracing Devices*

Interception requires that the conversation be overheard or recorded by means that are defined in Section 2510(5), namely, by "electronic, mechanical, or other devices." Thus, various forms of electronic surveillance may not come within Title I because of the method of electronic surveillance that is utilized. In United States v. New York Tel. Co., 434 U.S. 159 (1977), the Supreme Court held that the use of pen registers to record the date, time and numbers that were dialed on a telephone did not come within the meaning of Title I because such call tracing devices did not constitute an interception within Section 2510(4),(5), nor did they involve the "acquisition of the contents" of a wire communication within paragraph 8 of Section 2510.

All of the Courts of Appeals that had considered the pen registration issue had reached the conclusion that pen registrations are not within the scope of Title I. See *United States v. Illinois Bell Tel. Co.*, 531 F.2d 809 (7th Cir.1976); *United States v. Southwestern Bell Tel. Co.*, 546 F.2d 243 (8th Cir.1976), *cert. denied*, 434 U.S. 1008 (1978); *Michigan Bell Tel. Co. v. United States*, 565 F.2d 385 (6th Cir.1977); *Hodge v. Mountain States Tel. & Tel. Co.*, 555 F.2d 254 (9th Cir.1977); *United States v. Clegg*, 509 F.2d 605 (5th Cir.1975). In addition, four justices in dictum reached this conclusion in *United States v. Giordano*, 416 U.S. 505, 553–54 (1974) (decided on other grounds).

Courts have construed Title I similarly in respect to toll billing records. Such records reveal the numbers that have been called from a telephone. Acquiring this information is not viewed as the acquisition of the contents of a conversation for purposes of Title I. Therefore, there is no "interception" and no "acquisition of the contents" of a wire communication under Title I.

Recall that acquisition of information by the government through the use of a pen register does not constitute a fourth amendment search. See *Smith v. Maryland, supra* at page 87, and the discussion following the case. Toll records are viewed similarly under the federal constitution. See, *United States v. Fithian*, 452 F.2d 505, 506 (9th Cir.1971); *Reporters Comm. for Freedom of the Press v. American Tel. & Tel. Co.*, 593 F.2d 1030, 1043 (D.C.Cir.1978), *cert. denied*, 440 U.S. 949 (1979); *United States v. Baxter*, 492 F.2d 150, 167 (9th Cir.1973), *cert. denied*, 416 U.S. 940 (1974); *Di Piazza v. United States*, 415 F.2d 99, 103–04 (6th Cir.1969), *cert. denied*, 402 U.S. 949 (1971); *Szczuka v. Bellsouth Mobility, Inc.*, 189 Ga.App. 370, 375 S.E.2d 667 (1988). Governmental acquisition of toll records and pen registers without a court order has been found to violate some state constitutions. This development is examined in Chapter II. See the discussion in the notes following *State v. Hunt*, 91 N.J. 338, 450 A.2d 952 (1982), *supra*. See also *Commonwealth v. Melilli*, 521 Pa. 405, 555 A.2d 1254 (1989) (holding Pennsylvania Constitution extends to pen registers).

The interpretation of the statute to exclude data other than what is found in the contents of the conversation is an example of the second class status of transactional information or "communications attributes" in data privacy law. See discussion following *Smith v. Maryland* in Chapter Two.

The 1986 Amendments to the statute regulate the use of pen registers and trap and trace devices. These regulations are found in Title III of the ECPA, sections 3121–3126. The ECPA adopts an "accountability model" that relies on reporting of government use as the major vehicle for supervising this form of government surveillance. Court approval upon a proper application is required for a pen register or trap and trace device. The attorney or investigator must certify that the information is likely to be relevant to an ongoing criminal investigation and applications must be renewed after sixty days. The issuance of the order does not require an independent evaluation of the relevance of the information sought to be adduced by the pen register. Section 3123 states that the court "shall" enter an ex parte order if the court finds the requesting officer has "certified to the court" that the information obtained is likely to be relevant to an ongoing investigation. The court's role in issuing such orders is ministerial. Section 3125 requires the Attorney General to annually report to Congress on the number of pen register orders and orders for trap and trace devices that have been applied for by agencies of the Department of Justice. A person who knowingly violates section 3121 may be fined and/or imprisoned for less than one year. However, the right to suppress evidence procured in violation of Title III of the ECPA is not provided for in the statute, nor is a cause of action for damages available under Title III. Does the accountability model provide adequate legal protection for privacy?

m. Caller Identification and Other Advanced Call Management Services

Advancement in telephone switching technology has made it possible for telephone companies to provide the subscriber with a number of new services. This technology is called Custom Local Area Switching Service (CLASS). These call management services include: (1) call blocking—subscriber may screen calls by submitting a list of numbers and when calls come from these numbers the customer's phone will not ring; (2) priority call—the customer's phone has a distinct ring when calls come from a list of priority numbers; (3) call tracing—providing for the tracing of numbers by a customer after the customer has sent a printout to the telephone company of the calling and called number and the time of the call.

The most controversial of these new services is caller identification, where the subscriber can see the telephone number of the calling party displayed each time the phone rings. Both proponents and opponents of caller identification defend their positions in the name of privacy. Those who argue in favor of caller identification claim that it protects personal privacy by giving the recipient of the call the power to avoid harassing and obnoxious phone calls by screening them. Those who oppose the service argue that the unconsented-to dissemination of the phone number invades the privacy of the caller by depriving the caller of the ability to control the disclosure of personal information. Unlimited caller identification also would invade privacy through the disclosure of unpublished telephone numbers. Opponents also support their position on consequential grounds. They claim that caller identification will chill communications and seriously impede the acquiring of information in hotlines set up to deal with social problems such as child abuse and drug and alcohol abuse.

The caller identification debate raises a number of interesting questions. To what extent does caller identification protect the privacy of the recipient of the call? The privacy interest of the recipient of obnoxious or harassing phone calls is the interest in mental repose. Is this privacy interest weaker than an informational privacy interest? Also consider the distinction made by the *Nader* court, *infra*, Chapter Two, that tort privacy rights were limited to informational privacy interests and that the interest in preventing harassing phone calls and preserving mental equanimity was appropriately left to other tort remedies such as the tort of intentional infliction of emotional distress. Assuming that it is useful to think of the prevention of harassing and obnoxious phone calls as protecting privacy, to what extent does caller identification eliminate such calls? Once the use of the service becomes commonplace and well-known, would the caller avoid the risk of identification by using a public telephone?

Several serious questions are also raised concerning the extent to which there is a meaningful invasion of privacy by the publication of the caller's telephone number. To what extent does disclosing the number of a phone from which a call was made constitute an invasion of the privacy of the caller? Is the phone number from which you call "personal" or "intimate" information?

Consider Justice Stewart's comments in his dissenting opinion in *Smith v. Maryland* (the pen register case):

> Most private telephone subscribers may have their own numbers listed in a publicly distributed directory, but I doubt that there are any who would be happy to have broadcast to the world a list of the local or long distance numbers they have called. This is not because such a list might in some sense be incriminating, but because it easily could reveal the identities of the persons and the places called, and thus reveal the most intimate details of a person's life.

442 U.S. 735, 748 (1979).

Justice Stewart's view—that the telephone numbers that are called could reveal the identity of the persons and places called—seems unassailable in view of the fact that the objective of pen registers as an investigative tool is to identify the persons that the subject calls on her telephone. The potential for disclosing "intimate details" with a pen register results from the inference that may be drawn from knowledge of the identity of the caller and callee. Pen registers, unlike billing records, do not indicate whether the call was actually completed or the length and time of a conversation if the call was completed. In appropriate circumstances the existence of personal or political associations could be revealed from information acquired from a pen register. Numerous phone calls to the home of an employee during non-working hours might indicate the existence of an extra-marital relationship. Caller identification reveals less information than a pen register or billing records. Only the caller's identity is disclosed. Are "intimate details" of the caller's life likely to be discovered from the fact that a call was made to someone?

Professor Smith, in a leading article on informational privacy and caller identification, argues that the privacy interest in nondisclosure is relatively moderate. Smith views intimate facts as implicating privacy values because of the potential of such facts to have harmful or embarrassing consequences to the subject. The consequential features of the information that is revealed in caller identification do implicate privacy by raising the possibility that embarrassing facts about the caller will be revealed. However, Smith concludes that the small number of such calls and the options available to the caller to maintain anonymity—such as use of a telephone other than the caller's—greatly reduce the significance of the privacy interest of the caller. The other consequential feature of caller identification, the possibility of annoying or harassing phone calls, is not viewed as raising significant privacy concerns. Glenn Chatmas Smith, *We've Got Your Number! (Is it Constitutional to Give it Out?): Caller Identification Technology and the Right to Informational Privacy*, 37 U.C.L.A. L. Rev. 145, 213–15 (1989).

One way to protect the privacy interest of the caller is to provide notification of the caller identification service of the dialed number. If the caller knows that the phone she has called has caller identification, and still calls the phone, then the caller has chosen to disclose the telephone number from which the call is made. Under these circumstances there is a consensual disclosure of the information by the caller and no significant privacy problem. Would notifying the caller of the service at a particular telephone be satisfactory to the telephone company or to the subscriber of the service? What other potential invasion of informational privacy do caller identification kinds of telephone services represent?

Presumably, whatever information the telephone company could connect up with the telephone number could also be transmitted to the recipient of the call. Therefore, if the telephone company took the social security number of the lessee of the particular phone and found whatever information it could about that person through the use of the social security number and in public records, all of that information could be transmitted to the recipient of a call from that particular phone. Would there be a point where the risk to the caller from a particular phone of loss of informational privacy would be so great that the telephone company would lose customers because they would not wish to be part of this informational sharing system?

(1) The Current Legal Status of Caller Identification Services

Caller identification does not constitute an interception of a wire communication under Title I. This is because the content of the conversation is not acquired by the recipient of caller identification. The recipient receives *transactional data*—the phone number from which the call was made—and under the pen register cases is not a wire communication under Title I, see *United States v. New York Tel. Co.*, 434 U.S. 159, (1977).

Caller identification services are currently "Trap and Trace" devices under federal and state electronic eavesdropping statutes. The federal statute, Title III, defines a trap and trace device as "a device which captures the incoming electronic or other impulses which identifies the originating number of an instrument or device from which a wire or electronic communication was transmitted." 18 U.S.C.A. § 3124(b).

Title III prohibits the use of a trap and trace device without a court order but excepts from the court order requirement the use of a trap and trace devise, "when the consent of the user of that service has been obtained," (18 U.S.C.A. § 3122). For a time, two-party consent was required in Pennsylvania for caller ID because the Pennsylvania Electronic Eavesdropping Statute required the consent of both parties for the use of a trap and trace device in most circumstances. See, *Barasch v. Penna. Public Utility Commission*, 605 A.2d 1198 (Pa.1992) The Pennsylvania statute was amended to allow caller ID services.

Caller identification and other advanced call management services are currently available in every state. See Laura V. Eng, *Blocking Preemption: Convergence, Privacy and the FCC's Misguided Regulation of Caller ID*, 14 Cardozo Arts & Ent. L.J. 407 (1996).

Concerns about protecting the privacy of the caller have prompted proposals for federal legislation that would allow providers to make caller identification service available if the caller had the choice of blocking receipt of his or her telephone number. See the Telephone Privacy Act of 1991, S.652, 102d Cong. First Session, reprinted at 137 "Cong. Rec. S.3284" daily edition March 13, 1991, amending federal law to provide for caller identification services if they provide for blocking by the caller without charge. Providing the caller with the right to block the telephone number from being received by the recipient is consistent with providing privacy protection for both the caller and the recipient of the call. The caller controls whether the telephone from whom they are calling is disclosed and the recipient has control over whether to receive the call without the caller identification information. The personal information of the caller is protected by requiring that the caller consent to its disclosure and the interest in the recipient in mental anonymity and controlling who has access of them through a phone call is provided the recipient by simply not receiving the call.

There are two forms of blocking options available in a caller identification situation. "Per-call" blocking leaves the responsibility on the caller to block each individual call before calling (this is typically done with a star number). "Per-line" blocking presumes that calls are from a private line and not subject to caller identification unless the caller unblocks the call. Per-call presumes disclosure of the identity of the caller's number unless the caller blocks; per-line presumes non-disclosure unless the caller unblocks.

The Federal Communication Commission has adopted a rule that would only allow telephone common carriers to provide per-call blocking for interstate calls. See, Federal Communication Commission, § 64, 1601 and 1602.

n. *Electronic Tracking Devices: Beepers*

Transmitting devices attached to moving vehicles for the purpose of physically surveying particular suspects do not intercept the contents of communications within the ECPA. See *United States v. Moore*, 562 F.2d 106, 110 (1st Cir.1977), *cert. denied sub nom. Bobisink v. United States*, 435 U.S. 926 (1978). Such mobile tracking devices, however, may constitute a search within the meaning of the fourth amendment and be subject to the warrant requirement.

The Supreme Court has indicated that applicability of the warrant requirement of the fourth amendment would turn on whether the tracking device (beeper) was placed so that it tracked the public movements of the subject or was placed so as to track movement in areas such as a house wherein the subject has a legitimate expectation of privacy.

Compare *United States v. Knotts*, 460 U.S. 276 (1983) (beeper placed in container that was being transported in vehicle not subject to fourth amendment) with *United States v. Karo*, 468 U.S. 705 (1984) (warrant required for beeper placed inside house of subject). The full extent of constitutional restrictions on governmental use of beepers is beyond the scope of these materials. The question of whether the placement and monitoring of the beepers invades the subject's legitimate expectation of privacy and therefore constitutes a search turns on an examination of the circumstances of each case. The 1986 Amendments to the statute do not extend the reach of the act to beepers. Therefore, regulation occurs primarily through judicial construction of the fourth amendment. For a general discussion of the constitutional issues, see J. Carr, *The Law of Electronic Surveillance*, Section 3.2(c)(1) at 3–25 (Release #24, 3/99).

o. *Paging Devices*

LEGISLATIVE HISTORY: EXCERPT FROM REPORT OF THE COMMITTEE ON THE JUDICIARY ON THE ELECTRONIC COMMUNICATIONS PRIVACY ACT OF 1986, H.R. Rep. No. 647, 99th Cong., 2d Sess., 24–25 (1986)

An increasingly important adjunct to the telecommunications systems is the paging system. Radio paging is essentially a one-way message service. Recent estimates indicate that there are over 2.5 million pagers in operation; these numbers are expected to double within five years.

There are three basic types of paging devices; tone-only, digital, and voice. In a tone-only pager system an outside party places a telephone call to the paging service which in turn sends a signal to the user indicating that the user has a telephone call. The user must then call back a specific phone number (often an answering service). The digital or display pager permits the user to receive a digital or alphanumeric message on a display screen. A voice pager permits a person who wishes to communicate with the user to leave a recorded message which is then transmitted to the user. The user actually hears the voice message.

The only reported case on this technology, Dorsey v. State, involves a voice pager. In the Dorsey case, the court upheld the use of a scanner by the police to intercept voice messages transmitted over a paging system to an alleged drug dealer. The court held that these messages are neither wire nor oral communications and, therefore, such interceptions are lawful.

According to the United States Department of Justice, however, the three types of paging devices require different levels of statutory protection. The Department reasons that "tone only" pagers carry no reasonable expectation of privacy and therefore no court order is required for a government official to intercept or monitor such signals. The interception of "display pagers" is, according to the Department of Justice, also not within the gambit of Title III; the Department concedes, however, that because use of such devices encompasses a reasonable expectation of privacy, governmental interception of messages over such a system requires use of a search warrant under the Fourth Amendment. Finally, the Department of Justice concludes that a "voice pager" is simply the continuation of an original wire communication, and therefore a Title III court order is required.

p.   *Data Transmissions and Electronic Mail*

Electronic mail was one of the new technologies that Congress was concerned about in the enactment of the ECPA. Consider the following discussion of electronic mail from the legislative history:

LEGISLATIVE HISTORY: EXCERPT FROM REPORT OF THE COMMITTEE ON THE JUDICIARY ON THE ELECTRONIC COMMUNICATIONS PRIVACY ACT OF 1986, H.R. Rep. No. 647, 99th Cong., 2d Sess., 21–23 (1986)

DATA TRANSMISSIONS AND ELECTRONIC MAIL

When Congress enacted the Wiretap Act it specifically excluded the transmission of data from protection against private and governmental interceptions. In the intervening years, data transmission and computer systems have become a pervasive part of the business and home environments.

Computer and telephone technologies have merged; the resulting new communication techniques utilize computer terminals and video display screens and frequently transmit data over telephone lines.

The array of services include electronic bulletin boards, electronic data bases, videotext services, and remote computing. Some of these new services permit an individual to use a keyboard and telephone to transmit electronic messages and data and to receive interactive services featuring banking and other financial services, shopping, news, messages, and education. Many of these services also record the nature of the transactions engaged in by the user. Thus, the new technologies represent both an explosion in communication opportunities as well as surveillance possibilities.

One of the most popular new computer services is electronic mail, a service which combines features of the telephone and regular first class mail. Electronic mail can include telex, teletex, facsimile, voice mail and mixed systems that electronically transmit and store messages. Many e-mail users have found it a useful substitute for telephone calls, while others utilize it instead of the government postal service.

Electronic mail differs from regular mail in three ways. First, e-mail is provided by private parties and thus not subject to governmental control or regulation under the postal laws. Second, it is interactive in nature and can involve virtually instantaneous "conversations" more like a telephone call than mail. Finally, e-mail is different from regular mail because the electronic communication provider as part of the service may technically have access to the contents of the message and may retain copies of transmissions.

Any discussion of the application of current law governing interception of e-mail or the use of e-mail surveillance begins with the Fourth Amendment, which protects our reasonable expectation of privacy. There are no reported cases governing the acquisition of e-mail by the government, so an application of the Fourth Amendment to the interception of e-mail is speculative. It appears likely, however, that the courts would find that the parties to an e-mail transmission have a "reasonable expectation of privacy" and that a warrant of some kind is required.

As for statutory protection, while there may be some limits on government access to e-mail messages from an e-mail provider, there do not appear to be any [current] federal statutes which directly address this issue. Title III would not apply, since it is limited to the "aural acquisition" of the contents of a communication, and e-mail usually does not involve the transmission of audible sound. The Communications Act might have some limited application, excepting law enforcement officials. The Foreign Intelligence Surveillance Act, however, could be read to require federal law enforcement officials to obtain a court order before engaging in "electronic surveillance" that acquires the contents of e-mail communications. These criminal prohibitions do not apply to private persons.

(1) Current Status of Electronic Mail Under the ECPA

The Internet consists of a global system of linked computers. In the litigation challenging the federal Communication Decency Act, the federal district court and the Supreme Court took judicial notice of the explosion in the growth of the Internet. See *ACLU v. Reno*, 521 U.S. 844 (1997). There were nearly nine and one-half million computers linked in the Internet system and the Court estimated that there were over 40 million users. The expected use of the Internet by the end of the century is 200 million users.

A primary use of the Internet for businesses is for e-mail. Several current studies demonstrate how common employer monitoring of employee e-mail is. A 1993 survey of 301 businesses conducted by *MacWorld* magazine found that approximately 22% of participants have monitored employee e-mail, voice mail or computer files. Charles Piller, *Bosses With X-Ray Eyes*, MacWorld, Jul. 1993, at 118. A more recent study conducted in 1997 by the American Management Association reports an even higher percentage. The study of 906 companies found that approximately 35% of companies electronically monitor their employees, with 14.9% reporting that they store or review e-mail and 5.2% reporting that they review voice mail messages. Stuart Silverstein, *Careful—The Cubicles Have Ears,* L.A. Times, May 23, 1997, at D1. A similar 1998 survey, also conducted by the American Management Association, found that the percentage of employers electronically monitoring their employees jumped to 43%, with the number of participants reviewing e-mail rising to 20% and those reviewing voice mail messages remaining at approximately 5%. Michael Higgins, *High Tech, Low Privacy,* 85 A.B.A. J., May 1999 at 52. In 1999, the share of companies checking e-mail rose to 27%, with overall monitoring reported at 45%. According to the 1999 American Management Association survey, the three industries in which electronic monitoring is most common are the financial sector (68%), business and professional service providers (51%), and wholesalers and retailers (47%). American Management Association Press Release, Apr. 14, 1999.

While it is apparent that increased use of e-mail through the Internet and monitoring of e-mail by employers is occurring, case law on employer access to e-mail is sparse and unclear. Practices involving e-mail access are fraught with difficult legal issues.

(2) Government Access to E–Mail

Steve Jackson Games v. United States Secret Service, 36 F.3d 457 (5th Cir.1994), that follows this introductory text is currently the leading case on the status of e-mail under the ECPA, In examining *Steve Jackson Games*, it is important to consider how the analysis of the case affects access to stored voice mail. *Steve Jackson Games* also requires an examination of the language of Title II after the enactment of the ECPA (§§ 2701–2711). Review the overall structure and language of §§ 2701–2711 in Chapter Eight before reading the *Steve Jackson Games* case. *Steve Jackson Games* holds that the government access of stored e-mail violated § 2701 of Title II; but government access did not violate § 2511 of Title I (prohibiting interception of electronic communications).

STEVE JACKSON GAMES v. UNITED STATES SECRET SERVICE
36 F.3d 457 (5th Cir.1994).

BARKSDALE, J.

[The plaintiff, Steve Jackson Games, Inc. (SJG), publishes books, magazines, role-playing games, and related products. SJG began operating an electronic bulletin board in the mid–1980s called "Illuminati" (BBS), from one of their computers. The BBS offered customers the ability to send and receive private e-mail which was stored on the BBS computer's hard disk drive temporarily until the addressees called the BBS and read their mail. After reading their e-mail, recipients could choose to store it on a hard drive or delete it. In October of 1988, Henry Kluepfel, Director of Network Security Technology (an affiliate Bell Company), began investigating the unauthorized duplication of a computerized text file, containing information about Bell's emergency call system. In July, Kluepfel informed the Secret Service about the unauthorized distribution. Then in February 1990, Kluepfel learned that the document was available on the SJG's computer bulletin board which was operated by Loyd Blankenship, an SJG employee who had the power to review and delete any data on the BBS. Secret Service Agent Foley applied for a search warrant to search SJG's premises and Blankenship's residence for evidence of violation of statutes prohibiting interstate transportation of computer access information and interstate transportation of stolen property, 18 U.S.C. §§ 1030 and 2314. Among the items seized was the computer which operated the BBS which contained 162 items of unread e-mail at the time of the seizure. The plaintiff filed suit against the Secret Service in May 1991, alleging violations of the Privacy Protection Act, 42 U.S.C. § 2000aa, the Federal Wiretap Act, as amended by Title I and Title II of the Electronic Communication Privacy Act. The district court held that the Secret Service violated the Privacy Protection Act, and Title II of the ECPA but that they did not "intercept" the e-mail in violation of Title I of the ECPA.]

The narrow issue before us is whether the seizure of a computer, used to operate an electronic bulletin board system, and containing private electronic mail which had been sent to (stored on) the bulletin board, but not read (retrieved) by the intended recipients, constitutes an unlawful intercept under the Federal Wiretap Act, 18 U.S.C. § 2510, et seq., as amended by Title I of the Electronic Communications Privacy Act of 1986. We hold that it is not, and therefore AFFIRM.

. . .

Section 2511 was enacted in 1968 as part of Title III of the Omnibus Crime Control and Safe Streets Act of 1968, often referred to as the Federal Wiretap Act. Prior to the 1986 amendment by Title I of the ECPA, it covered only wire and oral communications. Title I of the ECPA extended that coverage to electronic communications . . .

The district court, relying on our court's interpretation of intercept in United States v. Turk, 526 F.2d 654 (5th Cir.), held that the Secret Service did not intercept the communications, because its acquisition of the contents of those communications was not contemporaneous with their transmission. In Turk, the government seized from a suspect's vehicle an audio tape of a prior conversation between the suspect and Turk. (Restated, when the conversation took place, it was not recorded contemporaneously by the government.) Our court held that replaying the previously recorded conversation was not an "intercept", because an intercept "require[s] participation by the one charged with an 'interception' in the contemporaneous acquisition of the communication through the use of the device".

Appellants agree with Turk's holding, but contend that it is not applicable, because it "says nothing about government action that both acquires the communication prior to its delivery, and prevents that delivery." . . .

Prior to the 1986 amendment by the ECPA, the Wiretap Act defined "intercept" as the "aural acquisition" of the contents of wire or oral communications through the use of a device. The ECPA amended this definition to include the "aural or other acquisition of the contents of . . . wire, electronic, or oral communications. . . ." The significance of the addition of the words "or other" in the 1986 amendment to the definition of "intercept" becomes clear when the definitions of "aural" and "electronic communication" are examined; electronic communications (which include the non-voice portions of wire communications), as defined by the Act, cannot be acquired aurally.

Webster's Third New International Dictionary (1986) defines "aural" as "of or relating to the ear" or "of or relating to the sense of hearing". And, the Act defines "aural transfer" as "a transfer containing the human voice at any point between and including the point of origin and the point of reception." This definition is extremely important for purposes of understanding the definition of a "wire communication", which is defined by the Act as any aural transfer made in whole or in part through the use of facilities for the transmission of communications by the aid of wire, cable, or other like connection between the point of origin and the point of reception (including the use of such connection in a switching station) . . . and such term includes any electronic storage of such communication.

In contrast, as noted, an "electronic communication" is defined as "any transfer of signs, signals, writing, images, sounds, data, or intelligence of any nature transmitted in whole or in part by a wire, radio, electromagnetic, photoelectronic or photooptical system . . . but does not include . . . any wire or oral communication. . . ." 18 U.S.C. § 2510(12) (emphasis added).

Critical to the issue before us is the fact that, unlike the definition of "wire communication", the definition of "electronic communication" does not include electronic storage of such communications.

Wire and electronic communications are subject to different treatment under the Wiretap Act. The Act's exclusionary rule, 18 U.S.C. § 2515, applies to the interception of wire communications, including such communications in electronic storage, see 18 U.S.C. § 2510(1), but not to the interception of electronic communications. See 18 U.S.C. § 2518(10)(a); And, the types of crimes that may be investigated by means of surveillance directed at electronic communications, 18 U.S.C. § 2516(3) ("any federal felony"), are not as limited as those that may be investigated by means of surveillance directed at wire or oral communications. See 18 U.S.C. § 2516(1) (specifically listed felonies). . . . The E-mail in issue was in "electronic storage". Congress' use of the word "transfer" in the definition of "electronic communication", and its omission in that definition of the phrase "any electronic storage of such communication" (part of the definition of "wire communication") reflects that Congress did not intend for "intercept" to apply to "electronic communications" when those communications are in "electronic storage".

[W]hen construing a statute, we do not confine our interpretation to the one portion at issue but, instead, consider the statute as a whole . . .

[T]he substantive and procedural requirements for authorization to intercept electronic communications are quite different from those for accessing stored electronic communications. For example, a governmental entity may gain access to the contents of electronic communications that have been in electronic storage for less than 180 days by obtaining a warrant. See 18 U.S.C. § 2703(a). But there are more stringent, complicated requirements for the interception of electronic communications; a court order is required. See 18 U.S.C. § 2518.

Second, other requirements applicable to the interception of electronic communications, such as those governing minimization, duration, and the types of crimes that may be investigated, are not imposed when the communications at issue are not in the process of being transmitted at the moment of seizure, but instead are in electronic storage....

Obviously, when intercepting electronic communications, law enforcement officers cannot know in advance which, if any, of the intercepted communications will be relevant to the crime under investigation, and often will have to obtain access to the contents of the communications in order to make such a determination. Interception thus poses a significant risk that officers will obtain access to communications which have no relevance to the investigation they are conducting. That risk is present to a lesser degree, and can be controlled more easily, in the context of stored electronic communications, because, as the Secret Service advised the district court, technology exists by which relevant communications can be located without the necessity of reviewing the entire contents of all of the stored communications. For example, the Secret Service claimed (although the district court found otherwise) that it reviewed the private E-mail on the BBS by use of key word searches.

Next, as noted, court orders authorizing an intercept of electronic communications are subject to strict requirements as to duration. An intercept may not be authorized "for any period longer than is necessary to achieve the objective of the authorization, nor in any event longer than thirty days". 18 U.S.C. § 2518(5). There is no such requirement for access to stored communications.

Finally, as also noted, the limitations as to the types of crimes that may be investigated through an intercept, see 18 U.S.C. § 2516, have no counterpart in Title II of the ECPA....

In light of the substantial differences between the statutory procedures and requirements for obtaining authorization to intercept electronic communications, on the one hand, and to gain access to the contents of stored electronic communications, on the other, it is most unlikely that Congress intended to require law enforcement officers to satisfy the more stringent requirements for an intercept in order to gain access to the contents of stored electronic communications.

At oral argument, appellants contended (for the first time) that Title II's reference in § 2701(c) to § 2518 (which sets forth the procedures for the authorized interception of wire, oral, or electronic communications) reflects that Congress intended considerable overlap between Titles I and II of the ECPA.

... Appellants overemphasize the significance of this reference to § 2518. [it] is clear that Congress intended to treat wire communications differently from electronic communications. Access to stored electronic communications may be obtained pursuant to a search warrant, ; but, access to stored wire communications requires a court order pursuant § 2518. Because § 2701 covers both stored wire and electronic commuı cations, it was necessary in subsection (c) to refer to the differeıⱴ provisions authorizing access to each.

Note

What is the practical significance of treating stored e-mail as exclusively regulated by the stored electronic communication section (Title II) and not covered by Title I—the Interception of Electronic Communication Section. As *Steve Jackson Games* indicates, the standards for governmental access to stored electronic communications under Title II §§ 2701–2711 are more lenient than the standards for governmental access to intercepted electronic communications under Title I §§ 2510–2518. Some of the major differences are: (1) government access of a stored electronic communication can be procured pursuant to a general search warrant issued under the federal rules of criminal procedure. These warrants do not contain the requirements of particularization and minimization that are required for a court ordered interception under § 2518—where there has been an interception of an electronic communication; (2) damages are less than for violation of the stored electronic communication section; (3) the exclusionary rule is different.

Steve Jackson Games holds that if the government acquires the contents of an e-mail communication while it is in flight, there is an interception of an electronic communication within Title I. Practically speaking what protection does Title I provide for e-mail under the severe limitations of the *Steve Jackson Games*?

In the section that follows we examine the scope of the ordinary business use exception to interceptions of wire, electronic and oral communications under title I. Does *Steve Jackson Games* make the ordinary business exception irrelevant to cases where the government or private persons have accessed e-mail? *Steve Jackson Games* has been the subject of a great deal of criticism in legal commentary.

(3) Employer Access to Employee E–Mail

Much of the concern about the privacy of e-mail has been over employer access to employee e-mail. In, *Vernars v. Young*, 539 F.2d 966 (3d Cir. 1976), the Third Circuit held that printed personal mail of an employee cannot be accessed by an employer without violating their common law right to privacy. Is e-mail sufficiently equivalent to a printed letter so that employee's privacy rights are violated by an employer's access? Or is e-mail more like a postcard than a letter? These are questions that are relevant to answering the issue of whether the employer's access violates an employee's right to privacy under the common law privacy intrusion tort, discussed in Chapter Five. But Title II is the federal statutory law for employer access to employee e-mail.

Section 2701(c) provides that it is not unlawful to access stored electronic communications if the access is authorized "by the person or entity providing a wire or electronic communications service."

This is generally referred to as the proprietary exception to accessing stored electronic communication. By this it is meant that the owner of the computer that stores the e-mail is the proprietor that is exempt from liability for accessing e-mail under § 2701 as long as the access was authorized by the proprietor (entity providing a wire or electronic communication service). There are no reported appellate court cases interpreting the proprietary exception to accessing e-mail, but a reasonable construction of the statutory language would be that employers have a right to access employee e-mail.

Even assuming that employers have a right to access employee e-mail under the proprietary exception of Title II, the privacy intrusion tort would still be a legal basis for a challenge by employees in an employer accessing of e-mail case. The crucial issue in common law intrusion privacy cases is whether an employee has a reasonable expectation of privacy in e-mail. The limited case law has indicated that employees have no legally recognized expectation of privacy in e-mail. In *Smyth v. Pillsbury Company*, 914 F.Supp. 97 (E.D.Pa.1996), the court rejected the claim of an employee that there was a reasonable expectation of privacy in e-mail. The court reasoned that once an employee had communicated comments to a second person—in this case, a supervisor—over an e-mail system that was utilized by the entire company, the employee's reasonable expectation of privacy was lost, 914 F.Supp. at 101. In an unreported California case, the court similarly rejected an employee's claim of reasonable expectation of privacy in e-mail. See *Bourke v. Nissan Motor Co.*, No. 68–705 (Cal. Ct. App. July 26, 1993). In that case, an employee of a car dealership accessed another employee's e-mail to illustrate the benefits of an e-mail system. The accessed e-mail was personal, sexual in nature and not business related. Subsequently, the e-mail messages of the employee were reviewed and several additional personal messages were discovered. A warning to the employee was issued for violating e-mail policy. When the employee protested about her e-mail being accessed, she was terminated. The court rejected the privacy intrusion tort claim by the employee on the basis that while a subjective expectation of privacy was present the expectation was not reasonable given the nature of e-mail communications.

In view of the meager case law interpreting the ECPA and the common law privacy intrusion tort in respect to employer access of e-mail, it is essential that employers establish an e-mail policy that provides notice to employees of when their e-mail will be accessed.

In discussing e-mail policies with a client/employer—it is important to emphasize the benefits of providing security for e-mail communications. The construction of the ECPA to provide for an employer proprietary exception for accessing e-mail may be a pyrrhic victory for the business community. If it becomes clear that e-mail communications by employees are not secure and like a post card, subject to public surveillance, then the content of communication over e-mail may be severely limited. This could substantially hinder the efficacy and use of electronically transmitted mail.

(4) Model Policies for Employer's Access to Employee E–Mail

Mark S. Dichter & Michael S. Burkhardt, Electronic Interaction In The Workplace: Monitoring, Retrieving and Storing Employee Communications In The Internet Age (October 2–5, 1996) <http://www.mlb.com/speech1.htm>

Policy

Employer is committed to providing an environment that encourages the use of computers and electronic information as essential tools to support Employer's business. It is the responsibility of each employee to ensure that this technology is used for proper business purposes and in a manner that does not compromise the confidentiality of proprietary or other sensitive information. This policy supplements, and should be read in conjunction with, Employer's policies regarding "Corporate Communications"; "Confidentiality"; and "Use of the Company's Communications Systems."

Coverage

All users of Employer's computer systems.

E-Mail Procedures

All E-mail correspondence is the property of Employer.

Employee E-mail communications are not considered private despite any such designation either by the sender or the recipient.

Messages sent to recipients outside of Employer, if sent over the Internet and not encrypted, are not secure.

Employer reserves the right to monitor its E-mail system—including an employee's mailbox—at its discretion in the ordinary course of business. Please note that in certain situations, Employer may be compelled to access and disclose messages sent over its E-mail system.

The existence of passwords and "message delete" functions do not restrict or eliminate Employer's ability or right to access electronic communications.

Employees shall not share an E-mail password, provide E-mail access to an unauthorized user, or access another user's E-mail box without authorization.

Employees shall not post, display or make easily available any access information, including, but not limited to, passwords.

Offensive, demeaning or disruptive messages are prohibited. This includes, but is not limited to, messages that are inconsistent with Employer's policies concerning "Equal Employment Opportunity"; and "Sexual Harassment and Other Unlawful Harassment."

Messages sent to all E-mail users require prior approval by an appropriate member of Employer.

Any employee who violates this policy shall be subject to discipline, up to and including discharge.

Internet Procedures

Employer's network, including its connection to the Internet, is to be used for business-related purposes only and not for personal use (or primarily for business-related purposes). Any unauthorized use of the

Internet is strictly prohibited. Unauthorized use includes, but is not limited to: connecting, posting, or downloading pornographic material; engaging in computer-"hacking" and other related activities; attempting to disable or compromise the security of information contained on Employer's computers (or otherwise using Employer's computers for personal use).

Internet messages should be treated as non-confidential. Anything sent through the Internet passes through a number of different computer systems, all with different levels of security. The confidentiality of messages may be compromised at any point along the way, unless the messages are encrypted.

Because postings placed on the Internet may display Employer's address, make certain before posting information on the Internet that the information reflects the standards and policies of Employer. Under no circumstances shall information of a confidential, sensitive or otherwise proprietary nature be placed on the Internet.

Subscriptions to news groups and mailing lists are permitted when the subscription is for a work-related purpose. Any other subscriptions are prohibited.

Information posted or viewed on the Internet may constitute published material. Therefore, reproduction of information posted or otherwise available over the Internet may be done only by express permission from the author or copyright holder.

Unless the prior approval of management has been obtained, users may not establish Internet or other external network connections that could allow unauthorized persons to gain access to Employer's systems and information. These connections include the establishment of hosts with public modem dial-ins, World Wide Web home pages and File Transfer Protocol (FTP).

All files downloaded from the Internet must be checked for possible computer viruses. If uncertain whether your virus-checking software is current, you must check with an authorized Information Systems Representative before downloading.

Offensive, demeaning or disruptive messages are prohibited. This includes, but is not limited to, messages that are inconsistent with Employer's policies concerning "Equal Employment Opportunity"; and "Sexual Harassment and Other Unlawful Harassment."

Any employee who violates this policy shall be subject to discipline, up to and including discharge.

ACKNOWLEDGMENT OF E–MAIL AND INTERNET ACCESS POLICY

As an employee of Employer, I understand that the confidentiality and protection of Employer's information is of the utmost importance. I have read and understand Employer's Policy on acceptable use of E-mail and Internet access.

If I receive a password for access to E-mail, the Internet or any other system of electronically-stored computer information, I will use it only for authorized purposes. I agree not to use a code, access a file or retrieve any stored communication other than where explicitly authorized unless there has been prior clearance by an authorized representative of Employer. I will notify Information Systems immediately if I believe that another person may have unauthorized access to my password.

I understand that all information stored in, transmitted or received through Employer's systems of printed or computer information is the property of Employer, and is to be used only for job-related purposes. I further understand that authorized representatives of Employer may monitor the use of Employer's systems of printed or computer information from time to time to ensure that such use is consistent with Employer's policies and interests. Further, I am aware that use of an Employer-provided password or code does not in any way restrict

Employer's right or ability to access electronic communications.

I am aware that any violation of Employer's E-mail or Internet Access Policy may subject me to disciplinary action, up to and including discharge from employment.

(Name)

(Signature)

(Date)

Compare the above model e-mail policy with the model e-mail policy in Perritt, *Law and the Information Superhighway*, Section 3.35, (Wiley, 1996).

§ 3.35 MODEL STATEMENT OF PRIVACY RIGHTS

The following model statement is intended to be disseminated to employees who use an internal E-mail system. It easily could be adapted for publication to other groups, like students and faculty, who use an institutional E-mail system:

As a general rule, your E-mail communications to other employees are private. Unless we get a report or complaint as described later in this statement, we do not generally monitor E-mail messages.*

You must keep your username and password to yourself, and change it frequently. You should use passwords conforming to the guidelines issued by the information services department to make it harder for an intruder to guess. If you use an easy-to-guess password, or if you allow your username and password to be discovered by others, the privacy of your E-mail and that of others is compromised.

You must not seek access to mailboxes other than your own or seek to read E-mail traffic not directed to you.

We reserve the privilege of accessing the content of your E-mail messages if we receive a complaint or report of misuse of the E-mail system or harmful messages or messages that intrude into another's privacy or property rights.

We reserve the privilege of monitoring information about your use of the E-mail system, other than the content of messages, on a routine basis and disclosing this information as we believe appropriate in the management of the business. You thus should understand that the people to whom you send messages and from whom you receive messages, the dates and times you exchange messages, and the volume of messages are not private.

You should be aware that when you exchange E-mail with persons outside this organization, through the Internet or otherwise, the privacy of your messages depends on policies and practices of serve providers and network managers not within the control of this organization.

§ 3.36 Sample E-mail and File Storage Agreement Provisos

This is a somewhat more formal and detailed statement, intended to have contractual effect.

1. Provider agrees to provide E-mail services and file storage and exchange services, totalling up to __ megabytes, for so long as subscriber adheres to its obligations under this agreement, including prompt payments of subscription fees according to the fee schedule as it may be revised from time to time.

2. In exchange for the services provided by provider to subscriber [student/faculty member/employee], subscriber agrees as follows:

    (a) Provider may access files stored on provider's system by subscriber in order to determine that subscriber is not

---

* This may seem like too broad a commitment of privacy to make, but it serves the institution because is makes it clear that the institution does not undertake to screen E-mail messages for harmful content.

storing illegal information or information likely to infringe the rights of third parties on provider's system.

(b) Provider may access subscriber's E-mail mailbox and
check the contents of messages contained therein in
order to determine that subscriber is not sending or
receiving E-mail messages likely to violate federal or
state law or to infringe the rights of third parties.

(c) Provider may disclose the contents obtained under paragraphs (a) or (b) as it reasonably deems appropriate to
report violations of federal or state law or to permit
third parties to assert their rights in appropriate forums.

(d) Provider may delete files or messages it reasonably
believes violate federal or state law or infringe the
rights of third parties.

(e) If provider deletes files or messages under paragraph
(d), it will notify subscriber and, if feasible, considering
the content of the files or messages, provide subscriber
with an opportunity to make archival copies of the files
or messages before they are deleted.

UNAUTHORIZED DISCLOSURE OF E–MAIL BY THE SERVICE PROVIDER

In *McVeigh v. Cohen*, 983 F.Supp. 215 (Dist.Ct. D.C. 1998) American
on Line (AOL) and the United States Navy were sued by Timothy R.
McVeigh (no relation to the Oklahoma City bombing defendant) under
Title II of the ECPA for the unauthorized disclosure and receipt of
stored electronic communications service records. McVeigh sought an
injunction against his discharge from the Navy for violation of the
"Don't Ask, Don't Tell, Don't Pursue" policy.

McVeigh alleged that AOL had identified McVeigh to Navy personnel as the customer who had sent an e-mail message with the alias
"boysrch" that was signed by a "Tim." The court held that both the
disclosure by AOL and the receipt of the information by the navy
violated the ECPA. The court interpreted Title II of the ECPA to restrict
government access to information from an online service provider to
instances where it: (1) obtained a search warrant under the Federal
Rules of Criminal Procedure or a state equivalent; or (2) gives prior
notice to the online subscriber and then issues a subpoena or receives a
court order authorizing disclosure under § 18 U.S.C.A. § 2703(b)(I)(A)-
(B), (c)(I)(B).

Section 2703(c)(1)(B) prohibits disclosure of electronic communication service records to the government unless the government obtains a
subpoena or warrant. The Government argued that this section restricted actions of service providers but not the government. The court
rejected this argument and found that the affirmative requirements

imposed upon the government to obtain a warrant or the like in § 2703(a) and (b) were to work in tandem with 2703(c) to protect consumer privacy. Therefore, the navy had violated the ECPA by soliciting a violation by AOL. Compare this analysis with *Tucker v. Waddell*, 83 F.3d 688 (4th Cir. 1996) (holding that § 2701(c)(I)(B) only prohibits the action of online providers, not the government).

(5) The Uneasy Status of Voicemail Under the ECPA

Voicemail and E-mail communications are technically quite similar. E-mail is a pure form of digital technology that involves only digital data in both the transmission and storage of the communication. Voicemail includes the voice at some point in the transmission of the communication. But when the voice message is stored in the computer network it is converted to digital data. *Steve Jackson Games* holds that the unauthorized access of stored E-mail is governed exclusively by Title II of the ECPA.

What is the status of voicemail under the ECPA? Voicemail seems clearly to be a wire communication under the ECPA. The definition of "wire communication" includes its electronic storage. Voicemail includes the human voice (at some point) and voicemail is a form of electronic storage. Title I prohibits the interception of wire communications (voicemail) and Title II prohibits the unauthorized access to stored wire communications (voicemail). Is the unauthorized access to voicemail (unlike E-mail) a violation of both Title I and Title II?

The Ninth Circuit considered this question in *United States v. Smith*, 155 F.3d 1051 (9th Cir. 1998). *Smith* involved the conviction of a corporate employee for insider trading in violation of federal securities law. Smith left an incriminating message on the voicemail of an employee (Bravo) in another corporate office. Without authorization, another employee (Gore) accessed the voicemail and forwarded it to her mailbox. Gore called her voicemail from her home and recorded the voicemail message with a hand-held audiotape. The tape was turned over to federal authorities. The ninth Circuit upheld Smith's conviction but held that the recording by Gore of the E-mail message was a violation of Title I. As such the E-mail message was found not to be admissible under the exclusionary rule of Title I.

In *Smith* the government argued that the *Steve Jackson Games* controlled and that interception under Title I was limited to acquiring the contents of the ·voicemail while in flight. Once voicemail was in storage it was exclusively regulated by the restrictions against unauthorized access under Title II. The court disagreed.

> It is not necessary, as the government assumes, either to rewrite or to ignore congressionally approved language to make sense of the Stored Communications Act and the Wiretap Act. Rather, the two statutes "admit[] a reasonable construction which gives effect to all of [their] provisions." The terms "intercept" and "access" are not, as the government claims, temporal-

ly different, with the former, but not the latter, requiring contemporaneity; rather, the terms are conceptually, or qualitatively, different. The word "intercept" entails actually acquiring the contents of a communication, whereas the word "access" merely involves being in position to acquire the contents of a communication. In other words, "access[]" is, for all intents and purposes, a lesser included offense (or tort, as the case may be) of "intercept|ion]." As applied to the facts of this case, Gore might have violated the Stored Communications Act's prohibition on "access[ing]" by simply making unauthorized use of Bravo's voicemail password and roaming about PDA's automated voicemail system, even had she never recorded or otherwise "intercepted" the contents of any given message. Once she retrieved and recorded Smith's message, however, she crossed the line between the Stored Communications Act and the Wiretap Act and violated the latter's prohibition on "intercept[ion]."

The court in *Smith* characterized its view as a holistic construction of the ECPA that permits Title I and Title II to "coexist peacefully." Do you agree with this assessment? Does *Smith* simply treat voicemail as a telephone conversation for purposes of Title I? If so, presumably the restrictions on an employer listening to the conversations of an employee that have developed under Title I would apply to voicemail. Review the ordinary course of business and consent defenses under Title I in *Spears*, infra. Does the distinction between putting oneself in a position to acquire the contents (access) and acquiring the contents (interception) hold up? Does *Smith* limit interception under Title I to the recording of a voicemail message? Would listening to a voicemail message be an interception under Title I or simple access under Title II? Would it violate Title I for an employer to authorize an employee to access (and listen) to an employee's voicemail? Under the lesser offense holding of *Smith* acts that constituted an interception of voicemail in violation of Title I would also include a violation of Title II. Would the party who left the voicemail message be able to recover damages under both Title I and Title II?

C. THE ORDINARY COURSE OF BUSINESS EXCEPTION

DEAL v. SPEARS

980 F.2d 1153 (8th Cir.1992).

BOWMAN, J.

[Defendants Newell and Juanita Spear owned and operated the White Oak Package Store near Camden, Arkansas The defendants live in a mobile home attached to the store. They had one incoming telephone line which was used for both their business and their residence. The plaintiff, Sibbie Deal, was employed at the defendant's store from

December 1988 until she was fired in August 1990. The defendants' store was burglarized in April of 1990 and the defendants suspected that it was an inside job. In the hopes of catching the suspect in an admission, the defendants installed a recording device on the extension phone in the mobile home which recorded all conversations made from both phones. The defendants taped calls from June 27, 1990, through August 13, 1990. Defendant Newell listened to virtually all twenty-two hours of the tapes he recorded, regardless of the nature of the calls or the content of the conversations. Nothing in the record indicated that the defendants learned anything about the burglary from listening to the tapes. They did learn other things, such as the fact that Sibbie Deal was having an extramarital-affair with the other plaintiff Calvin Lucas. The defendants also learned that Deal sold Lucas a keg of beer at cost which was against store policy. Afterwards, the defendants played a few seconds of the incriminating tape for Deal and then fired her. Deal and Lucas filed this action on August 29, 1990 alleging violation of the Omnibus Crime Control and Safe Streets Act (Title III). The court awarded the plaintiffs statutory damages and attorneys fees, but refused to award punitive damages. The appellate court affirmed.]

. . .

Under the relevant provisions of [Title III] criminal liability attaches and a federal civil cause of action arises when a person intentionally intercepts a wire or electronic communication or intentionally discloses the contents of the interception. . . . The successful civil plaintiff may recover actual damages plus any profits made by the violator. If statutory damages will result in a larger recovery than actual damages, the violator must pay the plaintiff "the greater of $100 a day for each day of violation or $10,000."[5] § 2520(c)(2)(B) (1988). Further, punitive damages, attorney fees, and "other litigation costs reasonably incurred" are allowed. § 2520(b)(2), (3) (1988).

The Spearses first claim they are exempt from civil liability because Sibbie Deal consented to the interception of calls that she made from and received at the store. Under the statute, it is not unlawful "to intercept a wire, oral, or electronic communication . . . where one of the parties to the communication has given prior consent to such interception," 18 U.S.C. § 2511(2)(d), and thus no civil liability is incurred. The Spearses contend that Deal's consent may be implied because Newell Spears had mentioned that he might be forced to monitor calls or restrict telephone privileges if abuse of the store's telephone for personal calls continued. They further argue that the extension in their home gave actual notice to Deal that her calls could be overheard, and that this notice resulted in her implied consent to interception. We find these arguments unpersuasive.

5. The District Court arrived at a total of $40,000 in statutory damages by awarding $10,000 each to Deal and Lucas, and against Newell Spears, for interception, and $10,000 each to Deal and Lucas, and against Juanita Spears, for disclosure. None of the parties appeals the quantum of statutory damages awarded.

There is no evidence of express consent here. Although constructive consent is inadequate, actual consent may be implied from the circumstances.

We do not believe that Deal's consent may be implied from the circumstances relied upon in the Spearses' arguments. The Spearses did not inform Deal that they were monitoring the phone, but only told her they might do so in order to cut down on personal calls. Moreover, it seems clear that the couple anticipated Deal would not suspect that they were intercepting her calls, since they hoped to catch her making an admission about the burglary, an outcome they would not expect if she knew her calls were being recorded. As for listening in via the extension, Deal testified that she knew when someone picked up the extension in the residence while she was on the store phone, as there was an audible "click" on the line.[6]

Given these circumstances, we hold as a matter of law that the Spearses have failed to show Deal's consent to the interception and recording of her conversations.

The Spearses also argue that they are immune from liability under what has become known as an exemption for business use of a telephone extension. The exception is actually a restrictive definition.

... Thus there are two essential elements that must be proved before [the business use] becomes a viable defense: the intercepting equipment must be furnished to the user by the phone company or connected to the phone line, and it must be used in the ordinary course of business. The Spearses argue that the extension in their residence, to which the recorder was connected, meets the equipment requirement, and the listening-in was done in the ordinary course of business. We disagree.

... [T]he recording device, and not the extension phone, is the instrument used to intercept the call. We do not believe the recording device falls within the statutory exemption. The recorder was purchased by Newell Spears at Radio Shack, not provided by the telephone company. Further, it was connected to the extension phone, which was itself the instrument connected to the phone line. There was no evidence that the recorder could have operated independently of the telephone.

We hold that the recording device, and not the extension phone, intercepted the calls. But even if the extension phone intercepted the calls, we do not agree that the interception was in the ordinary course of business.

We do not quarrel with the contention that the Spearses had a legitimate business reason for listening in: they suspected Deal's involvement in a burglary of the store and hoped she would incriminate herself

---

6. There was at least one occasion, however, when Deal was on the phone and did not hear Newell Spears pick up the extension. At the time, Deal was shouting to a beer delivery person as he was exiting the store, apparently about the keg of beer she was hoping to acquire, at cost, for Calvin Lucas.

in a conversation on the phone. Moreover, Deal was abusing her privileges by using the phone for numerous personal calls even, by her own admission, when there were customers in the store. The Spearses might legitimately have monitored Deal's calls to the extent necessary to determine that the calls were personal and made or received in violation of store policy.

But the Spearses recorded twenty-two hours of calls, and Newell Spears listened to all of them without regard to their relation to his business interests. Granted, Deal might have mentioned the burglary at any time during the conversations, but we do not believe that the Spearses' suspicions justified the extent of the intrusion. See Watkins, 704 F.2d at 583 ("We hold that a personal call may not be intercepted in the ordinary course of business under the exemption in section 2510(5)(a)(i), except to the extent necessary to guard against unauthorized use of the telephone or to determine whether a call is personal or not."); Briggs v. American Air Filter Co., 630 F.2d 414, 420 n. 9 (5th Cir.1980) ("A general practice of surreptitious monitoring would be more intrusive on employees' privacy than monitoring limited to specific occasions."). We conclude that the scope of the interception in this case takes us well beyond the boundaries of the ordinary course of business.

For the reasons we have indicated, the Spearses cannot avail themselves of the telephone extension/business use exemption of Title III. . . .

Finally, Deal and Lucas cross-appeal the District Court's failure to award punitive damages. See id. § 2520(b)(2). Punitive damages are unwarranted under Title III unless Deal and Lucas can prove "a wanton, reckless or malicious violation." It is difficult to conceive of a case less appropriate for punitive damages than this one.

The Spearses had lost $16,000 by theft in what must have been a serious blow to their business, and installed the recorder in hopes that they would be able to recover their loss, or at least catch the thief. They suspected an inside job and naturally they were anxious to find out whether the burglar was one of their employees. Further, despite warnings about abuse of the phone, the Spearses were paying a salary to an employee for the hours she spent on personal calls, including (as it turned out) her conversations with her lover. She sometimes carried on these conversations in the presence of the store's customers and apparently not infrequently used salacious language. The Spearses were not taping to get "dirt" on Lucas and Deal, but believed their business interests justified the recording. Moreover, before installing the recorder, Newell Spears inquired of a law enforcement officer and was told that the officer saw nothing wrong with Spears tapping his own phone. While the Spearses' reliance on the officer's statement does not absolve them of liability, it clearly demonstrates that the taping was neither wanton nor reckless. . . . Other than Sibbie Deal, those who testified as to direct knowledge of the disclosures apparently believed Juanita Spears had their best interests at heart and that the disclosures were in the manner of a warning to them and not malicious.

We agree with the District Court that defendants' conduct does not warrant the imposition of punitive damages.

The judgment of the District Court is affirmed in all respects.

Note: Further Comments on the "Use in the Ordinary Course of Business" Exception

Deal v. Spears and *United States v. Harpel*, 493 F.2d 346 (10th Cir. 1974), are the leading cases on the question of whether surreptitious monitoring of phone conversations is an ordinary use of a business phone and on the requirements of the consent defense under Title I. In *Harpel*, the court stated, "[w]e hold as a matter of law that a telephone extension used without authorization or consent to surreptitiously record a private telephone conversation is not used in the ordinary course of business." Id. at 351. Some courts have recognized a limited right for a business to surreptitiously monitor phone calls.

In business contexts the ordinary use exception, section 2510(5)(a)(i), has been found applicable to surreptitiously overheard conversations over a company extension telephone when the listener was acting solely to protect the company's interest in its business secrets, e.g., *Briggs v. American Air Filter Co.*, 630 F.2d 414 (5th Cir.1980). In *Briggs*, the court found that the branch manager of the defendant's company had particular suspicions that confidential information had been disclosed to a business competitor and had monitored a particular call from an agent of a competitor. The surreptitious monitoring of an employee's conversation was found to be an ordinary business use by the Eleventh Circuit in a subsequent case where the employee was suspected of making disparaging remarks about supervisors. See *Epps v. St. Mary's Hosp.*, 802 F.2d 412, 416–17 (11th Cir.1986). How would you state the scope of the limited exception that is represented by *Briggs* and *Epps*?

The Tenth Circuit has found that when notice is given to employees that conversations between employees and customers are to be monitored to assist in developing better customer relations skills, the ordinary business use exception is applicable. In *James v. Newspaper Agency Corp.*, 591 F.2d 579, 581 (10th Cir.1979), LaPriel B. James brought two causes of action against her former employer, Newspaper Agency Corp. The first alleged sex discrimination in conditions of employment under the Civil Rights Act of 1964 (42 U.S.C.A. § 2000e) and the second alleged the willful and unlawful interception of wire and oral communications in violation of 18 U.S.C.A. § 2510. James worked within the accounting/credit department of Newspaper Agency Corp. as a collector of transient advertising accounts. On January 5, 1972 Newspaper Agency Corp. decided to install a telephone monitoring system on the telephones in certain departments of the company, especially those departments dealing with the public. All affected personnel were notified of this decision in writing. The purpose of this installation was two-fold. First, supervisory personnel could monitor business calls to employees and thus provide training and instruction as to how to better deal with the public. Second, the monitoring system was to serve as a layer of protection for employees from abusive calls. The district court found that the second claim fell within the ordinary course of business exception provided within 18 U.S.C.A. § 2510(5)(a) and granted summary judgment in favor of the defendant. The Tenth Circuit affirmed.

The Eleventh Circuit takes the position that the intercepting device is the extension phone and not the device that records the conversation, see, *Epps v. Saint Mary's Hosp. of Athens*, 802 F.2d 412 (11th Cir.1986). What is the practical significance of this interpretation of Section 2510(1)? There is also support for the proposition that only business calls come within the ordinary course of business exception. See, *Watkins v. Berry*, 704 F.2d 577, 582 (11th Cir.1983), " . . . if the intercepted call was a business call, [the] monitoring was in the ordinary course of business. If it was a personal call, the monitoring was probably, but not certainly, not in the ordinary course of business."

D.   THE DOMESTIC CONFLICT EXCEPTION

1.   PRIVATE ELECTRONIC EAVESDROPPING IN DOMESTIC CONFLICTS: LIABILITY UNDER SECTION 2520

SIMPSON v. SIMPSON

490 F.2d 803 (5th Cir.), *cert. denied*, 419 U.S. 897 (1974).

Before BELL, COLEMAN and RONEY, CIRCUIT JUDGES.

BELL, CIRCUIT JUDGE:

[Uncertain as to his wife's faithfulness, a husband obtained a device for tapping and recording telephone conversations. He attached the device to phone lines within their home. The taped telephone conversations were mildly compromising and established that another man was making advances and that while the wife was resisting, she was not doing so in a firm and final fashion. Convinced that he had "caught her," the husband played the tapes, or portions thereof, to various neighbors and family members. He also played them for a lawyer, on whose advice the wife agreed to an uncontested divorce. After the divorce, she brought a civil action for damages under Section 2520 of Title III. The district court dismissed the suit and the Fifth Circuit affirmed.]

Title III of the Omnibus Act broadly prohibits the interception or disclosure of a wire communication subject to stated exceptions which are not relevant to this case. Violators are subject to criminal penalties of up to $10,000 or five years. They are also civilly liable to persons whose communications they intercept or disclose.

The naked language of Title III, by virtue of its inclusiveness, reaches this case. However, we are of the opinion that Congress did not intend such a far-reaching result, one extending into areas normally left to states, those of the marital home and domestic conflicts. We reach this decision because Congress has not, in the statute, committee reports, legislative hearings, or reported debates indicated either its positive intent to reach so far or an awareness that it might be doing so. Given the novelty of a federal remedy for persons aggrieved by the personal acts of their spouses within the marital home, and given the severity of the remedy seemingly provided by Title III, we seek such indications of congressional intent and awareness before extending Title III to this case.

Our independent search of legislative materials has been long, exhaustive, and inconclusive. To summarize the results, we have found no direct indications that Congress intended so much, and only several scattered suggestions that it was aware that the statute's inclusive language might reach this case. In support of this general statement, we now turn to a specific discussion of that statute and its history.

. . .

Of what testimony there was about private surveillance, only a minor portion was with reference to the marital setting. The only relevant passages which we have found, in hearings stretching over five years, are set forth in the margin.[14] It should be noted that the concerns

14. The following is from an article entitled "Is Big Brother Taping You?", [sic] by Arthur Whitman, from Tape Recording, Feb. 1965, reprinted in *Hearings* #II, pt. 1, at 18 (see note 10, *supra*):

Individuals involved in civil suits bug each others' premises to gather useful information and evidence. The prime area for this is divorce actions, particularly in states with restrictive codes. So little is sacred in this line of endeavor that bugs are routinely discovered under the beds of estranged husbands and wives who suspect each other of errant ways. The latest twist in this game is the installation of tiny radio transmitters in cars that relay to prying ears and tape recorders any conversations or other sounds produced by drivers and passengers.

Richard Gerstein, Dade County District Attorney:

Nonetheless, it is routine procedure in marital disagreements and other civil disputes for private detective agencies, generally with full knowledge of the lawyers, to tap telephones.

Hearings #II, pt. 2, at 1009 (see note 10, *supra*).

Bernard Spindel, private investigator/electronic technician (explaining the 10% of his work that he refers to as the "affirmative, defensive type of eavesdropping"):

In other words, it is restricted to defense in the sense that a man believes that there is some wrongdoing within his own premises; we will help him electronically obtain the evidence of such wrongdoing. But it is restricted within the confines of the law and within a man's own home or premises,

where he has absolute control, whether it be his office or his home or his factory.

Id., pt. 5, at 2262.

Ben Jamil, president of a firm which sold significant quantities of electronic surveillance equipment to persons other than public officials and license[d] private investigators:

I don't feel, however, that I am in any position to judge the rightness or wrongness of this mother eavesdropping on her daughter with one of my devices. Any more than I have the right to determine whether a suspicious husband or wife is entitled to snoop on his or her mate, a businessman is within his rights to determine whether an employee is guilty of pilferage. . . .

Id. at 2365.

John W. Leon, a private investigator, noted that 80% of his domestic work involved husbands spying on wives. He described the "10–day blitz," named for the fact that if it uncovers nothing within ten days you may as well forget the theory that your spouse is playing around. The blitz includes telephone taps, ear and room bugs, voice-activated tape recorders, and an automatic camera, all of which could be purchased for private use for $400. He testified that previously he would have employed the devices himself for a client, but no longer did so because of F.C.C. regulations.

When questioned about the ethics of these practices, he replied:

[W]e have found statistically that once the truth is out in any domestic squabble, there is a 50% better chance of a couple

and information in these passages are primarily directed towards the involvement of private investigators in marital conflicts. Indeed, were appellant seeking to recover from a third party, we could not, on the basis of this legislative history, accept the defense that the interceptions were authorized by the husband. However, to our minds a third-party intrusion into the marital home, even if instigated by one spouse, is an offense against a spouse's privacy of a much greater magnitude than is personal surveillance by the other spouse. The latter, it seems to us, is consistent with whatever expectations of privacy spouses might have vis-a-vis each other within the marital home.[15]

When we narrow our search to material relevant to this ultimate issue, that of whether Congress intended its regulations to invade the realm of personal acts within the marital home, we find very little indeed. We think that only two passages support appellant's case, these being the testimony of Ben Jamil and John W. Leon, quoted in note 14. These statements suggest congressional awareness that private individuals were using electronic surveillance techniques within their own homes. However, they do not support the proposition that Congress was concerned that such activities took place.

OTHER CONSIDERATIONS

Given this inconclusive legislative history, we think two other factors are important. First, it is clear that Congress did not intend to prohibit a person from intercepting a family member's telephone conversations by use of an extension phone in the family home—subsection (5)(a)(i) of section 2510 directly covers this point.[17] If there is a convincing distinction between this clearly acceptable overhear and the overhear accomplished by appellee, we fail to see it. In fact, we think the (5)(a)(i) exemption is indicative of Congress's intention to abjure from deciding a very intimate question of familial relations, that of the extent of privacy family members may expect within the home vis-a-vis each other.

---

being reconciled. Every time we make a case, I practically feel like a surgeon who is cutting out a cancer.

Id. at 2411.

15. We are aware that there is no statutory requirement of an expectation of privacy in wire communications. Compare Section 2510(1) note 2, *supra, with* Section 2510(2).

(2) "oral communication" means any oral communication uttered by a person exhibiting an expectation that such communication is not subject to interception under circumstances justifying such expectation;
. . .

We are here noting only that it is a large jump from a prohibition on third-party surveillance to one on personal spousal surveillance.

17. See note (1), *supra*.

The meaning of the phrase "being used by the subscriber or user in the ordinary course of its business" becomes clear in light of objections to the original version, which did not contain this phrase. Prof. Herman Schwartz, appearing for the A.C.L.U., stated his fear that the original version would permit intruders or other unauthorized persons to use extension phones without being subject to the prohibitions and penalties of the act. In the course of this objection, he made the following comment:

> I take it nobody wants to make it a crime for a father to listen in on his teenage daughter or some such related problem. . . . But this bill does not go to that and goes beyond that."

Hearings #VI, at 989 (see note 10, *supra*).

As should be obvious from the foregoing, we are not without doubts about our decision. However, we have concluded that the statute is not sufficiently definite and specific to create a federal cause of action for the redress of appellant's grievances against her former husband. Our decision is, of course, limited to the specific facts of this case. No public official is involved, nor is any private person other than appellee, and the locus in quo does not extend beyond the marital home of the parties.

Affirmed.

UNITED STATES v. JONES

542 F.2d 661 (6th Cir.1976).

Before CELEBREZZE, LIVELY and ENGEL, CIRCUIT JUDGES.

CELEBREZZE, CIRCUIT JUDGE.

This is an appeal by the Government from the dismissal of an indictment against William Allan Jones which charged him with intercepting telephone conversations of his estranged wife and using the contents of the intercepted communications in violation of 18 U.S.C. Sections 2511(1)(a) and (d) (1970). Relying principally on the decision of the Fifth Circuit in Simpson v. Simpson, the District Court held that Title III of the Omnibus Crime Control and Safe Streets Act of 1968 was not intended to reach interspousal wiretaps placed on telephones in the marital home [and dismissed the indictment]. . . .

. . .

We now turn to the basic contention of Appellee that he was exempt from prosecution under 18 U.S.C. Section 2511(1)(a). The language of 18 U.S.C. Section 2511(1)(a) and (d) is straightforward and comprehensive:

(1) Except as otherwise specifically provided in this chapter any person who—

(a) willfully intercepts, endeavors to intercept, or procures any other person to intercept or endeavor to intercept, any wire or oral communication;

. . .

(d) willfully uses, or endeavors to use, the contents of any wire or oral communication, knowing or having reason to know that the information was obtained through the interception of a wire or oral communication in violation of this subsection;

shall be fined not more than $10,000 or imprisoned not more than five years, or both.

. . .

Ordinarily a court will not refer to legislative history in construing a statute which is clear on its face. The language of Section 2511(1)(a) quite clearly expresses a blanket prohibition on all electronic surveillance except under circumstances specifically enumerated in the statute.

The natural presumption when construing a statute is that Congress meant what it said. However, the Simpson Court concluded that, despite the literal language of the section, the absence of the positive proof of congressional intent to include interspousal wiretaps in the Act's prohibitions indicated that Congress did not intend to reach that activity.... This conclusion is untenable because it contradicts both the explicit language of the statute and the clear intent of Congress expressed in the Act's legislative history.

... The Senate Report on the bill described the problem addressed by Title III:

> The tremendous scientific and technological developments that have taken place in the last century have made possible today the widespread use and abuse of electronic surveillance techniques. As a result of these developments, privacy of communication is seriously jeopardized by these techniques of surveillance. Commercial and employer-labor espionage is becoming widespread. It is becoming increasingly difficult to conduct business meetings in private. Trade secrets are betrayed. Labor and management plans are revealed. No longer is it possible, in short, for each man to retreat into his home and be left alone. Every spoken word [relative] to each man's personal, marital, religious, political, or commercial concerns can be interpreted by an unseen auditor and turned against the speaker to the auditor's advantage.

Although the primary target of the bill was organized crime, the Senate Report makes it clear that the purpose of the bill was to establish an across-the-board prohibition on all unauthorized electronic surveillance:

> Title III has as its dual purpose (1) protecting the privacy of wire and oral communications, and (2) delineating on a uniform basis the circumstances and conditions under which the interception of wire and oral communications may be authorized. To assure the privacy of oral and wire communications, Title III prohibits all wiretapping and electronic surveillance by persons other than duly authorized law enforcement officers engaged in the investigation or prevention of specified types of serious crimes, and only after authorization of a court order obtained after a showing and finding of probable cause.

The Simpson Court noted that the majority of the legislative history dealt with electronic surveillance by law enforcement officials and found the discussion of private surveillance to be inconclusive on the desired scope of the Act's prohibitions. However, the legislative history leaves no doubt that the Act was intended to reach private electronic surveillance and that Congress was aware that a major area of use for surveillance techniques was the preparation of domestic relations cases.[12] Professor

---

12. Congress held a number of hearings beginning in 1965, as part of a continuous legislative effort to revise federal law on electronic surveillance. This process culmi-

Robert Blakey, publicly credited with being the author of Title III, testified before the Subcommittee on Administrative Practice and Procedure of the Senate Judiciary Committee that:

> [P]rivate bugging in this country can be divided into two broad categories, commercial espionage and marital litigation.[14]

Congressional awareness that the Act's prohibition of private surveillance would be applicable to domestic relations investigations is reflected in the comments of Senator Hruska, one of the co-sponsors of the bill, which were joined by Senators Dirksen, Scott and Thurmond:

nated in the enactment of Title III of the Omnibus Crime Control and Safe Streets Act of 1968. For a list of Congressional hearings on the subject see *Simpson v. Simpson*, 490 F.2d at 807 n. 10.

In 1965, the Subcommittee on Administrative Practice and Procedure of the Senate Judiciary Committee held hearings on the need for legislation to protect the public's privacy against electronic surveillance. Hearings on Invasions of Privacy Before the Subcomm. on Administrative Practice & Procedure of the Senate Comm. on the Judiciary, 89th Cong. 1st Sess. (1965–66). Senator Long, the Chairman of the subcommittee, identified three major areas where private electronic surveillance was widespread:

> The three large areas of snooping in this [non-governmental] field are (1) industrial (2) *divorce cases*, and (3) politics. So far, we have heard no real justification for continuance of snooping in these three areas. If any justification exists, we will probably hear about it in the next few weeks as we expect to explore this terrain thoroughly.

Id. pt. 5 at 2261. (Emphasis added.) Senator Long included an article by Arthur Whitman entitled "*Is Big Brother Taping You*" in the record of the hearing which stated, in pertinent part, that:

> Individuals involved in civil suits bug each others' premises to gather useful information and evidence. The prime area for this is divorce actions, particularly in states with restrictive codes. So little is sacred in this line of endeavor that bugs are routinely discovered under the beds of estranged husbands and wives who suspect each other of errant ways. The latest twist in this game is the installation of tiny radio transmitters in cars that relay to prying ears and tape recorders any conversations or other sounds produced by drivers and passengers. . . .

14. *Hearings on The Right to Privacy Act of 1967 Before the Subcomm. on Administrative Practice & Procedure of the Senate*

Comm. on the Judiciary, 90th Cong., 1st Sess. pt. 2, at 413 (1967). In his testimony before the subcommittee, Professor Blakey praised the provisions in the Right to Privacy Act of 1967 which prohibited private electronic surveillance:

> The widespread use of electronic surveillance techniques in this country by private hands is an abomination. I can find no justification for their use and thus, I welcome the attempt of the Right of Privacy Act to strike at these practices.

Id. at 412. However, he questioned the wisdom of grounding the bill solely on the commerce power. *Id.* at 413. Comparing the two most frequent uses of electronic surveillance by private individuals—commercial espionage and domestic relations investigation—Professor Blakey mentioned a weakness of the Right to Privacy Act which could restrict its effectiveness in curbing private surveillance:

> But this [the interstate character of commercial espionage] is not true in the domestic relations investigation, which involves, moreover, a far more objectionable invasion of privacy [than commercial espionage]. It is, of course, one thing to overhear a business secret; it is a wholly different matter, however, to place under surveillance the marital relationship. Electronic surveillance by a private individual in another's bedroom cuts most sharply against the grain. But few, if any, of these investigations ever touch interstate commerce.

Id. at 442. *See also id.* at 413. As an alternative source of legislative authority, Professor Blakey suggested the draft statute he had prepared as a special consultant to the President's Commission on Law Enforcement and Administration of Justice which relied on section 5 of the Fourteenth Amendment to reach electronic surveillance in domestic relations cases. *Id.* at 442. This suggestion was adopted by Congress and incorporated into the Act's legislative history.

A broad prohibition is imposed on private use of electronic surveillance, particularly in domestic relations and industrial espionage situations.

Our review of the legislative history of this section, testimony at congressional hearings, and debates on the floor of Congress, inescapably lead to the conclusion that 18 U.S.C. Section 2511(1)(a) establishes a broad prohibition on all private electronic surveillance and that a principal area of congressional concern was electronic surveillance for the purposes of marital litigation.

The Simpson Court was privy to many of the same materials which were reviewed by this Court. However in Simpson their importance was discounted because the Court distinguished between unaided surveillance by a spouse and surveillance involving a third-party, even if instigated by the spouse. This distinction has been seized upon in a subsequent case. In our view, it is a classic "distinction without a difference." For purposes of federal wiretap law, it makes no difference whether a wiretap is placed on a telephone by a spouse or by a private detective in the spouse's employ. The end result is the same—the privacy of the unconsenting parties to the intercepted conversation has been invaded. It is important to recognize that it is not just the privacy of the targeted spouse which is being violated, but that of the other party to the conversation as well. . . .

. . . We also dispute the implication in Simpson that the limited attention given to private electronic surveillance in the legislative history, relative to that afforded surveillance by law enforcement personnel, reflects Congress' equivocation on the scope of Title III in the private sector. The more plausible explanation is that it was the consensus of Congress that there is "no justification" for private electronic surveillance so that debate centered on the more volatile issue of law enforcement surveillance.

. . .

Even if Simpson was correctly decided on its facts, this case is clearly distinguishable. In Simpson the Court was concerned about the scope of the civil remedies under Section 2520. The Court stated that Congress had not sought to create "a federal remedy for marital grievances" when it provided civil remedies for aggrieved persons. The Simpson Court based its decision, at least in part, on a desire to avoid a conflict between the civil remedies granted by the federal statute and the doctrine of interspousal immunity from civil action in tort recognized by many states. The Court concluded that Congress did not intend to override the doctrine of interspousal immunity and "intrude into the marital relation within the marital home," normally a subject for state law. This analysis is faulty when applied to this case in a number of respects. One problem is that state law is far from uniform on the doctrine of interspousal immunity. A number of states have decided the doctrine is antiquated and have abandoned it. There is also substantial doubt whether a doctrine of state tort law should have any influence in defining a cause of action expressly created by federal statute, particularly when Congress could have included a similar provision in the statute and failed to do so. The most telling difference between this case and Simpson however, is that we are here concerned with construing the scope of a criminal statute. Even in states which recognize interspousal immunity, the immunity does not apply to criminal prosecutions. As noted above, Title III protects the privacy of all parties to an intercepted communication, and the fact that one party to a tapped conversation is the spouse of the defendant should have no bearing whatsoever on the availability of criminal penalties.

This case is also distinguishable on its facts. In Simpson the wiretapping incident took place while the couple were living together as man and wife. Here, it is undisputed that Appellee and his wife were separated at the time of the electronic surveillance. Appellee had moved out of the house in July of 1974 and by October 18th when the surveillance device was installed he was under a restraining order from the Chancery Court to prevent him from "coming about" his wife. Also, in Simpson the Court stressed that "the locus in quo [of the wiretap] does not extend beyond the marital home of the parties." Here, it is doubtful whether there was a "marital home" within the Simpson Court's meaning of the term, and the surveillance was conducted from outside the residence where the telephone was located. While we are not convinced that the location of the surveillance device has any relevance in ascertaining the scope of the statute, we mention this only to emphasize that Appellee and his wife were not sharing a domicile at the time of the interception.

[Reversed and remanded.]

2. SPECIAL PROBLEMS OF THE ORDINARY BUSINESS EXCEPTION TO TITLE I COVERAGE

Surveillance of a conversation over the telephone which involves a use by the subscriber of that telephone in the ordinary course of business is not a violation of Title I. Under section 2510(5)(a)(1), such ordinary use in the course of business is not the acquisition of the content of the conversation by an "electronic, mechanical or other device." Therefore no "interception" has occurred. The ordinary use exception has come to be described as the extension phone/family member exception to Title I even though this interpretation is hardly derivable from the plain meaning of the text. How would the following problems be resolved after *Simpson* and *Jones*?

a. Problem 1

A and B were married in 1965. They separated seven years later and A's serious illness resulted in temporary custody of their two children being given to B. B had custody for two years until, upon A's full recovery, custody was transferred to A. During the two-year period when B had custody of their children, B recorded or simultaneously overheard all conversations that A had with their children in B's house by use of the following equipment. B purchased an automatic telephone answering machine which was plugged into the telephone and then played a recording of B's voice stating that callers had 45 seconds to identify themselves and leave a message. A loud speaker attached to the machine permitted anyone in the apartment to hear the callers identify themselves. B's purpose in installing this answering machine was to avoid speaking to A when A telephoned the children at B's apartment. If A was heard identifying herself on the machine one of the children rather than B would pick up the phone. B had instructed the children to turn a knob marked "record" on the machine whenever A called, thus, surreptitiously taping A's conversation. If B was at home, the loud speaker arrangement enabled B to hear the conversation in another room. If B was not at home, B could later play back the recording of the conversations. B alleged that the conversations were intended to be used against A in custody proceedings.

Consider the following questions:

(1) Was the projection of A's conversations over the loud speaker an interception of a wire or oral communication within Title I?

(2) Was the recording of A's conversation an interception of a wire or oral communication within Title I?

b. Problem 2

A and B are married. They separate and A, having left the marital home, establishes her own separate residence. B enters A's home and places a recording device on her telephone. He retrieves the device after it has been on her phone for one week.

c. Problem 3

A and B were lovers for a lengthy period of time. B was the mother of A's child. A hid for five days under B's house and electronically intercepted and taped all of her telephone conversations.

Do the actions of the parties in (2) and (3) constitute an interception of wire or oral communications within Title I?

Note

Federal cases following or consistent with *Jones* include *Kempf v. Kempf*, 868 F.2d 970, 973 (8th Cir.1989); *White v. Weiss*, 535 F.2d 1067 (8th Cir.1976); *Pritchard v. Pritchard*, 732 F.2d 372 (4th Cir.1984); *Heggy v. Heggy*, 944 F.2d 1537 (10th Cir.1991); *Nations v. Nations*, 670 F.Supp. 1432 (W.D.Ark.1987); *Kratz v. Kratz*, 477 F.Supp. 463 (E.D.Pa.1979).

Federal cases following *Simpson* include *Anonymous v. Anonymous*, 558 F.2d 677 (2d Cir.1977); *United States v. Schrimsher*, 493 F.2d 848 (5th Cir.1974) (distinguishing *Simpson* because victim and defendant were not married); *Perfit v. Perfit*, 693 F.Supp. 851 (C.D.Cal.1988); *Platt v. Platt*, 685 F.Supp. 208 (E.D.Mo.1988), *rev'd without opinion*, 873 F.2d 1447 (8th Cir.1989); *Lizza v. Lizza*, 631 F.Supp. 529 (E.D.N.Y.1986); *London v. Lon-*

don, 420 F.Supp. 944 (S.D.N.Y.1976); *Remington v. Remington*, 393 F.Supp. 898, 901 (E.D.Pa.1975). For a commentator supporting this view, see Stephens, *All's Fair: No Remedy under Title III for Interspousal Surveillance*, 57 Fordham L. Rev. 1035 (1989).

Even where *Simpson's* general approach to the domestic conflict exception is followed, there is general agreement that surveillance by a third party such as a private detective or a lawyer does not come within the exception. See *Anthony v. United States*, 667 F.2d 870 (10th Cir.1981), *cert. denied*, 419 U.S. 897 (1974); *Heyman v. Heyman*, 548 F.Supp. 1041 (N.D.Ill.1982); *Remington v. Remington*, 393 F.Supp. 898 (E.D.Pa.1975).

Even those courts and commentators that have been critical of the adoption of a domestic conflict exception to Title I have suggested that it would be inappropriate for the statute to be applied to the case of a parent listening to the conversation of a child in the family home over the extension phone. See James G. Carr, The Law of Electronic Surveillance, Section 3.6 (1991). If one were to take the position that listening to the conversation of a child by a parent is a "ordinary use" but listening to the conversation of a spouse is not, what would the principled basis for distinguishing between the two cases be? Suppose a parent suspects a child of drug use and also suspects the source of the child's exposure to drugs to be a particular friend of the child. Whenever the friend calls and the parent is home, the parent listens to their conversation over an extension phone. After listening to three conversations in which a purchase of marihuana is discussed, the parent anonymously informs the police of a prospective sale at the friend's house. The police arrest the child after he leaves the friend's house and find one pound of marihuana in his possession. Should the actions of the parent in listening to the conversations be viewed as a "ordinary use" of the telephone for purposes of a parent-child extension phone exception to Title I? See *Commonwealth v. Baldwin*, 282 Pa.Super. 82, 422 A.2d 838 (1980).

The first federal appellate court to squarely deal with the issue of whether a parent was exempt from liability under Title I for recording the conversation of a minor child has concluded that the eavesdropping was within the ordinary use exemption that is found in 2510 (5) (a) (i). See *Newcomb v. Ingle*, 944 F.2d 1534 (10th Cir.1991), *cert. denied*, 502 U.S. 1044 (1992). In *Newcomb* a divorced custodial parent taped conversations between her son and his father over the telephone in her home. After reaching majority the son brought an action under Title I for damages. In affirming the lower court's granting of summary judgment to the custodial parent Judge Anderson speaking for a unanimous court concluded that there was no "persuasive reason why Congress would exempt a business extension under 2510 (5) (a) (i) and not one in the home." Id. at 1536. The *Harpel* case, *supra*, was not discussed in *Newcomb*; the court did, however, invoke the testimony by Professor Herman Schwartz before the House Judiciary Committee holding hearings on The Federal Wiretap Statute in support of the holding ("I take it nobody wants to make it a crime for a father to listen in on his teenage daughter or some such related problem"). 944 F.2d at 1536. This testimony was also quoted by the *Simpson* court, *supra*.

Compare, *Newcomb* with *Anonymous v. Anonymous*, 558 F.2d 677 (2d Cir.1977).

Note: Electronic Surveillance of Conversations of Prisoners

Fourth amendment protection for the conversational privacy of prisoners has been addressed by the Supreme Court in two cases that have emerged as the controlling precedent. In *Lanza v. New York*, 370 U.S. 139 (1962), a majority of the Supreme Court assumed as a basis of its decision that the fourth amendment did not reach the electronic surveillance of a prisoner's conversation with his brother in an area that had been designated by the prison as a place for discussions with prisoners and persons from outside. The Court considered jail to be a public place that distinguished it from areas like a home, apartment, office, or automobile that were protected under the fourth amendment. *Lanza* was a pre-Katz decision. *Hudson v. Palmer*, 468 U.S. 517 (1984), further removed the reach of the Constitution. The Court held that a convicted prisoner has no reasonable expectation of privacy in her prison cell. *Lanza* and *Hudson* have generally been construed to hold that the electronic surveillance of the conversations of convicted prisoners within a prison with other prisoners or persons from the outside does not constitute a search under the federal constitution. This is also the case where fourth amendment claims are raised against governmental surveillance of conversations between prisoners or pre-trial detainees and those outside the prison over a telephone system. The visitor and the speaker on the phone outside the institution, as well as the prisoner and pre-trial detainee, are viewed as having no reasonable expectation of privacy in their conversations, see *United States v. Amen*, 831 F.2d 373 (2d Cir.1987), *cert. denied sub nom. Abbamonte v. United States*, 485 U.S. 1021 (1988); *United States v. Montgomery*, 675 F.Supp. 164 (S.D.N.Y.1987), *aff'd sub nom. United States v. Willoughby*, 860 F.2d 15 (2d Cir.1988), *cert. denied*, 488 U.S. 1033 (1989).

A similar analysis has been applied under Title I for the electronic surveillance of conversations within a prison. Where the surveillance involved oral communications, the absence of a reasonable expectation of privacy precludes application of Title I. However, Title I has been applied to some conversations by prisoners.

Although the legislative history of Title I cites *Lanza* as a case supporting the proposition that a prisoner has no reasonable expectation of privacy in a jail cell, Title I has been applied to the warrantless interception of conversations by prisoners on telephone systems that are connected to systems outside the prison. In *Campiti v. Walonis*, 611 F.2d 387 (1st Cir.1979), the court rejected the state's argument that the monitoring of conversations over a prison extension phone was exempt from statutory coverage. The court first rejected any blanket extension phone exception to Title I, noting that support for such an exception had been limited to domestic conflict cases. The central argument for the state was that the surveillance was not an interception within the meaning of 18 U.S.C.A. § 2510 (5)(a)(i) and (ii) which excludes surveillance by "an investigative or law enforcement officer in the ordinary course of his duty."

In rejecting the granting of a blanket exemption of recording of prisoners' telephone calls under the statute, the court found that the monitoring of the call was not part of the ordinary business of the prison officials but in fact was contrary to the monitoring practices that existed at the prison. The monitoring practice in Walpole prison was for a guard to stand next to the phone from which the prisoner was calling and the interception in this case was done without the consent or awareness of any of the participants and in violation of prison practice.

The Sixth Circuit applied the ordinary business law enforcement exemption to the monitoring of telephone conversations by prisoners in *United States v. Paul*, 614 F.2d 115 (6th Cir.1980), *cert. denied*, 446 U.S. 941 (1980). In *Paul*, the court relied heavily on the fact that the monitoring occurred pursuant to published federal and local prison rules and policies carefully drawn to protect the security of the prisoner. The *Paul* court distinguished *Campiti* on the basis that in that case the monitoring was not shown to be related to prison security and was not done pursuant to a posted prison regulation. The *Campiti* court specifically chose not to decide whether the ordinary business exception would apply to monitoring pursuant to an established prison policy of which prisoners had been informed. See *Campiti* at 392 n. 4.

The monitoring of calls which are made within a prison on a self-contained phone system would be subject to the analysis of oral communication within Title I. In those instances, where notice was given that calls were being monitored on a regular basis, the better argument would be that prisoners have no reasonable expectation of privacy regarding such calls. Telephone conversations between a federal prisoner and his attorney have been subject to a different analysis and found generally to be protected under Title I. This is because of a specific policy in the Federal Bureau of Prisons Regulations, 28 C.F.R. Section 540.101. See *Crooker v. United States Department of Justice*, 497 F.Supp. 500 (D.Conn.1980). The approach of the *Paul* court is also based upon a realistic assessment of the effect of applying the statute to telephone conversations in the prison context, namely, to eliminate telephone privileges to prisoners generally because of the restrictions of Title I. The interrelationship between the telephone privileges of prisoners and the monitoring of phone calls is illustrated by the following excerpts from the Federal Prison Regulations:

Subparts G–H—(Reserved)

Subpart 1—Telephone Regulations for Inmates Authority: 5 U.S.C. 301; 18 U.S.C. 4001, 4002, 4081, 4082, 5006–5024, 5039; 28 U.S.C. 509, 510; 28 C.F.R. 0.95–0.99.

Source: 44 FR 38249, June 29, 1979, unless otherwise noted.

28 C.F.R. sections 540.100 to 540.105 (1990).

Section 540.100 Purpose and scope.

An inmate may call a person of his choice outside the institution on a telephone provided for that purpose. Inmate telephone use is subject to limitations and restrictions which the Warden determines are necessary to insure the security, good order, and discipline of the institution and to protect the public. The Warden shall establish procedures and facilities for inmate telephone use. The Warden shall permit an inmate who has not been restricted from telephone use under Section 540.103 to make at least one telephone call each three months. Ordinarily, an inmate is allowed at least three minutes for each call.

Section 540.101 Monitoring of inmate telephone calls.

The Warden shall establish procedures that enable monitoring of telephone conversations on any telephone located within the institution, said monitoring to be done to preserve the security and orderly management of the institution and to protect the public. The Warden must provide notice to the inmate of the potential for monitoring. Staff may not monitor an inmate's properly placed call to an attorney. The Warden shall notify an inmate of the proper procedures to have an unmonitored telephone conversation with an attorney.

[48 FR 24622, June 1, 1983]

Section 540.102 Inmate telephone calls to attorneys.

The Warden may not apply frequency limitations on inmate telephone calls to attorneys when the inmate demonstrates that communication with attorneys by correspondence, visiting, or normal telephone use is not adequate.

Section 540.103 Responsibility for inmate misuse of telephones.

The inmate is responsible for any misuse of the telephone. The Warden shall refer incidents of unlawful inmate telephone use to law enforcement authorities. The Warden shall advise an inmate that violation of the institution's telephone regulations may result in institutional disciplinary action (See Part 541, Subpart B).

Section 540.104 Expenses of inmate telephone use.

An inmate is responsible for the expenses of inmate telephone use. Inmate calls shall ordinarily be made collect to the party called. Third party billing and electronic transfer of a call to a third party are not permitted. The Warden may direct the government to bear the expense of inmate telephone use under compelling circumstances such as when an inmate has lost contact with his family or has a family emergency. Another example is where the inmate experiences a lack of visits over an extended period of time. This is particularly true where there are no financial resources available either from the inmate or his family.

Section 540.105 Telephone calls for inmates in admission, holdover, segregation, or pre-trial status.

The Warden shall establish procedures for allowing inmates in admission, holdover or segregation status to make phone calls as provided in Section 540.100. Pre-trial inmates may make phone calls as provided in Part 551, Subpart J. Staff may not withhold phone privileges as a disciplinary measure except where the infraction for which disciplinary action is taken involves abuse, or a clear potential for abuse, of phone privileges.

[48 FR 24623, June 1, 1983]

The warrantless surveillance of conversations between a prisoner and his or her attorney constitutes a direct affront to the attorney/client privilege. Such practices arguably violate the Sixth Amendment right to counsel.

E. SEC. 2515 ADMISSIBILITY OF FRUITS OF EVIDENCE PROCURED BY ILLEGAL ELECTRONIC SURVEILLANCE

SCOPE OF SECTION 2515 AS APPLIED TO STATE DIVORCE AND CUSTODY PROCEEDINGS

If a jurisdiction follows *Jones* and not *Simpson* and interprets Title I not to carve out an exception for domestic conflicts, then the fairest reading of section 2515 would be that such evidence is not admissible in state divorce or custody proceedings. This is the view taken by the Florida appellate court in *Markham v. Markham*, 265 So.2d 59 (Fla.Dist. Ct.App.1972), *aff'd.*, 272 So.2d 813 (Fla.1973). The same result was reached in North Carolina in *Rickenbaker v. Rickenbaker*, 28 N.C.App. 644, 222 S.E.2d 463 (1976), *aff'd.*, 290 N.C. 373, 226 S.E.2d 347 (1976). In both of the above cases the wiretap was attempted to be introduced to establish the merits of the controversy. Suppose, however, a court took the view that section 2515 was generally applicable to state divorce or custody proceeding but what if the wiretap was introduced to establish that a provisional custody order was procured by fraud?

In *In re Marriage of Lopp*, 268 Ind. 690, 378 N.E.2d 414 (1978), the Supreme Court of Indiana held that it was not reversible error for a trial judge to hear wiretaps procured in violation of Title I where the wiretap victim claimed that the wiretaps were used by her spouse to blackmail her into signing a provisional custody order. The court decided that even if section 2515 generally required exclusion of wiretaps introduced to establish the merits of the controversy, the exclusionary rule was not applicable to conversations introduced to challenge the credibility of witnesses or to conversations that were pertinent to allegations of testimony defrauding a court. To apply the exclusionary rule of section 2515 to such cases would violate the due process clause and constitute an unconstitutional impairment of essential functions of state judges and state sovereignty.

The state sovereignty case relied upon in *Lopp* was *National League of Cities v. Usery*, 426 U.S. 833 (1976). *National League of Cities*, held that federal commerce clause legislation imposing a minimum wage requirement upon local government entities violated state sovereignty. The minimum wage holding of *National League of Cities* was overruled in *Garcia v. San Antonio Metropolitan Transit Authority*, 469 U.S. 528 (1985). However in two subsequent cases the Supreme Court has found federal legislation enacted under the commerce clause to violate state sovereignty. See *New York v. United States,* 505 U.S. 144 (1992) and *Printz v. United States*, 521 U.S. 898 (1997). Compare *Testa v. Katt*, 330 U.S. 386 (1947) (holding that federal legislation requiring state courts to enforce federally created causes of action does not violate state sovereignty). Is *Lopp* consistent with *Testa*?

F.   EXCEPTIONS IN TITLE I

1.   INTRODUCTION

Title I contains exceptions to the general prohibitions in the statute. A limited exception is provided for "provider[s] of wire or electronic communication service" in section 2511(2)(a), and for the Federal Communications Commission in section 2511(2)(b). A major exception is provided for persons acting under color of state law where a party to the conversation has given consent in section 2511–2(c). A more limited exception is given to private parties where consent has been given in section 2511–2(d). (An additional type of exception is contained in section 2518(7) for some emergencies providing a warrant is procured within 48 hours.)

2.   SECTION 2511–2(d) ONE PARTY CONSENT EXCEPTION TO LIABILITY FOR PRIVATE ELECTRONIC EAVESDROPPING

UNITED STATES v. PHILLIPS

540 F.2d 319 (8th Cir.1976), *cert. denied*, 429 U.S. 1000 (1976).

Before GIBSON, CHIEF JUDGE, and LAY and ROSS, CIRCUIT JUDGES.

ROSS, CIRCUIT JUDGE.

[Phillips was prosecuted for knowingly making false statements before a grand jury. The grand jury convened in December of 1971 to investigate a conspiracy involving certain organized crime members from Kansas City and certain nightclub owners from northeastern Oklahoma. The objective of the conspiracy was to establish illegal gambling and prostitution activities in the nightclubs by bribing local government officials in exchange for protection from the law.

Defendant Phillips, then a practicing attorney and Oklahoma state senator, was a close friend and political supporter of Frank Grayson, an Oklahoma district attorney. Grayson was providing protection for gambling at certain local clubs. Grayson testified before the grand jury that certain persons had told him that Phillips had stated that he could control Grayson with respect to illegal club operations. Specifically, Grayson testified that Charles Davis, owner of a major development named Shangri La Lodge, told him that Phillips stated he could arrange anything Davis needed in the way of local protection.

On August 1, 1972, Phillips was called before the grand jury. He repeatedly denied ever communicating to any individuals about an arrangement of protection from local law enforcement officials. He specifically denied that he made any related representations to persons affiliated with the Shangri La.

The critical evidence admitted at trial was a tape recorded meeting between Phillips, Davis, and George Overton, manager of the Shangri

La. This conversation was recorded by a private detective on July 7, 1971. At the time, Phillips was representing Davis and Overton before the Grand River Dam Authority regarding certain improvements in the Shangri La. Phillips, however, was not aware the conversation was recorded and the purpose for which the conversation was recorded is unknown.

The apparent purpose of the meeting was to settle on a fee arrangement between Phillips and the Shangri La management. During the conversation, Phillips told Davis and Overton that an illegal liquor and gambling operation could be run at the Shangri La on a limited basis. In an obvious reference to Grayson, Phillips stated, "I can control Frank."

Prior to trial, defendant filed a supplemental motion to suppress the tape recording on the grounds that the conversation was recorded in violation of Title III of the Omnibus Crime Control and Safe Streets Act of 1968, 18 U.S.C. Sections 2510, et seq. Defendant also moved to suppress the tape recording on the grounds that he was not admonished of his Miranda rights before the grand jury. Both motions were denied by Judge Duncan. At the conclusion of trial, defendant moved for a directed acquittal and a new trial. The motion was denied in all respects and the tape and its contents were admitted at trial.

The case was originally assigned to Judge Duncan who ruled on all pretrial motions and presided throughout the trial. At the conclusion of trial, defendant moved for a directed acquittal and a new trial. The motions were pending when Judge Duncan died on July 31, 1974. Judge Hunter was assigned to the case. Pursuant to Fed.R.Crim.P. 25(b), Judge Hunter certified that he could fairly and adequately dispose of the post-trial motions. After reviewing the record, Judge Hunter denied defendant's motions for acquittal and a new trial. Defendant alleged numerous points of error on this appeal.]

Title III of the Omnibus Crime Control and Safe Streets Act of 1968 sets forth a comprehensive legislative scheme regulating the interception of oral and wire communications. This legislation attempts to strike a delicate balance between the need to protect persons from unwarranted electronic surveillance and the preservation of law enforcement tools needed to fight organized crime.

Section 2511(1)(a) generally prohibits the willful interception of any wire or oral communication. Section 2511(2)(d) provides an exception and subexception to the general rule. That section reads as follows:

> It shall not be unlawful under this chapter for a person not acting under color of law to intercept a wire or oral communication where such person is a party to the communication or where one of the parties to the communication has given prior consent to such interception unless such communication is intercepted for the purpose of committing any criminal or tortious act in violation of the Constitution or laws of the United States or of any State or for the purpose of committing any other injurious act. (Emphasis supplied.)

This section was missing from Title III when the bill was first reported out of committee. At the urging of Senators Hart and McClellan however, Section 2511(2)(d) was added to the bill, 114 Cong. Rec. 14695 (May 28, 1968), " . . . to prohibit a one-party consent tap, [where the monitoring is conducted not under color of law,] except . . . for private persons who act in a defensive fashion." Id. at 14694. In the words of Senator Hart:

> . . . [W]henever a private person acts in such situations with an unlawful motive, he will violate the criminal provisions of Title III and will also be subject to a civil suit. Such one-party consent is also prohibited when the party acts in any way with an intent to injure the other party to the conversation in any other way. For example the secret consensual recording may be made for the purpose of blackmailing the other party, threatening him, or publicly embarrassing him. The provision would not, however, prohibit such activity when the party records information of criminal activity by the other party with the purpose of taking such information to the police as evidence. Nor does it prohibit such recording in other situations when the party acts out of legitimate desire to protect himself and his own conversations from later distortions or other unlawful or injurious uses by the other party.

18 U.S.C. Section 2515 imposes an evidentiary sanction to compel compliance with Section 2511. That section provides that any oral communication intercepted in violation of the Act shall not be received in evidence in any judicial proceeding. Section 2515 is not self-executing however. Section 2518(10)(a) provides that any aggrieved person may file a motion to suppress the contents of any unlawfully intercepted oral communication. This section " . . . provides the remedy for the right created by section 2515." Thus, as the government asserted at oral argument, whether the conversation was recorded for a permissible or impermissible purpose is a matter of suppression properly cognizable at a pretrial suppression hearing. Id.

Under traditional search and seizure law, "[t]he burden, is, of course, on the accused in the first instance to prove to the trial court's satisfaction that wire-tapping was unlawfully employed." The prima facie burden of proving the ultimate illegality should be distinguished from the burden to prove taint flowing from that illegality. " . . . [W]hen an illegal search has come to light, [the government] has the ultimate burden of persuasion to show that its evidence is untainted." (Emphasis supplied.)

Available legislative history in regard to Sections 2511(2)(d) and 2515 reflects no congressional desire to change the traditional burden of proof with respect to suppression of electronically gathered evidence. . . .

We perceive sound reasons for preserving the traditional allocation of burden of proof in this context. Sections 2511(2)(d) and 2515 require the exclusion of an intercepted communication if it was intercepted for any criminal, tortious or other injurious purpose. To require the government or any other party to prove as a matter of foundation that an interception was made for no criminal, tortious or other injurious purpose would create an impossible burden of proving three negatives. Logic requires that the party against whom the evidence is offered, the defendant here, carry the ultimate burden of alleging and proving the specific criminal, tortious, or other injurious purpose for which the interception was made.

... Indeed, in this case the fact to be proved, the purpose of the recording, has no relation to the act proscribed, the crime of perjury. Thus due process is not offended by requiring the defendant to shoulder the ultimate burden of proof under Sections 2511(2)(d) and 2515.

It is clear however that a party seeking to suppress such matter must be given a full and fair opportunity to meet his or her burden of proof. Our review of the record convinces us that defendant was effectively denied this opportunity in the court below.

Because of pretrial discovery, this point was not raised until the eve of trial. Nevertheless, at that time the defendant filed his supplemental motion to suppress claiming that the conversation was recorded for a tortious purpose. The motion was orally raised the next morning in the trial judge's chambers. The motion was summarily denied before defense counsel was given any opportunity to make a statement or offer evidence in support of the motion. The trial judge expressed the view at this time that any such evidence would be admissible for impeachment purposes only. At trial, defense counsel attempted to pursue the subject with George Overton, manager of the Shangri La. The government objected to this line of questioning on the grounds of irrelevancy and the objection was sustained. Thus, the dearth of evidence on the issue, which both parties acknowledge, was largely created by the unwillingness of the trial judge to allow defense counsel to pursue this line of inquiry. Under these circumstances, we find it necessary to remand to the district court for a hearing to determine the purpose for which the conversation was recorded. If the recording was made for a legitimate purpose, the judgment of conviction must be reinstated. If, however, the defendant proves by a preponderance of the evidence that the recording was made for a criminal, tortious or other injurious purpose, the tape must be suppressed. If the tape is suppressed, a new trial will be necessary under section 2511 (2) (d) if the recording was done for the purpose of causing "insult and injury" to the plaintiff, as alleged in the plaintiff's third count; this would be a question of fact for the jury.

Note

In *Moore v. Telfon Communications Corp.*, 589 F.2d 959 (9th Cir.1978), the Ninth Circuit held that a private nonconsensual recording of a telephone conversation did not violate Title I when the recorder did so out of a legitimate desire to protect himself (i.e., preserve evidence of extortion). Accord, *Meredith v. Gavin*, 446 F.2d 794 (8th Cir.1971), where the court reasoned that "[a] perfectly legitimate act may often be injurious," and held that the conduct Congress intended to prohibit was the "interception by a party to the conversation with an intent to use that interception against the non-consenting party in some harmful way and in a manner in which the offending party had no right to proceed." *Id.* at 799.

Section 2511(2)(d) was amended by the ECPA, and "or for the purpose of committing any other injurious act" was deleted from 2511(2)(d). The legislative history of this change indicates that the deletion of "any other injurious act" was intended to bring precision to the exception to one party consent in section (2)(d). The legislative history cites *Boddie v. American Broadcasting Co.*, 731 F.2d 333 (6th Cir.1984), as an example of judicial misconstruction of the deleted language. Report of the Committee on the Judiciary on the Electronic Communications Privacy Act of 1986, H.R. Rep. No. 647, 2d Sess., 39 (1986). In *Boddie* the plaintiff argued that the defendant violated the statute by recording a conversation between Boddie and a reporter even though the reporter consented to the recording. The court suggested that the consent of the reporter would not be a defense under section 2511(2)(d) if the recording was done for the purpose of causing "insult and injury" to the plaintiff, as alleged in the plaintiff's third count; this would be a question of fact for the jury.

With the amendment to section 2511(2)(d) under what circumstances other than recording a conversation for the purpose or blackmail or extortion would a recording of a conversation with the consent of one of the parties violate Title I?

G. EXPANDING INFORMATIONAL PRIVACY RIGHTS: BEYOND SEC. 2511 UNDER STATE ELECTRONIC EAVESDROPPING STATUTES.

STATE v. AYRES

118 N.H. 90, 383 A.2d 87 (1978).

Bois, J.

[The defendant was indicted for criminal solicitation under RSA 629:2 for unlawfully soliciting another person to commit murder. The charges arose out of an alleged meeting in a hotel room involving the defendant, his wife, a police informant, and a wired undercover police officer. It was at this meeting that the defendant allegedly solicited the undercover police officer to commit murder. The police officer wore an electronic device which transmitted the conversation to a tape recorder in the next room. At the defendant's trial, the tape recording was introduced into evidence. The defendant appeals.]

The recording of the conversation in this case did not violate the Federal Constitution. See United States v. White. See generally, United States v. Miller. New Hampshire RSA ch. 570–A, however, is a stricter wiretapping and eavesdropping law, and protects the individual's right to privacy to a greater degree than the United States Constitution or the federal statute, 18 U.S.C. Sections 2510–2520. This the State concedes. It is a comprehensive statute which prohibits, with a few exceptions, wiretapping and eavesdropping without prior court authorization. One exception to this prohibition, added in 1975 to RSA 570–A:2 reads:

> It shall not be unlawful for any law enforcement officer, when conducting investigations of or making arrests for offenses enumerated in this chapter, to carry with him on his person an electronic, mechanical or other device which intercepts oral communications and transmits such communications by radio.

The State conceded at oral argument that the actions of the police would have been illegal under RSA ch. 570–A without this exception, but claims the exception legalizes the police actions in this case. We agree that the interception of the oral communication herein was authorized by this exception. Our concern, however, is with the tape recording of the oral communication and the use of the tape at the defendant's trial. The State contends that because the interception is allowed its recordation and use are also allowed despite RSA 570–A:6. We do not agree.

An examination of the legislative history reveals that the proposal to amend RSA 570–A:2 to include this exception came from the attorney general. At oral argument the State explained that the amendment was designed for the protection of undercover police officers. The exception allows police officers who are outside the immediate vicinity of the criminal activity to monitor the criminal transaction. Should it become apparent that the safety of the undercover officer is in jeopardy, the police can come to his rescue. The State succinctly expressed the exception's purpose in these words: "It is to protect the safety of the officer and nothing more."

The history of this amendment does not indicate that the legislature intended to radically change the statute and do away with the protections afforded our citizens by the authorization procedures established by RSA ch. 570–A. The purpose was expressed as follows: "They tighten up loopholes in our present wiretapping law, . . . " If it were otherwise, a recording of a conversation transmitted from a bugged police officer could be used at trial, but a recording of the same conversation made by a tape recorder contained on the officer's person could not be used at trial unless prior authorization was obtained.

We do not believe that such a distinction was intended. It is our opinion that the legislature proposed to provide a narrow exception to the eavesdropping prohibition in order to protect the undercover police officer; it did not intend to allow a recording of the eavesdropping to be used as evidence. This is the only way in which the amendment can be construed consistently with the thrust of the entire chapter. See State v. Kay, 115 N.H. 696, 350 A.2d 336 (1975). If we are interpreting the legislature's intent incorrectly, it should take appropriate action. See e.g., Davis v. Manchester, 100 N.H. 335, 340, 126 A.2d 254, 258 (1956).

Because we hold the tape was improperly used as evidence at the defendant's trial and the order is for a new trial, we need not consider defendant's other contentions.

Defendant's exceptions sustained in part; remanded.

LAMPRON, J., did not sit; the others concurred.

Note: Expanding Informational Privacy Rights Under State Electronic Eavesdropping Statutes

As *State v. Ayres* illustrates, a state may provide greater legal protection against invasions of privacy by electronic surveillance than is provided for under the ECPA. State and federal authority to regulate electronic surveillance is an example of "cooperative federalism." Congress did not preempt the states from enacting regulatory legislation when the Federal Wiretap Act was adopted. Congress and the states maintain concurrent authority to legislate in the area as long as state legislation provides at least the same protection for privacy as the ECPA. Federal law is the floor of privacy protection but not the ceiling. State electronic surveillance statutes generally track the federal statute. As with the ECPA, state statutes are structured around the concepts of "interception of wire, oral or electronic communications" and generally deal with cases where one party has consented to the surveillance under sections in the statute that define the scope of exceptions from liability. In cases where invasions of privacy occur through electronic surveillance, it is important that the statute in the state where the surveillance occurred be examined carefully to determine if there are more restrictions on electronic surveillance under that state's law than there is under the ECPA.

The New Hampshire statute provides an example of one of the areas where state statutes depart from the federal statute and provide greater protection for privacy. There is essentially a blanket exception for responsibility under Title I if one party to the conversation has consented, yet under the New Hampshire statute the exception was limited to the transmission of a conversation by law enforcements officials. New Hampshire amended the electronics eavesdropping statute after *Ayres* to allow for greater warrantless surveillance of conversations where one party has consented. Such surveillance is allowed for investigations of specified crimes when there has been a determination by the Attorney General that there is "reasonable suspicion" that evidence of such crimes will be derived from the surveillance. N.H. Rev. Stat. Ann. Sections 570–A:1, A:2 (1986 & Supp. 1990).

State v. Ayres demonstrates that in participant monitoring cases it is especially important to research the state statutes' consent provisions. Pennsylvania is a state that has historically restricted electronic surveillance to a greater extent than The Federal Wiretap Act.

Consider the following portions of the Pennsylvania Wiretapping and Electronic Surveillance Control Act and compare the text of section 5704 (2) (i), (ii) of the Pennsylvania statute with section 2511 (2) (b), (c) of Title I.

18 Pa. C.S.A. Section 5703. CRIMES AND OFFENSES

Section 5703. Interception, disclosure or use of wire, electronic or oral
communications

Except as otherwise provided in this chapter, a person is guilty of a felony of the third degree if he:

(1) intentionally intercepts, endeavors to intercept, or procures any other person to intercept or endeavor to intercept any wire, electronic or oral communication;

(2) intentionally discloses or endeavors to disclose to any other person the contents of any wire, electronic or oral communication, or evidence derived therefrom, knowing or having reason to know that the information was obtained through the interception of a wire, electronic or oral communication; or

(3) intentionally uses or endeavors to use the contents of any wire, electronic or oral communication, or evidence derived therefrom, knowing or having reason to know, that the information was obtained through the interception of a wire, electronic or oral communication.

Section 5704. Exceptions to prohibition of interception and disclosure of communications

It shall not be unlawful under this chapter for:

(1) An operator of a switchboard, or an officer, agent or employee of a provider of wire or electronic communication service, whose facilities are used in the transmission of a wire communication, to intercept, disclose or use that communication in the normal course of his employment while engaged in any activity which is a necessary incident to the rendition of his service or to the protection of the rights or property of the provider of wire or electronic communication service. However, no provider of wire or electronic communication service shall utilize service observing or random monitoring except for mechanical or service quality control checks.

(2) Any investigative or law enforcement officer or any person acting at the discretion or request of an investigative or law enforcement officer to intercept a wire, electronic or oral communication involving suspected criminal activities where:

(i) such officer or person is a party to the communication; or

(ii) one of the parties to the communication has given prior consent to such interception. However, no interception under this paragraph shall be made unless the Attorney General or a deputy attorney general designated in writing by the Attorney General, or the district attorney, or an assistant district attorney designated in writing by the district attorney, of the county wherein the interception is to be made, has reviewed the facts and is satisfied that the consent is voluntary and has given prior approval for the interception; however such interception shall be subject to the recording and record keeping requirements of section 5714(a) (relating to recording of intercepted communications) and that the Attorney General, deputy attorney general, district attorney or assistant district attorney authorizing the interception shall be the custodian of recorded evidence obtained therefrom.

How would the following cases come out under the Pennsylvania Wiretapping and Electronic Surveillance Control Act?

1. A rapes B during a date at B's apartment. Shortly thereafter and before B has notified the police, B records a telephone call from A. In this

conversation A admits to forcing B to have sex but says it was because a was out of control because of A's love for B. In the subsequent prosecution of a for rape the prosecutor seeks to have the tape of the telephone conversation admitted into evidence. Is the tape admissible? (Assume that evidence procured in violation of the pennsylvania statute is inadmissible in civil or criminal proceedings.) Compare your answer with that of the court in *Commonwealth v. Jung*, 366 Pa.Super. 438, 531 A.2d 498 (1987). Does the taping of the conversation by b violate title III?

2.   A, an employer, is investigating the theft of equipment from the workplace. A calls B, an employee, into her office and secretly tapes the answers by B to questions asked of him by A and C, B's foreman. Does the taping of B's conversations with A and C in A's office violate the pennsylvania statute?

3.   A variation of 2. C Is not in the office and B secretly records A's interrogation of him about the alleged theft. Violation of the Pennsylvania statute? Compare your answer with that of the court in a similar case, *Commonwealth v. Henlen*, 522 Pa. 514, 564 A.2d 905 (1989).

H.   SECTIONS 2511 AND 2520 CRIMINAL AND CIVIL REMEDIES

1.   CRIMINAL SANCTIONS AND CIVIL REMEDIES FOR VIOLATIONS OF TITLE I

As previously noted, Title I subjects violators of the statute to a $10,000 fine and imprisonment for five years, authorizes the confiscation of illegal eavesdropping devices, and in some circumstances prohibits the manufacture, distribution and possession of interception devices. Section 2511 includes four categories of criminal offenses. Each of these categories includes an element of "willfulness" and "interception." Thus, for there to be a criminal penalty for violating Title I the defendant must have acted willfully and there must be an interception within the meaning of Section 2510(4).

2.   CIVIL REMEDIES: FAULT REQUIREMENT FOR LIABILITY AND THE "GOOD FAITH" DEFENSE UNDER SECTION 2520

Section 2520 grants a civil remedy for damages for violations of Title I. The section specifically fixes minimum damages and authorizes the awarding of attorneys' fees and litigation costs. As previously noted section 2511 of Title I limits criminal sanctions to willful violations of the statute. Although there was initially no reference to "willful" in section 2520, the weight of authority is that a demonstration that the defendant had "willfully" violated the statute is a prerequisite to recovery for damages under this section. See *Citron v. Citron*, 722 F.2d 14 (2d Cir.1983), *cert. denied*, 466 U.S. 973 (1984); *Kratz v. Kratz*, 477 F.Supp. 463 (E.D.Pa.1979). "Willfully" within the meaning of sections 2511 and 2520 is not limited to knowingly violating the statute; "willful" has the broader meaning of reckless disregard of a known legal duty. Accidental

or negligent violations of the statute will not satisfy the fault requirements of sections 2511 or 2520. However it is enough that the interception was done without justifiable excuse, stubbornly, obstinately, per-
versely or without ground for believing it was lawful or with careless
disregard whether or not one had the right to act. In addition to *Citron*
and *Kratz*, see *Heggy v. Heggy*, 944 F.2d 1537 (10th Cir.1991).

"Good faith" reliance on a court warrant or order, grand jury
subpoena or legislative or statutory authorization are specified as defenses to liability under the statute. However, a general defense of "good
faith" based upon a misunderstanding of the law is not allowed, see
Heggy, supra; *Campiti v. Walonis*, 611 F.2d 387, 394–95 (1st Cir.1979).

The ECPA substituted "intentional" for "willfully" in section 2511
and added intentional to portions of section 2520. This substitution is
not likely to change the fault requirements under sections 2511 and 2520
that are reflected in the law that existed prior to 1986 and that is
summarized above.

Injunctive relief is not generally available as a remedy under The
Federal Wiretap Act. The ECPA Amendments added section 2521 to
provide for injunctive relief in limited circumstances when the action is
brought by the Attorney General. Injunctive relief for illegal surveillance
may be available under the common law or a statute of the state or if
there is a violation of the Constitution. Examples of injunctive relief
under these alternative legal theories are discussed in other sections of
this book.

Liquidated Damages Under Title I

Section 2520(c)(2)(A), (B) provides that in most cases of violation of
Title I the court may assess damages whichever is the greater of:

> (A) the sum of the actual damages suffered by the plaintiff and
> any profits made by the violator as a result of the violation; or

> (B) statutory damages of whichever is greater of $100 a day for
> each day of violation or $10,000.

This language seems to clearly indicate that where actual damages
are not involved and liquidated damages are appropriate the damages
are to be base upon either a factor of $100 by 100 times or more or
$10,000 whichever is greater. One of the issues that has split the courts
is whether the number of offenses occurring in a day are to be taken into
account in determining liquidated damages. Another is whether there is
double recovery under the minimum liquidated damage recovery rule if
an offender violates Title I by both intercepting and disclosing the
contents of a Title I protected communication.

A minority of courts interpret (2)(B) to adopt only one inclusive
method for calculating damages—the number of days on which any
violation occurred and whether the number of days exceed 100. See
Desilets v. Wal–Mart Stores, 171 F.3d 711 (1st Cir. N.H.1999). Under the
Desilets rule it is irrelevant whether 100 violations of Title I occurred on

one day or 50 on another day or whether multiple violations occurred on any day. Damages are to be calculated on the basis of $100 per day or $10,000 in liquidated damages even though there may have been both interception and divulgence violations. The *Desilets* court's view is based upon the plain meaning rule. The court contends that had multiple minimum statutory amounts meant to be recoverable Congress would have employed "for each distinct type of violation (interception, disclosure of use)," in (2)(B).

The other view embraced by most courts that have considered the issue is that multiple recovery of the minimum statutory amounts may be recovered if there were different violations under Title I. See *Biton v. Menda* 812 F.Supp. 283 (D.P.R. 1993); *Romano v. Terdik* 939 F.Supp. 144, 150 (D.Conn.1996); *Rogers v. Wood*, 910 F.2d 444, 446 (7th Cir. 1990); *Dorris v. Absher*, 959 F.Supp. 813, 819 n.9 (M.D.Tenn.1997). The reasoning of these courts is that $10,000 may be awarded for interception and $10,000 may be awarded for interception and $10,000 may be awarded for disclosure because they are considered to be separate violations of section 2511 of Title I.

Which of these views of the liquidated damage provisions of section 2520 do you find more persuasive?

I. THE IDENTIFICATION AND NOTICE REQUIREMENTS OF TITLE I: SECTION 2518

1. SECTION 2518

Section 2518 is a central provision of Title I. This section delineates the procedures for applying for court approved interception of wire or oral communications, the content of applications, and the order(s) that are approved, as well as notice that must be sent after the fact to those persons whose conversations were intercepted. Additionally, section 2518(10)(a) grants a right to suppress evidence under specified circumstances. The identification, notice and inventory sections of Title I contained in section 2518 are to a considerable extent interdependent and have been the basis of considerable litigation.

2. THE IDENTIFICATION REQUIREMENT OF SECTION 2518(1)(b), (IV), AND (4)(a)

Section 2518 in the above quoted portions requires that the application for a court approved interception and the final order that follows from that application include "the identity of the person, if known, whose communications are to be intercepted." This identification requirement reflects a balance of crime control and informational privacy interests. On the one hand, a basic objective of law enforcement officials in the use of electronic surveillance is to identify and acquire incriminating evidence against participants in criminal endeavors who are unknown. Conversely, regulations of uses of electronic surveillance to protect informational privacy within the statutory scheme of the statute appears to be built to a considerable extent on the requirement that those persons whose conversations are to be intercepted pursuant to court order be identified. Inventory notice under section 2518 may be denied a person who is not identified; without such notice the ability to challenge surveillance in litigation is severely limited. Moreover, meaningful judicial review of their surveillance would seem to depend upon government identification of known persons whose conversations are to be recorded. The Supreme Court balancing of the two-fold interests of the identification section of section 2518 has produced critical commentary. See J. Carr, The Law of Electronic Surveillance, 176–179 (Clark–Boardman 1977).

In *United States v. Kahn*, 415 U.S. 143 (1974), the Supreme Court interpreted the identification provision of section 2518(1)(b)(iv) to mean that the only persons who must be named in an application under Title I are those the government has probable cause to believe are involved in a criminal activity and will be using the target phone. Thus, the spouse of a named individual and known user of the target phone did not have to be identified in the application because there was no probable cause to believe the individual was involved in criminal activity at the time of the application. The practical effect of *Kahn* is to severely limit the obligation to investigate known users of a target phone at the time of the application to determine whether probable cause to believe they are part of a criminal activity is present. See, e.g., *Orkin v. State*, 236 Ga. 176, 223 S.E.2d 61 (1976), *United States v. Moore*, 513 F.2d 485 (D.C.Cir. 1975), *vacated without opinion*, 556 F.2d 77 (D.C.Cir.1977).

3. THE INVENTORY AND NOTICE REQUIREMENT OF TITLE I

Section 2518(8)(d) entitles only those persons who were named in the court order to receive notice and inventory of the wire tap as a matter of right. Notice to all other persons, even though their conversations were overheard and they were identifiable, is left to judicial discretion in the interests of justice. In *United States v. Donovan*, 429 U.S. 413 (1977), the Supreme Court unanimously agreed with the Ninth Circuit's conclusion in *United States v. Chun*, 503 F.2d 533 (9th Cir. 1974), that the prosecutor "has the duty to classify all those whose conversations have been intercepted, and to transmit this information to the judge. Should the judge desire more information regarding these classes in order to exercise his statutory section 2518(8)(d) discretion . . . the government is also required to furnish such information that is available to it." *U.S. v. Donovan*, 429 U.S. 413 at 431 (citing *United States v. Chun*, 503 F.2d at 540). *Donovan* thus would require disclosure in many instances of individuals whose conversations were intercepted but who were not named in the court order to presiding judges so that the discretionary notice provision of section 2518 could be exercised with full information. This aspect of the *Donovan* decision alleviates, to some extent, the void created for protecting informational privacy that results from the discretionary inventory and notice aspect of section 2518. The discretionary nature of the notice and inventory requirement has been criticized. See, J. Carr, *The Law of Electronic Surveillance*, sections 5.13–5.13(a) (1991).

4. SUPPRESSION OF EVIDENCE WHERE THERE IS A VIOLATION OF THE IDENTIFICATION OR NOTICE AND INVENTORY PROVISION

Section 2515 of Title I expressly prohibits the use at trial, and at certain other proceedings, of the contents of any intercepted wire communication or any evidence derived therefrom "if the disclosure of that information would be in violation of this chapter." Thus, in terms of suppressing evidence procured from a tap in violation of section 2518, section 2515 incorporates section 2518 (10)(a) which enumerates the circumstances when suppression is warranted under section 2518. In *United States v. Donovan*, 429 U.S. 413 (1977), the Supreme Court was confronted with motions to suppress evidence obtained from a wiretap which did not conform to the identification and inventory and notice requirements of section 2518. Nevertheless, six members of the Court found that suppression of the evidence was not required because the identification and inventory and notice requirements did not "play a central, or even functional role in guarding against unwarranted use of wiretapping or electronic surveillance." The sorting out of violations of Title I for purposes of suppression of evidence in terms of violation of the statute which are "central and substantive" and violations which are "noncentral or nonsubstantive" originated in *United States v. Giordano*, 416 U.S. 505 (1974), and *United States v. Chavez*, 416 U.S. 562 (1974). *Giordano* concerned the provision in Title I requiring that an application for an intercept order be approved by the Attorney General or an assistant Attorney General specially designated by the Attorney General. The Court concluded that this provision played a substantive role in the statutory scheme of the statute and granted suppression of the evidence which had been obtained by an interception not so authorized. *Chavez* concerned the statutory requirement that the application for an intercept order specify the identity of the official authorizing the application on facts which involved misidentification of the individual. A majority of the Court concluded that mere misidentification of the official authorizing the application did not make the application unlawful for purposes of the suppression section of 2518 because the identification requirement did not play a "substantive role" in the regulatory scheme of Title I. 416 U.S. at 578. In *Chavez*, Justice Douglas, speaking for three other members of the Court in dissent, vigorously objected to the Court picking and choosing "among various statutory provisions, suppressing evidence only when they determine that a provision is "substantive," "central" or "directly and substantially" related to the congressional scheme." *Id.* at 584–85. Is there support for this bifurcated notion of suppression remedies for violation of section 2518 in the legislative history of the statute? After *Chavez, Giordano,* and *Donovan*, only violations of Title I which are "central and substantive" to the statutory scheme of Title I are "unlawful" within the meaning of section 2518(10)(a) for purposes of a motion to suppress. A substantial majority of lower courts had suppressed evidence that was procured in violation of the identification section of the statute prior to *Donovan*, see, e.g., *United States v. Bernstein*, 509 F.2d 996, 998 (4th Cir.1975), *vacated* 430 U.S. 902 (1977). Is there another basis upon which the evidence might have been suppressed in *Donovan* under section 2518(10)(a)? A violation of the notice and inventory requirement was also found in *Donovan*, but the notice and inventory requirement, like the identification requirement, was found not to be central or substantive to the statute for purposes of a motion to suppress.

In dictum, the Court in *Donovan* suggested that intentional failure to name individuals "for the purpose of keeping relevant information from the district court that might have prompted the court to conclude that probable cause was lacking" would be a different case for purposes of suppression of evidence. 429 U.S. at 436 n.23.

In footnote 26 of the opinion the Court stated, "[m]oreover respondents . . . were not prejudiced by their failure to receive postintercept notice under either of the District Court's inventory orders. As noted earlier, the Government made available to all defendants the intercept orders, applications, and related papers [a]nd in response to pretrial discovery motions, the Government produced transcripts of the intercepted conversations." 429 U.S. at 439 n.26. Lower federal courts have interpreted footnotes 23 and 26 to require that the violation of the identification and notice provisions be both intentional and prejudicial to the defendant for suppression. See *United States v. Fury*, 554 F.2d 522, 529 (2d Cir.1977), *United States v. Landmesser*, 553 F.2d 17, 21, 22 (6th Cir.1977), *cert. denied*, 434 U.S. 855 (1977). The burden of proof on the issue of prejudice is apparently on the party whom is moving to suppress. See *United States v. Fury*, 554 F.2d 522, 529 (2d Cir.1977).

Carr takes the position that even where there are intentional violations, if the defendant has received notice of the surveillance in any form, the Supreme Court would probably not find prejudice for purposes of a motion to suppress. See J. Carr, The Law of Electronic Surveillance, 178 (1991).

J.   THE MINIMIZATION REQUIREMENT, SECTION 2518(5)

Section 2518(5) of Title I requires that every court ordered interception of wire, oral or electronic communications be "conducted in such a way as to minimize the interception of communications not otherwise subject to interception." The "minimization" requirement of section 2518 is constitutionally compelled in governmental surveillance cases in order to prevent an electronic seizure of a conversation from becoming a general search. For the search of a conversation to be "reasonable," efforts must be made to prevent unnecessary invasions of privacy by the seizure of conversations that are not related to the criminal activity that is being investigated. Consider the discussion of the Supreme Court in *Berger, supra,* Chapter 2, on the minimization deficiency of the New York statute under the fourth amendment. See also Note, Minimization and the Fourth Amendment, 19 N.Y.L.F. 861 (1974).

The implementation of a minimization requirement dramaticizes the difference between a traditional fourth amendment search and the search of conversations over a telephone. Minimization is somewhat easy to administer with a traditional search. The search is generally limited to the particular evidence that is the subject of the search, i.e., weapons, drug paraphernalia, narcotics. It is much more difficult to minimize unnecessary intrusions with an electronic search of conversations. Whether a conversation implicates the speaker in criminal activity or includes information that would identify other possible criminals or the existence of a criminal conspiracy is virtually impossible to determine until the conversation has been in progress. It is difficult to particularize the kind of future conversations that will be relevant to criminal activity in the initial court order. Additionally, by implementing the surveillance while the conversation develops, it is very likely that conversations unrelated to the criminal activities that are the subject of the investigation will be overheard.

Given these practical difficulties, the question of whether the government has complied with the minimization requirement has proved to be a difficult one for the courts. The leading Supreme Court case, *Scott v. United States,* 436 U.S. 128 (1978), clarified the minimization standards under the statute, but has been criticized as not providing adequate protection for privacy. *Scott* arose from a narcotics investigation where court ordered wiretaps of a suspect's telephone for a one month period were involved. During the surveillance, no effort was made to exclude non-pertinent conversations. Only 40% of the intercepted conversations were narcotics-related. The defendant argued that the failure of government officials to make good faith efforts to exclude conversations that were unrelated to the investigation violated the minimization requirement of section 2518(5). A majority of the Court in *Scott,* speaking through Justice Rehnquist, rejected the view that section 2518(5) required officers to engage in good faith efforts to minimize the surveillance of non-pertinent conversations. Compliance with the minimization requirement was to be determined by an objective assessment of the reasonableness of the officers' conduct under the circumstances. The Court rejected the view that reasonableness is to be determined solely on the basis of the percentage of non-pertinent calls that are intercepted. Instead it suggested several factors to be taken into account in determining the reasonableness of the surveillance. These were: (1) the nature of the offense being investigated (large scale conspiracy in *Scott*); (2) the type and location of the device (bug or tap, public telephone or private residence); (3) the nature of the non-pertinent conversations that were overheard (short conversations, conversations early in the investigation).

Applying these factors the Court concluded that the record supported the appellate court's conclusion that the surveillance was reasonable. The Court noted that a number of the non-pertinent conversations were short, ambiguous and one-time calls that did not provide the agents with an opportunity to determine their innocence.

Justice Brennan and Justice Marshall dissented in *Scott*. They concluded that by a "linguistic tour de force the Court convert[ed] the mandatory language [in 2518(5)] that the interception 'shall be conducted' [in]to a precatory suggestion." *Id*. at 145–46. The dissenters contended that a duty to make "good faith" efforts to minimize was required in order to enforce the basic premise of the Act that "intrusions of privacy must be kept to the minimum." *Id*. at 145. Does the "post-hoc reconstruction" approach of the majority encourage the government to ignore minimization in the belief that a legally sufficient argument that the surveillance was reasonable will always be available after the fact?

The failure of the Court in *Scott* to require good faith efforts to minimize under Title I has been the subject of considerable criticism. See generally James G. Carr, *The Law of Electronic Surveillance*, section 5.7 (a), 5–27, 5–45 (1991); M. Goldsmith, *The Supreme Court and Title III: Rewriting the Law of Electronic Surveillance*, 74 J. Crim. L. & Crim. 1, 97–112 (1983).

Carr has summarized the cases interpreting *Scott* to include five factors as guides for determining the reasonableness of surveillance in the face of minimization issues. They are: (1) the nature of the offense and purpose of the investigation; (2) the type and location of the device; (1 and 2 noted above); (3) the suspects' apparent awareness of the possibility of surveillance and their use of countermeasures; (4) the officers' implementation of generally accepted and preferred minimization techniques; and (5) the degree of judicial supervision. Carr at 5–42.

Some states have rejected *Scott* and required good faith under state electronics eavesdropping statutes. See, e.g., *People v. Brenes*, 42 N.Y.2d 41, 47, 364 N.E.2d 1322, 1327, 396 N.Y.S.2d 629, 633 (1977).

1. ROVING ELECTRONIC SURVEILLANCE

A requirement of an applications for a court ordered interception of wire or oral communications under Title I is that the site of the targeted phone be identified. This is the statutory embodiment of the fourth amendment particularization requirement. In the case of surveillance of conversations in an automobile, the vehicle is identified as the site. The 1986 Electronic Communications Privacy Act amended the particularization requirement that the site be identified in applications for interceptions of wire or oral communications. Section 2518 (11) (a)(b) eliminates the requirement when there is a finding by the judge reviewing the application that the site identification requirement is "impractical." In wire communication, there must be a finding that the purpose of the person who is the subject of the surveillance is to thwart "interception by changing facilities."

The effect of these amendments in the ECPA is to authorize surveillance that roves to various sites where the suspects conversations are likely to take place. This authority for court ordered "roving surveillance" is unprecedented and has been challenged by privacy advocates and civil libertarians as violating the minimization and particuliarization requirement of the fourth amendment. For an interesting analysis of the constitutionality of "roving surveillance," see, Michael Goldsmith, *Eavesdropping Reform: The Legality of Roving Surveillance*, 1987 U. Ill. L. Rev. 401 (1987).

Chapter Four

COMPUTERS, DIGITAL TECHNOLOGY, THE INTERNET, AND PRIVACY

A. DATA PRIVACY PROTECTION

The revolution in communications and data processing that is occurring in the United States and much of the world has created a realm of activity popularly referred to as Cyberspace. The most conspicuous offshoot of the new information technology is the Internet. The Internet is an internationally linked system of computer networks on which the data flows. The Information Super Highway is a metaphor for the communication links of the Internet, while Cyberspace is a metaphor for the medium whereby data processing and communications between the computer networks occurs. Not only is there no central entity that manages the linked computer network of the Internet, the nature of Cyberspace also means that data is not in any geographical location but in space—the electronically linked computer networks.

Currently, the most popular way to access the Internet is through the World Wide Web (the Web). The Web consists of millions of Web sites. Each Web site is separate but interlinked and each Web site may have hundreds of Web pages. With proper software Internet users may create their own Web pages and post in digital form sound, images and text on the Web page. Internet users may also view the images and video, read the text and listen to the sound of other Web sites. Web browser's are used to access information on the Web.

Some idea of the dazzling pace of the new information processing order can be gleaned from the fact that in 1972 when Arthur Miller wrote the article that is printed in part below, he estimated there were one hundred thousand computers in operation. In 1995 it was estimated that there were nine and one half million host computers on the Internet alone. At the heart of the new order of communications and data processing is digital technology. The Information Super Highway, Cyberspace, and the Internet are possible because of digital technology. The use and importance of computer technology to the United States and the world has magnified the privacy issues that are raised by Arthur Miller and other writers in the 1970's. This chapter examines some of the important privacy issues raised by the new information technology to privacy and privacy law. First it is helpful to review some of the features of digital technology that account for the new order of information processing and communications.

1. ANALOG AND DIGITAL TECHNOLOGY

The central feature of the revolution in communication and data processing is the transformation in communications and data processing from analog to digital technology. Analog technology electronically transmits communications and images by an electronic representative of the actual communication or image. Analog technology is based upon replication of the form of the communication or image that is transmitted. The replicated phenomena is transmitted in a continuous uninterrupted form. For example, in analog based telephone communications, the sound wave produced by the voice is transmitted by an electronic signal with the same frequency as the voice. The whole replicated conversation is transmitted with analog technology.

Digital technology takes samples of the actual sound wave or image or text and converts the samples into arithmetic quantities that are expressed in binary digits or bits (with eight bits forming one "byte"). These bytes may be then packaged and transmitted. The package may consist of pieces of the sound wave, image, or text. In assembling the package bytes of sound waves, images or texts may be merged with and mixed with bytes of other sound waves, images or text. After transmission the bytes may be reassembled into samples of the original sound wave, image, or text. Because digital technology converts sounds, images and writing into data bytes with the universal logic of mathematics the converted data may instantaneously be electronically transmitted, monitored, copied, deleted, altered, merged, and updated. For an explanation of the basic technological terms and concepts of the new information technology, see, Perritt, *Law and the Information Superhighway*, Sec. 1.2 (Wiley Law 1996).

2. COMPUTER MATCHING, DATA ACQUISITION, DATA MERGING AND DATA PROFILING

Digital technology has dramatically increased the capacity to access data because computer data bases may be matched or linked and data instantaneously acquired. Once information is keyed into one computer, it may be transmitted to another computer without having to re-key the data. Digital technology makes it possible to merge and mix data.

The unprecedented capacity for loss of informational privacy is the result of the special features of digital technology in three phases of data processing: (1) data acquisition; (2) data merging and data matching; and (3) data profiling. Digital technology has tremendously increased the capacity for data acquisition. Once records have become computerized, unprecedented capacity to acquire data occurs through the matching of computerized records. Data in one record may instantaneously incorporate data from matched computerized records. The capacity to acquire data in the pre-digital era through the written transcription of factual information from the text of one record to the text of another is not comparable to the capacities for data acquisition through digital technology.

Computer matching allows for several kinds of data exchange. Factual information from various computers may be accumulated, merged, converted, deleted and altered. A list of the names and addresses of everyone who has purchased a new automobile in a particular area may be quickly accumulated if the computerized records of all new car retail establishments are matched. Since the text of the factual information is reduced to mathematically based data bytes, pieces of the factual information may be sorted out and be converted, altered or merged with other sorted out pieces of factual information in matched computers. Data from retail sales records, education, real estate title and tax records may be sorted out, merged and configured to create data profiles of an individual. The capacity to sort pieces of factual information and instantaneously merge and configure the pieces with pieces of data from other matched computers is limited only by the imagination of the software programmer. The capacity to merge has greatly enhanced the practice of data profiling and the capacity for personal surveillance.

3. THE CONCEPT OF DIGITAL PERSONA

Personal data that is acquired, merged and shared through connected networks like the Internet becomes a recognized form of behavior about the subject of the data. Roger Clarke argues that over a period of time the cumulative effect of this data behavior amounts to a digital persona that approximates personality:

> The digital persona is a construct, i.e., a rich cluster of inter-related concepts and implications. As a working definition [digital persona] . . . adopts the following meaning:

> The digital persona is a model of an individual's public personality based on data and maintained by transactions, and intended for use as a proxy for the individual. Roger Clarke, *The Digital Persona and Its Application to Data Surveillance*, The Information Society, 10, 2 (June 1994).

The meaning of the digital persona is determined by the data processing rules of the recipient of data. Clarke distinguishes between a "projected persona" based in part upon data created by the subject and which the individual has some control and "imposed persona" based on data created by others in which the individual has little influence.

Do current data privacy laws in the United States provide an opportunity for the creation of digital personae that are the basis upon which important decisions are made about an individual? Is a person's digital persona becoming more important than their natural persona in respect to important opportunities? If a person has rights to self determination in respect to their natural persona should a person have analogous rights to some degree of control over the creation of their digital persona? If so, what should those rights be?

4. TELEMARKETING AND SECONDARY USE OF INFORMATION

The capacity to match computers and mix and merge data adds to the value of information through "secondary use" of that information. "Secondary Use" is a term that refers to the use of information for a purpose other than the primary purpose for which the information was acquired. The practice of generating commercially valuable secondary information may be illustrated by a common use of digital technology. X calls an 800 number to purchase an item. A call tracing device, available because of digital technology, projects the number of the telephone from which the call originated onto a computer at the station of the operator who receives the call. Additional information relevant to the proposed transactions—a social security number or credit card number—is placed in the computer. All the information received from this call may then be merged with preexisting data systems and configured to create lists that are sold to telemarketing firms or businesses. What privacy interests are implicated by secondary use of information? Several options are available for providing some control to the individual over use of secondary information. The strongest privacy focussed rule would be to require written informed consent for secondary disclosure. This is the requirement in a few statutes that regulate especially sensitive health records—drug and alcohol and mental health treatment and HIV status records, see, for example, 42 C.F.R. Ch. 1, Sec. 2a.1 (1996). In respect to general business records there are two softer rules. One would be to prohibit secondary use unless the subject "opts in" by indicating that they consent to use of the information beyond the primary commercial purpose. Another approach is to presume that the subject agrees to secondary use of the information unless the subject "opts out" by indicating in writing to the entity that the subject does not authorize secondary use of personal information. There is no general legal requirement that a business entity adapt a "opting in" or "opting out" policy. Some state and federal statutes and regulations require authorization for secondary use.

The Family Educational Rights and Privacy Act (FERPA) adopts an opting out policy that allows students to inform their educational institution that they do not authorize the publication of directory information about them. The Video Privacy Protections Act adopts a opting out policy for video renters or purchasers.

Congress has addressed some telemarketing privacy issues. The 1991 Telephone Consumer Protection Act, 47 U.S.C.A. § 227, prohibits unsolicited facsimile advertisement and unsolicited prerecorded telephone calls. Prohibitions against prerecorded telephone solicitations under the 1991 Act and similar state laws have generally been found constitutional when challenged on first amendment grounds. In *Moser v. FCC*, 46 F.3d 970 (9th Cir.1995) the Court of Appeals reversed the district court and upheld the ban on automated telemarketing calls in the Telephone Consumer Protection Act against commercial speech right claims. Certiorari review was denied by the Supreme court, 515 U.S. 1161 (1995). The court concluded that the ban was narrowly tailored to advance governmental interests in residential privacy. See, also, *State of Minnesota v. Casino Marketing Group*, 491 N.W.2d 882 (Minn.1992) upholding a similar state statute against commercial speech challenges.

Under regulations adopted by the Federal Communications Commission implementing the 1991 Act telemarketers are required to refrain from calling consumers that ask not to be called, 47 C.F.R. § 64. 1200. Telemarketers are required to create and maintain lists of those customers who ask not to be called and to honor their requests, § 64. 1200 (e)(2). Consumers must sue in state courts to enforce these rights, see *Chairking Inc. v. Houston Cellular Corp.*, 131 F.3d 507 (5th Cir.1997) and *Szefczek v. Hillsborough Beacon*, 668 A.2d 1099 (1995) (awarding $2,000 for violation of the prohibition against calling customers who request to be placed on a no solicitation list.)

Rules promulgated by the Federal Trade Commission under the 1994 Telephone Disclosure and Resolution Act, 15 U.S.C.A. §§ 6101–6108, requires authorization by the consumer for access to a consumer's checking account, 16 C.F.R. § 310.3 (a)(3). Telemarketers are also required to disclose their identity and the purpose of the call. Telemarketing calls may only be made during the time period from 8:00 a.m. to 9:00 p.m., § 310.3 (a)(3), 310.4 (c). The Telemarketing and Consumer Fraud and Abuse Prevention Act authorizes the attorney general of each state to sue in federal court to enforce the FTC's rules, § 6103.

5. THE LOTUS INCIDENT

Where there are no restrictions by statute or in the contractual arrangement that generated the information secondary use without the consent of the subject is generally viewed as lawful. Does non-consensual secondary use of personal data constitute an invasion of privacy when the information was voluntarily disclosed and legally acquired? Recall that in *Nader v. GMC* and in the Supreme Court trilogy cases, *United States v. White, Smith v. Maryland* and *United States v. Miller,* discussed supra in Chapter 2, no legally protected expectation of privacy was recognized for information that is voluntarily disclosed to someone who agrees to share that information with someone else. In *Smith* and *Miller,* transactional data in telephone company and banking records was not given constitutional protection if the bank or telephone company shared the data with the government. Secondary use of transactional data is not legally prohibited as a general matter unless there is a specific statutory or contractual restriction. See, general discussion in Schwartz and Reidenberg, *Data Privacy Law,* § 14.2(b) (1996)

A well known incident involving the Lotus Development Corporation suggests that there are strong sentiments amongst the public that secondary use constitutes an invasion of privacy. In the spring of 1990,

Lotus Development Corporation and Equifax agreed to develop a database that would contain information on over one hundred million persons in the United States. Information in the database was to include, names and addresses, marital status, gender, age, type of dwelling and income of the household as well as purchasing power. The information was from public records and the records of business transactions. The database was entitled, Lotus Marketplace:Households and was to be made available for sale on CD–ROM. Announcement of the project precipitated a huge public outcry and the companies decided to abandon Lotus Marketplace:Households in January of 1991. The view that the public in general considers the sale of information acquired in business transactions to be an invasion of privacy is supported in a number of public opinion polls. For a useful account of the Lotus incident, see, Culnan, M.J. and Smith, H.J., *"Lotus" Marketplace: Households–Managing Information Privacy Concerns* in, *Computers, Ethics and Social Values,* (D.G. Johnson and H. Nissenbaum, eds. 1995).

6. THE ROLE OF RECORDS LAW IN COMPUTER PRIVACY LAW

Currently, there is no comprehensive federal statute regulating the security or privacy of data that is processed with computer technology. Most of current computer privacy law is found in laws that target specific records for regulation. Records law has an important role in protecting informational privacy in a computerized society because records contain most of the personal information about a person. This is a result of the importance of information sharing relationships in our society. Most of the relationships that afford persons opportunities to develop and achieve self-fulfillment are based upon requirements that individuals exchange information. The opportunity to work, acquire an education, practice a profession, travel, buy goods, vote, borrow books from the library, join a church as well as almost any other opportunity that is available requires individuals to give up information about themselves as a condition for entering into the relationship. Historically, the received information was stored in print or handwritten records. The benefits of digital technology has prompted the conversion of these records into computer databases.

7. GOVERNMENT RECORDS AND RECORDS IN THE PRIVATE SECTOR

As the material that follows indicates, there are differences in legal regulation of records controlled by the government (the public sector) and records in the control of non government entities (the private sector). Government records are subject to regulation under state and federal freedom of information and privacy statutes. Records in the private sphere do not generally come within the scope of freedom of information or privacy acts.

EXCERPTS FROM GEORGE B. TRUBOW, WATCHING THE WATCHERS: THE COORDINATION OF FEDERAL PRIVACY POLICY

3 Software L. J. 391, 392–97 (1989).

Modern technology makes it possible to collect, store, manipulate, and disseminate information at the speed of light and in quantity and quality never before imagined. The advent of miniaturization makes possible the micro or "personal" computer, so that for a few hundred dollars virtually anyone can own a sophisticated information processor. Modems allow computer users to connect their machines with data bases around the world, so that with appropriate identifiers one has a virtual central data base composed of information gleaned from distributed data bases in automated systems everywhere. The contents of the Library of Congress can be stored on a few discs, so that constraints of space regarding information storage have been all but eliminated.

. . .

There have been plenty of early warnings concerning the jeopardy to privacy resulting from the new technology. In 1971, Arthur Miller sounded the alarm in *The Assault on Privacy*. A. Westin and M. Baker, in 1972, clearly focused on the growing problem in their book, *Data Banks in a Free Society*. A special task force of the U.S. Department of Health, Education, and Welfare made the first in-depth government study of the problem and in 1973 issued its report, *Computers, Records, and the Rights of Citizens*, in which "principles of fair information practices" were first articulated; they were also reflected in the Privacy Act of 1974. In 1976, the Department of Justice issued guidelines regarding the security and privacy of criminal history records maintained in government data bases.

In 1977, after a comprehensive three-year study, the Privacy Protection Study Commission issued its report, *Personal Privacy in an Information Society*. The Commission made more than 160 recommendations for the protection of informational privacy, most of which have not been implemented because the Commission ceased to exist when its mission was completed and no other entity had responsibility to follow up its work. In 1981, the American Bar Association sponsored a National Symposium on Personal Privacy and Information Technology. The published report from the panel of distinguished participants emphasized the privacy threats and urged protective measures. A multitude of publications too numerous to catalogue here have echoed and re-echoed the previous warnings. Lisa Albinger, in the 1986 *Annual Survey of American Law*, succinctly summarized the nature of the problem:

> The right to privacy is integral to the American conception of the proper balance of power between the people and their government. As long as a citizen abides by the laws, his personal affairs should remain free from excessive governmental scru-

tiny. In recent years, however, this balance has shifted. Federal agencies today maintain vast amounts of computerized, easily accessible information on nearly every aspect of our lives. Unregulated access to this information threatens individual privacy interests. . . .

. . .

Because it is relatively easy and cheap to collect and store data, the limitations of cost that used to be a natural disincentive to the collection and storage of information have been markedly reduced. In 1981, based on data on using IBM mainframe systems, the United States Congress Office of Technology Assessment found that the cost of performing 100,000 calculations on a computer system had dropped from $1.26 in 1952, to $0.0025 in 1980. Though there has been no occasion for a more recent cost analysis, it is common knowledge that since 1980 the cost of computer systems has continued to drop in relation to the enormous increases in data processing capability.

The three billion files of personal information maintained by the federal government were but a small privacy threat when that information was manually stored and buried somewhere in stacks of paper archives. Today, as that information is converted to automated files, it is instantly available. What had been a theoretical threat to informational privacy has become a real one. The various automated data bases maintained by federal agencies can be linked together electronically so that, as the Office of Technology Assessment concluded in a recent report, in reality a virtually centralized data base on United States citizens is now available. To make matters worse, the Tax Reform Act of 1986 authorized the use of the Social Security number (SSN) for a wider range of personal files, and requires everyone over the age of five to have a SSN. Though directed at improving the efficiency and effectiveness of the government's tax programs, the law served to make the SSN an even more convenient and pervasive tool for locating, retrieving, and linking personal information in government files.

PRIVACY AND FAIR INFORMATIONAL PRACTICES, EXCERPTS FROM A PAPER BY TRUBOW, INFORMATIONAL PRIVACY LAW AND POLICY IN THE U.S., NATIONAL SYMPOSIUM ON PERSONAL PRIVACY AND INFORMATION TECHNOLOGY

1981.

A government report in 1973 often has been cited as the first major contribution to the development of a rational policy regarding personal information: "Records, Computers and the Rights of Citizens," by the Special Advisory Committee to the Secretary of Health, Education and Welfare. The report noted the significant growth of the use of computers to process information and proposed a set of "fair information practices" whose purpose was to enhance personal privacy by protecting the confidentiality of personal information. These principles may be distilled as follows:

1. Collect only that personal information necessary for a lawful purpose.

2. Use only decision making data that is relevant, accurate, timely, and complete.

3. Give the data subject access to information about himself and a procedure by which to challenge and correct the information.

4. Use data only for the purpose for which it was collected.

5. Protect the data against unauthorized loss, alteration, or disclosure.

The Privacy Protection Study Commission, established by the Privacy Act of 1974, conducted a thorough and comprehensive study of public and private record systems and issued some 166 specific recommendations to enhance informational privacy. While acknowledging the soundness of the foregoing principles, the Commission articulated three objectives of good information practice: (1) to minimize intrusiveness to the personal affairs of citizens, (2) to maximize fairness to individuals in the way personal information is managed, and (3) to legitimize expectations of the confidentiality of personal information.

PERSONAL PRIVACY IN AN INFORMATION SOCIETY, THE REPORT OF THE U.S. PRIVACY PROTECTION STUDY COMMISSION

3–6 (1977).

RECORD KEEPING AND PERSONAL PRIVACY

One need only glance at the dramatic changes in our country during the last hundred years to understand why the relationship between organizational record keeping and personal privacy has become an issue in almost all modern societies. The records of a hundred years ago tell little about the average American, except when he died, perhaps when and where he was born, and if he owned land, how he got his title to it. Three quarters of the adult population worked for themselves on farms or in small towns. Attendance at the village schoolhouse was not compulsory and only a tiny fraction pursued formal education beyond it. No national military service was required, and few programs brought individuals into contact with the Federal government. Local governments to be sure made decisions about individuals, but these mainly had to do with taxation, business promotion and regulation, prevention and prosecution of crime, and in some instances, public relief for the poor or the insane.

Record keeping about individuals was correspondingly limited and local in nature. The most complete record was probably kept by churches, who recorded births, baptisms, marriages, and deaths. Town officials and county courts kept records of similar activities. Merchants and bankers maintained financial accounts for their customers, and when they extended credit, it was on the basis of personal knowledge of the borrower's circumstances. Few individuals had insurance of any kind, and a patient's medical record very likely existed only in the doctor's memory. Records about individuals rarely circulated beyond the place they were made.

The past hundred years, and particularly the last three decades, have changed all that. Three out of four Americans now live in cities or their surrounding suburbs, only one in ten of the individuals in the workforce today is self-employed, and education is compulsory for every child. The yeoman farmer and small-town merchant have given way to the skilled workers and white-collar employees who manage and staff the organizations, both public and private, that keep society functioning.

In addition, most Americans now do at least some of their buying on credit, and most have some form of life, health, property, or liability insurance. Institutionalized medical care is almost universally available. Government social services programs now reach deep into the population along with government licensing of occupations and professions, Federal taxation of individuals, and government regulation of business and labor union affairs. Today, government regulates and supports large areas of economic and social life through some of the nation's largest bureaucratic organizations, many of which deal directly with individuals. In fact, many of the private-sector record-keeping relationships discussed in this report are to varying degrees replicated in programs administered or funded by Federal agencies.

A significant consequence of this marked change in the variety and concentration of institutional relationships with individuals is that record keeping about individuals now covers almost everyone and influences everyone's life, from the business executive applying for a personal loan to the school teacher applying for a national credit card, from the riveter seeking check-guarantee privileges from the local bank to the young married couple trying to finance furniture for its first home. All will have their credit worthiness evaluated on the basis of recorded information in the files of one or more organizations. So also with insurance, medical care, employment, education, and social services. Each of those relationships requires the individual to divulge information about himself, and usually leads to some evaluation of him based on information about him that some other record keeper has compiled.

The substitution of records for face-to-face contact in these relationships is what makes the situation today dramatically different from the way it was even as recently as 30 years ago. It is now commonplace for an individual to be asked to divulge information about himself for use by unseen strangers who make decisions about him that directly affect his everyday life. Furthermore, because so many of the services offered by organizations are, or have come to be considered, necessities, an individual has little choice but to submit to whatever demands for information about him an organization may make. Organizations must have some substitute for personal evaluation in order to distinguish between one individual and the next in the endless stream of otherwise anonymous individuals they deal with, and most organizations have come to rely on records as that substitute.

It is important to note, moreover, that organizations increasingly desire information that will facilitate fine-grained decisions about individuals. A credit-card issuer wants to avoid people who do not pay their bills, but it also strives to identify slow payers and well intentioned people who could easily get into debt beyond their ability to repay. Insurance companies seek to avoid people whose reputation or life style suggest that they may have more than the average number of accidents or other types of losses. Employers look for job applicants who give promise of being healthy, productive members of a work force. Social services agencies must sort individuals according to legally established eligibility criteria, but also try to see that people in need take advantage of all the services available to them. Schools try to take "the whole child" into account in making decisions about his progress, and government authorities make increasingly detailed evaluations of an individual's tax liability. Each individual plays a dual role in this connection—as an object of information gathering and as a consumer of the benefits and services that depend on it. Public opinion data suggest that most Americans treasure their personal privacy, both in the abstract and in their own daily lives, but individuals are clearly also willing to give information about themselves, or allow others to do so, when they can see a concrete benefit to be gained by it. Most of us are pleased to have the conveniences that fine-grained, record-based decisions about us make possible. It is the rare individual who will forego having a credit card because he knows that if he has one, details about his use of it will accumulate in the card issuer's files.

Often one also hears people assert that nobody minds organizational record-keeping practices "if you have nothing to hide," and many apparently like to think of themselves as having nothing to hide, not realizing that whether an individual does or not can be a matter of opinion. We live, inescapably, in an "information society," and few of us have the option of avoiding relationships with record-keeping organizations. To do so is to forego not only credit but also insurance, employment, medical care, education, and all forms of government services to individuals. This being so, each individual has, or should have, a concern that the records organizations make and keep about him do not lead to unfair decisions about him.

In a larger context, Americans must also be concerned about the long term effect record-keeping practices can have not only on relationships between individuals and organizations, but also on the balance of power between government and the rest of the society. Accumulations of information about individuals tend to enhance authority by making it easier for authority to reach individuals directly. Thus, growth in society's record-keeping capability poses the risk that existing power balances will be upset. Recent events illustrate how easily this can happen, and also how difficult it can be to preserve such balances once they are seriously threatened.

This report concentrates on the delicate balance between various types of organizations' need for information about individuals and each individual's desire to be secure and fairly treated. It also recognizes, however, that government's expanding role as regulator and distributor of largess gives it new ways to intrude, creating new privacy protection problems. By opening more avenues for collecting information and more decision-making forums in which it can employ that information, government has enormously broadened its opportunities both to help and to embarrass, harass, and injure the individual. These new avenues and needs for collecting information, particularly when coupled with modern information technology, multiply the dangers of official abuse against which the Constitution seeks to protect. Recent history reminds us that these are real, not mythical, dangers and that while our efforts to protect ourselves against them must ultimately be fashioned into law, the choices they require are not mere legal choices; they are social and political value choices of the most basic kind.

ARTHUR R. MILLER, COMPUTERS, DATA BANKS AND INDIVIDUAL PRIVACY: AN OVERVIEW

4 Colum. Human Rights L. Rev. 1, 1–10 (1972).

Concern over privacy is hardly irrational. In our increasingly computerized life, whenever a citizen files a tax return, applies for life insurance or a credit card, seeks government benefits or interviews for a job, a dossier is opened on him and his informational profile is sketched. It now has reached the point at which whenever we fly on a commercial airline, stay at one of the national hotel chains, or rent a car, we are likely to leave distinctive electronic tracks in the memory of a computer that can reveal much about our activities, habits and associations. Few people seem to appreciate the fact that modern technology is capable of monitoring, centralizing and evaluating these electronic entrees no matter how numerous and scattered they may be.

.   .   .

A brief recital of some of the blessings and blasphemies of the new technology makes the computer-privacy dilemma abundantly clear. In various medical centers, doctors are using computers to monitor physiological changes in the bodies of heart patients. The quest is to isolate those alterations in body chemistry that precede a heart attack, providing an early warning system so that treatment is not delayed until the actual heart attack has rendered the patient moribund for all practical purposes.

Other plans include giving everyone an identification number at birth for tax, banking, education, social security and draft purposes which would be done in conjunction with the computerization of a wide range of records. Thus, in the future, if a person falls ill away from home, a local doctor can use his identification number to retrieve the patient's medical history and drug reactions from a distant central data bank, thereby immensely speeding diagnosis and treatment.

. . .

But the same electronic sensors that can warn us of an impending heart attack can be used to locate us, track our movements, and measure our emotions and thoughts. For example, experiments are underway in the field of telemetry and similar breakthroughs are on the horizon. And some criminologists have already suggested that a prisoner be subjected to sensor implantation as a condition of parole. Law enforcement people then could monitor his activities and perhaps take him into custody should his *aggression level* become *too high*.

Similarly, the identification number given us at birth might become a leash around our necks, subjecting us to constant monitoring and making credible the fear of the fabled womb-to-womb dossier. In a computerized society those who control the recordation and preservation of personal data will have a degree of power over the individual that is at once unprecedented and subject to abuse.

Close scrutiny and evaluation of the implications of information technology on individual privacy are especially appropriate today because of the rising interest in many quarters for the establishment of governmental and private data centers. The extent to which federal agencies and private companies are using computers and microfilm technology to collect, store, and exchange information about the activities of private citizens is rapidly increasing. During the past year we have read of the Department of Housing and Urban Development's Adverse Information File, the National Science Foundation's data bank on scientists, the Customs Bureau's computerized data bank on *suspects*, the Civil Service Commission's *investigative* and *security* files, and the State Department's Passport Lookout Service. There also have been disturbing revelations about the Justice Department's intelligence bank, the Department of Transportation's National Driver Register of 2.6 million drivers, the Secret Service's dossiers on *undesirable*, *activists*, and *malcontents*, and the surveillance activities of the United States Army.

This list merely represents a sampling of the federal government's data banks that have been brought to light; even now only the tip of the iceberg may be visible. Still below the surface are the implications of several provisions in President Nixon's welfare reform proposal (the Family Assistance and Manpower Training Acts), which would give the Department of Health, Education and Welfare authority to computerize and exchange individualized data with state welfare agencies and lead to the establishment of a national job applicant data bank.

. . .

The emergence of a number of information systems in law enforcement magnifies both this threat to personal privacy and the potential *chilling effect* of informational surveillance. The FBI's constantly expanding National Crime Information Center (NCIC) provides state and city police forces with immediate access to computerized files on many people. Although until recently it only contained data on fugitives and stolen property, plans are underway to add arrest records and other types of sensitive information. Moreover, NCIC is the keystone of an emerging information network that will eventually tie together the nation's law enforcement information centers. By the end of 1969, it was exchanging data with state and local police agencies in every state except Alaska. State and local law enforcement surveillance systems also are becoming increasingly sophisticated—several with the aid of funding under the Law Enforcement Assistance Administration program of the Justice Department.

. . .

Data-gathering and dossier-building are as prevalent in private industry as in government. Personal information can be used for commercial purposes, such as generating a list of prospective consumers. *Reader's Digest* reportedly has used a computer to produce a mailing list consisting of its subscribers' neighbors, a tactic that proved surprisingly effective. "The approach had a kind of 'all the neighbors are doing it' quality," said one commentator, "but more significantly, the individual was pleased that *Reader's Digest* knew him and could relate him to others on his block."

The commercial use of cybernetics may go beyond this relatively benign method of soliciting business. The line between using the technology to communicate with a customer and employing it to manipulate his attitudes is nebulous and is likely to be transgressed frequently. For example, one New Jersey firm is developing a comprehensive data bank on doctors so that drug companies can promote their products in a way that will appeal to the habits and personality of individual doctors. And the nation's credit bureaus have been moving towards computerization since 1965; eventually, a computerized network will provide information instantaneously anywhere in the country....

Few people realize that they sign away a portion of their privacy when they apply for credit. Credit bureau and investigative agency files bulge with information on mortgages, make of car, salary, size of family; the resulting collage of data frequently produces an intimate sketch of the subject's economic life. To augment this file, many companies regularly comb newspapers, court records and other public files for bits of personal data that are thought to be relevant.

. . .

Perhaps the greatest dangers lie in the *information buddy system* that promotes the dissemination of personal information throughout the government and the private sector. It is a striking fact that many, if not most, bank and corporate security officers, private detectives, and field investigators for consumer reporting companies are former federal or local law enforcement agents. The result is a subterranean information exchange network that functions on a mutual back scratching basis or can be invoked for a fee. This network's existence means that decisions are being made about us based on reports from unknown sources we can never confront that contain information whose accuracy we can never challenge.

B. THE FAIR INFORMATION PRACTICES ACT MODEL FOR DATA PRIVACY PROTECTION

The five principles that are summarized in the article by George Trubow are the core concepts of the Fair Information Practices Act (FIPA model of data privacy protection). There are strong and weak examples of the FIPA model in the United States legal system. Strong senses of the model provide the subject of the data with meaningful control over the use of the data. A central rule of strong FIPA laws restricts secondary use without the written informed consent of the subject. The paradigm of this strong sense would be laws that regulate sensitive health records like drug and alcohol treatment records. Federal law regulating these records, for example, specifies the elements that are to be in a written consent form for release of health information and specifically requires the form to indicate that further disclosure is prohibited under law without the subject's written consent. Weaker data protection is found in other targeted records that adopt the FIPA model. One example would be the NAIC Insurance Information and Privacy Protection Model Act that has been adopted in a minority of states. The NAIC Model allows for redisclosure of information to a large number of persons and institutions, if disclosure furthers a business function and also for marketing purposes. See, National Association of Insurance Commissioners, NAIC Insurance Information and Privacy Protection Model Act (Kansas City: National Association of insurance Commissioners Model No. 670 (1992).

1. EUROPEAN DATA PRIVACY PROTECTION LAW

In *Data Privacy Law*, Schwartz and Reidenberg examine the differences between the European and American approaches to data privacy protection. As briefly summarized:

> In contrast to the diverse and targeted U.S. approach to fair information practice, most european countries have omnibus laws to regulate the use of personal information in the public and private sectors. European countries generally require the state to take an active role in protecting the fair treatment of personal information. Such laws establish comprehensive sets of rights and responsibilities that address the issues of data collection, storage, use and disclosure. Often, a single piece of legislation regulates both the public and private sectors. These laws are then supplemented by a series of laws and regulations that govern more narrow fields of processing activity. Legislative activity tends to be carried out in a complete and continuous fashion.

Within Europe, there is significant agreement on the essential principles of fair information practice. This consensus shows four elements: (a) the establishment of obligations and responsibilities for personal information; (b) the maintenance of transparent processing of personal information; (c) the creation of special protection for sensitive data; and (d) the establishment of enforcement rights and effective oversight of the treatment of personal information. These basic elements establish a comprehensive european approach to the protection of personal information. The complete set of basic principles is firmly established in existing national laws and in the Council of Europe Convention. They are also expressed in the European Union's 1995 directive on data processing and in the guidelines adopted by the Organization for Economic Co–Operation and Development. Schwartz and Reidenberg, *Data Privacy Law*, Chapter 2, Sec. 2.2, (1996).

Schwartz and Reidenberg define transparent processing as a "norm [that] requires that processing activities for personal information be structured in a manner that will be open and understandable ... [in] some cases [transparent processing] provides that consent from individuals must be obtained for certain kinds of processing of personal information." Schwartz and Reidenberg, *Data Privacy Law*, Section 2–2(b). For an extensive examination of comparative data privacy law, see, also, Colin J. Bennett, *Regulating Privacy,* (1992). See, also, Fred H. Cate, *Privacy and Telecommunications*, 33 Wake Forest L.Rev. 1, (1998) (comparing privacy protection between the European Union and the United States.

2. THE EUROPEAN UNION DIRECTIVE ON DATA PRIVACY PROTECTION

In 1995 the European Parliament and the Council of the European Union (EU) adopted a Directive designed to protect the privacy of personal data and increase the free flow of data amongst the fifteen Member States. See, "Directive 94/46/EC of the European Parliament and of the Council," Official Journal of the European Communities No. L. 281, 31–50 (November 23, 1995), <http://www2.echo.lu.>. The "Directive on the Protection of Individuals with Regard to the Processing of personal Data and on the Free Movement of Such Data" (Data Privacy Directive) became effective on October 25, 1998. As of that date only Greece, italy, Portugal, Sweden and the UK had implemented the Directive. All of the other member states were currently considering implementing legislation. The EU has indicated that the Directive will be applicable from the date the Directive became effective. When fully implemented the Directive will establish a uniform set of standards for the protection of personal data within the member states of the EU. The directive is important to American Business and privacy law because of the reciprocity principle in Article 25 that restricts transfer of personal data to a non-EU country unless the country ensures adequate levels of data protection.

The Directive contains a complex set of rights, restrictions and exemptions. The discussion and materials that follow are intended to highlight some of the privacy rights and issues that are raised by the Directive. For a fuller examination of the scope and implications of the Directive for data processing between the united States and Europe, see, Peter P. Swire and Robert E. Litan, *None of Your Business* (Brookings, 1998).

Scope

The Directive applies to the processing of all personal data subject to important exemptions found in Article 3. The Directive only applies to activities that may be the subject of legal regulation by the European Union and exempts processing operations concerning "public security, defense, State security, and criminal law activities of the State." The Directive also excludes data processed by a natural person "in the course of a purely personal or household activity." Swire and Litan interpret Article 3 and other sections of the Directive to limit the Directive's scope primarily to data processed in the private sector.

Data Quality and Legitimate Data Processing

The policies of the Directive are primarily implemented through legal restrictions on "controllers." A controller is the natural or legal person who determines the purposes and means of processing data (2(d). The legal requirements imposed upon the controller under the directive include adhering to the principles of data quality and legitimate data processing found in Article 6 and Article 7 and rights of subject access and control found in Article 12 and Article 14.

Article 6 adopts data quality principles. Controllers are required to limit collection of data to "specified, explicit and legitimate purposes" and to not process data in a way "incompatible" with those purposes" (6(b)). Data must be "adequate and, where necessary, kept up to date." Reasonable steps must be taken to ensure that incomplete or inadequate data (given the purpose of the data collection) be "erased or rectified" (6(d)) and kept in a form which permits identification of the subject for no longer than is necessary for the "purpose for which the data was collected" or processed. With appropriate safeguards data processed for "historical, statistical or scientific use" may be stored for longer periods (6(e)).

Do the data quality principles of Article 6 clearly prohibit nonconsensual secondary use of personal data?

The principles for legitimate processing of data contained in Article 7 generally prohibits the processing of data unless the data subject has "unambiguously given his consent" (7(a)). Processing without consent is allowed when "necessary" for "compliance with a legal obligation to which the controller is subject" or to "protect the vital interests of the data subject" or "for entering into or performing a contract with the data subject" or "necessary for performance of a task in the 'public interest' (7(b)-(e))."

Sensitive Information

The directive applies stricter privacy rules for data that reveals, "racial or ethnic origin, political opinions, religious or philosophical beliefs, trade union membership" and data "concerning health or sex life" (8(1)). "Explicit consent" is generally required for this data and a Member State may enact rules that would prohibit processing of sensitive data *even with the subject's consent* (8(2)(a)). Exceptions to these strict rules include data processing required in employment law, where the subject is physically or legally incapable of giving consent, to political philosophical, religious foundations and trade-unions (providing disclosure is limited to members or those regularly involved in the organizations) (8(2)(b)-(e)). A significant further exemption is for "preventive medicine, medical diagnosis," care or treatment, the management of health care services, health professionals subject to rules of 'professional secrecy' and other persons subject to 'equivalent obligation(s) of secrecy.' " (8(3)).

The Right to Know, The Right to Access and The Right to Object

Articles 10 and 11 require the controller to inform the subject of the identity of the controller, the purpose of processing and other information such as the existence of other rights in the direction such as rights to access and to rectify. These rights to know apply to data collected from the subject as well as data about the subject obtained from other sources.

Article 12 provides the subject with the right to access information from the controller about the source, category, recipients and purpose of personal data that is being processed about the subject, the right "as appropriate" to rectify, erase or block the processing of data that does not comply with the requirements of the Directive. When not impossible or requiring a "disproportionate" effort, the comptroller must notify third parties to whom data has been disclosed about any rectification, erasure or blocking of data.

Article 14 gives the right to object in some circumstances to the processing of data and where justified to prevent further processing.

Automated Individual Decisions

One of the most interesting sections of the Directive addresses the concerns by Clarke and others over the development of digital profiles (digital personae) that are the sole basis of important decisions affecting an individual. Article 15 generally grants:

> Every person has the right not, "to be subject to a decision which produces legal effects concerning him or significantly

affects him and which is based solely on automated processing of data intended to evaluate certain personal aspects relating to him such as his performance at work, credit worthiness, reliability, conduct, etc.''

The Consent Exceptions in Article 7 and Article 8

Note that the consent exception is described differently in Article 7 and Article 8. Article 2 defines, ''the data subject's consent'' as, ''any freely given specific and informed indication of his wishes by which the data subject signifies his agreement to personal data relating to him being processed.''

Would the unambiguous consent requirement of Article 7 and the ''explicit consent'' requirement of Article 8 be satisfied by an ''opt out'' rule. For an example of an opt out rule, see, Section 2710, (b)(2)(D)(i) (The Video Rental Privacy Act), *infra*, Chapter 8.

Free Speech and Privacy Rights

Article 9 requires Member States to develop exemptions for processing of personal data, ''carried out solely for journalistic purposes or the purpose of artistic or literary expression'' but ''only if the exemptions are necessary to reconcile the right to privacy with the rules governing freedom of expression.''

Does Article 9 give speech or privacy rights presumptive weight when they collide?

The Reciprocity Requirement

Article 25 provides that the transfer of personal data to a non-European country may take place only if the country ensures an adequate level of data protection. This article is designed to prevent the creation of data havens by third countries that would frustrate the purpose of the Directive. The adequacy of legal protection in a third country may be demonstrated by legal institutions and practices other than comparable legislation. Voluntary regulation by industry or contractual provisions that include promises of data security by the third country contractor may be sufficient to satisfy reciprocity requirements. Nevertheless, the lack of comprehensive national data privacy legislation in the United States and the ad hoc nature of state data privacy laws has raised serious questions about whether transfer of data from EU States to the United States violates Article 25.

Article 25 contains a limited number of exceptions where data transfer is permitted although the law of the non-European country does not provide adequate security. These include when the data subject has given ''unambiguous'' consent, where data is necessary to the exercise of defense of legal claims, or to the ''vital interest'' of the data subject. For a useful examination of the issues raised by the reciprocity requirement and recommendations on ways to avoid disruption of the flow of data under the Directive, see, Swire and Litan, None of Your Business, Chapter 8 (1998).

[*Editors note*. The current strategy of the United States is to comply with the Directive by voluntary action by U.S. entities not by enacting comprehensive federal data privacy legislation. On April 9, 1999, International Safe Harbor Privacy Principles were proposed by the Department of Commerce to the European Commission. These Safe Harbor Privacy Principles provide for entities to be eligible to receive personal data from EU countries if they agree to comply with the Safe Harbor Privacy Principles either by: (1) joining a private organization that complies with the principles; or (2) agreeing to comply with the principles in the contract with the entity transferring data from the EU country. Eligibility to receive personal data is also available to those entities that are subject to U.S. laws that require security for data privacy that is consistent with the Safe Harbor Privacy Principles. The Department of Commerce is currently in negotiations with the EU over whether the Safe Harbor Privacy Principles satisfy the data privacy requirements in the EU Data Privacy Directive.

If the Safe Harbor Privacy principle's concept is accepted by the EU, the result would be that personal data that migrates to and from the U.S. and EU countries would have greater privacy protection than most personal data that is collected and transmitted within the United States or between the United States and non-EU countries.]

C. BEYOND FAIR INFORMATION PRACTICES

An important book, *Technology and Privacy: The New landscape*, edited by Philip E. Agre and Marc Rotenberg, suggests that the privacy and digital technology debate is entering a new era. As explained by Professor Agre in the introduction:

> Our premise in organizing this volume is that the policy debate around technology and privacy has been transformed since the 1980's. Tectonic shifts in the technical, economic, and policy domains have brought us to a new landscape that is more variegated, more dangerous, and more hopeful than before. These shifts include the emergence of digital communication networks on a global scale; emerging technologies for protecting communications and personal identity; new digital media that support a wide range of social relationships; a generation of technologically sophisticated privacy activists; a growing body of practical experience in developing and applying data-protection laws; and the rapid globalization of manufacturing culture, and the policy process. Agre, Introduction 1, *Technology and Privacy; The New Landscape*, (Agre and Rotenberg, eds. 1997).

1. PRIVACY ENHANCING TECHNOLOGIES (PETS)

Herbert Burkert, *Privacy-Enhancing Technologies: Typology, Critique, Vision, in Technology and Privacy: The New Landscape*,125 (Agre and Rotenberg eds. 1997):

The term *privacy-enhancing technologies* (PETs) refers to technical and organizational concepts that aim at protecting personal identity. These concepts usually involve encryption in the form of (e.g.) digital signatures, blind signatures, or digital pseudonyms.

PETs have to be set apart from data-security technologies. It is one of the merits of the discussion on PETs that the concept of data security has been reclarified as to its limitations with regard to *privacy protection*. Data-security measures seek to render data processing safe regardless of the legitimacy of processing. Data security is a necessary but not a sufficient condition for privacy protection. PETs, on the other hand, seek to eliminate the use of personal data altogether or to give direct control over revelation of personal information to the person concerned. PETs are therefore closer to the social goals of privacy protection.

2.   ENCRYPTION AND ANONYMITY

Digital technology presents a paradox for data privacy. On the one hand, a linked system of computer networks greatly increases the sort of data and number of persons who have access to personal information. On the other hand, as suggested by Herbert Burkert, digital technology presents an opportunity for greater control over access to personal data through the use of Privacy Enhancing Technologies (P.E.T.s). One P.E.T.s is encryption. Cryptography is the science of secret writing through encryption and decryption of communications. With the revolution in modern communications and information technology cryptography is an academic discipline within applied mathematics. The cryptographers primary responsibility is to develop means for encrypting messages so that they are only understood by the recipients of the message. Encryption technology scrambles communications during transmission so that the content cannot be understood unless someone has a key that can unscramble the encrypted message. Encryption may protect privacy in two ways—preventing knowledge of the content of the communication or data and providing anonymity for the communicator or subject of the data. For a thorough examination of the history of public key cryptography see, Simon Garfinkel, *PGP: Pretty Good Privacy,* (1995).

Through the use of digital pseudonyms communications can be anonymous. It is common to use pseudonyms on the Internet. Anonymity obviously protects privacy because the data or information that is communicated is not identified with the actual person. The Supreme court has suggested that speech rights under the First Amendment include the right to speak anonymously. In *McIntyre v. Ohio Elections Comm.*, 514 U.S. 334 (1995) the Court found that an Ohio law that prohibited anonymous campaign literature violated the First Amendment. For an examination of the costs and benefits of anonymity, the prospects of anonymity protecting data privacy and the constitutional implications of regulating anonymous electronic communications, see,

Michael A. Froomkin, *Flood Control on the Information Ocean: Living With Anonymity, Cash, and Distributed Databases*, 15 J.L. & Comm. 395 (Spring 1996).

Export Restrictions on Encryption Technology

The federal government considers controlling the export of encryption technology to be a matter of national security. The concern is that the proliferation of encryption technology will hinder the United States Government's access to information it views as essential to national security. In addition, the availability of sophisticated encryption technology may threaten the secrecy of military communications and secrets. The export of nonmilitary encryption products and technology is governed by regulations promulgated by the Department of Commerce. See Export Administration Regulations (EAR), 61 Fed.Reg. 68, 572 (1996) (codified at C.F.R. Pts. 730–74). Under EAR regulations the "export" of certain encryption software require there is review of the application to determine whether the export would be "consistent with U.S. national security and foreign policy interests." 15 C.F.R. Sec. 742.15(b). Normally the review is within 90 days but if the application is referred to the President there is no time limit for the process. Final Administration decisions are not subject to judicial review. 25 C.F.R. Secs. 756.2(c)(1), 756.2(c)(2).

Daniel J. Bernstein, a professor in the computer science department of the University of Illinois at Chicago developed an encryption method that he dubbed "Snuffle." Bernstein was informed that he would need a license to export his work on "Snuffle." After an unsuccessful attempt to determine what the scope of the license requirements were, Bernstein brought a federal court lawsuit challenging the constitutionality of the licensing regulations. In *Bernstein v. United States Department of Justice; Department of Commerce, et al.*, 1999 WL 274111 (9th Cir. (Cal.)), the Ninth Circuit affirmed the grant of a summary judgment by a lower court to enjoin certain EAR regulations that limited Bernstein's ability to distribute the encryption software. The Ninth Circuit held that the EAR restrictions on Bernstein's encryption software in source code constituted a prior restraint that violated the first amendment.

A major issue in *Bernstein* was whether encryption software in its "source code" form is a form protected speech when employed by those in the field of cryptography. After reviewing statements from numerous cryptographers and computer programmers the court concluded that source code was a form of scientific expression because it provided cryptographers with a means to express their ideas in ways similar to the ways that mathematicians used equations and graphs to express their ideas. The court suggested that the EAR regulations were analogous to the government requiring mathematicians to obtain a prepublication license prior to publishing text that included mathematical equations. Characterizing the prepublication licensing scheme under the EAR as vesting unbridled discretion in government officials the court held the

EAR regulations constituted an unconstitutional prior restraint of scientific expression.

Judge Nelson dissented. He took the position that encryption source code was more like conduct than speech:

> Encryption source code is building tool. Academics and computer programmers can convey this source code to each other in order to reveal encryption machine they have built. But, the ultimate purpose of encryption code is, as its name suggests, to perform the function of encrypting messages. Thus, while encryption source code may occasionally be used in an expressive manner, it is inherently a functional device.

Which of the views on the speech status of encryption software in *Bernstein* do you find more persuasive?

Is There a Duty to Encrypt Cellular Phone Conversations? The ECPA (discussed in Chapter III) requires an intentional violation before civil and criminal sanctions of the ECPA come into play. Suppose a cellular phone service transmits a conversation that is intercepted but would not have been had the transmission been encrypted. Is the cellular phone service in violation of the ECPA? The only federal court of appeals to address this question said no. In *Shubert v. Metrophone*, 898 F.2d 401 (3rd Cir. 1990), the court held that the failure to provide encryption for a transmitted cellular phone conversation did not constitute an intentional violation of the ECPA.

3. THE DIGITAL TELEPHONY ACT

The Digital Telephony Act became law in 1994, see, Communications Assistance for Law Enforcement Act, Pub. L. No. 103–414, 108 Stat. 4279 (Oct. 25, 1994). The Act requires telecommunication providers to make the technological adjustments that are necessary to facilitate government interceptions of wire, oral, or electronic communications in view of the increasing influence of digital technology in telecommunications and data processing. Providers are also required to assist the government in executing legally authorized surveillance. The Act requires the government to pay for the cost of the technological conversions. Much controversy surrounded the adoption of the Digital Telephony Act. The proposition that citizens foot the bill for technological adjustments that would provide the government with more efficient ways to invade conversational and communication privacy was offensive to civil rights and privacy advocates. There was also concern that the authority granted to the government in the Act to access "call setup information" increased the capacity of the government to engage in data surveillance of citizens. For an account of the debate surrounding passage of the Act and evaluation of the significance of the Act to data privacy, see, Susan Freiwald, *Uncertain Privacy: Communications Attributes After the Digital Telephony Act*, 69 S. Cal. L. Rev. 949 (1996).

4. THE CLIPPER CHIP

In 1993 the Clinton Administration proposed a new national encryption standard that has come to be referred to as the Clipper Chip, see, 58 Fed. Reg. 40, 791 (July 30, 1993). Under this proposal an encryption standard difficult to breach would be implanted in telephone and computers systems. The standard would provide data security against decryption of communications by entities other than the government. The government would retain sole possession of a key that would allow for governmental decryption when appropriate—as in the case of a court order. To reduce the risk of potential abuse the key was to be in the possession of two separate governmental agencies. As of the time of this publication, the Clipper Chip proposal has not been enacted into law. For an account of the controversy surrounding the Clipper Chip proposal and the issues that the proposal has generated, see, Michael A. Froomkin, *The Metaphor Is The Key: Cryptography, The Clipper Chip, And The Constitution*, 143 U.Pa. L.Rev. 909 (1995).

Note: Wearable Computers

1. The portable "lap top" computer has made it possible to engage in sophisticated computing and communications virtually anywhere. Taking portability to another level, technologists are hard at work developing computers that people can wear. These "wearable computers" attach directly to the body or are embedded in clothing and accessories. Technologists hope to integrate human and computing functions as never before. Wearable computers will have extensive storage, sound, wireless links to the World Wide Web, and the power to record and display video.

One type of wearable computer under development consists of a Pentium computer with a tiny screen that rests over one eye and a one-handed keyboard strapped to the forearm. The Boeing Corporation and collaborators already market a wearable "humionics" computer system of this type for military and commercial applications. The Boeing DataSentinel offers voice-activated, hands-free operation, with an optional keyboard and mouse. The MicroOptical Corporation is developing ordinary looking eyeglasses that conceal a video or computer screen. Hoping to compete with more traditional field and mobile computer manufacturers, ViA, Inc. is marketing the ViA U PC, a wearable computer that attaches to the waist like a belt.

Most of the wearable computers currently under design and evaluation aim at highly efficient data collection and communication for business, medicine, law enforcement or the military. The express aim of the technology is first, to collect photographic images, live video and other factual data about what people are doing, saying, and experiencing; and second, to record and transmit such information. Often, the technology contemplates information transfers that are instantaneous, across great global distances, and without consent. The privacy implications of wearable computers are of concern both to some innovators in the field, and to outsiders from the fields of law, ethics and public policy who are just beginning to learn about wearable computer technology and its applications.

2. The first International Symposium on Wearable Computers sponsored by the IEEC was held October 13–14, 1997 in Cambridge,

Massachussetts. The IEEC's Second International Symposium on Wearable Computers was held October 19–20, 1998 in Pittsburgh, Pennsylvania. The program of the Pittsburg symposium featured a discussion of privacy concerns raised by the use of wearable computers, including remarks by Hank Strub, Thad Starner, Victoria Belloti and Anita L. Allen. Professor Allen observed that wearable computers potentially raise physical, information, propriety and decisional privacy concerns.

Specifically, a wearable computer that enabled the wearer to record or transmit visual images of third parties wishing to be alone will raise "physical privacy" concerns, particularly if the transmissions are more than momentary, are of identifiable parties, and are non-consensual. A person may regard it as an invasion of privacy that, while sitting in a quiet corner of a cafe in Paris, she is being observed via wearable camera technology and electronic links by someone in New York. A person required by her employer to attach a computing device to her body that revealed her location or monitored her bodily functions (heart rate, perspiration etc.) could complain of privacy invasion. Normally, "informational privacy" can be secured via secrecy, confidentiality, anonymity, data protection, locks and keys, or encryption. Wearables will allow wearers to collect vast amounts of information about individuals and enterprises very efficiently and very secretly, and then to pass the information on to others at lightning speed. This raises concerns about privacy, particularly if the information is of the sort people are inclined to view as personal, and if international data protection standards (like the European Community's 1998 Data Protection Directive) are flouted. "Proprietary privacy" is control over or ownership of one's own name, likeness and the attributes or repositories of personal identity—e.g., control over the use of photographs of oneself distinctive vocal traits, and publicity. Imagine that a person sitting in a theater watching a singer in concert, records or transmits the performance. The performer would have grounds for asserting privacy and publicity right violations; not to mention copyright rights. "Decisional privacy" denotes a person's ability to make important decisions relating to himself or herself autonomously, independently, or without interference from government or other unwanted third-parties. Family privacy, abortion privacy, and marital privacy are form of decisional privacy. If wearables with massive capacities to collect information about persons became commonplace, we could expect ordinary people to adopt modes of behavior that were less spontaneous and genuine. People could not act autonomously and independently in genuinely expressive ways if they thought they were on view, faced censure, or worse. The employers or government officials in control of the wearables that we were compelled to wear for their convenience would substantially control our lives. If it were difficult to detect when other people were wearing wearables embedded in glasses, vests, shoes, belts undergarments and the like, one could expect an increase in social anxiety. Suspicion and distrust might result, creating a market for a "counter-technology" that enabled one to detect or block other people's information gathering with the portable equivalent of a caller ID blocker.

3.   Some wearable computer innovators rightly stress that their devices enhance privacy rather than *diminish* it. For example, a wearable computer secreted in a fanny pack or in a pair of ordinary sunglasses could make it less obvious that a severely vision-impaired person was significantly disabled. The wearable computer could help an impaired person to keep a sensitive fact about herself more private than would otherwise be possible. Able-bodied people will someday wear computers utilized solely to improve the solitary experiences through sensory and cognitive enhancements. No privacy problems need arise, for example, where someone employed a wearable computer to facilitate her solitary hobbies of wilderness bird watching and listening to music.

4.   University of Toronto Professor Steve Mann is an artist and inventor who sees wearable computers and cameras as a technology for use against the pervasive forms of video surveillance conducted by government and business that *diminish* personal privacy. See *steve@media.mit.edu*. Subjected to public-safety and commercial video surveillance in the public streets, in locker rooms, retail establishments, and at work, Mann suggests that the general public "shoot back," using wearable cameras and video-capable computers that place the large institutions that study the public under surveillance by the public. See *Privacy Issues of Wearable Cameras Versus Surveillance Camera, http://wearcam.org/netcam-privacy-issues.html. Mann* advocates a "philosophical and tactical framework ... of appropriating the methodology of the oppressor ...[who] becomes the audience of a performance resulting from this new use of his or her own methodology." See Steve Mann, *'Reflectionism' and 'Diffusion': New Tactics for Deconstructing the Video Surveillance Superhighway*, 31 Leonardo 93 (1998), http://hi.eecg.toronto.edu/leonardo.

C.   FEDERAL DATA PRIVACY LEGISLATION

As previously explained, current federal data privacy legislation is expressed through records law that discretely target certain records for various degrees of protection. Some of the laws are directly traced to episodes. The Federal Video Privacy Protection Act is a response to attempts to acquire the video rental records of Judge Robert Bork during his confirmation process for Supreme Court Justice. Federal data privacy legislation is a fractured, episodic, record targeted patchwork of laws that leaves much of computerized data without legal regulation. See, generally, Robert M. Gellman, *Can Privacy Be Regulated Effectively on a National Level? Thoughts on the Possible Need for International Privacy Rules*, 41 Vill. L. Rev. 129 (1996). See also, Fred H. Cate, *Privacy and Telecommunications*, 33 Wake Forest L.Rev. 1 (1998).

A general overview of federal statutory laws follow with an examination of some of the fundamental features of selected statutes. For a comprehensive examination of federal and state data privacy law, see, the important book by Paul M. Schwartz and Joel R. Reidenberg, Data Privacy Law, (1996).

1. GENERAL OVERVIEW

On September 27, 1975, Congress passed the Privacy Act of 1974, the first comprehensive federal statute designed to protect the privacy of individuals with respect to the gathering and dissemination of personal information by federal executive agencies and departments. Prior to the Privacy Act, several federal statutes regulated informational privacy under limited circumstances.

The Omnibus Crime Control and Safe Streets Act of 1968, regulates the use of electronic eavesdropping devices to gather and disseminate information. 18 U.S.C.A. §§ 2510–2520 (1988).

The Fair Credit Reporting Act, 15 U.S.C.A. §§ 1681–1681t (1988), limits the circumstances under which consumer reporting agencies may disclose credit reports.

The Crime Control Act of 1973, 42 U.S.C.A. § 3789g (1988), requires states to adopt privacy and security programs to protect and regulate information in their criminal justice records systems.

The Family Educational Rights and Privacy Act of 1974, 20 U.S.C.A. § 1232g (1988), popularly known as the "Buckley Amendment," requires schools and colleges to give parents and students certain rights regarding personal information, and it sharply limits the disclosure of student records to third parties.

As the statutory vanguards of informational privacy, each of these statutes had its strengths and weaknesses; however, none of them provided the broad protection necessary to preserve informational privacy. *See generally* Project, *Government Information and the Rights of Citizens*, 73 Mich. L. Rev. 971 (1975). Subsequent to the Privacy Act of 1974, other federal legislation was enacted to deal with particular aspects of information protection.

The Right to Financial Privacy Act of 1978, 12 U.S.C.A. §§ 3401–3422 (1988), regulates the way in which federal agencies may gain access to bank records, giving the individual a privacy interest in his account information maintained by a bank. *See* George B. Trubow and Dennis L. Hudson, *The Right To Financial Privacy Act of 1978: New Protection from Federal Intrusion*, 12 John Marshall J. Prac. & Proc. 487 (1979).

The Privacy Protection Act of 1980, 42 U.S.C.A. § 2000aa (1988), establishes procedures for law enforcement agencies to get records and other information in the possession of newspapers. This law was passed in response to the case of *Zurcher v. Stanford Daily*, 436 U.S. 547 (1978), which upheld broader law enforcement access to a newspaper's files.

The Electronic Fund Transfer Act of 1980, 15 U.S.C.A. §§ 1693–1693r (1988), does not provide specific privacy protection to electronic transfers, but it does require a bank to notify a customer of any routine third party disclosure of personal records made by an automated transfer of money.

The Electronic Communications Privacy Act of 1986, 18 U.S.C.A. §§ 2510–2521 (1988), is an amendment to the 1968 Crime Control legislation. The ECPA makes criminal the interception of electronic communications, and provides civil remedies for invasions of privacy resulting from such interceptions.

The Video Privacy Protection Act of 1988, 18 U.S.C.A. § 2710 (1988), prohibits videocassette purveyors from disclosing what tapes had been rented or purchased by any customer. This law was in response to the disclosure, in connection with U.S. Senate confirmation hearings, of the titles and ratings of video movies that had been rented by Judge Robert Bork, a nominee for appointment to the Supreme Court. Judge Bork's nomination was defeated, principally because of his unsympathetic position regarding a constitutional right to privacy.

The Employee Polygraph Protection Act, 29 U.S.C.A. §§ 2001–2009 (1988), prevents private sector employers from using polygraph examinations of prospective or present employees except in certain enumerated circumstances.

The Computer Matching and Privacy Protection Act of 1988 (CMA), 5 U.S.C.A. § 552a (1988) is an amendment to the Privacy Act to close a gap in coverage. The CMA deals with the "matching" of automated files in separate electronic data bases. Federal agencies increasingly have been using the social security number or another identifier to link or compare different files pertaining to the same individual. The CMA establishes procedures to limit and monitor such practices by federal agencies.

In contrast to these privacy acts that may protect the confidentiality of certain personal information is the federal Freedom of Information Act (FOIA), 5 U.S.C.A. § 552 (1988), enacted in 1966, to guarantee public access to information maintained by federal agencies. The presumption of openness in the FOIA is often in conflict with the presumption of confidentiality in privacy legislation and the discussion and cases in this section will serve to explain how such conflicts are resolved. Here also follows a more detailed discussion of the significant privacy measures mentioned earlier.

2. THE PRIVACY ACT OF 1974

The Privacy Act applies generally to personal information that is part of a "record" contained in a government agency's "system of records." The Act provides to individuals the right to request access to records pertaining to them. 5 U.S.C.A. § 552a(d)(1). Once an individual makes such a request, the agency must inform her as to whether records pertaining to her are maintained in its system of records. The requestor then has a right to review and challenge the content of these records in terms of accuracy, relevance, completeness and timeliness of information, and to request correction of inaccurate information. 5 U.S.C.A. §§ 552a(d)(1), 552a(d)(2)(B). Agency and judicial review is available if an agency refuses to amend or denies access to the records. 5 U.S.C.A. §§ 552a(d)(3), 552a(g)(1)(A), 552a(g)(1)(B).

The purpose of the Privacy Act is to prevent agency disclosures of personal information to third parties without the consent of the data subject. The initial presumption of the confidentiality of such information can be overcome by one or more of twelve exceptions which permit the disclosure of information. 5 U.S.C.A. § 552a(b)(1)-(12). *See generally* George B. Trubow, *Privacy Law and Practice*, Vol. I, Ch. 2 (1987). Critical concepts in determining to what information the Act applies are "individual," "record," and "system of records."

a.   The Individual

The Privacy Act covers the "individual," which is defined as "a citizen of the United States or an alien lawfully admitted for permanent residence." 5 U.S.C.A. § 552a(a)(2). This definition is much narrower than applies to the FOIA, and thus does not include corporations or other legal entities seeking information in their own right. Individuals may, however, seek business or entrepreneurial information pertaining to them if other aspects of the Act are satisfied. *See Florida Medical Assoc. v. United States Dept., of Health, Educ. & Welfare*, 479 F.Supp. 1291 (M.D.Fla.1979).

b.   The Record

Section 552a(d) of the Privacy Act permits an individual access to records pertaining to him that are maintained by an agency. Personal notes or memoranda kept by an agency employee are not agency records. Any tangible information that reveals something about the data subject can be a record. In *Albright v. United States*, 631 F.2d 915 (D.C.Cir. 1980), the court held that a videotape showing a heated discussion between a supervisor and a discharged employee was an agency record. Some courts have said that to be a covered record the information must disclose something personal or private about the individual. For example, in *American Fed'n of Gov't. Employees v. NASA*, 482 F.Supp. 281, 283 (S.D.Tex.1980), the court held that employee sign-in sheets were not "information that is substantively, i.e., in and of itself, reflective of some quality or characteristic of an individual."

c.   The System of Records

Section 552a(b) of the 1974 Privacy Act prohibits the disclosure of "any record ... contained in a system of records" unless the information comes within one of the Act's enumerated exceptions. Thus, as a general matter, neither the access nor disclosure provisions of the Act are triggered unless the information in question is in a record which is part of a "system of records" within the meaning of the statute. Section 552a(a)(5) broadly defines "system of records" to include any group of records under agency control that can be retrieved by use of an individual's name or other identifier. Thus, even though information may pertain to a particular individual, if it is not indexed and retrieved in agency files by reference to that individual then it is not a record in a system of records. For instance, in *Smiertka v. United States Dept. of Treasury, I.R.S.*, 447 F.Supp. 221 (D.C. 1978), the court held that a supervisor's informal memoranda concerning a discharged federal employee's job performance were not within the agency's "system of records." *See also Savarese v. United States Dept. of Health, Educ. & Welfare*, 479 F.Supp. 304 (N.D.Ga.1979), *aff'd*, 620 F.2d 298 (5th Cir.1980), *cert. denied*, 449 U.S. 1078 (1981), where the court held that a supervisor's written comments about a discharged employee were not within the agency's "system of records." Arguably, in each of these cases the information sought was also not a "record" maintained by the agency.

Every agency is prohibited from maintaining any "record describing how any individual exercises rights guaranteed by the First Amendment unless expressly authorized by statute or by the individual ... or unless pertinent to and within the scope of an authorized law enforcement activity." 5 U.S.C.A. § 552a(e)(7). Because of the importance attached to the First Amendment, courts have allowed individuals to use the Privacy Act to pursue allegations of (e)(7) violation whether or not the records sought are part of the agencies "system of records." *See Albright*, *infra*, and *Clarkson v. I.R.S.*, 678 F.2d 1368 (11th Cir.1982), *cert. denied*, 481 U.S. 1031 (1987).

d.   Civil Remedies and Criminal Penalties

The Privacy Act provides for a civil remedy if an agency's willful violation of the disclosure provisions causes an adverse effect on the data subject. Injunctive relief is also available, but only when the data subject is denied his right to access or his right to amend his record prior to its disclosure to a third party. Civil actions must be brought in federal district court within two years subsequent to the alleged violation. Plaintiffs who have "substantially prevailed" in a Privacy Act action can obtain reasonable attorney's fees and court costs. 5 U.S.C.A. § 552a(g)(4).

If an agency willfully or intentionally violates the Act, actual damages of no less than one-hundred dollars, reasonable attorney's fees, and court costs may be awarded. Criminal penalties may be assessed against an officer or an employee of an agency who, by virtue of his position, has access to agency records that contain personal information and who knowingly and willfully discloses that information to an agency or a person not entitled to receive it. 5 U.S.C.A. § 552a(i). Such an officer is guilty of a misdemeanor and can be fined up to five-thousand dollars. This same criminal penalty extends to persons who knowingly and willfully request and obtain agency records containing personal information under false pretenses. 5 U.S.C.A. § 552a(i)(3).

e. Applying the Privacy Act

ALBRIGHT v. UNITED STATES

631 F.2d 915 (D.C.Cir.1980).

MIKVA, CIRCUIT JUDGE:

[Hearing and appeal analysts with the Bureau of Hearings and Appeal of the Social Security Administration, Department of Health, Education and Welfare, brought suit against the Department under the Privacy Act. The analysts alleged that a videotape of a meeting between the analysts and their supervisor, Brian Makoff, had been made without their consent or knowledge and was being kept by the defendant. The analysts claimed that this action by the Department constituted a violation of the Privacy Act's prohibition against the maintenance by governmental agencies of records describing how any individual exercises First Amendment rights, since the videotape showed employees complaining to their supervisor about work-related grievances.

The District Court entered summary judgment for the government, finding that the videotape was not incorporated into the government agency's "system of records" as that term is defined in the Act, and that therefore the Act was inapplicable to the agency's actions. The analysts appeal.]

The Privacy Act forbids any government agency that "maintains a system of records" from maintaining, collecting, using, or disseminating any record of the exercise of an individual's First Amendment rights. This case raises the issue whether an agency may make and keep such a record even if it is not subsequently incorporated into the agency's system of records. The district court held that incorporation is necessary to trigger the applicability of the act. We hold that the district court erred in its reading of the Act, and consequently we reverse.

I. BACKGROUND

Appellants are career Hearing and Appeal Analysts with the Bureau of Hearings and Appeal, Social Security Administration, United States Department of Health, Education and Welfare.[1] In the spring of 1977, several analysts were recommended for promotion to the GS–301 Grade, level 13. However, a subsequent classification determination by the Bureau's personnel division resulted in the downgrading of the GS–13 level positions to the GS–12 level. As a result, twenty-four analysts were denied the recommended promotions.

In order to explain the reclassification decision, R. Brian Makoff, the personnel officer responsible for the decision, called a meeting with the affected analysts. At the meeting, held in the Bureau's offices during business hours, there was a presentation by Makoff, followed by ques-

---

1. The Department of Health, Education and Welfare has been redesigned as the Department of Health and Human Services, 20 U.S.C.A. Section 3508 (Supp. 1980).

tions and answers and what has been described as a "heated exchange" between the analysts and Makoff. Although not announced to those present, the room in which the meeting was conducted contained video-taping equipment which was used to record the meeting. Afterwards the videotape was labeled "9/23/77, Brian Makoff Classification Address to Analysts" and placed in a locked file in the Bureau's office.

Having learned that the meeting had been videotaped, the analysts' union brought an unfair labor practice charge, and thereafter the tape was removed to a security branch office in Baltimore, Maryland. It is presently kept in a locked filing cabinet in a sealed envelope addressed to the chief of the security branch and marked "Confidential, Open by Addressee Only." The videotape has since been viewed on limited occasions in connection with this and the unfair labor practice proceeding.[3]

The analysts, after exhausting their administrative remedies, brought an action in the district court for monetary, declaratory, and injunctive relief, alleging a violation of subsection (e)(7) of the Privacy Act of 1974, 5 U.S.C. Section 552a(e)(7) (1976) and violations of the First and Fourth Amendments....

II. DISCUSSION

A. Interpretation of the Act

Subsection (e)(7) of the Privacy Act, under which the claim in this case was filed, provides in pertinent part:

> (e) ... Each agency that maintains a system of records shall—
>
>   . . .
>
> (7) maintain no record describing how any individual exercises rights guaranteed by the First Amendment unless expressly authorized by statute or by the individual about whom the record is maintained or unless pertinent to and within the scope of an authorized law enforcement activity.

5 U.S.C. Section 552a(e)(7)

The act defines a "record" as any item, collection, or grouping of information about an individual that is maintained by an agency, including, but not limited to, his education, financial transactions, medical history, and criminal or employment history and that contains his name, or the identifying number, symbol, or other identifying particular assigned to the individual, such as a finger or voice print or a photograph. 5 U.S.C. Section 552a(a)(4).

A "system of records" is defined as a group of any records under the control of any agency from which information is retrieved by the name of

---

3. A copy of the videotape was provided to the analysts' union pursuant to a request it filed in 1977 under the Freedom of Information Act.

the individual or by some identifying number, symbol, or other identifying particular assigned to the individual. 5 U.S.C. Section 552a(a)(5).

"Maintain" is defined to include "maintain, collect, use, or disseminate." 5 U.S.C. Section 552a(3).

In its interpretation of the statute, the district court emphasized that the prohibition against collecting records of First Amendment activities is, by the terms of subsection (e), applicable only to agencies that maintain a system of records. The court therefore inferred that subsection (e)(7)'s regulation of collection of records "pertains to records collected *with the intent to incorporate* them into the agency's system of records." That is, the court held, "Congress intended there be a nexus between the record collected (maintained, used, or disseminated) and the system of records maintained by the agency before the Privacy Act would apply. The court reasoned that if "the mere collection of records of individuals exercising their first amendment rights were the primary concern of Congress, it would have prohibited the collection of such records by any agency, not just those that maintain a system of records."

The district court found that the videotape in this case was not, and was not intended to be, indexed according to the name or any other identifying symbol of any of the analysts filmed. The court thus concluded that the record was not incorporated into the agency's system of records and consequently that the actions of the Bureau and Makoff in making the videotape did not fall within the subsection (e)(7) prohibition.

We do not agree with the district court's reading of the statute. The meaning of a statute must, in the first instance, be sought in the language of the statute itself. If the language is clear and unambiguous, a court must give effect to its plain meaning. The definition of "maintain" is the dispositive factor here. Subsection (e)(7) provides that any agency that maintains a system of records shall not "maintain [collect, use, or disseminate any] record describing how any individual exercises rights guaranteed by the First Amendment." When so read, the Act clearly prohibits even the mere collection of such a record, independent of the agency's maintenance, use, or dissemination of it thereafter. The district court's interpretation is thus inconsistent with the plain meaning of the language of the Act.

Our reading of the Act is also consistent with what we perceive to be the congressional intent. Congress is, of course, well aware of the special and sensitive treatment accorded First Amendment rights under the interpretive case law. The legislative history of the Act reveals Congress' own special concern for the protection of First Amendment rights, as borne out by statements regarding "the preferred status which the Committee intends managers of information technology to accord to information touching areas protected by the First Amendment of the Constitution." Thus, while other types of information may be "maintained" under the Act, there is a flat prohibition [with very limited exceptions] against maintenance of records regarding the exercise of

First Amendment rights. A requirement of incorporation, such as that imposed by the district court here, adds an ingredient that Congress did not provide. Information about an individual's exercise of his or her First Amendment rights can be retrieved even from records that are not incorporated into an agency's system of records and that do not identify that person by name.

The legislative history also reveals a concern for unwarranted collection of information as a distinct harm in and of itself. "[T]he section is directed to inquiries made for research or statistical purposes which, even though they may be accompanied by sincere pledges of confidentiality are, by the very fact that government make [sic] the inquiry, infringing on zones of personal privacy which should be exempted from unwarranted Federal inquiry."

Similarly, although not expressly provided for in the Constitution, courts have long recognized that "the First Amendment has a penumbra where privacy is protected from governmental intrusion." Griswold v. Connecticut. This penumbra of privacy can be invaded, under certain circumstances, by the mere inquiry of government into an individual's exercise of First Amendment rights. Thus it is not surprising that Congress would have provided in this Act, dedicated to the protection of privacy, that an agency may not so much as collect information about an individual's exercise of First Amendment rights except under very circumscribed conditions.[5]

We are not persuaded that a contrary congressional intent is revealed by the fact that the subsection (e)(7) prohibition is made applicable only to agencies that maintain a system of records. First, Congress need not treat every aspect of a problem in order to address any aspect of it. Furthermore, it would appear from the statement of purpose in the legislative history that the Act was intended to cover all of what were perceived to be the offending agencies. "The purpose of [the Act], as amended, is to promote governmental respect for the privacy of citizens

5. The Office of Management and Budget's (OMB) Privacy Act Guidelines, promulgated pursuant to Section 6 of the Privacy Act, Pub.L. No. 93-579, 88 Stat. 1896 (1974), also support our reading of the scope of subsection (e) (7). 40 Fed.Reg. 28949 (1975). The guidelines compare subsection (e) (7) with subsection (e) (1), which provides that an agency maintaining a system of records shall maintain in its records only such information about an individual as is relevant and necessary to accomplish a purpose of the agency required to be accomplished by statute or by executive order of the President. 5 U.S.C. Section 552a (e) (1). OMB reads "maintain" in this subsection to mean "collect" and then goes on to note that subsection (e) (7) "establishes an even more rigorous standard governing the maintenance of records regarding the exercise of First Amendment rights." 40 Fed.

Reg., at 28965. As another indication of subsection (e) (7)'s intended scope, the guidelines admonish agencies to "apply the broadest reasonable interpretation" in determining whether or not an activity constitutes the exercise of a First Amendment right. Id. These guidelines are owed the deference usually accorded interpretation of a statute by the agency charged with its administration, particularly when, as here, the regulation "involves a contemporaneous construction of a statute by the [persons] charged with the responsibility of setting its machinery in motion, of making the parts work efficiently and smoothly while they are yet untried and new." Zenith Radio Corp. v. United States, 437 U.S. 443, 450, 98 S.Ct. 2441, 2445, 57 L.Ed.2d 337 (1978) (quoting Norwegian Nitrogen Prods. Co. v. United States, 288 U.S. 294, 315, 53 S.Ct. 350, 358, 77 L.Ed. 796 (1933)).

by requiring all departments and agencies of the executive branch and their employees to observe certain constitutional rules in the computerization, collection, management, use, and disclosure of personal information about individuals."

. . . .

B. Applicability of the Act to This Case

Having determined that the district court erred in requiring a special nexus between a record of First Amendment activities and the agency's system of records, we must turn to an examination of whether the agency violated the Act by making the videotape of the meeting with the analysts. The threshold issue in this regard is whether the videotape is a record of the exercise of First Amendment rights. We do not think the fact that the means of storing information in this case was a videotape makes it any less a record for purposes of the Act. See Save the Dolphins v. United States Department of Commerce, 404 F. Supp. 407, 410–11 (N.D.Cal.1975) (holding that a motion picture film is a record for purposes of the Freedom of Information Act, 5 U.S.C. Section 552 (1976)). As long as the tape contains a means of identifying an individual by picture or voice, it falls within the definition of a "record" under the Privacy Act.

As to the content of the videotape, the analysts maintain that it depicts them questioning the Bureau's action and complaining of it in a heated fashion. Such complaining falls within the First Amendment rights of public employees. More specifically, "a petition by a federal employee to one above him in the executive hierarchy is covered by the First Amendment." Here, the videotape showed employees complaining to their employer about work-related grievances. It thus is a record of the exercise of First Amendment rights, and its creation violates subsection (e)(7) unless the agency can establish that one of the exceptions stated therein was met.

It is clear that no such exceptions apply in this case. The agency concedes that no statute expressly authorizes the making of the videotape. It is also undisputed that the participants in the meeting did not expressly consent to the videotaping, nor is there any assertion by the agency that the tape was made in connection with an authorized law enforcement activity. Thus, it would appear that the analysts do state a claim of a violation of subsection (e)(7).

This does not mean that the analysts must necessarily prevail on their claim below. First, there is some disagreement between the parties as to which, if any, of the analysts participating in this appeal were depicted by voice or picture in the videotape. Although we hold that if the voices or pictures were depicted, the videotape would constitute a record under the Act, we cannot, on the facts presented, determine that such was the case.

Second, in order to establish jurisdiction in the district court, the analysts would have to show that the making of this record had an adverse effect on them as required by subsection (g)(1)(D) of the Act. The analysts argue that they "properly alleged the adverse effect to them [in their complaint] since among other things . . . [they] have been identified as malcontents within the Agency. Accordingly, their promotion, transfer and assignment opportunities have been adversely affected." However, they concede that the district court did not rule on this question because of its holding that the Act was not applicable.

Finally, in order to be entitled to the damage remedy they seek, the analysts must establish that "the agency acted in a manner which was intentional or willful." 5 U.S.C. Section 552a(g)(4). The agency argues that its action was based on its desire to preserve a record of the meeting for other analysts affected by the classification decision who were unable to attend. The agency asserts that the idea to record the meeting actually came initially from one such analyst. The agency points out that it volunteered to destroy the tape when it became aware that the analysts were upset about its having been made, but the offer was refused by the analysts' union.

If these assertions are found to be true, we have serious doubts whether the agency action was a willful and intentional violation of the Act which would justify the assessment of damages. However, we are not in a position to decide this question. The factual disputes existing in this case must be decided by the district court on remand. Of course, even if the analysts are not entitled to damages, they may nevertheless be awarded some other remedy, such as destruction of the videotape.

III.   CONCLUSION

We hold that despite the absence of a nexus between the record and the agency's system of records, the Act applies to the videotape in this case. Since a number of factual questions must be resolved before a complete disposition of the case may be accomplished, we remand to the district court for further proceedings consistent with this opinion.

Reversed and remanded.

Note

The *Allbright* court's interpretation of (e)(7) was limited in *Clarkson v. IRS*, 678 F.2d 1368 (11th Cir.1982). Clarkson, an activist in organizations formed to protest federal tax laws sued the IRS for violation of 552a (e)(7) for collecting and maintaining surveillance reports, newsletters and other documents describing his exercise of First Amendment Rights. The documents were maintained in a separate file entitled "Tax Protest File" that was not part of the IRS's "system of records." The District Court did not follow *Allbright* and granted a summary judgment in favor of the IRS on the basis that (e)(7) did not apply to documents which are not contained in the agency's "system of records."

The Eleventh Circuit Court of Appeals reversed holding that (e)(7) might apply to records not maintained within agency's system of records. However, the court remanded the case for a determination of whether the "authorized law enforcement activity" exception in (e)(7) applied to surveillance of the tax protest meetings. On remand the District Court was advised that the law enforcement activities exception to (e)(7) did not authorize federal agencies to engage in "fishing expeditions" investigating citizen speech. The exception was limited to maintaining records relating to a "past or anticipated specific criminal act."

By this language, has the court prevented the law enforcement activity exception to (e)(7) from becoming a "loophole that threatens to swallow the rule?" For criticism of the breadth of this exception, see, Freedom of Information Privacy Acts, 46, 74–75 (R. Bouchard & J. Franklin, ed. 1980).

Note: Damages Under the Privacy Act

In order to recover damages under the Privacy Act, a plaintiff must allege that the disclosures of which he complains have caused him "an adverse effect." 5 U.S.C.A. § 552a(g)(1)(D). If the court determines that the agency acted in a manner which was intentional or willful, the United States shall be liable to the individual in an amount equal to the sum of:

> (A) [A]ctual damages sustained by the individual as a result of the refusal or failure, but in no case shall a person entitled to recovery receive less than the sum of $1,000; and

> (B) The costs of the action together with reasonable attorney fees as determined by the court.

5 U.S.C.A. § 552a(g)(4).

Courts disagree as to the meaning of the term "actual damages" under the Privacy Act. One view is that "actual damages" includes damages for physical and mental injury, as well as damages for out-of-pocket expenses. *See Johnson v. Dep't of Treasury, IRS*, 700 F.2d 971 (5th Cir.1983). In *Johnson*, the court found that the plain meaning of the term "actual damages" was uncertain. Therefore, the court focused on the legislative history, specifically the purposes of the Privacy Act, for illumination. The Fifth Circuit began its analysis by noting that Congress borrowed the remedy provision in the Privacy Act from the common law. The *Johnson* court referred to *Time, Inc. v. Hill*, 385 U.S. 374 (1967), a common law privacy action in which the Supreme Court indicated that the primary damage in "right to privacy" cases is mental distress. The *Johnson* court concluded that Congress chose the term "actual damages" to tailor the compensation to the nature of the privacy interest protected. "Obviously, mental distress is the normal and typical damage resulting from an invasion of privacy. . . ." *Johnson* at 977. Furthermore, the court reasoned that "[i]nterpreting 'actual damages' to include only out-of-pocket losses would not only preclude recovery in large numbers of cases but also run counter to Congress' intent to 'promote governmental respect for the privacy of citizens by requiring . . . agencies and their employees to observe . . . constitutional rules.' " *Id*.

The Tenth Circuit also interpreted the term "actual damages" to include mental distress in *Parks v. United States I.R.S.*, 618 F.2d 677 (10th Cir.1980). The *Parks* Court determined that invasion of privacy was a personal wrong which resulted in injury to the plaintiff's feelings and was actionable even though the plaintiff suffered no pecuniary loss nor physical harm. The essence of the action was the invasion of the right to privacy and thus mental distress or embarrassment was a natural and probable consequence. *Id*. at 683.

An alternative interpretation of the term "actual damages" limits the plaintiff's recovery to pecuniary losses only. In *Fitzpatrick v. I.R.S.*, 665 F.2d 327 (11th Cir.1982), the Eleventh Circuit reviewed the legislative history of the Privacy Act in an attempt to discern Congressional intent on the damages issue. The court observed that throughout the Privacy Act debate, a central concern was the scope of potential government liability for damages. *Id*. at 330. A Privacy Protection Commission study included in the final version of the Privacy Act found that the term "actual damages" was intended as a synonym for special damages as that term is used in defamation cases. *Id*. at 331. (In defamation cases special damages are limited to pecuniary losses). The *Fitzpatrick* court concluded that the legislative history supported a narrow reading of "actual damages." The court held that "actual damages" as used in the Privacy Act permits recovery only for pecuniary losses and not for generalized mental injuries, loss of reputation, embarrassment or other nonqualified injuries. However, it should be noted that in a footnote the court indicated that had the appellant introduced evidence of expenses for psychiatric care necessitated by the disclosure, he could have recovered those expenses. *Id*. at 331. A number of jurisdictions have limited "actual damages" to out-of-pocket expenses. *See Albright v. United States*, 558 F.Supp. 260 (D.C. 1982), *aff'd*, 732 F.2d 181 (D.C.Cir. 1984); *Houston v. United States Dep't. of Treasury*, 494 F.Supp. 24 (D.C. 1979), *Harper v. United States*, 423 F.Supp. 192 (D.S.C.1976). In each of these cases the plaintiffs failed to establish that they had suffered any adverse effects which would permit recovery. At first glance this lack of proof of adverse effects seems to be the obstacle preventing broader recovery under the Act. However, these courts have explicitly stated that under the Privacy Act damages for emotional distress are precluded in the absence of substantial physical injury.

f. *Social Security Numbers*

The Privacy Act prohibits agencies of federal, state or local government entities from denying the individual's rights, benefits or privileges solely on the basis that the individual has refused to disclose her social security number. The act has a grandfather clause and exempts required disclosures of social security numbers if the requirement existed before January 1, 1975, and was for the purpose of verifying the individual's identity. In addition, mandatory disclosure of social security numbers does not violate the Privacy Act if the disclosure is required by another federal law. *See* 5 U.S.C.A. § 552a(b)(7) (1988). This exception has been the basis for upholding requirements that recipients of federal welfare obtain social security numbers for their children. *See McElrath v. Califano,* 615 F.2d 434 (7th Cir.1980); *Green v. Philbrook*, 576 F.2d 440 (2d Cir.1978).

The Tax Reform Act of 1976 gives state and local government entities the authority to use social security numbers to verify individuals as part of administration of income tax returns at the state or local government level. The 1976 Act also provides that local government entities may use social security numbers in order to identify individuals that participate in public assistance programs or to identify individuals when issuing driver's licenses or motor vehicle registrations.

3. THE FAIR CREDIT REPORTING ACT

In 1970, Congress passed the Fair Credit Reporting Act (FCRA), 15 U.S.C.A. § 1681–1681t (1988). The purpose of the FCRA was to protect individuals from the misuse of personal information maintained by credit reporting agencies, but the permitted disclosures are so broad as to provide little confidentiality of information. A credit reporting agency may disclose consumer credit information in response to a court order or with the data subject's written consent; or, to a person who it has reason to believe intends to use the information in connection with an application by the individual for credit, employment, insurance, licensure or other governmental benefit; or, for an otherwise legitimate business need. 15 U.S.C.A. § 1681b. For instance, in *Hoke v. Retail Credit Corp.*, 521 F.2d 1079 (4th Cir.1975), *cert. denied*, 423 U.S. 1087 (1976), a state medical board's use of a credit report to review a doctor's license application was held to constitute an "employment purpose" under the FCRA.

Notice must be given to the consumer when the credit reporting agency is asked to procure an "investigative consumer report" on the data subject's character, general reputation, personal characteristics, or mode of living. 15 U.S.C.A. 1681(a)(1) (West 1982). The notice requirement is only triggered, however, if the "investigative report" is sought to determine the data subject's initial eligibility for insurance or for some government benefit. For example, it does not apply where an individual is already insured and the report is sought to determine the validity of some "disability" claim made by the insured. *See Cochran v. Metropolitan Life Ins. Co.*, 472 F.Supp. 827 (N.D.Ga.1979) (use of credit report in investigation of insurance claim was not application for insurance and thus did not trigger FCRA notice requirement). The consumer can then request information on the purpose of the reporting agency's disclosure, the nature and scope of the investigation, the sources of the information, and the identities of any of the credit report's recipients. 15 U.S.C.A. §§ 1681e, 1681g and 1681h (West 1982).

The consumer is entitled to have a copy of his credit report and any explanation necessary for him to understand the contents of the report. If the consumer disputes the completeness or accuracy of his report, he may inform the reporting agency of the discrepancy. Under Section 1681i, the agency must then reinvestigate the matter and correct any erroneous information. If this investigation does not resolve the issue, the consumer may file a brief statement setting forth his explanation of the matter, which must be included in his file for disclosure to anyone requesting a copy of his credit report. 15 U.S.C.A. § 1681i (West 1988).

An action for a violation of this Act can be brought in any district court without regard to the amount in controversy. 15 U.S.C.A. § 1681p (1988). If a reporting agency or report recipient willfully fails to comply with the Act, the civil liability includes any actual damages the consumer sustains due to the violation. These damages include any punitive damages the court may order, reasonable attorneys' fees and court costs in successful actions. 15 U.S.C.A. § 1681n (1988). Civil liability for negligent noncompliance includes actual damages, reasonable attorneys' fees, and court costs in successful actions. 15 U.S.C.A. § 1681o (1988). Any person who knowingly and willfully obtains credit information from a reporting agency under false pretenses, or who knowingly and willfully discloses such information to a person not authorized to receive it, is subject to a fine not more than $5,000 or may be imprisoned for not more than one year, or both. 15 U.S.C.A. § 1681q–1681r (1988). The criminal liability provisions of the Act can serve as a basis for a civil suit against an individual who obtains or releases a report under false pretenses. In *Hansen v. Morgan*, 582 F.2d 1214 (9th Cir.1978), the court held that an individual who obtained a report under false pretenses to damage a political opponent could be liable both criminally and civilly. Violations of the Act are deemed unfair or deceptive acts and are prosecutable by the Federal Trade Commission. 15 U.S.C.A. § 1681s (1988).

In *Peller v. Retail Credit Co.*, 359 F.Supp. 1235 (N.D.Ga.1973), *aff'd*, 505 F.2d 733 (5th Cir. 1974), the plaintiff was fired from his job when his present employer discovered that he had previously failed a pre-employment polygraph examination when applying for a job with another company. This information was obtained from plaintiff's credit report. The court ruled that neither his previous employer nor the polygraph examiner were "consumer reporting agencies" under the Act. The court also found that the results of the polygraph test were not "consumer credit reports" under the Act. The court also denied recovery under the state libel or slander laws, since there was no allegation of malice or willful intent. Furthermore, the court found that supplying this information to a credit reporting agency did not constitute an invasion of privacy. *Id.* at 1237.

In *Heath v. Credit Bureau of Sheridan, Inc.*, 618 F.2d 693 (10th Cir.1980), a credit reporting agency issued a union member's credit report to a union which sought to use the information for the purpose of humiliating him. The credit reporting agency was held to be potentially liable under either section 1681n or 1681o. The court ruled that the request was not "for employment purposes" as defined in section 1681b. The case was remanded for further proceedings to determine whether the credit reporting agency knew of the unlawful purpose for which the union had made its request.

.   .   .

Plaintiffs who file actions against consumer reporting agencies concerning the disclosure of information covered by sections 1681g, 1681h, or 1681m of the Act generally may not pursue common law actions for defamation, invasion of privacy, or negligence against the agency. 15 U.S.C.A. § 1681h(e). In this regard, the FCRA expressly preempts these common law actions. However, if the reporting agency provides false information with malice, or willful intent to injure the consumer, such actions can be brought at common law. *See, e.g., Thornton v. Equifax, Inc.*, 619 F.2d 700 (8th Cir.), *cert. denied*, 449 U.S. 835 (1980), (case remanded to determine whether malice or willful intent existed to allow defamation action when reporting agency disclosed false information to insurance agent concerning insured's live-in boyfriend).

It should also be noted that a person furnishing information about an individual based solely on its own experience or transactions with that person does not constitute the furnishing of a "consumer credit report" under the Act. 15 U.S.C.A. § 1681a(d) (1988). For example, in *Freeman v. Southern Nat'l Bank*, 531 F.Supp. 94 (S.D.Tex.1982), the court ruled that where a bank is furnishing information based on its own experience with a customer, the bank is not acting as a consumer reporting agency, and the information is not a consumer credit report under the Act.

The Consumer Credit Reporting Reform Act of 1996.

The above summary of FCRA needs to be read in conjunction with this brief highlight of important amendments to FCRA in 1996. Important changes were made to FCRA in the Consumer Credit Reporting Reform Act of 1996 (CCRRA). The 1996 act is codified at 15 U.S.C.A. secs. 1681a–1681t (West 1998). Some of the areas of changes under the CCRRA are (1) financial information that is outside of the scope of a "consumer report" is expanded. This allows for greater sharing of information on commercial transactions between affiliates-entities related by common ownership-without becoming a consumer reporting agency within the Act. See sec. 1681a (d)(2)(A); (2) new limitations are placed on the circumstances when credit reporting agencies may furnish credit reports or investigative consumer reports. See, for example, sec. 1681b(a)-(c). In this regard the CCRRA tightens the "legitimate business need" standard for release of credit reports. See sec. 1681b(a)(3)(F); (3) new rules for prescreening of credit reports to solicit customers have been established. See sec. 1681b. These include providing the customer with opt out rights after notifying the Consumer Reporting Agency. See sec. 1681b(c)(1)(B)(iii); (4) new obligations are imposed on business and creditors to insure that information furnished to Consumer Reporting Agencies is accurate and current sec. 1681s-2; (5) civil and criminal penalties are increased. See secs. 1681n–1681s.

The CCRRA addresses some of the problems that arose under FCRA regarding access by employers to sensitive information in credit reports. For example Under the CCRRA written consent of the employee is required before a credit report can be procured for employment purposes. See sec. 1681b(b)(2).

Under the FCRA state laws that were inconsistent with the statute were preempted. In sec. 1681t the CCRRA contains a more extensive preemption provision. For example any state regulation of the prescreening of consumer reports is preempted if the subject matter is regulated under the CCRRA. See sec. 1681t(b)(1)(A).

4. RIGHTS AND REMEDIES UNDER THE FAIR CREDIT RE-PORTING ACT

THOMPSON v. SAN ANTONIO RETAIL MERCHANTS ASS'N

682 F.2d 509 (5th Cir.1982).

Before RUBIN, JOHNSON and GARWOOD, CIRCUIT JUDGES.

PER CURIAM:

This case involves the liability of the San Antonio Retail Merchants Association (SARMA) for an inaccurate credit report. Gulf Oil Corporation (Gulf) and Montgomery Ward (Ward's) denied credit to William Douglas Thompson, III, on the basis of erroneous credit information furnished by SARMA. The district court, after a nonjury trial, entered judgement for Thompson in the sum of $10,000 actual damages and $4,485 attorneys' fees. SARMA appeals.

I. BACKGROUND

SARMA provides a computerized credit reporting service to local business subscribers. This service depends heavily upon credit history information fed into SARMA's files by subscribers. A key mechanism used by SARMA to update its files is a computerized "automatic capturing" feature. A subscriber must feed certain identifying information from its own computer terminal into SARMA's central computer in order to gain access to the credit history of a particular consumer. When presented with this identifying information, SARMA's computer searches its records and displays on the subscriber's terminal the credit history file that most nearly matches the consumer. The decision whether to accept a given file as being that of a particular consumer is left completely to the terminal operator. When a subscriber does accept a given file as pertaining to a particular consumer, however, the computer automatically captures into the file any information input from the subscriber's terminal that the central file did not already have.

The disadvantage of an automatic capturing feature is that it may accept erroneous information fed in by subscribers, unless special auditing procedures are built into the system. In the instant case, SARMA failed to check the accuracy of a social security number obtained by its automatic capturing feature. The social security number is the single most important identifying factor for credit-reference purposes. As a result, the computer erroneously began to report the bad credit history of "William Daniel Thompson, Jr.," to subscribers inquiring about "William Douglas Thompson, III."

In November, 1974, William Daniel Thompson, Jr., opened a credit account with Gordon's Jewelers (Gordon's) in San Antonio, listing his social security number as 457–68–5778, his address as 132 Baxter, his occupation as truck loader, and his marital status as single. He subsequently ran up a delinquent account of $77.25 at Gordon's that was ultimately charged off as a bad debt. When Gordon's voluntarily reported the bad debt, SARMA placed the information and a derogatory credit rating into file number 5867114, without any identifying social security number.

In early 1978, the plaintiff, William Douglas Thompson, III, applied for credit with Gulf and with Ward's in San Antonio. He listed his social security number as 407–86–4065, his address as 6929 Timbercreek, his occupation as groundskeeper, and his wife as Deborah C. On February 9, 1978, Gulf's terminal operator mistakenly accepted file number 5867114 as that of the plaintiff. SARMA's computer thereupon automatically captured various information about William Douglas Thompson, III, including his social security number, into file number 5867114. At that point, the original file, which was on Daniel Thompson, Jr., became a potpourri of information on both the plaintiff and the original William Daniel Thompson, Jr. The name of the file remained that of William Daniel Thompson, Jr. The social security number became that of the plaintiff, the current address and employer became that of the plaintiff, a former address and employer became that of William Daniel Thompson, Jr., and the wife's name became that of the plaintiff's wife. Shortly thereafter, Ward's terminal operator ran a credit check on the plaintiff, was given the garbled data, and accepted file number 5867114 as that of the plaintiff. As a result of the adverse information regarding the Gordon's account, Ward's denied the plaintiff credit. The plaintiff applied for credit at Ward's in May 1979 and was again rejected.

On February 21, 1978, Gulf requested a "revision" of file number 5867114, a procedure which entails a rechecking of information in a file with respect to a particular creditor or creditors. Following its usual procedures, SARMA would call Gordon's to verify in detail the information in the file. Although this was probably done, whoever contacted Gordon's apparently failed to check the social security number of Gordon's delinquent customer and take corrective action when it was received. Instead, the adverse information remained in the file under the plaintiff's social security number after Gulf's revision request, and Gulf denied the plaintiff credit.

The adverse information remained in the plaintiff's file during 1978 and the first five and a half months of 1979. During all of this time the plaintiff had thought he had been denied credit from Gulf and Ward's because of a 1976 Texas felony conviction for burglary. He had received a five-year probationary sentence, but subsequently gained fulltime employment and straightened out his life. In June of 1979, plaintiff's wife learned from her credit union in processing an application for a loan that her husband's adverse credit rating resulted from a bad debt at Gordon's. The plaintiff knew he had never had an account at Gordon's so he and his wife went directly to their place of business. After waiting some two hours he was informed that there had indeed been a mistake, their credit record was for William Daniel Thompson, Jr.

The plaintiff and his wife went to SARMA with this information in an attempt to purge the erroneous credit information. They spoke with an individual and showed birth registration and drivers license information revealing his name to be William Douglas Thompson, III. The entire process required some three hours. Nevertheless SARMA thereafter mailed appellee a letter addressed to William Daniel Thompson, III. Appellee's wife again returned to SARMA. Following this SARMA once again addressed a letter to William Daniel Thompson, III. Appellee once again returned to SARMA—yet again SARMA wrote still another letter with the same incorrect name. Further, though SARMA's policy was to send corrections made on a file to any subscribers who had made inquiry about it within the last six months, SARMA failed to notify Ward's of the corrections. The plaintiff filed an action in state court on October 4, 1979. It was not until October 16, 1979, that SARMA informed Ward's of the erroneous credit information. On November 5, 1979, the action was removed to the federal district court. After a bench trial, the district court found that denials of credit to the appellee by Gulf and Ward's were caused by SARMA's failure to follow reasonable procedures to assure the maximum possible accuracy of its files. The district court awarded plaintiff actual damages in the sum of $10,000 plus attorneys' fees in the sum of $4485.

II. THE LIABILITY ISSUE

Under 15 U.S.C. Section 1681o of the Fair Credit Reporting Act (Act), a "consumer reporting agency" is liable to "any consumer" for negligent failure to comply with "any requirement imposed" by the Act.[4] In the instant case, the district court determined that SARMA was liable under section 1681o for negligent failure to comply with section 1681e(b) of the Act, which provides:

> When a consumer reporting agency *prepares* a consumer report, it shall follow *reasonable procedures* to assure *maximum possible accuracy* of information concerning the individual about whom the report relates.

15 U.S.C. Section 1681e(b) (emphasis added).

Section 1681e(b) does not impose strict liability for any inaccurate credit report, but only a duty of reasonable care in preparation of the report. The duty extends to updating procedures, because "preparation" of a consumer report should be viewed as a continuing process and the

---

4. 15 U.S.C. Section 1681o provides:

Any consumer reporting agency or user of information which is negligent in failing to comply with any requirement imposed under this subchapter with respect to any consumer is liable to that consumer in an amount equal to the sum of—

(1) any actual damages sustained by the consumer as a result of the failure;

(2) in the case of any successful action to enforce any liability under this section, the costs of the action together with reasonable attorney's fees as determined by the court.

obligation to insure accuracy arises with every addition of information. The standard of conduct by which the trier of fact must judge the adequacy procedures is what a reasonably prudent person would do under the circumstances. Applying the reasonable-person standard, the district court found two acts of negligence in SARMA's updating procedures. First, SARMA failed to exercise reasonable care in programming its computer to automatically capture information into a file without requiring any minimum number of "points of correspondence" between the consumer and the file or having an adequate auditing procedure to foster accuracy. Second, SARMA failed to employ reasonable procedures designed to learn the disparity in social security numbers for the two Thompsons when it revised file number 5867114 at Gulf's request. This Court can reverse the district court on these findings of fact only if there is a definite and firm conviction that the judgment of the district court is clearly erroneous.

With respect to the first act of negligence, George Zepeda, SARMA's manager, testified that SARMA's computer had no minimum number of points of correspondence to be satisfied before an inquiring subscriber could accept credit information. Moreover, SARMA had no way of knowing if the information supplied by the subscriber was correct. Although SARMA did conduct spot audits to verify social security numbers, it did not audit all subscribers. With respect to the second act of negligence, SARMA's verification process failed to uncover the erroneous social security number even though Gulf made a specific request for a "revision" to check the adverse credit history to the plaintiffs. SARMA's manager, Mr. Zepeda, testified that what should have been done upon the request for revision, was to pick up the phone and check with Gordon's and learn, among other things, the social security number of William Daniel Thompson, Jr. It was the manager's further testimony that the social security number is the single most important information in a consumer's credit file. In light of this evidence, this Court cannot conclude that the district court was clearly erroneous in finding negligent violation of section 1681e(b).

III. AWARD OF DAMAGES

The district court's award of $10,000 in actual damages was based on humiliation and mental distress to the plaintiff. Even when there are no out-of-pocket expenses, humiliation and mental distress do constitute recoverable elements of damage under the Act. In the instant case, the amount of damages is a question of fact which may be reversed by this Court only if the district court's findings are clearly erroneous. Fed. R.Civ.P. 52(a).

SARMA asserts that Thompson failed to prove any actual damages, or at best proved only minimal damages for humiliation and mental distress. There was evidence, however, that Thompson suffered humiliation and embarrassment from being denied credit on three occasions. Thompson testified that the denial of credit hurt him deeply because of his mistaken belief that it resulted from his felony conviction:

I was trying to build myself back up, trying to set myself up, get back on my feet again. I was working sixty hours a week and sometimes seventy. I went back to school. I was going to school at night three nights a week, four nights a week, three hours a night, and [denial of credit] really hurt. It made me disgusted with myself.

... [I needed credit to] be able to obtain things that everybody else is able to obtain, to be able to buy clothes or be able to set myself up where I can show my ability to be trusted.

We didn't even have a bed. It was pretty bad. We were hurting. Everything we had to do, we had to save up and pay cash for strictly. It was just impossible to do it any other way.

Furthermore, the inaccurate information remained in SARMA's files for almost one and one-half years after the inaccurate information was inserted. Even after the error was discovered, Thompson spent months pressing SARMA to correct its mistakes and fully succeeded only after bringing a lawsuit against SARMA. This court is of the opinion that the trial judge was entitled to conclude that the humiliation and mental distress were not minimal but substantial.

SARMA contends that the instant damage award is excessive when compared to similar cases such as Millstone, 528 F.2d at 834–35 and Bryant, 487 F. Supp. at 1239–40. In Millstone, an insurance company canceled an automobile insurance policy after a consumer credit report alleged the insured was a political activist disliked by his neighbors. The insurer first canceled the insured's policy and then reinstated it when an agent discovered the insured was in fact a highly respected assistant managing editor of the St. Louis Post Dispatch. Even though the incorrect report involved a mere $68.00 insurance policy, the district court awarded $2,500 in actual damages for Millstone's mental anguish over the report. In Bryant, an inaccurate credit report was issued on a consumer in connection with a mortgage application for a house purchase. The credit report resulted in denial of the mortgage. The consumer called the inaccuracy to the attention of the credit reporting agency, yet the same inaccurate information was issued in connection with a later mortgage application. A jury determination of $8,000 in actual damages was sustained in that instance. The damage award in the instant case is not so out of line with Bryant and Millstone as to be clearly erroneous. The case *sub judice* was a trial before the court without a jury. The trial judge was in a position to weigh the credibility of testimony on humiliation and mental distress and, therefore, should be given considerable latitude; it cannot be said that his determination was clearly erroneous.

SARMA finally asserts that Thompson was required to mitigate his damages by first exhausting alternative remedies. SARMA cites section 1681i of the Act which sets forth a procedure for consumers to challenge the completeness or accuracy of any disputed information in this file.[6] The Act, however, does not require that a consumer pursue the remedies provided in section 1681i before bringing suit under section 1681o for violation of section 1681e. If a consumer can prove a violation of section 1681e, he can sue directly on that basis without first exhausting alternative remedies. Thompson was not required to mitigate his damages by formally disputing the accuracy of the information contained in his file.

IV.   AWARD OF ATTORNEY'S FEES

Section 1681o also allows an award of attorneys' fees. The district court may determine the amount of attorneys' fees on the basis of the guidelines set forth in Johnson v. Georgia Highway Express, Inc., 488 F.2d 714 (5th Cir.1974). The district court explicitly applied the Johnson criteria and awarded $4,485 in attorneys' fees based on 41.5 hours of work at $90 per hour and other special fees. The determination of a reasonable attorneys' fee is a matter within the discretion of the trial judge and should not be set aside absent clear abuse of discretion. This Court cannot say that the district court clearly abused its discretion.

The judgement of the district court is AFFIRMED.

Note

Other courts have held that failure to take reasonable action to verify adverse information is a violation of Section 1681e. *See Millstone v. O'Hanlon Reports, Inc.*, 383 F.Supp. 269 (E.D.Mo.1974), *aff'd*, 528 F.2d 829 (8th Cir.1976); *Miller v. Credit Bureau, Inc.* [1916–73 Transfer Binder] Cons. Credit Guide (CCH 99, 173 D.C. Superior Court 1972). *See also Lowry v. Credit Bureau, Inc.*, 444 F.Supp. 541 (N.D.Ga.1978).

5. THE FAMILY EDUCATIONAL RIGHTS AND PRIVACY ACT

In 1974, Congress passed The Family Educational Rights and Privacy Act of 1974 (FERPA), 20 U.S.C.A. § 1232g (1988), to regulate the disclosure of records that primary, secondary, and post-secondary educational institutions maintain concerning students and their parents. Included in the Act's scope of protection are parents' financial records, student's confidential letters of recommendation, and student's educational records. Federal funding is denied to any educational institution that releases a student's educational records without the prior written consent of his parents or without the student's consent if he is over eighteen years of age. 20 U.S.C.A. § 1232g(b)(1). However, no consent is required where disclosure is made to the officials of other school districts to which the student transfers, to the administrative head of the state educational authority, to state or local authorities, in connection with an application for financial aid for the student, or to accrediting bodies. *Id.*

Disclosing educational records without student or parental consent is also permitted under section 1232g(b)(1)(F) to an organization doing studies to develop, validate or administer predictive tests, administer

---

6. Both Gulf and Ward's notified the plaintiff of his right to make a written request from the consumer reporting agency of the reasons for the adverse action.

student aid programs, and improve instruction. However, such information may be released only where the studies are conducted in a manner that will prevent the personal identification of the student or his parents by persons outside the organization conducting the study, and only if the information is destroyed when no longer needed for the purpose of the study.

An educational institution may also make public disclosures of "directory information," i.e., name, address, birth place, date of birth, telephone, participation in sports, attendance records, degrees and awards received, about a student only after giving the student or his parents notice of the categories of information to be disclosed and allowing a reasonable time for them to object to the release. 20 U.S.C.A. § 1232g(a)(5)(A)-(B) (1988). An educational institution may only release personally identifiable information in the student's educational records, other than "directory information," when it has the parent's or student's written consent. This consent must specify the records to be released and the reason for the disclosure. Where a court order or subpoena mandates the release of student records, notice of the educational institution's intent to comply with the order must be given to the student or his parents. 20 U.S.C.A. § 1232g(b)(2)(A)-(B) (1988). Section 1232g(e) also places an affirmative duty on the educational agency to inform parents and students of their rights under the Act.

The Act's remedy provisions are limited. Parents and students seeking redress for violations under FERPA must first apply to the administrative head of the educational agency for a correction of the violation. 20 U.S.C.A. § 1232g(f) (1988). If the parents or student are not satisfied with the administrative head's resolution of the matter, they may petition the Secretary of Education. The only power the Secretary of Education has to redress a violation is to terminate federal funding to the educational institution. It is well settled that no private remedy is created by the Act. *See, e.g., Tarka v. Franklin,* 891 F.2d 102 (5th Cir.1989), *cert. denied,* 494 U.S. 1080 (1990).

Parents and other groups often use the Act to obtain educational records when pursuing legal actions against schools for inadequate educational training. For example, in *Rios v. Read,* 73 F.R.D. 589 (E.D.N.Y.1977), the District Court allowed parents to obtain educational records of students for use in a civil rights action against a school for failure to properly teach English to predominantly Hispanic children. The Court ordered that notice be provided to the parents of those students whose records would be disclosed, that disclosure must be limited to those connected with the litigation, and that there was no need to eliminate the names of the students from the records. The court further required that notice be sent in both Spanish and English.

In *In re Kryston v. Bd. of Educ.,* 77 A.D.2d 896, 430 N.Y.S.2d 688 (1980), the court allowed a parent to obtain test scores of his child's entire third-grade class. In order to protect the other students in the class, the court ordered the release of the test results in a scrambled order, with the students' names redacted. The court ruled that this was the best way to protect the privacy of the other seventy-five students who took the test. The court emphasized that disclosure in this non-identifying form was not an onerous burden on the school district.

In *Reeg v. Fetzer*, 78 F.R.D. 34 (W.D.Okla.1976), a doctor sought to use the Act to shield his hospital residency records from disclosure in a malpractice case. The records would have revealed that the doctor failed to complete orthopedic training. The court noted that the foundation of FERPA lies in notifying data subjects when a court orders release of their educational records, not in creating a privilege to bar access to such data. The court, however, did not order the release of the records. Instead, it concluded that such records were not the proper subject of discovery and would unfairly prejudice the jury.

6. THE RIGHT TO FINANCIAL PRIVACY ACT OF 1978

In 1976, the U.S. Supreme Court decided the case of *United States v. Miller*, 425 U.S. 435 (1976), wherein a bank's customer challenged the disclosure by his bank of personal financial information. The court held that the records belonged to the bank and were not the customer's papers protected by the fourth amendment. The court also held that the customer did not have a reasonable expectation of privacy regarding those records of negotiated checks because in writing a check he knew that the bank's employees would handle the checks and see the information on them. Further, the court held that the customer did not even have standing to raise the matter in court!

In 1978, Congress passed the Right to Financial Privacy Act (FPA), 12 U.S.C.A. § 3401–3422 (1988), as a response to the *Miller* decision. FPA regulates financial institution disclosures of personal financial information to federal agencies, recognizes the customer's privacy interest in his bank records and gives him rights regarding the disclosure of such records. The Act does not prohibit disclosures to the federal government, but rather it mandates specific procedures to be followed in government requests for disclosure, and it gives the customer rights to notice and challenge. Section 3402 grants federal agency's access to financial records if the government's request reasonably describes the records sought and either the customer authorizes disclosure or disclosure is in response to an administrative warrant or subpoena, a search warrant, or a judicial subpoena. The government can also access such records by filing a formal written request with the financial institution stating that the records sought are relevant to a legitimate law enforcement inquiry. The agency must also give advance notice to the customer. The only other requirement is that the head of the agency must create regulations authorizing the disclosure procedure. Section 3408.

Nothing in the Act precludes a financial institution from notifying the government of existing relevant information in its files, and often banks do report unusual transactions to the appropriate government agencies. Section 3403(c). Section 3413 of the act also permits supervisory bodies such as the FDIC, SEC, Federal Reserve, IRS, or state banking or securities departments to examine any financial records. No notice to the customer is required if disclosure to the government entity consists only of a customer's name, address, account number and type of account. Section 3413(g).

Under the Act, civil actions can be brought in district court within three years of the alleged violation or the customer's discovery of it. Section 3416. The civil remedies available include at least $100 in damages without regard to the volume of records involved, any actual damages resulting from disclosure, punitive damages if the court determines that the violation was willful, and reasonable attorney's fees and court costs if the plaintiff is successful. Section 3417(a). Injunctive relief with reasonable attorney's fees and court costs is also available. Section 3518.

There is a difference between a customer's bank transactions as recorded in a bank's business records and the customer's individual account records. Where the documents sought are the bank's own business records, the customer involved has no standing to challenge the disclosure. *See Clayton Brokerage Co. v. Clement*, 87 F.R.D. 569, 571 (D.Md.1980). However, the customer may challenge disclosures of his own deposit records.

The Congressional response was consistent with state court holdings regarding privacy and bank records. In *Burrows v. Superior Court*, 13 Cal.3d 238, 529 P.2d 590, 118 Cal.Rptr. 166 (1974), the California Supreme Court found that a bank customer did have a reasonable expectation of privacy with respect to his financial records and that this privacy right was protected under the California Constitution:

> Development of photocopying machines, electronic computers and other sophisticated instruments have accelerated the ability of government to intrude into areas which a person normally chooses to exclude from prying eyes and inquisitive minds. Consequently judicial interpretations of the reach of the constitutional protection of individual privacy must keep pace with the perils created by these new devices.

Id. at 248, 529 P.2d at 596, 118 Cal. Rptr. at 172.

A similar result was reached in *Commonwealth v. DeJohn*, 486 Pa. 32, 403 A.2d 1283 (1979), *cert. denied*, 444 U.S. 1032 (1980), where the Pennsylvania Supreme Court determined that a bank customer has a similar privacy right in his financial records under the Pennsylvania Constitution. *See also In re East Nat'l Bank*, 517 F.Supp. 1061 (D.Colo. 1981), holding that the Colorado Constitution affords a privacy right regarding a customer's bank records.

7. THE ELECTRONIC COMMUNICATIONS PRIVACY ACT

In 1986, Congress passed The Electronic Communications Privacy Act (ECPA) as an amendment to Title III of the Omnibus Crime Control and Safe Streets Act of 1968 (Crime Control Act). Pub. L. No. 99–508, 100 Stat. 1848 (codified as amended in various sections of 18 U.S.C.A. (1988)). The ECPA was enacted "to update and clarify Federal privacy protections and standards in light of dramatic changes in new computer and telecommunications technologies." S. Rep. No. 99–541, 99th Cong., 2d Sess. 1, *reprinted in* 1986 U.S. Code Cong. & Admin. News 3555 (hereinafter S. Rep. 541). The ECPA modified Title III by expanding the existing protection extended to oral and wire communications to include those transmitted by electronic devices. 18 U.S.C.A. § 2510(5) (1988). The ECPA brought various types of electronic devices within the purview of The Federal Wiretap Act. The new technologies protected by ECPA include electronic mail transmissions, communications transmitted between computers, cellular phone communications, and certain types of pagers. The ECPA is examined in Chapter III.

8. THE VIDEO PRIVACY PROTECTION ACT OF 1988

As mentioned, in response to disclosure by the media of a list of the movies rented by Judge Robert Bork, nominee to the U.S. Supreme Court, Congress enacted legislation to restrict access to consumer video-cassette rental and sales information—the Video Privacy Protection Act of 1988. 18 U.S.C.A. § 2710 (1988). The primary purpose of the Act is to keep "videotape service providers" from disclosing personally identifiable information concerning consumer videotape selections. Section 2710(b).

Videotape providers may disclose information to the consumer involved or his agent, Section 2710(b)(2)(a) and (b), or in compliance with a warrant or court order. Section 2710(b)(2)(C). They may also disclose the names and addresses of their customers provided that the customer has had an opportunity to prohibit such disclosure and the customer list does not reveal the content or subject matter of any videos rented. Section 2710(b)(2)(D)(i) and (ii).

The Act contains a civil remedy provision that allows an aggrieved party to bring an action in the United States District Court within two years of the date of discovery of an alleged violation, Section 2710(b)(3)(c)(2) and (3). Actual damages may be awarded for violating the statute. However, if actual damages are awarded, there is a liquidated damage provision requiring that the amount be at least $2,500. The court may also award punitive damages, attorney's fees and other equitable relief that it deems appropriate. Section 2710(b)(2)(3)(c)(2). The reach of the Video Privacy Protection Act is broad. The Act applies to any videotape service provider that is engaged in a business that affects interstate commerce. Section 2710 (a)(4).

Here is another example of narrowly-targeted legislation in response to an uproar arising out of media attention. The Congress did not take the time to consider, for instance, the related question of access to public library check-out information, though there have been reports of inquiries by the FBI or other law enforcement agencies concerning the kinds of books checked out of the public library by specific individuals. Might it be conjectured that more members of Congress patronize video stores than libraries? It is also interesting to note that the Act does not prohibit the video purveyors from selling customer lists.

9. THE COMPUTER MATCHING AND PRIVACY PROTECTION ACT OF 1988

In 1988, Congress passed the Computer Matching and Privacy Protection Act ("the Computer Matching Act"), 5 U.S.C.A. § 552a(*o*) (1988), as an amendment to the Privacy Act of 1974. The purpose of the Act is to regulate the practice of "matching" files pertaining to the same individual through the use of a personal identifier. A "computer match" may be accomplished by using a computer program that searches an agency's files for information associated with or indexed by a personal identifier such as a name or social security number. That information can then be compared with information in the files of another agency for discrepancies that might, for instance, detect payment errors or identify fraud in connection with government benefits. Though the elimination of fraud or abuse in government benefit programs is a legitimate end, computer matches implicitly conflict with the principle of the Privacy Act that information should be used only for the purpose for which it was gathered. The Act did not specifically address computer matching practices, however, and the unregulated sharing of information between agencies could result in significant invasions of informational privacy; Congress undertook to strike a balance between the individual's privacy and the legitimate pursuit of integrity in government service delivery. *See* Comment, *The Computer Matching and Privacy Protection Act of 1988: Necessary Relief From the Erosion of the Privacy Act of 1974*, 2 Software L.J. 391, 407 (1988).

The Computer Matching Act imposes several restrictions on federal agencies' computer matching practices. First, an agency that seeks to disclose information acquired from a computer match must enter a formal written agreement with the receiving entity. 5 U.S.C.A. § 552a(*o*)(1) (1988). Before taking any adverse action against the data subject of a computer match, the agency must independently verify the accuracy of the information. Section 552a(*o*)(1)(E). Every agency must publish notice prior to conducting or revising a computer match program. Section 552a(*o*)(1)(D). Finally, the Act requires that every federal agency establish a Data Integrity Board to monitor implementation of its provisions. Section 552a(u)(1). No matching program may exceed eighteen months unless a renewal is granted by the agency's Data Integrity Board. 552a(*o*)(2)(C).

a. The Matching Agreement

The matching agreement between the source and receiving agency must identify the legal authority for the match and the purpose and justification for it, describe the records that will be searched, and, specify the procedures for verifying the accuracy of the information used in the match. Section 552a(*o*)(1)(A-D).

b. The Notice Requirements

Any federal agency planning to participate in a computer match must publish notice in the Federal Register at least thirty days before conducting the match. This notice requirement applies even when a federal agency participates in a computer match with a non-federal entity. The data subject must be given additional notice prior to any termination of federal benefits resulting from the match program. Section 552a(p)(3). The notice must set forth the findings and advise the individual of procedures to contest the results. Section 552a(p)(3)(1)(A) and (B). Furthermore, no adverse action may be taken against the subject of a computer match until one of the agency's officers or employees independently verifies the accuracy of the information. Section 552a(p)(1).

c. Data Integrity Boards

The CMA requires the establishment of a Data Integrity Board within each agency that wishes to engage in match programs. Sections 552a(u)(1), and following. The members of the Boards are selected by the head of each agency from among its senior employees, and they are responsible for overseeing the agency's implementation of and compliance with the Act's provisions. The Board must submit an annual report to the Office of Management and Budget summarizing the matching activities in which the agency has participated.

10. THE FREEDOM OF INFORMATION ACT

a. The Interrelationship Between the Freedom of Information Act (FOIA) and the Privacy Act (PA)

As previously noted, the Privacy Act of 1974 provides for access by an individual to personal information in federal agency records. In 1966, Congress enacted the Freedom of Information Act (FOIA), 5 U.S.C.A. § 552 (1988). The purpose of FOIA is to provide the public with access to information in federal agency records. FOIA requires that agencies make information available for public inspection and copying, Sections 552(a)(2), and release information to "any person" making an appropriate request, Section 552(a)(3).

Procedures for access through FOIA are rather simple, and once a proper request has been made to an agency it must make the requested records available unless the agency establishes that the information sought comes within one of the Act's nine enumerated exemptions. The FOIA exemptions relevant to informational privacy are (b)(6) and (b)(7). Section 552(b)(6) exempts "personnel and medical files and similar files the disclosures of which would constitute a clearly unwarranted invasion of personal privacy." Section 552(b)(7) provides exemption for:

records or information compiled for law enforcement purposes, but only to the extent that the production of such law enforcement records or information (A) could reasonably be expected to interfere with enforcement proceedings, (B) would deprive a person of a right to a fair trial or an impartial adjudication, (C) could reasonably be expected to constitute an unwarranted invasion of personal privacy, (D) could reasonably be expected to disclose the identity of a confidential source ... and, in the case of a record or information compiled by a criminal law enforcement authority in the course of a criminal investigation or by an agency conducting a lawful national security intelligence investigation, information furnished by a confidential source, (E) would disclose techniques and procedures for law enforcement investigations ... , or (F) could reasonably be expected to endanger the life or physical safety of any individual....

The inherent conflict between the policies of protecting privacy under the PA and making information available to the public under FOIA is reconciled in the following way. The Privacy Act of 1974 became effective on September 27, 1975. Congress did not desire to upset the status quo regarding the availability of information under FOIA so information that must be disclosed pursuant to FOIA is expressly exempted from the scope of the Privacy Act's provisions. Section 552a(b)(2).

Since FOIA-mandated disclosures are exempt from the Privacy Act, FOIA litigation involving privacy interests focuses primarily on judicial interpretation of exemptions (b)(6) and (b)(7) when the information is contained in records that come within the coverage of both statutes. As a result, some of the most significant informational privacy questions in our legal system are found in litigation involving the two FOIA privacy exemptions.

Note that information generated, owned, and possessed by a private organization receiving federal funding for a specific project is not an "agency record" under FOIA and hence is not subject to the Act. In *Forsham v. Harris*, 445 U.S. 169 (1980), the University Group Diabetes Program had been given federal funding to study the effect of certain long-term diabetes treatments, and the results of the study had led the FDA to require labelling of certain drugs for diabetes with a warning of the increased risk of heart disease associated with the drugs. Nevertheless, the United States Supreme Court found that since the agency did not exercise its right to review the data or obtain custody of the data, the study was not part of an "agency record" under FOIA. In order for data generated by private institutions supported by federal funding to be an "agency record," it must be proven not only that the agency possesses such data but also that it owns the data and has subjected it to substantial government control and use. *See Ciba–Geigy Corp. v. Mathews*, 428 F.Supp. 523 (S.D.N.Y.1977).

b. Exemption (B)(6): the Threshold Question, Personnel, Medical and Similar Files

RURAL HOUSING ALLIANCE v. UNITED STATES DEP'T OF AGRICULTURE

498 F.2d 73 (D.C.Cir.1974).

Before BAZELON, CHIEF JUDGE, and ROBB and WILKEY, CIRCUIT JUDGES.

WILKEY, CIRCUIT JUDGE:

[The Rural Housing Alliance (RHA) brought an action against the United States Department of Agriculture (USDA) for alleged violation of the Freedom of Information Act (FOIA). In response to an RHA pamphlet charging racial and national origin discrimination in the awarding of government housing loans, USDA had investigated the allegations and had found no substantial evidence of discrimination. USDA refused RHA's request to obtain a copy of the investigative report on the grounds that FOIA exempted disclosure of the type of detailed and intimate case histories of specified persons contained therein. However, USDA indicated that it would disclose the requested material if RHA produced written release authorization from the particular individual named in any section. RHA did not seek to obtain such authorization and brought this FOIA action.

RHA subsequently filed a motion for summary judgment, which the district court denied. In order to ensure the omission of details which might permit identification of specific individuals, the district court ordered deletion of the names of applicants for loans, of the names of those who had complained to Congressmen, of the names of those who had been interviewed, of the names of attorneys and of others, of geographical references, of applications for loans, and of affidavits of applicants. USDA filed a motion to clarify or amend the court's order. In support of its motion, the Department provided a supporting affidavit of the Inspector General which emphasized the persistent risk that, notwithstanding the court-ordered deletions, the report contained sufficiently detailed information to allow ready identification of certain individuals by those familiar with the situation. The district court denied USDA's motion for clarification and, pending appeal by USDA, granted a stay.]

We have before us once again the question of the proper interpretation of several exemptions from disclosure under the Freedom of Information Act [FOIA]. At issue here is a report of a U.S. Department of Agriculture investigation of governmental housing discrimination in Florida, withheld from disclosure on the basis of exemptions 4, 5, 6, and 7. The District Court granted the plaintiff Rural Housing Alliance [RHA] motion for summary judgment after *in camera* inspection holding that the report was not within any exemption. We find the District Court applied incorrect legal standards in evaluating the applicability of the exemptions, hence reverse the judgment and remand for consideration consistent with this opinion.

I. THE NATURE OF THE GOVERNMENT REPORT

The USDA report and the investigation which spawned it were stimulated by an RHA pamphlet, "Studies in Bad Housing in America—Abuse of Power." Utilizing a method of case-history documentation, this RHA tract charged the Farmers Home Administration [FMHA] staff with racial and national origin discrimination in arranging government loans under the Rural Housing Program in two counties in Florida. The Office of Equal Opportunity of the USDA requested an investigation by the Department's Office of Inspector General [OIG]. After investigation, the OIG concluded in a 150–page report that there was no substantial evidence indicating discrimination.

RHA's request for a copy of the investigation report was denied. Instead, OIG made public the "Investigation Summary" and "Statistical Data" sections of the report. Citing exemptions 4, 5, 6, and 7 of FOIA as valid justification for keeping the remainder confidential, the Government did not release the remainder of the report because the Government felt that its form—detailed and intimate case histories of specified, named persons[4]—was inappropriate for disclosure. The Government did indicate that the material would be disclosed to RHA if it produced written authorization for release from the particular individual involved in any section. Rather than obtain such releases, RHA brought this FOIA suit.

The District Court, in considering RHA's motion for summary judgment, found that the report as a whole was not exempt from disclosure. However, the court recognized that there might be a need to delete details which would permit identification of the individuals involved. Consequently, the court ordered deletion of the names of applicants for loans, the names of those who complained to their Congressmen, those who were interviewed, attorneys, etc. Deletion of geographical references, applications for loans, and affidavits of applicants was likewise ordered.

USDA then filed a motion to clarify or amend the court's order. In support of the motion, USDA submitted an affidavit of the Inspector General, Nathaniel Kossack, explaining the Government's fear that the court order as framed would permit release of intimate details concerning persons who could be readily identified by those familiar with the

---

4. Inspector General Kossack's affidavit of 29 January 1973 stated that:

The report includes intimate details and information given by and with respect to borrowers and applicants for loans regarding the marital status of such borrowers and applicants, the number and the legitimacy of their children and grandchildren and the identity of the fathers of their children; information as to their medical condition and history, including statements as to surgery and the possibility of future pregnancies; information as to their occupations and work history and the amounts and sources of their annual income, including the amount of welfare payments received; information as to their habits with respect to the consumption of alcoholic beverages; information as to family fights which had occurred; information from their employers as to their reliability as employees; information as to their reputation in the community; information as to the risks involved in extending credit to them; and other information of a clearly personal and confidential nature.

situation, notwithstanding the deletions, thus exposing the individuals to embarrassment or possible reprisals. The District Judge, without explanation, denied the government motion for clarification. Pending appeal he granted a stay.

II. EXEMPTION 6: PERSONNEL, MEDICAL, AND SIMILAR FILES

The FOIA was enacted to ensure public access to a wide range of government reports and information. Recognizing that in certain circumstances disclosure realistically would not be in the public interest, Congress attempted to delineate a series of narrow exemptions. The sixth exemption provides that disclosure is unnecessary if the matters are "personnel and medical files and similar files the disclosure of which would constitute a clearly unwarranted invasion of personal privacy."

The District Court held that exemption 6 "has no application to this investigatory report." This holding was based on the view that the exemption "was designed to apply to detailed personal resumes and health records from agencies such as the Veterans Administration, welfare departments and the military." We think this statutory interpretation incorrect. We hold that exemption 6 is applicable to material such as the report here, hence we reverse the District Court and remand for appropriate review.

[1,2] While the District Judge provided no elaboration of his rationale in the form of findings, he implied that the report here could not be considered "similar files" under exemption 6. Looking to the purpose of exemption 6, on the contrary, we believe that the investigatory report comes well within the ambit of exemption 6. That exemption was designed to protect individuals from public disclosure of intimate details of their lives, whether the disclosure be of personnel files, medical files, or other similar files.[13] The exemption is not limited to Veterans' Administration or Social Security files, but rather is phrased broadly to protect individuals from a wide range of embarrassing disclosures.[14] As

---

13. The House Report on S. 1160, the bill which became the Freedom of Information Act, explains the broad purpose of exemption 6:

> Such agencies as the Veterans' Administration, Department of Health, Education, and Welfare, Selective Service, and Bureau of Prisons have great quantities of files containing intimate details about millions of citizens. Confidentiality of these records has been maintained by agency regulation but without statutory authority. A general exemption for the category of information is much more practical than separate statutes protecting each type of personal record. The limitation of a "clearly unwarranted invasion of personal privacy" provides a proper balance between the protection of an individual's right of privacy and the preservation of the public's right to Govern-

ment information by excluding those kinds of files the disclosure of which might harm the individual. The exemption is also intended to cover detailed Government records on an individual which can be identified as applying to that individual and not the facts concerning the award of a pension or benefit or the compilation of unidentified statistical information from personal records.

H.R. Rep.No.1497, 89th Cong., 2d Sess. 11 (1966).

14. Furthermore, the exemption should be read in conjunction with 5 U.S.C. Section 552(a)(2), which provides that

> To the extent required to prevent a clearly unwarranted invasion of personal privacy, an agency may delete identifying details when it makes available or publishes an opinion, statement of policy,

the materials here contain information regarding marital status, legitimacy of children, identity of fathers of children, medical condition, welfare payments, alcoholic consumption, family fights, reputation, and so on, it appears that the report involves sufficiently intimate details to be a "similar" file under exemption 6.

Of course, our interpretation of the statute, concluding that the investigatory report comes within the class of similar files which exemption 6 aimed at protecting, does not resolve the question whether exemption 6 dictates nondisclosure here, for exemption 6 specifically permits protection only of those files whose disclosure would result in "a clearly unwarranted invasion of personal privacy." On remand, it is for the District Judge to determine whether the files fall within that category.

. . .

These principles should be applied in evaluating the investigatory reports at issue here. The District Court should first determine the nature and extent of the invasion of the individuals' privacy. It should then consider the public interest purpose of RHA, and whether it could be achieved without this material. A balancing of these factors must thereafter be made.

One important factor which must be considered on remand is whether the deletions thus far ordered are sufficient to protect the privacy of the individuals. In construing the various exemptions, this court has often suggested deletions of certain protected matters so that the remainder of the document could be disclosed. The affidavit of Inspector General Kossack states, however, that the court order does not order adequate deletions, and that enough highly confidential material is left which would enable people with knowledge of the area to determine the identity of the individuals involved. The District Judge did not respond to this affidavit nor make any change in his order. On remand, the District Judge should reconsider and reevaluate this affidavit, and Kossack's prior affidavit submitted before the court's decision.

The District Judge should also consider any alternative sources of information which might be available. For example, the possibility of RHA asking individuals independently for similar information should be explored.

[Discussion of exemptions 4 and 7 omitted. Discussion of the effect of individual's consent to government disclosure omitted. Conclusion omitted.]

c. *The Supreme Court Approach: Total Rejection of the Strict View of "Similar Files"*

interpretation, or staff manual or instruction. However, in each case the justification for the deletion shall be explained fully in writing.

UNITED STATES DEP'T OF STATE
v. WASHINGTON POST CO.
456 U.S. 595 (1982).

[The Washington Post Company filed a request with the Department of State under the Freedom of Information Act for documents indicating whether certain Iranian nationals held valid United States passports. The State Department denied the request on the ground that the requested information was exempt from disclosure under Exemption 6 of the Act, which provides that the Act's disclosure requirements do not apply to "personnel and medical files and similar files the disclosure of which would constitute a clearly unwarranted invasion of personal privacy." Pending an ultimately unsuccessful administrative appeal, the Post brought an action in federal district court to enjoin the Department of State from withholding the requested documents, and the court granted summary judgment for the Post. The court of appeals affirmed, holding that because the citizenship status of the individuals in question was less intimate than information normally contained in personnel and medical files, it was not contained in "similar files" within the meaning of Exemption 6, and therefore there was no need to consider whether disclosure of the information would constitute a clearly unwarranted invasion of personal privacy. The Supreme Court reversed.]

REHNQUIST, J., delivered the opinion of the court, in which BURGER, C.J., and BRENNAN, WHITE, MARSHALL, BLACKMUN, POWELL, and STEVENS, JJ., joined. O'CONNOR, J., concurred in the judgment.

JUSTICE REHNQUIST delivered the opinion of the Court.

[Justice Rehnquist noted that in the lower court proceedings the Department of State had filed an affidavit that] explained that both Behzadnia and Yazdi were prominent figures in Iran's Revolutionary Government and that compliance with respondent's request would "cause a real threat of physical harm" to both men.[2]

· · ·

2. Petitioners' original affidavit stated:

There is intense anti-American sentiment in Iran and several Iranian revolutionary leaders have been strongly criticized in the press for their alleged ties to the United States. Any individual in Iran who is suspected of being an American citizen or of having American connections is looked upon with mistrust. An official of the Government of Iran who is reputed to be an American citizen would, in my opinion, be in physical danger from some of the revolutionary groups that are prone to violence. . . .

It is the position of the Department of State that any statement at this time by the United States Government which could be construed or misconstrued to indicate that any Iranian public official is currently a United States citizen is likely to cause a real threat of physical harm to that person.

Affidavit of Harold H. Saunders, Jan. 14, 1980, App. 17.

The affidavit reported that Yazdi, who has previously held the position of Foreign Minister, was currently a member of the Revolutionary Council and was responsible for solving problems in various regions of Iran. It also indicated that Behzadnia had been a senior official in the Ministry of National Guidance, but that the State Department had not received any report of his activities in recent weeks. Ibid. A supplemental affidavit, executed three months after the first affidavit, stated that Yazdi had been elected to the Iranian National Assembly, but that the activities of Behzadnia were still unreported. Supplemental Affidavit of Harold H. Saunders, April 22, 1980, App. 41.

The language of Exemption 6 sheds little light on what Congress meant by "similar files." Fortunately, the legislative history is somewhat more illuminating. The House and Senate Reports, although not defining the phrase "similar files," suggest that Congress' primary purpose in enacting Exemption 6 was to protect individuals from the injury and embarrassment that can result from the unnecessary disclosure of personal information. After referring to the "great quantities of [Federal Government] files containing intimate details about millions of citizens," the House Report explains that the exemption is "general" in nature and seeks to protect individuals:

> A *general exemption* for [this] category of information is much more practical than separate statutes protecting each type of personal record. The limitation of a "clearly unwarranted invasion of personal privacy" provides a proper balance between the protection of an individual's right of privacy and the preservation of the public's right to Government information *by excluding those kinds of files the disclosure of which might harm the individual*.

H.R. Rep. No. 1497, 89th Cong., 2nd Sess., 11 (1966) (emphasis added).

Similarly, the Senate Judiciary Committee reached a "consensus that these [personal] files should not be opened to the public, and ... decided upon a *general exemption* rather than a number of specific statutory authorizations for various agencies." S. Rep. No. 813, 89th Cong., 1st Sess., 9 (1965) (emphasis added). The Committee concluded that the balancing of private against public interests, not the nature of the files in which the information was contained, should limit the scope of the exemption: "It is believed that the scope of the exemption is held within bounds by the use of the limitation of 'a clearly unwarranted invasion of personal privacy.'" Ibid. Thus, "the primary concern of Congress in drafting Exemption 6 was to provide for the confidentiality of personal matters."

Respondent relies upon passing references in the legislative history to argue that the phrase "similar files" does not include all files which contain information about particular individuals, but instead is limited to files containing "intimate details" and "highly personal" information. See H.R. Rep. No. 1497, supra, at 11; S. Rep. No. 813, supra, at 9. We disagree. Passing references and isolated phrases are not controlling when analyzing a legislative history. Congress' statements that it was creating a "general exemption" for information contained in "great quantities of files," H.R. Rep. No. 1497, supra, at 11, suggest that the phrase "similar files" was to have a broad, rather than a narrow, meaning. This impression is confirmed by the frequent characterization of the "clearly unwarranted invasion of personal privacy" language as a "limitation" which holds Exemption 6 "within bounds." S. Rep. No. 813, supra, at 9. See also, H.R. Rep. No. 1497, supra, at 11; S. Rep. No. 1219, 88th Cong., 2d Sess., 14 (1964). Had the words "similar files" been intended to be only a narrow addition to "personnel and medical files," there would seem to be no reason for concern about the exemption's being "held within bounds," and there surely would be clear suggestions in the legislative history that such a narrow meaning was intended. We have found none.

A proper analysis of the exemption must also take into account the fact that "personnel and medical files," the two benchmarks for measuring the term "similar files," are likely to contain much information about a particular individual that is not intimate. Information such as place of birth, date of birth, date of marriage, employment history, and comparable data is not normally regarded as highly personal, and yet respondent does not disagree that such information, if contained in a "personnel" or "medical" file, would be exempt from any disclosure that would constitute a clearly unwarranted invasion of personal privacy. The passport information here requested, if it exists, presumably would be found in files containing much of the same kind of information. Such files would contain at least the information that normally is required from a passport applicant. See 22 U.S.C. Section 213. It strains the normal meaning of the word to say that such files are not "similar" to personnel or medical files.

We agree with petitioners' argument that adoption of respondent's limited view of Exemption 6 would produce anomalous results. Under the plain language of the exemption, nonintimate information about a particular individual which happens to be contained in a personnel or medical file can be withheld if its release would constitute a clearly unwarranted invasion of personal privacy. And yet under respondent's view of the exemption, the very same information, being nonintimate and therefore not within the "similar files" language, would be subject to mandatory disclosure if it happened to be contained in records other than personnel or medical files. "[T]he protection of an individual's right of privacy" which Congress sought to achieve by preventing "the disclosure of [information] which might harm the individual," H.R. Rep. No. 1497, supra, at 11, surely was not intended to turn upon the label of the file which contains the damaging information. In Department of Air Force v. Rose, 425 U.S. 352, 372 (1976), we recognized that the protection of Exemption 6 is not determined merely by the nature of the file in which the requested information is contained:

> Congressional concern for the protection of the kind of confidential personal data usually included in a personnel file is abundantly clear. But Congress also made clear that nonconfidential matter was not to be insulated from disclosure merely because it was stored by an agency in "personnel" files.

By the same reasoning, information about an individual should not lose the protection of Exemption 6 merely because it is stored by an agency in records other than "personnel" or "medical" files.

In sum, we do not think that Congress meant to limit Exemption 6 to a narrow class of files containing only a discrete kind of personal information. Rather, "[t]he exemption [was] intended to cover detailed Government records on an individual which can be identified as applying to that individual." H.R. Rep. No. 1497, supra, at 11.[3] When disclosure of information which applies to a particular individual is sought from Government records, courts must determine whether release of the information would constitute a clearly unwarranted invasion of that person's privacy.[4] The citizenship information sought by respondent satisfies the "similar files" requirement of Exemption 6, and petitioners' denial of the request should have been sustained upon a showing by the Government that release of the information would constitute a clearly unwarranted invasion of personal privacy. The Court of Appeals expressly declined to consider the effect of disclosure upon the privacy interests of Behzadnia and Yazdi, and we think that such balancing should be left to the Court of Appeals or to the District Court on remand. The judgment of the Court of Appeals is reversed, and the case is remanded for further proceedings consistent with this opinion.

It is so ordered.

JUSTICE O'CONNOR concurs in the judgment.

Note: Scope of the Concept of "Similar Files" After Washington Post

Does *Washington Post* resolve the conflict in federal court opinions about what is necessary for a file to be "similar" to a medical or personnel file within the meaning of (b)(6)? *Washington Post* applied the broadest possible construction to the concept of "similar files." Unambiguously the Court stated that all information in an agency record which "applies to a particular individual" is a "similar" file within (b)(6), 456 U.S. at 602. Consider the implications of this interpretation of the concept of "similar files" under (b)(6) when it is combined with the analysis of the Court in *Reporters Committee, infra.*

Rural Housing Alliance, supra, and *Wine Hobby, infra,* suggest the following dichotomy in evaluating the privacy implications of information in (b)(6) cases. Some information significantly implicates privacy values because it discloses "intimate" facts about an individual. These are facts

---

3. This view of Exemption 6 was adopted by the Attorney General shortly after enactment of the FOIA in a memorandum explaining the meaning of the Act to various federal agencies:

It is apparent that the exemption is intended to exclude from the disclosure requirements all personnel and medical files, *and all private or personal information contained in other files* which, if disclosed to the public, would amount to a clearly unwarranted invasion of the privacy of any person.

Attorney General's Memorandum on the Public Information Section of the Administrative Procedure Act 36 (June 1967) (emphasis added).

4. This construction of Exemption 6 will not render meaningless the threshold requirement that information be contained in personnel, medical, and similar files by reducing it to a test which fails to screen out any information that will not be screened out by the balancing of private against public interests. As petitioners point out, there are undoubtedly many Government files which contain information not personal to any particular individual, the disclosure of which would nonetheless cause embarrassment to certain persons. Information unrelated to any particular person presumably would not satisfy the threshold test.

involving family, sexual, or personal relationships or about the physical condition and health of a person. Other facts implicate privacy because they are "personal." Their disclosure will produce consequences that in a reasonably foreseeable way might cause harm to the person. The name and address of someone under the *Wine Hobby* analysis may be the paradigm of "personal" information. The disclosure of such information may invade privacy because in the hands of the business or political entrepreneur the person may be subjected to unsolicited phone calls or mailings. This loss of privacy is to a person's mental equanimity or mental repose. *Washington Post* seems clearly to reject this sorting out of information in terms of privacy values on the threshold question in (b)(6) cases.

Consider a recent decision in the D.C. Circuit Court of Appeals. In *New York Times Co. v. NASA*, 852 F.2d 602 (D.C.Cir.1988), the D.C. Circuit upheld a district court opinion in a FOIA action to disclose the tape recording of the last words of the crew of the ill fated Challenger space shuttle. The (b)(6) privacy defense to disclosure was rejected because the recording was not a "similar" file. The majority of the court found the threshold requirement of (b)(6) not to be satisfied because the tape "contains no information about any astronaut beyond participation in the launch," Id. at 606. Judge Ginsburg in dissent thought an opposite ruling was required by Washington Post because it was "inconceivable that the 'sound and inflection' of a person's voice during the last seconds of his or her life is not information that 'somehow relates to an individual's life,' " 852 F.2d at 609. In your view, does New York Times Co. v. NASA suggest that courts might resist the broad indiscriminate approach of the Court in Washington Post to the concept of "similar" files under (b)(6)? Does the information sought in New York Times Co. v. NASA implicate privacy in the "intimate" or "personal" senses of privacy that are discussed above?

Does *Washington Post* at least require that the requested information identify a specific individual? Consider *Arieff v. Department of Navy*, 712 F.2d 1462 (D.C.Cir.1983) (request for list of drugs used by some of a group of 600 persons).

d. Balancing the Interests

(1) The Significance of a Purely Private Business Interest

WINE HOBBY USA, INC. v. UNITED STATES IRS
502 F.2d 133 (3d Cir.1974)

[Wine Hobby, a distributor of amateur wine-making equipment, brought an action under the Freedom of Information Act to obtain names and addresses of persons filing forms with the Bureau of Alcohol, Tobacco and Firearms for the purpose of being permitted to produce wine for the use of their families without paying tax. The district court ordered that names and addresses be disclosed, and the Government appeals, contending that the material sought is within exemption 6 of the Act, which excludes from the Act's coverage "personnel and medical files and similar files the disclosure of which would constitute a clearly unwarranted invasion of privacy."]

Before KALODNER, ROSENN and HUNTER, CIRCUIT JUDGES.

OPINION OF THE COURT

ROSENN, CIRCUIT JUDGE.

. . . Under the Internal Revenue Code and the Federal Alcohol Administration Act, persons who produce wine are subject to certain permit, bonding, and tax requirements. Criminal penalties are provided for noncompliance. An exception to these requirements is provided by statute in the case of a "duly registered head of any family" who produces "for family use and not for sale an amount of wine not exceeding 200 gallons per annum."

Pursuant to regulations, registration under the statutory exception is effected by filing Form 1541 with the Bureau of Alcohol, Tobacco and Firearms. Upon determination that the person is qualified, Form 1541 is stamped, one copy is returned to the registrant and the remaining copy is placed in the Bureau's files. Records of the Bureau indicate that in fiscal year 1973, 64,756 Forms 1541 were filed, including 2,846 in the Mid–Atlantic region. In fiscal year 1974, as of February 1974, 41,585 Forms 1541 were on file, including 4,000 in the Mid–Atlantic region.

Wine Hobby is engaged in the business of selling and distributing amateur winemaking equipment and supplies to amateur winemakers through franchises, wholly owned retail stores, and by mail order. Wine Hobby has stipulated in the district court that its purpose in obtaining the names and addresses of the Form 1541 registrants is "to enable plaintiff to forward catalogues and other announcements to these persons regarding equipment and supplies that the plaintiff offers for sale."

. . .

The Government relies on Exemption (6) as the basis for refusing to supply the information requested by Wine Hobby. The district court reluctantly concluded that despite the potential for abuse, the names and addresses sought here were not subject to this exemption as an invasion of privacy. The court also held that it had no power to exercise its equitable discretion to withhold and no alternative but to grant the request. We hold that the names and addresses sought are within the exemption and we therefore reverse.

To qualify under Exemption (6), the requested information must consist of "personnel, medical or similar files," and the disclosure of the material must constitute a "clearly unwarranted invasion of personal privacy."

We believe that the list of names and addresses is a "file" within the meaning of Exemption (6). A broad interpretation of the statutory term to include names and addresses is necessary to avoid a denial of statutory protection in a case where release of requested materials would result in clearly unwarranted invasion of personal privacy. Since the thrust of the exemption is to avoid unwarranted invasions of privacy, the term "files" should not be given an interpretation that would often preclude inquiry into this more crucial question.

Furthermore, we believe the list of names and addresses is a file "similar" to the personnel and medical files specifically referred to in the exemption. The common denominator in "personnel and medical and similar files" is the personal quality of information in the file, the disclosure of which may constitute a clearly unwarranted invasion of personal privacy. We do not believe that the use of the term "similar" was intended to narrow the exemption from disclosure and permit the release of files which would otherwise be exempt because of the resultant invasion of privacy.

We now turn to the Government's contention that disclosure of the names and addresses to Wine Hobby would result in a "clearly unwarranted invasion of personal privacy." Because of an apparent conflict in the circuits, we must first consider whether the statutory language, which clearly demands an examination of the invasion of privacy, also requires inquiry into the interest in disclosure.

Our examination of the statute and its legislative history leads us to conclude, in the language of the District of Columbia Circuit, that "Exemption (6) necessarily requires the court to balance a public interest purpose for disclosure of personal information against the potential invasion of individual privacy." On its face, the statute, by the use of the term "unwarranted," compels a balancing of interests. The interpretation, moreover, is supported by the legislative history. . . .

To apply the balancing test to the facts of this case we must determine whether release of the names and addresses would constitute an invasion of personal privacy and, if so, balance the seriousness of that invasion with the purpose asserted for release. Turning to the first consideration, we conclude that disclosure would involve an invasion of privacy. As the Government points out in its brief, there are few things which pertain to an individual in which his privacy has traditionally been more respected than his own home. Mr. Chief Justice Burger recently stated: "The ancient concept that 'a man's home is his castle' into which 'not even the king may enter' has lost none of its vitality. . . ." Rowan v. United States Post Office Dept., 397 U.S. 728, 737, 90 S.Ct. 1484, 1491, 25 L.Ed.2d 736 (1970). Disclosure of the requested lists would involve a release of each registrant's home address, information that the individual may fervently wish to remain confidential or only selectively released. One consequence of this disclosure is that a registrant will be subjected to unsolicited and possibly unwanted mail from Wine Hobby and perhaps offensive mail from others. Moreover, information concerning personal activities within the home, namely wine-making, is revealed by disclosure. Similarly, disclosure reveals information concerning the family status of the registrant, including the fact that he is not living alone and that he exercises family control or responsibility in the household. Disclosure of these facts concerning the home and private activities within it constitutes an "invasion of personal privacy."

We must now balance the seriousness of this invasion of privacy against the public interest purpose asserted by the plaintiff. As noted, the sole purpose for which Wine Hobby has stipulated that it seeks the information is for private commercial exploitation. Wine Hobby advanced no direct or indirect public interest purpose in disclosure of these lists and indeed, we can conceive of none. The disclosure of names of potential customers for commercial business is wholly unrelated to the purposes behind the Freedom of Information Act and was never contemplated by Congress in enacting the Act. In light of this failure by Wine Hobby to assert a public interest purpose for disclosure, we conclude that the invasion of privacy caused by disclosure would be "clearly unwarranted," even though the invasion of privacy in this case is not as serious as that considered by the court in other cases, see, e.g., Rose v. Dept. of the Air Force, 495 F.2d 261 (2d Cir.1974). On balance, therefore, we believe that the list of names and addresses of the Form 1541 registrants is exempted from disclosure under Section 552(b)(6) in the circumstances of this case.

The judgment of the district court will be reversed.

Notes

The *Wine Hobby* court's emphasis on the requestor's commercial purpose in seeking the information exposes a basic conflict between the purpose of FOIA and the courts' interpretation of exemption six's privacy exemption. Presumably FOIA's purpose is to grant the public broad access to government-held information. The requestor's motives or purposes for seeking the information are generally irrelevant when interpreting the Act's disclosure provisions. Kronman, *The Privacy Exemption to the Freedom of Information Act*, 9 J. Legal Studies 727, 743 (1980) (hereinafter *Privacy Exemption*). However, when balancing the public interest in disclosure against a data subject's privacy interest courts often factor in the requestor's purpose for seeking the information when determining the weight to be given to the public interest side of the equation. *See, e.g., Ditlow v. Shultz*, 517 F.2d 166 (D.C.Cir.1975) (disclosure under FOIA can be limited to the purpose for which the requester seeks the information). In effect, this interpretation of FOIA places on the requestor the burden of proving a legitimate right of access. This was clearly not the intent of the legislature when it passed the FOIA. See 5 U.S.C.A. § 552(a)(4)(B) (19) (" . . . the burden is on the agency to sustain its action."). However, it is a necessary burden in weighing the interests of the requestor against any privacy rights inherent in the information stored in a record.

In *Schwaner v. Dep't of Air Force*, 898 F.2d 793 (D.C.Cir.1990), the United States District Court for the District of Columbia attempted to explain this conflict.

> While a commercially-minded requester is as entitled to information as any other, the existence of a commercial motivation is not to be equated with "the public interest." Appellant's commercial motivation does not make him less worthy of receiving information about the government, but "the disclosure of names of potential customers for commercial business is wholly unrelated to the purposes behind the FOIA and was never contemplated by Congress in enacting the act." (citing *Wine Hobby USA v. IRS*, 502 F.2d 133,

137 (3d Cir.1974)). This simply means that a commercial purpose for a request is not enough, by itself, to satisfy the public interest exception to exemption 2.

Id. at 800.

Commentators suggest that exemption six is an exception to the general rule forbidding consideration of the motives of the requester. Note, *The FOIA—The Parameters of the Exemptions,* 62 Geo. L.J. 177, 197–98 (1973). It has been suggested that the balancing necessary to determine at what point a "clearly unwarranted" invasion of privacy occurs requires at least some consideration of the purpose for which the requester seeks the information. *Privacy Exemption,* supra at 743 n.60.

(2) Characterizing the Privacy Interest

ROBLES v. EPA

484 F.2d 843 (4th Cir.1973).

Before CRAVEN, RUSSELL and WIDENER, CIRCUIT JUDGES.

DONALD RUSSELL, CIRCUIT JUDGE:

This is a bizarre case, illustrative of the ignorance by even scientists of the dangerous properties of radioactive waste materials and of the hazards that may result from such ignorance. It arose out of the practice by a uranium processing plant of making available free of charge its uranium tailings for use as clean fill dirt in connection with construction of private and public structures in the community of Grand Junction, Colorado, where the uranium processing plant was located. The practice, begun in 1950, continued until 1966, when the hazards incident to the use of such tailings were belatedly recognized. In the meantime, these tailings had been extensively used. Because of the obvious dangers connected with such use, the Environmental Protection Agency (hereinafter referred to as EPA), with the assistance of the Colorado Department of Health, undertook in 1970 to monitor the radiation levels in the homes and public structures where any of these tailings had been used. In addition, the homes and business or public structures were tested for radioactive emissions. In the course of this monitoring, some 15,000 homes were surveyed. The survey was extensive. In some of the homes an air sampler was placed for a week at a time on each of six occasions in the course of a year as a part of what was described as an "(I)ndoor radon daughter concentration level." In order to secure approval for such a survey from a homeowner, the government surveyors were instructed to advise orally the homeowner or occupier that the results of the survey would not be released to any one other than the owner or occupier and federal officials working on the problem. When the surveys were completed, the results were made available by the EPA to the Colorado Department of Health, in conjunction with which the survey was made. Through an arrangement with the Colorado Department of Health, the Development Director of the community can secure and make available to any "proper party" the results of the tests made on any specific structure. In addition, each owner of a structure surveyed has been given the results of the survey of his building.

The plaintiffs at first made formal request upon the defendant for the results of the survey as it applied to all public and private structures in the community. It later modified this request to cover only those structures in which the radiation levels exceeded the Surgeon General's "safety guidelines." [sic] The agency responded to this request by offering to provide the results but with the names and addresses of homeowners or occupiers deleted. It based its refusal to supply any of this information upon the exemptions set forth in subdivisions (4) and (6) of Section 552(b), 5 U.S.C. This was unacceptable to the plaintiffs, who then filed this action under the Freedom of Information Act to compel disclosure. The defendant entered a motion to dismiss, and, in the alternative, a motion for summary judgement. The plaintiffs then submitted their cross-motion for summary judgment. When the motions came on for hearing, the District Court denied plaintiffs' cross-motion and granted the defendant's motion for summary judgment, finding that disclosure, though not exempt under subdivision (4), was exempted under subdivision (6) of the Act. The plaintiffs appeal.

... Accordingly, the sole issue here is whether the District Court was correct in finding that the defendant agency had sustained its burden of establishing a right to exemption from disclosure of the requested information under exemption (6) of the Act.

Exemption (6) is as follows:

(6) personnel and medical files and similar files the disclosure of which would constitute a clearly unwarranted invasion of personal privacy.

Obviously, the information requested was not included in any "personnel" or "medical" files as such. The basis for a claim of exemption must accordingly be found in the phrase, "similar files the disclosure of which would constitute a clearly unwarranted invasion of personal privacy." The term "similar" was used, it seems, to indicate that, while the exemption was not limited to strictly medical or personnel files, the files covered in this third category must have the same characteristics of confidentiality that ordinarily attach to information in medical or personnel files; that is, to such extent as they contain " 'intimate details' of a 'highly personal' nature," they are within the umbrella of the exemption.... It would seem to follow that the exemption applies only to information which relates to a specific person or individual, to "intimate details" of a "highly personal nature" in that individual's employment record or health history or the like, and has no relevancy to information that deals with physical things, such as structures as in this case. The agency contends, however, that this is too simplistic an approach to the unique situation in this case. It is true, the agency argues, that while the information sought by the plaintiffs relates strictly to the condition of structures, of buildings, and real estate, it was gathered, analyzed, and is of interest only as it relates to the possible effect of that condition on the health and well-being of the occupants of those structures, i.e., of specific persons and individuals. So viewed, in this broad context, the information, the agency contends, comes within the definition of information of a "highly personal nature," as contemplated in exemption (6).

It must be conceded that there is a certain persuasiveness to this argument. The survey of the homes in the community was engaged in because of concern for personal health and safety; it was not an engineering survey to determine the structural adequacy or nature of the structures. And the reason for the health concern was the possibility that continued occupancy of the building might expose the occupants and even their progeny to hazards of health and even biological impairments. It is suggested that these potential health impairments could affect adversely employment opportunities and might even reduce marriage possibilities of the occupants.

Assuming, however, that it is possible to analogize these records to health records, it does not follow automatically that such records are exempt from disclosure. The statutory exemption does not simply cover any files that may be regarded as "similar" to health files. "Similar files," in order to qualify under the exemption, must fit the additional qualifications set forth in the exemption, i.e., they must contain information "the disclosure of which would constitute a clearly unwarranted invasion of personal privacy." The use of the term "clearly" in this qualification, which was not inadvertent but purposeful on the part of the Congress, was, itself, a "clear" instruction to the Courts that, in determining the issue whether a disclosure would constitute "a clearly unwarranted invasion of personal privacy," [sic] they should "tilt the balance in favor of disclosure."

In resolving against disclosure, the District Court relied strongly on the fact that the agency had in some instances promised the householder that the results of the survey would be kept confidential. While, perhaps, a promise of confidentiality is a factor to be considered, it is not enough to defeat the right of disclosure that the agency "received the file under a pledge of confidentiality to the one who supplied it. Undertakings of that nature cannot, in and of themselves, override the Act." Particularly in this case is the alleged promise of confidentiality unveiling as an excuse. In the first place, the promise was given by the door-to-door surveyors only where confidentiality was specifically inquired about by a householder. The agency has offered no proof of how many householders in the community had received such promise. Even more important is the fact that the information has not been held in confidence. The results of the survey are available to the Colorado Department of Health. This Department, seemingly with the approval of EPA, readily makes available on request the results of the survey as to any specific structure through the City Director of Development. This practice is well known to the EPA, which offers proof of the practice in support of its claim to exemption by reason of its promise of confidentiality. And it is of some significance that, so far as the record indicates, no householder has objected to this disclosure by the City Director of Development. Finally, it should be pointed out that this claim, that a promise of confidentiality supports the award of an exemption, is entirely inapplicable to public buildings.

.   .   .

The agency suggests that the information sought is of such a recondite scientific nature that the ordinary citizen could not properly evaluate or understand it. No one would question the ignorance of the general public—and perhaps, the scientific world, too—as to the possible harmful aspects of radioactive materials. The same could no doubt be said of much governmental information. Even census data is subject to misinterpretation and has prompted violent controversy even among experts. But the mere circumstance that information may not be fully understood is not among the "specific" exemptions authorized under the Act. Actually, it may well be that the very fact that the government so adamantly opposes release may give free rein to unbridled fear for the worst on the part of the people of this community; whereas, the release of the surveys, even though not fully understood, may have a beneficial, calming effect on the reasonable apprehensions of these citizens.

The Government has, it developed, embarked recently since discovery of the danger on a remedial program intended to remove or minimize the hazard of radioactive injury to the occupiers of these structures. The District Court felt that such a program militated against a determination that there was any public need for or benefit to result from disclosure. In balancing equities, it thought this of moment. But, as we have already observed, the right to disclosure under the Act is not to be resolved by a balancing of equities or a weighing of need or even benefit. The only ground for denial of disclosure in this situation is that the disclosure would represent a "clearly unwarranted invasion of personal privacy." For the reasons given, we are unable to find any reasonable basis for finding such a "clearly unwarranted basis."

Reversed, with direction to the District Court to enter a decree granting disclosure.

WIDENER, CIRCUIT JUDGE (concurring and dissenting):

I must respectfully dissent with respect to those who made an agreement with the government in good faith that the information disclosed about their "private homes" would be kept confidential, particularly those who are yet in possession of the premises involved. What I say does not apply to "public buildings." The words "private homes" and "public buildings" are quoted from the complaint.

I am of opinion that the statute does not require blanket disclosure, to complete strangers, of information which the government obtained under a good faith agreement that it would not be disclosed. For persons who so agreed, I believe the files of information concerning their homes are " . . . similar files, the disclosure of which would constitute a clearly unwarranted invasion of personal privacy." 5 U.S.C. Section 552(b)(6).

There is no question but that giving out this information promiscuously to strangers is an invasion of personal privacy. Disclosure of a specifically agreed upon confidential communication from citizen to sovereign may be considered no less. The question is whether or not it is clearly unwarranted. If the person seeking the information has any colorable interest in obtaining it, I think it may not be the clearly unwarranted invasion contemplated by the statute. These plaintiffs, however, insist that they need have no connection with the premises involved, no matter how remote, in order to get the information sought. Webster's New International Dictionary, 2nd Edition, defines unwarranted as "Not warranted; being without warrant, authority, or guaranty." Plaintiffs' right to interfere, having no interest they have chosen to disclose, is, in my opinion, clearly without warrant or authority, and ought not to be allowed.

With respect to these particular plaintiffs, in their search for information about the private homes of others, I agree with the district court when it stated: "As the House Report accompanying this legislation indicated, a citizen must be able to confide in his Government. When the Government has obligated itself in good faith not to disclose documents or information which it receives, it should be able to honor this obligation."

Note

The exhaustion of administrative remedies rule under the Freedom of Information Act is also applicable to the 1974 Privacy Act and enforcement of rights generally in the 1964 and 1968 Civil Rights Acts. Exhaustion of administrative remedies is a general precondition to challenge of agency action on federal statutory grounds. A plaintiff is not required to exhaust administrative remedies in suits brought under Section 1983 of Title 42 and Section 1331 of Title 28 of the United States Code for violation by administrative agencies of the fourteenth amendment. *See Monroe v. Pape*, 365 U.S. 167, 183 (1961); *York v. Story*, 324 F.2d at 452–56; Jeffrey M. Shaman & Richard C. Turkington, *Huffman v. Pursue, Ltd.: The Federal Courthouse Door Closes Further*, 56 B.U.L. Rev. 907, 919–22 (1976).

(3) Characterizing the Public Interest

GETMAN v. NLRB
450 F.2d 670 (D.C.Cir.1971).

[Plaintiffs-appellees, law professors engaged in research regarding voting patterns, brought an action under the Freedom of Information Act (FOIA) to compel disclosure of National Labor Relations Board (NLRB) lists containing the names and addresses of employees eligible to vote in certain elections. The plaintiffs desired access to the lists for purposes of conducting surveys among union members to determine their attitudes about union elections. The NLRB refused disclosure on the grounds that FOIA exempted disclosure of the requested information, and plaintiffs filed this action. Both parties filed motions for summary judgment, and the district court granted plaintiffs motion for summary judgment. Defendant NLRB appeals.]

Before WRIGHT, MACKINNON and ROBB, CIRCUIT JUDGES.

J. SKELLY WRIGHT, CIRCUIT JUDGE.

. . .

Exemption (6) applies to "personnel and medical files and similar files the disclosure of which would constitute a clearly unwarranted invasion of personal privacy." Assuming that the Excelsior lists may be characterized as "personnel and medical files and similar files," it is still only a disclosure constituting a "clearly unwarranted invasion of personal privacy" that falls within the scope of Exemption (6). Exemption (6) requires a court reviewing the matter *de novo* to balance the right of privacy of affected individuals against the right of the public to be informed; and the statutory language "clearly unwarranted" instructs the court to tilt the balance in favor of disclosure.

In carrying out the balance of interests required by Exemption (6), our first inquiry is whether disclosure of the names and addresses of employees constitutes an invasion of privacy and, if so, how serious an invasion. We find that, although a limited number of employees will suffer an invasion of privacy in losing their anonymity and in being asked over the telephone if they would be willing to be interviewed in connection with the voting study, the loss of privacy resulting from this particular disclosure should be characterized as relatively minor. Both the House and Senate reports on the bill which became the Freedom of Information Act indicate that the real thrust of Exemption (6) is to guard against unnecessary disclosure of files of such agencies as the Veterans Administration or the Welfare Department or Selective Service or Bureau of Prisons, which would contain "intimate details" of a "highly personal" nature. The giving of names and addresses is a very much lower degree of disclosure; in themselves a bare name and address give no information about an individual which is embarrassing. In the conduct of the appellees' study, any disclosure of information more personal than a name and address is wholly consensual within the control of the employee. Appellees represent that any employee that does not wish to undergo an interview may refuse, and that employees have in fact done so in connection with the pilot studies conducted to date. Although four pilot studies had been conducted at the time briefs were submitted, there is no indication whatever in the record of any harassment of employees who declined to cooperate. Thus assuming *arguendo* that the disclosure of Excelsior lists constitutes disclosure of a "file" within the meaning of Exemption (6), and while recognizing that such disclosure does involve some invasion of privacy, we find that the invasion itself is to a very minimal degree.

In determining whether this relatively minor invasion of privacy is "clearly unwarranted," we must also weigh the public interest purpose of appellees' NLRB voting study, the quality of the study itself, and the possibility that appellees could pursue their study without the Excelsior lists. As previously indicated, the Board has established complicated rules and enforcement procedures governing the behavior of the parties during election campaigns. The costs of Board regulation are great. The proportion of elections in which the losing party has filed objections has risen to almost one in seven in recent years, and such objections require expensive and time consuming investigation, hearings and rulings. Interference with the "laboratory conditions" required to conduct these elections may indeed result in elections being set aside, as the Board contends. But there is no proof to support the contention. It will be time enough to consider the relief to which the Board is entitled if and when a showing of disruption of Board functions is made.

. . . The public interest need for such an empirical investigation into the assumptions underlying the Board's regulation of campaign tactics has for some time been recognized by labor law scholars. This particular study has been reviewed and supported by virtually every major scholar in the labor law field. The record is also replete with testimonials from leading management and union representatives and Government officials. Appellees' research has also been approved by the prestigious National Science Foundation, which has awarded appellees the largest grant ever made available for law related research.

Without reviewing the practical workings of the NLRB voting study in detail here, the court notes that appellees Getman and Goldberg are both highly qualified specialists in labor law, that they have designed their study carefully and in collaboration with scholars in the field of survey research over the past two years, and that they have selected and trained their interviewers carefully to avoid biasing effects in the questioning process. The interview part of the study has been tested in three pilot elections and evaluation reveals no evidence which would support the Board's fears that the interviewing might have the effect of confusing or inhibiting the employees. According to the uncontested statement of appellees, no employee who has consented to an initial interview has yet declined to schedule a second interview or to vote in the subsequent election. No employee has brought a complaint concerning the study to either appellees or the Board. Followup checks have shown that employees have been answering truthfully such "sensitive" questions as whether they had signed a union authorization card and how they voted.

In striking the balance necessary to determine whether disclosure of Excelsior lists would constitute a clearly unwarranted invasion of privacy, it is also significant that appellees are asking for the names and addresses of employees in only 35 out of the approximately 15,000 elections which the Board will supervise during the next two years and that appellees have no other source for obtaining the names and addresses consistent with their goal of an unbiased and successful study. . . .

Having considered and weighed all of the above factors, we find it impossible to say that disclosure of the Excelsior lists would constitute a clearly unwarranted invasion of employee privacy under Exemption (6) of the Freedom of Information Act. If anything, our finding is that disclosure for purposes of appellees' study is clearly warranted. The invasion of employee privacy strikes us as very minimal, and the possible detrimental effects of the study in terms of delaying the election process as highly speculative. On the other hand, the study holds out an unusual promise. . . .

Affirmed.

Note: FOIA Decisions As Illuminators of Informational Privacy Values

Because subsections 552(b)(6) and (7)(c) require courts to consider information on the basis of privacy values, these subsection cases contain some very extensive and insightful discussions of informational privacy. The extent to which specific types of information implicate privacy often may be a by-product of two interrelated factors: the intrinsic and consequential features of the information. Intrinsic features involve the degree of intimacy of the information. Consequential features involve the potential for harm to the subject if the information is disclosed. Information may not be intimate, and yet may be considered "highly personal" by a reasonable person because of the fear that disclosure would bring harmful or embarrassing consequences. Do the (b)(6) and (7)(c) cases in this section provide support for this notion? What information is properly characterized as "intimate"?

e.   Exemption (B)(7)(c): Accessibility of "Rap Sheets"

UNITED STATES DEP'T OF JUSTICE v. REPORTERS COMMITTEE FOR FREEDOM OF PRESS
489 U.S. 749 (1989).

[Plaintiffs, a CBS news correspondent and the Reporters Committee for Freedom of the Press, filed a Freedom of Information Act (FOIA) request to obtain information maintained by the Federal Bureau of Investigation (FBI) concerning the criminal records of four members of the Medico family. The FOIA request sought disclosure of rap sheets detailing any arrests, indictments, acquittals, convictions, and sentences of any of the four Medicos. The Pennsylvania Crime Commission had identified the family's company as a legitimate business dominated by organized crime figures. Although the FBI ultimately provided the requested data concerning three of the family members following their deaths, it refused disclosure of the information pertaining to the fourth member.

Plaintiffs proceeded to file this action against the United States Department of Justice for the FBI's alleged violation of FOIA. The parties filed cross-motions for summary judgment. The district court granted summary judgment for defendant on the grounds that 28 U.S.C. Section 534 prohibits the release of such information to members of the public and that such information is included within the category of "personnel and medical files and similar files the disclosure of which would constitute an unwarranted invasion of privacy," thereby rendering applicable Exemptions 3 and 6, respectively, of FOIA.

The court of appeals reversed and remanded. It held that an individual's privacy interest in criminal history information that is a matter of public record is minimal, at best. Noting the absence of any statutory standards by which to judge the public interest in disclosure, the court of appeals concluded that it should be bound by the state and local determinations that such information should be made available to the general public. Accordingly, it held that Exemptions 6 and 7(c) were inapplicable. Furthermore, it found Exemption 3 to be inapplicable on the grounds that 28 U.S.C. Section 534 does not qualify as a statute "specifically" exempting rap sheets from disclosure.]

JUSTICE STEVENS delivered the opinion of the Court.

The Federal Bureau of Investigation (FBI) has accumulated and maintains criminal identification records, sometimes referred to as "rap sheets," on over 24 million persons. The question presented by this case is whether the disclosure of the contents of such a file to a third party "could reasonably be expected to constitute an unwarranted invasion of personal privacy" within the meaning of the Freedom of Information Act (FOIA), 5 U.S.C. Section 552(b)(7)(c).

In 1924 Congress appropriated funds to enable the Department of Justice (Department) to establish a program to collect and preserve fingerprints and other criminal identification records. 43 Stat. 217. That statute authorized the Department to exchange such information with "officials of States, cities and other institutions." Ibid. Six years later Congress created the FBI's identification division, and gave it responsibility for "acquiring, collecting, classifying, and preserving criminal identification and other crime records and the exchanging of said criminal identification records with the duly authorized officials of governmental agencies, of States, cities, and penal institutions." Rap sheets compiled pursuant to such authority contain certain descriptive information, such as date of birth and physical characteristics, as well as a history of arrests, charges, convictions, and incarcerations of the subject. Normally a rap sheet is preserved until its subject attains age 80. Because of the volume of rap sheets, they are sometimes incorrect or incomplete and sometimes contain information about other persons with similar names.

The local, state, and federal law enforcement agencies throughout the Nation that exchange rap-sheet data with the FBI do so on a voluntary basis. The principal use of the information is to assist in the detection and prosecution of offenders; it is also used by courts and corrections officials in connection with sentencing and parole decisions. As a matter of executive policy, the Department has generally treated rap sheets as confidential and, with certain exceptions, has restricted their use to governmental purposes. Consistent with the Department's basic policy of treating these records as confidential, Congress in 1957 amended the basic statute to provide that the FBI's exchange of rap-sheet information with any other agency is subject to cancellation "if dissemination is made outside the receiving departments or related agencies."

As a matter of Department policy, the FBI has made two exceptions to its general practice of prohibiting unofficial access to rap sheets. First, it allows the subject of a rap sheet to obtain a copy and second, it occasionally allows rap sheets to be used in the preparation of press releases and publicity designed to assist in the apprehension of wanted persons or fugitives.

In addition, on three separate occasions Congress has expressly authorized the release of rap sheets for other limited purposes. In 1972 it provided for such release to officials of federally chartered or insured banking institutions and "if authorized by State statute and approved by the Attorney General, to officials of State and local governments for purposes of employment and licensing. . . ." In 1975, in an amendment to the Securities Act, Congress permitted the Attorney General to release rap sheets to self-regulatory organizations in the securities industry. And finally, in 1986 Congress authorized release of criminal-history information to licensees or applicants before the Nuclear Regulatory Commission. These three targeted enactments—all adopted after the FOIA was passed in 1966—are consistent with the view that Congress understood and did not disapprove the FBI's general policy of treating rap sheets as nonpublic documents.

Although much rap-sheet information is a matter of public record, the availability and dissemination of the actual rap sheet to the public is limited. Arrests, indictments, convictions, and sentences are public events that are usually documented in court records. In addition, if a person's entire criminal history transpired in a single jurisdiction, all of the contents of his or her rap sheet may be available upon request in that jurisdiction. That possibility, however, is presently in only three States. All of the other 47 States place substantial restrictions on the availability of criminal-history summaries even though individual events in those summaries are matters of public record. Moreover, even in Florida, Wisconsin, and Oklahoma, the publicly available summaries may not include information about out-of-state arrests or convictions.

. . .

Congress exempted nine categories of documents from the FOIA's broad disclosure requirements. Three of those exemptions are arguably relevant to this case. Exemption 3 applies to documents that are specifically exempted from disclosure by another statute. Section 552(b)(3). Exemption 6 protects "personnel and medical files and similar files the disclosure of which would constitute a clearly unwarranted invasion of personal privacy." Section 552(b)(6). Exemption 7(c) excludes records or information compiled for law enforcement purposes, "but only to the extent that the production of such [materials] . . . could reasonably be expected to constitute an unwarranted invasion of personal privacy." Section 552(b)(7)(c).

Exemption 7(c)'s privacy language is broader than the comparable language in Exemption 6 in two respects. First, whereas Exemption 6 requires that the invasion of privacy be "clearly unwarranted," the adverb "clearly" is omitted from Exemption 7(c). This omission is the product of a 1974 amendment adopted in response to concerns expressed by the President. Second, whereas Exemption 6 refers to disclosures that "would constitute" an invasion of privacy, Exemption 7(c) encompasses any disclosure that "could reasonably be expected to constitute" such an invasion. This difference is also the product of a specific amendment. Thus, the standard for evaluating a threatened invasion of privacy interests resulting from the disclosure of records compiled for law-enforcement purposes is somewhat broader than the standard applicable to personnel, medical, and similar files.

. . .

Exemption 7(c) requires us to balance the privacy interest in maintaining, as the Government puts it, the "practical obscurity" of the rap sheets, against the public interest in their release.

The preliminary question is whether Medico's interest in the nondisclosure of any rap sheet the FBI might have on him is the sort of "personal privacy" interest that Congress intended Exemption 7(c) to protect.[13] As we have pointed out before, "[t]he cases sometimes characterized as protecting 'privacy' have in fact involved at least two different kinds of interests. One is the individual interest in avoiding disclosure of personal matters, and another is the interest in independence in making certain kinds of important decisions." [Whalen v. Roe.] Here, the former interest, "in avoiding disclosure of personal matters," is implicated. Because events summarized in a rap sheet have been previously disclosed to the public, respondents contend that Medico's privacy interest in avoiding disclosure of a federal compilation of these events approaches zero. We reject respondents' cramped notion of personal privacy.

To begin with, both the common law and the literal understandings of privacy encompass the individual's control of information concerning his or her person. In an organized society, there are few facts that are not at one time or another divulged to another. Thus the extent of the protection accorded a privacy right at common law rested in part on the degree of dissemination of the allegedly private fact and the extent to which the passage of time rendered it private. According to Webster's initial definition, information may be classified as "private" if it is "intended for or restricted to the use of a particular person or group or class of persons: not freely available to the public." Recognition of this

---

13. The question of the statutory meaning of privacy under FOIA is, of course, not the same as the question whether a tort action might lie for invasion of privacy or the question whether an individual's interest in privacy is protected by the Constitution. See, e.g., Cox Broadcasting Corp. v. Cohn, 420 U.S. 469, 95 S.Ct. 1029, 43 L.Ed.2d 328 (1975) (Constitution forbids State from penalizing publication of name of deceased rape victim obtained from public records); Paul v. Davis, 424 U.S. 693, 712–714, 96 S.Ct. 1155, 1165–1167, 47 L.Ed.2d 405 (1976) (no constitutional privacy right affected by publication of name of arrested but untried shoplifter).

attribute of a privacy interest supports the distinction, in terms of personal privacy, between scattered disclosure of the bits of information contained in a rap sheet and revelation of the rap sheet as a whole. The very fact that federal funds have been spent to prepare, index, and maintain these criminal-history files demonstrates that the individual items of information in the summaries would not otherwise be "freely available" either to the officials who have access to the underlying files or to the general public. Indeed, if the summaries were "freely available," there would be no reason to invoke the FOIA to obtain access to the information they contain. Granted, in many contexts the fact that information is not freely available is no reason to exempt that information from a statute generally requiring its dissemination. But the issue here is whether the compilation of otherwise hard-to-obtain information alters the privacy interest implicated by disclosure of that information. Plainly there is a vast difference between the public records that might be found after a diligent search of courthouse files, county archives, and local police stations throughout the country and a computerized summary located in a single clearinghouse of information.

. . .

In sum, the fact that "an event is not wholly 'private' does not mean that an individual has no interest in limiting disclosure or dissemination of the information." Rehnquist, Is an Expanded Right of Privacy Consistent with Fair and Effective Law Enforcement?, Nelson Timothy Stephens Lectures, University of Kansas Law School, pt. 1, p. 13 (Sept. 26–27, 1974). The privacy interest in a rap sheet is substantial. The substantial character of that interest is affected by the fact that in today's society the computer can accumulate and store information that would otherwise have surely been forgotten long before a person attains the age of 80, when the FBI's rap sheets are discarded.

V

Exemption 7(c), by its terms, permits an agency to withhold a document only when revelation "could reasonably be expected to constitute an unwarranted invasion of personal privacy."

. . .

Thus whether disclosure of a private document under Exemption 7(c) is warranted must turn on the nature of the requested document and its relationship to "the basic purpose of the Freedom of Information Act 'to open agency action to the light of public scrutiny[,]' " rather than on the particular purpose for which the document is being requested. . . . Official information that sheds light on an agency's performance of its statutory duties falls squarely within that statutory purpose. That purpose, however, is not fostered by disclosure of information about private citizens that is accumulated in various governmental files but that reveals little or nothing about an agency's own conduct. In this case—and presumably in the typical case in which one private citizen is seeking information about another—the requester does not intend to discover anything about the conduct of the agency that has possession of the requested records. Indeed, response to this request would not shed any light on the conduct of any Government agency or official.

. . . What we have said should make clear that the public interest in the release of any rap sheet on Medico that may exist is not the type of interest protected by the FOIA. Medico may or may not be one of the 24 million persons for whom the FBI has a rap sheet. If respondents are entitled to have the FBI tell them what it knows about Medico's criminal history, any other member of the public is entitled to the same disclosure—whether for writing a news story, for deciding whether or not to employ Medico, to rent a house to him, to extend credit to him, or simply to confirm or deny a suspicion. There is, unquestionably, some public interest in providing interested citizens with answers to their questions about Medico. But that interest falls outside the ambit of the public interest that the FOIA was enacted to serve.

. . .

VI

Both the general requirement that a court "shall determine the matter de novo" and the specific reference to an "unwarranted" invasion of privacy in Exemption 7(c) indicate that a court must balance the public interest in disclosure against the interest Congress intended the Exemption to protect. Although both sides agree that such a balance must be undertaken, *how* such a balance should be done is in dispute. The Court of Appeals majority expressed concern about assigning federal judges the task of striking a proper case-by-case, or ad hoc, balance between individual privacy interests and the public interest in the disclosure of criminal-history information without providing those judges standards to assist in performing that task. Our cases provide support for the proposition that categorical decisions may be appropriate and individual circumstances disregarded when a case fits into a genus in which the balance characteristically tips in one direction. . . .

. . . [W]e conclude today, upon closer inspection of Exemption 7(c), that for an appropriate class of law-enforcement records or information a categorical balance may be undertaken there as well.

. . .

. . . The privacy interest in maintaining the practical obscurity of rap-sheet information will always be high. When the subject of such a rap sheet is a private citizen and when the information is in the Government's control as a compilation, rather than as a record of "what the Government is up to," the privacy interest protected by Exemption 7(c) is in fact at its apex while the FOIA-based public interest in disclosure is at its nadir. Such a disparity on the scales of justice holds for a class of cases without regard to individual circumstances; the standard virtues of bright-line rules are thus present, and the difficulties attendant to ad hoc adjudication may be avoided. Accordingly, we hold as a categorical matter that a third party's request for law-enforcement records or information about a private citizen can reasonably be expected to invade that citizen's privacy, and that when the request seeks no "official information" about a Government agency, but merely records that the Government happens to be storing, the invasion of privacy is "unwarranted." The judgment of the Court of Appeals is reversed.

JUSTICE BLACKMUN, with whom JUSTICE BRENNAN joins, concurring in the judgment.

I concur in the result the Court reaches in this case, but I cannot follow the route the Court takes to reach that result. In other words, the Court's use of "categorical balancing" under Exemption 7(c), I think, is not basically sound. Such a bright-line rule obviously has its appeal, but I wonder whether it would not run aground on occasion, such as in a situation where a rap sheet discloses a congressional candidate's conviction of tax fraud five years before. Surely, the FBI's disclosure of that information could not "reasonably be expected" to constitute an invasion of personal privacy, much less an unwarranted invasion, inasmuch as the candidate relinquished any interest in preventing the dissemination of this information when he chose to run for Congress. In short, I do not believe that Exemption 7(c)'s language and its legislative history, or the case law, support interpreting that provision as exempting all rap-sheet information from FOIA's disclosure requirements.

Note: The Impact of Reporters Committee on Construction of the Scope of (b)(6) and (7)(c)

(i) The Court in *Reporters Committee* viewed FOIA's primary purpose as promoting governmental accountability and concluded that the disclosure of a "rap sheet" would not further this "watchdog" function. Additionally, in balancing the interests, the court said that the Pennsylvania Crime Commission had identified the Medicos as a family whose business was dominated by organized crime and who had obtained governmental contracts through improper arrangements with a corrupt Congressman. In view of these circumstances, is the release to the media of the rap sheet of a member of the Medico family an example of informational disclosure which promotes governmental accountability? Consider the analysis of *Reporters Committee* concerning the kind of information which, if disclosed, would promote FOIA's watchdog function.

(ii) What significance does *Reporters Committee* have for judicial construction of exceptions (b)(6) and (7)(c) in FOIA litigation? Consider two possibilities: (a) *Reporters Committee* is limited to its strict holding: that "rap sheets" are law enforcement records which are per se exempt from disclosure under (7)(c), or (b) *Reporters Committee* has broader significance: in cases where disclosure would not further FOIA's core purpose (holding governmental officials and agencies accountable) but would reveal significant sensitive information about the individual involved, the current Court will limit disclosure through expanded use of a per se approach and in balancing the interests emphasize informational privacy over the diminished public interest.

The United States Court of Appeals for the District of Columbia appears to have viewed *Reporters Committee* as having broad significance in FOIA actions. In *Federal Labor Relations Authority v. United States Dep't of the*

Treasury, Financial Management Serv., 884 F.2d 1446 (D.C.Cir.1989), *cert. denied,* 110 S. Ct. 863 (1990), the court held that (b)(6) precluded disclosure of the names and home addresses of federal governmental agency employees working in certain bargaining units when such information was requested under FOIA by labor unions. Several circuit courts prior to *Reporters Committee* had required disclosure upon determining that the special public interest in advancing collective bargaining outweighed the privacy interests of employees. In *Federal Labor Relations Authority,* the court found that assigning this significance to the interest in advancing collective bargaining was inconsistent with *Reporters Committee* because the "Court made clear that under FOIA the disclosure interest must be measured in terms of its relation to FOIA's central purpose—'to ensure that the Government's activities be opened to the sharp eye of public scrutiny.'" *Id.* at 1451. Since the request for information in the case was to further an interest other than the public's interest in "knowing what their government is up to," it was of diminished significance in the balancing under (b)(6). On the other hand, the privacy interests of employees were predominant since they might be subject to an unwarranted barrage of mailings and personal solicitations by potential users of the name and address list.

Applying a similar analysis, the District of Columbia Court of Appeals denied access to the names and addresses of retired or disabled federal employees. In *National Ass'n of Retired Federal Employees (NARFE) v. Horner,* 879 F.2d 873 (D.C.Cir.1989), the court concluded that the public interest in disclosure of the list to the Labor Union was zero, while the privacy interest was significant because the list would impliedly disclose that the listed persons received a monthly annuity check from the government and those on the list might be subject to unwarranted mailings and solicitations.

Do you find the interpretation of *Reporters Committee* by the United States Court of Appeals for the District of Columbia to be warranted? Would you buy the argument that because of the linguistic differences in (b)(6) and (7)(c), *Reporters Committee* has no bearing on (b)(6) cases? Does the linguistic difference in the two sections weigh only on the privacy side of the balance? Do any of the (b)(6) cases that are included in this section survive *Reporters Committee*?

Is the minimal value assigned to non-government watchdog interests limited to cases where (b)(6) and (7)(c) are implicated? In *United States Dept. of Justice v. Tax Analysts,* 492 U.S. 136, (1989), the Supreme Court held that FOIA requires the Department of Justice to release its compilations of district court tax decisions to the publisher of *Tax Notes,* a weekly magazine. The information requested in *Tax Analysts* was available from other sources but the compilation by the Justice Department provided the relevant information to the publication at a lower cost. Thus, as Justice Blackmun indicated in dissent, the disclosure did not further the core government watchdog purpose of FOIA. In *Tax Analysts,* the presumption in favor of disclosure under FOIA required disclosure without a separate demonstration that a public interest was furthered by the disclosure.

Judge Ginsberg of the District of Columbia Court of Appeals finds the results in *Tax Analysts* and *Reporters Committee* anomalous:

[T]he juxtaposition of *Tax Analysts* and our decision today reveals a tension in the Supreme Court's interpretation of the FOIA: the Information Act, in the first instance, demands no showing at all of "public interest": yet, once a privacy interest, however modest, is implicated, the Act forbids disclosure of information that advances a significant public interest (here, the interest in informed collective bargaining), if that interest is unrelated to FOIA's "core purpose."

Federal Labor Relations Authority v. United States Dept. of the Treasury, Financial Management Serv., 884 F.2d at 1459 (concurring opinion).

U.S. Department of Defense v. F.L.R.A.

Any doubt as to whether the reasoning in *Reporters Committee* extended to (b)(6) cases was resolved by the Supreme Court in *U.S. Dept. of Defense v. F.L.R.A.* 510 U.S. 487 (1994). The Fifth Circuit had required the release of the home addresses of federal employees to labor unions representing the bargaining units of the employees. The court concluded that since the request for the names was initiated under a federal labor statute and not FOIA, *Reporters Committee* was not controlling. In such cases it was appropriate to balance the public interest underlying the statute. On balance the public interest in effective collective bargaining in the public sphere outweighed the privacy interests of employees under (b)(6).

The Supreme Court reversed holding that *Reporters Committee* was controlling in any case where disclosure ultimately turned on the availability of a (7)(C) or (b)(6) exemption. Justice Thomas wrote the opinion for the Court. The only relevant public interest in disclosure in (b)(6) or (7)(C) cases is whether the disclosure would serve the "core purpose of the FOIA." Since the disclosure of the names would not inform the public of what the agency was up to the "relevant public interest" supporting disclosure in the case was negligible. On the other hand the Court concluded that federal employees had some "non trivial" privacy interest in avoiding union mailing, visits and phone calls by union and other parties that would have access under FOIA. Even if communications were limited to mailings, employees had an interest in preventing unwanted mail sent to their home and the Court was reluctant to "disparage the privacy of the home, which is accorded special consideration in our constitution laws and traditions."

After *Reporters Committee* and *F.L.R.A.* under what circumstances would personal data ever be disclosable under FOIA in (b)(c) and (7)(C) cases when disclosure would not further a "core FOIA purpose?" Does *Getman v. NLRB*, supra, survive *Reporters Committee* and *F.L.R.A.*?

Note: Technology, Privacy and Rap Sheets

In *Reporter's Committee* the Supreme Court said that because the various pieces of criminal history information had been compiled into a dossier by electronic collation, that the assembled profile had a special privacy value. The Court acknowledged a privacy interest in this data even though the various items of information in the rap sheet are themselves of public record at the law enforcement agency by which they were supplied. In reality, the Court said that the whole was greater than the sum of its parts, at least in terms of informational privacy. Recall Judge Breitel's similar analysis in *Nader v. General Motors, infra*:

> Although acts performed in "public," especially if taken singly or in small numbers, may not be confidential, at least arguably a right to privacy may nevertheless be invaded through extensive or exhaustive monitoring and cataloguing of acts normally disconnected and anonymous.

255 N.E.2d 765, 772, 307 N.Y.S.2d 647, 657.

In a study commissioned by the U.S. Department of Justice and published in 1978, *Privacy and Security of Criminal History Information: An Analysis of Privacy Issues*, by George B. Trubow, (U.S.G.P.O. No. 027–000–00712–1) p. 18, the same point was made:

> To argue that because the aggregate is merely a collection of public transactions there is no need to restrict access, misses the point about dossiers. It is the very marshalling of separate and discrete transactions into a single file that can change the nature and potential [of] the resulting information.

Reporter's Committee actually brings to fruition the recognition of this issue as announced earlier by the Court in *Whalen v. Roe*:

> We are not unaware of the threat to privacy implicit in the accumulation of vast amounts of personal information in computerized databanks or other massive government files. . . . The right to collect and use such data for public purposes is typically accompanied by a concomitant statutory or regulatory duty to avoid unwarranted disclosures.

449 U.S. 589, 605.

In his concurring opinion in *Whalen*, Justice Brennan emphasized that data in electronic form "vastly increases the potential for abuse of that information." *Id.* at 607.

The ever-increasing proliferation of personal information in automated data banks emphasizes the significance of the foregoing observations and the holding in the *Reporter's Committee* case. The impact of this rationale extends far beyond government data banks and FOIA inquiries but is relevant as well to the vast array of private sector data banks containing personal information. We already visited this matter in the section on Computers, Technology and Privacy, *supra* pp. 323–330.

Compare the court's analysis of the privacy interest in rap sheets in *Reporters Committee* with the court's analysis of the privacy interest of a rape victim in her name when it is acquired from public records in *Florida Star v. B.J.F.*, 491 U.S. 524 (1989), *supra*.

In the foregoing cases a privacy interest has been balanced against the public or societal interest in the information, as the FOIA is construed to require. An interesting conflict of personal interests was involved in *Ferri v. Bell*, 645 F.2d 1213 (3d Cir.1981), wherein the plaintiff brought an FOIA action for access to the rap sheet of one Lynn Dunn. Ferri had been convicted of the federal offense of mail fraud and Dunn had been a principle witness for the prosecution. Ferri sought Dunn's rap sheet to impeach Dunn's testimony on the basis that Dunn had made a deal with the federal prosecutor, in which case Ferri could be entitled to a new trial under the "Brady rule," from the case of *Brady v. Maryland*, 373 U.S. 83 (1963). In allowing disclosure of the rap sheet, the court said, "The public at large has an important stake in ensuring that criminal justice is fairly administered; to the extent disclosure may remedy and deter Brady violations, society stands to gain."

f. Reverse FOIA Actions

When a private party who has submitted information to the federal government sues under FOIA to restrain disclosure, the action is called a "reverse FOIA action." The leading case on reverse FOIA actions to restrain disclosure of trade secrets, *Chrysler Corp. v. Brown*, 441 U.S. 281 (1979), should govern exemption 6 cases. For a general analysis of the issues that arise in reverse FOIA actions, *see* Allan Robert Adler, *Litigation Under the Federal Open Government Laws*, 89–99 (1991).

g. State Freedom of Information Acts

Many states have formulated their own Freedom of Information Acts, usually patterned after the federal statute discussed previously. As in the federal law, the states list a variety of exceptions to a FOIA's general disclosure requirement, one of which is usually the general privacy exemption for "personnel and medical files and *similar files* the disclosure of which would constitute a clearly unwarranted invasion of personal privacy." 5 U.S.C.A. § 552(b)(6) (1982) (emphasis supplied).

In applying such a provision the states also use a balancing test, as in federal cases, to determine what information is exempt from disclosure by weighing an individual's privacy interest against the public's interest in the information. Thus, in *Child Protection Group v. Cline*, 350 S.E.2d 541 (W.Va.1986), a parent's group was permitted access under the West Virginia FOIA to the medical records of a school bus driver when the driver's behavior created concern over his ability to safely operate his vehicle.

In addition to disagreements in the balance of interests, state courts display the same disparities as federal courts in deciding what are "similar files" for privacy exemption purposes. In contrast to the general exemption, a number of state statutes specify in some detail which records are subject to a privacy exemption. *See, e.g.*, Haw. Rev. Stat. sec. 92F–14 (1988 & Supp. 1990); Ill. Ann. Stat. ch. 116, para. 207 (Smith–Hurd 1988); N.Y. Public Officers Law sec. 89 (McKinney 1988). An examination of a few of the common topics of the privacy exemption in state FOIA litigation will illustrate the divergence in results.

A major area of litigation concerns access to personnel files, particularly with respect to performance evaluations of government employees. In *Chairman, Criminal Justice Commission v. Freedom of Information Commission,* the Supreme Court of Connecticut decided that the state FOIA privacy exemption should be construed liberally with regard to public officials. 217 Conn. 193, 585 A.2d 96, 99 (1991). As a result, the court held that the performance evaluation of a state's attorney was not subject to disclosure as he had a reasonable expectation of privacy concerning the report. To the same effect is *Pawtucket Teachers Alliance v. Brady*, 556 A.2d 556 (R.I.1989), where the job performance of a school principal was held not subject to disclosure.

On the other hand, some states have held that performance reports or work records do not fall within their FOIA privacy exemption. In *Buffalo News v. Buffalo Municipal Housing Authority,* 163 A.D.2d 830, 558 N.Y.S.2d 364 (1990), the payroll and disciplinary records of housing authority employees were ruled not to come within the FOIA privacy exemption. Similarly, in *Rainey v. Levitt,* 138 Misc.2d 962, 525 N.Y.S.2d 551 (1988), the court held that New York's FOIA privacy exemption should be construed narrowly and that plaintiff police officer was entitled to the examination grades of Black and Hispanic officers on a supplementary list for promotion to sergeant.

Public policy concerns are often the decisive factor in determining when access to a personnel file is warranted. In cases involving discipline of teachers guilty of sexual misconduct with students, for instance, the courts universally allow disclosure of information relating to action taken. For example, in *Brouillet v. Cowles Pub. Co.*, 114 Wash. 2d 788, 791 P.2d 526 (1990), plaintiff sought access to files of the Superintendent of Public Instruction regarding the revocation of teaching certificates because of sexual misconduct. The court allowed access to the files in spite of the state's FOIA privacy exemption, though it did order the deletion of the identity of students.

Another area of frequent litigation involves access to government employees mailing lists and the subsequent ability to reach individuals in their homes. The state courts are split on this issue, depending on the interpretation of their particular FOIA. In *Providence Journal Co. v. Kane*, the Supreme Court of Rhode Island refused a newspaper's request for access to state records that would "uniquely identify" state employees by name, address, race, and employment history. 577 A.2d 661 (R.I.1990). In *Healey v. Teachers Retirement Service*, 200 Ill.App.3d 240, 558 N.E.2d 766 (1990), the court said that names and addresses of government employees are *per se* exempt under the FOIA privacy provision because they reveal practically nothing about the government. Nonetheless, other courts hold that disclosure of the home addresses of government employees is not exempt under their FOIA, as in *State*

Employees Association v. Department of Management and Budget, 428 Mich. 104, 404 N.W.2d 606 (1987).

Kestenbaum v. Michigan State University, 414 Mich. 510, 327 N.W.2d 783 (1982), is a leading case on the effect of state FOIA privacy exemptions on requests for "directory" information about students in state universities. The Supreme Court of Michigan was equally divided as to whether significant privacy interests would be implicated by disclosure of computerized records containing the names, addresses, telephone numbers and course numbers of students at Michigan State University. As a result of the division in the Supreme Court, the lower court's decision to exempt the computerized directory from disclosure was affirmed.

Since a printed directory of the information about the students was available under the state act, the privacy analysis turns on whether the disclosure of the information on *computerized tape* raised different and more serious privacy issues.

Chief Justice Fitzgerald, speaking for two other justices, concluded that:

> Form, not just content, affects the nature of information. Seemingly benign data in an intrusive form takes on quite different characteristics than if it were merely printed.... The very existence of information in computer-ready form may serve to motivate an invasion of privacy.... The university was not wrong in concluding that the release of names and addresses on magnetic tape was a more serious invasion of privacy than disclosure in directory form.

Id. at 532, 327 N.W.2d at 789.

Justice Ryan, joined by two other justices, took a contrary view:

> Our brother holds that nondisclosure of the magnetic tape is justified because it converts "seemingly benign data" into "an intrusive form." It is obvious that the magnetic tape form makes the information more *usable* for the purposes contemplated by the plaintiff.... But to equate usefulness with intrusiveness is to turn the FOIA on its head. A public body should not be allowed to thwart legislative uses of public information by releasing the information in a format difficult or expensive to use.

Id., at 559, 327 N.W.2d at 801–802.

Apart from FOIA statutes, the states also have a variety of specific laws governing certain record-keeping authority and procedures; these may take precedence over an FOIA regarding access to government records containing personal information.

A good example concerns access to the state's motor vehicle records and the clash between the privacy exclusion of a state FOIA and another state statute opening these records to public inspection. The majority of courts hold that, taken alone, personal information contained in Department of Motor Vehicle records is exempt from FOIA disclosure, as in *Jordan v. Motor Vehicles Division, State of Oregon*, 308 Or. 433, 781 P.2d 1203 (1989), where the court said that disclosure of home addresses from Motor Vehicle Division records would be an unreasonable invasion of privacy. Yet, some courts have required disclosure because of other state statutes that may preempt the privacy exemption of the FOIA, as in *Dunhill v. Director, District of Columbia Department of Transportation*, 416 A.2d 244 (1980).

With regard to autopsy records, for instance, the courts generally hold that there is no privacy right in this information because that right belongs to the individual and ends at death, though in some instances disclosure has been ordered because of other statutes. Similarly, access to names, addresses and other information about jurors is routinely controlled by the state's judiciary law and not the FOIA. Accordingly, the laws of each state must be examined carefully regarding access to any specific record system to determine whether the FOIA may be superseded.

Chapter Five

COMMON LAW TORT PRIVACY RIGHTS

A. PRIVACY INTRUSION TORT

In 1965 William Prosser published an article in the California Law Review that has greatly influenced the formulation of common law privacy rights. The article is discussed in Chapter I. Prosser argued that four torts had developed from the large body of common law decisions. Although the torts were commonly called privacy, Prosser contended the torts involved different kinds of invasions and different interests. The disparate tort theory and four-part interest analysis that Prosser developed was incorporated into Section 652 of the Second Restatement of Torts. The Restatement is generally embraced by courts as an initial premise in analysis of tort privacy claims. Two of the torts—Intrusion (652B) and Private Facts (652D)—are examined in this chapter. The Appropriation (652C) and False Light (652E) torts are examined in Chapter Six.

1. COMMON LAW RIGHT

RHODES v. GRAHAM
238 Ky. 225, 37 S.W.2d 46 (1931).

Rees, J.

Defendants tapped telephone company appliances and telephone company lines leading to and from Rhodes' house without authority. Defendants connected a line to the house where they all resided. Defendants listened in on many of Rhodes' conversations and employed a stenographer to listen to and transcribe conversations. The lower court sustained a demurrer to the petition and dismissed the plaintiff's petition; the high court (Court of Appeals) reversed.

There is much conflict in the authorities as to whether or not an unwarranted invasion of the right of privacy may be made the subject of an action in tort where no property or contractual right is involved. This court has adopted the rule that an unwarranted invasion of the right of privacy constitutes a legal injuria for which redress will be granted.... In Brents v. Morgan, ... the court said: "He is entitled to recover substantial damages, although the only damages suffered by him resulted from mental anguish. The fact that the damages cannot be measured by a pecuniary standard is not a bar to his recovery." A person is entitled to the privacy of his home as against the unwarranted invasion of others, and a violation thereof will give rise to an action. It is the legal right of every man to enjoy social and business relations with his friends, neighbors, and acquaintances, and he is entitled to converse with them without molestation by intruders.

In an article entitled "The Right of Privacy," published in the Fourth Harvard Law Review, after describing the gradual growth of the common law to meet the changing demands of society, the authors said: "Recent inventions and business methods call attention to the next step which must be taken for the protection of the person, and for securing to the individual what Judge Cooley calls the right 'to be let alone.' Instantaneous photographs and newspaper enterprise have invaded the sacred precincts of private and domestic life; and numerous mechanical devices threaten to make good the prediction that 'what is whispered in the closet shall be proclaimed from the house tops.' "

The evil incident to the invasion of the privacy of the telephone is as great as that occasioned by unwarranted publicity in newspapers and by other means of a man's private affairs for which courts have granted the injured person redress. Whenever a telephone line is tapped the privacy of those talking over the line is invaded and conversations, wholly proper and confidential, may be overheard. Wire tapping is akin to eavesdropping, which was an indictable offense at common law, and while it has not been made a punishable offense by statute in this state, we conclude that the facts alleged in the petition in this case constitute a wrong done to appellant for which the law affords a remedy by an action for damages.

a. Privacy: Section 652B—Intrusion Upon Seclusion

(1) Invasion of Privacy

Section 652B Intrusion Upon Seclusion

One who intentionally intrudes, physically or otherwise, upon the solitude or seclusion of another or his private affairs or concerns, is subject to liability to the other for invasion of his privacy, if the intrusion would be highly offensive to a reasonable person.

(2) Comment

(a) The form of invasion of privacy covered by this Section does not depend upon any publicity given to the person whose interest is invaded or to his affairs. It consists solely of an intentional interference with his interest in solitude or seclusion, either as to his person or as to his private affairs or concerns, of a kind that would be highly offensive to a reasonable man.

(b) The invasion may be by physical intrusion into a place in which the plaintiff has secluded himself, as when the defendant forces his way into the plaintiff's room in a hotel or insists over the plaintiff's objection in entering his home. It may also be by the use of defendant's senses, with or without mechanical aids, to oversee or overhear the plaintiff's private affairs, as by looking into his upstairs windows with binoculars, or tapping his telephone wires. It may be by some other form of investigation or examination into his private concerns, as by opening his private and personal mail, searching his safe or his wallet, examining his private bank account, or compelling him by a forged court order to permit an inspection of his personal documents. The intrusion itself makes the defendant subject to liability, even though there is no publication or other use of any kind of the photograph or information outlined.

2. DIVULGENCE, PUBLICATION

HAMBERGER v. EASTMAN

106 N.H. 107, 206 A.2d 239 (1964).

KENISON, C.J. . . . .

The plaintiffs, husband and wife, brought companion suits for invasion of their privacy against the defendant, who rented a dwelling house to the plaintiffs. The plaintiffs alleged that the defendant concealed "a listening and recording device" in their bedroom, that this device was connected to the defendant's adjacent residence, and that ever since discovering the device they had suffered humiliation, embarrassment and severe mental distress. The defendant moved to dismiss both actions on the grounds that neither suit stated a cause of action. The court reserved judgment and transferred the cases to the Supreme Court of New Hampshire without ruling. The Supreme Court denied the motion to dismiss and remanded the case.

The Restatement, Torts Section 867 provides that "a person who unreasonably and seriously interferes with another's interest in not having his affairs known to others . . . is liable to the other." As is pointed out in comment *d* "liability exists only if the defendant's conduct was such that he should have realized that it would be offensive to persons of ordinary sensibilities. It is only where the intrusion has gone beyond the limits of decency that liability accrues. These limits are exceeded where intimate details of the life of one who has never manifested a desire to have publicity are exposed to the public. . . . "

The defendant contends that the right of privacy should not be recognized on the facts of the present case as they appear in the pleadings because there are no allegations that anyone listened or overheard any sounds or voices originating from the plaintiffs' bedroom.

The tort of intrusion on the plaintiffs' solitude or seclusion does not require publicity and communication to third persons although this would affect the amount of damages. . . . The defendant also contends that the right of privacy is not violated unless something has been published, written or printed and that oral publicity is not sufficient. . . .

If the peeping Tom, the big ear and the electronic eavesdropper (whether ingenious or ingenuous) have a place in the hierarchy of social values, it ought not to be at the expense of a married couple minding their own business in the seclusion of their bedroom who have never asked for or by their conduct deserved a potential projection of their private conversations and actions to their landlord or to others. Whether actual or potential such "publicity with respect to private matters of purely personal concern is an injury to personality. It impairs the mental peace and comfort of the individual and may produce suffering more acute than that produced by a mere bodily injury." . . .

3. NOTES

a. *The Privacy Intrusion Tort*

Electronic surveillance in the form of wiretaps or tape recorders surreptitiously placed in residential dwellings are core examples of invasions of privacy that constitute intrusions into seclusion or private affairs in violation of common law privacy rights as formulated in 652B. It is clearly settled that the privacy intrusions tort may be committed without publication of personal information by the defendant. The major role of the tort is to reach invasions of privacy by business entities or private persons that occur through the *acquiring of information* about an individual. Are there cases where the tort is committed even though no information has been acquired about an individual? Suppose a place of public accommodation installs see-through panels in public rest rooms. If a user of the bathroom discovers the existence of the panels does she have a cause of action under the privacy intrusion tort without alleging that someone had observed her through the panels? For an affirmative answer to this question, *see Harkey v. Abate*, 131 Mich.App. 177, 346 N.W.2d 74 (1983). What is the basis for concluding that the installation of a hidden viewing device by itself constitutes an invasion of privacy?

Suppose A poses for pictures as a centerfold for Playboy magazine. Two months after the publication, B, a compulsive peeping Tom, sneaks under A's bedroom window and observes her lying naked in bed. It seems clear that B has invaded A's privacy. Has B intruded upon A's seclusion or private affairs? Has B acquired information about A that was not already public?

Consider Dean Bloustein's comment on the underlying basis for rights in tort and constitutional law for invasions of privacy through intrusive actions:

The fundamental fact is that our Western culture defines individuality as including the right to be free from certain types of intrusions. This measure of personal isolation and personal control over the conditions of its abandonment is of the very essence of personal freedom and dignity, is part of what our culture means by these concepts. A man whose home may be entered at the will of another, whose conversation may be overheard at the will of another, whose marital and familial intimacies may be overseen at the will of another, is less of a man, has less human dignity, on that account. He who may intrude upon another at will is the master of the other and, in fact, intrusion is a primary weapon of the tyrant.

I contend that the gist of the wrong in the intrusion cases is not the intentional infliction of mental distress but rather a blow to human dignity, an assault on human personality. Eavesdropping and wiretapping, unwanted entry into another's home, may be the occasion and cause of distress and embarrassment but that is not what makes these acts of intrusion wrongful. They are wrongful because they are demeaning of individuality, and they are such whether or not they cause emotional trauma.

Edward J. Bloustein, *Privacy as an Aspect of Human Dignity: An Answer to Dean Prosser*, 39 N.Y.U. L.Rev. 962, 973–74 (1964).

b. Sexual Harassment and the Intrusion Tort

An Alabama employer made a practice of forcing a female janitorial worker into his office behind locked doors several times a week to inquire about her sex life. Knowing that her family was dependent upon her salary, he demanded (without success) that she have oral sex with him. Once he swatted her "across the bottom." When the employee attempted to return to work one day she was told she had been "laid off."

These are the facts of *Phillips v. Smalley Maintenance Services, Inc.*, 435 S.2d 705 (Ala.1983). The Alabama Supreme Court held that the employer's conduct easily qualified as intrusion upon seclusion within the meaning of the Restatement (Second) of Torts Sec. 652B. Employer Smalley did not act surreptitiously, publicize Phillip's private affairs to third parties, or get the sexual facts and favors he persistently sought. In what sense was there an "intrusion upon seclusion"?

The *Smalley* court rejected the view that "acquiring information" or "surreptitious actions" were *sine qua nons* for recovery under the Privacy Intrusion Tort. The court concluded that Smalley had intruded into the plaintiff's private affairs because:

Smalley's intrusive and coercive sexual demands upon Brenda Phillips were ... "an examination" into her "private concerns," ... [and] improper inquiries into her personal sexual proclivities and personality.

Smalley, 435 S.2d at 711.

Are all forms of conduct commonly termed "sexual harassment" also invasions of privacy? *See generally* Anita L. Allen, *Uneasy Access: Privacy for Women in a Free Society*, 128 (1988). Professor Allen argues that many forms of sexual harassment—leering, insulting, prying, and offensive touching—are also invasions of privacy.

4. DAMAGES: GENERAL, PUNITIVE

MONROE v. DARR

221 Kan. 281, 559 P.2d 322 (1977).

PRAGER, JUSTICE . . .

[The plaintiff sought to recover damages under Section 652B of the Second Restatement of Torts—intrusion upon seclusion—following a non-consensual entry into Monroe's apartment by sheriff's deputies. The deputies entered the apartment in search of an unknown person who might have been involved in an attempted robbery one hour before. The victim had described his assailant's vehicle as a 1960–61 Dodge Lancer. Sheriff's deputies observed a 1960–61 Plymouth Valiant parked outside Monroe's apartment building, and told the apartment manager that the vehicle seemed to match the description of one used in an attempted robbery. They also told the manager that the assailant had been described as a six-foot white male with long brown hair and a long beard. The manager stated that this sounded like the people who lived in the basement apartment downstairs and arranged for the officers to enter the apartment when they received no response to a knock on the door. The plaintiff was asleep, and awoke to see a deputy pointing a shotgun at him. According to Monroe, the deputy advised him that he was looking for a black man with a beard. The officers left Monroe's apartment two minutes later, having decided that he was not involved in the robbery. The plaintiff appeals from the dismissal of the case on the ground that the plaintiff's evidence failed to show that he had sustained any damages.]

Monroe's first point on the appeal is that the trial court erred in striking his claim for punitive damages before he was afforded an opportunity to introduce evidence on that issue. The record discloses that in the prayer of his petition plaintiff sought to recover $5,000 exemplary damages in addition to $5,000 actual damages. The plaintiff continued to assert his claim for punitive damages at the pretrial conference. The pretrial order specifically states that a mixed question of law and fact to be determined is whether or not the plaintiff is entitled to recover punitive damages. Plaintiff maintains that it was prejudicial error for the trial court to strike his claim for punitive damages before trial without affording plaintiff an opportunity to prove his claim.

The general rule is that punitive damages may be recovered for an invasion of the right of privacy where the defendant has acted with malice. A plaintiff seeking to recover punitive damages has the burden of proving malice on part of the defendant. In the present case the trial court prematurely entered its order striking the plaintiff's claim for punitive damages before the plaintiff had an opportunity to introduce evidence on that issue. However, at the trial the plaintiff, in order to show the factual circumstances surrounding the invasion of his apartment by the sheriff's deputies, offered into evidence statements taken from various sheriff's deputies who were involved in the affair. The plaintiff accepted the statements of these officers as true and rested his case upon them. In these statements the sheriff's deputies stated unequivocally that they entered the Monroe apartment because they were in search of an unknown person who might have been involved in the attempted robbery of Maurice Hackworth approximately one hour before. Although the actions of the deputy sheriffs could well be described as overly zealous in invading Monroe's apartment without first obtaining a search warrant, there is nothing contained in the evidence relied upon by Monroe which shows that the sheriff's deputies acted with malice or were chargeable with willful or wanton misconduct. We have held that exemplary or punitive damages are not recoverable from a sheriff unless fraud, malice, oppression or improper motives are shown. We have concluded that, although the district court acted prematurely in striking plaintiff's claim for punitive damages before trial, in view of the fact that the undisputed evidence offered by plaintiff at the trial fails as a matter of law to show malice or improper motive plaintiff was not prejudiced by the ruling of the district court. On the undisputed facts Monroe is not entitled to recover punitive damages from Sheriff Darr or his surety. We, therefore, hold that Monroe's first point does not justify a reversal of the case.

Monroe's second point on the appeal is that the trial court erred in directing a verdict in favor of the defendants at the close of the plaintiff's case. The defendants moved to dismiss the case and for a directed verdict for three reasons: (1) Probable cause for entry into the plaintiff's apartment by the sheriff's deputies had been shown; (2) since the sheriff could not discharge the deputies at his pleasure, he was not liable for the deputies' acts; and (3) plaintiff's evidence failed to show that he had sustained any damages. The district court overruled the motion on the first two grounds but held it should be sustained for the reason that proof of damages was remote and speculative and therefore the plaintiff's evidence failed to show that he had sustained any damages.

. . . An invasion of privacy action is primarily concerned with compensation for injured feelings or mental suffering of the injured party. The gist of the cause of action for invasion of privacy is for direct wrongs of a personal character which result in injury to the plaintiff's feelings.

Kunz v. Allen, 102 Kan. 883, 172 P. 532 (1918), was the first Kansas case to recognize an action for the breach of privacy. That case involved a demurrer sustained by the trial court on the ground that plaintiff failed to prove any actual damages from the invasion. This court reversed saying it was not necessary for the plaintiff to prove the amount of her damages in dollars and cents as long as the evidence tended to show the effect of the wrong upon the plaintiff. A similar rule is applied in cases of assault and battery.... [A]lthough a plaintiff in a privacy suit can recover without proof of special damages and is not required to show general damages in specific amounts, he is required to introduce some evidence to show that he suffered anxiety, embarrassment, or some other form of mental anguish. In the present case the trial court in sustaining the defendant's motion for a directed verdict held that Monroe's evidence was insufficient to show that he had suffered general damages by way of mental distress as a result of the invasion of his privacy. We have concluded that the trial court erred in this regard. Although somewhat skimpy, the evidence was sufficient to submit the issue of general damages to the jury.

At the trial the plaintiff Monroe took the stand and testified that since the incident he could not sleep well at night, that he was more nervous than he was before, that he had feelings of apprehension, and no longer felt safe. Monroe's wife testified that since the incident her husband had become extremely nervous, hears noises at night, has had more attacks of asthma than he had before the incident, has trouble going to sleep, and that he does not trust law enforcement officers any more. She further testified as to his mental distress on the date the incident occurred. It was not necessary for the plaintiff to call medical witnesses to testify as to his condition and to show his mental anxiety and suffering. It was not necessary for him to introduce evidence to show the value of his mental distress in dollars and cents. The amount of damages which should be allowed for the plaintiff's mental distress was a question for the determination of the jury. The district court in our judgment erred in taking the case away from the jury and entering judgment in favor of the defendants since the plaintiff introduced evidence showing that he suffered mental distress and anxiety as a result of the incident. The case must be reversed and remanded to the district court for a new trial.

Note: Compensatory and Punitive Damages

Compensatory damages in tort include general and special damages. Special damages are out-of-pocket economic losses such as medical expenses and lost wages that are caused by the conduct that constitutes the tort. General damages include physical and emotional pain and suffering that is caused by the tortious conduct and, in lawsuits for torts like defamation or false light, damage to the plaintiff's reputation.

Consider Warren and Brandeis' comment that "[e]ven in the absence of special damages, substantial compensation could be allowed for injury to feelings as in the action of slander and libel." Warren and Brandeis, *The Right to Privacy*, 4 Harv. L. Rev. 193, 219 (1890).

Do the damage rules from defamation actions in libel or slander apply to common law privacy tort actions? The answer to that question may be important in privacy intrusion actions because in certain defamation actions—libel and slander per se—damages are presumed. Presumed damages in defamation means that there is a legal presumption that general damages have occurred where defamation has occurred in a certain way. *Monroe v. Darr* is a leading case on damage standards in privacy intrusion and public disclosure tort actions. The court rejects the view that damages are presumed in privacy tort actions. The plaintiff is required to introduce some credible evidence of emotional distress in order to recover general damages.

Consider the evidence the court viewed as sufficient to establish mental distress in the case. Does the court impose significant evidentiary burdens on the recovery of general damages in privacy cases? Compare *Trevino v. Southwestern Bell Tel. Co.*, 582 S.W.2d 582 (Tex. Civ. App. 1979), where the court upheld a $50.00 nominal damages award to the plaintiff in an intrusion action based upon the defendant entering the premises of the plaintiff's place of business and removing two business phones. In *Trevino*, evidence of the plaintiff's emotional distress was limited to his testimony that he was very upset because the telephones had been stolen.

Compare Post, *The Social Foundations of Privacy: Community and Self in the Common Law Tort*, 77 Calif. L. Rev. 957, 963–65 (1989), where the author argues that the intrusion tort cases are best read as allowing the plaintiff to recover general damages without demonstrating that the invasion of privacy caused emotional distress.

Consider the Second Restatement of Torts section on damages in privacy cases. (Section 652H.) Does the Second Restatement of Torts support the view that damages may be recoverable without a demonstration of either emotional distress or economic loss flowing from the invasion of privacy?

Section 652H. Damages

One who has established a cause of action for invasion of his privacy is entitled to recover damages for

(a) the harm to his interest in privacy resulting from the invasion;

(b) his mental distress proved to have been suffered if it is of a kind that normally results from such an invasion; and

(c) special damage of which the invasion is a legal cause.

Comment:

a. A cause of action for invasion of privacy, in any of its four forms, entitles the plaintiff to recover damages for the harm to the particular element of his privacy that is invaded. Thus one who suffers an intrusion upon his solitude or seclusion under section 652B, may recover damages for the deprivation of seclusion.

Although the plaintiff in *Monroe v. Darr* did not recover punitive damages, the court expresses the general view on the requirement imposed upon the plaintiff for recovery of punitive damages in a privacy tort action: the plaintiff must establish malice or willful and wanton misconduct.

5. EXPECTATION OF PRIVACY PRINCIPLE

NADER v. GENERAL MOTORS CORPORATION

25 N.Y.2d 560, 307 N.Y.S.2d 647, 255 N.E.2d 765 (1970).

FULD, CHIEF JUDGE.

[The plaintiff, an author and lecturer on automotive safety, had been a severe critic of the defendant's products. The plaintiff alleged in his complaint that the defendant's agents conducted a campaign of intimidation against him to suppress his criticism by: (1) conducting interviews with the plaintiff's acquaintances and questioning them about his views and habits; (2) keeping him under surveillance in public; (3) causing him to be accosted by girls for the purpose of entrapping him into illicit relationships; (4) making threatening telephone calls to his home; (5) tapping his telephone; and (6) conducting a continuing investigation of him. The complaint pleaded four causes of action, two for invasion of privacy, one for intentional infliction of severe emotional distress and one for interference with the plaintiff's economic advantage. The defendant appeals from the denial of its motion to dismiss the invasion of privacy counts for failure to state a cause of action.]

On this appeal, taken by permission of the Appellate Division on a certified question, we are called upon to determine the reach of the tort of invasion of privacy as it exists under the law of the District of Columbia.

. . .

The threshold choice of law question requires no extended discussion. In point of fact, the parties have agreed—at least for purposes of this motion—that the sufficiency of these allegations is to be determined under the law of the District of Columbia. The District is the jurisdiction in which most of the acts are alleged to have occurred, and it was there, too, that the plaintiff lived and suffered the impact of those acts. It is, in short, the place which has the most significant relationship with the subject matter of the tort charged.

Turning, then, to the law of the District of Columbia, it appears that its courts have not only recognized a common-law action for invasion of privacy but have broadened the scope of that tort beyond its traditional limits. Thus, in the most recent of its cases on the subject, Pearson v. Dodd, the Federal Court of Appeals for the District of Columbia declared (p.704):

> We approve the extension of the tort of invasion of privacy to instances of *intrusion*, whether by physical trespass or not, into spheres from which an ordinary man in a plaintiff's position could reasonably expect that the particular defendant should be excluded. (Italics supplied.)

It is this form of invasion of privacy—initially termed "intrusion" by Dean Prosser in 1960—on which the two challenged causes of action are predicated.

. . .

It should be emphasized that the mere gathering of information about a particular individual does not give rise to a cause of action under this theory. Privacy is invaded only if the information sought is of a confidential nature and the defendant's conduct was unreasonably intrusive. Just as a common-law copyright is lost when material is published, so, too, there can be no invasion of privacy where the information sought is open to public view or has been voluntarily revealed to others. In order to sustain a cause of action for invasion of privacy, therefore, the plaintiff must show that the appellant's conduct was truly "intrusive" and that it was designed to elicit information which would not be available through normal inquiry or observation.

. . . At most, only two of the activities charged to the appellant are, in our view, actionable as invasions of privacy under the law of the District of Columbia. However, since . . . two counts include allegations which are sufficient to state a cause of action, we could—as the concurring opinion notes—merely affirm the order before us without further elaboration. To do so, though, would be a disservice both to the judge who will be called upon to try this case and to the litigants themselves. In other words, we deem it desirable, nay essential, that we go further and, for the guidance of the trial court and counsel, indicate the extent to which the plaintiff is entitled to rely on the various allegations in support of his privacy claim.

. . .

Turning, then, to the particular acts charged in the complaint, we cannot find any basis for a claim of invasion of privacy, under District of Columbia law, in the allegations that the appellant, through its agents or employees, interviewed many persons who knew the plaintiff, asking questions about him and casting aspersions on his character. Although those inquiries may have uncovered information of a personal nature, it is difficult to see how they may be said to have invaded the plaintiff's privacy. Information about the plaintiff which was already known to others could hardly be regarded as private to the plaintiff. Presumably, the plaintiff had previously revealed the information to such other persons, and he would necessarily assume the risk that a friend or acquaintance in whom he had confided might breach the confidence. If, as alleged, the questions tended to disparage the plaintiff's character, his remedy would seem to be by way of an action for defamation, not for breach of his right to privacy.

Nor can we find any actionable invasion of privacy in the allegations that the appellant caused the plaintiff to be accosted by girls with illicit proposals, or that it was responsible for the making of a large number of threatening and harassing telephone calls to the plaintiff's home at odd hours. Neither of these activities, howsoever offensive and disturbing, involved intrusion for the purpose of gathering information of a private and confidential nature.

As already indicated, it is manifestly neither practical nor desirable for the law to provide a remedy against any and all activity which an individual might find annoying. On the other hand, where severe mental pain or anguish is inflicted through a deliberate and malicious campaign of harassment or intimidation, a remedy is available in the form of an action for the intentional infliction of emotional distress—the theory underlying the plaintiff's third cause of action. But the elements of such an action are decidedly different from those governing the tort of invasion of privacy, and just as we have carefully guarded against the use of the prima facie tort doctrine to circumvent the limitations relating to other established tort remedies, we should be wary of any attempt to rely on the tort of invasion of privacy as a means of avoiding the more stringent pleading and proof requirements for an action for infliction of emotional distress.

Apart, however, from the foregoing allegations which we find inadequate to spell out a cause of action for invasion of privacy under the District of Columbia law, the complaint contains allegations concerning other activities by the appellant or its agents which do satisfy the requirements for such a cause of action. The one which most clearly meets those requirements is the charge that the appellant and its codefendants engaged in unauthorized wiretapping and eavesdropping by mechanical and electronic means....

There are additional allegations that the appellant hired people to shadow the plaintiff and keep him under surveillance. In particular, he claims that, on one occasion, one of its agents followed him into a bank, getting sufficiently close to him to see the denomination of the bills he was withdrawing from his account. From what we have already said, it is manifest that the mere observation of the plaintiff in a public place does not amount to an invasion of his privacy. But, under certain circumstances, surveillance may be so "overzealous" as to render it actionable. Whether or not the surveillance in the present case falls into this latter category will depend on the nature of the proof. A person does not automatically make public everything he does merely by being in a public place, and the mere fact that Nader was in a bank did not give anyone the right to try to discover the amount of money he was withdrawing. On the other hand, if the plaintiff acted in such a way as to reveal that fact to any casual observer, then, it may not be said that the appellant intruded into his private sphere. In any event, though, it is enough for present purposes to say that the surveillance allegation is not insufficient as a matter of law.

．　．　．

The order appealed from should be affirmed, with costs, and the question certified answered in the affirmative.

BREITEL, JUDGE (concurring in result).

True, scholars, in trying to define the elusive concept of the right of privacy, have, as of the present, subdivided the common law right into separate classifications, most significantly distinguishing between unreasonable intrusion and unreasonable publicity. This does not mean, however, that the classifications are either frozen or exhausted, or that several of the classifications may not overlap.

. . . [I]t does not strain credulity or imagination to conceive of the systematic "public" surveillance of another as being the implementation of a plan to intrude on the privacy of another. Although acts perf—— in "public," especially if taken singly or in small numbers, ι confidential, at least arguably a right to privacy may never, invaded through extensive or exhaustive monitoring and catalε acts normally disconnected and anonymous.

. . .

There is still further difficulty. In this State thus far there h no recognition of a common law right of privacy, but only tha derives from a statute of rather limited scope. Consequently, th must undertake the hazardous task of applying what is at pre quite different law of the District of Columbia. True, this ma court's burden eventually, if the case were to return to it for rev trial, especially if the plaintiff were to prevail upon such a trial er, there is no occasion to advance, now, into a complicated, sτ still-changing field of law of another jurisdiction, solely to ε before trial the relevancy and allocability among pleaded causes or projected but not yet offered items of evidence. . . .

Note: Intrusion Limited by the Expectation of Privacy I

In the instant case, Judge Fuld in dictum interprets the right under the law of the District of Columbia as not applicable to th harassing and obnoxious telephone calls. This is so because, as J explains, the privacy tort of intrusion is limited to activities which purpose the gathering of confidential information. Judge Fuld con the intrusion tort is not implicated where there is an allegation on the part of the defendant which consists of interviewing and ε acquaintances of Ralph Nader about his racial and religious views sexual proclivity, and other personal habits. Although the purpε activity was to acquire information, by sharing that informatio quaintances, Nader has assumed the risk that the information published and, therefore, the information is not confidential. Th of the surveillance in public places was rejected on the grounds would not reasonably expect that public places were areas where lar defendant would be excluded.

Judge Fuld's concept of the privacy intrusion tort merges t constitutional standards for privacy by grafting the expectatio test and the assumption of risk doctrine onto the tort. The restrictive view of the privacy intrusion tort which would limit protecting only informational privacy interests.

The Restatement of Torts (comment *b*, illustration 5, Section 652B), Dean Prosser and several jurisdictions have adopted a more expansive view of the intrusion tort than the view of the *Nader* court. Under this expansive view, the tort is available in cases of repeated intimidating and harassing phone calls and surveillance. Such activities constitute a nonphysical intrusion into mental solitude. The leading cases are *Pinkerton Nat'l Detective Agency, Inc. v. Stevens*, 108 Ga.App. 159, 132 S.E.2d 119 (1963), *Carey v. Statewide Finance Co.*, 3 Conn. Cir. Ct. 716, 223 A.2d 405 (1966), and *Housh v. Peth*, 99 Ohio App. 485, 59 Ohio Op. 330, 135 N.E.2d 440 (1955), *aff'd*, 165 Ohio St. 35, 59 Ohio Op. 60, 133 N.E.2d 340 (1956). The latter two cases involve repetitious and harassing phone calls by creditors to the plaintiffs at home and, in *Carey*, also at the hospital. In *Pinkerton Nat'l Detective Agency*, repeated acts of surveillance and eavesdropping by a detective agency employed by an insurance company were found to violate the subject's tort right of privacy. In *Vescovo*, the intermediate California appellate court decision that follows, use of the privacy right of intrusion in tort to protect mental repose is carried to its outer limits.

The availability of an intrusion privacy tort action for protection of mental repose depends upon the extensiveness of the intrusion into solitude in terms of both the nature and repetitiveness of the conduct. Some leading cases distinguishing *Pinkerton*, *Carey* and *Housh* on this basis are *Windsor v. General Motors Acceptance Corp.*, 295 Ala. 80, 323 So.2d 350 (1975); *Catania v. Eastern Airlines, Inc.*, 381 So.2d 265 (Fla.Dist.Ct.App.1980); *Jackson v. Peoples Federal Credit Union*, 25 Wash. App. 81, 604 P.2d 1025 (1979).

Note: The Shadowing Cases

The majority opinion in *Nader* is but another example of where the public/private dichotomy defines the scope of privacy rights (acquiring information about someone in a public place is not actionable). However, even under Judge Fuld's view, overzealous public surveillance may cross over into the sphere of the private and constitute an actionable invasion of privacy. This was the basis for preserving Nader's count on the surveillance in the bank: his actions in the bank were public but the amount of his deposit or in his account was private and confidential.

Judge Breitel's concurring opinion in *Nader* questions the clearness of the line drawn by the court between surveillance of public and private acts:

> Although acts performed in "public," especially if taken singly or in small numbers, may not be confidential, at least arguably a right to privacy may nevertheless be invaded through extensive or exhaustive monitoring and cataloguing of acts normally disconnected and anonymous.

25 N.Y.2d at 572, 255 N.E.2d at 772, 307 N.Y.S.2d at 657.

The opinions of Judge Fuld and Judge Breitel in *Nader* reflect two bases upon which the close shadowing and monitoring of public acts may become sufficiently "overzealous" to be actionable under the privacy intrusion tort. One is where public surveillance results in the acquiring of "private information"; the other is where the accumulation of public facts provides a composite of the person that reveals sufficiently "more" about the person to be an invasion of privacy that is actionable.

In *Galella v. Onassis*, 353 F.Supp. 196 (S.D.N.Y.1972), the federal district court found that the surveillance of President John Kennedy's widow by the photographer Galella was sufficiently overzealous to satisfy the requirements under the privacy intrusion tort of either Judge Fuld or Judge Breitel. Despite a court order requiring that Galella cease surveillance and following and remain at least 50 yards from the family and 100 yards away from their home, he continued to follow their car and harass them, armed with his camera, when they would leave the car. He waited outside their home at all hours. He intruded into the children's schools, hid in bushes and behind coat racks in restaurants, sneaked into beauty salons, bribed door-men, hatcheck girls, chauffeurs, fishermen in Greece, hairdressers and schoolboys, romanced employees, and questioned stores and restaurants about purchases. *Id.* at 228. Although New York courts had not yet recognized the tort of intrusion, the district court reasoned that the state court would have under these circumstances, which it describes as a "torrent of almost unrelieved abuse into the privacy of everyday activity." Id. at 227, 229.

The injunction against Galella was affirmed by the Second Circuit on appeal but the scope of the injunction was modified, *Galella v. Onassis*, 487 F.2d 986, 998–99 (2d Cir.1973). The court of appeals assumed as a basis of its holding that the lower court was correct in its interpretation of the right to privacy under New York law but sustained the injunction under a New York criminal statute that prohibited harassment. 487 F.2d at 995.

a. *"Rough Shadowing" in Personal Injury Investigations*

The claim that excessive surveillance (rough shadowing) of the plaintiff constitutes an invasion of privacy has arisen in response to investigations by insurance companies of plaintiffs who initiate personal injury actions in tort or under worker compensation law.

In an interesting commentary on the subject of privacy intrusions in personal injury cases the author summarizes some of the most intrusive surveillance techniques:

> One technique is known as "duping the subject." The subject is the plaintiff making the personal injury claim. A typical situation involving duping would begin by establishing that a plaintiff frequents a particular establishment and in-structing an investigator assigned to the case to strike up an acquaintance. What generally follows is some sort of setup whereby the "duped" plaintiff is enticed to engage in certain activities which are filmed, to reveal the extent of the physical activity or injuries. For example, having gained the plaintiff's confidence and friendship, an investigator takes the plaintiff to an amusement park and has her walk across an expansion bridge, which he causes to shake and sway in an attempt to detect the extent of her injuries. While this activity is being

created another investigator is taking motion pictures of the situation to be used later . . . .

"Roping" is a manufactured setting designed to encourage physical activity. An example of roping a subject is the situation where the plaintiff, out of work because of his injury and thus in need of funds, is offered temporary work such as planting shrubbery or raking leaves. The work usually is done at a location where the plaintiff's physical activities can be photographed over a two or three day period. Generally the plaintiff is offered such attractive hourly wages that he would be reluctant to refuse them . . . .

Aggravating the subject into a "statement of activity" is another technique that has been used. The object is to obtain motion pictures of the plaintiff performing a strenuous activity such as changing the tire on his car. Since a flat tire is a relatively rare occurrence, the surveillance team will intentionally deflate the plaintiff's tire, conceal themselves, and then film the plaintiff's activities. Techniques employed to cause the plaintiff's tire to go flat include using a valve cap with a long inverted nipple which loosens the tire's valve core, puncturing the tire with a sharp instrument, or firing a pellet gun at the tire . . . .

A technique called the "mess" involves some form of sticky rubbish, usually a mixture of flour, plaster-of-paris, shellac, ink and the like. The investigators will throw this mixture on the windshield of the plaintiff's automobile. This draws the plaintiff out into the open to clean it before he can continue on his way, giving the investigator a good view from which to take still or motion pictures of particular capabilities of the plaintiff in a near-normal situation.

The "delivery" is a technique whereby the investigator contrives to obstruct the driveway, porch, or similar necessary access area at the plaintiff's home. The investigator might telephone a building supply firm while the plaintiff is off the premises and, in the plaintiff's name, order several pounds of sand or some other object that is left in a place where the plaintiff must remove it immediately upon arriving home. At this point, the investigator is positioned to film the activities involved in removing the object.

George A. LaMarca, *Overintrusive Surveillance of Plaintiffs in Personal Injury Cases*, 9 A. J. Trial Advoc. 1, 608 (1985).

Pinkerton Nat'l Detective Agency, Inc. v. Stevens, 108 Ga.App. 159, 132 S.E.2d 119 (1963), illustrates the excesses in surveillance that will result in liability under the intrusion tort. In *Pinkerton*, private investigators were hired by the insurance company to follow the plaintiff and report on her injury. For several months, the detective kept a constant surveillance, parking at the plaintiff's home and following her car, especially at night. The detectives frequently snooped and eavesdropped at her window, sneaked through her woods, and cut a hole through her hedge. Twice they entered her home posing as legitimate visitors. The court found that this course of conduct went beyond what was reasonable as a means of investigation. There is no bright line that sorts out cases where investigations go beyond what is reasonable to become excessive surveillance and unreasonable shadowing and a violation of the privacy intrusion tort.

A leading case upholding the legality of surveillance is *Saldana v. Kelsey–Hayes Co.,* 178 Mich.App. 230, 443 N.W.2d 382 (1989), where the Michigan Court of Appeals upheld the granting of summary judgment in favor of an employer and supervisor for an invasion of privacy claim brought by their employee. In *Saldana,* the employer hired a private investigator to observe an employee that had filed a work-related accident claim because the employer suspected that the employee was malingering. Using not only his naked eye but also a high powered camera lens the investigator watched the plaintiff at home from the end of the street, the sidewalk and through the window. Other actions included telephoning his home, questioning recent visitors to his home, posing as a process-server to enter his home and tailing him as he went to doctor appointments.

Michigan adopts a three part test for the privacy intrusion tort. The plaintiff must show (1) an intrusion by the defendant; (2) into a matter in which the plaintiff has a right of privacy; (3) by a means or method that is objectionable to a reasonable person. The court in *Saldana* found that the defendants' actions in observing the plaintiff in his home and in entering the home under false pretenses established an intrusion and presented a factual question as to whether these methods would be objectionable to a reasonable person. However, the court held as a matter of law that the plaintiff had no right to privacy in the matter that was intruded upon. This was because the employer had a legitimate interest in investigating matters that are potential sources of legal liability. 178 Mich. App. at 235, 443 N.W.2d at 385.

Does the *Saldana* court's view of the privacy intrusion tort suggest that persons who initiate personal injury lawsuits no longer have legitimate expectations of privacy in respect to information that is relevant to the case regardless of how the information is acquired?

b. Litigation Strategy—Nader v. General Motors

The activities of General Motors and their agents, which Ralph Nader claimed violated his tort rights of privacy, occurred in Connecticut, the District of Columbia, Iowa, Massachusetts, New Hampshire, Pennsylvania and New York. Given the contacts with these jurisdictions,

Ralph Nader had the option of initiating the lawsuit in either the federal district or state court in all of these jurisdictions.

Stewart Speiser, Ralph Nader's lawyer, has written about the strategy that went into the decision to sue in a state court in New York in a very interesting book. *See* S. Stewart Speiser, *Lawsuit* (1980). In the determination to sue in a state court in New York, there were considerations of several factors. A suit in the state court in New York had the difficulty of being brought in a state which did not recognize a tort privacy right that would cover the activities of General Motors in the *Nader* case. In addition, in New York courts, parties could get interlocutory appeals which were not available as a possible dilatory tactic in a federal court action.

c. The Choice of Law Issues in the Nader Case

Although New York did not recognize a cause of action in privacy which would provide relief to Ralph Nader, the other jurisdictions where the alleged violations of privacy occurred did recognize the privacy intrusion tort. Under prevailing choice of law principles, the New York court would, as it did, apply the law of the state with the most significant relationship to Mr. Nader's claims. That would be his residency, the District of Columbia, where most of the alleged illegal actions occurred. The Second Restatement of Conflicts adopts a presumption that the domicile of the plaintiff in a defamation or privacy tort action is the jurisdiction that has the most significant relationship because it is the center of the plaintiff's reputation and personhood interests. *See* Restatement (Second) of Conflicts, Sections 150, 153 (1971) (Section 150 Multi–State Defamation; Section 153 Multi–State Invasion of Privacy).

The feature of suing in the state of New York, which proved to be the most enticing to the *Nader* litigation team, was the tradition in New York of liberal liability and damage awards. Mr. Speiser indicates that this factor was the one that turned the decision in favor of the suit in New York state courts. According to Speiser the largest damage judgment that had been rendered in a common law privacy action until the *Nader* case was for $12,500. Since the *Nader* decision there have been a number of judgments based upon privacy claims under the common law, constitution and federal statutes that exceed six figures.

d. The Settlement in the Nader Litigation

Ralph Nader asked for $2,000,000 in compensatory damages and $5,000,000 in punitive damages. He ultimately settled with General Motors for $425,000. One of the supreme ironies of the *Nader* litigation is that the money from the settlement was a major financial source for Ralph Nader's consumer protection movement.

6. THE PRIVACY INTRUSION TORT GENERALLY BEYOND NADER: PRIVACY TORT PROTECTION FOR MENTAL REPOSE

VESCOVO v. NEW WAY ENTERPRISES, LTD.

60 Cal.App.3d 582, 130 Cal.Rptr. 86 (1976)

ASHBY, J.

[Plaintiffs Norma Jean and Albert Vescovo are the parents of plaintiff Frankie Renee Vescovo, a minor. Defendants are publishers of the Los Angeles Free Press. In 1973, the following classified advertisement appeared in the Free Press: "Hot Lips—Deep Throat—Sexy young bored housewife—Norma—[plaintiffs' address]." After the ad appeared, Norma received letters from inmates in penal institutions and numerous other persons soliciting her to perform sexual acts. In excess of 250 persons entered the plaintiffs' property without permission, demanding to see Norma, or cruised by the property in their vehicles harassing the plaintiffs. The plaintiffs' complaint alleged that neither Norma nor anyone representing her placed the advertisement and set forth ten causes of action, including libel (Norma), invasion of privacy (all plaintiffs), and intentional and negligent infliction of emotional distress (Frankie). The trial court sustained the defendants' demurrers to the causes of action for invasion of privacy (intrusion upon solitude or seclusion) by Frankie.

ISSUES PRESENTED

The question on this appeal is whether the first amended complaint stated a valid cause of action on behalf of Frankie for invasion of privacy, intentional infliction of emotional harm, and negligent infliction of emotional harm. We hold that the complaint, although hardly a model of pleading, adequately alleges the three causes of action. Therefore we reverse.

.   .   .

INVASION OF PRIVACY

In the fifth cause of action it is alleged that "[a]s a direct and proximate result of the publication of said classified advertisement, plaintiff Frankie Renee Vescovo's right to privacy has been violated in that said plaintiff's physical solitude and home have been wrongfully invaded by innumerable undesirable and unsavory persons, who in responding to said malicious advertisement, have harassed, annoyed and frightened plaintiff Frankie Renee Vescovo, all of which have resulted in the disruption of said plaintiff's life and the peace and tranquility of her mind, and have made her subject to contempt and ridicule of her neighbors and friends, and who have invaded and impaired the seclusion of said plaintiff's private life and her said residence, and have caused and will continue to cause plaintiff Frankie Renee Vescovo injury to her mental health, strength, activity and body and have caused and will continue to cause said plaintiff great mental, physical and nervous pain and suffering, all to her general damage in the sum of $50,000.00.''

Plaintiffs contend that the fifth cause of action adequately states a cause of action for that aspect of invasion of privacy involving intrusion of the plaintiff's physical solitude or seclusion.

Defendants contend that there is no relational right to privacy, i.e., even a close relative may not recover for the invasion of privacy of another. In this respect defendants' argument misses the mark. Frankie does not seek to recover based upon the derogatory information implied about Norma in the advertisement. Frankie seeks to recover for the physical intrusion by various unsavory characters on her own solitude in her own home. . . .

It is alleged in the first amended complaint that defendants published the advertisement "with intent and design to injure, disgrace and aggrieve plaintiff Frankie Renee Vescovo and disregarding the comfort of said plaintiff's life and the peace and tranquility of her mind, and to invade and impair the seclusion of said plaintiff's private life. . . .'' Under the circumstances a cause of action for invasion of privacy was stated.

Note: Intentional Intrusions

Vescovo involves an allegation of invasion of privacy by the fourteen year old daughter of the woman whose address was included in the published ad. In sustaining the privacy claim on behalf of the daughter, for purposes of a motion on the pleading, did the court decide that under the privacy intrusion tort in California an action is available without any showing of intent on the part of the defendant? Does the allegation in the complaint satisfy the requirement that the defendant intentionally intrude upon the solitude of the plaintiff daughter?

Did the publication of the advertisement constitute the "intrusion" into the daughter's solitude? The intrusion tort almost always involves direct encroachment upon the solitude, seclusion or private affairs of the plaintiff by the defendant's actions. In *Vescovo*, the publication combined with the actions of numerous readers to bring about the alleged intrusion. Does the court adequately discuss the difference between a direct intrusion and indirect intrusion case? Suppose a newspaper mistakenly publishes the phone number of a person in an advertisement which reads: "Used color televisions for sale. Call between 11 and 12 p.m.'' The plaintiff for two nights receives numerous phone calls inquiring about the availability and price of the merchandise in the ad. Is this advertisement a violation of the intrusion tort under California law? If you were counsel for a newspaper that sold space for personal advertisements, what advice would you give your client to avoid potential liability after *Vescovo*?

7. THE PRIVACY INTRUSION TORT IN OTHER CONTEXTS: INVASIONS OF PRIVACY BY UNAUTHORIZED SURVEILLANCE OR ACQUISITION OF PERSONAL INFORMATION

a. De May v. Roberts Revisited

KNIGHT v. PENOBSCOT BAY MEDICAL CENTER
420 A.2d 915 (Me.1980).

Before Mckusick, C. J., AND Wernick, Godfrey, Glassman AND Roberts, JJ.

WERNICK, JUSTICE.

Plaintiffs William and Kathleen Knight, husband and wife, have appealed from a judgment of the Superior Court (Waldo County) entered on a jury verdict finding that none of the defendants (Penobscot Bay Medical Center, Sandra Robie, Theodore Robie and Albert J. Lantinen, Jr.) had invaded "privacy" rights of, or engaged in "outrageous" conduct causing severe emotional distress to, either of the plaintiffs. The appeals are taken from only that part of the judgment denying the claimed invasion of privacy. Two points are raised, each directed to an allegedly erroneous instruction to the jury by the presiding justice.

We deny the appeals and affirm the Superior Court judgment.

Late in the morning of January 8, 1977, plaintiff, Kathleen Knight, expecting to give birth, was admitted to the defendant hospital (Pen Bay). Kathleen had been accompanied by her husband, who left after she had been admitted. Two doctors were caring for Kathleen during her pregnancy, one of whom, the defendant Albert J. Lantinen, Jr., was on duty at the hospital when Kathleen was admitted. Another of the defendants, Sandra Robie, a registered nurse, was also there, on duty. She had completed her regular shift but was obliged to remain on duty because a severe snowstorm had delayed the arrival of the nurse who had the next duty.

Nurse Robie's husband, the defendant Theodore Robie, anticipating that his wife would leave the hospital at the end of her regular shift, had come to the hospital to meet her and take her home. When he learned that she would be detained, he decided to stay at the hospital until she finished her work. To give her husband something interesting to do while he was waiting for her, Nurse Robie asked Dr. Lantinen for permission to have her husband witness a birth. Dr. Lantinen had two patients waiting to give birth, a Mrs. Allen and the plaintiff, Kathleen Knight. Having sought, and obtained, the permission of Mrs. Allen for Mr. Robie to observe her giving birth, Dr. Lantinen told Mr. Robie that he could observe Mrs. Allen's delivery.[1]

---

1. Dr. Lantinen had spent the previous four years, until about six months before   the date in question, as an obstetrical resident at a teaching hospital in Columbus,

Mrs. Allen's pregnancy had been difficult. As the time approached for her to deliver, Dr. Lantinen realized that he would face complications. He decided that it would be better to have Mr. Robie witness a normal birth, and so he stationed Mr. Robie, who had put on hospital attire, where he could watch Kathleen Knight instead of Mrs. Allen.

Mr. Robie stood behind a viewing window in the surgical corridor, approximately twelve feet from the delivery table. From where he stood, Mr. Robie had a side view of Mrs. Knight's body, and her body was entirely covered by draping, except for her face and hands. Hence, Mr. Robie did not witness the actual process of delivering; what he saw was the baby being lifted up and then being placed on the mother's abdomen.

Meanwhile, Mr. Knight had returned to the hospital at about 5:00 p.m., and he then had someone call the delivery area. Kathleen was informed by Nurse Robie that Mr. Knight had returned to the hospital, and she requested that her husband come to the delivery room. Nurse Robie arranged for Mr. Knight to come to the delivery area. When he arrived there, Nurse Robie assisted him in putting on hospital attire and then brought him into the delivery room. Both Mr. and Mrs. Knight were positioned where they could see Mr. Robie observing through the window.

Dr. Lantinen had arranged for Nurse Robie, the more experienced nurse, to be with Mrs. Knight while he and Debra Strout, a licensed practical nurse, stayed with Mrs. Allen. Dr. Lantinen thought Mrs. Allen would deliver before Kathleen Knight, but Kathleen did the unexpected and began to deliver at the same time as Mrs. Allen. Nurse Robie asked Mr. Knight to go to the next room and ask Dr. Lantinen to attend to Kathleen. For some reason, Mr. Knight was unable to comply, so Nurse Robie motioned to her husband observing at the window and said something to him about going to get the doctor.[2] Dr. Lantinen came in and took over for Nurse Robie. Kathleen Knight gave birth, uneventfully, to a healthy baby girl who was normal in all respects.

Both Mr. and Mrs. Robie testified that they believed that Mr. Robie's presence had been authorized, that they were entirely unaware that his presence in the surgical corridor was offensive or intrusive to either patient, and that they had no intent to intrude. Similarly, Dr. Lantinen testified that he had no intention to "intrude upon anyone's privacy." During her stay in the hospital, Kathleen Knight never expressed any concern about Fred Robie's having been present at the window in the delivery area.

1.

Plaintiff's first point on appeal is that the presiding justice erred in failing to give one of several instructions plaintiffs had requested be

Ohio, where people routinely viewed deliveries.

2. The two nurses and Dr. Lantinen were the only people on duty in the delivery area at the time. It was undisputed that this was adequate staffing.

given.[3] We reject this contention.

. . .

More specifically, the justice acted correctly in refusing to instruct in accordance with plaintiff's requested instruction #8 because it was erroneous in three respects.

First, it failed to refer to the essential element that the defendant must *intend* as the result of his conduct that there be an intrusion upon another's solitude or seclusion.

Second, in reference to whether Mr. Robie's presence in the delivery area was "unnecessary" to serve the functional purpose involved, requested instruction #8 was couched in the language of a case decided almost a century ago.[4] It erroneously stated that Mr. Robie's "unnecessary" presence in the delivery area was *sufficient, without more,* to establish *as a matter of law* that Mr. Robie had unlawfully intruded upon the plaintiff's interest in seclusion.

Third, requested instruction #8 failed to differentiate between Kathleen Knight's interest in solitude or seclusion while giving birth and her husband's separate interest as arising from his being present at the time of birth. Since the interest in solitude or seclusion is protected as a *personal* interest, Mr. Knight could not properly claim an invasion of his separate personal interest merely because he was Kathleen Knight's husband. Thus, for example, if plaintiff Kathleen Knight had consented to the presence of Mr. Robie, it would be open to serious question whether it was also necessary to procure her husband's consent, even if it could be anticipated that he might be present in the delivery room. To focus upon this issue in yet another way, suppose that the third person "unnecessarily" present in the delivery area was unable to see Mrs. Knight but could see only her husband's reaction as he observed the delivery. Could it fairly be said that the fact alone of another's person's "unnecessary" presence was enough to establish as a matter of law that the husband's interest in being secluded at that time had been tortiously violated? Rather, would it not be that, at best, the issue is a question of fact, to be resolved in light of all the circumstances, more particularly because it is an essential element of the tort that the intrusion be such as would be "highly offensive to a reasonable person"?

3. The requested instruction at issue (numbered 8 among those plaintiffs requested) was the following:

8. The occasion of the birth of a child is one of the most sacred in our society and no one has the right to intrude unless invited or because of some real and pressing necessity. There is no pretense that such a necessity existed in this case. Mrs. Knight had a legal right to the privacy of the delivery room at such a time and the law secured this to her and to her hus-band after he joined her and the law requires others to observe it and to abstain from its violation. *De May v. Roberts,* 46 Mich. 160 [9 N.W. 146] (1881).

4. The language was from the case of *De May v. Roberts, supra,* n.3., decided even prior to the celebrated law review article of Brandeis and Warren, identifying "privacy" as an interest protected by law, at least in some of its aspects. L. Brandeis and S. Warren, "The Right to Privacy," 4 Harv. L.Rev. 193 (1890).

Note: Mr. Knight's Privacy

Consider the *Knight* court's analysis of the privacy interest of Mr. Knight, the husband of the person giving birth. The court finds that the jury could properly have concluded Mr. Knight's privacy rights were not violated because his rights are personal and not derived from Mrs. Knight's rights. Whether his solitude or seclusion had been invaded depended upon an assessment of all of the circumstances including the determination as to whether the intrusion would be "highly offensive to a reasonable person." The *Knight* court also states, "since the interest in solitude or seclusion is protected as a personal interest, Mr. Knight could not properly claim an invasion of his separate personal interests merely because he was Kathleen Knight's husband." *Knight v. Penobscot Bay Medical Center* at 918. Is the court wrong about Mr. Knight's personal privacy interest? Does the observation of the natural father's assistance in childbirth involve the acquiring of "intimate information" about him? Is *Knight* much ado about nothing? Is the unarticulated premise of the case that childbirth in a modern hospital setting is too public to grant privacy rights to the parents?

Note: the Intention Requirement as Viewed by the Courts in Vescovo and Knight

The court in *Vescovo* assumed that the causes of action in privacy that withstood the pleadings motions contained sufficient allegations of intention for the privacy intrusion tort to be a basis for a recovery. An analysis of intention in *Vescovo* under the general standard of intent in tort goes like this: the newspaper in publishing the ad knew with substantial certainty that the acts of harassment and intrusion into solitude would follow from the publication. Therefore, the newspaper "intended" the consequences which are the basis of the privacy intrusion tort. In addition, mistake of fact is not a defense to intent in tort and any argument invoked by the newspaper that the publication was based upon a mistaken view of the identity of the plaintiff would not be a defense.

The Restatement (Second) of Torts, Section 8A states:

> The word "intent" is used throughout the Restatement of this Subject to denote that the actor desires to cause consequences of his act, or that he believes that the consequences are substantially certain to result from it.

This section indicates that intent may be established two ways: by demonstrating that the defendant's purpose (desire) was to bring about the consequences that were the basis of tort or by demonstrating belief or knowledge on the part of the defendant that the consequences would occur from the act. The former may be described as "specific" intent and the latter "general" intent.

The unexamined concept of intention which the *Vescovo* court appears to be adopting for the intrusion tort is the general standard of intent.

Does the *Knight* court adopt a stricter view of intention? Does *Knight* require the plaintiff to establish that the defendant knew that consent was not given for the observation of childbirth, and he knew that it would be highly offensive to the plaintiff for the observation to occur, in order to show that the defendant intended to intrude into the solitude or seclusion of the plaintiff? Like the *Vescovo* court, the *Knight* court does not thoroughly examine the concept of intent that it is applying in the privacy tort action and the relationship of the concept to the general intent standards applicable to intentional torts.

Compare the Third Circuit's analysis in *O'Donnell v. United States*, 891 F.2d 1079 (3d Cir.1989). In *O'Donnell*, the court held that intrusion action was not available under Pennsylvania law against a psychiatrist that disclosed information under a mistaken but honest belief that he had the consent of the patient. In interpreting Section 652B of the Restatement as applied to the intrusion tort the court concluded, "that an actor commits an *intentional* intrusion only if he believes, or is substantially certain, that he lacks the necessary legal or personal permission to commit the intrusive act. We emphasize that the intrusion, as well as the action, must be intentional." 891 F.2d at 1083. Would you describe the strong sense of intent adopted by *O'Donnell* as the intent to wrong the plaintiff?

8. SURVIVAL

WELLER v. HOME NEWS PUBLISHING COMPANY

112 N.J.Super. 502, 271 A.2d 738 (1970).

Furman, J.S.C.

Defendants move for summary judgment (R. 4:46). The complaint filed December 3, 1968 and the pretrial order entered September 12, 1969, allege libel of Mrs. Weller, who died on August 19, 1970, and of her daughter and son-in-law, Mr. and Mrs. Semple, and invasion of Mrs. Weller's right of privacy. The facts, which are substantially undisputed, are unusual.

Mrs. Weller in 1967 was a paying patient in defendant hospital suffering from a heart affliction. Defendant Murray as its public relations director prepared a series of three articles dealing with charity patient care. Defendant newspaper published these articles. The second had as its central figure Prudence "Grandmom" Pickett, a charity patient not eligible for Medicare, cheerful, unselfish and destitute. "Grandmom" Pickett was fictitious, although the article, which was published on Sunday, December 10, 1967, did not so state. The accompanying photograph, captioned "Grandmom" Pickett, was that of Mrs. Weller in a walker in a profile view.

A release entitled "Photographic Consent" is alleged but not relied upon by defendants on this motion. Plaintiffs deny such consent.

As to Mrs. Weller's causes of action for libel and invasion of privacy, defendants urge their abatement upon her death during the pendency of the litigation. The authority cited is Alpaugh v. Conkling, 88 N. J. L. 64 (Sup.Ct. 1915), which held that the survival statute did not apply to a cause of action for slander by the decedent, who died during the pendency of the litigation. Justice Parker stated broadly that "the conclusion that the Legislature did not intend that libel or slander, considered purely as injurious to the feelings and reputation and apart from special damage, should survive to the personal representative."

. . .

Dean Prosser has pressed the view that

... the modern trend is definitely toward the view that tort causes of action and liabilities are as fairly a part of the estate of either plaintiff or defendant as contract debts, and that the question is rather one of why a fortuitous event such as death should extinguish a valid action. Accordingly, survival statutes gradually are being extended; and it may be expected that ultimately all tort actions will survive to the same extent as those founded on contract.

. . .

The survival statute abrogating the common law rule preserved a decedent's cause of action for trespass to person or property and a cause of action against a decedent for trespass to person or property without stated exceptions. To construe trespass to person as not encompassing libel or invasion of the right of privacy is to import a limitation into the survival statute which is not expressed. The term "trespass" in the statute is equated with "tort." It should not be modified by implication to exclude torts in which damages for emotional distress, not physical injury, are sought. Any such distinction is arbitrary. Damages for mental suffering and nervous anguish without physical injury were recoverable at common law in several causes of action arising out of trespass on the case, e.g., libel, slander, malicious prosecution and alienation of affections. Nor is there any logical basis for Justice Parker's dictum in *Alpaugh* that defamation actions alleging special damages, that is, property or money losses, are within the survival statute, although defamation actions alleging general damages are not.

The survival statute is, therefore, construed to apply to the torts of libel and invasion of the right of privacy resulting in damage to reputation and emotional distress without special damages. Alpaugh is specifically not followed. The motion for summary judgment on the two counts brought by Mrs. Weller, now deceased, is denied.

In their briefs defendants and plaintiffs have argued in favor of and opposing a summary judgment on a cause of action by Mr. and Mrs. Semple for invasion of their right of privacy. No such cause of action may be fairly said to be framed in the complaint or pretrial order.

In any event, there is no recognized cause of action for invasion of a relational right of privacy, except in some factual circumstances when the relative is deceased at the time of the tort. Note, "Relational Right of Privacy," 21 Rutgers L. Rev. 74 (1966); Hanson, Libel and Related Torts, paragraph 265 at 212 (1969).

Finally, defendants contend that the count by the Semples sounding in libel should be struck down. They urge that the courts have disallowed as a matter of law vicarious defamation actions arising out of a defamation of a relative, absent special damage or damage to plaintiff's reputation by necessary implication, e.g., that her child is illegitimate.

These authorities, apparently unimpeachable, are not governing. The theory of plaintiffs Semple is that they were libelled because the readers of defendant newspaper recognized the photograph of her mother, identified as a charity patient, and considered that her daughter and son-in-law were derelict in their obligation to her and had defrauded defendant hospital by representing that they were impoverished themselves. Neither the intent to defame nor the naming of the plaintiff is a necessary element in an action for libel.

Thus it appears that a fact question for the trier of fact would be raised if the proofs in their most favorable aspect would support findings that the relationship of plaintiffs Semple with decedent Mrs. Weller was known to an appreciable number of the readers of defendant newspaper and her identification as a charity patient reasonably understood by them as damaging plaintiff's reputations.

The motion for summary judgment on the cause of action in libel by plaintiffs Semple is, therefore, likewise denied.

Note: Survival Under Common Law Privacy Tort Actions

The *Weller* survival rule was reaffirmed by the New Jersey Supreme Court in *Canino v. New York News, Inc.*, 96 N.J. 189, 475 A.2d 528 (1984).

9. CONSENT/ASSUMPTION OF THE RISK

DIETEMANN v. TIME, INC.

449 F.2d 245 (9th Cir.1971).

Before CARTER and HUFSTEDLER, CIRCUIT JUDGES, and VON DER HEYDT, DISTRICT JUDGE.

HUFSTEDLER, CIRCUIT JUDGE . . .

This is an appeal from a judgment for plaintiff in an action for invasion of privacy. Jurisdiction was grounded in diversity. The parties agreed that California law governed. After a court trial plaintiff was awarded $1000 general damages. On appeal we are asked to consider significant questions involving the relationship between personal privacy and the freedom of the press.

The district court's decision is reported in Dietemann v. Time, Inc., 284 F. Supp. 925 (1968). The facts, as narrated by the district court, are these:

> Plaintiff, a disabled veteran with little education, was engaged in the practice of healing with clay, minerals, and herbs— as practiced, simple quackery.

> Defendant, Time, Incorporated, a New York corporation, publishes Life Magazine. Its November 1, 1963 edition carried an article entitled "Crackdown on Quackery." The article de-

picted plaintiff as a quack and included two pictures of him. One picture was taken at plaintiff's home on September 20, 1963, previous to his arrest on a charge of practicing medicine without a license, and the other taken at the time of his arrest.

Life Magazine entered into an arrangement with the District Attorney's Office of Los Angeles County whereby Life's employees would visit plaintiff and obtain facts and pictures concerning his activities. Two employees of Life, Mrs. Jacki Metcalf and Mr. William Ray, went to plaintiff's home on September 20, 1963. When they arrived at a locked gate, they rang a bell and plaintiff came out of his house and was told by Mrs. Metcalf and Ray that they had been sent there by a friend, a Mr. Johnson. The use of Johnson's name was a ruse to gain entrance. Plaintiff admitted them and all three went into the house and into plaintiff's den.

The plaintiff had some equipment which could at best be described as gadgets, not equipment which had anything to do with the practice of medicine. Plaintiff, while examining Mrs. Metcalf, was photographed by Ray with a hidden camera without the consent of plaintiff. One of the pictures taken by him appeared in Life Magazine showing plaintiff with his hand on the upper portion of Mrs. Metcalf's breast while he was looking at some gadgets and holding what appeared to be a wand in his right hand. Mrs. Metcalf had told plaintiff that she had a lump in her breast. Plaintiff concluded that she had eaten some rancid butter 11 years, 9 months, and 7 days prior to that time. Other persons were seated in the room during this time.

The conversation between Mrs. Metcalf and plaintiff was transmitted by radio transmitter hidden in Mrs. Metcalf's purse to a tape recorder in a parked automobile occupied by Joseph Bride, Life Employee, John Miner of the District Attorney's Office, and Grant Leake, an investigator of the State Department of Public Health. While the recorded conversation was not quoted in the article in Life, it was mentioned that Life correspondent Bride was making notes of what was being received via the radio transmitter, and such information was at least referred to in the article.

The foregoing events were photographed and recorded by an arrangement among Miner of the District Attorney's Office, Leake of the State Department of Public Health, and Bride, a representative of Life. It had been agreed that Life would obtain pictures and information for use as evidence, and later could be used by Life for publication.

Prior to the occurrences of September 20, 1963, on two occasions the officials had obtained recordings of conversations in plaintiff's home; however, no pictures had been secured. Life employees had not participated in obtaining the recordings on these occasions.

On October 15, 1963, plaintiff was arrested at his home on a charge of practicing medicine without a license in violation of Section 26280, California Health and Safety Code. At the time of his arrest, many pictures were made by Life of plaintiff at his home. Plaintiff testified that he did not agree to pose for the pictures but allowed pictures because he thought the officers could require it. Also present were newspaper men who had also been invited by the officials to be present at the time of arrest.

Defendant contends that plaintiff posed for pictures at the time of his arrest and thus permission was given to take those pictures. As hereinafter pointed out, it is unnecessary to decide whether or not permission was given to take pictures at the time of his arrest.

Plaintiff, although a journeyman plumber, claims to be a scientist. Plaintiff had no listings and his home had no sign of any kind. He did not advertise, nor did he have a telephone. He made no charges when he attempted to diagnose or to prescribe herbs and minerals. He did accept contributions.

Life's article concerning plaintiff was not published until after plaintiff was arrested but before his plea on June 1, 1964 of nolo contendere for violations of Section 2141 of the California Business and Professions Code and Section 26280 of the California Health and Safety Code (misdemeanors).

. . .

Defendant's claim that the plaintiff's house was open to the public is not sustained by the evidence. The plaintiff was administering his so-called treatments to people who visited him. He was not a medical man of any type. He did not advertise. He did not have a phone. He did have a lock on his gate. To obtain entrance it was necessary to ring a bell. He conducted his activities in a building which was his home. The employees of defendant gained entrance by a subterfuge.

The district court concluded:

The publication in Life Magazine on November 1, 1963 of plaintiff's picture taken without his consent in his home on September 20, 1963 was an invasion of his privacy under California law for which he is entitled to damages. The acts of defendant also constituted an invasion of plaintiff's right to privacy guaranteed by the Constitution of the United States which would entitle him to relief under Section 1983, Title 42, United States Code.

The court awarded $1,000 general damages "for injury to [Dietemann's] feelings and peace of mind". Time appeals from that decision.

The appeal presents three ultimate issues: (1) Under California law, is a cause of action for invasion of privacy established upon proof that defendant's employees, by subterfuge, gained entrance to the office portion of plaintiff's home wherein they photographed him and electronically recorded and transmitted to third persons his conversation without his consent as a result of which he suffered emotional distress? (2) Does the First Amendment insulate defendant from liability for invasion of privacy because defendant's employees did those acts for the purpose of gathering material for a magazine story and a story was thereafter published utilizing some of the material thus gathered? (3) Were the defendant's employees acting as special agents of the police and, if so, did their acts violate the First, Fourth, and Fourteenth Amendments of the Federal Constitution, thereby subjecting defendant to liability under the Civil Rights Act (42 U.S.C. Section 1983)? Because we hold that plaintiff proved a cause of action under California law and that the First Amendment does not insulate the defendant from liability, we do not reach the third issue.

Were it necessary to reach the Civil Rights Act questions, we would be obliged to explore the relationship between the defendant's employees and the police for the purpose of ascertaining the existence of the "color of law" element of the Act. Because we do not reach the issue, we can and do accept the defendant's disclaimer that its employees were acting for or on behalf of the police.

In jurisdictions other than California in which a common law tort for invasion of privacy is recognized, it has been consistently held that surreptitious electronic recording of a plaintiff's conversation causing him emotional distress is actionable. Despite some variations in the description and the labels applied to the tort, there is agreement that publication is not a necessary element of the tort, that the existence of a technical trespass is immaterial, and that proof of special damages is not required.

Although the issue has not been squarely decided in California, we have little difficulty in concluding that clandestine photography of the plaintiff in his den and the recordation and transmission of his conversation without his consent resulting in his emotional distress warrants recovery for invasion of privacy in California.

... It does not become such a license simply because the person subjected to the intrusion is reasonably suspected of committing a crime.

Defendant relies upon the line of cases commencing with New York Times Co. v. Sullivan (1964) 376 U.S. 254, 84 S.Ct. 710, 11 L.Ed.2d 686 and extending through Rosenbloom v. Metromedia, Inc. (1971) 403 U.S. 29, 91 S.Ct. 1811, 29 L.Ed.2d 296 (1971) to sustain its contentions that (1) publication of news, however tortiously gathered, insulates defendant from liability for the antecedent tort, and (2) even if it is not thus shielded from liability, those cases prevent consideration of publication as an element in computing damages.

As we previously observed, publication is not an essential element of plaintiff's cause of action. Moreover, it is not the foundation for the invocation of a privilege. Privilege concepts developed in defamation cases and to some extent in privacy actions in which publication is an essential component are not relevant in determining liability for intrusive conduct antedating publication. . . .

No interest protected by the First Amendment is adversely affected by permitting damages for intrusion to be enhanced by the fact of later publication of the information that the publisher improperly acquired. Assessing damages for the additional emotional distress suffered by a plaintiff when the wrongfully acquired data are purveyed to the multitude chills intrusive acts. It does not chill freedom of expression guaranteed by the First Amendment. A rule forbidding the use of publication as an ingredient of damages would deny to the injured plaintiff recovery for real harm done to him without any countervailing benefit to the legitimate interest of the public in being informed. The same rule would encourage conduct by news media that grossly offends ordinary men.

The judgment is affirmed.

JAMES M. CARTER, CIRCUIT JUDGE (concurring and dissenting).

I concur in all of the majority opinion except that portion refusing to meet the issue of the liability of defendants' agents, acting as agents of the police.

Note: Media Liability for Invasions of Privacy in the Information Gathering Phase of Investigatory Reporting

As *Dietemann* illustrates, the intrusion tort may impose responsibility on the media for invasions of privacy that occur in the information gathering phase of investigatory reporting. The *Dietemann* court makes a clear distinction between the first amendment protection that is afforded the media in *acquiring* information and the first amendment protection afforded the media in *publishing* information after it has been acquired. In a passage that is often cited, Judge Hufstedler indicates that the constitutional protection for the former is considerably less than that for the latter:

> The defendant claims that the First Amendment immunizes it from liability for invading plaintiff's den with a hidden camera and its concealed electronic instruments because its employees were gathering news and its instrumentalities are "indispensable tools of investigative reporting." We agree that news gathering is an integral part of news dissemination. We strongly disagree, however, that the hidden mechanical contrivances are "indispensable tools" of newsgathering. Investigative reporting is an ancient art; its successful practice long antecedes the invention of miniature cameras and electronic devices. . . . The First Amendment is not a license to trespass, to steal, or to intrude by electronic means into the precincts of another's home or office. It does not become such a license simply because the person subjected to the intrusion is reasonably suspected of committing a crime.

449 F.2d 245, 249 (9th Cir.1971)

When the acquired information becomes published as part of a story, the availability of a cause of action in tort for the publication depends upon whether the requirements of the public disclosure tort are satisfied. *See* materials *infra*. In public disclosure tort actions, if the information is "newsworthy," no liability in tort attaches for its publication. Is the information in the story published by *Time* newsworthy? Although the *Dietemann* court found that there was no separate tort liability against *Time* for the publication alone, the court would allow the extent of publication to be considered as a factor in assessing damages. If the first amendment protects the media in the publication of the information, has the *Dietemann* court adequately explained why it would not violate the first amendment to consider the publication in determining damages under the intrusion tort action? Compare the *Dietmann* court's view of the publication damage issue with that of the *Food Lion* court *infra*.

Note: Requirement that the Media Directly Participate in the Intrusion

There are a number of cases that have dealt with the question of the liability of the media for publishing information that has been received from someone who has acquired the information under circumstances that constitute a violation of the intrusion tort. In these cases, courts have generally determined that no liability attaches to the media recipient of the information. Although the discussion in the cases is inadequate, the results are consistent with tort standards of responsibility. Unless the media defendant directly participates in the intrusion activity or enters into a contractual arrangement for acquiring the information through tortious means, the defendant has not committed the action necessary for liability and is not a joint tortfeasor. As innocent recipients of the information after the fact, two of the elements necessary for recovery under the intrusion tort may not be satisfied against the media: that the actions of the media caused the intrusion and that the media intended to intrude upon the solitude, seclusion or private affairs of the plaintiff. Such cases are distinguishable from *Dietemann* because *Time* actively participated in the intrusion. *See, e.g.,* *Pearson v. Dodd*, 410 F.2d 701 (D.C.Cir.), *cert. denied*, 395 U.S. 947 (1969); *Liberty Lobby, Inc. v. Pearson*, 390 F.2d 489 (D.C.Cir.1967); *Griffith v. Rancocas Valley Hosp.*, 8 Media L. Rep. (BNA) 1760 (N.J.Super.1982); *Bilney v. Evening Star Newspaper Co.*, 43 Md.App. 560, 406 A.2d 652 (1979).

In *Pearson v. Dodd*, the court explained the reason why the media was not liable for the mere receipt of the fruits of intrusion:

> In an untried and developing area of tort law, we are not prepared to go so far. A person approached by an eavesdropper with an offer to share in the information gathered through the eavesdropping would perhaps play the nobler part should he spurn the offer and shut his ears. However, it seems to us that at this point, it would place to great a strain on human weakness to hold one liable in damages who merely succumbs to temptation and listens. *Id.* at 704.

On facts similar to *Pearson*, could the media be responsible under laws making the receipt of stolen property a crime? Note that the *Pearson* court held that the personal data photocopied from Dodd's file was not his property for purposes of the tort of conversion. *Id* at 708. Would a law making it a crime to publish information that was illegally acquired violate the first amendment. Consider *Florida Star* and discussion in notes, infra .

Compare *Dietemann* with *In re Mack*, 386 Pa. 251, 126 A.2d 679 (1956), *cert. denied*, 352 U.S. 1002 (1957), where the Supreme Court of Pennsylvania upheld a contempt citation against the media for taking the picture of a prisoner in violation of a court rule while he was within ten feet of the courthouse.

Suppose a newspaper wrote a series of articles on pornography and published pictures of local citizens perusing sexually explicit magazines and purchasing sexual aids in an adult book store. The pictures were taken with a hidden camera by a newspaper employee who posed as a prospective customer. Would the newspaper be liable to the subjects of the photographs under the privacy intrusion tort?

Media Ride–Alongs

WILSON v. LAYNE

1999 WL 320817.

CHIEF JUSTICE REHNQUIST delivered the opinion of the Court.

[In the execution of an arrest warrant for Dominic Wilson for violation of probation for violent felonies, United States Marshals and policemen from Montgomery County, Maryland invited a reporter and photographer from the Washington Post to accompany them. The arrest warrants were addressed to "any duly authorized peace officer." Unknown to the police the address on the arrest warrants was that of Dominic Wilson's parents. At 6:45 a.m. the officers with media representation in tow entered the home while the Wilsons were in bed; Charles Wilson clad in a pair of briefs was subdued on the floor after angrily demanding that the officers state their business; Geraldine Wilson wearing only a nightgown observed the restraint of her husband by the police. The Washington Post photographer took numerous pictures and the reporter observed the confrontation between the police and Charles Wilson but they were never involved in the execution of the arrest warrant. The Wilsons sued the federal marshals for damages under a *Bivens* theory and the state offices under § 1983. (The photographer, reporter and Washington Post were not defendants in the case.) The District Court denied defendants motion for summary judgment on the basis of qualified immunity. The Fourth Circuit Court of Appeals heard the case three times; initially a divided panel reversed holding that the officers were entitled to qualified immunity; twice thereafter the Fourth Circuit reheard the case *en banc* and concluded that because the right not to have the media present during execution of an arrest warrant was not clearly established, the officers were entitled to qualified immunity.

Five judges dissented, contending that the Fourth Amendment was violated and qualified immunity was not a defense to the officers.]

Although this case involves suits under both § 1983 and Bivens, the qualified immunity analysis is identical under either cause of action. A court evaluating a claim of qualified immunity 'must first determine whether the plaintiff has alleged the deprivation of an actual constitutional right at all, and if so, proceed to determine whether that right was clearly established at the time of the alleged violation.'

We now turn to the Fourth Amendment question.

[Justice Rehnquist summarized English precedent on the value of privacy in the home.]

The Fourth Amendment embodies this centuries-old principle of respect for the privacy of the home....

Our decisions have applied these basic principles ... to situations, like those in this case, in which police enter a home under the authority of an arrest warrant in order to take into custody the suspect named in the warrant. In *Payton v. New York*, we noted that ... the common-law tradition at the time of the drafting of the Fourth Amendment was ambivalent on the question of whether police could enter a home without a warrant. We were ultimately persuaded that the "overriding respect for the sanctity of the home that has been embedded in our traditions since the origins of the Republic" meant that absent a warrant or exigent circumstances, police could not enter a home to make an arrest. We decided that "an arrest warrant founded on probable cause implicitly carries with it the limited authority to enter a dwelling in which the suspect lives when there is reason to believe the suspect is within."

Here, of course, the officers had such a warrant, and they were undoubtedly entitled to enter the Wilson home in order to execute the arrest warrant for Dominic Wilson. But it does not necessarily follow that they were entitled to bring a newspaper reporter and a photographer with them. In *Horton v. California*, we held "[i]f the scope of the search exceeds that permitted by the terms of a validly issued warrant or the character of the relevant exception from the warrant requirement, the subsequent seizure is unconstitutional without more." While this does not mean that every police action while inside a home must be explicitly authorized by the text of the warrant, see *Michigan v. Summers*, (Fourth Amendment allows temporary detainer of homeowner while police search the home pursuant to warrant), the Fourth Amendment does require that police actions in execution of a warrant be related to the objectives of the authorized intrusion.

Certainly the presence of reporters inside the home was not related to the objectives of the authorized intrusion. Respondents concede that the reporters did not engage in the execution of the warrant, and did not assist the police in their task. The reporters therefore were not present for any reason related to the justification for police entry into the home—the apprehension of Dominic Wilson.

Respondents argue that the presence of the Washington Post reporters in the Wilsons' home nonetheless served a number of legitimate law enforcement purposes. They first assert that officers should be able to exercise reasonable discretion about when it would "further their law enforcement mission to permit members of the news media to accompany them in executing a warrant." But this claim ignores the importance of the right of residential privacy at the core of the Fourth Amendment. It may well be that media ride-alongs further the law enforcement objectives of the police in a general sense, but that is not the same as furthering the purposes of the search. Were such generalized 'law enforcement objectives' themselves sufficient to trump the Fourth Amendment, the protections guaranteed by that Amendment's text would be significantly watered down.

Respondents next argue that the presence of third parties could serve the law enforcement purpose of publicizing the government's efforts to combat crime, and facilitate accurate reporting on law enforcement activities. There is certainly language in our opinions interpreting the First Amendment which points to the importance of 'the press' in informing the general public about the administration of criminal justice. In *Cox Broadcasting Corp. v. Cohn*, for example, we said 'in a society in which each individual has but limited time and resources with which to observe at first hand the operations of his government, he relies necessarily upon the press to bring to him in convenient form the facts of those operations. No one could gainsay the truth of these observations, or the importance of the First Amendment in protecting press freedom from abridgement by the government. But the Fourth Amendment also protects a very important right, and in the present case it is in terms of that right that the media ride-alongs must be judged.

Surely the possibility of good public relations for the police is simply not enough, standing alone, to justify the ride-along intrusion into a private home. And even the need for accurate reporting on police issues in general bears no direct relation to the constitutional justification for the police intrusion into a home in order to execute a felony arrest warrant.

Finally, respondents argue that the presence of third parties could serve in some situations to minimize police abuses and protect suspects, and also to protect the safety of the officers. While it might be reasonable for police officers to themselves videotape home entries as par of a "quality control" effort to ensure that the rights of homeowners are being respected, or even to preserve evidence, cf. *Ohio v. Robinette*, 519 U.S. 33, 35 (1996) (noting the use of a "mounted video camera" to record the details of a routine traffic stop), such a situation is significantly different from the media presence in this case. The Washington Post reporters in the Wilsons' home were working on a story for their own purposes. They were not present for the purpose of protecting the officers, much less the Wilsons. A private photographer was acting for private purposes, as evidenced in part by the fact that the newspaper and not the police retained the photographs. Thus, although the presence of third parties during the execution of a warrant may in some circumstances by constitutionally permissible, the presence of these third parties was not.

The reasons advanced by respondents, taken in their entirety, fall short of justifying presence of media inside a home. We hold that it is a violation of the Fourth Amendment for police to bring members of the media or other third parties into a home during the execution of a warrant when the presence of the third parties in the home was not in aid of the execution of the warrant.

Since the police action in this case violated the petitioners' Fourth Amendment right, we now must decide whether this right was clearly established at the time of the search. What [qualified immunity] means in practice is that 'whether an official protected by qualified immunity may be held personally liable for an allegedly unlawful official action generally turns on the 'objective legal reasonableness' of the action, assessed in light of the legal rules that were 'clearly established' at the time it was taken. . . .

'Clearly established' for purposes of qualified immunity means that '[t]he contours of the right must be sufficiently clear that a reasonable official would understand that what he is doing violates that right. This is not to say that an official action is protected by qualified immunity unless the very action in question has previously been held unlawful, but it is to say that in the light of pre-existing law the unlawfulness must be apparent.'

In this case, the appropriate question is the objective inquiry of whether a reasonable officer could have believed hat bringing members of the media into a home during the execution of an arrest warrant was lawful, in light of clearly established law and the information the officers possessed.

We hold that it was not unreasonable for a police officer in April 1992 to have believed that bringing media observers along during the execution of an arrest warrant (even in a home) was lawful. First, the constitutional question presented by this case is by no means open and shut. The Fourth Amendment protects the rights of homeowners from entry without a warrant, but there was a warrant here. The question is whether the invitation to the media exceeded the scope of the search authorized by the warrant. Accurate media coverage of police activities serves an important public purpose, and it is not obvious from the general principles of the Fourth Amendment that the conduct of the officers in this case violated the Amendment.

Second, although media ride-alongs of one sort or another had apparently become a common police practice, in 1992 there were no judicial opinions holding that this practice became unlawful when it entered a home. The only published decision directly on point was a state intermediate court decision which, though it did not engage in an extensive Fourth Amendment analysis, nonetheless held that such conduct was not unreasonable. . . .

Petitioners have not brought to our attention any cases of controlling authority in their jurisdiction at the time of the incident which clearly established the rule on which they seek to rely, nor have they identified a consensus of cases of persuasive authority such that a reasonable officer could not have believed that his actions were lawful.

Finally, important to our conclusion was the reliance by the United States marshals in this case on a Marshal's Service ride-along policy which explicitly contemplated that media who engaged in ride-alongs might enter private homes with their cameras as part of fugitive apprehension arrests. Such a policy, of course, could not make reasonable a belief that was contrary to a decided body of case law. But here the state of the law as to third parties accompanying police on home entries was at best undeveloped, and it was not unreasonable for law enforcement officers to look and rely on their formal ride-along policies.

Between the time of the events of this case and today's decision, a split among the Federal Circuits in fact developed on the question whether media ride-alongs that enter homes subject the police to money damages. If judges thus disagree on a constitutional question, it is unfair to subject police to money damages for picking the losing side of the controversy.

For the foregoing reasons, the judgment of the Court of Appeals is affirmed.

[Justice Stevens dissented on the qualified immunity holding.] Stevens disagreed with the majority's bare assertion that the constitutional question was not open and shut noting that every federal appellate judge and all members of the Court agreed that media ride-alongs violated the fourth amendment. He found the majority's view inconsistent with *United States v. Lanier*, 520 U.S. 259 (1997) where the Court held that a state judge had fair warning that extorting sexual favors from a potential litigant violated the constitution even though there was no specific judicial holding on the issue. Justice Stevens concludes that the Court's restricted concept of clearly established constitutional rights under the qualified immunity doctrine erodes Fourth Amendment protection for privacy of the home:

> The conduct in this case, as the Court itself reminds us, contravened the Fourth Amendment's core protection of the home. In shielding this conduct as if it implicated only the unsettled margins of our jurisprudence, the Court today authorizes one free violation of the well-established rule it reaffirms.

Note: Media Liability in Ride-Along Cases

As noted by the Court in *Wilson v. Layne* there was general agreement in the federal appellate courts that media ride-alongs violated the fourth amendment. However the circuits were split on the question whether qualified immunity as a matter of law was available as a defense to the law enforcement officers. Compare, *Ayeni v. Motolla*, 35 F.3d 680 (2d Cir. 1994) with the Ninth Circuit case that was appealed in *Wilson v. Layne*. The question of Media Liability in a *Bivens* or section 1983 case was not decided in *Wilson v. Layne* because the media were not sued. Recall that in *Dietemann*, supra, the media was sued along with the police. But the court declined to find the media to be sufficiently involved with law enforcement to be acting under color of state law (state action) for purposes of section 1983. If the media in a ride-along case is not the state then liability under *Bivens* or section 1983 would not attach. As discussed later, liability would turn on whether the media violated a common law tort or state or federal statute. What if the media were sufficiently involved with the police action to be viewed as acting under color of state law (state action)? Would the media have the same qualified immunity as the police officers?

This issue was litigated in *Berger v. Hanlon*, 129 F.2d 505 (9th Cir. 1997). In *Berger*, federal agents entered into a contract with Cable News Network and Turner Broadcasting System which authorized the filming and recording of a search of Paul and Emma Bergers' ranch for broadcasting of environmental television shows. The filming was motivated by CNN's desire to demonstrate that Paul Berger was poisoning eagles; the federal government wanted the positive publicity that would come from the television exposure. A search warrant was issued for the Bergers' ranch by judge that had no knowledge of the agreement between the federal government and CNN to film the search. More than eight hours of video and audio recordings were made by CNN during the execution of the search warrant; the video and audio recording was broadcast by CNN. The Bergers sued the federal agents and CNN in *Bivens* action. The Ninth Circuit held that qualified immunity did not protect the federal officials. CNN was found to be acting as the government because of the contractual relation and therefore subject to potential liability under *Bivens* However, on the basis of *Richardson v. Mcknight*, 117 S.Ct. 2100 (1997) the court held that CNN was not entitled to the qualified immunity defense that the federal agents were. In *Richardson* the court held that the prison guards employed by a private firm that had been hired by the state of Tennessee to manage its correctional facilities were not entitled to qualified immunity action in a 1983 action. CNN appealed the ruling. The Supreme Court denied the writ of certiorari. See *CNN v. Berger*, 1999 WL 343316 (U.S.). The effect of the denial is to uphold the decision of the Ninth Circuit. Does it make sense to treat CNN as the government for purposes of the fourth amendment claim but not for purposes of the qualified immunity defense? See *Richardson*, Id., for the Court's answer. What defense, if any would be available to CNN to the damage action?

Note: Ambush Journalism

Are the tort and constitutional theories as interpreted in *Dietemann* and *Wilson v. Layne* adequate protection for persons who have been investigated by the media with methods that have come to be described in the media as "ambush journalism?" While not precisely defined, "ambush journalism" refers to techniques of investigative reporting that include various forms of misrepresentation by the media to acquire information that is subsequently published as a form of investigative journalism. Most commonly as in *Dietemann* employees or agents of the media will be sent to places of business with hidden cameras and tape recorders impersonating potential customers, clients or employees. In these cases consent is given for the agent to be on the property. But the question is whether the consent is vitiated by the tacit misrepresentation by the agent as to the reason for their presence. Another form of ambush journalism is where the media procures consent for a video or audio taped interviews but misrepresents the ultimate use of the information that is acquired in the interview.

Wilson v. Layne represents perhaps the easiest of the cases involving forms of "ambush journalism." Court authorized law enforcement searches of the home have a long standing history of circumscribed conditions for appropriate reasonableness under the fourth amendment. The idea of strangers to those in law enforcement being present during the execution of a search or arrest warrant in the home is, as *Wilson v. Layne* suggests, clearly contrary to this tradition. As noted by Justice Stevens in dissent all of the federal appellate court judges and a unanimous Court found that media ride-alongs violated the fourth amendment. See, for example, *Ayeni v. Mottola*, 35 F.3d 680 (2d Cir. 1994).

Cases decided since *Dietemann* that have involved media investigations independent of law enforcement searches suggest that the evolving law is more complicated. If *Dietemann* is read to stand for the hard proposition that the first amendment does not provide the media with a privilege to commit torts in the fact or information gathering process, the tactics of ambush journalism described above might subject the media to liability for trespass to land, privacy intrusion, fraudulent misrepresentation or intentional infliction of emotional distress. Suits by individuals in ambush journalism cases based upon the *Dietemann* principle has received a mixed reception by courts.

a. *Desnick v. ABC*

Popular investigative television programs like ABC's Prime Time Live (PTL) and CBS's Street Stories have been sued under a variety of tort theories, including trespass to land, privacy intrusion and fraud. PTL was the defendant in an important case that reached the Seventh Circuit. In *Desnick v. ABC*. 44 F.3d 1345 (7th Cir.1995), the court speaking through Chief Judge Posner dismissed trespass to property, privacy intrusion and fraud claims brought against PTL and their star reporter Sam Donaldson by Dr. Desnick and two ophthalmolic surgeons. Dr. Desnick's company had twenty-five offices and performed more than 10,000 cataract operations a year. PTL had contacted Dr. Desnick for a story on large cataract practices. Desnick was informed that the program would not involve "ambush" interviews or "undercover surveillance" and that it would be "fair and balanced." Without Dr. Desnick's knowledge ABC sent agents with concealed cameras as "test patients" to two offices other than where the consented to interview took place. The secret videotapes of examinations of the "test patients" was the basis for a PTL program whose general theme was that unnecessary cataract operations were performed in Dr. Desnick's offices.

The court held that the consent given for entry to the premises was a valid defense to the trespass and privacy intrusion tort claims even though consent was procured through misrepresentation. In a remarkable line of reasoning the court found that the fraudulent consent in the case was closer to those cases where the law gave effect to consent procured by fraud than it was to the consent in *Dietemann*. Illustrative of the cases upholding fraudulently gained consent were that of a restaurant critic who conceals her identity when ordering a meal and an example in the Second Restatement of Torts of a man who obtains consent to sexual intercourse with a woman but pays her with counterfeit currency. Judge Posner posited that consent was legally valid in these cases because the underlying interests of the torts of trespass and battery were not implicated. The misrepresentation about the validity of the currency did not make the consent an affront to dignity since she had consented to the sexual contact. The misrepresentation to the restaurant owner did not implicate trespass interests because the owner wanted customers.

Cases such as *Dietemann, De May v. Roberts* and those involving sexual intercourse with a psychotherapist where misrepresentation vitiated consent were distinguishable. These cases were viewed as implicating privacy and battery interests because they involved a violation of the doctor-patient privilege and invasion of a person's private space. The surreptitious videotaping in the ophthalmologists' offices did not implicate trespass or privacy interests. There was no disruption of the activities of the office, violation of the doctor-patient privilege or eavesdropping on private conversations—only those between the consenting testor and staff were recorded.

Do you find Judge Posner's "underlying interest" approach an adequate basis for distinguishing the activities of the media in *Dietemann*? Are physicians' offices and restaurants private or public places for purposes of the privacy intrusion tort? Does the analysis of the court in *Dietemann* support limiting the ruling to surreptitious video and audio surveillance in a private residence? The *Desnick* court suggests that *Dietemann* is limited to private residents or apartments.

PTL was involved in another suit where their agent accepted a job as a "tele-psychic" without any relevant experience and videotaped the business operations and secretly taped two of her conversations with tele-psychic Mark Sanders. The taping took place at two of the numerous three-sided cubicles that were provided for tele-psychics in a large room. Each cubicle was five feet high and a conversation could be overheard between cubicles. Sanders was awarded 1.2 million dollars after the trial court, relying in part on *Dietemann* had instructed the jury that California recognized a "sub-tort"—the right to be free from photographic invasion. The judgment was reversed on appeal because Sanders had no reasonable expectation of privacy in conversation and images in an open work area. The *Dietemann* principle was limited to the surreptitious videotaping in private places such as: (1) homes and apartments; (2) changing areas; and (2) closed rooms where employees receive work evaluations. *Sanders v. ABC*, 60 Cal.Rptr.2d 595, 597–98 (Cal.Ct.App. 1997).

In dissent Justice Spencer would have affirmed the judgment but not on the basis of the sub-tort of photographic privacy. Rather, the deceitful gaining of entrance and surreptitious videotaping violated Sanders' right of autonomy privacy in the workplace. Justice Spencer relied upon the elaboration of the constitutional right to privacy under the California constitution in *Hill v. NCAA*, discussed in Chapter Two. In *Hill* the court recognized two legally protected privacy interests— informational privacy and autonomy privacy. Autonomy privacy includes "unwarranted . . . observation . . . to certain private matters." (The *Sanders* court did not have the issue of trespass or fraud before it.)

Compare the Court's analysis of fraudulently induced consent in *Desnick* with *Food Lion Inc. v. Capital Cities/ABC*, 887 F.Supp. 811 (M.D.N.C.1995). In *Food Lion* the Court held that a retail food supermarket chain had stated a claim for trespass, fraud and unfair business practices under North Carolina law against PTL. Food Lion alleged that PTL staff members had fabricated employment applications and identities in order to gain employment and surreptitiously videotape conversations with food Lion employees and conditions in the supermarkets. Of the 50 hours of hidden camera footage taken by PTL agents, five or six minutes were aired in a PTL story critical of Food Lion. Following the broadcast Food Lion alleged that retail sales suffered and that Food Lion's public stock value decreased. Consent to PTL's agents entry was found not to be a defense to the trespass, fraud and unfair business practices claims because under North Carolina law consent was negated by the abuse and excess of the authority to enter that had occurred by the subsequent wrongful acts of PTL.

For a thorough examination of *Food Lion*, *Desnick* and legal issues raised by surreptitious newsgathering generally, see, David Logan, *Naked Media: Judges, Juries, and the Law of Surreptitious Newsgathering*, 83 Iowa L. Rev. 161 (1997). Logan rejects granting an immunity for newsgathering activities but argues for a liability and damage regime in which judges and jurors would take into account the value of the story and apply practical doctrine tools of general tort law to limit compensatory or punitive damages. One practical doctrinal tool is the general restriction in tort against recovering damages for "pure economic harm." Others include judicial supervision through jury instructions and the review of jury awards to limit consequential economic loss to predictable economic damages that are caused by the tortious conduct. Excessive punitive damages would be controlled by legislative caps and judicial review of jury awards.

b. *Shulman v. Group W Productions, Inc.*

As noted, supra 177, the Supreme Court of California interpreted the state constitutional right to privacy to extend to private action in *Hill v. NCAA*. As a result privacy law in California is unique amongst the states. The constitutional privacy right is a norm that reaches many private activities that also come within the reach of statutory regulation or the common law privacy torts. Developing a rational and unified concept of the right to privacy in view of this multilayered privacy law will be a challenge to the courts in California. *Hill* involved mandatory drug testing of an athlete at a private university (Stanford). The court adopted a different test under the state constitution for invasion of privacy in the private and public sphere. Government invasions of privacy were subject to strict scrutiny; invasions of privacy in the private sphere were subject to a less rigorous balancing of interest test: the plaintiff first demonstrates serious invasion by the defendant of a legally protected privacy interest, then the defendant must demonstrate a competing interest that justifies the invasion.

The balancing test adopted by the *Hill* court to uphold the mandatory drug testing rule is similar to the balancing test applied by the United States Supreme Court in fourth amendment drug testing cases. It is also similar to the balancing test that some courts have applied to challenges to drug testing in the private sector under the privacy intrusion tort. Therefore, *Hill* did not require the court to elaborate much on the relationship between the constitutional right to privacy and the privacy intrusion tort in California.

In *Shulman v. Group W Productions, Inc.*, 955 P.2d 469 (Cal.1998) the court spoke more fully on this relationship in an important case that is of general significance to privacy law. Mrs. Shulman and her son sued a television producer that videotaped them after an automobile accident and while they were transported to a hospital. Portions of the videotape were used in a documentary on medical rescues. The lawsuit was brought for violation of the intrusion tort, private facts torts and for violation of a California statute prohibiting recording of "confidential" communication. A majority of the court held that summary judgment was proper on the private facts cause of action but not on the intrusion or statutory cause of action.

Ruth and Wayne Shulman were injured when the car in which they were riding flew off the highway and tumbled into a drainage ditch. Both had to be freed from the upside down vehicle by a device called "the jaws of life." A rescue helicopter with a nurse (Carnahan), medic and a video camera operator (Cooke) aboard arrived at the scene. Nurse Carnahan wore a wireless microphone that picked up her conversations with Ruth and rescue personnel. Cooke videotaped the rescue scene. The videotape was edited to a nine minute piece and was broadcast five days after the accident as a segment of a program named, "On Scene: Emergency Response."

The program included video and narrative overlay of the helicopter on the way and at the accident scene and while Ruth is being moved from the helicopter to the hospital. The court summarizes portions of the segment at the accident scene:

> "This is terrible. Am I dreaming?" She also asks what happened and where the rest of her family is, repeating the questions even after being told she was in an accident and the other family members are being cared for. While being loaded

into the helicopter on a stretcher, Ruth says: "I just want to die." Carnahan reassures her that she is "going to do real well," but Ruth repeats: "I just want to die. I don't want to go through this .."

The helicopter flight segment included nurse Carnahan speaking into a microphone about Ruth's vital signs—saying that Ruth had no sensation in her feet. Ruth's face is shown for a few seconds covered by an oxygen mask.

As a result of the accident, Ruth Shulman is a paraplegic. When Ruth saw the televised segment in her hospital room she testified that she was, "shocked, so to speak, that this would be run and I would be exploited, have my privacy invaded, which is what I felt had happened."

[This discussion is limited to the court's discussion of the privacy intrusion tort.]

The Intrusion Tort Analysis

A majority of the court concurred with the privacy intrusion tort analysis in Justice Wedegar's opinion. The *Shulman* court acknowledged that in earlier cases it had recognized a relationship between the tort and constitutional right to privacy. But these cases had not suggested that the, "constitutional framework developed for resolving claims under the California Constitution . . . supplanted . . . or precluded the independent development of [the] common law [of privacy]."

Justice Wedegar then summarized California law on the requirements for establishing the intrusion and highly offensive elements of the intrusion tort. The intrusion element requires the plaintiff to demonstrate that the defendant penetrated some "zone of physical or sensory privacy surrounding, or obtained unwanted access to data about, the plaintiff." The element is proven only if the "plaintiff had an objectively reasonable expectation of seclusion or solitude in the place, conversation or data source."

The intrusion element had not been demonstrated by Ruth Shulman and her son in respect to the filming at the scene of the accident. The presence of the cameraman and his filming at the scene were not "physical or sensory" intrusions on the plaintiff's seclusion—they had no right or possessory interest in the property where the injury took place and no reasonable expectation that the media would be excluded from the scene.

Both the plaintiffs did raise triable issues of fact as to whether they had a reasonable expectation of privacy in the *video and audio recording in the helicopter* because the helicopter functioned as an ambulance and no custom or law permitted the press to ride in ambulances or enter hospital rooms during treatment without the patient's consent.

Triable issues of fact had also been presented as to whether Ruth Shulman had reasonable expectations of privacy in certain conversations at the accident scene. The court observed that the rescue did not take place "on a heavily traveled highway" but in a ditch below and some distance from the superhighway. It was unlikely that any passerby could have observed the rescue or heard Ruth's conversations with Carnahan. The conversations between Ruth and the medical team and between the medical team and the hospital that could not be overheard by persons passing by the accident were not public as was the general accident scene.

In stating the "highly offensive" means element of the tort the court reiterated the standard developed in an earlier appellate court case, *Miller v. National Broadcasting Co.*, 187 Cal.App.3d 1463 (1986) (upholding an intrusion tort action against the media for entering the Miller home with a paramedic team and videotaping the unsuccessful attempt to revise Miller after he suffered a heart attack). Under the *Miller* standard, "all of the circumstances of the intrusion, including its degree and setting and the intruders "motives and objectives" were to be evaluated in determining the "offensiveness" of the intrusion. The *Miller* court had concluded that reasonable persons could conclude the filming of emergency treatment in the patient's home a "cavalier disregard for ordinary citizens 'rights' of privacy" and therefore highly offensive.

Applying the *Miller* standard to the case the California Supreme Court concluded that a jury might conclude that the placement of a microphone on a medical rescuer (nurse Carnahan), the recording of conversations from Shulman to Carnahan and the filming in the air ambulance was "highly offensive to a reasonable person."

The Significance of Shulman

Shulman is a significant decision for a number of reasons. California is a state with a large entertainment and media industry. The news gathering activities of these industries has been the basis of numerous suits in which privacy and first amendment values have clashed. *Shulman* is currently the most thorough and thoughtful appellate court examination of the intrusion tort and first amendment/privacy conflicts in our legal system.

Defacto Balancing of Interests

Shulman rejects a first amendment defense to the media for news gathering in intrusion cases citing *Dietemann, Cohen v. Cowles* and *Branzburg v. Hayes*. The privacy intrusion tort like the contract law in *Cohen* and the grand jury investigation in *Branzburg* is a law of general applicability with only an incidental burden on the press. The court rejected the view that hidden mechanical contrivances of the kind used by the media in *Dietemann* or *Shulman* were "indispensable tools" of news gathering. Do you agree with the court?

Although the court rejects a straightforward balancing of press and privacy interests in news gathering intrusion tort cases, it does recognize that the interests of the press will be taken into account and balanced against the plaintiff's loss of privacy in the "highly offensive means" dimension of the tort. As discussed above the intruder's "motives and objectives" are pertinent to the highly offensive element of the tort. The "reporter's motive" may reduce the offensiveness of the intrusion.

Does the defacto balancing of interest test that is contained within the concept of "highly offensive means" significantly undercut the value of the intrusion tort in protecting privacy? Is a jury equipped to sort out "routine" news gathering techniques from news gathering activities that constitute "highly offensive disrespect for the patient's personal privacy"? Compare the *Shulman* court's approach to balancing in the highly offensive means element with *Luedtke v. Nabors Alaska Drilling, Inc.*, 768 P.2d 1123 (Alaska 1989) (testing employees for drug and alcohol use not "offensive method" of intrusion).

c. The Publication Damage to Reputation Issue

When privacy intrusion, fraud or trespass actions are successful in ambush journalism cases, what damages are recoverable? Suppose, for example, that a court views the fraudulently gained entrance and surreptitious videorecording to constitute one of the above torts. The plaintiff alleges that the subsequent television program costs lost business and depreciates the value of the business' stock. These out of pocket losses, if demonstrated, are a form of "special damages" that are generally recoverable in a tort action. But in this case, the theory of economic loss is: the fruit of the tortious conduct was the basis of the program; the publicity from the program damaged the reputation of the plaintiff and this damage caused economic loss. Should the presence of the element of publication damages to the plaintiff's reputation limit the damages that are recoverable?

Two Supreme Court cases bear on the answer to this question, *Cohen v. Cowles Media Co.*, 501 U.S. 663, (1991) and *Hustler Magazine v. Falwell*, 485 U.S. 46 (1988). These cases are summarized, *infra*. In *Cohen* the Court upheld a $200,000 damage award against the press for publishing the name of a source for a story after a reporter had promised confidentiality. The award was based upon the promissory estoppel doctrine under Minnesota contract law. In rejecting the first amendment claim, the Court applied what it characterized as the well established principle that laws of general applicability do not violate the first amendment simply because they have an incidental effect on speech. Fraud, trespass and privacy intrusion laws are of general application and if *Cohen* is read as standing for the above principle special damages flowing from the tortious conduct including publication reputational damages ought to be recoverable.

Hustler arguably supports limiting recovery for special damages that flow from publication damages to reputation. In *Hustler*, the Court held that a $150,000 damage award against Hustler Magazine based upon the tort of intentional infliction of emotional distress violated the first amendment. The basis of the intentional infliction action was a parody of

Reverend Jerry Falwell, a public figure. The Court held that public figures could not recover damages for intentional infliction of emotional distress based upon a publication unless they satisfied the first amendment requirements in defamation cases—that the publication contains a false statement of fact and is published with constitutional malice. *Hustler* may be read for the broad proposition that a plaintiff may not recover for reputation damages by using general tort law to avoid the strict first amendment requirements of defamation law. Under this view of *Hustler* arguably economic loses flowing from publication damages to reputation should not be recoverable without satisfying the strict first amendment requirements of a defamation claim.

In *Food Lion*, discussed above, the court read *Hustler* to limit *Cohen* and held that the Food Lion could recover economic damages caused by the trespass, fraud and unfair business practices claim but could not recover damages for injury to reputation caused by the PTL broadcast without establishing falsity and malice. What's left of damage claims if Food Lion is required to show that the loss of business and stock value was caused by the trespass, fraud and violation of the state fair business practices act and not by the PTL broadcast? (In the damage phase of *Food Lion* the jury awarded $1,402 in compensation damages and $5.5 million in punitive damages, reduced to $315,000 by the trial judge. See, Logan, supra at pp. 177–78.) In *Cohen* the plaintiff was fired by his employer after his name was identified as the source of negative information about a gubernatorial candidate. The contract damage award upheld by the court was based upon the firing and his lower earning capacity—both resulting from the publication. How is *Food Lion's* special damage theory different from *Cohen's*? Aren't Cohen's economic losses the result of publication damages to reputation?

The *Shulman* court, supra, did not decide whether compensatory damages resulting from publication of material acquired through actionable intrusion would be recoverable under California law. In footnote 18 the court noted that this publication damage issue that was decided by *Food Lion* was not before the court on the summary judgment motion.

ESTATE OF BERTHIAUME v. PRATT

365 A.2d 792 (Me.1976).

POMEROY, JUSTICE.

The appellee is a physician and surgeon practicing in Waterville, Maine. It was established at trial without contradiction that the deceased, Henry Berthiaume, was suffering from a cancer of his larynx. Appellee, an otolaryngologist, had treated him twice surgically. A laryngectomy was performed; and later, because of a tumor which had appeared in his neck, a radical neck dissection on one side was done. No complaint is made with respect to the surgical interventions.

During the period appellee was serving Mr. Berthiaume as a surgeon, many photographs of Berthiaume had been taken by appellee or under his direction. The jury was told that the sole use to which these photographs were to be put was to make the medical record for the appellee's use. There is nothing in the case to suggest that the photographs were to be shown to students for teaching purposes or were to be used as illustrative photographs in any text books or papers. The only persons to whom the photographs were available were those members of appellee's staff and the appropriate hospital personnel who had duties to perform with respect to the medical records.

Although at no time did the appellee receive any written consent for the taking of photographs from Berthiaume or any members of his family, it was appellee's testimony that Berthiaume had always consented to having such photographs made.

At all times material hereto Mr. Berthiaume was the patient of a physician other than appellee. Such other physician had referred the patient to appellee for surgery. On September 2, 1970, appellee saw the patient for the last time for the purpose of treatment or diagnosis. The incident which gave rise to this lawsuit occurred on September 23, 1970.

It was also on that day that Mr. Berthiaume died.

Although appellee disputed the evidence appellant produced at trial in many material respects, the jury could have concluded from the evidence that shortly before Mr. Berthiaume died on the 23rd, the appellee and a nurse appeared in his hospital room. In the presence of Mrs. Berthiaume and a visitor of the patient in the next bed, either Dr. Pratt or the nurse, at his direction, raised the dying Mr. Berthiaume's head and placed some blue operating room toweling under his head and beside him on the bed. The appellee testified that this toweling was placed there for the purpose of obtaining a color contrast for the photographs which he proposed to take. He then proceeded to take several photographs of Mr. Berthiaume.

The jury could have concluded from the testimony that Mr. Berthiaume protested the taking of pictures by raising a clenched fist and moving his head in an attempt to remove his head from the camera's range. The appellee himself testified that before taking the pictures he had been told by Mrs. Berthiaume when he talked with her in the corridor before entering the room that she "didn't think that Henry wanted his picture taken."

It is the raising of the deceased's head in order to put the operating room towels under and around him that appellant claims was an assault and battery. It is the taking of the pictures of the dying Mr. Berthiaume that appellant claims constituted the actionable invasion of Mr. Berthiaume's right to privacy.

At the close of all the evidence, the presiding justice, acting on a motion seeking such action, directed a verdict for the defendant, as he is permitted to do under the provisions of Rule 50(a), M.R.Civ.P. This seasonably filed appeal followed.

We sustain the appeal.

The announced rationale of the presiding justice for the action taken may best be summed up by quoting two statements he made when he explained to the jury why he was withdrawing the case from their consideration and directing a verdict. At one point, while addressing the jury, he said:

> The mere fact the taking of pictures, under the best circumstances, in other words, assuming that the pictures were taken without consent as the plaintiff-administratrix complains, the mere taking of pictures is not invasion of privacy. There is no proof they were published; no proof they were used for any purpose other than their intended use in the record-keeping process by the doctor in the care of the patient that he had.

Later, while addressing the jury he said:

> The law says in the course of his treating a patient, the doctor has the right to lay his hand on you in order to provide you with treatment for which you have sought his advice, and his attention and care and treatment.

> Although the taking of pictures is not necessarily treatment, it is part of the overall medical care, an association, a relationship between the doctor and the patient, and as the doctor has testified, I think medical science must have some information in its effort to track down and search for a cure.

. . .

In this case we are concerned only with a claimed intrusion upon the plaintiff's intestate's physical and mental solitude or seclusion. The jury had a right to conclude from the evidence that plaintiff's intestate was dying. It could have concluded he desired not to be photographed in his hospital bed in such condition and that he manifested such desire by his physical motions. The jury should have been instructed, if it found these facts, that the taking of pictures without decedent's consent or over his objection was an invasion of his legally protected right to privacy, which invasion was an actionable tort for which money damages could be recovered.

Instead, a directed verdict for the defendant was entered, obviously premised on the presiding justice's announced incorrect conclusion that the taking of pictures without consent did not constitute an invasion of privacy and the further erroneous conclusion that no tort was committed in the absence of "proof they [the photographs] were published."

. . .

As to the claimed assault and battery, on the state of the evidence, the jury should have been permitted to consider the evidence and return a verdict in accordance with its fact finding. It should have been instructed that consent to a touching of the body of a patient may be implied from the patient's consent to enter into a physician-patient relationship whenever such touching is reasonably necessary for the diagnosis and treatment of the patient's ailments while the physician-patient relationship continues. Quite obviously also, there would be no actionable assault and battery if the touching was expressly consented to. Absent express consent by the patient or one authorized to give consent on the patient's behalf, or absent consent implied from the circumstances, including the physician-patient relationship, the touching of the patient in the manner described by the evidence in this case would constitute assault and battery if it was part of an undertaking which, in legal effect, was an invasion of the plaintiff's intestate's "right to be let alone."

It has been urged upon us that great benefit inures to medical science from the taking and preservation of photographs. The evidence discloses that the appellee had taken photographs at various stages during the course of Berthiaume's fatal illness and had made these photographs a part of appellee's medical record of the case. It is argued that by looking at Berthiaume's photographs appellee would be better able to evaluate and predict the progress of a malignancy of the same type and nature in other patients similarly afflicted. We are urged to declare as a matter of law that it was the physician's right to complete the photographic record by capturing on film Berthiaume's appearance in his final dying hours, even without the patient's consent or over his objections. This we are unwilling to do.

We recognize the benefit to the science of medicine which comes from the making of photographs of the treatment and of medical abnormalities found in patients. However, we agree with the reasoning expressed by Alessandroni, J., sitting in the Court of Common Pleas in Pennsylvania, when in writing of a fact situation almost identical to that now before us, he said in Clayman v. Bernstein, 38 Pa.D. & C. 543 (1940):

> The court recognized that an individual has the right to decide whether that which is his shall be given to the public and not only to restrict and limit but also to withhold absolutely his talents, property, or other subjects of the right of privacy from all dissemination. The facial characteristics or peculiar caste of one's features, whether normal or distorted, belong to the individual and may not be reproduced without his permission. Even the photographer who is authorized to take a portrait is not justified in making or retaining additional copies for himself.

> A man may object to any invasion, as well as to an unlimited invasion. Widespread distribution of a photograph is not essential nor can it be said that publication in its common usage or in its legal meaning is necessary. It may be conceded that the doctrine of privacy in general is still suffering the pains of its birth and any doctrine in its inception borrows from established precedent. An analogy to the laws of libel, however, is not justified under the circumstances of this case. The author of a libel is the creator and there can be no offense until the contents are communicated to another. One cannot invade the

rights of another merely by expressing his thoughts on paper. Two persons are necessary. One's right of privacy, however, may be invaded by a single human agency. Plaintiff's picture was taken without her authority or consent. Her right to decide whether her facial characteristics should be recorded for another's benefit or by reason of another's capriciousness has been violated. The scope of the authorization defines the extent of the acts necessary to constitute a violation. If plaintiff had consented to have her photograph taken only for defendant's private files certainly he would have no right to exhibit it to others without her permission. Can it be said that his rights are equally extensive when even that limited consent has not been given?

Id., at 546–47.

Because there were unresolved, disputed questions of fact, which, if decided by the factfinder in favor of the plaintiff, would have justified a verdict for the plaintiff, it was reversible error to have directed a verdict for the defendant.

The entry must be:

Appeal sustained.

New trial ordered.

All Justices concurring.

d. More on the Unauthorized Taking of Pictures

In *Estate of Berthiaume v. Pratt, supra*, and *Clayman v. Bernstein*, 38 Pa. D. & C. 543 (1940) (cited in *Pratt*), the courts adopted the principle that the unauthorized taking of a picture in a private place constitutes an actionable invasion of privacy. *Accord, Barber v. Time, Inc.*, 348 Mo. 1199, 159 S.W.2d 291 (1942) (newspaper photographer in hospital).

The unauthorized taking of an employee's picture while the employee is engaged in the discharge of his duties is generally not actionable. *See, e.g., Thomas v. General Elec. Co.*, 207 F.Supp. 792 (W.D.Ky.1962); *DeLury v. Kretchmer*, 66 Misc.2d 897, 322 N.Y.S.2d 517 (1971). The employer must have a legitimate business purpose in taking the photograph and apparently mere curiosity is not sufficient. No privacy action was available to a governmental employee even though the employee objected, was not consulted or informed of the use of the picture, and was not compensated in *Truxes v. Kenco Enters., Inc.*, 80 S.D. 104, 119 N.W.2d 914 (1963).

10. WHAT DETERMINES THE BOUNDARIES OF PLACES THAT ARE PUBLIC AND PLACES THAT ARE PRIVATE?

As several of the cases in this section indicate, the question of whether information is acquired of the plaintiff in a public or private place is crucial in privacy intrusion tort actions. However, it has sometimes been possible to recover for privacy intrusions that occur in public places. *See, e.g., Bennett v. Norban*, 396 Pa. 94, 151 A.2d 476 (1959). In *Bennett*, the court validated an intrusion claim brought by an innocent shop-lifting suspect searched in an open parking lot. However, in a more recent case, a Maryland court ruled against a union official who sought to bring unreasonable intrusion claims after he learned that he had been "shadowed" by his enemies in an effort to uncover evidence of adultery. *See Pemberton v. Bethlehem Steel Corp.*, 66 Md.App. 133, 502 A.2d 1101, 1117, *cert. denied*, 306 Md. 289, 508 A.2d 488, *cert. denied,* 479 U.S. 984 (1986). The court made an issue of the fact that the plaintiff had not been aware of the surveillance at the time. What difference should the awareness of the intrusion make in privacy actions? The court's more fundamental concern was that the defendant had not been in a place of seclusion at the time of the alleged intrusions, but in places open to the public.

Some "public" places are nonetheless highly "private." Places of public accommodation in which disrobing is likely, such as dressing rooms and toilet facilities, are generally considered private places. *See Harkey v. Abate*, 131 Mich.App. 177, 346 N.W.2d 74 (1983), *appeal denied*, 419 Mich. 912 (1984). However, courts have indicated that private property owners may have legitimate interests in observing patrons in restrooms and dressing rooms. No unlawful invasion of privacy was found where a retail manager observed the restroom of his store through a crack in the ceiling to investigate customer complaints of criminal sodomy. *See Elmore v. Atlantic Zayre, Inc.*, 178 Ga.App. 25, 341 S.E.2d 905, 906 (1986). Warnings of possible surveillance are not a condition of immunity from privacy liability. However, retailers have escaped liability in cases in which they posted advanced warnings of possible surveillance. *See Lewis v. Dayton Hudson Corp.*, 128 Mich.App. 165, 339 N.W.2d 857 (1983). An older Wisconsin case in which a bar owner escaped liability after photographing a woman while she was in the restroom and later circulated the pictures among bar patrons is exceptional. *See Yoeckel v. Samonig*, 272 Wis. 430, 75 N.W.2d 925 (1956). For a general examination of the extent to which the public place limitation has limited the privacy intrusion tort, see, Andrew Joy McClurg, *Bringing Privacy Law Out of the Closet: A Tort Theory of Liability For Intrusions in Public Places*, 73 N.C.L. Rev. 938 (1995). McClurg argues for a right to "public privacy."

11. EXPECTATIONS OF PRIVACY IN MAIL

In many cases, the question of whether conduct constitutes an intrusion into "seclusion or private affairs" under the intrusion torts turns upon whether the plaintiff had a reasonable expectation of privacy in the information that was acquired. The reasonable expectation of privacy principle defines the boundaries of the public and private under the intrusion tort. Do employees have a reasonable expectation of privacy in mail that is sent to them at their place of employment? In

Vernars v. Young, 539 F.2d 966 (3d Cir. 1976), the court of appeals held that a cause of action had been stated under Pennsylvania law for intrusion upon seclusion where a letter addressed to the plaintiff and marked "personal" had been opened by a corporate officer without the plaintiff's consent. The court concluded that since persons have a reasonable expectation that their telephone conversations will not be surreptitiously intercepted, "they also have a reasonable expectation that their personal mail will not be opened and read by unauthorized persons." *Id*. at 969. The court in *Vernars* analogizes mail to telephone conversations. Would the result be different if the employer had a "reasonable suspicion" that the employee was sharing company secrets with competitors? Compare *Vernars* with *Briggs v. American Air Filter Co.*, 630 F.2d 414 (5th Cir.1980), and other cases involving the scope of the ordinary course of business exception to The Federal Wiretap Act, *supra*, Chapter III. Would an employee have a reasonable expectation of privacy in personal e-mail communications that were sent to her place of employment? The current status of legal protection for e-mail is examined in Chapter III.

B.   TORT PROTECTION AGAINST INVASIONS OF PRIVACY THROUGH THE DISSEMINATION OF INFORMATION: THE PUBLIC DISCLOSURE TORT/PRIVATE FACTS TORT

1.   INTRODUCTION

The focus of the Warren and Brandeis article was on invasions of privacy through dissemination of personal or intimate information by the print media:

> Instantaneous photographs and newspaper enterprise have invaded the secret precincts of private and domestic life; and numerous mechanical devices threaten to make good the predictions that "what is whispered in the closet shall be proclaimed from the house-tops." . . .

> . . . The press is overstepping in every direction the obvious bounds of propriety and of decency. Gossip is no longer the resource of the idle and of the vicious, but has become a trade, which is pursued with industry as well as effrontery. . . . [S]olitude and privacy have become more essential to the individual; but modern enterprise and invention have, through invasion upon his privacy, subjected him to mental pain and distress, far greater than could be inflicted by mere bodily injury.

Warren & Brandeis, *The Right to Privacy*, 4 Harv. L. Rev. 193, 195–6 (1890).

The core of the tort that was advocated by Warren and Brandeis was damage recovery for emotional distress caused by public dissemination of information about one's private life. Yet judicial recognition of a common law tort right to privacy that would encompass this type of invasion of privacy did not occur until nearly four decades after the publication of the article. In *Brents v. Morgan*, 221 Ky. 765, 299 S.W. 967 (1927), a debtor was successful in a common law privacy action against a creditor who had publicly posted a notice of an overdue account. In upholding the cause of action the court relied extensively on the analysis in the Warren and Brandeis article. Recall that judicial recognition of a common law right to privacy for the commercial exploitation of a person's name to advertise a commercial product had occurred earlier in *Pavesich v. New England Life Ins. Co.*, discussed in Chapter I.

The common law tort that developed is referred to by the short-hand expressions "the public disclosure tort" or "private facts tort." Both expressions are employed in this book. One of the central features of this tort is that an action in damages may be available against the media even though what is published is true. Consider one of Warren and Brandeis' comments:

> The truth of the matter published does not afford a defense. Obviously this branch of the law should have no concern with the truth or falsehood of the matters published. It is not for injury to the individual's character that redress or prevention is sought, but for injury to the right of privacy. For the former, the law of slander and libel provides perhaps a sufficient safeguard. The latter implies the right not merely to prevent inaccurate portrayal of private life, but to prevent its being depicted at all.

Warren and Brandeis, *The Right to Privacy*, 4 Harv. L. Rev. 193, 218 (1890).

Consider the positive values that are promoted by the dissemination of truthful information. Protecting truthful speech against government censorship is at the heart of the first amendment. In his seminal treatise on the first amendment, Professor Thomas Emerson summarizes the central functions that are performed in a democracy by a system of free expression as no less than (1) assurance of individual self-fulfillment, (2) advancement of knowledge and the discovery of truth, (3) facilitation of participation in the political process, and (4) maintenance of the appropriate balance between stability and change. *See* Thomas I. Emerson, *The System of Freedom of Expression* 1, 6 (1970). First amendment limitations on the public disclosure tort will be examined in a latter part of this section. Is the public disclosure tort primarily directed at the purveyor of gossip? Is there value to gossip in society? Professor Diane Zimmerman, in an important article that is critical of the "Warren–Brandeis Privacy Tort," suggests that many of the values historically performed by person to person gossip in small rural communities are performed by modern journalism in urbanized, less intimate societies. She argues that Warren and Brandeis were wrong in their values and perceptions about gossip:

Students of the phenomenon claim that gossip, and the rules governing who participates and who is privy to what information about whom, helps mark out social groupings and establish community ties. By providing people with a way to learn about social groups to which they do not belong, gossip increases intimacy and a sense of community among disparate individuals and groups. Gossip may also foster the development of relationships by giving two strangers the means to bridge a gap of silence when they are thrown together in a casual social situation.

Thus, from the perspective of the anthropologist and sociologist, gossip is a basic form of information exchange that teaches about other lifestyles and attitudes, and through which community values are changed or reinforced. This description is a far cry from that of Warren and Brandeis. . . .

Gossip thus appears to be a normal and necessary part of life for all but the rare hermit among us. Perceived in this way, gossip contributes directly to the first amendment "marketplace of ideas," and the comparative weight assigned to an interest in its limitation merits careful consideration.

Diane Zimmerman, *Requiem for a Heavyweight: A Farewell to Warren and Brandeis's Privacy Tort*, 68 Cornell L. Rev. 291, 333–34 (1983).

In public disclosure tort actions, privacy is pitted against a host of positive values which are promoted by the dissemination of truthful information. As a result, the circumstances under which the tort is actionable are limited. Public disclosure is a tort for which the limitations on recovery are featured in the case law and commentary, as well as in the formulation of legal doctrine.

RESTATEMENT OF TORTS, SECOND, SECTION 652D. PUBLICITY GIVEN TO PRIVATE LIFE

One who gives publicity to a matter concerning the private life of another is subject to liability to the other for invasion of his privacy, if the matter publicized is of a kind that

(a) would be highly offensive to a reasonable person, and

(b) is not of legitimate concern to the public.

2. PRIVATE FACTS

The second Restatement has had considerable influence in the development of the public disclosure tort by state courts. The Restatement formulation limits recovery to publicity of matters concerning the "private life" of another. No liability attaches to disclosure of public information. Comment *b* to Section 652 D further unpacks the Restatement's concept of "private fact":

b. *Private life.* . . . There is no liability when the defendant merely gives further publicity to information about the plaintiff that is already public. Thus there is no liability for giving publicity to facts about the plaintiff's life that are matters of public record, such as the date of his birth, the fact of his marriage, his military record, the fact that he is admitted to the practice of medicine or is licensed to drive a taxicab, or the pleadings that he has filed in a lawsuit. On the other hand, if the record is one not open to public inspection, as in the case of income tax returns, it is not public and there is an invasion of privacy when it is made so.

. . .

Every individual has some phases of his life and his activities and some facts about himself that he does not expose to the public eye, but keeps entirely to himself or at most reveals only to his family or to close personal friends. Sexual relations, for example, are normally entirely private matters, as are family quarrels, many unpleasant or disgraceful or humiliating illnesses, most intimate personal letters, most details of a man's life in his home, and some of his past history that he would rather forget.

One of the areas where the private fact requirement of the public disclosure tort has been placed in issue is when the plaintiff has disclosed the information to others. Does the disclosure of information to others by the plaintiff result in the information being public? In many instances the answer is yes. Recall *Nader v. General Motors Corp.*, discussed in an earlier section on the privacy intrusion tort. In *Nader*, information that had been disclosed by Ralph Nader to his friends was not viewed as part of his private affairs for purposes of an intrusion tort action against General Motors for the acquiring of the information. A similar analysis is made when the public disclosure tort is invoked for the dissemination of such information. In *Cummings v. Walsh Constr. Co.*, 561 F.Supp. 872 (S.D.Ga.1983), the plaintiff was held to have no cause of action against the defendant for disclosing the fact they had sexual relations because she had informed others and therefore waived her right not to have the information disclosed by the defendant. The facts disclosed to others were public for purposes of the public disclosure tort.

Similarly, disclosure of information about the public activities of someone has been found not to be actionable. An illustrative case is *Tellado v. Time–Life Books, Inc.*, 643 F.Supp. 904 (D.N.J.1986). In *Tellado*, a Vietnam veteran sued the publishers on various theories in tort for the massive dissemination, in numerous publications, of a picture taken of him in Vietnam. The photograph, taken in 1966, depicted the plaintiff and other infantrymen while under sniper fire just moments after they had experienced a fierce encounter where six soldiers had been killed and twelve others had been wounded. The photograph accurately portrayed the anguish, agony and fear of the plaintiff. The plaintiff, a janitor, saw the photograph in a discarded brochure while emptying a trash can in 1986. Five million copies of the brochure were published. The court summarized the plaintiff's feelings on seeing the photograph by quoting from the plaintiff's deposition:

> I was kind of freaked out. Here I look into a trash can, almost 20 years later and I see myself there. Here's something I've been trying to avoid for the past 19 years and all of a sudden I find myself back under the same situation.

Id. at 907.

The court concluded that the photograph depicted soldiers in a "clearly public setting" during a combat mission in Vietnam, and therefore the facts disclosed about the plaintiff were "public" and no cause of action under the public disclosure tort would lie. Put yourself in the position of Tellado. Would you consider the publication of your picture in identical circumstances to be an invasion of privacy?

Would the voluntary disclosure of information by the plaintiff in all situations result in the characterization of the information as public for purposes of the public disclosure tort? Suppose a woman saw a man in her apartment when she discovered the nude dead body of her roommate. She waited outside the apartment on the street while police investigated and later was questioned at a neighbor's house and in a restaurant by the police. She described the man to the police and told certain friends, neighbors and family members that she discovered the body and saw the murderer. The police did not release her name to the press because of concerns about her safety. A reporter obtained her name from an unknown person in the coroner's office. In a story about the rape and murder, the plaintiff was identified by name as the discoverer of the victim. Is there publicity of a private fact? *See Times Mirror Co. v. Superior Court*, 198 Cal.App.3d 1420, 244 Cal.Rptr. 556 (1988), *cert. dismissed*, 489 U.S. 1094 (1989). *Sports Illustrated* publishes a story about surfing that features plaintiff as a conspicuous member of a group of men who enjoy the hazardous sport of body surfing. The story includes pictures of the plaintiff and information obtained from an extensive interview with a reporter. The story also contains details about the plaintiff's daredevil escapades that were not connected to surfing. Upon learning that the proposed story was to contain unflattering information beyond that provided by the plaintiff in the interview involving his surfing activities, the plaintiff revoked consent to use the information in the interview. Is there publication of private facts? *See Virgil v. Time, Inc.*, 527 F.2d 1122 (9th Cir.1975), *cert. denied*, 425 U.S. 998 (1976); *see also Virgil v. Sports Illustrated*, 424 F.Supp. 1286 (S.D.Cal.1976). Is there a principled way to distinguish *Cummings* and *Tellado* (public facts) from *Times Mirror* and *Virgil* (private facts)? For the view that "private fact" cases are those where the plaintiff has communicated the information to a "small, select group of persons," see the useful discussion by J. McCarthy, *The Rights of Publicity and Privacy*, Sections 5.9[C](2), at 5–88 (1991). Consider the public-private fact issue in the cases discussing the "public records" and "implied consent" and "public figure" defenses to the public disclosure tort, *supra*. Is the inability of the courts to sort out information as "private" or "public" in a clear way a reason to junk the tort altogether? Is it a reason to rely on other elements of the Restatement formulation to provide the appropriate balance between privacy and truthful discourse?

Suppose a health care professional disclosed the fact that a patient in the hospital where he was employed was infected with HIV to a group of persons at a social gathering. Would the voluntary disclosure of the patient's condition to his physician at the hospital make the information "public" for purposes of the public disclosure tort? What affect does the breach of confidentiality tort have on all of this? Consider *Harris v. Easton Publishing Co.*, and the "publicity" requirement of the public disclosure tort, *infra*, p. 459.

"THE RED KIMONO" CASE

Shortly after the Kentucky high court recognized the private facts tort in *Brents v. Morgan*, the issue was presented to an appellate court in California. But in this instance the dissemination was by a media defendant. In *Melvin v. Reid*, 112 Cal.App. 285, 297 P. 91 (1931), the plaintiff, Gabrielle Melvin, sued the distributors of a motion picture entitled "The Red Kimono" for violation of her right to privacy. The theory of the plaintiff's privacy claim was that the use of her maiden name, Gabrielle Darley, in the picture, and the plot of depicting the true story of plaintiff's previous life as a prostitute, as it was revealed in a criminal prosecution, unjustifiably invaded the plaintiff's privacy. In overruling the lower court's granting of a demurrer to the defendants, the intermediate appellate court stated:

> [T]he use of the incidents from the life of appellant in the moving picture is in itself not actionable. These incidents appeared in the records of her trial for murder which is a public record open to the perusal of all. The very fact that they were contained in a public record is sufficient to negative the idea that their publication was a violation of a right of privacy. When the incidents of a life are so public as to be spread upon a public record they come within the knowledge and into the possession of the public and cease to be private. Had respondents, in the story of "The Red Kimono," stopped with the use of those incidents from the life of appellant which were spread upon the record of her trial, no right of action would have accrued. They went further and in the formation of the plot used the true maiden name of appellant. If any right of action exists it arises from the use of this true name in connection with the true incidents from her life together with their advertisements in which they stated that the story of the picture was taken from true incidents in the life of Gabrielle Darley who was Gabrielle Darley Melvin.

112 Cal. App. at 290–91, 297 P. at 93.

The court added that the public policy of encouraging efforts of persons to rehabilitate themselves provided a further reason for the view that the publication of facts of the previous life of the plaintiff was not justified. *Melvin v. Reid* was the first of a number of court decisions in California to interpret the common law of that state to provide protection against invasions of privacy. California has one of the richest jurisprudence in our legal system in all facets of the right to privacy.

Precisely what were the "private facts" that were published by the media in *Melvin v. Reid*?

3.   "OFFENSIVE INFORMATION"

DAILY TIMES DEMOCRAT v. GRAHAM
276 Ala. 380, 162 So.2d 474 (1964).

HARWOOD, JUSTICE.

[Flora Bell Graham lived her whole life in Cullam County, Alabama. She was married and had two young children. Her family resided in a rural community where her husband was engaged in the business of raising chickens. Graham took her two children to the county fair. After her boys expressed fear about going through the "Fun House" alone, she accompanied them. Graham had never been through a Fun House before and had no knowledge that there was a device that blew jets of air up from the platform of the Fun House upon exit. As she was leaving her dress was blown up by air jets on the platform at the exit, and her body was exposed from the waist down with the exception of that portion covered by her "panties." At that moment a Daily Times Democrat photographer took a picture of her. This was done without Graham's knowledge or consent. Four days later the picture was published on the front page of the newspaper. The Daily Times Democrat published five thousand newspapers daily. Although Graham's back was largely toward the camera, her sons were in the picture and the photograph was recognized by many of Graham's friends and acquaintances. As a result of the publication Graham became embarrassed, self-conscious, upset, and cried on occasion. Graham brought an action for invasion of privacy. The Circuit Court entered judgment for Graham. Damages were assessed by the jury at $4,166.00. On appeal, the Supreme Court of Alabama affirmed.]

Counsel contends that as a matter of law the publication of the photograph was a matter of legitimate news of interest to the public; that the publishing of the picture was in connection with a write-up of the Fair, which was a matter of legitimate news. . . .

. . . We can see nothing of legitimate news value in the photograph. Certainly it discloses nothing as to which the public is entitled to be informed. . . . Mr. Prosser in his article on "Privacy" observes:

It may nevertheless be suggested that there must be yet some undefined limits of common decency as to what can be published about anyone; and that a photograph of indecent exposure, for example, can never be legitimate "news."

In the Restatement of the Law of Torts . . . it is provided:

> . . . "These limits" (justifiable invasion of privacy) "are exceeded where . . . *photographs of a person in an embarrassing pose are surreptitiously taken and published.*" (Emphasis ours.)

Not only was this photograph embarrassing to one of normal sensibilities, we think it could properly be classified as obscene, in that "obscene" means "offensive to modesty or decency." . . .

. . .

Counsel further argues that . . . [since] appellee's picture was taken at the time she was a part of a public scene . . . the publication of the photograph could not therefore be deemed an invasion of her privacy as a matter of law.

. . .

To hold that one who is involuntarily and instantaneously enmeshed in an embarrassing pose forfeits her right of privacy merely because she happened at the moment to be part of a public scene would be illogical, wrong, and unjust.

One who is part of a public scene may be lawfully photographed as an incidental part of that scene in his ordinary status. Where the status he expects to occupy is changed without his volition to a status embarrassing to an ordinary person of reasonable sensitivity, then he should not be deemed to have forfeited his right to be protected from an indecent and vulgar intrusion of his right of privacy merely because misfortune overtakes him in a public place. *See* Gautier v. Pro–Football, Inc., et al., 304 N.Y. 354, 107 N.E.2d 485; Jacova v. Southern Radio and Television Co., Fla., 83 So.2d. 34.

Note

Are you persuaded by Justice Harwood's response to the newspaper's contention that no cause of action would lie because the picture of the plaintiff contained public information? How does one determine whether information is or is not "an incidental part of the public scene in its ordinary status"? Consider the two cases cited by the court. In *Gautier v. Pro–Football, Inc.,* 304 N.Y. 354, 107 N.E.2d 485 (1952), the half-time performance of a well-known animal trainer at a professional football game was televised without his consent. The New York Court of Appeals found that the publication did not constitute the use of plaintiff's name or picture for purposes of advertisement or trade within the statutory right to privacy in New York because the telecast was in connection with an item of news. Judge Froessal, writing for a majority of the Court, explained:

> One traveling upon the public highway may expect to be televised, but only as an incidental part of the general scene. So one attending a public event such as a professional football game may

expect to be televised in the status in which he attends. If a mere spectator, he may be taken as part of the general audience, but may not be picked out of the crowd alone, thrust upon the screen and unduly featured for public view.... Here plaintiff ... [became] a part of the spectacle as a whole by appearing between the halves, and voluntarily occupying the very center of attraction for several minutes. Under these circumstances, it can hardly be said that his right of privacy was invaded.

107 N.E.2d at 489, 304 N.Y. at 360.

The other case, *Jacova v. Southern Radio & Television Co.*, 83 So.2d 34 (Fla.1955), denied relief to a plaintiff for the use of the plaintiff's picture in a "canned" telecast of a gambling raid on a restaurant on the theory that the plaintiff, an involuntary bystander, was an actor in a newsworthy event.

Note: *Consent to Publication*

Compare the analysis of the court in *Neff v. Time, Inc.*, 406 F.Supp. 858 (W.D.Pa.1976), where the court granted summary judgment in favor of defendant Time against Neff in a public disclosure action based upon a picture of him with the zipper of his trousers open which was used in an article in *Sports Illustrated* about Pittsburgh Steelers football fans. Neff knew that his picture was being taken at a game between the Pittsburgh Steelers and Cleveland Browns at Cleveland but was unaware that he was unzipped. Neff's picture had been selected as one of three photographs out of 7,200 to be included in an article entitled, "A Strange Kind of Love." Although the court found that the magazine had deliberately exhibited Neff in an embarrassing manner, it denied recovery, in part because a "photograph taken at a public event ... with the knowledge and implied consent of the subject ... is not a matter concerning a private fact." *Id*. at 862. Suppose Neff had been intoxicated at the time he was photographed. Should the summary judgement motion have been granted? Is a member of the general public entitled to rely on the expectation that the media will not publish consensually obtained photographs if they are not in good taste?

Note: the Requirement That the Information Be "Highly Offensive to a Person of Ordinary Sensibilities"

Courts are in general agreement that for the disclosure of private facts to be actionable, the disclosure must contain the kind of factual information that an ordinary, reasonable person would find highly offensive if disclosed about him or her. In comment *c* to Section 652D, the Restatement indicates that publishing that someone has done "her washing yesterday" or the accurate details of family events like a wedding would not be actionable because disclosure of this information would not satisfy the "highly offensive" standard. Courts have a fondness for citing the following statement of this feature of the tort from the leading hornbook on torts:

The law is not for the protection of the hypersensitive, and all of us must, to some reasonable extent, lead lives exposed to the public gaze. Anyone who is not a hermit must expect the more or less casual observation of his neighbors and the passing public as to what he is and does, and some reporting of his daily activities. The ordinary reasonable person does not take offense at mention in a newspaper of the fact he has returned home from a visit, or gone camping in the woods, or given a party at his house for his friends. It is quite a different matter when the details of sexual relations are spread before the public eye, or there is highly personal portrayal of his intimate private characteristics or conduct.

W. Page Keeton, *Prosser and Keeton on the Law of Torts* sec. 117, at 857 (5th Ed. 1984).

This requirement is the threshold device for sorting out private publicized facts that are not actionable because they are factual disclosures that members of the community expect and accept will be made about the normal everyday events of their lives. The idea of a community standard determining whether disclosures are actionable is reflected in the hypothetical ordinary reasonable person standard. The *Daily Times Democrat* court also considered the degree to which the published facts offended community standards of decency in considering whether the disclosure constituted "legitimate news." Reconsider this feature of the court's analysis in the section that examines the concept of "legitimate public concern," *infra*.

Note: Post's Thesis, the Privacy Intrusion and Public Disclosure Torts' Role in Safeguarding Rules of Civility and the Values of Community

Part of the underpinnings of prevailing theories of the right to privacy is the notion that rights like privacy pit the individual against society. In an important article Professor Robert Post challenges this view and contends that the privacy intrusion and public disclosure torts safeguard "rules of civility that in some significant measure constitute both individuals and community," Robert C. Post, *The Social Foundations of Privacy: Community and Self in the Common Law Tort*, 77 Calif. L. Rev. 957, 959 (1989). Post's intricate analysis incorporates the ideas of sociologist Erving Goffman. He summarizes Goffman's views as identifying two rules of social conduct that function as "bindings of society." These are rules of deference and demeanor. Observance of these rules are means by which individual personality is constituted. Post calls the personality that observance of rules of deference and demeanor uphold "social personality." Post views the legal requirements of the privacy intrusion and public disclosure torts that the method of intrusion and public disclosure be "offensive" to the ordinary person as "instantiation[s]" of community norms that reflect relevant rules of deference and demeanor (civility rules). These requirements condition relief under the privacy torts upon the plaintiff demonstrating a violation of social norms that if observed protect the integrity of social personality. They shift the focus of privacy law from the injury to the individual to the protection of social personality.

In his article Professor Post examines a range of issues involving the privacy intrusion and public disclosure torts in terms of his account of the social foundations of privacy. He concludes that the public disclosure tort has a much more limited role in preserving rules of civility than the privacy intrusion tort. The former's attempt to control communications runs into a long standing theory of public accountability (one is accountable for the public sphere) and "once persons or events are made public, the logic of public accountability will all but displace rules of civility." *Id.* at 1006. This explains decisions like *Sidis, infra* p. 467, where the court adopts an expansive view of the concept of public figure for purposes of determining whether the details of Sidis' life were newsworthy.

Do the "private life" and "highly offensive" requirements of the public disclosure tort reflect more than a concern about the content of information? Consider Professor Robert Post's comment:

> [T]hese two criteria do not concern merely the information that may be contained in a communication. They serve instead as standards for the evaluation of communicative acts, and are used to assess not merely communicative content, but also varied aspects of these acts as their timing, justification, addresses, form, and general context.

Post, supra at 979.

HARRIS v. EASTON PUBLISHING CO.

335 Pa.Super. 141, 483 A.2d 1377 (1984).

Before ROWLEY, MONTEMURO and JOHNSON, JJ.

JOHNSON, JUDGE.

We are called upon to review the summary dismissal of an action for invasion of privacy where a newspaper of general circulation published facts concerning the private lives of an applicant for public welfare benefits and her family on information supplied by the Department of Public Welfare. The appeal is from an order granting summary judgment in favor of Easton Publishing Company (Company). Since we find that the pleadings raise genuine issues of material fact concerning publicity given to private life, we reverse and remand.

Appellants filed a complaint in trespass on September 10, 1980 alleging that a column appearing in the Company's newspaper on April 25, 1979 had revealed personal facts of appellants. The complaint alleged that publication of the column constituted an invasion of privacy as (1) an unreasonable intrusion upon appellants' seclusion and (2) publicity given to appellants' private lives. . . .

The record establishes that appellant Brigitte Harris was born in Germany, married a U.S. enlisted man and gave birth to three children in Germany. She subsequently moved to the United States and gave birth to a fourth child. In January of 1979, Brigitte filled out an application for medical assistance and food stamps on behalf of herself, her granddaughter Rebekah, and pregnant daughter Phyllis all of whom occupied the same household, along with Brigitte's son James and daughter Janis. Brigitte refused to sign the application and subsequently withdrew it because (1) she refused to permit the caseworker to photocopy certain documents which bore a written prohibition against photocopying and (2) there was some question regarding household size and the income of her son, James.

On February 21, 1979, Brigitte Harris telephoned the Department of Public Welfare (Department) and discussed with an employee her difficulties in applying for benefits. The Department subsequently altered some of the facts in order to disguise appellants' identities and fashioned a fictionalized account of the inquiry. This account was sent to various newspapers in northeast Pennsylvania for inclusion as part of a public service column regularly provided by the Department. The purpose of the column was to create more public understanding of the Department's operations, policies and available services.

The column, consisting of a question and response, stated:

Welfare Corner

Q.   I recently applied for medical assistance and food stamps for myself, grandson, and my youngest daughter who is 17 and lives with me. She is pregnant and needs the help of a doctor. The welfare office told me I would have to let them make a copy of my naturalization papers. I was born in Germany, married a G.I. and had four children in Germany by him. Then we came to this country and my youngest child, now 17, was born in New Jersey. The trouble is that the welfare office didn't want to give me medical assistance because I refused to let them copy my naturalization papers. It already says on this paper that it must not be copied. My daughter has a birth certificate in this country which I showed them and they wanted to copy that also.

I called the Immigration Service in Washington and they referred me to you. Can you help?

A.   The county assistance office supervisor reported to this office that you decided not to sign the application and, therefore, it is being held pending your decision. The worker stated that she could waive the copying of the naturalization papers even though it is customary to establish proof of age. An examination of your daughter's birth certificate was sufficient to establish her age as a minor child, although we now make copies of these to maintain proper documentation. We were also informed that you had a 19–year old son who works intermittently for a company which has irregular work. Since he and a young grandson of yours also live in your home, your total family income (all those presently living in the home) will have to be established to determine your eligibility. From what you have stated, you are probably eligible for food stamps as well as medical assistance, but complete information must be given.

We were also informed that a letter had recently been sent to you urging you to come back so that your eligibility and that of your daughter, in particular, can be determined. We hope you will do this for your daughter and her unborn child's sake. At the time your completion of the application and the determination of eligibility is made, you should also ask your worker about sources of other kinds of help for your daughter. Please be sure that we want you to have the assistance your family needs if you are entitled to it.

The above column, as sent to the Company by the Department prior to its appearance in the newspaper, set forth the initials and address "J.S., Reading" following the sentence "Can you help?" The initials and address were not included by the Company when it published the column. A disclaimer was also regularly included by the Department with the proposed columns which stated, inter alia, that the information in the column is disguised and that attempts should not be made to identify specific persons from the information provided. This disclaimer was also not published with the column.

The complaint alleged that from the information which appeared in the column, numerous persons had indicated to appellants and to others that from reading the column, they had immediately recognized appellants as the purportedly fictional characters in the account. In response to interrogatories, appellants listed seventeen persons who had so identified them from reading the column.

. . .

Appellants' first privacy claim alleges intrusion upon seclusion.

. . .

The facts alleged to constitute the invasion of privacy in the instant case were not obtained by the Company by means of any intentional intrusion. Brigitte Harris voluntarily exposed the facts to the Board of Assistance and the Department. Also, the Company received these facts unsolicited from the Department. Hence, the trial court properly granted summary judgment as to this portion of the complaint. . . ."

[The court then discusses the sufficiency of the complaint in respect to the public disclosure tort claim.]

. . .

We must initially determine whether the evidence as presented satisfies the element of publicity, as a matter of law. The evidence indicates that the column appeared in the Company's general circulation newspaper. However, this fact alone is insufficient to establish publicity. For a fact concerning a complainant's private life to be communicated to anyone, the disclosed facts must necessarily be identified with the complainant. Absent an ability to identify the complainant, there can be no communication and hence, no publicity.

The column in the instant case did not, on its face, reveal appellants' identities. The fact that the complainant was not specifically named in a defamatory publication or utterance does not prevent recovery in a libel action. In such circumstances, the court must initially decide whether the defamatory material was capable of being reasonably understood as intended to refer to the complainant. The same analysis should be accorded to an alleged [public disclosure] tort action [on the element of publicity]. . . .

The evidence establishes that seventeen individuals did in fact identify appellants from the column. Hence, the allegedly private facts were communicated by the appearance of the column in the newspaper to those seventeen individuals. A question of law arises as to whether the communication to seventeen individuals is a large enough group that the matter must be regarded as substantially certain to become one of public knowledge. We hold that, under the facts of this case, communication to a group of seventeen individuals is large enough to constitute publicity as a matter of law. Therefore, we hold that the element of publicity has been established.

The second element, private facts, is shown by the allegations in the complaint which set forth the details in the column which correspond to the private lives of the appellants. The fact question at issue here involves whether the seventeen individuals who "recognized" appellants from the information in the column did so with or without prior knowledge of these facts. The use of the term "recognize" should not, on its face, be considered to limit the averment in the complaint where no further allegations in any of the pleadings set forth that these individuals had prior knowledge of any or all of the facts revealed in the column.

The extent of the knowledge held by the seventeen individuals, or others, prior to publication is a matter for proof and factual determination. Of course, there can be no recovery of damages on the basis of the publication of "private facts" that were already known to the recipients of the publication prior to publication. We disagree with the trial court's determination that the facts were not private because they have been made public by the Department's distribution of the column to various newspapers for publication. Such a distribution does not constitute publicity so as to render private facts public where the general public is not privy to such distributions and the column as distributed is anonymous. Also, the Company has made no allegation that anyone in receipt of the article as distributed by the Department was able to identify appellants.

The third element requires the publicity given to private facts be highly offensive to a reasonable person. This element finds support from both the protection afforded welfare applicants pursuant to . . . the Public Welfare Code and from a common sense analysis of the type of information at issue.

Section 404 of the Public Welfare Code states:

Section 404. Regulations for protection of information

(a) The department shall have the power to make and enforce regulations:

(1) To protect the names of applicants for and recipients of public assistance from improper publication, and to restrict the use of information furnished to other agencies or persons to purposes connected with the administration of public assistance. Upon request by an adult resident of the Commonwealth, the department may furnish the address and amount of assistance with respect to persons about whom inquiry is made; but, information so obtained shall not be used for commercial or political purposes; and, no information shall be furnished regarding any person's application for, or receipt of, medical assistance.

The fourth element requires that the publicity given to private facts not involve a subject of legitimate public concern. There can be no doubt as to the benefits inherent in the publication of information to aid those eligible for public assistance who encounter difficulties in applying for assistance or continuing their receipt thereof. However, there is no legitimate public concern in giving publicity to the actual circumstances of a person's application for assistance where intimate personal facts are revealed (1) in such a way as to imply that those facts are true and (2) where the personal facts are unnecessary to aid those interested in receiving advice in their applications for assistance.

The article in question consisted of a purported letter from a medical assistance and food stamp applicant and a response from the Department. The letter requested aid concerning a specific problem: the propriety of copying naturalization papers by the welfare office. Various personal facts unrelated to this question appeared in both the letter and the response, such as (1) the pregnancy of the seventeen-year-old daughter of the applicant, (2) the pregnant daughter's need of help from a doctor, (3) the fact that the applicant was born in Germany, married a G.I. and had four children in Germany by him, (4) the failure of the applicant to sign the application, and (5) the fact that the applicant had a nineteen-year-old son working intermittently. None of this information was necessary to understand or respond to the letter's request for aid. The form and tone of the article clearly implied that the facts were true. Therefore, there was no legitimate public concern in giving publicity to the intimate personal facts set forth in this article.

Note: The "Publicity Requirement"

Consider the comment from the Second Restatement of Torts section 652D that follows.

Comment:

a. *Publicity.* The form of invasion of the right of privacy covered in this Section depends upon publicity given to the private life of the individual. "Publicity," as it is used in this Section, differs from "publication," as that term is used in Section 577 in connection with liability for defamation. "Publication," in that sense, is a word of art, which includes any communication by the defendant to a third person. "Publicity," on the other hand, means that the matter is made public, by communicating it to the public at large, or to so many persons that the matter must be regarded as substantially certain to become one of public knowledge. The difference is not one of the means of communication, which may be oral, written or by any other means. It is one of a communication that reaches, or is sure to reach, the public.

Thus it is not an invasion of the right of privacy, within the rule stated in this Section, to communicate a fact concerning the plaintiff's private life to a single person or even to a small group of persons. On the other hand, any publication in a newspaper or a magazine, even of small circulation, or in a handbill distributed to a large number of persons, or any broadcast over the radio, or statement made in an address to a large audience, is sufficient to give publicity within the meaning of the term as it is used in this Section. The distinction, in other words, is one between private and public communication.

Illustrations:

1. A, a creditor, writes a letter to the employer of B, his debtor, informing him that B owes the debt and will not pay it. This is not an invasion of B's privacy under this Section.

2. A, a creditor, posts in the window of his shop, where it is read by those passing by on the street, a statement that B owes a debt to him and has not paid it. This is an invasion of B's privacy.

3. A, a motion picture exhibitor, wishing to advertise a picture to be exhibited, writes letters to a thousand men in which he makes unprivileged and objectionable statements concerning the private life of B, an actress. This is an invasion of B's privacy.

QUESTIONS

At a chamber of commerce luncheon, employer "A" tells three people at a table during lunch that employee "B" has AIDS. Is this sufficient publicity for an action to lie under the Public Disclosure Tort? Consider the discussion of the breach of confidentiality tort, *infra*, this Chapter and in Chapter Two. Would a cause of action for breach of confidentiality be available on these facts?

Would oral publications ever satisfy the publicity requirement of the public disclosure tort? Consider Warren and Brandeis' comment:

The law would probably not grant any redress for the invasion of privacy by oral publication in the absence of special damage.

The same reasons exist for distinguishing between oral and written publications of private matters, as is afforded in the law of defamation by the restricted liability for slander as compared with liability for libel. The injury resulting from such oral communications would ordinarily be so trifling that the law might well, in the interest of free speech, disregard it altogether.

Warren and Brandeis, *The Right To Privacy,* 4 Harv. L. Rev. 193, 217 (1890).

a. The Special Relationship Exception to the Publicity Requirement

As the comments from the Restatement make clear, the public disclosure tort reaches disclosures of private facts to the "public." Limited disclosure is not enough, although there may be reasonable differences as to whether disclosures initially communicated to a small group would be regarded as "substantially certain" to be communicated to the public at large.

Should the number of persons to whom the disclosure is made exclusively determine whether the disclosure is to the public? If the publicity requirement is designed to exempt social discourse between a few people from public disclosure actions because the invasion of privacy is not significant enough, should disclosures that involve serious invasions of privacy, but are only communicated to a few persons, be actionable? The Michigan Supreme Court thinks so. In *Beaumont v. Brown*, 401 Mich. 80, 257 N.W.2d 522 (1977), the court reversed a summary judgment that had been granted by the court below in part because of the failure of the plaintiff to establish publicity. The public disclosure tort action was based upon a letter that included derogatory information about the plaintiff that had been sent by the defendant to an office of the Army Reserve. In rejecting the requirement that the plaintiff had to allege that the defendant had disclosed the facts that were contained in the letter to a large number of persons, the Court stated:

> "communication to the general public" is somewhat ambiguous because a communication rarely, if ever, reaches everyone. It is therefore in order to consider the significance of communicating to the public. Communication of embarrassing facts about an individual to a public not concerned with that individual and with whom the individual is not concerned obviously is not a "serious interference" with plaintiff's right to privacy.... An invasion of a plaintiff's right to privacy is important if it exposes private facts to a public whose knowledge of those facts would be embarrassing to the plaintiff. Such a public might be the general public, if the person were a public figure, or a particular public such as fellow employees, club members, church members, family, or neighbors, if the person were not a public figure.

257 N.W.2d at 531.

The above language was cited in *Miller v. Motorola, Inc.*, 202 Ill.App.3d 976, 980–81, 560 N.E.2d 900, 903 (1990), to stand for the proposition that, "the public disclosure requirement may be satisfied by proof that the plaintiff has a special relationship with the "public" to whom the information is disclosed." The *Miller* court found that the plaintiff had stated a cause of action under the public disclosure tort against her employer for disclosing to her coworkers that she had mastectomy surgery.

4. MATTERS OF LEGITIMATE PUBLIC CONCERN

The major vehicle for accommodating privacy and the values promoted by truthful speech is the denial of recovery under the public disclosure tort for information that is a matter of legitimate public concern. This principle is embraced in the Restatement formulation and in the Warren and Brandeis article. It is clear from the article and from discussions in the cases that the legitimate public concern concept is an expression of the values that are embodied in the first amendment. However, the first Supreme Court case to hold that the first amendment restricted state tort law was *New York Times Co. v. Sullivan*, 376 U.S. 254 (1964). Prior to 1964, the notion of legitimate public concern, while reflecting first amendment values, was a matter of state common law.

Public Figures

WARREN & BRANDEIS, THE RIGHT TO PRIVACY
4 Harv. L. Rev. 193, 214–16 (1890).

The right to privacy does not prohibit any publication of matter which is of public or general interest.

In determining the scope of this rule, aid would be afforded by the analogy, in the law of libel and slander, of cases which deal with the qualified privilege of comment and criticism on matters of public and general interest. There are of course difficulties in applying such a rule. . . . The design of the law must be to protect those persons with whose affairs the community has no legitimate concern, from being dragged into an undesirable and undesired publicity and to protect all persons, whatsoever their position or station, from having matters which they may properly prefer to keep private, made public against their will. It is the unwarranted invasion of individual privacy which is reprehended, and to be, so far as possible, prevented. The distinction, however, noted in the above statement is obvious and fundamental. There are persons who may reasonably claim as a right, protection from the notoriety entailed by being made the victims of journalistic enterprise. There are others who, in varying degrees, have renounced the right to live their lives screened from public observation. Matters which men of the first class may justly contend, concern themselves alone, may in those of the second be the subject of legitimate interest to their fellow-citizens. Peculiarities of manner and person, which in the ordinary individual should be free from comment, may acquire a public importance, if found in a candidate for political office. Some further discrimination is necessary, therefore, to class facts or deeds as public or private according to a standard to be applied to the fact or deed *per se*. To publish of a modest and retiring individual that he suffers from an impediment in his speech or that he cannot spell correctly, is an unwarranted, if not an unexampled, infringement of his rights, while to state and comment on the same characteristics found in a would-be congressman could not be regarded as beyond the pale of propriety.

The general object in view is to protect the privacy of private life, and to whatever degree and in whatever connection a man's life has ceased to be private, before the publication under consideration has been made, to that extent the protection is to be withdrawn. Since, then, the propriety of publishing the very same facts may depend wholly upon the person concerning whom they are published, no fixed formula can be used to prohibit obnoxious publications. Any rule of liability adopted must have in it an elasticity which shall take account of the varying circumstances of each case,—a necessity which unfortunately renders such a doctrine not only more difficult of application, but also to a certain extent uncertain in its operation and easily rendered abortive. Besides, it is only the more flagrant breaches of decency and propriety that could in practice be reached, and it is not perhaps desirable even to attempt to repress everything which the nicest taste and keenest sense of the respect due to private life would condemn.

In general, then, the matters of which the publication should be repressed may be described as those which concern the private life, habits, acts, and relations of an individual, and have no legitimate connection with his fitness for a public office which he seeks or for which he is suggested, or for any public or quasi public position which he seeks or for which he is suggested, and have no legitimate relation to or bearing upon any act done by him in a public or quasi public capacity. The foregoing is not designed as a wholly accurate or exhaustive definition, since that which must ultimately in a vast number of cases become a question of individual judgment and opinion is incapable of such definition; but it is an attempt to indicate broadly the class of matters referred to. Some things all men alike are entitled to keep from popular curiosity, whether in public life or not, while others are only private because the persons concerned have not assumed a position which makes their doings legitimate matters of public investigation.

SIDIS v. F–R PUBLISHING CORP.

113 F.2d 806 (2d Cir.), *cert. denied,* 311 U.S. 711 (1940).

Before SWAN, CLARK, and PATTERSON, CIRCUIT JUDGES

CLARK, CIRCUIT JUDGE.

[William James Sidis was a famous child prodigy in 1910. At the age of eleven, he lectured to distinguished mathematicians on the subject of Four–Dimensional Bodies; at the age of sixteen, he graduated from Harvard. In August, 1937, Sidis was the unwilling subject of a biographical sketch and cartoon printed in the New Yorker that was part of that magazine's features on current and past personalities entitled, "Where Are They Now?" The article on Sidis was subtitled "April Fool" and recounted his early accomplishments in mathematics, the wide-spread attention he received, the breakdown he suffered, and his strenuous attempts to conceal his identity and withdraw from the public view in the years that followed. The author also described Sidis' choice of a career as a clerk who would not need to employ unusual mathematical talents. The article closed with an account of an interview with Sidis at his present lodgings, described as "a hall bedroom of Boston's shabby south end." The untidiness of his room, his curious laugh, his manner of speech, and other personal habits were commented upon at length, as was the curious manifestations of his genius by such things as the study of the lore of the Okamakammessett Indians. Accompanying the biography was a small cartoon showing an eleven year old lecturing to a group of astounded professors. Further references were made to Sidis in a newspaper advertisement announcing the issue. Sidis brought an action in federal district court against the publisher for invasion of privacy under state law for both the public disclosure and appropriation torts. The Second Circuit affirmed the dismissal of the privacy claims by the district court.]

Warren and Brandeis realized that the interest of the individual in privacy must inevitably conflict with the interest of the public in news. Certain public figures, they conceded, such as holders of public office, must sacrifice their privacy and expose at least part of their lives to public scrutiny as the price of the powers they attain. But even public figures were not to be stripped bare. "In general, then, the matters of which the publication should be repressed may be described as those which concern the private life, habits, acts, and relations of an individual, and have no legitimate connection with his fitness for a public office.... Some things all men alike are entitled to keep from popular curiosity, whether in public life or not, while others are only private because the persons concerned have not assumed a position which makes their doings legitimate matters of public investigation." [Warren and Brandeis].

It must be conceded that under the strict standards suggested by these authors plaintiff's right of privacy has been invaded. Sidis today is neither politician, public administrator, nor statesman. Even if he were, some of the personal details revealed were of the sort that Warren and Brandeis believed "all men alike are entitled to keep from popular curiosity."

But despite eminent opinion to the contrary, we are not yet disposed to afford to all of the intimate details of private life an absolute immunity from the prying of the press. Everyone will agree that at some point the public interest in obtaining information becomes dominant over the individual's desire for privacy. Warren and Brandeis were willing to lift the veil somewhat in the case of public officers. We would go further, though we are not yet prepared to say how far. At least we would permit limited scrutiny of the "private" life of any person who has achieved, or has thrust upon him, the questionable and indefinable status of a "public figure."

William James Sidis was once a public figure. As a child prodigy, he excited both admiration and curiosity. Of him great deeds were expected. In 1910, he was a person about whom the newspapers might display a legitimate intellectual interest, in the sense meant by Warren and Brandeis, as distinguished from a trivial and unseemly curiosity. But the precise motives of the press we regard as unimportant. And even if Sidis had loathed public attention at that time, we think his uncommon achievements and personality would have made the attention permissible. Since then Sidis has cloaked himself in obscurity, but his subsequent history, containing as it did the answer to the question of whether or not he had fulfilled his early promise, was still a matter of public concern. The article in The New Yorker sketched the life of an unusual personality, and it possessed considerable popular news interest.

We express no comment on whether or not the news worthiness of the matter printed will always constitute a complete defense. Revelations may be so intimate and so unwarranted in view of the victim's position as to outrage the community's notions of decency. But when focused upon public characters, truthful comments upon dress, speech, habits, and the ordinary aspects of personality will usually not transgress this line. Regrettably or not, the misfortunes and frailties of neighbors and "public figures" are subjects of considerable interest and discussion to the rest of the population. And when such are the mores of the community, it would be unwise for a court to bar their expression in the newspapers, books, and magazines of the day.

Note

Sidis is the leading case on the limited privacy rights of public figures. Is the real principle that emanates from *Sidis* that once someone is a public figure he is always a public figure? What are concrete examples of revelations about public figures that are "so intimate" and "so unwarranted" as to "outrage the community's notion of decency"? Why did Sidis lose his case while the plaintiff in *Melvin v. Reid*, *supra*, won hers? Sidis, too, had a past he wanted to forget.

Note: Public Figures

To what extent is the denial of recovery to public figures in public disclosure cases based upon consent theory? Does the answer to that question depend upon the type of public figure involved? The concept of "public figure" developed by the Supreme Court in first amendment defamation cases includes two types: "all purpose" and "limited purpose" public figures. The former are those who have acquired such celebrity status that they are household names and the latter are persons who have voluntarily interjected themselves into a public controversy to influence its outcome. *See Gertz v. Robert Welch, Inc.*, 418 U.S. 323, 324 (1974), *cert. denied*, 459 U.S. 1226 (1983). Is the basis for limiting rights in public disclosure actions that those who seek publicity and recognition in the community impliedly waive their right to privacy? Kenneth Karst rejects this view; he contends it is mistaken because the express withholding of consent in public figure cases would not change the result. Implied consent is a "seductive" notion that obscures the real basis for limiting recovery—that publicity is justified in the public interest. This interesting analysis is found in Kenneth Karst, "The

Files": *Legal Controls Over the Accuracy and Accessibility of Stored Personal Data*, 31 Law & Contemp. Probs. 342, 344–45 (1966).

5. COMMUNITY STANDARDS OF DECENCY AS THE LIMIT-ING PRINCIPLE IN DISCLOSURE CASES

If there is anything approaching a consensus in public disclosure cases it is that recovery should be allowed for disclosures that so exceed community standards of decency as to be shocking. Professor Alfred Hill's support of this view is often cited, *e.g.*, Alfred Hill, *Defamation and Privacy Under the First Amendment*, 76 Colum. L. Rev. 1205, 1258 (1976); an interesting argument elaborating upon this view and drawing upon the Supreme Court's obscenity cases is found in Linda N. Woito & Patrick McNulty, *The Private Disclosure Tort and the First Amendment: Should the Community Decide Newsworthiness?*, 64 Iowa L. Rev. 185 (1979). As noted above, the Second Circuit in *Sidis* adopts an "outrage the community's notion of decency" test. The Ninth Circuit followed *Sidis* in *Virgil v. Time, Inc.*, 527 F.2d 1122 (9th Cir.1975) *cert. denied*, 425 U.S. 998 (1976), and invoked comment *h* of Section 652D of the Second Restatement of Torts:

> In determining what is a matter of legitimate public inter-est account must be taken of the customs and conventions of the community; and in the last analysis what is proper becomes a matter of community mores. The line is to be drawn when the publicity ceases to be the giving of information to which the public is entitled, and becomes a morbid and sensational prying into private lives for its own sake, with which a reasonable member of the public, with decent standards, would say that he had no concern.

527 F.2d at 1129.

Is the "shocking to community standards of decency" approach the ultimate answer to the problem of defining the newsworthy or public interest standard in a way that adequately protects first amendment values and privacy? Diane Zimmerman contends the test is essentially unworkable because the determination of what is "unconscionable" in view of standards of decency is ultimately a subjective one. *See* Diane Zimmerman, *Requiem for a Heavyweight: A Farewell to Warren and Brandeis' Privacy Tort*, 68 Cornell L. Rev. 291, 362 (1983). Do you agree?

BRISCOE v. READER'S DIGEST ASS'N

4 Cal.3d 529, 483 P.2d 34, 93 Cal.Rptr. 866 (1971).

PETERS, JUSTICE.

[Marvin Briscoe brought an action for invasion of privacy against Reader's Digest after the defendant published an article disclosing that Briscoe had committed a "hijacking" of a truck. Although the facts pertaining to Briscoe which were set forth in the article were true,

Briscoe contended that the use of his name was not "newsworthy" and constituted an invasion of his privacy because the incident had occurred eleven years before the article was written, and because he had since rehabilitated himself and assumed a respectable place in society. Briscoe also claimed that since the publication of the article, his eleven-year-old daughter and his friends had become aware of his past and had thereafter scorned and abandoned him. Reader's Digest filed special and general demurrers which were sustained without leave to amend.]

[W]e are presented simply with a pleading problem—does the complaint state a cause of action?

. . .

Conceding the truth of the facts published in defendant's article, plaintiff claims that the public disclosure of these private facts has humiliated him and exposed him to contempt and ridicule. Conceding that the *subject* of the article may have been "newsworthy," he contends that the use of his *name* was not, and that the defendant has thus invaded his right to privacy.

. . . In many respects a person had less privacy in the small community of the 18th century than he did in the urbanizing late 19th century or he does today in the modern metropolis. Extended family networks, primary group relationships, and rigid communal mores served to expose an individual's every deviation from the norm and to straitjacket him in a vise of backyard gossip. Yet Warren and Brandeis perceived that it was mass exposure to public gaze, as opposed to backyard gossip, which threatened to deprive men of the right of "scratching wherever one itches." (Westin, *Science, Privacy, and Freedom: Issues and Proposals for the 1970's*, 66 Colum.L.Rev. 1003, 1025 (1966).)

Acceptance of the right to privacy has grown with the increasing capability of the mass media and electronic devices with their capacity to destroy an individual's anonymity, intrude upon his most intimate activities, and expose his most personal characteristics to public gaze.

In a society in which multiple, often conflicting role performances are demanded of each individual, the original etymological meaning of the word "person"—mask—has taken on new meaning. Men fear exposure not only to those closest to them; much of the outrage underlying the asserted right to privacy is a reaction to exposure to persons known only through business or other secondary relationships. The claim is not so much one of total secrecy as it is of the right to *define* one's circle of intimacy—to choose who shall see beneath the quotidian mask. Loss of control over which "face" one puts on may result in literal loss of self-identity (Westin, supra, at p. 1023; cf. Fried, Privacy (1968) 77 Yale L.J. 475), and is humiliating beneath the gaze of those whose curiosity treats a human being as an object.

. . .

The central purpose of the First Amendment "is to give every voting member of the body politic the fullest possible participation in the understanding of those problems with which the citizens of a self-governing society must deal.... '' Nor is freedom of the press confined to comment upon public affairs and those persons who have voluntarily sought the public spotlight. "Freedom of discussion ... must embrace all issues about which information is needed or appropriate to enable the members of society to cope with the exigencies of their period.... '' The scope of the privilege thus extends to almost all reporting of recent events, even though it involves the publication of a purely private individual's name or likeness.

Particularly deserving of First Amendment protection are reports of "hot news," items of possible immediate public concern or interest. The need for constitutional protection is much greater under these circumstances, where deadlines must be met and quick decisions made, than in cases where more considered editorial judgments are possible....

There can be no doubt that reports of current criminal activities are the legitimate province of a free press. The circumstances under which crimes occur, the techniques used by those outside the law, the tragedy that may befall the victims—these are vital bits of information for people coping with the exigencies of modern life. Reports of these events may also promote the values served by the constitutional guarantee of a public trial. Although a case is not to be "tried in the papers," reports regarding a crime or criminal proceedings may encourage unknown witnesses to come forward with useful testimony and friends or relatives to come to the aid of the victim.

It is also generally in the social interest to identify adults currently charged with the commission of a crime. While such an identification may not presume guilt, it may legitimately put others on notice that the named individual is suspected of having committed a crime. Naming the suspect may also persuade eye witnesses and character witnesses to testify. For these reasons, while the suspect or offender obviously does not consent to public exposure, his right to privacy must give way to the overriding social interest.

In general, therefore, truthful reports of *recent* crimes and the names of suspects or offenders will be deemed protected by the First Amendment.

The instant case, however, compels us to consider whether reports of the facts of *past* crimes and the identification of past offenders serve these same public-interest functions.

We have no doubt that reports of the facts of past crimes are newsworthy. Media publication of the circumstances under which crimes were committed in the past may prove educational in the same way that reports of current crimes do. The public has a strong interest in enforcing the law, and this interest is served by accumulating and disseminating data cataloguing the reasons men commit crimes, the methods they use, and the ways in which they are apprehended. Thus in an article on truck hijackings, Reader's Digest certainly had the right to report the facts of plaintiff's criminal act.

However, identification of the *actor* in reports of long past crimes usually serves little independent public purpose. Once legal proceedings have terminated, and a suspect or offender has been released, identification of the individual will not usually aid the administration of justice. Identification will no longer serve to bring forth witnesses or obtain succor for victims. Unless the individual has reattracted the public eye to himself in some independent fashion, the only public "interest" that would usually be served is that of curiosity.

There may be times, of course, when an event involving private citizens may be so unique as to capture the imagination of all. In such cases—e.g., the behavior of the passengers on the sinking *Titanic*, the heroism of Nathan Hale, the horror of the Saint Valentine's Day Massacre—purely private individuals may by an accident of history lose their privacy regarding that incident for all time. There need be no "reattraction" of the public eye because the public interest never wavered. An individual whose name is fixed in the public's memory, such as that of the political assassin, never becomes an anonymous member of the community again. But in each case it is for the trier of fact to determine whether the individual's infamy is such that he has never left the public arena; we cannot do so as a matter of law.

. . .

Another factor militating in favor of protecting the individual's privacy here is the state's interest in the integrity of the rehabilitative process. . . .

. . .

One of the premises of the rehabilitative process is that the rehabilitated offender can rejoin that great bulk of the community from which he has been ostracized for his anti-social acts. In return for becoming a "new man," he is allowed to melt into the shadows of obscurity.

We are realistic enough to recognize that men are curious about the inner sanctums of their neighbors—that the public will create its heroes and villains. We must also be realistic enough to realize that full disclosure of one's inner thoughts, intimate personal characteristics, and past life is neither the rule nor the norm in these United States. We have developed a variegated panoply of professional listeners to whom we confidentially "reveal all"; otherwise we keep our own counsel. The masks we wear may be stripped away upon the occurrence of some event of public interest. But just as the risk of exposure is a concomitant of urban life, so too is the expectation of anonymity regained. It would be a crass legal fiction to assert that a matter once public never becomes private again. Human forgetfulness over time puts today's "hot" news in tomorrow's dusty archives. In a nation of 200 million people there is ample opportunity for all but the most infamous to begin a new life.

Plaintiff is a man whose last offense took place 11 years before, who has paid his debt to society, who has friends and an 11–year-old daughter who were unaware of his early life—a man who has assumed a position in "respectable" society. Ideally, his neighbors should recognize his present worth and forget his past life of shame. But men are not so divine as to forgive the past trespasses of others, and plaintiff therefore endeavored to reveal as little as possible of his past life. Yet, as if in some bizarre canyon of echoes, petitioner's past life pursues him through the pages of Reader's Digest, now published in 13 languages and distributed in 100 nations, with a circulation in California alone of almost 2,000,000 copies.

In a nation built upon the free dissemination of ideas, it is always difficult to declare that something may not be published. But the great general interest in an unfettered press may at times be outweighed by other great societal interests. As a people we have come to recognize that one of these societal interests is that of protecting an individual's right to privacy. The right to know and the right to have others not know are, simplistically considered, irreconcilable. But the rights guaranteed by the First Amendment do not require total abrogation of the right to privacy. The goals sought by each may be achieved with a minimum of intrusion upon the other.

. . . Thus a truthful publication is constitutionally protected if (1) it is newsworthy and (2) it does not reveal facts so offensive as to shock the community's notions of decency.

. . .

On the assumed set of facts before us we are convinced that a jury could reasonably find that plaintiff's identity as a former hijacker was not newsworthy. First, as discussed above, a jury could find that publication of plaintiff's identity in connection with incidents of his past life was in this case of minimal social value. There was no independent reason whatsoever for focusing public attention on Mr. Briscoe as an individual at this time. A jury could certainly find that Mr. Briscoe had once again become an anonymous member of the community. Once legal proceedings have concluded, and particularly once the individual has reverted to the lawful and unexciting life led by the rest of the community, the public's interest in knowing is less compelling.

Second, a jury might find that revealing one's criminal past for all to see is grossly offensive to most people in America. Certainly a criminal background is kept even more hidden from others than a humiliating disease (Barber v. Time, Inc., supra) or the existence of business debts (Trammell v. Citizens News Co., Inc., supra; Tollefson v. Price, supra). The consequences of revelation in this case—ostracism, isolation, and the alienation of one's family—make all too clear just how deeply offensive to most persons a prior crime is and thus how hidden the former offender must keep the knowledge of his prior indiscretion.

Third, in no way can plaintiff be said to have voluntarily consented to the publicity accorded him here. He committed a crime. He was punished. He was rehabilitated. And he became, for 11 years, an obscure and law-abiding citizen. His every effort was to forget and have others forget that he had once hijacked a truck.

Finally, the interests at stake here are not merely those of publication and privacy alone, for the state has a compelling interest in the efficacy of penal systems in rehabilitating criminals and returning them as productive and law-abiding citizens to the society whence they came. A jury might well find that a continuing threat that the rehabilitated offender's old identity will be resurrected by the media is counterproductive to the goals of this correctional process.

Mindful that "the balance is always weighted in favor of free expression," and that we must not chill First Amendment freedoms through uncertainty, we find it reasonable to require a plaintiff to prove, in each case, that the publisher invaded his privacy with reckless disregard for the fact that reasonable men would find the invasion highly offensive.

We do not hold today that plaintiff must prevail in his action. It is for the trier of fact to determine (1) whether plaintiff had become a rehabilitated member of society, (2) whether identifying him as a former criminal would be highly offensive and injurious to the reasonable man, (3) whether defendant published this information with a reckless disregard for its offensiveness, and (4) whether any independent justification for printing plaintiff's identity existed. We hold today only that, as pleaded, plaintiff has stated a valid cause of action, sustaining the demurrer to plaintiff's complaint was improper, and that the ensuing judgment must therefore be reversed.

WRIGHT, C.J., and McCOMB, TOBRINER, MOSK, BURKE, and SULLIVAN, JJ.,concur.

Note

Briscoe represents one of the most ambitious attempts by a court to delineate factors that ought to count in sorting out information that is "newsworthy" and of "legitimate public concern" from information that is not. Does *Cox Broadcasting Corp. v. Cohn*, 420 U.S. 469 (1975), and the first amendment cases decided after *Cox, infra,* leave the precedential value of *Briscoe* seriously in doubt?

Consider the role of the court and jury in the determination of newsworthiness under the *Briscoe* approach. Are first amendment values adequately protected by leaving the question of newsworthiness to the jury to the extent that the *Briscoe* court does? One way to think about *Briscoe* is to view the court as looking at public disclosure cases as essentially tort actions with important first amendment dimensions that may be adequately addressed within the traditional tort litigation process. For current purposes suppose we speak of this notion of *Briscoe* as the "It's a Tort Case" model. Under this perspective, the question of the newsworthiness of published private facts is dealt with by threshold rulings by the court sorting out nonactionable disclosures and submission of the remaining cases to the jury for factual determinations with careful instructions.

Barber v. Time, Inc., 348 Mo. 1199, 159 S.W.2d 291 (1942), represents the extreme end of the spectrum of "Its a Tort Case" perspective. In *Barber*, the Supreme Court of Missouri upheld a damage judgment against *Time* for publishing a story in its weekly magazine which described the plaintiff's eating disorder in detail. The article was entitled, "Starving Glutton" and included a picture of the plaintiff in bed in a hospital gown. The court concluded it was properly a jury question as to whether the publication was of legitimate public concern, adding, "while plaintiff's ailment may have been a matter of some public interest ... the identity of [the plaintiff] ... was not." *Id*. at 1207, 159 S.W. 2d at 295. Compare *Barber* with *Dietemann v. Time*, *supra*. (Note that in *Barber*, the action was brought against the newspaper for publishing the photograph in connection with an article, not against the newspaper or the photographer for the taking of the photograph.)

Examine the Court's approach in *Cox Broadcasting Corp. v. Cohn*, below, on the role of the court and jury in public disclosure actions against media defendants. Does the Supreme Court adopt a different perspective of these cases, namely, that public disclosure cases are primarily first amendment cases (couched in tort theory)? Under the "It's a First Amendment Case" model, the question of whether true factual disclosures are newsworthy is for media editors and not for courts or juries (the risk of juries imposing their personal tastes on the press in findings of "newsworthiness" produces self-censorship and "chills" speech). Diane Zimmerman, a noted critic of the public disclosure tort, expresses this thought as the "Leave-it-to-the-Press" model. *See* Diane Zimmerman, *Requiem For A Heavyweight: A Farewell To Warren And Brandeis' Privacy Tort*, 68 Corn. L. Rev. 291, 353–55 (1983). Under this perspective the question of who determines "newsworthiness" is crucial. Primacy is given to first amendment values because of the perception by courts that a heavy tax is imposed on free speech by jury determinations of "newsworthiness." Most of the Court's rulings on the newsworthiness or legitimate public concern issue are best viewed as examples of this model.

a. Truth as a Constitutional Defense

COX BROADCASTING CORP. v. COHN

420 U.S. 469 (1975).

Mr. Justice White delivered the opinion of the Court.

[In August, 1971, Cohn's 17–year-old daughter died after being raped. In April, 1972 six defendants appeared in court to enter their pleas. A reporter (one of the appellants) covering the proceedings for his employer learned the name of the victim from an examination of the indictments, which were made available to him in the courtroom as public records. Later that day, and on the following day, the reporter broadcast on appellant Cox Broadcasting's television station a news report concerning the court proceedings and naming the victim of the crime. In May, 1972 Cohn brought an action for damages against the appellants relying on the Georgia Code Section 26–99001 which makes it a misdemeanor to publish or broadcast the name or identity of a rape victim.[1] Cohn also claimed that his right to privacy had been invaded by the television broadcasts giving the name of his deceased daughter. Appellants claimed the broadcasts were privileged under both state law and the first and fourteenth amendments. The trial court held that the Georgia statute gave a civil remedy to those injured by its violation and granted summary judgment to Cohn as to liability, with the determination of damages to await trial by jury. On appeal, the Georgia Supreme Court initially held that the trial court had erred in construing Section 26–9901 to extend a civil cause of action for invasion of privacy but ruled that the complaint stated a cause of action for common law invasion of privacy. The Georgia Supreme Court later denied a motion for rehearing on the ground that the Georgia statute declared a state policy that a rape victim's name was not a matter of public concern, and sustained the statute as a legitimate limitation on freedom of expression. The newspaper and the reporter appeal.]

The issue before us in this case is whether consistently with the First and Fourteenth Amendments, a State may extend a cause of action for damages for invasion of privacy caused by the publication of the name of a deceased rape victim which was publicly revealed in connection with the prosecution of the crime.

. . .

Georgia stoutly defends both Section 26–9901 and the State's common law privacy action challenged here. Her claims are not without force, for powerful arguments can be made, and have been made, that however it may be ultimately defined, there is a zone of privacy surrounding every individual, a zone within which the State may protect him from intrusion by the press, with all its attendant publicity. Indeed, the central thesis of the root article by Warren and Brandeis, The Right to Privacy, 4 Harv. L. Rev. 193, 196 (1890), was that the press was overstepping its prerogatives by publishing essentially private information and that there should be a remedy for the alleged abuses.

More compellingly, the century has experienced a strong tide running in favor of the so-called right of privacy. In 1967, we noted that

---

1. It shall be unlawful for any news media or any other person to print and publish, broadcast, televise, or disseminate through any other medium of public dissemination or cause to be printed and published, broadcast, televised, or disseminated in any newspaper, magazine, periodical or other publications published in this State or through any radio or television broadcast originating in the State the name or identity of any female who may have been raped or upon whom an assault with intent to commit rape may have been made. Any person or corporation violating the provisions of this section shall, upon conviction, be punished as for a misdemeanor.

Three other States have similar statutes. See Fla. Stat. Ann. Sections 794.03, 794.04; S.C. Code Section 16–81; Wis. Stat. Ann. Section 942.02. The Wisconsin Supreme Court upheld the constitutionality of the Wisconsin statute in State v. Evjue, 253 Wis. 146, 33 N.W.2d 305 (1948). The South Carolina statute was involved in Nappier v. Jefferson Standard Life Insurance Co., 322 F.2d 502, 505 (C.A.4 1963), but no constitutional challenge to the statute was made. In Hunter v. Washington Post, 102 Daily Washington L. Rptr. 1561 (1974), the D.C. Superior Court denied the defendant's motion for judgment on the pleadings based upon constitutional grounds in an action brought for invasion of privacy resulting from the defendant's publication identifying the plaintiff as a rape victim and giving her name, age, and address.

"[i]t has been said that a 'right of privacy' has been recognized at common law in 30 States plus the District of Columbia and by statute in four States." . . .

These are impressive credentials for a right of privacy, but we should recognize that we do not have at issue here an action for the invasion of privacy involving the appropriation of one's name or photograph, a physical or other tangible intrusion into a private area, or a publication of otherwise private information that is also false although perhaps not defamatory. The version of the privacy tort now before us— termed in Georgia—"the tort of public disclosure,"—is that in which the plaintiff claims the right to be free from unwanted publicity about his private affairs, which although wholly true, would be offensive to a person of ordinary sensibilities. Because the gravamen of the claimed injury is the publication of information, whether true or not, the dissemination of which is embarrassing or otherwise painful to an individual, it is here that claims of privacy most directly confront the constitutional freedoms of speech and press. The face-off is apparent, and the appellants urge upon us the broad holding that the press may not be made criminally or civilly liable for publishing information that is neither false nor misleading but absolutely accurate, however damaging it may be to reputation or individual sensibilities.

[Justice White then summarized the defamation and false light first amendment cases, noting that the question of whether truth was an absolute defense in cases involving private plaintiffs had been left open.]

Those precedents, as well as other considerations, counsel similar caution here. In this sphere of collision between claims of privacy and those of the free press, the interests on both sides are plainly rooted in the traditions and significant concerns of our society. Rather than address the broader question whether truthful publications may ever be subjected to civil or criminal liability consistently with the First and Fourteenth Amendments, or to put it another way, whether the State may ever define and protect an area of privacy free from unwanted publicity in the press, it is appropriate to focus on the narrower interface between press and privacy that this case presents, namely, whether the State may impose sanctions on the accurate publication of the name of a rape victim obtained from public records—more specifically, from judicial records which are maintained in connection with a public prosecution and which themselves are open to public inspection. We are convinced that the State may not do so.

In the first place, in a society in which each individual has but limited time and resources with which to observe at first hand the operations of his government, he relies necessarily upon the press to bring to him in convenient form the facts of those operations. Great responsibility is accordingly placed upon the news media to report fully and accurately the proceedings of government, and official records and documents open to the public are the basic data of governmental operations. Without the information provided by the press most of us and many of our representatives would be unable to vote intelligently or to register opinions on the administration of government generally. With respect to judicial proceedings in particular, the function of the press serves to guarantee the fairness of trials and to bring to bear the beneficial effects of public scrutiny upon the administration of justice.

Appellee has claimed in this litigation that the efforts of the press have infringed his right to privacy by broadcasting to the world the fact that his daughter was a rape victim. The commission of crime, prosecutions resulting from it, and judicial proceedings arising from the prosecutions, however, are without question events of legitimate concern to the public and consequently fall within the responsibility of the press to report the operations of government.

. . .

The developing law surrounding the tort of invasion of privacy recognizes a privilege in the press to report the events of judicial proceedings. The Warren and Brandeis article, supra, noted that the proposed new right would be limited in the same manner as actions for libel and slander where such a publication was a privileged communication: "the right to privacy is not invaded by any publication made in a court of justice . . . and (at least in many jurisdictions) reports of any such proceedings would in some measure be accorded a like privilege."

. . .

Thus even the prevailing law of invasion of privacy generally recognizes that the interests in privacy fade when the information involved already appears on the public record. . . .

. . .

We are reluctant to embark on a course that would make public records generally available to the media but forbid their publication if offensive to the sensibilities of the supposed reasonable man. Such a rule would make it very difficult for the media to inform citizens about the public business and yet stay within the law. The rule would invite timidity and self-censorship and very likely lead to the suppression of many items that would otherwise be published and that should be made available to the public. At the very least, the First and Fourteenth Amendments will not allow exposing the press to liability for truthfully publishing information released to the public in official court records. If there are privacy interests to be protected in judicial proceedings, the States must respond by means which avoid public documentation or other exposure of private information. Their political institutions must weigh the interests in privacy with the interests of the public to know and of the press to publish. Once true information is disclosed in public court documents open to public inspection, the press cannot be sanctioned for publishing it. In this instance as in others reliance must rest upon the judgment of those who decide what to publish or broadcast. See Miami Herald Publishing Co. v. Tornillo, 418 U.S., at 258.

Appellant Wassell based his televised report upon notes taken during the court proceedings and obtained the name of the victim from the indictments handed to him at his request during a recess in the hearing. Appellee has not contended that the name was obtained in an improper fashion or that it was not on an official court document open to public inspection. Under these circumstances, the protection of freedom of the press provided by the First and Fourteenth Amendments bars the State of Georgia from making appellants' broadcast the basis of civil liability.

Reversed.

MR. CHIEF JUSTICE BURGER concurs in the judgment.

MR. JUSTICE POWELL, concurring.

I join in the Court's opinion, as I agree with the holding and most of its supporting rationale. My understanding of some of our decisions concerning the law of defamation, however, differs from that expressed in today's opinion. Accordingly, I think it appropriate to state separately my views.

... I think that the constitutional necessity of recognizing a defense of truth is equally implicit in our statement of the permissible standard of liability for the publication or broadcast of defamatory statements whose substance makes apparent the substantial danger of injury to the reputation of a private citizen.

In *Gertz* we held that the First Amendment prohibits the States from imposing strict liability for media publication of allegedly false statements that are claimed to defame a private individual. While providing the required "breathing space" for First Amendment freedoms, the *Gertz* standard affords the States substantial latitude in compensating private individuals for wrongful injury to reputation. "[S]o long as they do not impose liability without fault, the States may define for themselves the appropriate standard of liability for a publisher or broadcaster of defamatory falsehood injurious to a private individual." 418 U.S., at 347.... It is fair to say that if the statements are true, the standard contemplated by *Gertz* cannot be satisfied.

. . .

MR. JUSTICE REHNQUIST, dissenting.

Because I am of the opinion that the decision which is the subject of this appeal is not a "final" judgment or decree, as that term is used in 28 U.S.C. Section 1257, I would dismiss this appeal for want of jurisdiction.

Note

In *Cox*, the court says in dicta that "the defense of truth is constitutionally required where the subject of the publication is a public official or public figure," but specifically leaves open the question of whether awarding damages to a private plaintiff in a public disclosure action would violate the first amendment. Justice Powell believes that *Gertz v. Robert Welch, Inc.*,

418 U.S. 323 (1974), *cert. denied,* 459 U.S. 1226 (1983), implicitly imposes a constitutional defense of truth even if the plaintiff is a private individual.

In *Gertz*, discussed *supra*, the Court held that in private plaintiff defamation cases, the first amendment requires that the plaintiff suing the media defendant establish that the defendant published the *false* utterance negligently, and establish by credible evidence that as a consequence of the publication the plaintiff suffered emotional injury or damage to her reputation. What difficulties would arise if the Court were to decide to adopt the "negligence-actual injury" standard of *Gertz* in public disclosure cases brought by private persons against media defendants? The basic question is whether the fault standard in first amendment cases dealing with false information has any relevance to first amendment cases when the tort action is based upon publication of *true facts*. Is the attempt to transport first amendment concepts from defamation to public disclosure cases an example of that insidious intellectual disease, "the fallacy of the category transplant"? *See* Moffatt Hancock, *Fallacy of the Transplanted Category*, 37 Can. B. Rev. 535 (1959).

Note: Truth as an Absolute Defense

As suggested above, the Supreme Court has rejected the invitation to hold that the first amendment dictates that truth be an absolute defense in all tort actions. Two excellent articles presenting different views as to whether truth ought to be an absolute defense are Marc A. Franklin, *The Origins and Constitutionality of Limitations on Truth as a Defense in Tort Law*, 16 Stan. L. Rev. 789 (1963) (yes) and Melville G. Nimmer, *The Right to Speak from Times to Time: First Amendment Theory Applied to Libel and Misapplied to Privacy*, 56 Calif. L. Rev. 935 (1968) (no).

Note: Should Malice be an Element of the Public Disclosure Tort?

Consider Warren and Brandeis' comment:

The absence of "malice" in the publisher does not afford a defence.

Personal ill will is not an ingredient of the offence, any more than in an ordinary case of trespass to person or to property. Such malice is never necessary to be shown in an action for libel or slander at common law, except in rebuttal of some defence, *e.g.*, that the occasion rendered the communication privileged, or, under the statutes in this State and elsewhere, that the statement complained of was true. The invasion of the privacy that is to be protected is equally complete and equally injurious, whether the motives by which the speaker or writer was actuated are, taken by themselves, culpable or not.... Viewed as a wrong to the individual, this rule is the same pervading the whole law of torts....

Warren and Brandeis, *The Right To Privacy*, 4 Harv. L. Rev. 193, 218–19 (1890).

Recall that in *Briscoe v. Reader's Digest, supra*, the Supreme Court of California required the plaintiff to demonstrate publication by the defendant with "reckless disregard for the offensiveness of the information" and viewed this determination to be for the jury. There is additional support in the cases for requiring "malicious" publication in private fact cases as an additional way to provide adequate protection for the press. Again the analogy is to first amendment defamation cases. *Taylor v. K.T.V.B. Inc.*, 96 Idaho 202, 525 P.2d 984 (1974) is an example of judicial use of the malice requirement in public disclosure cases.

In *Taylor*, a television station in Boise, Idaho showed Taylor being arrested on an evening news broadcast. Taylor had brandished a weapon in his house and was ordered into the street by the police. He left the house completely nude, and was arrested and covered with a blanket by the police officers after being handcuffed. The video of the arrest which showed the buttocks and genitals of Taylor for a fraction of one second was shown on the telecast. The Idaho Supreme Court reversed the judgment of $15,000 that had been awarded Taylor by the jury in his public disclosure tort action against the station. However, the court rejected the defendant's arguments that the facts were public, newsworthy and of legitimate public interest as a matter of law. The remand was solely because the trial court had failed to instruct the jury that Taylor was required to prove there was "malicious" disclosure of the private details of the arrest. Malicious disclosure consisted of disclosure done either for the "purpose" of embarrassing or humiliating Taylor or "with reckless disregard" as to whether the disclosure would result in embarrassment or humiliation. The court concluded that the malice rule was required by the holdings of the Supreme Court in defamation and false light first amendment cases.

Chief Justice Sheppard dissented:

I am unable to agree that what had been made available to public view by the plaintiff himself could constitute private facts. . . .

Under the fact situation presented herein where the plaintiff has voluntarily displayed himself in the nude while in the course of committing criminal offenses and while he was being placed under arrest, I would hold that he has waived any privilege he might have had to the privacy of his privates. In my judgment, any arrest is or can be argued to be embarrassing and humiliating. Even the most veteran felon is undoubtedly embarrassed, if nothing else, at being apprehended.

Criminal behavior and its consequences, while perhaps involving elements of privacy of victims, cannot be said to be beyond the legitimate interest of society in general since the conduct is offensive and proscribed by society in general. I discern no standard by which our lower courts can be guided in future when faced with such cases.

Note

What credible testimony could the defendant give before the jury that would convince them that the decision to televise the arrest was made without the defendant knowing that the telecast would be embarrassing to the defendant?

(1) Lawfully Acquired Public Information

FLORIDA STAR v. B.J.F.

491 U.S. 524 (1989).

JUSTICE MARSHALL delivered the opinion of the Court.

[The Florida Star is a newspaper which publishes a "Police Reports" section containing brief articles describing local criminal incidents under police investigation. After appellee B.J.F.[2] reported to the Sheriff's Department that she had been robbed and sexually assaulted, the Department prepared a report on the incident which identified B.J.F. by her full name. The Department then placed the report in its press room. A Florida Star reporter-trainee sent to the press room copied the police report word for word, including B.J.F.'s full name, and a Florida Star reporter then prepared an article about the crime, also including B.J.F.'s full name. B.J.F. filed suit against the Sheriff's Department and The Florida Star, alleging that both parties had negligently violated Florida Stat. Section 794.03 (1987) making it unlawful to print, publish or broadcast "in any instrument of mass communication" the name of the victim of a sexual offense. Before trial, the Department settled with B.J.F. for $2,500. The Florida Star moved to dismiss, claiming that imposing civil sanctions on the newspaper pursuant to Section 794.03 violated the first amendment. The trial judge rejected the motion.

At the trial, B.J.F. testified that she had suffered emotional distress from the publication of her name, that she had heard about the article from fellow workers and acquaintances, that her mother had received several phone calls from a man who stated that he would rape B.J.F. again, and that these events had forced B.J.F. to change her residence and phone number. She also stated that she had been forced to seek police protection and to obtain mental health counseling. At the close of the newspaper's defense, the judge granted B.J.F.'s motion for a directed verdict on the issue of negligence, finding the Florida Star per se negligent based upon its violation of the statute. The judge then instructed the jury that it could award B.J.F. punitive damages if it found that the newspaper had "acted with reckless indifference to the rights of others." The jury awarded B.J.F. $75,000 in compensatory damages and $25,000 in punitive damages. The First District Court of Appeal affirmed; the Supreme Court of Florida denied discretionary review. The Florida Star appeals.]

The tension between the right which the First Amendment accords to a free press ... and the protections which various statutes and common-law doctrines accord to personal privacy against the publication of truthful information ... is a subject we have addressed several times

---

2. In filing a lawsuit, appellee used her full name in the caption of this case. On appeal, the Florida District Court of Appeals sua sponte revised the caption, stating that it would refer to the appellee by her first initials, "in order to preserve [her] privacy interests." Respecting those interests, we too, refer to appellee by her first initials, both in the caption and in our discussion.

in recent years.... [A]lthough our decisions have without exception upheld the press' right to publish, we have emphasized each time that we were resolving this conflict only as it arose in a discrete factual context....

... [In] Smith v. Daily Mail Publishing Co., 443 U.S. 97 (1979), we found unconstitutional the indictment of two newspapers for violating a state statute forbidding newspapers to publish, without written approval of the juvenile court, the name of any youth charged as a juvenile offender. The papers had learned about a shooting by monitoring a police band radio frequency, and had obtained the name of the alleged juvenile assailant from witnesses, the police, and a local prosecutor.

Appellant takes the position that this case is indistinguishable from *Cox Broadcasting*. Alternatively, it urges that ... the press may never be punished, civilly or criminally, for publishing the truth.... [A]ppellee urges that *Cox Broadcasting* be overruled and replaced with a categorical rule that publication of the name of a rape victim never enjoys constitutional protection.

We conclude that imposing damages on appellant for publishing B.J.F.'s name violates the First Amendment, although not for either of the reasons appellant urges. Despite the strong resemblance this case bears to *Cox Broadcasting*, that case cannot fairly be read as controlling here. The name of the rape victim in that case was obtained from courthouse records that were open to public inspection.... Significantly, one of the reasons we gave in *Cox Broadcasting* for invalidating the challenged damages award was the important role the press plays in subjecting trials to public scrutiny and thereby helping guarantee their fairness. That role is not directly compromised where, as here, the information in question comes from a police report prepared and disseminated at a time at which not only had no adversarial criminal proceedings begun, but no suspect had been identified.

Nor need we accept appellant's invitation to hold broadly that truthful publication may never be punished consistent with the First Amendment. Our cases have carefully eschewed reaching this ultimate question, mindful that the future may bring scenarios which prudence counsels our not resolving anticipatorily.... We continue to believe that the sensitivity and significance of the interests presented in clashes between First Amendment and privacy rights counsel relying on limited principles that sweep no more broadly than the appropriate context of the instant case.

In our view, this case is appropriately analyzed with reference to such a limited First Amendment principle. It is the one, in fact, which we articulated in *Daily Mail* in our synthesis of prior cases involving attempts to punish truthful publication: "[I]f a newspaper lawfully obtains truthful information about a matter of public significance then state officials may not constitutionally punish publication of the information, absent a need to further a state interest of the highest order." According the press the ample protection provided by that principle is supported by at least three separate considerations, in addition to, of course, the overarching " 'public interest, secured by the Constitution, in the dissemination of truth.' " ... [Quote from *Cox Broadcasting*]

First, because the *Daily Mail* formulation only protects the publication of information which a newspaper has "lawfully obtain[ed]," the government retains ample means of safeguarding significant interests upon which publication may impinge, including protecting a rape victim's anonymity. To the extent sensitive information rests in private hands, the government may under some circumstances forbid its nonconsensual acquisition, thereby bringing outside of the Daily Mail principle the publication of any information so acquired. To the extent sensitive information is in the government's custody, it has even greater power to forestall or mitigate the injury caused by its release. The government may classify certain information, establish and enforce procedures ensuring its redacted release, and extend a damages remedy against the government or its officials where the government's mishandling of sensitive information leads to its dissemination. Where information is entrusted to the government, a less drastic means than punishing truthful publication almost always exists for guarding against the dissemination of private facts.

A second consideration undergirding the *Daily Mail* principle is the fact that punishing the press for its dissemination of information which is already publicly available is relatively unlikely to advance the interests in the service of which the State seeks to act. It is not, of course, always the case that information lawfully acquired by the press is known, or accessible, to others. But where the government has made certain information publicly available, it is highly anomalous to sanction persons other than the source of its release.... The *Daily Mail* formulation reflects the fact that it is a limited set of cases indeed where, despite the accessibility of the public to certain information, a meaningful public interest is served by restricting its further release by other entities, like the press....

A third and final consideration is the "timidity and self-censorship" which may result from allowing the media to be punished for publishing certain truthful information....

Applied to the instant case, the *Daily Mail* principle clearly commands reversal.... It is undisputed that the news article describing the assault on B.J.F. was accurate. In addition, appellant lawfully obtained B.J.F.'s name. Appellee's argument to the contrary is based on the fact that under Florida law, police reports which reveal the identity of the victim of a sexual offense are not among the matters of "public record" which the public, by law, is entitled to inspect. But the fact that state officials are not required to disclose such reports does not make it unlawful for a newspaper to receive them when furnished by the government. Nor does the fact that the Department apparently failed to fulfill its obligation under 794.03 not to "cause or allow to be ... published" the name of a sexual offense victim make the newspaper's ensuing receipt of this information unlawful. Even assuming the Constitution permitted a State to proscribe *receipt* of information, Florida has not taken this step. It is, clear, furthermore, that the news article concerned "a matter of public significance," in the sense in which the *Daily Mail* synthesis of prior cases used that term. That is, the article generally, as opposed to the specific identity contained within it, involved a matter of paramount public import: the commission, and investigation, of a violent crime which had been reported to authorities. The second inquiry is whether imposing liability on appellant pursuant to Section 794.03 serves "a need to further a state interest of the highest order." Appellee argues that a rule punishing publication furthers three closely related interests: the privacy of victims of sexual offenses; the physical safety of such victims, who may be targeted for retaliation if their names become known to their assailants; and the goal of encouraging victims of such crimes to report these offenses without fear of exposure.

At a time in which we are daily reminded of the tragic reality of rape, it is undeniable that these are highly significant interests, a fact underscored by the Florida Legislature's explicit attempt to protect these interests by enacting a criminal statute prohibiting much dissemination of victim identities. We accordingly do not rule out the possibility that, in a proper case, imposing civil sanctions for publication of the name of a rape victim might be so overwhelmingly necessary to advance these interests as to satisfy the *Daily Mail* standard. For three independent reasons, however, imposing liability for publication under the circumstances of this case is too precipitous a means of advancing these interests to convince us that there is a "need" within the meaning of the *Daily Mail* formulation for Florida to take this extreme step.

First is the manner in which appellant obtained the identifying information in question. As we have noted, where the government itself provides information to the media, it is most appropriate to assume that the government had, but failed to utilize, far more limited means of guarding against dissemination than the extreme step of punishing truthful speech. That assumption is richly borne out in this case. B.J.F.'s identity would never have come to light were it not for the erroneous, if inadvertent, inclusion by the Department of her full name in an incident report made available in a press room open to the public. Florida's policy against disclosure of rape victims' identities, reflected in Section 794.03, was undercut by the Department failure to abide by this policy. Where, as here, the government has failed to police itself in disseminating information, it is clear ... that the imposition of damages against the press for its subsequent publication can hardly be said to be a narrowly tailored means of safeguarding anonymity. Once the government has placed such information in the public domain, "reliance must rest upon the judgment of those who decide what to publish or broadcast," and hopes for restitution must rest upon the willingness of the government to compensate victims for their loss of privacy, and to protect them from the other consequences of its mishandling of the information which these victims provided in confidence.

That appellant gained access to the information in question through a government news release makes it especially likely that, if liability were to be imposed, self-censorship would result.... The government's issuance of such a release, without qualification, can only convey to recipients that the government considered dissemination lawful, and indeed expected the recipients to disseminate the information further. Had appellant merely reproduced the news release prepared and released by the Department, imposing civil damages would surely violate the First Amendment. The fact that appellant converted the police report into a news story by adding the linguistic connecting tissue necessary to transform the report's facts into full sentences cannot change this result.

A second problem with Florida's imposition of liability for publication is the broad sweep of the negligence *per se* standard applied under the civil cause of action implied from Section 794.03. Unlike claims based on the common law tort of invasion of privacy, see Restatement (Second) of Torts Section 652D (1977), civil actions based on Section 794.03 require no case-by-case findings that the disclosure of a fact about a person's private life was one that a reasonable person would find highly offensive. On the contrary, under the *per se* theory of negligence by the courts below, liability follows automatically from publication. This is so regardless of whether the identity of the victim is already known throughout the community; whether the victim has voluntarily called public attention to the offenses; or whether the identity of the victim has otherwise become a reasonable subject of publication concern—because, perhaps, questions have arisen whether the victim fabricated an assault by a particular person. Nor is there a scienter requirement of any kind under Section 794.03, engendering the perverse result that truthful publications challenged pursuant to this cause of action are less protected by the First Amendment than even the least protected defamatory falsehoods: those involving purely private figures, where liability is evaluated under a standard, usually applied by a jury, of ordinary negligence....

Third, and finally, the facial underinclusiveness of Section 794.03 raises serious doubts about whether Florida is, in fact, serving, with this statute, the significance interests which appellee invokes in support of affirmance. Section 794.03 prohibits the publication of identifying information only if this information appears in an "instrument of mass communication," a term the statute does not define. Section 794.03 does not prohibit the spread by other means of the identities of victims of sexual offenses. An individual who maliciously spreads word of the identity of a rape victim is thus not covered, despite the fact that the communication of such information to persons who live near, or work with, the victim may have consequences equally devastating as the exposure of her name to large numbers of strangers.

When a State attempts the extraordinary measure of punishing truthful publication in the name of privacy, it must demonstrate its commitment to advancing this interest by applying its prohibition even-handedly, to the smalltime disseminator as well as the media giant.

Where important First Amendment interests are at stake, the mass scope of disclosure is not an acceptable surrogate for injury.... Without more careful and inclusive precautions against alternative forms of dissemination, we cannot conclude that Florida's selective ban on publication by the mass media satisfactorily accomplishes its stated purpose.

Our holding today is limited. We do not hold that truthful publication is automatically constitutionally protected, or that there is no zone of personal privacy within which the State may protect the individual from intrusion by the press, or even that a State may never punish publication of the name of a victim of a sexual offense. We hold only that where a newspaper publishes truthful information which it has lawfully obtained, punishment may lawfully be imposed, if at all, only when narrowly tailored to a state interest of the highest order, and that no such interest is satisfactorily served by imposing liability under Section 794.03 to appellant under the facts of this case. The decision below is therefore

Reversed.

Justice Scalia, concurring in part and concurring in the judgment.

Justice White, with whom The Chief Justice and Justice O'Connor join, dissenting.

"Short of homicide, [rape] is the 'ultimate violation of self.' " For B.J.F., however, the violation she suffered at a rapist's knifepoint marked only the beginning of her ordeal. A week later, while her assailant was still at large, an account of this assault—identifying by name B.J.F. as the victim—was published by the Florida Star. As a result, B.J.F. received harassing phone calls, required mental health counseling, was forced to move from her home, and was even threatened with being raped again. Yet today, the Court holds that a jury award of $75,000 to compensate B.J.F. for the harm she suffered due to the Star's negligence is at odds with the First Amendment. I do not accept this result.

The Court reaches its conclusion based on an analysis of three of our precedents and a concern with three particular aspects of the judgment against appellant. I consider each of these points in turn, and then consider some of the larger issues implicated by today's decision.

. . .

At issue in this case is whether there is any information about people, which—though true—may not be published in the press. By holding that only "a state interest of the highest order" permits the State to penalize the publication of truthful information, and by holding that protecting a rape victim's right to privacy is not among those state interests of the highest order, the Court accepts appellant's invitation to obliterate one of the most note-worthy legal inventions of the 20th-Century: the tort of the publication of private facts. Even if the Court's opinion does not say as much today, such obliteration will follow inevitably from the Court's conclusion here. If the First Amendment prohibits wholly private persons (such as B.J.F.) from recovering for the publication of the fact that she was raped, I doubt that there remain any "private facts" which persons may assume will not be published in the newspapers, or broadcast on television.[4]

Of course, the right to privacy is not absolute. Even the article widely relied upon in cases vindicating privacy rights, Warren & Brandeis, The Right to Privacy, recognized that this right inevitably conflicts with the public's right to know about matters of general concern—and that sometimes, the latter must trump the former. Resolving this conflict is a difficult matter, and I do not fault the Court for attempting to strike an appropriate balance between the two, but rather, for according too little weight to B.J.F.'s side of equation, and too much on the other.

. . .

Ironically, this Court, too, had occasion to consider this same balance just a few weeks ago, in United States Department of Justice v. Reporters Committee for Freedom of the Press. There, we were faced with a press request, under the Freedom of Information Act, for a "rap sheet" on a person accused of bribing a Congressman—presumably, a person whose privacy rights would be far less than B.J.F.'s. Yet this Court rejected the media's request for disclosure of the "rap sheet," saying:

> The privacy interest in maintaining the practical obscurity of rap-sheet information will always be high. When the subject of such a rap sheet is a private citizen and when the information is in the Government's control as a compilation, rather than as a record of "what the government is up to," the privacy interest . . . is . . . at its apex while the . . . public interest in disclosure is at its nadir.

The Court went on to conclude that disclosure of rap sheets "categorical[ly]" constitutes an "unwarranted" invasion of privacy. The same surely must be true—indeed, much more so—for the disclosure of a rape victim's name.

---

4. The consequences of the Court's ruling—that a State cannot prevent the publication of private facts about its citizens which the State inadvertently discloses—is particularly troubling when one considers the extensive powers of the State to collect information. One recent example illustrates this point.

In *Boettger v. Loverro*, 555 A.2d 1234 (Pa.1989), police officers had lawfully "tapped" the telephone of a man suspected of bookmaking. Under Pennsylvania law transcripts of the conversations intercepted this way may not be disclosed. 18 Pa.C.S. Section 5703. . . . Nonetheless, in a preliminary court hearing, a prosecutor inadvertently attached a transcript of the phone conversations to a document filed with the court. A reporter obtained a copy of the transcript due to this error, and his paper published a version of the remarks disclosed by the telephone tap. On appeal, the Supreme Court of Pennsylvania upheld a civil liability award of $1,000 against the paper for its unlawful disclosure of the contents of the phone conversations, concluding that individuals' rights to privacy outweighed the interest in public disclosure of such private telephone communications. *Boettger*, 555 A.2d, at 1239–1240.

The Court's decision today suggests that this ruling by the Pennsylvania Court was erroneous. In light of the substantial privacy interest in such communications, though, *cf. Katz v. United States*, 389 U.S. 347, 88 S.Ct. 507, 19 L.Ed.2d 576 (1967), I would strike the balance as the Pennsylvania Supreme Court did.

I do not suggest that the Court's decision today is radical departure from a previously charted course. The Court's ruling has been foreshadowed. In Time, Inc. v. Hill, we observed that—after a brief period early in this century where Brandeis' view was ascendant—the trend in "modern" jurisprudence has been to eclipse an individual's right to maintain private any truthful information that the press wished to publish. More recently, in *Cox Broadcasting*, we acknowledged the possibility that the First Amendment may prevent a State from ever subjecting the publication of truthful but private information to civil liability. Today, we hit the bottom of the slippery slope.

I would find a place to draw the line higher on the hillside: a spot high enough to protect B.J.F.'s desire for privacy and peace-of-mind in the wake of a horrible personal tragedy. There is no public interest in publishing the names, addresses, and phone numbers of persons who are the victims of crime—and no public interest in immunizing the press from liability in the rare cases where a State's efforts to protect a victim's privacy have failed. Consequently, I respectfully dissent.

HALL v. POST

323 N.C. 259, 372 S.E.2d 711 (1988).

Mitchell, Justice.

[A public disclosure tort action was initiated against the Salisbury Post for publication of two articles that focused on the efforts of the natural mother of the plaintiff, Susie Hall, to locate her after having abandoned her shortly after birth. The first article described the unsuccessful efforts of the natural mother to locate the plaintiff after seventeen years and issued a call to the community for assistance in the search. The second article reported that the mother had located the child with the aid of the responses from the earlier article. This article identified the child as Susie Hall and identified her adoptive mother as Mary Hall and described in detail a telephone conversation between the adoptive parent and natural mother and the emotions of both families. In the lawsuit by Mary and Susie Hall, the plaintiffs alleged that they fled their home in order to avoid public attention resulting from the article and that they sought and received psychiatric care for the emotional and mental distress caused by the incident. The trial court granted summary judgement to the defendants; the Court of Appeals reversed; the North Carolina Supreme Court reversed.

After summarizing the Warren and Brandeis article and the English Common Law, Justice Mitchell noted that the public disclosure branch of tort privacy has not been recognized in England. He also observed that the application of the first amendment to the states and as a restriction on state tort law followed the publication of the article and could not have been contemplated by the authors. Justice Mitchell then canvassed some of the criticism of the public disclosure tort that had appeared in scholarship and judicial opinions. He noted that much of this criticism focused on the first amendment tension that is created by the fact the tort is available for publication of true information against media defendants. Justice Mitchell concluded:]

The same two basic concerns which prevented our adoption of the tort of false light invasion of privacy strongly favor our rejecting the tort of invasion of privacy by publishing private facts, as to which not even truth is a defense. First, decisions of the Supreme Court of the United States, scholarly articles and the Restatement make it clear that the private facts branch of the invasion of privacy tort is, at the very best, constitutionally suspect. Therefore, it would be entirely unrealistic to suggest that adoption of the private facts tort would do other than "add to the tension already existing between the First Amendment and the law of torts." Second, the constitutionally suspect private facts branch of the invasion of privacy will almost never provide a plaintiff with any advantage not duplicated or overlapped by the tort of intentional infliction of emotional distress and possibly by other torts such as trespass or intrusive invasion of privacy. We reemphasize here, however, that in this case we do not consider or decide the "broader question" of whether any other tort is constitutional or cognizable at law upon facts such as those presented here.

Note

Rejection of the public disclosure tort is, of course, the final solution for dealing with the first amendment difficulties that are created by public disclosure tort actions. The concerns expressed by the *Hall* court and critics of the public disclosure tort were dealt with in a somewhat less brutal way by the Oregon Supreme Court in *Anderson v. Fisher Broadcasting Cos.*, 300 Or. 452, 712 P.2d 803 (1986). In *Anderson*, the plaintiff sued under the public disclosure tort for the broadcasting of a video which showed the plaintiff bleeding and in pain while receiving emergency treatment after an automobile accident. In a unanimous opinion written by Justice Linde, the court held that the publication of truthful facts about a person, even if the facts are not newsworthy, does not give rise to a common law action for emotional distress "unless the manner or purpose of defendant's conduct is wrongful in some respect apart from causing the plaintiff's hurt feelings." *Id.* at 469, 712 P.2d at 814.

Some of the examples given by the court of "independent wrongful conduct disclosures" which might be actionable were, (1) publication of information wrongfully obtained, (2) purposely inflicting emotional distress by publishing information in a socially intolerable way, and (3) publication in violation of duties under a statute or duties of confidentiality. Does Anderson represent de facto rejection of the public disclosure tort?

Note: *Landmark Communications, Inc. v. Virginia*
435 U.S. 829 (1978).

Florida Star and *Cox Broadcasting Corp. v. Cohn* involved the use of civil tort law by the state to protect personal privacy. *Landmark* involved the use of criminal sanctions against the press for invading personal privacy. Landmark was criminally prosecuted for publishing the names of judges and other information about an inquiry pending before a judicial review commission into allegations of judicial misconduct. The Virginia Constitution specifically provided that the information before such commissions was to be confidential. The Supreme Court found that the prosecution violated the first amendment. In reviewing the prosecution the Court said that the criminal prosecution of the dissemination of true information would only be constitutional if the state could demonstrate that the dissemination constituted an imminent danger to an important state interest. In that determination the Court would not defer to the legislature's judgment on the imminence of the danger or the importance of the interest and would also consider whether other methods less damaging to speech would serve the state's interest.

Two of the asserted state interests—protecting the reputation of judges and maintaining the institutional integrity of courts—were held not to be sufficient interests to justify criminal punishment of *Landmark*. The third interest, the fair and orderly administration of justice, was found to be a significant interest. However, the Court found that publication of information about proceedings investigating judicial misconduct did not constitute a sufficiently imminent threat to a fair determination by the commission to justify punishing the press, citing Supreme Court cases holding the imposition of a gag rule on the press in criminal prosecutions unconstitutional. The leading case is *Nebraska Press Ass'n v. Stuart*, 427 U.S. 539 (1976).

Note

Florida Star and *Landmark* taken together represent an important departure from the analysis in *Cox*. These cases evaluate the constitutionality of regulation by standards that have developed in traditional first amendment cases that have not involved media torts. In these cases, the Court has strictly scrutinized state law by using a balancing of interests test that is weighed heavily in favor of speech and the press. If there are alternatives that are available to the state that would further the state interest with less detriment to the first amendment interest, the laws will generally be found unconstitutional. Notice the role of the "less detrimental alternative" principle in the Court's analysis of the constitutionality of the tort action in *Florida Star*. What were the alternatives that the Court indicated were available to the state of Florida to protect the privacy of a rape victim that would be less detrimental to freedom of speech and of the press? Reconsider *Harris v. Easton Publishing Co.*, *supra*. Suppose that case were looked at under the *Florida Star* test. The state argues that the common law public disclosure action furthers the state's interest in protecting personal privacy. Is that a significant interest? Assuming that it is, are there alternative means available to Pennsylvania that would protect the Harris' interest in personal privacy that are less detrimental to freedom of the press?

Note: What's Left of the Public Disclosure Tort?

In addition to *Cox Broadcasting Corp. v. Cohn*, *Smith v. Daily Mail Publishing Co.*, 443 U.S. 97 (1979), *Landmark Communications, Inc. v. Virginia*, and *Florida Star*, the Supreme Court has found unconstitutional a state court's pretrial order enjoining the media from publishing the name or photograph of an 11–year-old boy in connection with juvenile proceedings involving that child which reporters had attended. *See Oklahoma Publishing Co. v. District Court*, 430 U.S. 308 (1977).

What is left of the public disclosure tort? The Supreme Court is careful to indicate in dicta that each of its decisions in which a first amendment defense is raised by the media in respect to the publication of truthful information is limited to its facts. However, the Court has invalidated all of the attempts by the states to impose civil and criminal responsibility on the media that have reached the Court, except where the appropriation tort was the basis of the civil action. See *Zacchini v. Scripps–Howard Broadcasting Co.*, 433 U.S. 562 (1977), discussed *infra* p. 554.

Therefore, as the dissenting justices in *Florida Star* suggest, a serious question has in fact been raised as to whether the public disclosure tort has any vitality in the face of the first amendment jurisprudence of the Supreme Court. Does *Briscoe v. Reader's Digest*, supra, survive *Florida Star*?

Consider the following: A is a transsexual. She was born in Puerto Rico in 1942, a male. In 1975, successful surgery was performed to change A's gender to female. A kept her surgery a secret from all of her immediate family and closest friends. A changed her name to one commonly given to a female. A enrolled in a college in 1975 and was elected student body president of the college for the 1977–78 academic year, the first female to hold the office. In the middle of her term as student body president, A became embroiled in a controversy in which she charged the college administrators with abuse of student funds. Shortly after this controversy, B, a reporter for the college newspaper, was informed by a confidential source that A had been born a man and was still listed as a male in official records. B checked local police records and discovered that A was arrested in 1971 for soliciting an undercover police officer, a misdemeanor. The arrest record listed A as a male. After learning of this B wrote a column in the college newspaper which said in part, "The students at the college will be surprised to learn their student body president 'A' is no lady, but is in fact a man. I realize, that in these times, such a matter is no big deal, but I suspect his female classmates may wish to make other bathroom and showering arrangements." Does A have a cause of action against the college newspaper for violation of the public disclosure tort? *Cf., Diaz v. Oakland Tribune, Inc.*, 139 Cal.App.3d 118, 188 Cal.Rptr. 762 (1983). Does *Taylor v. K.T.V.B., Inc.*, supra survive *Florida Star* and *Cox Broadcasting Co. v. Cohn*?

(2) Resuscitation of the Private Facts Tort After Florida Star

As discussed, supra, California has rejected newsworthiness and first amendment defenses in several private facts tort cases. Most notable of these cases are, *Melvin v. Reid, Briscoe v. Reader's Digest* and *Diaz v. Oakland Tribune*, supra. In *Shulman v. Group W. Productions, Inc.*, supra, pp. 438–39, the Supreme Court of California reaffirmed the continued validity of *Reid, Briscoe* and *Diaz* after *Florida Star*. The procedural history, facts and intrusion tort analysis of *Shulman* are discussed, supra.

The court in *Shulman* rejected the private facts cause of action holding that the televised segments of the rescue and transportation of Ruth Shulman and her son from an accident scene to the hospital were newsworthy as a matter of law.

In examining California precedent in light of *Florida Star* the court observed that the Court in *Florida Star* had specifically not held that truthful publications may never be the subject of civil liability and thus had not banished the private facts tort completely. Yet the Court had provided little guidance as to what is, and what is not, "a matter of public significance." The court in *Shulman* viewed its private facts tort precedent on the tort and first amendment defense of newsworthiness to be consistent with the federal constitution, but could not be sure until further guidance from the Court.

The *Shulman* court summarized the newsworthiness concept in California to involve to some degree a normative evaluation of the "social value" of a publication. Newsworthiness requires a "reasonable proportion between the events that make the individual a public figure and the private facts to which the publicity is given." In the case of a limited involuntary public figure, like Briscoe or Shulman or Diaz, newsworthiness depended upon the relevance of the identity of the plaintiff to the newsworthy subject. In such cases there must be a substantial connection between the identity of the plaintiff and the newsworthy event. This connection was not established when Briscoe was identified as a former criminal, Reid as a former prostitute, or Diaz as a transsexual in the publications that were the basis of their private facts actions.

In applying the substantial connection test, the *Shulman* court concluded that Ruth Shulman's appearance and words as she was rescued at the accident and transported to the hospital were substantially connected to the subject which made the story newsworthy. This subject was the risky and demanding work of those who are in charge of leading medical assistance to accident victims and communications between accident victims, emergency personnel and the hospital base.

Does the *Shulman* connection test provide sufficient certainty so as to avoid the problem of chilling protected speech that the Supreme Court has identified in cases like *Cox v. Cohn* and *Florida Star* where the media is found liable in tort for publishing truthful speech? Review the Court's analysis in *Florida Star* as to whether publishing the alleged rape victim's name was a matter of public significance. The *Shulman* connection test requires a court or jury to sort out speech that is of public concern or newsworthy on the basis of evaluating the relationship of the identity of the plaintiff to the newsworthy subject of the story. Is such an evaluation consistent with the Court's concept of matters of public significance in *Florida Star*?

Further Commentary: The Privileged Communication Defense to the Public Disclosure Tort

Consider Warren and Brandeis' view on the relationship between the defenses in defamation and privacy.

> The right to privacy does not prohibit the communication of any matter, though in its nature private, when the publication is made under circumstances which would render it a privileged communication according to the law of slander and libel.

> Under this rule, the right to privacy is not invaded by any publication made in a court of justice, in legislative bodies, or the committees of those bodies; in municipal assemblies, or the committees of such assemblies, or practically by any communication made in any other public body, municipal or parochial, or in any body quasi public, like the large voluntary associations formed for almost every purpose of benevolence, business, or other general interest; and (at least in many jurisdictions) reports of any such proceedings would in some measure be accorded a like privilege. Nor would the rule prohibit any publication made by one in the discharge of some public or private duty, whether legal or moral, or in conduct of one's own affairs, in matters where his own interest is concerned.

Warren and Brandeis, *The Right to Privacy*, 4 Harv. L. Rev. 193, 216 (1890).

To what extent does the test in *Florida Star* for determining the scope of first amendment protection for information in a public record differ from Warren and Brandeis' suggested limitations on the tort?

In *Young v. Jackson*, 572 So.2d 378 (Miss.1990), the Supreme Court of Mississippi invoked the language from the Warren and Brandeis article that is noted above and held that public disclosure tort actions are subject to common law privilege defenses to the same extent that defamation actions are. The public disclosure tort action was brought by an employee against a co-worker and others for disclosing the fact of her operation for a partial hysterectomy to other workers. The court concluded that the disclosure was privileged because the co-workers had a legitimate interest in knowing that the plaintiff's hospitalization was not caused by radiation exposure in the plant. The qualified privilege in *Young* would have been exceeded if there was evidence that the disclosure was made with "ill will or spite" or published beyond those persons with a legitimate interest in the information. See also *Senogles v. Security Benefit Life Ins. Co.*, 536 P.2d 1358, 1361–62 (Kan.1975). Compare *Young v. Jackson* with *Miller v. Motorola, Inc.*, 560 N.E.2d 900 (Ill. App. Ct. 1990). The court in *Miller* found that allegations that an employer had disclosed the fact of plaintiff's mastectomy to her co-workers stated a cause of action under the public disclosure tort.

C. INJUNCTIVE REMEDIES FOR INVASIONS OF PRIVACY

Requests for injunctive relief in public disclosure tort cases are seldom granted. Historically the Supreme Court has found injunctions directed at media publications to be "prior restraints" of the press that are subject to the highest first amendment concerns. A leading prior restraint case is *Nebraska Press Ass'n v. Stuart*, 427 U.S. 539 (1976). *Nebraska Press* held that a gag order imposed upon the press in a pending criminal prosecution was an unconstitutional prior restraint. Chief Justice Burger speaking for a unanimous Court emphasized the special place prior restraints have in first amendment cases by contrasting government action that threatens civil or criminal sanctions after publication with government action that prohibits the publication itself (prior restraints). The former " 'chills' speech, [while the latter] 'freezes' it at least for the time." *Id.* at 559.

In the "Titicut Follies" case, *Commonwealth v. Wiseman*, 356 Mass. 251, 249 N.E.2d 610 (1969), *cert. denied*, 398 U.S. 960 (1970), an injunction against the dissemination of the documentary "Titicut Follies" was granted in an action brought on behalf of institutionalized persons for invasion of privacy. The documentary contained powerful and intimate images of persons in a Massachusetts institute for the criminally insane. The filmmaker exceeded the permission for filming that had been granted by the state. An action to enjoin the distribution of the film was brought on behalf of the subjects of the film by the Commonwealth of Massachusetts. The Supreme Court of Massachusetts affirmed the lower court's holding that the filming invaded the privacy of the intimate lives of institutionalized persons and also agreed with the lower court that the state had standing to assert the privacy rights of institutionalized persons under the doctrine of parens patriae.

In determining the appropriate scope of injunctive relief the court balanced the interests in privacy of the subjects of the documentary with the right to know of the public. The result of this balancing produced a limited injunction in *Wiseman*. The injunction was limited to prohibiting the distribution of the documentary for general commercial purposes. The documentary could be distributed to mental health professionals, educators, and policy makers.

The public interest in disclosure to specialized audiences for purposes of rehabilitation and research outweighed the privacy interests of the inmates because in part the "character of such audiences" greatly reduced the likelihood of humiliation of inmates. 249 N.E.2d at 618.

The injunction against commercial distribution of Titicut Follies was not lifted until 1991.

An injunction may be an appropriate remedy in privacy intrusion cases where first amendment concerns are not significant and where the invasion of privacy occurs through repeated actions. *See Galella v. Onassis*, 487 F.2d 986 (2d Cir.1973), *supra.*

D.   LEGAL REMEDIES FOR DISCLOSURE OF OR PUBLICATION OF CONFIDENTIAL INFORMATION

1.   DISCLOSURE IN JUDICIAL PROCEEDINGS

RASMUSSEN v. SOUTH FLORIDA BLOOD SERVICE

500 So.2d 533 (Fla.1987).

BARKETT, JUSTICE.

[While hospitalized as a result of an automobile accident Rasmussen received fifty-one units of blood. Approximately one year later he was diagnosed as having "Acquired Immune Deficiency Syndrome" (AIDS). He died of AIDS one year after the diagnosis. As part of his personal injury litigation arising from the automobile accident his estate subpoenaed the blood supplier for the hospital. In an effort to establish that he incurred AIDS as part of the necessary medical service arising from the accident, they sought "any and all records, documents and other material indicating the names and addresses of the [51] blood donors." The blood supplier was not a party to the underlying personal injury litigation and there was no allegation of negligence on their part. The trial court ordered the supplier to disclose the subpoenaed information. The circuit court reversed, and the Supreme Court approved the circuit court decision.]

Although we agree with respondent's contention that Rasmussen's blood donors' rights of privacy are protected by state and federal constitutions, we need not engage in the stricter scrutiny mandated by constitutional analysis. We find that the interests involved here are adequately protected under our discovery rules....

The potential for invasion of privacy is inherent in the litigation process. Under the Florida discovery rules, any nonprivileged matter that is relevant to the subject matter of the action is discoverable. The discovery rules also confer broad discretion on the trial court to limit or prohibit discovery in order to "protect a party or person from annoyance, embarrassment, oppression, or undue burden or expense." Under this authority, a court may act to protect the privacy of the affected person.

... Thus, the discovery rules provide a framework for judicial analysis of challenges to discovery on the basis that the discovery will result in undue invasion of privacy....

Accordingly, we must assess all of the interests that would be served by the granting or denying of discovery.... We begin by examining the nature and importance of the donors' rights.

In Whalen v. Roe, the Supreme Court specifically recognized that the right to privacy encompassed at least two different kinds of interests, "the individual interest in avoiding disclosure of personal matters, and . . . the interest in independence in making certain kinds of important decisions." In Nixon v. Administrator of General Services, the Supreme Court reaffirmed the confidentiality strand of privacy. Lower federal courts have recognized that the essential core of this zone of privacy is the right "to prevent disclosure of . . . identity in a damaging context." These cases clearly establish that the federal right to privacy extends protection in some circumstances against disclosure of personal matters.

Moreover, in Florida, a citizen's right to privacy is independently protected by our state constitution. Art V, sec. 23, Fla.Const.[3] . . .

. . . [A] principle aim of the constitutional provision is to afford individuals some protection against increasing collection, retention, and use of information relating to all facets of an individual's life.

. . . .

As the district court recognized, petitioner needs more than just the names and addresses of the donors. His interest is in establishing that one or more of the donors has AIDS or is in a high risk group. Petitioner argues that his inquiry *may* never go beyond comparing the donors' names against other public records (e.g. conviction records in order to determine whether any of the donors is a known drug user). He contends that as a limited inquiry may reveal the information he seeks, with no invasion of privacy, the donors' privacy rights are not yet at issue. We find this argument disingenuous. . . . [T]he subpoena in question gives petitioner access to the names and addresses of the blood donors with no restrictions on their use. There is nothing to prohibit petitioner from conducting an investigation without the knowledge of the persons in question. We cannot ignore, therefore, the consequences of disclosure to nonparties, including the possibility that a donor's coworkers, friends, employers, and others may be queried as to the donor's sexual preferences, drug use, or general life-style.

The threat posed by the disclosure of the donors' identities goes far beyond the immediate discomfort occasioned by third party probing into sensitive areas of the donors' lives. . . . As the district court recognized:

> AIDS is the modern equivalent of leprosy. AIDS, or a suspicion of AIDS, can lead to discrimination in employment, education, housing and even medical treatment.

We wish to emphasize that although the importance of protecting the privacy of the donor information does not depend on the special stigma associated with AIDS, public response to the disease does make this a

---

3. Article I, section 23, Florida Constitution, provides:

Right of Privacy—Every natural person has the right to be let alone and free from governmental intrusion into his private life except as otherwise provided herein.

This section shall not be construed to limit the public's right of access to public records and meetings as provided by law.

more critical matter.[9] ... We conclude, therefore, that the disclosure sought here implicates constitutionally protected privacy interests.

Our analysis of the interests to be served by denying discovery does not end with the effects of disclosure on the private lives of the fifty-one donors implicated in this case. Society has a vital interest in maintaining a strong volunteer blood supply, a task that has become more difficult with the emergence of AIDS. The donor population has been reduced by the necessary exclusion of potential blood donors through AIDS screening and testing procedures as well as by the unnecessary reduction in the donor population as a result of the widespread fear donation itself can transmit the disease. In light of this, it is clearly "in the public interest to discourage any serious disincentive to volunteer blood donation." Because there is little doubt that the prospect of inquiry into one's private life and potential association with AIDS will deter blood donation, we conclude that society's interest in a strong and healthy blood supply will be furthered by the denial of the discovery in this case.

In balancing the competing interests involved, we do not ignore Rasmussen's interest in obtaining the requested information in order to prove aggregation of his injuries and obtain full recovery.... [W]e find that the discovery order requested here would do little to advance that interest. The probative value of the discovery sought by Rasmussen is dubious at best. The potential of significant harm to most if not all, of the fifty-one unsuspecting donors in permitting such a fishing expedition is great and far outweighs the plaintiff's need under these circumstances.

2.   EXTRA JUDICIAL DISCLOSURE

HAMMONDS v. AETNA CASUALTY & SURETY COMPANY

243 F.Supp. 793 (N.D.Ohio 1965).

CONNELL, CHIEF JUDGE.

[Hammonds was engaged in litigation for an injury allegedly sustained due to a hospital's negligence. Hammonds was being treated for the injury by a Dr. Ling, for whom Aetna Casualty provided malpractice insurance. The hospital was represented by an attorney for whom Aetna Casualty allegedly secured confidential information from Dr. Ling on the pretext that Hammonds was contemplating a malpractice suit against Dr. Ling. Hammonds brought suit against Aetna for inducing Dr. Ling to divulge confidential information gained through a doctor-patient relationship. Aetna Casualty moves for reconsideration of a District Court order overruling a motion to dismiss the complaint or in the alternative for summary judgment.]

---

9. Social hostility to the disease has been extended to individuals associated with the disease, however tangentially, even though they do not in fact have AIDS. *See,* *e.g.,* N.Y. City Commission on Human Rights, *Gay and Lesbian Discrimination Documentation Project* (1984).

The defendant argues that, since there was no common law privilege clothing communications between doctor and patient with confidentiality, there can be no common law action for the breach of confidence nor for the inducement of such a breach. The privileged communication statute, according to the defendant, merely precludes a doctor from testifying in court as to communications received while treating a patient; as far as the law and the statute are concerned, the doctor is uninhibited in his private discussions about his patient and the insurance company is perfectly free to promote a full discussion in private of any communication made by the patient to the doctor. . . . Modern public policy, not the archaic whims of common law, demands that doctors obey their implied promise of secrecy.

This is not the first time, nor will it be the last, that a court, confronted with a unique situation, must, after an unsuccessful search for binding precedent on point, repair to the dictates of public policy to do justice between litigants at the bar of justice. . . .

. . .

We see this concomitant policy reflected in three separate indicia: the promulgated code of ethics adopted by the medical profession on which the public has a right to rely; the privileged communication statute, which precludes the doctor from testifying in open court; and that part of the State Medical Licensing Statute which seals the doctor's lips in private conversation.

In all medical jurisprudence there are few problems which have deserved and received more concentrated attention than the protection of the personal information which a patient remits to his physician. This relationship "is one of trust and confidence. . . ." To foster the best interest of the patient and to insure a climate most favorable to a complete recovery, men of medicine have urged that patients be totally frank in their discussions with their physicians. To encourage the desired candor, men of law have formulated a strong policy of confidentiality to assure patients that only they themselves may unlock the doctor's silence in regard to those private disclosures. . . .

The defendant generously concedes that the Hippocratic Oath embodies some restriction on a doctor's right to discuss the condition of, and communications from, his patient. The Oath of Hippocrates, in so far as here pertinent, provides:

> Whatever in connection with my professional practice or not in connection with it I see or hear in the life of men which ought not to be spoken abroad I will not divulge as recommending that all such should be kept secret.

We agree with the defendant that there are some situations[3] where divulgence will inure to the benefit of the public at large or even to the

---

3. For example, where a doctor discovers that his patient is afflicted with a communicable disease, he must report that fact to proper authorities. In Ohio he is specifically absolved by statute from liability for such disclosure. When a doctor discovers

patient himself, but we have no such situation before us. The plaintiff here was engaged in litigation for an injury (which Dr. Ling was treating) allegedly sustained at the negligent hand of the Euclid–Glenville Hospital, which was represented by an attorney for whom the defendant here allegedly secured confidential information from Dr. Ling. In this adversary judicial system, with its intensity heightened by the continuing friction between insurance companies and claimants, is there no impropriety in a doctor discussing the case of his patient-plaintiff with the lawyer of the defending insurance company? Who would dare say so?

. . .

It cannot be questioned that part of a doctor's duty of total care requires him to offer his medical testimony on behalf of his patient if the patient becomes involved in litigation over the injury or illness which the doctor treated. Thus, during the course of such litigation, in addition to the duty of secrecy, there arises the duty of undivided loyalty. Should a doctor breach either of these two duties, the law must afford the patient some legal recourse against such perfidy. We should not suffer a wrong without a remedy, especially when the wrong complained of involves the abuse of a fiduciary position.

. . .

Any time a doctor undertakes the treatment of a patient, and the consensual relationship of physician and patient is established, two jural obligations (of significance here) are simultaneously assumed by the doctor. Doctor and patient enter into a simple contract, the patient hoping that he will be cured and the doctor optimistically assuming that he will be compensated. As an implied condition of that contract, the Court is of the opinion that the doctor warrants that any confidential information gained through the relationship will not be released without the patient's permission. Almost every member of the public is aware of the promise of discretion contained in the Hippocratic Oath, and every patient has a right to rely upon this warranty of silence. The promise of secrecy is as much an express warranty as the advertisement of a commercial entrepreneur. Consequently, when a doctor breaches his duty of secrecy, he is in violation of part of his obligations under the contract.

When a patient seeks out a doctor and retains him, he must admit him to the most private part of the material domain of man. Nothing material is more important or more intimate to man than the health of his mind and body. Since the layman is unfamiliar with the road to recovery, he cannot sift the circumstances of his life and habits to determine what is information pertinent to his health. As a consequence, he must disclose all information in his consultations with his doctor—

that one of the parties to a contemplated marriage has contracted a venereal disease, he may, without fear of legal ramifications, make that fact known to certain specified persons. Some jurisdictions require that doctors report all wounds inflicted by bullet, knife or other weapon.

even that which is embarrassing, disgraceful or incriminating. To promote full disclosure, the medical profession extends the promise of secrecy referred to above. The candor which this promise elicits is necessary to the effective pursuit of health; there can be no reticence, no reservation, no reluctance when patients discuss their problems with their doctors. But the disclosure is certainly intended to be private. If a doctor should reveal any of these confidences, he surely effects an invasion of the privacy of his patient. We are of the opinion that the preservation of the patient's privacy is no mere ethical duty on the part of the doctor; there is a legal duty as well. The unauthorized revelation of medical secrets, or any confidential communication given in the course of treatment, is tortious conduct which may be the basis for an action in damages.

. . .

From all these authorities, both primary and secondary, we draw the necessary conclusion that a doctor may be legally culpable for an intentional, unauthorized divulgence of confidences.

II.

However, we are not critically concerned here solely with the alleged disclosure by a doctor since the complaint accuses Dr. Ling only of a misfeasance predicated on misinformation and directs its plea for redress not against the doctor but against the defendant insurance company which allegedly supplied this inaccurate information. The defendant here has also challenged, in its Motion for Reconsideration, the Court's finding that one who induces a physician's treachery may also be held liable for damages. This finding was predicated upon the holding that the physician-patient relationship is a confidential one which imposes fiduciary obligations upon the physician. As we have noted above, the patient necessarily reposes a great deal of trust not only in the skill of the physician but in his discretion as well. The introduction into the relationship of this aura of trust, and the expectation of confidentiality which results therefrom, imposes the fiduciary obligations upon the doctor. As a consequence, all reported cases dealing with this point hold that the relationship of physician and patient is a fiduciary one.

If the analogy expressed in the Court's earlier opinion (comparing the relationship of physician and patient to that of trustee and principal and comparing the confidences exchanged between doctor and patient to a trust res) is offensive to the defendant, it comes as no surprise to the medical profession. The Code of Medical Ethics itself recommends the following attitude:

> The confidences ... should be held as a trust and should never be revealed except when imperatively required by the laws of the state.

Principles of Medical Ethics of A.M.A. Ch. II, Section 1 (1943).

Nor does the imposition of a trustee's duties upon a physician as a fiduciary fashion any new doctrine in American jurisprudence. By its very definition the term "fiduciary relationship" imports the notion that "[i]f a wrong arises, the same remedy exists against the wrongdoer on behalf of the principal as would exist against a trustee on behalf of the *cestui que trust*." Therefore it is readily apparent that the legal obligations of a trustee are imposed upon any person working in a fiduciary capacity and the same principles of law governing the behavior of a trustee are applicable to all fiduciaries.

It also follows that the same principles of law governing third party participation in breaches of trust must also apply to one who participates in or induces the breach of any fiduciary duty. The law is settled in Ohio and elsewhere that a third party who induces a breach of a trustee's duty of loyalty, or participates in such a breach, or knowingly accepts any benefit from such a breach, becomes directly liable to the aggrieved party. Therefore, we reaffirm our earlier finding that when one induces a doctor to divulge confidential information in violation of the doctor's legal responsibility to his patient, the third party may also be held liable in damages to the patient.

The defendant's Motion for Reconsideration of the Court's earlier opinion is accordingly overruled.

3. MORE ON THE BREACH OF CONFIDENTIALITY THEORY: THE SCOPE OF LEGAL PROTECTION FOR INVASION OF PATIENT AND CLIENT PRIVACY BY UNAUTHORIZED EXTRA–LEGAL DISCLOSURE OF HEALTH CARE INFORMATION

a. *The Breach of Confidentiality Theory*

The breach of confidentiality theory utilized by the *Hammonds* court was the basis upon which the high court in Maryland protected the privacy of bank records in *Suburban Trust*, discussed in an earlier section of these materials. Invasions of privacy by extra-legal disclosure of information that is acquired in the course of a health care professional-patient or client relationship has been a source of considerable recent litigation and the focus of much legislation. Virtually all of the courts that have addressed the broad question of whether a cause of action may be available for the unauthorized extra-legal disclosure of health care information have concluded that a common law cause of action may be available.

b. *The Breach of Confidentiality Tort*

Most courts utilize three interrelated theories as the basic approach to protecting the privacy of health care information that is disclosed extra-judicially. These theories combine doctrines from several areas of law as well as ethical concepts of the health care profession. The result is an emerging recognition in our legal system of a cause of action for the unauthorized disclosure of health care information and recovery of demonstrable tort damages. One commentator has aptly described this emerging jurisprudence as the breach of confidentiality tort. *See* Note, *Breach of Confidence: An Emerging Tort*, 82 Colum. L. Rev. 1426 (1982).

c. Implied Contract Theory of Recovery

One approach to granting the patient or client recovery against the health care practitioner is to incorporate the ethical standards of confidentiality of the medical profession into the service contract between the professional and patient or client and to imply a duty not to disclose as part of the contract. In addition to *Hammonds, see also Horne v. Patton*, 291 Ala. 701, 287 So.2d 824 (1973) (physician liable to patient for disclosing health care information to patient's employer).

d. Public Policy Theory

Some courts, in addition to the implied contract theory, view the public policy of the state as evidenced by the law of that state (constitutional and statutory), the code of ethics adopted by the profession of that state, and the state licensing statute as collectively imposing a legal duty upon the professional not to gratuitously disclose confidential information. In addition, divulgence of health care information is viewed as a palpable wrong which state courts have the inherent power and duty to remedy. In addition to *Hammonds, see also, Smith v. Driscoll*, 94 Wash. 441, 162 P. 572 (1917) (law provides remedies for so palpable a wrong as physician's divulgence of confidential communication) (dicta).

e. The Breach of Fiduciary Relationship Theory

The breach of fiduciary relationship theory utilized by the *Hammonds* court is the most expansive of the approaches that have been adopted. Under this analysis, the relationship between the physician and patient is viewed as a fiduciary one so that disclosure of health care information would constitute a breach of the fiduciary relationship. This theory is borrowed from the law of estates and is available against third parties. By analogizing to the law of estates, a third party who induced the breach of the physician's professional duty of loyalty would likewise be liable to the patient for the breach of the fiduciary duty. *Hammonds* is the leading case imposing liability on third parties.

f. Exceptions to and Limitations on the Breach of Confidentiality Cause of Action

It is useful to organize the cases which have examined the scope of the breach of confidentiality cause of action for unauthorized disclosure of health care information by health professionals into the following groups: (1) disclosure that is not associated with pending or imminent litigation; (2) disclosure that is associated with pending or imminent litigation.

(1) Disclosure that is Not Associated With Pending or Imminent Litigation

There is general agreement that in the absence of justification, unauthorized disclosure of health care information is actionable. Several jurisdictions have recognized a cause of action for breach of confidentiality when the health professional disclosed information to employers or family members without the authorization of the patient or client: (1) Massachusetts, *Alberts v. Devine*, 395 Mass. 59, 479 N.E.2d 113, *cert. denied*, 474 U.S. 1013 (1985) (psychiatrist of priest to superior and Bishop); (2) New York, *MacDonald v. Clinger*, 84 A.D.2d 482, 446 N.Y.S.2d 801 (1982) (psychiatrist to spouse); (3) South Dakota, *Schaffer v. Spicer*, 88 S.D. 36, 215 N.W.2d 134 (1974) (psychiatrist to spouse); (4) Oregon, *Humphers v. First Interstate Bank*, 298 Or. 706, 696 P.2d 527 (1985) (physician of natural mother to adopted daughter); (5) Alabama, *Horne v. Patton*, 291 Ala. 701, 287 So.2d 824 (1973) (physician to employer). Decisions to the contrary are rare. *See Collins v. Howard*, 156 F.Supp. 322 (S.D.Ga.1957) (no legally protected confidential relationship breached by disclosure of blood test by hospital to employer). Doubt was raised as to whether a cause of action for breach of confidentiality was available in *Mikel v. Abrams*, 541 F.Supp. 591 (W.D.Mo.1982), *aff'd without op.*, 716 F.2d 907 (8th Cir.1983) (general principle that spouse is entitled to information regarding medical condition of other spouse precluded recovery for disclosure to wife by physician of husband's substance abuse).

Florida has rejected the breach of confidentiality theory at least in respect to disclosures by health professionals. In *Coralluzzo By and Through Coralluzzo v. Fass*, 450 So.2d 858 (Fla.1984), the Supreme Court of Florida found that there was no violation of Holly Coralluzzo's legal rights by the ex parte disclosure of health care information by physicians that had or were currently treating her. Justice Ehrlich speaking for a majority of the court observed:

> No law statutory or common [law], prohibits—even by implication—respondent's actions. We note that no evidentiary rule of physician/patient confidentiality exists in Florida and that, although several statutes preserve confidentiality in certain medical records, petitioner has failed to identify a specific statute respondents have infringed. Likewise, no rule of procedure or rule of professional responsibility proscribes respondents' interview with Dr. Magnacca. . . .

> The focal point of petitioner's distress seems to be Dr. Magnacca's failure to fulfill his fiduciary duty toward his patient. . . . Whether he [Dr. Magnacca] violated the ethical standards of his profession is a matter to be addressed by the profession itself. Such standards have not been codified and we therefore have no jurisdiction on this matter. Any violation of the fiduciary relationship with Holly Coralluzzo must be addressed in appropriate proceedings to which Dr. Magnacca is a party.

Id. at 959.

(2) *Defenses to the Breach of Confidentiality Cause of Action*

(A) JUSTIFICATION

As the previous section indicates, where health care information is disclosed, there is a presumptive cause of action for breach of confidentiality. Disclosure of health care information may not be actionable if the health professional can demonstrate that the disclosure was justified. The New York Court of Appeals has said, "Disclosure of confidential information by a psychiatrist to a spouse will be justified whenever there is danger to the patient, the spouse or another person; otherwise, information should not be disclosed without authorization." *MacDonald v. Clinger*, 84 A.D.2d 482, 446 N.Y.S.2d 801 (1982). Although the *MacDonald* decision involved a psychiatrist, the breach of confidentiality cause of action is not limited to psychotherapist-client relationships. Recall *Humphers v. First Interstate Bank*, 298 Or. 706, 696 P.2d 527 (1985) and *Horne v. Patton*, 291 Ala. 701, 287 So.2d 824 (1973) (physicians in traditional physician-patient relationship), noted in section C of this chapter.

Consider the arguments that you would raise in support of disclosure in those cases referred to in the previous note where a cause of action was allowed. Would disclosure be justified under the *MacDonald* standard: to protect the patient or others against "danger"? In *Tarasoff v. Regents of University of California*, 17 Cal.3d 425, 551 P.2d 334, 131 Cal.Rptr. 14 (1976), the Supreme Court of California imposed a common law duty on psychotherapists to disclose threats of harm by their patients to third parties in limited circumstances. Does *MacDonald* simply incorporate a *Tarasoff* defense to the breach of confidentiality cause of action? Consider the Pennsylvania statute regulating the confidentiality of "Confidential HIV Related Information" in the statutory appendix to these materials. If that statute were controlling in those cases noted in [1] where a cause of action was allowed for breach of confidentiality, and the information that was disclosed to the various persons was the fact of HIV infection, would a cause of action be available against the health professional?

(B) THE IMPLIED CONSENT AND IMPENDING LITIGATION DEFENSES

The breach of confidentiality cause of action has been brought against health professionals in numerous cases where the patient has initiated litigation that is pending when the disclosure by the health professional occurs. As a general matter, a person who initiates litigation and brings into question her physical or mental condition is viewed as waiving any testimonial or evidentiary privilege that is based upon a professional client relationship. As a practical matter this means that the defendant in such cases will have access to health care information about the litigant through compelled disclosure in discovery or at trial. When litigation is pending and there is unauthorized disclosure by the health professional to agents of the defendant's insurance company, or to the defendant's lawyer, should the disclosure be actionable if the disclosure has not been compelled by the court managing the litigation? There is a divergence of judicial responses to the resolution of this question. *Hammonds v. Aetna Casualty & Surety Corp., supra,* rejected a pending litigation defense and imposed liability where the physician disclosed information to the lawyer of a hospital that the patient was suing. Other courts have agreed with Hammonds in not justifying disclosure and requiring that the party seeking information do so pursuant to a court order or statute.

Still other courts have viewed the initiation of litigation by the patient as a waiver of a cause of action for breach of confidentiality and have not allowed recovery for disclosure to the attorney of the defendant even though the defendant has not sought disclosure through discovery. *See Mull v. String,* 448 So.2d 952 (Ala.1984); *Moses v. McWilliams,* 379 Pa.Super. 150, 549 A.2d 950 (1988), *appeal denied,* 521 Pa. 630, 558 A.2d 532 (1989); *Tooley v. Provident Life & Accident Ins. Co.,* 244 La. 1019, 156 So.2d 226 (1963). In *Moses,* the plaintiff in the breach of confidentiality action (Moses) had initially brought an action against a hospital for negligence. The attorney for the hospital requested information about the plaintiff's medical condition from a physician who had performed surgery on Moses at another hospital. The physician (not a defendant in Moses' lawsuit) disclosed the requested information to the attorney without notifying Moses.

In rejecting Moses' cause of action for breach of confidentiality, the court stated:

> Given a patient's qualified right to privacy in his or her medical records and an individual's reduced expectation of privacy as a result of filing a civil suit for personal injuries in conjunction with policies supporting both the physician-patient privilege statute and the absolute immunity from civil liability granted to witnesses in judicial proceedings, we will not recognize the cause of action for breach of confidentiality as pled in this case.

Id. at 157, 549 A.2d at 953–54.

The physician-patient testimonial privilege in Pennsylvania specifically excludes patient's medical information "in civil matters brought by such patient for damages on account of personal injuries," 42 Pa. Cons. Stat. Ann. section 5929 (Purdon 1982).

FURTHER QUESTIONS

Which approach to the pending litigation or implied waiver defense is correct?

Compare the breach of confidentiality cause of action with the common law public intrusion and public disclosure torts that have been examined. Will a common law tort action always be available in cases where the breach of confidentiality cause of action is available?

(c) First Amendment Defenses to the Breach of Confidentiality Tort

Suppose a newspaper receives information that is derogatory about a political candidate by someone associated with the opposition candidate. The information is provided under the condition that the newspaper promises not to disclose the name of the source. A subsequent story about the political race discloses the source's name. The source is fired from his employment because of the story. Would the awarding of damages against the media for breach of contract in the disclosure of the source's name violate the first amendment? Consider the following possibilities:

(1) The balancing test of *Florida Star* governs the case. Since the information has been lawfully acquired the media may not be subject to tort liability unless the state demonstrates that civil liability furthers an interest of the highest order. Under *Florida Star* would the state's interest in enforcing the newspaper's promise of confidentiality outweigh the first amendment interest in dissemination of truthful information about someone associated with a candidate for political office leaking negative information about an opposition candidate? Is the information lawfully acquired?

(2) *Dietemann* controls and there is no first amendment violation because the first amendment does not give the media the right to commit a tort or breach a contract. Is *Dietemann* distinguishable because in that case the tort was based exclusively on the actions of the media involved in *acquiring* information for a story, where in the hypothetical case contract liability is based upon the breach of promise in the *publication* of information in the story?

On similar facts in *Cohen v. Cowles Media Co.*, 501 U.S. 663 (1991), a bare majority of the Supreme Court upheld a contract action in the face of first amendment challenges. Justice White speaking for the majority rejected a balancing of interests approach as appropriate in the case. Instead it upheld the law by applying the general principle that the application of a general law (contracts) with only an incidental effect on speech does not violate the first amendment. The dissenters would have found the law unconstitutional under the balancing test under the holding of *Hustler Magazine, Inc. v. Falwell*, 485 U.S. 46 (1988). In *Hustler* a damage award was granted against the press for the tort of intentional infliction of emotional distress. The basis of the tort action was a caricature of Rev. Jerry Falwell in Hustler magazine that depicted the Reverend as engaging in sexual improprieties with his mother. The court found that the imposition of liability for the tort of intentional infliction of emotional distress for the publication of an opinion about a public figure violated the first amendment. If *Hustler* is based upon the proposition that civil liability may not be based upon speech or expression about a public figure that is not false without violating the first amendment, does it control the first amendment question raised by *Cohen v. Cowles*?

The breach of confidentiality tort cases that are discussed in this chapter generally involve breach of implied promises not to disclose by individuals (not the media) who are in a fiduciary relationship with the plaintiff. Does *Cohen v. Cowles* clearly establish that there are no first amendment violations for tort damages that are recovered in breach of confidentiality actions?

Chapter Six

PRIVACY PROTECTION FOR PERSONALITY, IDENTITY AND REPUTATION

WARREN & BRANDEIS, THE RIGHT TO PRIVACY
4 Harv. L. Rev. 193 (1890).

[Warren and Brandeis rejected the view that property rights were the basis of common law cases granting relief for the publication of letters, manuscripts, lectures, and etchings. Review the section of the article in Chapter 1, *supra*, in which the authors argue that the common law cases were really about vindicating the principle of inviolate personality and not about private property.]

A. SECOND RESTATEMENT OF TORTS

SECTION 652C APPROPRIATION OF NAME OR LIKENESS

One who appropriates to his own use or benefit the name or likeness of another is subject to liability to the other for invasion of his privacy.

Comment:

    a. The interest protected by the rule stated in this Section is the interest of the individual in the exclusive use of his own identity, in so far as it is represented by his name or likeness, and in so far as the use may be of benefit to him or to others. Although the protection of his personal feelings against mental distress is an important factor leading to a recognition of the rule, the right created by it is in the nature of a property right, for the exercise of which an exclusive license may be given to a third person, which will entitle the licensee to maintain an action to protect it. The right of such a third person has sometimes been called a "right of publicity."

    b. How invaded. The common form of invasion of privacy under the rule here stated is the appropriation and use of the plaintiff's name or likeness to advertise the defendant's business or product, or for some similar commercial purpose. Apart from statute, however, the rule stated is not limited to commercial appropriation. It applies also when the defendant makes use of the plaintiff's name or likeness for his own purposes and benefit, even though the benefit sought to be obtained is not a pecuniary one. Statutes in some states have, however, limited the liability to commercial uses of the name or likeness.

B.   IS APPROPRIATION A PRIVACY TORT?

MELVILLE B. NIMMER, THE RIGHT OF PUBLICITY

19 Law and Contemporary Problems 203 (1954).

This article will attempt to outline the inadequacy of traditional legal theories in protecting publicity values, and will then discuss the probable substance of and limitations on the right of publicity, followed by an examination of the extent of judicial recognition thus far accorded to this new right.

INADEQUACY OF PRIVACY

Those persons and enterprises in the entertainment and allied industries wishing to control but not prohibit the use by others of their own or their employees' names and portraits will find, for the reasons indicated below, that the right of privacy is generally an unsatisfactory means of assuring such control.

Waiver by Celebrities. It is generally the person who has achieved the somewhat ephemeral status of "celebrity" who must cope with the unauthorized use by others of his name and portrait, since the fact of his fame makes such use commercially attractive to others. Yet, when such a person seeks to invoke the right of privacy to protect himself from such unauthorized use, he finds that by the very fact of his being a celebrity "he has dedicated his life to the public and thereby waived his right to privacy."[12] . . .

. . .

Some courts have taken a more limited approach to the doctrine of waiver by celebrities. These courts hold that the mere fact that the plaintiff is a celebrity will not affect his right of privacy, but that if a person consents to appear or perform before a limited audience (e.g., a live audience in the immediate presence of the performer), then such person cannot complain of an invasion of privacy if by means of motion pictures, still pictures or live television persons other than the limited audience also view the performance or appearance. However, even this limited waiver can be highly injurious to a professional performer. Thus,

---

12. Leon R. Yankwich, Chief Judge, United States District Court for the Southern District of California, in his article, The Right of Privacy, 27 Notre Dame Law, 499 (1952).

in *Gautier v. Pro–Football, Inc.*[19] the plaintiff, having consented to perform before an audience of thirty-five thousand persons during the half time of a professional football game, was held to have waived his privacy with respect to the persons who might view this performance by television. Certainly one cannot quarrel with the court's conclusion that plaintiff by performing in the football stadium had consented to the loss of his "privacy," but to conclude that the plaintiff had thereby waived any right to control and profit from the reproduction of his image on television seems to be unnecessarily harsh. . . .

Offensive Use. It is reported that Brandeis and Warren first became interested in the problem of privacy and decided to write their article as a direct result of a Boston newspaper's practice of reporting in lurid detail the activities of Samuel Warren and his wife.[28] Thus, the doctrine of privacy was evolved as a means of preventing offensive (as distinguished from non-offensive) publicity. To this day most courts recognize the rule of the *Restatement of Torts* that in a privacy action "liability exists only if the defendant's conduct was such that he should have realized that it would be offensive to persons of ordinary sensibilities. It is only where the intrusion has gone beyond the limits of decency that liability accrues."

In attempting to control and profit from the use of publicity values connected with the use of his name, photograph, and likeness, the well known personality will usually find it difficult to invoke such protection under the right of privacy for the reason that usually such publicity cannot be considered such as "would be offensive to persons of ordinary sensibilities" or as an intrusion "beyond the limits of decency." Situations may of course occur where exploitation of a plaintiff's publicity values will prove humiliating or embarrassing to him,[30] but in most situations one who has achieved such prominence as to give a publicity value to the use of his name, photograph and likeness cannot honestly claim that he is humiliated or offended by their use before the public. The fact that he wishes to be paid for such use does not indicate that use without payment is so offensive as to give a right of action in privacy. . . .

.   .   .

Non-assignable. In most jurisdictions it is well established that a right of privacy is a personal right rather than a property right and

---

19. 304 N.Y. 354, 107 N.E. 2d 485 (1952).

28. Mason, Brandeis, *A Free Man's Life* 70 (1946).

30. For example, in Sinclair v. Postal Telegraph and Cable Co., 72 N.Y.S.2d 841 (1935), the defendant used a photograph of the plaintiff (an actor) which had been taken in connection with a motion picture photoplay in which plaintiff appeared. Defendant's use of the photo made it appear that plaintiff was notifying his "enthusiastic ad-

mirers" by telegraph that he was about to appear in a motion picture at a given theatre. Plaintiff brought an action under the New York privacy act arguing that defendant's use of his photograph was humiliating to plaintiff in that it put him in an undignified light, in the same manner as an attorney would appear if he telegraphed his friends requesting that they attend a court room where he was about to participate in a case. Plaintiff recovered.

consequently is not assignable. The publicity value of a prominent person's name and portrait is greatly restricted if this value cannot be assigned to others. Moreover, persons willing to pay for such publicity values will usually demand that in return for payment they obtain an exclusive right. Yet since the right of privacy is non-assignable, any agreement purporting to grant the right to use the grantor's name and portrait (as in connection with a commercial endorsement or tie-up) is construed as constituting merely a release as to the purchaser and as not granting the purchaser any right which he can enforce as against a third party. Thus, if a prominent motion picture actress should grant to a bathing suit manufacturer the right to use her name and portrait in connection with its product and if subsequently a competitive manufacturer should use the same actress's name and portrait in connection with its product, the first manufacturer cannot claim any right of action on a privacy theory against its competitor since the first manufacturer cannot claim to "own" the actress' right of privacy. Assuming the second manufacturer acted with the consent of the actress, it is possible that the first manufacturer would have a cause of action for breach of contract against the actress, but this would present a remedy in damages only and in some instances even recovery of damages might be doubtful. Therefore, if a prominent person is found merely to have a personal right of privacy and not a property right of publicity, the important publicity values which he has developed are greatly circumscribed and thereby reduced in value.

Limited to Human Beings. It is common knowledge that animals often develop important publicity values. Thus, it is obvious that the use of the name and portrait of the motion picture dog Lassie in connection with dog food would constitute a valuable asset. Yet an unauthorized use of this name could not be prevented under a right of privacy theory, since it has been expressly held that the right of privacy "does not cover the case of a dog or a photograph of a dog."[51] Not only animals but business enterprises as well are unprotected under the right of privacy,[52] and this applies to both partnerships[53] and corporations.[54] Yet as in the case of animals so also with business enterprises, the economic realities are such that the use of a business name may have a considerable publicity value. . . .

SUBSTANCE OF AND LIMITATIONS ON THE RIGHT OF PUBLICITY

. . .

51. Lawrence v. Ylla, 184 Misc. 807, 55 N.Y.S. 2d 343 (Sup. Ct. 1945).

52. Shubert v. Columbia Pictures Corp., 189 Misc. 734, 72 N.Y.S. 2d 851 (Sup. Ct. 1947); Gautier v. Pro–Football, 278 App. Div. 431, 106 N.Y.S. 2d 553 (1st Dep't 1951), *aff'd*, 304 N.Y. 354, 107 N.E. 2d 485 (1952); Maysville Transit Co. v. Ort, 296 Ky. 524, 177 S.W.2d 369 (1943).

53. Rosenwasser v. Ogoglia, 172 App. Div. 107, 158 N.Y.S. 56 (2d Dep't 1916).

54. Vassar College v. Loose–Wiles Biscuit Co., 197 Fed. 982 (W.D.Mo.1912). See also Jaggard v. R.H. Macy & Co., 176 Misc. 88, 26 N.Y.S. 2d 829 (Sup. Ct. 1941), *aff'd*, 265 App. Div. 15, 37 N.Y.S. 2d 570 (1st Dep't 1942).

The nature of the inadequacy of the traditional legal theories dictates in large measure the substance of the right of publicity. The right of publicity must be recognized as a property (not a personal) right, and as such capable of assignment and subsequent enforcement by the assignee. Furthermore, appropriation of publicity values should be actionable regardless of whether the defendant has used the publicity in a manner offensive to the sensibilities of the plaintiff. Usually the use will be non-offensive, since such a use is more valuable to the defendant as well as to the plaintiff. Likewise, the measure of damages should be computed in terms of the value of the publicity appropriated by defendant rather than, as in privacy, in terms of the injury sustained by the plaintiff. There must be no waiver of the right by reason of the plaintiff being a well known personality. Indeed, the right usually becomes important only when the plaintiff (or potential plaintiff) has achieved in some degree a celebrated status. Moreover, since animals, inanimate objects, and business and other institutions all may be endowed with publicity values, the human owners of these non-human entities should have a right of publicity (although no right of privacy) in such property, and this right should exist (unlike unfair competition) regardless of whether the defendant is in competition with the plaintiff, and regardless of whether he is passing off his own products as those of the plaintiff.

It is not possible to set forth here in any detail the necessary limitations on the right of publicity which only the unhurried occurrence of actual cases will clearly establish. Yet some few suggestions can be made. In privacy cases there is a tendency by some courts to confuse or at least fail to distinguish between the defense of waiver by a well known personality and the defense of "news" or public interests. Although, as indicated *supra*, the defense of waiver by celebrities should not be recognized in a publicity action, the defense of public interest should be no less effective in a publicity action than in a privacy action. Where use of a person's name, photograph, or likeness is made in the dissemination of news or in a manner required by the public interest, that person should not be able to complain of the infringement of his right of publicity.

C. IS APPROPRIATION A PROPERTY TORT?

WILLIAM L. PROSSER, PRIVACY
48 Calif. L. Rev. 383 (1960).

APPROPRIATION

It seems sufficiently evident that appropriation is quite a different matter from intrusion, disclosure of private facts, or a false light in the public eye. The interest protected is not so much a mental as a proprietary one, in the exclusive use of the plaintiff's name and likeness as an aspect of his identity. It seems quite pointless to dispute over whether such a right is to be classified as "property." If it is not, it is at least, once it is protected by the law, a right of value upon which the plaintiff can capitalize by selling licenses. Its proprietary nature is clearly indicated by a decision of the Second Circuit that an exclusive license has what has been called a "right of publicity," which entitles him to enjoin the use of the name or likeness by a third person. Although this decision has not yet been followed, it would seem clearly to be justified.

EDWARD J. BLOUSTEIN, PRIVACY AS AN ASPECT OF HUMAN DIGNITY: AN ANSWER TO DEAN PROSSER

39 N.Y.U. L. Rev. 962 (1964).

The third "distinct tort" involving a "distinct interest" which Dean Prosser isolates turns on the commercial exploitation of a person's name or likeness. This group of cases is designed, he says, to protect an interest which "is not so much a mental as a proprietary one, in the exclusive use of the plaintiff's name and likeness as an aspect of identity."

. . . .

. . . In *Pavesich v. New England Life Ins. Co.*, the plaintiff's photograph was used, without his consent, in a newspaper advertisement for life insurance, which proclaimed to the world that Pavesich had bought life insurance and was the better man for it. There was no suggestion in the case that the plaintiff sought to vindicate a proprietary interest, that he sought recompense for the commercial value of the use of his name; since he was not well known, the use of his name or picture could hardly command even a fraction of the cost of the lawsuit. Nor did Pavesich claim, as the plaintiff in the *Roberson* case did, that he suffered severe nervous shock as a result of the publication.

The basis of recovery in the case was rather "a trespass upon Pavesich's right of privacy." . . .

The *Pavesich* case has probably been cited more often than any other case in the history of the development of the right to privacy, and it has been cited not only in cases involving use of name or likeness but also in the so-called intrusion cases and the public disclosure cases. To my mind, *Pavesich* and the other use of name or likeness cases are no different in the interest they seek to protect than the intrusion and public disclosure cases. That interest is not, as Dean Prosser suggests, a "proprietary one," but rather the interest in preserving individual dignity.

The use of a personal photograph or a name for advertising purposes has the same tendency to degrade and humiliate as has publishing details of personal life to the world at large; in the *Pavesich* court's words, the use of a photograph for commercial purposes brings a man "to a realization that his liberty has been taken away from him" and "that he is no longer free." Thus, a young girl whose photograph was used to promote the sale of dog food complained of "humiliation," "loss of respect and admiration" and co-incident "mental anguish," and the Illinois court which upheld her cause of action cited the Illinois constitutional guarantee of life, liberty and pursuit of happiness as the basis of recovery. Similarly, where a lawyer's name was used for the purposes of advertising photocopy equipment, where a young woman's picture in a bathing suit was used to advertise a slimming product, or where the plaintiff's photograph was used to advertise Doan's pills, the wrong complained of was mortification, humiliation and degradation rather than any pecuniary or property loss.

. . .

One possible cause for confusion concerning the interest which underlies these cases is that the use of name or likeness is held to be actionable in many of the cases precisely because it is a use for commercial or trade purposes. This seems to suggest that the value or interest threatened is a proprietary or commercial one. Such a conclusion is mistaken, however, because, in the first place, as I noted above, the name or likeness which is used in most instances has no true commercial value, or it has a value which is only nominal and hardly worth the lawsuit. In fact, it has been held that general rather than special damages are recoverable and this, in itself, is a refutation of the conclusion that the interest concerned is a proprietary one.

In the second place, the conclusion that the plaintiff seeks to vindicate a proprietary right in these cases overlooks the true role of the allegation that the plaintiff's name or picture was used commercially. The reason that the commercial use of a personal photograph is actionable, while—under many circumstances, such as where consent to publication is implied from the fact the photograph was taken in a public place—the use of the same photograph in a news story would not be, is that it is the very commercialization of a name or photograph which does injury to the sense of personal dignity. As one court has stated, "the right protected is the right to be protected against the commercial exploitation of one's personality."

No man wants to be "used" by another against his will, and it is for this reason that commercial use of a personal photograph is obnoxious. Use of a photograph for trade purposes turns a man into a commodity and makes him serve the economic needs and interest of others. In a community at all sensitive to the commercialization of human values, it is degrading to thus make a man part of commerce against his will.

Some have said that in such cases a "right of publicity" rather than a right of privacy is involved. It is a mistake, however, to conclude from these "right of publicity" cases that all the cases involving commercial use of name or likeness are founded on a proprietary interest. Moreover, the very characterization of these cases as involving a "right to publicity" disguises the important fact that name and likeness can only begin to command a commercial price in a society which recognizes that there is a right to privacy, a right to control the conditions under which name and likeness may be used. Property becomes a commodity subject to be bought and sold only where the community will enforce an individual's right to maintain use and possession of it as against the world. Similarly, unless an individual has a right to prevent another from using his name or likeness commercially, even where the use of that name or likeness has no commercial value, no name or likeness could ever command a price.

Thus, there is really no "right to publicity"; there is only a right, under some circumstances, to command a commercial price for abandoning privacy. Every man has a right to prevent the commercial exploitation of his personality, not because of its commercial worth, but because it would be demeaning to human dignity to fail to enforce such a right. A price can be had in the market place by some men for abandoning it, however. If a commercial use is made of an aspect of the personality of such a man without his consent, he has indeed suffered a pecuniary loss, but the loss concerned is the price he could command for abandoning his right to privacy. The so-called "right to publicity" is merely a name for the price for which some men can sell their right to maintain their privacy.

. . .

I agree with Dean Prosser that, in one sense, it is "quite pointless to dispute over whether such a right is to be classified as 'property'"; as Warren and Brandeis long ago pointed out, there is a sense in which there inheres "in all . . . rights recognized by the law . . . the quality of being owned or possessed—and (as that is the distinguishing attribute of property) there may be some propriety in speaking of those rights as property."

But in one sense it is very important, as Warren and Brandeis saw, to decide whether the right to damages for the commercial use of name or likeness is called a property right. The importance resides in finding the common ground between the use of name and likeness cases, the public disclosure cases, and the intrusion cases. In Dean Prosser's view the interest vindicated in each of these classes of cases is a different one. In my view the interest protected in each is the same, it is human dignity and individuality or, in Warren and Brandeis' words, "inviolate personality."

HYMAN GROSS, THE CONCEPT OF PRIVACY
42 N.Y.U. L. Rev. 34 (1967).

Dean Prosser's "Several Torts" Thesis

Dean Prosser's position is that what is called "invasion of privacy" may be any one of four distinct torts, each wrongful conduct with respect to one of three distinct interests.

. . .

The fourth tort distinguished is appropriation of a name or image— the very attributes of personality—for the benefit of the one who appropriates them. The victim here, it is asserted, has his proprietary interest in his personality violated. The range of cases of such commercial usage extends from advertising to work of literary and graphic art.

. . .

Appropriation cases involve a use for the defendant's advantage, while other types do not.—It is true, of course, that the "appropriation" cases all involve a use for the defendant's advantage, for (as before) if they did not they would not be so classified by Dean Prosser. But is the use of plaintiff's name or likeness for defendant's advantage in derogation of a *proprietary* right of plaintiff in his identity, as Dean Prosser indicates? I suggest that this is a serious mislocation of the gravamen of the wrong. The offense is to sensibility; and, more particularly, to those sensibilities of a person which are offended by another's use of his personality *regardless of any advantage*. Qualifications requiring a use for defendant's advantage do indeed exist. But when there is this requirement for a cause of action it is only to insure that a particular offense to privacy is unredeemed by a paramount public interest in unhindered communication—that the assault on privacy has been perpetrated merely to promote some selfish interest. The requirement represents a balance struck between a public interest and an interest in privacy, not an element of definition of the interest in privacy. Pursuing the inessential character of "appropriation" further, we might consider the New York statute which makes invasion of privacy in that jurisdiction a classic variety of "appropriation" in Dean Prosser's sense—uses "for advertising purposes, or for the purpose of trade." There are a number of cases under this statute in which there is no value ascribable to the particular name or picture used—an appropriate name or picture selected at random could have been substituted and it would have made no difference to the user. Nor was any loss of value in his name suffered by the plaintiff. Yet a good prima facie case was made under the statute. Clearly, then, it is not the value of the name to user or to bearer which matters here, but the unauthorized use itself. "Appropriation," then, is nothing more than unauthorized use, and this species of invasion of privacy is nothing more than unauthorized publicity given to a person's name or image.

D. THE SIGNIFICANCE OF LABELING THE TORT "PRIVACY" OR "PUBLICITY"

As the preceding articles demonstrate, there has been a heated debate by commentators and jurists about what the appropriate characterization of a claim brought in tort for the unauthorized use of a person's name, picture or likeness ought to be. This debate has been around for the whole century since the publication of the Warren and Brandeis article. Recall that some of the common law authority relied upon by Warren and Brandeis involved the unauthorized use of photographs and of etchings of a member of the royal family. These decisions and others that granted legal protection against the unauthorized use of lectures and letters were characterized by the courts as property and contracts cases. Warren and Brandeis contended that they were really privacy cases. The two major privacy cases decided after the publication of the Warren and Brandeis article featured the New York Court of Appeals and the Georgia Supreme Court disagreeing over whether the essence of such claims was rooted in harm to inviolate personality or personal dignity or in monetary harm through commercial exploitation of something akin to property.

The Second Circuit Court of Appeals was the first court to refer to the claim for unauthorized commercial use of a person's name and photograph as the "right of publicity." In *Haelan Laboratories, Inc. v. Topps Chewing Gum*, 202 F.2d 866 (2d Cir.) *cert. denied*, 346 U.S. 816 (1953), a company engaged in selling chewing gum asked a federal court to enjoin a competitor from using the photograph of a baseball player. Haelan had contracted with the player for use of his photograph and argued that the contract assigned Haelan a legal interest in the player's photograph that was protected under the New York statutory right to privacy. Topps argued that the right to privacy was personal and not assignable by contract.

Judge Jerome Frank wrote for a majority of the court:

> Whether it be labelled a "property" right is immaterial; for here, as often elsewhere, the tag "property" simply symbolizes the fact that courts enforce a claim which has pecuniary worth.

> This right might be called a "right of publicity."

Id. at 868.

Shortly after the *Haelan* decision, Melville B. Nimmer published an article that has been characterized by a leading commentator on the subject as the "foundation stone" of the right to publicity. J. McCarthy, *The Rights of Publicity and Privacy*, Section 1.8 at 1–34 to 1–34.1 (Release #11, 4/94). Review the arguments of Professor Nimmer in this important article as well as the views expressed by the various scholars in the articles that precede and follow his in the section above. What is the practical significance of the label that one attaches to the tort (publicity, appropriation, privacy)?

Professor McCarthy, a leading commentator on the right to publicity, has observed:

> While much judicial confusion has been expressed over the years as to the difference between the Right of Publicity and the appropriation form of the right of privacy, the dimensions of the difference are today fairly well spelled out by many courts and commentators. . . .

> Simplistically put, while the appropriation branch of the right of privacy is invaded by an injury to the psyche, the Right of Publicity is infringed by an injury to pocketbook.

McCarthy, *supra*, Section 5.8[C], 5–69.

Professor McCarthy then charts the differences in the publicity and appropriation-privacy theories:

[D]   Chart of Comparison Between "Appropriation Privacy" and the "Right of Publicity"

	Appropriation Privacy	Right of Publicity
Infringing Act	Unpermitted Use of Identity	Unpermitted Use of Identity
Impact	Upon Personal Dignity	Upon Property Right in Persona
Measure of Damage	Mental/Physical Injury	Damage to the Value of Identity/Persona

Id., Section 5.8 [D] at 5–72.

7.   Appropriation and Publicity as a Privacy Based Right—California View

LUGOSI v. UNIVERSAL PICTURES

25 Cal.3d 813, 603 P.2d 425, 160 Cal.Rptr. 323 (1979).

BY THE COURT:

[Bram Stoker's 1897 novel *Dracula* has always been in the public domain. Universal Pictures'[1] film *Dracula*, however, was copyrighted after the studio had purchased the motion picture rights from Stoker's heir, and from Hamilton Deane and John Balderston, the authors of the 1927 stage play *Dracula*. In September 1930, the actor Bela Lugosi and Universal Pictures entered into a written agreement for the production of the film *Dracula*, in which Lugosi was to play, and did play, the title role. The agreement contained a grant of rights to the producer to photograph and otherwise reproduce, exhibit, distribute and exploit in connection with the film any and all of Lugosi's acts, poses, plays and appearances of any kind.[2] The right to record, reproduce, and exploit

---

1. Appellant Universal Pictures, a Division of Universal City Studios, Inc., is the survivor of Universal Pictures Company, Inc. Appellant and its predecessor corporation are referred to herein collectively as Universal.

2. The producer shall have the right to photograph and/or otherwise produce, reproduce, transmit, exhibit, distribute and *exploit in connection with* the said photo-

play any and all of the artist's acts, poses, plays and appearances of any and all kinds hereunder, and *shall further have the right to record, reproduce, transmit, exhibit, distribute, and exploit in connection with* said photoplay the artist's voice, and all instrumental, musical, and other sound effects produced by the artist in connection with such acts, poses, plays and appearances. The producer shall likewise have the right

Lugosi's voice as well as to use and give publicity to his name and likeness in connection with the film was also granted.

Lugosi died in 1956. In 1960, Universal began to enter into many licensing agreements which authorized the licensees to use the Count Dracula character. The plaintiffs, Lugosi's widow and surviving son (Lugosi's heirs), sought to recover the profits made by Universal in its licensing and to enjoin Universal from making any additional grants without their consent. The trial court concluded that during his lifetime, Lugosi had a protectible property right in his facial characteristics and the individual manner of his likeness and appearance as Count Dracula. The court further held that this property right did not terminate with Lugosi's death but descended to his heirs, who thus acquired all right, title and interest in and to such property under the actor's will. The plaintiffs recovered a judgment for damages and an injunction. Universal appeals.]

We granted a hearing in this case in order to consider the important issues raised. After an independent study of these issues, we have concluded that the thoughtful opinion of presiding Justice Roth for the Court of Appeal, Second Appellate District, in this case correctly treats the issues, and accordingly adopt it as our own. [The Court then incorporates the edited version of the court of appeals opinion, some of which follows.]

. . .

Assuming arguendo that Lugosi, in his lifetime, based upon publicity he received and/or because of the nature of his talent in exploiting his name and likeness in association with the Dracula character, had established a business under the name of Lugosi Horror Pictures and sold licenses to have "Lugosi as Dracula" imprinted on shirts, and in so doing built a large public acceptance and/or good will for such business, product or service, there is little doubt that Lugosi would have created during his lifetime a business or a property wholly apart from the rights he granted to Universal to exploit his name and likeness in the characterization of the lead role of Count Dracula in the picture Dracula.

However, even on the above assumption, whether Lugosi's heirs would have succeeded to such property depends entirely on how it was managed before Lugosi died. Lugosi may have sold the property and spent the consideration before he died, or sold it for installment payments and/or royalties due after his death, in which latter event such payments and/or royalties would, of course, be a part of his estate.

. . .

When the right invaded was more strictly the privilege "to be let alone," the courts in this state have refused to extend to the heirs of the

to use and give publicity to the *artist's name and likeness*, photographic or otherwise, and to recordations and reproductions of the artist's voice and all instrumental, musical, and other sound effects produced by the artist hereunder, *in connection with the advertising and exploitation of said photoplay. (Italics added).*

(potential) plaintiff the right to recover for the invasion of that right: "It is well settled that the right of privacy is purely a personal one; it cannot be asserted by anyone other than the person whose privacy has been invaded, that is, plaintiff must plead and prove that *his* privacy has been invaded. Further, the right does not survive but dies with the person."

There is good reason for the rule. The very decision to exploit name and likeness is a personal one. It is not at all unlikely that Lugosi and others in his position did not during their respective lifetimes exercise their undoubted right to capitalize upon their personalities, and transfer the value thereof into some commercial venture, for reasons of taste or judgment or because the enterprise to be organized might be too demanding or simply because they did not want to be bothered.

It seems to us rather novel to urge that because one's immediate ancestor did not exploit the flood of publicity and/or other evidence of public acceptance he received in his lifetime for commercial purposes, *the opportunity* to have done so is property which descends to his heirs. Yet [plaintiffs'] claim boils down to this: now that Bela Lugosi is dead, they are the only ones who should have the opportunity to exploit their ancestor's personality.

If the opportunities of a person to exploit a name or likeness in one's lifetime is inheritable property, may it be assumed that if the first heirs thereof, like their immediate ancestor, do not exploit similar opportunities the right to do so is automatically transferred to succeeding heirs? [May the remote descendants of historic public figures obtain damages for the unauthorized commercial use of the name or likeness of their distinguished ancestors? If not, where is the line to be drawn, and who should draw it? ... Certainly the Legislature by appropriate amendment to Civil Code ... might recognize a right of action on behalf of the family or immediate heirs of persons such as Lugosi. For the reasons stated above, however, we decline to adopt judicially any such rule.

Thus, under present law,] upon Lugosi's death anyone, related or unrelated to Lugosi, with the imagination, the enterprise, the energy and the cash could, in [his or her] own name or in a fictitious name, or a trade name coupled with that of Lugosi, have impressed a name so selected with a secondary meaning and realized a profit or loss by so doing depending upon the value of the idea, its acceptance by the public and the management of the enterprise undertaken. After Lugosi's death, his name was in the public domain. Anyone, including [plaintiffs], or either of them, or Universal, could use it for a legitimate commercial purpose.

We are not prepared to say, however, that [plaintiffs] or any person other than Universal could have attempted to build a business with a secondary meaning, which business exploited the name Lugosi, and coupled *Lugosi's name* with that of Dracula. That question is not before us.

The learned trial judge, in holding that the name and likeness are "property" which can pass to the heirs, relied on a line of cases which purport to recognize such a "property right" as opposed to the right of privacy founded in tort [e.g., Haelan Laboratories v. Topps Chewing Gum].

The question which these cases pose is this: if the right to exploit name and likeness can be assigned because it is a "property" right (Haelan), is there any reason why the same right cannot pass to the heirs?

Assignment of the right to exploit name and likeness by the "owner" thereof is synonymous with its exercise. In all of the above cases *the owner* of the right did assign it in his lifetime and, too, Lugosi did precisely this in his lifetime when he assigned his name and likeness to Universal for exploitation in connection with the picture *Dracula*.... Thus, whether or not the right sounds in tort or property, and we think with Dean Prosser that a debate over this issue is pointless, what is at stake is the question whether this right is or ought to be personal.

The so-called right of publicity means in essence that the reaction of the public to name and likeness, which may be fortuitous or which may be managed or planned, endows the name and likeness of the person involved with commercially exploitable opportunities. The protection of name and likeness from unwarranted intrusion or exploitation is the heart of the law of privacy.

If rights to the exploitation of artistic or intellectual property never exercised during the lifetime of their creators were to survive their death, neither society's interest in the free dissemination of ideas nor the artist's rights to the fruits of his own labor would be served....

We hold that the right to exploit name and likeness is personal to the artist and must be exercised, if at all, by him during his lifetime. [End of Court of Appeal opinion.]

The judgment is reversed and the trial court is directed to enter a new judgment in favor of Universal for its costs. Plaintiffs' cross-appeal is dismissed as moot. Universal shall recover its costs of appeal.

Mosk, Justice, concurring.

With the majority of my colleagues I concur in the judgement, and in the opinion of Presiding Justice Roth. Because this is a matter of first impression in our court, I am impelled to add some observations.

Factually and legally this is a remarkable case. Factually: not unlike the horror films that brought him fame, Bela Lugosi rises from the grave 20 years after death to haunt his former employer. Legally: his vehicle is a strained adaptation of a common law cause of action heretofore unknown either in a statute or case law in California.

The plaintiffs, and my dissenting colleagues, erroneously define the fundamental issue, and consistently define the fundamental issue, and consistently repeat their misconception. We are not troubled by the nature of Lugosi's right to control the commercial exploitation of *his* likeness. That right has long been established. The issue here is the right of Lugosi's successors to control the commercialization of a likeness of a dramatic character—i.e., Count Dracula—created by a novelist and portrayed for compensation by Lugosi in a film version produced by a motion picture company under license from the successor of the novelist. The error in discerning the problem pervades the trial court's conclusion. Inevitably one who asks the wrong question gets the wrong answer.

Bela Lugosi was a talented actor. But he was an actor, a practitioner of the thespian arts; he was not a playwright, an innovator, a creator or an entrepreneur. . . .

Merely playing a role under the foregoing circumstances creates no inheritable property right in an actor, absent a contract so providing. Indeed, as the record discloses, many other actors have portrayed the same role, notably Lon Chaney and John Carradine; the first movie was a European version released in 1922 with Max Schreck as the Count. Thus neither Lugosi during his lifetime nor his estate thereafter owned the exclusive right to exploit Count Dracula any more than Gregory Peck possesses or his heirs could possess common law exclusivity to General MacArthur, George C. Scott to General Patton, James Whitmore to Will Rogers and Harry Truman, or Charlton Heston to Moses.

I do not suggest that an actor can never retain a proprietary interest in a characterization. An original creation of a fictional figure played exclusively by its creator may well be protectible. Thus Groucho Marx just being Groucho Marx, with his moustache, cigar, slouch and leer, cannot be exploited by others. Red Skelton's variety of self-devised roles would appear to be protectible, as would the unique personal creations of Abbott and Costello, Laurel and Hardy and others of that genre. . . .

Here it is clear that Bela Lugosi did not portray himself and did not create Dracula, he merely acted out a popular role that had been garnished with the patina of age, as had innumerable other thespians over the decades. His performance gave him no more claim on Dracula than that of countless actors on Hamlet who have portrayed the Dane in a unique manner.

. . .

Finally, I must comment briefly on the problems my dissenting colleagues face when they attempt to determine the temporal limitations of their version of the right of publicity. May the descendants of George Washington sue the Secretary of the Treasury for placing his likeness on the dollar bill? May the descendants of Abraham Lincoln obtain damages for the commercial exploitation of his name and likeness by the Lincoln National Life Insurance Company or the Lincoln division of the Ford Motor Company? May the descendants of James and Dolly Madison recover for the commercialization of Dolly Madison confections?

Although conceding it is inherently a policy decision, and without statutory guidance or case authority, the dissent, by mere *ipse dixit* selects the copyright period, i.e., the author's life plus 50 years. . . .

. . .

BIRD, C.J.—I respectfully dissent. . . .

I conclude that Universal Picture's licensing of Lugosi's image was unauthorized and infringed on Lugosi's proprietary interest in his likeness. Since that interest is inheritable, the trial court correctly held that plaintiffs are entitled to damages and injunctive relief.

. . .

II.   THE RIGHT OF PUBLICITY

The fundamental issue in this case is the nature of Lugosi's right to control the commercial exploitation of his likeness. The trial court found Universal's licensing agreements constituted a tortious interference with Lugosi's proprietary or property interest in the commercial use of his likeness, an interest which had descended to plaintiffs. Universal asserts that Lugosi's interest is protected only under the rubric of the right of privacy. Since that right is personal and ceased with Lugosi's death, plaintiffs cannot recover damages based on Universal's conduct. Accordingly, the critical question is whether an individual's interest in the commercial use of his likeness is protected solely as an aspect of the right of privacy or whether additional or alternative protection exists.

A.   Privacy or Publicity

The common law right of privacy creates a cause of action for "an interference with the right of the plaintiff . . . 'to be let alone.' " "The gist of the cause of action in a privacy case is . . . a direct wrong of a personal character resulting in injury to the feelings. . . . The injury is mental and subjective. It impairs the mental peace and comfort of the person and may cause suffering much more acute than that caused by a bodily injury." . . .

. . .

Today, it is commonplace for individuals to promote or advertise commercial services and products or, as in the present case, even have their identities infused in the products. Individuals prominent in athletics, business, entertainment and the arts, for example, are frequently involved in such enterprises. When a product's promoter determines that the commercial use of a particular person will be advantageous, the promoter is often willing to pay handsomely for the privilege. As a result, the sale of one's persona in connection with the promotion of commercial products has unquestionably become big business.

Such commercial use of an individual's identity is intended to increase the value or sales of the product by fusing the celebrity's identity with the product and thereby siphoning some of the publicity value or good will in the celebrity's persona into the product. This use is premised, in part, on public recognition and association with that person's name or likeness, or an ability to create such recognition. The commercial value of a particular person's identity thus primarily depends on that person's public visibility and the characteristics for which he or she is known.

Often considerable money, time and energy are needed to develop one's prominence in a particular field. Years of labor may be required before one's skill, reputation, notoriety or virtues are sufficiently developed to permit an economic return through some medium of commercial promotion. . . .

. . .

Accordingly, the gravamen of the harm flowing from an unauthorized commercial use of a prominent individual's likeness in most cases is the loss of potential financial gain, not mental anguish. The fundamental objection is not that the commercial use is offensive, but that the individual has not been compensated. Indeed, the representation of the person will most likely be flattering, since it is in the user's interest to project a positive image. The harm to feelings, if any, is usually minimal.

The individual's interest thus threatened by most unauthorized commercial uses is significantly different than the personal interests protected under the right of privacy. Recognition of this difference has prompted independent judicial protection for this economical interest. The individual's interest in the commercial value of his identity has been regarded as proprietary in nature and sometimes denominated a common law "right of publicity." This right has won increasing judicial recognition, as well as endorsements by legal commentators.

The right of publicity has been regarded as "the right of each person to control and profit from the publicity values which he created or purchased." [citing language from Professor Nimmer's article.] . . .

. . .

B.   *The Scope of the Right of Publicity*

The parameters of the right of publicity must now be considered. This case presents two questions: (1) whether the right extends to the likeness of an individual in his portrayal of the fictional character; and (2) whether the right dies with the individual or may be passed to one's heirs or beneficiaries.

. . .

In summary, I would hold that a prominent person's interest in the economic value of commercial uses of his or her name and likeness is protected under the common law. This interest is denominated a right of publicity and is assignable. The right is descendible and is accorded legal protection during the individual's lifetime and for a period of 50 years thereafter. Having found Universal licensed Lugosi's likeness in his distinctive portrayal of Count Dracula, the trial court properly held such use infringed on Lugosi's right of publicity. Since plaintiffs inherited that right upon Lugosi's death, they are entitled to relief for Universal's tortious conduct.

. . .

V.   Conclusion

Judicial recognition and protection of the proprietary interest in one's name and likeness is not an unjustified foray by the judiciary into the legislative domain but a recognition of the common law's sensitivity to the evolution of societal needs and its ability to adapt to new conditions. The trial court properly found Lugosi had a right of publicity in his likeness in his portrayal of Count Dracula and that the right descended to plaintiffs as his beneficiaries.

The right of publicity is distinct from the right of privacy. The majority's effort to squeeze the former into the traditional parameters of the latter is ultimately destructive of both rights. To accommodate the right of privacy to the realities of the commercial use of a celebrity's identity, the majority hastily provided that the right was assignable. Yet, the right of privacy has heretofore been considered a personal, nonassignable right. In characterizing a prominent individual's interest in the commercial uses of his identity as solely affecting the right of privacy, the majority has failed to confront the dual nature of such appropriations. In the process, the individual's interest has been undervalued, and a salutary development in the common law—hailed in other jurisdictions—has been aborted.

I would reverse the judgement and remand the cause to the trial court with directions to modify the damage award and injunction consistent with the views expressed herein. In all other respects, I would affirm the judgement.

TOBRINER and MANUEL, JJ., concur.

Note: *Lugosi*

Lugosi is an example of how confusing issues of assignability and descendibility can be to appellate courts. The disparate views of the Justices in *Lugosi* demonstrate that the clean distinctions between the appropriation and publicity torts that are contained in the summary by Professor McCarthy are not always recognized by courts.

Lugosi illustrates a factual pattern where the label that is given to the right has practical consequences. Heirs assert rights to control the use of a celebrity's name, picture or likeness after her death. If one's interest in deciding whether one's picture or likeness will be used is akin to property, then it would become part of an individual's estate upon death and, like other assets, descend to the heirs. If it is an interest or right to privacy, then the claim of heirs confronts the long standing and generally embraced rule that privacy rights are in that class of personal rights that do not survive the death of the person that held them. We examined this non-survival of privacy rights view earlier in these materials. *See, Weller* and note following, *supra*. Does the *Lugosi* decision adequately explain why the heirs have no rights? Does the majority in *Lugosi* adopt the approach of the Restatement of Torts to the privacy appropriation tort? Consider Professor Nimmer's view of the right to publicity. Are the references to and discussions of the concept by the various Justices in *Lugosi* consistent with the views of Professor Nimmer?

Two days after *Lugosi* was decided, the California Supreme Court in *Guglielmi v. Spelling–Goldberg Productions*, 25 Cal.3d 860, 603 P.2d 454, 160 Cal.Rptr. 352 (1979), reaffirmed its holding in *Lugosi* that the publicity right does not survive the owner's death. However, the court made no reference to the "exploitation during lifetime" qualification on descendibility as it had in *Lugosi*. This omission created some confusion as to the state of California law. This confusion was addressed by the Second Circuit in *Groucho Marx Productions v. Day and Night Company, Inc.*, 689 F.2d 317 (2d Cir.1982). The court held that under California law the right to exploit one's name and likeness is a personal, not a property right, and that if the owner of the publicity right did not exploit it during his lifetime with respect to a *particular commercial venture*, his heirs could not assert the deceased's interest in his name or likeness being used in that particular commercial venture after his death. *Id.* at 321–322. The Second Circuit reasoned that the California courts would reject the view that if the owner of the publicity right was exploited with respect to *any commercial venture*, his heirs could assert his publicity right after his death against any commercial venture using the owner's name or likeness. *Id.* at 322.

E. PUBLICITY AS AN ASSIGNABLE AND DESCENDIBLE PROPERTY BASED RIGHT

The vast majority of courts that have considered the right to publicity view it as a property-based right. Most of these courts find this property-based publicity right freely assignable by its owner during his lifetime and fully descendible to his heirs after his death regardless of whether he used his right during his lifetime. *See, e.g., Martin Luther King, Jr., Center for Social Change, Inc. v. American Heritage Prods., Inc.*, 694 F.2d 674 (11th Cir.1983); *Motschenbacher v. R. J. Reynolds Tobacco Co.*, 498 F.2d 821 (9th Cir.1974); *Ettore v. Philco Television Broadcasting Corp.*, 229 F.2d 481 (3d Cir.1956), *cert. denied*, 351 U.S. 926 (1956); *Gee v. CBS, Inc.*, 471 F.Supp. 600 (E.D.Pa.), *aff'd without op.*, 612 F.2d 572 (3d Cir.1979); *Uhlaender v. Henricksen*, 316 F.Supp. 1277 (D.Minn.1970).

A few courts find that the property-based publicity right is descendible only if the owner of the right used it during his lifetime with respect to any commercial venture. *See, e.g., Estate of Presley v. Russen*, 513 F.Supp. 1339 (D.N.J.1981); *Hicks v. Casablanca Records, Inc.*, 464 F.Supp. 426 (S.D.N.Y.1978). The death of Elvis Presley spawned a number of lawsuits that raised the issue of whether the right to publicity descended to his heirs. Initially the right to publicity in Tennessee was viewed by the federal courts to be property-based, assignable and yet not descendible. *See, e.g., Factors, Etc., Inc. v. Pro Arts, Inc.*, 652 F.2d 278 (2d Cir.1981), *cert. denied*, 456 U.S. 927 (1982) (applying Tennessee law); *Memphis Dev. Found. v. Factors, Etc., Inc.*, 616 F.2d 956 (6th Cir.), *cert. denied*, 449 U.S. 953 (1980) (applying Tennessee law). These courts applying Tennessee law reasoned that to recognize a right of publicity during a celebrity's lifetime inspires creative endeavors but to recognize such a right after the celebrity's death does not.

The survivability or descendibility of rights in commercial use of identity, name, or likeness has been specifically dealt with in a number of states by statute. In California, legislation was enacted to overrule the *Lugosi* decision and provide for a post mortem right of publicity. The statute applies to personalities that died within fifty years of the statute's effective date and extends those rights to fifty years after their death. Cal. Civ. Code Sec. 990 (West 1985). Tennessee enacted legislation providing that the right to publicity in that state is transferable and that the right continues for ten years after the death of the person. Tenn. Cod Ann. Sec. 1104 (1988). The statutes in both California and Tennessee indicate clearly that post mortem rights to publicity accrue even though the right was not commercially exploited during the life of the person. For a summary of the approach of various states under common law developments and statutes on the descendibility issue, see J. McCarthy, *supra*, sec. 9.5 [A], 9–31.

1. MUST NAME OR LIKENESS HAVE "COMMERCIAL VALUE"?

Under the Restatement view of the appropriation tort, misappropriation of a person's name or likeness for personal use is actionable. Numerous courts have found tort violations for non-commercial appropriations of the plaintiff's name or picture. Often cited examples are *Vanderbilt v. Mitchell*, 72 N.J.Eq. 910, 67 A. 97 (1907) (plaintiff's name used as father of illegitimate child), and *Battaglia v. Adams*, 164 So.2d 195 (Fla.1964) (plaintiff's name entered in presidential primary). *See generally* David A. Elder, *The Law of Privacy*, Sec. 6:3 at 387 (1991).

A few courts that have characterized the right to publicity as a property right assert that only persons whose name or likeness have commercial value and who could have exploited this commercial value are entitled to bring an action against those who misappropriate their name or likeness without their consent for commercial purposes. For example, in *Pierson v. News Group Publications, Inc.*, 549 F.Supp. 635 (S.D.Ga.1982), the Southern District Court of Georgia found that a soldier whose picture was taken during "prisoner of war" training could not sue a publisher for using the picture in a news article under the right of publicity. The district court stated that the soldier could not commercially exploit his name or likeness himself, noting that he had failed to show that his name or likeness had commercial value and that army regulations required him to allow his name and photo to be used without payment when his superiors permitted the training photos to be taken for the news article. Does the requirement that the name or likeness have "commercial value" limit the right to publicity to celebrities?

The view that the right is limited to celebrities is expressed mostly in dicta in cases where celebrities bring right to publicity actions. In

Martin Luther King Center v. American Heritage Prods., Inc., 250 Ga. 135, 296 S.E.2d 697 (1982), a majority of the Supreme Court of Georgia held that under Georgia law, a celebrity like Martin Luther King had a common law right to publicity that is inheritable and devisable regardless of whether it is exploited during the celebrity's lifetime. Summarizing the cases in Georgia, Justice Hill stated:

> In *Pavesich*, this right not to have another appropriate one's photograph was denominated the right of privacy; in *Cabaniss v. Hipsley*, it was the right of publicity. Mr. Pavesich was not a public figure; Ms. Hipsley was. We conclude that while private citizens have the right of privacy, public figures have a similar right of publicity, and that the measure of damages to a public figure for violation of his or her right of publicity is the value of the appropriation to the user.

Id. at 143, 296 S.E.2d at 703. *See also Ali v. Playgirl, Inc.*, 447 F.Supp. 723, 729 (S.D.N.Y.1978).

Other cases also suggest in dicta that only persons whose names have commercial value have publicity rights. However, the issue in these cases is clouded by the fact that the plaintiff's likeness was used as part of promotion and advertisement of media publications and the primary basis for denying relief was that the use of plaintiff's name was incidental to a newsworthy story. *See Valentine v. C.B.S.*, 698 F.2d 430 (11th Cir.1983); *Fogel v. Forbes, Inc.*, 500 F.Supp. 1081 (E.D.Pa.1980); *Lawrence v. A.S. Abell Co.*, 299 Md. 697, 475 A.2d 448 (1984); *Anderson v. Fisher Broadcasting Cos.*, 300 Or. 452, 469, 712 P.2d 803, 814 (1986).

Limiting publicity rights to celebrities is supported by some commentators. *See* George B. Trubow, *Privacy Law and Practice*, Sec. 1.03[5], at 1–21 (1991); Peter L. Felcher & Edward L. Rubin, *Privacy, Publicity and the Portrayal of Real People by the Media*, 88 Yale L.J. 1577, 1591 n.78 (1979). Others have argued that non-celebrity status should go to the measure of their pecuniary damages, not to whether non-celebrities have a property right for publicity. *See* Nimmer, *supra*, at 217; J. McCarthy, *supra*, sec. 4.3[G], at 4–19. There is considerable support in the case law for this view. *See, e.g., Motschenbacher v. R.J. Reynolds Tobacco Co.*, 498 F.2d 821 (9th Cir.1974); *Tellado v. Time–Life Books*, 643 F.Supp. 904, 913 (D.N.J.1986). Consider the number of companies that prefer to have their products endorsed by non-celebrities because they want to appeal to the average consumers. The use of a non-celebrity to advertise a product seems clearly to be of commercial value to the seller of the product and that value ought to be demonstrable. Where the publicity right is part of the privacy appropriation tort, may celebrities recover emotional distress damages for indignities? Where publicity is viewed as a separate tort, are emotional distress damages recoverable by celebrities for indignities? Is it credible for a celebrity who has endorsed several commercial products to claim that the unauthorized use of her name to endorse a commercial product is an affront to her dignity? Review the treatment of these questions by the various commentators whose articles are excerpted in the beginning of this chapter and by the courts in the decisions that follow.

2. BEYOND NAME OR LIKENESS: "COMMERCIAL IDENTITY"

CARSON v. HERE'S JOHNNY PORTABLE TOILETS, INC.

698 F.2d 831 (6th Cir.1983).

Before KENNEDY, CIRCUIT JUDGE, BROWN and SWYGERT, SENIOR CIRCUIT JUDGES.

BAILEY BROWN, SENIOR CIRCUIT JUDGE.

[Appellant John W. Carson is the well-known host of "The Tonight Show." Since he began hosting the show in 1962, he has been introduced by the phrase "Here's Johnny" which is generally associated with Carson by the television viewing public. Carson has authorized the use of this phrase by three outside business ventures including appellant Johnny Carson Apparel, Inc. The phrase has never been registered by appellants as a trademark or service mark. Appellee is a Michigan corporation which shortly after going into business began using the "Here's Johnny" phrase, aware that it was the introductory slogan for "The Tonight Show." The appellants to whom use of the phrase had been permitted brought various actions, including invasion of privacy and publicity rights, seeking damages and an injunction prohibiting further use of the phrase. The district court held that the right to privacy and publicity rights extended only to a "name or likeness" and not to the "Here's Johnny" phrase.]

The appellants also claim that the appellee's use of the phrase "Here's Johnny" violates the common law right of privacy and right of publicity.[1] The confusion in this area of the law requires a brief analysis of the relationship between these two rights.

In an influential article, Dean Prosser delineated four distinct types of the right of privacy: (1) intrusion upon one's seclusion or solitude, (2) public disclosure of embarrassing private facts, (3) publicity which places one in a false light, and (4) appropriation of one's name or likeness for the defendant's advantage. This fourth type has become known as the "right of publicity." Henceforth we will refer to Prosser's last, or fourth, category as the "right of publicity."

Dean Prosser's analysis has been a source of some confusion in the law. His first three types of the right of privacy generally protect the right "to be let alone," while the right of publicity protects the celebri-

---

1. Michigan law, which governs these claims, has not yet clearly addressed the right of publicity. But the general recognition of the right, see W. Prosser, *Handbook of the Law of Torts* Section 117, at 805 (4th ed. 1971), suggests to us that the Michigan courts would adopt the right. Michigan has recognized a right of privacy, *Beaumont v. Brown*, 401 Mich. 80, 257 N.W.2d 522 (1977).

ty's pecuniary interest in the commercial exploitation of his identity. Thus, the right of privacy and right of publicity protect fundamentally different interests and must be analyzed separately.

We do not believe that Carson's claim that his right of privacy has been invaded is supported by the law or the facts. Apparently, the gist of this claim is that Carson is embarrassed by and considers it odious to be associated with the appellee's product. Clearly, the association does not appeal to Carson's sense of humor. But the facts here presented do not, it appears to us, amount to an invasion of any of the interests protected by the right of privacy. In any event, our disposition of the claim of an invasion of the right of publicity makes it unnecessary for us to accept or reject the claim of an invasion of the right of privacy.

The right of publicity has developed to protect the commercial interest of celebrities in their identities. The theory of the right is that a celebrity's identity can be valuable in the promotion of products, and the celebrity has an interest that may be protected from the unauthorized commercial exploitation of that identity. . . .

The district court dismissed appellants' claim based on the right of publicity because appellee does not use Carson's name or likeness. It held that it "would not be prudent to allow recovery for a right of publicity claim which does not more specifically identify Johnny Carson." We believe that, on the contrary, the district court's conception of the right of publicity is too narrow. The right of publicity, as we have stated, is that a celebrity has a protected pecuniary interest in the commercial exploitation of his identity. If the celebrity's identity is commercially exploited, there has been an invasion of his right whether or not his "name or likeness" is used. Carson's identity may be exploited even if his name, John W. Carson, or his picture is not used.

. . .

In this case, Earl Braxton, president and owner of Here's Johnny Portable Toilets, Inc., admitted that he knew that the phrase "Here's Johnny" had been used for years to introduce Carson. Moreover, in the opening statement in the district court, appellee's counsel stated:

> Now, we've stipulated in this case that the public tends to associate the words "Johnny Carson," the words "Here's Johnny" with plaintiff, John Carson and, Mr. Braxton, in his deposition, admitted that he knew that and probably absent that identification, he would not have chosen it.

App. 68. That the "Here's Johnny" name was selected by Braxton because of its identification with Carson was the clear inference from Braxton's testimony irrespective of such admission in the opening statement.

We therefore conclude that, applying the correct legal standards, appellants are entitled to judgment. The proof showed without question that appellee had appropriated Carson's identity in connection with its corporate name and its product.

. . .

CORNELIA G. KENNEDY, CIRCUIT JUDGE, dissenting.

I respectfully dissent from that part of the majority's opinion which holds that appellee's use of the phrase "Here's Johnny" violates appellant Johnny Carson's common law right of publicity. While I agree that an individual's identity may be impermissibly exploited, I do not believe that the common law right of publicity may be extended beyond an individual's name, likeness, achievements, identifying characteristics or actual performances, to include phrases or other things which are merely associated with the individual, as is the phrase "Here's Johnny." The majority's extension of the right of publicity to include phrases or other things which are merely associated with the individual permits a popular entertainer or public figure, by associating himself or herself with a common phrase, to remove those words from the public domain.

The phrase "Here's Johnny" is merely associated with Johnny Carson, the host and star of "The Tonight Show" broadcast by the National Broadcasting Company. Since 1962, the opening format of "The Tonight Show," after the theme music is played, is to introduce Johnny Carson with the phrase "Here's Johnny." The words are spoken by an announcer, generally Ed McMahon, in a drawn out and distinctive manner. Immediately after the phrase "Here's Johnny" is spoken, Johnny Carson appears to begin the program.[1] This method of introduction was first used by Johnny Carson in 1957 when he hosted a daily television show for the American Broadcasting Company. This case is not transformed into a "name" case simply because the diminutive form of John W. Carson's given name and the first name of his full stage name, Johnny Carson, appears in it. The first name is so common, in light of the millions of persons named John, Johnny or Jonathan that no doubt inhabit this world, that, alone, it is meaningless or ambiguous at best in identifying Johnny Carson, the celebrity. In addition, the phrase containing Johnny Carson's first stage name was certainly selected for its value as a double entendre. Appellee manufactures portable toilets. The value of the phrase to appellee's product is in the risque meaning of "john" as a toilet or bathroom. For this reason, too, this is not a "name" case.

Appellee has stipulated that the phrase "Here's Johnny" is associated with Johnny Carson and that absent this association, he would not have chosen to use it for his product and corporation, Here's Johnny Portable Toilets, Inc. I do not consider it relevant that appellee intentionally chose to incorporate into the name of his corporation and product a phrase that is merely associated with Johnny Carson. What is

1. It cannot be claimed that Johnny Carson's appearances on "The Tonight Show" are the only times at which a performer is introduced with the phrase "Here's _____." Numerous other performers are introduced with the phrase "Here's _____," using their first name, last name or full name.

not protected by law is not taken from public use. Research reveals no case in which the right of publicity has been extended to phrases or other things which are merely associated with an individual and are not part of his name, likeness, achievements, identifying characteristics or actual performances. Both the policies behind the right of publicity and countervailing interests and considerations indicate that such an extension should not be made.

I.   Policies Behind Right of Publicity

The three primary policy considerations behind the right of publicity are succinctly stated in Hoffman, *Limitations on the Right of Publicity*, 28 Bull. Copr. Soc'y, 111, 116–22 (1980). First, "the right of publicity vindicates the economic interests of celebrities, enabling those whose achievements have imbued their identities with pecuniary value to profit from their fame." Second, the right of publicity fosters "the production of intellectual and creative works by providing the financial incentive for individuals to expend the time and resources necessary to produce them." Third, "[t]he right of publicity serves both individual and societal interests by preventing what our legal tradition regards as wrongful conduct: unjust enrichment and deceptive trade practices."

None of the above-mentioned policy arguments supports the extension of the right of publicity to phrases or other things which are merely associated with an individual. First, the majority is awarding Johnny Carson a windfall, rather than vindicating his economic interests, by protecting the phrase "Here's Johnny" which is merely associated with him. . . . There is nothing in the record to suggest that "Here's Johnny" has any nexus to Johnny Carson other than being the introduction to his personal appearances. The phrase is not part of an identity that he created. In its content "Here's Johnny" is a very simple and common introduction. The content of the phrase neither originated with Johnny Carson nor is it confined to the world of entertainment. The phrase is not said by Johnny Carson, but said of him. Its association with him is derived, in large part, by the context in which it is said—generally by Ed McMahon in a drawn out and distinctive voice[5] after the theme music to "The Tonight Show" is played, and immediately prior to Johnny Carson's own entrance. Appellee's use of the content "Here's Johnny," in light of its value as a double entendre, written on its product and corporate name, and therefore outside of the context in which it is associated with Johnny Carson, does little to rob Johnny Carson of something which is unique to him or a product of his own efforts.

The second policy goal of fostering the production of creative and intellectual works is not met by the majority's rule because in awarding publicity rights in a phrase neither created by him nor performed by him, economic reward and protection is divorced from personal incentive to produce on the part of the protected and benefited individual. Johnny

---

5.   Ed McMahon arguably has a competing publicity interest in this same phrase because it is said by him in a distinctive and drawn out manner as his introduction to entertainers who appear on "The Tonight Show," including Johnny Carson.

Carson is simply reaping the rewards of the time, effort and work product of others....

. . .

II. COUNTERVAILING INTERESTS AND CONSIDERATIONS

The right of publicity, whether tied to name, likeness, achievements, identifying characteristics or actual performances, etc., conflicts with the economic and expressive interests of others. Society's interests in free enterprise and free expression must be balanced against the interests of an individual seeking protection in the right of publicity where the right is being expanded beyond established limits. In addition, the right to publicity may be subject to federal preemption where it conflicts with the provisions of the Copyright Act of 1976.

. . .

Protection under the right of publicity confers a monopoly on the protected individual that is potentially broader, offers fewer protections and potentially competes with federal statutory monopolies. As an essential part of three federal monopoly rights, copyright, trademark and patents, notice to the public is required in the form of filing with the appropriate governmental office and use of an appropriate mark. This apprises members of the public of the nature and extent of what is being removed from the public domain and subject to claims of infringement. The right of publicity provides limited notice to the public of the extent of the monopoly right to be asserted, if one is to be asserted at all. As the right of privacy is expanded beyond protections of name, likeness and actual performances, which provide relatively objective notice to the public of the extent of an individual's rights, to more subjective attributes such as achievements and identifying characteristics, the public's ability to be on notice of a common law monopoly right, if one is even asserted by a given famous individual, is severely diminished. Protecting phrases and other things merely associated with an individual provides virtually no notice to the public at all of what is claimed to be protected. By ensuring the invocation of the adjudicative process whenever the commercial use of a phrase or other associated thing is considered to have been wrongfully appropriated, the public is left to act at their peril. The result is a chilling effect on commercial innovation and opportunity.

. . .

... The protected tangible expressions are asserted to not run afoul of first amendment challenges because the notice requirements and limited duration of copyright protection balances the interest of individuals seeking protection under the copyright clause and first amendment. Because the phrase "Here's Johnny" is more akin to an idea or concept of introducing an individual than an original protectible fixed expression of that idea and because the right of publicity in this instance is not complemented by saving notice or duration requirements, phrases such as "Here's Johnny" should not be entitled to protection under the right of publicity as a matter of policy and concern for the first amendment.

Apart from the possibility of outright federal preemption, public policy requires that the public's interest in free enterprise and free expression take precedence over any interest Johnny Carson may have in a phrase associated with his person.

. . .

Accordingly, neither policy nor case law supports the extension of the right of publicity to encompass phrases and other things merely associated with an individual as in this case. I would affirm the judgment of the District Court on this basis as well.

WHITE v. SAMSUNG ELECTRONICS AMERICA, INC.

971 F.2d 1395 (9th Cir.1992).

[Vanna White, the well known hostess of the popular television game show, the Wheel of Fortune, sued Samsung Electronics America, Inc. for appropriation of identity based upon the corporation displaying a robot, dressed in a wig, gown and jewelry that was chosen to resemble the television star's hair and clothes in an advertisement for their products. The advertisement was part of a series of adds that were set in the twenty-first century and placed an item from current culture with a Samsung product and were united by the theme that Samsung products would still be in use. Attention was drawn to the product with humor by projecting outrageous future scenarios for the culture items. One ad depicted a raw steak with the caption: "Revealed to be health food. 2010 A.D." The look-alike robot in the ad in question was standing next to a Wheel of Fortune-like game board with the caption: "Longest-running game show. 2012 A.D."

The district court granted summary judgment against White on all of her claims—common law publicity, California statutory publicity, and the federal Lanham Act. On appeal the Ninth Circuit reversed on the common law publicity claim relying to a great extent on the reasoning of *Carson* stating, "It is not important how the defendant has appropriated the plaintiff's identity but whether the defendant has done so." The court rejected the "parody" defense on the basis that the primary message in the ad was to buy Samsung products and the spoof of Vanna White and the game show was tangential to this purely commercial purpose.[1]]

JUDGE KOZINSKI'S DISSENT FROM DENIAL OF THE PETITION FOR REHEARING

Samsung's petition for a rehearing en banc was denied by a majority of the Judges in the Ninth Circuit. Portions of Judge Kozinski's dissent which was joined by Judges O'Scannlain and Kleinfeld follows. The dissent is found in 989 F.2d 1512 (9th Cir.1993).

---

1. The Ninth Circuit also reversed the summary judgment on the Lanham Act claim.

KOZINSKI, CIRCUIT JUDGE, with whom CIRCUIT JUDGES O'SCANNLAIN and KLEINFELD join, dissenting from the order rejecting the suggestion for rehearing en banc.

Saddam Hussein wants to keep advertisers from using his picture in unflattering contexts. Clint Eastwood doesn't want tabloids to write about him. Rudolf Valentino's heirs want to control his film biography. The girl Scouts don't want their image soiled by association with certain activities. Pepsico doesn't singers to use the word "Pepsi" in their songs. Guy Lombardo wants an exclusive property right to ads that show big bands playing on New Year's Eve. Uri Geller thinks he should be paid for ads showing psychics bending metal through telekinesis. Paul Prud-homme, that household name, thinks the same about ads featuring corpulent bearded chefs. And scads of copyright holders see purple when their creations are made fun of.

Something very dangerous is going on here. Private property, in-cluding intellectual property, is essential to our way of life. It provides an incentive for investment and innovation; it stimulates the flourishing of our culture; it protects the moral entitlements of people to the fruits of their labors. But reducing too much to private property can be bad medicine. Private land, for instance is far more useful if separated from other private land by public streets, roads and highways. Public parks utility rights of way and sewers reduce the amount of land in private hands, but vastly enhance the value of the property that remains.

So too it is with intellectual property. Overprotecting intellectual property is as harmful as underprotecting it. Creativity is impossible without a rich public domain. Nothing today, likely nothing since we tamed fire, is genuinely new: Culture like science and technology, grows by accretion, each new creator building on the works of those who came before. Overprotection stifles the very creative forces it's supposed to nurture.

The district judge quite reasonably held that, because Samsung didn't use White's name, likeness, voice or signature, it didn't violate her right of publicity. Not so, says the panel majority: The California right of publicity can't possibly be limited to name and likeness. If it were, the majority reasons, a "clever advertising strategist" could avoid using White's name or likeness but nevertheless remind people of her with impunity, "effectively eviscerat[ing]" her rights. To prevent this "evis-ceration," the panel majority holds that the right of publicity must extend beyond name and likeness, to any "appropriation" of White's "identity"—anything that "evoke[s]" her personality.

But what does "evisceration" mean in intellectual property law? Intellectual property rights aren't like some constitutional rights, abso-lute guarantees protected against all kinds of interference, subtle as well as blatant. They cast no penumbras, emit no emanations: the very point of intellectual property laws is that they protect only against certain specific kinds of appropriation. I can't publish unauthorized copies of, say, *Presumed Innocent;* I can't make a movie out of it. But I'm perfectly free to write a book about an idealistic young prosecutor on trial for a crime he didn't commit. So what if I got the idea from *Presumed Innocent*? So, what if it reminds readers of the original? Have I "eviscerated" Scott Turow's intellectual property rights? Certainly not. A creators draw in part on the work of those who came before, referring to it, building on it, poking fun at it; we call this creativity, not piracy.

The majority isn't in fact, preventing the "evisceration" of Vanna White's existing rights; it's creating a new and much broader property right, a right unknown in California law. It's replacing the existing balance between the interests of the celebrity and those of the public by a different balance, one substantially more favorable to the celebrity. Instead of having an exclusive right in her name, likeness, signature or voice, every famous person now has an exclusive right to *anything that reminds the viewer of her*. After all, that's all Samsung did. It used an inanimate object to remind people of White, to "evoke [her identity]."

Consider how sweeping this new right is. What is it about the ad that makes people think of White? It's not the robot's wig, clothes or jewelry; there must be ten million blond women (many of them quasi-famous) who wear dresses and jewelry like White's. It's that the robot is posed near the "Wheel of Fortune" game board. Remove the game board from the ad, and no one would think of Vanna White. But once you include the game board, anybody standing beside it—a brunette woman, a man wearing women's clothes, a monkey in a wig and gown—would evoke White's image, precisely the way the robot did. It's the "Wheel of Fortune" set, not the robot's face or dress or jewelry that evokes White's image. The panel is giving White an exclusive right not in what she looks like or who she is, but in what she does for a living.

This is entirely the wrong place to strike the balance. Intellectual property rights aren't free. They're imposed at the expense of future creators and of the public at large. Where would we be if Charles Lindbergh had an exclusive right in the concept of a heroic solo aviator? If Arthur Conan Doyle had gotten a copyright in the idea of the detective story, or Albert Einstein had patented the theory of relativity? If every author and celebrity had been given the right to keep people from mocking them or their work? Surely this would have made the world poorer, not richer, culturally as well as economically.

This is why intellectual property law is full of careful balances between what's set aside for the owner and what's left in the public domain for the rest of us: The relatively short life of patents; the longer, but finite, life of copyrights; copyright's idea-expression dichotomy; the fair use of doctrine; the prohibition on copyrighting facts; the compulsory license of television broadcasts and musical compositions; federal preemption of overbroad state intellectual property laws; the nominative use of doctrine in trademark law; the right to make soundalike recordings. All of these diminish an intellectual property owner's rights. All let the public use something created by someone else. But all are necessary to maintain a free environment in which creative genius can flourish.

The intellectual property right created by the panel here has none of these essential limitations: No fair use exception; no right to parody; no idea-expression dichotomy. It impoverishes the public domain, to the detriment of future creators and the public at large. . . .

Finally, I can't see how giving White the power to keep others from evoking her image in the public's mind can be squared with the First Amendment. Where does White get this right to control our thoughts? The majority's creation goes way beyond the protection given a trademark or a copyrighted work, or a person's name or likeness. All those things control one particular way of expressing an idea, one way of referring to an object or a person. But not allowing *any* means of reminding people of someone? That's a speech restriction unparalleled in First Amendment law.

What's more, I doubt even a name and likeness-only right of publicity can stand without a parody exception. The First Amendment isn't just about religion or politics—it's also about protecting the free development of our national culture. Parody, humor, irreverence are all vital components of the marketplace of ideas. The last thing we need, the last thing the First Amendment will tolerate, is a law that lets public figures keep people from mocking them, or from "evok[ing]" their images in the mind of the public.[29]

The majority dismisses the First Amendment issue out of hand because Samsung's ad was commercial speech. So what? Commercial speech may be less protected by the First Amendment than noncommercial speech, but less protected means protected nonetheless. . . .

And there are very good reasons for this. Commercial speech has a profound effect on our culture and our attitudes. Neutral-seeming ads influence people's social and political attitudes, and themselves arouse political controversy. "Where's the Beef?" turned from an advertising catchphrase into the only really memorable thing about the 1984 presidential campaign. Four years later, Michael Dukakis called George Bush "the Joe Isuzu of American politics."

In our pop culture, where salesmanship must be entertaining and entertainment must sell, the line between the commercial and noncommercial has not merely blurred; it has disappeared. Is the Samsung parody any different from a parody on Saturday Night Live or in Spy Magazine? Both use a celebrity's identity to sell things—one to sell VCRs, the other to sell advertising. Both mock their subjects. Both try to make people laugh. Both add something, perhaps something worthwhile and memorable, perhaps not, to our culture. Both are things that the people being portrayed might dearly want to suppress. . . .

---

29. The majority's failure to recognize a parody exception to the right of publicity would apply equally to parodies of politicians as of actresses. Consider the case of Wok Fast, a Los Angeles Chinese food delivery service, which put up a billboard with a picture of then-L.A. Police Chief Daryl Gates and the Text "When you can't leave the office. Or won't." (This was an allusion to Chief Gates's refusal to retire despite pressure from Mayor Tom Bradley.) Gates forced the restaurant to take the billboard down by threatening a right of publicity lawsuit.

Commercial speech is a significant, valuable part of our national discourse. The Supreme Court has recognized as much, and has insisted that lower courts carefully scrutinize commercial speech restrictions, but the panel totally fails to do this. The panel majority doesn't even purport to apply the *Central Hudson* test, which the Supreme Court devised specifically for determining whether a commercial speech restriction is valid. The majority doesn't ask, as *Central Hudson* requires, whether the speech restriction is justified by a substantial state interest. It doesn't ask whether the restriction directly advances the interest. It doesn't ask whether the restriction is narrowly tailored to the interest. . . . These are all things the Supreme court told us—in no uncertain terms—we must consider; the majority opinion doesn't even mention them. . . .

Maybe applying the test would have convinced the majority to change its mind; maybe going through the factors would have shown that its rule was too broad, or the reasons for protecting White's "identity" too tenuous. Maybe not. But we shouldn't thumb our nose at the Supreme Court by just refusing to apply its test.

For better or worse, we *are* the Court of Appeals for the Hollywood Circuit. Millions of people toil in the shadow of the law we make, and much of their livelihood is made possible by the existence of intellectual property rights. But much of their livelihood—and much of the vibrancy of our culture—also depends on the existence of other intangible rights. The right to draw ideas from a rich and varied public domain, and the right to mock, for profit as well as fun, the cultural icons of our time.

In the name of avoiding the "evisceration" of a celebrity's rights in her image, the majority diminishes the rights of copyright holders and the public at large. In the name of fostering creativity, the majority suppresses it. Vanna White and those like her have been given something they never had before, and they've been given it at our expense. I cannot agree.]

a. *Beyond Name or Likeness: Right of Publicity Protection for "Commercial Identity"*

Initially, the appropriation tort action was used to redress those publicity right violations involving only the unauthorized commercial exploitation of a person's "name or likeness"; however, several courts in addition to *Carson* have extended this protection to all of those characteristics of a public figure's personality and public image which make up the public figure's commercial identity. In *Hirsch v. S.C. Johnson & Son*, 90 Wis.2d 379, 280 N.W.2d 129 (1979), the Wisconsin Supreme Court found that the famous professional football player, Elroy Hirsch, could sue a company under the right of publicity for use of his nickname "Crazylegs" to promote shaving gel for women. The Court said that the fact that others might be known by that nickname does not vitiate the publicity action but it may effect the quantum of damages awarded. *Id.* at 398, 280 N.W.2d at 137. And in *Ali v. Playgirl*, 447 F.Supp. 723 (S.D.N.Y.1978), the Southern District Court of New York found boxer

Mohammed Ali's publicity right to be imitated when a magazine used Ali's identifying phrase "The Greatest" in connection with a drawing of a nude black boxer labeled the "Mystery Man." *See also Motschenbacher v. R.J. Reynolds Tobacco Co.*, 498 F.2d 821 (9th Cir.1974) (professional race car driver can sue for publicity violation for use of car with distinctive decorations like those on his car in television cigarette commercial although his name or likeness was not used); *Onassis v. Christian Dior–New York, Inc.*, 122 Misc.2d 603, 472 N.Y.S.2d 254 (1984) (look-alike professional model in advertisement constitutes use of "picture and portrait" of Jacqueline Onassis within the meaning of New York statutory right to privacy).

Live performances which imitate a public figure's or entertainer's distinctive performing style have been found to be publicity right violations. In *Estate of Presley v. Russen*, 513 F.Supp. 1339 (D.N.J.1981), the district court found that the record before the court of a live stage production mimicking Elvis Presley's live performing style had demonstrated a publicity violation. The court distinguished between entertainment which is a copy or imitation of an entertainer's performing style and not a creative use, and entertainment that provided sufficient additional information to have its own creative component and have significant value as pure entertainment. *Id.* at 1359. The former constituted a publicity violation while the latter was protected under the first amendment.

Also, in *Groucho Marx Productions, Inc. v. Day and Night Company, Inc.*, 523 F.Supp. 485 (S.D.N.Y.1981), the federal district court found that the musical play "A Day in Hollywood/A Night in the Ukraine" exploited the rights of publicity in the characters that the Marx Brothers had created. The performers in the play dressed similarly to the Marx Brothers and imitated their comedic style although the Marx Brothers' names were not used. The production was not a parody, satire or critical review of the entertainers which would have been protected under the first amendment. On appeal, the Second Circuit reversed but on the basis that the court had incorrectly applied New York law to the case. Under the applicable law—California—the right to publicity was not descendible and therefore the court concluded that it was unnecessary to consider the "substantial" first amendment issues raised by imposing liability under the publicity tort to the play. *Groucho Marx Productions, Inc. v. Day & Night Company, Inc.*, 689 F.2d 317, 319 n. 2 (2d Cir.1982).

However, not all courts have extended publicity right protection to commercial imitations of an entertainer's style. In *Lombardo v. Doyle, Dane & Bernbach, Inc.*, 58 A.D.2d 620, 396 N.Y.S.2d 661 (1977), a New York court found that an imitation of a New Year's Eve party on a television commercial for car sales in which a man who did not look like Guy Lombardo imitated his band-leading style and in which the song "Auld Lang Syne" was used was not a publicity right violation since it did not commercially exploit Guy Lombardo's "name or likeness." And in *Guglielmi v. Spelling–Goldberg Prod.*, 25 Cal.3d 860, 603 P.2d 454, 160 Cal.Rptr. 352 (1979), the California Supreme Court stated that the right of publicity derives from "public prominence" and "does not confer a shield to ward off caricature, parody, and satire. Rather, prominence invites creative comment." *Id.* at 869, 603 P.2d at 460, 160 Cal. Rptr. at 358.

Is the deliberate imitation of the distinctive voice of a celebrity to sell a product actionable use of the commercial identity of the celebrity for purposes of the appropriation or publicity tort? There is some authority for restricting appropriation and publicity rights to use of the actual voice of the celebrity and not to voice imitations. In *Booth v. Colgate–Palmolive Company*, 362 F.Supp. 343 (S.D.N.Y.1973), the federal court rejected actress Shirley Booth's right to publicity claim under the statutory right to privacy in New York for the intentional imitation of her voice in an advertisement that featured a cartoon of a character (Hazel) she had played in a television series. The court concluded that the actress's publicity rights were not violated because her name or likeness was not used to "identify her as the source of the voice of Hazel." *Id.* at 347. The court suggested that extension of rights to commercial identity to voice impressions would frustrate policies of promoting the arts.

The Ninth Circuit broke new ground and recognized a cause of action for the intentional imitation of a celebrity's voice to sell a commercial product. In *Midler v. Ford Motor Co.*, 849 F.2d 460 (9th Cir.1988), the well-known actress and singer Bette Midler was found to have a cause of action under the common law right of publicity in California against an automobile manufacturer that used a singer to imitate her voice in an advertisement for the sale of Ford products. Judge Noonan for the Court found that, "The singer manifests herself in the song. To impersonate her voice is to pirate her identity." *Id.* at 463.

F. THE NEW YORK STATUTORY PUBLICITY RIGHT

1. INTRODUCTION

In this section, cases and developments under the New York statutory right of privacy are examined. The New York statute, N.Y. Civil Rights Act Sections 50–51, was enacted shortly after the New York Court of Appeals refused to recognize a right of privacy in the common law of the state in *Roberson v. Rochester Folding Box Co.*, 171 N.Y. 538, 64 N.E. 442 (1902).

The combination of the high state court rejecting a common law right to privacy and the legislature enacting a statutory right to privacy has caused confusion as to both the parameters and source of privacy rights in New York. Does the statutory right to privacy encompass the four common law privacy torts that are embraced in the Restatement? Does the statutory right include the privacy appropriation tort or the publicity tort or both? Is there a common law right to publicity that is independent of the statutory right? The New York Court of Appeals answered some of these questions in *Stephano v. News Group Publications, Inc.*, 64 N.Y.2d 174, 474 N.E.2d 580, 485 N.Y.S.2d 220 (1984):

> Since the "right of publicity" is encompassed under the Civil Rights Law as an aspect of the right of privacy, which, as noted, is exclusively statutory in this state, the plaintiff cannot claim an independent common-law right of publicity.

Id. at 193, 474 N.E.2d at 584, 485 N.Y.S.2d at 224.

The law that has evolved in New York plays an important role in the national law of appropriation and publicity rights. New York is a center of finance and entertainment and the statutory right of privacy has been the subject of litigation there for nearly a century. Consequently, New York has a rich case law and jurisprudence regarding privacy. New York courts have dealt with a number of issues which have not been litigated elsewhere. The cases construing Sections 50 and 51 of the Civil Rights Act are therefore a source of guidance to the courts of other states in appropriation and publicity cases that are brought under state common law or statutory claims.

N.Y. CIVIL RIGHTS LAW SECTION 50–51

(McKinney 1976 & Supp. 1991).

a. Section 50. Right of privacy

A person, firm or corporation that uses for advertising purposes, or for the purposes of trade, the name, portrait or picture of any living person without having first obtained the written consent of such person, or if a minor of his or her parent or guardian, is guilty of a misdemeanor.

b. Section 51. Action for injunction and for damages

Any person whose name, portrait or picture is used within this state for advertising purposes or for the purposes of trade without the written consent first obtained as above provided may maintain an equitable action in the supreme court of this state against the person, firm or corporation so using his name, portrait or picture, to prevent and restrain the use thereof; and may also sue and recover damages for any injuries sustained by reason of such use and if the defendant shall have knowingly used such person's name, portrait or picture in such manner as is forbidden or declared to be unlawful by section fifty of this article, the jury, in its discretion, may award exemplary damages. But nothing contained in this article shall be so construed as to prevent any person, firm or corporation from selling or otherwise transferring any material containing such name, portrait or picture in whatever medium to any user of such name, portrait or picture, or to any third party for sale or transfer directly or indirectly to such a user, for use in a manner lawful under this article; nothing contained in this article shall be so construed as to prevent any person, firm or corporation, practicing the profession of photography, from exhibiting in or about his or its establishment specimens of the work of such establishment, unless the same is continued by such person, firm or corporation after written notice objecting thereto has been given by the person portrayed; and nothing contained in this article shall be so construed as to prevent any person, firm or corporation from using the name, portrait or picture of any manufacturer or dealer in connection with the goods, wares and merchandise manufactured, produced or dealt in by him which he has sold or disposed of with such name, portrait or picture used in connection therewith; or from using the name, portrait or picture of any author, composer or artist in connection with his literary, musical or artistic productions which he has sold or disposed of with such name, portrait or picture used in connection therewith.

2. SECTIONS 50, 51: LIKENESS "FOR ADVERTISING PURPOSES OR PURPOSES OF TRADE"

NEGRI v. SCHERING CORPORATION
333 F.Supp. 101 (S.D.N.Y.1971).

FREDERICK van PELT BRYAN, DISTRICT JUDGE:

[Plaintiff Pola Negri, a motion picture actress, brought an action under Sections 50 and 51 of the New York Civil Rights Law seeking damages from defendant Schering Corporation for using a photograph of her in an advertisement for one of its products without her consent or authorization. The advertisement contained a photograph of a full length likeness of Negri with clear and characteristic features as she appeared in a silent movie. The photograph was recognized by friends of Negri's who brought the advertisement to her attention. Schering admits to publishing the advertisement in seven magazines without Negri's consent, but argues that it is entitled to summary judgment because the photograph was not used for advertising purposes or purposes of trade and because it was not a recognizable likeness of Negri as required under the statute.]

Schering argues that recovery is precluded under the New York Civil Rights Law because (1) the photograph as it appeared in the advertisement was not a recognizable likeness of Pola Negri and (2) that the photograph of Miss Negri in the advertisement was not used for advertising purposes or purposes of trade. Both of these arguments are devoid of merit.

It is plain that a picture used for advertising purposes is not actionable under the statute unless it is a recognizable likeness of the plaintiff. The picture used must be a clear representation of the plaintiff, recognizable from the advertisement itself. . . .

. . . Pola Negri's picture, as used in the Schering advertisement, is an individual, full length likeness of her, approximately 9 inches high, with features that are quite clear and characteristic. It is a clear representation of the famous motion picture star, easily recognizable as a picture of her. For example, it was recognized by the physician and friend who brought the advertisement to her attention and by four others, who were even able to identify the film from which it was taken. If there were any doubts as to the recognizability of the photograph as that of Miss Negri, and there are none, the fact that she is shown recommending POLAramine to her leading man, Conway Tearle, whose picture is shown next to hers, plainly point toward recognition.

. . .

... It is plain that, beyond her friends and acquaintances, Miss Negri's features were well known to millions of persons comprising her motion picture public. It may well be that since a number of years have elapsed since Miss Negri was at the height of her career, many persons who have seen her films are by no means as young as they once were and memories undoubtedly grow dim. But I fail to see that this is any reason to suppose that many of Miss Negri's public would not still easily recognize her as depicted in the Schering advertisement. In any event, the number of people who recognized the photograph in the advertisement as Miss Negri, while it may be relevant on the question of damages, is not material on the issue of liability. On that issue the question is whether the figure is recognizable, not the number of people who recognized it.

. . .

No doubt, Miss Negri's appearance at this writing differs substantially from what she looked like in 1922 when the picture was taken. But this, again, is beside the point. The policy underlying the New York statute is to protect "any living person" against the unauthorized use of his or her name or picture for commercial exploitation. If a picture so used is a clear and identifiable likeness of a living person, he or she is entitled to recover damages suffered by reason of such use, whether or not his or her appearance has altered through the passage of time.

. . .

In the case at Bar, there was no attempt to obscure or blur Miss Negri's features, nor did any obscuring or blurring occur. Anyone familiar with her appearance at the time the photograph was taken would have no difficulty recognizing her from the Schering advertisement. I hold that plaintiff has established that the photograph in the Schering advertisement is a recognizable likeness of the plaintiff.

. . .

Defendant's cross motion for summary judgment is in all respects denied. Since there are no material questions of fact to be tried on the issue of liability, plaintiff's motion for summary judgment on that issue is granted and the case will proceed to trial on the issue of damages.

It is so ordered.

a. The Identifiability Requirement

Since the essence of appropriation and publicity tort actions is the appropriation of identity, it is necessary for the plaintiff to demonstrate that the public identifies the plaintiff in the use by the defendant that is the basis of the tort claim. When a celebrity's name or picture is used to sell a commercial product, identifiability will not be a significant issue. Identifiability is a crucial issue in the cases discussed in the prior note following the *Carson* decision because the use does not involve literal reproduction of the plaintiff's name or picture. Is identifiability an important issue in *Negri*? How does the issue of identifiability arise under the New York statute? How is the issue of identifiability different in the *Midler* case discussed *supra*.

3. SECTIONS 50, 51: INJUNCTIVE RELIEF

ROSEMONT ENTERPRISES v. CHOPPY PRODUCTIONS

74 Misc.2d 1003, 347 N.Y.S.2d 83 (1972).

JACOB MARKOWITZ, JUSTICE:

[Plaintiff Howard R. Hughes alleged that defendants manufactured, distributed or sold without his consent various clothing merchandise bearing his name, purported signature or likeness. Hughes settled with two of the defendants, and was granted preliminary relief against the remaining three. The affidavits submitted by the remaining defendants confirmed that a joint venture had been created to manufacture and sell articles bearing Hughes' name and images of Hughes with corresponding comical or satirical comments. Hughes moves for summary judgment against all the defendants. The defendants move to dismiss the complaint.]

Defendant . . . after what is basically a general denial, alleged in its answer that plaintiff Hughes may be dead or may lack the capacity to bring the action and that defendant's action is protected by the First Amendment to the United States Constitution. . . .

. . .

I find no validity in their argument that the violation is protected by the constitutional right of free speech. The authorities they cite do not bear them out in the type of situation presently before the court; and this court, affirmed by the Appellate Division, has heretofore held to the contrary.

Plaintiff is presumed to be alive. On the proof submitted in his behalf in support of the motion he is entitled to a permanent injunction with an assessment of damages to the extent that he seeks reimbursement for attorneys' fees and disbursements, and the counterclaim will be dismissed.

4. INTENTION: PUNITIVE DAMAGES

WELCH v. MR. CHRISTMAS, INC.

57 N.Y.2d 143, 440 N.E.2d 1317, 454 N.Y.S.2d 971 (1982).

MEYER, JUDGE.

[Welch, a professional actor, brought an action under section 51 of the New York Civil Rights Law for damages resulting from the unauthorized use of a television commercial he had made for the defendant corporation. Welch had entered into a one year contract with the corporation to appear in a commercial advertising Christmas trees during 1973. The contract contained an option for the use of the commercial in 1974. Welch cautioned the corporation in 1975 that the term of permissible use had expired, but the commercial was aired in 1975 by a local distributor without Welch's knowledge or consent. There was no evidence to indicate that the corporation had arranged for this airing of the commercial. There was also no evidence to indicate that the corporation had taken steps to recall the commercial or limit its distribution. Testimony that use of the commercial by distributors was encouraged and was unrestricted was offered by the president of the corporation.

The jury awarded Welch $1,000 compensatory damages and $25,000 for exemplary damages. The trial judge reduced the exemplary damages to $15,000 and denied defendant's motion for judgment notwithstanding the verdict. The Appellate Division affirmed. The defendant appeals.]

Knowledge is not an element of the cause of action for compensatory damages or injunctive relief under the statute. This necessarily follows from its express requirement as to exemplary damages that "defendant shall have knowingly used" another's name, portrait or picture without consent, and the omission in the earlier portion of the same sentence dealing with compensatory damages of any modifier similarly limiting the use made compensable. Whether the claimed lack of knowledge concerns . . . the use or . . . the absence of consent is, as to compensatory damages, irrelevant in view of the wording of the statute. Nor need it be shown that defendant arranged for or directed use of the commercial by its Rochester distributor in 1975. The evidence that defendant actively encouraged maximum use of the commercial by its distributors who were expected to make their own arrangements for air time and neither placed any restriction upon the period within which it was to be used by the distributors nor made any effort at the expiration of the consent period or following the March, 1975 warning from the Screen Actors Guild to recall prints of the commercial from the distributors furnished a more than sufficient basis for holding defendant responsible for the unauthorized 1975 use.

. . .

The Appellate Division held that, defendant having been warned that the permissible period of use for the commercial had expired, the evidence was sufficient to support the conclusion that defendant acted knowingly within the meaning of the statute's exemplary damage provision. We do not find it necessary to reach that question. The jury was charged that it could award exemplary damages if it found that defendant "used plaintiff's picture, knowing that plaintiff had not consented to the use, or in reckless disregard of whether plaintiff had consented to the use." No exception was taken to that charge. It was, therefore, the law of the case that plaintiff's right to exemplary damages turned on whether defendant knew plaintiff had not consented rather than whether defendant itself knowingly caused the commercial to be aired. Because, as the Appellate Division noted, there was evidence to support a finding that defendant, having been warned, knew that plaintiff had not consented to use of the commercial in 1975, the jury's award of exemplary damages must be upheld under the law of the case.

For the foregoing reasons, the order of the Appellate Division should be affirmed, with costs.

COOKE, C.J., and JASEN, GABRIELLI, JONES, WACHTLER and Fuchsberg, JJ., CONCUR.

a. Is Intent an Element of the Appropriation and Publicity Torts?

Notice that section 652C of the Restatement of Torts does not specifically refer to intent in the definition of the appropriation tort. "One who *appropriates to his own use or benefit* the name or likeness of another" is liable. Restatement (Second) of Torts section 652C (1977) (emphasis added). Appropriation of commercial identity may occur without any intention to violate a person's right to privacy or publicity. This would be the case, for example, if the picture of a celebrity were used to advertise a commercial product under a good faith but mistaken view that there was consent to do so.

The holding in *Welch* that intention is not a requirement for recovery of compensatory damages under the New York statute was based upon the absence of an express requirement of "knowing use" in the section of the statute that addressed compensatory damages. The sparse discussion of the intent issue in common law appropriation and publicity cases is consistent with the holding in *Welch* that compensatory damages are recoverable without a demonstration that the defendant has intentionally misappropriated the plaintiff's identity or that the defendant used the plaintiff's name, picture or likeness knowing that there was no consent for her to do so. *See, e.g., Fairfield v. American Photocopy Equipment*, 138 Cal.App.2d 82, 87, 291 P.2d 194, 197 (1955).

Recall the discussion following *Monroe v. Darr, infra* pp. 242–243, about the availability of punitive damages in common law tort actions for invasions of privacy. Such damages are generally recoverable if the plaintiff can establish that the defendant acted with "malice" or engaged in willful and wanton misconduct toward the plaintiff. Does *Welch* interpret the New York statute to require a demonstration of less fault for punitive damages than is required under common law principles?

The defendant's state of mind in respect to intention or whether there is ill-will or malice toward the plaintiff may be relevant to a number of issues other than those addressed by the court in *Welch*. Does the defendant have to have intent in respect to the identification requirement that was addressed in the *Negri* decision, *infra*? Professor McCarthy concludes that knowledge that the public would identify the plaintiff is not a requirement in publicity actions. However, he argues that if intent to identify is established, that should be probative evidence of the fact of identification. McCarthy, section 3.6[D][2] at 3–30.

5. DEFENSE: USE OF NAME OR LIKENESS IN CONNECTION WITH NEWS

FRIEDAN v. FRIEDAN

414 F.Supp. 77 (S.D.N.Y.1976).

EDWARD WEINFELD, DISTRICT JUDGE.

[Plaintiff Friedan brought an action for recovery of damages resulting from the unauthorized use of his name and photograph in an article written by his former wife for New York Magazine. Plaintiff named his wife and the magazine as defendants and also brought an action against three broadcasting companies for the use of his photograph in an advertisement for the magazine. The photograph is of plaintiff, his former wife and their son in 1949. Plaintiff's wife is a well known leader of the feminist movement and the article and accompanying picture contrasted her life as a housewife in 1949 with her present status and views. Defendants move for summary judgment in this action.]

The theme of the magazine issue was a twenty-five year throwback to the year 1949 described as "The Year We Entered Modern Times" with a series of articles. The Betty Friedan article, describing her life as a housewife in that year, was illustrated by the photograph, which pictured the author, her then husband, plaintiff Carl Friedan, and their son Danny in 1949.

Defendant Betty Friedan, as a leader of the feminist movement, is a public figure. All incidents of her life, including those which contrast with her present status and views, are significant in terms of the interest of the public in news. Thus, her connubial life and experience twenty five years ago is a matter of public interest, and those who played a part in her life then may be referred to publicly.

Her former husband's right of privacy is subordinated to the public interest in news. In a family picture, which in a sense invades her then husband's privacy as one of the three shown in the picture, plaintiff cannot be separated from the other members of his family. As was put in Sidis v. F–R Pub. Corp.: "Everyone will agree that at some point the public interest in obtaining information becomes dominant over the individual's desire for privacy."

The picture of plaintiff together with his former wife and their child was related to and illustrative of the article describing her life twenty-five years ago, which was a matter of public interest. In this circumstance it cannot be considered used for the purpose of trade or advertising within the prohibition of the New York Civil Rights statute....

On the other hand, the use of plaintiff's photograph on television in commercials advertising the New York Magazine issue in which his former wife's article appeared was clearly "for advertising purposes." However, it has long been held that, under New York law, an advertisement, the purpose of which is to advertise the article, "shares the privilege enjoyed by the article" if the "article itself was unobjectionable."

Thus, although plaintiff alleges he has made every effort to disassociate himself from his former wife's public status to preserve his identity as a private person, he does not assert a cause of action under the New York Civil Rights Act.... Matters of public interest may and often do involve wholly private individuals and may still be reported or depicted without entailing liability under section 51. While plaintiff here has not acted affirmatively to make himself newsworthy, within the limited context of his past relationship to defendant Betty Friedan, who is a public figure, such a role has been thrust upon him.

Since plaintiff has failed to state a claim under the New York Civil Rights Act upon which his complaint is exclusively grounded, the defendant's motion for summary judgment is granted.

a.   Incidental Use of Identification: In Connection with a Newsworthy Story

Courts have historically recognized the potential tension between privacy appropriation tort claims and first amendment values. In *Pavesich v. New England Life Ins. Co.*, 122 Ga. 190, 50 S.E. 68 (1905), *supra*, the first court to recognize a privacy appropriation claim rejected the argument that the imposition of tort liability for the unauthorized use of the plaintiff's picture in a media advertisement for insurance violated freedom of speech and of the press. The first amendment was not found by the Supreme Court to restrict state tort law until 1964. Judicial recognition of first amendment values in early cases such as *Pavesich* were expressed in the state common law development of the tort. Use of the names or pictures of celebrities or ordinary folks is the heart of the news published in the print and electronic media. Furthermore, much of the media are commercial enterprises. If appropriation of identity is a tort, and if the reporting and publishing of stories about people is at the heart of freedom of speech and the press, then courts must sort out those commercial uses of identity that are tortious and those that are protected expression. In a very crude way this sorting out distinguishes between the use of identity to sell a stock commercial product, such as flour or insurance, and the use of identity as part of the selling of media products, such as a newspaper or magazine. As the cases that follow illustrate, this distinction is often difficult to make.

The *Friedan* case illustrates how the issue was dealt with for a long time under the New York statute. The first amendment questions were subsumed as part of the construction and meaning of statutory concepts. If the use of identity was made in conjunction with—or was incidental to—a newsworthy story or was part of the advertisement of a newsworthy story, the use was not for "advertising purposes, or for the purposes of trade," within the meaning of the statute.

The Restatement (Second) of Torts has been influential in developing an exception to liability in common law appropriation and publicity tort actions for uses that are "incidental" because the plaintiff's identity is part of a newsworthy story or is a matter of public interest:

> The value of plaintiff's name is not appropriated by mere mention of it, or by reference to it in connection with legitimate mention of his public activities; nor is the value of his likeness appropriated when it is published for purposes other than taking advantage of his reputation, prestige, or other value associated with him, for purposes of publicity.... It is only when the publicity is given for the purpose of appropriating to the defendant's benefit the commercial or other values associated with the name or the likeness that the right of privacy is invaded.

Restatement (Second) of Torts sec. 652C comment *d* (1977)

The incidental use doctrine and the first amendment newsworthy defense sometimes overlap. As illustrated by the cases that follow *Friedan* in the materials, courts are now inclined to address the first amendment issues more directly and explicitly recognize the privilege to publish newsworthy matters of public interest as a defense in appropriation or publicity actions brought under statutes or the common law. As indicated in *Friedan*, if the story is protected because it is newsworthy, advertisements about the story are also protected.

Use of a person's name or likeness in an unauthorized biography of that person has been held to be protected under the first amendment as "newsworthy." *See Meeropol v. Nizer*, 381 F.Supp. 29 (S.D.N.Y.1974), *petition denied*, 508 F.2d 837 (2d Cir. 1975), *aff'd*, 560 F.2d 1061 (2d Cir.1977), *cert. denied*, 434 U.S. 1013 (1978). *See also Frosch v. Grosset and Dunlap, Inc.*, 75 A.D.2d 768, 427 N.Y.S.2d 828 (1980). Use of a mental patient's likeness in a television film documentary of conditions in mental health facilities was found to be incidental to the "newsworthy" documentary and protected under the first amendment. *Delan by Delan v. C.B.S., Inc.*, 91 A.D.2d 255, 458 N.Y.S.2d 608 (1983). Also, use of a person's name in connection with a fictionalized book or movie based in part on that person's real-life, "newsworthy" incidents has been held to be a "newsworthy" use under the first amendment. *Leopold v. Levin*, 45 Ill.2d 434, 259 N.E.2d 250 (1970).

(1) First Amendment Restrictions on the Appropriation and False Light Privacy Torts

Some of the first amendment issues that are raised by common law tort privacy actions have been explored in the earlier portions of these materials. The most significant restrictions occur in public disclosure privacy tort actions where tort claims are brought against media defendants for the dissemination of truthful information. Significant first amendment issues are raised in tort actions brought under the appropriation (right of publicity) and false light theories as well. The first amendment jurisprudence formally originated in the seminal Supreme Court case, *New York Times v. Sullivan*, 376 U.S. 254 (1964). *Sullivan* was the first case in which the Supreme Court construed the first amendment to be a restriction on the civil tort reparation system of the states. A fundamental premise of *Sullivan* is that a jury award for compensatory and punitive damages against the media in a defamation action is government action that regulates first amendment activities sufficiently to bring the federal constitution into play. Prior to *Sullivan* the first amendment was viewed as protecting the press only from direct government sanctions against the press that were part of the prosecution of penal laws. *Sullivan* extended the first amendment to the indirect regulation of the press through damage awards in civil actions.

The first amendment issues in *Sullivan* were presented to the Court in a defamation action. In such an action, the speech that is the basis of the tort action is false and discredits the plaintiff's reputation. In the first amendment defamation cases following *Sullivan*, the Court has balanced the interest in reputation and the first amendment interests by imposing a number of requirements on the states in defamation actions. First, in cases where the plaintiff is a public official or public figure, the plaintiff must establish malice in the publication of the false and defamatory utterance. Malice entails a demonstration that the defendant either published the statement knowing that it was false or acted with reckless disregard as to whether it was false. Second, in cases where the plaintiff is not a public official or public figure (private plaintiff cases), the plaintiff must demonstrate that the falsehood was published negligently and that the plaintiff suffered actual injury. Third, in all cases, malice must be demonstrated before *punitive* damages may be recovered against the media. The negligence-actual injury rule in private defamation cases was established in *Gertz v. Robert Welch, Inc.*, 418 U.S. 323 (1974); the Court refined the requirements for establishing actual injury in *Time v. Firestone*, 424 U.S. 448 (1976).

In *Dun & Bradstreet v. Greenmoss Builders, Inc.*, 472 U.S. 749 (1985), the Supreme Court ruled that in private plaintiff defamation cases where the publication was not a matter of public concern the first amendment did not limit state defamation law. The Court was divided in *Greenmoss* and none of the opinions in the case enjoyed the support of a majority of the Justices. However, a majority of the Court would remove some defamation actions from the protection of the first amendment because the speech that was the basis of the defamation action is a "matter of purely private concern," *Id.* at 759–60. Whether the speech is a matter of private concern or a matter of public concern is to be determined by examining the content, form and context of the published utterance. The speech found to be a matter of private and not public concern in *Greenmoss* was contained in a credit report that had been provided to five subscribers who were restricted from disseminating the information further under the agreement with Dun & Bradstreet; the test for determining whether speech is private or public in *Greenmoss* is ambiguous. However, it is likely that speech that is disseminated by the media to the public generally would not be a matter of private concern within the meaning of the *Greenmoss* decision and the first amendment restrictions developed in *Sullivan* and *Gertz* would therefore apply to defamation actions brought against media defendants.

(2) Time v. Hill: The False Light First Amendment Case

As the subsequent materials in this section illustrate, the false light privacy tort tracks the tort of defamation in many respects. The Supreme Court has only decided two false light privacy cases in the post-*Sullivan* era. These two cases are *Time v. Hill*, 385 U.S. 374 (1967), and *Cantrell v. Forest City Publishing Co.*, 419 U.S. 245 (1974). The more important of these is *Time v. Hill*. The Hill family sued *Life* magazine for what was said about them in a story about the stage play *The Desperate Hours*. The plot of the play revolved around a family that was held hostage in their home by three escaped convicts. In the play members of the family are physically and sexually abused by their captors. The story in *Life* reported that the play was based upon the real life experience of the Hill family. In the real life event the family had been held hostage but no sexual or physical assault had occurred. The action was brought under the New York privacy statute on the theory that by reporting the fictionalized events of the play as true events in the lives of the Hill family, *Life* had placed the family in "false light." *Life* argued that the constitutional malice requirement of *Sullivan* applied to the publication. A majority of the Supreme Court agreed that the first amendment required a "private" plaintiff to demonstrate constitutional malice in a false light tort privacy action involving a matter of public interest. *Gertz v. Robert Welch*, discussed in the note above, was decided after *Time v. Hill*. In *Gertz*, the Supreme Court held that the first amendment required only that a private plaintiff in a defamation action demonstrate negligence in the publication of the false defamatory utterance. Does the *Gertz* negligence-actual injury rule apply to false light cases? Consider the view expressed by the *Braun* court in the case that follows.

(3) Zacchini v. Scripps—Howard Broadcasting Co.: The Appropriation–Publicity First Amendment Case

As of this date, the Supreme Court has only decided one case in which the first amendment was raised by the media as a defense to a right of appropriation action. The case involved the showing during the eleven o'clock news of the entire performance of Zacchini at a county fair as he was shot from a cannon. The 15 second video had been taped earlier during the performance and was shown on the television station without Zacchini's permission. Zacchini sued the station for violation of the right of appropriation in Ohio, and the Ohio Supreme Court found that the showing was part of a news report that was of legitimate public interest, and, therefore, was not actionable. The Supreme Court reversed in a closely divided opinion. Justice White, speaking for a bare majority of five justices, limited the holding of the case to the proposition that the first amendment did not protect the media in the broadcasting of a "performer's entire act." *Zacchini v. Scripps—Howard Broadcasting Co.*, 433 U.S. 562, 575 (1977).

The dissent, written by Justice Powell, would have held that the use of the film as part of the "routine portion of a regular program" was protected under the first amendment. *Id.* at 581. How often is a performer's entire act shown on a newscast? What significance does *Zacchini* have on the first amendment analysis in the decisions in *Lerman* and *Cher* which follow?

6. FIRST AMENDMENT DEFENSES

LERMAN v. FLYNT DISTRIBUTING CO., INC.

745 F.2d 123 (2d Cir. 1984), *cert. denied*, 471 U.S. 1054 (1985).

Before VAN GRAAFEILAND and CARDAMONE, CIRCUIT JUDGES, and BONSAL, DISTRICT JUDGE.

CARDAMONE, CIRCUIT JUDGE:

[Plaintiff Lerman brought an action alleging libel, violation of New York's Civil Rights Law Sections 50–51 and invasion of her common law right to publicity. Photographs of an anonymous actress appearing topless and in an "orgy" scene from a movie Lerman and her husband had written and produced were printed in the May 1980 issue of *Adelina* magazine. The magazine misidentified Lerman as the actress in the photographs and the cover of the magazine stated that nude photographs of Lerman were contained within. Lerman initially commenced an action against the publisher and national distributor of the magazine seeking an injunction and damages. The distributor attempted to recall all unsold copies of the magazine, but the publisher used the photographs in two separate subscription solicitation efforts in June 1980 and January 1981.

Shortly after the original lawsuit was commenced, but after the magazine was in the channels of distribution, Flynt Distributing Company purchased the contract to distribute *Adelina*. Flynt was then joined as a party defendant. Liability was determined in Lerman's favor against the original defendants before trial and a jury returned a special verdict determining that Flynt Distributing was liable for $7 million in compensatory damages and $33 million in exemplary damages for the May 1980 publication. The trial court struck $30 million from the exemplary award and Flynt now appeals the $10 million verdict.]

Freedom of expression preserves all other liberties so inseparably that freedom of the press and a free society either prosper together or perish together. Yet, because of its enormous power, the contemporary press is under heavy attack because of a widely held perception that it uses its special First Amendment status as a license to invade individual privacy. This case illustrates the complexity of the concerns when these interests clash.

. . .

B.   NEW YORK'S RIGHT OF PRIVACY STATUTE

. . .

1.   Advertising Purposes Under Section 51

Where the use of plaintiff's name is solely for the purpose of soliciting purchasers for defendant's products the advertising purposes prong of the statute is violated. . . .

. . .

The June 1980 and January 1981 uses could be viewed as for advertising purposes since they solicited orders for back issues of *Adelina*. But, the republications in the June 1980 and January 1981 subscription solicitations were incidental to the May 1980 publication. Because the solicitations were designed simply to convey the nature and content of past *Adelina* issues, they cannot form the basis for an independent claim under the advertising use prong of Section 51.

2.   Trade Purposes Under Section 51

Next, we examine whether the uses of plaintiff's name were for "purposes of trade" under the statute. Because the media in reporting the news routinely uses names and likenesses without consent, New York courts early recognized the need to encourage the free exchange of ideas and created a broad privilege for the legitimate dissemination to the public of news and information. The trade purposes prong of the statute may not be used to prevent comment on matters in which the public has a right to be informed. . . . Where plaintiff is a public personage or an actual participant in a newsworthy event, the use of his name or likeness is not for purposes of trade within the meaning of Section 51. . . . Since "newsworthiness" and "public interest" are to be "freely defined," the use of plaintiff's name in connection with the movie "The World is Full of Married Men" is a matter in which the public plainly has a legitimate interest.

Plaintiff may still be entitled to obtain the sanctions of Section 51 under the trade purposes prong even where the use is in conjunction with a report on a matter of public interest, but in order to do so must meet one of two tests. First, a plaintiff may attempt to demonstrate that the use of plaintiff's name or likeness has no real relationship to the discussion, and thus is an advertisement in disguise. Alternatively, a plaintiff may claim that defendant forfeited the privilege for reporting matters on which the public has the right to be informed by proving that the defendant's use was infected with material and substantial fiction or falsity. Even when so infected, for defendant to lose the newsworthy privilege plaintiff must prove that defendant acted with some degree of fault regarding the fictionalization or falsification.

We cannot accept plaintiff's first argument that the photo in this case has "no real relationship" to any discussion in *Adelina*. Ms. Lerman wrote the book and screenplay that contained scenes of nudity for the film "The World is Full of Married Men." While the article in *Adelina* was vapid it did relate to the growing use of nudity in films. Insofar as the use of the name "Jackie Collins" is concerned the May 1980 use must be considered incidental to the story, and hence not objectionable as a "disguised advertisement" under Section 51. Further, plaintiff's status as an author and screenwriter of a film in the erotic genre makes her claim of "no connection" with these particular photographs unpersuasive.... Ms. Lerman was not an innocent bystander without any relationship to the subject matter of the article and to the photograph.

Plaintiff's reliance on the alternative basis for defeating the newsworthy privilege rests on firmer ground, that is, the fictionalization or falsification ground....

. . .

... When presented with a factual error which brings an otherwise privileged newsworthy use within the trade purpose prohibition, the Supreme Court and the New York Court of Appeals have required that there be a finding of fault.

We agree that plaintiff's name in all three *Adelina* issues is fictionalized or false and therefore loses the privilege that ordinarily extends to reporting matters in which the public has an interest. Further, the degree of falsity here was severe since plaintiff was not the actress pictured. Were it not for constitutional concerns this falsity would permit a properly instructed jury to find the uses here to be for trade purposes under Section 51 of the New York Civil Rights Law. But, precisely because of First Amendment guarantees Flynt Distributing cannot be held liable for the use of plaintiff's name unless it acted with the requisite fault, and it is on this last point that plaintiff's proof fails as we will later explain.

[The court's discussion of the common law right to publicity is omitted.]

D. FALSE LIGHT TORT DISTINGUISHABLE FROM RIGHT TO PUBLICITY

[W]e undertake a brief analysis of the false light tort because it is essential to an understanding of the application of the First Amendment to Section 51. While not specifically alleged in her complaint, Ms. Lerman's action presents a classic false light claim. . . .

. . .

Assuming the requisite proof of fault, the facts of this case state a cause of action under section 652E [Restatement Second false light tort]. The nude actress pictured was not Ms. Lerman. Whether or not this misidentification is defamatory to Ms. Lerman, we cannot conclude that such publicity is not "highly offensive to a reasonable person." . . .

In a false light case, however styled under a state statute or common law, the gravamen of the tort is falsity; not, as here, simply a factual error. Further, regardless of whether Ms. Lerman's cause of action is cast in terms of libel or false light or under the falsified trade purposes prong of Section 51, the same constitutional protections apply. Therefore, we must address the federal constitutional question to determine the appropriate standard of fault plaintiff should have been required to meet and to evaluate plaintiff's proof under that constitutional standard. . . .

III. CONSTITUTIONAL ISSUES

A. *Public or Private Figure*

[The court discussed the first amendment defamation cases from *New York Times v. Sullivan,* to *Gertz v. Robert Welch*; these and other cases are discussed in the note preceding this case.] These holdings provide a frame to determine what constitutes a "limited purpose public figure." A defendant must show the plaintiff has: (1) successfully invited public attention to his views in an effort to influence others prior to the incident that is the subject of litigation; (2) voluntarily injected himself into a public controversy related to the subject of the litigation; (3) assumed a position of prominence in the public controversy; and (4) maintained regular and continuing access to the media. Having ascertained what the basic test is, we apply it.

The record before us reveals that Ms. Lerman has achieved international renown as the author of nine novels. Her books are decidedly controversial in nature because of her firm conviction—made the focal point of her comments to the press—that there is pervasive inequality in the treatment accorded to females vis-a-vis males. This topic greatly appeals to the public since her books sell in the millions, are full of descriptions of sex, including deviate sex and orgies, and are heavily laden with four-letter words. Ms. Lerman is quick to point out that some of her novels have been banned in Australia—a distinction similar to being banned in Boston. She has achieved a world-wide following, frequently appears as a guest on national TV and readily grants interviews to the mass media. On such occasions, one example of sexual inequality that Ms. Lerman uses refers to the fact that women more frequently than men appear unclad in films and magazines. This is unfair she claims because men have more opportunity to view undressed women than vice versa. She advocates "equal nudes for all."

Ms. Lerman's photograph is prominently displayed on the jackets of her novels that enjoy good reviews despite—or perhaps, because of—their description as "shocking," "racy," "sexy" and the like. She admits her books are considered "pornographic." Her first novel was translated into 32 languages. Movies have been made of several and, as earlier noted, the picture of the nude actress that is the subject of this litigation came from the film based on her novel "The World is Full of Married Men." Quite plainly Ms. Lerman is today in the forefront of women writing about sex and what is perceived of as a continuing double-standard in sexual mores. Thus, for plaintiff, seeking publicity both for herself and her books is part and parcel of her professional endeavors as a writer. The record plainly reflects her undoubted success in this effort. Her organized and ongoing effort to maintain media access, in order to call attention to her writings and disseminate her views on current sexual standards, helps to sell her novels and screenplays like the one "commented upon" in the May 1980 *Adelina*.

No doubt defendant has shown that plaintiff successfully invited public attention to her views and has maintained continuing access to the media. Nonetheless, we agree with the district court that Ms. Lerman is not that rare person the Gertz decision identifies as an all purpose public figure. As the Court there noted, "Absent clear evidence of general fame or notoriety in the community, and pervasive involvement in the affairs of society, an individual should not be deemed a public personality for all aspects of his life."

But, we believe Ms. Lerman is a limited purpose public figure required to satisfy the *New York Times* standard of fault. By voluntarily devoting herself to the public's interest in sexual mores, through extensive writing on this topic, reaping profits and wide notoriety for herself in the process, Ms. Lerman must be deemed to have purposefully surrendered part of what would otherwise have been her protectible privacy rights, at least those related in some way to her involvement in writing her books and screenplays.

The difficult question is whether Ms. Lerman injected herself into a "public controversy" related to the offending publication. The district court rejected defendants' argument that Ms. Lerman was a public figure for the limited purpose of commenting on sex and nudity in films. The court reasoned that such a topic is merely a matter of interest, but not a true public controversy. We disagree. The relations between the sexes and public nudity are topics of continued and general public interest and may be considered "public controversies" even though not involving political debate or criticism of public officials. A public "controversy" is any topic upon which sizeable segments of society have different, strongly held views. Certainly various groups today have vastly divergent views on the propriety of female or male nudity in films and in the print media generally. In the public controversies that daily swirl about—be they politics, pocketbook issues, or, as here, contemporary standards regarding nudity—some plunge into the arena and enter the fray. Plaintiff, as a controversial, outspoken authoress and screenwriter advocating equal nudity, was such a willing participant in this public controversy.

B.   NEWSWORTHINESS FOR FIRST AMENDMENT PURPOSES

The district court adopted plaintiff's argument that an actual malice standard of fault does not apply even if plaintiff is a public figure because the use was "completely exploitive" and outside the broad category of matters of public interest and therefore not newsworthy. This led it erroneously to conclude that the distributor could be held strictly liable for disseminating the magazine without treading on the First Amendment. On the contrary, *Adelina* falls far short of crossing the line that would cause it to forfeit First Amendment protection.... The factual error in this case would be actionable only if the distribution of *Adelina* loses First Amendment protection under a standard analogous to that which causes libelous speech to lose such protection. We cannot accept a view that a publication must meet an independent standard of newsworthiness to stand under the umbrella of First Amendment protection. Even "vulgar" publications are entitled to such guarantees. It makes no difference that *Adelina* may have few redeeming features, that it may express a point of view far afield from what one might consider the community's standard of decency, or that an ordinary reader may find it distasteful. The compass of the First Amendment covers a vast spectrum of tastes, views, ideas and expressions. To hold otherwise would draw a tight noose around the throat of public discussion choking off media First Amendment rights.

The *Adelina* article unquestionably would have been within the broad definition of a newsworthy matter or a matter of public interest or concern had Ms. Lerman in fact been the "starlet" pictured. That there was a factual error does not alter the subject matter of the offending publication. As noted earlier, New York law must yield in this context to First Amendment concerns which protect the media from liability for such errors, absent proof of fault. Courts are, and should be reluctant to attempt to define newsworthiness. The Supreme Court in *Gertz* expressly warned against "committing this task to the conscience of judges." (nor should the task be undertaken by legislators since a statute that attempts to prohibit reproductions of United States obligations unless made for newsworthy purposes is held violative of the First Amendment). Rather, the factual error is only actionable against defendant distributor if made with the *Gertz* required fault. What then is the appropriate standard of fault in cases involving distributors?

C.   PROOF OF ACTUAL MALICE

1.   *Actual Malice of Distributors*

First Amendment guarantees have long been recognized as protecting distributors of publications....

But, a public figure plaintiff may only recover compensatory damages where a distributor acts with "actual malice," and no plaintiff—

public figure or private individual—may recover punitive damages unless the New York Times v. Sullivan standard is met.

2. *Actual Malice in This Case*

Flynt Distributing may be held liable only if plaintiff presented clear and convincing evidence that some high level employee of the corporation acted with reckless disregard of the fact that false matter had been published by Chuckleberry. The only evidence pointing in that direction is the conceded fact that Flynt Distributing knew of plaintiff's lawsuit against Chuckleberry and Publishers Distributing for the May 1980 issue, plus a claimed failure thereafter by it to investigate. Plaintiff cites no other evidence in her brief, and careful examination of the voluminous record in this case reveals none.

Absent are any facts demonstrating that anyone in the defendant distributing company had a subjective awareness of probable falsity. Notice of the lawsuit regarding the May issue standing alone certainly is not clear and convincing evidence as to knowledge for June and January, especially given the miniscule mention of plaintiff in those issues. Moreover, mere failure to investigate, while relevant, is also not itself sufficient to show actual malice.... Consequently, we hold as a matter of law that a properly instructed jury could not fairly and rationally conclude upon clear and convincing evidence that this defendant's uses were knowing or made with actual malice.

IV. THE DAMAGE AWARDS

The jury awarded plaintiff a total of seven million dollars in compensatory damages, which the trial court refused to reduce. No doubt such an enormous verdict chills media First Amendment rights. But a verdict of this size does more than chill an individual defendant's rights, it deepfreezes that particular media defendant permanently. Putting aside First Amendment implications of "megaverdicts" frequently imposed by juries in media cases, the compensatory damages awarded shock the conscience of this Court. They are grossly excessive and obviously a product of plaintiff's counsel's appeals to the passion and prejudice of the jury. It cannot seriously be contended that Ms. Lerman's lacerated feelings are worth anything close to $7 million. No proof was offered that she sought or needed professional help because of these publications and the fact she completed a novel between March and September in 1980 refutes her contention that she was unable to work. In any event, damages under the New York statute often are only nominal since they are designed primarily to compensate for injury to feelings....

Finally, we note that reputational damage to Ms. Lerman could not have been great. Only the readers of *Adelina*, a magazine of relatively modest circulation that Ms. Lerman describes as "sordid" and "obscene" would have seen the offending material. In fact, given the number of famous persons portrayed in this fashion, one wonders whether such pictures are even capable of producing genuine reputational harm. Even assuming the word would get around to those whose esteem of plaintiff would be diminished, the main source of publicity for the pictures came not from the magazine's publication, but from Ms. Lerman's lawsuit and statements to the press.

The jury also awarded a total of $33 million in punitive damages, more than plaintiff demanded in her complaint and over six times greater than plaintiff's counsel requested in his summation. This award also shocks our conscience and reinforces our conclusion that the verdicts represent appeals to passion or prejudice.

V. CONCLUSION

The availability of damages depends on plaintiff's ability to satisfy the actual malice standard of New York Times v. Sullivan that plaintiff as a limited purpose public figure was required to meet. Since Ms. Lerman cannot present clear and convincing evidence of defendant's requisite fault with respect to the factual error disseminated, the judgment awarding her ten million dollars in compensatory and punitive damages is reversed as a matter of law and her complaint against Flynt Distributing is dismissed.

a. *Advertisement in Disguise: Use Unconnected With a Newsworthy Event*

As the *Lerman* court indicates, the incidental use doctrine is qualified by the requirement that the name, picture or likeness must have a "real relationship" to the newsworthy story or report of an event that is of public interest. This requirement is apparently designed to prevent disguised use of someone's identity to advertise a product by including that person's name or likeness where there is no connection with a newsworthy article. Courts have been liberal in finding a sufficient connection to satisfy the "real relationship" test. Some of the most difficult cases have involved pictures taken of persons in public places that were used as part of the background for an article. A leading case is *Arrington v. New York Times*, 55 N.Y.2d 433, 434 N.E.2d 1319, 449 N.Y.S.2d 941 (1982), where the court held that the photograph taken of a black male on a public street had a real relationship to a story about successful middle class blacks having little interest in the fortunes of poor and less successful blacks. The use of a picture of individuals at a Miami airport counter which was used in connection with a news article on the exporting of United States products through Miami Airport to Latin America was deemed merely incidental to showing the merchandise to be exported in the picture. *Fogel v. Forbes, Inc.*, 500 F.Supp. 1081 (E.D.Pa.1980).

A recent pronouncement by the New York Court of Appeals adopts a generous view of when the use of plaintiff's name or likeness has a sufficient relationship to the story to come within the protection of the newsworthy concept of the statute. In *Finger v. Omni Publications International*, 77 N.Y.2d 138, 566 N.E.2d 141, 564 N.Y.S.2d 1014, (1990), Joseph and Ida Finger sued Omni on behalf of themselves and their six children for the non-consensual publication of a photograph of the family in conjunction with an article discussing caffeine-aided fertilization. The article described research that indicated that in vitro fertilization rates may be enhanced by exposing sperm to high concentrations of caffeine. Beneath the family photograph was the caption, "Want a big family? Maybe your sperm needs a cup of java in the morning. Tests reveal that caffeine-spiritized sperm swim faster, which may increase the chances for in vitro fertilization." The plaintiffs' name was not mentioned nor did the article indicate that the Finger children were produced through in vitro fertilization. The Court of Appeals upheld the dismissal of plaintiffs' complaint under the "newsworthiness exception" to the New York Civil Rights Act, noting that the exception should be liberally applied and that questions of "newsworthiness" are better left to "reasonable editorial judgment and discretion," *Id.* at 143, 566 N.E.2d at 144, 564 N.Y.S.2d at 1017. Given this liberal view, there was a real relationship between the picture of the plaintiff's large family and the fertility theme of the article.

Where the use of plaintiff's picture as background for an article produces a substantial falsehood about the plaintiff because of the content of the story, courts have found that the relationship link between the use of identity and newsworthiness of the story is not satisfied. *See, e.g., Metzger v. Dell Pub. Co.,* 207 Misc. 182, 136 N.Y.S.2d 888 (1955) (plaintiff's picture as part of story about gangs falsely portrayed plaintiff as a gang member).

CHER v. FORUM INTERNATIONAL, LTD.

692 F.2d 634 (9th Cir.1982), *cert. denied,* 462 U.S. 1120 (1983).

Before CHAMBERS and GOODWIN, CIRCUIT JUDGES, EAST, DISTRICT JUDGE.

GOODWIN, CIRCUIT JUDGE.

[A well-known female entertainer who performs under the name of "Cher" had given an interview to a radio talk show host named Fred Robbins with the understanding that the interview was to appear in *Us* magazine. Robbins regularly interviews celebrities and sells the interviews, or parts of them, to as many magazines as possible. After her meeting with Robbins, however, Cher did not feel that the interview sufficiently emphasized her new band and wished to cancel its publication. At her request, the editors of *Us* magazine did not run the interview, and returned it to Robbins, paying him a "kill" fee. Robbins, however, then sold the interview to a magazine published under the name of *Forum* and to News Group Publications, Inc., the publishers of a tabloid called the *Star.* Both sources published the interview. The major stockholder of *Forum,* a magazine called *Penthouse International,* also ran advertisements which publicized Cher's interview in *Forum.* Cher then brought claims against Robbins, News Group Publications, Inc., Forum International, Ltd., and Penthouse International, Ltd. Cher did not allege that the published text of the interview was false or defamatory. Instead her complaint charged breach of contract, unfair competition, misappropriation of name and likeness, misappropriation of right to publicity, and violations of the Lanham Act. The trial court awarded general and punitive damages against all defendants.]

(1) Fred Robbins

Robbins taped the interview with Cher with her consent and cooperation. She now says she gave that consent under the mistaken belief that the interview would appear as a cover story in *Us* magazine and that she did not consent to other uses of the interview. The trial court found that Cher had no contract with Robbins. We accept that finding. Moreover, it was stipulated that Robbins had never promised any interviewee approval rights over an interview. Accordingly, any liability of Robbins to Cher must be predicated upon a finding that Robbins participated in one or more of the tortious actions of the publisher defendants.

Robbins had no part in the publishing, advertising or marketing of the articles in question. Accordingly, the judgment against Robbins is clearly erroneous and must be vacated.

(2) News Group Publications, Inc.

News Group Publications, Inc. publishes, among other things, a tabloid called *Star*. *Star* published portions of the Robbins interview in its March 17 and 24, 1981, issues and printed Cher's picture and these words on its March 17 cover: "Exclusive Series," followed by "Cher: My life, my husbands and my many, many men."

Cher's theory against News Group was that her image as a major celebrity was degraded by the suggestion that she would give an exclusive interview to that publication. Cher also claimed that News Group had wrongfully appropriated Cher's implied endorsement of *Star* for commercial purposes.

We note first that it was stipulated that "exclusive" interviews with Cher had previously appeared in *Star* a number of times. We also note that Cher conceded at trial that she had never been paid for an interview, and that *Star* had never paid an interviewee for an interview. Whether the article itself was an "exclusive," it was stipulated that the *Star* article had not previously appeared in any other publication. Even if some of the material in *Star* had already appeared in *Forum*, Cher did not suffer any damage from *Star's* exaggerated claims of exclusivity.

Star bought an interview with a public figure from a free-lance writer and published portions of it. This activity is protected by the First and Fourteenth Amendments in the absence of a showing that the publishers knew that their statements were false or published them in reckless disregard of the truth. Cher makes no claim that *Star* published any statements from the interview with knowledge that they were false or with reckless disregard for their truth.

Cher's theory was that by using the words "Exclusive Series" and "Cher: My life, my husbands and my many, many men" on the cover of

Star, the magazine was falsely representing to the public that Cher had given *Star* an exclusive interview.

Star was entitled to inform its readers that the issue contained an article about Cher, that the article was based on an interview with Cher herself, and that the article had not previously appeared elsewhere. It sought to do so by the use of words, including "Exclusive Series." The use of these words cannot support a finding of the knowing or reckless falsity required under Time, Inc. v. Hill.

Neither do the words in question constitute a false claim that Cher endorsed *Star* magazine. There is no evidence in the record to support such a theory.

. . .

The California statute governing the use of another's name or likeness for commercial purposes contains an express exception for news accounts.

The California Supreme Court has subjected the "right of publicity" under California law to a narrowing interpretation which accords with First Amendment values. The Court has acknowledged that "the right of publicity has not been held to outweigh the value of free expression. Any other conclusion would allow reports and commentaries on the thoughts and conduct of public and prominent persons to be subject to censorship under the guise of preventing the dissipation of the publicity value of a person's identity."

The judgment against News Group is reversed.

(3) Forum International, Ltd.

Forum International, Ltd., a New York corporation, published part of the Robbins interview in the March 1981 issue of *Forum*, identifying Robbins as the interviewer but changing the text so that *Forum* appeared as the poser of questions and Cher appeared as the respondent (apparently a common practice in the industry). The magazine printed Cher's picture on its cover with the words: "Exclusive: Cher Talks Straight." *Forum* also caused to be published advertising copy referring to Cher which is discussed below. Cher sued Forum International on two theories: (1) falsely creating and exploiting the impression that Cher had in fact given an exclusive interview directly to *Forum* when she had not; and (2) exploiting Cher's celebrity value to sell magazines without her consent by implying that she endorsed *Forum*.

Cher concedes that *Forum's* publication of the interview was protected by the First Amendment. As explained above with reference to News Group, this protection extends to *Forum's* use of headlines and cover display so long as the headlines and promotional devices were true or were not published with knowledge that they were false or in reckless disregard for their truth. It was stipulated that the photos used by *Forum* were purchased from an independent agency which owned them. Unlike *Star*, however, *Forum* also engaged in explicit advertising using

Cher's name and picture. This advertising provided an alternate basis for liability.

Forum carried inside its March 1981 issue a subscription "tear out" opposite the following legend: "There are certain things that Cher won't tell *People* and would never tell *Us*. She tells *Forum*." This message was printed above a picture of Cher. The text of the ad included the following sentence: "So join Cher and FORUM's hundreds of thousands of other adventurous readers today."

The same legend and picture were used in an ad appearing in the February 1981 issue of *Penthouse*. The text of that ad included the sentence: "So take a tip from Cher and hundreds of thousands of other adventurous people and subscribe to *Forum*."

Forum was also the beneficiary of a display advertisement in the *New York Daily News* on February 18, 1981, which, next to her picture, stated: "Cher Never Told Anyone How She Played Kiss and Tell with Rock Star Gene Simmons.... She Told *Forum* Magazine." The court found that both Forum International and Penthouse International participated in concocting and placing the above described advertising copy and concluded that they were liable for falsely implying that Cher had endorsed *Forum*.

. . .

Constitutional protection extends to the truthful use of a public figure's name and likeness in advertising which is merely an adjunct of the protected publication and promotes only the protected publication. Advertising to promote a news medium, accordingly, is not actionable under an appropriation of publicity theory so long as the advertising does not falsely claim that the public figure endorses that news medium. *Forum* would have been entitled to use Cher's picture and to refer to her truthfully in subscription advertising for the purpose of indicating the content of the publication, because such usage is protected by the First Amendment. But *Forum* was not content with honest exploitation of the fact that it possessed some pictures of Cher and an interview that she had given a writer. *Forum* falsely proclaimed to the readers of its advertising copy that Cher "tells *Forum*" things that she "would never tell *Us*." In view of the fact that Cher had intended to "tell" the rival magazine, *Us*, the very words in the interview, and had not "told" *Forum* anything, the advertising copy was patently false. This kind of mendacity is not protected by the First Amendment, and those defendants responsible for the placement and circulation of the challenged advertising copy must look elsewhere for their protection.

The trial court found in effect that *Forum* or *Penthouse* published the ads in question with knowledge that they were false or in reckless disregard for their truth. Cher maintains that *Forum* falsely stated that Cher had actually endorsed that magazine. *Forum* contends that the statements which form the basis of Cher's complaint are vague and subject to numerous interpretations. For example, "So join Cher and FORUM's hundreds of thousands of other adventurous readers today" may readily be interpreted in several ways. The reader may understand this as an invitation to enjoy reading about Cher along with other readers or to read about Cher and other readers in *Forum*, which as a regular feature prints a large number of letters from readers. Similarly, "so take a tip from Cher ..." is equivocal and could be interpreted to refer to what the reader will learn from reading about Cher in *Forum* magazine. Cher's own expert admitted that the other language in the ads—*e.g.,* "There are certain things that Cher won't tell *People* and would never tell *Us*. She tells *Forum*"—does not constitute an express endorsement. Nevertheless, the trier found that there was an implied endorsement of *Forum* in the words of the advertisement.

Because of the First Amendment implications in this case, we have examined the trier's findings with the extra care required in such cases. We are satisfied that the trier could find, from the record as a whole, that no matter how carefully the editorial staff of *Forum* may have trod the border between the actionable and the protected, the advertising staff engaged in the kind of knowing falsity that strips away the protection of the First Amendment. Whether we agree with the trier's finding of knowing falsity, or fall back a step to reckless disregard for the truth, there is enough evidence to support the material findings under Fed. R.Civ.P. 52 against Forum International, Ltd.

(4) PENTHOUSE INTERNATIONAL, LTD.

Cher's theory against Penthouse International was based on two aspects of Penthouse International's involvement with Forum International: (1) Penthouse International owns 80% of the stock of Forum International; and (2) *Penthouse's* staff participated in the preparation of the advertisements which appeared in *Forum* and in *Penthouse* ... There was enough participation in the false advertising to permit Penthouse International to share Forum International's liability.

The remaining questions have to do with the measure of damages.

The challenged judgment provides that Cher:

> (1) recover of defendants Forum International, Ltd., Penthouse International, Ltd., and Fred Robbins, jointly and severally, as special damages, the sum of $100,000, with interest;

> (2) recover of defendants Forum International, Ltd. and Fred Robbins, jointly and severally, as general damages, the additional sum of $69,117, with interest;

> (3) recover of defendant Forum International, Ltd., as exemplary damages, the additional sum of $100,000 with interest;

> (4) recover of defendants News Group Publications, Inc. and Fred Robbins, jointly and severally, as special and general damages, the additional sum of $169,117, with interest;

> (5) recover of defendant News Group Publications, Inc., as exemplary damages, the additional sum of $200,000, with interest;

(6) recover of defendant Fred Robbins, as exemplary damages, the additional sum of $25,000, with interest; together with costs against all defendants jointly and severally.

Because Fred Robbins did not participate in the activities found by the trial court to be wrongful, all portions of the judgment against Robbins are vacated.

We find no substantial flaw in the manner in which the trier found general and special damages against Penthouse International and Forum International. Accordingly, those parts of items (1) and (2) which impose general and special damages against Penthouse International and Forum International, with interest from January 15, 1982, at seven percent, are affirmed.

Some exemplary damages can be supported as punishment for the false advertising and promotional misrepresentations of those defendants. In view of the dollar amounts that were discussed in the evidence concerning situations when celebrities agree to commercialize their publicity value, we cannot say that the trier's assessment of $100,000 exemplary damages in item (3) against *Forum* is clearly erroneous.

All portions of the judgment against News Group Publications, Inc., are vacated.

Reversed in part, affirmed in part, and modified in part.

b. First Amendment Defenses to the Appropriation and Publicity Torts

The courts in *Lerman* and *Cher* assume that the first amendment jurisprudence that developed in the defamation area will apply to appropriation and publicity tort actions where the essence of the case is that there has been material false factual statements published about the plaintiff. For first amendment purposes, should the name of the tort that is the basis of a suit against the media make a difference if the essence of the tortious action is false speech about the plaintiff? In *Zacchini*, discussed *supra*, the Supreme Court rejected the first amendment defense that was raised by the media defendant. Are the courts in *Lerman* and *Cher* warranted in extending first amendment doctrine beyond the facts of *Zacchini* to appropriation and publicity claims based upon false factual representations?

c. Use of a Celebrity's Name to Falsely Endorse a Media Product

In deciding the first amendment issues in the case, the court in *Cher* distinguished between the use of the celebrity Cher's name to advertise a story in the *Forum* magazine and the use of her name to falsely endorse the magazine. What is the theoretical basis for this distinction? Consider the following possibility: The use of Cher's name in advertising furthers first amendment values by informing the public about the contents of a story that is newsworthy. It informs the public about where they may learn more about Cher. To falsely say that Cher endorses the magazine exploits Cher's commercial identity to sell the general commercial enterprise. The reference to Cher in the endorsement does not inform the public about where they can find out more about Cher but rather hawks the commercial product that happens to contain a story about the celebrity. Is the false claim of endorsement by Cher like using Elvis's name to sell a guitar or Elvis Doll without his consent?

Consider the comments by Peter L. Felcher and Edward L. Rubin on the scope of first amendment protection for the media in publicity and privacy cases:

> A careful reading of the existing cases suggests that there are a number of social policies at work, of which the First Amendment is the most important. In light of these policies, two principles that courts actually use in reaching their decisions can be discerned. The primary principle, derived directly from First Amendment considerations, centers on the purpose of the portrayal: if it serves an informative or cultural function, it will be immune from liability; if it serves no such function but merely exploits the individual portrayed, immunity will not be granted. In the latter case, courts then look to the second principle, which is based on the concept of identifiable harm: if the portrayed individual can demonstrate some observable injury, of a generally accepted nature, courts will grant relief; if no such harm is apparent, relief will be denied. These two principles account for court decisions regarding media portrayals more consistently than any rules that can be stated solely in terms of the rights of privacy and publicity.

Peter Felcher and Edward Rubin, *Privacy, Publicity, and the Portrayal of Real People by the Media*, 88 Yale L.J. 1577, 1596.

Do the two principles identified by Felcher and Rubin account for the *Cher* court decision?

G.   REPUTATION

1.   RESTATEMENT (SECOND) OF TORTS SECTION 652E

a.   *Section 652E: Publicity Placing Person in False Light*

One who gives publicity to a matter concerning another that places the other before the public in a false light is subject to liability to the other for invasion of his privacy, if

(a) the false light in which the other was placed would be highly offensive to a reasonable person, and

(b) the actor had knowledge of or acted in reckless disregard as to the falsity of the publicized matter and the false light in which the other would be placed.

Comment:

(1) Nature of Section

The form of invasion of privacy covered by the rule stated in this section does not depend upon making public any facts concerning the private life of the individual. On the contrary, it is essential to the rule stated in this section that the matter published concerning the plaintiff is not true. The rule stated here is, however, limited to the situation in which the plaintiff is given publicity. On what constitutes publicity and the publicity of application to a simple disclosure, see section 652C, comment *a*, which is applicable to the rule stated here.

(2) Relation to Defamation

The interest protected by this section is the interest of the individual in not being made to appear before the public in an objectionable false light or false position, or in other words, otherwise than as he is. In many cases to which the rule stated here applies, the publicity given to the plaintiff is defamatory, so that he would have an action for libel or slander under the rules stated in Chapter 24 of the Restatement (Second) of Torts. In such a case the action for invasion of privacy will afford an alternative or additional remedy, and the plaintiff can proceed upon either theory, or both, although he can have but one recovery for a single instance of publicity.

It is not, however, necessary to the action for invasion of privacy that the plaintiff be defamed. It is enough that he is given unreasonable and highly objectionable publicity that attributes to him characteristics, conduct or beliefs which are false, and so is placed before the public in false position. When this is the case and the matter attributed to the plaintiff is not defamatory, the rule here stated affords a different remedy, not available in an action for defamation.

2. RECOGNITION OF THE RIGHT

LEVERTON v. CURTIS PUB. CO.

192 F.2d 974 (3d Cir.1951).

GOODRICH, CIRCUIT JUDGE.

This case involves the extent of the right of privacy. Plaintiff had a judgment in the District Court. The defendant challenges both her right to recover and the amount awarded to her by the jury verdict.

The facts are simple and almost undisputed. The plaintiff in 1947, when she was a child of ten, was involved in a street accident in the city of Birmingham, Alabama. A motor car nearly ran over her. A newspaper photographer who happened to be on the spot took a photograph of the child being lifted to her feet by a woman bystander. The picture was dramatic and its effect was heightened by the fact that it was an action picture, not one posed for the camera.

The photograph appeared in a Birmingham newspaper the day following. Twenty months later it was used by the Curtis Publishing Company as an illustration for an article on traffic accidents, with emphasis on pedestrian carelessness, under the title, "They Ask To Be Killed" by David G. Wittels. The print was purchased by Curtis from a supplier of illustration material. Plaintiff claims that the publication of her picture this long after the accident in which she was involved, was a violation of her right of privacy.

The suit was brought in the federal court on diversity of citizenship only. We take our law, therefore, from the courts of the State of Pennsylvania....

. . .

It is well to delineate with as much exactness as we can the very thing which we have here to decide. The defendant admits the existence of the right of privacy both generally and particularly under the law of Pennsylvania and Alabama.

The plaintiff, on the other hand, admits that the original publication in the Birmingham newspaper on the day following her accident, was not an actionable invasion of her right of privacy. This admission is well taken for as pointed out in the Restatement, one who is the subject of a striking catastrophe is the object of legitimate public interest. This has nothing to do with waiver or consent, obviously. The result is the same as where one does waive his right of privacy by voluntarily getting into the public eye but the reason is different....

. . .

... It is agreed on all sides that the original publication of the picture of this traffic accident was not actionable. If it invaded the right of the plaintiff to stay out of public attention, it was a privileged invasion, her interest in being left alone being overbalanced by the general public interest in being kept informed. As we see the questions in this case, they are two. (1) Is the privilege involved in the original publication lost by the lapse of time between the date of the original publication immediately following the accident and the reappearance of the plaintiff's picture in the Saturday Evening Post twenty months later? (2) The second question is whether, if the privilege has not been lost by lapse of time, it is lost by the using of the plaintiff's picture, not in connection with a news story, but as an illustration heading an article on pedestrian traffic accidents?

On the first point the plaintiff urges language from the comment of the Restatement of Torts, Section 867. That comment, after dealing with writers, candidates for public office, and so on, mentions "One who unwillingly comes into the public eye because of his own fault, as in the case of a criminal,...." Then it goes on to say: "Community custom achieves the same result with reference to one unjustly charged with crime or the subject of a striking catastrophe. Both groups of persons are the objects of legitimate public interest during a period of time after their conduct or misfortune has brought them to the public attention; until they have reverted to the lawful and unexciting life led by the great bulk of the community, they are subject to the privileges which publishers have to satisfy the curiosity of the public as to their leaders, heroes, villains and victims."

It could be easily agreed that the plaintiff in this case, because she was once involved in an automobile accident does not continue throughout her life to have her goings and comings made the subject of newspaper stories. That, however, is a long way from saying that the occasion of her once becoming a subject of public interest cannot be brought again to public attention later on. Suppose the same newspaper which printed the plaintiff's photograph the day after her accident printed a resume sometime later of traffic accidents and supplied pictures dealing with them, including this one, which photographers on its staff had compiled. We cannot think that their publication under those circumstances would subject the publisher to liability.

. . .

We conclude that the immunity from liability for the original publication was not lost through lapse of time when the same picture was again published.

Now to the second point. The first publication of the plaintiff's photograph was purely news. The second publication was a sort of a dramatic setting for the discussion of a traffic problem by Mr. Wittels. Does that much of a change in the purpose of the publication lose the privilege?

Something was made at the argument of the point that the use of the photograph by Curtis was "commercial." Of course it was. So was the original publication in the Birmingham newspaper. People who run newspapers and magazines as commercial enterprises, run them to make profit if they can. What adds to reader interest adds to circulation and that adds to profit. . . . The publication in this case was not an appropriation for a commercial use.

Nevertheless, we think this particular publication was an actionable invasion of plaintiff's right of privacy. Granted that she was "newsworthy" with regard to her traffic accident. Assume, also, that she continued to be newsworthy with regard to that particular accident for an indefinite time afterward. This use of her picture had nothing at all to do with her accident. It related to the general subject of traffic accidents and pedestrian carelessness. Yet the facts, so far as we know them in this case, show that the little girl, herself, was at the time of her accident not careless and the motorist was. The picture is used in connection with several headings tending to say that this plaintiff narrowly escaped death because she was careless of her own safety. That is not libelous; a count for defamation was dropped out in the course of the trial. But we are not talking now about liability for defamation. We are talking about the privilege to invade her interest in being left alone.

The heading of the article was called "They Ask To Be Killed." Underneath the picture of the little girl was the heading "Safety education in schools has reduced child accidents measurably, but unpredictable darting through traffic still takes a sobering toll." In a box beside the title appears the following: "Do you invite massacre by your own carelessness? Here's how thousands have committed suicide by scorning laws that were passed to keep them alive." The sum total of all this is that this particular plaintiff, the legitimate subject for publicity for one particular accident, now becomes a pictorial, frightful example of pedestrian carelessness. This, we think, exceeds the bounds of privilege. An analogous case, though admittedly not right on point, is Mau v. Rio Grande Oil. There a man who was a holdup victim had his unhappy experience translated into a radio program with garnishment and embellishment appropriate for that form of entertainment. The news account of the holdup was, of course, comparable to a news account of a traffic accident. But when his account came to be the basis for public entertainment, the Court considered the bounds of the privilege exceeded. We think the same is true here.

Defendant complains of the amount of the judgment. It was for $5,000. We agree that the jury was pretty liberal with the defendant's money. But we have often expressed the limitation of our authority in controlling the amount of verdicts unless they are so high as to shock the judicial conscience. The trial judge heard the case and also heard and passed upon a motion raising the point of the alleged excessiveness of the recovery. We do not think that this case is strong enough to call upon us to substitute our judgment for either his or that of the jury.

The judgment of the District Court will be affirmed.

BRAUN v. FLYNT

726 F.2d 245 (5th Cir.1984).

Before POLITZ and JOLLY, CIRCUIT JUDGES, and HUNTER, DISTRICT JUDGE.

E. GRADY JOLLY, CIRCUIT JUDGE:

[Jeannie Braun brought a diversity action against Larry C. Flynt and *Chic* Magazine, Inc. for the alleged unauthorized, libelous publication of her picture in the December 1977 issue of *Chic* magazine. The dominant theme of *Chic* magazine is "female nudity." Mrs. Braun's photograph was placed within a section of the magazine which contained drawings, cartoons, pictures, and brief stories which either directly concerned sex or were of an overtly sexual nature. The picture which was placed in the magazine was of Mrs. Braun and "Ralph, the Diving Pig." Mrs. Braun worked for Aquarena Springs amusement park in San Marcos, Texas and part of her job included working in a novelty act with "Ralph." Mrs. Braun had signed a release authorizing Aquarena's use of pictures of Ralph and herself. Aquarena then made pictures and postcards of Ralph and Mrs. Braun.

In May 1977, Henry Nuwer, an editor of *Chic*, went to the amusement park and saw Ralph and Mrs. Braun, as well as a postcard containing the picture in question. Nuwer called Ms. Jennifer Benton, Aquarena's public relations director, and requested consent to use the picture as well as transparencies or negatives of the picture. Benton was not familiar with *Chic* and inquired about the nature of the magazine. Nuwer replied that *Chic* was a men's magazine containing fashion, travel, and humor. At trial, Nuwer stated that "the idea of nudity never came up."

A jury trial returned a judgment for $5,000 actual damages and $25,000 punitive damages for defamation. Under the invasion of privacy claim, a judgement was entered for $15,000 actual damages and $50,000 punitive damages. The Fifth Circuit remanded the case on the issue of damages.]

. . .

The dominant theme of *Chic* magazine is "female nudity." According to *Chic*'s editor, the magazine depicts "unchastity in women." The associate editor admitted that the caricatures found in the magazine are "indecent." The particular issue of the magazine with which the case is involved contained numerous explicit photographs of female genitalia. Suffice to say that *Chic* is a glossy, oversized, hard-core men's magazine. One of the opening sections of the magazine, entitled "*Chic* Thrills," contains brief stories about current "events." In the issue of the magazine in question, twenty-one vignettes were included in "*Chic* Thrills." Most of these either concerned sex overtly or were accompanied by a photograph or cartoon of an overtly sexual nature.

This is the context in which Mrs. Braun's picture was published. Mrs. Braun was employed by Aquarena Springs amusement park in San Marcos, Texas. Part of Mrs. Braun's job included working in a novelty act with "Ralph, the Diving Pig." In the act, Mrs. Braun, treading water in a pool would hold out a bottle of milk with a nipple on it. Ralph would dive into the pool and feed from the bottle.

Pictures and postcards were made of Ralph and Mrs. Braun's act, showing Ralph, in good form, legs fully extended, tail curled, diving toward Mrs. Braun, who is shown in profile holding the bottle.

Mrs. Braun had signed a release authorizing Aquarena Spring's use of the picture. The release provided that

> I [Jeannie Braun] in consideration of the fact that I am employed and paid by Aquarena Springs, Inc., agree as part of my employment that all photos of me can be used by Aquarena Springs and their advertising and publicity agents. It is to be understood that all photographs are to be in good taste and without embarrassment to me and my family. . . .

On the same page on which Mrs. Braun's picture appeared were stories about "10 Things that P _____ Off Woman" with an accompanying cartoon of a woman whose large breasts are partially exposed; a story entitled "Mammaries Are Made of This" about men whose breasts have been enlarged by exposure to a synthetic hormone, with an accompanying cartoon showing a man with large breasts; and a story entitled "Chinese Organ Grinder" about the use of sexual organs from deer, dogs and seals as a Chinese elixir. On the facing page is a picture showing a nude female model demonstrating naval jewelry and an article on "Lust Rock Rules" about a "throbbing paean" to sex written by "the Roman Polanski of rock." The cover of the issue shows a young woman sitting in a chair with her shirt open so as partially to reveal her breasts, one hand to her mouth and the other hand in her tightly-fitting, unzipped pants.

Mrs. Braun learned of her inclusion in *Chic* on November 23, 1977, when she stopped at a drive-in grocery store in Maxwell, Texas, which lies between San Marcos and her home town of Lockhart, Texas. She walked into the store and a stranger walked up to her and said, "Hey, I know you," explaining that he recognized her from her picture in *Chic*. Mrs. Braun stated that

> ... [H]e went and got the magazine. And I stood there because I was really really terrified. I thought something is going to happen, my picture is not in this magazine. My legs were like jelly, I couldn't untrack. I was petrified. And he was thumbing through these pictures. I was raised in a private Catholic school and I had never seen anything like this. And I was terrified, I didn't know what he had in mind. I thought something horrible was going to happen to me. He flipped through that book and my picture was in that book. I didn't believe it. I stood there like a dummy.

Mrs. Braun testified that she "was very upset" and "felt like crawling in a hole and never coming out." She stated that she did not want to return to work, and that she suffered "embarrassment and humiliation."[3] ...

We turn initially to the determination of whether *Chic*'s publication of Mrs. Braun's picture with piglet merits protection under the rigorous first amendment standard applied to publications regarding public figures. If such protection were due, as *Chic* strenuously claims, the verdict below would have to be reversed.

The protection due publishers by the first amendment against claims of libel has progressed from the first "modern" case of New York Times Co. v. Sullivan, through Gertz v. Robert Welch, Inc., and subsequent cases. It is clear that publications alleged to constitute invasions of privacy merit the same constitutional protections as do publications alleged to be defamatory. We hold that *Chic*'s publication of Mrs.

---

3. *Chic* presented evidence in the jury showing that Mrs. Braun participated as a "barrel racer" at a local rodeo on the same night that she discovered her picture in *Chic*.

Braun's picture is not entitled to constitutional protection under those standards.

. . .

. . . In *Gertz*, which laid to rest consideration of the newsworthiness of the publication in determining the standard of liability, the Court set forth the following rubric:

> That designation [as public official/public figure] may rest on either of two alternative bases. In some instances an individual may achieve such pervasive fame or notoriety that he becomes a public figure for all purposes and in all contexts. More commonly, an individual voluntarily injects himself or is drawn into a particular public controversy and thereby becomes a public figure for a limited range of issues.

Under these various definitions, Mrs. Braun clearly was not a public figure. It is true that she voluntarily undertook a public job; however, the mere fact that she had limited public exposure does not suffice to expose her to the increased burdens and lessened protections of those who fall within the *Gertz* standard. She was involved in no public controversy and had no hand in determining the outcome of any important public issues. She certainly cannot be said to have relinquished interest in protecting her name and reputation by force of her limited role as an entertainer. "A private individual is not automatically transformed into a public figure just by becoming involved in or associated with a matter that attracts public attention." Wolston v. Reader's Digest Assn., Inc.

We therefore conclude that Mrs. Braun is a private individual and that *Chic* is not entitled to the protection of the first amendment applicable to public figures as such standard was enunciated by New York Times v. Sullivan and its progeny.

In determining the standard to be applied here, we start with the premise that *Gertz* leaves to the states the task of defining a standard of liability for the defamation of a private individual. The states are not free, however, to impose liability without fault, nor are they free to award compensation greater than the actual injury suffered by a plaintiff.

Because the prospect of punitive damage awards might tend to inhibit the exercise of legitimate first amendment rights, the Court in *Gertz* held that the states could not allow such awards in the absence of recklessness or actual knowledge of falsity. The states' interest in protecting private individuals from defamation was held not to extend to "securing for plaintiffs . . . gratuitous awards of money damages far in excess of any actual injury." *Gertz* allows only those remedies which go "no farther than is necessary to protect the legitimate interest involved."

In this case, we are faced with a single wrongful publication which has given rise to two separate causes of action under Texas law.

Moreover, the plaintiff was allowed to recover damages under both theories even though the two actions contained identical elements of damages. It has become obvious, with the expansion of privacy law, that a "false light" invasion of privacy action will often arise from the same circumstances which yield a cause of action for defamation. Federal courts have frequently noted the similarities between the two causes of action and have often carried over elements of state defamation law into their consideration of false-light invasion actions. The policy which motivates the holding of *Gertz* requires that there be only a single recovery where the same items of damages are alleged under both defamation and invasion of privacy theories. We must, therefore, look to the jury awards in this case to determine if Mrs. Braun has been doubly compensated for her injuries. Although we recognize that the principle element of injury in a defamation action is impairment of reputation, while an invasion of privacy claim is founded on mental anguish, under Texas law, Mrs. Braun was entitled to recover actual damages for mental anguish under both causes of action. She was also entitled to recover actual damages for the impugnment of her reputation under either theory. See Time, Inc. v. Hill. The elements of damages allowed under the two actions are overlapping.[7]

Having examined the jury instructions and the special verdict in the case, we find that the elements constituting the basis of damages of each of the two causes of action were not sufficiently distinguished from one another to assure that there was not double compensation. Indeed, from the evidence offered on the damage issue, it is, as a practical matter, impossible to distinguish between damages Mrs. Braun suffered from defamation and from invasion of privacy. Very little evidence was offered to show that Mrs. Braun's reputation in her community actually was harmed by the publication, nor was there evidence of tangible economic damage to Mrs. Braun. The evidence supporting the award of damages in this case deals almost exclusively with Mrs. Braun's personal pain and suffering over the appearance of her photograph in *Chic*. Thus it would appear that the jury, in making the award based on Mrs. Braun's defamation cause of action, was primarily compensating her for the embarrassment and humiliation she suffered, the same harms for which the jury was instructed to compensate her under the invasion of privacy cause of action. The $5,000 award for defamation was made in response to an interrogatory regarding damage to reputation; however, the jury was instructed that it could consider Mrs. Braun's personal humiliation, mental anguish and suffering in making both the defamation and

---

7. The jury in this case was instructed as follows with respect to damages:

In order to recover damages to compensate for the defamation, Mrs. Braun must show that she has suffered or will suffer an impairment of her reputation or standing in her community, personal humiliation or mental anguish and suffering as a direct result of the publication of her picture in *Chic*.

If you find that Mrs. Braun's privacy was wrongfully invaded, then you may consider an award of compensatory damages. Do not consider the elements of the causes of action for defamation in awarding damages for invasion of privacy. In awarding compensatory damages, you may consider Mrs. Braun's personal humiliation, mental anguish and suffering.

invasion of privacy awards. Because of the manner in which the jury was instructed, it is impossible for us to determine to what exact extent the compensatory damage awards are overlapping. In view of the jury instructions, however, and the evidence presented, we are convinced that there is a substantial likelihood that the defamation award, at least in part, was intended to compensate Mrs. Braun for harms also compensated for by the invasion award.

With respect to punitive damages awarded for loss of reputation, we are persuaded beyond any doubt that they duplicate those awarded for invasion of privacy. The conduct upon which each award is based is the same: *Chic's* misrepresentations to the personnel of Aquarena Springs and its reckless disregard for the false impression its publication created of Mrs. Braun. Additionally, public policy reasons which support the award of punitive damages in libel actions do not justify punitive damages under both causes of action; that is, punitive damages seek to punish and to prevent future occurrences of a type of conduct, and here, punitive damages on one cause of action clearly fulfills that purpose. Indeed, it is doubtful whether we could ever uphold an award of punitive damages for both invasion of privacy and defamation based on the same reckless conduct.

Given our determination that there can be only a single recovery for any item of damages in a case such as this one, we are compelled to remand the case for a new trial on damages. To do so is the only way that Mrs. Braun is compensated to the fullest extent allowed by law. On the evidence presented in the record before us, however, it appears that Mrs. Braun, on retrial, would be able to prove only nominal damages for loss of reputation independent of that for which she has been compensated for invasion of privacy. If so, retrial would be futile. This decision, however, is not one which we are free to make for the plaintiff; but the plaintiff has the alternative of accepting the compensatory damage award with respect to one of her causes of action. We can uphold one of the awards without running afoul of the rights of *Chic* against a double recovery. This is true because the jury was appropriately instructed with respect to the actual elements of damages allowable separately under each cause of action; it is merely the confluence of the two which infects the verdict and award in this case. We would, therefore, be able to uphold an entry of judgment on one of the compensatory awards and the correlative punitive damages if the jury's verdict is otherwise supportable in law and fact. Because the facts of this case and the nature of the damages suffered—primarily, personal humiliation, embarrassment, pain and suffering—fit more precisely the "false light" invasion of privacy theory than they do the defamation theory, we review the invasion of privacy award. If Mrs. Braun elects to waive her right to retrial, no further appeal by *Chic* will be necessary. We accordingly do not reach the various challenges which *Chic* raises to the defamation award.

The question to which we now turn is whether the evidence supports the jury verdict finding *Chic* liable to Mrs. Braun for invasion of privacy under Texas law. In our analysis, because of the paucity of Texas cases concerning false-light invasion of privacy and because of the similarity of the two causes of action, we will, as have other jurisdictions, rely to some extent on Texas defamation cases.

... The branch of privacy law under which Mrs. Braun recovered involves the right of an individual to be free from publicity which places her in a false light in the public eye. The Restatement (Second) of Torts Section 652(e) (1977) provides that:

> One who gives publicity to a matter concerning another that places the other before the public in a false light is subject to liability to the other for invasion of his privacy, if
>
>> (a) the false light in which the other was placed would be highly offensive to a reasonable person, and
>>
>> (b) the actor had knowledge of or acted in reckless disregard as to the falsity of the publicized matter and the false light in which the other would be placed.

The special verdict indicates that the jury found both that *Chic* published Mrs. Braun's picture in a manner highly offensive to a reasonable person, that *Chic* acted in willful or reckless disregard of Mrs. Braun's right to be free from unwarranted publicity, and that *Chic*'s publication created a false impression of Mrs. Braun. Having examined the record, we hold that a reasonable jury could conclude that Mrs. Braun's right to privacy under Texas law had been violated.

Although we find no Texas cases directly on point, our examination of Texas defamation law and the law of privacy in other states which have adopted the Second Restatement formulation, as Texas has, convinces us that *Chic* is liable to Mrs. Braun for its publication of her picture.

Although under Texas law the court must make a threshold determination whether the complained-of publication is capable of conveying defamatory or false meaning, whether the publication does actually place the subject in a false light and whether that false light would be highly offensive to a reasonable person are questions of fact....

Although *Chic* urges the contrary position, we hold that the evidence in this case supports the conclusion that the publication of Mrs. Braun's picture in the "*Chic* Thrills" section of the magazine was fully capable of creating a false impression of Mrs. Braun. Similarly, we are unpersuaded by *Chic*'s argument that no reasonable person would find the publication of Mrs. Braun's picture in that context to be both false and highly offensive. Having examined the evidence presented, we hold that a reasonable person could have arrived at the same conclusion as did the jurors in this case. In reaching our conclusion, we have remained ever mindful that we sit as a court reviewing the verdict of Mrs. Braun's peers; we do not, cannot, and should not sit as jurors whose job it is ultimately to determine whether the publication was false and offensive.

Chic urges that its publication of Mrs. Braun's picture was substantially true and that Mrs. Braun failed to establish falsity, a necessary element of the false-light invasion of privacy action. *Chic* argues that the picture and caption should have been considered by the jury separately and apart from the other portions of the magazine in determining whether they created a false impression of Mrs. Braun. This argument was raised before the district court in *Chic's* motion in limine to exclude from the jury the "unrelated contents" of the magazine. The court denied the motion and held that the entire magazine could be considered by the jury. Thus, in determining whether Mrs. Braun was presented in a false light, we must decide whether the picture of her should have been considered in isolation or in the context of the entire magazine.

. . .

According to *Chic's* argument, context has no bearing on whether Mrs. Braun was libeled; we should cut out Mrs. Braun's picture and look solely at it to determine whether she had been defamed or cast in a false light. Common sense dictates that the context and manner in which a statement or picture appears determines to a large extent the effect which it will have on the person reading or seeing it.

Texas law supports a realistic view which not only allows but requires presentation of proof which comports with the world outside the courtroom. That is where and how the alleged defamation occurred. If the construction which the ordinary reader would give to Mrs. Braun's picture depended solely on her picture, then the proof should have been limited solely to her picture. That is not the case, however. We cannot therefore find that the court erred in admitting the entire magazine into evidence.

Chic urges that under Texas's law of defamation, consent by an individual to publication of his or her picture for commercial purposes is a defense to libel....

The jury expressly found that Mr. Nuwer misrepresented the true nature of the magazine to Ms. Benton and that consent was not obtained. While there was some dispute as to the exact nature of Mr. Nuwer's representation, sufficient evidence was presented at trial to support the jury's finding.

Chic cites Virginia, Oregon and New York cases for the proposition that, because the jury found that consent was deceitfully induced, rather than exceeded, Mrs. Braun's action lies not in defamation or libel, but must be brought against Aquarena Springs for breach of the consent given by Mrs. Braun to it.

No Texas case is cited on this point, nor have we found authority for this proposition. The gist of the argument, as we (we think) understand it, is that Mrs. Braun gave her release to Aquarena, qualified by the proviso that any pictures (and, implicitly, the use of any pictures) not be embarrassing to her or her family. Aquarena, by allowing itself to be misled by *Chic*, violated the terms of that release and is therefore liable to Mrs. Braun. Any cause of action against *Chic* should have been brought by Aquarena.

We decline to accept this tortuous, caustic argument. The question here is not one of agency or privity or of other relationships among the parties. The question is whether *Chic had consent to publish.* Aquarena, acting in good faith and on the basis of the information the jury determined had been given to it by *Chic,* gave fraudulently induced consent, which is the legal equivalent of no consent. All of *Chic's* tap dancing aside, *Chic* published the picture with no consent: Mrs. Braun was placed in a false light, and *Chic* cannot now hide behind Aquarena's skirts . . . .

VACATED and REMANDED

APPENDIX TO OPINION
RECORD ON APPEAL—VOLUME 1
No. 82–1235—Braun v. Flynt
PAGE 000020–000023

1. Do you find that *Chic* defamed Mrs. Braun?

Answer yes or no: *yes*

2. Do you find that the picture published by *Chic* left a false impression as to Mrs. Braun's reputation, integrity or virtue?

Answer yes or no: *yes*

If you answered No. 1 and No. 2 "yes," answer No. 3.

3. Do you find that *Chic* knew or should have known that the impression left was false?

Answer yes or no: *yes*

4. What sum of money, if paid now in cash, will fairly and reasonably compensate Mrs. Braun for the damage to her reputation?

Answer in dollars and cents or none: *$5,000.00*

If you answered No. 3 "yes," answer No. 5.

5. Do you find that *Chic* acted in willful or reckless disregard of Mrs. Braun's reputation by publishing her picture?

Answer yes or no: *yes*

6. What sum of money, if paid now in cash, should be awarded against *Chic* as exemplary or punitive damages for injuring Mrs. Braun's reputation?

Answer in dollars and cents or none: *$25,000.00*

7. Do you find that *Chic's* publication of Mrs. Braun's picture created a false impression of her or was an unauthorized appropriation of her picture, reputation or accomplishments?

Answer yes or no: *yes*

8. Do you find that *Chic* published Mrs. Braun's picture in a manner highly offensive to a reasonable person?

Answer yes or no: *yes*

9.   Do you find that *Chic* received a valid consent from Aquarena Springs to publish Mrs. Braun's picture? In answering this question, consider whether Mr. Nuwer misrepresented the nature of the magazine.

Answer yes or no: *no*

10.   What sum of money, if paid now in cash, will fairly and reasonably compensate Mrs. Braun for the invasion of her privacy?

Answer in dollars and cents or none: *$15,000.00*

11.   Do you find that *Chic* acted in willful or reckless disregard of Mrs. Braun's right to be free from unwarranted publicity?

Answer yes or no: *yes*

12.   What sum of money, if paid now in cash, should be awarded against *Chic* as exemplary or punitive damages for invading Mrs. Braun's privacy?

Answer in dollars and cents or none: *$50,000.00*

POLITZ, CIRCUIT JUDGE, specially concurring:

I concur in the result insofar as it relates to the invasion of privacy claim, but would reach and specifically address defamation and reverse as to that issue. The truth of the matter published is a defense to a defamation action. It is conceded that the report regarding Ralph the diving pig and Mrs. Braun was factually accurate and that neither the picture nor the caption was distorted or offensive. That factual accuracy and non-distortion forecloses consideration of the issue of damages based on alleged defamation.

Note: Is False Light a Superfluous Tort? Is the False Light Tort Unconstitutional As Well?

Defamation is a tort that has a long history under the common law of protecting the integrity of reputation. Privacy has a much shorter history as a common law tort and is traditionally viewed as vindicating affronts to human dignity. Reputational interests are relational in the sense that damage to reputation is manifested in the reaction of others to a person. Dignity interests are personal in the sense that damage to personal dignity is manifested by the offensiveness of the tortious action to the person. Although the theoretical foundations for the false light privacy and defamation torts are different, the *Braun* decision demonstrates that the two torts track each other in many respects. The gravamen of both torts is material false statements about a person and in many states the compensatory damages that are recoverable under both torts include the dollar value of both the emotional distress and damage to reputation that is caused by the tortious conduct.

The duplication of defamation and the false light torts in substantive content and damage recovery raises the following issues: (1) If false light tracks defamation in substantive content and in compensation for damage to reputation, is the false light tort superfluous and therefore unnecessary? (2) Given the reputational interests that are implicated by material false statements about someone, is false light really a privacy tort?

The judicial inefficiency produced by the duplicative nature of the false light and defamation torts was one of the grounds upon which the Supreme Court of North Carolina in *Renwick v. News and Observer Publishing Company*, 310 N.C. 312, 312 S.E.2d 405 (1984), rejected the tort as part of the common law of the state. Justice Mitchell speaking for the majority gave two reasons for not recognizing a false light tort:

> First, any right to recover for a false light invasion of privacy will often either duplicate an existing right of recovery for libel or slander or involve a good deal of overlapping with such rights. Second, the recognition of a separate tort of false light invasion of privacy, to the extent it would allow recovery beyond that permitted in actions for libel or slander, would tend to add to the tension already existing between the First Amendment and law of torts in cases of this nature.

Id. at 323, 312 S.E.2d at 412.

Justice Mitchell's complaint that the false light tort constitutes a greater threat to first amendment values than defamation is grounded on features of the false light tort that differ from defamation and in some instances allow for recovery under the tort when a defamation action would fail. For a thorough account of the differences between the torts see D. Elder, *The Law of Privacy*, sections 4.1, 4.4, 4.5, at 261–69, 281–99, 299–305 (1991). One of the advantages of the false light tort is that there is no requirement that the plaintiff demonstrate "special damages" (out of pocket losses), where in some defamation actions special damages must be demonstrated in order for the plaintiff to recover compensatory damages. An important additional advantage is that "placing the plaintiff in false light" does not require a demonstration that the plaintiff's reputation be discredited as is the case in defamation. False representations that would be highly offensive to a reasonable person are actionable under the false light tort even though they do not seriously impugn the character or reputation of the plaintiff. *Time v. Hill, supra,* the leading Supreme Court case dealing with the false light tort, is often given as an example of this generous feature of the tort. In that case, the false light action was based upon the defendant misrepresenting that the Hill family had experienced physical and verbal abuse during a siege of their home where they were held hostage for nineteen hours. However, the family was portrayed as courageously and bravely responding to the danger. Courts will accept that it might be offensive to a reasonable person to think that people thought they were placed in a demeaning or pathetic situation even if they were victims. There are a number of cases like *Time v. Hill* where false light actions have been brought by victims of criminal conduct for representations that are arguably complimentary about their character but highly offensive within the meaning of the false light tort because they show the plaintiff in demeaning or degrading situations. *Leverton, supra,* is another example of the expansive nature of the false light tort. Falsely saying that a child was careless was not defamatory but it did place the plaintiff in a false light. Some commentators have argued that extending false light recovery beyond defamation in these cases places unacceptable strains on the freedom of the press. In an important article, Professor Diane Zimmerman develops this and other arguments in support of states either eliminating the false light tort altogether or reducing its scope significantly. *See* Diane Zimmerman, *False Light Invasion of Privacy: The Light That Failed*, 64 N.Y.U. L. Rev. 364 (1989). *See also, Proposal for the Reform of Libel Law: The Report of the Libel Reform Project of the Annenberg Washington Program*, 15 (1988) (recommending abolition of the false light tort). Other commentators have rejected the view that once the false light tort breaks away from the historic moorings of defamation, serious problems are created for the tort reparation system or for the first amendment. *See Elder, supra*, at 261–63 ("circumvention of ... anachronistic restrictions [in the law of defamation] may constitute no great loss"). Despite eloquent calls for its abandonment and some expression of judicial disfavor with the tort, the false light privacy tort appears to be alive and well in our legal system. *See Elder, supra* at 261–340, (discussion of the large number of recent cases).

a. *First Amendment Restrictions on the False Light Tort*

Cher, Lerman, and *Braun* assume that the first amendment limitations on defamation that have been developed by the Supreme Court in cases from *New York Times* to *Greenmoss* apply to false light cases. As noted in the summary of this development, *supra, Time v. Hill,* the leading false light first amendment case, suggested that the first amendment limitations would be the same for both torts but applied the requirement of actual malice to a private plaintiff in that false light case. Subsequently, the Court in *Gertz* required less than malice—negligence—in private plaintiff defamation actions. *Cher, Lerman,* and *Braun* reflect the general view that the law developed in *Gertz* and *Greenmoss*— that negligence and actual injury be demonstrated before a private plaintiff may recover compensatory damage for false representations in a publication that is a matter of public concern—also would apply to false light tort actions. The Restatement of Torts incorporates the *Time v. Hill* holding in the definition of liability for the privacy false light tort but specifically does not take a position on whether the *Gertz* negligence actual injury standard applies to the false light tort. Restatement (Second) of Torts section 652E, Caveat (1977).

Do the differences in the theoretical foundations for the two torts provide support for the view that malice ought to be required in private plaintiff false light tort action? Consider the comments of Judge Posner:

> There is, incidentally, some question whether a plaintiff in a false-light case, merely because he (or she) is not a public figure, is relieved from having to prove malice, as would be true in a defamation case.... An argument can be made that the injury that being cast in a false light creates is less serious than that created by being defamed, and therefore the plaintiff should have a tougher road to hoe.

Douglass v. Hustler Magazine, Inc., 769 F.2d 1128, 1141 (7th Cir.1985).

Compare Judge Posner's statement with the California Supreme Court's view in *Fellows v. National Enquirer, Inc.*, 42 Cal.3d 234, 721 P.2d 97, 228 Cal.Rptr. 215 (1986). In *Fellows*, the court held that the special damage requirements in defamation cases should apply to false light cases. The lower court would not have applied the special damage rule in false light cases because it viewed the torts as protecting different interests. Justice Broussard, speaking for the California Supreme Court, indicated that the conceptual differences between the two torts did not warrant making a statement that was protected under defamation law actionable simply because the media defendant was sued under the false light tort. The breathing space that must be given false statements in defamation actions in order to insure "vigorous debate and free dissemination of the news" should not be viewed as less necessary in false light cases simply because the false statement contained a "privacy-invading element." *Id.* at 270, 721 P.2d at 106, 228 Cal. Rptr. at 225.

Chapter Seven

PRIVACY, AUTONOMY
AND INTIMACY

A. DECISIONAL PRIVACY

So far this book has examined laws primarily aimed at protecting three of the four basic dimensions of privacy: informational, physical, and proprietary. Chapters 2, 3, 4 and 5 focused on the privacy and confidentiality of information contained in records, conversations, computer systems and the media. These chapters, especially Chapters 2 and 5, also focused on physical privacy concerns relating to efforts to shield our bodies, belongings, and certain of our intimate activities from observation. Chapter 6 highlighted the proprietary privacy and publicity interests celebrities and ordinary people assert with respect to personality, identity and reputation. The important area of law relating to a fourth and final dimension of privacy is the subject of this chapter: the decisional dimension.

In the United States the phrase "right to privacy" commonly denotes a right of unfettered, independent decision-making about private life. The materials gathered in this chapter explore legal protection afforded decision-making respecting aspects of sexuality, reproduction, parenting, families, lifestyles, and medical care. This chapter will feature federal and state case law whose role in the development in the United States of a jurisprudence of decision-making about private life has been paramount.

The Supreme Court has noted that its privacy cases involve protection of what are often called "autonomy" interests in making certain kinds of decisions independently, as well as interests in avoiding unwanted disclosures. *See Whalen v. Roe*, 429 U.S. 589, 599–600 (1977). What is autonomy? In one familiar philosophical sense of the term, "autonomy" refers, first, to the capacity of rational persons to *discern* what ought to be done; and second, to the freedom or liberty to *do* what ought to be done. Moral individuals ascertain rational moral law and live by it. See J.B. Schneewind, *The Invention of Autonomy: A History of Modern Moral Philosophy* 483 (1998). Judicial recognition of autonomy interests in privacy cases serves as a practical shield against unwanted interference with the freedom of individuals to make personal decisions that conform to their moral values.

Personal decision-making is not the exclusive domain of individuals acting independently. The decisions we make are surely shaped, at least in part, by social and cultural factors beyond our control. Moreover, people in close personal relationships often agree to make decisions together. Married couples, families, tribes and religious congregations act in concert to make decisions for common and reciprocal purposes. It may be useful to speak of the "aggregate autonomy" of these and similar groupings, to underscore the claims they may assert to separate themselves from the wider society and to be self-governing. The ascription of aggregate autonomy is consistent with the sense many share that the ultimate value of decisional privacy is its ability to foster intimacy–affectional, sexual, familial, spiritual or cultural intimacy with others. Cf. Patricia Boling, *Privacy and the Politics of Intimate Life* (1996). Yet the interpretation of decisional privacy rights as matters of aggregate autonomy is controversial. Philosophical liberals and libertarians are disposed to believe that safeguarding the rights and interests of individuals rather than groups is the surest foundation for a society that aspires to be just, free and democratic. It has been argued, for example, that "marital" and "family" privacy rights grant easily abused powers of domination to husbands over their wives and parents over their children. See, e.g., June A. Eichbaum, *Towards an Autonomy–Based Theory of Constitutional Privacy: Beyond the Ideology of Familial Privacy*, 14 Harvard Civil Rights–Civil liberties Law Review 361 (1979).

Theorists have placed autonomy and intimacy at the moral core of discussions of legal privacy, along with concerns for toleration and limited government. See generally Linda McClain, *Toleration, Autonomy, and Governmental Promotion of Good Lives: Beyond 'Empty' Toleration to Toleration as Respect*, 59 Ohio State Law Journal 19 (1998). These background moral concerns may help to explain the designation of privacy as a " fundamental" constitutional right and protected liberty interest . Indeed, in the face of concern about devolution to "natural law" jurisprudence and the proliferation of unenumerated constitutional rights, many courts and commentators have defended interpretations of the Fourteenth Amendment's express guarantee of "life, *liberty* and due process" as firm textual support for a substantive, free-standing constitutional privacy right.

For more than three decades, judges deciding constitutional cases and commentators defending rights of personal decision-making about pregnancy, homosexuality and the right to refuse medical care have relied heavily on the concept of privacy. The concept of privacy has also figured prominently in legal analysis of the right to choose one's own spouse; to rear children in accordance with one's own moral or religious values; and to possess sexually explicit films or literature in one's own home.

Not every decisional privacy claim has fared well in the courts. Recent state courts applying state and federal constitutional principles have uniformly rejected claims that privacy rights to consensual adult sex immunize persons charged with prostitution from criminal prosecution, even when the sexual activity takes place in the home. *See infra at* 731, State v. Mueller, 671 P.2d 1351 (1983). *See also Blyther v. United States*, 577 A. 2d 1154 (D.C. Ct. App. 1990) (prostitution occurring in a private home may be criminalized, subject only to constitutional standards of government intrusion). *See generally* Timothy O. Lenz, *"Rights Talk" About Privacy in State Courts*, 60 Albany L. Rev. 1613 (1997). The Supreme Court has held that fundamental rights to private decision-making must be either "implicit in the concept of ordered liberty," citing *Palko v. Connecticut*, 302 U.S. 319, 325, 326 (1937) overruled on other grounds by 395 U.S. 784 (1969), or "deeply rooted in this Nation's history and tradition," as called for by *Moore v. East Cleveland*, 431 U.S. 494, 503 (1977) (opinion of Powell, J.). *See, e.g., Bowers v. Hardwick*, 478 U.S. 186 (1986) (upholding Georgia's criminal sodomy statute); *but see Powell v. State*, 270 Ga. 327, 510 S.E.2d 18 (1998) (invalidating Georgia's criminal sodomy statute under state law).

In the initial years following *Griswold v. Connecticut*, 381 U.S. 479 (1965) and *Roe v. Wade*, 410 U.S. 113 (1973), the landmark cases invalidating statutes criminalizing birth-control and abortion, the Court frequently embraced substantive due-process jurisprudence, to this extent. The Court characterized reproductive rights of private decision-making as (1) fundamental rights guaranteed by the 14th Amendment; (2) inviolate against any but compelling state interests and narrowly tailored remedies; and (3) requiring strict judicial scrutiny of restrictive legislation. In recent cases the Court's analyses of reproductive rights of private decision-making have rejected or modified its prior substantive due process jurisprudence. In the 1980s and 1990s Justice Sandra Day O'Connor urged modification of the abortion privacy doctrine in a number of significant cases. She argued that strict scrutiny review of abortion-related statutes is not required where challenged legislation does not "unduly burden" a fundamental right. *See Planned Parenthood v. Casey,* 505 U.S. 833 (1992), *Planned Parenthood v. Ashcroft*, 462 U.S. 476 (1983). In the "right to die" context, Chief Justice Rehnquist has construed privacy rights claimed by patients, family members, guardians, and doctors as cherished liberty interests to be weighed and balanced against the legitimate and compelling interests of local, state and federal government. *See, e.g., Washington v. Glucksberg,* 521 U.S. 702 (1997); *Cruzan v. Director, Missouri Dep't Pub. Health*, 497 U.S. 261 (1990).

This chapter traces the development of legal protection for private decision-making, primarily in the context of federal constitutional law. The starting point will be philosophical perspectives on the concept of autonomy and the normative basis of decisional privacy rights in the law. We emphasize autonomy here because it has been of special concern to privacy advocates and privacy scholars. However, we also include perspectives on personal decision-making that do not rest on the ideal of autonomy, and that challenge that ideal. The emphasis on autonomy should not be permitted to obscure the extent to which cases included in this chapter may concern protecting interests in socially valuable intimate relationships and constraints on government, as much as or more than they concern protecting interests in individual choice.

1. THE CASE FOR AND AGAINST AUTONOMY

The idea of an explicit legal right to privacy protecting personal autonomy is a product of the twentieth century. However, the intellectual roots of the notion that society should be organized to include a sphere for independent decision-making run deep into Greek and Roman antiquity. Influenced by Immanuel Kant and the Enlightenment, modern philosophers have argued that individual autonomy has special moral significance for rational human beings. See J.B. Schneewind, *The Invention of Autonomy: A History of Modern Moral Philosophy* (1998). As the material included below reveals, recent philosophers have both identified privacy with autonomy and designated it as one of the essential preconditions of autonomy. Philosophers also have argued that recognition of a right to privacy is an essential feature of just government. See Judith Wagner DeCew, *In Pursuit of Privacy: Law, Ethics and the Rise of Technology* (1997).

Some theorists have cautioned, however, against over-valuing autonomy at the expense of competing goods relating to public welfare, health and safety. Autonomous choice, they warn, can be used for good or evil, for just or unjust purposes. Legal scholars associated with critical legal studies and feminist legal theory have been especially critical of the applications in law of the concepts of autonomy and a private sphere for autonomous decision-making. They view the liberal emphasis on autonomy as a mistake of fact (because human beings are not generally autonomous decision-makers) and value (because intimacy and community are more desirable than separation and autonomy).

In this section, leading theorists attempt to explicate the meaning of autonomy and its moral significance for individuals, viewed both in isolation from others and in personal, intimate relationships with others. This chapter will also include perspectives critical of attempts to divide social life neatly into public and private spheres.

a. *The Definition of Autonomy*

GERALD DWORKIN, THE THEORY AND PRACTICE OF AUTONOMY
12–13 (1988).

. . . The central idea that underlies the concept of autonomy is indicated by the etymology of the terms: *autos* (self) and *nomos* (rule or law). The term was first applied to the Greek city state. A city had *autonomia* when its citizens made their own laws, as opposed to being under the control of some conquering power.

There is then a natural extension to persons as being autonomous when their decisions and actions are their own; when they are self-determining. The impetus for this extension occurs first when questions of following one's conscience are raised by religious thinkers. Aquinas, Luther, and Calvin placed great stress on the individual acting in accordance with reason as shaped and perceived by the person. This idea is then taken up by the Renaissance humanists. Pico della Mirandola expresses the idea clearly in his "Oration on the Dignity of Man." God says to Adam:

> We have given thee, Adam, no fixed seat, no form of thy very own, no gift peculiarly thine, that . . . thou mayest . . . possess as thine own the seat, the form, the gift which thou thyself shalt desire . . . thou wilt fix the limits of thy nature for thyself . . . thou . . . are the molder and the maker of thyself.

The same concept is presented by [Isaiah] Berlin under the heading of "positive liberty":

> I wish to be an instrument of my own, not other men's acts of will. I wish to be a subject, not an object . . . deciding, not being decided for, self-directed and not acted upon by external nature or by other men as if I were a thing, or an animal, or a slave incapable of playing a human role, that is, of conceiving goals and policies of my own and realizing them. . . .

b. *Autonomy as a Precondition of Moral Agency*

Gerald Dworkin, The Theory and Practice of Autonomy
34–37 (1988).

. . . There is a philosophical view about morality that is shared by moral philosophers as divergent as Kant, Kierkegaard, Nietzsche, [and] Sartre. . . . It is a view of the moral agent as necessarily autonomous. . . . I speak of a view and not a thesis because the position involves not merely a conception of autonomy, but connected views about the nature of moral principles, of moral epistemology, of rationality, and of responsibility. . . .

. . . The most general formulation of moral autonomy is: A person is morally autonomous if and only if his [or her] moral principles are his own. . . .

. . . How could a person's moral principles not be his own? Not by being at the same time someone else's. For the fact that we share a common set of principles no more shows them not to be my own than our sharing a taste for chocolate shows that my taste is not my own. . . .

. . . One suggestion is that we create or invent our moral principles. Sartre speaks of a young man deciding between joining the Free French or staying with his aged mother as being "obliged to invent the law for himself." Kant says that the will "must be considered as also making the law for itself."

... If this is what moral autonomy demands, then it is impossible on both empirical and conceptual grounds. On empirical grounds this view denies our history. We are born in a given environment with a given set of biological endowments. We mature more slowly than other animals and are deeply influenced by parents, siblings, peers, culture, class, climate, schools, accident, genes, and the accumulated history of the species. It makes no more sense to suppose we invent the moral law for ourselves than to suppose that we invent the language we speak for ourselves....

... A central feature of moral principles is their social character. By this I mean, partly, that their interpretation often bears a conventional character. What my duties are as a parent, how close a relative must be to be owed respect, what duties of aid are owed to another, how one expresses regret or respect, are to some extent relative to the understandings of a given society. In addition, moral rules often function to provide solutions to a coordination problem—a situation in which what one agent chooses to do depends upon his expectations of what other agents will do—agents whose choices are in turn dependent on what the first agent will do. Such conventions depend upon the mutual convergence of patterns of behavior. The principles of morality are also social in that they have what H.L.A. Hart calls an internal aspect. They provide common standards that are used as the basis of criticism and demands for obedience. All of these preclude individual invention....

... What is valuable about autonomy is that the commitments and promises a person makes be ones he views as his, as part of the person he wants to be, so that he defines himself via those commitments. But whether they be long-term or short, prima facie or absolute, permanent or temporary, is not what contributes to their value....

In my conception, the autonomous person can be a tyrant or a slave, a saint or a sinner, a rugged individualist or champion of fraternity, a leader or a follower. But I believe that there are contingent connections between being autonomous and the substantive nature of such a person's values. Although there are no a priori truths about the content of an autonomous person's values, one can speculate about psychological and sociological connections. It seems plausible that those who practice in their daily life a critical reflection on their own value structure will tend to be suspicious of modes of thought that rely on the uncritical acceptance of authority, tradition, and custom. They will be disposed to value the kind of substantive independence ranked so highly by philosophers like John Stuart Mill....

c. *Privacy as Essential for Autonomy*

JOSEPH KUPFER, PRIVACY, AUTONOMY, AND SELF–CONCEPT
24 American Philosophical Quarterly 81, 82 (1987).

[P]rivacy is essential to the development and maintenance of an autonomous self.... While there is a good deal more to autonomy, it necessarily includes a concept of oneself as determining his course of action, his life-plan....

An autonomous self-concept requires identifying with a particular body whose thoughts, purposes, and actions are subject to one's control.... It is not enough simply to be free from others' interference; autonomy requires awareness of control over one's relation to others, including their access to us. An individual who was free from interference by others but did not realize it, for example, would hardly be autonomous. His [or her] choices and actions would still be determined from without, by his perception of the desires and purposes of others. No matter how free from external restraint, an individual is not in control of his life, is not self-determining, unless he conceives of himself as such. Which is just to say that autonomy requires an autonomous self-concept.

Developing a conception of self as autonomous through the exercise of choice in ends and their pursuit, however, requires that others affirm the social boundaries of this self.... Autonomy, therefore, is a social product, the result of various social practices which encourage self-determination, including those forming the institution of privacy.

It should be noted that I am not arguing here for the value of autonomy; in a sense I assume it. I grant its rather recent emergence in Western civilization as a value and I also grant that some societies may be better off without widespread autonomy. But these concessions are really beside the present point. What is to the point is the place self-concept occupies in autonomy and the necessity of privacy for both. Of course, in societies which can in some sense flourish without autonomy, privacy will be of little value. But that does nothing to weaken the claim being advanced here.

d. *Autonomy for the Sake of Intimacy*

JULIE INNESS, PRIVACY, INTIMACY AND ISOLATION

91 (1992).

[P]rivacy ... amounts to the state of the agent having control over decisions concerning matters that draw their meaning and value from the agent's love, caring or liking. These decisions cover choices on the agent's part about access to herself, the dissemination of information about herself, and her actions. Since matters draw their meaning and value from the agent's love, liking, or care according to the role they play for the agent, the construction of intimacy lies on the agent's shoulders. Therefore privacy claims are claims to possess autonomy with respect to our expression of love, liking and care.

e. *Autonomy as a Legal Value*

JOEL FEINBERG, AUTONOMY, SOVEREIGNTY AND PRIVACY: MORAL IDEALS IN THE CONSTITUTION?

58 Notre Dame L. Rev. 445, 446–90 (1983).

The word "autonomy" . . . can be rendered at least approximately by such terms as "self-rule," "self-determination," "self-government," and "independence." These phrases are all familiar to us from their more frequent, and often more exact, application to states and other political institutions. Indeed it is plausible to suppose that the original applications and denials of these notions were to states and that their attribution to individuals is derivative, in which case "personal autonomy" is a political metaphor.

When applied to individual persons the word "autonomy" can refer to either (i) the *capacity* to govern oneself, which of course is a matter of degree; or (ii) the actual *condition* of self-government and its associated virtues; or (iii) an *ideal of character* derived from that conception; or (iv) (on the analogy to a political state) the *sovereign authority* to govern oneself, which is absolute within one's own moral "boundaries." This fourth sense of "autonomy," . . . is suggested by the language of international law in which autonomous nation-states are said to have the sovereign right of self-determination. . . .

. . . The kernel of the idea of autonomy is the right to make choices and decisions—what to put into my body, what contacts with my body to permit, where and how to move my body through public space, how to use my chattels and physical property, what personal information to disclose to others, what information to conceal, and more. Some of these rights are more basic and more plausibly treated as indispensable than others. Put compendiously, the most basic autonomy-right is the right to decide how one is to live one's life, in particular how to make the critical life-decisions—what course of study to take, what skills and virtues to cultivate, what career to enter, whom or whether to marry, which church if any to join, whether to have children, and so on. . . .

. . . [T]he [Supreme] Court, in its various ways, has circumscribed as "private" those decisions that involve the most *basic* of the self-regarding decisions. . . . The boundary line . . . tends to follow, however erratically, the line of those liberties which are most fecund, those exercised in the pivotally central life decisions and thereby underlying and supporting all the others.

f. *Autonomy as Myth*

GARY PELLER, THE METAPHYSICS OF AMERICAN LAW
73 Calif. L. Rev. 1151, 1178 (1985).

... It is necessary to resist the image of social relations as simple products of individual intent and choice. Rather, we must recognize and articulate the social and external aspects inherent in so-called private relations. The image of private social relations and "individual" choice depends on the metaphysic of presence. "Private" relations are "private" to the extent that they are represented as not constituted or influenced by "absent" public or social forces; "individual will" is "individual" to the extent that it is self-present and not dependent on the practices of others. The metaphysic of privacy and self-presence accordingly denies the politics of the social construction of the self and the other by finding the origin of the relation ... in a mythical moment of purity from the public world.

On the other hand, we must take care to avoid attributing the same positive presence to the group or public realm. Against the notion that communication and social relations objectively develop as if by some "natural" force autonomous from people, it is necessary to pose the dependence of this social power on social subjects, on people actually acting and conceiving of the world.

g. *Critical Legal Theory and the Rejection of Liberal Autonomy*

ANTHONY COOK, BEYOND CRITICAL LEGAL STUDIES: THE RECONSTRUCTIVE THEOLOGY OF DR. MARTIN LUTHER KING, JR.,
103 Harvard Law Review 985, 1009–10 (1990).

Many CLS [Critical Legal Studies] scholars see the liberal conception of community as heavily dependent on the faith that the state can and does set community-defining boundaries that establish the limits of collective action through the neutral application of objective and determinate principles. Although sovereignty is theoretically vested in "the people," the specific nature and conditions of that sovereignty are the subject of a "legal" text and subject to the interpretation of a "judicial aristocracy" of federal judges. CLS asks, "On what grounds can the people be legitimately robbed of this sovereignty?" One response is that the courts must enforce the boundaries articulated by the Constitution that define the spheres of privacy within which the collective cannot intrude.

This enforcement requires a delicate balancing between individual rights and duties. The apparatus of liberal rights mediates the relationship between ourselves and others whose cooperation both threatens and is indispensable to our survival. Under liberal theory, the process of mediation requires the establishment of private spheres of autonomy into which others are not permitted to intrude. A liberal discourse of abstract rights and duties purports to map out the borders of these private spheres of autonomy and to set the conditions under which they may be justifiably disregarded.

The most troubling aspect of this story of neutrality and dispassionate adjudication is that those in power draw the line between public and private to preserve the distributions of wealth and power that limit transformative change and preserve hierarchies directly or indirectly benefitting them. How does CLS respond to this problem? One way is by showing the inherent indeterminacy of line-drawing. We have examined this approach; it deconstructs ideology at the level of both social and legal theory. Another way is by offering an alternative vision of community, a new way of drawing the lines between rights and duties....

The alternative vision begins with a different conception of the self. Because liberal theory is thought to legitimize its social order by deducing it from specific conceptions of human nature, some have thought it necessary to posit a different conception of human nature in order to deduce a different conception of community transcending the limitations of liberalism. That alternative conception of human nature rejects the conceptions offered by classical and contemporary liberal theory. It implies that liberal theory has mistaken the symptoms of the individual's condition for its causes. That is, what Hobbes and Locke describe as natural merely reflects the individual's alienation from his true nature. The individual is not, by nature, an autonomous and acquisitive being desiring to dominate others and appropriate property. Rather, her alienation and loneliness are socially produced. Individuals long for a genuine connection with others, a mutual acknowledgment of their humanity and need for empowerment. However, socially imposed roles temper their desires for connection with fears of rejection. The regime of liberal rights establishes many of these roles through the distribution of abstract rights and duties that distance us from ourselves and others whom we long to experience in more meaningful ways than our present social existence permits.

Some would contend, for instance, that when we speak of the individual's right to privacy versus the right of the community to pass laws regarding the use of contraception and abortion, or the rights of individual property owners to be free from the pollution of their water supply versus the rights of individuals to dispose of their property as they see fit, or the rights of African–Americans to attend nonsegregated schools versus the right of white Americans to attend neighborhood schools, or when we describe the collective picketing of the South African embassy as an exercise of a first amendment right, much is lost through the abstractions used to express the underlying realities. Once filled with life, suffering, pain, joy, and hope, these realities are filtered through the desensitizing and sterilizing discourse of rights, and appear as reified pronouncements of law whose detachment from underlying realities only further entrenches our own sense of detachment and loneliness, and rationalizes our continued oppression.

We are lonely because our relationships with each other are distorted by these abstractions, and thus the potential for genuine connection is always limited by the socially contrived roles we adopt. Landlord/tenant, employer/laborer, professor/student, bank teller/customer, and judge/lawyer are all roles that distance us, diminish our intersubjectivity, and decrease the likelihood of a sustained sense of community. The liberal state, however, provides us with an alternative community that really is no community at all. To mediate the threat posed by others to ourselves, the state fosters an illusion of a community consisting of rights-bearing citizens said to be equal before the law and thus members of a community of equals. This is problematic because at one level we perceive others as the bearers of rights, as equals in a community of equals. At a different level, that of the market for instance, we perceive others as a threat, something to be dominated or neutralized in the acquisitive world of "dog-eat-dog." The day-to-day realities of our private loneliness and alienation belie the image of our communitarian existence as equal political citizens. The illusory liberal community is held together by the manipulation of political symbols by elites through their access to the mass media and our utter need to believe in community, even when it is utterly absent. That is, we long for community so desperately that a chief executive's invasion of a small island, bombing of an African country, and general rhetoric of American patriotism shape our conception of community and fill the emptiness we experience daily.

Given the pervasive sense of alienation characterizing their interactions with others, then, individuals place great faith in the capacity of the state to define the nature of community. Part of that definition consists of the state's ability to articulate and enforce neutral boundaries defining the liberal equality of individuals, their equal freedom within private spheres of autonomy protecting them from the arbitrary incursion of private and collective forces. When a careful "trashing" of legal doctrine reveals, however, that all things are infused with both public and private qualities, there no longer exists any supposed objective criterion by which to logically characterize all things as either public or private. Under the weight of this analysis, the private-public dichotomy collapses and with it the artificial limitations imposed upon the possibilities of collective action needed to create alternative forms of community. We need not maintain faith in a state, "a passivizing illusion—actually a hallucination," proven incapable of objectively mediating the contradiction between public and private life.

The prescription of some, therefore, is to eliminate the state as we know it and, along with it, the artificially generated social roles that limit the possibilities of our communitarian impulses. In short, some call for a type of decentralized socialism where one need not hide behind the private for either protection or self-aggrandizement. Communities where relationships might be just "us, you and me, and the rest of us," deciding for ourselves what we want, without the alienating third of the state. In that setting ... we might even make group decisions about reproduction, replacing our pervasive alienation and fear of one another with something more like mutual trust, or love.

... Nothing about law or our present social order is sacrosanct or compelled by forces independent of our own capacities to envision and construct alternative forms of community. Deconstruction that demonstrates the indeterminacy of both legal doctrine and the political assumptions undergirding legal doctrine emphasizes that the kind of community in which we live remains a matter of choice—the important question being who will make those choices.

h. *Autonomy: Men's Existential Predicament*

ROBIN WEST, JURISPRUDENCE AND GENDER
55 U. of Chi. L. Rev. 1 (1988).

What is a human being? ... [V]irtually all modern legal theorists, like most moral and political philosophers, either explicitly or implicitly embrace what I will call the 'separation thesis' about what it means to be a human being. A 'human being,' whatever else he is, is physically separate from all other human beings....

According to liberal legalism, the inevitability of the individual's material separation from the 'other,' entails ... an existential state of highly desirable and much valued freedom.... This existential condition of freedom in turn entails the liberal's conception of value. Because we are all free and we are each equally free, we should be treated by our government as free, and as equally free....

Autonomy and freedom are both entailed by the separation thesis, and autonomy and freedom both feel very good.... [A]ccording to liberal legalism, each of us is physically separate from every other, and because of that separation, we value our autonomy from the other and fear our annihilation by him. According to critical legal theory, we are indeed physically separate from the other, but what that existentially entails is that we dread the alienation and isolation from the separate other, and long for connection with him....

... Underlying both radical and cultural feminism is a conception of women's existential state that is grounded in women's potential for physical, material connection to human life. Just as underlying both liberal and critical legalism is a conception of men's existential state that is grounded in the inevitability of men's physical separation from the species. I will call the shared conception of women's existential lives the "connection thesis." ...

The "connection thesis" is simply this: Women are actually or potentially materially connected to other human life. [They are connected through sexual intercourse, pregnancy and breast-feeding.] Men aren't. This material fact has existential consequences. While it may be true for men that the individual is "epistemically and morally prior to the collectivity," it is not true for women. The potential for material connection with the other defines women's subjective, phenomenological and existential state, just as surely as the inevitability of material separation from the other defines men's....

2. DEMARCATING THE PUBLIC AND THE PRIVATE

As Jurgen Habermas and Hannah Arendt observed, supra Chapter One ____, decision-making respecting reproduction, family life and personal affairs has been a historic prerogative of actors within the socially constructed "private sphere" since classical antiquity. The controversial distinction between "the public" and "the private" made today has much—though not everything—in common with ancient Greek and Roman conceptions. One important commonality is that the home is the presumptive center of the appropriately private sphere. A second, equally important, is that the biological family is deemed to have its seat in the private domain. Theorists are increasingly challenging prior assumptions about the relative value attributed to the public and private aspects of life. Critical legal scholars and many feminist legal theorists believe that it is no longer possible, if ever it was possible, to sustain a cogent distinction between "public" and "private." Jean Elshtain, below, defends a revised version of the public/private split as essential for humane child-rearing.

a. We Still Need a Private Sphere

JEAN B. ELSHTAIN, PUBLIC MAN, PRIVATE WOMAN
322–28 (1981).

To talk of an ideal of the private world within the context of contemporary American society is to talk about the family. The family is the linchpin in all visions of future alternatives, often as something to be reformed or overthrown....

[One] variation of the end-of-family ideology grew out of the counterculture commune movement in the 1960s, one to which many social rebels turned as an alternative to the nuclear family. The motivations for these moves lay primarily in restructuring male-female relations and presuming, from a stance lacking in moral concern and reflexivity, that these changes would a fortiori be "good for the children" as the child would be the "child of all" and not the "possession of two." ...

Another claim and aim of social critics in family elimination or radical transformation is an instrumentalist one: in order for other political ends to be achieved. The idea here is that devotion to the family and to private ties and purposes ... takes the edge off radical commitments to change.

... [F]amilial ties and modes of child-rearing are essential to establish the minimal foundation of human, social existence. What we call human capacities could not exist outside a familial mode; for human beings to flourish a particular ideal of the family is necessary.... But first, the family's status as a moral imperative derives from its universal, pan-cultural existence in all known past and present societies. We are not dealing with a tangential, episodic cultural form but a transhistorical one. To state a presumptive case for familial ties, to argue that they are required to make us minimally human, is *not* to detail the specific forms within which the creation and nourishment of humanity may take place. Aristotle and all other political theorists down through the centuries who asserted the primacy of politics, and viewed man (the male, at any rate, if not generic humanity) as preeminently a political animal even as they downgraded or simply took for granted the private sphere, were guilty of a serious distortion. It is the family which "pervades all our perceptions of social reality." It is the family that constitutes our "common humanity," for our use of language, the basis of that humanness, has its origin in family forms. This makes the family "the universal basis of human culture.... As language constitutes the essence of man as a species, and not reason, so the family and not the social order, is the setting that humanizes him."....

Children will incur an assault to their humanness, an affront they will know in the tissue of their bio-psychic beings, if they suffer from the diseases of neglect and nonattachment.... [T]he knowledge we now have of what happens to children *in the absence of strong, early attachments to specific adult others*, allows us to assert that we are dealing with a categorical imperative of human existence.

b. What is Considered Private?

The concept of a "right to privacy" has its most distinctive application in the law today where at stake are interests in autonomy within the realms of what are presumed to be personal or private affairs. Chiefly, these realms encompass sex, reproduction and family life. "Privacy" and cognate expressions also appear where the liberty or autonomy at issue is freedom from intrusion, especially, governmental intrusion, into the presumed commercial and professional realms of life. The freedom to enter into legally enforceable contracts at will, and the freedom to acquire, enjoy and alienate "private" property are sometimes described as privacy.

A degree of legally protected personal and economic privacy has been the ideal and reality for many in the United States since its founding. This basic truth is unaffected by a constitutional history which reflects that state and federal lawmakers have erected significant barriers to private decisionmaking by white women, non-whites, non-heterosexuals and the poor of every race and sexual orientation.

Privacy rights presuppose that governmental actors and non-governmental actors ought to share decision-making about individual and group conduct. How ought society allocate the power to decide? It is obviously only a tautology to say that the proper sphere of official decision-making is the public sphere; the sphere of appropriately private decision-making, the private sphere.

While contemporary conventional paradigms can be cited of what is personal on the one hand, and commercial or professional on the other, legal debate over privacy often arises precisely because citizens disagree about whether a particular range of decisions and conduct are personal and thus appropriately left to the choices of private actors.

The debate over the criminalization of prostitution is an apt example. While sex is paradigmatic personal conduct appropriately protected by the law in the name of personal autonomy, accepting payment for a service is paradigmatic commercial conduct normally subject to a broad range of state regulation in the public interest.

Professional or commercial enterprises that are not themselves within the socially constructed sphere of the personal, may nonetheless fall within the reach of legal privacy. Courts have recognized that protecting personal privacy sometimes requires protecting commercial and professional privacy. For example, it is widely acknowledged that personal autonomy for users of birth control presupposes a degree of professional autonomy for their physicians, as well as commercial autonomy for the pharmaceutical industry.

The recognition of the right to privacy implies that unconstrained control of individual and group life is a political evil—a kind of totalitarianism. Yet unconstrained autonomous conduct is also an evil. Community life presupposes collective decision-making, compromise and constraint. The quest for privacy-as-autonomy is most often a quest for greater relative freedom in a discrete realm of decision and action, not absolute freedom from interference.

The rules of criminal and civil law reflect the popular understanding that injurious intentional, reckless and negligent acts are justifiably constrained. The primary focus of laws constraining autonomous conduct is conduct that directly and seriously injures others. Laws prohibiting homicide, assault, and theft are examples. However, the law prohibits many acts that directly injure only the actor and the actor's intimates. Thus state laws criminalize the possession of a quantity of marijuana grown at home for personal use. They also make a husband liable for raping his wife; and permit legal intervention on behalf of abused children. For better or worse, many such laws have been challenged on privacy, marital privacy and family privacy grounds. Also challenged have been laws prohibiting acts, like consensual sodomy and same-sex marriage, that directly harm no one, but merely offend certain standards of moral decency.

No aspect of "private" life is wholly free from "public" regulation. Is the public/private distinction thus ultimately, as critics claim, a kind of "fairy tale"? *See* Howard B. Radest, *The Public and the Private: An American Fairy Tale*, 89 Ethics 280, 280–91 (1979), supra 11. See generally, Elizabeth Mensch and Allen Freeman, *The Public-Private Distinction in American Law*, 36 Buffalo L. Rev. 237 (1987) (critical legal studies perspective challenging the public/private split); David Kairys, ed., *The Politics of Law* (1998) (progressive critiques of liberal legal theory).

3. CONSTITUTIONAL PRIVACY AND AUTONOMY

To understand the constitutional right of decisional privacy, it is essential to understand its origins. The right to privacy was slow to gain recognition as a distinct right under common law and the Constitution. Its rapid development in state and federal constitutional law after 1965 was a testament to the appeal of judicial limitations on legislative interference with valued forms of private decision-making.

Yet, even sympathetic observers such as Joel Feinberg, *supra*, have expressed concern about the erratic boundaries of the autonomous domain seemingly posited by the courts. Have the courts gone too far? Have they refused to go far enough? On what non-arbitrary basis can courts in a complex, regulated, democratic, multicultural society like our own carve out appropriate spheres for private decision-making? Does the express recognition of privacy rights protecting autonomy render all state regulation suspect? What standards of review should courts apply in cases brought to challenge governmental regulation of allegedly private life?

Under the privacy rubric, supporters defend the recognition of autonomy claims by appeal to a panoply of values. The case for privacy-as-autonomy evokes the value of limited government, self-rule, moral personhood, and individualism on the one hand; group identity, selective intimacy and freedom of association on the other.

In the excerpt that follows, Jed Rubenfeld summarizes the history of the constitutional privacy doctrine from the founding of the nation through the late twentieth century, noting its close connection with ideals of sex and sexuality. Many of the cases Professor Rubenfeld cites are excerpted and presented for further discussion and analysis later in this chapter. The idea of privacy rights, especially fundamental constitutional privacy rights promoting autonomy, has been controversial among lawyers and judges from its inception. Professor Henkin, below, explains some of the reasons why.

a. *A Brief History of Constitutional Privacy Rights*

JED RUBENFELD, THE RIGHT OF PRIVACY
102 Harv. L. Rev. 737, 740–47 (1989)(footnotes omitted).

I. A GENEALOGY OF PRIVACY

The emergence of this substantive right to privacy, and hence the constitutional protection of the conduct to which it applies, is of very recent origin. The doctrine is only some twenty years old. Its genealogy, however, extends as far back as constitutional law reaches in this country. Indeed its most venerable ancestor is the decision that rendered constitutional law itself possible: *Marbury v. Madison. Marbury* is a progenitor of the right-to-privacy decisions because it too belongs to the diverse series of cases in which the Supreme Court has reached out beyond the express language of the Constitution and struck down on constitutional grounds some piece of federal or state legislation. A brief history of this family of cases follows.

A. Pre–Privacy Case Law

The earliest and most authoritative articulation of the idea that fundamental rights exist unspecified in the Constitution is of course in the ninth amendment, which provides: "The enumeration in the Constitution, of certain rights, shall not be construed to deny or disparage others retained by the people." The earliest judicial statement of this idea followed soon after the Constitution was ratified. In *Calder v. Bull*, Justice Chase advanced the proposition that legislation might be held invalid under natural law even if the legislation does not violate any specific constitutional principles or provisions. Justice Iredell, however, disagreed, and his views have, at least ostensibly, prevailed. From the early 1800's to the present, the Court has generally paid lip service to the idea that it should not use its constitutional power to invalidate legislation except where specific constitutional provisions supply the principle of invalidity.

Yet the Court has never practiced what it preached. Through one device or another, the Court has always managed to read into the Constitution limits on legislative power that can hardly be gathered from within that document's four corners. In the antebellum period, the Court accomplished this task principally through ingenious interpretations of the contract clause, one of the few constitutional provisions then applicable against the states....

After the Civil War, the passage of the fourteenth amendment gave the Court a great deal more constitutional material to consider. Curiously, the provision of that amendment containing what appears to be the most explicit and potent substantive limitations on state legislative powers—the privileges and immunities clause—proved too much for the Court to swallow. In a series of early post-War cases, the Court gave an extremely narrow reading to that clause, and this reading remains in effect today. Instead, the Court seized on a much more unlikely provision—the due process clause—for the strength to take on the state legislatures.

Although the phrase "due process" might seem to pertain only to procedural interests, the Court began to read substantive guarantees into the clause as well. From the late 1870's to the turn of the century, the Court formulated an interpretation of due process in which the predominant figure was a fundamental, potentially inviolate "liberty of contract" with which legislatures had no power to interfere. Armed with this "liberty of contract," guaranteed as a matter of substantive due process, the Court was prepared in this century to do considerable damage to state economic regulation. Thus, in *Lochner v. New York*, the Court invalidated a maximum-hours law for bakers on the ground that it interfered with "the freedom of master and employee to contract." On similar grounds the Court later condemned, for example, prohibitions of anti-union clauses in labor contracts, price-fixing regulations of employment agencies, and a fair-wage law for women.

In the same period, the Court also relied on the due process clause to invalidate two state laws regulating the education of children. In *Meyer v. Nebraska*, the Court held that a state could not prohibit the teaching of foreign languages in elementary school, and in *Pierce v. Society of Sisters,* the Court struck down a requirement that all children attend public school. Although *Meyer* and *Pierce* resemble the other *Lochner*-era cases in analytic form, in content they are closer to modern privacy case law. Indeed, for reasons that will emerge more clearly below, these two cases may be seen as the true parents of the privacy doctrine, and today they are frequently classified together with other privacy decisions.

The climax of the *Lochner*-era jurisprudence was President Franklin Roosevelt's retaliatory plan to increase the number of Justices on the Supreme Court. Although the plan did not succeed as designed, it apparently put sufficient pressure on the Court to change the course of Constitutional law. In *West Coast Hotel Co. v. Parrish*, the Court renounced its freedom of contract/substantive due process jurisprudence. A year later, in *United States v. Carolene Products Co.*, the Court held that state economic regulations were entitled to a presumption of constitutionality. In the ensuing decades, the Court repeatedly held that states were free to regulate "their internal commercial and business affairs, so long as their laws do not run afoul of some specific constitutional prohibition, or of some valid federal law."

Even while repudiating its substantive due process jurisprudence, however, the Court expressly noted that its newfound self-restraint might not extend beyond the economic realm. Indeed, in an important line of cases involving individual liberties not overtly economic in nature, the Court has continued to strike down state laws found to violate fundamental rights nowhere specified in the Constitution. These cases elaborate the right-to-privacy doctrine.

B.   The Privacy Cases

The great peculiarity of the privacy cases is their predominant, though not exclusive, focus on sexuality—not "sex" as such, of course, but sexuality in the broad sense of that term: the network of decisions and conduct relating to the conditions under which sex is permissible, the social institutions surrounding sexual relationships, and the procreative consequences of sex. Nothing in the privacy cases says that the doctrine must gravitate around sexuality. Nevertheless, it has.

The Court first announced the new privacy doctrine in [1965] in *Griswold v. Connecticut*. In *Griswold* the Court invalidated statutes prohibiting the use and distribution of contraceptive devices. Eschewing an approach explicitly grounded in Lochnerian substantive due process, the Court stated that a "right to privacy" could be discerned in the "penumbras" of the first, third, fourth, fifth, and ninth amendments.

This right included the freedom of married couples to decide for themselves what to do in the "privacy" of their bedrooms.

Two years later, in *Loving v. Virginia*, the Court struck down a law criminalizing interracial marriage. The Court ruled that states could not interfere in that manner with an individual's choice of whom to marry. On similar grounds, the Court also invalidated laws restricting the ability of poor persons to marry or to divorce.

Although it remained possible after *Loving* to understand the new privacy doctrine as limited (for some unelaborated reason) to marital decisions, in *Eisenstadt v. Baird* the Court extended its *Griswold* holding to protect the distribution of contraceptives to unmarried persons as well. "If the right to privacy means anything," the Court stated, "it is the right of the *individual*, married or single, to be free from unwarranted governmental intrusion into matters so fundamentally affecting a person as the decision whether to bear or beget a child." The next year, the Court took a further step from the confines of marriage and delivered its most controversial opinion since *Brown v. Board of Education*. Justice Blackmun, with only two Justices dissenting, wrote in *Roe v. Wade* that the right to privacy was "broad enough to encompass a woman's decision whether or not to terminate her pregnancy." Subsequent cases have reaffirmed *Roe* in the context of state efforts to "regulate" abortions, but the Court's support of *Roe* appears to be rapidly diminishing.

The right to privacy was further expanded in the 1977 case of *Moore v. City of East Cleveland*, in which the Court struck down a zoning ordinance that limited occupancy of dwelling units to members of a nuclear family—the "nominal head of a household," his or her spouse, and their parents and children. Although there was no majority opinion, the four-Justice plurality expressly relied on the *Griswold* line of cases, as well as *Meyer* and *Pierce*, emphasizing the "private realm of family life which the state cannot enter."

... [In] *Bowers v. Hardwick*, ... a 5–4 majority held that a state could make homosexual sodomy a criminal offense without violating the right to privacy. The *Hardwick* decision ... may foretoken a considerable narrowing of the privacy doctrine.

b. Can There Be a Fundamental Constitutional Right of Privacy?

LOUIS HENKIN, PRIVACY AND AUTONOMY
74 Colum. L. Rev. 1410, 1419–31 (1974).

... From the beginning, indisputably, the Constitution has protected some elements of "privacy".... The fourth amendment provides that the "right of the people to be secure in their persons, houses, papers, and effects against unreasonable searches and seizures shall not be violated." There is that happily forgotten third amendment that limits the Government's right to quarter soldiers in any house in time of peace without the consent of the owner. Some might include in privacy a person's right under the fifth amendment not be compelled to be witness against himself. Rights not themselves strictly rights of privacy have been held to imply other rights that approach "hard-core privacy." Freedoms of speech and press include the freedom not to speak or publish and the freedom to speak or publish anonymously.... The freedom of religion includes the right not to disclose one's religion. The freedoms of speech and assembly, or something else in that large first amendment, include a right to associate; and the right to associate includes the right not to associate, to select one's associates and associations, and the right not to disclose one's associations....

Primarily and principally the new right of privacy is a zone of prima facie autonomy, of presumptive immunity from regulation.... The zone, Justice Blackmun told us, [in *Roe v. Wade*] consists of "personal rights" that can be deemed "fundamental," that are "implicit in the concept of ordered liberty." ...

... We are not told the basis—in language, history, or whatever else may be relevant to constitutional interpretation—for concluding that "liberty" includes some individual autonomy that is "fundamental" and much that is not. We are not told what is the touchstone for determining "fundamentality." We are not told why privacy satisfies that test (unless privacy is a tautology for fundamentality); we are not told, precisely and persuasively, what that privacy is and includes. The zone of privacy, we are told, includes rights that are "personal," "fundamental," "essential to ordered liberty," but if these apparently aspire to some kind of justification, they hardly provide definition. Surely the zone of autonomy-privacy is not defined by that authoritative and appealing formula, "the right to be let alone." Is that not a reasonable translation of *laissez faire*, which is surely *not* what the right of privacy signifies today? What, then, is it that makes my right to use contraceptives a right of privacy, and fundamental, but my right to contract to work 16 hours a day or pay more for milk than the law fixes, not a right of privacy and not fundamental? ...

. . .

The Court's creation of an additional zone of individual autonomy to include some (perhaps all) it has recently put into it, and more to come, does not, I think, clearly exceed the bounds of proper judicial innovation. That the Court has adequately rationalized and justified what it has done is less clear.

Jurisprudential uncertainties are aggravated, I think, because consideration has focused on defining the private right of privacy, with little regard to our other balance, the competing "public good." There are, we have seen, intimations that the new zone of privacy is characterized by activity done "in private," and sexual relations, to be sure, are usually conducted "in private," even today; but other activities are also generally secreted, done "in private," from burglary to espionage and conspiracies to overthrow governments. There are intimations that the right of privacy extends to activities that are intimate, and sexual relations, to be sure, are intimate, even today; but so are they in situations of statutory rape, prostitution, adultery, incest, homosexuality and other forms of sodomy, which are still in almost every criminal code. (The law also regulates marriage, divorce and other "intimate" family relationships, and often disregards friendship and other intimacies.) Control over one's body—made much of in the abortion debates—has not included the right to commit suicide, to reject medical treatment or vaccination, to refuse to make that body available to military service, or one's child's body and mind to compulsory elementary education.

. . .

. . . [N]ow that we have added a new, expandable zone of autonomy, fundamental but not absolute, a jurisprudence of balancing of rights and goods cries for thinking about public goods. The Court has not told us which assertions of governmental authority promote purposes that are not permissible or not public, or not good, which public goods are "insufficient," which are "acceptable," which are "compelling." It is not clear whether "compelling" means "weighty," or "clear," or both, or something else. Are there preferred goods as there are preferred rights? Are there fundamental public goods . . . ?

c. *Privacy, Equality and Public Goods*

The dramatic appearance in American jurisprudence of privacy rights protecting autonomy interests has been accompanied by concern about four separate issues. First, do courts have the constitutional authority to demarcate a right of private decisionmaking? Second, can one define "privacy" sufficient to dispel conceptual confusion surrounding its usage? Third, how viable are the public/private distinction and the idea of a private safe haven for family and intimacy? And fourth, whom can privacy rights and privacy rights discourse help and whom can they harm?

We have not yet fully considered substantive concerns about what Henkin called "public goods," or the potentially negative impact of privacy-as-autonomy rights on particular segments of society. Some legal commentators reproach judicially expanded privacy rights on the grounds that autonomous decision-making for some entails cognizable injury and neglect for others, especially women and children. Feminists, including Catherine Mackinnon, have argued that contemporary constitutional privacy jurisprudence applied to reproductive rights is in tension with the very ideals of equality that it purports to further. *But see* Anita L. Allen, *The Proposed Equal Protection Fix for Abortion Law*, 18 Harv. J. Law and P.P. 419 (1995). Importantly, abortion rights opponents have argued that women's right to privacy deprives the unborn of their right to life.

If privacy is crucial to personhood, are the poor less likely to flourish as persons than the affluent? Consider this perspective:

In our own society, the constitutional guarantee of privacy has increasingly come to be thought of as protecting dignity and free development of personality . . . .

The war on poverty, however, has focused attention on the fact that the indispensable conditions of privacy, dignity, and freedom are lacking for millions of Americans. Thus, while the Constitution's guarantees presuppose the existence of these indispensable conditions, their actual non-existence tends to reduce the guarantees themselves to mere suppositions.

.... [I]f poverty is at war with the Constitution, the Constitution is equally at war with poverty.... [P]ersons in our society have a constitutional right to privacy and to the conditions which are indispensable to its realization.

Albert M. Bendich, *Privacy, Poverty and the Constitution*, 54 California Law Review 407, 407–9 (1966).

Has the Supreme Court subscribed to Bendich's idea that the constitution broadly protects the indispensable "conditions" of privacy? What might those conditions be? Is a home of one's own such a condition? If so, does it follow that the poor have a constitutional privacy interest in publicly subsidized housing; that the homeless have a constitutional privacy interest in temporary shelters? How about sexual and reproductive autonomy? Are they among the conditions indispensable to the realization of privacy and personhood? *Cf. Harris v. McRae*, 448 U.S. 297 (1980). In *Harris* the Court held that the Constitution does not mandate federal funding for abortions, since "[a]lthough the liberty protected by the Due Process Clause affords protection against unwarranted government interference with freedom of choice in the context of certain personal decisions, it does not confer an entitlement to such funds as may be necessary to realize all the advantages of that freedom." 448 U.S. at 317–18. The upshot of *Harris* seems to be that a person's ability to engage in *effective* autonomous decision-making is to a significant extent going to be a function of his or her economic class. See Dorothy Roberts, *Rust v. Sullivan and the Control of Knowledge*, 61 George Washington l. Rev 587 (1993).

Questions about public goods Professor Louis Henkin raised in 1974, are still being raised today. How cogent is the idea of a broad, general right of citizens to immunity from public regulation aimed at furthering public goods? A workable liberal democracy presupposes constraints on the ability of individuals to do as they please. Regulation for the public good is part of the vision of government and citizenship reflected in the structural provisions of the Constitution and the Bill of Rights. Does this mean that privacy rights construed as presumptions against constrained autonomy are untenable?

d. *De-linking Privacy and Autonomy*

Can we theorize about privacy apart from autonomy? Dr. Arnold H. Modell, who writes about the private self from a psychoanalytic perspective, argues that the connection between private selves and autonomy goes back at least to Aristotle . Aristotle "recognized that we can achieve autonomy through a passionate commitment to personal moral values" and "observed that although we are not masters of our impulses, we are in control of our moral choices." *See Arnold H. Modell, The Private Self* 62 (1993).

While "the link between privacy and autonomy is now so familiar as to seem natural," Michael Sandel has argued from a neo-republican perspective that "through most of history in American Law, the right of privacy has implied neither the ideal of the neutral state nor the ideal of a self freely choosing its aims and attachments." See Michael Sandel, *Democracy's Discontent* 93 (1996). In the excerpt below, Sandel identifies an alternative to the concept of privacy-as-autonomy. Sandel argues for for a broad understanding of privacy rights as protective of identity and non-voluntary relationships, such as families and religions, rather than purely autonomous individual choices.

e. *Privacy Rights Protect Important Relationships*

MICHAEL SANDEL, *DEMOCRACY'S DISCONTENT*

93 (1996)(footnotes omitted).

. . . Through most of its history in American law, the right to privacy has implied neither the ideal of the neutral state nor the ideal of a self freely choosing its aims and attachments. That the meaning of privacy has in recent years come to carry these assumptions reflects their growing prominence in our moral and political culture.

Where the contemporary right of privacy is the right to engage in certain conduct without government restraint, the traditional version is the right to keep certain personal facts from public view. The new privacy protects a person's "independence in making certain kinds of important decisions," whereas the old privacy protects a person's interest in "avoiding disclosure of personal matters."

The tendency to identify privacy with autonomy not only obscures these shifting understandings of privacy; it also restricts the range of reasons for protecting it. Although the new privacy typically relies on voluntarist justifications, it can also be justified in other ways. A right to be free of governmental interference in matters of marriage, for example, can be defended not only in the name of individual choice but also in the name of intrinsic value or social importance of the practice it protects.

As the Court has sometimes acknowledged, "certain kinds of personal bonds have played a critical role in the culture and traditions of the Nation by cultivating and transmitting shared ideals and beliefs; they thereby foster diversity and act as critical buffers between the individual and the power of the state. The Court's greater tendency, however, has been to view privacy in voluntarist terms, as protecting, "The ability independently to define one's identity."

f. Constitutional Privacy Forestalls Totalitarian Government

Michael Sandel's analysis of privacy has proven to be provocative. *See, e.g.*, the wide-ranging critical perspectives of Mary Shanley, Robin West, Andrew Seigel, and Linda McClain and James Fleming in Anita L. Allen and Milton Regan (eds.) *Debating Democracy's Discontent* (1998). Is Sandel correct that the privacy-as-autonomy idea is "new" when compared to the idea of privacy-as-non-disclosure? Would it be more accurate to say that these ideas have existed side by side, though one (non-disclosure) came expressly into law under the "right to privacy" rubric sooner than the other (autonomy)?

Some of Sandel's critics worry that de-linking privacy from autonomy threatens contemporary efforts to use privacy jurisprudence to protect non-traditional relationships, such as gay marriages, no less than traditional ones. Is Sandel's non-voluntarist conception of privacy inherently more "conservative" and the voluntarist inherently more "liberal"? When reading the landmark privacy cases below, look for evidence of Sandel's contention that the voluntarist direction of the Supreme Court's thinking about privacy has been the "greater tendency."

Like Sandel, Jed Rubenfeld has defended an analysis of privacy that rejects the idea of government giving maximal sway to autonomy. Rubenfeld asks us to consider the kind of government we want rather than the kind of persons we want. Since the autonomous person can choose to be either a saint or a tyrant, society has no categorical reason to place a high value on individual autonomy. See J. Rubenfeld, the Right to Privacy, supra 600. Rubenfeld maintains that The point of decisional privacy rights is to prevent government from becoming totalitarian. The main social goal behind constitutional privacy rights, he argues, is the harnessing of public authority to prevent abuse and domination:

> What, then is the right to privacy? What does it protect? A number of commentators seem to think that they have it when they add the word "autonomy" to the privacy vocabulary. But to call an individual "autonomous" is simply another way of saying that he is morally free, and to say that the right to privacy protects freedom adds little to our understanding of the doctrine. . . .
>
> Privacy takes its stand at the outer boundaries of the legitimate exercise of state power. It is to be invoked only where the

government threatens to take over or occupy our lives–to exert its power in some way over the totality of our lives.

... The anti-totalitarian right to privacy, it might be said, prevents the state from imposing on individuals a defined identity, whereas the personhood right to privacy ensures that individuals are free to define their own identities. [but the freedom to define oneself is a chimera. We are powerfully influenced and cannot, as individuals, define our own identities.]

Id. At 750, 785, 792. Protecting autonomy and curbing government are indeed different goals. However, traditional liberals who fear the loss of moral autonomy when privacy is threatened, also tend to fear totalitarian styles of government precisely because totalitarian governments suppress the human potential for genuine morally autonomous conduct.

4. VEXING CONCEPTUAL ISSUES

Some analytical legal philosophers sharply criticize the courts for the practice of styling rights of autonomous decision-making as "privacy" rights. They insist that "privacy" is a misnomer as applied to decision-making about reproduction, families and personal life. They recommend that its use be abandoned to clear up conceptual confusion in the law. How important are definitional debates over the meaning of privacy? Why do they persist? Does how an interest is labeled have any bearing on whether or how forcefully courts are willing to protect it?

Criticism of the idea that autonomy interests are protected by privacy rights is sometimes premised on the belief that "autonomy" is not a synonym, or not a proper synonym, for "privacy." Scholars in this camp typically assert that the condition of non-interference, suggested by terms like "autonomy," "liberty," and "freedom" is not the core referential meaning of "privacy." They argue that, in its paradigmatic uses, "privacy" refers to control over information, or, restricted access to persons and personal information.

Ruth Gavison and like-minded analytic philosophers believe that, as compared to "privacy," either "liberty" or "freedom" better captures the nature of our legal interests in effective decision-making. Even where the autonomy interests in question relate to intimate, personal affairs, the argument goes, it is confusing to refer to the absence of regulation or other interference as "privacy."

The Court's use of "privacy" as a rough synonym for "autonomy", "liberty" and "freedom" has numerous defenders. See, e.g., Judith Decew, *Defending the 'Private' in Constitutional Privacy*, Journal of Value Inquiry 21: 171–184, 180 (1987), arguing that "the view that no privacy interests are at stake in the constitutional cases is unhelpful at best and question-begging [as to the meaning of privacy] at worst."

a. *"Liberty" Is Not a True Synonym for "Privacy"*

RUTH GAVISON, PRIVACY AND THE LIMITS OF LAW
89 Yale L.J. 421, 428, 438–39 (1980).

... [I]dentifying privacy as noninterference with private action, often in order to avoid an explicit return to "substantive due process," may obscure the nature of the legal decision and draw attention away from important considerations. The limit of state interference with individual action is an important question that has been with us for centuries. The usual terminology for dealing with this question is that of "liberty of action." It may well be that some cases pose a stronger claim for noninterference than others, and that the intimate nature of certain decisions affects these limits. This does not justify naming this set of concerns "privacy," however. A better way to deal with these issues may be to treat them as involving questions of liberty, in which enforcement may raise difficult privacy issues.

b. *"Freedom" is Not a True Synonym for "Privacy"*

STANLEY I. BENN, A THEORY OF FREEDOM
292–93 (1988).

Privacy is frequently referred to as a kind, or a part, of freedom. In a trivial sense it is true: Someone who enjoys privacy is free from observation. But in that sense any valued state, such as health, would be a part of freedom—freedom from its opposite, disease. That is hardly a substantial reason for associating freedom and privacy.

John Stuart Mill's distinction in *On Liberty* between self-and other-regarding actions is sometimes taken as defining the scope of private affairs, in which neither government nor society could have a legitimate interest. So in the debate on victimless crimes, such as (in some jurisdictions) homosexual acts, the private use of narcotic drugs, or pornography, it is often claimed that the criminal law is improperly invading privacy. The famous formulation of a right of privacy, first by Judge Cooley, then by Warren and Brandeis, as "the right to be let alone" has tended to encourage this association.

Yet Mill's essay is not about privacy, in the sense of a right not to have to share information, places, and so on with unwanted intruders. It is about criteria for public regulation of individuals' actions, whether done in private or in public. Victimless crimes do not qualify for regulation by Mill's criteria because they are held not to be "other-regarding"; Mill would claim, on that account, that they are not to be interfered with, that one is at liberty to do as one likes in those matters. He does not claim that one has a special interest in excluding intruders, voyeurs, or reporters when one does such acts. If smoking were a strictly self-damaging vice, legislating to prohibit it would violate not a right to privacy but the general principle of freedom from interference, grounded on the principle of respect for persons. . . .

Admittedly, not all the paradigm invasions of privacy (for instance, harassment by debt collectors) could be accurately described as attempts to "get acquainted" with private affairs, but there is a reasonably determinate set of problems having to do with the collection of information by observation or inquiry, and its dissemination, which is not naturally subsumed under considerations of freedom of action, rights of property, or personal security, while having certain things in common with all three. It will be more convenient, therefore, to confine discussion of interests in privacy to this narrower determinate set rather than to adopt a more inclusive interpretation. The analytical edge of the concept of privacy will be blunted if, even in respect of intimate, personal relations and activities, it is invoked to restrain not only access to information, publication, and physical intrusion, but also regulation of the relations and the practices themselves. The problem of determining rights to privacy is complex enough, without subsuming under it the entire question of the limits of state interference.

c. *Privacy is Not Autonomy, Freedom or Liberty*

RAYMOND WACKS, THE POVERTY OF PRIVACY
96 Law Quarterly Review 73, 78–81 (1980).

The pervasive tendency to treat "privacy" as synonymous with individual autonomy or, indeed, with freedom itself, is especially manifest in recent Supreme Court decisions on sexual freedom and obscene material, but this by no means exhausts the application of the concept which, most recently, has been invoked to vindicate the "right to die."

This alarming development may be attributable to two factors. The first harks back to the Warren and Brandeis thesis that the proposition that the essence of the "right to privacy" is the "right to be let alone"— a sweeping phrase which is as comprehensive as it is vague. If "privacy" consists in being "let alone" then every physical assault would constitute an invasion of privacy.

Secondly, since the Constitution is silent on the subject of "privacy," the Supreme Court has, in its determination to protect this "fundamental personal right" discovered in the provisions of the Bill of Rights, or even outside them, ample flexibility and scope for the development of implied "rights to privacy." Once this right is declared to emanate "from the totality of the constitutional scheme under which we live," it is not surprising that it has come to approximate what Mill in *On Liberty* understood by "privacy" in the widest possible sense when he said: "Over himself, over his own body and mind, the individual is sovereign." But what is in issue here is not "privacy" but the limits of the law in regulating the individual's freedom of action. [This is the stuff of the well ventilated Hart/Devlin debate. *See* H.L.A. Hart, *Law Liberty and Morality* (1963); P. Devlin, *The Enforcement of Morals* (1965).] This principle—that there is a sphere of thought and action that should be free from public interference—may well constitute "the central idea of liberalism," but for the purposes of the legal recognition of a "right to privacy" it is only an ultimate norm which underpins the narrower and more specific right.

d. The Political Force of "Privacy"

ANITA L. ALLEN, UNEASY ACCESS: PRIVACY FOR WOMEN IN A FREE SOCIETY

33–34 (1988).

... The definition assigned to "privacy" constrains what one can term a condition of privacy, an invasion of privacy, and a loss of privacy. The moral rhetoric of fundamental rights of constitutional proportions and the rhetoric of privacy have helped to keep reproductive rights concerns near the top of the public policy agenda. To define reproductive issues beyond the realm of privacy discourse carries with it the threat that these concerns will seem less urgent. It is conceivable that the desire to take women's issues out of the public eye has even on occasion been a motive for insisting that "privacy" be narrowly defined to exclude reproductive concerns.

... [T]he close ties between reproductive liberties and personal privacy take much of the point away from insisting that political advocacy of permissive abortion policies be purged of privacy talk. Privacy diminution [i.e., increased surveillance, information losses, less time alone at home] is part of what is wrong with governmentally imposed obstacles to decision-making respecting birth control, abortion, and the discharge of childcare duties. Women understand that their liberty, their equality, their moral authority, but also their privacy is at stake.

B. REPRODUCTIVE AUTONOMY

Introduction

Meyer v. Nebraska, 262 U.S. 390 (1923) and *Pierce v. Society of Sisters*, 268 U.S. 510 (1925) may be the "true parents of the privacy doctrine" found in reproductive rights cases. *See* Jed Rubenfeld *The Right to Privacy*, 102 Harv. L. Rev. 737, 746 (1985). No explicit mention of a general right of constitutional privacy appeared in either *Meyer* or *Pierce*. Both cases were Fourteenth Amendment challenges to state statutes regulating childrearing and education, rather than reproduction.

However, these cases testing the limits of "public" interference with "private" decision-making assumed that, in the words of Justice Reynolds in *Meyer*, "the individual has certain fundamental rights which must be respected" by state law. 262 U.S. at 401. As the source of fundamental rights, *Meyer* pointed to the Fourteenth Amendment provision that "No State shall deprive any person of life, liberty, or property, without due process of law." *Id*. at 399. *Meyer* urged that Fourteenth Amendment liberty surely includes what many would regard as rights of autonomous, private decision-making: "the right of the individual to contract, to engage in any of the common occupations of life, to acquire useful knowledge, to marry, establish a home and bring up children, to worship God according to the dictates of his own conscience, and generally to enjoy those privileges long recognized at common law as essential to the orderly pursuit of happiness by free men." *Id*. at 399. To describe constitutional rights as fundamental means that even "highly advantageous" public policies cannot be coerced. *Id*. The State may "go very far"—but only so far—"in order to improve the quality of its citizens, physically, mentally and morally." *Id*. at 401.

Courts first distinctly recognized a fundamental right to privacy forty years after *Meyer* in celebrated cases announcing autonomy rights to reproductive choice and services. Does the Constitution permit states to ban the use, distribution or advertising of contraceptives? May states prohibit abortion? It was in the course of answering "no" to these questions that the Supreme Court in the 1960s and 1970s developed the explicit doctrine of fundamental privacy rights requiring strict judicial scrutiny.

In the United States, laws expressly regulating contraception and abortion date back only to the second half of the nineteenth century. The period that followed of relative public quietude over government regulation of reproduction was not to last a hundred years. How did public regulation of contraception and abortion begin? What were its goals and consequences? Consider Michael Grossberg's interesting history of the origin of U.S. law prohibiting contraception and abortion.

1. CONTRACEPTION

MICHAEL GROSSBERG, GOVERNING THE HEARTH: LAW AND THE FAMILY IN NINETEENTH CENTURY AMERICA

157–159 (1985).

Though it is difficult to pierce the privacy surrounding family limitation, at the beginning of the nineteenth century, husbands and wives apparently still relied on age-old methods of birth control such as delayed marriage, breast feeding, and abstinence (as well as *coitus interruptus* and other active practices). The growing determination to control fertility encouraged innovation; the popularizer of one method, the douche, ignited the first legal confrontation over contraception.

A Massachusetts country doctor, Charles Knowlton, published the first American medical treatise on contraception in 1832. . . .

Knowlton's slim volume, *Fruits of Philosophy*, offered the most detailed explanation of contraception and reproduction popularly available in the English language. . . . The *Boston Medical Journal* reacted to the volume sternly: "The less is known by the public at large, the better it will be for the whole moral community." Local officials responded more aggressively: [several towns, including Cambridge] indicted Knowlton for peddling obscenity. His publisher ... also ran afoul of the law for distributing *Fruits of Philosophy*.

... [T]here were no common law precedents or statutory directives labeling the distribution of contraceptive information as either immoral or illegal. The doctor protested that he had written *Fruits of Philosophy* to improve health and morality.... The physician claimed far-reaching benefits from following his advice: less poverty, fewer illegitimate births, and improved feminine health....

... [One court] fined him $50 and $27.50 court costs, [another] sentenced him to three months of hard labor in the house of corrections, and [a third] added another jail sentence.... [Knowlton's] cause stirred little public sympathy.

... Only an 1847 Massachusetts obscenity statute turned [popular pronatalism] into a formal prohibition.... For most Americans, birth control remained a private affair, but its public advocacy became associated with indecency and sexual radicalism....

The reception of Knowlton's book documents this divergence of thought and practice.... By 1881 over 277,000 copies had been published.... For much of the century, birth control remained beyond the reach of the law .....

Self-appointed purity campaigners led the drive against contraception. New Yorkers created the first purity society in 1872, the New York Society for the Suppression of Vice. Though founded and funded by elite city residents such as banker Morris K. Jessup, who also headed the YMCA, the society's point man for purity reform was a little known ex-dry goods salesman, Anthony Comstock. The son of devout Connecticut parents, he tried unsuccessfully to make his fortune as a businessman in New York City. The flagrant vices he encountered in the city shocked him into a highly publicized vigilante campaign. It culminated in his appointment as the antivice society's chief agent, thus launching his career as late nineteenth-century America's self-avowed savior of public morals.

... Comstock began to lobby for tougher laws. In 1872 he convinced the antivice society to send him to Washington to press for a rigorous national statute.

In Washington the vice crusader succeeded beyond his wildest expectations.... Comstock enlisted the aid of Vice President Henry Wilson and Supreme Court Justice William Strong to draft a new obscenity law. The bill passed with little debate and became law on 1 March 1873....

... Federal authorities capped the statute's passage by appointing Comstock a special postal agent charged with enforcing the law.

The federal act, quickly dubbed the Comstock Law, was the center-piece of the drive against obscenity, but purity crusaders also prodded state legislators into action. Antivice societies, and after 1885 the Social Purity Alliance, succeeded in persuading twenty-two legislatures to enact general obscenity laws and another twenty-four to specifically ban birth control and abortion.

ACT OF JULY 12, 1876

19 Stat. 90, amending 17 Stat. 598–99.

"THE COMSTOCK LAW"

Be it enacted by the Senate and House of Representatives of the United States of America in Congress assembled. That section thirty eight hundred and ninety-three of the Revised Statutes shall be, and is hereby, amended so as to read as follows:

Every obscene, lewd, or lascivious book, pamphlet, picture, paper, writing, print, or other publication of an indecent character, and every article or thing designed or intended for the prevention of conception or procuring of abortion, and every article or thing intended or adapted for any indecent or immoral use, and every written or printed card, circular, book, pamphlet, advertisement, or notice of any kind giving information, directly or indirectly, where, or how, or of whom, or by what means, any of the hereinbefore mentioned matters, articles or things may be obtained or made, and every letter upon the envelope of which, or postal card upon which, indecent, lewd, obscene, or lascivious delineations, epithets, terms, or language may be written or printed, are hereby declared to be non-mailable matter, and shall not be conveyed in the mails, nor delivered from any post-office nor by any letter-carrier....

Act of July 12, 1876, 19 Stat. 90.

Note: The Comstock Laws

Congress passed the original Comstock Law, "An Act for the Suppression of, Trade in, and Circulation of, Obscene Literature and Articles of immoral Use," 17 Stat. 598–99, on March 3, 1873. The Law made it a crime to sell, lend, give away, publish or possess devices or literature pertaining to birth control or abortion. The Law was amended in 1876. *See* Act of July 12, 1876, 19 Stat. 90, *supra.* The 1876 Amendment appeared to narrow the scope of the Act. Focusing on the use of the United States mails, the amended Act declared contraception and abortion information, along with "obscene, lewd, or lascivious" articles to be "unmailable matter." The amended Act provided that offenders would be "fined not less than one hundred dollars nor more than five thousand dollars, or imprisoned at hard labor not less than one year no more than ten years, or both...." *Id.*

POE v. ULLMAN

367 U.S. 497 (1961).

[Note: Justice Harlan's dissent in *Poe v. Ullman* would have a profound impact on subsequent constitutional law. The case began with a Connecticut statute dating from 1879, "An Act Concerning Offenses Against Decency, Morality and Humanity." The Comstock era statute provided that: "Any person who uses any drug, medicinal article or instrument for the purpose of preventing conception shall be fined not less than fifty dollars or imprisoned not less than sixty days nor more than one year or be both fined and imprisoned." Connecticut law also provided that: "Any person who assists, abets, counsels, causes, hires or commands another to commit any offense may be prosecuted and punished as if he were the principal offender."

The statute appeared to prohibit a Planned Parenthood physician, Dr. C. Lee Buxton, from providing birth control information to the fictitiously named plaintiff-appellant, Pauline Poe. Poe, whose action sought a declaratory judgment that the Connecticut contraception prohibitions were unconstitutional, had previously given birth to three short-lived infants with multiple congenital abnormalities. Neither Poe nor her physician had been prosecuted under the seldom enforced law, and the Court held that the case was not ripe for constitutional adjudication on the merits. Justice Harlan dissented on the grounds that the statute, which would be struck down four years later in *Griswold v. Connecticut*, 381 U.S. 479 (1965), violated constitutional privacy rights guaranteed by the Bill of Rights and Fourteenth Amendment.]

MR. JUSTICE HARLAN, dissenting.

. . . I believe that a statute making it a criminal offense for *married couples* to use contraceptives is an intolerable and unjustifiable invasion of privacy in the conduct of the most intimate concerns of an individual's personal life. . . .

Due process has not been reduced to any formula; its content cannot be determined by reference to any code. The best that can be said is that through the course of this Court's decisions it has represented the balance which our Nation, built upon postulates of respect for the liberty of the individual, has struck between that liberty and the demands of organized society. If the supplying of content to this Constitutional concept has of necessity been a rational process, it certainly has not been one where judges have felt free to roam where unguided speculation might take them. The balance of which I speak is the balance struck by this country, having regard to what history teaches are the traditions from which it developed as well as the traditions from which it broke. That tradition is a living thing. A decision of this Court which radically departs from it could not long survive, while a decision which builds on what has survived is likely to be sound. No formula could serve as a substitute, in this area, for judgment and restraint.

It is this outlook which has led the Court continuingly [sic] to perceive distinctions in the imperative character of Constitutional provisions, since that character must be discerned from a particular provision's larger context. And inasmuch as this context is one not of words, but of history and purposes, the full scope of the liberty guaranteed by the Due Process Clause cannot be found in or limited by the precise terms of the specific guarantees elsewhere provided in the Constitution. This "liberty" is not a series of isolated points pricked out in terms of the taking of property; the freedom of speech, press, and religion; the right to keep and bear arms; the freedom from unreasonable searches and seizures; and so on. It is a rational continuum which, broadly speaking, includes a freedom from all substantial arbitrary impositions and purposeless restraints....

As was said in Meyer v. Nebraska, 262 U.S. 390, 399, "this Court has not attempted to define with exactness the liberty thus guaranteed ... Without doubt, it denotes not merely freedom from bodily restraint...." Thus, for instance, when in that case and in Pierce v. Society of Sisters, the Court struck down laws which sought not to require what children must learn in schools, but to prescribe, in the first case, what they must *not* learn, and in the second, *where* they must acquire their learning, I do not think it was wrong to put those decisions on "the right of the individual to ... establish a home and bring up children," Meyer v. Nebraska, or on the basis that "The fundamental theory of liberty upon which all governments in this Union repose excludes any general power of the State to standardize its children by forcing them to accept instruction from public teachers only," Pierce v. Society of Sisters. I consider this so, even though today those decisions would probably have gone by reference to the concepts of freedom of expression and conscience assured against state action by the Fourteenth Amendment, concepts that are derived from the explicit guarantees of the First Amendment against federal encroachment upon freedom of speech and belief.... For it is the purposes of those guarantees and not their text, the reasons for their statement by the Framers and not the statement itself, see United States v. Carolene Prods., 304 U.S. 144, 152–153, which have led to their present status in the compendious notion of "liberty" embraced in the Fourteenth Amendment....

... The State ... asserts that it is acting to protect the moral welfare of its citizenry, both directly, in that it considers the practice of contraception immoral in itself, and instrumentally, in that the availability of contraceptive materials tends to minimize "the disastrous consequence of dissolute action," that is fornication and adultery....

Yet the very inclusion of the category of morality among state concerns indicates that society is not limited in its objects only to the physical well-being of the community, but has traditionally concerned itself with the moral soundness of its people as well. Indeed to attempt a line between public behavior and that which is purely consensual or solitary would be to withdraw from community concern a range of subjects with which every society in civilized times has found it necessary to deal. The laws regarding marriage which provide both when the sexual powers may be used and the legal and societal context in which children are born and brought up, as well as laws forbidding adultery, fornication and homosexual practices which express the negative of the proposition, confining sexuality to lawful marriage, form a pattern so deeply pressed into the substance of our social life that any Constitutional doctrine in this area must build upon that basis. . . .

It is in this area of sexual morality, which contains many proscriptions of consensual behavior having little or no direct impact on others, that the State of Connecticut has expressed its moral judgment that all use of contraceptives is improper. Appellants cite an impressive list of authorities who, from a great variety of points of view, commend the considered use of contraceptives by married couples. What they do not emphasize is that not too long ago the current of opinion was very probably quite the opposite, and that even today the issue is not free of controversy. Certainly, Connecticut's judgment is no more demonstrably correct or incorrect than are the varieties of judgment, expressed in law, on marriage and divorce, on adult consensual homosexuality, abortion, and sterilization, or euthanasia and suicide. . . .

Precisely what is involved here is this: the State is asserting the right to enforce its moral judgment by intruding upon the most intimate details of the marital relation with the full power of the criminal law. Potentially, this could allow the deployment of all the incidental machinery of the criminal law, arrests, searches and seizures; inevitably, it must mean at the very least the lodging of criminal charges, a public trial, and testimony as to the *corpus delicti*. Nor could any imaginable elaboration of presumptions, testimonial privileges, or other safeguards, alleviate the necessity for testimony as to the mode and manner of the married couples' sexual relations, or at least the opportunity for the accused to make denial of the charges. In sum, the statute allows the State to enquire into, prove and punish married people for the private use of their marital intimacy.

This, then, is the precise character of the enactment whose Constitutional measure we must take. The statute must pass a more rigorous Constitutional test than that going merely to the plausibility of its underlying rationale. . . . This enactment involves what, by common understanding throughout the English-speaking world, must be granted to be a most fundamental aspect of "liberty," the privacy of the home in its most basic sense, and it is this which requires that the statute be subjected to "strict scrutiny."

That aspect of liberty which embraces the concept of the privacy of the home receives explicit Constitutional protection at two places only. These are the Third Amendment, relating to the quartering of soldiers, and the Fourth Amendment, prohibiting unreasonable searches and seizures. . . .

It is clear, of course, that this Connecticut statute does not invade the privacy of the home in the usual sense, since the invasion involved here may, and doubtless usually would, be accomplished without any physical intrusion whatever into the home. What the statute undertakes to do, however, is to create a crime which is grossly offensive to this privacy, while the Constitution refers only to methods of ferreting out substantive wrongs, and the procedure it requires presupposes that substantive offenses may be committed and sought out in the privacy of the home. But such an analysis forecloses any claim to Constitutional protection against this form of deprivation of privacy, only if due process in this respect is limited to what is explicitly provided in the Constitution, divorced from the rational purposes, historical roots, and subsequent developments of the relevant provisions....

It would surely be an extreme instance of sacrificing substance to form were it to be held that the Constitutional principle of privacy against arbitrary official intrusion comprehends only physical invasions by the police. To be sure, the times presented the Framers with two particular threats to that principle, the general warrant, see Boyd v. United States, and the quartering of soldiers in private homes. But though "Legislation, both statutory and constitutional, is enacted, ... from an experience of evils, ... its general language should not, therefore, be necessarily confined to the form that evil had theretofore taken.... (A) principle to be vital must be capable of wider application than the mischief which gave it birth." Weems v. United States, 217 U.S. 349, 373.

Although the form of intrusion here—the enactment of a substantive offense—does not, in my opinion, preclude the making of a claim based on the right of privacy embraced in the "liberty" of the Due Process Clause, it must be acknowledged that there is another sense in which it could be argued that this intrusion on privacy differs from what the Fourth Amendment, and the similar concept of the Fourteenth, were intended to protect: here we have not an intrusion into the home so much as on the life which characteristically has its place in the home. But to my mind such a distinction is so insubstantial as to be captious: if the physical curtilage of the home is protected, it is surely as a result of solicitude to protect the privacies of the life within. Certainly the safeguarding of the home does not follow merely from the sanctity of property rights. The home derives its pre-eminence as the seat of family life. And the integrity of that life is something so fundamental that it has been found to draw to its protection the principles of more than one explicitly granted Constitutional right....

Of course, just as the requirement of a warrant is not inflexible in carrying out searches and seizures, so there are countervailing considerations at this more fundamental aspect of the right involved. "[T]he family ... is not beyond regulation," and it would be an absurdity to suggest either that offenses may not be committed in the bosom of the family or that the home can be made a sanctuary for crime. The right of privacy most manifestly is not an absolute. Thus, I would not suggest that adultery, homosexuality, fornication and incest are immune from criminal enquiry, however privately practiced. So much has been explicitly recognized in acknowledging the State's rightful concern for its people's moral welfare. But not to discriminate between what is involved in this case and either the traditional offenses against good morals or crimes which, though they may be committed anywhere, happen to have been committed or concealed in the home, would entirely misconceive the argument that is being made.

Adultery, homosexuality and the like are sexual intimacies which the State forbids altogether, but the intimacy of husband and wife is necessarily an essential and accepted feature of the institution of marriage, an institution which the State not only must allow, but which always and in every age it has fostered and protected. It is one thing when the State exerts its power either to forbid extra-marital sexuality altogether, or to say who may marry, but it is quite another when, having acknowledged a marriage and the intimacies inherent in it, it undertakes to regulate by means of the criminal law the details of that intimacy.

In sum, even though the State has determined that the use of contraceptives is as iniquitous as any act of extra-marital sexual immorality, the intrusion of the whole machinery of the criminal law into the very heart of marital privacy, requiring husband and wife to render account before a criminal tribunal of their uses of that intimacy, is surely a very different thing indeed from punishing those who establish intimacies which the law has always forbidden and which can have no claim to social protection.

GRISWOLD v. CONNECTICUT
381 U.S. 479 (1965).

(This case is in Chapter One of these materials.)

Notes: Jus Tertii Standing

As a general rule, individuals have standing only to challenge government action that proximately causes their own injuries. *Jus tertii*, or third-party, standing may be available where the right asserted is inextricably bound up with the activity of the litigant or where there is a "genuine obstacle" to the third party asserting their own rights. *See Singleton v. Wulff*, 428 U.S. 106 (1976).

As *Griswold* illustrates, parties have been granted standing to assert the privacy rights of affected individuals not before the court. *See generally*, Robert Allen Sedler, *Standing to Assert Constitutional Jus Tertii in the Supreme Court*, 71 Yale L.J. 599 (1962); Note, *Standing to Assert Constitutional Jus Tertii*, 88 Harv. L. Rev. 423 (1974). *Jus tertii* standing has been utilized in other significant autonomy cases. *See, e.g., Pierce v. Society of Sisters*, 268 U.S. 510 (1925).

Why did the Court make *jus tertii* standing available to appellants in the *Griswold* case? The direct constitutional injury suffered by appellant health care providers in *Griswold* was a loss of their own personal property. Both had been ordered to pay $100 fines. However, the Court permitted the health care providers to assert derivative claims based on Planned Parenthood patients' constitutional injuries. The Court held that the constitutional right of privacy of married couples includes use of medically prescribed contraception.

What standard of review would the Court have applied if the health care providers in *Griswold* had been limited to challenging the law on the basis of their personal constitutional injury? Compare the strict scrutiny standard of review applied in right to privacy cases to the deferential rational basis standard that was adopted by the Court to uphold an Oklahoma law that deprived opticians of liberty to engage in their profession and of their property in *Williamson v. Lee Optical Co.*, 348 U.S. 483 (1955).

Many of the Supreme Court's abortion cases have relied upon *jus tertii* standing rules. Women's privacy rights have been asserted by reproductive services organizations in, for example, *Planned Parenthood v. Casey*, 505 U.S. 833 (1992). *See also Planned Parenthood of Central Missouri v. Danforth*, 428 U.S. 52 (1976); *Thornburgh v. American College of Obstetricians and Gynecologists*, 476 U.S. 747 (1986); *Akron v. Akron Center for Reproductive Health, Inc.*, 462 U.S. 416 (1983).

A more restrictive standing rule is utilized in fourth amendment cases and other areas of informational privacy laws. This personal standing rule was examined in Chapter II.

Notes: The Penumbra Metaphor

(1) The *Griswold* case is widely regarded as having established a fundamental right of constitutional privacy. Among lawyers, the majority opinion in *Griswold* is perhaps best known and most criticized for Justice Douglas' "penumbra" metaphor of the foundations of privacy rights. Douglas first expressed the idea that a right of privacy can be found in the "penumbra" of the Bill of Rights in his dissent in *Poe v. Ullman*, 367 U.S. 497, 517 (1961).

(2) Compare Justice Douglas' penumbral conception of the right of privacy with Justice Holmes' in his dissent in *Olmstead v. United States*, 277 U.S. 438 (1928) (government wiretapping withstands Fourth and Fifth Amendment challenges). Holmes stressed that the government wiretap was illegal under the laws of the state of Washington and argued that evidence obtained illegally should not be used in a federal criminal prosecution:

> My brother Brandeis has given this case so exhaustive an examination that I desire to add but a few words. While I do not deny it, I am not prepared to say that the *penumbra* of the Fourth and Fifth Amendments covers the defendant, although I fully agree that the Courts are apt to err by sticking too closely to the words of a law where those words import a policy that goes beyond them....

277 U.S. at 485. (emphasis added)

Justice Brandeis' often-quoted dissent in *Olmstead* referred to by Holmes, above, characterized the right to privacy as "the right to be left alone—the most comprehensive of rights and the right most valued by civilized men." *Id.* at 478.

(3) Justice Harlan declined to concur in the opinion of Justice Douglas in *Griswold*, although he concurred in the judgment. Did Harlan at least implicitly rely upon a penumbral privacy theory in his *Poe* dissent as well? Is, for example, Harlan's argument that the Court must look to "a particular provision's larger context" to discern constitutional imperatives, tantamount to an appeal to the "penumbras" of specific constitutional guarantees?

(4) As noted, critics accuse Justice Douglas of excessive reliance in *Griswold* upon the imagery of "penumbra" and "emanations." Douglas maintained that penumbral zones of privacy give "form and substance" to enumerated rights. But his phraseology was ambiguous. His language suggests both that privacy functions to protect enumerated rights and that privacy and explicit fundamental rights are interdependent; that one cannot thrive without the other. Less imagery and more elaboration of the role of privacy rights in protecting other constitutional values could perhaps have shielded Douglas from criticism like the following:

> The accordion-like qualities of the emanations-and-penumbra theory, and the ease with which it can be used in the same broad way in which the fundamental rights theory has been used, become evident when one considers its application to areas where the Court in recent years has limited the sphere of constitutional protection. The point is made that since liberty of contract is not mentioned in the Constitution, it should not be a constitutionally protected right. Yet, since the body of the Constitution protects against the impairment of the obligations of contracts, it does not require a far-fetched application of the emanations-and-penumbra theory to suggest that implicit in the contracts clause (or at least radiating from it) is a constitutional right to enter into contracts. Likewise, it may be suggested that since the fifth amendment protects property against expropriation without compensation, there is surely a penumbra of rights emanating from this which would include the right to acquire and enjoy the use of property without arbitrary interference by the government. I am not suggesting that the Court will arrive at these results through the application of the peripheral-emanations-penumbra idea. The only point I wish to make is that in extending the specifics to the periphery, and in finding rights derived from the total scheme of the Bill of Rights, the Court is applying essentially the same process as that used in the fundamental rights approach, but dignifying it with a different name and thereby creating the illusion of greater objectivity.

Paul C. Kauper, *Penumbras, Peripheries, Emanations, Things Fundamental and Things Forgotten: The Griswold Case*, 64 Mich. L. Rev. 235, 253 (1965).

EISENSTADT v. BAIRD
405 U.S. 438 (1972).

MR. JUSTICE BRENNAN delivered the opinion of the Court.

Appellee William Baird was convicted at a bench trial in the Massachusetts Superior Court under Massachusetts General Laws Ann., c. 272,

Section 21, first, for exhibiting contraceptive articles in the course of delivering a lecture on contraception to a group of students at Boston University and, second, for giving a young woman a package of Emko vaginal foam at the close of his address. . . .

Massachusetts General Laws Ann., c. 272, Section 21, under which Baird was convicted, provides a maximum five-year term of imprisonment for "whoever . . . gives away . . . any drug, medicine, instrument or article whatever for the prevention of conception," except as authorized in Section 21A. Under Section 21A, "[a] registered physician may administer to or prescribe for any married person drugs or articles intended for the prevention of pregnancy or conception. [And a] registered pharmacist actually engaged in the business of pharmacy may furnish such drugs or articles to any married person presenting a prescription from a registered physician." . . .

The question for our determination in this case is whether there is some ground of difference that rationally explains the different treatment accorded married and unmarried persons under Massachusetts General Laws Ann., c. 272, Sections 21 and 21A. For the reasons that follow, we conclude that no such ground exists. . . .

It would be plainly unreasonable to assume that Massachusetts has prescribed pregnancy and the birth of an unwanted child as punishment for fornication, which is a misdemeanor under Massachusetts General Laws Ann., c. 272, Section 18. Aside from the scheme of values that assumption would attribute to the State, it is abundantly clear that the effect of the ban on distribution of contraceptives to unmarried persons has at best a marginal relation to the proffered objective. What Mr. Justice Goldberg said in Griswold v. Connecticut, [concurring opinion], concerning the effect of Connecticut's prohibition on the use of contraceptives in discouraging extramarital sexual relations, is equally applicable here. "The rationality of this justification is dubious, particularly in light of the admitted widespread availability to all persons in the State of Connecticut, unmarried as well as married, of birth-control devices for the prevention of disease, as distinguished from the prevention of conception." . . .

If under *Griswold* the distribution of contraceptives to married persons cannot be prohibited, a ban on distribution to unmarried persons would be equally impermissible. It is true that in *Griswold* the right of privacy in question inhered in the marital relationship. Yet the marital couple is not an independent entity with a mind and heart of its own, but an association of two individuals each with a separate intellectual and emotional makeup. If the right of privacy means anything, it is the right of the *individual*, married or single, to be free from unwarranted governmental intrusion into matters so fundamentally affecting a person as the decision whether to bear or beget a child. See Stanley v. Georgia. See also Skinner v. Oklahoma; Jacobson v. Massachusetts.

On the other hand, if *Griswold* is no bar to a prohibition on the distribution of contraceptives, the State could not, consistently with the

Equal Protection Clause, outlaw distribution to unmarried but not to married persons. In each case the evil, as perceived by the State, would be identical, and the underinclusion would be invidious....

... We hold that by providing dissimilar treatment for married and unmarried persons who are similarly situated, Massachusetts General Laws Ann., c. 272, Sections 21 and 21A, violate the Equal Protection Clause....

MR. JUSTICE DOUGLAS, concurring.

While I join the opinion of the Court, there is for me a narrower ground for affirming the Court of Appeals. This to me is a simple First Amendment case, that amendment being applicable to the States by reason of the Fourteenth.

Under no stretch of the law as presently stated could Massachusetts require a license for those who desire to lecture on planned parenthood, contraceptives, the rights of women, birth control, or any allied subject, or place a tax on that privilege....

Had Baird not "given away" a sample of one of the devices whose use he advocated, there could be no question about the protection afforded him by the First Amendment. A State may not "contract the spectrum of available knowledge." [citing Griswold]....

First Amendment rights are not limited to verbal expression. The right to petition often involves the right to walk. The right of assembly may mean pushing or jostling. Picketing involves physical activity as well as a display of a sign. A sit-in can be a quiet, dignified protest that has First Amendment protection even though no speech is involved.... Putting contraceptives on display is certainly an aid to speech and discussion. Handing an article under discussion to a member of the audience is a technique known to all teachers and is commonly used. A handout may be on such a scale as to smack of a vendor's marketing scheme. But passing one article to an audience is merely a projection of the visual aid and should be a permissible adjunct of free speech. Baird was not making a prescription nor purporting to give medical advice. Handing out the article was not even a suggestion that the lady use it. At most it suggested that she become familiar with the product line.

I do not see how we can have a Society of the Dialogue, which the First Amendment envisages, if time-honored teaching techniques are barred to those who give educational lectures.

Notes: Minors' Access to Contraception

(1) Do minors possess a constitutional right to contraception, comparable to the right of married and unmarried adults? Minors' right to contraception access was strongly implied by the abortion case, *Planned Parenthood of Cent. Missouri v. Danforth*, 428 U.S. 52 (1976). There the Supreme Court held that "a State may not impose a blanket provision ... requiring the consent of a parent or person *in loco parentis* as a condition for abortion of an unmarried minor during the first 12 weeks of her pregnancy." *Id.* at 74. A year later, in *Carey v. Population Services International*, 431 U.S. 678

(1977), the Court affirmed the unconstitutionality of provisions of the New York Education Law making it a crime to sell or distribute contraceptives to minors under the age of sixteen. The invalidated statute had also made it unlawful for anyone other than a licensed pharmacist to distribute contraceptives to adults, and for anyone, even pharmacists, to advertise or display contraceptives.

Appellant State of New York argued that *Griswold* accorded *use* of contraceptives the status of a fundamental right, not their *distribution*. Writing for the majority, Justice Brennan responded that:

> The fatal fallacy in this argument is that it overlooks the underlying premise of those decisions that the Constitution protects "the right of the individual ... to be free from unwarranted governmental intrusion into ... the decision whether to bear or beget a child." [*Eisenstadt*, *Roe v. Wade*, and *Whalen v. Roe*] put *Griswold* in proper perspective. *Griswold* may no longer be read as holding only that a State may not prohibit a married couple's use of contraceptives. Read in the light of its progeny, the teaching of *Griswold* is that the Constitution protects individual decisions in matters of childbearing from unjustified intrusion by the State.

Restrictions on the distribution of contraceptives clearly burden the freedom to make such decisions.... Insofar as [the statute] applies to nonhazardous contraceptives, it bears no relation to the State's interest in protecting health. Nor is the interest in protecting potential life implicated in state regulation of contraceptives.

Carey, at 687–90. As for minors' rights to acquire contraceptives, the Court found that:

> ... [T]he right to privacy in connection with decisions affecting procreation extends to minors as well as adults.... State restrictions inhibiting privacy rights of minors are valid only if they serve "any significant state interest ... that is not present in the case of an adult." ...

> Since the state may not impose a blanket prohibition, or even a blanket requirement of parental consent, on the choice of a minor to terminate her pregnancy, the constitutionality of a blanket prohibition of the distribution of contraceptives to minors is *a fortiori* foreclosed. The State's interests in protection of the mental and physical health of the pregnant minor, and in protection of potential life are clearly more implicated by the abortion decision than by the decision to use a nonhazardous contraception.

Id. at 693–94.

New York argued that "advertisements of contraceptive products would be offensive and embarrassing to those exposed to them, and that permitting them would legitimize sexual activity of young people." Brennan rejoined that "these are classically not justifications validating the suppression of [commercial] expression protected by the First Amendment." And,

> ... As for the possible "legitimation" of illicit sexual behavior, whatever might be the case if the advertisements directly incited

illicit sexual activity among the young, none of the advertisements in this record can even remotely be characterized as "directed to inciting or producing imminent lawless action and . . . likely to incite or produce such action."

Id. at 701. Often over-simplified in the advocacy context, the motives and social contexts of teenage pregnancy are still or partly understood. Cf. Judith S. Musick, *Young, Poor and pregnant: The Psychology of Teenage Motherhood* (1993); Nancy Chodorow, The Reproduction of Mothering: Psychoanalysis and the Sociology of Gender (1978). After *Carey* minors clearly have a right to acquire contraceptives. States are not obligated, however, to provide contraception for minors who could not otherwise afford it; nor are states required to permit the distribution of contraceptives in public high schools.

Notes: Birth Control Technology and Safety

(1) Once the Court cleared away legal barriers to the use, distribution and advertising of contraceptives, the pharmaceutical industry presented consumers in every state with a growing array of birth control products. Condoms, topical spermicides, and diaphragms provided relatively low cost birth control with few health risks. The major drawbacks of these products was their inconvenience and high rate of failure—sexually active women still exposed themselves to significant risk of unwanted pregnancy. Studies indicate that 20% to 30% of the women who use diaphragms and contraceptive sponges become pregnant.

The oral contraceptive hit the mass market in the early 1960s. Viewed in some quarters as a miracle drug, "the pill" provided easy to use, highly reliable protection against pregnancy. Available by prescription, women taking oral contraceptives were required to ingest one tiny tablet for 21 consecutive days each month.

Very early versions of the oral contraceptive contained higher doses of estrogen than necessary to prevent pregnancy. Women complained of weight gain, headache and emotional changes. A few deaths from cardiovascular complications were attributed to the birth control pill. Although subsequently developed oral contraceptives have had a good record of safety, use of the pill may increase some women's risk of blood clotting, heart disease and certain cancers. A major long-term study reported in January 1999 showed no overall increase in the incidence of cancer, stroke or heart disease among women who used oral contraceptives for ten years.

The intrauterine device, the "IUD," emerged as a popular form of birth control in the 1960s and 1970s. Nearly as effective as oral contraceptives, it seemed for a while to pose fewer health risks. Litigation brought by users of the "Dalkon Shield" IUD greatly reduced the supply of—and demand for—intrauterine devices in the United States. In thousands of suits filed against Dalkon Shield manufacturer A.H. Robins, its insurer Aetna Casualty and Surety Company, hospitals, and physicians, plaintiffs alleged that the defective design of the IUD led to pelvic inflammatory disease, sterility or death. Plaintiffs injured in the 1970s recovered punitive damage awards as high as $9 million. In 1985, after paying out over $500 million in claims, A.H. Robins filed for bankruptcy under Chapter 11 of the federal Bankruptcy Code. Litigation resulted in the creation of a $2.48 billion trust from which Dalkon

Shield victims could be compensated. Nearly 200,000 eventual claims on the funds were anticipated.

By 1990 public and private research spending on birth control had declined. The number of firms manufacturing contraceptives dramatically decreased. But the industry remained profitable. The sale of oral contraceptives alone reached $900,000,000 in 1988, with Ortho Pharmaceutical Corporation and Wyeth–Ayerst Laboratories holding the largest shares of the market. Industry observers cited fear of product liability lawsuits and political boycotts as factors countermanding investment in research. Still, research on a few new oral contraceptives and sub-dermal contraceptive implants was reported as patent protection for older products began to run out and government studies linked oral contraceptives to an increased risk of breast cancer. The Food and Drug Administration approved a product called "Norplant," the first sub-dermal implant, for commercial use late in 1990.

Soon after Norplant appeared on the market in 1990, a judge in Visalia, California ordered that a 27–year old African American woman who pled guilty to child abuse use the novel drug as a condition of her probation. See Steven S. Spitz, *The Norplant Debate: Birth Control or Woman Control?* 25 Colum. Hum. Rits. L. Rev. 131 (1993); Kristyn M. Walker, *Judicial Control of Reproductive Freedom: The Use of Norplant as a Condition of Probation*, 78 Iowa L. Rev. 779 (1993).

Norplant consists of five matchbook-sized tubes of a pharmaceutical contraceptive inserted under the skin of a woman's upper arm in a fan-shaped pattern. Norplant provides several years of potentially "care free" contraceptive protection. Although many believed Norplant would prove popular, consumer interest in the drug waned substantially after only a few years. The process of inserting, arranging and removing Norplant proved tedious for busy physicians, nurses and patients; the process sometimes caused pain, discomfort and scarring. Some woman using the drug reported unpleasant side affects and embarrassment when the implanted tubes of medication were detected by others through the skin.

(2) In the 1980s a drug developed in France by Etienne–Emile Baulieu, known as mifepristone or RU 486 (after manufacturer Roussel Uclaf) was heralded as a breakthrough in family planning. Surgical abortion has been legal in France since 1975. RU 486 has been legal in France since 1988 when it was described by French Minister of Health Claude Evin as "the moral property of women, not just the property of the drug company."

(3) Abortion rights opponents disparage mifepristone as an "abortion pill" because it acts to expel fertilized eggs from the womb. The initial effort to bring an "abortion pill" to the United States with Food and Drug Administration was clouded by concerns among abortion rights opponents and proponents that the drug might have undisclosed side effects or risks. When used with prostaglandins and under close medical supervision, RU 486 established a record of safety in clinical studies in Europe. Safe for the overwhelming majority of users, a study suggests that one case of RU 486 usage in 1000 will result in side affects ranging from dizziness, nausea, and

painful contractions to hemorrhaging requiring hospitalization and blood transfusions. U.S. trials of mifepristone are expected to yield an equivalent or better safety record.

(4) Read narrowly, *Griswold* invalidated state laws erecting barriers to access to the use of nonhazardous contraception. The case left open for *Roe v. Wade* the question of whether states may prohibit abortion. Arguably, the principle behind *Griswold* is privacy protection for decisions about whether to remain pregnant as well as decisions about whether to become pregnant. However, preventing pregnancy and ending pregnancy are often thought to pose very different regulatory issues. Even the courts have sometimes assumed that abortion implicates the state's interest in unborn life and women's psychological well-being in ways contraception does not.

A regulatory scheme that aims to take a permissive stance toward contraception and a prohibitive stance toward abortion encounters an important difficulty: how to distinguish between contraception and abortion. Some regard the moment an egg is fertilized as conception. However, the American College of Obstetricians and Gynecologists defines conception, not as fertilization, but as implantation. Following this definition, a device or chemical that prevented ovulation or fertilization is a contraceptive, but so is a device or chemical that acted to block the successful implantation of a fertilized egg.

Many birth control devices labeled "contraception" act against the implantation of fertilized eggs. Although the birth control pill generally succeeds at preventing ovulation, ovulation sometimes occurs in pill users and fertilized eggs are expelled from the body with menstruation. Widely regarded as a contraceptive device, the IUD may actually function in many instances by rendering the uterine wall inhospitable to a fertilized egg—it may abort pregnancy in its very earliest stages rather than prevent conception.

Dr. Baulieu has urged the public (without success) to regard RU 486 as neither contraception nor abortion, but rather "contragestation." "Contragestation" denotes the action of the drug in blocking the chemical events needed to permit any fertilized egg which may be present in the uterus following sexual intercourse from attaching itself to the uterine wall. Dr. Baulieu has denied that contragestation is baby-killing, in either moral or physical terms.

Compare mifepristone to another drug currently under use in the United States for early abortions, methotrexate. This drug was originally approved by the FDA as a cancer treatment. Physicians prescribe methotrexate for the treatment of cancer, psoriasis and arthritis. When injected into a pregnant woman, the drug will halt embryo cell division, terminating pregnancy within a few days time. Advocates of non-surgical abortions using drugs like mifepristone and methotrexate say such abortions enhance women's privacy by eliminating both the need for a physically invasive procedure and the need for a trip to an abortion specialty clinic. Whereas first trimester surgical abortions take only a few minutes to complete, however, medical abortions by pill or injection require up to a week to complete, during which time cramping and bleeding may occur.

Is one likely to escape the politics of the abortion debate in the United States by characterizing mifepristone as "contragestation" rather than abortion?

2. ABORTION

When and how did American law come to include the abortion bans that *Roe v. Wade* would invalidate? Professor Rhode provides a little history. See also, Ricki Solinger (ed.), *Abortion Wars: A Half Century of Struggle*, 1950–2000 (1998); Reva Siegel, *Reasoning from the Body: A Historical Perspective on Abortion Regulation and Questions of Equal Protection*, 44 Stanford L. Rev. 261 (1992).

DEBRA RHODE, JUSTICE AND GENDER

202–207 (1989).

... Early English and American common law followed the view [of Christian theologians that the fetus did not acquire a soul until it had "quickened," that is, until it had begun to move of its own accord].

This doctrinal development had practical as well as spiritual underpinnings. Until the point of fetal movement, medical knowledge was not sophisticated enough to determine whether a woman was definitely pregnant. The first American statutes, enacted between 1820 and 1840, typically codified case law and prohibited only post-quickening abortions. Although a second wave of legislation between 1840 and 1860 was more inclusive, enforcement remained lax. Since early court decisions placed high burdens of proof on prosecutors, even statutes that did not distinguish in theory between early and late abortions often did so in practice.

Various cultural trends that began in the mid-nineteenth century contributed to a more stringent regulatory climate. Increased advertising of birth control and abortion made these practices even more visible; expanded opportunities for women outside the domestic sphere made such techniques more desirable. The shift from rural to urban industrial society meant that large numbers of children were no longer an economic asset but rather an impediment to a family's rising standard of living. As middle-and upper-middle class Protestant wives increasingly turned to abortion and contraception as a means of limiting fertility, the resulting decline in birth rates sparked widespread concern. At the end of the century, estimates suggest that almost three-quarters of women practiced some method of fertility control, and that the ratio of abortions to live births was between one to three and one to five. As a result, the birth rate was about half of what it had been in 1800.

Opposition to these abortion and contraception practices reflected various concerns. Some critics feared that any separation of sex from procreation would result in increased venereal disease, psychological "derange[ment]," and social instability. The decline in fertility among the "better" classes coupled with substantial population growth among immigrants, prompted fears of "race suicide." ...

... [L]eaders of the organized medical profession had special reasons for mobilizing against abortion. The issue provided doctors with a means of asserting technical, ethical, and social superiority over their competitors, particularly midwives and other practitioners who had not

graduated from approved educational programs.... By lobbying for
statutes that prohibited abortions unless necessary to save the life of the
mother, the organized medical profession could criminalize much of its
competition.

The crusade was largely effective.... In 1873 Congress passed the
Comstock Law, which prohibited dissemination of information about
abortion or contraception. Over the next several decades, all but one
state made abortion a felony, and such statutes remained largely un-
changed until the late 1960s....

Legal restraints on birth control gradually weakened in response to
various cultural forces.... The military's distribution of condoms to
prevent venereal disease during World War I increased the supply and
ultimately the demand for such products. Liberalization of sexual mores
in the post-World War I era further expanded the market. Other factors
contributed to that trend; opportunities for nonmarital sexual contacts
in automobiles, dance halls and the like during the 1920s; greater
economic pressures to curtail fertility during the Depression in the
thirties; and increased female labor-force participation in the forties and
fifties. After 1960 the availability of an oral contraceptive helped liberal-
ize public attitudes and practices, and concerns over global overpopula-
tion had similar effects. [By 1967] federal agencies were spending close
to 30 million dollars on contraceptive programs at home and abroad.

Beginning in the mid–1960s, the Supreme Court issued a series of
decisions that reflected and reinforced these trends.

ROE v. WADE
410 U.S. 113 (1973).

[Note: This is one of the best known Supreme Court decisions of all
time. The Court held that states may not ban abortion. "Jane Roe"—
Norma McCorvey—was a poor Dallas woman who had allegedly become
pregnant as a result of rape. A Texas statute criminalized abortion and
provided for prison terms of up to 10 years. Unable to obtain a legal
abortion in Texas, McCorvey carried the pregnancy to term and placed
the child for adoption. In her landmark law suit against the State of
Texas, she was joined by plaintiffs "John and Mary Doe," a married
couple, and a Dr. Hallford, a licensed physician. They alleged that the
Texas abortion statute violated rights of personal privacy protected by
the First, Fourth, Fifth, Ninth, and Fourteenth Amendments. The Court
invalidated the Texas statute under a streamlined Fourteenth amendment analysis.]

MR. JUSTICE BLACKMUN delivered the opinion of the Court.

. . .

The principal thrust of appellant's attack on the Texas statutes is
that they improperly invade a right, said to be possessed by the pregnant
woman, to choose to terminate her pregnancy. Appellant would discover

this right in the concept of personal "liberty" embodied in the Fourteenth Amendment's Due Process Clause; or in personal, marital, familial, and sexual privacy said to be protected by the Bill of Rights or its penumbras, see Griswold v. Connecticut; Eisenstadt v. Baird; *id.*, at 460 (White, J., concurring in result); or among those rights reserved to the people by the Ninth Amendment, Griswold v. Connecticut, 381 U.S. at 486 (Goldberg. J., concurring). Before addressing this claim, we feel it desirable briefly to survey, in several aspects, the history of abortion, for such insight as that history may afford us, and then to examine the state purposes and interests behind the criminal abortion laws....

It is thus apparent that at common law, at the time of the adoption of our Constitution, and throughout the major portion of the 19th century, abortion was viewed with less disfavor than under most American statutes currently in effect. Phrasing it another way, a woman enjoyed a substantially broader right to terminate a pregnancy than she does in most States today. At least with respect to the early stage of pregnancy, and very possibly without such a limitation, the opportunity to make this choice was present in this country well into the 19th century. Even later, the law continued for some time to treat less punitively an abortion procured in early pregnancy.

... When most criminal abortion laws were first enacted, the procedure was a hazardous one for the woman. This was particularly true prior to the development of antiseptics. Antiseptic techniques, of course, were based on discoveries by Lister, Pasteur, and others first announced in 1867, but were not generally accepted and employed until about the turn of the century. Abortion mortality was high. Even after 1900, and perhaps until as late as the development of antibiotics in the 1940's, standard modern techniques such as dilation and curettage were not nearly so safe as they are today. Thus, it has been argued that a State's real concern in enacting a criminal abortion law was to protect the pregnant woman, that is, to restrain her from submitting to a procedure that placed her life in serious jeopardy.

Modern medical techniques have altered this situation. Appellants and various *amici* refer to medical data indicating that abortion in early pregnancy, that is, prior to the end of the first trimester, although not without its risk, is now relatively safe. Mortality rates for women undergoing early abortions, where the procedure is legal appear to be as low as or lower than the rates for normal childbirth. Consequently, any interest of the State in protecting the woman from an inherently hazardous procedure, except when it would be equally dangerous for her to forgo it, has largely disappeared. Of course, important state interests in the area of health and medical standards do remain. The State has legitimate interest in seeing to it that abortion, like any other medical procedure, is performed under circumstances that insure maximum safety for the patient. This interest obviously extends at least to the performing physician and his staff, to the facilities involved, to the availability of after-care, and to adequate provision for any complication or emergency that might arise. The prevalence of high mortality rates at illegal "abortion mills" strengthens, rather than weakens, the State's interest in regulating the conditions under which abortions are performed. Moreover, the risk to the woman increases as her pregnancy continues. Thus, the State retains a definite interest in protecting the woman's own health and safety when an abortion is proposed at a late stage of pregnancy.

. . . The State's interest and general obligation to protect life then extends, it is argued, to prenatal life. Only when the life of the pregnant mother herself is at stake, balanced against the life she carries within her, should the interest of the embryo or fetus not prevail. Logically, of course, a legitimate state interest in this area need not stand or fall on acceptance of the belief that life begins at conception or at some other point prior to live birth. In assessing the State's interest, recognition may be given to the less rigid claim that as long as at least *potential* life is involved, the State may assert interests beyond the protection of the pregnant woman alone.

The Constitution does not explicitly mention any right of privacy. In a line of decisions, however, going back perhaps as far as Union Pacific R. Co. v. Botsford, 141 U.S. 250, 251 (1891), the Court has recognized that a right of personal privacy, or a guarantee of certain areas or zones of privacy, does exist under the Constitution. In varying contexts, the Court or individual Justices have, indeed, found at least the roots of that right in the First Amendment, Stanley v. Georgia; in the Fourth and Fifth Amendments, Terry v. Ohio, Katz v. United States; Boyd v. United States, see Olmstead v. United States, (Brandeis J., dissenting); in the penumbras of the Bill of Rights, Griswold v. Connecticut; in the Ninth Amendment, *id.,* (Goldberg. J., concurring); or in the concept of liberty guaranteed by the first section of the Fourteenth Amendment, see Meyer v. Nebraska. These decisions make it clear that only personal rights that can be deemed "fundamental" or "implicit in the concept of ordered liberty," Palko v. Connecticut, are included in this guarantee of personal privacy. They also make it clear that the right has some extension to activities relating to marriage, Loving v. Virginia; procreation, Skinner v. Oklahoma; contraception, Eisenstadt v. Baird, (White J., concurring in result); family relationships, Prince v. Massachusetts, 321 U.S. 158, 166 (1944); and child rearing and education, Pierce v. Society of Sisters, Meyer v. Nebraska, *supra.*

This right of privacy, whether it be founded in the Fourteenth Amendment's concept of personal liberty and restrictions upon state action, as we feel it is, or, as the District Court determined, in the Ninth Amendment's reservation of rights to the people, is broad enough to encompass a woman's decision whether or not to terminate her pregnancy. The detriment that the State would impose upon the pregnant woman by denying this choice altogether is apparent. Specific and direct harm medically diagnosable even in early pregnancy may be involved. Maternity, or additional off-spring, may force upon the woman a distressful life and future. Psychological harm may be imminent. Mental and physical health may be taxed by child care. There is also the distress, for all concerned, associated with the unwanted child, and there is the problem of bringing a child into a family already unable, psychologically and otherwise, to care for it. In other cases, as in this one, the additional difficulties and continuing stigma of unwed motherhood may be involved. All these are factors the woman and her responsible physician necessarily will consider in consultation.

On the basis of elements such as these, appellant and some *amici* argue that the woman's right is absolute and that she is entitled to terminate her pregnancy at whatever time, in whatever way, and for whatever reason she alone chooses. With this we do not agree. Appellant's arguments that Texas either has no valid interest at all in regulating the abortion decision, or no interest strong enough to support any limitation upon the woman's sole determination are unpersuasive. The Court's decisions recognizing a right of privacy also acknowledge that some state regulation in areas protected by that right is appropriate. As noted above, a State may properly assert important interests in safeguarding health, in maintaining medical standards, and in protecting potential life. At some point in pregnancy, these respective interests become sufficiently compelling to sustain regulation of the factors that govern the abortion decision. The privacy right involved, therefore, cannot be said to be absolute. . . .

Where certain "fundamental rights" are involved, the Court has held that regulation limiting these rights may be justified only by a "compelling state interest," Kramer v. Union Free School District, 395 U.S. 621, 627 (1969); Shapiro v. Thompson, 394 U.S. 618, 634 (1969), Sherbert v. Verner, 374 U.S. 398, 406 (1963), and that legislative enactments must be narrowly drawn to express only the legitimate state interests at stake. Griswold v. Connecticut; . . . see Eisenstadt v. Baird, (White, J., concurring in result). . . .

A. The appellee and certain *amici* argue that the fetus is a "person" within the language and meaning of the Fourteenth Amendment. In support of this, they outline at length and in detail the well-known facts of fetal development. If this suggestion of personhood is established, the appellant's case of course, collapses, for the fetus' right to life would then be guaranteed specifically by the Amendment. The appellant conceded as much on reargument. On the other hand, the appellee conceded on reargument that no case could be cited that holds that a fetus is a person within the meaning of the Fourteenth Amendment.

The Constitution does not define "person" in so many words. Section 1 of the Fourteenth Amendment contains three references to "person." The first, in defining "citizens," speaks of "persons born or naturalized in the United States." The word also appears both in the Due Process Clause and in the Equal Protection Clause. "Person" is used in other places in the Constitution: in the listing of qualifications for Representatives and Senators; in the Apportionment Clause; in the Migration and Importation provision; in the Emolument Clause; in the provision outlining qualifications for the office of President; in the

Extradition provisions, and the superseded Fugitive Slave Clause; and in the Fifth, Twelfth, and Twenty-second Amendments, as well as in ... the Fourteenth Amendment. But in nearly all these instances, the use of the word is such that it has application only postnatally. None indicates, with any assurance, that it has any possible pre-natal application.

All this, together with our observation, *supra*, that throughout the major portion of the 19th century prevailing legal abortion practices were far freer than they are today, persuades us that the word "person," as used in the Fourteenth Amendment, does not include the unborn....

B. The pregnant woman cannot be isolated in her privacy. She carries an embryo and, later, a fetus, if one accepts the medical definitions of the developing young in the human uterus. See *Dorland's Illustrated Medical Dictionary* 478–479, 547 (24th ed. 1965). The situation therefore is inherently different from marital intimacy, or bedroom possession of obscene material, or marriage, or procreation, or education, with which *Eisenstadt*, and *Griswold*, *Stanley*, *Loving*, *Skinner*, and *Pierce*, and *Meyer* were respectively concerned. As we have intimated above, it is reasonable and appropriate for a State to decide that at some point in time another interest, that of health of the mother or that of potential human life, becomes significantly involved. The woman's privacy is no longer sole and any right of privacy she possesses must be measured accordingly.

Texas urges that, apart from the Fourteenth Amendment, life begins at conception and is present throughout pregnancy, and that, therefore, the State has a compelling interest in protecting that life from and after conception. We need not resolve the difficult question of when life begins. When those trained in the respective disciplines of medicine, philosophy, and theology are unable to arrive at any consensus, the judiciary at this point in the development of man's knowledge, is not in a position to speculate as to the answer....

In areas other than criminal abortion, the law has been reluctant to endorse any theory that life, as we recognize it, begins before live birth or to accord legal rights to the unborn except in narrowly defined situations and except when the rights are contingent upon live birth. For example, the traditional rule of tort law denied recovery for prenatal injuries even though the child was born alive. That rule has been changed in almost every jurisdiction. In most States, recovery is said to be permitted only if the fetus was viable, or at least quick, when the injuries were sustained, though few courts have squarely so held. In a recent development, generally opposed by the commentators, some States permit the parents of a stillborn child to maintain an action for wrongful death because of prenatal injuries. Such an action, however, would appear to be one to vindicate the parents' interest and is thus consistent with the view that the fetus, at most, represents only the potentiality of life. Similarly, unborn children have been recognized as acquiring rights or interests by way of inheritance or other devolution of property and have been represented by guardians *ad litem*. Perfection of the interests involved, again, has generally been contingent upon live birth. In short, the unborn have never been recognized in the law as persons in the whole sense.

In view of all this, we do not agree that, by adopting one theory of life, Texas may override the rights of the pregnant woman that are at stake. We repeat, however, that the State does have an important and legitimate interest in preserving and protecting the health of the pregnant woman, whether she be a resident of the State or a nonresident who seeks medical consultation and treatment there, and that it has still *another* important and legitimate interest in protecting the potentiality of human life. These interests are separate and distinct. Each grows in substantiality as the woman approaches term and, at a point during pregnancy, each becomes "compelling."

With respect to the State's important and legitimate interest in the health of the mother, the "compelling" point, in the light of present medical knowledge, is at approximately the end of the first trimester. This is so because of the now-established medical fact, referred to above . . . , that until the end of the first trimester mortality in abortion may be less than mortality in normal childbirth. It follows that, from and after this point, a State may regulate the abortion procedure to the extent that the regulation reasonably relates to the preservation and protection of maternal health. Examples of permissible state regulation in this area are requirements as to the qualifications of the person who is to perform the abortion; as to the licensure of that person; as to the facility in which the procedure is to be performed, that is, whether it must be a hospital or may be a clinic or some other place of less-than-hospital status; as to the licensing of the facility; and the like.

This means, on the other hand, that for the period of pregnancy prior to this "compelling" point, the attending physician, in consultation with his patient, is free to determine, without regulation by the State, that, in his medical judgment, the patient's pregnancy should be terminated. If that decision is reached, the judgment may be effectuated by an abortion free of interference by the State.

With respect to the State's important and legitimate interest in potential life, the "compelling" point is at viability. This is so because the fetus then presumably has the capability of meaningful life outside the mother's womb. State regulation protective of fetal life after viability thus has both logical and biological justifications. If the State is interested in protecting fetal life after viability, it may go so far as to proscribe abortion during that period, except when it is necessary to preserve the life or health of the mother. . . .

To summarize and to repeat:

1.   A state criminal abortion statute of the current Texas type, that excepts from criminality only a *life-saving* procedure on behalf of the mother, without regard to pregnancy stage and without recognition of the other interests involved, is violative of the Due Process Clause of the Fourteenth Amendment.

(a) For the stage prior to approximately the end of the first trimester, the abortion decision and its effectuation must be left to the medical judgment of the pregnant woman's attending physician.

(b) For the stage subsequent to approximately the end of the first trimester, the State, in promoting its interest in the health of the mother, may, if it chooses, regulate the abortion procedure in ways that are reasonably related to maternal health.

(c) For the stage subsequent to viability, the State in promoting its interest in the potentiality of human life may, if it chooses, regulate, and even proscribe, abortion except where it is necessary, in appropriate medical judgment, for the preservation of the life or health of the mother.

2. The State may define the term "physician," as it has been employed in the preceding paragraphs of this Part XI of this opinion, to mean only a physician currently licensed by the State, and may proscribe any abortion by a person who is not a physician as so defined. . . .

MR. JUSTICE REHNQUIST, dissenting. . . .

. . . I have difficulty in concluding, as the Court does, that the right of "privacy" is involved in this case. Texas, by the statute here challenged, bars the performance of a medical abortion by a licensed physician on a plaintiff such as Roe. A transaction resulting in an operation such as this is not "private" in the ordinary usage of that word. Nor is the "privacy" that the Court finds here even a distant relative of the freedom from searches and seizures protected by the Fourth Amendment to the Constitution, which the Court has referred to as embodying a right to privacy.

If the Court means by the term "privacy" no more than that the claim of a person to be free from unwanted state regulation of consensual transactions may be a form of "liberty" protected by the Fourteenth Amendment, there is no doubt that similar claims have been upheld in our earlier decisions on the basis of that liberty. . . . But that liberty is not guaranteed absolutely against deprivation, only against deprivation without due process of law. The test traditionally applied in the area of social and economic legislation is whether or not a law such as that challenged has a rational relation to a valid state objective. . . . The Due Process Clause of the Fourteenth Amendment undoubtedly does place a limit, albeit a broad one, on legislative power to enact laws such as this. If the Texas statute were to prohibit an abortion even where the mother's life is in jeopardy, I have little doubt that such a statute would lack a rational relation to a valid state objective under the test stated in Williamson. . . .

. . . As in *Lochner* and similar cases applying substantive due process standards to economic and social welfare legislation, the adoption of the compelling state interest standard will inevitably require this Court to examine the legislative policies and pass on the wisdom of these policies in the very process of deciding whether a particular state interest put forward may or may not be "compelling." The decision here to break pregnancy into three distinct terms and to outline the permissible restrictions the State may impose in each one, for example, partakes more of judicial legislation than it does of a determination of the intent of the drafters of the Fourteenth Amendment.

Note: Roe v. Wade and Doe v. Bolton

In the companion case to *Roe v. Wade* decided the same day, *Doe v. Bolton*, 410 U.S. 179 (1973), the Supreme Court addressed another set of criminal abortion laws, these from Georgia. Because the statutes were based on the American Law Institute's Model Penal Code and were similar to laws enacted in one quarter of the states, the Court addressed them separately from those struck down in *Roe*.

The Georgia statute imposed fewer restrictions on abortion than the categorically prohibitive Texas statute invalidated in *Roe*. The Georgia statute permitted abortions performed "in the best clinical judgment" of a physician, where pregnancy would endanger the woman's life or "seriously and permanently injure her health"; the fetus would be born with "grave, permanent, and irremediable mental or physical defect[s]"; or "[t]he pregnancy resulted from forcible or statutory rape." 410 U.S. at 183. The District Court, anticipating *Roe*'s holding, granted the plaintiff relief with regard to the limitations on when she could permissibly choose an abortion and thus invalidated those portions of the statute forbidding abortions except in the three situations outlined. *Id.* at 186. But the trial court refused to invalidate those portions of the statute that regulated the manner and location for the performance of abortions. It upheld (1) residency requirements for would-be abortion patients, (2) requirements that all abortions be performed in accredited hospitals, and (3) procedures requiring that all abortions be approved in advance by hospital staff committees and physicians.

In the Supreme Court, Justice Blackmun writing for the majority reiterated *Roe*'s "conclusion that a pregnant woman does not have an absolute constitutional right to an abortion on her own demand." *Id.* at 189. The court struck down several provisions regarding accreditation of the facility, three doctors' concurrence, and review of abortion decisions by hospital committees as not "reasonably related" to the safety or necessity of the abortion. *Id.* at 194, 198, 200. However, the Court went on to uphold the portion of the statute requiring that one doctor certify to the necessity of the abortion and reemphasized the paramount role it found for medical care providers in *Roe*.

Together, *Roe v. Wade* and *Doe v. Bolton* announced a constitutional right of medical abortion for women who could afford to pay for it. In the months and years after these decisions the Court's action was praised for ushering in a future of increased moral autonomy and social equality for women:

> The traditional condemnation of abortion fails, at a deep ethical level, to take seriously the moral independence of women as free and rational persons, lending the force of law to theological ideas of biological naturalness and gender hierarchy that degrade the constructive moral powers of women themselves to establish the mean-

ing of their sexual and reproductive life histories. The underlying conception appears to be not discontinuous with the sexist idea that women's minds and bodies are not their own, but the property of others, namely, men or their masculine God, who may use them and their bodies for the greater good. The abortion choice is thus one of the choices essential to the just moral independence of women, centering their lives in a body image and aspirations expressive of their moral powers.

David A.J. Richards, *Toleration and the Constitution*, 268 (1986).

But the Court was condemned as well, for endorsing "infanticide" and devaluing of women's unique biological capacity. In the eyes of some, abortion remains "a radical invasion of the woman's body," a kind of unnatural "mutilation," and, at the very least, the "denial of one of those powers which make women women." *See* Paige C. Cunningham, *Pro Life: Is Abortion a Women's Issue?*, 5 Update on Law–Related Education 6, 46 (Fall 1981) (quoting Janet E. Smith, *Abortion as a Feminist Concern*, 4 Hum. Life Rev. 62, 67 (1978)). Far from being an advance for women, some critics viewed abortion rights as a step backward. Where some saw "freedom of choice" for women, others saw "freedom from responsibility" for sexually active men, women and the male-dominated medical establishment.

Judges and lawyers who opposed *Roe* and *Doe* expressed concern about the implications of these cases for constitutional jurisprudence and the role of the Courts. Even a sympathetic academic observer like David A.J. Richards, *supra*, could see that the right to privacy doctrine of *Roe* posed a conundrum: "How can constitutional privacy, a right which is not textually rooted in any clause of the written constitution, be inferred with judicial fidelity to the interpretation of the terms of the Constitution?" Moreover, "assuming the right is textually based in some form, how can such textual inference b[e] squared with the basic premises of the political theory of democratic self-rule that sharply limit the scope of proper judicial invalidation of majority rule?" Id. Another academic critic, John Hart Ely, *infra*, described *Roe's* constitutional privacy argument as "frightening."

Notes: The Legacy of Lochner

Justice Rehnquist blasted the detailed trimester analysis of abortion rights included in the *Roe* decision as "judicial legislation" of an abortion code. Some legal scholars agreed and further condemned *Roe v. Wade* and *Griswold v. Connecticut* as a return to the disfavored approach of *Lochner v. New York*, 198 U.S. 45 (1905). *See, e.g.*, John Hart Ely, *The Wages of Crying Wolf: A Comment on Roe v. Wade*, 82 Yale L.J. 920 (1973), *infra*, p. 639. On the face of it, *Roe* and *Griswold* have little in common with *Lochner*, a case in which the Supreme Court invalidated a New York statute establishing maximum hour limitations on the weekly employment of bakers. Justice Douglas took pains in *Griswold* to distinguish the jurisprudence of fundamental privacy from the jurisprudence of *Lochner*, but to no avail.

The holding of *Lochner* has come to symbolize substantive judicial intervention premised on constitutional principles of due process, property rights and liberty. *Cf.* Cass R. Sunstein, *Lochner's Legacy*, 87 Colum. L. Rev.

873 (1987); Laurence H. Tribe, *The Puzzling Persistence of Process–Based Constitutional Theories*, 89 Yale L.J. 1063 (1980); McCloskey, *Economic Due Process and the Supreme Court: An Exhumation and Reburial*, 1962 Sup. Ct. Rev. 54. For more than thirty years after *Lochner*, the Court frequently engaged in substantive analysis of state and federal legislation regulating economic relations. The Court as an institution met with severe criticism during the *Lochner* era. To further the social and economic goals of the New Deal, President Franklin D. Roosevelt attempted to undercut judicial "Lochnerizing" through a failed "court packing" plan. New appointments to the Court and changes of position by some Justices eventually produced *West Coast Hotel v. Parrish*, 300 U.S. 379 (1937). In that decision, Chief Justice Hughes, and Justices Roberts, Brandeis, Cardozo, and Stone upheld a minimum wage law for women and children constitutional, effectively bringing an end to a generation of *Lochner-style* substantive assessment of legislation enacted pursuant to federal and state police powers.

Lochner is one of the most thoroughly discredited decisions of the Supreme Court. Yet, while there is general agreement that the Court went wrong, there is a great deal of disagreement about precisely how it went wrong. If there is a leading view, it probably is that the primary evil of *Lochner* was in the attempt by the Court to, "fasten on the country . . . a pattern of [laissez faire] economic regulation believed by the Court to be essential to the fullest development of the nation's economy." Only Justice Holmes, in dissent, clearly isolated the view. *See generally*, Bernard H. Siegan, *Economic Liberties and the Constitution* 23 (1980); Frank R. Strong, *The Economic Philosophy of Lochner: Emergence, Embrasure and Emasculation*, 15 Ariz. L. Rev. 419 (1973); Sunstein, *Naked Preferences and the Constitution*, 84 Colum. L. Rev. 1689, 1697, 1718 (1984); Laurence H. Tribe, *Foreward: Toward a Model of Rules in the Due Process of Life and Law*, 87 Harv. L. Rev. 1 (1973).

The pair of excerpts that follow are contrasting perspectives on the legitimacy of the *Roe* decision in light of the legacy of *Lochner*.

JOHN HART ELY, THE WAGES OF CRYING WOLF: A COMMENT ON ROE v. WADE

82 Yale L.J. 920, 923–44 (1973).

Let us not underestimate what is at stake: Having an unwanted child can go a long way toward ruining a woman's life. And at bottom *Roe* signals the Court's judgment that this result cannot be justified by any good that anti-abortion legislation accomplishes. This surely is an understandable conclusion—indeed it is one with which I agree—but ordinarily the Court claims no mandate to second-guess legislative balances, at least not when the Constitution has designated neither of the values in conflict as entitled to special protection. But even assuming it would be a good idea for the Court to assume this function, *Roe* seems a curious place to have begun. Laws prohibiting the use of "soft" drugs or, even more obviously, homosexual acts between consenting adults can stunt "the preferred life styles" of those against whom enforcement is threatened in very serious ways. It is clear such acts harm no one besides the participants, and indeed the case that the participants are harmed is a rather shaky one. Yet such laws survive, on the theory that there exists a societal consensus that the behavior involved is revolting or at any rate immoral. Of course the consensus is not universal but it is sufficient, and this is what is counted crucial, to get the laws passed and keep them on the books. Whether anti-abortion legislation cramps the life style of an unwilling mother more significantly than anti-homosexuality legislation cramps the life style of a homosexual is a close question. But even granting that it does, the *other* side of the balance looks very different. For there is more than simple societal revulsion to support legislation restricting abortion: Abortion ends (or if it makes a difference, prevents) the life of a human being other than the one making the choice. . . .

. . . The Burger Court, like the Warren Court before it, has been especially solicitous of the right to travel from state to state, demanding a compelling state interest if it is to be inhibited. Yet nowhere in the Constitution is such a right mentioned. It is, however, as clear as such things can be that this right was one the framers intended to protect, most specifically by the Privileges and Immunities Clause of Article IV. The right is, moreover, plausibly inferable from the system of government, and the citizen's role therein, contemplated by the Constitution. The Court in *Roe* suggests an inference of neither sort—from the intent of the framers, or from the governmental system contemplated by the Constitution—in support of the constitutional right to an abortion.

What the Court does assert is that there is a general right of privacy granted special protection—that is, protection above and beyond the baseline requirement of "rationality"—by the Fourteenth Amendment, and that that right "is broad enough to encompass" the right to an abortion. . . .

[The physical, psychological and economic burden of pregnancy] ought to be taken very seriously. But it has nothing to do with privacy in the Bill of Rights sense or any other the Constitution suggests. I suppose there is nothing to prevent one from using the word "privacy" to mean the freedom to live one's life without governmental interference. But the Court obviously does not so use the term. Nor could it, for such a right is at stake in *every* case. Our life styles are constantly limited, often seriously, by governmental regulation; and while many of us would prefer less direction, granting that desire the status of a preferred constitutional right would yield a system of "government" virtually unrecognizable to us and only slightly more recognizable to our forefathers. . . .

But perhaps the inquiry should not end even there. In his famous *Carolene Products* footnote, Justice Stone suggested that the interests to which the Court can responsibly give extraordinary constitutional protection include not only those expressed in the Constitution but also those that are unlikely to receive adequate consideration in the political process, specifically the interests of "discrete and insular minorities" unable to form effective political alliances. There can be little doubt that such considerations have influenced the direction, if only occasionally the rhetoric, of the recent Courts. My repeated efforts to convince my students that sex should be treated as a "suspect classification" have convinced me it is no easy matter to state such considerations in a "principled" way. But passing that problem, *Roe* is not an appropriate case for their invocation.

Compared with men, very few women sit in our legislatures, a fact I believe should bear some relevance—even without an Equal Rights Amendment—to the appropriate standard of review for legislation that favors men over women. But *no* fetuses sit in our legislatures.... Compared with men, women may constitute such a "minority"; compared with the unborn, they do not. I'm not sure I'd know a discrete and insular minority if I saw one, but confronted with a multiple choice question requiring me to designate (a) women or (b) fetuses as one, I'd expect no credit for the former answer.

. . . At times the inferences the Court has drawn from the values the Constitution marks for special protection have been controversial, even shaky, but never before has its sense of an obligation to draw one been so obviously lacking.

Not in the last thirty-five years at any rate. For, as the received learning has it, this sort of thing did happen before, repeatedly. From its 1905 decision in *Lochner v. New York* into the 1930's the Court, frequently though not always under the rubric of "liberty of contract," employed the Due Process Clauses of the Fourteenth and Fifth Amendments to invalidate a good deal of legislation.

. . .

. . . The Constitution has little say about contract, less about abortion, and those who would speculate about which the framers would have been more likely to protect may not be pleased with the answer. The Court continues to disavow the philosophy of *Lochner*. Yet as Justice Stewart's concurrence admits, it is impossible candidly to regard *Roe* as the product of anything else.

That alone should be enough to damn it. Criticism of the *Lochner* philosophy has been virtually universal and will not be rehearsed here. I would, however, like to suggest briefly that although *Lochner* and *Roe* are twins to be sure, they are not identical. While I would hesitate to argue the one is more defensible than the other in terms of judicial style, there *are* differences in that regard that suggest *Roe* may turn out to be the more dangerous precedent.

PHILIP B. HEYMANN & DOUGLAS E. BARZELAY, THE FOREST AND THE TREES: ROE v. WADE AND ITS CRITICS

53 B.U.L. Rev. 765, 765–774 (1973).

... [T]he ... Court's opinion in *Roe* is amply justified both by precedent and by those principles that have long guided the Court in making the ever-delicate determination of when it must tell a state that it may not pursue certain measures, because to do so would impinge on those rights of individuals that the Constitution explicitly or implicitly protects. The language of the Court's opinion in *Roe* too often obscures the full strength of the four-step argument that underlies its decision.

(1) Under the fourteenth amendment to the Constitution, there are certain interests of individuals, long called "fundamental" in judicial decisions, that a state cannot abridge without a very good reason.

(2) The Court has never limited this set of "fundamental" interests to those explicitly mentioned elsewhere in the Constitution.

(3) One set of nonenumerated but fundamental rights, which the Court has recognized for 50 years but has only more recently begun calling aspects of "privacy," includes rights of individual choice as to marriage, procreation and child rearing.

(4) Since the issue of a right to terminate a pregnancy falls squarely within this long-established area of special judicial concern, the Court was obligated to determine in *Roe* whether the states did in fact have a sufficiently compelling reason for abridging the individual's freedom of choice as to abortion.

Notes: Regulating Abortion by Statute and Constitutional Amendment

(1) **Congressional efforts to "overrule" Roe**. After the *Roe* decision in 1973, several attempts were made in the House and Senate to bring about an amendment to the Constitution to undermine the effect of *Roe*. Needless to say, the attempts were unsuccessful. The attempts were of two broad types. The first type was a "states' rights" approach. In 1983, for example, a proposed Senate resolution provided that "A right to abortion is not secured by the Constitution." If added to the Constitution, this language would imply that the states are free to restrict abortions. See S.J. Res. 3, 98th Cong. 1st Sess. (1983). The Senate rejected the states' rights amendment 50–49 on June 28, 1983. The second type was a "right to life" approach, an attempt to expand the definition of "person" under the due process and equal protection clauses of the Fifth and Fourteenth Amendments. Proposals in this category usually declared that the right to personhood attaches from the moment of conception. For an example, *see* S.J. Res. 130, 93rd Cong. 2nd Sess. (1983). Introduced by Senator Jesse Helms, this unsuccessful proposal attempted to protect human life from the moment of conception.

(2) **Congressional efforts to enact Roe**. In the wake of *Webster v. Reproductive Health Servs.*, 492 U.S. 490 (1989), the first major Supreme

Court decision after *Roe v. Wade* upholding restrictions on abortion, members of Congress sought to guarantee a federal right of abortion privacy by statute. The Freedom of Choice Act was introduced in Congress on November 18, 1989, with 22 co-sponsors in the Senate and 101 in the House. The Act would have prohibited states from enacting restrictions on the right to abortion before fetal viability.

(3) **Congressional Efforts to Restrict Second–Trimester and Third–Trimester Abortion Bans.** In 1995 and again in 1997 members of Congress introduced legislation aimed at preventing certain abortions. In 1996, President Bill Clinton vetoed the Partial–Birth Abortion Ban Act of 1995, a bill passed by Congress that would have imposed criminal penalties for a specific, so called "late term," abortion procedure dubbed "partial-birth abortion." Efforts to override the President's veto failed. See 142 Cong. Rec. S11227–01. Would such a statute have been constitutional under *Roe*? Consider whether the ban would have been constitutional under *Casey*, infra, p. 657, which expressly rejected the trimester analysis of abortion rights found in *Roe*. See 143 Cong. Rec. S4517–01, S4568, for Congressional debate on the issue of the constitutionality of the proposed ban. New York lawmakers introduced a copy-cat partial-birth abortion ban statute in 1997, see 1997 NY A.B. 5463 (SN). Lawmakers in Nebraska asked their state Attorney General for an opinion on whether a state ban on partial-birth abortion would be constitutional. See Neb. Op. Atty. Gen. No. 96043, May 29, 1996.

(4) **State efforts to enact *Roe*.** The *Webster* decision prompted legislative action in Connecticut that led to the enactment in April 1990 of a statute framed in the language of *Roe* guaranteeing the right to abortion as a matter of state law. By contrast, *Webster's* validation of abortion restraints led Louisiana officials to consider enforcing anti-abortion statutes never repealed but presumed unenforceable immediately after *Roe*. *See Weeks v. Connick*, 733 F. Supp. 1036 (E. La. 1990) (motion to dissolve injunction against enforcement of anti-abortion statute).

a. *Comparative Perspectives*

In *Abortion and Divorce Law in Western Law: American Failures, European Challenges* (1989), Mary Ann Glendon observed that: "In contrast to the current American situation, it is worth noting that the French statute *names* the underlying problem as one involving human life, not as a conflict involving a woman's individual liberty or privacy and a non-person. While showing great concern for the pregnant woman, it tries, through legal provisions of a type that have been struck down in a series of American cases, to make her aware of alternatives without either frightening or unduly burdening her." *Id*. at 19. Professor Glendon characterizes American abortion law as "singular" among Western nations, "not only because it requires no protection of unborn life at any stage of pregnancy, ... but also because our abortion policy was not worked out in the give-and-take of the legislative process." She continues, "Our basic approach to, and our regulation of, abortion was established by the United States Supreme Court in a series of cases that rendered the abortion legislation of all states wholly or partly unconstitutional and severely limited the scope of future state regulation of abortion." *Id.* at 24–25. Glendon's observation that the Court "severely" limited state regulation of abortion is arguably obsolete now that the Court has tempered *Roe* in both *Webster* (in 1989) and *Planned Parenthood v. Casey (in 1992).*

In *Morgenthaler v. Queen,* (1988), the Supreme Court of Canada found that provisions of the Criminal Code infringed provisions of the Canadian Charter of Rights and Freedoms promising "life, liberty and security of the person." The Court held that: "State interference with bodily integrity and serious state-imposed psychological stress, at least in the criminal context, constitutes a breach of the security of the person. Section 251 clearly interferes with a woman's physical and bodily integrity. Forcing a woman by threat of criminal sanction, to carry a foetus to term unless she meets certain criteria unrelated to her own priorities and aspirations, is a profound interference with a woman's body and thus an infringement of security of the person." Did the Canadian decision go even further than *Roe* in seemingly placing concern for women's autonomy above concern for unborn life?

b. *Regulation of Self–Induced Abortion*

Should states criminalize self-induced abortions? Would legislation criminalizing first-trimester, self-induced abortions be constitutional?

(1) Nearly 1.5 million American women obtained legal abortions in the United States each year in the decade of the 1980's. The number declined, but only slightly, in the latter half of the 1990's. When abortion was illegal, it is vaguely estimated that between 200,000 and 2,000,000 criminal abortions were performed annually in the United States. See Harold Rosen, *Abortion in America,* 180 (1967).

For the most part, contemporary legislators aim proposed anti-abortion measures at the abortion provider. However, in the past abortion statutes appeared to criminalize pregnant women's own participation in abortion—inducing, seeking to obtain, or obtaining abortions. Criminalizing self-induced abortion poses special problems of law enforcement. Self-induced abortion has often involved insertion of items such as extended wire "coat hangers" or knitting needles through the cervix, caustic douches, ingestion of toxins and self-inflicted battery. It is speculated that a rash of desperate abortion attempts would be the inevitable result of laws prohibiting all legal, medically safe abortion.

(2) The possibility of self-help—non-medical abortion safely performed in the privacy of one's own home—is represented by the technique of "menstrual extraction" developed in the early 1970s in Los Angeles by members of a self-help clinic. *See* "Menstrual Extraction," *A New View of a Woman's Body,* 121–27 (Federation of Feminist Women's Health Centers, 1981):

> ... The group found that menstrual extraction was not difficult to learn and that the introduction of a sterile four-millimeter cannula into the uterus was not traumatic because it did not require that the cervix be dilated. There was no cutting or scraping; anesthetics

were not necessary; and the suction was sufficient to extract all or most of a woman's flow in around 20 to 30 minutes. . . .

The contents of the uterus—blood, clots or small bits of tissue— are examined in a shallow dish or glass. If chorionic villi, the yellowish material with branchlike structures which is the beginning of the placenta, are present, then it is a good sign that the menstrual extraction ended the pregnancy.

(3) Should menstrual extraction be illegal? If a woman does not know for certain that she is pregnant, is menstrual extraction abortion? How might a state enforce legislation banning self-induced abortion through menstrual extraction?

Notes: Third–Party Consent and Notification

(1) **Spousal Consent.** The Court invalidated both spousal and parental consent requirements in the abortion context in *Planned Parenthood of Cent. Missouri v. Danforth*, 428 U.S. 52 (1976). Justice Blackmun wrote for the Court that, "since the State cannot regulate or proscribe abortion during the first stage, when the physician and his patient make that decision, the State cannot delegate authority to any particular person, even the spouse, to prevent abortion during that same period." Acknowledging that abortion without spousal consent permits women the right to act "unilaterally," Blackmun also observed that "[s]ince it is the woman who physically bears the child and who is the more directly and immediately affected by the pregnancy, as between the two, the balance weighs in her favor."

(2) **Parental Consent.** As for parental consent requirements, the Court in *Danforth* held that: "the State may not impose a blanket provision . . . requiring the consent of a parent or person *in loco parentis* as a condition for abortion of an unmarried minor during the first 12 weeks of her pregnancy." (428 U S. at 74.) Again, Blackmun argued that "the State does not have the constitutional authority to give a third party an absolute, and possibly arbitrary, veto over the decision of the physician and his patient to terminate the patient's pregnancy, regardless of the reason for withholding the consent." *Id*. Recognizing that "The Court . . . has recognized that the State has somewhat broader authority to regulate the activities of children than of adults," Blackmun nonetheless concluded that there is no "significant state interest in conditioning an abortion on the consent of a parent or person *in loco parentis* that is not present in the case of an adult." *Id*. at 74–75.

In a companion case to *Danforth*, *Bellotti v. Baird*, 428 U.S. 132 (1976), the Supreme Court abstained from deciding the constitutionality of a Massachusetts statute which contained a provision allowing for the obtaining of a consent order by a judge "for good cause shown" if the parents refused consent to a minor's abortion. In remanding the case to the Supreme Judicial Court of Massachusetts to determine whether the "for good cause" provision meant that judicial consent would be given to a minor who was found to be mature enough to be capable of consenting, Justice Blackmun indicated that such an interpretation would make the statute "fundamentally" different from the statute in *Danforth* which created a "parental veto."

In 1983, the Supreme Court, relying on *Danforth* and *Bellotti*, struck down a city's requirement that abortion only be performed on women under the age of 15 years with the written consent of their parents or a court order. The court reasoned that the city regulation did not provide for a procedure to individually determine whether a minor was sufficiently mature or emancipated to make the decision for herself. *Akron v. Akron Center for Reproductive Health, Inc.,* 462 U.S. 416 (1983), overruled by *Planned Parenthood v. Casey,* 505 U.S. 833 (1992). On the same day, the Supreme Court upheld a Missouri requirement of parental consent in respect to unemancipated minors where there was a judicial alternative available which would allow an unemancipated minor female to decide to have an abortion where she is sufficiently mature or where the abortion is in her best interests. *Planned Parenthood Ass'n v. Ashcroft,* 462 U.S. 476 (1983). *See Planned Parenthood v. Danforth,* 428 U.S. 52 (1976); *Bellotti v. Baird* (I), 428 U.S. 132 (1976); *Bellotti v. Baird* (II), 443 U.S. 622 (1979); *H.L. v. Matheson,* 450 U.S. 398 (1981).

Although the Court took the position that minors could terminate their pregnancies without parental consent, it did not grant minors an unqualified right to abort without protective measures such as parental notification and waiting periods. On the contrary, the Court has upheld states' efforts to involve parents in the abortion decision through statutes requiring that minors or health care providers contact parents in advance of the procedure. *Hodgson v. Minnesota,* 497 U.S. 417 (1990). Critics argued that parental notice was not needed since most minors alert parents of pregnancy other than where tantamount to a parental veto.

(3) **Consent Requirements Under State Constitutions.** The Florida Supreme Court has invalidated that state's parental consent requirement, but relying upon the state constitution. *In re T.W.,* 551 So. 2d 1186 (Fla. 1989). In doing so it also made plain that Florida would recognize a fundamental abortion right even if *Roe v. Wade* were overruled:

> The citizens of Florida opted for more protection from governmental intrusion [than the federal Constitution provides] when they approved article I, section 23, of the Florida Constitution. This amendment is an independent, freestanding constitutional provision which declares the fundamental right to privacy.... The drafters of the amendment rejected the use of the words "unreasonable" or "unwarranted" before the phrase "governmental intrusion" in order to make the privacy right as strong as possible.... [T]he amendment embraces more privacy interests, and extends more protection to the individual in those interests, than does the federal Constitution.

> . . .

> Florida's privacy provision is clearly implicated in a woman's decision of whether or not to continue her pregnancy. We can conceive of few more personal or private decisions concerning one's body that one can make in the course of a lifetime, except perhaps the decision of the terminally ill in their choice of whether to discontinue necessary medical treatment....

... Minors are natural persons in the eyes of the law and "[c]onstitutional rights do not mature and come into being magically only when one attains the state-defined age of majority." ...

[W]here parental rights over a minor child are concerned, society has recognized additional state interests—protection of the immature minor and preservation of the family unit.... [W]e find that neither of these interests is sufficiently compelling under Florida law to override Florida's privacy amendment.

551 So. 2d at 1191–94.

(4) **Spousal Notification.** As recently as 1990, state legislatures adopted spousal notification requirements. Pennsylvania required that a woman wait twenty-four hours and notify her husband prior to abortion. The Supreme Court invalidated Pennsylvana's spousal notification requirement in *Planned Parenthood v. Casey*, 505 U.S. 833 (1992). (The Court upheld the waiting period, however.)

(5) **Parental Notification** . The decision of the Fourth Circuit in *Planned Parenthood of the Blue Ridge v. Camblos,* 155 F.3d 352 (1998) to let stand a statute requiring abortion providers to notify an unemancipated minor's parent or guardian twenty four hours prior to an abortion in the abssence of a judicial by-pass is consistent with leading Supreme Court authority. In *Hodgson v. Minnesota*, 497 U.S. 417 (1990), and *Ohio v. Akron Center for Reproductive Health*, 497 U.S. 502 (1990), the Court approved parental notification requirements in states that also provided minors a "judicial by-pass." *Hodgson v. Minnesota* affirmed the judgment of the 8th Circuit that one of two alternative sections of the Minnesota Minors Consent to Health Services Act was constitutional. The constitutional section required that two-parent notification and a 48 hour waiting period precede minors' abortions, except where a court determines either that a minor is mature and capable of informed consent or that parental notification would not be in the minor's best interest. The unconstitutional section provided for no judicial override or by-pass.

Akron Center reversed the Court of Appeal to uphold an Ohio statute that made it a crime for a physician to perform an abortion on an unmarried, unemancipated minor without first obtaining a court order or notifying one of the minor's parents. The Court found the Ohio law, including its judicial by-pass provisions, fully consistent with the court's five previous decisions involving parental notification and consent statutes.

One of those cases, *H. L. v. Matheson*, 450 U.S. 398 (1981), narrowly upheld a Utah law requiring physicians to "notify, if possible, the parents or guardians of any minor upon whom an abortion is to be performed." The Court validated the statute as applied to an unemancipated minor female who is living with and dependent upon her parents and who can not prove to the Court her maturity status. On the threshold question of whether the notice requirement unduly burdens the decision to terminate pregnancy, the majority opinion by Chief Justice Burger stated that the Utah law "created no veto power over the minor's abortion decision," but was reasonably calculated to protect immature and unemancipated minors by "enhancing the parental consultation concerning a decision that has potentially traumatic and permanent consequences.''

The majority reasoned that the possibility that the notice requirement may inhibit some minors from seeking abortions is not a valid basis to void the Statute, and argued that "the Constitution does not compel a state to fine-tune its statutes so as to encourage or facilitate abortions." Justice Marshall's dissent, which was joined by Justices Brennan and Blackmun, said that the parental notice requirement unconstitutionally burdens the minor's privacy right. Marshall agreed that the state intrusion occasioned by the notice requirement is an unwarranted interference with the normal functioning of the family, and is "hardly likely to resurrect parental authority that the parents themselves are unable to preserve." Justices Powell and Stewart, who joined the majority opinion, were careful to emphasize that the decision in the case left open the constitutionality of such a parental consent provision as applied to mature minors. Justice Stevens' concurrence, however, stated that the Utah law was constitutional on its face as applied to all minors due to the "State's interest in protecting a young pregnant woman from the consequences of an incorrect abortion decision."

MAHER v. ROE

432 U.S. 464 (1977).

[Note: This case was the first in an important line of cases establishing that government need not treat the decision to bear a child and the decision to terminate a pregnancy equally for purposes of allocating public resources.]

MR. JUSTICE POWELL delivered the opinion of the Court.

. . .

The Constitution imposes no obligation on the States to pay the pregnancy-related medical expenses of indigent women, or indeed to pay any of the medical expenses of indigents. But when a State decides to alleviate some of the hardships of poverty by providing medical care, the manner in which it dispenses benefits is subject to constitutional limitations. Appellees' claim is that Connecticut must accord equal treatment to both abortion and childbirth, and may not evidence a policy preference by funding only the medical expenses incident to childbirth. This challenge to the classifications established by the Connecticut regulation presents a question arising under the Equal Protection Clause of the Fourteenth Amendment. . . .

This case involves no discrimination against a suspect class. An indigent woman desiring an abortion does not come within the limited category of disadvantaged classes so recognized by our cases. Nor does the fact that the impact of the regulation falls upon those who cannot pay lead to a different conclusion. In a sense, every denial of welfare to an indigent creates a wealth classification as compared to nonindigents who are able to pay for the desired goods or services. But this Court has never held that financial need alone identifies a suspect class for purposes of equal protection analysis. Accordingly, the central question in this case is whether the regulation "impinges upon a fundamental right explicitly or implicitly protected by the Constitution." The District Court read our decisions in Roe v. Wade, and the subsequent cases applying it, as establishing a fundamental right to abortion and therefore concluded that nothing less than a compelling state interest would justify Connecticut's different treatment of abortion and childbirth. We think the District Court misconceived the nature and scope of the fundamental right recognized in *Roe*.

... *Roe* did not declare an unqualified "constitutional right to an abortion," as the District Court seemed to think. Rather, the right protects the woman from unduly burdensome interference with her freedom to decide whether to terminate her pregnancy. It implies no limitation on the authority of a State to make a value judgment favoring childbirth over abortion, and to implement that judgment by the allocation of public funds.

Mr. Justice Brennan, with whom Mr. Justice Marshall and Mr. Justice Blackmun join, dissenting.

... [A] distressing insensitivity to the plight of impoverished pregnant women is inherent in the Court's analysis. The stark reality for too many, not just "some," indigent pregnant women is that indigency makes access to competent licensed physicians not merely "difficult" but "impossible." As a practical matter, many indigent women will feel they have no choice but to carry their pregnancies to term because the State will pay for the associated medical services, even though they would have chosen to have abortions if the State had also provided funds for that procedure, or indeed if the State had provided funds for neither procedure. This disparity in funding by the State clearly operates to coerce indigent pregnant women to bear children they would not otherwise choose to have, and just as clearly, this coercion can only operate upon the poor, who are uniquely the victims of this form of financial pressure.

Roe v. Wade and cases following it hold that an area of privacy invulnerable to the State's intrusion surrounds the decision of a pregnant woman whether or not to carry her pregnancy to term. The Connecticut scheme clearly impinges upon that area of privacy by bringing financial pressures on indigent women that force them to bear children they would not otherwise have. That is an obvious impairment of the fundamental right established by Roe v. Wade.

Notes: Should Government Fund Abortions?

(1) *Maher, supra,* established that the federal Constitution permits states to deny abortion funding to indigent women, in furtherance of non-neutral policies aimed at encouraging childbirth. New Jersey has invalidated state legislation limiting access to public funds for abortion, on *state* constitutional grounds. *See Right to Choose v. Byrne,* 91 N.J. 287, 450 A.2d 925 (1982).

(2) A later Supreme Court case holding that public hospitals need not provide abortion services relied on *Maher. See Poelker v. Doe,* 432 U.S. 519 (1977):

Respondent Jane Doe, an indigent, sought unsuccessfully to obtain a nontherapeutic abortion at Starkloff Hospital, one of two city-owned public hospitals in St. Louis, Mo. She subsequently brought this class action under 42 U.S.C. Section 1983 against the Mayor of St. Louis and the Director of Health and Hospitals, alleging that the refusal by Starkloff Hospital to provide the desired abortion violated her constitutional rights....

. . .

... [T]he constitutional question presented here is identical in principle with that presented by a State's refusal to provide medic-aid benefits for abortions while providing them for childbirth. This was the issue before us in *Maher v. Roe*.... [W]e find no constitu-tional violation by the city of St. Louis in electing, as a policy choice, to provide publicly financed hospital services for childbirth without providing corresponding services for nontherapeutic abortions.

432 U.S. at 519–21.

(3) Congress has enacted legislation restricting the use of federal funds for the reimbursement of abortion costs under the Medicare program. Under the various Hyde Amendments from 1976 to 1982, federal Medicare funds are not available to pay for abortions except where the mother's life would be endangered, or where the mother was a victim of rape or incest who reported the rape or incest promptly to an official agency. The Amendment also provided that the several states "shall remain free not to fund abortions to the extent that they in their sole discretion deem appropriate." Hyde Amendment of 1982, Pub. L. No. 97–12, 95 Stat. 96.

In a 5–to–4 decision in *Harris v. McRae*, 448 U.S. 297 (1980), the Supreme Court upheld the federal Hyde Amendment under constitutional attack under the Due Process and Equal Protection Clauses of the Fifth Amendment and the First Amendment Free Exercise and Establishment Clauses. Justice Stewart for the majority stated that "[a]lthough the liberty protected by the Due Process Clause affords protection against unwarranted governmental interference with freedom of choice in the context of certain personal decisions, it does not confer an entitlement to such funds as may be necessary to realize all the advantages of that freedom." 448 U.S. at 317–18. Applying a "rational basis" test to the Hyde Amendment under the Equal Protection Clause, Justice Stewart argued that the Amendment, "by encour-aging childbirth except in the most urgent circumstances, is rationally related to the legitimate governmental objective of protecting potential life." 448 U.S. at 325. Justice Stewart additionally stated that the Establishment Clause of the First Amendment is not violated simply because the pro-life policy behind the Amendment parallels the tenets of some organized reli-gions; the Free Exercise Claim was rejected because the plaintiff had failed to show any "coercive effect" on her beliefs due to the funding restrictions on abortion.

(4) *Rust v. Sullivan*, 889 F.2d 401 (2d Cir. 1989) *aff'd*. 500 U.S.173 (1991), upheld a "Title X" regulation promulgated by Secretary of Health and Human Services that "None of the funds appropriated [for family planning] under this subchapter shall be used in programs where abortion is

a method of family planning"). On appeal before the Supreme Court appellants in *Rust* unsuccessfully argued that the Secretary's implementation of Congress's decision not to fund abortion counseling, referral or advocacy constituted a violation of the First Amendment rights of health care providers or of women to free speech.

(5) *Webster v. Reproductive Health Services*, 492 U.S. 490 (1989), involved challenges to three of Missouri's statutory efforts to regulate abortions. One of the challenged statutes prohibited the use of public funds, employees or facilities for the purpose of "encouraging or counseling" a woman to have an abortion not necessary to save her life. The Court upheld the prohibition along with a requirement that physicians ascertain whether a fetus was "viable" by performing "such medical examinations and tests as are necessary to a finding of (the fetus') gestational age, weight and lung maturity," in abortions performed on any woman whom the physician has reason to believe is 20 or more weeks pregnant. The Court declined to find unconstitutional the declaration in the preamble of the statute that "(the) life of each human being begins at conception," and that "unborn children have protectible interests in life, health and well being." The preamble required that all state laws be interpreted to provide unborn children with the same rights enjoyed by other persons, subject to the Federal Constitution and Supreme Court precedent. A majority of the justices found the preamble to be "precatory" and thus that its constitutionality was not part of the justiciable controversy that was before the court.

c. *Other Indirect Constraints*

Since *Roe*, many states and the territory of Guam have sought to discourage abortion—if not prohibit it—through regulation. Third-party notification or consent requirements, and public funding restrictions are two effective means of "indirectly" constraining abortion choice that have been brought before the Court. States have attempted to control abortion through restrictions on advertising; zoning restrictions on abortion facilities; record-keeping and reporting requirements; the requirement of pre-abortion "informed consent" counseling by physicians; mandatory pre-abortion waiting periods; bans on abortions for sex selection; the requirement of the presence of a second physician during the abortion procedure; the requirement that a method of abortion calculated to spare fetal life be employed in post viability abortions; the requirement that all tissue removed during an abortion be sent to a laboratory for analysis by a certified pathologist; the requirement that insurance companies offer at a lower cost insurance that does not cover most elective abortions; legislating a state-wide information campaign to communicate an official state policy against abortion; legislating criminal sanctions for physicians who knowingly abort viable fetuses; and a requirement that some or all abortions after the first trimester be performed in a hospital.

Some abortion restrictions appear difficult to enforce, including restrictions on self-induced abortions. Are criminal restrictions on abortion for sex selection, for example, purely symbolic? This questions takes of special urgency, now that ultrasound imaging and prenatal genetic testing has made selective abortion for sex, disability and other conditions more feasible and popular.

In *Akron v. Akron Center for Reproductive Health, Inc.*, 462 U.S. 416 (1983), the Supreme Court invalidated a city's requirement that any abortion performed after the first trimester be performed in a hospital (as opposed to a free-standing outpatient facility). Relying heavily on then current standards of the American College of Obstetricians and Gynecologists, the Court noted that various techniques permit safe outpatient abortions through most, and perhaps all, of the second trimester. The court concluded that Akron's hospitalization requirement "imposed a heavy, and unnecessary, burden on women's access to a relatively inexpensive, otherwise accessible, and safe abortion procedure . . . [and] therefore unreasonably infringes upon a woman's constitutional right to obtain an abortion." *Id.* at 438–39. The Supreme Court in *Planned Parenthood Ass'n v. Ashcroft*, 462 U.S. 476 (1983), invalidated a similar requirement that abortions after 12 weeks of pregnancy be performed in a hospital. However, in *Ashcroft*, a five-Justice majority of the Court upheld a requirement that a second physician be present for abortions performed after viability, noting that this requirement reasonably furthers the State's compelling interest in protecting the life of viable fetuses "in the comparatively few instances of live birth that occur." *Id.* at 486. This majority also upheld a requirement that any tissue removed during the abortion be examined by a pathologist who must file a report with the state, stating that such a "tissue examination does not significantly burden a pregnant woman's abortion decision." *Id.* at 490. The dissenting Justices argued that the state had not proven that either the second physician requirement or the pathology report requirement was "tailored to protect the State's legitimate interests." *Id.* at 501. In *Simopoulos v. Virginia*, 462 U.S. 506 (1983), the Supreme Court upheld Virginia's hospitalization requirement for second trimester abortions, since the Virginia statute defined "in hospital" to include licensed outpatient hospitals and clinics.

The Court's first major pronouncement on the problem of indirect constraints on abortion rights was *Thornburgh v. American College of Obstetricians and Gynecologists*, 476 U.S. 747 (1986), affirmed in part, reversed in part by 61 F.3d 1493 (1995). A divided Court held unconstitutional several provisions of Pennsylvania's Abortion Control Act of 1982. The invalid provisions required what the Court characterized as elaborate and burdensome forms of "voluntary and informed consent," physician reporting, and special precautions in post-viability abortions. Justice Blackmun wrote for the majority:

> In the years since this Court's decision in *Roe*, States and municipalities have adopted a number of measures seemingly designed to prevent a woman, with the advice of her physician, from exercising her freedom of choice. . . . The States are not free, under the guise of protecting maternal health or potential life, to intimidate women into continuing pregnancies. Appellants claim that the statutory provisions before us today further legitimate compelling interests of the Commonwealth. Close

analysis of those provisions, however, shows that they wholly subordinate constitutional privacy interests and concerns with maternal health in an effort to deter a woman from making a decision that, with her physician, is hers to make. . . .

Our cases long have recognized that the Constitution embodies a promise that a certain private sphere of individual liberty will be kept largely beyond the reach of government. That promise extends to women as well as to men. Few decisions are more personal and intimate, more properly private, or more basic to individual dignity and autonomy, than a woman's decision—with the guidance of her physician and within the limits specified in *Roe*—whether to end her pregnancy. A woman's right to make that choice freely is fundamental. Any other result, in our view, would protect inadequately a central part of the sphere of liberty that our law guarantees equally to all.

Id. at 759–72.

Blackmun's account of the jurisprudence of abortion privacy was far more lucid and self-assured in *Thornburgh* than in *Roe*. It inspired an equally lucid dissent by Justice White, reproduced, in part, below. White argues that *Roe v. Wade* should be overturned. Justice O'Connor's dissent searched for a middle ground. She would have upheld provisions of the Pennsylvania Abortion Control Act, but on the ground that they did not "unduly" burden women's fundamental right to privacy.

THORNBURGH v. AMERICAN COLLEGE OF OBSTETRICIANS AND GYNECOLOGISTS

476 U.S. 747 (1986).

[Justice White, whom Justice Rehnquist joined, dissenting]

In my view, the time has come to recognize that Roe v. Wade, . . . "departs from a proper understanding" of the Constitution and to overrule it. . . . That the flaws in an opinion were evident at the time it was handed down is hardly a reason for adhering to it. . . .

In most instances, the substantive protection afforded the liberty or property of an individual by the Fourteenth Amendment is extremely limited: State action impinging on individual interests need only be rational to survive scrutiny under the Due Process Clause, and the determination of rationality is to be made with a heavy dose of deference to the policy choices of the legislature. Only "fundamental" rights are entitled to the added protection provided by strict judicial scrutiny of legislation that impinges upon them. . . . I can certainly agree with the proposition—which I deem indisputable—that a woman's ability to choose an abortion is a species of "liberty" that is subject to the general protections of the Due Process Clause. I cannot agree, however, that this liberty is so "fundamental" that restrictions upon it call into play anything more than the most minimal judicial scrutiny.

Fundamental liberties and interests are most clearly present when the Constitution provides specific textual recognition of their existence and importance. Thus, the Court is on relatively firm ground when it deems certain of the liberties set forth in the Bill of Rights to be fundamental and therefore finds them incorporated in the Fourteenth Amendment's guarantee that no State may deprive any person of liberty without due process of law. When the Court ventures further and defines as "fundamental" liberties that are nowhere mentioned in the Constitution (or that are present only in the so-called "penumbras" of specifically enumerated rights), it must, of necessity, act with more caution, lest it open itself to the accusation that, in the name of identifying constitutional principles to which the people have consented in framing their Constitution, the Court has done nothing more than impose its own controversial choices of value upon the people.

. . .

The Court has justified the recognition of a woman's fundamental right to terminate her pregnancy by invoking decisions upholding claims of personal autonomy in connection with the conduct of family life, the rearing of children, marital privacy, and the use of contraceptives, and the preservation of the individual's capacity to procreate.... However one answers the metaphysical or theological question whether the fetus is a "human being" or the legal question whether it is a "person" as that term is used in the Constitution, one must at least recognize, first, that the fetus is an entity that bears in its cells all the genetic information that characterizes a member of the species *homo sapiens* and distinguishes an individual member of that species from all others, and second, that there is no nonarbitrary line separating a fetus from a child or, indeed, an adult human being. Given that the continued existence and development—that is to say, the *life*—of such an entity are so directly at stake in the woman's ... decision whether or not to terminate her pregnancy, that decision must be recognized as *sui generis*, different in kind from the others that the Court has protected under the rubric of personal or family privacy and autonomy. Accordingly, the decisions cited by the Court both in *Roe* and in its opinion today as precedent for the fundamental nature of the liberty to choose abortion do not, even if all are accepted as valid, dictate the Court's classification
. . . . .

If the woman's liberty to choose an abortion is fundamental, then, it is not because any of our precedents (aside from *Roe* itself) command or justify that result; it can only be because protection for this unique choice is itself "implicit in the concept of ordered liberty" or, perhaps, "deeply rooted in this Nation's history and tradition." It seems clear to me that it is neither. The Court's opinion in *Roe* itself convincingly refutes the notion that the abortion liberty is deeply rooted in the history or tradition of our people, as does the continuing and deep division of the people themselves over the question of abortion. As for the notion that choice in the matter of abortion is implicit in the concept of ordered liberty, it seems apparent to me that a free, egalitarian, and democratic society does not presuppose any particular rule or set of rules with respect to abortion. And again, the fact that many men and women of good will and high commitment to constitutional government place themselves on both sides of the abortion controversy strengthens my own conviction that the values animating the Constitution do not compel recognition ... of the abortion liberty as fundamental. In so denominating that liberty, the Court engages not in constitutional interpretation, but in the unrestrained imposition of its own, extraconstitutional value preferences.

B.

A second, equally basic error infects the Court's decision in Roe v. Wade. The detailed set of rules governing state restrictions on abortion that the Court first articulated in *Roe* and has since refined and elaborated presupposes not only that the woman's liberty to choose an abortion is fundamental, but also that the State's countervailing interest in protecting fetal life (or, as the Court would have it, "potential human life," 410 U.S., at 159) becomes "compelling" only at the point at which the fetus is viable. As Justice O'Connor pointed out three years ago in her dissent in Akron v. Akron Center for Reproductive Health, the Court's choice of viability as the point at which the State's interest becomes compelling is entirely arbitrary. The Court's "explanation" for the line it has drawn is that the State's interest becomes compelling at viability "because the fetus then presumably has the capacity of meaningful life outside the mother's womb." ...

The governmental interest at issue is in protecting those who will be citizens if their lives are not ended in the womb.... The State's interest is in the fetus as an entity in itself, and the character of this entity does not change at the point of viability under conventional medical wisdom. Accordingly, the State's interest, if compelling after viability, is equally compelling before viability.[4]

Both the characterization of the abortion liberty as fundamental and the denigration of the State's interest in preserving the lives of nonvia-

---

4. Further, it is self-evident that neither the legislative decision to assert a state interest in fetal life before viability nor the judicial decision to recognize that interest as compelling constitutes an impermissible "religious" decision merely because it coincides with the belief of one or more religions. Certainly the fact that the prohibition of murder coincides with one of the Ten Commandments does not render a State's interest in its murder statutes less than compelling, nor are legislative and judicial decisions concerning the use of the death penalty tainted by their correspondence to varying religious views on that subject. The simple, and perhaps unfortunate, fact of the matter is that in determining whether to assert an interest in fetal life, a State cannot avoid taking a position that will correspond to some religious beliefs and contradict others. The same is true to some extent with respect to the choice this Court faces in characterizing an asserted state interest in fetal life, for denying that such an interest is a "compelling" one necessarily entails a negative resolution of the "religious" issue of the humanity of the fetus, whereas accepting the State's interest as compelling reflects at least tolerance for a state decision that is congruent with the equally "religious" position that human life begins at conception. Faced with such a decision, the most appropriate course of action for the Court is to defer to a legislative resolution of the issue: in other words, if a state legislature asserts an interest in protecting fetal life, I can see no satisfactory basis for *denying* that it is compelling....

ble fetuses are essential to the detailed set of constitutional rules devised by the Court to limit the States' power to regulate abortion. If either or both of these facets of Roe v. Wade were rejected, a broad range of limitations on abortion (including outright prohibition) that are now unavailable to the States would again become constitutional possibilities.

In my view, such a state of affairs would be highly desirable from the standpoint of the Constitution. Abortion is a hotly contested moral and political issue. Such issues, in our society, are to be resolved by the will of the people, either as expressed through legislation or through the general principles they have already incorporated into the Constitution they have adopted. Roe v. Wade implies that the people have already resolved the debate by weaving into the Constitution the values and principles that answer the issue. As I have argued, I believe it is clear that the people have never—not in 1787, 1791, 1868, or at any time since—done any such thing. I would return the issue to the people by overruling Roe v. Wade.

JUSTICE O'CONNOR, with whom JUSTICE REHNQUIST joins, dissenting,

. . . The State has compelling interests in ensuring maternal health and in protecting potential human life, and these interests exist "throughout pregnancy." Under this Court's fundamental-rights jurisprudence, judicial scrutiny of state regulation of abortion should be limited to whether the state law bears a rational relationship to legitimate purposes such as the advancement of these compelling interests, with heightened scrutiny reserved for instances in which the State has imposed an "undue burden" on the abortion decision. An undue burden will generally be found "in situations involving absolute obstacles or severe limitations on the abortion decision," not wherever a state regulation "may 'inhibit' abortions to some degree." And if a state law does interfere with the abortion decision to an extent that is unduly burdensome, so that it becomes "necessary to apply an exacting standard of review," the possibility remains that the statute will withstand the stricter scrutiny. . . .

The Court today goes well beyond mere distortion of the "unduly burdensome" standard. By holding that each of the challenged provisions is facially unconstitutional as a matter of law, and that no conceivable facts appellants might offer could alter this result, the Court appears to adopt as its new test a *per se* rule under which any regulation touching on abortion must be invalidated if it poses "an unacceptable danger of deterring the exercise of that right." Under this prophylactic test, it seems that the mere possibility that some women will be less likely to choose to have an abortion by virtue of the presence of a particular state regulation suffices to invalidate it. Simultaneously, the Court strains to discover "the anti-abortion character of the statute," . . . and, as Justice White points out, invents an unprecedented canon of construction under which "in cases involving abortion, a permissible reading of a statute is to be avoided at all costs." I shall not belabor the dangerous extravagance of this dual approach, because I hope it represents merely a temporary aberration rather than a portent of lasting change in settled principles of constitutional law. Suffice it to say that I dispute not only the wisdom but also the legitimacy of the Court's attempt to discredit and pre-empt state abortion regulation regardless of the interests it serves and the impact it has.

PLANNED PARENTHOOD v. CASEY

505 U.S. 833 (1992).

[Note: Like the *Thornburgh* case, this began as a challenge to the Pennsylvania Abortion Control Act. State lawmakers originally enacted the Act 1982, amending it in 1988 and 1989. Planned Parenthood challenged five provisions of the Act. The Act contained an informed consent requirement, a 24–hour waiting period requirement, a spousal notification requirement, a parental consent requirement, and a reporting requirement. Because of changes in the ideological composition of the Court and the holding of the *Webster* decision permitting additional regulation of abortion under a weakened standard of review, the public anticipated that the Court might use *Casey* as an occasion for overruling *Roe v. Wade*. Instead, the Court affirmed what it repeatedly termed the "essential holding" of *Roe*. In declining to overrule *Roe*, the Court also emphasized the importance to judicial legitimacy of the principle of *stare decisis* and the reality of reliance on the abortion right for nearly two decades. Critics argued that the Court eviscerated *Roe*, though, by supplanting *Roe*'s strict scrutiny standard of review with Justice O'Connor's "undue burden" analysis, and by repudiating *Roe's* trimester framework on the ground that the State may assert a legitimate interest in unborn life during all stages of pregnancy. Justices O'Connor, joined by Kennedy and Souter, announced the plurality judgment of the Court.]

. . . We are led to conclude this: the essential holding of Roe v. Wade should be retained and once again reaffirmed.

It must be stated at the outset and with clarity that Roe's essential holding . . . has three parts. First is a recognition of the right of the woman to choose to have an abortion before viability and to obtain it without undue interference from the State. Before viability, the State's interests are not strong enough to support a prohibition of abortion or the imposition of a substantial obstacle to the woman's effective right to elect the procedure. Second is a confirmation of the State's power to restrict abortions after fetal viability, if the law contains exceptions for pregnancies which endanger the woman's life or health. And third is the principle that the State has legitimate interests from the outset of the pregnancy in protecting the health of the woman and the life of the fetus that may become a child. . . .

Constitutional protection of the woman's decision to terminate her pregnancy derives from the Due Process clause of the Fourteenth Amendment.... The controlling word ...is "liberty." [I]t is settled that the due process clause of the Fourteenth amendment applies to matters of substantive law as well as to matters of procedure....

Men and women of good conscience can disagree ... about the profound moral and spiritual implications of terminating pregnancy, even in its earliest stage....

It is conventional constitutional doctrine that where reasonable people disagree the government can adopt one position or the other.... That theorem, however, assumes a state of affairs in which the choice does not intrude upon a protected liberty. ...

Our law affords constitutional protection to personal decisions relating to marriage, procreation, contraception, family relationships, child rearing, and education.... At the heart of liberty is the right to define one's own concept of existence, of meaning, of the universe, and of the mystery of human life. Beliefs about these matters could not define the attributes of personhood were they formed under compulsion of the State....

... The mother who carries a child to full term is subject to anxieties, to physical constraints, to pain that only she must bear. That these sacrifices have from the beginning of the human race been endured by woman with a pride that ennobles her in the eyes of others and gives to an infant a bond of love cannot alone be grounds for the state to insist she make the sacrifice....

Her suffering is too intimate and personal for the State to insist, without more, on its own vision of the woman's role, however dominant that vision has been in the course of our history and our culture. The destiny of the woman must be shaped to a large extent on her own conception of her spiritual imperatives and her place in history.

... Although Roe has engendered opposition, it has in no sense proven "unworkable" ...

No evolution of legal principle has left Roe's doctrinal footings weaker than they were in 1973....

... An entire generation has come of age free to assume Roe's concept of liberty in defining the capacity of women to act in society and to make reproductive decisions; no erosion of principle going to liberty or personal autonomy has left Roe's central holding a doctrinal remnant; Roe portends no developments at odds with other precedent for the analysis of personal liberty; and no changes have rendered viability more or less appropriate as the point at which the balance of interests tips. Within the bounds of normal stare decisis analysis. ... the stronger argument is for affirming Roe's central holding ... not for overruling it.

... A decision to overrule Roe's essential holding under the existing circumstances would address error, if error there was, at the cost of both profound and unnecessary damage to the Court's legitimacy, and to the

Nations' commitment to the rule of law. It is therefore imperative to adhere to the essence of Roe's original decision as we do so today.

. . . Roe established a trimester framework to govern abortion regulations. Under this elaborate but rigid construct, almost no regulation at all is permitted during the first trimester of pregnancy. . . .

. . . Though the woman has a right to choose to terminate or continue her pregnancy before viability, it does not at all follow that the State is prohibited from taking steps to ensure that this choice is thoughtful and informed. Even in the earliest stages of pregnancy, the state may enact rules and regulations designed to encourage her to know that there are philosophic and social arguments of great weight that can be brought to bear in favor of continuing the pregnancy to full term and that there are procedures and institutions to allow adoption of unwanted children as well as a certain degree of state assistance. . . .

. . . We [therefore] reject the trimester framework, which we do not consider to be part of the essential holding of Roe. . . .

A finding of an undue burden is a shorthand for the conclusion that a state regulation has the purpose or effect of placing a substantial obstacle in the path of a woman seeking an abortion of a nonviable fetus. A statute with this purpose is invalid. . . .

d. *Abortion Protest and Clinic Violence*

(1) Abortion is as much a political, moral and religious issue as a legal one. The abortion question has spawned a number of injunctive and damage actions that pit claims to political and religious free expression against claims to access to abortion services. *See Schenck v. Pro-Choice Network of Western New York*, 519 U.S. 357 (1997). Women seeking abortion free from physical dangers and harassment, clinics seeking freedom from unruly trespassers, and cities seeking to be rid of public nuisances have joined in actions against aggressive anti-abortion protesters. *See New York State N.O.W. v. Terry*, 886 F.2d 1339 (2d Cir. 1989) (upholding injunction) (First Amendment does not grant Randall Terry and "Operation Rescue" right to engage in activities designed to deny access to abortion clinics). *See also Eanes v. State*, 569 A.2d 604, 318 Md. 436 (1990) (state law proscribing "loud and unseemly" noises constitutional under first Amendment when applied against religiously motivated anti-abortion demonstration in front of abortion clinic on congested street), *cert. denied*, 498 U.S. 938 (1990).

(2) On December 30, 1994, two women were killed and several other people wounded at Planned Parenthood and Preterm Health Services clinics in Brookline, Massachusetts by John C. Salvi, who was a strong opponent of abortion. On July 29, 1994, Paul Hill shot Dr. John Britton, a Florida abortion provider, and two elderly pro-choice volunteer escorts. Britton and one of the escorts died. Hill, a former Presbyterian minister, was the director of the violence-advocating anti-abortion group, Defensive Action.

(3) When enacted in the mid–1990's, the federal Freedom of Access to Clinic Entrances ("FACE") Act, 18 U.S.C.S. 248 (1997), converted trespass, harassment, intimidation, assault and battery at abortion clinic entrances into serious federal offenses punishable by civil and criminal penalties including fines and imprisonment for up to 10 years for the most serious repeat offenders.

(4) Should a pharmacist who opposes abortion on moral grounds be legally entitled to refuse to fill a prescription for the "morning after pill" or another medication he or she believes a customer and her doctor (the prescribing physician) intend for use as an abortifacient?

e. Control Over Fetal Remains

Does the right to obtain an abortion entail a right to determine the fate of the aborted fetal tissue or fetus? Several states have enacted statutes expressly addressing the disposal of fetal remains. *See* Nicolas P. Terry, *"Alas! Poor Yorick," I Knew Him Ex Utero: The Regulation of Embryo and Fetal Experimentation and Disposal in England and the United States*, 39 Vand. L. Rev. 419, 427 (1986). These statutes typically stipulate that abortion providers insure that "fetal remains . . . are disposed of in a fashion similar to that in which other tissue is disposed." Terry, at 427. *See, e.g.*, Ark. Stat. Ann. Sec. 82–436 (Supp. 1985). Fetal disposal statutes have been invalidated on constitutional grounds both in Ohio and Louisiana.

In *Akron v. Akron Center for Reproductive Health, Inc.*, 462 U.S. 416 (1983), the Supreme Court held that, although the municipality had a legitimate interest in proper fetal disposal, the statute under review was unconstitutionally vague for failure to specify procedures. A statute requiring women obtaining abortions to specify fetal burial or cremation was invalidated in *Margaret S. v. Treen*, 597 F. Supp. 636 (E.D. La. 1984), for unconstitutionally burdening women's abortion choice. *See also Margaret S. v. Edwards*, 488 F. Supp. 181 (E.D. La. 1980). Indeed, presenting women with the choice of a burial or cremation could lead some to believe that all abortions result in the extraction of a dead infant. In this country the vast majority of abortions—90%—are performed in the first trimester of pregnancy, when extracted tissue does not resemble a baby.

Fetal tissue and fetuses are commonly utilized for research purposes. Elective medical abortions have provided researchers with a supply of fetuses and fetal tissue for research. The tissue of fetuses, particularly those less than 16 weeks, promises to have a role in the treatment of diseases including diabetes, leukemia, Alzheimer's disease and Parkinson's disease. Fetal tissue may also have a valuable role in the field of bone marrow and other transplants. *See* D. Lehrman, *Summary: Fetal Research and Fetal Tissue Research* (Washington: Association of American Medical College, 1988); U.S. Congress Office of Technology Assessment, New Developments in Biotechnology: Ownership of Human Tissues and Cells—Special Report (Washington: U.S. Government Printing Office, 1987). Is it ethical to create and destroy human embryos for biomedical research relating to human health?

Should public policy ascribe women who abort a legal, proprietary interest in their fetal tissue or fetuses? *Cf. Moore v. Regents of University of California*, 51 Cal. 3d 120, 271 Cal. Rptr. 146, 793 P.2d 479 (1990) (leukemia patient had no property interest in lucrative research made possible through secret use of tissue appropriated in course of medical care), *cert. denied*, 111 S.Ct. 1388 (1991). Should women, on an individual basis, have a right to veto unwanted research on their fetal tissues or fetuses? State and federal law does not broach these questions. Federal funding regulations provide only that fetal experimentation and research be conducted "in accordance with any applicable state or local laws regarding such activities." 45 C.F.R. Sec. 46.210 (1986). Research involving fetal tissue and fetuses is governed in the states by statutes patterned after the Uniform Anatomical Gift Act. Sec. 1(b) of The Act defines "decedent" to include "a stillborn infant or fetus." Sec. 2(b) authorizes either parent to donate fetal remains for therapeutic transplantation.

3. PREGNANCY AND CHILDBIRTH

a. *"Fetal Rights" v. Women's Autonomy?*

Women's rights of privacy and equal protection are cited as grounds for limiting government regulation of the conduct of pregnant women and the recognition of "fetal rights". *See* Janet Gallagher, *Prenatal Invasions & Interventions: What's Wrong with Fetal Rights*, 10 Harv. Women's L. J. 9 (1987); Dawn E. Johnsen, *The Creation of Fetal Rights: Conflicts with Women's Constitutional Rights to Liberty, Privacy, and Equal Protection*, 95 Yale L.J. 599, 600 (1986). However, some commentators favor legal recognition of fetal interests during all stages of pregnancy. Comment, *Maternal Substance Abuse: The Need to Provide Legal Protection for the Fetus*, 60 S. Cal. L. Rev. 1209 (1987) (authored by Sam Balisy). *Cf.* Patricia A. King, *The Juridical Status of the Fetus: A Proposal for the Legal Protection of the Unborn*, 77 Mich. L. Rev. 1647, 1674 (1979).

Commentators go further, arguing that women who decide against terminating pregnancy, should be held to enforceable standards of responsibility for the health of their unborn children. *See* John A. Robertson, *Procreative Liberty and the Control of Contraception, Pregnancy, and Childbirth*, 69 Va. L. Rev. 405 (1983); Jeffrey A. Parness, *The Duty to Prevent Handicaps: Laws Promoting the Prevention of Handicaps to Newborns*, 5 Western New Eng. L. Rev. 431 (1983). In addition to criminal and tort liability, proposed forms of regulation include the extension of child abuse and neglect principles from family law to the care female parents give the unborn.

Three situations have raised concern. The first is where a pregnant woman engages in lawful conduct that poses a health risk to the fetus, such as smoking cigarettes, consuming alcoholic beverages, or failing to heed her physician's advice about sexual intercourse, prescription drugs, nutrition or prenatal care. Use of alcohol during pregnancy has been associated with retarded development, disorders of the central nervous system, and facial abnormalities. *See* Barbara Shelly, *Maternal Substance Abuse: The Next Step in the Protection of Fetal Rights*, 92 Dickinson L. Rev. 691 (1988). Infants born to mothers who smoked during pregnancy may suffer from the effects of low birth weight, notably, Sudden Infant Death Syndrome, retarded development, breathing difficulty, hypoglycemia and jaundice. *Id.* at 707. Smokers incur an increased risk of miscarriage.

The second situation is where a pregnant woman knowingly ingests illegal drugs—most commonly, crack cocaine or heroin. See Dorothy Roberts, *Punishing Drug Addicts Who Have Babies: Women of Color, Equality, and the Right to Privacy*, 104 Harv. L. Rev. 1419 (1991). The long-term effects of *in utero* heroin exposure are uncertain. However, heroin addicts typically give birth to heroin addicted, and sometimes, still-born babies. Heroin addicted infants experience seizures, vomiting, diarrhea and other symptoms of sudden drug withdrawal. The newborns of cocaine addicted women are prone to Sudden Death Syndrome, undersized skulls, and neurological damage.

The third context of concern is where pregnant women refuse medical care that physicians recommend, such as blood transfusion or Caesarian surgical delivery. *See Jefferson v. Griffin Spalding County Hosp. Authority*, 247 Ga. 86, 274 S.E.2d 457 (1981) (hospital authorized to perform surgical delivery without patient consent); *Raleigh Fitkin–Paul Memorial Hosp. v. Anderson*, 42 N.J. 421, 201 A.2d 537 (1964), *cert. denied*, 377 U.S. 985 (1964) (hospital authorized to perform blood transfusion without patient consent).

As prenatal screening and fetal therapy become increasingly available, pressure may mount to subject pregnant women to legal sanctions for refusing testing and care for themselves and their fetuses. The medical and scholarly community has already begun to debate whether mandatory prenatal testing and therapy for the human immunodeficiency virus antibody associated with the AIDS disease is warranted. AIDS is but one transmittable disease or congenital abnormality for which tests or treatments exist, or are likely to be developed. *See generally*, M. Henifin, R. Hubbard, J. Norsigian, "Prenatal Screening," in *Reproductive Laws for the 1990s*, 155, 158, 165, 166 (1989):

> An aspect of individual liberty and privacy is the right to be free from coerced physical intrusion, including coerced medical treatment.... However, the Supreme Court has not yet decided whether procreative choice and bodily integrity protect the right to use or refuse new reproductive technologies.

> At present the incidence of inborn diseases is on the order of 3 to 4 percent.... As it becomes possible to screen for a growing number of genetically transmitted health problems, it is important that prospective parents be offered a range of options and

full information and counselling about them, so that they can evaluate various alternatives.

Since scientists first developed prenatal tests 20 years ago to detect sex and Down syndrome, more than 4000 genetic traits have been catalogued, and prenatal tests now exist for over 300 of them with new tests being developed all the time. Most of these tests are used to detect rare diseases, not to screen routinely for common difficulties, and can be useful only when there is a family history of a particular disease.... Screening of prospective parents can become problematic when a particular racial, age, or occupational group has a higher incidence of a particular genetic condition and therefore is singled out for testing. Associating Down syndrome with the pregnancies of older women, Tay–Sachs disease with Jews, and sickle cell anemia with blacks are examples of this phenomenon....

Through prenatal diagnosis, the fetus has become a new category of patient for whom experimental therapies are being developed. A pregnant woman may feel compelled to accept every opportunity physicians offer to diagnose and "treat" her fetus despite the risks involved. In a recent review of advances in pediatric surgery, researchers noted that treatment is becoming available for a number of fetal impairments. Detection of a fetal disability may now suggest a change in the timing of delivery, a change in the mode of delivery, or even prenatal treatment. For example, ultra-sonography can be used to diagnose fetal urinary tract obstruction or intestinal blockage, leading the obstetrician to recommend an early delivery.... Other conditions can be treated by injecting medications and nutrients directly into the amniotic fluid. Most drastically, fetal surgery is recommended for several anatomic disorders....

Presently women do not face governmental intervention when making a decision of whether or not to undergo prenatal screening. But some legal commentators suggest that a pregnant woman who is at risk of delivering a baby with a disability and refuses screening should be liable for "prenatal abuse." Others recommend maternal tort liability. Both of these types of legal liability would severely limit the degree of autonomy experienced by women during pregnancy to make decisions about medical treatment and procreation.

What is an appropriate response to behavior that places the well-being of the unborn seriously at risk? In the last decade, in highly publicized cases, pregnant and recently-pregnant women were indicted, jailed, and forced to undergo rehabilitation for failure to take medical advice or for prenatal use of drugs. In 1988, a Washington, D.C. judge ordered pregnant cocaine user Brenda Vaughan jailed in lieu of probation for second degree theft. In 1986, Pamela Rae Stewart was indicted by San Diego prosecutors who alleged that her baby boy's death resulted from prenatal conduct that included her use of barbiturates, sexual intercourse with her husband, and failure to seek prompt medical attention for vaginal hemorrhaging.

Controversy remains over whether women who refuse caesarian surgery, and smoke or drink in moderation are necessarily negligent. It is argued that physicians prescribe caesarian deliveries out of fear of malpractice liability. Indeed the medical profession has been criticized for dramatic increases in the rate of caesarian delivery. Still, drug addiction and other prenatal behavior is undeniably risky for pregnant women and their unborn children. Applauded in some quarters, punitive responses to the problem of prenatal negligence is viewed in others as reducing women to the status of mere "vessels" for the unborn. *See generally* Gallagher, "Fetus as Patient," in *Reproductive Laws for the 1990s*, 185, 188, 211, (1989) According to Gallagher, "[c]alls for court-ordered surgery and for legal punishment for negligent behavior in pregnancy or 'fetal abuse' are unacceptable given the unavailability of even the most basic prenatal and obstetrical health care for many pregnant women." In a widely publicized incident in 1997, the body of a brain dead pregnant woman was maintained on heart and lung life-support for months, solely to permit her non-viable fetus to grow to viability. Once physicians delivered the fetus via Caesarian section, they immediately removed the woman from life support, and she quickly expired. The infant was placed in the custody of its maternal grandmother, its putative father wanting no hand in the matter. Is this case of a dead woman "giving birth" evidence of Gallagher's thesis that women are considered vessels for the unborn?

IN RE A.C.

573 A.2d 1235 (D.C. Ct. App. 1990).

[This case came before the trial court when George Washington University Hospital petitioned the emergency judge in chambers for declaratory relief as to how it should treat its patient, A.C., who was close to death from cancer and was twenty-six and one-half weeks pregnant with a viable fetus. After a hearing lasting approximately three hours, which was held at the hospital (though not in A.C.'s room), the court ordered that a caesarean section be performed on A.C. to deliver the fetus. Counsel for A.C. immediately sought a stay in this court, which was unanimously denied by a hastily assembled division of three judges. *In Re A.C.*, 533 A.2d 611 (D.C. 1987). The caesarean was performed, and a baby girl, L.M.C., was delivered. Tragically, the child died within two and one-half hours, and the mother died two days later.]

[JUDGE TERRY]

. . .

A.   INFORMED CONSENT AND BODILY INTEGRITY

. . . [O]ur analysis of this case begins with the tenet common to all medical treatment cases: that any person has the right to make an informed choice, if competent to do so, to accept or forego medical treatment. The doctrine of informed consent, based on this principle and rooted in the concept of bodily integrity, is ingrained in our common law.

Under the doctrine of informed consent, a physician must inform the patient, "at a minimum," of "the nature of the proposed treatment, any alternative treatment procedures, and the nature and degree of risks and benefits inherent in undergoing and in abstaining from the proposed treatment." To protect the right of every person to bodily integrity, courts uniformly hold that a surgeon who performs an operation without the patient's consent may be guilty of a battery, or that if the surgeon obtains an insufficiently informed consent, he or she may be liable for negligence. . . .

In the same vein, courts do not compel one person to permit a significant intrusion upon his or her bodily integrity for the benefit of another person's health. Bonner v. Moran, (parental consent required for skin graft from fifteen-year-old for benefit of cousin who had been severely burned); McFall v. Shimp. In *McFall* the court refused to order Shimp to donate bone marrow which was necessary to save the life of his cousin, McFall. . . . It has been suggested that fetal cases are different because a woman who "has chosen to lend her body to bring [a] child into the world" has an enhanced duty to assure the welfare of the fetus, sufficient even to require her to undergo caesarean surgery. Robertson, *Procreative Liberty*, 69 Va. L. Rev. at 456. Surely, however, a fetus cannot have rights in this respect superior to those of a person who has already been born.

. . .

Courts have generally held that a patient is competent to make his or her own medical choices when that patient is capable of "the informed exercise of a choice, and that entails an opportunity to evaluate knowledgeably the options available and the risks attendant upon each." Canterbury v. Spence. . . . Thus competency in a case such as this turns on the patient's ability to function as a decision-maker, acting in accordance with her preferences and values. . . .

This court has recognized as well that, above and beyond common law protections, the right to accept or forego medical treatment is of constitutional magnitude. . . .

Decisions of the Supreme Court, while not explicitly recognizing a right to bodily integrity, seem to assume that individuals have the right, depending on the circumstances, to accept or refuse medical treatment or other bodily invasion. . . .

This court and others, while recognizing the right to accept or reject medical treatment, have consistently held that the right is not absolute. . . . In some cases, especially those involving life-or-death situations or incompetent patients, the courts have recognized four countervailing interests that may involve the state as *parens patriae*: preserving life, preventing suicide, maintaining the ethical integrity of the medical profession, and protecting third parties. Neither the prevention of suicide nor the integrity of the medical profession has any bearing on this case. Further, the state's interest in preserving life must be truly compelling to justify overriding a competent person's right to refuse medical treatment. This is equally true for incompetent patients, who have just as much right as competent patients to have their decisions made while competent respected, even in a substituted judgment framework.

In those rare cases in which a patient's right to decide her own course of treatment has been judicially overridden, courts have usually acted to vindicate the state's interest in protecting third parties, even if in fetal state. *See* Jefferson v. Griffin Spalding County Hosp. Authority (ordering that caesarean section be performed on a woman in her thirty-ninth week of pregnancy to save both the mother and the fetus); Raleigh Fitkin–Paul Morgan Memorial Hosp. v. Anderson (ordering blood transfusions over the objection of a Jehovah's Witness, in her thirty-second week of pregnancy, to save her life and that of the fetus); In re Jamaica Hosp., (ordering the transfusion of blood to a Jehovah's Witness eighteen weeks pregnant, who objected on religious grounds, and finding that the state's interest in the not-yet-viable fetus outweighed the patient's interests); Crouse Irving Memorial Hosp. v. Paddock, (ordering transfusions as necessary over religious objections to save the mother and a fetus that was to be prematurely delivered); *cf.* In re President & Directors of Georgetown College, (ordering a transfusion, *inter alia*, because of a mother's parental duty to her living minor children). *But see* Taft v. Taft (vacating an order which required a woman in her fourth month of pregnancy to undergo a "purse-string" operation, on the ground that there were no compelling circumstances to justify overriding her religious objections and her constitutional right of privacy).

What we distill from the cases discussed in this section is that every person has the right, under the common law and the Constitution, to accept or refuse medical treatment.14 This right of bodily integrity belongs equally to persons who are competent and persons who are not. Further, it matters not what the quality of a patient's life may be; the right of bodily integrity is not extinguished simply because someone is ill, or even at death's door. To protect that right against intrusion by others—family members, doctors, hospitals, or anyone else, however well-intentioned—we hold that a court must determine the patient's wishes by any means available, and must abide by those wishes unless there are truly extraordinary or compelling reasons to override them. When the patient is incompetent, or when the court is unable to determine competency, the substituted judgment procedure must be followed.

From the record before us, we simply cannot tell whether A.C. was ever competent, after being sedated, to make an informed decision one way or the other regarding the proposed caesarean section. The trial court never made any finding about A.C.'s competency to decide....

We think it is incumbent on any trial judge in a case like this, unless it is impossible to do so, to ascertain whether a patient is competent to make her own medical decisions. Whenever possible, the judge should personally attempt to speak with the patient and ascertain her wishes directly, rather than relying exclusively on hearsay evidence, even from doctors. It is improper to presume that a patient is incompetent. We have no reason to believe that, if competent, A.C. would or would not have refused consent to a caesarean. We hold, however, that without a competent refusal from A.C. to go forward with the surgery, and without a finding through substituted judgment that A.C. would not have consented to the surgery, it was error for the trial court to proceed to a balancing analysis, weighing the rights of A.C. against the interests of the state.

.   .   .

B.   Substituted Judgment

.   .   .

Under the substituted judgment procedure, the court as decision-maker must "substitute itself as nearly as may be for the incompetent, and . . . act upon the same motives and considerations as would have moved her . . . ."

.   .   .

We begin with the proposition that the substituted judgment inquiry is primarily a subjective one: as nearly as possible, the court must ascertain what the patient would do if competent. Due process strongly suggests (and may even require) that counsel or a guardian *ad litem* should be appointed for the patient unless the situation is so urgent that there is no time to do so.

.   .   .

After A.C. was informed of the court's decision, she consented to the caesarean; moments later, however, she withdrew her consent. The trial court did not then make a finding as to whether A.C. was competent to make the medical decision or whether she had made an informed decision one way or the other. Nor did the court then make a substituted judgment for A.C. Instead, the court said that it was "still not clear what her intent is" and again ordered the caesarean.

It is that order which we must now set aside. What a trial court must do in a case such as this is to determine, if possible, whether the patient is capable of making an informed decision about the course of her medical treatment. If she is, and if she makes such a decision, her wishes will control in virtually all cases. If the court finds that the patient is incapable of making an informed consent (and thus incompetent), then the court must make a substituted judgment. This means that the court must ascertain as best it can what the patient would do if faced with the particular treatment question. Again, in virtually all cases the decision of the patient, albeit discerned through the mechanism of substituted judgment, will control. . . .

.   .   .

Note: Dead Dads

It is now possible to harvest and preserve the sperm of deceased men for later use. In 1999 newspapers announced the birth of a baby girl whose biological father had died more than two years prior to her birth. Sperm from the healthy infant's biological father was extracted from his corpse by physicians at the request of his grieving widow two days after the man's unexpected death.

According to lawyer and bioethicist Lori B. Andrews, harvesting sperm from dead and comatose men is no longer rare. See Lori Andrews, *The Sperminator: Dead Man Father's Child!* The New York Times Magazine, Sunday March 28, 1999. Widows, girlfriends and parents have sought to preserve the procreative potential of deceased men. A mechanical technique known as "electroejaculation" has been used to stimulate ejaculation of sperm, although ordinary masturbation by a family member has been a low-tech alternative. Does removing sperm from a dead man raise ethical or legal issues? Professor Andrews likens the practice to rape. Is it like rape? Are the men in such cases simply being used? Does a widow's constitutional right to procreation extend to the use of her dead husband's sperm?

CLEVELAND BOARD OF EDUCATION v. LAFLEUR

414 U.S. 632 (1974).

MR. JUSTICE STEWART delivered the opinion of the Court.

. . .

I

Jo Carol LaFleur and Ann Elizabeth Nelson, the respondents in No. 72–777, are junior high school teachers employed by the Board of Education of Cleveland, Ohio. Pursuant to a rule first adopted in 1952, the school board requires every pregnant school teacher to take maternity leave without pay, beginning five months before the expected birth of her child. . . .

. . .

II

This Court has long recognized that freedom of personal choice in matters of marriage and family life is one of the liberties protected by the Due Process Clause of the Fourteenth Amendment. . . .

By acting to penalize the pregnant teacher for deciding to bear a child, overly restrictive maternity leave regulations can constitute a heavy burden on the exercise of these protected freedoms. Because public school maternity leave rules directly affect "one of the basic civil rights of man," Skinner v. Oklahoma, *supra*, at 541, the Due Process Clause of the Fourteenth Amendment requires that such rules must not needlessly, arbitrarily, or capriciously impinge upon this vital area of a teacher's constitutional liberty. . . .

. . .

The mandatory termination provisions of the Cleveland and Chesterfield County rules surely operate to insulate the classroom from the presence of potentially incapacitated pregnant teachers. But the question is whether the rules sweep too broadly. See Shelton v. Tucker, 364 U.S. 479. That question must be answered in the affirmative, for the provisions amount to a conclusive presumption that every pregnant teacher who reaches the fifth or sixth month of pregnancy is physically incapable of continuing. There is no individualized determination by the teacher's doctor—or the school board's—as to any particular teacher's ability to continue at her job. The rules contain an irrebuttable presumption of physical incompetency, and that presumption applies even when the medical evidence as to an individual woman's physical status might be wholly to the contrary.

As the Court noted last Term in Vlandis v. Kline, 412 U.S. 441, 446, "permanent irrebuttable presumptions have long been disfavored under the Due Process Clauses of the Fifth and Fourteenth Amendments." . . .

. . . .

These principles control our decision in the cases before us. While the medical experts in these cases differed on many points, they unanimously agreed on one—the ability of any particular pregnant woman to continue at work past any fixed time in her pregnancy is very much an individual matter. Even assuming, *arguendo*, that there are some women who would be physically unable to work past the particular cutoff dates embodied in the challenged rules, it is evident that there are large numbers of teachers who are fully capable of continuing work for longer than the Cleveland and Chesterfield County regulations will allow. Thus, the conclusive presumption embodied in these rules, like that in Vlandis, is neither "necessarily [nor] universally true," and is violative of the Due Process Clause.

The school boards have argued that the mandatory termination dates serve the interest of administrative convenience, since there are many instances of teacher pregnancy, and the rules obviate the necessity for case-by-case determinations. . . .

While it might be easier for the school boards to conclusively presume that all pregnant women are unfit to teach past the fourth or fifth month or even the first month, of pregnancy, administrative convenience alone is insufficient to make valid what otherwise is a violation of due process of law. The Fourteenth Amendment requires the school boards to employ alternative administrative means, which do not so broadly infringe upon basic constitutional liberty, in support of their legitimate goals.

We conclude, therefore, that neither the necessity for continuity of instruction nor the state interest in keeping physically unfit teachers out of the classroom can justify the sweeping mandatory leave regulations that the Cleveland and Chesterfield County School Boards have adopted. While the regulations no doubt represent a good faith attempt to achieve a laudable goal, they cannot pass muster under the Due Process Clause of the Fourteenth Amendment, because they employ irrebuttable presumptions that unduly penalize a female teacher for deciding to bear a child.

DEMAY v. ROBERTS

46 Mich. 160, 9 N.W. 146 (1881).

CHIEF JUSTICE MARSTON.

The declaration in this case ... sets forth that the plaintiff was ... a poor married woman, and being confined in child-bed and a stranger, employed in a professional capacity defendant DeMay who was a physician; .... [D]efendant visited the plaintiff as such, and against her desire and intending to deceive her wrongfully, etc., introduced and caused to be present at the house and lying-in room of the plaintiff while she was in the pains of parturition the defendant Scattergood, who intruded upon the privacy of the plaintiff, indecently, wrongfully and unlawfully laid hands upon her and assaulted her, the said Scattergood, which was well known to defendant DeMay, being a young unmarried man, a stranger to plaintiff and utterly ignorant of the practice of medicine....

... [E]vidence was given tending to show that Scattergood very reluctantly accompanied Dr. DeMay ... that the night was a dark and stormy one, the roads ... so bad that a horse could not be ridden or driven over them; that the doctor was sick and very much fatigued from overwork, and therefore asked the defendant Scattergood to accompany and assist him in carrying a lantern, umbrella and certain [other] articles....

. . .

Dr. DeMay therefore took an unprofessional young unmarried man with him, introduced and permitted him to remain in the house of the plaintiff, when it was apparent that he could hear at least, if not see all that was said and done.... It would be shocking to our sense of right, justice and propriety to doubt even but that for such an act the law would afford an ample remedy. To the plaintiff the occasion was a most sacred one and no one had a right to intrude unless invited or because of some real and pressing necessity.... The plaintiff had a legal right to the privacy of her apartment at such a time, and the law secures to her this right.... In obtaining admission at such a time and under such circumstances without fully disclosing his true character, both parties were guilty of deceit, and the wrong thus done entitles the injured party to damages afterwards sustained, from shame and mortification.

KNIGHT v. PENOBSCOT BAY MEDICAL CENTER

420 A.2d 915 (Me. 1980).

(This case is in Chapter Five of these materials.)

Note: The Childbirth Environment

DeMay v. Roberts may be the oldest American case making reference to a right of privacy. Was the interest at issue in *DeMay* best understood as an interest in physical seclusion during childbirth, or an autonomy interest in controlling the conditions of childbirth? Was the female plaintiff's privacy claim in *DeMay* stronger than the female plaintiff's claim in *Knight* because the former delivered at home? What other factors might have been relevant?

Once the rule, home birth and midwife-assisted birth are now the exceptions. Most American women give birth in hospitals. Only one percent of all pregnant women deliver at home. Hospitals insure access to hygienic medical and nursing services. Many women doubtless view homebirth as medically risky for mother and child. However, hospital births inject strangers into the birthing process. Moreover, they burden families with webs of regulation. Advocates urge that women are entitled to more decisional and physical privacy in childbirth than traditional hospitals afford. *See* Barbara Katz Rothman, *In Labor: Women and Power in the Birthplace* (1982).

Do women have a legal interest, over and above common law privacy interests, in giving birth in intimate settings free from unwanted contact with strangers and regulation? Home birth and mid-wifery have been said to raise "two basic constitutional claims—that home birth is encompassed within the ... right of privacy, and that the right of privacy includes one's choice of an unlicensed birth attendant." Charles Wolfson, *Midwives and Home Birth: Social, Medical, and Legal Perspectives*, 37 Hastings L.J. 909, 929 n. 117 (1986). *See* Note, *Respecting Liberty and Preventing Harm: Limits of State Intervention in Prenatal Choice*, 8 Harv. J.L. & Pub. Pol'y 19 (1985).

In *People v. Rosburg*, 805 P.2d 432 (Colo. 1991), the Supreme Court of Colorado rejected claims made by Jean Rosburg and Barbara Parker that state laws prohibiting the practice of midwifery without a license violated the right of privacy of pregnant women to choose their method of childbirth. Although the court agreed that the lay midwives had standing to assert the privacy rights of pregnant women, it held that women's privacy and equal protection were not violated by a statute limiting the practice of midwifery to licensed midwives. *Cf. Leigh v. Board of Registration in Nursing*, 506 N.E. 2d 91, 399 Mass. 558 (1987) (upholding statute limiting births attended by nonphysicians to licensed facilities and certified nurse midwives) ("Although we recognize that homebirths are safe in many circumstances, we also note that, in many other cases, back-up assistance and emergency facilities must be immediately available.").

4. FORCED STERILIZATION

SKINNER v. OKLAHOMA
316 U.S. 535 (1942).

MR. JUSTICE DOUGLAS delivered the opinion of the Court.

This case touches a sensitive and important area of human rights. Oklahoma deprives certain individuals of a right which is basic to the perpetuation of a race—the right to have offspring. Oklahoma has decreed the enforcement of its law against petitioner, overruling his claim that it violated the Fourteenth Amendment. Because that decision raised grave and substantial constitutional questions, we granted the petition for certiorari.

The statute involved is Oklahoma's Habitual Criminal Sterilization Act. The Act defines an "habitual criminal" as a person who, having been convicted two or more times for crimes "amounting to felonies involving moral turpitude," either in an Oklahoma court or in a court of any other State, is thereafter convicted of such a felony in Oklahoma and is sentenced to a term of imprisonment in an Oklahoma penal institution. Machinery is provided for the institution by the Attorney General of a proceeding against such a person in the Oklahoma courts for a judgement that such person shall be rendered sexually sterile. Notice, an opportunity to be heard, and the right to a jury trial are provided. The issues triable in such a proceeding are narrow and confined. If the court or jury finds that the defendant is an "habitual criminal" and that he "may be rendered sexually sterile without detriment to his or her general health," then the court "shall render judgement to the effect that said defendant be rendered sexually sterile" by the operation of vasectomy in case of a male, and of salpingectomy in case of a female. Only one other provision of the Act is material here, and that is Section 195, which provides that "offenses arising out of the violation of the prohibitory laws, revenue acts, embezzlement, or political offenses, shall not come or be considered within the terms of this Act."

Petitioner was convicted in 1926 of the crime of stealing chickens, and was sentenced to the Oklahoma State Reformatory. In 1929 he was convicted of the crime of robbery with firearms, and was sentenced to the reformatory. In 1934 he was convicted again of robbery with fire-arms, and was sentenced to the penitentiary. He was confined there in 1935 when the Act was passed. In 1936 the Attorney General instituted proceedings against him. . . .

Several objections to the constitutionality of the Act have been pressed upon us. It is urged that the Act cannot be sustained as an exercise of the police power, in view of the state of scientific authorities respecting inheritability of criminal traits. It is argued that due process is lacking because ... no opportunity to be heard on the issue as to whether he is the probable potential parent of socially undesirable offspring. It is also suggested that the Act is penal in character and that the sterilization provided for is cruel and unusual punishment and violative of the Fourteenth Amendment. We pass those points without intimating an opinion on them, for there is a feature of the Act which clearly condemns it. That is, its failure to meet the requirements of the equal protection clause of the Fourteenth Amendment.

We do not stop to point out all of the inequalities in this Act. A few examples will suffice. . . . A person who enters a chicken coop and steals chickens commits a felony; and he may be sterilized if he is thrice convicted. If, however, he is a bailee of the property and fraudulently appropriates it, he is an embezzler. Hence, no matter how habitual his proclivities for embezzlement are and no matter how often his conviction, he may not be sterilized. . . .

. . .

... [T]he instant legislation runs afoul of the equal protection clause, though we give Oklahoma that large deference which the rule of the foregoing cases requires. We are dealing here with legislation which involves one of the basic civil rights of man. Marriage and procreation are fundamental to the very existence and survival of the race. The power to sterilize, if exercised, may have subtle, far-reaching and devastating effects. In evil or reckless hands it can cause races or types which are inimical to the dominant group to wither and disappear. There is no redemption for the individual whom the law touches. Any experiment which the State conducts is to his irreparable injury. He is forever deprived of a basic liberty. We mention these matters not to reexamine the scope of the police power of the States. We advert to them merely in emphasis of our view that strict scrutiny of the classification which a State makes in a sterilization law is essential, lest unwittingly, or otherwise, invidious discriminations are made against groups or types of individuals in violation of the constitutional guaranty of just and equal laws. The guaranty of "equal protection of the laws is a pledge of the protection of equal laws." When the law lays an unequal hand on those who have committed intrinsically the same quality of offense and sterilized one and not the other, it has made as invidious a discrimination as if it had selected a particular race or nationality for oppressive treatment.... Oklahoma's line between larceny by fraud and embezzlement is determined, as we have noted, "with reference to the time when the fraudulent intent to convert the property to the taker's own use" arises. We have not the slightest basis for inferring that that line has any significance in eugenics.... The equal protection clause would indeed be a formula of empty words if such conspicuously artificial lines could be drawn.

Notes: Temporary and Permanent Sterilization

(1) **Court-Ordered Birth Control**. Does *Skinner v. Oklahoma* entail opposition to court-ordered birth control? Consider the following, which occurred just one month after the Food and Drug Administration approved the sale of Norplant, a contraceptive device consisting of match-sized rubber tubes containing synthetic hormones that suppress ovulation when surgically inserted in the upper arm of a fertile woman:

> A [27 year old black] mother who pleaded guilty to child abuse has agreed to have a birth control device implanted under her arm as part of a sentence of probation.

> [The woman], Darlene Johnson, who is pregnant, is to serve one year in jail before starting three years of probation, when a device that releases hormones to block pregnancy is to be implanted.

> Her lawyer, Charles Rothbaum, said today that he was shocked at the sentence imposed on Wednesday by Superior Court Judge Howard Broadman [in Vasalia California].

The police charged Ms. Johnson, who lives in Tulare, with beating two of her children with a belt and electrical cord in September. The children are now living in foster homes.

"Woman Agrees to Sentence That Requires Birth Control," *The New York Times*, January 4, 1991.

(2) Nonconsensual Procedures. A slight majority of courts hold there is no inherent authority to judicially compel the sterilization of legally incompetent persons, such as mentally retarded women. *See Sparkman v. McFarlin*, 552 F.2d 172 (7th Cir. 1977), *rev'd sub nom., Stump v. Sparkman*, 435 U.S. 349 (1978); *Wade v. Bethesda Hosp.*, 337 F. Supp. 671 (S.D. Ohio 1971); *Guardianship of Tulley*, 83 Cal. App. 3d 698, 146 Cal. Rptr. 266 (1978), *cert. denied*, 440 U.S. 967 (1979); *Guardianship of Kemp*, 43 Cal. App. 3d 758, 118 Cal. Rptr. 64 (1974); *In re S.C.E.*, 378 A.2d 144 (Del. Ch. 1977); *A.L. v. G.R.H.*, 163 Ind. App. 636, 325 N.E.2d 501 (1975), *cert. denied*, 425 U.S. 936 (1976); *Holmes v. Powers*, 439 S.W.2d 579 (Ky. App. 1968); *In re M.K.R.*, 515 S.W.2d 467 (Mo. 1974); *Application of A.D.*, 90 Misc. 2d 236, 394 N.Y.S.2d 139 (1977), *aff'd on other grounds*, 64 A.D.2d 898, 408 N.Y.S.2d 104 (1978); *Smith v. Command*, 231 Mich. 409, 204 N.W. 140 (1925); *Frazier v. Levi*, 440 S.W.2d 393 (Tex. Civ. App. 1969).

The emerging yet still minority rule is to allow for judicially approved sterilization provided that appropriate procedural safeguards are followed. Leading cases include *In re Matter of C.D.M.*, 627 P.2d 607 (Alaska 1981); *In re Grady*, 426 A.2d 467 (N.J. 1981); *In re Matter of Moe*, 385 Mass. 555, 432 N.E.2d 712 (1982); *In re A.W.*, 637 P.2d 366 (Colo. 1981).

5. CONTRACT PREGNANCY

Ideals of reproductive autonomy might suggest that competent adult women should be legally free to become commercial surrogate mothers at will. Infertile couples, some scholars argue, have a correlative constitutional privacy right to decide to hire surrogate mothers. How should courts resolve disputes that arise when surrogate mothers wish to void surrogacy contracts and parent children originally intended for others? In *Johnson v. Calvert*, below, The California Supreme Court adopted Professor Marjorie Shultz's theory that the intent of the contracting parties should govern dispute resolution to show the highest regard for women as autonomous choosers. But see Margaret Jane Radin, *Contested Commodities: The Trouble with Trade in Sex, Children, Body Parts and Other Things* 131–153 (1996). Ethical values other than autonomy may be pertinent to decisions about the conditions of pregnancy and parenting. See, e.g., Melinda Roberts, *Child v. Childmaker: Future Persons and Present Duties in Ethics and the Law* (1998). The New Jersey high court has chosen to invalidate contract parenting agreements as tantamount to unlawful commercial adoption and contrary to sound public policy.

MARJORIE SHULTZ, REPRODUCTIVE TECHNOLO-GY AND INTENT-BASED PARENTHOOD: AN OP-PORTUNITY FOR GENDER NEUTRALITY

Wis. L. Rev. 297, 300–03, 319–21 (1990).

Greater individual choice ordinarily implies a welcome potential for greater fulfillment. However, these particular choices are highly controversial. The issues of procreation, marriage, sexuality and child rearing are profoundly bound up with the individual and societal beliefs and values. Some object strenuously to changes wrought by technology in the basic procreative process. Others fear the flexible, pluralist and non-conventional family arrangements that are a likely result of the expansion of choice.

Whatever the doubts, the trend toward conscious choice about and management of reproduction seems certain to continue and expand. Both the evolving techniques and the issues they raise are fundamental. . . .

. . . I propose that legal rules governing modern procreative arrangements and parental status should recognize the importance and legitimacy of individual efforts to project intentions and decisions into the future. Where such intentions are deliberate, explicit and bargained for, where they are the catalyst for reliance and expectations, as is the case in technologically-assisted reproductive arrangements, they should be honored. If these propositions are accepted, contractual perspectives, doctrines and concepts could become important tools for solution of the legal issues raised by modern reproductive technologies.

By embracing the emerging opportunities provided by advancing technology, the law would enhance individual freedom, fulfillment and responsibility. Important additional gains would also accrue. Rules that would determine legal parenthood on the basis of individual intentions about procreation and parenting—at least in the context of reproductive technology—would recognize, encourage and reinforce men's choices to nurture children. By adopting a sex-neutral criterion such as intention, the law would partially offset the biological disadvantages men experience in accessing child-nurturing opportunities. . . .

. . . For the most part our society eagerly embraces the ideology of autonomy. . . . Many would admit that although we are liberated and energized by options, we also draw stability and comfort from boundaries. Choice brings moral responsibility, and with it the possibility of blame or inadequacy. . . . Ironically, however, the availability of choice is not something we control; our decisions are about how fully to recognize and exercise it.

. . .

While legal assignment of parental status has typically drawn legitimacy from its reflection of and alignment with biological givens, adoption has long constituted an important, albeit partial, exception. Adoption provides an avenue to parenthood through legally recognized intention rather than through biological connection. Individual intentions ... are the trigger both for surrendering a child and for adopting one. However, the legal system of adoption has traditionally mimicked ... the conventional nuclear family....

Standard adoption procedures substitute the adoptive for the biological parents.... All records of the parties and the circumstances are buried in secret files of a "go-between," never to be revealed to any of the parties. No ties of knowledge, name or personal contact are to remain after the initial redefinition takes place. This approach has been understood and justified as being for the welfare of all concerned. But it may also be analyzed as a limitation unnecessarily imposed by concepts too readily assumed to be mandatory. [Variations on the conventional nuclear biological family are deemed aberrant.] Therefore, facts must be altered and suppressed in order to make what began as intention mirror as closely as possible the standard model of socially legitimated biology....

In recent years, the efforts of adopted children to find their "real" parents, the resistance of some mothers who are giving up their babies to being utterly eliminated from the lives of their children, the conflict between rights of birth parents and those of adoptive parents, as well as an increase in private adoptions that do not necessarily honor the norms of mainstream adoption all suggest [non-traditional preferences and needs]. Intention, rather than biology, is the basis for giving up or adopting a child.... Thus, while adoption is a partial exception to the generalization that legal parenthood has traditionally tracked biological fate and fact, the exception is much attenuated.

JOHNSON v. CALVERT

5 Cal. 4th 84, 19 Cal.Rptr.2d 494, 851 P.2d 776.

PANELLI, J.

. . .

Mark and Crispina Calvert are a married couple who desired to have a child. Crispina was forced to undergo a hysterectomy in 1984. Her ovaries remained capable of producing eggs, however, and the couple eventually considered surrogacy. In 1989 Anna Johnson heard about Crispina's plight from a coworker and offered to serve as a surrogate for the Calverts.

On January 15, 1990, Mark, Crispina, and Anna signed a contract providing that an embryo created by the sperm of Mark and the egg of Crispina would be implanted in Anna and the child born would be taken into Mark and Crispina's home "as their child." Anna agreed she would relinquish "all parental rights" to the child in favor of Mark and Crispina. In return, Mark and Crispina would pay Anna $10,000 in a series of installments, the last to be paid six weeks after the child's birth.

Mark and Crispina were also to pay for a $200,000 life insurance policy on Anna's life. [Anna gave birth to a healthy male infant who was the genetic offspring of the Calverts. Anna did not want to be bound by the surrogacy contract and brought an action seeking parental rights ordinarily accorded birth mothers.]

. . .

Although [a California statute] recognizes both genetic consanguinity and giving birth as means of establishing a mother and child relationship, when the two means do not coincide in one woman, she who intended to procreate the child—that is, she who intended to bring about the birth of a child that she intended to raise as her own—is the natural mother under California law.

. . .

Anna urges that surrogacy contracts violate several social policies. Relying on her contention that she is the child's legal, natural mother, she cites the public policy . . . prohibiting the payment for consent to adoption of a child. She argues further that the policies underlying the adoption laws of this state are violated by the surrogacy contract because it in effect constitutes a prebirth waiver of her parental rights.

We disagree. Gestational surrogacy differs in crucial respects from adoption and so is not subject to the adoption statutes. The parties voluntarily agreed to participate in in vitro fertilization and related medical procedures before the child was conceived; at the time when Anna entered into the contract, therefore, she was not vulnerable to financial inducements to part with her own expected offspring. As discussed above, Anna was not the genetic mother of the child. The payments to Anna under the contract were meant to compensate her for her services in gestating the fetus and undergoing labor, rather than for giving up "parental" rights to the child. Payments were due both during the pregnancy and after the child's birth. We are, accordingly, unpersuaded that the contract used in this case violates . . . public policies . . . and the adoption statutes. For the same reasons, we conclude these contracts do not implicate the policies underlying the statutes governing termination of parental rights. . . .

It has been suggested that gestational surrogacy may run afoul of prohibitions on involuntary servitude. (See U.S. Const., Amend. XIII; Cal. Const., art. I, § 6; Pen.Code, § 181.). . . . We see no potential for that evil in the contract at issue here, and extrinsic evidence of coercion or duress is utterly lacking. We note that although at one point the contract purports to give Mark and Crispina the sole right to determine whether to abort the pregnancy, at another point it acknowledges: "All parties understand that a pregnant woman has the absolute right to abort or not abort any fetus she is carrying. Any promise to the contrary is unenforceable." We therefore need not determine the validity of a surrogacy contract purporting to deprive the gestator of her freedom to terminate the pregnancy.

Finally, Anna and some commentators have expressed concern that surrogacy contracts tend to exploit or dehumanize women, especially women of lower economic status. Anna's objections center around the psychological harm she asserts may result from the gestator's relinquishing the child to whom she has given birth. Some have also cautioned that the practice of surrogacy may encourage society to view children as commodities, subject to trade at their parents' will.

. . .

We are unpersuaded that gestational surrogacy arrangements are so likely to cause the untoward results Anna cites as to demand their invalidation on public policy grounds. Although common sense suggests that women of lesser means serve as surrogate mothers more often than do wealthy women, there has been no proof that surrogacy contracts exploit poor women to any greater degree than economic necessity in general exploits them by inducing them to accept lower-paid or otherwise undesirable employment. We are likewise unpersuaded by the claim that surrogacy will foster the attitude that children are mere commodities; no evidence is offered to support it. The limited data available seem to reflect an absence of significant adverse effects of surrogacy on all participants.

IN THE MATTER OF BABY M

109 N.J. 396, 537 A.2d 1227 (1988).

WILENTZ, C.J.

. . .

I. FACTS

In February 1985, William Stern and Mary Beth Whitehead entered into a surrogacy contract. It recited that Stern's wife, Elizabeth, was infertile, that they wanted a child, and that Mrs. Whitehead was willing to provide that child as the mother with Mr. Stern as the father.

The contract provided that through artificial insemination using Mr. Stern's sperm, Mrs. Whitehead would become pregnant, carry the child to term, bear it, deliver it to the Sterns, and thereafter do whatever was necessary to terminate her maternal rights so that Mrs. Stern could thereafter adopt the child. Mrs. Whitehead's husband, Richard, was also a party to the contract; Mrs. Stern was not. Mr. Whitehead promised to do all acts necessary to rebut the presumption of paternity under the Parentage Act. N.J.S.A. 9:17–43a(1),–44a. [Subsequent to the trial court proceedings, Mr. and Mrs. Whitehead were divorced, and soon thereafter Mrs. Whitehead remarried.] Although Mrs. Stern was not a party to the surrogacy agreement, the contract gave her sole custody of the child in the event of Mr. Stern's death. Mrs. Stern's status as a nonparty to the surrogate parenting agreement presumably was to avoid the application of the baby-selling statute to this arrangement. N.J.S.A. 9:3–54.

Mr. Stern, on his part, agreed to attempt the artificial insemination and to pay Mrs. Whitehead $10,000 after the child's birth, on its delivery to him. In a separate contract, Mr. Stern agreed to pay $7,500 to the Infertility Center of New York ("ICNY"). The Center's advertising campaigns solicit surrogate mothers and encourage infertile couples to consider surrogacy. ICNY arranged for the surrogacy contract by bringing the parties together, explaining the process to them, furnishing the contractual form, and providing legal counsel.

The history of the parties' involvement in this arrangement suggests their good faith. William and Elizabeth Stern were married in July 1974, having met at the University of Michigan, where both were Ph.D candidates. Due to financial considerations and Mrs. Stern's pursuit of a medical degree and residency, they decided to defer starting a family until 1981. Before then, however, Mrs. Stern learned that she might have multiple sclerosis and that the disease in some cases renders pregnancy a serious health risk. Her anxiety appears to have exceeded the actual risk, which current medical authorities assess as minimal. Nonetheless that anxiety was evidently quite real, Mrs. Stern fearing that pregnancy might precipitate blindness, paraplegia, or other forms of debilitation. Based on the perceived risk, the Sterns decided to forego having their own children. The decision had a special significance for Mr. Stern. Most of his family had been destroyed in the Holocaust. As the family's only survivor, he very much wanted to continue his bloodline.

Initially the Sterns considered adoption, but were discouraged by the substantial delay apparently involved and by the potential problem they saw arising from their age and their differing religious backgrounds. They were most eager for some other means to start a family.

The paths of Mrs. Whitehead and the Sterns to surrogacy were similar. Both responded to advertising by ICNY. The Sterns' response, following their inquiries into adoption, was the result of their long-standing decision to have a child. Mrs. Whitehead's response apparently resulted from her sympathy with family members and others who could have no children (she stated that she wanted to give another couple the "gift of life"); she also wanted the $10,000 to help her family.

Both parties, undoubtedly because of their own self-interest, were less sensitive to the implications of the transaction than they might otherwise have been. Mrs. Whitehead, for instance, appears not to have been concerned about whether the Sterns would make good parents for her child; the Sterns, on their part, while conscious of the obvious possibility that surrendering the child might cause grief to Mrs. Whitehead, overcame their qualms because of their desire for a child. At any rate, both the Sterns and Mrs. Whitehead were committed to the arrangement; both thought it right and constructive.

Mrs. Whitehead had reached her decision concerning surrogacy before the Sterns, and had actually been involved as a potential surrogate mother with another couple. After numerous unsuccessful artificial inseminations, that effort was abandoned. Thereafter, the Sterns learned of the Infertility Center, the possibilities of surrogacy, and of Mary Beth Whitehead. The two couples met to discuss the surrogacy arrangement and decided to go forward. On February 6, 1985, Mr. Stern and Mr. and Mrs. Whitehead executed the surrogate parenting agreement. After several artificial inseminations over a period of months, Mrs. Whitehead became pregnant. The pregnancy was uneventful and on March 27, 1986, Baby M was born.

Not wishing anyone at the hospital to be aware of the surrogacy arrangement, Mr. and Mrs. Whitehead appeared to all as the proud parents of a healthy female child. Her birth certificate indicated her name to be Sara Elizabeth Whitehead and her father to be Richard Whitehead. In accordance with Mrs. Whitehead's request, the Sterns visited the hospital unobtrusively to see the newborn child.

Mrs. Whitehead realized, almost from the moment of birth, that she could not part with this child. She had felt a bond with it even during pregnancy. Some indication of the attachment was conveyed to the Sterns at the hospital when they told Mrs. Whitehead what they were going to name the baby. She apparently broke into tears and indicated that she did not know if she could give up the child. She talked about how the baby looked like her daughter, and made it clear that she was experiencing great difficulty with the decision.

Nonetheless, Mrs. Whitehead was, for the moment, true to her word. Despite powerful inclinations to the contrary, she turned her child over to the Sterns on March 30 at the Whiteheads' home.

The Sterns were thrilled with their new child. They had planned extensively for its arrival, far beyond the practical furnishing of a room for her. It was a time of joyful celebration—not just for them but for their friends as well. The Sterns looked forward to raising their daughter, whom they named Melissa. While aware by then that Mrs. Whitehead was undergoing an emotional crisis, they were as yet not cognizant of the depth of that crisis and its implications for their newly-enlarged family.

Later in the evening of March 30, Mrs. Whitehead became deeply disturbed, disconsolate, stricken with unbearable sadness. She had to have her child. She could not eat, sleep, or concentrate on anything other than her need for her baby. The next day she went to the Sterns' home and told them how much she was suffering.

The depth of Mrs. Whitehead's despair surprised and frightened the Sterns. She told them that she could not live without her baby, that she must have her, even if only for one week, that thereafter she would surrender her child. The Sterns, concerned that Mrs. Whitehead might indeed commit suicide, not wanting under any circumstances to risk that, and in any event believing that Mrs. Whitehead would keep her word, turned the child over to her. It was not until four months later, after a series of attempts to regain possession of the child, that Melissa was returned to the Sterns, having been forcibly removed from the home where she was then living with Mr. and Mrs. Whitehead, the home in Florida owned by Mary Beth Whitehead's parents.

The struggle over Baby M began when it became apparent that Mrs. Whitehead could not return the child to Mr. Stern. Due to Mrs. Whitehead's refusal to relinquish the baby, Mr. Stern filed a complaint seeking enforcement of the surrogacy contract. He alleged, accurately, that Mrs. Whitehead had not only refused to comply with the surrogacy contract but had threatened to flee from New Jersey with the child in order to avoid even the possibility of his obtaining custody. The court papers asserted that if Mrs. Whitehead were to be given notice of the application for an order requiring her to relinquish custody, she would, prior to the hearing, leave the state with the baby. And that is precisely what she did. After the order was entered, *ex parte*, the process server, aided by the police, in the presence of the Sterns, entered Mrs. Whitehead's home to execute the order. Mr. Whitehead fled with the child, who had been handed to him through a window while those who came to enforce the order were thrown off balance by a dispute over the child's current name.

The Whiteheads immediately fled to Florida with Baby M. They stayed initially with Mrs. Whitehead's parents, where one of Mrs. Whitehead's children had been living. For the next three months, the Whiteheads and Melissa lived at roughly twenty different hotels, motels, and homes in order to avoid apprehension. From time to time Mrs. Whitehead would call Mr. Stern to discuss the matter; the conversations, recorded by Mr. Stern on advice of counsel, show an escalating dispute about rights, morality, and power, accompanied by threats of Mrs. Whitehead to kill herself, to kill the child, and falsely to accuse Mr. Stern of sexually molesting Mrs. Whitehead's other daughter.

Eventually the Sterns discovered where the Whiteheads were staying, commenced supplementary proceedings in Florida, and obtained an order requiring the Whiteheads to turn over the child. Police in Florida enforced the order, forcibly removing the child from her grandparents' home. She was soon thereafter brought to New Jersey and turned over to the Sterns. The prior order of the court, issued *ex parte*, awarding custody of the child to the Sterns *pendente lite*, was reaffirmed by the trial court after consideration of the certified representations of the parties (both represented by counsel) concerning the unusual sequence of events that had unfolded. Pending final judgment, Mrs. Whitehead was awarded limited visitation with Baby M.

The Sterns' complaint, in addition to seeking possession and ultimately custody of the child, sought enforcement of the surrogacy contract. Pursuant to the contract, it asked that the child be permanently placed in their custody, that Mrs. Whitehead's parental rights be terminated, and that Mrs. Stern be allowed to adopt the child, *i.e.*, that, for all purposes, Melissa become the Sterns' child.

The trial took ... two months.... It held that the surrogacy contract was valid; ordered that Mrs. Whitehead's parental rights be terminated and that sole custody of the child be granted to Mr. Stern; and, after hearing brief testimony from Mrs. Stern, immediately entered an order allowing the adoption of Melissa by Mrs. Stern, all in accordance with the surrogacy contract. Pending the outcome of the appeal, we granted a continuation of visitation to Mrs. Whitehead, although slightly more limited than the visitation allowed during the trial.

. . .

Mrs. Whitehead appealed. This Court granted direct certification. 107 N.J. 140 (1987)....

. . .

II. INVALIDITY AND UNENFORCEABILITY OF SURROGACY CONTRACT

We have concluded that this surrogacy contract is invalid. Our conclusion has two bases: direct conflict with existing statutes and conflict with the public policies of this State, as expressed in its statutory and decisional law.

One of the surrogacy contract's basic purposes, to achieve the adoption of a child through private placement, though permitted in New Jersey "is very much disfavored." Its use of money for this purpose—and we have no doubt whatsoever that the money is being paid to obtain an adoption and not, as the Sterns argue, for the personal services of Mary Beth Whitehead—is illegal and perhaps criminal. In addition to the inducement of money, there is the coercion of contract: the natural mother's irrevocable agreement, prior to birth, even prior to conception, to surrender the child to the adoptive couple. Such an agreement is totally unenforceable in private placement adoption. Even where the adoption is through an approved agency, the formal agreement to surrender occurs only after birth ... and then, by regulation, only after the birth mother has been counseled.

The [surrogacy contract's provisions] not only directly conflict with New Jersey statutes, but also offend long-established State policies....

A. *Conflict with Statutory Provisions*

The surrogacy contract conflicts with: (1) laws prohibiting the use of money in connection with adoptions; (2) laws requiring proof of parental unfitness or abandonment before termination of parental rights is ordered or an adoption is granted; and (3) laws that make surrender of custody and consent to adoption revocable in private placement adoptions.

. . .

B. *Public Policy Considerations*

The surrogacy contract's invalidity ... is further underlined when its goals and means are measured against New Jersey's public policy. The contract's basic premise, that the natural parents can decide in advance of birth which one is to have custody of the child, bears no relationship to the settled law that the child's best interests shall determine custody. The fact that the trial court remedied that aspect of the contract through the "best interests" phrase does not make the contractual provision any less offensive to the public policy of this State.

The surrogacy contract guarantees permanent separation of the child from one of its natural parents. Our policy, however, has long been that to the extent possible, children should remain with and be brought up by both of their natural parents. . . .

. . .

The surrogacy contract violates the policy of this State that the rights of natural parents are equal concerning their child, the father's right no greater than the mother's. "The parent and child relationship extends equally to every child and to every parent, regardless of the marital status of the parents."

The policies expressed in our comprehensive laws governing consent to the surrender of a child, discussed *supra* at 429–434, stand in stark contrast to the surrogacy contract and what it implies. Here there is no counseling, independent or otherwise, of the natural mother, no evaluation, no warning.

. . .

Under the contract, the natural mother is irrevocably committed before she knows the strength of her bond with her child. She never makes a totally voluntary, informed decision, for quite clearly any decision prior to the baby's birth is, in the most important sense, uninformed, and any decision after that, compelled by a pre-existing contractual commitment, the threat of a lawsuit, and the inducement of a $10,000 payment, is less than totally voluntary. Her interests are of little concern to those who controlled this transaction.

Although the interest of the natural father and adoptive mother is certainly the predominant interest, realistically the *only* interest served, even they are left with less than what public policy requires. They know little about the natural mother, her genetic makeup, and her psychological and medical history. Moreover, not even a superficial attempt is made to determine their awareness of their responsibilities as parents.

Worst of all, however, is the contract's total disregard of the best interests of the child. There is not the slightest suggestion that any inquiry will be made at any time to determine the fitness of the Sterns as custodial parents, of Mrs. Stern as an adoptive parent, their superiority to Mrs. Whitehead, or the effect on the child of not living with her natural mother.

This is the sale of a child, or, at the very least, the sale of a mother's right to her child, the only mitigating factor being that one of the purchasers is the father. Almost every evil that prompted the prohibition of the payment of money in connection with adoptions exists here.

. . .

In the scheme contemplated by the surrogacy contract in this case, a middle man, propelled by profit, promotes the sale. Whatever idealism may have motivated any of the participants, the profit motive predominates, permeates, and ultimately governs the transaction. The demand for children is great and the supply small. . . .

Intimated, but disputed, is the assertion that surrogacy will be used for the benefit of the rich at the expense of the poor. . . . [The] Sterns are not rich and the Whiteheads not poor. Nevertheless, it is clear to us that it is unlikely that surrogate mothers will be as proportionately numerous among those women in the top twenty percent income bracket as among those in the bottom twenty percent. . . . Put differently, we doubt that infertile couples in the low-income bracket will find upper income surrogates.

In any event, even in this case one should not pretend that disparate wealth does not play a part simply because the contrast is not the dramatic "rich versus poor." At the time of trial, the Whiteheads' net assets were probably negative—Mrs. Whitehead's own sister was foreclosing on a second mortgage. Their income derived from Mr. Whitehead's labors. Mrs. Whitehead is a homemaker, having previously held part-time jobs. The Sterns are both professionals, she a medical doctor, he a biochemist. Their combined income when both were working was about $89,500 a year and their assets sufficient to pay for the surrogacy contract arrangements.

The point is made that Mrs. Whitehead *agreed* to the surrogacy arrangement, supposedly fully understanding the consequences. Putting aside the issue of how compelling her need for money may have been, and how significant her understanding of the consequences, we suggest that her consent is irrelevant. There are, in a civilized society, some things that money cannot buy. In America, we decided long ago that merely because conduct purchased by money was "voluntary" did not mean that it was good or beyond regulation and prohibition. . . .

The long-term effects of surrogacy contracts are not known, but feared—the impact on the child who learns her life was bought, that she is the offspring of someone who gave birth to her only to obtain money; the impact on the natural mother as the full weight of her isolation is felt along with the full reality of the sale of her body and her child; the impact on the natural father and adoptive mother once they realize the consequences of their conduct. Literature in related areas suggests these are substantial considerations, although, given the newness of surrogacy, there is little information.

. . .

Beyond that is the potential degradation of some women that may result from this arrangement. In many cases, of course, surrogacy may bring satisfaction, not only to the infertile couple, but to the surrogate mother herself. The fact, however, that many women may not perceive surrogacy negatively but rather see it as an opportunity does not diminish its potential for devastation to other women.

In sum, the harmful consequences of this surrogacy arrangement appear to us all too palpable. In New Jersey the surrogate mother's agreement to sell her child is void. Its irrevocability infects the entire contract, as does the money that purports to buy it.

. . .

III.

TERMINATION

We have already noted that under our laws termination of parental rights cannot be based on contract, but may be granted only on proof of the statutory requirements....

. . .

Nothing in this record justifies a finding that would allow a court to terminate Mary Beth Whitehead's parental rights under the statutory standard. It is not simply that obviously there was no "intentional abandonment or very substantial neglect of parental duties without a reasonable expectation of reversal of that conduct in the future," quite the contrary, but furthermore that the trial court never found Mrs. Whitehead an unfit mother and indeed affirmatively stated that Mary Beth Whitehead had been a good mother to her other children.

Although the best interests of the child is dispositive of the custody issue in a dispute between natural parents, it does not govern the question of termination. It has long been decided that the mere fact that a child would be better off with one set of parents than with another is an insufficient basis for terminating the natural parent's rights....

. . .

... We therefore conclude that the natural mother is entitled to retain her rights as a mother.

IV.

CONSTITUTIONAL ISSUES

Both parties argue that the Constitutions—state and federal—mandate approval of their basic claims. The source of their constitutional arguments is essentially the same: the right of privacy, the right to procreate, the right to the companionship of one's child, those rights flowing either directly from the fourteenth amendment or by its incorporation of the Bill of Rights, or from the ninth amendment, or through the penumbra surrounding all of the Bill of Rights. They are the rights of personal intimacy, of marriage, of sex, of family, of procreation. Whatever their source, it is clear that they are fundamental rights protected by both the federal and state Constitutions. The right asserted by the Sterns is the right of procreation; that asserted by Mary Beth Whitehead is the right to the companionship of her child. We find that the right of procreation does not extend as far as claimed by the Sterns. As for the right asserted by Mrs. Whitehead, since we uphold it on other grounds (*i.e.*, we have restored her as mother and recognized her right, limited by the child's best interests, to her companionship), we need not decide that constitutional issue, and for reasons set forth below, we should not.

. . .

The right to procreate, as protected by the Constitution, has been ruled on directly only once by the United States Supreme Court. *See* Skinner v. Oklahoma (forced sterilization of habitual criminals violates equal protection clause of fourteenth amendment). Although Griswold v. Connecticut is obviously of a similar class, strictly speaking it involves the right *not* to procreate. The right to procreate very simply is the right to have natural children, whether through sexual intercourse or artificial insemination. It is no more than that. Mr. Stern has not been deprived of that right. Through artificial insemination of Mrs. Whitehead, Baby M is his child. The custody, care, companionship, and nurturing that follow birth are not parts of the right to procreation; they are rights that may also be constitutionally protected, but that involve many considerations other than the right of procreation. To assert that Mr. Stern's right of procreation gives him the right to the custody of Baby M would be to assert that Mrs. Whitehead's right of procreation does *not* give her the right to the custody of Baby M; it would be to assert that the constitutional right of procreation includes within it a constitutionally protected contractual right to destroy someone else's right of procreation.

We conclude that the right of procreation is best understood and protected if confined to its essentials, and that when dealing with rights concerning the resulting child, different interests come into play. There is nothing in our culture or society that even begins to suggest a fundamental right on the part of the father to the custody of the child as part of his right to procreate when opposed by the claim of the mother to the same child. We therefore disagree with the trial court: there is no constitutional basis whatsoever requiring that Mr. Stern's claim to the custody of Baby M be sustained. Our conclusion may thus be understood as illustrating that a person's rights of privacy and self-determination are qualified by the effect on innocent third persons of the exercise of those rights.

Mr. Stern also contends that he has been denied equal protection of the laws by the State's statute granting full parental rights to a husband in relation to the child produced, with his consent, by the union of his wife with a sperm donor. N.J.S.A. 9:17–44. The claim really is that of Mrs. Stern. It is that she is in precisely the same position as the husband in the statute: she is presumably infertile, as is the husband in the statute; her spouse by agreement with a third party procreates with the understanding that the child will be the couple's child. The alleged unequal protection is that the understanding is honored in the statute when the husband is the infertile party, but no similar understanding is honored when it is the wife who is infertile.

It is quite obvious that the situations are not parallel. A sperm donor simply cannot be equated with a surrogate mother. The State has more than a sufficient basis to distinguish the two situations—even if the only difference is between the time it takes to provide sperm for artificial insemination and the time invested in a nine-month pregnancy—so as to justify automatically divesting the sperm donor of his parental rights without automatically divesting a surrogate mother. Some basis for an equal protection argument might exist if Mary Beth Whitehead had contributed her egg to be implanted, fertilized or otherwise, in Mrs. Stern, resulting in the latter's pregnancy. That is not the case here, however.

Mrs. Whitehead, on the other hand, asserts a claim that falls within the scope of a recognized fundamental interest protected by the Constitution. As a mother, she claims the right to the companionship of her child. This is a fundamental interest, constitutionally protected. Furthermore, it was taken away from her by the action of the court below. Whether that action under these circumstances would constitute a constitutional deprivation, however, we need not and do not decide. By virtue of our decision Mrs. Whitehead's constitutional complaint—that her parental rights have been unconstitutionally terminated—is moot. We have decided that both the statutes and public policy of this state require that that termination be voided and that her parental rights be restored. It therefore becomes unnecessary to decide whether that same result would be required by virtue of the federal or state Constitutions. . . .

Having held the contract invalid and having found no other grounds for the termination of Mrs. Whitehead's parental rights, we find that nothing remains of her constitutional claim. It seems obvious to us that since custody and visitation encompass practically all of what we call "parental rights," a total denial of both would be the equivalent of termination of parental rights. That, however, as will be seen below, has not occurred here. We express no opinion on whether a prolonged suspension of visitation would constitute a termination of parental rights, or whether, assuming it would, a showing of unfitness would be required.[16]

. . .

16. On such quantitative differences, constitutional validity can depend, where the statute in question is justified as serving a compelling state interest. The quality of the interference with the parents' right of companionship bears on these issues: if a statute, like the surrogacy contract before us, made the consent given prior to conception irrevocable, it might be regarded as a greater interference with the fundamental right than a statute that gave that effect only to a consent executed, for instance, more than six months after the child's birth. There is an entire spectrum of circumstances that strengthen and weaken the fundamental right involved, and a similar spectrum of state interests that justify or does not justify particular restrictions on that right. We do not believe it would be wise for this Court to attempt to identify various combinations of circumstances and interests, and attempt to indicate which combinations might and which might not constitutionally permit termination of parental rights.

We will say this much, however: a parent's fundamental right to the companionship of one's child can be significantly eroded by that parent's consent to the surrender of that child. That surrender, if voluntarily and knowingly made, may reduce the strength of that fundamental right to the point where a statute awarding custody and all parental rights to an adoptive couple, especially one that includes a parent of the child, would be valid.

V.

Custody

Having decided that the surrogacy contract is illegal and unenforceable, we now must decide the custody question without regard to the provisions of the surrogacy contract that would give Mr. Stern sole and permanent custody. (That does not mean that the existence of the contract and the circumstances under which it was entered may not be considered to the extent deemed relevant to the child's best interests.) With the surrogacy contract disposed of, the legal framework becomes a dispute between two couples over the custody of a child produced by the artificial insemination of one couple's wife by the other's husband. Under the Parentage Act the claims of the natural father and the natural mother are entitled to equal weight, *i.e.*, one is not preferred over the other solely because it is the father or the mother. The applicable rule given these circumstances is clear: the child's best interests determine custody.

. . .

There were eleven experts who testified concerning the child's best interests, either directly or in connection with matters related to that issue. Our reading of the record persuades us that the trial court's decision awarding custody to the Sterns (technically to Mr. Stern) should be affirmed since "its findings ... could reasonably have been reached on sufficient credible evidence present in the record." ... More than that, on this record we find little room for any different conclusion. The trial court's treatment of this issue is both comprehensive and, in most respects, perceptive. We agree substantially with its analysis with but few exceptions that, although important, do not change our ultimate views.

Our custody conclusion is based on strongly persuasive testimony contrasting both the family life of the Whiteheads and the Sterns and the personalities and characters of the individuals. The stability of the Whitehead family life was doubtful at the time of trial. Their finances were in serious trouble (foreclosure by Mrs. Whitehead's sister on a second mortgage was in process). Mr. Whitehead's employment, though relatively steady, was always at risk because of his alcoholism, a condition that he seems not to have been able to confront effectively. Mrs. Whitehead had not worked for quite some time, her last two employments having been part-time. One of the Whiteheads' positive attributes was their ability to bring up two children, and apparently well, even in so vulnerable a household. Yet substantial question was raised even about that aspect of their home life. The expert testimony contained criticism of Mrs. Whitehead's handling of her son's educational difficulties. Certain of the experts noted that Mrs. Whitehead perceived herself as omnipotent and omniscient concerning her children. She knew what they were thinking, what they wanted, and she spoke for them. As to Melissa, Mrs. Whitehead expressed the view that she alone knew what that child's cries and sounds meant. Her inconsistent stories about various things engendered grave doubts about her ability to explain honestly and sensitively to Baby M—and at the right time—the nature of her origin. Although faith in professional counseling is not a *sine qua non* of parenting, several experts believed that Mrs. Whitehead's contempt for professional help, especially professional psychological help, coincided with her feelings of omnipotence in a way that could be devastating to a child who most likely will need such help. In short, while love and affection there would be, Baby M's life with the Whiteheads promised to be too closely controlled by Mrs. Whitehead. The prospects for a wholesome, independent psychological growth and development would be at serious risk.

The Sterns have no other children, but all indications are that their household and their personalities promise a much more likely foundation for Melissa to grow and thrive. There is a track record of sorts—during the one-and-a-half years of custody Baby M has done very well, and the relationship between both Mr. and Mrs. Stern and the baby has become very strong. The household is stable, and likely to remain so. Their finances are more than adequate, their circle of friends supportive, and their marriage happy. Most important, they are loving, giving, nurturing, and open-minded people. They have demonstrated the wish and ability to nurture and protect Melissa, yet at the same time to encourage her independence. Their lack of experience is more than made up for by a willingness to learn and to listen, a willingness that is enhanced by their professional training, especially Mrs. Stern's experience as a pediatrician. They are honest; they can recognize error, deal with it, and learn from it. They will try to determine rationally the best way to cope with problems in their relationship with Melissa. When the time comes to tell her about her origins, they will probably have found a means of doing so that accords with the best interests of Baby M. All in all, Melissa's future appears solid, happy, and promising with them.

Based on all of this we have concluded, independent of the trial court's identical conclusion, that Melissa's best interests call for custody in the Sterns. . . .

It seems to us that given her predicament, Mrs. Whitehead was rather harshly judged—both by the trial court and by some of the experts. She was guilty of a breach of contract, and indeed, she did break a very important promise, but we think it is expecting something well beyond normal human capabilities to suggest that this mother should have parted with her newly born infant without a struggle. Other than survival, what stronger force is there? We do not know of, and cannot conceive of, any other case where a perfectly fit mother was expected to surrender her newly born infant, perhaps forever, and was then told she was a bad mother because she did not.

. . .

Some comment is required on the initial *ex parte* order awarding custody pendente lite to the Sterns (and the continuation of that order after a plenary hearing). The issue, although irrelevant to our disposition of this case, may recur; and when it does, it can be of crucial importance. When father and mother are separated and disagree, at birth, on custody, only in an extreme, truly rare, case should the child be taken from its mother pendente lite, i.e., only in the most unusual case should the child be taken from its mother before the dispute is finally determined by the court on its merits. The probable bond between mother and child, and the child's need, not just the mother's, to strengthen that bond, along with the likelihood, in most cases, of a significantly lesser, if any, bond with the father—all counsel against temporary custody in the father. A substantial showing that the mother's continued custody would threaten the child's health or welfare would seem to be required.

. . .

VI.

VISITATION

. . .

For the benefit of all concerned, especially the child, we would prefer to end these proceedings now, once and for all. It is clear to us, however, that it would be unjust to do so and contrary to precedent. . . .

We have decided that Mrs. Whitehead is entitled to visitation at some point, and that question is not open to the trial court on this remand. The trial court will determine what kind of visitation shall be granted to her, with or without conditions, and when and under what circumstances it should commence. It also should be noted that the guardian's recommendation of a five-year delay is most unusual—one might argue that it begins to border on termination. Nevertheless, if the circumstances as further developed by appropriate proofs or as reconsidered on remand clearly call for that suspension under applicable legal principles of visitation, it should be so ordered.

. . .

If the Legislature decides to address surrogacy, consideration of this case will highlight many of its potential harms. We do not underestimate the difficulties of legislating on this subject. In addition to the inevitable confrontation with the ethical and moral issues involved, there is the question of the wisdom and effectiveness of regulating a matter so private, yet of such public interest. Legislative consideration of surrogacy may also provide the opportunity to begin to focus on the overall implications of the new reproductive biotechnology—*in vitro* fertilization, preservation of sperm and eggs, embryo implantation and the like. The problem is how to enjoy the benefits of the technology—especially for infertile couples—while minimizing the risk of abuse. The problem can be addressed only when society decides what its values and objectives are in this troubling, yet promising, area.

Notes: Surrogate Motherhood

1. The New Jersey Supreme Court Rejected the Chancery Court's Finding that the Sterns had constitutional privacy rights validating their surrogacy contract with Whitehead. Professor Robertson agreed with the Chancery court:

> The constitutional right of married couples to family and procreative autonomy should ... give them a fundamental right to produce a child with the help of collaborators. This right would extend to arranging ... ordinary adoption.... [I]t would [also] extend to arranging with others to provide the sperm, egg, gestational services, or any combination necessary to produce a child for them to rear.

Single persons arguably should and possibly would enjoy the same right.

John A. Robertson, *Procreative Liberty and the Control of Conception, Pregnancy, and Childbirth*, 69 Va. L. Rev. 405, 459 (1983). *But see* Anita L. Allen, *Privacy, Surrogacy and the Baby M Case*, 76 Georgetown L.J. 1759 (1988), (arguing that appeal to constitutional privacy rights of surrogate and biological parents cannot resolve contract and child custody issues raised by commercial surrogacy).

2. In February 1988, two weeks after the New Jersey high court awarded custody of "Baby M" to the Sterns, Mary Beth Whitehead and her former husband settled a separate civil lawsuit they had brought alleging that the infertility Center of New York negligently selected Mrs. Whitehead to serve as a surrogate mother. Assuming there was a *prima facie* tort, was there contributory negligence? Did Whitehead assume the risk of the injury she suffered? Did the outcome of the custody suit make settlement more likely?

Suppose the New Jersey high court had held, on privacy grounds, that the surrogacy contract was valid. Could the Infertility Center have asserted the privacy rights of the Sterns by way of defense, *jus tertii*?

3. Chief Judge Wilenz wrote the opinion of the court in the *Baby M* case. He expressed concern that the practice of surrogacy might exacerbate economic inequities between poorer and more affluent segments of society. Indeed, during the pendency of *Baby M* and in its aftermath, many raised concern over the possibility that poor and "Third World" women would someday be unfairly used as a class of routine surrogate gestators for wealthy Whites. *Cf.* Katharine T. Bartlett, *Re-Expressing Parenthood*, 98 Yale L.J. 293, 334 (1988). According to Bartlett, surrogacy may help dilute the stereotype of women in nuclear families confined to the roles of mother and homemaker, but "depends upon a continued underclass of women—the surrogates—who will continue to be bound to their role as babymakers." A few even urged that surrogacy was a kind of slavery. *See, e.g.*, Schneider, *Mothers Urge Ban on Surrogacy as a form of "Slavery,"* N.Y. Times, Sept. 1, 1987, at A13, col. 1. *Cf.* Allen, *Surrogacy, Slavery and the Ownership of Life*, 13 Harv. J.L. & Pub. Pol'y 139 (1990) (drawing parallels between surrogacy and American slavery).

4. Should gestational surrogate mothers have the same legal rights as genetic surrogate mothers? *See* Anita Allen, *The Black Surrogate Mother*, 8 Harvard Blackletter Journal 17 (1991). A surrogate mother can now be hired

to gestate a donated or "adopted' embryo, resulting in a child without genetic ties either to the surrogate mother, or to the man, woman or couple who hires her.

5. Many states have banned commercial surrogacy arrangements. In *Johnson v. Calvert*, Judge Parslow recommended that California enact comprehensive legislation regulating the practice of surrogate gestation. One of his recommendations for lawmakers was the adoption of a requirement that first-time surrogates be second-time mothers. Would such a requirement reduce the number of disputes between surrogates and their employers? Anna Johnson already had a daughter when she gave birth to the Calvert's genetic son. The child called "Baby M" was Mary Beth Whitehead's *third* child.

C. FAMILY AUTONOMY

Introduction

MARTHA MINOW, MAKING ALL THE DIFFERENCE: INCLUSION, EXCLUSION AND AMERICAN LAW

269–70 (1990).

Traditional family law, forged in the eighteenth and nineteenth centuries, treated the white male head of household as a family's representative to the state. Rights in this context attached to the man, who exercised suffrage, held the family property, and entered into contracts. His wife and minor children were generally excluded from the right to sue or be sued, to enter into contracts, or to hold property or earnings. The head of household secured, under law, powers over the property and services of his wife and children, including the power to discipline them. The traditional allocation of power in the family permeated legal rules about marriage, giving the husband legal power to select the marital domicile and to serve as head of the household, as well as the legal obligation to support the family financially. In return, the wife under the traditional marriage agreement was to provide domestic services as housewife, mother, sexual partner, and companion.

Besides enforcing gender-based roles, traditional family law embraced a particular notion of family autonomy which barred the legal system from invading the private enclave of the family and the sphere of power reserved to the head of the family. Influenced largely by religious teachings and by the conception of the family as the stable reserve for child rearing, the law treated marriage as a permanent and indissoluble union. Well past the middle of the nineteenth century, marriage represented a permanent bond that the state should protect. The state would not make its courts available for resolving disputes between husband and wife or among other family members. This was to be a realm where affection and mutual commitment would resolve disagreements.

1. REARING AND EDUCATING CHILDREN

MEYER v. NEBRASKA

262 U.S. 390 (1923).

MR. JUSTICE MCREYNOLDS delivered the opinion of the Court.

Plaintiff in error was tried and convicted in the District Court for Hamilton County, Nebraska, under an information which charged that on May 25, 1920, while an instructor in Zion Parochial School, he unlawfully taught the subject of reading in the German language to Raymond Parpart, a child of ten years who had not attained and successfully passed the eighth grade. The information is based upon "An act relating to the teaching of foreign languages in the State of Nebraska," approved April 9, 1919, which follows....

The Supreme Court of the State affirmed the judgement of conviction. 107 Neb. 657. It declared the offense charged and established was "the direct and intentional teaching of the German language as a distinct subject to a child who had not passed the eighth grade," in the parochial school maintained by Zion Evangelical Lutheran Congregation, a collection of Biblical stories being used therefor. And it held that the statute forbidding this did not conflict with the Fourteenth Amendment, but was a valid exercise of the police power. The following excerpts from the opinion sufficiently indicate the reasons advanced to support the conclusion.

The salutary purpose of the statute is clear. The legislature had seen the baneful effects of permitting foreigners, who had taken residence in this country, to rear and educate their children in the language of their native land. The result of that condition was found to be inimical to our own safety. To allow the children of foreigners, who had emigrated here, to be taught from early childhood the language of the country of their parents was to rear them with that language as their mother tongue. It was to educate them so that they must always think in that language, and, as a consequence, naturally inculcate in them the ideas and sentiments foreign to the best interests of this country. The statute, therefore, was intended not only to require that the education of all children be conducted in the English language, but that until they had grown into that language and until it had become a part of them, they should not in the schools be taught any other language. The obvious purpose of this statute was that the English language should be and become the mother tongue of all children reared in this state. The enactment of such a statute comes reasonably within the police power of the state....

. . .

While this court has not attempted to define with exactness the liberty thus guaranteed, the term has received much consideration and some of the included things have been definitely stated. Without doubt, it denotes not merely freedom from bodily restraint but also the right of the individual to contract, to engage in any of the common occupations of life, to acquire useful knowledge, to marry, establish a home and bring up children, to worship God according to the dictates of his own conscience, and generally to enjoy those privileges long recognized at common law as essential to the orderly pursuit of happiness by free men. . . .

. . .

Practically, education of the young is only possible in schools conducted by especially qualified persons who devote themselves thereto. The calling always has been regarded as useful and honorable, essential, indeed, to the public welfare. Mere knowledge of the German language cannot reasonably be regarded as harmful. Heretofore it has been commonly looked upon as helpful and desirable. Plaintiff in error taught this language in school as part of his occupation. His right thus to teach and the right of parents to engage him so to instruct their children, we think, are within the liberty of the Amendment.

. . .

It is said the purpose of the legislation was to promote civic development by inhibiting training and education of the immature in foreign tongues and ideals before they could learn English and acquire American ideals; and "that the English language should be and become the mother tongue of all children reared in this State." It is also affirmed that the foreign born population is very large, that certain communities commonly use foreign words, follow foreign leaders, move in a foreign atmosphere, and that the children are thereby hindered from becoming citizens of the most useful type and the public safety is imperiled.

That the State may do much, go very far, indeed, in order to improve the quality of its citizens, physically, mentally and morally, is clear; but the individual has certain fundamental rights which must be respected. The protection of the Constitution extends to all, to those who speak other languages as well as to those born with English on the tongue. Perhaps it would be highly advantageous if all had ready understanding of our ordinary speech, but this cannot be coerced by methods which conflict with the Constitution—a desirable end cannot be promoted by prohibited means.

. . .

The desire of the legislature to foster a homogeneous people with American ideals prepared readily to understand current discussions of civic matters is easy to appreciate. Unfortunate experiences during the late war and aversion toward every characteristic of truculent adversaries were certainly enough to quicken that aspiration. But the means adopted, we think exceed the limitations upon the power of the State and conflict with rights assured to plaintiff in error. The interference is plain enough and no adequate reason therefore in time of peace and domestic tranquility has been shown.

. . .

Mr. Justice Holmes, dissenting.

. . . Youth is the time when familiarity with a language is established and if there are sections in the State where a child would hear only Polish or French or German spoken at home I am not prepared to say that it is unreasonable to provide that in his early years he shall hear and speak only English at school. But if it is reasonable it is not an undue restriction of the liberty either of teacher or scholar. . . . I think I appreciate the objection to the law but it appears to me to present a question upon which men reasonably might differ and therefore I am unable to say that the Constitution of the United States prevents the experiment being tried.

PRINCE v. MASSACHUSETTS

321 U.S. 158 (1944).

Mr. Justice Rutledge delivered the opinion of the Court.

. . .

[Massachusetts' comprehensive child labor law provides that:] "No boy under twelve and no girl under eighteen shall sell, expose or offer for sale any newspapers, magazines, periodicals or any other articles of merchandise of any description, or exercise the trade of bootblack or scavenger, or any other trade, in any street or public place." . . .

. . . Mrs. [Sarah] Prince, [a Jehovah's Witness] living in Brockton, is the mother of two young sons. She also has legal custody of Betty Simmons, who lives with them. The children too are Jehovah's Witnesses and both Mrs. Prince and Betty testified they were ordained ministers. The former was accustomed to go each week in the streets of Brockton to distribute "Watchtower" and "Consolation," according to the usual plan. She had permitted the children to engage in this activity previously, and had been warned against doing so by the school attendance officer, Mr. Perkins. . . .

. . . Mrs. Prince permitted the children "to engage in the preaching work with her upon the sidewalks." That is, with specific reference to Betty, she and Mrs. Prince took positions about twenty feet apart near a street intersection. Betty held up in her hand, for passers-by to see, copies of "Watch Tower" and "Consolation." From her shoulder hung the usual canvas magazine bag, on which was printed: "Watchtower and Consolation 5 cents per copy." . . .

. . . It may be added that testimony, by Betty, her aunt and others, was offered at the trials, and was excluded, to show that Betty believed it was her religious duty to perform this work and failure would bring condemnation "to everlasting destruction at Armageddon."

. . .

To make accommodation between these freedoms and an exercise of state authority always is delicate. It hardly could be more so than in such a clash as this case presents. On one side is the obviously earnest claim for freedom of conscience and religious practice. With it is allied the parent's claim to authority in her own household and in the rearing of her children. The parent's conflict with the state over control of the child and his training is serious enough when only secular matters are concerned. It becomes the more so when an element of religious conviction enters. Against these sacred private interests, basic in a democracy, stand the interests of society to protect the welfare of children, and the state's assertion of authority to that end, made here in a manner conceded valid if only secular things were involved. The last is no mere corporate concern of official authority. It is the interest of youth itself, and of the whole community, that children be both safeguarded from abuses and given opportunities for growth into free and independent well-developed men and citizens....

... It is cardinal with us that the custody, care and nurture of the child reside first in the parents, whose primary function and freedom include preparation for obligations the state can neither supply nor hinder. Pierce v. Society of Sisters. And it is in recognition of this that these decisions have respected the private realm of family life which the state cannot enter.

But the family itself is not beyond regulation in the public interest, as against a claim of religious liberty. Reynolds v. United States, 98 U.S. 145. And neither rights of religion nor rights of parenthood are beyond limitation. Acting to guard the general interest in youth's well being, the state as *parens patriae* may restrict the parent's control by requiring school attendance, regulating or prohibiting the child's labor and in many other ways. Its authority is not nullified merely because the parent grounds his claim to control the child's course of conduct on religion or conscience. Thus, he cannot claim freedom from compulsory vaccination for the child more than for himself on religious grounds. The right to practice religion freely does not include liberty to expose the community or the child to communicable disease or the latter to ill health or death. The catalogue need not be lengthened. It is sufficient to show what indeed appellant hardly disputes, that the state has a wide range of power for limiting parental freedom and authority in things affecting the child's welfare; and that this includes, to some extent, matters of conscience and religious conviction.

. . .

The state's authority over children's activities is broader than over like actions of adults. This is peculiarly true of public activities and in matters of employment. A democratic society rests, for its continuance, upon the healthy, well-rounded growth of young people into full maturity as citizens, with all that implies. It may secure this against impeding restraints and dangers within a broad range of selection. Among evils most appropriate for such action are the crippling effects of child employment, more especially in public places, and the possible harms arising from other activities subject to all the diverse influences of the street. . . .

. . .

. . . The zealous though lawful exercise of the right to engage in propagandizing the community, whether in religious, political or other matters, may and at times does create situations difficult enough for adults to cope with and wholly inappropriate for children, especially of tender years, to face. Other harmful possibilities could be stated, of emotional excitement and psychological or physical injury. Parents may be free to become martyrs themselves. But it does not follow they are free, in identical circumstances, to make martyrs of their children before they have reached the age of full and legal discretion when they can make that choice for themselves. [Judgment Affirmed.]

MR. JUSTICE MURPHY, dissenting:

. . .

. . . Reference is made in the majority opinion to "the crippling effects of child employment, more especially in public places, and the possible harms arising from other activities subject to all the diverse influences of the street." . . . Yet there is not the slightest indication in this record, or in sources subject to judicial notice, that children engaged in distributing literature pursuant to their religious beliefs have been or are likely to be subject to any of the harmful "diverse influences of the street." Indeed, if probabilities are to be indulged in, the likelihood is that children engaged in serious religious endeavor are immune from such influences. . . .

. . . From ancient times to the present day, the ingenuity of man has known no limits in its ability to forge weapons of oppression for use against those who dare to express or practice unorthodox religious beliefs. And the Jehovah's Witnesses are living proof of the fact that even in this nation, conceived as it was in the ideals of freedom, the right to practice religion in unconventional ways is still far from secure.

WISCONSIN v. YODER

406 U.S. 205 (1972).

MR. CHIEF JUSTICE BURGER delivered the opinion of the Court.

On petition of the State of Wisconsin, we granted the writ of certiorari in this case to review a decision of the Wisconsin Supreme Court holding that respondents' convictions of violating the State's compulsory school-attendance law were invalid under the Free Exercise Clause of the First Amendment to the United States Constitution made applicable to the States by the Fourteenth Amendment. For the reasons hereafter stated we affirm the judgement of the Supreme Court of Wisconsin.

Respondents Jonas Yoder and Wallace Miller are members of the Old Order Amish religion, and respondent Adin Yutzy is a member of the Conservative Amish Mennonite Church. They and their families are residents of Green County, Wisconsin. Wisconsin's compulsory school-attendance law required them to cause their children to attend public or private school until reaching age 16 but the respondents declined to send their children, ages 14 and 15, to public school after they completed the eighth grade. . . .

. . . The trial testimony showed that respondents believed, in accordance with the tenants of Old Order Amish communities generally, that their children's attendance at high school, public or private, was contrary to the Amish religion and way of life. They believed that by sending their children to high school, they would not only expose themselves to the danger of the censure of the church community, but, as found by the county court, also endanger their own salvation and trait of their children. The State stipulated that respondents' religious beliefs were sincere.

. . .

Amish objection to formal education beyond the eighth grade is firmly grounded in these central religious concepts. They object to the high school, and higher education generally, because the values they teach are in marked variance with Amish values and the Amish way of life; they view secondary school education as an impermissible exposure of their children to a "worldly" influence in conflict with their beliefs. The high school tends to emphasize intellectual and scientific accomplishments, self-distinction, competitiveness, worldly success, and social life with other students. Amish society emphasizes informal learning-through-doing; a life of "goodness," rather than a life of intellect; wisdom, rather than technical knowledge; community welfare, rather than competition; and separation from, rather than integration with, contemporary worldly society.

Formal high school education beyond the eighth grade is contrary to Amish beliefs, not only because it places Amish children in an environment hostile to Amish beliefs with increasing emphasis on competition in class work and sports and with pressure to conform to the styles, manners, and ways of the peer group, but also because it takes them away from their community, physically and emotionally, during the crucial and formative adolescent period of life. During this period, the children must acquire Amish attitudes favoring manual work and self-reliance and the specific skills needed to perform the adult role of an Amish farmer or housewife. They must learn to enjoy physical labor. Once a child has learned basic reading, writing, and elementary mathematics, these traits, skills, and attitudes admittedly fall within the category of those best learned through example and "doing" rather than in a classroom. And, at this time in life, the Amish child must also grow in his faith and his relationship to the Amish community if he is to be prepared to accept the heavy obligations imposed by adult baptism. In short, high school attendance with teachers who are not of the Amish faith—and may even be hostile to it—interposes a serious barrier to the integration of the Amish child into the Amish religious community. Dr. John Hostetler, one of the experts on Amish society, testified that the modern high school is not equipped, in curriculum or social environment, to impart the values promoted by Amish society.

. . .

On the basis of such considerations, Dr. Hostetler testified that compulsory high school attendance could not only result in great psychological harm to Amish children, because of the conflicts it would produce, but would also, in his opinion, ultimately result in the destruction of the Old Order Amish church community as it exists in the United States today. . . .

. . .

I

There is no doubt as to the power of a State, having a high responsibility for education of its citizens, to impose reasonable regulations for the control and duration of basic education. See, e.g., Pierce v. Society of Sisters. Providing public schools ranks at the very apex of the function of a State. . . .

. . .

The State advances two primary arguments in support of its system of compulsory education. It notes, as Thomas Jefferson pointed out early in our history, that some degree of education is necessary to prepare citizens to participate effectively and intelligently in our open political system if we are to preserve freedom and independence. Further, education prepares individuals to be self-reliant and self-sufficient participants in society. We accept these propositions.

However, the evidence adduced by the Amish in this case is persuasively to the effect that an additional one or two years of formal high school for Amish children in place of their long-established program of informal vocational education would do little to serve those interests. Respondents' experts testified at trial, without challenge, that the value of all education must be assessed in terms of its capacity to prepare the child for life. It is one thing to say that compulsory education for a year or two beyond the eighth grade may be necessary when its goal is the preparation of the child for life in modern society as the majority live, but it is quite another if the goal of education be viewed as the preparation of the child for life in the separated agrarian community that is the keystone of the Amish faith. See Meyer v. Nebraska.

The State attacks respondents' position as one fostering "ignorance" from which the child must be protected by the State. No one can question the State's duty to protect children from ignorance but this argument does not square with the facts disclosed in the record. Whatever their idiosyncrasies as seen by the majority, this record strongly shows that the Amish community has been a highly successful social unit within our society, even if apart from the conventional "mainstream." Its members are productive and very law-abiding members of society;

they reject public welfare in any of its usual modern forms. The Congress itself recognized their self-sufficiency by authorizing exemption of such groups as the Amish from the obligation to pay social security taxes.

It is neither fair nor correct to suggest that the Amish are opposed to education beyond the eighth grade level. What this record shows is that they are opposed to conventional formal education of the type provided by a certified high school because it comes at the child's crucial adolescent period of religious development. Dr. Donald Erickson, for example, testified that their system of learning-by-doing was an "ideal system" of education in terms of preparing Amish children for life as adults in the Amish community. . . .

. . .

The State, however, supports its interest in providing an additional one or two years of compulsory high school education to Amish children because of the possibility that some children will choose to leave the Amish community, and that if this occurs they will be ill-equipped for life. . . .

There is nothing in this record to suggest that the Amish qualities of reliability, self-reliance, and dedication to work would fail to find ready markets in today's society. Absent some contrary evidence supporting the State's position, we are unwilling to assume that persons possessing such valuable vocational skills and habits are doomed to become burdens on society should they determine to leave the Amish faith, nor is there any basis in the record to warrant a finding that an additional one or two years of formal school education beyond the eighth grade would serve to eliminate any such problem that may exist.

Insofar as the State's claim rests on the view that a brief additional period of formal education is imperative to enable the Amish to participate effectively and intelligently in our democratic process, it must fall. The Amish alternative to formal secondary school education has enabled them to function effectively in their day-to-day life under self-imposed limitations on relations with the world, and to survive and prosper in contemporary society as a separate, sharply identifiable and highly self-efficient community for more than 200 years in this country. In itself this is strong evidence that they are capable of fulfilling the social and political responsibilities of citizenship without compelled attendance beyond the eighth grade at the price of jeopardizing their free exercise of religious belief. . . .

The requirement of compulsory education beyond the eighth grade is a relatively recent development in our history. Less than 60 years ago, the educational requirements of almost all of the States were satisfied by completion of the elementary grades, at least where the child was regularly and lawfully employed. The independence and successful social functioning of the Amish community for a period approaching almost three centuries and more than 200 years in this country are strong evidence that there is at best a speculative gain, in terms of meeting the duties of citizenship, from an additional one or two years of compulsory formal education. Against this background it would require a more particularized showing from the State on this point to justify the severe interference with religious freedom such additional compulsory attendance would entail. [Affirmed]. . . .

Mr. Justice Douglas, dissenting in part.

I

I agree with the Court that the religious scruples of the Amish are opposed to the education of their children beyond the grade schools, yet I disagree with the Court's conclusion that the matter is within the dispensation of parents alone. The Court's analysis assumes that the only interest at stake in the case are those of the Amish parents on the one hand, and those of the State on the other. The difficulty with this approach is that, despite the Court's claim, the parents are seeking to vindicate not only their own free exercise claims, but also those of their high-school-age children.

. . .

. . . Frieda Yoder has in fact testified that her own religious views are opposed to high-school education. I therefore join the judgement of the Court as to respondent Jonas Yoder. But Frieda Yoder's views may not be those of Vernon Yutzy or Barbara Miller. I must dissent, therefore, as to respondents Adin Yutzy and Wallace Miller as their motion to dismiss also raised the question of their children's religious liberty.

. . .

II

The views of the two children in question were not canvassed by the Wisconsin courts. The matter should be explicitly reserved so that new hearings can be held on remand of the case.

RUNYON v. McCRARY

427 U.S. 160 (1976).

Mr. Justice Stewart delivered the opinion of the Court.

The principal issue presented by these consolidated cases is whether a federal law, namely 42 U.S.C. Section 1981, prohibits private schools from excluding qualified children solely because they are Negroes.

. . .

In Meyer v. Nebraska, the Court held that the liberty protected by the Due Process Clause of the Fourteenth Amendment includes the right "to acquire useful knowledge, to marry, establish a home and bring up children," and, concomitantly, the right to send one's children to a private school that offers specialized training—in that case, instruction in the German language. In Pierce v. Society of Sisters, the Court applied "the doctrine of Meyer v. Nebraska," to hold unconstitutional an

Oregon law requiring the parent, guardian, or other person having custody of a child between eight and 16 years of age to send that child to public school on pain of criminal liability.... In Wisconsin v. Yoder, the Court stressed the limited scope of *Pierce*, pointing out that it lent "no support to the contention that parents may replace state educational requirements with their own idiosyncratic views of what knowledge a child needs to be a productive and happy member of society" but rather "held simply that while a State may posit [educational] standards, it may not preempt the educational process by requiring children to attend public schools." (White, J., concurring).

It is clear that the present application of Section 1981 infringes no parental right recognized in *Meyer*, *Pierce*, *Yoder*, or *Norwood*. No challenge is made to the petitioners schools' right to operate their private schools or the right of parents to send their children to a particular private school rather than a public school. Nor do these cases involve a challenge to the subject matter which is taught at any private school. Thus, the Fairfax–Brewster School and Bobbe's Private School and members of the intervenor association remain presumptively free to inculcate whatever values and standards they deem desirable. *Meyer* and its progeny entitle them to no more.

. . .

The court has held that in some situations the Constitution confers a right to privacy. See Roe v. Wade, Eisenstadt v. Baird, Stanley v. Georgia, Griswold v. Connecticut. See also Loving v. Virginia, Skinner v. Oklahoma ex rel. Williamson.

While the application of Section 1981 to the conduct at issue here—a private school's adherence to a racially discriminatory admissions policy—does not represent governmental intrusion into the privacy of the home or a similarly intimate setting, it does implicate parental interests. These interests are related to the procreative rights protected in Roe v. Wade, *supra*, and Griswold v. Connecticut, *supra*. A person's decision whether to bear a child and a parent's decision concerning the manner in which his child is to be educated may fairly be characterized as exercises of familial rights and responsibilities. But it does not follow that because government is largely or even entirely precluded from regulating the child-bearing decision, it is similarly restricted by the Constitution from regulating the implementation of parental decisions concerning a child's education.

The Court has repeatedly stressed that while parents have a constitutional right to send their children to private schools and a constitutional right to select private schools that offer specialized instruction, they have no constitutional right to provide their children with private school education unfettered by reasonable government regulation. See Wisconsin v. Yoder, *supra*; Pierce v. Society of Sisters, *supra*; Meyer v. Nebraska.[15] Indeed, the Court in *Pierce* expressly acknowledged "the

15. The *Meyer–Pierce–Yoder* "parental" right and the privacy right, while dealt with separately in this opinion, may be no more than verbal variations of a single constitu-

power of the State reasonably to regulate all schools, to inspect, supervise and examine them, their teachers and pupils...." 268 U.S., at 534. See also Prince v. Massachusetts.

. . .

For the reasons stated in this opinion, the judgement of the Court of Appeals is in all respects affirmed.

MR. JUSTICE WHITE, with whom MR. JUSTICE REHNQUIST joins, dissenting.

. . .

The majority's holding that 42 U.S.C. Section 1981 prohibits all racially motivated contractual decisions ... threatens to embark the Judiciary on a treacherous course. Whether such conduct should be condoned or not, whites and blacks will undoubtedly choose to form a variety of associational relationships pursuant to contracts which exclude members of the other race. Social clubs, black and white, and associations designed to further the interests of blacks or whites are but two examples.

PALMORE v. SIDOTI

466 U.S. 429 (1984).

CHIEF JUSTICE BURGER delivered the opinion for the Court.

We granted certiorari to review a judgment of a state court divesting a natural mother of the custody of her infant child because of her remarriage to a person of a different race.

. . .

When petitioner Linda Sidoti Palmore and respondent Anthony J. Sidoti, both Caucasians, were divorced in May 1980 in Florida, the mother was awarded custody of their 3–year-old daughter.

In September 1981 the father sought custody of the child by filing a petition to modify the prior judgment because of changed conditions. The change was that the child's mother was then cohabiting with a Negro, Clarence Palmore, Jr., whom she married two months later.

. . .

The question ... is whether the reality of private biases and the possible injury they might inflict are permissible considerations for removal of an infant child from the custody of its natural mother. We have little difficulty concluding that they are not. The Constitution cannot control such prejudices but neither can it tolerate them. Private biases may be outside the reach of the law, but the law cannot, directly or indirectly, give them effect. "Public officials sworn to uphold the

tional right. See *Roe v. Wade*, 410 U.S. 113, 152–153 (citing *Meyer v. Nebraska* and *Pierce v. Society of Sisters* for the proposition that this court has recognized a constitutional right of privacy.)

Constitution may not avoid a constitutional duty by bowing to the hypothetical effects of private racial prejudice that they assume to be both widely and deeply held." Palmer v. Thompson, 403 U.S. 217, 260–261 (1971) (WHITE, J., dissenting).

DESHANEY v. WINNEBAGO COUNTY DEPARTMENT OF SOCIAL SERVICES

489 U.S. 189 (1989).

CHIEF JUSTICE REHNQUIST delivered the opinion of the Court.

. . .

In March 1984, Randy DeShaney beat 4–year-old Joshua so severely that he fell into a life-threatening coma. Emergency brain surgery revealed a series of hemorrhages caused by traumatic injuries to the head inflicted over a long period of time. Joshua did not die, but he suffered brain damage so severe that he is expected to spend the rest of his life confined to an institution for the profoundly retarded. Randy DeShaney was subsequently tried and convicted of child abuse.

Joshua and his mother brought this action under 42 U.S.C. Sec. 1983 in the United States District Court for the Eastern District of Wisconsin against respondents Winnebago County, DSS, and various individual employees of DSS. The complaint alleged that respondents had deprived Joshua of his liberty without due process of law, in violation of his rights under the Fourteenth Amendment, by failing to intervene to protect him against a risk of violence at his father's hands of which they knew or should have known. The District Court granted summary judgment for respondents.

The Court of Appeals for the Seventh Circuit affirmed. . . .

We now affirm.

II

The Due Process Clause of the Fourteenth Amendment provides that "[n]o State shall ... deprive any person of life, liberty, or property, without due process of law." Petitioners contend that the State deprived Joshua of his liberty interest in "free[dom] from ... unjustified intrusions on personal security," see Ingraham v. Wright, 430 U. S. 651, 673 (1977), by failing to provide him with adequate protection against his father's violence. The claim is one invoking the substantive rather than procedural component of the Due Process Clause; petitioners do not claim that the State denied Joshua protection without according him appropriate procedural safeguards, but that it was categorically obligated to protect him in these circumstances.

But nothing in the language of the Due Process Clause itself requires the State to protect the life, liberty, and property of its citizens against invasion by private actors. The Clause is phrased as a limitation on the State's power to act, not as a guarantee of certain minimal levels of safety and security. It forbids the State itself to deprive individuals of life, liberty, or property without "due process of law," but its language cannot fairly be extended to impose an affirmative obligation on the State to ensure that those interests do not come to harm through other means. Nor does history support such an expansive reading of the constitutional text. Like its counterpart in the Fifth Amendment, the Due Process Clause of the Fourteenth Amendment was intended to prevent government "from abusing [its] power, or employing it as an instrument of oppression." . . . Its purpose was to protect the people from the State, not to ensure that the State protected them from each other. The Framers were content to leave the extent of governmental obligation in the latter area to the democratic political processes.

Consistent with these principles, our cases have recognized that the Due Process Clauses generally confer no affirmative right to governmental aid, even where such aid may be necessary to secure life, liberty, or property interests of which the government itself may not deprive the individual. See, e.g., Harris v. McRae (no obligation to fund abortions or other medical services) (discussing Due Process Clause of Fifth Amendment); Lindsey v. Normet, 405 U.S. 56, 74 (1972) (no obligation to provide adequate housing) (discussing Due Process Clause of Fourteenth Amendment). As we said in Harris v. McRae, "[a]lthough the liberty protected by the Due Process Clause affords protection against unwarranted *government* interference . . ., it does not confer an entitlement to such [governmental aid] as may be necessary to realize all the advantages of that freedom." If the Due Process Clause does not require the State to provide its citizens with particular protective services, it follows that the State cannot be held liable under the Clause for injuries that could have been averted had it chosen to provide them. As a general matter, then, we conclude that a State's failure to protect an individual against private violence simply does not constitute a violation of the Due Process Clause.

Petitioners contend, however, that even if the Due Process Clause imposes no affirmative obligation on the State to provide the general public with adequate protective services, such a duty may arise out of certain "special relationships" created or assumed by the State with respect to particular individuals. Petitioners argue that such a "special relationship" existed here because the State knew that Joshua faced a special danger of abuse at his father's hands, and specifically proclaimed, by word and by deed, its intention to protect him against that danger. Having actually undertaken to protect Joshua from this danger—which petitioners concede the State played no part in creating—the State acquired an affirmative "duty," enforceable through the Due Process Clause, to do so in a reasonably competent fashion. Its failure to discharge that duty, so the argument goes, was an abuse of governmental power that so "shocks the conscience," Rochin v. California, as to constitute a substantive due process violation.

We reject this argument. . . .

... [W]hen the State takes a person into its custody and holds him there against his will, the Constitution imposes upon it a corresponding duty to assume some responsibility for his safety and general well-being. See Youngberg v. Romeo, *supra*, at 317 ("When a person is institutionalized—and wholly dependent on the State[,] ... a duty to provide certain services and care does exist"). The rationale for this principle is simple enough: when the State by the affirmative exercise of its power so restrains an individual's liberty that it renders him unable to care for himself, and at the same time fails to provide for his basic human needs—*e.g.*, food, clothing, shelter, medical care, and reasonable safety—it transgresses the substantive limits on state action set by the Eighth Amendment and the Due Process Clause. The affirmative duty to protect arises not from the State's knowledge of the individual's predicament or from its expressions of intent to help him, but from the limitation which it has imposed on his freedom to act on his own behalf. In the substantive due process analysis, it is the State's affirmative act of restraining the individual's freedom to act on his own behalf—through incarceration, institutionalization, or other similar restraint of personal liberty—which is the "deprivation of liberty" triggering the protections of the Due Process Clause, not its failure to act to protect his liberty interests against harms inflicted by other means.

... Petitioners concede that the harm Joshua suffered did not occur while he was in the State's custody, but while he was in the custody of his natural father, who was in no sense a state actor. While the State may have been aware of the dangers that Joshua faced in the free world, it played no part in their creation, nor did it do anything to render him any more vulnerable to them. That the State once took temporary custody of Joshua does not alter the analysis, for when it returned him to his father's custody, it placed him in no worse position than that in which he would have been had it not acted at all; the State does not become the permanent guarantor of an individual's safety by having once offered him shelter. Under these circumstances, the State had no constitutional duty to protect Joshua.

It may well be that, by voluntarily undertaking to protect Joshua against a danger it concededly played no part in creating, the State acquired a duty under state tort law to provide him with adequate protection against that danger. But the claim here is based on the Due Process Clause of the Fourteenth Amendment, which, as we have said many times, does not transform every tort committed by a state actor into a constitutional violation.

2. MARRIAGE AND DIVORCE

Marriage is the quintessentially "private" relationship and yet government extensively regulates when we may marry, how we may marry, and the persons whom we may marry. Some of the limitations on marriage, such as the ban on incestuous marriages are not controversial. Laws banning bigamy and polygamy have few serious opponents, although new immigrants from African nations, in which polygamy is a venerated tradition have raised serious questions about the legitimacy of legal non-recognition of the practice on U.S. soil.

The greatest challenge to traditional marriage laws in the U.S. today is the idea of same-sex marriages. The concept appears to be gaining legal ground for the first time in American history. See William N. Eskridge, Jr., *The Case for Same–Sex marriage* (1996). Cf. John Finnis, *The Good of Marriage and the Morality of Sexual Relations: Some Philosophical and Historical Observations*, 42 Am J. Jur. 97 (1997), As you read the cases and notes below, carefully consider whether the reasons courts have given for upholding some marriage restrictions and topping others are consistent and sound.

REYNOLDS v. UNITED STATES

98 U.S. 145 (1878).

[T]he plaintiff in error, the accused, proved that at the time of his alleged second marriage he was, and for many years before had been, a member of the Church of Jesus Christ of Latter Day Saints, commonly called the Mormon Church, and a believer in its doctrines; that it was an accepted doctrine of the church "that it was the duty of male members of said church, circumstances permitting, to practise [sic] polygamy . . . ."

Upon this proof he asked the court to instruct the jury that if they found from the evidence that he "was married . . . in pursuance of and in conformity with what he believed at the time to be a religious duty, that the verdict must be 'not guilty.' " . . .

Congress cannot pass a law for the government of the Territories which shall prohibit the free exercise of religion. The first amendment to the Constitution expressly forbids such legislation. . . .

Polygamy has always been odious among the northern and western nations of Europe, and until the establishment of the Mormon Church, was almost exclusively a feature of the life of Asiatic and of African people. . . .

In our opinion, the statute . . . is within the legislative power of Congress. . . .

Laws are made for the government of actions, and while they cannot interfere with mere religious belief and opinions, they may with practices. Suppose one believed that human sacrifices were a necessary part of religious worship . . . ? Or if a wife religiously believed it was her duty to burn herself upon the funeral pile of her dead husband . . . ?

. . . Congress in 1862 (12 Stat. 501), saw fit to make bigamy a crime in the Territories. This was done because of the evil consequences that were supposed to flow from plural marriages. . . .

Upon a careful consideration of the whole case, we are satisfied that no error was committed by the court below.

LOVING v. VIRGINIA

388 U.S. 1 (1967).

MR. CHIEF JUSTICE WARREN delivered the opinion of the Court.

.   .   .

In June 1958, two residents of Virginia, Mildred Jeter, a Negro woman, and Richard Loving, a white man, were married in the District of Columbia pursuant to its laws. Shortly after their marriage, the Lovings returned to Virginia and established their marital abode in Caroline County. At the October Term, 1958, of the Circuit Court of Caroline County, a grand jury issued an indictment charging the Lovings with violating Virginia's ban on interracial marriages. On January 6, 1959, the Lovings pleaded guilty to the charge and were sentenced to one year in jail; however, the trial judge suspended the sentence for a period of 25 years on the condition that the Lovings leave the State and not return to Virginia together for 25 years. He stated in an opinion that:

> Almighty God created the races white, black, yellow, malay and red, and he placed them on separate continents. And but for the interference with his arrangement there would be no cause for such marriages. The fact that he separated the races shows that he did not intend for the races to mix.

After their convictions, the Lovings took up residence in the District of Columbia. . . .

.   .   .

The two statutes under which appellants were convicted and sentenced are part of a comprehensive statutory scheme aimed at prohibiting and punishing interracial marriages. The Lovings were convicted of violating Section 20–58 of the Virginia Code:

> **Leaving State to evade law**—If any white person and colored person shall go out of this State, for the purpose of being married, and with the intention of returning, and be married out of it, and afterwards return to and reside in it, cohabiting as man and wife, they shall be punished as provided in Section 20–59, and the marriage shall be governed by the same law as if it had been solemnized in this State. The fact of their cohabitation here as man and wife shall be evidence of their marriage.

Section 20–50, which defines the penalty for miscegenation, provides:

> **Punishment for marriage**—If any white person intermarry with a colored person, or any colored person intermarry with a white person, he shall be guilty of a felony and shall be punished by confinement in the penitentiary for not less than one nor more than five years.

Other central provisions in the Virginia statutory scheme are Section 20–57, which automatically voids all marriages between "a white person and a colored person" without any judicial proceeding, and Sections 20–54 and 1–14 which, respectively define "white persons" and "colored persons and Indians" for purposes of the statutory prohibitions. The Lovings have never disputed in the course of this litigation that Mrs. Loving is a "colored person" or that Mr. Loving is a "white person" within the meanings given those terms by the Virginia statutes.

Virginia is now one of 16 States which prohibit and punish marriages on the basis of racial classifications. Penalties for miscegenation arose as an incident to slavery and have been common in Virginia since the colonial period. The present statutory scheme dates from the adoption of the Racial Integrity Act of 1924, passed during the period of extreme nativism which followed the end of the First World War. The central features of this Act, and current Virginia law, are the absolute prohibition of a "white person" marrying other than another "white person," a prohibition against issuing marriage licenses until the issuing official is satisfied that the applicants' statements as to their race are correct, certificates of "racial composition" to be kept by both local and state registrars, and the carrying forward of earlier prohibitions against racial intermarriage.

I

In upholding the constitutionality of these provisions in the decision below, the Supreme Court of Appeals of Virginia referred to its 1955 decision in Naim v. Naim, 197 Va. 80, 87 S.E.2d 749, as stating the reasons supporting the validity of these laws. In Naim, the state court concluded that the State's legitimate purposes were "to preserve the racial integrity of its citizens," and to prevent "the corruption of blood," "a mongrel breed of citizens," and "the obliteration of racial pride," obviously an endorsement of the doctrine of White Supremacy. *Id.*, at 90, 87 S.E.2d at 756. The court also reasoned that marriage has traditionally been subject to state regulation without federal intervention, and, consequently, the regulation of marriage should be left to exclusive state control by the Tenth Amendment.

... [T]he State contends that, because its miscegenation statutes punish equally both the white and the Negro participants in an interracial marriage, these statutes, despite their reliance on racial classifications, do not constitute an invidious discrimination based upon race....

.   .   .

There can be no question but that Virginia's miscegenation statutes rest solely upon distinctions drawn according to race. The statutes proscribe generally accepted conduct if engaged in by members of different races. Over the years, this Court has consistently repudiated "[d]istinctions between citizens solely because of their ancestry" as being "odious to a free people whose institutions are founded upon the doctrine of equality." Hirabayashi v. United States, 320 U.S. 81, 100 (1943). At the very least, the Equal Protection Clause demands that racial classifications, especially suspect in criminal statutes, be subjected to the "most rigid scrutiny," Korematsu v. United States, 323 U.S. 214, 216 (1944), and, if they are ever to be upheld, they must be shown to be necessary to the accomplishment of some permissible state objective, independent of the racial discrimination which it was the object of the Fourteenth Amendment to eliminate. Indeed, two members of this Court have already stated that they "cannot conceive of a valid legislative purpose ... which makes the color of a person's skin the test of whether his conduct is a criminal offense." McLaughlin v. Florida, supra, at 198 (Stewart, J., joined by Douglas J., concurring).

There is patently no legitimate overriding purpose independent of invidious racial discrimination which justifies this classification. The fact that Virginia prohibits only interracial marriages involving white persons demonstrates that the racial classifications must stand on their own justification, as measures designed to maintain White Supremacy. We have consistently denied the constitutionality of measures which restrict the rights of citizens on account of race. There can be no doubt that restricting the freedom to marry solely because of racial classifications violates the central meaning of the Equal Protection Clause.

ZABLOCKI v. REDHAIL

434 U.S. 374 (1978).

MR. JUSTICE MARSHALL delivered the opinion of the Court.

. . .

On September 27, 1974, appellee Redhail filed an application for a marriage license with appellant Zablocki, the County Clerk of Milwaukee County, and a few days later the application was denied on the sole ground that appellee had not obtained a court order granting him permission to marry, as required by Section 245.10. Although appellee did not petition a state court thereafter, it is stipulated that he would not have been able to satisfy either of the statutory prerequisites for an order granting permission to marry. First, he had not satisfied his support obligations to his illegitimate child, and as of December 1974 there was an arrearage in excess of $3,700. Second, the child had been a public charge since her birth, receiving benefits under the Aid of Families with Dependent Children program. It is stipulated that the child's benefit payments were such that she would have been a public charge even if appellee had been current in his support payments.

. . .

The leading decision of this Court on the right to marry is Loving v. Virginia . . . . .

It is not surprising that the decision to marry has been placed on the same level of importance as decisions relating to procreation, childbirth, child-rearing, and family relationships. As the facts of this case illustrate, it would make little sense to recognize a right of privacy with respect to other matters of family life and not with respect to the decision to enter the relationship that is the foundation of the family in our society. The woman whom appellee desired to marry had a fundamental right to seek an abortion of their expected child, or to bring the child into life to suffer the myriad social, if not economic, disabilities that the status of illegitimacy brings. Surely, a decision to marry and raise the child in a traditional family setting must receive equivalent protection. And, if appellees right to procreate means anything at all, it must imply some right to enter the only relationship in which the State of Wisconsin allows sexual relations legally to take place.

. . .

When a statutory classification significantly interferes with the exercise of a fundamental right, it cannot be upheld unless it is supported by sufficiently important state interests and is closely tailored to effectuate only those interests. Appellant asserts that two interests are served by the challenged statute: the permission-to-marry proceeding furnishes an opportunity to counsel the applicant as to the necessity of fulfilling his prior support obligations; and the welfare of the out-of-custody children is protected. We may accept for present purposes that these are legitimate and substantial interests, but, since the means selected by the State for achieving these interests unnecessarily impinge on the right to marry, the statute cannot be sustained.

The statutory classification created by Sections 245.10(1),(4),(5) thus cannot be justified by the interests advanced in support of it. The judgment of the District Court is, accordingly, AFFIRMED.

Notes: Same–Sex Marriage

(1) The general rule in the United States is that persons of the same sex are not permitted to marry. Most recent cases prove the rule, see e.g., Dean v. District of Columbia, 653 A. 2d 307 (D.C. 1995); one notable case breaks ground, see Baehr v. Lewin, 74 Haw. 530, 852 P. 2d 44 (1993), remanded for a demonstration that under a strict scrutiny standard that a statutory ban on same-sex marriage furthers a compelling state interest and is narrowly tailored. See also *Baehr v. Miike*, 1996 WL 694235 (Hawai'i Cir.Ct.) (sex-based classification in marriage statute violates state constitution's equal protection provisions; Baehr v. Miike, 80 Hawai'i 341, 910 P.2d 112 (1996).

The Baehr decision has spawned vigorous scholarly and legislative debate about whether gay marriage bans can survive strict scrutiny. Also of great interest is whether a gay marriage valid under the laws of one state (such as hawaii) would have to be recognized in other states. See Mark Strasser, *Statutory Construction, Equal Protection, and the Amendment Process: On Romer, Hunter, and Efforts to Tame Baehr*, 45 Buffalo L. Rev. 739 (1997); Mark Strasser, *For Whom the Bells Toll: on Subsequent Domiciles' Refusing to Recognize Same–Sex Marriages*, 66 U. Cin. L. Rev. 39 (1998); Rebecca S. Paige, *Wagging the Dog–If the State of Hawaii Accepts Same-sex Marriage Will Other States Have To? An Examination of Conflicts of Laws and Escape Devices*, 47 Am. U. L. Rev. 165 (1997); Michael Mandell, *Same Sex Marriages: Arizona Reacts to a Perceived Threat to Traditional Marriages*, 29 Arizona State Law Journal 623 (1997).

(2) In *Singer v. Hara*, 11 Wash. App. 247, 522 P.2d 1187 (1974), two men appealed a trial court's order denying their motion that county officials issue them a marriage license. Relying, *inter alia*, on *Loving v. Virginia* and the state Equal Rights Amendment ("ERA"), the couple contested the constitutionality of applicable marriage statutes, interpreted by the county and the trial court as prohibiting same-sex marriages. According to the state ERA, "Equality of rights and responsibility under the law shall not be denied or abridged on account of sex." The court dispensed with the appeal by denying the analogy to racial classifications invalidated by the Supreme Court in *Loving*. The Court also resorted to what it took to be the "obvious" definition of marriage: "the legal union of one man and one woman." *Id*. at 264, 522 P.2d at 1197. The relationship proposed by the appellants, said the court, quoting *Jones v. Hallahan*, 501 S.W.2d at 590, "is not a marriage." *Id*. at 255, 522 P.2d at 1192.

Note: Transsexuals and Marriage

When a male non-commissioned army officer married another man believing him to be a woman, a New York court declared "that the so-called marriage ceremony ... did not in fact or in law create a marriage contract and that the plaintiff and the defendant [who underwent a sex change operation after the alleged marriage] are not and have not ever been 'husband and wife' or parties to a valid marriage." *Anonymous v. Anonymous*, 67 Misc. 2d 982, 325 N.Y.S.2d 499 (1971).

However, another state court refused to void a marriage between a man and the post-operative transsexual whom he had knowingly courted, married and made a home. *M.T. v. J.T.*, 140 N.J. Super. 77, 355 A.2d 204 (1976). The court reasoned that:

> Plaintiff has become physically and psychologically unified and fully capable of sexual activity consistent with her reconciled sexual attributes of gender and anatomy. Consequently, plaintiff should be considered a member of the female sex for marital purposes. It follows that such an individual would have the capacity to enter into a valid marriage relationship with a member of the opposite sex and did so here. In so ruling we do no more than give legal effect to a *fait accompli*, based upon medical judgment and action which are irreversible. Such recognition will promote the individual's quest for inner peace and personal happiness, while in no way disserving any societal interest, principle of public order or precept of morality.

Id. at 89–90, 355 A.2d at 211. Is this court's concern for the "inner peace and happiness" of transsexuals consistent with most courts' stand regarding same-sex marriage?

BODDIE v. CONNECTICUT
401 U.S. 371 (1971).

MR. JUSTICE HARLAN delivered the opinion of the Court.

Appellants, welfare recipients residing in the State of Connecticut, brought this action in the Federal District Court ... on behalf of themselves and others similarly situated, challenging ... certain state procedures for the commencement of litigation, including requirements for payment of court fees and costs for service of process, that restrict their access to the courts in their effort to bring an action for divorce.

It appears from the briefs and oral argument that the average cost to the litigant for bringing an action for divorce is $60.... An additional $15 is usually required for the service of process by the sheriff, although as much as $40 or $50 may be necessary where notice must be accomplished by publication.

. . .

... Our conclusion is that, given the basic position of the marriage relationship in this society's hierarchy of values and the concomitant state monopolization of the means for legally dissolving their relationship, due process does prohibit a State from denying, solely because of inability to pay, access to its courts to individuals who seek judicial dissolution of their marriages.

. . .

In concluding that the Due Process Clause of the Fourteenth Amendment requires that these appellants be afforded an opportunity to go into court to obtain a divorce, we wish to re-emphasize that we go no further than necessary to dispose of the case before us, a case where the *bona fides* of both appellants' indigency and desire for divorce are here beyond dispute.

Note: Residency Requirements for Divorce

In *Sosna v. Iowa*, 419 U.S. 393 (1975), the Court upheld an Iowa statute imposing a one-year residency requirement on persons seeking divorce in the state. The reasonable grounds for the limitation recognized by the Court included budgetary considerations, administrative convenience, comity, and the state's desire to avoid becoming a "divorce mill."

3. MAINTAINING FAMILY TIES

STANLEY v. ILLINOIS

405 U.S. 645 (1972).

Mr. Justice White delivered the opinion of the Court.

Joan Stanley lived with Peter Stanley intermittently for 18 years, during which time they had three children. When Joan Stanley died, Peter Stanley lost not only her but also his children. Under Illinois law, the children of unwed fathers become wards of the State upon the death of the mother. Accordingly, upon Joan Stanley's death, in a dependency proceeding instituted by the State of Illinois, Stanley's children were declared wards of the State and placed with court-appointed guardians. Stanley appealed, claiming that he had never been shown to be an unfit parent and that since married fathers and unwed mothers could not be deprived of their children without such a showing, he had been deprived of the equal protection of the laws guaranteed him by the Fourteenth Amendment. The Illinois Supreme Court accepted the fact that Stanley's own unfitness had not been established but rejected the equal protection claim, holding that Stanley could properly be separated from his children upon proof of the single fact that he and the dead mother had not been married. Stanley's actual fitness as a father was irrelevant.

Stanley presses his equal protection claim here. The State continues to respond that unwed fathers are presumed unfit to raise their children and that it is unnecessary to hold individualized hearings to determine whether particular fathers are in fact unfit parents before they are separated from their children. We granted certiorari to determine whether this method of procedure by presumption could be allowed to stand in light of the fact that Illinois allows married fathers—whether divorced, widowed, or separated—and mothers—even if unwed—the benefit of the presumption that they are fit to raise their children.

I.

. . .

In considering this procedure under the Due Process Clause, we recognize, as we have in other cases, that due process of law does not require a hearing "in every conceivable case of government impairment of private interest." Cafeteria Worker v. McElroy, 367 U.S. 886, 894 (1961). That case explained that "[t]he very nature of due process negates any concept of inflexible procedures universally applicable to every imaginable situation" and firmly established that "what procedures due process may require under any given set of circumstances must begin with a determination of the precise nature of the government function involved as well as of the private interest that has been affected by governmental action." *Id.*, at 895, Goldberg v. Kelly, 397 U.S. 245, 263 (1970).

The private interest here, that of a man in the children he has sired and raised, undeniably warrants deference and, absent a powerful countervailing interest, protection. It is plain that the interest of a parent in the companionship, care, custody, and management of his or her children "come[s] to this Court with a momentum for respect lacking when appeal is made to liberties which derive merely from shifting economic arrangements."

The Court has frequently emphasized the importance of the family. The rights to conceive and to raise one's children have been deemed "essential," [Meyer v. Nebraska], "basic civil rights of man," [Skinner v. Oklahoma], and "[r]ights far more precious . . . than property rights," [May v. Anderson]. "It is cardinal with us that the custody, care and nurture of the child reside first in the parents, whose primary function and freedom include preparation for obligations the state can neither supply nor hinder." [Prince v. Massachusetts.] The integrity of the family unit has found protection in the Due Process Clause of the Fourteenth Amendment, [Meyer v. Nebraska], the Equal Protection

Clause of the Fourteenth Amendment, [Skinner v. Oklahoma], and the Ninth Amendment, [Griswold v. Connecticut (Goldberg, J., concurring)].

Nor has the law refused to recognize those family relationships unlegitimized by a marriage ceremony. The Court has declared unconstitutional a state statute denying natural, but illegitimate, children a wrongful-death action for the death of their mother, emphasizing that such children cannot be denied the right of other children because familial bonds in such cases were often as warm, enduring, and important as those arising within a more formally organized family unit. Levy v. Louisiana, 391 U.S. 68, 71–72 (1968). "To say that the test of equal protection should be the 'legal' rather than the biological relationship is to avoid the issue. For the Equal Protection Clause necessarily limits the authority of a State to draw such 'legal' lines as it chooses." Glona v. American Guarantee Co., 391 U.S. 73, 75–76 (1968).

These authorities make it clear that, at the least, Stanley's interest in retaining custody of this children is cognizable and substantial.

For its part, the State has made its interest quite plain: Illinois has declared that the aim of the Juvenile Court Act is to protect "the moral, emotional, mental, and physical welfare of the minor and the best interests of the community" and to "strengthen the minor's family ties whenever possible, removing him from the custody of his parents only when his welfare or safety or the protection of the public cannot be adequately safeguarded without removal. . . ." These are legitimate interests, well within the power of the State to implement. We do not question the assertion that neglectful parents may be separated from their children.

But we are here not asked to evaluate the legitimacy of the state ends, rather, to determine whether the means used to achieve these ends are constitutionally defensible. What is the state interest in separating children from fathers without a hearing designed to determine whether the father is unfit in a particular disputed case? We observe that the State registers no gain towards its declared goals when it separates children from the custody of fit parents. Indeed, if Stanley is a fit father, the State spites its own articulated goals when it needlessly separates him from his family.

. . .

Procedure by presumption is always cheaper and easier than individualized determination. But when, as here, the procedure forecloses the determinative issues of competence and care, when it explicitly disdains present realities in deference to past formalities, it needlessly risks running roughshod over the important interest of both parent and child. It therefore cannot stand.

Bell v. Burson held that the State could not, while purporting to be concerned with fault in suspending a driver's license, deprive a citizen of his license without a hearing that would assess fault. Absent fault, the State's declared interest was so attenuated that administrative convenience was insufficient to excuse a hearing where evidence of fault could be considered. That drivers involved in accidents, as a statistical matter, might be very likely to have been wholly or partially at fault did not foreclose hearing and proof in specific cases before licenses were suspended.

We think the Due Process Clause mandates a similar result here. The State's interest in caring for Stanley's children is *de minimis* if Stanley is shown to be a fit father. It insists on presuming rather than proving Stanley's unfitness solely because it is more convenient to presume than to prove. Under the Due Process Clause that advantage is insufficient to justify refusing a father a hearing when the issue at stake is the dismemberment of his family.

III.

The state of Illinois assumes custody of the children of married parents, divorced parents, and unmarried mothers only after a hearing and proof of neglect. The children of unmarried fathers, however, are declared dependent children without a hearing on parental fitness and without proof of neglect. Stanley's claim in the state courts and here is that failure to afford him a hearing on his parental qualifications while extending it to other parents denied him equal protection of the laws. We have concluded that all Illinois parents are constitutionally entitled to a hearing on their fitness before their children are removed from their custody. It follows that denying such a hearing to Stanley and those like him while granting it to other Illinois parents is inescapably contrary to the Equal Protection Clause.

The judgement of the Supreme Court of Illinois is reversed and the case is remanded to that court for proceedings not inconsistent with this opinion. It is so ordered.

MICHAEL H. v. GERALD D.
491 U.S. 110 (1989).

JUSTICE SCALIA delivered the opinion of the court

The facts of this case are, we must hope, extraordinary. On May 9, 1976, in Las Vegas, Nevada, Carole D., an international model, and Gerald D., a top executive in a French oil company, were married. The couple established a home in Playa del Rey, California, in which they resided as husband and wife when one or the other was not out of the country on business. In the summer of 1978, Carole became involved in an adulterous affair with a neighbor.

Michael H. In September 1980, she conceived a child, Victoria D., who was born on May 11, 1981. Gerald was listed as father on the birth certificate and has always held Victoria out to the world as his daughter. Soon after delivery of the child, however, Carole informed Michael that she believed he might be the father.

In the first three years of her life, Victoria remained always with Carole, but found herself within a variety of quasifamily units. In

October 1981, Gerald moved to New York City to pursue his business interests, but Carole chose to remain in California. At the end of that month, Carole and Michael had blood tests of themselves and Victoria, which showed a 98.07% probability that Michael was Victoria's father. In January 1982, Carole visited Michael in St. Thomas, where his primary business interests were based. There Michael held Victoria out as his child. In March, however, Carole left Michael and returned to California. . . .

Michael raises two related challenges to the constitutionality of § 621. First, he asserts that requirements of procedural due process prevent the State from terminating his liberty interest in his relationship with his child without affording him an opportunity to demonstrate his paternity in an evidentiary hearing. We believe this claim derives from a fundamental misconception of the nature of the California statute. While § 621 is phrased in terms of a presumption, that rule of evidence is the implementation of a substantive rule of law. California declares it to be, except in limited circumstances, irrelevant for paternity purposes whether a child conceived during, and born into, an existing marriage was begotten by someone other than the husband and had a prior relationship with him. As the Court of Appeal phrased it: " 'The conclusive presumption is actually a substantive rule of law based upon a determination by the Legislature as a matter of overriding social policy, that given a certain relationship between the husband and wife, the husband is to be held responsible for the child, and that the integrity of the family unit should not be impugned.' " 191 Cal. App. 3d, at 1005, 236 Cal. Rptr., at 816. . . .

Of course the conclusive presumption not only expresses the State's substantive policy but also furthers it, excluding inquiries into the child's paternity that would be destructive of family integrity and privacy. This Court has struck down as illegitimate certain "irrebuttable presumptions." See, e. g., Stanley v. Illinois, 405 U.S. 645 (1972); Vlandis v. Kline, 412 U.S. 441 (1973); Cleveland Board of Education v. LaFleur, 414 U.S. 632 (1974). Those holdings did not, however, rest upon procedural due process. A conclusive presumption does, of course, foreclose the person against whom it is invoked from demonstrating, in a particularized proceeding, that applying the presumption to him will in fact not further the lawful governmental policy the presumption is designed to effectuate. But the same can be said of any legal rule that establishes general classifications, whether framed in terms of a presumption or not. In this respect there is no difference between a rule which says that the marital husband shall be irrebuttably presumed to be the father, and a rule which says that the adulterous natural father shall not be recognized as the legal father. Both rules deny someone in Michael's situation a hearing on whether, in the particular circumstances of his case, California's policies would best be served by giving him parental . Thus, as many commentators have observed, see, e. g., Bezanson, Some Thoughts on the Emerging Irrebuttable Presumption Doctrine, 7 Ind. L. Rev. 644 (1974); Nowak, Realigning [*121] the

Standards of Review Under the Equal Protection Guarantee—Prohibited, Neutral, and Permissive Classifications, 62 Geo. L. J. 1071, 1102–1106 (1974); Note, Irrebuttable Presumptions: An Illusory Analysis, 27 Stan. L. Rev. 449 (1975); Note, The Irrebuttable Presumption Doctrine in the Supreme Court, 87 Harv. L. Rev. 1534 (1974), our "irrebuttable presumption" cases must ultimately be analyzed as calling into question not the adequacy of procedures but—like our cases involving classifications framed in other terms, see, e. g., Craig v. Boren, 429 U.S. 190 (1976); Carrington v. Rash, 380 U.S. 89 (1965)—the adequacy of the "fit" between the classification and the policy that the classification serves. See LaFleur, supra, at 652 (Powell, J., concurring in result); Vlandis, supra, at 456–459 (White, J., concurring), 466–469 (Rehnquist, J., dissenting); Weinberger v. Salfi, 422 U.S. 749 (1975). We therefore reject Michael's procedural due process challenge and proceed to his substantive claim.

Michael contends as a matter of substantive due process that, because he has established a parental relationship with Victoria, protection of Gerald's and Carole's marital union is an insufficient state interest to support termination of that relationship. This argument is, of course, predicated on the assertion that Michael has a constitutionally protected liberty interest in his relationship with Victoria.

It is an established part of our constitutional jurisprudence that the term "liberty" in the Due Process Clause extends beyond freedom from physical restraint. See, e. g., Pierce v. Society of Sisters, 268 U.S. 510 (1925); Meyer v. Nebraska, 262 U.S. 390 (1923). Without that core textual meaning as a limitation, defining the scope of the Due Process Clause "has at times been a treacherous field for this Court," giving "reason for concern lest the only limits to ... judicial intervention become the predilections of those who happen at the time to be Members of this Court." Moore v. East Cleveland, 431 U.S. 494, 502 (1977). The need for restraint has been cogently expressed by Justice White: "That the Court has ample precedent for the creation of new constitutional rights should not lead it to repeat the process at will. The Judiciary, including this Court, is the most vulnerable and comes nearest to illegitimacy when it deals with judge-made constitutional law having little or no cognizable roots in the language or even the design of the Constitution. Realizing that the present construction of the Due Process Clause represents a major judicial gloss on its terms, as well as on the anticipation of the Framers ..., the Court should be extremely reluctant to breathe still further substantive content into the Due Process Clause so as to strike down legislation adopted by a State or city to promote its welfare. Whenever the Judiciary does so, it unavoidably pre-empts for itself another part of the governance of the country without express constitutional authority." Moore, supra, at 544 (dissenting opinion).

In an attempt to limit and guide interpretation of the Clause, we have insisted not merely that the interest denominated as a "liberty" be "fundamental" (a concept that, in isolation, is hard to objectify), but also that it be an interest traditionally protected by our society. As we have put it, the Due Process Clause affords only those protections "so rooted in the traditions and conscience of our people as to be ranked as fundamental." Snyder v. Massachusetts, 291 U.S. 97, 105 (1934) (Cardozo, J.). Our cases reflect "continual insistence upon respect for the teachings of history [and] solid recognition of the basic values that underlie our society...." Griswold v. Connecticut, 381 U.S. 479, 501 (1965) (Harlan, J., concurring in judgment).

This insistence that the asserted liberty interest be rooted in history and tradition is evident, as elsewhere, in our cases according constitutional protection to certain parental rights. Michael reads the landmark case of Stanley v. Illinois, 405 U.S. 645 (1972), and the subsequent cases of Quilloin v. Walcott, 434 U.S. 246 (1978), Caban v. Mohammed, 441 U.S. 380 (1979), and Lehr v. Robertson, 463 U.S. 248 (1983), as establishing that a liberty interest is created by biological fatherhood plus an established parental relationship—factors that exist in the present case as well. We think that distorts the rationale of those cases. As we view them, they rest not upon such isolated factors but upon the historic respect—indeed, sanctity would not be too strong a term—traditionally accorded to the relationships that develop within the unitary family.... In Stanley, for example, we forbade the destruction of such a family when, upon the death of the mother, the State had sought to remove children from the custody of a father who had lived with and supported them and their mother for 18 years. As Justice Powell stated for the plurality in Moore v. East Cleveland, supra, at 503: "Our decisions establish that the Constitution protects the sanctity of the family precisely because the institution of the family is deeply rooted in this Nation's history and tradition."

The presumption of legitimacy was a fundamental principle of the common law. H. Nicholas, Adulturine Bastardy 1 (1836). Traditionally, that presumption could be rebutted only by proof that a husband was incapable of procreation or had had no access to his wife during the relevant period. Id., at 9–10 (citing Bracton, De Legibus et Consuetudinibus Angliae, bk. i, ch. 9, p. 6; bk. ii, ch. 29, p. 63, ch. 32, p. 70 (1569)). As explained by Blackstone, nonaccess could only be proved "if the husband be out of the kingdom of England (or, as the law somewhat loosely phrases it, extra quatuor maria [beyond the four seas]) for above nine months...." 1 Blackstone's Commentaries 456 (J. Chitty ed. 1826). And, under the common law both in England and here, "neither [*125] husband nor wife [could] be a witness to prove access or nonaccess." J. Schouler, Law of the Domestic Relations § 225, p. 306 (3d ed. 1882); R. Graveson & F. Crane, A Century of Family Law: 1857–1957, p. 158 (1957). The primary policy rationale underlying the common law's severe restrictions on rebuttal of the presumption appears to have been an aversion to declaring children illegitimate, see Schouler, supra, § 225, at 306–307; M. Grossberg, Governing the Hearth 201 (1985), thereby depriving them of rights of inheritance and succession, 2 J. Kent, Commentaries on American Law *175, and likely making them wards of the state. A secondary policy concern was the interest in promoting the "peace and tranquillity of States and families," Schouler, supra, § 225, at 304, quoting Boullenois, Traite des Status, bk. 1, p. 62, a goal that is obviously impaired by facilitating suits against husband and wife asserting that their children are illegitimate. Even though, as bastardy laws became less harsh, "[j]udges in both [England and the United States] gradually widened the acceptable range of evidence that could be offered by spouses, and placed restraints on the 'four seas rule'. [,] the law retained a strong bias against ruling the children of married women illegitimate." Grossberg, supra, at 202.

We have found nothing in the older sources, nor in the older cases, addressing specifically the power of the natural father to assert parental rights over a child born into a woman's existing marriage with another man. Since it is Michael's burden to establish that uch a power (at least where the natural father has established a relationship with the child) is so deeply embedded within our traditions as to be a fundamental right, the lack of evidence alone might defeat his case. But the evidence shows that even in modern times—when, as we have noted, the rigid protection of the marital family has in other respects been relaxed—the ability of a person in Michael's position to claim paternity has not been generally acknowledged. For example, a 1957 annotation on the subject: "Who may dispute presumption of legitimacy of child conceived or born during wedlock," 53 A. L. R. 2d 572, shows three States (including California) with statutes limiting standing to the husband or wife and their descendants, one State (Louisiana) with a statute limiting it to the husband, two States (Florida and Texas) with judicial decisions limiting standing to the husband, and two States (Illinois and New York) with judicial decisions denying standing even to the mother. Not a single decision is set forth specifically according standing to the natural father, and "express indications of the nonexistence of any ... limitation" upon standing were found only "in a few jurisdictions." Id., at 579.

Moreover, even if it were clear that one in Michael's position generally possesses, and has generally always possessed, standing to challenge the marital child's legitimacy, that would still not establish Michael's case. As noted earlier, what is at issue here is not entitlement to a state pronouncement that Victoria was begotten by Michael. It is no conceivable denial of constitutional right for a State to decline to declare facts unless some legal consequence hinges upon the requested declaration. What Michael asserts here is a right to have himself declared the natural father and thereby to obtain parental prerogatives. What he must establish, therefore, is not that our society has traditionally allowed a natural father in his circumstances to establish paternity, but that it has traditionally accorded such a. father parental rights, or at least has not traditionally denied them. Even if the law in all States had always been that the entire world could challenge the marital presumption and obtain a declaration as to who was the natural father, that would not advance Michael's claim. Thus, it is ultimately irrelevant, even for purposes of determining current social attitudes towards the alleged substantive right Michael asserts, that the present law in a number of States appears to allow the natural father—including the natural father who has not established a relationship with the child—the theoretical power to rebut the marital presumption, see Note, Rebutting the Marital Presumption: A Developed Relationship Test, 88 Colum. L. Rev. 369, 373 (1988). What counts is whether the States in fact award substantive parental rights to the natural father of a child conceived within, and born into, an extant marital union that wishes to embrace the child. We are not aware of a single case, old or new, that has done so. This is not the stuff of which fundamental rights qualifying as liberty interests are made.

In Lehr v. Robertson, a case involving a natural father's attempt to block his child's adoption by the unwed mother's new husband, we observed that "[t]he significance of the biological connection is that it offers the natural father an opportunity that no other male possesses to develop a relationship with his offspring," 463 U.S., at 262, and we assumed that the Constitution might require some protection of that opportunity, id., at 262–265. Where, however, the child is born into an extant marital family, the natural father's unique opportunity conflicts with the similarly unique opportunity of the husband of the marriage; and it is not unconstitutional for the State to give categorical preference to the latter. In Lehr we quoted approvingly from Justice Stewart's dissent in Caban v. Mohammed, 441 U.S., at 397, to the effect that although " '[i]n some circumstances the actual relationship between father and child may suffice to create in the unwed father parental interests comparable to those of the married father,' " " 'the absence of a legal tie with the mother may in such circumstances appropriately place a limit on whatever substantive constitutional claims might otherwise exist.' " 463 U.S., at 260, n. 16. In accord with our traditions, a limit is also imposed by the circumstance that the mother is, at the time of the child's conception and birth, married to, and cohabitating with, another man, both of whom wish to raise the child as the offspring of their union. It is a question of legislative policy and not constitutional law whether California will allow the presumed parenthood of a couple desiring to retain a child conceived within and born into their marriage to be rebutted.

We do not accept Justice Brennan's criticism that this result "squashes" the liberty that consists of "the freedom not to conform." Post, at 141. It seems to us that reflects the erroneous view that there is only one side to this controversy—that one disposition can expand a "liberty" of sorts without contracting an equivalent "liberty" on the other side. Such a happy choice is rarely available. Here, to provide protection to an adulterous natural father is to deny protection to a marital father, and vice versa. If Michael has a "freedom not to conform" (whatever that means), Gerald must equivalently have a "freedom to conform." One of them will pay a price for asserting that "freedom"— Michael by being unable to act as father of the child he has adulterously begotten, or Gerald by being unable to preserve the integrity of the traditional family unit he and Victoria have established. Our disposition does not choose between these two "freedoms," but leaves that to the people of California. Justice Brennan's approach chooses one of them as the constitutional imperative, on no apparent basis except that the unconventional is to be preferred.

. . . Victoria's due process challenge is, if anything, weaker than Michael's. Her basic claim is not that California has erred in preventing her from establishing that Michael, not Gerald, should stand as her legal father. Rather, she claims a due process right to maintain filial relationships with both Michael and Gerald. This assertion merits little discussion . . .

Victoria claims in addition that her equal protection rights have been violated because, unlike her mother and presumed father, she had no opportunity to rebut the presumption of her legitimacy. We find this argument wholly without merit.

JUSTICE WHITE, with whom JUSTICE BRENNAN joins, dissenting.

Like Justices Brennan, Marshall, Blackmun, and Stevens, I do not agree with the plurality opinion's conclusion that a natural father can never "have a constitutionally protected interest in his relationship with a child whose mother was married to, and cohabiting with, another man at the time of the child's conception and birth." Ante, at 133 (Stevens, J., concurring in judgment). Prior cases here have recognized the liberty interest of a father in his relationship with his child. In none of these cases did we indicate that the father's rights were dependent on the marital status of the mother or biological father. The basic principle enunciated in the Court's unwed father cases is that an unwed father who has demonstrated a sufficient commitment to his paternity by way of personal, financial, or custodial responsibilities has a protected liberty interest in a relationship with his child. . . .

In the case now before us, Michael H. is not a father unwilling to assume his responsibilities as a parent. To the contrary, he is a father who has asserted his interests in raising and providing for his child since the very time of the child's birth. In contrast to the father in Lehr, Michael had begun to develop a relationship with his daughter. There is no dispute on this point. Michael contributed to the child's support. Michael and Victoria lived together. . . .

California plainly denies Michael this protection, by refusing him the opportunity to rebut the State's presumption that the mother's husband is the father of the child. California law not only deprives Michael of a legal parent-child relationship with his daughter Victoria but even denies him the opportunity to introduce blood-test evidence to rebut the demonstrable fiction that Gerald is Victoria's father. . . . Michael has not been denied notice. He has, most definitely, however, been denied any real opportunity to be heard. The grant of summary judgment against Michael was based on the conclusive presumption of Cal. Evid. Code Ann. § 621 (West Supp. 1989), which denied him the opportunity to prove that he is Victoria's biological father. The Court gives its blessing to § 621 by relying on the State's asserted interests in the integrity of the family (defined as Carole and Gerald) and in protecting Victoria from the stigma of illegitimacy and by balancing away Michael's interest in establishing that he is the father of the child.

The interest in protecting a child from the social stigma of illegitimacy lacks any real connection to the facts of a case where a father is seeking to establish, rather than repudiate, paternity. The "stigma of illegitimacy" argument harks back to ancient common law when there were no blood tests to ascertain that the husband could not "by the laws of nature" be the child's father. Judicial process refused to declare that a child born in wedlock was illegitimate unless the proof was positive. The only such proof was physical absence or impotency. But we have now clearly recognized the use of blood tests . . .

The State's professed interest in the preservation of the existing marital unit is a more significant concern. To be sure, the intrusion of an outsider asserting that he is the father of a child whom the husband believes to be his own would be disruptive to say the least. On the facts of this case, however, Gerald was well aware of the liaison between Carole and Michael. The conclusive presumption of evidentiary rule § 621 virtually eliminates the putative father's chances of succeeding in his effort to establish paternity, but it by no means prevents him from asserting the claim. It may serve as a deterrent to such claims but does not eliminate the threat. . . .

As the Court has said: "The significance of the biological connection is that it offers the natural father an opportunity that no other male possesses to develop a relationship with his offspring. If he grasps that opportunity and accepts some measure of responsibility for the child's future, he may enjoy the blessings of the parent-child relationship. . . .

SMITH v. ORGANIZATION OF FOSTER FAMILIES FOR EQUALITY AND REFORM

431 U.S. 816 (1977).

JUSTICE BRENNAN delivered the opinion of the court.

[Appellees, individual foster parents and a foster parents' organization, sought declaratory and injunctive relief against New York officials alleging that state regulations establishing procedures for the removal of foster children were constitutionally invalid. Appellees' contentions that the State's 10–day notice, agency conference and appeal procedures were inadequate relied, in part, on the Fourteenth Amendment's "right to familial privacy."]

. . .

It is, of course, true that "freedom of personal choice in matters of . . . family life is one of the liberties protected by the Due Process Clause of the Fourteenth Amendment." Cleveland Bd. of Ed. v. LaFleur. There does exist a "private realm of family life which the state cannot enter," Prince v. Massachusetts, that has been afforded both substantive and procedural protection. But is the relation of foster parent to foster child sufficiently akin to the concept of "family" recognized in our precedents to merit similar protection? . . .

First, the usual understanding of "family" implies biological relationships. . . .

A biological relationship is not present in the case of the usual foster family. But the biological relationships are not the exclusive determination of the existence of a family. . . .

. . . [T]he importance of the familial relationship to the individuals involved and to the society, stems from the emotional attachments that derive from the role it plays in "promot[ing] a way of life" through the instruction of children, Wisconsin v. Yoder, as well as from the fact of blood relationship. . . . At least where a child has been placed in foster care as an infant, has never known his natural parents, and has remained continuously for several years in the care of the same foster parents, it is natural that the foster family should hold the same place in the emotional life of the foster child, and fulfill the same socializing functions, as a natural family. For this reason, we cannot dismiss the foster family as a mere collection of unrelated individuals.

But there are also important distinctions between the foster family and the natural family. First, unlike the earlier cases recognizing a right to family privacy, the State here seeks to interfere, not with a relationship having its origins entirely apart from the power of the State, but rather with a foster family which has its source in state law and contractual arrangements. . . . [W]hatever emotional ties may develop between foster parent and foster child have their origins in an arrangement in which the State has been a partner from the outset. . . .

. . .

. . . We are persuaded that, even on the assumption that appellees have a protected "liberty interest," the District Court erred in holding that the preremoval procedures presently employed by the State are constitutionally defective.

Notes: The Impact of Incarceration

(1) What happens to rights of reproductive and parental privacy when individuals are incarcerated? How far must government go to accommodate the idea that rights to bear and rear children are constitutionally "fundamental"? Are incarcerated persons entitled to state-funded abortions, procreative sex, and in-prison parenting of small children?

Inmates do not shed their privacy rights at the jailhouse door. Prisoners are not beyond the reach of the Constitution. They must be "accorded those rights not fundamentally inconsistent with imprisonment itself or incompatible with the objectives of incarceration." See Hudson v. Palmer, 468 U.S. 517 (1984) (unannounced cell-searches warranted for discipline and safety, but physical searches impact bodily integrity and implicate Fourth Amendment values); Bell v. Wolfish, 441 U.S. 520 (1979) (upholding body-cavity searches after inmates had "contact visits" with outsiders).

The Court has indicated over the years that safety, health, discipline and fiscal constraints can provide reasonable grounds for diminished privacy in the prisons. In recent years health has emerged as an increasingly important addition to the list of administrative rationales courts tolerate for diminishing privacy in prison. Inmates challenging lost privacy or breach of confidentiality concerning their HIV status have generally failed to recover for injury alleged under tort or constitutional theories.

Does the "right of privacy" applied to the marital relationship suggest that married individuals ought to have access to their incarcerated husbands and wives—access that includes physical intimacy, so-called "conjugal visitation"? Although they are in custody, do prisoners themselves have privacy rights to intimate seclusion with spouses—or perhaps lovers, or members of the opposite sex—that prison officials are bound to respect? *See* Norman Elliot Kent, *The Legal and Sociological Dimensions of Conjugal Visitation in Prisons*, 2 New Eng. J. Prison L. 47 (1975); Note, *Conjugal Visitation Rights and the Appropriate Standard of Judicial Review for Prison Regulations*, 73 Mich. L. Rev. 398 (1974).

D. PERSONAL AUTONOMY

1. DOMESTIC ASSOCIATION

The "right of privacy" is sometimes broadly construed to include the right to a home and a life of one's own design, free from governmental interference or penalty. Official impediments exist to some efforts to form households based on affectional ties or practical necessity.

Notes: Living Arrangements

(1) **Shared Households and Food Stamp Eligibility**. In *U.S. Department of Agriculture v. Moreno*, 413 U.S. 528 (1973) (Rehnquist, J., dissenting), the Supreme Court considered the constitutionality of federal legislation denying Food Stamp eligibility to unrelated individuals who share common living quarters. Under Section 3(e) of the Food Stamp Act of 1964, as amended, 84 Stat. 2048, 7 U.S.C. Section 2012(e), no household, other than an institution or boarding house, consisting in whole or in part of non-family members, was eligible to participate in the federal government's food-purchase subsidy program. Thus, administrators ruled that a family that sheltered a 20–year old girl with emotional problems, and another that moved into an apartment with a single woman to acquire affordable accommodations near a deaf daughter's special school, were ineligible for food stamps under the amended statute.

The Court held that the classification, "households of related persons versus households containing one or more unrelated persons,"—challenged in a class action on equal protection grounds—was not rationally related to the state's legitimate interest in the prevention of welfare fraud. 413 U.S. at 534. The Court determined that the Congressional intent to deny benefits to "hippies" and "hippie communes" could not sustain the statute. In invalidating the statute the Court noted that other provisions of the statute could serve as a deterrent to fraud. Section 5 (c) of the Act denied benefits to certain households containing "an able bodied adult person between the ages of eighteen and sixty-five." Moreover, Sections 14 (b) and (c) imposed strict criminal penalties for fraudulently obtaining food stamp benefits.

(2) **Zoning Restrictions**. A year after the *Moreno* case, the Court upheld a Long Island, New York zoning ordinance restricting land use to "one-family dwellings excluding lodging houses, boarding houses, fraternity houses, or multiple dwelling housing." *See Village of Belle Terre v. Boraas*, 416 U.S. 1 (1974). The ordinance had been challenged by co-owners and tenants of a house leased to six unrelated college students. The ordinance defined a "family" as:

> [O]ne or more persons related by blood, adoption, or marriage, living and cooking together as a single housekeeping unit, exclusive of household servants. A number of persons but not exceeding two (2) living and cooking together as a single housekeeping unit though not related by blood, adoption, or marriage shall be deemed to constitute a family.

Id. at 2.

In his dissent, Justice Marshall argued for strict judicial scrutiny since the classification inherent in the ordinance "burdens the students' fundamental rights of association and privacy guaranteed by the First and Fourteenth Amendments." *Id.* at 13.

> According to Marshall:

> Zoning officials properly concern themselves with the uses of land [including] the number and kind of dwellings to be constructed in a certain neighborhood or the number of persons who can reside in those dwellings. But zoning authorities cannot validly consider who those persons are, what they believe, or how they choose to live, whether they are Negro or white, Catholic or Jew, Republican or Democrat, married or unmarried.

Id. at 14–15.

Distinguishing *Village of Belle Terre* on the grounds that the ordinance at issue there barred households of *unrelated* individuals, the Court invalidated a zoning ordinance limiting occupancy of a residential dwelling to a single "family" in *Moore v. East Cleveland*, 431 U.S. 494 (1977). In doing so, the Court overturned the conviction of an Ohio grandmother whose only "crime" was to have lived with her son and grandson in violation of the statute. The appellant grandmother had been sentenced to five days in jail and fined $25. The Court depicted the rejected statute's narrow definition of "family" as intruding deeply into lives of actual families:

> When a city undertakes such intrusive regulation of the family ... the usual judicial deference to the legislature is inappropriate. This Court has long recognized that freedom of personal choice in matters of marriage and family life is one of the liberties protected by the Due Process Clause of the Fourteenth Amendment.

. . .

The city seeks to justify [the ordinance] as a means of preventing overcrowding, minimizing traffic and parking congestion, and avoiding an undue financial burden on East Cleveland's school system. Although these are legitimate goals, the ordinance before us serves them marginally at best. [The history of the *Lochner* era] counsels caution and restraint. But it does not require ... cutting off any protection of family rights at the first convenient, if arbitrary boundary—the boundary of the nuclear family.

Id. at 499–500, 502.

(3) **Unmarried Cohabitation**. United States Civil Service Commission Regulations prior to 1975 permitted the dismissal of federal employees who engaged in "immoral conduct." In 1975, the Commission adopted the "rational nexus" test of *Norton v. Macy*, 417 F.2d 1161 (D.C. Cir. 1969), which approved dismissal only where employees' off-duty conduct had an adverse effect on job performance and on the efficiency of the agency's service. *See* 5 C.F.R. Section 731.202(b) (1983). Federal employees are deemed to have a "property interest" in their jobs under the due process clause of the fifth amendment if they can prove a "legitimate entitlement" based on written contracts or "implied understandings." *Perry v. Sinderman*, 408 U.S. 593 (1972).

Most dismissals of federal employees because of unmarried cohabitation have been invalidated as a violation of this property interest since a "rational nexus" between cohabitation and job performance cannot be made. *See Mindel v. United States Civil Service Commission*, 312 F. Supp. 485 (N.D. Cal. 1970).

Most state and local governmental discrimination cases involving dismissals of employees involved in unmarried cohabitation also have invalidated these dismissals relying on the "rational nexus" test. In *Briggs v. North Muskegon Police Department*, 563 F. Supp. 585 (W.D. Mich. 1983), *aff'd without opinion*, 746 F.2d 1475 (6th Cir. 1984), *cert. denied*, 473 U.S. 909 (1985), the District Court held the dismissal of a part-time police officer who lived with a woman other than his wife was an unconstitutional violation of his privacy and associational rights and had no rational nexus with his job performance. The court dismissed a state statute criminalizing "cohabitation of unmarried persons in a lewd and lascivious manner" as unconstitutionally vague. It has also been held that questioning a police officer about his cohabitation without marriage with a woman was a violation of his privacy rights where the questions are beyond the scope of a reasonable investigation by the police department. *Schuman v. Philadelphia*, 470 F. Supp. 449 (E.D. Pa. 1979). The District Court in *Schuman* ordered the reinstatement with a back pay award of the officer who was dismissed due to his refusal to answer the questions.

A few courts have utilized the "rational nexus" test with respect to cohabiting public school teachers and have found that the cohabitation does not adversely affect the teacher's job performance or the efficiency of the school. *See Thompson v. Southwest School Dist.*, 483 F. Supp. 1170 (W.D. Mo. 1980). These courts stress the seriousness of the privacy and associational interest that would be infringed by dismissal, and the lack of any evidence proffered by the community or school administrators that the teacher's cohabitation adversely affects students, parents, or the community.

In past cases involving small communities where cohabiting employees were in a position to influence young people, i.e., public school teachers or librarians, courts often upheld employee dismissals. In *Hollenbaugh v. Carnegie Free Library*, 436 F. Supp. 1328 (W.D. Pa. 1977), *aff'd without opinion*, 578 F.2d 1374 (3d Cir. 1978), *cert. denied*, 439 U.S. 1052 (1978), the discharge of two library employees in a small community was upheld by the District Court which reasoned that "there is no fundamental right for two persons, one of whom is already married, to live together." The *Hollenbaugh* Court found no privacy violation and no equal protection violation as the employees failed to allege "state action" in their dismissal. In *Sullivan v. Meade Independent School District*, 530 F.2d 799 (8th Cir. 1976), the Eighth Circuit upheld the dismissal of an elementary school teacher in a small mobile home park community of one hundred persons when it was discovered that she was cohabiting with a male without the benefit of marriage. The court was concerned about the effect of this revelation on the teacher's ability to teach her students in view of the substantial public reaction against her continued employment. *Id*. at 803. The Court also expressed a concern about the adverse effects of her cohabitation on her students in the future, noting the testimony of two expert witnesses on this adverse effect. *Id*. The Court concluded that the state has a vital concern "in the well-being of its youth and in preserving parental rights in the upbringing of their children," and that there was no privacy right to cohabit without marriage. *Id*. at 804.

2. USE AND DISPLAY OF SEXUALLY EXPLICIT MATERIAL

STANLEY v. GEORGIA
394 U.S. 557 (1969).

MR. JUSTICE MARSHALL delivered the opinion of the Court.

An investigation of appellants' alleged bookmaking activities led to the issuance of a search warrant for appellant's home. Under authority of this warrant, federal and state agents secured entrance. They found very little evidence of bookmaking activity, but ... found three reels of eight-millimeter film. Using a projector and screen found in an upstairs living room, they viewed the films. The state officer concluded that they were obscene and seized them.... [Appellant was placed under arrest and later indicted for "knowingly" possessing "obscene matter" in violation of Georgia law.]

        . . .

... Th[e] right to receive information and ideas, regardless of their social worth, is fundamental to our free society. Moreover, in the context of this case—a prosecution for mere possession of printed or filmed matter in the privacy of a person's home—that right takes on added dimension. For also fundamental is the right to be free, except in very limited circumstances, from unwanted governmental intrusions into one's privacy.... [citing Olmstead v. United States (Brandeis, J., dissenting), and Griswold v. Connecticut.]

These are the rights that appellant is asserting in the case before us. He is asserting the right to read or observe what he pleases—the right to satisfy his intellectual and emotional needs in the privacy of his own home. He is asserting the right to be free from state inquiry into the contents of his library.... Georgia justifies this assertion by arguing that the films in the present case are obscene.... Whatever may be the justifications for other statutes regulating obscenity, we do not think they reach into the privacy of one's own home. If the First Amendment means anything, it means that a State has no business telling a man, sitting alone in his own house, what books he may read or films he may watch. Our whole constitutional heritage rebels at the thought of giving government the power to control men's minds.

.   .   .

We hold that the First and Fourteenth Amendments prohibit making mere private possession of obscene materials a crime.

Note: Sex and Nudity on the Internet

Men and women with access to the Internet can enjoy sexually explicit reading materials and images in the privacy of their homes or offices, effectively by-passing the problem of easy detection faced by the appellant in *Stanley v. Georgia*, who stored hard copies of obscene materials in his home. Already Internet users are claiming privacy interests in access to Internet pornography. Concerns about child pornography and juvenile access to pornography have led to calls for regulation of Internet "indecency." *See* Timothy Bass, *Obscenity in Cyberspace: Some Reasons for Retaining the Local Community Standard*, 1996 U. of Chi. Legal Forum 471 (1996); C. Dianne Martin and Joseph M. Reagle, *An Alternative to Government Regulation and Censorship: Content Advisory Systems for the Internet*, 15 Cardozo Arts and Ent. L.J. (409) (1997).

In a different vein, concerns have been raised about the voluntary loss of privacy experienced by the young women with websites inviting site visitors to take an intimate look at their at lives and bodies. *See* Anita L. Allen, Coercing Privacy, 40 William and Mary Law Review 723 (1999), discussing the privacy implications of the Jennicam , Saracam and similar websites. *Cf.* Keith A. Ditthavong, *Paving the Way for Women on the Information Super-Highway; Curbing Sexism Not Freedoms*, 4 Am. U. J. Gender & Law 455 (1996).

ERZNOZNIK v. CITY OF JACKSONVILLE
422 U.S. 205 (1975).

MR. JUSTICE POWELL delivered the opinion of the Court.

This case presents a challenge to the facial validity of a Jacksonville, Fla. ordinance that prohibits showing films containing nudity by a drive-in movie theatre when its screen is visible from a public street or place.

[The manager of a drive-in theatre was charged with violating a municipal ordinance prohibiting exhibiting a motion picture visible from public streets in which "female buttocks and bare breasts were shown." He appealed.]

II.

. . .

Appellee's primary argument is that it may protect its citizens against unwilling exposure to materials that may be offensive....

This court has considered analogous issues—pitting the First Amendment rights of speakers against the privacy rights of those who may be unwilling viewers or auditors—in a variety of contexts....

. . .

The Jacksonville ordinance discriminates among movies solely on the basis of content. Its effect is to deter drive-in theatres from showing movies containing any nudity, however innocent or even educational. This discrimination cannot be justified as a means of preventing significant intrusions on privacy. The ordinance seeks only to keep these films from being seen from public streets and places where the offended viewer readily can avert his eyes. In short, the screen of a drive-in theater is not "so obtrusive as to make it impossible for an unwilling individual to avoid exposure to it." [Redrup v. New York.] Thus, we conclude that the limited privacy interest of persons on the public streets cannot justify the censorship of otherwise protected speech on the basis of its content.

[The court goes on to consider and reject as overbroad a defense of the ordinance premised on the ground that the city has an interest in protecting youth.]

. . .

... We hold ... that the present ordinance does not satisfy the rigorous constitutional standards that apply when government attempts to regulate expression.

Note: Public Breast-Feeding

Ten women in Rochester, New York were arrested in July 1989, for appearing bare-breasted at a public beach to protest the attitude that the display of women's breasts is offensive. One of the arrested women was breast-feeding an infant.

"These days breast-feeding of a baby in a public place is considered by many as being 'offensive to ... modesty,' vulgar and indecent." *Burns v. State*, 256 Ark. 1008, 1023, 512 S.W.2d 928, 936 (1974). *Cf. Settoon v. St. Paul Fire and Marine Insurance Co.* 331 So. 2d 73 (La. Ct. App. 1976), (alleging that a physician invaded the privacy of patient whose hospital room he entered while she breast-fed her infant).

In 1981, a woman who breast-fed her infant in a department store parking lot was warned by police, and later by the St. Louis, Missouri city counselor, that she could be cited for indecent exposure. Citation would be warranted if the manner in which she nursed exceeded the "bounds of decorum as determined by local standards of decency." In 1987, the City

Council of Dubuque, Iowa rescinded an indecent exposure ordinance enacted in haste after a woman repeatedly exposed her breasts to passing motorists. Public uproar persuaded the Council that the ordinance could be interpreted to outlaw breast-feeding in public. A north Carolina Public indecency statute specifically excludes breast-feeding. *See State v. Fly*, 501 S.E.2d 656, 659, 348 N.C. 556 (1998)(quoting Act of 7 July 1993, ch. 301, sec. 1, 1993 N.C. Sess. Laws 586, 587: "Notwithstanding any other provision of law, a woman may breast feed in any public or private location where she is otherwise authorized to be, irrespective of whether the nipple of the mother's breast is uncovered during or incidental to the breast feeding.").

3. CONSENSUAL AND NONCONSENSUAL SEX

Note: Marital Rape

At common law, a man could not be found guilty of raping his wife. Her consent was imputed as a matter of law. *Cf. Shunn v. State*, 742 P.2d 775 (Wyo. 1987) (history of common law marital exemption for spousal rape). Numerous courts have held on equal protection grounds that the marital exemption for spousal rape should be abandoned. *Cf. Merton v. State*, 500 So. 2d 1301 (Ala. Crim. App. 1986) (outlining equal protection analysis supporting elimination of exemption for marital rape).

In 1985, Randy Shoemaker was convicted by a jury of spousal sexual assault under the newly created Pennsylvania Spousal Assault Statute. *See Commonwealth v. Shoemaker*, 359 Pa. Super. 111, 518 A.2d 591 (1986). His estranged wife testified that:

> ... she and appellant engaged in a heated argument regarding custody arrangements for their child. She told him to leave the apartment and when he didn't comply, she went to the door to call for help.... [T]he two engaged in pushing and shoving resulting in an injury [to her].... [A]ppellant came at the victim with a sharp kitchen knife, threatened to harm both her and the child and proceeded to engage in oral and vaginal intercourse with the victim without her consent.

Id. at 114, 518 A.2d at 592–93. Shoemaker was sentenced to an 18 month jail term and appealed. On appeal he argued that the Pennsylvania Spousal Sexual Assault Statute violated his constitutional right to privacy. The court held that marital rape and involuntary deviate sexual intercourse are crimes of violence the Constitution does not protect.

STATE v. MUELLER
66 Haw. 616, 671 P.2d 1351 (1983).

JUSTICE NAKAMURA

I.

The defendant was charged in the District Court of the First Circuit that she "did engage in, or agree to engage in, sexual conduct with another person, in return for a fee, in violation of Section 712–1200 of the Hawaii Revised Statutes." She moved to dismiss the charge, asserting a "constitutional right to privacy for activities that were conducted in the privacy of her own home." At the hearing on the motion the parties entered into a stipulation of facts, agreeing that the activity in question took place in Lauren Mueller's apartment, the participants were willing adults, and there were "no signs of advertising" anywhere in the apartment building.

The case proceeded to trial, and the State offered the testimony of several police officers, including that of the officer responsible for arranging the assagnation leading to her arrest.

II.

The sole issue posed on appeal is whether the proscriptions of Hawaii Revised Statutes (HRS) Sec. 712–1200 may be applied to an act of sex for a fee that took place in a private apartment. With Roe v. Wade, as the point of departure, the defendant argues the privacy guaranteed by the federal and state constitutions prevented a valid application of the statute to the act in question . .

. . .

IV.

The defendant asserts *Griswold, et al.*, and the State Constitution placed the act for which she was prosecuted beyond the reach of HRS Sec. 712–1200 because it was sexual activity carried on in private between two consenting adults and it was not preceded by public solicitation. There was, she claims, no state interest that compelled her prosecution under these circumstances.

Since the guaranteed freedom from intrusion extends to sexual activity among unmarried adult couples as Eisenstadt v. Baird suggests and to autoeroticism in the home as Stanley v. Georgia implies, we would have to agree there is room for argument that the right encompasses any decision to engage in sex at home with another willing adult.

The defendant has directed us to nothing suggesting a decision to engage in sex for hire at home should be considered basic to ordered liberty. Our review of Supreme Court case law in the relevant area leaves us with a distinct impression to the contrary, for we perceive no inclination on the part of the Court to exalt sexual freedom per se or to promote an anomic society. And until we learn from the Court's pronouncements that we have been misinformed, we shall continue to assume there is a "social interest in order and morality," [Chaplinsky v. New Hampshire], that enables a state legislature to act in this area.…

The drafters of the Hawaii Penal Code justified the enactment of HRS Sec. 712–1200 on "the need for public order. .We would not dispute that it was reasonable for the legislature to act on that basis. A large segment of society undoubtedly regards prostitution as immoral and degrading, and the self-destructive or debilitating nature of the practice, at least for the prostitute, is often given as a reason for outlawing it. We could not deem these views irrational. . . .

The sum of experience, including that of the past two decades, affords an ample basis for legislatures to conclude that a sensitive, key relationship of human existence, central to family life, community welfare, and the development of human personality, can be debased and distorted by crass commercial exploitation of sex. Nothing in the Constitution prohibits a State from reaching such a conclusion and acting on it legislatively simply because there is no conclusive evidence or empirical data.

BOWERS v. HARDWICK

478 U.S. 186, *reh'g denied*, 478 U.S. 1039 (1986).

JUSTICE WHITE delivered the opinion of the Court.

In August 1982, respondent . . . was charged with violating the Georgia statute criminalizing sodomy[1] by committing that act with another adult male in the bedroom of respondent's home. . . . [The statute defined sodomy as performing or submitting to "any sex act involving the sex organs of one person and the mouth or anus of another."]

Respondent then brought suit in the Federal District Court, challenging the constitutionality of the statute insofar as it criminalized consensual sodomy.[2] He asserted that he was a practicing homosexual. . . .

This case does not require a judgment on whether laws against sodomy between consenting adults in general, or between homosexuals in particular, are wise or desirable. It raises no question about the right or propriety of state legislative decisions to repeal their laws that criminalize homosexual sodomy, or of state court decisions invalidating those laws on state constitutional grounds. The issue presented is whether the Federal Constitution confers a fundamental right upon homosexuals to engage in sodomy and hence invalidates the laws of the many States that still make such conduct illegal and have done so for a very long time. The case also calls for some judgment about the limits of the Court's role in carrying out its constitutional mandate.

We first register our disagreement with the Court of Appeals and with respondent that the Court's prior cases have construed the Consti-

---

1. Georgia Code Ann. sec. 16–6–2 (1984) provides in pertinent part, as follows:

(a) a person commits the offense of sodomy when he performs or submits to any sexual act involving the sex organs of one person and the mouth or anus of another. . . .

(b) A person convicted of the offense of sodomy shall be punished by imprison-

ment for not less than one nor more than 20 years. . . .

2. . . . . The only claim properly before the Court, therefore, is Hardwick's challenge to the Georgia statute as applied to consensual homosexual sodomy. We express no opinion on the constitutionality of the Georgia statute as applied to other acts of sodomy.

tution to confer a right of privacy that extends to homosexual sodomy and for all intents and purposes have decided this case. The reach of this line of cases was sketched in Carey v. Population Services International. Pierce v. Society of Sisters, and Meyer v. Nebraska, were described as dealing with child rearing and education; Prince v. Massachusetts, with family relationships; Skinner v. Oklahoma ex rel. Williamson, with procreation; Loving v. Virginia, with marriage; Griswold v. Connecticut, *supra*, and Eisenstadt v. Baird, *supra*, with contraception; and Roe v. Wade, with abortion. The latter three cases were interpreted as construing the Due Process Clause of the Fourteenth Amendment to confer a fundamental individual right to decide whether or not to beget or bear a child.

. . . [W]e think it evident that none of the rights announced in these cases bear any resemblance to the claimed constitutional right of homosexuals to engage in acts of sodomy that is asserted in this case. No connection between family, marriage or procreation on the one hand and homosexual activity on the other has been demonstrated, either by the Court of Appeals or by respondent. Moreover, any claim that these cases nevertheless stand for the proposition that any kind of private consensual sexual conduct between consenting adults is constitutionally protected is unsupportable. . . .

Precedent aside, however, respondent would have us announce . . . a fundamental right to engage in homosexual sodomy. This we are quite unwilling to do. . . .

Striving to assure itself and the public that announcing rights not readily identifiable in the Constitution's text involves much more than the imposition of the Justices' own choice of values on the States and the Federal Government, the Court has sought to identify the nature of the rights qualifying for heightened judicial protection. In Palko v. Connecticut, it was said that this category includes those fundamental liberties that are "implicit in the concept of ordered liberty," such that "neither liberty nor justice would exist if [they] were sacrificed." A different description of the fundamental liberties appeared in Moore v. East Cleveland, (opinion of Powell, J.), where they are characterized as those liberties that are "deeply rooted in this Nation's history and tradition."

It is obvious to us that neither of these formulations would extend a fundamental right to homosexuals to engage in acts of consensual sodomy. Proscriptions against that conduct have ancient roots. Sodomy was a criminal offense at common law and was forbidden by the laws of the original 13 States when they ratified the Bill of Rights. In 1868, when the Fourteenth Amendment was ratified, all but 5 of the 37 States in the Union had criminal sodomy laws. In fact, until 1961, all 50 States outlawed sodomy, and today 24 States and the District of Columbia continue to provide criminal penalties for sodomy performed in private between consenting adults. Against this background, to claim that a right to engage in such conduct is "deeply rooted in this Nation's history and tradition" or "implicit in the concept of ordered liberty" is, at best, facetious.

Nor are we inclined to take a more expansive view of our authority to discover new fundamental rights imbedded in the Due Process Clause. The Court is most vulnerable and comes nearest to illegitimacy when it deals with judge-made constitutional law having little or no cognizable roots in the language or design of the Constitution. . . .

Respondent . . . relies upon Stanley v. Georgia, where the Court held that the First Amendment prevents conviction for possessing and reading obscene material in the privacy of one's home. . . .

Stanley did not protect conduct that would not have been protected outside the home, and partially prevented the enforcement of state obscenity laws; but the decision was firmly grounded in the First Amendment. The right pressed upon us here has no similar support in the text of the Constitution, and does not qualify for recognition under the prevailing principles for construing the Fourteenth Amendment. Its limits are also difficult to discern. Plainly enough, otherwise illegal conduct is not immunized whenever it occurs in the home. Victimless crimes such as the possession or use of illegal drugs, do not escape the law where they are committed at home. . . .

. . . [R]espondent asserts that there must be a rational basis for the law and that there is none in this case other than the presumed belief of a majority of the electorate in Georgia that homosexual sodomy is immoral and unacceptable. This is said to be an inadequate rationale to support the law. The law, however, is constantly based on notions of morality, and if all laws representing essentially moral choices are to be invalidated under the Due Process Clause, the courts will be very busy indeed. . . .

CHIEF JUSTICE BURGER, concurring.

. . .

This is essentially not a question of personal "preferences" but rather of the legislative authority of the State. . . . [Holding] that the act of homosexual sodomy is somehow protected as a fundamental right would be to cast aside millennia of moral teaching. [N]othing in the Constitution [deprives] a State of the power to enact the statute challenge here.

JUSTICE POWELL, concurring.

. . .

. . . I agree with the Court. . . . This is not to suggest, however, that respondent may not be protected by the Eighth Amendment of the Constitution. The Georgia statute . . . authorizes a court to imprison a person for up to 20 years for a single private, consensual act of sodomy. In my view a prison sentence for such conduct—certainly a sentence of long duration—would create a serious Eighth Amendment issue. . . .

JUSTICE BLACKMUN, with whom JUSTICE BRENNAN, JUSTICE MARSHALL, and JUSTICE STEVENS join, dissenting.

. . .

This case is no more about "a fundamental right to engage in homosexual sodomy," as the Court purports to declare, than Stanley v. Georgia was about a fundamental right to watch obscene movies, or Katz v. United States, was about a fundamental right to place interstate bets from a telephone booth. Rather this case is about "the most comprehensive of rights and the right most valued by civilized men," namely," the right to be let alone.". . . .

. . . [T]he Court's almost obsessive focus on homosexual activity is particularly hard to justify in light of the broad language Georgia has used. . . . The sex or status of the persons who engage in the act is irrelevant as a matter of state law.

Notes: Homosexuality and Sodomy

(1) Does Romer v. Evans, 517 U.S. 1620 (1996) have adverse implications for the future of the *Bowers*? *See* S.I. Strong, *Romer v. Evans and the Permissibility of Morality Legislation*, 39 Ariz. L. Rev. 1259 (1997). Is *Bowers* likely to be overruled? *See Powell v. State*, 270 Ga. 327, 510 S.E.2d 18 (1998) (invalidating criminal sodomy statute on state law privacy grounds); Commonwealth v. Wasson, 842 S.W.2d 487, 501 (Ky. 1992) (invalidating sodomy statute under state constitutions's guarantees of privacy and equal protection grounds). In *Romer* the Court held violative of equal protection an amendment to the Colorado constitution that singled out homosexuals, lesbians and bi-sexuals as ineligible for "any minority status, quota preferences, protected status or claim of discrimination." The State asserted that the amendment simply denied homosexuals "special rights." Justice Kennedy for the Court concluded, however, that : "To the contrary, the amendment imposes a special disability upon those persons alone. Homosexuals are forbidden the safeguards that others enjoy or may seek without constraint. . . . The Amendment classifies homosexuals not to further a proper legislative end, but to make them unequal to everyone else."

(2) **Pre-Bowers Challenges to Sodomy Statutes**. The Supreme Court held in *Bowers v. Hardwick* that the Constitution does not afford privacy protection to homosexuals who engage in sodomy in violation of state law. Prior to *Bowers*, several courts had upheld sodomy rights. *See, e.g., People v. Onofre*, 51 N.Y.2d 476, 415 N.E.2d 936, 434 N.Y.S.2d 947 (1980) (holding that statute making consensual sodomy a crime is unconstitutional), *cert. denied*, 451 U.S. 987 (1981); *Baker v. Wade*, 553 F. Supp. 1121 (N.D. Texas 1982) (holding that statute prohibiting deviate sexual intercourse between consenting homosexuals, but not between consenting adults of the opposite sex, is unconstitutional), *appeal dismissed*, 743 F.2d 236 (5th Cir. 1984); *Commonwealth v. Bonadio*, 490 Pa. 91, 415 A.2d 47 (1980) (holding Pennsylvania Voluntary Deviate Sexual Intercourse Act unconstitutional).

The "right to privacy" has been only one of three legal bases for challenges to sodomy laws. "Vagueness" and "cruel and unusual punishment" are two additional constitutional grounds upon which "victimless crimes" in the area of sexual freedom have been challenged.

In *Harris v. State*, 457 P.2d 638 (Alaska 1969), the Alaskan Supreme Court declared the statutory term "crime against nature" void for vagueness. But the court found differently respecting the term "sodomy" as applied to the defendant's act of inserting his penis in the rectum of another without consent. 457 P.2d at 649 (affirming the conviction). In dicta, the Court indicated that had the case at bar concerned private, consensual conduct with no visible impact on other persons, a right to privacy defense might be available. *See also, Franklin v. State*, 257 So. 2d 21 (Fla. 1971). However, two other courts have upheld the statutory expression "crime against nature" as lacking defective vagueness in view of ample judicial construction. *See State v. Crawford*, 478 S.W.2d 314 (Mo. 1972), *appeal dismissed*, 409 U.S. 811 (1972); *Hogan v. State*, 84 Nev. 372, 441 P.2d 620 (1968).

Other statutory language has survived constitutional review prompted by vagueness claims. Citing the Alaska Supreme Court's *Harris* decision, *Jones v. State*, 55 Wis. 2d 742, 200 N.W.2d 587 (1972), stated in dicta that a prior statute defining sodomy as a "crime against nature" was vague. The court went on to hold that the current statute prohibiting acts of sex by oral or anal intercourse was valid. A statute prohibiting any person from "willfully commit[ting], in an unnatural manner, any lewd or lascivious act upon or with the body or any part or member thereof of a male or female person with the intent of arousing ... lust," was held not void for vagueness in *State v. Jones*, 8 Ariz. App. 381, 383, 446 P.2d 487,489 (1968). A different term, "act of gross indecency" was determined not to be unconstitutionally vague in *People v. Haggerty*, 27 Mich. App. 594, 183 N.W.2d 862 (1970).

In his concurring opinion in *Bowers*, Justice Powell suggested that *imprisoning* (but not prosecuting) sodomy offenders may constitute cruel and usual punishment within the meaning of the Eighth Amendment. Lower courts have universally rejected the argument that prosecution for sodomy violates the Eight Amendment. *See People v. Stevenson*, 28 Mich. App. 538, 184 N.W.2d 541 (1970); *State v. Stubbs*, 266 N.C. 295, 145 S.E.2d 899 (1966) (also rejecting argument that homosexuality is an illness); *People v. Roberts*, 256 Cal. App. 2d 488, 64 Cal. Rptr. 70 (1967); *State v. Phillips*, 102 Ariz. 377, 430 P.2d 139 (1967) (on grounds that sex crimes of child molestation require the sternest of measures).

Before *Bowers* a number of courts had upheld criminal sodomy statutes. *See, e.g., People v. Penn*, 70 Mich. App. 638, 247 N.W.2d 575 (1976) (upholding statute that prohibited "gross indecency between males"); *Witherspoon v. State*, 278 So. 2d 611 (Fla. 1973) (upholding statute that prohibited unnatural and lascivious acts with another person); *Neville v. State*, 290 Md. 364, 430 A.2d 570 (1981) (upholding a Maryland perverted practices statute).

A federal court upheld the constitutionality of a Virginia statute that made sodomy a crime in *Doe v. Commonwealth's Attorney for City of Richmond*, 403 F. Supp. 1199 (E.D. Va 1975), *aff'd*, 425 U.S. 901 (1976). The statute provided that:

> If any person shall carnally know in any manner any brute animal, or carnally know any male or female person by the anus or by or with the mouth, or voluntarily submit to such carnal knowledge, he

or she shall be guilty of a felony and shall be confined in the penitentiary not less than one year nor more than three years.

Id. at 1280.

Plaintiffs relied on *Griswold's* privacy jurisprudence. But the court construed *Griswold* as pointing "unequivocally" to the conclusion that "homosexual intimacy is denunciable by the State." The court also invoked Justice Harlan's dissent in *Poe v. Ullman*, 367 U.S. 497, 553 (1961), which had asserted that "Adultery, homosexuality and the like are sexual intimacies which [unlike marital intimacy] the State forbids...."

Relying in part on *Doe v. Commonwealth's Attorney for City of Richmond*, the United States Court of Appeals interpreted the right of privacy restrictively in *Dronenburg v. Zech*, 741 F.2d 1388 (D.C. Cir. 1984). In *Dronenburg* the court upheld the discharge of a career navy serviceman because of his homosexual activities. Dronenburg was honorably discharged in 1981 after he admitted being homosexual and engaging in homosexual conduct with another serviceman in violation of Navy regulations. Judge Robert Bork, speaking for the majority, said that the Supreme Court has never extended the right of privacy to include homosexual conduct, [741 F.2d at 1391], because, citing *Doe*, such conduct "bears no relation to marriage, procreation, or family." 741 F.2d at 1392. Judge Bork went on to say that since the constitutional right does not extend to homosexual conduct, then the only question is whether the "regulation bears a rational relationship to a permissible end." 741 F.2d at 1398. Bork applied this test and found that the regulation was related to a permissible end. The Navy did not have to supply quantitative data that homosexual conduct by Navy personnel is harmful to morale and discipline, since "common sense and common experience demonstrate" that it is harmful. 741 F.2d at 1398. A year before *Bowers*, the Supreme Court affirmed the constitutionality of the provisions of an Oklahoma statute that allowed for the dismissal of homosexual teachers. *See National Gay Task Force v. Bd. of Educ.*, 729 F.2d 1270 (10th Cir.1984), *aff'd*, 470 U.S. 903 (1985). The Court upheld Oklahoma Statute Title 70 Section 6–103.5, allowing for dismissal of teachers who committed public homosexual acts, but, on first amendment grounds, struck down the part of the statute allowing for dismissal of teachers who advocate, solicit or promote homosexual activity. The court held that not allowing a teacher to advocate such activity deters legitimate expression. Even where sodomy is illegal, teachers have a protected interest in advocating such conduct as long as such advocacy does not incite imminent action. 729 F.2d at 1274. The court recognized the state's interest in protecting students, but said that teachers' right to free expression clearly outweighs the state's interest.

(2) **Public and Military Employment**. The United States Supreme Court has long recognized that federal and state government employees may have protected "property" interests in their jobs of which they may not be deprived without certain procedural due process safeguards. *See Board of Regents v. Roth*, 408 U.S. 564, 577 (1972) (professor at state university has property interest protected under due process clause if he can show a "legitimate claim of entitlement" to job); *Perry v. Sinderman*, 408 U.S. 593 (1972) (legitimate claim of entitlement to government job can be proven if

employee can show that governmental "rules or mutual explicit understandings" support expectation of entitlement).

In *Shahar v. Bowers*, 70 F.3d 1218 (11th Cir. 1995) a woman's employment offer was rescinded by the Georgia Department of Law after the Attorney General learned of her plans to marry another woman. Applying strict scrutiny, the Court held that the loss of employment opportunity based on statements about future plans violated the First Amendment rights of the lesbian plaintiff to freedom of association.

In *Norton v. Macy*, 417 F.2d 1161 (D.C. Cir. 1969), which involved a federal employee who was dismissed under a United States Civil Service regulation on "immoral conduct" because of his homosexuality, the Circuit Court of the District of Columbia established a "rational nexus" test that would be used thereafter in the vast majority of homosexual employment discrimination cases. Under this test, an employee can be dismissed only if his homosexuality bears a rational nexus to the poor performance of his duties or the inefficiency of the agency's service. *Id.* at 1164.

This "rational nexus" test was adopted by the United States Civil Service Commission in its "Suitability Guidelines for Federal Employment" in 1975 and it is still extant. *See* 5 C.F.R. Section 731.202(b) "Infamous or Notoriously Disgraceful Conduct" (1983). The Office of Personnel Management (the current version of the U.S. Civil Service Commission) has also issued a policy memorandum for use by all federal governmental agencies prohibiting discrimination on the basis of conduct which does not adversely affect the performance of employees or applicants for employment. *See also* Memorandum/Policy Statement on Discrimination on the Basis of Conduct Which Does Not Adversely Affect the Performance of Employees or Applicants for Employment (O.P.M. May 12, 1980). Even a non-civil service, federal employee who is a homosexual has been found to have a "property" interest in his job which cannot be taken away from him unless the procedural due process safeguards of notice and a hearing are used and only if his dismissal is based on a job-related reason and not solely on his homosexuality. *Ashton v. Civiletti*, 613 F.2d 923 (D.C. Cir. 1979).

It has been held that the federal government can inquire on an employment application about the applicant's homosexuality if it is relevant to his job performance. In *Richardson v. Hampton*, 345 F. Supp. 600 (D.C. Cir. 1972), the District Court stated that the government does not have the unfettered right to inquire about a particular applicant's private sexual habits but may ask about his homosexuality where the applicant was previously terminated from federal employment due to perceived emotional instability as evidenced in his admission of homosexuality and frequent emotional outbursts.

Even prior to the adoption of its "Don't Ask, Don't Tell" policy, codified as 10 USCA Sec 654 (b) (1994 Supp.), the military had a long tradition of proscribing homosexuals from both military service and civilian employment in a military branch. *Cf. Philips v. Perry*, 106 F. 3d 1420 (9th Cir. 1997), upholding the "Don't Ask, Don't Tell" policy as applied in the discharge of an enlisted naval service member who informed his division officer of his gay sexual orientation. Ironically, the government has cited the privacy interests of heterosexuals as a reason to ban gays from the military. *See Able v. U.S.*,

88 F.3d 1280 (2d Cir. 1996); 155 F.3d 628 (2d Cir.1998) (Reversing lower court holding that the "Don't Ask, Don't Tell" policy's "imposition of unequal conditions on homosexuals as a prerequisite to serving their country in the armed forces is invalid under the equal protection component of the Fifth Amendment to the Constitution").

Under the Uniform Code of Military Justice, 10 U.S.C. Section 801–940 [West 1983], homosexuals are discharged, usually dishonorably, from military service when their homosexuality is discovered under any one or a combination of three articles of the Code: Article 125 (10 U.S.C. Section 925) prohibiting sodomy, Article 80 (10 U.S.C. Section 880) prohibiting attempts to commit a punishable offense, or Article 134 (10 U.S.C. Section 934) prohibiting conduct of a nature to bring discredit upon the Armed Forces.

Relying on the United States Supreme Court's summary of affirmance of *Doe v. Commonwealth's Attorney for Richmond*, 403 F. Supp. 1199 (E.D. Va. 1975), *aff'd* 425 U.S. 901 (1976), some district courts have found no privacy right to engage in homosexual activity in cases involving the dismissals or refusals of reenlistment of military personnel. *See Matlovich v. Secretary of Air Force*, 414 F. Supp. 690 (D.C. 1976), *vac'd and rem'd*, 591 F.2d 852 (D.C. Cir. 1978) (remanded to see if homosexual airman's activity impaired his ability to perform military service); *Saal v. Middendorf*, 427 F. Supp. 192 (N.D. Cal. 1977) (rational nexus used to invalidate refusal of reenlistment of homosexual), *rev'd sub nom., Beller v. Middendorf*, 632 F.2d 788 (9th Cir. 1980). In cases specifically involving the refusal of a homosexual's reenlistment, courts have also often found no property right under the due process clause to reenlist. In *Miller v. Rumsfeld*, 647 F.2d 80 (9th Cir. 1981), *cert. denied sub. nom. Miller v. Weinberger,* 454 U.S. 855 (1981), the majority upheld as constitutional a navy regulation discharging any member who engaged in homosexual activity without regard to individual fitness for service. Thus far, courts have been willing to uphold such discriminatory discharge regulations, reasoning that the military branches have a great interest in protecting national defense, in maintaining discipline, and in upholding obedience under the peculiar conditions of military life which outweighs any privacy or free speech rights of the discharged military personnel.

In the unusual case of *benShalom v. Secretary of Army*, 489 F. Supp. 964 (E.D. Wis. 1980), *aff'd in part, vac'd in part, remanded*, 776 F.2d 1049 (7th Cir. 1985) (opinion not reported), a district court invalidated an Army regulation discharging any soldier evidencing homosexual desires, tendencies, or interests. The Court held that such discharges violated the discharged reserve officer's first amendment free speech and associational rights and of her right to privacy. Although the district court found no "property right" under the due process clause of the fifth amendment in her continued service and no "liberty" interest in wrongful reputation loss due to her discharge, it found that her discharge placed an unconstitutional "chill" on her freedom of speech to openly admit her homosexuality, to receive information and ideas about homosexuality, and to associate freely with other homosexuals. *Id.* at 971–72, 974.

The *benShalom* court noted that, although the soldier openly admitted her homosexuality, there was no evidence of her involvement in homosexual activity. *Id.* at 973. Many courts dealing with employment discrimination against homosexuals make a distinction between "latent" homosexuals, those that profess to be homosexual but about whom there is no evidence of homosexual activity, and "overt" homosexuals, those about whom there is evidence of homosexual activity. This distinction is based on the reality that many states and the military still have criminal laws against homosexual acts, including sodomy. The *benShalom* court characterized the soldier as having only a homosexual personality and stated that the "privacy of one's personality," "the essence of one's identity," is an "interest so fundamental or 'implicit in the concept of ordered liberty' as to merit constitutional protection." *Id.* at 975. The *benShalom* Court concluded that the soldier had a good record of service and that absent the Army's showing of a rational "nexus" between her sexual preference and her military capabilities, she could not be dismissed. *Id.* at 976.

In the context of state and local government employment, several courts have utilized the "rational nexus" test of *Norton v. Macy, supra,* when dealing with employment discrimination against homosexual state and local government employees. In *McConnell v. Anderson*, 316 F. Supp. 809 (D. Minn. 1970), *rev'd*, 451 F.2d 193 (8th Cir. 1971), the district court used the rational nexus test to find that a homosexual applicant for a librarian's job in a state university was denied due process under the fourteenth amendment where there was no showing that his homosexuality would impair his efficiency on the job. The *McConnell* court stressed that the librarian would not be "exposed to children of tender years, would not be subject to blackmail because he was open about his homosexuality, and would not be dealing with classified information of national security," and concluded that · the applicant's homosexuality would not affect his job performance. The *McConnell* court also reasoned that although the applicant did not have an inalienable property right to be employed by the state, he did have a legitimate entitlement under the due process clause in not being discriminated against in the application process. The *McConnell* court also found a "liberty interest" under the due process clause of the fourteenth amendment in that the applicant's reputation was injured wrongfully by the refusal of his application.

Challenges to homosexuals teaching in public schools have been particularly controversial. While some courts have used the *Norton* "rational nexus" test to save homosexual teachers from dismissal by arguing that their homosexuality has no effect on their "fitness to teach," other courts have used the "rational nexus" test to authorize the dismissal of homosexual teachers, particularly where there is evidence that the students are young and impressionable and that the community is in an uproar over the teacher's homosexuality. *See Morrison v. State Bd. of Educ.*, 1 Cal. 3d 214, 82 Cal. Rptr. 175, 461 P.2d 375 (1969) (homosexual special education teacher is not "unfit to teach"); *Gaylord v. Tacoma School Dist.*, 88 Wash. 2d 286, 559 P.2d 1340, *cert. denied*, 434 U.S. 879 (1977) (evidence that one student and three fellow teachers objected to homosexual teacher's remaining on teaching staff enough to show adverse effect of his homosexuality on his teaching ability and required his dismissal despite a record of good teaching for twenty years). In *Gaylord, supra,* the Supreme Court of Washington *en banc* reasoned that "a teacher's efficiency is determined by his relationship with students, their parents, fellow teachers, and administrators," and that after a teacher's homosexual status became known, his teaching ability would be impaired due to the atmosphere of "fear, confusion, suspicion, parental concern and pressure on the administration by parents, students, and other teachers." *Id*. at 1350. *See also Gish v. Board of Educ.*, 145 N.J. Super. 96, 366 A.2d 1337 (1976), *cert. denied*, 74 N.J. 251, 377 A.2d 658 (1977), *cert. denied*, 434 U.S. 879 (1977). The *Gaylord* Court declared that homosexuality has been "immoral" since biblical times although Washington's Statute on lewdness and sodomy was repealed just prior to the court's decision, *id*. at 1345–46, and the court worried that the teacher's retention would signal "adult approval of homosexuality" to the "impressionable, adolescent minds" of high school students. *Id*. at 1347.

In homosexual teacher discrimination cases, courts have often made the "overt"-"latent" homosexuality distinction. This appears to be because school boards often express the concern that a teacher should not be an example of a lawbreaker to the students. *Id*. at 1342. Courts have also looked to see whether teachers openly "flaunt" homosexuality, allowing the classroom to become a forum for discussing homosexuality. *Id*. at 1347. *See also Safransky v. State Personnel Bd.*, 62 Wis. 2d 464, 215 N.W.2d 379 (1974) (court upheld dismissal of homosexual house parent in state institution for teenage retarded boys where house parent openly discussed and joked about his homosexuality in front of retarded boys).

Courts have upheld the dismissal of homosexual teachers where it is found that they deliberately withheld information about homosexuality on their employment applications. *Acanfora v. Board of Educ.*, 491 F.2d 498 (4th Cir. 1974), *cert. denied*, 419 U.S. 836 (1974). Courts have also ordered homosexual teachers to undergo psychiatric examination prior to teaching because it was believed that their homosexuality displayed deviance from normal mental health that might affect their teaching ability. *See Gish*, *supra*. And courts have often dismissed homosexual teachers under state regulations proscribing "immoral behavior" for teachers. *See Gaylord*, *supra*. Only a few courts have challenged such "immorality" standards as unconstitutionally vague. *Burton v. Cascade School Dist.*, 353 F. Supp. 254 (D. Or. 1973), *aff'd* 512 F.2d 850 (9th Cir.), *cert. denied*, 423 U.S. 839 (1975).

Another litigated area of state and local employment discrimination against homosexuals involves police officers. In *Childers v. Dallas Police Department*, 513 F. Supp. 134 (N.D. Tex. 1981), the District Court held that the police department's refusal of a homosexual applicant did not violate the applicant's first amendment free speech and associational rights nor his right to privacy. The court found no "legitimate entitlement" and hence, no due process property interest in a mere application for a job and no reputational loss to constitute a due process liberty deprivation. The Court pointed to the Texas criminal statute prohibiting certain homosexual activities and concluded that the right to engage in homosexual activity was not a "fundamental right." The *Childers* court also found no equal protection violation and stated that homosexuals were not a "suspect class." Finally, the court applied the *Norton* "rational nexus" test and concluded that the position the applicant applied for involved the investigation and prosecution of illegal homosexual activities and that his job performance and the harmony in that department among the other officers would be affected by his own homosexuality.

The California Supreme Court was the first state court to use its own state constitutional equal protection clause to protect the employment rights of homosexuals in state and local government. *Gay Law Students Ass'n v. Pacific Tel. & Tel. Co.*, 24 Cal. 3d 458, 595 P.2d 592, 156 Cal. Rptr. 14 (1979). In this case, the Court found a state-regulated public utility's firing of a homosexual employee to be "state action" which violated the equal protection clause of the California Constitution.

(3) **Private Employment**. Title VII of the Civil Rights Act of 1964, 42 U.S.C. Section 2000e–2(a)(1) [West 1983] prohibits private employment discrimination because of an individual's sex. Several homosexuals have attempted to use Title VII to redress private employment discrimination based on sexual preference; most of these attempts have been unsuccessful. *See, e.g., Smith v. Liberty Mutual Ins. Co.*, 395 F. Supp. 1098 (N.D. Ga. 1975) (sexual preference not protected under Title VII) *aff'd*, 569 F.2d 325 (5th Cir. 1978); *Voyles v. Ralph K. Davies Medical Center*, 403 F. Supp. 456 (N.D. Cal. 1975) (Title VII does not protect homosexuals, transsexuals, or bisexuals), *aff'd without opinion*, 570 F.2d 354 (9th Cir. 1978); *DeSantis v. Pacific Tel. & Tel. Co.*, 608 F.2d 327 (9th Cir. 1979) (sexual preference not covered by Title VII); *Blum v. Gulf Oil Corp.*, 597 F.2d 936 (5th Cir. 1979) (Title VII does not protect homosexuals); *Grossman v. Bernards Township*, 538 F.2d 319 (3rd Cir. 1976), (Title VII does not protect transsexuals) *cert. denied*, 429 U.S. 897 (1976); *Sommers v. Budget Mktg. Inc.*, 667 F.2d 748 (8th Cir. 1982) (Title VII does not include sexual preferences). From 1975 to 1977, several bills were introduced into the House to amend Title VII to include sexual preference but none were successful. *See Holloway v. Arthur Andersen & Co.*, 566 F.2d 659, 662 n.6 (9th Cir. 1977).

However, a district court has held that a dismissal of an employee because he refuses homosexual advances made on him by his superior is redressable under Title VII. *Wright v. Methodist Youth Services*, 511 F. Supp. 307 (N.D. Ill. 1981). In this case, the court importantly realized that sexual harassment in the work place involving either heterosexual or homosexual persons constitutes a violation of Title VII since the advances occurred only because of the employee's sex. *Id.* at 310. *But see Barnes v. Costle*, 561 F.2d 983 (D.C. Cir. 1977) (sexual harassment by bisexual is not remedial under Title VII since it can potentially affect both males and females.) Also the argument has also been made that employment discrimination against homosexuals is gender discrimination remediable under Title VII since statistically more homosexuals are men, and therefore, discrimination against homosexuals has a "disproportionate impact" on males. This argument was rejected by the Ninth Circuit in *DeSantis, supra*.

Several states with private employment discrimination statutes modeled from Title VII have also found that "sex" discrimination in the state statutes does not include discrimination on the basis of sexual preference. *See Macauley v. Massachusetts Comm'n Against Discrimination*, 379 Mass. 279, 397 N.E.2d 670 (1979); *Gay Law Students Ass'n v. Pacific Tel. & Tel. Co.*, 24 Cal. 3d 458, 595 P.2d 592, 156 Cal. Rptr. 14 (1979). *But see Gay Rights Coalition v. Georgetown University*, 536 A.2d 1 (1987), holding that the eradication of sexual orientation discrimination is a compelling governmental interest articulated in the Human Rights Statute of the District of Columbia, D.C.Code 1981, 1–2501.

For a detailed discussion of homosexual rights through the 1970s, *see*, Rhonda R. Rivera, *Our Straight-laced Judges: The Legal Position of Homosexual Persons in the United States*, 30 Hastings L. Rev. 799 (1979) (part of a Symposium on Sexual Preference and Gender Identity); Rhonda R. Rivera, *Recent Developments in Sexual Preference Law*, 30 Drake L. Rev. 311 (1980–81) (follow-up to Hastings' article); Annot., 42 A.L.R.Fed. 189 (1979).

Note: Marital Sodomy

Bowers left uncertain whether the Constitution permits criminal convictions of persons who engage in sodomy with their spouses. In *Cotner v. Henry*, 394 F.2d 873 (7th Cir. 1968), *cert. denied*, 393 U.S. 847 (1968), the Seventh Circuit reversed the conviction of a man jailed after pleading guilty to his wife's charge that he had engaged in "the abominable and detestable crime against nature." *Id.* at 874. It was not clear from the record whether the sodomy had been with or without the woman's consent. The court explained that:

> Under *Griswold* Indiana courts could not interpret the [sodomy] statute constitutionally as making private consensual physical relations between married persons a crime absent a clear showing that the state had an interest in preventing such relations, which outweighed the constitutional right to marital privacy.... [Even so] the protection of the *Griswold* rule would not be available to Cotner if there was a showing that Cotner employed force.

Id. at 875–76.

In another pre-*Bowers* case involving a married couple, *Lovisi v. Slayton*, 539 F.2d 349 (4th Cir. 1976), *cert. denied*, 429 U.S. 977 (1976), a husband and wife were convicted of violating state sodomy laws after "carelessly exposing erotic pictures of their sexual activity to [Mrs. Lovisi's young daughters]." *Id.* at 350. The photographs were discovered when one daughter reportedly appeared in school with an erotic photograph. Acting on a search warrant, the police found hundreds of erotic photographs of the Lovisis and adult companions. The Fourth Circuit affirmed the conviction and endorsed the rationale that the couple had waived their constitutional right of privacy by admitting the adult "swingers" they identified through advertisements into their bedroom to observe intimacies.

4. EXPANDED STATE CONSTITUTIONAL PROTECTION

STATE v. PILCHER

242 N.W.2d 348 (Iowa 1976).

Mason, Justice.

Defendant, Robert Eugene Pilcher, appeals from judgment imposed following his conviction by a jury of the crime of sodomy in violation of section 705.1, The Code. Although several issues are presented for review, defendant primarily challenges the constitutionality of this statute. . . .

I. Defendant contends the trial court erred in overruling his demurrer and motion to dismiss directed at the constitutionality of sections 705.1 and 705.2. These statutes provide in pertinent part:

705.1 Definition. Whoever shall have carnal copulation in any opening of the body except sexual parts, with another human being, . . . , shall be deemed guilty of sodomy.

705.2 Punishment. Any person who shall commit sodomy shall be imprisoned in the penitentiary not more than ten years. . . .

Defendant's attack upon the constitutionality of these statutes is based on the assumption the facts occurred as described by Roma Waterhouse although a witness defendant denied involvement in the case. Viewed in this light, Pilcher is charged with having committed, in privacy, carnal copulation per se with an adult person of the opposite sex, not his spouse.

Pilcher first points out section 705.1 makes all sodomy illegal, whether the persons married or unmarried, between opposite sexes. It draws no distinction between public and private acts. Likewise, the age of the parties is not relevant. However, he specifically states he is not asking the court to consider homosexual activity or carnal copulation per anum. . . .

The main and most compelling thrust of any argument against a sodomy statute's constitutionality entails assertion that the emerging right of privacy protects private sexual activity between consenting adults of the opposite sex not married to each other.

The Supreme Court has recognized the right to privacy as it applies to sexual relations. Thus, in Griswold v. Connecticut, supra, a statute prohibiting the use and distribution of contraceptives was struck down on the basis it operated " . . . directly on an intimate relation of husband wife and their physician's role in one aspect of that relation." . . .

The next step taken in this area is that the State may not interfere with the private sexual actions of consenting adults of the opposite sex not married to each other. This reasoning has often found its basis in Eisenstadt v. Baird, a case which held the different treatment accorded married and unmarried persons as to the availability of contraceptives was not grounded on a rational difference. Thus, the statute violated equal protection. The Court, through Justice Brennan, reasoned this was so under either of two situations: (1) If under *Griswold* the distribution of contraceptives to married persons could not be prohibited due to the right of privacy, then such right would inhere equally to individuals; (2) if *Griswold* does not bar the state's prohibition on the distribution of contraceptives, the state could not allow married persons such a right but deny it to unmarried individuals.

The *Eisenstadt* court further stated: " . . . It is true that in *Griswold* the right of privacy in question inhered in the marital relationship. Yet the marital couple is not an independent entity with a mind and heart of its own, but an association of two individuals each with a separate intellectual and emotional makeup...."

Thus, it may be said the Equal Protection Clause insures one's right to privacy in the individual sense. Governmental intrusion into "fundamental matters" cannot be distinguished on the basis of marital status.

In our opinion, the rationale expressed in *Eisenstadt* extends to protect the manner of sexual relations performed in private between consenting adults of the opposite sex not married to each other.

Before the state each encroach into recognized areas of fundamental rights, such as the personal right of privacy, there must exist a subordinating interest which is compelling and necessary, not merely related, to the accomplishment of a permissible state policy. [Griswold v. Connecticut, (Goldberg, J., concurring).] The State has not shown the existence of any such interest here.

Defense counsel has referred the court to numerous publications which might be adequately described as "sex manuals." As suggested in Carter v. State, we do not deem these publications to be of such compelling force or effect that we may take judicial notice of the supposed data, arguments and recommendation of the authors (even though they may have been bestsellers). These publications have no place in a quest involving determination of the constitutional validity of a criminal statute. We have not considered this material in reaching our decision.

We hold section 705.1 in its present form is unconstitutional as an invasion of fundamental rights, such as the personal right of privacy, to the extent it attempts to regulate through use of criminal penalty consensual sodomitical practices performed in private by adult persons of the opposite sex.

We are convinced in light of the decisions considered herein and the authorities cited in those opinions that the right of privacy extends to sexual relations between husband and wife. Consequently, if sections 705.1 and 705.2 are applied to sexual acts committed in private between consenting married couples, the statutes are unconstitutional.

We point out what should be obvious that in reaching the foregoing decision we are dealing with section 705.1 as presently in force and in no way touch the power of the legislature to enact statutes which otherwise pass constitutional muster providing for regulation rendering criminal sexual acts of any nature in public, bestiality, adult corruption of children or forcible nonconsenting sexual behavior between adults. We do not reach the question of homosexuality since the applicability of the statute to such conduct was not made an issue in this case....

RAWLINGS, REES, HARRIS and McCORMICK, JJ., concur.

REYNOLDSON, J., MOORE, C.J., LEGRAND and UHLENHOPP, JJ., dissent.

Of course, majority's holding that the right of privacy per se is a fundamental right creates potentially infinite implications. From now on, whenever a litigant challenges a statute on the basis of his right to privacy, the State will have the constitutional burden to prove it has a *compelling interest* in enforcement of the statute. The State would be hard pressed to show a compelling State interest in making arrest records public (see chapter 68A, The Code); or prohibiting use of marijuana in the home (see chapter 204, The Code). The State could also be forced to come up with a compelling interest in prohibiting keeping a house of ill fame (section 724.3, The Code), regulating massage parlors, prohibiting adultery (section 702.1, The Code), and bigamy (section 703.1, The Code), and statutory proscriptions in any number of other areas states have traditionally regulated. The possibilities are limited only by the fertile imagination of our practicing bar. . . .

In overview, it is clear the majority opinion pushes the protection of the United States Constitution far beyond any point suggested by United States Supreme Court decisions. It unnecessarily engineers in complex moral and social areas better left to the legislature. It effectively leaves citizens without deterrent protection from the most offensive of violent crimes. However much in good faith, it accomplishes these results by failing to utilize the legislation-salvaging devices we have readily applied in similar situations, and by failing to appreciate the careful limiting language in *Griswold* and *Eisenstadt*.

I would affirm the judgment below.

5. DRUG USE

Notes: Possession and Sale of Narcotics

(1) Although efforts to legalize marijuana for medical purposes have met with some success in California and elsewhere, courts have generally rejected claims that criminal drug laws violate privacy rights. *See, e.g., State v. Mallan*, 86 Haw. 440, 950 P.2d 178 (1998) (holding that the express right to privacy in article 1 sec. 6 of the Hawai'i state constitution does not encompass a right to possess and use marijuana).

In *Ravin v. State*, 537 P.2d 494 (Alaska 1975), a man arrested for possession of marijuana attacked statutes criminalizing the narcotic as, *inter alia*, violative of his right of privacy under the Alaska and the federal constitutions. The Alaska Supreme Court held that a basic right to privacy in the home encompasses "the possession and ingestion of substances such as marijuana in a purely personal, non-commercial context in the home." *But see State v. Kantner*, 53 Haw. 327, 493 P.2d 306 (1972) (marijuana use not clearly within class of interests accorded highest protection of state and federal constitutions), *cert. denied*, 409 U.S. 948 (1972). The Court declined to count enforcement of traffic laws and public health concerns as raising a legitimate state interest sufficient to warrant blanket criminalization of marijuana use or possession.

(2) Shortly after it decided the *Ravin* case, the Alaska Supreme Court decided a case involving the sale of two pounds of marijuana by a juvenile and an adult accessory to an undercover agent. *Belgarde v. State*, 543 P.2d 206 (Alaska 1975). The adult accessory had appealed on constitutional

grounds a lower court's order denying his motion to dismiss the indictment. The court affirmed the order, citing *Ravin*, which had expressly distinguished mere possession of drugs for private use from buying, selling, or public use of drugs.

EMPLOYMENT DIV., DEP'T OF HUMAN RES. v. SMITH

494 U.S. 872 (1990).

JUSTICE SCALIA delivered the opinion of the Court.

This case requires us to decide whether the Free Exercise Clause of the First Amendment permits the State of Oregon to include religiously inspired peyote use within the reach of its general criminal prohibition on use of that drug, and thus permits the State to deny unemployment benefits to persons dismissed from their jobs because of such religiously inspired use.

I

Oregon law prohibits the knowing or intentional possession of a "controlled substance" unless the substance has been prescribed by a medical practitioner. Ore. Rev. Stat. section 475.992(4) (1987). The law defines "controlled substance" as a drug classified in Schedule I through V of the Federal Controlled Substances Act, 21 U.S.C. sections 811–812 (1982 ed. and Supp. V), as modified by the State Board of Pharmacy. Ore. Rev. Stat. section 475.005(6) (1987). Persons who violate this provision by possessing a controlled substance listed on Schedule I are "guilty of a Class B felony." section 475.992(4)(a). As compiled by the State Board of Pharmacy under its statutory authority, see Ore. Rev. Stat. section 475.035 (1987), Schedule I contains the drug peyote, a hallucinogen derived from the plant *Lophophorawilliamsii Lemaire*. Ore. Admin. Rule 855–80–021(3)(s) (1988).

Respondents Alfred Smith and Galen Black were fired from their jobs with a private drug rehabilitation organization because they ingested peyote for sacramental purposes at a ceremony of the Native American Church, of which both are members. When respondents applied to petitioner Employment Division for unemployment compensation, they were determined to be ineligible for benefits because they had been discharged for work-related "misconduct." The Oregon Court of Appeals reversed that determination, holding that the denial of benefits violated respondents' free exercise rights under the First Amendment.

On appeal to the Oregon Supreme Court, petitioner argued that the denial of benefits was permissible because respondents' consumption of peyote was a crime under Oregon law. The Oregon Supreme Court reasoned, however, that the criminality of respondents' peyote use was irrelevant to resolution of their constitutional claim—since the purpose of the "misconduct" provision under which respondents had been disqualified was not to enforce the State's criminal laws but to preserve the financial integrity of the compensation fund, and since that purpose was inadequate to justify the burden that disqualification imposed on respondents' religious practice. . . . [T]he court concluded that respondents were entitled to payment of unemployment benefits.

Before this Court in 1987, petitioner continued to maintain that the illegality of respondents' peyote consumption was relevant to their constitutional claim. We agreed, concluding that "if a State has prohibited through its criminal laws certain kinds of religiously motivated conduct without violating the First Amendment, it certainly follows that it may impose the lesser burden of denying unemployment compensation benefits to persons who engage in that conduct." (Smith I). We noted, however, that the Oregon Supreme Court had not decided whether respondents' sacramental use of peyote was in fact proscribed by Oregon's controlled substance law, and that this issue was a matter of dispute between the parties. Being "uncertain about the legality of the religious use of peyote in Oregon," we determined that it would not be "appropriate for us to decide whether the practice is protected by the Federal Constitution." Accordingly, we vacated the judgment of the Oregon Supreme Court and remanded for further proceedings. On remand, the Oregon Supreme Court held that respondents' religiously inspired use of peyote fell within the prohibition of the Oregon statute, which "makes no exception for the sacramental use" of the drug. It then considered whether that prohibition was valid under the Free Exercise Clause, and concluded that it was not. The court therefore reaffirmed its previous ruling that the State could not deny unemployment benefits to respondents for having engaged in that practice.

We again granted certiorari.

II

Respondents' claim for relief rests on our decisions . . . , in which we held that a State could not condition the availability of unemployment insurance on an individual's willingness to forgo conduct required by his religion. As we observed in *Smith I*, however, the conduct at issue in those cases was not prohibited by law. We held that distinction to be critical, for "if Oregon does prohibit the religious use of peyote, and if that prohibition is consistent with the Federal Constitution, there is no federal right to engage in that conduct in Oregon," and "the State is free to withhold unemployment compensation from respondents for engaging in work-related misconduct, despite its religious motivation." Now that the Oregon Supreme Court has confirmed that Oregon does prohibit the religious use of peyote, we proceed to consider whether that prohibition is permissible under the Free Exercise Clause.

A

The Free Exercise Clause of the First Amendment, which has been made applicable to the States by incorporation into the Fourteenth Amendment, see Cantwell v. Connecticut, provides that "Congress shall make no law respecting an establishment of religion, or *prohibiting the free exercise thereof. . . .*" U.S. Const. Am. I (emphasis added). The free exercise of religion means, first and foremost, the right to believe and profess whatever religious doctrine one desires. Thus, the First Amendment obviously excludes all "governmental regulation of religious *beliefs* as such." [Sherbert v. Verner.] The government may not compel affirmation of religious belief, see Torcaso v. Watkins, (1961), punish the expression of religious doctrines it believes to be false, United States v. Ballard, impose special disabilities on the basis of religious views or religious status, see McDaniel v. Paty; Fowler v. Rhode Island; cf. Larson v. Valente, or lend its power to one or the other side in controversies over religious authority or dogma, see Presbyterian Church v. Hull Church; Kedroff v. St. Nicholas Cathedral; Serbian Eastern Orthodox Diocese v. Milivojevich.

But the "exercise of religion" often involves not only belief and profession but the performance of (or abstention from) physical acts: assembling with others for a worship service, participating in sacramental use of bread and wine, proselytizing, abstaining from certain foods or certain modes of transportation. It would be true, we think (though no case of ours has involved the point), that a state would be "prohibiting the free exercise [of religion]" if it sought to ban such acts or abstentions only when they are engaged in for religious reasons, or only because of the religious belief that they display. It would doubtless be unconstitutional, for example, to ban the casting of "statutes that are to be used for worship purposes," or to prohibit bowing down before a golden calf.

Respondents in the present case, however, seek to carry the meaning of "prohibiting the free exercise [of religion]" one large step further. They contend that their religious motivation for using peyote places them beyond the reach of a criminal law that is not specifically directed at their religious practice, and that is concededly constitutional as applied to those who use the drug for other reasons. They assert, in other words, that "prohibiting the free exercise [of religion]" includes requiring any individual to observe a generally applicable law that requires (or forbids) the performance of an act that his religious belief forbids (or requires)....

... We have never held that an individual's religious beliefs excuse him from compliance with an otherwise valid law prohibiting conduct that the State is free to regulate. On the contrary, the record of more than a century of our free exercise jurisprudence contradicts that proposition. As described succinctly by Justice Frankfurter in Minersville School Dist. Bd. of Ed. v. Gobitis: "Conscientious scruples have not, in the course of the long struggle for religious toleration, relieved the individual from obedience to a general law not aimed at the promotion or restriction of religious beliefs. The mere possession of religious convictions which contradict the relevant concerns of a political society does not relieve the citizen from the discharge of political responsibilities (footnote omitted)." We first had occasion to assert that principle in Reynolds v. United States, where we rejected the claim that criminal laws against polygamy could not be constitutionally applied to those whose religion commanded the practice....

. . .

The only decisions in which we have held that the First Amendment bars application of a neutral, generally applicable law to religiously motivated action have involved not the Free Exercise Clause alone, but the Free Exercise Clause in conjunction with other constitutional protections, such as freedom of speech and of the press, see Cantwell v. Connecticut (invalidating a licensing system for religious and charitable solicitations under which the administrator had discretion to deny a license to any cause he deemed nonreligious); Murdock v. Pennsylvania, (invalidating a flat tax on solicitation as applied to the dissemination of religious ideas); Follett v. McCormick, or the right of parents, acknowledged in Pierce v. Society of Sisters, to direct the education of their children, see Wisconsin v. Yoder, (invalidating compulsory school-attendance laws as applied to Amish parents who refused on religious grounds to send their children to school).[1] Some of our cases prohibiting compelled expression, decided exclusively upon free speech grounds, have also involved freedom of religion....

The present case does not present such a hybrid situation, but a free exercise claim unconnected with any communicative activity or parental right....

B

Respondents argue that even though exemption from generally applicable criminal laws need not automatically be extended to religiously motivated actors, at least the claim for a religious exemption must be evaluated under the balancing test set forth in Sherbert v. Verner. Under the Sherbert test, governmental actions that substantially burden a religious practice must be justified by a compelling governmental interest....

Even if we were inclined to breathe into Sherbert some life beyond the unemployment compensation field, we would not apply it to require exemptions from a generally applicable criminal law.

. . .

The "compelling government interest" requirement seems benign, because it is familiar from other fields. But using it as the standard that must be met before the government may accord different treatment on the basis of race, see, e.g., Palmore v. Sidoti, or before the government may regulate the content of speech . . . , is not remotely comparable to using it for the purpose asserted here. What it produces in those other

---

1. ...
Yoder said that "the Court's holding in Pierce stands as a charter of the rights of parents to direct the religious upbringing of their children. And, when the interests of parenthood are combined with a free exercise claim of the nature revealed by this record, more than merely a 'reasonable relation to some purpose within the competency of the State' is required to sustain the validity of the State's requirement under the First Amendment." 406 U.S. at 233, 92 S.Ct. at 1542.

fields—equality of treatment, and an unrestricted flow of contending speech—are constitutional norms; what it would produce here—a private right to ignore generally applicable laws—is a constitutional anomaly.

Nor is it possible to limit the impact of respondents' proposal by requiring a "compelling state interest" only when the conduct prohibited is "central" to the individual's religion.... Repeatedly and in many different contexts, we have warned that courts must not presume to determine the place of a particular belief in a religion or the plausibility of a religious claim.

. . .

... It is ... not surprising that a number of States have made an exception to their drug laws for sacramental peyote use. But to say that a nondiscriminatory religious-practice exemption is permitted, or even that it is desirable, is not to say that it is constitutionally required, and that the appropriate occasions for its creation can be discerned by the courts. It may fairly be said that leaving accommodation to the political process will place at a relative disadvantage those religious practices that are not widely engaged in; but that unavoidable consequence of democratic government must be preferred to a system in which each conscience is a law unto itself or in which judges weigh the social importance of all laws against the centrality of all religious beliefs....

... Oregon may, consistent with the Free Exercise Clause, deny respondents unemployment compensation when their dismissal results from use of the drug. The decision of the Oregon Supreme Court is accordingly reversed.

. . .

JUSTICE O'CONNOR, with whom JUSTICE BRENNAN, JUSTICE MARSHALL, and JUSTICE BLACKMUN join as to Parts I and II, concurring in the judgment. [JUSTICES BRENNAN and MARSHALL join Parts I and II of the opinion, but do not concur in the judgment.]

. . .

The Court today, however, interprets the Clause to permit the government to prohibit, without justification, conduct mandated by an individual's religious beliefs, so long as that prohibition is generally applicable.... A person who is barred from engaging in religiously motivated conduct is barred from freely exercising his religion. Moreover, that person is barred from freely exercising his religion regardless of whether the law prohibits the conduct only when engaged in for religious reasons, only by members of that religion, or by all persons. It is difficult to deny that a law that prohibits religiously motivated conduct, even if the law is generally applicable, does not at least implicate First Amendment concerns.

... If the First Amendment is to have any vitality, it ought not be construed to cover only the extreme and hypothetical situation in which a State directly targets a religious practice. As we have noted in a slightly different context, "[s]uch a test has no basis in precedent and relegates a serious First Amendment value to the barest level of minimum scrutiny that the Equal Protection Clause already provides." Hobbie v. Unemployment Appeals Comm'n of Florida.

To say that a person's right to free exercise has been burdened, of course, does not mean that he has an absolute right to engage in the conduct....

. . .

... [T]he Court today suggests that the disfavoring of minority religions is an "unavoidable consequence" under our system of government and that accommodation of such religions must be left to the political process. In my view, however, the First Amendment was enacted precisely to protect the rights of those whose religious practices are not shared by the majority and may be viewed with hostility. The history of our free exercise doctrine amply demonstrates the harsh impact majoritarian rule has had on unpopular or emerging religious groups such as the Jehovah's Witnesses and the Amish....

. . .

[Nevertheless,] ... I believe that granting a selective exemption in this case would seriously impair Oregon's compelling interest in prohibiting possession of peyote by its citizens. Under such circumstances, the Free Exercise Clause does not require the State to accommodate respondents' religiously motivated conduct. See, e.g., Thomas, 450 U.S. at 719....

. . .

I would therefore adhere to our established free exercise jurisprudence and hold that the State in this case has a compelling interest in regulating peyote use by its citizens and that accommodating respondents' religiously motivated conduct "will unduly interfere with fulfillment of the governmental interest." Lee, 455 U.S. at 259. Accordingly, I concur in the judgment of the Court.

JUSTICE BLACKMUN, WITH WHOM JUSTICE BRENNAN AND JUSTICE MARSHALL JOIN, DISSENTING.

. . .

... [A] distorted view of our precedents leads the majority to conclude that strict scrutiny of a state law burdening the free exercise of religion is a "luxury" that a well-ordered society cannot afford, *ante*, at 1605, and that the repression of minority religions is an "unavoidable consequence of democratic government." *Ante*, at 1606. I do not believe the Founders thought their dearly bought freedom from religious persecution a "luxury," but an essential element of liberty—and they could not have thought religious intolerance "unavoidable," for they drafted the Religion Clauses precisely in order to avoid that intolerance.

. . .

The State proclaims an interest in protecting the health and safety of its citizens from the dangers of unlawful drugs. It offers, however, no evidence that the religious use of peyote has ever harmed anyone.

The fact that peyote is classified as a Schedule I controlled substance does not, by itself, show that any and all uses of peyote, in any circumstance, are inherently harmful and dangerous. The Federal Government, which created the classifications of unlawful drugs from which Oregon's drug laws are derived, apparently does not find peyote so dangerous as to preclude an exemption for religious use.[5] Moreover, other Schedule I drugs have lawful uses.

The carefully circumscribed ritual context in which respondents used peyote is far removed from the irresponsible and unrestricted recreational use of unlawful drugs. The Native American Church's internal restrictions on, and supervision of, its members' use of peyote substantially obviate the State's health and safety concerns.

Not only does the Church's doctrine forbid nonreligious use of peyote; it also generally advocates self-reliance, familial responsibility, and abstinence from alcohol.

.   .   .

The State's apprehension of a flood of other religious claims is purely speculative. Almost half the States, and the Federal Government, have maintained an exemption for religious peyote use for many years, and apparently have not found themselves overwhelmed by claims to other religious exemptions. . . .

.   .   .

III

Finally, although I agree with Justice O'Connor that courts should refrain from delving into questions of whether, as a matter of religious doctrine, a particular practice is "central" to the religion, *ante*, at 1614, I do not think this means that the courts must turn a blind eye to the severe impact of a State's restrictions on the adherents of a minority religion. . . .

6. PERSONAL APPEARANCE

Few dimensions of personal appearance are unalterable. Those that are alterable are commonly altered to reflect personal taste and cultural norms. Cosmetic plastic surgery, tatoos, elaborate hair styles, body piercing, Botox and collagen injections were popular in the 1990s. In earlier decades, the right to wear hairstyles and clothing reflective of

---

5. . . .

Moreover, 23 States, including many that have significant Native American populations, have statutory or judicially crafted exemptions in their drug laws for religious use of peyote. See Smith v. Employment Division, 307 Ore. 68, 73, n. 2, 763 P.2d 146, 148, n. 2 (1988). Although this does not prove that Oregon must have such an exception too, it is significant that these States, and the Federal Government, all find their (presumably compelling) interests in controlling the use of dangerous drugs compatible with an exemption for religious use of peyote.

one's own identity and personality was sometimes styled as a privacy right.

KELLEY v. JOHNSON
425 U.S. 238 (1976).

[Note: In 1971, just as longer hair styles gained in popularity, a regulation promulgated by the Suffolk County Police Department "was directed at the style and length of hair, sideburns, and mustaches; beards and goatees were prohibited, except for medical reasons; and wigs conforming to the regulation could be worn for cosmetic reasons." A patrolman attacked the new regulation as violative of his right of free expression under the First Amendment and guarantees of due process and equal protection under the Fourteenth Amendment, stressing that the regulation was "not based upon the generally accepted standard of grooming in the community" and placed "an undue restriction" on him as a member of the community.]

MR. JUSTICE REHNQUIST delivered the opinion of the Court.

. . . .

The [Fourteenth Amendment] "liberty" interest claimed by respondent here, of course, is distinguishable from those protected by the Court in Roe v. Wade, Eisenstadt v. Baird, Stanley v. Illinois, Griswold v. Connecticut, and Meyer v. Nebraska. Each of these cases involved a substantial claim of infringement on the individual's freedom of choice with respect to certain basic matters of procreation, marriage, and family life. But whether the citizenry at large has some sort of "liberty" interest within the Fourteenth Amendment in matters of personal appearance is a question on which this Court's cases offer little, if any, guidance. We can, nevertheless, assume an affirmative answer for purposes of deciding this case, because we find that assumption insufficient to carry the day for respondent's claim.

Respondent has sought the protection of the Fourteenth Amendment not as a member of the citizenry at large, but on the contrary as an employee of the police force of Suffolk County, a subdivision of the State of New York. . . .

The hair-length regulation here touches respondent as an employee of the county and, more particularly, as a policeman. Respondent's employer has, in accordance with its well-established duty to keep the peace, placed myriad demands upon the members of the police force, duties which have no counterpart with respect to the public at large. Respondent must wear a standard uniform, specific in each detail. When in uniform he must salute the flag. He cannot take an active role in local political affairs by way of being a party delegate or contributing or soliciting political contributions. He may not smoke in public. All of these and other regulations of the Suffolk County Police Department infringe on respondent's freedom of choice in personal matters, and it was apparently the view of the Court of Appeals that the burden is on the State to prove a "genuine public need" for each and every one of these regulations. . . .

... We believe, however, that the hair-length regulation cannot be viewed in isolation, but must be rather considered in the context of the county's chosen mode of organization for its police force.

The promotion of safety of persons and property is unquestionably at the core of the State's police power, and virtually all state and local governments employ a uniformed police force to aid in the accomplishment of that purpose. Choice of organization, dress, and equipment for law enforcement personnel is a decision entitled to the same sort of presumption of legislative validity as are state choices designed to promote other aims within the cognizance of the State's police power.... Thus the question is not, as the Court of Appeals conceived it to be, whether the State can "establish" a "genuine public need" for the specific regulation. It is whether respondent can demonstrate that there is no rational connection between the regulation, based as it is on petitioner's method of organizing its police force, and the promotion of safety of persons and property.

... The overwhelming majority of state and local police of the present day are uniformed. This fact itself testifies to the recognition by those who direct those operations, and by the people of the States and localities who directly or indirectly choose such persons, that similarity in appearance of police officers is desirable. This choice may be based on a desire to make police officers readily recognizable to the members of the public, or a desire for the esprit de corps which such similarity is felt to inculcate within the police force itself. Either one is a sufficiently rational justification for regulations so as to defeat respondent's claim based on the liberty guaranty of the Fourteenth Amendment....

Mr. Justice Marshall, with whom Mr. Justice Brennan joins, dissenting.

. . .

... It seems to me manifest that that "full range of conduct" must encompass one's interest in dressing according to his own taste. An individual's personal appearance may reflect, sustain, and nourish his personality and may well be used as a means of expressing his attitude and lifestyle. In taking control over a citizen's personal appearance, the government forces him to sacrifice substantial elements of his integrity and identity as well. To say that the liberty guarantee of the Fourteenth Amendment does not encompass matters of personal appearance would be fundamentally inconsistent with the values of privacy, self-identity, autonomy, and personal integrity that I have always assumed the Constitution was designed to protect. See Roe v. Wade; Stanley v. Georgia; Griswold v. Connecticut; Olmstead v. United States (Brandeis, J., dissenting).

If little can be found in past cases of this Court or indeed in the Nation's history on the specific issue of a citizen's right to choose his own personal appearance, it is only because the right has been so clear as to be beyond question....

This Court, too, has taken as an axiom that there is a right in one's personal appearance. Indeed, in 1958 we used the existence of that right as support for our recognition of the right to travel:

> The right to travel is a part of the "liberty" of which the citizen cannot be deprived without the due process of law under the Fifth Amendment.... It may be as close to the heart of the individual as the choice of what he eats, or wears, or reads.

Kent v. Dulles, 357 U.S. 116, 125–126 (1958) (emphasis added).

To my mind, the right in one's personal appearance is inextricably bound up with the historically recognized right of "every individual to the possession and control of his own person," Union Pacific R. Co. v. Botsford, and perhaps even more fundamentally, with "the right to be let alone—the most comprehensive of rights and the right most valued by civilized men." Olmstead v. United States, supra, at 478 (Brandeis, J., dissenting). In an increasingly crowded society in which it is already extremely difficult to maintain one's identity and personal integrity, it would be distressing, to say the least, if the Government could regulate our personal appearance unconfined by any constitutional strictures whatsoever....

... And even if one accepted the argument that substantial similarity in appearance would increase a force's esprit de corps, I simply do not understand how implementation of this regulation could be expected to create any increment in similarity of appearance among members of a uniformed police force. While the regulation prohibits hair below the ears or the collar and limits the length of sideburns, it allows the maintenance of any type of hairstyle, other than a ponytail. Thus, as long as their hair does not go below their collars, two police officers, with an "Afro" hair style and the other with a crewcut could both be in full compliance with the regulation.

... I see no connection between the regulation and the offered rationales and would accordingly affirm the judgment of the Court of Appeals.

Note: Appearance Codes Under Title VII

In 1988, a reservation agent at the J.W. Marriott Hotel in Washington, D.C. filed a complaint with the D.C. Office of Human Rights. A twenty-five year old black female who wore her hair in a "cornrow" braided style, Pamela Mitchell alleged that she had been threatened with dismissal because of her race and appearance. Marriott managers characterized Mitchell's hair style as "extreme or faddish" in violation of company policy.

Aside from any valid claim she may have had under District of Columbia law, did Mitchell have a valid Title VII claim? Mitchell's attorney stated in a press interview that, "If you ask a black woman to take her cornrows out, you're asking her to take away part of her African heritage." He also noted that cornrows are not faddish, but thousands of years old. Had Marriott not backed down and been found guilty of violating the human rights statute, all of its local business licenses would have been in jeopardy. *See* Lynne Duke,

"Worker Files Complaint with City Over Cornrows," *Washington Post*, p. B8 (January 6, 1988).

The question of an employee's rights to a preferred hairstyle was raised outside of the privacy context—but with significant implications for personal autonomy—in *EEOC. v. Greyhound Lines, Inc.*, 635 F.2d 188 (3d Cir. 1980). The issue was whether Greyhound's facially neutral no-beard job qualification policy had a discriminatory effect (against black male workers with a painful and disfiguring condition called pseudo-folliclitis barbae) in violation of Title VII of the Civil Rights Act of 1964, 42 U.S.C. sections 2000e to 2000e–17. The majority held that: "no violation of Title VII can be grounded on the disparate impact theory without proof that the questioned policy or practice has had a disproportionate impact on the employer's workforce." 635 F.2d at 192. The dissent concluded that the existing proof of disproportionate impact was ample, since the skin malady in question is unique to men with kinky hair.

STULL v. SCHOOL BOARD OF WESTERN BEAVER JR.-SR. H.S.

459 F.2d 339 (3d Cir. 1972).

Edward R. Becker, District Judge.

I

The School Board of the Western Beaver Junior–Senior High School (Board), like so many of its counterparts throughout the land, has promulgated a dress code which, *inter alia*, proscribes the wearing of hair covering the ears and below the collar line. James Robert Stull (James), a fifteen year old schoolboy, like so many of his peers, has adopted a hairstyle which offends the cited provisions of the code.

. . .

James has come before us asserting his right to control his own personal appearance and lifestyle, and to develop, as it were, his own individuality. The Board's dress code restricts that right in a manner which extends beyond school hours, for his hair, long or short, is with him twenty-four hours a day, seven days a week, twelve months a year. The right asserted is directly related to one's personal liberty.... However, the principal question raised by the courts which have refused to interfere with school regulations prohibiting long hairstyles is not whether the right to control one's hairstyle is a function of one's personal liberty, but whether that right is sufficiently substantial to be accorded constitutional protection....

James' counsel has suggested three principal bases for the claim of a constitutionally protected right. One of them may be disposed of quickly. It is asserted that the action of the school authorities, without adequate justification, disturbs the "delicately balanced relationship of members of a family" and interferes with the rights of parents in rearing a child to "decide what hair style their son should wear." Whether or not the regulations violate a constitutional right of James' parents to govern the raising of their family or whether or not the Fourteenth Amendment forbids state intrusion into the parent-child relationship is not before us here, for there is no indication in the record that James' parents were responsible for his choice of hairstyle. The decision to wear long hair was James'. While the parents have arduously supported his right to govern his personal appearance, the record fails to establish any direct invasion of their rights. Moreover, James' own rights are sufficient to support his claim within the language of Tinker v. Des Moines Ind. Comm. School Dist., 393 U.S. 503 (1969)....

. . .

... [W]e therefore prefer to follow it and hold that the governance of the length and style of one's hair is implicit in the liberty assurance of the Due Process Clause of the Fourteenth Amendment....

The foregoing does not end the discussion of the constitutionality of the school dress code under attack, for it is fundamental that personal freedoms are not absolute. Accordingly, we must ... assess the reasonableness of the regulation in relation to its subject, to reconcile the protected right with the legitimate interests of the community.

... [T]here is no evidence that long hair worn by James or any other student has caused disruption of any kind either before or after adoption of the code. There is no evidence in this case that long hair was hazardous to anyone's health. With the exception of safety considerations in the shop classes, when the Board's evidence is boiled down, it amounts to a contention, which has generally been rejected, that long hair is bad for the "academic atmosphere." Whether or not this phrase, uttered by the school principal, is a euphemism for an establishmentarian distaste for long hair is beside the point. The fact is that there is no evidence in this record that long hair has any effect on the academic accomplishments of James or of other "longhairs" or their classmates.

The exception which we have noted does, however, require further consideration, for the evidence which was developed with respect to the metal and wood shop classes, if credited, might well justify the enforcement of regulations pertaining to the length, or at least the management, of hair as a condition of taking the various shop courses at the school. For instance, perhaps nets or head bands could provide the requisite safety in such class, or other measures could be adopted which are designed to assure that their legitimate purpose—safety—is accomplished, as long as they are as limited as possible so as not to overly burden the exercise of a protected right.

With the exception of the shop class situation, the school administration failed to supply persuasive reason or proof to support the promulgation and enforcement of the Board's regulation limiting the length of the hair of male students. It has demonstrated no outweighing state interest justifying the intrusion. We have before us only the facts of this case. On the basis of those facts, and in view of our discussion of the constitutional issues involved, we hold the Board's regulation, except as applied to the shop classes, invalid and its terms unenforceable.

7. NAMES AND NAMING

Note: the Right to Name One's Child

Names can be a matter of identity and naming an expression of heritage, taste and autonomy. A Nebraska statute, Neb. Rev. Stat. 71–640.01, limits the ability of parents to name their own children. The statute was challenged in *Henne v. Wright*, 904 F.2d 1208 (8th Cir. 1990), *cert. denied*, 498 U.S. 1032 (1991). As an initial matter, the court determined that no fundamental right of privacy to give one's child a surname other than one's own, one's husband's, or the child's father's is found in the history or tradition of the nation. The court then determined that the Nebraska legislation prohibiting parents from giving children surnames without a legally recognized parental connection furthered legitimate state interests in promoting child welfare, in deterring misappropriation of names, and in efficient record-keeping. *But see Jech v. Burch*, 466 F. Supp. 714 (D.C. Hawaii 1979).

KRUZEL v. PODELL

67 Wis.2d 138, 226 N.W.2d 458 (1975).

HEFFERNAN, J.

. . .

Kathleen Rose Harney married Joseph Michael Kruzel on July 31, 1971. She is an art teacher in the Milwaukee school system and was issued a teacher's certificate under her birth-given surname. She was employed by the Milwaukee school system under that name and exhibited works of art under the name Harney. She at all times used the name Harney and not Kruzel.

The Milwaukee School Board insisted, however, for group insurance purposes, that Kathleen either use her husband's surname or "legally" change her surname to Harney . . . . .

Obviously, the conditions that led to the practice of having women adopt their husband's surnames no longer have their foundation in existing law. In Wisconsin law, since the passage of the Married Woman's Property Act, ch. 44 of the Laws of 1850, and of ch. 529, Laws of 1921, granting women equal rights, and the constitutional amendment permitting women to vote, married women have been emancipated from the common law rules which held them, in effect, in bondage to their husbands and deprived them of all property rights. Insofar as this state is concerned, the obligations of the married woman differ little from the obligations of a married man. Each of them, of course, is limited in the same way under the laws of marriage and divorce promulgated by the legislature. Certainly, this court, bearing in mind the history of our society, should not at this time impose a common law rule that compels a married woman to take her husband's surname when never before has this been required by law in this jurisdiction. . . .

We conclude that the statutes of Wisconsin are consistent with the common law, which does not require a wife to assume her husband's surname and when the husband's surname was acquired, it was the result of usage and her holding out to the world that the surname is the same as the husband's.

8.   THE RIGHT TO DIE: WITHDRAWING TREATMENT, REFUSING TREATMENT AND ASSISTED SUICIDE

In the last decades courts have been asked to resolve fundamental moral and social issues involving incompetent or terminally-ill persons. Appellate courts have had to decide whether life-limiting procedures such as sterilization or kidney removal are to be performed on incompetent persons. There have been numerous decisions in which appellate courts have decided whether life-prolonging procedures such as kidney dialysis and the respirator are to be utilized in respect to terminally ill persons.

Unprecedented developments—improvements—in medical technology and techniques have spawned the litigation in this area. The development of the respirator, mechanical ventilator, and hemodialysis, and improved technology and techniques in chemotherapy and organ transplants have placed intolerable stress on some of our most venerable legal concepts. The most direct assault has been on the traditional legal test for death: cessation of the heart/lung functions. Depriving the brain of oxygen from four to six minutes may cause the death of all cognitive and conscious functions. However, the brain stem which naturally performs the functions of respiration and circulation is likely to be alive unless the brain is deprived of oxygen for from 10 to 20 minutes. What this means is that with the increased availability of effective resuscitation procedures persons who suffer traumatic injury, heart attacks or drug-related harm can be revived prior to the death of the brain stem. Such persons will continue to breathe but often will be in what has come to be known as a "persistent vegetative state" with no likely prospect of ever becoming cognitive or conscious again. Moreover, even if death of the brain stem appears imminent, a mechanical respirator can be utilized to continue to perform the job of the brain stem artificially.

Even though the brain stem has been destroyed, mechanical maintenance of the heartbeat and circulation can be continued for a limited period of time. It is this limited period of time that distinguishes between technical brain death and the persistent vegetative non-cognitive state. It is also this limited period of time that is the crucial period for organ removal for transplants. The brain death test is the emerging criteria for determining precisely when death legally occurs. A majority of the states have now adopted brain death statutes. In a few states a brain test for death has been adopted by judicial decision. In an effort to harmonize various statutes and to clarify the interrelation between the concept of brain death and the more traditional definition of death as the cessation of respiration and circulation, the National Conference of Commissioners on Uniform State Laws developed the Uniform Determination of Death Act in 1980.

Some of the best known and legally significant "right to die" cases are included in this section. Consider whether and what ideals of privacy and autonomy are at issue in these tragic cases.

IN RE QUINLAN

70 N.J. 10, 355 A.2d 647, *cert. denied*, 429 U.S. 922 (1976).

HUGHES, C.J.

The central figure in this tragic case is Karen Ann Quinlan, a New Jersey resident. At the age of 22, she lies in debilitated and allegedly moribund state at Saint Clare's Hospital in Denville, New Jersey. The litigation has to do, in final analysis, with her life,—its continuance or cessation,—and the responsibilities, rights and duties, with regard to any fateful decision, concerning it, of her family, her guardian, her doctors, the hospital, the State through its law enforcement authorities, and finally the courts of justice.

. . .

The matter is of transcendent importance, involving questions related to the definition and existence of death; the prolongation of life through artificial means developed by medical technology undreamed of in past generations of the practice of the healing arts; the impact of such durationally indeterminate and artificial life prolongation on the rights of the incompetent, her family and society in general; the bearing of constitutional right and the scope of judicial responsibility, as to the appropriate response of an equity court of justice to the extraordinary prayer for relief of the plaintiff. Involved as well is the right of the plaintiff, Joseph Quinlan, to guardianship of the person of his daughter.

. . .

. . . [I]n addition to being comatose [Karen] is in a chronic and persistent "vegetative" state, having no awareness of anything or anyone around her and existing at a primitive reflex level. Although she does have some brain stem function (ineffective for respiration) and has other reactions one normally associates with being alive, such as moving, reacting to light, sound and noxious stimuli, blinking her eyes, and the like the quality of her feeling impulses is unknown. She grimaces, makes stereotyped cries and sounds and has chewing motions. Her blood pressure is normal.

Karen remains in the intensive care unit at Saint Clare's Hospital, receiving 24–hour care by a team of four nurses. . . .

Her posture is described as fetal-like and grotesque; there is extreme flexion-rigidity of the arms, legs and related muscles and her joints are severely rigid and deformed.

. . . Severe brain and associated damage, albeit of uncertain etiology, has left Karen in a chronic and persistent vegetative state. No form of treatment which can cure or improve that condition is known or available. As nearly as may be determined, considering the guarded area of remote uncertainties characteristic of most medical science predictions, she can *never* be restored to cognitive or sapient life. . . .

... [N]o physician risked the opinion that she could live more than a year and indeed she may die much earlier.... Her life accordingly is sustained by the respirator and tubal feeding, and removal from the respirator would cause her death soon, although the time cannot be stated with more precision.

. . .

... The character and general suitability of Joseph Quinlan as guardian for his daughter, in ordinary circumstances, could not be doubted. The record bespeaks the high degree of familial love which pervaded the home of Joseph Quinlan and reached out fully to embrace Karen although she was living elsewhere at the time of her collapse....

To confirm the moral rightness of the decision he was about to make he consulted with his parish priest and later with the Catholic chaplain of Saint Clare's Hospital. He would not, he testified, have sought termination if that act were to be morally wrong or in conflict with the tenets of the religion he so profoundly respects. He was disabused of doubt however, when the position of the Roman Catholic Church was made known to him as it is reflected in the record in this case. While it is not usual for matters of religious dogma or concepts to enter a civil litigation (except as they may bear upon constitutional right, or sometimes, familial matters), they were rightly admitted in evidence here. The judge was bound to measure the character and motivations in all respects of Joseph Quinlan as prospective guardian; and insofar as these religious matters bore upon them, they were properly scrutinized and considered by the court.

. . .

Constitutional and Legal Issues

At the outset we note the dual role in which plaintiff comes before the Court. He not only raises, derivatively, what he perceives to be the constitutional and legal rights of his daughter Karen, but he also claims certain rights independently as parent.

Although generally litigant may assert only his own constitutional rights, we have no doubt that plaintiff has sufficient standing to advance both positions.

. . .

The father of Karen Quinlan is certainly no stranger to the present controversy. His interests are real and adverse and he raises questions of surpassing importance. Manifestly, he has standing to assert his daughter's constitutional rights, she being incompetent to do so....

I.   The Free Exercise of Religion

We think the contention as to interference with religious beliefs or rights may be considered and dealt with without extended discussion....

. . .

We think, ... that, ranged against the State's interest in the preservation of life, the impingement of religious belief, much less religious "neutrality" as here, does not reflect a constitutional question, in the circumstances at least of the case presently before the Court. Moreover, like the trial court, we do not recognize an independent parental right of religious freedom to support the relief requested.

II.   Cruel and Unusual Punishment

Similarly inapplicable to the case before us is the Constitution's Eighth Amendment protection against cruel and unusual punishment which as held by the trial court, is not relevant to situations other than the imposition of penal sanctions....

. . .

III.   The Right of Privacy

It is the issue of the constitutional right of privacy that has given us most concern, in the exceptional circumstances of this case. Here a loving parent, *qua* parent and raising the rights of his incompetent and profoundly damaged daughter, probably irreversibly doomed to no more than a biologically vegetative remnant of life, is before the court. He seeks authorization to abandon specialized technological procedures which can only maintain for a time a body having no potential for resumption or continuance of other than a "vegetative" existence.

We have no doubt, in these unhappy circumstances, that if Karen were herself miraculously lucid for an interval (not altering the existing prognosis of the condition to which she would soon return) and perceptive of her irreversible condition, she could effectively decide upon discontinuance of the life-support apparatus, even if it meant the prospect of natural death....

We have no hesitancy in deciding, in the instant diametrically opposite case, that no external compelling interest of the State could compel Karen to endure the unendurable, only to vegetate a few measurable months with no realistic possibility of returning to any semblance of cognitive or sapient life. We perceive no thread of logic distinguishing between such a choice on Karen's part and a similar choice which, under the evidence in this case, could be made by a competent patient terminally ill, riddled by cancer and suffering great pain; such a patient would not be resuscitated or put on a respirator in the example described by Dr. Korein, and *a fortiori* would not be kept *against his will* on a respirator.

. . .

The U.S. Supreme Court in Griswold v. Connecticut found the unwritten constitutional right of privacy to exist in the penumbra of specific guarantees of the Bill of Rights "formed by emanations from those guarantees that help give them life and substance." Presumably this right is broad enough to encompass a patient's decision to decline medical treatment under certain circumstances, in much the same way as it is broad enough to encompass a woman's decision to terminate pregnancy under certain conditions. Roe v. Wade, (1973).

Nor is such right of privacy forgotten in the New Jersey Constitution. N.J. Const. (1947), Art. I, par. 1.

The claimed interests of the State in this case are essentially the preservation and sanctity of human life and defense of the right of the physician to administer medical treatment according to his best judgment. In this case the doctors say that removing Karen from the respirator will conflict with their professional judgment. The plaintiff answers that Karen's present treatment serves only maintenance function; that the respirator cannot cure or improve her condition but at best can only prolong her inevitable slow deterioration and death; and that the interests of the patient, as seen by her surrogate, the guardian, must be evaluated by the court as predominant, even in the face of an opinion *contra* by the present attending physicians. Plaintiff's distinction is significant. The nature of Karen's care and the realistic chances of her recovery are quite unlike those of the patients discussed in many of the cases where treatments were ordered. In many of those cases the medical procedure required (usually a transfusion) constituted a minimal bodily invasion and the chances of recovery and return to functioning life were very good. We think that the State's interest *contra* weakens and the individual's right to privacy grows as the degree of bodily invasion increases and the prognosis dims. Ultimately there comes a point at which the individual's rights overcome the State interest. It is for that reason that we believe Karen's choice, if she were competent to make it, would be vindicated by the law. Her prognosis is extremely poor,—she will never resume cognitive life. And the bodily invasion is very great,— she requires 24 hour intensive nursing care, antibiotics, the assistance of a respirator, a catheter and feeding tube.

Our affirmation of Karen's independent right of choice, however, would ordinarily be based upon her competency to assert it. The sad truth, however, is that she is grossly incompetent and we cannot discern her supposed choice based on the testimony of her previous conversations with friends, where such testimony is without sufficient probative weight. Nevertheless we have concluded that Karen's right of privacy may be asserted on her behalf by her guardian under the peculiar circumstances here present.

If a putative decision by Karen to permit this non-cognitive, vegetative existence to terminate by natural forces is regarded as a valuable incident of her right of privacy, as we believe it to be, then it should not be discarded solely on the basis that her condition prevents her conscious exercise of the choice. The only practical way to prevent destruction of the right is to permit the guardian and family of Karen to render their best judgment, subject to the qualifications hereinafter stated, as to whether she would exercise it in these circumstances. If their conclusion is in the affirmative this decision should be accepted by a society the overwhelming majority of whose members would, we think, in similar circumstances, exercise such a choice in the same way for themselves or for those closest to them. It is for this reason that we determine that Karen's right of privacy may be asserted in her behalf, in this respect, by her guardian and family under the particular circumstances presented by this record.

Regarding Mr. Quinlan's right of privacy, we agree with Judge Muir's conclusion that there is no parental constitutional right that would entitle him to a grant of relief *in propria persona*. Insofar as a parental right of privacy has been recognized, it has been in the context of determining the rearing of infants and as Judge Muir put it, involved "continuing life styles." Karen Quinlan is a 22 year old adult. Her right of privacy in respect of the matter before the Court is to be vindicated by Mr. Quinlan as guardian, as hereinabove determined.

IV. The Medical Factor

Having declared the substantive legal basis upon which plaintiff's rights as representative of Karen must be deemed predicated, we face and respond to the assertion on behalf of defendants that our premise unwarrantably offends prevailing medical standards. . . .

. . .

. . . [L]aw, equity and justice must not themselves quail and be helpless in the face of modern technological marvels presenting questions hitherto unthought of. Where a Karen Quinlan, or a parent, or a doctor, or a hospital, or a State seeks the process and response of a court, it must answer with its most informed conception of justice in the previously unexplored circumstances presented to it. That is its obligation and we are here fulfilling it, for the actors and those having an interest in the matter should not go without remedy.

. . .

. . . [W]e conclude that the state of the pertinent medical standards and practices which guided the attending physicians in this matter is not such as would justify this Court in deeming itself bound or controlled thereby in responding to the case for declaratory relief established by the parties on this record before us.

V. Alleged Criminal Liability

. . . We are aware that such termination of treatment would accelerate Karen's death. The County Prosecutor and the Attorney General maintain that there would be criminal liability for such acceleration. Under the statutes of this State, the unlawful killing of another human being is criminal homicide. N.J.S.A. 2A:113–1, 2, 5. We conclude that there would be no criminal homicide in the circumstances of this case. We believe, first, that the ensuing death would not be homicide but rather expiration from existing natural causes. Secondly, even if it were to be regarded as homicide, it would not be unlawful.

These conclusions rest upon definitional and constitutional bases. The termination of treatment pursuant to the right of privacy is, within the limitations of this case *ipso facto* lawful. Thus, a death resulting from such an act would not come within the scope of the homicide statutes proscribing only the unlawful killing of another. There is a real and in this case determinative distinction between the unlawful taking of the life of another and the ending of artificial life support systems as a matter of self-determination.

Furthermore, the exercise of a constitutional right such as we have here found is protected from criminal prosecution. *See* Stanley v. Georgia. We do not question the State's undoubted power to punish the taking of human life, but that power does not encompass individuals terminating medical treatment pursuant to their right of privacy. The Constitutional protection extends to third parties whose action is necessary to effectuate the exercise of that right where the individuals themselves would not be subject to prosecution or the third parties are charged as accessories to an act which could not be a crime. Eisenstadt v. Baird, Griswold v. Connecticut. And, under the circumstances of this case, these same principles would apply to and negate a valid prosecution for attempted suicide were there still such a crime in this State.

VI.   The Guardianship of the Person

. . .

The trial court was apparently convinced of the high character of Joseph Quinlan and his general suitability as guardian under other circumstances, describing him as "very sincere, moral, ethical and religious." The court felt, however, that the obligation to concur in the medical care and treatment of his daughter would be a source of anguish to him and would distort his "decision-making processes." We disagree, for we sense from the whole record before us that while Mr. Quinlan feels a natural grief, and understandably sorrows because of the tragedy which has befallen his daughter, his strength of purpose and character far outweighs these sentiments and qualifies him eminently for guardianship of the person as well as the property of his daughter. Hence we discern no valid reason to overrule the statutory intendment of preference to the next of kin.

. . .

CONCLUSION

We therefore remand this record to the trial court to . . . appoint Joseph Quinlan as guardian of the person of Karen Quinlan with full power to make decisions with regard to the identity of her treating physicians.

We repeat for the sake of emphasis and clarity that upon the concurrent of the guardian and family of Karen, should the responsible attending physicians conclude that there is no reasonable possibility of Karen's ever emerging from her present comatose condition to a cognitive, sapient state and that the life-support apparatus now being administered to Karen should be discontinued, they shall consult with the hospital "Ethics Committee" or like body of the institution in which

Karen is then hospitalized. If that consultative body agrees that there is no reasonable possibility of Karen's ever emerging from her present comatose condition to a cognitive, sapient state, the present life-support system may be withdrawn and said action shall be without any civil or criminal liability therefor on the part of any participant, whether guardian, physician hospital or others.

BROPHY v. NEW ENGLAND SINAI HOSP., INC.
398 Mass. 417, 497 N.E.2d 626 (1986).

[Note: The family of Paul Brophy, a man in a "persistent vegetative state," sought to discontinue food and water introduced through a silicone "G-tube" physicians attached to his stomach to keep him alive. His wife and legal guardian wanted Brophy to be allowed to die. The hospital objected. The court held that the "substituted judgment" of a person in a "persistent vegetative state" to forego artificial nutrition and hydration should be honored when supported by his guardian and family, even if opposed by physicians. Dissenting Justice Nolan said the court's decision "affront[ed] logic, ethics and the dignity of the human person."]

LYNCH J. (dissenting in part)

. . .

. . . The State has an interest in the prevention of suicide. The underlying State interest in this area is the prevention of irrational self-destruction. . . . We have stated that an adult's refusing medical treatment is not necessarily suicide because "(1) in refusing treatment the patient may not have the specific intent to die, and (2) even if he did, to the extent that the cause of death was from natural causes the patient did not set the death producing agent in motion with the intent of causing his own death." Here, Brophy is not terminally ill, and death is not imminent, and the judge specifically found that Paul Brophy's decision would be to terminate his life by declining food and water. The judge also found that "Brophy's decision, if he were competent to make it, would primarily be based upon the present quality of life possible for him, and would not be based upon the burdens imposed upon him by receiving food and water through a G-tube, which burdens are relatively minimal. . . ." Where treatment is burdensome and invasive, no such specific intent is normally at issue because, whether or not the patient seeks to die, the patient primarily seeks to end invasive or burdensome treatment. There is no question that the intent here is to end a life that is "over." Moreover, death here would not be from natural causes, i.e., causes he or his agents did not set in motion by a volitional act with the intent to cause death.

Suicide is primarily a crime of commission, but can, and indeed must, also be conceived as an act of omission at times. See In re Caulk (suicide can be committed by starvation [or dehydration]). If nutrition and hydration are terminated, it is not the illness which causes the death but the decision (and act in accordance therewith) that the illness makes life not worth living. There is no rational distinction between suicide by deprivation of hydration or nutrition in or out of a medical setting—both are suicide.

Notes

In *Rutherford v. United States*, 438 F. Supp. 1287 (W.D. Okla. 1977), the District Court found no state interest asserted was sufficiently compelling to justify regulating access to Laetrile in the face of the assertion of a terminally-ill cancer patient's privacy right. Laetrile was found to be "nontoxic." In *Suenram v. Society of Valley Hospital*, 155 N.J. Super. 593, 383 A.2d 143 (N.J. Super., Law Div. 1977), the intermediate appellate court in New Jersey enjoined a private hospital from interfering with a terminally-ill cancer patient's decision, under the advice of her doctor, to use Laetrile and forego further orthodox chemotherapy treatments. The court concluded that since the patient's right of privacy included the right to refuse treatment for her cancer altogether, she had a right to select unorthodox, nontoxic treatment.

In *People v. Privitera*, 23 Cal. 3d 697, 591 P.2d 919, 153 Cal. Rptr. 431 (*en banc* 1979), *cert. denied*, 444 U.S. 949 (1979), the Supreme Court of California did not follow the view expressed in *Suenram* and *Rutherford*. The court held that the right of privacy does not encompass the right of access to drugs of unproven efficacy and that the criminal convictions of those conspiring to sell the drug were constitutional.

SUPERINTENDENT OF BELCHERTOWN
v. SAIKEWICZ

373 Mass. 728, 370 N.E.2d 417 (1977).

LLACOS, J.

. . .

I.

The judge below found that Joseph Saikewicz, at the time the matter arose, was sixty-seven years old, with an I.Q. of ten and a mental age of approximately two years and eight months. He was profoundly mentally retarded. The record discloses that, apart from his leukemia condition, Saikewicz enjoyed generally good health. He was physically strong and well built, nutritionally nourished, and ambulatory. He was not, however, able to communicate verbally—resorting to gestures and grunts to make his wishes known to others and responding only to gestures or physical contacts. . . .

. . . Saikewicz was diagnosed as suffering from acute myeloblastic monocytic leukemia. Leukemia is a disease of the blood. It arises when organs of the body produce an excessive number of white blood cells as well as other abnormal cellular structures, in particular undeveloped and immature white cells. . . . The particular form of the disease present in this case, acute myeloblastic monocytic leukemia is . . . invariably fatal.

Chemotherapy, as was testified to at the hearing in the Probate Court, involves the administration of drugs over several weeks, the purpose of which is to kill the leukemia cells. This treatment unfortunately affects normal cells as well.... [T]he patient immediately becomes much "sicker" with the commencement of chemotherapy, and there is a possibility that infections during the initial period of severe anemia will prove fatal. Moreover, while most patients survive chemotherapy, remission of the leukemia is achieved in only thirty to fifty per cent of the cases.... According to the medical testimony before the court below, persons over age sixty have more difficulty tolerating chemotherapy and the treatment is likely to be less successful than in younger patients. The prognosis may be compared with the doctors' estimates that, left untreated, a patient in Saikewicz's condition would live for a matter of weeks or, perhaps, several months. According to the testimony, a decision to allow the disease to run its natural course would not result in pain for the patient, and death would probably come without discomfort.

. . .

[Without receiving chemotherapy] Saikewicz died on September 4, 1976, at the Belchertown State School hospital. Death was due to bronchial pneumonia, a complication of the leukemia. Saikewicz died without pain or discomfort.

II.

. . .

A.

It is clear that the most significant of the asserted State interests is that of the preservation of human life. Recognition of such an interest, however, does not necessarily resolve the problem where the affliction or disease clearly indicates that life will soon, and inevitably, be extinguished. The interest of the State in prolonging a life must be reconciled with the interest of an individual to reject the traumatic cost of that prolongation.... The constitutional right to privacy, as we conceive it, is an expression of the sanctity of individual free choice and self-determination as fundamental constituents of life. The value of life as so perceived is lessened not by a decision to refuse treatment, but by the failure to allow a competent human being the right of choice.

A second interest of considerable magnitude, which the State may have some interest in asserting, is that of protecting third parties, particularly minor children, from the emotional and financial damage which may occur as a result of the decision of a competent adult to refuse life-saving or life-prolonging treatment. Thus in Holmes v. Silver Cross Hosp., the court held that, while the State's interest in preserving an individual's life was not sufficient, by itself, to outweigh the individual's interest in the exercise of free choice, the possible impact on minor children would be a factor which might have a critical effect on the outcome of the balancing process....

The last State interest requiring discussion is that of the maintenance of the ethical integrity of the medical profession as well as allowing hospitals the full opportunity to care for people under their control. The force and impact of this interest is lessened by the prevailing medical ethical standards. Prevailing medical ethical practice does not, without exception, demand that all efforts toward life prolongation be made in all circumstances.... Recognition of the right to refuse necessary treatment in appropriate circumstances is consistent with existing medical mores; such a doctrine does not threaten either the integrity of the medical profession, the proper role of hospitals in caring for such patients or the State's interest in protecting the same. It is not necessary to deny a right of self-determination to a patient in order to recognize the interests of doctors, hospitals, and medical personnel in attendance on the patient. Also, if the doctrines of informed consent and right of privacy have as their foundations the right to bodily integrity, see Union Pac. Ry. v. Botsford, and control of one's own fate, then those rights are superior to the institutional considerations.

B.

. . .

Karen Quinlan's situation, however, must be distinguished from that of Joseph Saikewicz. Saikewicz was profoundly mentally retarded. His mental state was a cognitive one but limited in his capacity to comprehend and communicate. Evidence that most people choose to accept the rigors of chemotherapy has no direct bearing on the likely choice that Joseph Saikewicz would have made. Unlike most people, Saikewicz had no capacity to understand his present situation or his prognosis. The guardian ad litem gave expression to this important distinction in coming to grips with this "most troubling aspect" of withholding treatment from Saikewicz: "If he is treated with toxic drugs he will be involuntarily immersed in a state of painful suffering, the reason for which he will never understand. Patients who request treatment know the risks involved and can appreciate the painful side-effects when they arrive. They know the reason for the pain and their hope makes it tolerable." To make a worthwhile comparison, one would have to ask whether a majority of people would choose chemotherapy if they were told merely that something outside of their previous experience was going to be done to them, that this something would cause them pain and discomfort, that they would be removed to strange surroundings and possibly restrained for extended periods of time, and that the advantages of this course of action were measured by concepts of time and mortality beyond their ability to comprehend.

To put the above discussion in proper perspective, we realize that an inquiry into what a majority of people would do in circumstances that truly were similar assumes an objective viewpoint not far removed from a "reasonable person" inquiry. While we recognize the value of this kind of indirect evidence, we should make it plain that the primary test is subjective in nature—that is, the goal is to determine with as much accuracy as possible the wants and needs of the individual involved. This may or may not conform to what is thought wise or prudent by most people. The problems of arriving at an accurate substituted judgment in matters of life and death vary greatly in degree, if not in kind, in different circumstances. For example, the responsibility of Karen Quinlan's father to act as she would have wanted could be discharged by drawing on many years of what was apparently an affectionate and close relationship. In contrast, Joseph Saikewicz was profoundly retarded and noncommunicative his entire life, which was spent largely in the highly restrictive atmosphere of an institution. While it may thus be necessary to rely to a greater degree on objective criteria, such as the supposed inability of profoundly retarded persons to conceptualize or fear death, the effort to bring the substituted judgment into step with the values and desires of the affected individual must not, and need not, be abandoned.

The "substituted judgment" standard which we have described commends itself simply because of its straightforward respect for the integrity and autonomy of the individual. We need not, however, ignore the substantial pedigree that accompanies this phrase. The doctrine of substituted judgment had its origin over 150 years ago in the area of the administration of the estate of an incompetent person. Ex parte Whitbread in re Hinde, a Lunatic, 35 Eng. Rep. 878 (1816). The doctrine was utilized to authorize a gift from the estate of an incompetent person to an individual when the incompetent owed no duty of support. The English court accomplished this purpose by substituting itself as nearly as possible for the incompetent, and acting on the same motives and considerations as would have moved him. . . .

In modern times the doctrine of substituted judgment has been applied as a vehicle of decision in cases more analogous to the situation presented in this case. In a leading decision on this point, Strunk v. Strunk, 445 S.W.2d 145 (Ky. Ct. App. 1969), the court held that a court of equity had the power to permit removal of a kidney from an incompetent donor for purposes of effectuating a transplant. The court concluded that, due to the nature of their relationship, both parties would benefit from the completion of the procedure, and hence the court could presume that the prospective donor would, if competent, assent to the procedure.

With this historical perspective, we now reiterate the substituted judgment doctrine as we apply it in the instant case. We believe that both the guardian ad litem in his recommendation and the judge in his decision should have attempted (as they did) to ascertain the incompetent person's actual interests and preferences. In short, the decision in cases such as this should be that which would be made by the incompetent person, if that person were competent, but taking into account the present and future incompetency of the individual as one of the factors which would necessarily enter into the decision-making process of the competent person. Having recognized the right of a competent person to make for himself the same decision as the court made in this case, the question is, do the facts on the record support the proposition that

Saikewicz himself would have made the decision under the standard set forth. We believe they do.

C.

We turn now to a consideration of the procedures appropriate for reaching a decision where a person allegedly incompetent is in a position in which a decision as to the giving or withholding of life-prolonging treatment must be made....

. . .

The course of proceedings in such a case is readily determined by reference to the applicable statutes. The first step is to petition the court for the appointment of guardian or a temporary guardian.... At the hearing on the appointment of a guardian or temporary guardian, the issues before the court are (1) whether the person involved is mentally retarded within the meaning of the statute and (2) if the person is mentally retarded, who shall be appointed guardian. As an aid to the judge in reaching these two decisions, it will often be desirable to appoint a guardian ad litem, sua sponte or on motion, to represent the interests of the person. Moreover, we think it appropriate, and highly desirable, in cases such as the one before us to charge the guardian ad litem with an additional responsibility to be discharged if there is a finding of incompetency. This will be the responsibility of presenting to the judge, after as thorough an investigation as time will permit, all reasonable arguments in favor of administering treatment to prolong the life of the individual involved. This will ensure that all viewpoints and alternatives will be aggressively pursued and examined at the subsequent hearing where it will be determined whether treatment should or should not be allowed. The report of the guardian or temporary guardian will, of course, also be available to the judge at this hearing on the ultimate issue of treatment. Should the probate judge then be satisfied that the incompetent individual would, as determined by the standards previously set forth, have chosen to forgo potentially life-prolonging treatment, the judge shall issue the appropriate order. If the judge is not so persuaded, or finds that the interests of the State require it, then treatment shall be ordered.

Commensurate with the powers of the Probate Court already described, the probate judge may, at any step in these proceedings, avail himself or herself of the additional advice or knowledge of any person or group. We note here that many health care institutions have developed medical ethics committees or panels to consider many of the issues touched on here. Consideration of the findings and advice of such groups as well as the testimony of the attending physicians and other medical experts ordinarily would be a great assistance to a probate judge faced with such a difficult decision. We believe it desirable for a judge to consider such views wherever available and useful to the court. We do not believe, however, that this option should be transformed by us into a required procedure. We take a dim view of any attempt to shift the ultimate decision-making responsibility away from the duly established courts of proper jurisdiction to any committee, panel or group, ad hoc or permanent. Thus, we reject the approach adopted by the New Jersey Supreme Court in the *Quinlan* case of entrusting the decision whether to continue artificial life support to the patient's guardian, family, attending doctors, and hospital "ethics committee."

We do not view the judicial resolution of this most difficult and awesome question—whether potentially life-prolonging treatment should be withheld from a person incapable of making his own decision—as constituting a "gratuitous encroachment" on the domain of medical expertise. Rather, such questions of life and death seem to us to require the process of detached but passionate investigation and decision that forms the ideal on which the judicial branch of government was created. Achieving this ideal is our responsibility and that of the lower court, and is not to be entrusted to any other group purporting to represent the "morality and conscience of our society," no matter how highly motivated or impressively constituted.

III.

Finding no State interest sufficient to counterbalance a patient's decision to decline life-prolonging medical treatment in the circumstances of this case, we conclude that the patient's right to privacy and self-determination is entitled to enforcement. Because of this conclusion, and in view of the position of equality of an incompetent person in Joseph Saikewicz's position, we conclude that the probate judge acted appropriately in this case.

CRUZAN v. DIRECTOR, MISSOURI DEPARTMENT OF HEALTH

497 U.S. 261 (1990).

REHNQUIST, C. J., delivered the opinion of the Court....

. . .

On the night of January 11, 1983, Nancy Cruzan lost control of her car as she traveled down Elm Road in Jasper County, Missouri. The vehicle overturned, and Cruzan was discovered lying face down in a ditch without detectable respiratory or cardiac function. Paramedics were able to restore her breathing and heartbeat at the accident site, and she was transported to a hospital in an unconscious state. An attending neurosurgeon diagnosed her as having sustained probable cerebral contusions compounded by significant anoxia (lack of oxygen). The Missouri trial court in this case found that permanent brain damage generally results after 6 minutes in an anoxic state; it was estimated that Cruzan was deprived of oxygen from 12 to 14 minutes. She remained in a coma for approximately three weeks and then progressed to an unconscious state in which she was able to orally ingest some nutrition. In order to ease feeding and further the recovery, surgeons implanted a gastrostomy feeding and hydration tube in Cruzan with the consent of her then husband. Subsequent rehabilitative efforts proved unavailing. She now lies in a Missouri state hospital in what is commonly referred to as a persistent vegetative state: generally, a condition in which a person exhibits motor reflexes but evinces no indications of significant cognitive function. The State of Missouri is bearing the cost of her care.

After it had become apparent that Nancy Cruzan had virtually no chance of regaining her mental faculties her parents asked hospital employees to terminate the artificial nutrition and hydration procedures. All agree that such a removal would cause her death. The employees refused to honor the request without court approval. The parents then sought and received authorization from the state trial court for termination. The court found that a person in Nancy's condition had a fundamental right under the State and Federal Constitutions to refuse or direct the withdrawal of "death prolonging procedures." The court also found that Nancy's "expressed thoughts at age twenty-five in somewhat serious conversation with a housemate friend that if sick or injured she would not wish to continue her life unless she could live at least halfway normally suggests that given her present condition she would not wish to continue on with her nutrition and hydration."

The Supreme Court of Missouri reversed by a divided vote. The court recognized a right to refuse treatment embodied in the common-law doctrine of informed consent, but expressed skepticism about the application of that doctrine in the circumstances of this case. The court also declined to read a broad right of privacy into the State Constitution which would "support the right of a person to refuse medical treatment in every circumstance," and expressed doubt as to whether such a right existed under the United States Constitution. It then decided that the Missouri Living Will statute, Mo. Rev. Stat. section 459.010 *et seq.* (1986), embodied a state policy strongly favoring the preservation of life. The court found that Cruzan's statements to her roommate regarding her desire to live or die under certain conditions were "unreliable for the purpose of determining her intent, and thus insufficient to support the co-guardians claim to exercise substituted judgment on Nancy's behalf." It rejected the argument that Cruzan's parents were entitled to order the termination of her medical treatment, concluding that "no person can assume that choice for an incompetent in the absence of the formalities required under Missouri's Living Will statutes or the clear and convincing, inherently reliable evidence absent here." The court also expressed its view that "[b]road policy questions bearing on life and death are more properly addressed by representative assemblies" than judicial bodies.

We granted certiorari to consider the question of whether Cruzan has a right under the United States Constitution which would require the hospital to withdraw life-sustaining treatment from her under these circumstances.... The informed consent doctrine has become firmly entrenched in American tort law.

The logical corollary of the doctrine of informed consent is that the patient generally possesses the right not to consent, that is, to refuse treatment. Until about 15 years ago and the seminal decision in In re Quinlan, ... the number of right-to-refuse-treatment decisions were relatively few. Most of the earlier cases involved patients who refused medical treatment forbidden by their religious beliefs, thus implicating First Amendment rights as well as common law rights of self-determination. More recently, however, with the advance of medical technology capable of sustaining life well past the point where natural forces would have brought certain death in earlier times, cases involving the right to refuse life-sustaining treatment have burgeoned.

. . .

After *Quinlan*, ... most courts have based a right to refuse treatment either solely on the common law right to informed consent or on both the common law right and a constitutional privacy right. In Superintendent of Belchertown State School v. Saikewicz, the Supreme Judicial Court of Massachusetts relied on both the right of privacy and the right of informed consent....

In In re Storar 52 N.Y.2d 363, 420 N.E.2d 266, *cert. denied*, 454 U.S. 858, 102 S.Ct. 309, 70 L.Ed.2d 153 (1981), the New York Court of Appeals declined to base a right to refuse treatment on a constitutional privacy right. Instead, it found such a right "adequately supported" by the informed consent doctrine. In In re Eichner (decided with In re Storar, supra) an 83–year-old man who had suffered brain damage from anoxia entered a vegetative state and was thus incompetent to consent to the removal of his respirator. The court, however, found it unnecessary to reach the question of whether his rights could be exercised by others since it found the evidence clear and convincing from statements made by the patient when competent that he "did not want to be maintained in a vegetative coma by use of a respirator." ...

Many of the later cases build on the principles established in *Quinlan*, *Saikewicz* and *Storar/Eichner*. For instance, in In re Conroy, the same court that decided Quinlan considered whether a nasogastric feeding tube could be removed from an 84–year-old incompetent nursing-home resident suffering irreversible mental and physical ailments. While recognizing that a federal right of privacy might apply in the case, the court, contrary to its approach in *Quinlan*, decided to base its decision on the common-law right to self-determination and informed consent.

. . .

In contrast to *Conroy*, the Court of Appeals of New York recently refused to accept less than the clearly expressed wishes of a patient before permitting the exercise of her right to refuse treatment by a surrogate decisionmaker. In re Westchester County Medical Center on behalf of O'Connor, 72 N.Y.2d 517, 534 N.Y.S.2d 886, 531 N.E. 2d 607 (1988) (O'Connor). There, the court, over the objection of the patient's family members, granted an order to insert a feeding tube into a 77–year-old woman rendered incompetent as a result of several strokes. While continuing to recognize a common-law right to refuse treatment, the court rejected the substituted judgment approach for asserting it "because it is inconsistent with our fundamental commitment to the notion that no person or court should substitute its judgment as to what would be an acceptable quality of life for another. Consequently, we adhere to the view that, despite its pitfalls and inevitable uncertainties, the inquiry must always be narrowed to the patient's expressed intent, with every effort made to minimize the opportunity for error." The court held that the record lacked the requisite clear and convincing evidence of the patient's expressed intent to withhold life-sustaining treatment.

.   .   .

As these cases demonstrate, the common-law doctrine of informed consent is viewed as generally encompassing the right of a competent individual to refuse medical treatment. Beyond that, these decisions demonstrate both similarity and diversity in their approach to decisions of what all agree is a perplexing question with unusually strong moral and ethical overtones. State courts have available to them for decision a number of sources—state constitutions, statutes, and common law—which are not available to us. In this Court, the question is simply and starkly whether the United States Constitution prohibits Missouri from choosing the rule of decision which it did. This is the first case in which we have been squarely presented with the issue of whether the United States Constitution grants what is in common parlance referred to as a "right to die." . . .

The Fourteenth Amendment provides that no State shall "deprive any person of life, liberty, or property, without due process of law." The principle that a competent person has a constitutionally protected liberty interest in refusing unwanted medical treatment may be inferred from our prior decisions. In Jacobson v. Massachusetts, for instance, the Court balanced an individual's liberty interest in declining an unwanted smallpox vaccine against the State's interest in preventing disease. Decisions prior to the incorporation of the Fourth Amendment into the Fourteenth Amendment analyzed searches and seizures involving the body under the Due Process Clause and were thought to implicate substantial liberty interests. . . .

.   .   .

But determining that a person has a "liberty interest" under the Due Process Clause does not end the inquiry; "whether respondent's constitutional rights have been violated must be determined by balancing his liberty interests against the relevant state interests." . . .

Petitioners insist that under the general holdings of our cases, the forced administration of life-sustaining medical treatment, and even of artificially-delivered food and water essential to life, would implicate a competent person's liberty interest. Although we think the logic of the cases discussed above would embrace such a liberty interest, the dramatic consequences involved in refusal of such treatment would inform the inquiry as to whether the deprivation of that interest is constitutionally permissible. But for purposes of this case, we assume that the United

States Constitution would grant a competent person a constitutionally protected right to refuse lifesaving hydration and nutrition.

Petitioners go on to assert that an incompetent person should possess the same right in this respect as is possessed by a competent person. They rely primarily on our decisions in Parham v. J.R., *supra*, and Youngberg v. Romeo. In *Parham*, we held that a mentally disturbed minor child had a liberty interest in "not being confined unnecessarily for medical treatment," but we certainly did not intimate that such a minor child, after commitment, would have a liberty interest in refusing treatment. In *Youngberg*, we held that a seriously retarded adult had a liberty interest in safety and freedom from bodily restraint. *Youngberg*, however, did not deal with decisions to administer or withhold medical treatment.

The difficulty with petitioners' claim is that in a sense it begs the question: an incompetent person is not able to make an informed and voluntary choice to exercise a hypothetical right to refuse treatment or any other right. Such a "right" must be exercised for her, if at all, by some sort of surrogate. Here, Missouri has in effect recognized that under certain circumstances a surrogate may act for the patient in electing to have hydration and nutrition withdrawn in such a way as to cause death, but it has established a procedural safeguard to assure that the action of the surrogate conforms as best it may to the wishes expressed by the patient while competent. Missouri requires that evidence of the incompetent's wishes as to the withdrawal of treatment be proved by clear and convincing evidence. The question, then, is whether the United States Constitution forbids the establishment of this procedural requirement by the State. We hold that it does not.

Whether or not Missouri's clear and convincing evidence requirement comports with the United States Constitution depends in part on what interests the State may properly seek to protect in this situation. Missouri relies on its interest in the protection and preservation of human life, and there can be no gainsaying this interest. As a general matter, the States—indeed, all civilized nations—demonstrate their commitment to life by treating homicide as serious crime. Moreover, the majority of States in this country have laws imposing criminal penalties on one who assists another to commit suicide. We do not think a State is required to remain neutral in the face of an informed and voluntary decision by a physically-able adult to starve to death.

But in the context presented here, a State has more particular interests at stake. The choice between life and death is a deeply personal decision of obvious and overwhelming finality. We believe Missouri may legitimately seek to safeguard the personal element of this choice through the imposition of heightened evidentiary requirements. It cannot be disputed that the Due Process Clause protects an interest in life as well as an interest in refusing life-sustaining medical treatment. Not all incompetent patients will have loved ones available to serve as surrogate decisionmakers. And even where family members are present, "[t]here will, of course, be some unfortunate situations in which family members will not act to protect a patient." A State is entitled to guard against potential abuses in such situations. Similarly, a State is entitled to consider that a judicial proceeding to make a determination regarding an incompetent's wishes may very well not be an adversarial one, with the added guarantee of accurate factfinding that the adversary process brings with it. Finally, we think a State may properly decline to make judgments about the "quality" of life that a particular individual may enjoy, and simply assert an unqualified interest in the preservation of human life to be weighed against the constitutionally protected interests of the individual.

In our view, Missouri has permissibly sought to advance these interests through the adoption of a "clear and convincing" standard of proof to govern such proceedings. "The function of a standard of proof, as that concept is embodied in the Due Process Clause and in the realm of factfinding, is to 'instruct the factfinder concerning the degree of confidence our society thinks he should have in the correctness of factual conclusions for a particular type of adjudication.' " ... Addington v. Texas. "This Court has mandated an intermediate standard of proof— 'clear and convincing evidence'—when the individual interests at stake in a state proceeding are both 'particularly important' and 'more substantial than mere loss of money.' " Santosky v. Kramer. Thus, such a standard has been required in deportation proceedings, in denaturalization proceedings, in civil commitment proceedings, and in proceedings for the termination of parental rights. Further, this level of proof, "or an even higher one, has traditionally been imposed in cases involving allegations of civil fraud, and in a variety of other kinds of civil cases involving such issues as ... lost wills, oral contracts to make bequests, and the like."

We think it self-evident that the interests at stake in the instant proceedings are more substantial, both on an individual and societal level, than those involved in a run-of-the-mine civil dispute. But not only does the standard of proof reflect the importance of a particular adjudication, it also serves as "a societal judgment about how the risk of error should be distributed between the litigants." Santosky, Addington. The more stringent the burden of proof a party must bear, the more that party bears the risk of an erroneous decision. We believe that Missouri may permissibly place an increased risk of an erroneous decision on those seeking to terminate an incompetent individual's life-sustaining treatment....

It is also worth noting that most, if not all, States simply forbid oral testimony entirely in determining the wishes of parties in transactions which, while important, simply do not have the consequences that a decision to terminate a person's life does. At common law and by statute in most States, the parole evidence rule prevents the variations of the terms of a written contract by oral testimony. The statute of frauds makes unenforceable oral contracts to leave property by will, and statutes regulating the making of wills universally require that those instruments be in writing. . . .

In sum, we conclude that a State may apply a clear and convincing evidence standard in proceedings where a guardian seeks to discontinue nutrition and hydration of a person diagnosed to be in a persistent vegetative state. We note that many courts which have adopted some sort of substituted judgment procedure in situations like this, whether they limit consideration of evidence to the prior expressed wishes of the incompetent individual, or whether they allow more general proof of what the individual's decision would have been, require a clear and convincing standard of proof for such evidence.

The Supreme Court of Missouri held that in this case the testimony adduced at trial did not amount to clear and convincing proof of the patient's desire to have hydration and nutrition withdrawn. In so doing, it reversed a decision of the Missouri trial court which had found that the evidence "suggest[ed]" Nancy Cruzan would not have desired to continue such measures, App. to Pet. for Cert. A98, but which had not adopted the standard of "clear and convincing evidence" enunciated by the Supreme Court. The testimony adduced at trial consisted primarily of Nancy Cruzan's statements made to a housemate about a year before her accident that she would not want to live should she face life as a "vegetable," and other observations to the same effect. The observations did not deal in terms with withdrawal of medical treatment or of hydration and nutrition. We cannot say that the Supreme Court of Missouri committed constitutional error in reaching the conclusion that it did.

Petitioners alternatively contend that Missouri must accept the "substituted judgment" of close family members even in the absence of substantial proof that their views reflect the views of the patient. . . .

No doubt is engendered by anything in this record but that Nancy Cruzan's mother and father are loving and caring parents. If the State were required by the United States Constitution to repose a right of "substituted judgment" with anyone, the Cruzans would surely qualify. But we do not think the Due Process Clause requires the State to repose judgment on these matters with anyone but the patient herself. Close family members may have a strong feeling—a feeling not at all ignoble or unworthy, but not entirely disinterested, either—that they do not wish to witness the continuation of the life of a loved one which they regard as hopeless, meaningless, and even degrading. But there is no automatic assurance that the view of close family members will necessarily be the same as the patient's would have been had she been confronted with the prospect of her situation while competent. All of the reasons previously discussed for allowing Missouri to require clear and convincing evidence of the patient's wishes lead us to conclude that the State may choose to defer only to those wishes, rather than confide the decision to close family members.

The judgment of the Supreme Court of Missouri is Affirmed.

Notes: Cruzan, Quill and Glucksberg

(1) The *Cruzan* decision was 5–4, holding that the Constitution is not violated by a state's procedural demand that petitioners bear the burden of proving by clear and convincing evidence that an incompetent in a persistent vegetative state would prefer death. Justice Rehnquist's opinion quietly rejected the popular perspective adopted by lower courts that "the right to die" is a fundamental privacy right. Nancy Cruzan was instead ascribed a liberty interest appropriately balanced against "relevant state interests."

Justice O'Connor's concurrence in *Cruzan* asserted that the state may sometimes have a constitutional duty to protect a patient's liberty interest in refusing medical treatment by respecting the delegated authority of a duly-appointed surrogate. However, she agreed with the majority that the Constitution does not require states to permit unauthorized parents to substitute their judgment for that of incompetent adult children.

According to Justice Scalia in a second concurring opinion, American law accords to the state the power to prevent suicide, "by force if necessary." The federal courts have no business making law in the "suicide" field, he wrote, since "The point at which means to preserve it become 'extraordinary' or 'inappropriate' are neither set forth in the Constitution, nor are known to the nine Justices of the court any better than they are known to nine people picked at random from the Kansas City telephone directory. . . ."

The Court issued two dissenting opinions in *Cruzan*. Justice Brennan's dissent, joined by Justices Marshall and Blackmun, was a plea for Cruzan's fundamental liberty to die with her dignity and bodily integrity intact. The word "privacy" was not invoked, but the concept of privacy was present in his eerie depiction of Nancy Cruzan as a woman trapped in a publicly mandated "twilight zone."

Justice Brennan argued that the liberty interest in refusing medical treatment, conceded by the Court, "must be fundamental." Referring to a right to be free of unwanted medical attention, including artificial delivery of food and water, he characterized it as one of the "basic civil rights of a man," a right "deeply rooted in this nation's tradition." Because death is personal and profound, he argued, Missouri's interest is solely a *parens patriae* interest in providing Nancy Cruzan, now incompetent, with as accurate as possible a determination of how she would exercise her rights under these circumstances. Brennan criticized the Missouri court for "categorical exclusion of relevant evidence" of Nancy Cruzan's wishes, especially conversations with family members.

Urging that "[l]ives do not exist in abstraction from persons," Justice Stevens' dissent was a frank, broad appeal to the jurisprudence of family, domestic and personal privacy. He reasoned that the injustice and unconstitutionality of Missouri's treatment of Nancy Cruzan stemmed from the state's misguided attempt to define the boundaries of life. Compounding its error, Stevens continued, Missouri chose a definition that is "uncommon," "aberrant" and "anomalous." The meaning and completion of Cruzan's life should be controlled by persons who have her best interests at heart—not by a state legislature concerned only with the "preservation of human life." Accordingly, he concluded, the Court must have an affirmative role in empowering private decisionmaking about life and death.

(2) The Court issued decisions in two physician-assisted suicide cases in 1997. In *Quill v. Vacco*, infra, a New York statute banning physician-assisted suicide was challenged on Equal Protection grounds. In *Washington v. Glucksberg*, infra, a Washington statute banning physician-assisted suicide was challenged on substantive due-process grounds. The Court upheld both state statutes, in the face of arguments that *Cruzan*, *Planned Parenthood v. Casey* and logic dictated recognizing a federal constitutional right of terminally ill private citizens to elect physician-assisted death .

(3) After reading the opinion of the Chief Justice in *Glucksberg*, below, compare it with the majority opinions in *Bowers v. Hardwick* and *Michael H v. Gerald D., supra*. All three cases are striking for their positivistic rendering of the test for whether an asserted right or liberty is fundamental. Is this positivism defensible when public attitudes have undergone change and what is at stake are arguably the most profound intimacies of mind, body and identity?

(4) Do you agree with Justice Rehnquist that "assisting suicide" and "withdrawing life-sustaining treatment" are rationally distinct?

VACCO v. QUILL

521 U.S. 793 (1997).

CHIEF JUSTICE REHNQUIST delivered the opinion of the Court.

In New York, as in most States, it is a crime to aid another to commit or attempt suicide, but patients may refuse even lifesaving medical treatment. The question presented by this case is whether New York's prohibition on assisting suicide therefore violates the Equal Protection Clause of the Fourteenth Amendment. We hold that it does not . . .

New York's statutes outlawing assisting suicide affect and address matters of profound significance to all New Yorkers alike. They neither infringe fundamental rights nor involve suspect classifications. These laws are therefore entitled to a "strong presumption of validity."

On their faces, neither New York's ban on assisting suicide nor its statutes permitting patients to refuse medical treatment treat anyone differently than anyone else or draw any distinctions between persons. Everyone, regardless of physical condition, is entitled, if competent, to refuse unwanted lifesaving medical treatment; no one is permitted to assist a suicide. Generally speaking, laws that apply evenhandedly to all "unquestionably comply" with the Equal Protection Clause.

The Court of Appeals, however, concluded that some terminally ill people—those who are on life-support systems—are treated differently than those who are not, in that the former may "hasten death" by ending treatment, but the latter may not "hasten death" through physician-assisted suicide. This conclusion depends on the submission that ending or refusing lifesaving medical treatment "is nothing more nor less than assisted suicide." Unlike the Court of Appeals, we think the distinction between assisting suicide and withdrawing life-sustaining treatment, a distinction widely recognized and endorsed in the medical profession and in our legal traditions, is both important and logical; it is certainly rational.

The distinction comports with fundamental legal principles of causation and intent. First, when a patient refuses life-sustaining medical treatment, he dies from an underlying fatal disease or pathology; but if a patient ingests lethal medication prescribed by a physician, he is killed by that medication.

Furthermore, a physician who withdraws, or honors a patient's refusal to begin, life sustaining medical treatment purposefully intends, or may so intend, only to respect his patient's wishes and "to cease doing useless and futile or degrading things to the patient when [the patient] no longer stands to benefit from them" ... The same is true when a doctor provides aggressive palliative care; in some cases, painkilling drugs may hasten a patient's death, but the physician's purpose and intent is, or may be, only to ease his patient's pain. A doctor who assists a suicide, however, "must, necessarily and indubitably, intend primarily that the patient be made dead." Similarly, a patient who commits suicide with a doctor's aid necessarily has the specific intent to end his or her own life, while a patient who refuses or discontinues treatment might not.

The law has long used actors' intent or purpose to distinguish between two acts that may have the same result. Put differently, the law distinguishes actions taken "because of" a given end from the actions taken "in spite of" their unintended but foreseen consequences ...

Logic and contemporary practice support New York's judgment that the two acts are different, and New York may therefore, consistent with the Constitution, treat them differently. By permitting everyone to refuse unwanted medical treatment while prohibiting anyone from assisting a suicide, New York law follows a longstanding and rational distinction ...

WASHINGTON v. GLUCKSBERG
521 U.S. 702 (1997).

CHIEF JUSTICE REHNQUIST delivered the opinion of the Court.

. . .

The question presented in this case is whether Washington's prohibition against "caus[ing]" or "aid[ing]" a suicide offends the Fourteenth Amendment to the United States Constitution. We hold that it does not. . . .

We begin, as we do in all due-process cases, by examining our Nation's history, legal traditions, and practices. In almost every State—indeed, in almost every western democracy—it is a crime to assist a suicide. The States' assisted-suicide bans are not innovations. Rather, they are longstanding expressions of the States' commitment to the protection and preservation of all human life.

More specifically, for over 700 years, the Anglo–American common-law tradition has punished or otherwise disapproved of both suicide and assisting suicide ...

Against this backdrop of history, tradition, and practice, we now turn to respondents' constitutional claim.

The Due Process Clause guarantees more than fair process, and the "liberty" it protects includes more than the absence of physical restraint. The Clause also provides heightened protection against government interference with certain fundamental rights and liberty interests. In a long line of cases, we have held that, in addition to the specific freedoms protected by the Bill of Rights, the "liberty" specially protected by the Due Process Clause includes the rights to marry; to have children; to direct the education and upbringing of one's children; to marital privacy; to use contraception; to bodily integrity, and to abortion. We have also assumed, and strongly suggested, that the Due Process Clause protects the traditional right to refuse unwanted lifesaving medical treatment.

Our established method of substantive-due-process analysis has two primary features: First, we have regularly observed that the Due Process Clause specially protects those fundamental rights and liberties which are, objectively, "deeply rooted in this Nation's history and tradition," and "implicit in the concept of ordered liberty," such that "neither liberty nor justice would exist if they were sacrificed," Second, we have required in substantive-due-process cases a "careful description" of the asserted fundamental liberty interest. Our Nation's history, legal traditions, and practices thus provide the crucial "guideposts for responsible decisionmaking," that direct and restrain our exposition of the Due Process Clause ...

In our view, however, the development of this Court's substantive-due-process jurisprudence, has been a process whereby the outlines of the "liberty" specially protected by the Fourteenth Amendment—never fully clarified, to be sure, and perhaps not capable of being fully clarified—have at least been carefully refined by concrete examples involving fundamental rights found to be deeply rooted in our legal tradition. This approach tends to rein in the subjective elements that are necessarily present in due-process judicial review. In addition, by establishing a threshold requirement—that a challenged state action implicate a fundamental right—before requiring more than a reasonable relation to a legitimate state interest to justify the action, it avoids the need for complex balancing of competing interests in every case.

Turning to the claim at issue here, respondents assert a "liberty to choose how to die" and a right to "control of one's final days," and describe the asserted liberty as "the right to choose a humane, dignified death," and "the liberty to shape death.". .

We now inquire whether this asserted right has any place in our Nation's traditions. Here we are confronted with a consistent and almost universal tradition that has long rejected the asserted right, and continues explicitly to reject it today, even for terminally ill, mentally competent adults. To hold for respondents, we would have to reverse centuries of legal doctrine and practice, and strike down the considered policy choice of almost every State . . .

Respondents contend that in *Cruzan* we "acknowledged that competent, dying persons have the right to direct the removal of life-sustaining medical treatment and thus hasten death," and that "the constitutional principle behind recognizing the patient's liberty to direct the withdrawal of artificial life support applies at least as strongly to the choice to hasten impending death by consuming lethal medication."

The right assumed in *Cruzan*, however, was not simply deduced from abstract concepts of personal autonomy. Given the common-law rule that forced medication was a battery, and the long legal tradition protecting the decision to refuse unwanted medical treatment, our assumption was entirely consistent with this Nation's history and constitutional traditions. The decision to commit suicide with the assistance of another may be just as personal and profound as the decision to refuse unwanted medical treatment, but it has never enjoyed similar legal protection. Indeed, the two acts are widely and reasonably regarded as quite distinct . . .

Respondents also rely on *Casey*. We held, first, that a woman has a right, before her fetus is viable, to an abortion "without undue interference from the State"; second, that States may restrict post-viability abortions, so long as exceptions are made to protect a woman's life and health; and third, that the State has legitimate interests throughout a pregnancy in protecting the health of the woman and the life of the unborn child. [R]espondents emphasize the statement in *Casey* that: "At the heart of liberty is the right to define one's own concept of existence, of meaning, of the universe, and of the mystery of human life. Beliefs about these matters could not define the attributes of personhood were they formed under compulsion of the State."

By choosing this language, the Court's opinion in *Casey* described, in a general way and in light of our prior cases, those personal activities and decisions that this Court has identified as so deeply rooted in our history and traditions, or so fundamental to our concept of constitutionally ordered liberty, that they are protected by the Fourteenth Amendment. The opinion moved from the recognition that liberty necessarily includes freedom of conscience and belief about ultimate considerations to the observation that "though the abortion decision may originate within the zone of conscience and belief, it is more than a philosophic exercise." That many of the rights and liberties protected by the Due Process Clause found in personal autonomy does not warrant the sweeping conclusion that any and all important, intimate, and personal decisions are so protected, and *Casey* did not suggest otherwise.

The Constitution also requires, however, that Washington's assisted-suicide ban be rationally related to legitimate government interests. This requirement is unquestionably met here. Washington's assisted-suicide ban implicates a number of state interests.

First, Washington has an "unqualified interest in the preservation of human life". The State's prohibition on assisted suicide, like all homicide laws, both reflects and advances its commitment to this interest. This interest is symbolic and aspirational as well as practical ...

Those who attempt suicide—terminally ill or not—often suffer from depression or other mental disorders. Research indicates, however, that many people who request physician-assisted suicide withdraw that request if their depression and pain are treated. Thus, legal physician-assisted suicide could make it more difficult for the State to protect depressed or mentally ill persons, or those who are suffering from untreated pain, from suicidal impulses.

The State also has an interest in protecting the integrity and ethics of the medical profession.

Next, the State has an interest in protecting vulnerable groups— including the poor, the elderly, and disabled persons—from abuse, neglect, and mistakes. We have recognized the real risk of subtle coercion and undue influence in end-of-life situations. *Cruzan*. If physician-assisted suicide were permitted, many might resort to it to spare their families the substantial financial burden of end-of-life health-care costs.

The State's interest here goes beyond protecting the vulnerable from coercion; it extends to protecting disabled and terminally ill people from prejudice, negative and inaccurate stereotypes, and "societal indifference." The State's assisted-suicide ban reflects and reinforces its policy that the lives of terminally ill, disabled, and elderly people must be no less valued than the lives of the young and healthy, and that a seriously disabled person's suicidal impulses should be interpreted and treated the same way as anyone else's.

Finally, the State may fear that permitting assisted suicide will start it down the path to voluntary and perhaps even involuntary euthanasia ... Thus, it turns out that what is couched as a limited right to "physician-assisted suicide" is likely, in effect, a much broader license, which could prove extremely difficult to police and contain. Washington's ban on assisting suicide prevents such erosion ...

We need not weigh exactly the relative strengths of these various interests. They are unquestionably important and legitimate, and Washington's ban on assisted suicide is at least reasonably related to their promotion and protection.

Justice Souter, concurring in the judgment.

... When the physicians claim that the Washington law deprives them of a right falling within the scope of liberty that the Fourteenth Amendment guarantees against denial without due process of law, they are not claiming some sort of procedural defect in the process through which the statute has been enacted or is administered. Their claim, rather, is that the State has no substantively adequate justification for barring the assistance sought by the patient and sought to be offered by the physician. Thus, we are dealing with a claim to one of those rights sometimes described as rights of substantive due process and sometimes as unenumerated rights, in view of the breadth and indeterminacy of the "due process" serving as the claim's textual basis. The doctors accordingly arouse the skepticism of those who find the Due Process Clause an unduly vague or oxymoronic warrant for judicial review of substantive state law, just as they also invoke two centuries of American constitutional practice in recognizing unenumerated, substantive limits on governmental action. The persistence of substantive due process in our cases points to the legitimacy of the modern justification for such judicial review found in Justice Harlan's dissent in *Poe* [*v. Ullman*].

My understanding of unenumerated rights in the wake of the *Poe* dissent and subsequent cases avoids the absolutist failing of many older cases without embracing the opposite pole of equating reasonableness with practice. That understanding begins with a concept of "ordered liberty," *Poe*,(Harlan, J.); comprising a continuum of rights to be free from "arbitrary impositions and purposeless restraints," *Poe* (Harlan, J., dissenting).

After the *Poe* dissent, as before it, this enforceable concept of liberty would bar statutory impositions even at relatively trivial levels when governmental restraints are undeniably irrational as unsupported by any imaginable rationale. Such instances are suitably rare. The claims of arbitrariness that mark almost all instances of unenumerated substantive rights are those resting on "certain interests requir[ing] particularly careful scrutiny of the state needs asserted to justify their abridgment." In the face of an interest this powerful a State may not rest on threshold rationality or a presumption of constitutionality, but may prevail only on the ground of an interest sufficiently compelling to place within the realm of the reasonable a refusal to recognize the individual right asserted.

This approach calls for a court to assess the relative "weights" or dignities of the contending interests, and to this extent the judicial method is familiar to the common law. Common law method is subject, however, to two important constraints in the hands of a court engaged in substantive due process review. First, such a court is bound to confine the values that it recognizes to those truly deserving constitutional stature, either to those expressed in constitutional text, or those exemplified by "the traditions from which [the Nation developed," or revealed by contrast with "the traditions from which it broke." *Poe* (Harlan, J., dissenting).

The second constraint, again, simply reflects the fact that constitutional review, not judicial lawmaking, is a court's business here. The weighing or valuing of contending interests in this sphere is only the first step, forming the basis for determining whether the statute in questions falls inside or outside the zone of what is reasonable in the way it resolves the conflict between the interests of state and individual. It is no justification for judicial intervention merely to identify a reasonable resolution of contending values that differs from the terms of the legislation under review. It is only when the legislation's justifying principle, critically valued, is so far from being commensurate with the individual interest as to be arbitrarily or pointlessly applied that the statute must give way. Only if this standard points against the statute can the individual claimant be said to have a constitutional right ...

When identifying and assessing the competing interests of liberty and authority, for example, the breadth of expression that a litigant or a judge selects in stating the competing principles will have much to do with the outcome and may be dispositive ...

Just as results in substantive due process cases are tied to the selections of statements of the competing interests, the acceptability of the results is a function of the good reasons for the selections made. It is here that the value of common-law method becomes apparent, for the usual thinking of the common law is suspicious of the all-or-nothing analysis that tends to produce legal petrification instead of an evolving boundary between the domains of old principles. Common-law method tends to pay respect instead to detail, seeking to understand old principles afresh by new examples and new counter-examples. The "tradition is a living thing," *Poe*, (Harlan, J., dissenting), albeit one that moves by moderate steps carefully taken. "The decision of an apparently novel claim must depend on grounds which follow closely on well-accepted principles and criteria. The new decision must take its place in relation to what went before and further [cut] a channel for what is to come." Exact analysis and characterization of any due process claim is critical to the method and to the result.

So, in *Poe*, Justice Harlan viewed it as essential to the plaintiffs' claimed right to use contraceptives that they sought to do so within the privacy of the marital bedroom. This detail in fact served two crucial and complementary functions, and provides a lesson for today. It rescued the individuals' claim from a breadth that would have threatened all state regulation of contraception or intimate relations; extramarital intimacy, no matter how privately practiced, was outside the scope of the right Justice Harlan would have recognized in that case. It was, moreover, this same restriction that allowed the interest to be valued as an aspect of a broader liberty to be free from all unreasonable intrusions into the privacy of the home and the family life within it, a liberty exemplified in constitutional provisions such as the Third and Fourth Amendments, in prior decisions of the Court involving unreasonable intrusions into the home and family life, and in the then-prevailing status of marriage as the sole lawful locus of intimate relations.

On the other side of the balance, the State's interest in *Poe* was not fairly characterized simply as preserving sexual morality, or doing so by regulating contraceptive devices ... It was assumed that the State might legitimately enforce limits on the use of contraceptives through laws regulating divorce and annulment, or even through its tax policy, but not necessarily be justified in criminalizing the same practice in the marital bedroom, which would entail the consequence of authorizing state enquiry into the intimate relations of a married couple who chose to close their door.

The same insistence on exactitude lies behind questions, in current terminology, about the proper level of generality at which to analyze claims and counter-claims, and the demand for fitness and proper tailoring of a restrictive statute is just another way of testing the legitimacy of the generality at which the government sets up its justification. We may therefore classify Justice Harlan's example of proper analysis in any of these ways: As applying concepts of normal critical reasoning, as pointing to the need to attend to the levels of generality at which countervailing interest are stated, or as examining the concrete application of principles for fitness with their own ostensible justifications ... For here we are faced with an individual claim not to a right on the part of just anyone to help anyone else commit suicide under any circumstances, but to the right of a narrow class to help others also in a narrow class under a set of limited circumstances. And the claimants are met with the State's assertion, among others, that rights of such narrow scope cannot be recognized without jeopardy to individuals whom the State may concededly protect through its regulations ...

I do not understand the argument to rest on any assumption that rights either to suicide or to assistance in committing it are historically based as such. Respondents, rather, acknowledge the prohibition of each historically, but rely on the fact that to a substantial extent the State has repudiated that history. The result of this, respondents say, is to open the door to claims of such a patient to be accorded one of the options open to those with different, traditionally cognizable claims to autonomy in deciding how their bodies and minds should be treated.

It is in the abortion cases that the most telling recognitions of the importance of bodily integrity and the concomitant tradition of medical assistance have occurred ... Without physician assistance in abortion, the woman's right would have too often amounted to nothing more than a right to self-mutilation, and without a physician to assist in the suicide of the dying, the patient's right will often be confined to crude methods of causing death, most shocking and painful to the decedent's survivors.

There is, finally, one more reason for claiming that a physician's assistance here would fall within the accepted tradition of medical care in our society ... For, in the course of holding that the decision to perform an abortion called for a physician's assistance, the Court recognized that the good physician is not just a mechanic of the human body whose services have no bearing on a person's moral choices, but one who does more than treat symptoms, one who ministers to the patient. This idea of the physician as serving the whole person is a source of the high value traditionally placed on the medical relationship. Its value is surely as apparent here as in the abortion cases.

The State has put forward several interests to justify the Washington law as applied to physicians treating terminally ill patients, even those competent to make responsible choices: protecting life generally, discouraging suicide even if knowing and voluntary, and protecting terminally ill patients from involuntary suicide and euthanasia, both voluntary and nonvoluntary.

It is not necessary to discuss the exact strengths of the first two claims of justification in the present circumstances, for the third is dispositive for me. That third justification is different from the first two, for it addresses specific features of respondents' claim, and it opposes that claim not with a moral judgment contrary to respondents', but with a recognized state interest in the protection of nonresponsible individuals and those who do not stand in relation either to death or to their physicians as do the patients whom respondents describe. The State claims interests in protecting patients from mistakenly and involuntarily deciding to end their lives, and in guarding against both voluntary and involuntary euthanasia. Leaving aside any difficulties in coming to a clear concept of imminent death, mistaken decisions may result from inadequate palliative care or a terminal prognosis that turns out to be error; coercion and abuse may stem from the large medical bills that family members cannot bear or unreimbursed hospitals decline to shoulder. Voluntary and involuntary euthanasia may result once doctors are authorized to prescribe lethal medication in the first instance, for they might find it pointless to distinguish between patients who administer their own fatal drugs and those who wish not to, and their compassion for those who suffer may obscure the distinction between those who ask for death and those who may be unable to request it. The argument is that a progression would occur, obscuring the line between the ill and the dying, and between the responsible and the unduly influenced, until ultimately doctors and perhaps others would abuse a limited freedom to aid suicides by yielding to the impulse to end another's suffering under conditions going beyond the narrow limits the respondents propose. The State thus argues, essentially, that respondent's claim is not as narrow as it sounds, simply because no recognition of the interest they assert could be limited to vindicating those interests and affecting no others. The State says that the claim, in practical effect, would entail consequences that the State could, without doubt, legitimately act to prevent.

Respondents propose an answer to all this, the answer of state regulation with teeth. Legislation proposed in several States, for example, would authorize physician-assisted suicide but require two qualified physicians to confirm the patient's diagnosis, prognosis, and competence; and would mandate that the patient make repeated requests witnessed by at least two others over a specified time span; and would impose reporting requirements and criminal penalties for various acts of coercion.

But at least at this moment there are reasons for caution in predicting the effectiveness of the teeth proposed. Respondents' proposals, as it turns out, sound much like the guidelines now in place in the Netherlands, the only place where experience with physician-assisted suicide and euthanasia has yielded empirical evidence about how such regulations might affect actual practice. Dutch physicians must engage in consultation before proceeding, and must decide whether the patient's decision is voluntary, well considered, and stable, whether the request to die is enduring and made more than once, and whether the patient's future will involve unacceptable suffering. There is, however, a substantial dispute today about what the Dutch experience shows. Some commentators marshall evidence that the Dutch guidelines have in practice failed to protect patients from involuntary euthanasia and have been violated with impunity. The day may come when we can say with some assurance which side is right, but for now it is the substantiality of the factual disagreement, and the alternatives for resolving it, that matter. They are, for me, dispositive of the due process claim at this time.

JUSTICE O'CONNOR, concurring.

Death will be different for each of us. For many, the last days will be spent in physical pain and perhaps the despair that accompanies physical deterioration and a loss of control of basic bodily and mental functions. Some will seek medication to alleviate that pain and other symptoms.

The Court frames the issue in this case as whether the Due Process Clause of the Constitution protects a "right to commit suicide which itself includes a right to assistance in doing so," and concludes that our Nation's history, legal traditions, and practices do not support the existence of such a right. I join the Court's opinions because I agree that there is no generalized right to "commit suicide." But respondents urge us to address the narrower question whether a mentally competent person who is experiencing great suffering has a constitutionally cognizable interest in controlling the circumstances of his or her imminent death. I see no need to reach that question in the context of the facial challenges to the New York and Washington laws at issue here. The parties and *amici* agree that in these States a patient who is suffering from a terminal illness and who is experiencing great pain has no legal barriers to obtaining medication, from qualified physicians, to alleviate that suffering, even to the point of causing unconsciousness and hastening death. In this light, even assuming that we would recognize such an interest, I agree that the State's interests in protecting those who are not truly competent or facing imminent death, or those whose decisions to hasten death would not truly be voluntary, are sufficiently weighty to justify a prohibition against physician-assisted suicide.

In sum, there is no need to address the question whether suffering patients have a constitutionally cognizable interest in obtaining relief from the suffering that they may experience in the last days of their lives. There is no dispute that dying patients in Washington and New York can obtain palliative care, even when doing so would hasten their deaths. The difficulty in defining terminal illness and the risk that a dying patient's request for assistance in ending his or her life might not be truly voluntary justifies the prohibitions on assisted suicide we uphold here.

JUSTICE STEVENS, concurring in the judgments.

The Court ends its opinion with the important observation that our holding today is fully consistent with a continuation of the vigorous debate about the "morality, legality, and practicality of physician-assisted suicide" in a democratic society. I write separately to make it clear that there is also room for further debate about the limits that the Constitution places on the power of the States to punish the practice ...

Today, the Court decides that Washington's statute prohibiting assisted suicide is not invalid "on its face," that is to say, in all or most cases in which it might be applied. That holding, however, does not foreclose the possibility that some applications of the statute might well be invalid ...

History and tradition provide ample support for refusing to recognize an open-ended constitutional right to commit suicide. Much more than the State's paternalistic interest in protecting the individual from the irrevocable consequences of an ill-advised decision motivated by temporary concerns is at stake. There is truth in John Donne's observation that "No man is an island". The State has an interest in preserving and fostering the benefits that every human being may provide to the community—a community that thrives on the exchange of ideas, expressions of affection, shared memories and humorous incidents as well as on the material contributions that its members create and support. The value to others of a person's life is far too precious to allow the individual to claim a constitutional entitlement to complete autonomy in making a decision to end that life. Thus, I fully agree with the Court that the "liberty" protected by the Due Process Clause does not include a categorical "right to commit suicide which itself includes a right to assistance in doing so."

In *Cruzan* the Court assumed that the interest in liberty protected by the Fourteenth Amendment encompassed the right of a terminally ill patient to direct the withdrawal of life-sustaining treatment. As the Court correctly observes today, that assumption "was not simply deduced from abstract concepts of personal autonomy." Instead, it was supported by the common-law tradition protecting the individual's general right to refuse unwanted medical treatment.

[The]   common-law right to protection from battery, which included the right to refuse medical treatment in most circumstances, did not mark "the outer limits of the substantive sphere of liberty" that supported the Cruzan family's decision to hasten Nancy's death. *Planned Parenthood of Southeastern Pa. v. Casey* [Text, p.468]. Those limits have never been precisely defined. They are generally identified by the importance and character of the decision confronted by the individual. Whatever the outer limits of the concept may be, it definitely includes protection for matters "central to personal dignity and autonomy." *Casey.* It includes, "the individual's right to make certain unusually important decisions that will affect his own, or his family's destiny. .

The *Cruzan* case demonstrated that some state intrusions on the right to decide how death will be encountered are also intolerable. The now-deceased plaintiffs in this action may in fact have had a liberty interest even stronger than Nancy Cruzan's because, not only were they terminally ill, they were suffering constant and severe pain. Avoiding intolerable pain and the indignity of living one's final days incapacitated and in agony is certainly "[a]t the heart of [the] liberty ... to define one's own concept of existence, of meaning, of the universe, and of the mystery of human life." *Casey.*

While I agree with the Court that *Cruzan* does not decide the issue presented by these cases, *Cruzan* did give recognition, not just to vague, unbridled notions of autonomy, but to the more specific interest in making decisions about how to confront an imminent death ... The liberty interest at stake in a case like this differs from, and is stronger than, both the common-law right to refuse medical treatment and the unbridled interest in deciding whether to live or die. It is an interest in deciding how, rather than whether, a critical threshold shall be crossed.

JUSTICE GINSBURG, concurring in the judgements

I concur in the Court's judgments in these cases substantially for the reasons stated by Justice O'Connor in her concurring opinion.

JUSTICE BREYER, concurring in the judgments.

I agree with the Court in *Vacco v. Quill* that the articulated state interests justify the distinction drawn between physician assisted suicide and withdrawal of life-support. I also agree with the Court that the critical question in both of the cases before us is whether "the 'liberty' specially protected by the Due Process Clause includes a right" of the sort that the respondents assert. *Washington v. Glucksberg.* I do not agree, however, with the Court's formulation of that claimed "liberty" interest. The Court describes it as a "right to commit suicide with another's assistance." But I would not reject the respondents' claim without considering a different formulation, for which our legal tradition may provide greater support. That formulation would use words roughly like a "right to die with dignity." But irrespective of the exact words used, at its core would lie personal control over the manner of death, professional medical assistance, and the avoidance of unnecessary and severe physical suffering—combined.

As Justice Souter points out, Justice Harlan's dissenting opinion in *Poe v. Ullman* offers some support for such a claim. In that opinion, Justice Harlan referred to the "liberty" that the Fourteenth Amendment protects as including "a freedom from all substantial arbitrary impositions and purposeless restraints" and also as recognizing that "certain interests require particularly careful scrutiny of the state needs asserted to justify their abridgment." The "certain interests" to which Justice Harlan referred may well be similar (perhaps identical) to the rights, liberties, or interest that the Court today, as in the past, regards as "fundamental".

Justice Harlan concluded that marital privacy was such a "special interest." He found in the Constitution a right of "privacy of the home''—with the home, the bedroom, and ''intimate details of the marital relation'' at its heart—by examining the protection that the law had earlier provided for related, but not identical, interests described by such words as ''privacy,'' ''home,'' and ''family.'' The respondents here essentially ask us to do the same. They argue that one can find a ''right to die with dignity'' by examining the protection the law has provided for related, but not identical, interests relating to personal dignity, medical treatment, and freedom from state-inflicted pain.

I do not believe, however, that this Court need or now should decide whether or not such a right is ''fundamental.'' That is because, in my view, the avoidance of severe physical pain (connected with death) would have to comprise an essential part of any successful claim and because, as Justice O'Connor points out, the laws before us do not force a dying person to undergo that kind of pain . . .

Medical technology, we are repeatedly told, makes the administration of pain-relieving drugs sufficient, except for a very few individuals for whom the effectiveness of pain control medicines can mean, not pain, but the need for sedation which can end in a coma. We are also told that there are many instances in which patients do not receive the palliative care that, in principle, is available, but that is so for institutional reasons or inadequacies or obstacles, which would seem impossible to overcome, and which do not include a prohibitive set of laws.

This legal circumstance means that the state laws before us do not infringe directly upon the (assumed) central interest (what I have called the core of the interest in dying with dignity) as, by way of contrast, the state anticontraceptive laws at issue in *Poe* did interfere with the central interest there at stake—by bringing the State's police powers to bear upon the marital bedroom.

Were the legal circumstances different—for example, were state law to prevent the provision of palliative care, including the administration of drugs as needed to avoid pain at the end of life—then the law's impact upon serious and otherwise unavoidable pain (accompanying death) would be more directly at issue. And as Justice O'Connor suggests, the Court might have to revisit its conclusions in these cases.

Notes on Glucksberg: Living and Dying with Dignity

1. Justice O'Connor argued that although there is no constitutional ''right to suicide'' there may be a constitutional right against laws that bar access to potentially lethal medication to alleviate grave pain. If ''living one's final days incapacitated and in agony'' is really an indignity, as the Justice implied, is there any reason to prefer palliative lethal medication to direct acts of assisted suicide?

2. Justice Breyer's appeal to Harlan's dissent in *Poe v. Ullman*, suggests that the decision to ''die with dignity'' is as much a protected liberty as the decision to use birth control. Is using contraception a way of, one might say, living with dignity? Does the idea of human dignity, even better than the idea of autonomy, capture the ethic of decisional privacy in the assisted suicide and other ''right to die'' cases? Is autonomy the moral core of human dignity? Is respect for autonomy at least a part of what respect for human dignity requires?

Chapter Eight

STATUTORY APPENDIX

A. TITLE I OF THE ELECTRONIC COMMUNI-CATIONS PRIVACY ACT OF 1986 (PUB.L. 99–508) (CODIFIED AT 18 U.S.C.A. §§ 2510–2521

1. PROVISIONS OF THE STATUTE

CHAPTER 119—WIRE AND ELECTRONIC COMMUNICATIONS INTERCEPTION AND INTERCEPTION OF ORAL COMMUNICATIONS

Section 2510. Definitions

As used in this chapter—

(1) "wire communication" means any aural transfer made in whole or in part through the use of facilities for the transmission of communications by the aid of wire, cable, or other like connection between the point of origin and the point of reception (including the use of such connection in a switching station) furnished or operated by any person engaged in providing or operating such facilities for the transmission of interstate or foreign communications or communications affecting interstate or foreign commerce and such term includes any electronic storage of such communication;

(2) "oral communication" means any oral communication uttered by a person exhibiting an expectation that such communication is not subject to interception under circumstances justifying such expectation, but such term does not include any electronic communication;

(3) "State" means any State of the United States, the District of Columbia, the Commonwealth of Puerto Rico, and any territory or possession of the United States;

(4) "intercept" means the aural or other acquisition of the contents of any wire, electronic, or oral communication through the use of any electronic, mechanical, or other device;

(5) "electronic, mechanical, or other device" means any device or apparatus which can be used to intercept a wire, oral, or electronic communication other than—

(a) any telephone or telegraph instrument, equipment or facility, or any component thereof, (i) furnished to the subscriber or user by a provider of wire or electronic communication service in the ordinary course of its business and being used by the subscriber or user in the ordinary course of its business or furnished by such subscriber or user for connection to the facilities of such service and used in the ordinary course of its business; or (ii) being used by a provider of wire or electronic communication service in the ordinary course of its business, or by an investigative or law enforcement officer in the ordinary course of his duties;

(b) a hearing aid or similar device being used to correct subnormal hearing to not better than normal;

(6) "person" means any employee, or agent of the United States or any State or political subdivision thereof, and any individual, partnership, association, joint stock company, trust, or corporation;

(7) "Investigative or law enforcement officer" means any officer of the United States or of a State or political subdivision thereof, who is empowered by law to conduct investigations of or to make arrests for offenses enumerated in this chapter, and any attorney authorized by law to prosecute or participate in the prosecution of such offenses;

(8) "contents", when used with respect to any wire, oral, or electronic communication, includes any information concerning the substance, purport, or meaning of that communication;

(9) "Judge of competent jurisdiction" means—

(a) a judge of a United States district court or a United States court of appeals; and

(b) a judge of any court of general criminal jurisdiction of a State who is authorized by a statute of that State to enter orders authorizing interceptions of wire, oral, or electronic communications;

(10) "communication common carrier" shall have the same meaning which is given the term "common carrier" by section 153(h) of title 47 of the United States Code;

(11) "aggrieved person" means a person who was a party to any intercepted wire, oral, or electronic communication or a person against whom the interception was directed;

(12) "electronic communication" means any transfer of signs, signals, writing, images, sounds, data, or intelligence of any nature transmitted in whole or in part by a wire, radio, electromagnetic, photoelectronic or photooptical system that affects interstate or foreign commerce, but does not include—

(A) any wire or oral communication;

(B) any communication made through a tone-only paging device;

(C) any communication from a tracking device (as defined in section 3117 of this title); or

(D) electronic fund transfer information stored by a financial institution used for the electronic storage and transfer of fund;

(13) "user" means any person or entity who—

(A) uses an electronic communication service; and

(B) is duly authorized by the provider of such service to engage in such use;

(14) "electronic communications system" means any wire, radio, electromagnetic, photooptical or photoelectronic facilities for the transmission of electronic communications, and any computer facilities or related electronic equipment for the electronic storage of such communications;

(15) "electronic communication service" means any service which provides to users thereof the ability to send or receive wire or electronic communications;

(16) "readily accessible to the general public" means, with respect to a radio communication, that such communication is not—

(A) scrambled or encrypted:

(B) transmitted using modulation techniques whose essential parameters have been withheld from the public with the intention of preserving the privacy of such communication;

(C) carried on a subcarrier or other signal subsidiary to a radio transmission;

(D) transmitted over a communication system provided by a common carrier, unless the communication is a tone only paging system communication; or

(E) transmitted on frequencies allocated under part 25, subpart D, E, or F of part 74, or part 94 of the Rules of the Federal Communications Commission, unless, in the case of a communication transmitted on a frequency allocated under part 74 that is not exclusively allocated to broadcast auxiliary services, the communication is a two-way voice communication by radio;

(17) "electronic storage" means—

(A) any temporary, intermediate storage of a wire or electronic communication incidental to the electronic transmission thereof; and

(B) any storage of such communication by an electronic communication service for purposes of backup protection of such communication; and

(18) "aural transfer" means a transfer containing the human voice at any point between and including the point of origin and the point of reception.

Section 2511. Interception and disclosure of wire, oral, or electronic communications prohibited

(1) Except as otherwise specifically provided in this chapter any person who—

(a) intentionally intercepts, endeavors to intercept, or procures any other person to intercept or endeavor to intercept, any wire, oral, or electronic communication;

(b) intentionally uses, endeavors to use, or procures any other person to use or endeavor to use any electronic, mechanical, or other device to intercept any oral communication when—

(i) such device is affixed to, or otherwise transmits a signal through, a wire, cable, or other like connection used in wire communication; or

(ii) such device transmits communications by radio, or interferes with the transmission of such communication; or

(iii) such person knows, or has reason to know, that such device or any component thereof has been sent through the mail or transported in interstate or foreign commerce; or

(iv) such use or endeavor to use (A) takes place on the premises of any business or other commercial establishment the operations of which affect interstate or foreign commerce; or (B) obtains or is for the purpose of obtaining information relating to the operations of any business or other commercial establishment the operations of which affect interstate or foreign commerce; or

(v) such person acts in the District of Columbia, the Commonwealth of Puerto Rico, or any territory or possession of the United States;

(c) intentionally discloses, or endeavors to disclose, to any other person the contents of any wire, oral, or electronic communication, knowing or having reason to know that the information was obtained through the interception of a wire, oral, or electronic communication in violation of this subsection;

(d) intentionally uses, or endeavors to use, the contents of any wire, oral, or electronic communication, knowing or having reason to know that the information was obtained through the interception of a wire, oral, or electronic communication in violation of this subsection; or

(e)(i) intentionally discloses, or endeavors to disclose, to any other person the contents of any wire, oral, or electronic communication, intercepted by means authorized by sections 2511(2)(a)(ii), 2511(2)(b) to (c), 2511(2)(e), 2516, and 2518 of this chapter, (ii) knowing or having reason to know that the information was obtained through the interception of such a communication in connection with a criminal investigation, (iii) having obtained or received the information in connection with a criminal investigation, and (iv) with intent to improperly obstruct, impede, or interfere with a duly authorized criminal investigation,

shall be punished as provided in subsection (4) or shall be subject to suit as provided in subsection (5).

(2)(a)(i) It shall not be unlawful under this chapter for an operator of a switchboard, or an officer, employee, or agent of a provider of wire or electronic communication service, whose facilities are used in the transmission of a wire communication or electronic communication, to intercept, disclose, or use that communication in the normal course of his employment while engaged in any activity which is a necessary incident to the rendition of his service or to the protection of the rights or property of the provider of that service, except that a provider of wire communication service to the public shall not utilize service observing or random monitoring except for mechanical or service quality control checks.

(ii) Notwithstanding any other law, providers of wire or electronic communication service, their officers, employees, and agents, landlords, custodians, or other persons, are authorized to provide information, facilities, or technical assistance to persons authorized by law to intercept wire, oral, or electronic communications or to conduct electronic surveillance, as defined in section 101 of the Foreign Intelligence Surveillance Act of 1978, if such provider, its officers, employees, or agents, landlord, custodian, or other specified person, has been provided with—

 (A) a court order directing such assistance signed by the authorizing judge, or

 (B) a certification in writing by a person specified in section 2518(7) of this title of (sic) the Attorney General of the United States that no warrant or court order is required by law, that all statutory requirements have been met, and that the specified assistance is required,

setting forth the period of time during which the provision of the information, facilities, or technical assistance is authorized and specifying the information, facilities, or technical assistance required. No provider of wire or electronic communication service, officer, employee, or agent thereof, or landlord, custodian, or other specified person shall disclose the existence of any interception or surveillance or the device used to accomplish the interception or surveillance with respect to which the person has been furnished a court order or certification under this chapter, except as may otherwise be required by legal process and then only after prior notification to the Attorney General or to the principal prosecuting attorney of a State or any political subdivision of a State, as may be appropriate. Any such disclosure, shall render such person liable for the civil damages provided for in section 2520. No cause of action shall lie in any court against any provider of wire or electronic communication service, its officers, employees, or agents, landlord, custodian, or other specified person for providing information, facilities, or assistance in accordance with the terms of a court order or certification under this chapter.

(b) It shall not be unlawful under this chapter for an officer, employee, or agent of the Federal Communications Commission, in the normal course of his employment and in discharge of the monitoring responsibilities exercised by the Commission in the enforcement of chapter 5 of title 47 of the United States Code, to intercept a wire or electronic communication, or oral communication transmitted by radio, or to disclose or use the information thereby obtained.

(c) It shall not be unlawful under this chapter for a person acting under color of law to intercept a wire, oral, or electronic communication, where such person is a party to the communication or one of the parties to the communication has given prior consent to such interception.

(d) It shall not be unlawful under this chapter for a person not acting under color of law to intercept a wire, oral, or electronic communication where such person is a party to the communication or where one of the parties to the communication has given prior consent to such interception unless such communication is intercepted for the purpose of committing any criminal or tortious act in violation of the Constitution or laws of the United States or of any State.

(e) Notwithstanding any other provision of this title or section 705 or 706 of the Communications Act of 1934, it shall not be unlawful for an officer, employee, or agent of the United States in the normal course of his official duty to conduct electronic surveillance, as defined in section 101 of the Foreign Intelligence Surveillance Act of 1978, as authorized by that Act.

(f) Nothing contained in this chapter or chapter 121, or section 705 of the Communications Act of 1934, shall be deemed to affect the acquisition by the United States Government of foreign intelligence information from international or foreign communications, or foreign intelligence activities conducted in accordance with otherwise applicable Federal law involving a foreign electronic communications system, utilizing a means other than electronic surveillance as defined in section 101 of the Foreign Intelligence Surveillance Act of 1978, and procedures in this chapter and the Foreign Intelligence Surveillance Act of 1978 shall be the exclusive means by which electronic surveillance, as defined in section 101 of such Act, and the interception of domestic wire and oral communications may be conducted.

(g) It shall not be unlawful under this chapter or chapter 121 of this title for any person—

(i) to intercept or access an electronic communication made through an electronic communication system that is configured so that such electronic communication is readily accessible to the general public;

(ii) to intercept any radio communication which is transmitted—

(I) by any station for the use of the general public, or that relates to ships, aircraft, vehicles, or persons in distress;

(II) by any governmental, law enforcement, civil defense, private land mobile, or public safety communications system, including police and fire, readily accessible to the general public;

(III) by a station operating on an authorized frequency within the bands allocated to the amateur, citizens band, or general mobile radio services; or

(IV) by any marine or aeronautical communications system;

(iii) to engage in any conduct which—

(I) is prohibited by section 633 of the Communications Act of 1934; or

(II) is excepted from the application of section 705(a) of the Communications Act of 1934 by section 705(b) of that Act;

(iv) to intercept any wire or electronic communication the transmission of which is causing harmful interference to any lawfully operating station or consumer electronic equipment, to the extent necessary to identify the source of such interference; or

(v) for other users of the same frequency to intercept any radio communication made through a system that utilizes frequencies monitored by individuals engaged in the provision or the use of such system, if such communication is not scrambled or encrypted.

(h) It shall not be unlawful under this chapter—

(i) to use a pen register or a trap and trace device (as those terms are defined for the purposes of chapter 206 (relating to pen registers and trap and trace devices) of this title); or

(ii) for a provider of electronic communication service to record the fact that a wire or electronic communication was initiated or completed in order to protect such provider, another provider furnishing service toward the completion of the wire or electronic communication, or a user of that service, from fraudulent, unlawful or abusive use of such service.

(3)(a) Except as provided in paragraph (b) of this subsection, a person or entity providing an electronic communication service to the public shall not intentionally divulge the contents of any communication (other than one to such person or entity, or an agent thereof) while in transmission on that service to any person or entity other than an addressee or intended recipient of such communication or an agent of such addressee or intended recipient.

(b) A person or entity providing electronic communication service to the public may divulge the contents of any such communication—

(i) as otherwise authorized in section 2511(2)(a) or 2517 of this title;

(ii) with the lawful consent of the originator or any addressee or intended recipient of such communication;

(iii) to a person employed or authorized, or whose facilities are used, to forward such communication to its destination; or

(iv) which were inadvertently obtained by the service provider and which appear to pertain to the commission of a crime, if such divulgence is made to a law enforcement agency.

(4)(a) Except as provided in paragraph (b) of this subsection or in subsection (5), whoever violates subsection (1) of this section shall be fined under this title or imprisoned not more than five years, or both.

(b) If the offense is a first offense under paragraph (a) of this subsection and is not for a tortious or illegal purpose or for purposes of direct or indirect commercial advantage or private commercial gain, and the wire or electronic communication with respect to which the offense under paragraph (a) is a radio communication that is not scrambled, encrypted, or transmitted using modulation techniques the essential parameters of which have been withheld from the public with the intention of preserving the privacy of such communication, then—

(i) if the communication is not the radio portion of a cellular telephone communication, a cordless telephone communication that is transmitted between the cordless telephone handset and the base unit, a public land mobile radio service communication or a paging service communication, and the conduct is not that described in subsection (5), the offender shall be fined under this title or imprisoned not more than one year, or both; and

(ii) if the communication is the radio portion of a cellular telephone communication, a cordless telephone communication that is transmitted between the cordless telephone handset and the base unit, a public land mobile radio service communication or a paging service communication, the offender shall be fined under this title.

(c) Conduct otherwise an offense under this subsection that consists of or relates to the interception of a satellite transmission that is not encrypted or scrambled and that is transmitted—

(i) to a broadcasting station for purposes of retransmission to the general public; or

(ii) as an audio subcarrier intended for redistribution to facilities open to the public, but not including data transmissions or telephone calls,

is not an offense under this subsection unless the conduct is for the purposes of direct or indirect commercial advantage or private financial gain.

(5)(a)(i) If the communication is—

(A) a private satellite video communication that is not scrambled or encrypted and the conduct in violation of this chapter is the private viewing of that communication and is not for a tortious or illegal purpose or for purposes of direct or indirect commercial advantage or private commercial gain; or

(B) a radio communication that is transmitted on frequencies allocated under subpart D of part 74 of the rules of the Federal Communications Commission that is not scrambled or encrypted and the conduct in violation of this chapter is not for a tortious or illegal purpose or for purposes of direct or indirect commercial advantage or private commercial gain,

then the person who engages in such conduct shall be subject to suit by the Federal Government in a court of competent jurisdiction.

(ii) In an action under this subsection—

(A) if the violation of this chapter is a first offense for the person under paragraph (a) of subsection (4) and such person has not been found liable in a civil action under section 2520 of this title, the Federal Government shall be entitled to appropriate injunctive relief; and

(B) if the violation of this chapter is a second or subsequent offense under paragraph (a) of subsection (4) or such person has been found liable in any prior civil action under section 2520, the person shall be subject to a mandatory $500 civil fine.

(b) The court may use any means within its authority to enforce an injunction issued under paragraph (ii)(A), and shall impose a civil fine of not less than $500 for each violation of such an injunction.

Section 2512. Manufacture, distribution, possession, and advertising of wire, oral, or electronic communication intercepting devices prohibited

(1) Except as otherwise specifically provided in this chapter, any person who intentionally—

(a) sends through the mail, or sends or carries in interstate or foreign commerce, any electronic, mechanical, or other device, knowing or having reason to know that the design of such device renders it primarily useful for the purpose of the surreptitious interception of wire, oral, or electronic communications;

(b) manufactures, assembles, possesses, or sells any electronic, mechanical, or other device, knowing or having reason to know that the design of such device renders it primarily useful for the purpose of the surreptitious interception of wire, oral, or electronic communications, and that such device or any component thereof has been or will be sent through the mail or transported in interstate or foreign commerce; or

(c) places in any newspaper, magazine, handbill, or other publication any advertisement of—

(i) any electronic, mechanical, or other device knowing or having reason to know that the design of such device renders it primarily useful for the purpose of the surreptitious interception of wire, oral, or electronic communications; or

(ii) any other electronic, mechanical, or other device, where such advertisement promotes the use of such device for the purpose of the surreptitious interception of wire, oral, or electronic communications,

knowing or having reason to know that such advertisement will be sent through the mail or transported in interstate or foreign commerce,

shall be fined under this title or imprisoned not more than five years, or both.

(2) It shall not be unlawful under this section for—

(a) a provider of wire or electronic communication service or an officer, agent, or employee of, or a person under contract with, such a provider, in the normal course of the business of providing that wire or electronic communication service, or

(b) an officer, agent, or employee of, or a person under contract with, the United States, a State, or a political subdivision thereof, in the normal course of the activities of the United States, a State, or a political subdivision thereof,

to send through the mail, send or carry in interstate or foreign commerce, or manufacture, assemble, possess, or sell any electronic, mechanical, or other device knowing or having reason to know that the design of such device renders it primarily useful for the purpose of the surreptitious interception of wire, oral, or electronic communications.

(3) It shall not be unlawful under this section to advertise for sale a device described in subsection (1) of this section if the advertisement is mailed, sent, or carried in interstate or foreign commerce solely to a domestic provider of wire or electronic communication service or to an agency of the United States, a State, or a political subdivision thereof which is duly authorized to use such device.

Section 2513. Confiscation of wire, oral, or electronic communication intercepting devices

Any electronic, mechanical, or other device used, sent, carried, manufactured, assembled, possessed, sold, or advertised in violation of section 2511 or section 2512 of this chapter may be seized and forfeited to the United States. All provisions of law relating to (1) the seizure, summary and judicial forfeiture, and condemnation of vessels, vehicles, merchandise, and baggage for violations of the customs laws contained in title 19 of the United States Code, (2) the disposition of such vessels, vehicles, merchandise, and baggage or the proceeds from the sale thereof, (3) the remission or mitigation of such forfeiture, (4) the compromise of claims, and (5) the award of compensation to informers in respect of such forfeitures, shall apply to seizures and forfeitures incurred, or alleged to have been incurred, under the provisions of this section, insofar as applicable and not inconsistent with the provisions of this section; except that such duties as are imposed upon the collector of customs or any other person with respect to the seizure and forfeiture of vessels, vehicles, merchandise, and baggage under the provisions of the customs laws contained in title 19 of the United States Code shall be performed with respect to seizure and forfeiture of electronic, mechanical, or other intercepting devices under this section by such officers, agents, or other persons as may be authorized or designated for that purpose by the Attorney General.

Section 2515. Prohibition of use as evidence of intercepted wire or oral communications

Whenever any wire or oral communication has been intercepted, no part of the contents of such communication and no evidence derived therefrom may be received in evidence in any trial, hearing, or other proceeding in or before any court, grand jury, department, officer, agency, regulatory body, legislative committee, or other authority of the United States, a State, or a political subdivision thereof if the disclosure of that information would be in violation of this chapter.

Section 2516. Authorization for interception of wire, oral, or electronic communications

(1) The Attorney General, Deputy Attorney General, Associate Attorney General, or any Assistant Attorney General, any acting Assistant Attorney General, or any Deputy Assistant Attorney General or acting Deputy Assistant Attorney General in the Criminal Division specially designated by the Attorney General, may authorize an application to a Federal judge of competent jurisdiction for, and such judge may grant in conformity with section 2518 of this chapter an order authorizing or approving the interception of wire or oral communications by the Federal Bureau of Investigation, or a Federal agency having responsibility for the investigation of the offense as to which the application is made, when such interception may provide or has provided evidence of—

(a) any offense punishable by death or by imprisonment for more than one year under sections 2274 through 2277 of title 42 of the United States Code (relating to the enforcement of the Atomic Energy Act of 1954), section 2284 of title 42 of the United States Code (relating to sabotage of nuclear facilities or fuel), or under the following chapters of this title: chapter 37 (relating to espionage), chapter 90 (relating to protection of trade secrets), chapter 105 (relating to sabotage), chapter 115 (relating to treason), chapter 102 (relating to riots), chapter 65 (relating to malicious mischief), chapter 111 (relating to destruction of vessels), or chapter 81 (relating to piracy);

(b) a violation of section 186 or section 501(c) of title 29, United States Code (dealing with restrictions on payments and loans to labor organizations), or any offense which involves murder, kidnapping, robbery, or extortion, and which is punishable under this title;

(c) any offense which is punishable under the following sections of this title: section 201 (bribery of public officials and witnesses), section 215 (relating to bribery of bank officials), section 224 (bribery in sporting contests), subsection (d), (e), (f), (g), (h), or (i) of section 844 (unlawful use of explosives), section

1032 (relating to concealment of assets), section 1084 (transmission of wagering information), section 751 (relating to escape), section 1014 (relating to loans and credit applications generally; renewals and discounts), sections 1503, 1512, and 1513 (influencing or injuring an officer, juror, or witness generally), section 1510 (obstruction of criminal investigations), section 1511 (obstruction of State or local law enforcement), section 1751 (Presidential and Presidential staff assassination, kidnapping, and assault), section 1951 (interference with commerce by threats or violence), section 1952 (interstate and foreign travel or transportation in aid of racketeering enterprises), section 1958 (relating to use of interstate commerce facilities in the commission of murder for hire), section 1959 (relating to violent crimes in aid of racketeering activity), section 1954 (offer, acceptance, or solicitation to influence operations of employee benefit plan), section 1955 (prohibition of business enterprises of gambling), section 1956 (laundering of monetary instruments), section 1957 (relating to engaging in monetary transactions in property derived from specified unlawful activity), section 659 (theft from interstate shipment), section 664 (embezzlement from pension and welfare funds), section 1343 (fraud by wire, radio, or television), section 1344 (relating to bank fraud), sections 2251 and 2252 (sexual exploitation of children), sections 2312, 2313, 2314, and 2315 (interstate transportation of stolen property), section 2321 (relating to trafficking in certain motor vehicles or motor vehicle parts), section 1203 (relating to hostage taking), section 1029 (relating to fraud and related activity in connection with access devices), section 3146 (relating to penalty for failure to appear), section 3521(b)(3) (relating to witness relocation and assistance), section 32 (relating to destruction of aircraft or aircraft facilities), section 1963 (violations with respect to racketeer influenced and corrupt organizations), section 115 (relating to threatening or retaliating against a Federal official), and section 1341 (relating to mail fraud), section 351 (violations) with respect to congressional, Cabinet, or Supreme Court assassinations, kidnaping, and assault), section 831 (relating to prohibited transactions involving nuclear materials), section 33 (relating to destruction of motor vehicles or motor vehicle facilities), section 175 (relating to biological weapons) section 1992 (relating to wrecking trains), a felony violation of section 1028 (relating to production of false identification documentation), section 1425 (relating to the procurement of citizenship or nationalization unlawfully), section 1426 (relating to the reproduction of naturalization or citizenship papers), section 1427 (relating to the sale of naturalization or citizenship papers), section 1541 (relating to passport issuance without authority), section 1542 (relating to false statements in passport applications), section 1543 (relating to forgery or false use of passports), section 1544 (relating to misuse of passports), or section

1546 (relating to fraud and misuse of visas, permits, and other documents);

(d) any offense involving counterfeiting punishable under section 471, 472, or 473 of this title;

(e) any offense involving fraud connected with a case under title 11 or the manufacture, importation, receiving, concealment, buying, selling, or otherwise dealing in narcotic drugs, marihuana, or other dangerous drugs, punishable under any law of the United States;

(f) any offense including extortionate credit transactions under sections 892, 893, or 894 of this title;

(g) a violation of section 5322 of title 31, United States Code (dealing with the reporting of currency transactions);

(h) any felony violation of sections 2511 and 2512 (relating to interception and disclosure of certain communications and to certain intercepting devices) of this title;

(i) any felony violation of chapter 71 (relating to obscenity) of this title;

(j) any violation of section 60123(b) (relating to destruction of a natural gas pipeline) or section 46502 (relating to aircraft piracy) of title 49;

(k) any criminal violation of section 2778 of title 22 (relating to the Arms Export Control Act);

(*l*) the location of any fugitive from justice from an offense described in this section;

(m) a violation of section 274, 277, or 278 of the Immigration and Nationality Act (8 U.S.C. 1324, 1327, or 1328) (relating to the smuggling of aliens);

(n) any felony violation of sections 922 and 924 of title 18, United States Code (relating to firearms);

(o) any violation of section 5861 of the Internal Revenue Code of 1986 (relating to firearms);

(p) [1]a felony violation of section 1028 (relating to production of false identification documents), section 1542 (relating to false statements in passport applications), section 1546 (relating to fraud and misuse of visas, permits, and other documents) of this title or a violation of section 274, 277, or 278 of the Immigration and Nationality Act (relating to the smuggling of aliens);

(p) [1]any conspiracy to commit any offense described in any subparagraph of this paragraph.

(2) The principal prosecuting attorney of any State, or the principal prosecuting attorney of any political subdivision thereof, if such attorney is authorized by a statute of that State to make application to a State court judge of competent jurisdiction for an order authorizing or approv-

---

1. any conspiracy to commit any offense described in any subparagraph of this paragraph.

ing the interception of wire, oral, or electronic communications, may apply to such judge for, and such judge may grant in conformity with section 2518 of this chapter and with the applicable State statute an order authorizing, or approving the interception of wire, oral, or electronic communications by investigative or law enforcement officers having responsibility for the investigation of the offense as to which the application is made, when such interception may provide or has provided evidence of the commission of the offense of murder, kidnapping, gambling, robbery, bribery, extortion, or dealing in narcotic drugs, marihuana or other dangerous drugs, or other crime dangerous to life, limb, or property, and punishable by imprisonment for more than one year, designated in any applicable State statute authorizing such interception, or any conspiracy to commit any of the foregoing offenses.

(3) Any attorney for the Government (as such term is defined for the purposes of the Federal Rules of Criminal Procedure) may authorize an application to a Federal judge of competent jurisdiction for, and such judge may grant, in conformity with section 2518 of this title, or order authorizing or approving the interception of electronic communications by an investigative or law enforcement officer having responsibility for the investigation of the offense as to which the application is made, when such interception may provide or has provided evidence of any Federal felony.

Section 2517. Authorization for disclosure and use of intercepted wire, oral, or electronic communications

(1) Any investigative or law enforcement officer who, by any means authorized by this chapter, has obtained knowledge of the contents of any wire, oral, or electronic communication, or evidence derived therefrom, may disclose such contents to another investigative or law enforcement officer to the extent that such disclosure is appropriate to the proper performance of the official duties of the officer making or receiving the disclosure.

(2) Any investigative or law enforcement officer who, by any means authorized by this chapter, has obtained knowledge of the contents of any wire, oral, or electronic communication or evidence derived therefrom may use such contents to the extent such use is appropriate to the proper performance of his official duties.

(3) Any person who has received, by any means authorized by this chapter, any information concerning a wire, oral, or electronic communication, or evidence derived therefrom intercepted in accordance with the provisions of this chapter may disclose the contents of that communication or such derivative evidence while giving testimony under oath or affirmation in any proceeding held under the authority of the United States or of any State or political subdivision thereof.

(4) No otherwise privileged wire, oral, or electronic communication intercepted in accordance with, or in violation of, the provisions of this chapter shall lose its privileged character.

(5) When an investigative or law enforcement officer, while engaged in intercepting wire, oral, or electronic communications in the manner authorized herein, intercepts wire, oral, or electronic communications relating to offenses other than those specified in the order of authorization or approval, the contents thereof, and evidence derived therefrom, may be disclosed or used as provided in subsections (1) and (2) of this section. Such contents and any evidence derived therefrom may be used under subsection (3) of this section when authorized or approved by a judge of competent jurisdiction where such judge finds on subsequent application that the contents were otherwise intercepted in accordance with the provisions of this chapter. Such application shall be made as soon as practicable.

Section 2518. Procedure for interception of wire, oral, or electronic communications

(1) Each application for an order authorizing or approving the interception of a wire, oral, or electronic communication under this chapter shall be made in writing upon oath or affirmation to a judge of competent jurisdiction and shall state the applicant's authority to make such application. Each application shall include the following information:

(a) the identity of the investigative or law enforcement officer making the application, and the officer authorizing the application;

(b) a full and complete statement of the facts and circumstances relied upon by the applicant, to justify his belief that an order should be issued, including (i) details as to the particular offense that has been, is being, or is about to be committed, (ii) except as provided in subsection (11), a particular description of the nature and location of the facilities from which or the place where the communication is to be intercepted, (iii) a particular description of the type of communications sought to be intercepted, (iv) the identity of the person, if known, committing the offense and whose communications are to be intercepted;

(c) a full and complete statement as to whether or not other investigative procedures have been tried and failed or why they reasonably appear to be unlikely to succeed if tried or to be too dangerous;

(d) a statement of the period of time for which the interception is required to be maintained. If the nature of the investigation is such that the authorization for interception should not automatically terminate when the described type of communication has been first obtained, a particular description of facts establishing probable cause to believe that additional communications of the same type will occur thereafter;

(e) a full and complete statement of the facts concerning all previous applications known to the individual authorizing and making the application, made to any judge for authorization to intercept, or for approval of interceptions of, wire, oral, or electronic communications involving any of the same persons, facilities or places specified in the application, and the action taken by the judge on each such application; and

(f) where the application is for the extension of an order, a statement setting forth the results thus far obtained from the interception, or a reasonable explanation of the failure to obtain such results.

(2) The judge may require the applicant to furnish additional testimony or documentary evidence in support of the application.

(3) Upon such application the judge may enter an ex parte order, as requested or as modified, authorizing or approving interception of wire, oral, or electronic communications within the territorial jurisdiction of the court in which the judge is sitting (and outside that jurisdiction but within the United States in the case of a mobile interception device authorized by a Federal court within such jurisdiction), if the judge determines on the basis of the facts submitted by the applicant that—

(a) there is probable cause for belief that an individual is committing, has committed, or is about to commit a particular offense enumerated in section 2516 of this chapter;

(b) there is probable cause for belief that particular communications concerning that offense will be obtained through such interception;

(c) normal investigative procedures have been tried and have failed or reasonably appear to be unlikely to succeed if tried or to be too dangerous;

(d) except as provided in subsection (11), there is probable cause for belief that the facilities from which, or the place where, the wire, oral, or electronic communications are to be intercepted are being used, or are about to be used, in connection with the commission of such offense, or are leased to, listed in the name of, or commonly used by such person.

(4) Each order authorizing or approving the interception of any wire, oral, or electronic communication under this chapter shall specify—

(a) the identity of the person, if known, whose communications are to be intercepted;

(b) the nature and location of the communications facilities as to which, or the place where, authority to intercept is granted;

(c) a particular description of the type of communication sought to be intercepted, and a statement of the particular offense to which it relates;

(d) the identity of the agency authorized to intercept the communications, and of the person authorizing the application; and

(e) the period of time during which such interception is authorized, including a statement as to whether or not the interception shall automatically terminate when the described communication has been first obtained.

An order authorizing the interception of a wire, oral, or electronic communication under this chapter shall, upon request of the applicant, direct that a provider of wire or electronic communication service, landlord, custodian or other person shall furnish the applicant forthwith all information, facilities, and technical assistance necessary to accomplish the interception unobtrusively and with a minimum of interference with the services that such service provider, landlord, custodian, or person is according the person whose communications are to be intercepted. Any provider of wire or electronic communication service, landlord, custodian or other person furnishing such facilities or technical assistance shall be compensated therefor by the applicant for reasonable expenses incurred in providing such facilities or assistance. Pursuant to section 2522 of this chapter, an order may also be issued to enforce the assistance capability and capacity requirements under the Communications Assistance for Law Enforcement Act.

(5) No order entered under this section may authorize or approve the interception of any wire, oral, or electronic communication for any period longer than is necessary to achieve the objective of the authorization, nor in any event longer than thirty days. Such thirty-day period begins on the earlier of the day on which the investigative or law enforcement officer first begins to conduct an interception under the order or ten days after the order is entered. Extensions of an order may be granted, but only upon application for an extension made in accordance with subsection (1) of this section and the court making the findings required by subsection (3) of this section. The period of extension shall be no longer than the authorizing judge deems necessary to achieve the purposes for which it was granted and in no event for longer than thirty days. Every order and extension thereof shall contain a provision that the authorization to intercept shall be executed as soon as practicable, shall be conducted in such a way as to minimize the interception of communications not otherwise subject to interception under this chapter, and must terminate upon attainment of the authorized objective, or in any event in thirty days. In the event the intercepted communication is in a code or foreign language, and an expert in that foreign language or code is not reasonably available during the interception period, minimization may be accomplished as soon as practicable after such interception. An interception under this chapter may be conducted in whole or in part by Government personnel, or by an individual operating under a contract with the Government, acting under the supervision of an investigative or law enforcement officer authorized to conduct the interception.

(6) Whenever an order authorizing interception is entered pursuant to this chapter, the order may require reports to be made to the judge who issued the order showing what progress has been made toward achievement of the authorized objective and the need for continued interception. Such reports shall be made at such intervals as the judge may require.

(7) Notwithstanding any other provision of this chapter, any investigative or law enforcement officer, specially designated by the Attorney General, the Deputy Attorney General, the Associate Attorney General or by the principal prosecuting attorney of any State or subdivision thereof acting pursuant to a statute of that State, who reasonably determines that—

    (a) an emergency situation exists that involves—

        (i) immediate danger of death or serious physical injury to any person,

        (ii) conspiratorial activities threatening the national security interest, or

        (iii) conspiratorial activities characteristic of organized crime,

that requires a wire, oral, or electronic communication to be intercepted before an order authorizing such interception can, with due diligence, be obtained, and

    (b) there are grounds upon which an order could be entered under this chapter to authorize such interception,

may intercept such wire, oral, or electronic communication if an application for an order approving the interception is made in accordance with this section within forty-eight hours after the interception has occurred, or begins to occur. In the absence of an order, such interception shall immediately terminate when the communication sought is obtained or when the application for the order is denied, whichever is earlier. In the event such application for approval is denied, or in any other case where the interception is terminated without an order having been issued, the contents of any wire, oral, or electronic communication intercepted shall be treated as having been obtained in violation of this chapter, and an inventory shall be served as provided for in subsection (d) of this section on the person named in the application.

(8)(a) The contents of any wire, oral, or electronic communication intercepted by any means authorized by this chapter shall, if possible, be recorded on tape or wire or other comparable device. The recording of the contents of any wire, oral, or electronic communication under this subsection shall be done in such way as will protect the recording from editing or other alterations. Immediately upon the expiration of the period of the order, or extensions thereof, such recordings shall be made available to the judge issuing such order and sealed under his directions. Custody of the recordings shall be wherever the judge orders. They shall not be destroyed except upon an order of the issuing or denying judge and in any event shall be kept for ten years. Duplicate recordings may be made for use or disclosure pursuant to the provisions of subsections (1) and (2) of section 2517 of this chapter for investigations. The presence of the seal provided for by this subsection, or a satisfactory explanation for the absence thereof, shall be a prerequisite for the use or disclosure of the contents of any wire, oral, or electronic communication or evidence derived therefrom under subsection (3) of section 2517.

(b) Applications made and orders granted under this chapter shall be sealed by the judge. Custody of the applications and orders shall be wherever the judge directs. Such applications and orders shall be disclosed only upon a showing of good cause before a judge of competent jurisdiction and shall not be destroyed except on order of the issuing or denying judge, and in any event shall be kept for ten years.

(c) Any violation of the provisions of this subsection may be punished as contempt of the issuing of (sic) denying judge.

(d) Within a reasonable time but not later than ninety days after the filing of an application for an order of approval under section 2518(7)(b) which is denied or the termination of the period of an order or extensions thereof, the issuing or denying judge shall cause to be served, on the persons named in the order or the application, and such other parties to intercepted communications as the judge may determine in his discretion that is in the interest of justice, an inventory which shall include notice of—

(1) the fact of the entry of the order or the application;

(2) the date of the entry and the period of authorized, approved or disapproved interception, or the denial of the application; and

(3) the fact that during the period wire, oral, or electronic communications were or were not intercepted.

The judge, upon the filing of a motion, may in his discretion make available to such person or his counsel for inspection such portions of the intercepted communications, applications and orders as the judge determines to be in the interest of justice. On an ex parte showing of good cause to a judge of competent jurisdiction the serving of the inventory required by this subsection may be postponed.

(9) The contents of any wire, oral, or electronic communication intercepted pursuant to this chapter or evidence derived therefrom shall not be received in evidence or otherwise disclosed in any trial, hearing, or other proceeding in a Federal or State court unless each party, not less than ten days before the trial, hearing, or proceeding, has been furnished with a copy of the court order, and accompanying application, under which the interception was authorized or approved. This ten-day period may be waived by the judge if he finds that it was not possible to furnish the party with the above information ten days before the trial,

hearing, or proceeding and that the party will not be prejudiced by the delay in receiving such information.

(10)(a) Any aggrieved person in any trial, hearing, or proceeding in or before any court, department, officer, agency, regulatory body, or other authority of the United States, a State, or a political subdivision thereof, may move to suppress the contents of any wire or oral communication intercepted pursuant to this chapter, or evidence derived therefrom, on the grounds that—

> (i) the communication was unlawfully intercepted;
>
> (ii) the order of authorization or approval under which it was intercepted is insufficient on its face; or
>
> (iii) the interception was not made in conformity with the order of authorization or approval.

Such motion shall be made before the trial, hearing, or proceeding unless there was no opportunity to make such motion or the person was not aware of the grounds of the motion. If the motion is granted, the contents of the intercepted wire or oral communication, or evidence derived therefrom, shall be treated as having been obtained in violation of this chapter. The judge, upon the filing of such motion by the aggrieved person, may in his discretion make available to the aggrieved person or his counsel for inspection such portions of the intercepted communication or evidence derived therefrom as the judge determines to be in the interests of justice.

> (b) In addition to any other right to appeal, the United States shall have the right to appeal from an order granting a motion to suppress made under paragraph (a) of this subsection, or the denial of an application for an order of approval, if the United States attorney shall certify to the judge or other official granting such motion or denying such application that the appeal is not taken for purposes of delay. Such appeal shall be taken within thirty days after the date the order was entered and shall be diligently prosecuted.
>
> (c) The remedies and sanctions described in this chapter with respect to the interception of electronic communications are the only judicial remedies and sanctions for nonconstitutional violations of this chapter involving such communications.

(11) The requirements of subsections (1)(b)(ii) and (3)(d) of this section relating to the specification of the facilities from which, or the place where, the communication is to be intercepted do not apply if—

> (a) in the case of an application with respect to the interception of an oral communication—
>
> > (i) the application is by a Federal investigative or law enforcement officer and is approved by the Attorney General, the Deputy Attorney General, the Associate Attorney

General, an Assistant Attorney General, or an acting Assistant Attorney General;

(ii) the application contains a full and complete statement as to why such specification is not practical and identifies the person committing the offense and whose communications are to be intercepted; and

(iii) the judge finds that such specification is not practical; and

(b) in the case of an application with respect to a wire or electronic communication—

(i) the application is by a Federal investigative or law enforcement officer and is approved by the Attorney general, the Deputy Attorney General, the Associate Attorney General, an Assistant Attorney General, or an acting Assistant Attorney General;

(ii) the application identifies the person believed to be committing the offense and whose communications are to be intercepted and the applicant makes a showing that there is probable cause to believe that the person's actions could have the effect of thwarting interception from a specified facility;

(iii) the judge finds that such showing has been adequately made; and

(iv) the order authorizing or approving the interception is limited to interception only for such time as it is reasonable to presume that the person identified in the application is or was reasonably proximate to the instrument through which such communication will be or was transmitted.

(12) An interception of a communication under an order with respect to which the requirements of subsections (1)(b)(ii) and (3)(d) of this section do not apply by reason of subsection (11)(a) shall not begin until the place where the communication is to be intercepted is ascertained by the person implementing the interception order. A provider of wire or electronic communications service that has received an order as provided for in subsection (11)(b) may move the court to modify or quash the order on the ground that its assistance with respect to the interception cannot be performed in a timely or reasonable fashion. The court, upon notice to the government, shall decide such a motion expeditiously.

Section 2519. Reports concerning intercepted wire, oral, or electronic communications

(1) Within thirty days after the expiration of an order (or each extension thereof) entered under section 2518, or the denial of an order

approving an interception, the issuing or denying judge shall report to the Administrative Office of the United States Courts—

(a) the fact that an order or extension was applied for;

(b) the kind of order or extension applied for (including whether or not the order was an order with respect to which the requirements of sections 3518(1)(b)(ii) and 2518(3)(d) of this title did not apply by reason of section 2518(11) of this title);

(c) the fact that the order or extension was granted as applied for, was modified, or was denied;

(d) the period of interceptions authorized by the order, and the number and duration of any extensions of the order;

(e) the offense specified in the order or application, or extension of an order;

(f) the identity of the applying investigative or law enforcement officer and agency making the application and the person authorizing the application; and

(g) the nature of the facilities from which or the place where communications were to be intercepted.

(2) In January of each year the Attorney General, an Assistant Attorney General specially designated by the Attorney General, or the principal prosecuting attorney of a State, or the principal prosecuting attorney for any political subdivision of a State, shall report to the Administrative Office of the United States Courts—

(a) the information required by paragraphs (a) through (g) of subsection (1) of this section with respect to each application for an order or extension made during the preceding calendar year;

(b) a general description of the interceptions made under such order or extension, including (i) the approximate nature and frequency of incriminating communications intercepted, (ii) the approximate nature and frequency of other communications intercepted, (iii) approximate number of persons whose communications were intercepted, and (iv) the approximate nature, amount, and cost of the manpower and other resources used in the interceptions;

(c) the number of arrests resulting from interceptions made under such order or extension, and the offenses for which arrests were made;

(d) the number of trials resulting from such interceptions;

(e) the number of motions to suppress made with respect to such interceptions, and the number granted or denied;

(f) the number of convictions resulting from such interceptions and the offenses for which the convictions were obtained and a general assessment of the importance of the interceptions; and

(g) the information required by paragraphs (b) through (f) of this subsection with respect to orders or extensions obtained in a preceding calendar year.

(3) In April of each year the Director of the Administrative Office of the United States Courts shall transmit to the Congress a full and complete report concerning the number of applications for orders authorizing or approving the interception of wire, oral, or electronic communications pursuant to this chapter and the number of orders and extensions granted or denied pursuant to this chapter during the preceding calendar year. Such report shall include a summary and analysis of the data required to be filed with the Administrative Office by subsections (1) and (2) of this section. The Director of the Administrative Office of the United States Courts is authorized to issue binding regulations dealing with the content and form of the reports required to be filed by subsections (1) and (2) of this section.

Section 2520. Recovery of civil damages authorized

(a) In general.—Except as provided in section 2511(2)(a)(ii), any person whose wire, oral, or electronic communication is intercepted, disclosed, or intentionally used in violation of this chapter may in a civil action recover from the person or entity which engaged in that violation such relief as may be appropriate.

(b) Relief.—In an action under this section, appropriate relief includes—

(1) such preliminary and other equitable or declaratory relief as may be appropriate;

(2) damages under subsection (c) and punitive damages in appropriate cases; and

(3) a reasonable attorney's fee and other litigation costs reasonably incurred.

(c) Computation of damages.—(1) In an action under this section, if the conduct in violation of this chapter is the private viewing of a private satellite video communication that is not scrambled or encrypted or if the communication is a radio communication that is transmitted on frequencies allocated under subpart D of part 74 of the rules of the Federal Communications Commission that is not scrambled or encrypted and the conduct is not for a tortious or illegal purpose or for purposes of direct or indirect commercial advantage or private commercial gain, then the court shall assess damages as follows:

(A) If the person who engaged in that conduct has not previously been enjoined under section 2511(5) and has not been found liable in a prior civil action under this section, the court shall assess the greater of the sum of actual damages suffered by the plaintiff, or statutory damages of not less than $50 and not more than $500.

(B) If, on one prior occasion, the person who engaged in that conduct has been enjoined under section 2511(5) or has been found liable in a civil action under this section, the court shall assess the greater of the sum of actual damages suffered by the plaintiff, or statutory damages of not less than $100 and not more than $1000.

(2) In any other action under this section, the court may assess as damages whichever is the greater of—

(A) the sum of the actual damages suffered by the plaintiff and any profits made by the violator as a result of the violation; or

(B) statutory damages of whichever is the greater of $100 a day for each day of violation or $10,000.

(d) **Defense.**—A good faith reliance on—

(1) a court warrant or order, a grand jury subpoena, a legislative authorization, or a statutory authorization;

(2) a request of an investigative or law enforcement officer under section 2518(7) of this title; or

(3) a good faith determination that section 2511(3) of this title permitted the conduct complained of;

is a complete defense against any civil or criminal action brought under this chapter or any other law.

(e) **Limitation.**—A civil action under this section may not be commenced later than two years after the date upon which the claimant first has a reasonable opportunity to discover the violation.

Section 2521. Injunction against illegal interception

Whenever it shall appear that any person is engaged or is about to engage in any act which constitutes or will constitute a felony violation of this chapter, the Attorney General may initiate a civil action in a district court of the United States to enjoin such violation. The court shall proceed as soon as practicable to the hearing and determination of such an action, and may, at any time before final determination, enter such a restraining order of prohibition, or take such other action, as warranted to prevent a continuing and substantial injury to the United States or to any person or class of persons for whose protection the action is brought. A proceeding under this section is governed by the Federal Rules of Civil Procedure, except that, if an indictment has been returned against the respondent, discovery is governed by the Federal Rules of Criminal Procedure.

B. TITLE II OF THE ELECTRONIC COMMUNI-CATIONS PRIVACY ACT OF 1986 (P.L. 99–508) (CODIFIED AT 18 U.S.C.A § 2701–2711 (1994))

2. CHAPTER 121. STORED WIRE AND ELECTRONIC COMMUNICATIONS AND TRANSACTIONAL RECORDS ACCESS

Section 2701. Unlawful access to stored communications

(a) Offense.—Except as provided in subsection (c) of this section whoever—

> (1) intentionally accesses without authorization a facility through which an electronic communication service is provided; or

> (2) intentionally exceeds an authorization to access that facility;

and thereby obtains, alters, or prevents authorized access to a wire or electronic communication while it is in electronic storage in such system shall be punished as provided in subsection (b) of this section.

(b) Punishment.—The punishment for an offense under subsection (a) of this section is—

> (1) if the offense is committed for purposes of commercial advantage, malicious destruction or damage, or private commercial gain—

>> (A) a fine under this title or imprisonment for not more than one year, or both, in the case of a first offense under this subparagraph; and

>> (B) a fine under this title or imprisonment for not more than two years, or both, for any subsequent offense under this subparagraph; and

> (2) a fine of not more than $5,000 or imprisonment for not more than six months, or both, in any other case.

(c) Exceptions.—Subsection (a) of this section does not apply with respect to conduct authorized—

(1) by the person or entity providing a wire or electronic communications service;

(2) by a user of that service with respect to a communication of or intended for that user; or

(3) in section 2703, 2704 or 2518 of this title.

Section 2702. Disclosure of contents

(a) Prohibitions.—Except as provided in subsection (b)—

(1) a person or entity providing an electronic communication service to the public shall not knowingly divulge to any person or entity the contents of a communication while in electronic storage by that service; and

(2) a person or entity providing remote computing service to the public shall not knowingly divulge to any person or entity the contents of any communication which is carried or maintained on that service—

(A) on behalf of, and received by means of electronic transmission from (or created by means of computer processing of communications received by means of electronic transmission from), a subscriber or customer of such service; and

(B) solely for the purpose of providing storage or computer processing services to such subscriber or customer, if the provider is not authorized to access the contents of any such communications for purposes of providing any services other than storage or computer processing.

(b) Exceptions.—A person or entity may divulge the contents of a communication—

(1) to an addressee or intended recipient of such communication or an agent of such addressee or intended recipient;

(2) as otherwise authorized in section 2517, 2511(2)(a), or 2703 of this title;

(3) with the lawful consent of the originator or an addressee or intended recipient of such communication, or the subscriber in the case of remote computing service;

(4) to a person employed or authorized or whose facilities are used to forward such communication to its destination;

(5) as may be necessarily incident to the rendition of the service or to the protection of the rights or property of the provider of that service; or

(6) to a law enforcement agency,

(A) if such contents—

(i) were inadvertently obtained by the service provider; and

(ii) appear to pertain to the commission of a crime; or

(B) if required by section 227 of the Crime Control Act of 1990 [42 U.S.C.A. § 13032].

Section 2703. Requirements for governmental access

(a) Contents of electronic communications in electronic storage.—A governmental entity may require the disclosure by a provider of electronic communication service of the contents of an electronic communication, that is in electronic storage in an electronic communications system for one hundred and eighty days or less, only pursuant to a warrant issued under the Federal Rules of Criminal Procedure or equivalent State warrant. A governmental entity may require the disclosure by a provider of electronic communications services of the contents of an electronic communication that has been in electronic storage in an electronic communications system for more than one hundred and eighty days by the means available under subsection (b) of this section.

(b) Contents of electronic communications in a remote computing service.—(1) A governmental entity may require a provider of remote computing service to disclose the contents of any electronic communication to which this paragraph is made applicable by paragraph (2) of this subsection—

(A) without required notice to the subscriber or customer, if the governmental entity obtains a warrant issued under the Federal Rules of Criminal Procedure or equivalent State warrant; or

(B) with prior notice from the governmental entity to the subscriber or customer if the governmental entity—

(i) uses an administrative subpoena authorized by a Federal or State statute or a Federal or State grand jury or trial subpoena; or

(ii) obtains a court order for such disclosure under subsection (d) of this section; except that delayed notice may be given pursuant to section 2705 of this title.

(2) Paragraph (1) is applicable with respect to any electronic communication that is held or maintained on that service—

(A) on behalf of, and received by means of electronic transmission from (or created by means of computer processing of communications received by means of electronic transmission from), a subscriber or customer of such remote computing service; and

(B) solely for the purpose of providing storage or computer processing services to such subscriber or customer, if the provider is not authorized to access the contents of any such communications for the purposes of providing any services other than storage or computer processing.

(c) Records concerning electronic communication service or remote computing service.—(1)(A) Except as provided in subparagraph (B), a provider of electronic communication service or remote computing service may disclose a record or other information pertaining to a subscriber to or customer of such service (not including the contents of communications covered by subsection (a) or (b) of this section) to any person other than a governmental entity.

(B) A provider of electronic communication service or remote computing service shall disclose a record or other information pertaining to a subscriber to or customer of such service (not including the contents of communications covered by subsection (a) or (b) of this section) to a governmental entity only when the governmental entity—

(i) obtains a warrant issued under the Federal Rules of Criminal Procedure or equivalent State warrant;

(ii) obtains a court order for such disclosure under subsection (d) of this section;

(iii) has the consent of the subscriber or customer to such disclosure; or

(iv) submits a formal written request relevant to a law enforcement investigation concerning telemarketing fraud for the name, address, and place of business of a subscriber or customer of such provider, which subscriber or customer is engaged in telemarketing (as such term is defined in section 2325 of this title).

(C) A provider of electronic communication service or remote computing service shall disclose to a governmental entity the name, address, local and long distance telephone toll billing records, telephone number or other subscriber number or identity, and length of service of a subscriber to or customer of such service and the types of services the subscriber or customer utilized, when the governmental entity uses an administrative subpoena authorized by a Federal or State statute or a Federal or State grand jury or trial subpoena or any means available under subparagraph (B).

(2) A governmental entity receiving records or information under this subsection is not required to provide notice to a subscriber or customer.

(d) Requirements for court order.—A court order for disclosure under subsection (b) or (c) may be issued by any court that is a court of competent jurisdiction described in section 3127(2)(A) and shall issue only if the governmental entity offers specific and articulable facts showing that there are reasonable grounds to believe that the contents of a wire or electronic communication, or the records or other information sought, are relevant and material to an ongoing criminal investigation. In the case of a State governmental authority, such a court order shall not issue if prohibited by the law of such State. A court issuing an order pursuant to this section, on a motion made promptly by the service provider, may quash or modify such order, if the information or records requested are unusually voluminous in nature or compliance with such order otherwise would cause an undue burden on such provider.

(e) No cause of action against a provider disclosing information under this chapter.—No cause of action shall lie in any court against any provider of wire or electronic communication service, its officers, employees, agents, or other specified persons for providing information, facilities, or assistance in accordance with the terms of a court order, warrant, subpoena, or certification under this chapter.

(f) Requirement to preserve evidence.—

(1) In general.—A provider of wire or electronic communication services or a remote computing service, upon the request of a governmental entity, shall take all necessary steps to preserve records and other evidence in its possession pending the issuance of a court order or other process.

(2) Period of retention.—Records referred to in paragraph (1) shall be retained for a period of 90 days, which shall be extended for an additional 90–day period upon a renewed request by the governmental entity.

Section 2704. Backup preservation

(a) Backup preservation.—(1) A governmental entity acting under section 2703(b)(2) may include in its subpoena or court order a requirement that the service provider to whom the request is directed create a backup copy of the contents of the electronic communications sought in order to preserve those communications. Without notifying the subscriber or customer of such subpoena or court order, such service provider shall create such backup copy as soon as practicable consistent with its regular business practices and shall confirm to the governmental entity that such backup copy has been made. Such backup copy shall be created within two business days after receipt by the service provider of the subpoena or court order.

(2) Notice to the subscriber or customer shall be made by the governmental entity within three days after receipt of such confirmation, unless such notice is delayed pursuant to section 2705(a).

(3) The service provider shall not destroy such backup copy until the later of—

(A) the delivery of the information; or

(B) the resolution of any proceedings (including appeals of any proceeding) concerning the government's subpoena or court order.

(4) The service provider shall release such backup copy to the requesting governmental entity no sooner than fourteen days after the governmental entity's notice to the subscriber or customer if such service provider—

(A) has not received notice from the subscriber or customer that the subscriber or customer has challenged the governmental entity's request; and

(B) has not initiated proceedings to challenge the request of the governmental entity.

(5) A governmental entity may seek to require the creation of a backup copy under subsection (a)(1) of this section if in its sole discretion such entity determines that there is reason to believe that notification under section 2703 of this title of the existence of the subpoena or court order may result in destruction of or tampering with evidence. This determination is not subject to challenge by the subscriber or customer or service provider.

(b) Customer challenges.—(1) Within fourteen days after notice by the governmental entity to the subscriber or customer under subsection (a)(2) of this section, such subscriber or customer may file a motion to quash such subpoena or vacate such court order, with copies served upon the governmental entity and with written notice of such challenge to the service provider. A motion to vacate a court order shall be filed in the court which issued such order. A motion to quash a subpoena shall be filed in the appropriate United States district court or State court. Such motion or application shall contain an affidavit or sworn statement—

(A) stating that the applicant is a customer or subscriber to the service from which the contents of electronic communications maintained for him have been sought; and

(B) stating the applicant's reasons for believing that the records sought are not relevant to a legitimate law enforcement inquiry or that there has not been substantial compliance with the provisions of this chapter in some other respect.

(2) Service shall be made under this section upon a governmental entity by delivering or mailing by registered or certified mail a copy of the papers to the person, office, or department specified in the notice which the customer has received pursuant to this chapter. For the purposes of this section, the term "delivery" has the meaning given that term in the Federal Rules of Civil Procedure.

(3) If the court finds that the customer has complied with paragraphs (1) and (2) of this subsection, the court shall order the governmental entity to file a sworn response, which may be filed in camera if the governmental entity includes in its response the reasons which make in camera review appropriate. If the court is unable to determine the motion or application on the basis of the parties' initial allegations and response, the court may conduct such additional proceedings as it deems appropriate. All such proceedings shall be completed and the motion or application decided as soon as practicable after the filing of the governmental entity's response.

(4) If the court finds that the applicant is not the subscriber or customer for whom the communications sought by the governmental entity are maintained, or that there is a reason to believe that the law enforcement inquiry is legitimate and that the communications sought are relevant to that inquiry, it shall deny the motion or application and order such process enforced. If the court finds that the applicant is the subscriber or customer for whom the communications sought by the governmental entity are maintained, and that there is not a reason to believe that the communications sought are relevant to a legitimate law enforcement inquiry, or that there has not been substantial compliance with the provisions of this chapter, it shall order the process quashed.

(5) A court order denying a motion or application under this section shall not be deemed a final order and no interlocutory appeal may be taken therefrom by the customer.

Section 2705. Delayed notice

(a) **Delay of notification.**—(1) A governmental entity acting under section 2703(b) of this title may—

(A) where a court order is sought, include in the application a request, which the court shall grant, for an order delaying the notification required under section 2703(b) of this title for a period not to exceed ninety days, if the court determines that there is reason to believe that notification of the existence of the court order may have an adverse result described in paragraph (2) of this subsection; or

(B) where an administrative subpoena authorized by a Federal or State statute or a Federal or State grand jury subpoena is obtained, delay the notification required under section 2703(b) of this title for a period not to exceed ninety days upon the execution of a written certification of a supervisory official that there is reason to believe that notification of the existence of the subpoena may have an adverse result described in paragraph (2) of this subsection.

(2) An adverse result for the purposes of paragraph (1) of this subsection is—

(A) endangering the life or physical safety of an individual;

(B) flight from prosecution;

(C) destruction of or tampering with evidence;

(D) intimidation of potential witnesses; or

(E) otherwise seriously jeopardizing an investigation or unduly delaying a trial.

(3) The governmental entity shall maintain a true copy of certification under paragraph (1)(B).

(4) Extensions of the delay of notification provided in section 2703 of up to ninety days each may be granted by the court upon application, or by certification by a governmental entity, but only in accordance with subsection (b) of this section.

(5) Upon expiration of the period of delay of notification under paragraph (1) or (4) of this subsection, the governmental entity shall serve upon, or deliver by registered or first-class mail to, the customer or subscriber a copy of the process or request together with notice that—

(A) states with reasonable specificity the nature of the law enforcement inquiry; and

(B) informs such customer or subscriber—

(i) that information maintained for such customer or subscriber by the service provider named in such process or request was supplied to or requested by that governmental authority and the date on which the supplying or request took place;

(ii) that notification of such customer or subscriber was delayed;

(iii) what governmental entity or court made the certification or determination pursuant to which that delay was made; and

(iv) which provision of this chapter allowed such delay.

(6) As used in this subsection, the term "supervisory official" means the investigative agent in charge or assistant investigative agent in charge or an equivalent of an investigating agency's headquarters or regional office, or the chief prosecuting attorney or the first assistant prosecuting attorney or an equivalent of a prosecuting attorney's headquarters or regional office.

(b) Preclusion of notice to subject of governmental access.—
A governmental entity acting under section 2703, when it is not required
to notify the subscriber or customer under section 2703(b)(1), or to the
extent that it may delay such notice pursuant to subsection (a) of this
section, may apply to a court for an order commanding a provider of
electronic communications service or remote computing service to whom
a warrant, subpoena, or court order is directed, for such period as the
court deems appropriate, not to notify any other person of the existence
of the warrant, subpoena, or court order. The court shall enter such an
order if it determines that there is reason to believe that notification of
the existence of the warrant, subpoena, or court order will result in—

(1) endangering the life or physical safety of an individual;

(2) flight from prosecution;

(3) destruction of or tampering with evidence;

(4) intimidation of potential witnesses; or

(5) otherwise seriously jeopardizing an investigation or unduly delaying a trial.

Section 2706. Cost reimbursement

(a) Payment.—Except as otherwise provided in subsection (c), a
governmental entity obtaining the contents of communications, records,
or other information under section 2702, 2703, or 2704 of this title shall
pay to the person or entity assembling or providing such information a
fee for reimbursement for such costs as are reasonably necessary and
which have been directly incurred in searching for, assembling, reproducing, or otherwise providing such information. Such reimbursable
costs shall include any costs due to necessary disruption of normal
operations of any electronic communication service or remote computing
service in which such information may be stored.

(b) Amount.—The amount of the fee provided by subsection (a)
shall be as mutually agreed by the governmental entity and the person
or entity providing the information, or, in the absence of an agreement,
shall be as determined by the court which issued the order for production of such information (or the court before which a criminal prosecution relating to such information would be brought, if no court order was
issued for production of the information).

(c) Exception.—The requirement of subsection (a) of this section
does not apply with respect to records or other information maintained
by a communications common carrier that relate to telephone toll
records and telephone listings obtained under section 2703 of this title.
The court may, however, order a payment as described in subsection (a)
if the court determines the information required is unusually voluminous in nature or otherwise caused an undue burden on the provider.

Section 2707. Civil action

(a) Cause of action.—Except as provided in section 2703(e), any
provider of electronic communication service, subscriber, or customer

aggrieved by any violation of this chapter in which the conduct constituting the violation is engaged in with a knowing or intentional state of mind may, in a civil action, recover from the person or entity which engaged in that violation such relief as may be appropriate.

(b) Relief.—In a civil action under this section, appropriate relief includes—

(1) such preliminary and other equitable or declaratory relief as may be appropriate;

(2) damages under subsection (c); and

(3) a reasonable attorney's fee and other litigation costs reasonably incurred.

(c) Damages.—The court may assess as damages in a civil action under this section the sum of the actual damages suffered by the plaintiff and any profits made by the violator as a result of the violation, but in no case shall a person entitled to recover receive less than the sum of $1,000. If the violation is willful or intentional, the court may assess punitive damages. In the case of a successful action to enforce liability under this section, the court may assess the costs of the action, together with reasonable attorney fees determined by the court.

(d) Disciplinary actions for violations.—If a court determines that any agency or department of the United States has violated this chapter and the court finds that the circumstances surrounding the violation raise the question whether or not an officer or employee of the agency or department acted willfully or intentionally with respect to the violation, the agency or department concerned shall promptly initiate a proceeding to determine whether or not disciplinary action is warranted against the officer or employee.

(e) Defense.—A good faith reliance on—

(1) a court warrant or order, a grand jury subpoena, a legislative authorization, or a statutory authorization;

(2) a request of an investigative or law enforcement officer under section 2518(7) of this title; or

(3) a good faith determination that section 2511(3) of this title permitted the conduct complained of;

is a complete defense to any civil or criminal action brought under this chapter or any other law.

(f) Limitation. A civil action under this section may not be commenced later than two years after the date upon which the claimant first discovered or had a reasonable opportunity to discover the violation.

Section 2708. Exclusivity of remedies

The remedies and sanctions described in this chapter are the only judicial remedies and sanctions for nonconstitutional violations of this chapter.

Section 2709. Counterintelligence access to telephone toll and transactional records

(a) **Duty to provide.**—A wire or electronic communication service provider shall comply with a request for subscriber information and toll billing records information, or electronic communication transactional records in its custody or possession made by the Director of the Federal Bureau of Investigation under subsection (b) of this section.

(b) **Required certification.**—The Director of the Federal Bureau of Investigation, or his designee in a position not lower than Deputy Assistant Director, may—

(1) request the name, address, length of service, and local and long distance toll billing records of a person or entity if the Director (or his designee in a position not lower than Deputy Assistant Director) certifies in writing to the wire or electronic communication service provider to which the request is made that—

(A) The name, address, length of service, and toll billing records sought are relevant to an authorized foreign counterintelligence investigation; and

(B) there are specific and articulable facts giving reason to believe that the person or entity to whom the information sought pertains is a foreign power or an agent of a foreign power as defined in section 101 of the Foreign Intelligence Surveillance Act of 1978 (50 U.S.C. 1801); and

(2) request the name, address, and length of service of a person or entity if the Director (or his designee in a position not lower than Deputy Assistant Director) certifies in writing to the wire or electronic communication service provider to which the request is made that—

(A) the information sought is relevant to an authorized foreign counterintelligence investigation; and

(B) there are specific and articulable facts giving reason to believe that communication facilities registered in the name of the person or entity have been used, through the services of such provider, in communication with—

(i) an individual who is engaging or has engaged in international terrorism as defined in section 101(c) of the Foreign Intelligence Surveillance Act or clandestine intelligence activities that involve or may involve a violation of the criminal statutes of the United States; or

(ii) a foreign power or an agent of a foreign power under circumstances giving reason to believe that the communication concerned international terrorism as defined in section 101(c) of the Foreign Intelligence Surveillance Act or clandestine intelligence activities that involve or may involve a violation of the criminal statutes of the United States.

(c) Prohibition of certain disclosure.—No wire or electronic communication service provider, or officer, employee, or agent thereof, shall disclose to any person that the Federal Bureau of Investigation has sought or obtained access to information or records under this section.

(d) Dissemination by bureau.—The Federal Bureau of Investigation may disseminate information and records obtained under this section only as provided in guidelines approved by the Attorney General for foreign intelligence collection and foreign counterintelligence investigations conducted by the Federal Bureau of Investigation, and, with respect to dissemination to an agency of the United States, only if such information is clearly relevant to the authorized responsibilities of such agency.

Section 2710. Wrongful disclosure of video tape rental or sale records

(a) Definitions.—For purposes of this section—

(1) the term "consumer" means any renter, purchaser, or subscriber of goods or services from a video tape service provider;

(2) the term "ordinary course of business" means only debt collection activities, order fulfillment, request processing, and the transfer of ownership;

(3) the term "personally identifiable information" includes information which identifies a person as having requested or obtained specific video materials or services from a video tape service provider; and

(4) the term "video tape service provider" means any person engaged in the business, in or affecting interstate or foreign commerce, of rental, sale, or delivery of prerecorded video cassette tapes or similar audio visual materials, or any person or other entity to whom a disclosure is made under subparagraph (D) or (E) of subsection (b)(2), but only with respect to the information contained in the disclosure.

(b) Video tape rental and sale records.—(1) A video tape service provider who knowingly discloses, to any person, personally identifiable information concerning any consumer of such provider shall be liable to the aggrieved person for the relief provided in subsection (d).

(2) A video tape service provider may disclose personally identifiable information concerning any consumer—

(A) to the consumer;

(B) to any person with the informed, written consent of the consumer given at the time the disclosure is sought;

(C) to a law enforcement agency pursuant to a warrant issued under the Federal Rules of Criminal Procedure, an equivalent State warrant, a grand jury subpoena, or a court order;

(D) to any person if the disclosure is solely of the names and addresses of consumers and if—

(i) the video tape service provider has provided the consumer with the opportunity, in a clear and conspicuous manner, to prohibit such disclosure; and

(ii) the disclosure does not identify the title, description, or subject matter of any video tapes or other audio visual material; however, the subject matter of such materials may be disclosed if the disclosure is for the exclusive use of marketing goods and services directly to the consumer.

(E) to any person if the disclosure is incident to the ordinary course of business of the video tape service provider; or

(F) pursuant to a court order, in a civil proceeding upon a showing of compelling need for the information that cannot be accommodated by any other means, if—

(i) the consumer is given reasonable notice, by the person seeking the disclosure, of the court proceeding relevant to the issuance of the court order; and

(ii) the consumer is afforded the opportunity to appear and contest the claim of the person seeking the disclosure.

If an order is granted pursuant to subparagraph (C) or (F), the court shall impose appropriate safeguards against unauthorized disclosure.

(3) Court orders authorizing disclosure under subparagraph (C) shall issue only with prior notice to the consumer and only if the law enforcement agency shows that there is probable cause to believe that the records or other information sought are relevant to a legitimate law enforcement inquiry. In the case of a State government authority, such a court order shall not issue if prohibited by the law of such State. A court issuing an order pursuant to this section, on a motion made promptly by the video tape service provider, may quash or modify such order if the information or records requested are unreasonably voluminous in nature or if compliance with such order otherwise would cause an unreasonable burden on such provider.

(c) Civil action.—(1) Any person aggrieved by any act of a person in violation of this section may bring a civil action in a United States district court.

(2) The court may award—

(A) actual damages but not less than liquidated damages in an amount of $2,500;

(B) punitive damages;

(C) reasonable attorneys' fees and other litigation costs reasonably incurred; and

(D) such other preliminary and equitable relief as the court determines to be appropriate.

(3) No action may be brought under this subsection unless such action is begun within 2 years from the date of the act complained of or the date of discovery.

(4) No liability shall result from lawful disclosure permitted by this section.

(d) Personally identifiable information.—Personally identifiable information obtained in any manner other than as provided in this section shall not be received in evidence in any trial, hearing, arbitration, or other proceeding in or before any court, grand jury, department, officer, agency, regulatory body, legislative committee or other authority of the United States, a State, or a political subdivision of a State.

(e) Destruction of old records.—A person subject to this section shall destroy personally identifiable information as soon as practicable, but no later than one year from the date the information is no longer necessary for the purpose for which it was collected and there are no pending requests or orders for access to such information under subsection (b)(2) or (c)(2) or pursuant to a court order.

(f) Preemption.—The provisions of this section preempt only the provisions of State or local law that require disclosure prohibited by this section.

Section 2711. Definitions for chapter

As used in this chapter—

(1) the terms defined in section 2510 of this title have, respectively, the definitions given such terms in that section; and

(2) the term "remote computing service" means the provision to the public of computer storage or processing services by means of an electronic communications system.

3. SEARCHES AND SEIZURES [18 U.S.C.A. § 3117 (LAW. COOP. 1979 & SUPP. 1991)]

Section 3117. Mobile tracking devices.

Section 3117. Mobile tracking devices

(a) In general.—If a court is empowered to issue a warrant or other order for the installation of a mobile tracking device, such order may authorize the use of that device within the jurisdiction of the court, and outside that jurisdiction if the device is installed in that jurisdiction.

(b) **Definition.**—As used in this section, the term "tracking device" means an electronic or mechanical device which permits the tracking of the movement of a person or object.

C. TITLE III OF THE ELECTRONIC COMMUNICATIONS PRIVACY ACT OF 1986 (PUB.L. 99–508) (CODIFIED AT 18 U.S.C.A. §§ 3121–3127 (1994))

4. CHAPTER 206. PEN REGISTERS AND TRAP AND TRACE DEVICES

Section

Section 3121. General prohibition on pen register and trap and trace device use; exception

(a) **In general.**—Except as provided in this section, no person may install or use a pen register or a trap and trace device without first obtaining a court order under section 3123 of this title or under the Foreign Intelligence Surveillance Act of 1978 (50 U.S.C.A. § 1801 et seq.).

(b) **Exception.**—The prohibition of subsection (a) does not apply with respect to the use of a pen register or a trap and trace device by a provider of electronic or wire communication service—

(1) relating to the operation, maintenance, and testing of a wire or electronic communication service or to the protection of the rights or property of such provider, or to the protection of users of that service from abuse of service or unlawful use of service; or

(2) to record the fact that a wire or electronic communication was initiated or completed in order to protect such provider, another provider furnishing service toward the completion of the wire communication, or a user of that service, from fraudulent, unlawful or abusive use of service; or

(3) where the consent of the user of that service has been obtained.

(c) Limitation.—A government agency authorized to install and use a pen register under this chapter or under State law shall use technology reasonably available to it that restricts the recording or decoding of electronic or other impulses to the dialing and signaling information utilized in call processing.

(d) Penalty.—Whoever knowingly violates subsection (a) shall be fined under this title or imprisoned not more than one year, or both.

Section 3122. Application for an order for a pen register or a trap and trace device

(a) Application.—(1) An attorney for the Government may make application for an order or an extension of an order under section 3123 of this title authorizing or approving the installation and use of a pen register or a trap and trace device under this chapter, in writing under oath or equivalent affirmation, to a court of competent jurisdiction.

(2) Unless prohibited by State law, a State investigative or law enforcement officer may make application for an order or an extension of an order under section 3123 of this title authorizing or approving the installation and use of a pen register or a trap and trace device under this chapter, in writing under oath or equivalent affirmation, to a court of competent jurisdiction of such State.

(b) Contents of application.—An application under subsection (a) of this section shall include—

(1) the identity of the attorney for the Government or the State law enforcement or investigative officer making the application and the identity of the law enforcement agency conducting the investigation; and

(2) a certification by the applicant that the information likely to be obtained is relevant to an ongoing criminal investigation being conducted by that agency.

Section 3123. Issuance of an order for a pen register or a trap and trace device

(a) In general.—Upon an application under section 3122 of this title, the court shall enter an ex parte order authorizing the installation and use of a pen register or a trap and trace device within the jurisdiction of the court if the court finds that the attorney for the Government or the State law enforcement or investigative officer has certified to the court that the information likely to be obtained by such installation and use is relevant to an ongoing criminal investigation.

(b) Contents of order.—An order issued under this section—

(1) shall specify—

(A) the identity, if known, of the person to whom is leased or in whose name is listed the telephone line to which the pen register or trap and trace device is to be attached;

(B) the identity, if known, of the person who is the subject of the criminal investigation;

(C) the number and, if known, physical location of the telephone line to which the pen register or trap and trace device is to be attached and, in the case of a trap and trace device, the geographic limits of the trap and trace order; and

(D) a statement of the offense to which the information likely to be obtained by the pen register or trap and trace device relates; and

(2) shall direct, upon the request of the applicant, the furnishing of information, facilities, and technical assistance necessary to accomplish the installation of the pen register or trap and trace device under section 3124 of this title.

(c) Time period and extensions.—(1) An order issued under this section shall authorize the installation and use of a pen register or a trap and trace device for a period not to exceed sixty days.

(2) Extensions of such an order may be granted, but only upon an application for an order under section 3122 of this title and upon the judicial finding required by subsection (a) of this section. The period of extension shall be for a period not to exceed sixty days.

(d) Nondisclosure of existence of pen register or a trap and trace device.—An order authorizing or approving the installation and use of a pen register or a trap and trace device shall direct that—

(1) the order be sealed until otherwise ordered by the court; and

(2) the person owning or leasing the line to which the pen register or a trap and trace device is attached, or who has been ordered by the court to provide assistance to the applicant, not disclose the existence of the pen register or trap and trace device or the existence of the investigation to the listed subscriber, or to any other person, unless or until otherwise ordered by the court.

Section 3124. Assistance in installation and use of a pen register or a trap and trace device.

(a) Pen registers.—Upon the request of an attorney for the government or an officer of a law enforcement agency authorized to install and use a pen register under this chapter, a provider of wire or electronic communication service, landlord, custodian, or other person shall furnish such investigative or law enforcement officer forthwith all information, facilities, and technical assistance necessary to accomplish the installation of the pen register unobtrusively and with a minimum of interference with the services that the person so ordered by the court accords the party with respect to whom the installation and use is to take place, if such assistance is directed by a court order as provided in section 3123(b)(2) of this title.

(b) Trap and trace device.—Upon the request of an attorney for the Government or an officer of a law enforcement agency authorized to receive the results of a trap and trace device under this chapter, a provider of a wire or electronic communication service, landlord, custodian, or other person shall install such device forthwith on the appropriate line and shall furnish such investigative or law enforcement officer all additional information, facilities and technical assistance including installation and operation of the device unobtrusively and with a minimum of interference with the services that the person so ordered by the court accords the party with respect to whom the installation and use is to take place, if such installation and assistance is directed by a court order as provided in section 3123(b)(2) of this title. Unless otherwise ordered by the court, the results of the trap and trace device shall be furnished, pursuant to section 3123(b) or section 3125 of this title, to the officer of a law enforcement agency, designated in the court order, at reasonable intervals during regular business hours for the duration of the order.

(c) Compensation.—A provider of a wire or electronic communication service, landlord, custodian, or other person who furnishes facilities or technical assistance pursuant to this section shall be reasonably compensated for such reasonable expenses incurred in providing such facilities and assistance.

(d) No cause of action against a provider disclosing information under this chapter.—No cause of action shall lie in any court against any provider of a wire or electronic communication service, its officers, employees, agents, or other specified persons for providing information, facilities, or assistance in accordance with the terms of a court order under this chapter or request pursuant to section 3125 of this title.

(e) Defense.—A good faith reliance on a court order, under this chapter, a request pursuant to section 3125 of this title, a legislative authorization, or a statutory authorization is a complete defense against any civil or criminal action brought under this chapter or any other law.

Section 3125. Emergency pen register and trap and trace device installation

(a) Notwithstanding any other provision of this chapter [18 U.S.C.A. §§ 3121 et seq.], any investigative or law enforcement officer, specially designated by the Attorney General, the Deputy Attorney General, the Associate Attorney General, any Assistant Attorney General, any acting Assistant Attorney General, or any Deputy Assistant Attorney General, or by the principal prosecuting attorney of any State or subdivision thereof acting pursuant to a statute of that State, who reasonably determines that—

(1) an emergency situation exists that involves—

(A) immediate danger of death or serious bodily injury to any person; or

(B) conspiratorial activities characteristic of organized crime, that requires the installation and use of a pen register or a trap and trace device before an order authorizing such installation and use can, with due diligence, be obtained, and

(2) there are grounds upon which an order could be entered under this chapter [18 U.S.C.A. §§ 3121 et seq.] to authorize such installation and use may have installed and use a pen register or trap and trace device if, within forty-eight hours after the installation has occurred, or begins to occur, an order approving the installation or use is issued in accordance with section 3123 of this title.

(b) In the absence of an authorizing order, such use shall immediately terminate when the information sought is obtained, when the application for the order is denied or when forty-eight hours have lapsed since the installation of the pen register or trap and trace device, whichever is earlier.

(c) The knowing installation or use by any investigative or law enforcement officer of a pen register or trap and trace device pursuant to subsection (a) without application for the authorizing order within forty-eight hours of the installation shall constitute a violation of this chapter [18 U.S.C.A. §§ 3121 et seq.].

(d) A provider for a wire or electronic service, landlord, custodian, or other person who furnished facilities or technical assistance pursuant to this section shall be reasonably compensated for such reasonable expenses incurred in providing such facilities and assistance.

Section 3126. Reports concerning pen registers and trap and trace devices.

The Attorney General shall annually report to Congress on the number of pen register orders and orders for trap and trace devices applied for by law enforcement agencies of the Department of Justice.

Section 3127. Definitions for chapter.

As used in this chapter—

(1) the terms "wire communication," "electronic communication," and "electronic communication service" have the meanings set forth for such terms in section 2510 of this title;

(2) the term "court of competent jurisdiction" means—

(A) a district court of the United States (including a magistrate of such a court) or a United States Court of Appeals; or

(B) a court of general criminal jurisdiction of a State authorized by the law of that State to enter orders authorizing the use of a pen register or a trap and trace device;

(3) the term "pen register" means a device which records or decodes electronic or other impulses which identify the numbers dialed or otherwise transmitted on the telephone line to which such device is attached, but such term does not include any device used by a provider or customer of a wire or electronic communication service for billing, or recording as an incident to billing, for communications services provided by such provider or any device used by a provider or customer of a wire communication service for cost accounting or other like purposes in the ordinary course of its business;

(4) the term "trap and trace device" means a device which captures the incoming electronic or other impulses which identify the originating number of an instrument or device from which a wire or electronic communication was transmitted;

(5) the term "attorney for the Government" has the meaning given such term for the purposes of the Federal Rules of Criminal Procedure; and

(6) the term "State" means a State, the District of Columbia, Puerto Rico, and any other possession or territory of the United States.

D.   FEDERAL FREEDOM OF INFORMATION ACT 5 U.S.C.A. § 552 (WEST 1996)

§ 552.   Public information; agency rules, opinions, orders, records, and proceedings

(a) Each agency shall make available to the public information as follows:

(1) Each agency shall separately state and currently publish in the Federal Register for the guidance of the public—

(A) descriptions of its central and field organization and the established places at which, the employees (and in the case of a uniformed service, the members) from whom, and the methods whereby, the public may obtain information, make submittals or requests, or obtain decisions;

(B) statements of the general course and method by which its functions are channeled and determined, including the nature and requirements of all formal and informal procedures available;

(C) rules of procedure, descriptions of forms available or the places at which forms may be obtained, and instructions as to the scope and contents of all papers, reports, or examinations;

(D) substantive rules of general applicability adopted as authorized by law, and statements of general policy or interpretations of general applicability formulated and adopted by the agency; and

(E) each amendment, revision, or repeal of the foregoing.

Except to the extent that a person has actual and timely notice of the terms thereof, a person may not in any manner be required to resort to, or be adversely affected by, a matter required to be published in the Federal Register and not so published. For the purpose of this paragraph, matter reasonably available to the class of persons affected thereby is deemed published in the Federal Register when incorporated by reference therein with the approval of the Director of the Federal Register.

(2) Each agency, in accordance with published rules, shall make available for public inspection and copying—

(A) final opinions, including concurring and dissenting opinions, as well as orders, made in the adjudication of cases;

(B) those statements of policy and interpretations which have been adopted by the agency and are not published in the Federal Register;

(C) administrative staff manuals and instructions to staff that affect a member of the public;

(D) copies of all records, regardless of form or format, which have been released to any person under paragraph (3) and which, because of the nature of their subject matter, the agency determines have become or are likely to become the subject of subsequent requests for substantially the same records; and

(E) a general index of the records referred to under subparagraph (D);

unless the materials are promptly published and copies offered for sale. For records created on or after November 1, 1996, within one year after such date, each agency shall make such records available, including by computer telecommunications or, if computer telecommunications means have not been established by the agency, by other electronic means. To the extent required to prevent a clearly unwarranted invasion of personal privacy, an agency may delete identifying details when it makes available or publishes an opinion, statement of policy, interpretation, staff manual, instruction, or copies of records referred to in subparagraph (D). However, in each case the justification for the deletion shall be explained fully in writing, and the extent of such deletion shall be indicated on the portion of the record which is made available or published, unless including that indication would harm an interest protected by the exemption in subsection (b) under which the deletion is made. If technically feasible, the extent of the deletion shall be indicated at the place in the record where the deletion was made. Each agency shall also maintain and make available for public inspection and copying current indexes providing identifying information for the public as to any matter issued, adopted, or promulgated after July 4, 1967, and required by this paragraph to be made available or published. Each agency shall promptly publish, quarterly or more frequently, and distribute (by sale or otherwise) copies of each index or supplements thereto unless it determines by order published in the Federal Register that the publication would be unnecessary and impracticable, in which case the agency shall nonetheless provide copies of such index on request at a cost not to exceed the direct cost of duplication. Each agency shall make the index referred to in subparagraph (E) available by computer telecommunications by December 31, 1999. A final order, opinion, statement of policy, interpretation, or staff manual or instruction that affects a member of the public may be relied on, used, or cited as precedent by an agency against a party other than an agency only if—

> **(i)** it has been indexed and either made available or published as provided by this paragraph; or

> **(ii)** the party has actual and timely notice of the terms thereof.

(3)(A) Except with respect to the records made available under paragraphs (1) and (2) of this subsection, each agency, upon any request for records which (i) reasonably describes such records and (ii) is made in accordance with published rules stating the time, place, fees (if any), and procedures to be followed, shall make the records promptly available to any person.

(B) In making any record available to a person under this paragraph, an agency shall provide the record in any form or format requested by the person if the record is readily reproducible by the agency in that form or format. Each agency shall make reasonable efforts to maintain its records in forms or formats that are reproducible for purposes of this section.

(C) In responding under this paragraph to a request for records, an agency shall make reasonable efforts to search for the records in electronic form or format, except when such efforts would significantly interfere with the operation of the agency's automated information system.

(D) For purposes of this paragraph, the term "search" means to review, manually or by automated means, agency records for the purpose of locating those records which are responsive to a request.

(4)(A)(i) In order to carry out the provisions of this section, each agency shall promulgate regulations, pursuant to notice and receipt of public comment, specifying the schedule of fees applicable to the processing of requests under this section and establishing procedures and guidelines for determining when such fees should be waived or reduced. Such schedule shall conform to the guidelines which shall be promulgated, pursuant to notice and receipt of public comment, by the Director of the Office of Management and Budget and which shall provide for a uniform schedule of fees for all agencies.

(ii) Such agency regulations shall provide that—

(I) fees shall be limited to reasonable standard charges for document search, duplication, and review, when records are requested for commercial use;

(II) fees shall be limited to reasonable standard charges for document duplication when records are not sought for commercial use and the request is made by an educational or noncommercial scientific institution, whose purpose is scholarly or scientific research; or a representative of the news media; and

(III) for any request not described in (I) or (II), fees shall be limited to reasonable standard charges for document search and duplication.

(iii) Documents shall be furnished without any charge or at a charge reduced below the fees established under clause (ii) if disclosure of the information is in the public interest because it is likely to contribute significantly to public understanding of the operations or activities of the government and is not primarily in the commercial interest of the requester.

(iv) Fee schedules shall provide for the recovery of only the direct costs of search, duplication, or review. Review costs shall include only the direct costs incurred during the initial examination of a document for the purposes of determining whether the documents must be disclosed under this section and for the purposes of withholding any portions exempt from disclosure under this section. Review costs may not include any costs incurred in resolving issues of law or policy that may be raised in the course of processing a request under this section. No fee may be charged by any agency under this section—

(I) if the costs of routine collection and processing of the fee are likely to equal or exceed the amount of the fee; or

(II) for any request described in clause (ii)(II) or (III) of this subparagraph for the first two hours of search time or for the first one hundred pages of duplication.

(v) No agency may require advance payment of any fee unless the requester has previously failed to pay fees in a timely fashion, or the agency has determined that the fee will exceed $250.

(vi) Nothing in this subparagraph shall supersede fees chargeable under a statute specifically providing for setting the level of fees for particular types of records.

(vii) In any action by a requester regarding the waiver of fees under this section, the court shall determine the matter de novo: *Provided*, That the court's review of the matter shall be limited to the record before the agency.

(B) On complaint, the district court of the United States in the district in which the complainant resides, or has his principal place of business, or in which the agency records are situated, or in the District of Columbia, has jurisdiction to enjoin the agency from withholding agency records and to order the production of any agency records improperly withheld from the complainant. In such a case the court shall determine the matter de novo, and may examine the contents of such agency records in camera to determine whether such records or any part thereof shall be withheld under any of the exemptions set forth in subsection (b) of this section, and the burden is on the agency to sustain its action. In addition to any other matters to which a court accords substantial weight, a court shall accord substantial weight to an affidavit of an agency concerning the agency's determination as to technical feasibility under paragraph (2)(C) and subsection (b) and reproducibility under paragraph (3)(B).

(C) Notwithstanding any other provision of law, the defendant shall serve an answer or otherwise plead to any complaint made under this subsection within thirty days after service upon the defendant of the pleading in which such complaint is made, unless the court otherwise directs for good cause shown.

[**(D)** Repealed. Pub.L. 98–620, Title IV, § 402(2), Nov. 8, 1984, 98 Stat. 3357]

(E) The court may assess against the United States reasonable attorney fees and other litigation costs reasonably incurred in any case under this section in which the complainant has substantially prevailed.

(F) Whenever the court orders the production of any agency records improperly withheld from the complainant and assesses against the United States reasonable attorney fees and other litigation costs, and the court additionally issues a written finding that the circumstances surrounding the withholding raise questions whether agency personnel acted arbitrarily or capriciously with respect to the withholding, the Special Counsel shall promptly initiate a proceeding to determine whether disciplinary action is warranted against the officer or employee who was primarily responsible for the withholding. The Special Counsel, after investigation and consideration of the evidence submitted, shall submit his findings and recommendations to the administrative authority of the agency concerned and shall send copies of the findings and recommendations to the officer or employee or his representative. The administrative authority shall take the corrective action that the Special Counsel recommends.

(G) In the event of noncompliance with the order of the court, the district court may punish for contempt the responsible employee, and in the case of a uniformed service, the responsible member.

(5) Each agency having more than one member shall maintain and make available for public inspection a record of the final votes of each member in every agency proceeding.

(6)(A) Each agency, upon any request for records made under paragraph (1), (2), or (3) of this subsection, shall—

(i) determine within 20 days (excepting Saturdays, Sundays, and legal public holidays) after the receipt of any such request whether to comply with such request and shall immediately notify the person making such request of such determination and the reasons therefor, and of the right of such person to appeal to the head of the agency any adverse determination; and

(ii) make a determination with respect to any appeal within twenty days (excepting Saturdays, Sundays, and legal public holidays) after the receipt of such appeal. If on appeal the denial of the request for records is in whole or in part upheld, the agency shall notify the person making such request of the provisions for judicial review of that determination under paragraph (4) of this subsection.

(B)(i) In unusual circumstances as specified in this subparagraph, the time limits prescribed in either clause (i) or clause (ii) of subparagraph (A) may be extended by written notice to the person making such request setting forth the unusual circumstances for such extension and the date on which a determination is expected to be dispatched. No such notice shall specify a date that would result in an extension for more than ten working days, except as provided in clause (ii) of this subparagraph.

(ii) With respect to a request for which a written notice under clause (i) extends the time limits prescribed under clause (i) of subparagraph (A), the agency shall notify the person making the request if the request cannot be processed within the time limit specified in that clause and shall provide the person an opportunity to limit the scope of the request so that it may be processed within that time limit or an opportunity to arrange with the agency an alternative time frame for processing the request or a modified request. Refusal by the person to reasonably modify the request or arrange such an alternative time frame shall be considered as a factor in determining whether exceptional circumstances exist for purposes of subparagraph (C).

(iii) As used in this subparagraph, "unusual circumstances" means, but only to the extent reasonably necessary to the proper processing of the particular requests—

(I) the need to search for and collect the requested records from field facilities or other establishments that are separate from the office processing the request;

(II) the need to search for, collect, and appropriately examine a voluminous amount of separate and distinct records which are demanded in a single request; or

(III) the need for consultation, which shall be conducted with all practicable speed, with another agency having a substantial interest in the determination of the request or among two or more components of the agency having substantial subject-matter interest therein.

(iv) Each agency may promulgate regulations, pursuant to notice and receipt of public comment, providing for the aggregation of certain requests by the same requestor, or by a group of requestors acting in concert, if the agency reasonably believes that such requests actually constitute a single request, which would otherwise satisfy the unusual circumstances specified in this subparagraph, and the requests involve clearly related matters. Multiple requests involving unrelated matters shall not be aggregated.

(C)(i) Any person making a request to any agency for records under paragraph (1), (2), or (3) of this subsection shall be deemed to have exhausted his administrative remedies with respect to such request if the agency fails to comply with the applicable time limit provisions of this paragraph. If the Government can show exceptional circumstances exist and that the agency is exercising due diligence in responding to the request, the court may retain jurisdiction and allow the agency additional time to complete its review of the records. Upon any determination by an agency to comply with a request for records, the records shall be made promptly available to such person making such request. Any notification of denial of any request for records under this subsection shall set forth the names and titles or positions of each person responsible for the denial of such request.

(ii) For purposes of this subparagraph, the term "exceptional circumstances" does not include a delay that results from a predictable agency workload of requests under this section, unless the agency demonstrates reasonable progress in reducing its backlog of pending requests.

(iii) Refusal by a person to reasonably modify the scope of a request or arrange an alternative time frame for processing a request (or a modified request) under clause (ii) after being given an opportunity to do so by the agency to whom the person made the request shall be considered as a factor in determining whether exceptional circumstances exist for purposes of this subparagraph.

(D)(i) Each agency may promulgate regulations, pursuant to notice and receipt of public comment, providing for multitrack processing of requests for records based on the amount of work or time (or both) involved in processing requests.

(ii) Regulations under this subparagraph may provide a person making a request that does not qualify for the fastest multitrack processing an opportunity to limit the scope of the request in order to qualify for faster processing.

(iii) This subparagraph shall not be considered to affect the requirement under subparagraph (C) to exercise due diligence.

(E)(i) Each agency shall promulgate regulations, pursuant to notice and receipt of public comment, providing for expedited processing of requests for records—

(I) in cases in which the person requesting the records demonstrates a compelling need; and

(II) in other cases determined by the agency.

(ii) Notwithstanding clause (i), regulations under this subparagraph must ensure—

(I) that a determination of whether to provide expedited processing shall be made, and notice of the determination shall be provided to the person making the request, within 10 days after the date of the request; and

(II) expeditious consideration of administrative appeals of such determinations of whether to provide expedited processing.

(iii) An agency shall process as soon as practicable any request for records to which the agency has granted expedited processing under this subparagraph. Agency action to deny or affirm denial of a request for expedited processing pursuant to this subparagraph, and failure by an agency to respond in a timely manner to such a request shall be subject to judicial review under paragraph (4), except that the judicial review shall be based on the record before the agency at the time of the determination.

(iv) A district court of the United States shall not have jurisdiction to review an agency denial of expedited processing of a request for records after the agency has provided a complete response to the request.

(v) For purposes of this subparagraph, the term "compelling need" means—

(I) that a failure to obtain requested records on an expedited basis under this paragraph could reasonably be expected to pose an imminent threat to the life or physical safety of an individual; or

(II) with respect to a request made by a person primarily engaged in disseminating information, urgency to inform the public concerning actual or alleged Federal Government activity.

(vi) A demonstration of a compelling need by a person making a request for expedited processing shall be made by a statement certified by such person to be true and correct to the best of such person's knowledge and belief.

(F) In denying a request for records, in whole or in part, an agency shall make a reasonable effort to estimate the volume of any requested matter the provision of which is denied, and shall provide any such estimate to the person making the request, unless providing such estimate would harm an interest protected by the exemption in subsection (b) pursuant to which the denial is made.

(b) This section does not apply to matters that are—

(1) (A) specifically authorized under criteria established by an Executive order to be kept secret in the interest of national defense or foreign policy and (B) are in fact properly classified pursuant to such Executive order;

(2) related solely to the internal personnel rules and practices of an agency;

(3) specifically exempted from disclosure by statute (other than section 552b of this title), provided that such statute (A) requires that the matters be withheld from the public in such a manner as to leave no discretion on the issue, or (B) establishes particular criteria for withholding or refers to particular types of matters to be withheld;

(4) trade secrets and commercial or financial information obtained from a person and privileged or confidential;

(5) inter-agency or intra-agency memorandums or letters which would not be available by law to a party other than an agency in litigation with the agency;

(6) personnel and medical files and similar files the disclosure of which would constitute a clearly unwarranted invasion of personal privacy;

(7) records or information compiled for law enforcement purposes, but only to the extent that the production of such law enforcement records or information (A) could reasonably be expected to interfere with enforcement proceedings, (B) would deprive a person of a right to a fair trial or an impartial adjudication, (C) could reasonably be expected to constitute an unwarranted invasion of personal privacy, (D) could reasonably be expected to disclose the identity of a confidential source, including a State, local, or foreign agency or authority or any private institution which furnished information on a confidential basis, and, in the case of a record or information compiled by criminal law enforcement authority in the course of a criminal investigation or by an agency conducting a lawful national security intelligence investigation, information furnished by a confidential source, (E) would disclose techniques and procedures for law enforcement investigations or prosecutions, or would disclose guidelines for law enforcement investigations or prosecutions if such disclosure could reasonably be expected to risk circumvention of the law, or (F) could reasonably be expected to endanger the life or physical safety of any individual;

(8) contained in or related to examination, operating, or condition reports prepared by, on behalf of, or for the use of an agency responsible for the regulation or supervision of financial institutions; or

(9) geological and geophysical information and data, including maps, concerning wells.

Any reasonably segregable portion of a record shall be provided to any person requesting such record after deletion of the portions which are exempt under this subsection. The amount of information deleted shall be indicated on the released portion of the record, unless including that indication would harm an interest protected by the exemption in this subsection under which the deletion is made. If technically feasible, the amount of the information shall be indicated at the place in the record where such deletion is made.

(c)(1) Whenever a request is made which involves access to records described in subsection (b)(7)(A) and—

> **(A)** the investigation or proceeding involves a possible violation of criminal law; and

> **(B)** there is reason to believe that (i) the subject of the investigation or proceeding is not aware of its pendency, and (ii) disclosure of the existence of the records could reasonably be expected to interfere with enforcement proceedings,

the agency may, during only such time as that circumstance continues, treat the records as not subject to the requirements of this section.

> **(2)** Whenever informant records maintained by a criminal law enforcement agency under an informant's name or personal identifier are requested by a third party according to the informant's name or personal identifier, the agency may treat the records as not subject to the requirements of this section unless the informant's status as an informant has been officially confirmed.

> **(3)** Whenever a request is made which involves access to records maintained by the Federal Bureau of Investigation pertaining to foreign intelligence or counterintelligence, or international terrorism, and the existence of the records is classified information as provided in subsection (b)(1), the Bureau may, as long as the existence of the records remains classified information, treat the records as not subject to the requirements of this section.

(d) This section does not authorize withholding of information or limit the availability of records to the public, except as specifically stated in this section. This section is not authority to withhold information from Congress.

(e)(1) On or before February 1 of each year, each agency shall submit to the Attorney General of the United States a report which shall cover the preceding fiscal year and which shall include—

> **(A)** the number of determinations made by the agency not to comply with requests for records made to such agency under subsection (a) and the reasons for each such determination;

(B)(i) the number of appeals made by persons under subsection (a)(6), the result of such appeals, and the reason for the action upon each appeal that results in a denial of information; and

(ii) a complete list of all statutes that the agency relies upon to authorize the agency to withhold information under subsection (b)(3), a description of whether a court has upheld the decision of the agency to withhold information under each such statute, and a concise description of the scope of any information withheld;

(C) the number of requests for records pending before the agency as of September 30 of the preceding year, and the median number of days that such requests had been pending before the agency as of that date;

(D) the number of requests for records received by the agency and the number of requests which the agency processed;

(E) the median number of days taken by the agency to process different types of requests;

(F) the total amount of fees collected by the agency for processing requests; and

(G) the number of full-time staff of the agency devoted to processing requests for records under this section, and the total amount expended by the agency for processing such requests.

(2) Each agency shall make each such report available to the public including by computer telecommunications, or if computer telecommunications means have not been established by the agency, by other electronic means.

(3) The Attorney General of the United States shall make each report which has been made available by electronic means available at a single electronic access point. The Attorney General of the United States shall notify the Chairman and ranking minority member of the Committee on Government Reform and Oversight of the House of Representatives and the Chairman and ranking minority member of the Committees on Governmental Affairs and the Judiciary of the Senate, no later than April 1 of the year in which each such report is issued, that such reports are available by electronic means.

(4) The Attorney General of the United States, in consultation with the Director of the Office of Management and Budget, shall develop reporting and performance guidelines in connection with reports required by this subsection by October 1, 1997, and may establish additional requirements for such reports as the Attorney General determines may be useful.

(5) The Attorney General of the United States shall submit an annual report on or before April 1 of each calendar year which shall include for the prior calendar year a listing of the number of cases arising under this section, the exemption involved in each case, the disposition of such case, and the cost, fees, and penalties assessed under subparagraphs (E), (F), and (G) of subsection (a)(4). Such report shall also include a description of the efforts undertaken by the Department of Justice to encourage agency compliance with this section.

(f) For purposes of this section, the term—

(1) "agency" as defined in section 551(1) of this title includes any executive department, military department, Government corporation, Government controlled corporation, or other establishment in the executive branch of the Government (including the Executive Office of the President), or any independent regulatory agency; and

(2) "record" and any other term used in this section in reference to information includes any information that would be an agency record subject to the requirements of this section when maintained by an agency in any format, including an electronic format.

(g) The head of each agency shall prepare and make publicly available upon request, reference material or a guide for requesting records or information from the agency, subject to the exemptions in subsection (b), including—

(1) an index of all major information systems of the agency;

(2) a description of major information and record locator systems maintained by the agency; and

(3) a handbook for obtaining various types and categories of public information from the agency pursuant to chapter 35 of title 44, and under this section.

. . .

E. FEDERAL PRIVACY ACT, 5 U.S.C.A. § 552a (WEST 1996)

§ 552a. Records maintained on individuals

(a) Definitions.—For purposes of this section—

(1) the term "agency" means agency as defined in section 552(e) of this title;

(2) the term "individual" means a citizen of the United States or an alien lawfully admitted for permanent residence;

(3) the term "maintain" includes maintain, collect, use, or disseminate;

(4) the term "record" means any item, collection, or grouping of information about an individual that is maintained by an agency, including, but not limited to, his education, financial transactions, medical history, and criminal or employment history and that contains his name, or the identifying number, symbol, or other identifying particular assigned to the individual, such as a finger or voice print or a photograph;

(5) the term "system of records" means a group of any records under the control of any agency from which information is retrieved by the name of the individual or by some identifying number, symbol, or other identifying particular assigned to the individual;

(6) the term "statistical record" means a record in a system of records maintained for statistical research or reporting purposes only and not used in whole or in part in making any determination about an identifiable individual, except as provided by section 8 of title 13;

(7) the term "routine use" means, with respect to the disclosure of a record, the use of such record for a purpose which is compatible with the purpose for which it was collected;

(8) the term "matching program"—

(A) means any computerized comparison of—

(i) two or more automated systems of records or a system of records with non-Federal records for the purpose of—

(I) establishing or verifying the eligibility of, or continuing compliance with statutory and regulatory requirements by, applicants for, recipients or beneficiaries of, participants in, or providers of services with respect to, cash or in-kind assistance or payments under Federal benefit programs, or

(II) recouping payments or delinquent debts under such Federal benefit programs, or

(ii) two or more automated Federal personnel or payroll systems of records or a system of Federal personnel or payroll records with non-Federal records,

(B) but does not include—

(i) matches performed to produce aggregate statistical data without any personal identifiers;

(ii) matches performed to support any research or statistical project, the specific data of which may not be used to make decisions concerning the rights, benefits, or privileges of specific individuals;

(iii) matches performed, by an agency (or component thereof) which performs as its principal function any activity pertaining to the enforcement of criminal laws, subsequent to the initiation of a specific criminal or civil law enforcement investigation of a named person or persons for the purpose of gathering evidence against such person or persons;

(iv) matches of tax information (I) pursuant to section 6103(d) of the Internal Revenue Code of 1986, (II) for purposes of tax administration as defined in section 6103(b)(4) of such Code, (III) for the purpose of intercepting a tax refund due an individual under authority granted by section 404(e), 464, or 1137 of the Social Security Act; or (IV) for the purpose of intercepting a tax refund due an individual under any other tax refund intercept program authorized by statute which has been determined by the Director of the Office of Management and Budget to contain verification, notice, and hearing requirements that are substantially similar to the procedures in section 1137 of the Social Security Act;

(v) matches—

(I) using records predominantly relating to Federal personnel, that are performed for routine administrative purposes (subject to guidance provided by the Director of the Office of Management and Budget pursuant to subsection (v)); or

(II) conducted by an agency using only records from systems of records maintained by that agency;

if the purpose of the match is not to take any adverse financial, personnel, disciplinary, or other adverse action against Federal personnel

(vi) matches performed for foreign counterintelligence purposes or to produce background checks for security clearances of Federal personnel or Federal contractor personnel; or

(vii) matches performed incident to a levy described in section 6103(k)(8) of the Internal Revenue Code of 1986;

(9) the term "recipient agency" means any agency, or contractor thereof, receiving records contained in a system of records from a source agency for use in a matching program;

(10) the term "non-Federal agency" means any State or local government, or agency thereof, which receives records contained in a system of records from a source agency for use in a matching program;

(11) the term "source agency" means any agency which discloses records contained in a system of records to be used in a matching program, or any State or local government, or agency thereof, which discloses records to be used in a matching program;

(12) the term "Federal benefit program" means any program administered or funded by the Federal Government, or by any agent or State on behalf of the Federal Government, providing cash or in-kind assistance in the form of payments, grants, loans, or loan guarantees to individuals; and

(13) the term "Federal personnel" means officers and employees of the Government of the United States, members of the uniformed services (including members of the Reserve Components), individuals entitled to receive immediate or deferred retirement benefits under any retirement program of the Government of the United States (including survivor benefits).

(b) Conditions of disclosure.—No agency shall disclose any record which is contained in a system of records by any means of communication to any person, or to another agency, except pursuant to a written request by, or with the prior written consent of, the individual to whom the record pertains, unless disclosure of the record would be—

(1) to those officers and employees of the agency which maintains the record who have a need for the record in the performance of their duties;

(2) required under section 552 of this title;

(3) for a routine use as defined in subsection (a)(7) of this section and described under subsection (e)(4)(D) of this section;

(4) to the Bureau of the Census for purposes of planning or carrying out a census or survey or related activity pursuant to the provisions of title 13;

(5) to a recipient who has provided the agency with advance adequate written assurance that the record will be used solely as a statistical research or reporting record, and the record is to be transferred in a form that is not individually identifiable;

(6) to the National Archives and Records Administration as a record which has sufficient historical or other value to warrant its continued preservation by the United States Government, or for evaluation by the Archivist of the United States or the designee of the Archivist to determine whether the record has such value;

(7) to another agency or to an instrumentality of any governmental jurisdiction within or under the control of the United States for a civil or criminal law enforcement activity if the activity is authorized by law, and if the head of the agency or instrumentality has made a written request to the agency which maintains the record specifying the particular portion desired and the law enforcement activity for which the record is sought;

(8) to a person pursuant to a showing of compelling circumstances affecting the health or safety of an individual if upon such disclosure notification is transmitted to the last known address of such individual;

(9) to either House of Congress, or, to the extent of matter within its jurisdiction, any committee or subcommittee thereof, any joint committee of Congress or subcommittee of any such joint committee;

(10) to the Comptroller General, or any of his authorized representatives, in the course of the performance of the duties of the General Accounting Office;

(11) pursuant to the order of a court of competent jurisdiction; or

(12) to a consumer reporting agency in accordance with section 3711(e) of title 31.

(c) Accounting of certain disclosures.—Each agency, with respect to each system of records under its control, shall—

(1) except for disclosures made under subsections (b)(1) or (b)(2) of this section, keep an accurate accounting of—

(A) the date, nature, and purpose of each disclosure of a record to any person or to another agency made under subsection (b) of this section; and

(B) the name and address of the person or agency to whom the disclosure is made;

(2) retain the accounting made under paragraph (1) of this subsection for at least five years or the life of the record, whichever is longer, after the disclosure for which the accounting is made;

(3) except for disclosures made under subsection (b)(7) of this section, make the accounting made under paragraph (1) of this subsection available to the individual named in the record at his request; and

(4) inform any person or other agency about any correction or notation of dispute made by the agency in accordance with subsection (d) of this section of any record that has been disclosed to the person or agency if an accounting of the disclosure was made.

(d) Access to records.—Each agency that maintains a system of records shall—

(1) upon request by any individual to gain access to his record or to any information pertaining to him which is contained in the system, permit him and upon his request, a person of his own choosing to accompany him, to review the record and have a copy made of all or any portion thereof in a form comprehensible to him, except that the agency may require the individual to furnish a written statement authorizing discussion of that individual's record in the accompanying person's presence;

(2) permit the individual to request amendment of a record pertaining to him and—

    (A) not later than 10 days (excluding Saturdays, Sundays, and legal public holidays) after the date of receipt of such request, acknowledge in writing such receipt; and

    (B) promptly, either—

        (i) make any correction of any portion thereof which the individual believes is not accurate, relevant, timely, or complete; or

        (ii) inform the individual of its refusal to amend the record in accordance with his request, the reason for the refusal, the procedures established by the agency for the individual to request a review of that refusal by the head of the agency or an officer designated by the head of the agency, and the name and business address of that official;

(3) permit the individual who disagrees with the refusal of the agency to amend his record to request a review of such refusal, and not later than 30 days (excluding Saturdays, Sundays, and legal public holidays) from the date on which the individual requests such review, complete such review and make a final determination unless, for good cause shown, the head of the agency extends such 30–day period; and if, after his review, the reviewing official also refuses to amend the record in accordance with the request, permit the individual to file with the agency a concise statement setting forth the reasons for his disagreement with the refusal of the agency, and notify the individual of the provisions for judicial review of the reviewing official's determination under subsection (g)(1)(A) of this section;

(4) in any disclosure, containing information about which the individual has filed a statement of disagreement, occurring after the filing of the statement under paragraph (3) of this subsection, clearly note any portion of the record which is disputed and provide copies of the statement and, if the agency deems it appropriate, copies of a concise statement of the reasons of the agency for not making the amendments requested, to persons or other agencies to whom the disputed record has been disclosed; and

(5) nothing in this section shall allow an individual access to any information compiled in reasonable anticipation of a civil action or proceeding.

(e) Agency requirements.—Each agency that maintains a system of records shall—

(1) maintain in its records only such information about an individual as is relevant and necessary to accomplish a purpose of the agency required to be accomplished by statute or by executive order of the President;

(2) collect information to the greatest extent practicable directly from the subject individual when the information may result in adverse determinations about an individual's rights, benefits, and privileges under Federal programs;

(3) inform each individual whom it asks to supply information, on the form which it uses to collect the information or on a separate form that can be retained by the individual—

(A) the authority (whether granted by statute, or by executive order of the President) which authorizes the solicitation of the information and whether disclosure of such information is mandatory or voluntary;

(B) the principal purpose or purposes for which the information is intended to be used;

(C) the routine uses which may be made of the information, as published pursuant to paragraph (4)(D) of this subsection; and

(D) the effects on him, if any, of not providing all or any part of the requested information;

(4) subject to the provisions of paragraph (11) of this subsection, publish in the Federal Register upon establishment or revision a notice of the existence and character of the system of records, which notice shall include—

(A) the name and location of the system;

(B) the categories of individuals on whom records are maintained in the system;

(C) the categories of records maintained in the system;

(D) each routine use of the records contained in the system, including the categories of users and the purpose of such use;

(E) the policies and practices of the agency regarding storage, retrievability, access controls, retention, and disposal of the records;

(F) the title and business address of the agency official who is responsible for the system of records;

(G) the agency procedures whereby an individual can be notified at his request if the system of records contains a record pertaining to him;

(H) the agency procedures whereby an individual can be notified at his request how he can gain access to any record pertaining to him contained in the system of records, and how he can contest its content; and

(I) the categories of sources of records in the system;

(5) maintain all records which are used by the agency in making any determination about any individual with such accuracy, relevance, timeliness, and completeness as is reasonably necessary to assure fairness to the individual in the determination;

(6) prior to disseminating any record about an individual to any person other than an agency, unless the dissemination is made pursuant to subsection (b)(2) of this section, make reasonable efforts to assure that such records are accurate, complete, timely, and relevant for agency purposes;

(7) maintain no record describing how any individual exercises rights guaranteed by the First Amendment unless expressly authorized by statute or by the individual about whom the record is maintained or unless pertinent to and within the scope of an authorized law enforcement activity;

(8) make reasonable efforts to serve notice on an individual when any record on such individual is made available to any person under compulsory legal process when such process becomes a matter of public record;

(9) establish rules of conduct for persons involved in the design, development, operation, or maintenance of any system of records, or in maintaining any record, and instruct each such person with respect to such rules and the requirements of this section, including any other rules and procedures adopted pursuant to this section and the penalties for noncompliance;

(10) establish appropriate administrative, technical, and physical safeguards to insure the security and confidentiality of records and to protect against any anticipated threats or hazards to their security or integrity which could result in substantial harm, embarrassment, inconvenience, or unfairness to any individual on whom information is maintained;

(11) at least 30 days prior to publication of information under paragraph (4)(D) of this subsection, publish in the Federal Register notice of any new use or intended use of the information in the system, and provide an opportunity for

interested persons to submit written data, views, or arguments to the agency; and

(12) if such agency is a recipient agency or a source agency in a matching program with a non-Federal agency, with respect to any establishment or revision of a matching program, at least 30 days prior to conducting such program, publish in the Federal Register notice of such establishment or revision.

(f) Agency rules.—In order to carry out the provisions of this section, each agency that maintains a system of records shall promulgate rules, in accordance with the requirements (including general notice) of section 553 of this title, which shall—

(1) establish procedures whereby an individual can be notified in response to his request if any system of records named by the individual contains a record pertaining to him;

(2) define reasonable times, places, and requirements for identifying an individual who requests his record or information pertaining to him before the agency shall make the record or information available to the individual;

(3) establish procedures for the disclosure to an individual upon his request of his record or information pertaining to him, including special procedure, if deemed necessary, for the disclosure to an individual of medical records, including psychological records, pertaining to him;

(4) establish procedures for reviewing a request from an individual concerning the amendment of any record or information pertaining to the individual, for making a determination on the request, for an appeal within the agency of an initial adverse agency determination, and for whatever additional means may be necessary for each individual to be able to exercise fully his rights under this section; and

(5) establish fees to be charged, if any, to any individual for making copies of his record, excluding the cost of any search for and review of the record.

The Office of the Federal Register shall biennially compile and publish the rules promulgated under this subsection and agency notices published under subsection (e)(4) of this section in a form available to the public at low cost.

(g)(1) Civil remedies.—Whenever any agency

(A) makes a determination under subsection (d)(3) of this section not to amend an individual's record in accordance with his request, or fails to make such review in conformity with that subsection;

(B) refuses to comply with an individual request under subsection (d)(1) of this section;

(C) fails to maintain any record concerning any individual with such accuracy, relevance, timeliness, and completeness as is necessary to assure fairness in any determination relating to the qualifications, character, rights, or opportunities of, or benefits to the individual that may be made on the basis of such record, and consequently a determination is made which is adverse to the individual; or

(D) fails to comply with any other provision of this section, or any rule promulgated thereunder, in such a way as to have an adverse effect on an individual,

the individual may bring a civil action against the agency, and the district courts of the United States shall have jurisdiction in the matters under the provisions of this subsection.

(2)(A) In any suit brought under the provisions of subsection (g)(1)(A) of this section, the court may order the agency to amend the individual's record in accordance with his request or in such other way as the court may direct. In such a case the court shall determine the matter de novo.

(B) The court may assess against the United States reasonable attorney fees and other litigation costs reasonably incurred in any case under this paragraph in which the complainant has substantially prevailed.

(3)(A) In any suit brought under the provisions of subsection (g)(1)(B) of this section, the court may enjoin the agency from withholding the records and order the production to the complainant of any agency records improperly withheld from him. In such a case the court shall determine the matter de novo, and may examine the contents of any agency records in camera to determine whether the records or any portion thereof may be withheld under any of the exemptions set forth in subsection (k) of this section, and the burden is on the agency to sustain its action.

(B) The court may assess against the United States reasonable attorney fees and other litigation costs reasonably incurred in any case under this paragraph in which the complainant has substantially prevailed.

(4) In any suit brought under the provisions of subsection (g)(1)(C) or (D) of this section in which the court determines that the agency acted in a manner which was intentional or willful, the United States shall be liable to the individual in an amount equal to the sum of—

(A) actual damages sustained by the individual as a result of the refusal or failure, but in no case shall a person entitled to recovery receive less than the sum of $1,000; and

(B) the costs of the action together with reasonable attorney fees as determined by the court.

(5) An action to enforce any liability created under this section may be brought in the district court of the United States in the district in which the complainant resides, or has his principal place of business, or in which the agency records are situated, or in the District of Columbia, without regard to the amount in controversy, within two years from the date on which the cause of action arises, except that where an agency has materially and willfully misrepresented any information required under this section to be disclosed to an individual and the information so misrepresented is material to establishment of the liability of the agency to the individual under this section, the action may be brought at any time within two years after discovery by the individual of the misrepresentation. Nothing in this section shall be construed to authorize any civil action by reason of any injury sustained as the result of a disclosure of a record prior to September 27, 1975.

(h) Rights of legal guardians.—For the purposes of this section, the parent of any minor, or the legal guardian of any individual who has been declared to be incompetent due to physical or mental incapacity or age by a court of competent jurisdiction, may act on behalf of the individual.

(i)(1) Criminal penalties.—Any officer or employee of an agency, who by virtue of his employment or official position, has possession of, or access to, agency records which contain individually identifiable information the disclosure of which is prohibited by this section or by rules or regulations established thereunder, and who knowing that disclosure of the specific material is so prohibited, willfully discloses the material in any manner to any person or agency not entitled to receive it, shall be guilty of a misdemeanor and fined not more than $5,000.

(2) Any officer or employee of any agency who willfully maintains a system of records without meeting the notice requirements of subsection (e)(4) of this section shall be guilty of a misdemeanor and fined not more than $5,000.

(3) Any person who knowingly and willfully requests or obtains any record concerning an individual from an agency under false pretenses shall be guilty of a misdemeanor and fined not more than $5,000.

(j) General exemptions.—The head of any agency may promulgate rules, in accordance with the requirements (including general notice) of sections 553(b)(1), (2), and (3), (c), and (e) of this title, to exempt any system of records within the agency from any part of this section except subsections (b), (c)(1) and (2), (e)(4)(A) through (F), (e)(6), (7), (9), (10), and (11), and (i) if the system of records is—

(1) maintained by the Central Intelligence Agency; or

(2) maintained by an agency or component thereof which performs as its principal function any activity pertaining to the enforcement of criminal laws, including police efforts to prevent, control, or reduce crime or to apprehend criminals, and the activities of prosecutors, courts, correctional, probation, pardon, or parole authorities, and which consists of (A) information compiled for the purpose of identifying individual criminal offenders and alleged offenders and consisting only of identifying data and notations of arrests, the nature and disposition of criminal charges, sentencing, confinement, release, and parole and probation status; (B) information compiled for the purpose of a criminal investigation, including reports of informants and investigators, and associated with an identifiable individual; or (C) reports identifiable to an individual compiled at any stage of the process of enforcement of the criminal laws from arrest or indictment through release from supervision.

At the time rules are adopted under this subsection, the agency shall include in the statement required under section 553(c) of this title, the reasons why the system of records is to be exempted from a provision of this section.

(k) Specific exemptions.—The head of any agency may promulgate rules, in accordance with the requirements (including general notice) of sections 553(b)(1), (2), and (3), (c), and (e) of this title, to exempt any system of records within the agency from subsections (c)(3), (d), (e)(1), (e)(4)(G), (H), and (I) and (f) of this section if the system of records is—

(1) subject to the provisions of section 552(b)(1) of this title;

(2) investigatory material compiled for law enforcement purposes, other than material within the scope of subsection (j)(2) of this section: *Provided, however*, That if any individual is denied any right, privilege, or benefit that he would otherwise be entitled by Federal law, or for which he would otherwise be eligible, as a result of the maintenance of such material, such material shall be provided to such individual, except to the extent that the disclosure of such material would reveal the identity of a source who furnished information to the Government under an express promise that the identity of the source would be held in confidence, or, prior to the effective date of this section, under an implied promise that the identity of the source would be held in confidence;

(3) maintained in connection with providing protective services to the President of the United States or other individuals pursuant to section 3056 of title 18;

(4) required by statute to be maintained and used solely as statistical records;

(5) investigatory material compiled solely for the purpose of determining suitability, eligibility, or qualifications for Federal civilian employment, military service, Federal contracts, or access to classified information, but only to the extent that the disclosure of such material would reveal the identity of a source who furnished information to the Government under an express promise that the identity of the source would be held in confidence, or, prior to the effective date of this section, under an implied promise that the identity of the source would be held in confidence;

(6) testing or examination material used solely to determine individual qualifications for appointment or promotion in the Federal service the disclosure of which would compromise the objectivity or fairness of the testing or examination process; or

(7) evaluation material used to determine potential for promotion in the armed services, but only to the extent that the disclosure of such material would reveal the identity of a source who furnished information to the Government under an express promise that the identity of the source would be held in confidence, or, prior to the effective date of this section, under an implied promise that the identity of the source would be held in confidence.

At the time rules are adopted under this subsection, the agency shall include in the statement required under section 553(c) of this title, the reasons why the system of records is to be exempted from a provision of this section.

(*l*)(1) **Archival records.**—Each agency record which is accepted by the Archivist of the United States for storage, processing, and servicing in accordance with section 3103 of title 44 shall, for the purposes of this section, be considered to be maintained by the agency which deposited the record and shall be subject to the provisions of this section. The Archivist of the United States shall not disclose the record except to the agency which maintains the record, or under rules established by that agency which are not inconsistent with the provisions of this section.

(2) Each agency record pertaining to an identifiable individual which was transferred to the National Archives of the United States as a record which has sufficient historical or other value to warrant its continued preservation by the United States Government, prior to the effective date of this section, shall, for the purposes of this section, be considered to be maintained by the National Archives and shall not be subject to the provisions of this section, except that a statement generally describing such records (modeled after the requirements relating to records subject to subsections (e)(4)(A) through (G) of this section) shall be published in the Federal Register.

(3) Each agency record pertaining to an identifiable individual which is transferred to the National Archives of the

United States as a record which has sufficient historical or other value to warrant its continued preservation by the United States Government, on or after the effective date of this section, shall, for the purposes of this section, be considered to be maintained by the National Archives and shall be exempt from the requirements of this section except subsections (e)(4)(A) through (G) and (e)(9) of this section.

(m)(1) Government contractors.—When an agency provides by a contract for the operation by or on behalf of the agency of a system of records to accomplish an agency function, the agency shall, consistent with its authority, cause the requirements of this section to be applied to such system. For purposes of subsection (i) of this section any such contractor and any employee of such contractor, if such contract is agreed to on or after the effective date of this section, shall be considered to be an employee of an agency.

(2) A consumer reporting agency to which a record is disclosed under section 3711(e) of title 31 shall not be considered a contractor for the purposes of this section.

(n) Mailing lists.—An individual's name and address may not be sold or rented by an agency unless such action is specifically authorized by law. This provision shall not be construed to require the withholding of names and addresses otherwise permitted to be made public.

(o) Matching agreements.—**(1)** No record which is contained in a system of records may be disclosed to a recipient agency or non-Federal agency for use in a computer matching program except pursuant to a written agreement between the source agency and the recipient agency or non-Federal agency specifying—

(A) the purpose and legal authority for conducting the program;

(B) the justification for the program and the anticipated results, including a specific estimate of any savings;

(C) a description of the records that will be matched, including each data element that will be used, the approximate number of records that will be matched, and the projected starting and completion dates of the matching program;

(D) procedures for providing individualized notice at the time of application, and notice periodically thereafter as directed by the Data Integrity Board of such agency (subject to guidance provided by the Director of the Office of Management and Budget pursuant to subsection (v)), to—

(i) applicants for and recipients of financial assistance or payments under Federal benefit programs, and

(ii) applicants for and holders of positions as Federal personnel, that any information provided by such applicants, recipients, holders, and individuals may be subject to verification through matching programs;

(E) procedures for verifying information produced in such matching program as required by subsection (p);

(F) procedures for the retention and timely destruction of identifiable records created by a recipient agency or non-Federal agency in such matching program;

(G) procedures for ensuring the administrative, technical, and physical security of the records matched and the results of such programs;

(H) prohibitions on duplication and redisclosure of records provided by the source agency within or outside the recipient agency or the non-Federal agency, except where required by law or essential to the conduct of the matching program;

(I) procedures governing the use by a recipient agency or non-Federal agency of records provided in a matching program by a source agency, including procedures governing return of the records to the source agency or destruction of records used in such program;

(J) information on assessments that have been made on the accuracy of the records that will be used in such matching program; and

(K) that the Comptroller General may have access to all records of a recipient agency or a non-Federal agency that the Comptroller General deems necessary in order to monitor or verify compliance with the agreement.

(2)(A) A copy of each agreement entered into pursuant to paragraph (1) shall—

(i) be transmitted to the Committee on Governmental Affairs of the Senate and the Committee on Government Operations of the House of Representatives; and

(ii) be available upon request to the public.

(B) No such agreement shall be effective until 30 days after the date on which such a copy is transmitted pursuant to subparagraph (A)(i).

(C) Such an agreement shall remain in effect only for such period, not to exceed 18 months, as the Data Integrity Board of the agency determines is appropriate in light of the purposes, and length of time necessary for the conduct, of the matching program.

(D) Within 3 months prior to the expiration of such an agreement pursuant to subparagraph (C), the Data Integrity Board of the agency may, without additional review, renew the matching agreement for a current, ongoing matching program for not more than one additional year if—

(i) such program will be conducted without any change; and

(ii) each party to the agreement certifies to the Board in writing that the program has been conducted in compliance with the agreement.

(p) Verification and opportunity to contest findings.—**(1)** In order to protect any individual whose records are used in a matching program, no recipient agency, non-Federal agency, or source agency may suspend, terminate, reduce, or make a final denial of any financial assistance or payment under a Federal benefit program to such individual, or take other adverse action against such individual, as a result of information produced by such matching program, until—

(A)(i) the agency has independently verified the information; or

(ii) the Data Integrity Board of the agency, or in the case of a non-Federal agency the Data Integrity Board of the source agency, determines in accordance with guidance issued by the Director of the Office of Management and Budget that—

(I) the information is limited to identification and amount of benefits paid by the source agency under a Federal benefit program; and

(II) there is a high degree of confidence that the information provided to the recipient agency is accurate;

(B) the individual receives a notice from the agency containing a statement of its findings and informing the individual of the opportunity to contest such findings; and

(C)(i) the expiration of any time period established for the program by statute or regulation for the individual to respond to that notice; or

(ii) in the case of a program for which no such period is established, the end of the 30–day period beginning on the date on which notice under subparagraph (B) is mailed or otherwise provided to the individual.

(2) Independent verification referred to in paragraph (1) requires investigation and confirmation of specific information relating to an individual that is used as a basis for an adverse action against the individual, including where applicable investigation and confirmation of—

(A) the amount of any asset or income involved;

(B) whether such individual actually has or had access to such asset or income for such individual's own use; and

(C) the period or periods when the individual actually had such asset or income.

(3) Notwithstanding paragraph (1), an agency may take any appropriate action otherwise prohibited by such paragraph if the agency determines that the public health or public safety may be adversely affected or significantly threatened during any notice period required by such paragraph.

(q) **Sanctions.**—(1) Notwithstanding any other provision of law, no source agency may disclose any record which is contained in a system of records to a recipient agency or non-Federal agency for a matching program if such source agency has reason to believe that the requirements of subsection (p), or any matching agreement entered into pursuant to subsection (o), or both, are not being met by such recipient agency.

(2) No source agency may renew a matching agreement unless—

(A) the recipient agency or non-Federal agency has certified that it has complied with the provisions of that agreement; and

(B) the source agency has no reason to believe that the certification is inaccurate.

(r) **Report on new systems and matching programs.**—Each agency that proposes to establish or make a significant change in a system of records or a matching program shall provide adequate advance notice of any such proposal (in duplicate) to the Committee on Government Operations of the House of Representatives, the Committee on Governmental Affairs of the Senate, and the Office of Management and Budget in order to permit an evaluation of the probable or potential effect of such proposal on the privacy or other rights of individuals.

(s) **Biennial report.**—The President shall biennially submit to the Speaker of the House of Representatives and the President pro tempore of the Senate a report—

(1) describing the actions of the Director of the Office of Management and Budget pursuant to section 6 of the Privacy Act of 1974 during the preceding 2 years;

(2) describing the exercise of individual rights of access and amendment under this section during such years;

(3) identifying changes in or additions to systems of records;

(4) containing such other information concerning administration of this section as may be necessary or useful to the Congress in reviewing the effectiveness of this section in carrying out the purposes of the Privacy Act of 1974.

(t)(1) Effect of other laws.—No agency shall rely on any exemption contained in section 552 of this title to withhold from an individual any record which is otherwise accessible to such individual under the provisions of this section.

(2) No agency shall rely on any exemption in this section to withhold from an individual any record which is otherwise accessible to such individual under the provisions of section 552 of this title.

(u) Data Integrity Boards.—**(1)** Every agency conducting or participating in a matching program shall establish a Data Integrity Board to oversee and coordinate among the various components of such agency the agency's implementation of this section.

(2) Each Data Integrity Board shall consist of senior officials designated by the head of the agency, and shall include any senior official designated by the head of the agency as responsible for implementation of this section, and the inspector general of the agency, if any. The inspector general shall not serve as chairman of the Data Integrity Board.

(3) Each Data Integrity Board—

(A) shall review, approve, and maintain all written agreements for receipt or disclosure of agency records for matching programs to ensure compliance with subsection (*o*), and all relevant statutes, regulations, and guidelines;

(B) shall review all matching programs in which the agency has participated during the year, either as a source agency or recipient agency, determine compliance with applicable laws, regulations, guidelines, and agency agreements, and assess the costs and benefits of such programs;

(C) shall review all recurring matching programs in which the agency has participated during the year, either as a source agency or recipient agency, for continued justification for such disclosures;

(D) shall compile an annual report, which shall be submitted to the head of the agency and the Office of Management and Budget and made available to the public on request, describing the matching activities of the agency, including—

(i) matching programs in which the agency has participated as a source agency or recipient agency;

(ii) matching agreements proposed under subsection (*o*) that were disapproved by the Board;

(**iii**) any changes in membership or structure of the Board in the preceding year;

(**iv**) the reasons for any waiver of the requirement in paragraph (4) of this section for completion and submission of a cost-benefit analysis prior to the approval of a matching program;

(**v**) any violations of matching agreements that have been alleged or identified and any corrective action taken; and

(**vi**) any other information required by the Director of the Office of Management and Budget to be included in such report;

(**E**) shall serve as a clearinghouse for receiving and providing information on the accuracy, completeness, and reliability of records used in matching programs;

(**F**) shall provide interpretation and guidance to agency components and personnel on the requirements of this section for matching programs;

(**G**) shall review agency recordkeeping and disposal policies and practices for matching programs to assure compliance with this section; and

(**H**) may review and report on any agency matching activities that are not matching programs.

(**4**)(**A**) Except as provided in subparagraphs (B) and (C), a Data Integrity Board shall not approve any written agreement for a matching program unless the agency has completed and submitted to such Board a cost-benefit analysis of the proposed program and such analysis demonstrates that the program is likely to be cost effective.

(**B**) The Board may waive the requirements of subparagraph (A) of this paragraph if it determines in writing, in accordance with guidelines prescribed by the Director of the Office of Management and Budget, that a cost-benefit analysis is not required.

(**C**) A cost-benefit analysis shall not be required under subparagraph (A) prior to the initial approval of a written agreement for a matching program that is specifically required by statute. Any subsequent written agreement for such a program shall not be approved by the Data Integrity Board unless the agency has submitted a cost-benefit analysis of the program as conducted under the preceding approval of such agreement.

(**5**)(**A**) If a matching agreement is disapproved by a Data Integrity Board, any party to such agreement may appeal the disapproval to the Director of the Office of Management and

Budget. Timely notice of the filing of such an appeal shall be provided by the Director of the Office of Management and Budget to the Committee on Governmental Affairs of the Senate and the Committee on Government Operations of the House of Representatives.

(B) The Director of the Office of Management and Budget may approve a matching agreement notwithstanding the disapproval of a Data Integrity Board if the Director determines that—

    (i) the matching program will be consistent with all applicable legal, regulatory, and policy requirements;

    (ii) there is adequate evidence that the matching agreement will be cost-effective; and

    (iii) the matching program is in the public interest.

(C) The decision of the Director to approve a matching agreement shall not take effect until 30 days after it is reported to committees described in subparagraph (A).

(D) If the Data Integrity Board and the Director of the Office of Management and Budget disapprove a matching program proposed by the inspector general of an agency, the inspector general may report the disapproval to the head of the agency and to the Congress.

(6) The Director of the Office of Management and Budget shall, annually during the first 3 years after the date of enactment of this subsection and biennially thereafter, consolidate in a report to the Congress the information contained in the reports from the various Data Integrity Boards under paragraph (3)(D). Such report shall include detailed information about costs and benefits of matching programs that are conducted during the period covered by such consolidated report, and shall identify each waiver granted by a Data Integrity Board of the requirement for completion and submission of a cost-benefit analysis and the reasons for granting the waiver.

(7) In the reports required by paragraphs (3)(D) and (6), agency matching activities that are not matching programs may be reported on an aggregate basis, if and to the extent necessary to protect ongoing law enforcement or counterintelligence investigations.

    (v) Office of Management and Budget responsibilities.—The Director of the Office of Management and Budget shall—

(1) develop and, after notice and opportunity for public comment, prescribe guidelines and regulations for the use of agencies in implementing the provisions of this section; and

(2) provide continuing assistance to and oversight of the implementation of this section by agencies.

. . .

F.   CHAPTER 22—EMPLOYEE POLYGRAPH PROTECTION ACT OF 1988

29 U.S.C.A. § 2001 to 2009
(West Supp. 1991)

Sec.

Sec. 2001. Definitions

As used in this chapter:

(1) **Commerce.**—The term "commerce" has the meaning provided by section 203(b) of this title.

(2) **Employer**.—The term "employer" includes any person acting directly or indirectly in the interest of an employer in relation to an employee or prospective employee.

(3) **Lie detector**.—The term "lie detector" includes a polygraph, deceptograph, voice stress analyzer, psychological stress evaluator, or any other similar device (whether mechanical or electrical) that is used, or the results of which are used, for the purpose of rendering a diagnostic opinion regarding the honesty or dishonesty of an individual.

(4) **Polygraph**.—The term "polygraph" means an instrument that—

(A) records continuously, visually, permanently, and simultaneously changes in cardiovascular, respiratory, and electrodermal patterns as minimum instrumentation standards; and

(B) is used, or the results of which are used, for the purpose of rendering a diagnostic opinion regarding the honesty or dishonesty of an individual.

(5) **Secretary**.—The term, "Secretary" means the Secretary of Labor. (Pub.L. 100–347, Sec. 2, June 27, 1988, 102 Stat. 646.)

Sec. 2002. Prohibitions on lie detector use

Except as provided in section 2006 and 2007 of this title, it shall be unlawful for any employer engaged in or affecting commerce or in the production of goods for commerce—

(1) directly or indirectly, to require, request, suggest, or cause any employee or prospective employee to take or submit to any lie detector test;

(2) to use, accept, refer to, or inquire concerning the results of any lie detector test of any employee or prospective employee;

(3) to discharge, discipline, discriminate against in any manner, or deny employment or promotion to, or threaten to take any such action against—

(A) any employee or prospective employee who refuses, declines, or fails to take or submit to any lie detector test, or

(B) any employee or prospective employee of the basis of the results of any lie detector test; or

(4) to discharge, discipline, discriminate against in any manner, or deny employment or promotion to, or threaten to take any such action against, any employee or prospective employee because—

(A) such employee or prospective employee has filed any complaint or instituted or caused to be instituted any proceeding under or related to this chapter,

(B) such employee or prospective employee has testified or is about to testify in any such proceeding, or

(C) of the exercise by such employee or prospective employee, on behalf of such employee or another person, of any right afforded by this chapter. (Pub.L. 100–347, Sec. 3, June 27, 1988, 102 Stat. 646.)

Sec. 2003. Notice of protection

The Secretary shall prepare, have printed, and distribute a notice setting forth excerpts from, or summaries of, the pertinent provisions of this chapter. Each employer shall post and maintain such notice in conspicuous places on its premises where notices to employees and applicants to employment are customarily posted. (Pub.L. 100–347, Sec. 4, June 27, 1988, 102 Stat. 647.)

Sec. 2004. Authority of the Secretary

(a) **In general**

The Secretary shall—

(1) issue such rules and regulations as may be necessary or appropriate to carry out this chapter;

(2) cooperate with regional, State, local, and other agencies, and cooperate with and furnish technical assistance to employers, labor organizations, and employment agencies to aid in effectuating the purposes of this chapter; and

(3) make investigations and inspections and require the keeping of records necessary or appropriate for the administration of this chapter.

(b) **Subpoena authority**

For the purpose of any hearing or investigation under this chapter, the Secretary shall have the authority contained in sections 49 and 50 of Title 15. (Pub.L. 100–347, Sec. 5, June 27, 1988, 102 Stat. 647.)

Sec. 2005. Enforcement provisions

(a) **Civil penalties**

(1) **In general**

Subject to paragraph (2), any employer who violates any provision of this chapter may be assessed a civil penalty of not more than $10,000.

(2) **Determination of amount**

In determining the amount of any penalty under paragraph (1), the Secretary shall take into account the previous record of the person in terms of compliance with this chapter and the gravity of the violation.

(3) Collection

Any civil penalty assessed under this subsection shall be collected in the same manner as is required by subsections (b) through (e) of section 1853 of this title with respect to civil penalties assessed under subsection (a) of such section.

(b) Injunctive actions by the Secretary

The Secretary may bring an action under this section to restrain violations of this chapter. The Solicitor of Labor may appear for and represent the Secretary in any litigation brought under this chapter. In any action brought under this section, the district courts of the United States shall have jurisdiction, for cause shown, to issue temporary or permanent restraining orders and injunctions to require compliance with this chapter, including such legal or equitable relief incident thereto as may be appropriate, including, but not limited to, employment, reinstatement, promotion, and the payment of lost wages and benefits.

(c) Private civil actions

(1) Liability

An employer who violates this chapter shall be liable to the employee or prospective employee affected by such violation. Such employer shall be liable for such legal or equitable relief as may be appropriate, including, but not limited to, employment, reinstatement, promotion, and the payment of lost wages and benefits.

(2) Court

An action to recover the liability prescribed in paragraph (1) may be maintained against the employer in any Federal or State court of competent jurisdiction by an employee or prospective employee for or on behalf of such employee, prospective employee, and other employees or prospective employees similarly situated. No such action may be commenced more than 3 years after the date of the alleged violation.

(3) Costs

The court, in its discretion, may allow the prevailing party (other than the United States) reasonable costs, including attorney's fees.

(d) Waiver of rights prohibited

The rights and procedures provided by this chapter may not be waived by contract or otherwise, unless such waiver is part of a written settlement agreed to and signed by the parties to the pending action or complaint under this Chapter. (Pub.L. 100–347, Sec. 6, June 27, 1988, 102 Stat. 647.)

Sec. 2006. Exemptions

(a) No application to Governmental employers

This chapter shall not apply with respect to the United States Government, any State or local government, or any political subdivision of a State or local government.

(b) National defense and security exemption

(1) National defense

Nothing in this chapter shall be construed to prohibit the administration, by the Federal Government, in the performance of any counterintelligence function, of any lie detector test to—

(A) any expert or consultant under contract to the Department of Defense or any employee of any contractor of such Department; or

(B) any expert or consultant under contract with the Department of Energy in connection with the atomic energy defense activities of such Department or any employee of any contractor of such Department in connection with such activities.

(2) Security

Nothing in this chapter shall be construed to prohibit the administration, by the Federal Government, in the performance of any intelligence or counterintelligence function, of any lie detector test to—

(A)(i) any individual employed by, assigned to, or detailed to, the National Security Agency, the Defense Intelligence Agency, or the Central Intelligence Agency,

(ii) any expert or consultant under contract to any such agency,

(iii) any employee of a contractor to any such agency,

(iv) any individual applying for a position in any such agency, or

(v) any individual assigned to a space where sensitive cryptologic information is produced, processed, or stored for any such agency; or

(B) any expert, or consultant (or employee of such expert or consultant) under contract with any Federal Government department, agency, or program whose duties involve access to information that has been classified at the level of top secret or designated as being within a special access program under section 4.2(a) of Executive Order 12356 (or a successor Executive order).

(c) FBI contractors exemptions

Nothing in this chapter shall be construed to prohibit the administration, by the Federal Government, in the performance of any counterintelligence function, of any lie detector test to an employee of a contractor of the Federal Bureau of Investigation of the Department of Justice who is engaged in the performance of any work under the contract with such Bureau.

(d) **Limited exemption for ongoing investigations**

Subject to sections 2007 and 2009 of this title, this chapter shall not prohibit an employer from requesting an employee to submit to a polygraph test if—

(1) the test is administered in connection with an ongoing investigation involving economic loss or injury to the employer's business, such as theft, embezzlement, misappropriation, or an act of unlawful industrial espionage or sabotage;

(2) the employee had access to the property that is the subject of the investigation;

(3) the employer has a reasonable suspicion that the employee was involved in the incident or activity under investigation; and

(4) the employer executes a statement, provided to the examinee before the test, that—

(A) sets forth with particularity the specific incident or activity being investigated and the basis for testing particular employees,

(B) is signed by a person (other than a polygraph examiner) authorized to legally bind the employer,

(C) is retained by the employer for at least 3 years, and

(D) contains at a minimum—

(i) an identification of the specific economic loss or injury to the business of the employer,

(ii) a statement indicating that the employee had access to the property that is the subject of the investigation, and

(iii) a statement describing the basis of the employer's reasonable suspicion that the employee was involved in the incident or activity under investigation.

(e) **Exemption for security services**

(1) **In general**

Subject to paragraph (2) and sections 2007 and 2009 of this title, this chapter shall not prohibit the use of polygraph tests on prospective employees by any private employer whose primary business purpose consists of providing armored car personnel, personnel engaged in the design, installation, and maintenance of security alarm systems, or other uniformed or plainclothes security personnel and whose function includes protection of—

(A) facilities, materials, or operations having a significant impact on the health or safety of any State or political subdivision thereof, or the national security of the United States, as determined under rules and regulations issued by the Secretary within 90 days after June 27, 1988, including—

(i) facilities engaged in the production, transmission, or distribution of electric or nuclear power,

(ii) public water supply facilities,

(iii) shipments or storage of radioactive or other toxic waste materials, and

(iv) public transportation, or

(B) currency, negotiable securities, precious commodities or instruments, or proprietary information.

(2) **Access**

The exemption provided under this subsection shall not apply if the test is administered to a prospective employee who would not be employed to protect facilities, materials, operations, or assets referred to in paragraph (1).

(f) **Exemption for drug security, drug theft, or drug diversion investigations**

(1) **In general**

Subject to paragraph (2) and sections 2007 and 2009 of this title, this chapter shall not prohibit the use of a polygraph test by any employer authorized to manufacture, distribute, or dispense a controlled substance listed in schedule I, II, III, or IV of section 812 of Title 21.

(2) **Access**

The exemption provided under this subsection shall apply—

(A) if the test is administered to a prospective employee who would have direct access to the manufacture, storage, distribution, or sale of any such controlled substance; or

(B) in the case of a test administered to a current employee, if—

(i) the test is administered in connection with an ongoing investigation of criminal or other misconduct involving, or potentially involving, loss or injury to the manufacture, distribution, or dispensing of any such controlled substance by such employer, and

(ii) the employee had access to the program or property that is the subject of the investigation. (Pub.L. 100–347, Sec. 7, June 27, 1988, 102 Stat. 648.)

Sec. 2007. Restrictions on use of exemptions

(a) Test as basis for adverse employment action

(1) Under ongoing investigations exemption

Except as provided in paragraph (2), the exemption under subsection (d) of section 2006 of this title shall not apply if an employee is discharged, disciplined, denied employment or promotion, or otherwise discriminated against in any manner on the basis of the analysis of a polygraph test chart or the refusal to take a polygraph test, without additional supporting evidence. The evidence required by such subsection may serve as additional supporting evidence.

(2) Under other exemptions

In the case of an exemption described in subsection (e) or (f) of such section, the exemption shall not apply if the results of an analysis of a polygraph test chart are used, or the refusal to take a polygraph test is used, as the sole basis upon which an adverse employment action described in paragraph (1) is taken against an employee or prospective employee.

(b) Rights of examinee

The exemptions provided under subsections (d), (e), and (f) of section 2006 of this title shall not apply unless the requirements described in the following paragraphs are met:

(1) All phases

Throughout all phrases of the test—

(A) the examinee shall be permitted to terminate the test at any time;

(B) the examinee is not asked questions in a manner designed to degrade, or needlessly intrude on, such examinee;

(C) the examinee is not asked any questions concerning—

(i) religious beliefs or affiliations,

(ii) beliefs or opinions regarding racial matters,

(iii) political beliefs or affiliations,

(iv) any matter relating to sexual behavior; and

(v) beliefs, affiliations, opinions, or lawful activities regarding unions or labor organizations; and

(D) the examiner does not conduct the test if there is sufficient written evidence by a physician that the examinee is suffering from a medical or psychological condition or undergoing treatment that might cause abnormal responses during the actual testing phase.

(2) **Pretest phase**

During the pretest phase, the prospective examinee—

(A) is provided with reasonable written notice of the date, time, and location of the test, and of such examinee's right to obtain and consult with legal counsel or an employee representative before each phase of the test;

(B) is informed in writing of the nature and characteristics of the tests and of the instruments involved;

(C) is informed, in writing—

(i) whether the testing area contains a two-way mirror, a camera, or any other device through which the test can be observed,

(ii) whether any other device, including any device for recording or monitoring the test, will be used, or

(iii) that the employer or the examinee may (with mutual knowledge) make a recording of the test;

(D) is read and signs a written notice informing such examinee—

(i) that the examinee cannot be required to take the test as a condition of employment,

(ii) that any statement made during the test may constitute additional supporting evidence for the purposes of an adverse employment action described in subsection (a) of this section,

(iii) of the limitations imposed under this section,

(iv) of the legal rights and remedies available to the examinee if the polygraph test is not conducted in accordance with this chapter, and

(v) of the legal rights and remedies of the employer under this chapter (including the rights of the employer under section 2008(c)(2) of this title); and

(E) is provided an opportunity to review all questions to be asked during the test and is informed of the right to terminate the test at any time.

(3) **Actual testing phase**

During the actual testing phase, the examiner does not ask such examinee any question relevant during the test that was not presented in writing for review to such examinee before the test.

(4) **Post-test phase**

Before any adverse employment action, the employer shall—

(A) further interview the examinee on the basis of the results of the test; and

(B) provide the examinee with—

(i) a written copy of any opinion or conclusion rendered as a result of the test, and

(ii) a copy of the questions asked during the test along with the corresponding charted responses.

(5) Maximum number and minimum duration of tests

The examiner shall not conduct and complete more than five polygraph tests on a calendar day on which the test is given, and shall not conduct any such test for less than a 90–minute duration.

(c) Qualifications and requirements of examiners

The exemptions provided under subsections (d), (e), and (f) of section 2006 of this title shall not apply unless the individual who conducts the polygraph test satisfies the requirements under the following paragraphs:

(1) Qualifications

The examiner—

(A) has a valid and current license granted by licensing and regulatory authorities in the State in which the test is to be conducted, if so required by the State; and

(B) maintains a minimum of a $50,000 bond or equivalent amount of professional liability coverage.

(2) Requirements

The examiner—

(A) renders any opinion or conclusion regarding the test—

(i) in writing and solely on the basis of an analysis of polygraph test charts,

(ii) that does not contain information other than admissions, information, case facts, and interpretation of the charts relevant to the purpose and stated objectives of the test, and

(iii) that does not include any recommendation concerning the employment of the examinee; and

(B) maintains all opinions, reports, charts, written questions, lists, and other records relating to the test for a minimum period of 3 years after administration of the test. (Pub.L. 100–347, Sec. 8, June 27, 1988, 102 Stat. 650.)

Sec. 2008. Disclosure of information

(a) In general

A person, other than the examinee, may not disclose information obtained during a polygraph test, except as provided in this section.

(b) **Permitted disclosures**

A polygraph examiner may disclose information acquired from a polygraph test only to—

> (1) the examinee or any other person specifically designated in writing by the examinee;

> (2) the employer that requested the test; or

> (3) any court, governmental agency, arbitrator, or mediator, in accordance with due process of law, pursuant to an order from a court of competent jurisdiction.

(c) **Disclosure to employer**

An employer (other than employer described in subsection (a), (b), or (c) of section 2006 of this title) for whom a polygraph test is conducted may disclose information from the test only to—

> (1) a person in accordance with subsection (b) of this section; or

> (2) a governmental agency, but only insofar as the disclosed information is an admission of criminal conduct. (Pub.L. 100–347, Sec. 9, June 27, 1988, 102 Stat. 652.)

Sec. 2009. Effect on other laws and agreements

Except as provided in subsections (a), (b), and (c) of section 2006 of this title, this chapter shall not preempt any provision of any State or local law or of any negotiated collective bargaining agreement that prohibits lie detector tests or is more restrictive with respect to lie detector tests than any provision of this chapter. (Pub.L. 100–347, Sec. 10, June 27, 1988, 102 Stat. 653.)

G. 35 P.S. SECS. 7601–7612 (1991)

I. CHAPTER 45. [Pennsylvania] CONFIDENTIALITY OF HIV–RELATED INFORMATION ACT

Sec.

Sec. 7601. Short title

This act shall be known and may be cited as the Confidentiality of HIV–Related Information Act.

1990, Nov. 29, P.L. 585, No. 148, Sec. 1, effective in 90 days.

Sec. 7602. Legislative intent

(a) **Findings**.—The General Assembly finds that the incidence of acquired immune deficiency syndrome (AIDS) is increasing in this Commonwealth at a significant rate. Controlling the incidence of this disease is aided by providing testing and counseling activities for those persons who are at risk of exposure to or who are carrying the human immunodeficiency virus (HIV), which is the causative agent of AIDS. Testing and counseling are promoted by establishing confidentiality requirements which protect individuals from inappropriate disclosure and subsequent misuse of confidential HIV-related information. The General Assembly also finds that, since certain specific behaviors place a person at risk of contracting the virus, testing and counseling of persons who are at risk of exposure to the virus makes an efficient use of available funding.

(b) **Further findings**.—The General Assembly further finds that individual health care providers are increasingly concerned about occupational exposure to human immunodeficiency virus (HIV), the causative agent for acquired immune deficiency syndrome (AIDS). Due to the nature of their work, individual health care providers and first responders frequently come into contact with the blood and/or body fluids of individuals whose HIV infection status is not known. Regardless of the use of universal precautions to prevent HIV transmission between patients and individual health care providers, there will be instances of significant exposure to the blood and/or body fluids of patients.

(c) **Intent**.—It is the intent of the General Assembly to promote confidential testing on an informed and voluntary basis in order to encourage those most in need to obtain testing and appropriate counseling.

(d) **Further intent**.—It is the further intent of the General Assembly to provide a narrow exposure notification and information mechanism for individual health care providers or first responders, who experience a significant exposure to a patient's blood and/or body fluids, to learn of a patient's HIV infection status and thereby obtain the means to make informed decisions with respect to modes and duration of therapy as well as measures to reduce the likelihood of transmitting an infection to others.

1990, Nov. 29, P.L. 585, No. 148, Sec. 2, effective in 90 days.

Sec. 7603. Definitions

The following words and phrases when used in this act shall have the meanings given to them in this section unless the context clearly indicates otherwise:

"**AIDS**." Acquired immune deficiency syndrome.

"**Available blood.**" Blood that is in the possession of the institutional health care provider or the source patient's physician pursuant to a valid authorization.

"**CDC**." The Centers for Disease Control of the United States Public Health Service.

"**Confidential HIV-related information**." Any information which is in the possession of a person who provides one or more health or social services or who obtains the information pursuant to a release of confidential HIV-related information and which concerns whether an individual has been the subject of an HIV-related test, or has HIV, HIV-related illness or AIDS; or any information which identifies or reasonably could identify an individual as having one or more of these conditions, including information pertaining to the individual's contacts.

"**Contact**." A sex-sharing or needle-sharing partner of the subject.

"**Department**." The Department of Health of the Commonwealth.

"**First responder**." Police, firefighters, rescue personnel or any other person who provides emergency response, first aid or other medically related assistance either in the course of their occupational duties or as a volunteer, which may expose them to contact with a person's bodily fluids.

"**Health care provider**." An individual or institutional health care provider.

"**HIV**." The human immunodeficiency virus.

"**HIV-related test**." Any laboratory test or series of tests for any virus, antibody, antigen or etiologic agent whatsoever thought to cause or to indicate the presence of HIV infection.

"**Home care agency**." Any organization or part of an organization which is staffed and equipped to provide in-home health care services. The term includes, but is not limited to, Pennsylvania-licensed home health agencies, home health aide agencies or private duty care agencies.

"**Individual health care provider**." A physician, nurse, emergency medical services worker, chiropractor, optometrist, psychologist, nurse-midwife, physician assistant, dentist or other person, including a professional corporation or partnership, providing medical, nursing, drug or alcohol rehabilitation services, mental health services, other health care services or an employee or agent of such individual or an institutional health care provider.

"**Institutional health care provider**." A hospital, nursing home, hospice, clinic, blood bank, plasmapheresis or other blood product center, organ or tissue bank, sperm bank, clinical laboratory, residential or outpatient drug and alcohol rehabilitation service, mental health facility, mental retardation facility, home care agency as defined in this act, or any health care institution required to be licensed in this Commonwealth whether privately or publicly operated.

"**Insurer**." Any insurance company, association or exchange authorized to do business in this Commonwealth under the act of May 17, 1921 (P.L. 682, No. 284), known as The Insurance Company Law of 1921,[1] any entity subject to 40 Pa. C.S. Ch. 61 (relating to hospital plan corporations) or 63 (relating to professional health services plan corporations), the act of December 29, 1972 (P.L. 1701, No. 364), known as the Health Maintenance Organization Act,[2] or the act of July 29, 1977 (P.L. 105, No. 38), known as the Fraternal Benefit Society Code.[3]

"**Significant exposure**." Direct contact with blood or body fluids of a patient in a manner which, according to the most current guidelines of the Centers for Disease Control, is capable of transmitting human immunodeficiency virus, including, but not limited to, a percutaneous injury (e.g., a needle stick or cut with a sharp object), contact of mucous membranes or contact of skin (especially when the exposed skin is chapped, abraded or afflicted with dermatitis) or if the contact is prolonged or involves an extensive area.

"**Source patient**." Any person whose body fluids have been the source of a significant exposure to an individual health care provider.

"**Subject**." An individual or a guardian of the person of that individual.

"**Substitute decisionmaker**." Any guardian or person who by law or medical practice is authorized to consent on behalf of an incompetent person for medical treatment.

1990, Nov. 29, P.L. 585, No. 148, Sec. 3, effective in 90 days.

Sec. 7604. Prevention of transmission of infectious disease

The department shall, by regulation, require the use of protective measures and equipment by individuals, persons and institutions not covered by regulations promulgated by the Occupational Safety and Health Administration governing such protective measures and equip-

---

1. 40 P.S. Sec. 341 et seq.
2. 40 P.S. Sec. 1551 et seq.
3. 40 P.S. Sec. 1141–101 et seq.

ment. The department shall develop such regulations pursuant to guidelines established by the CDC. For health care providers covered by the provisions of the Occupational Safety and Health Administration governing such protective measures and equipment, the department shall encourage compliance with approved standards. This section shall not preclude the department from exercising rulemaking authority granted under any other act.

1990, Nov. 29, P.L. 585, No. 148, Sec. 4, effective in 90 days.

Sec. 7605. Consent to HIV-related test

(a) **Consent**.—Except as provided in section 6 with respect to the involuntary testing of a source patient, no HIV-related test shall be performed without first obtaining the informed written consent of the subject. Any consent shall be preceded by an explanation of the test, including its purpose, potential uses, limitations and the meaning of its results.

(b) **Pretest counseling**.—No HIV-related test may be performed without first making available to the subject information regarding measures for the prevention of, exposure to and transmission of HIV.

(c) **Confirmatory test**.—No test result shall be determined as positive, and no positive test result shall be revealed, without confirmatory testing if it is required by generally accepted medical standards.

(d) **Notice of test result**.—The physician who ordered the test, the physician's designee or a successor in the same relationship to the subject shall make a good faith effort to inform the subject of the result regardless of whether the result is positive or negative.

(e) **Post-test counseling**.—

(1) No positive or negative test result shall be revealed to the subject without affording the subject the immediate opportunity for individual, face-to-face counseling about:

(i) The significance of the test results.

(ii) Measures for the prevention of the transmission of HIV.

(iii) The benefits of locating and counseling any individual by whom the subject may have been exposed to HIV and the availability of any services with respect to locating and counseling such individual.

(2) No positive test result shall be revealed to the subject without, in addition to meeting the requirements of paragraph (1), also affording the subject the immediate opportunity for individual, face-to-face counseling about:

(i) The availability of any appropriate health care services, including mental health care, and appropriate social and support services.

(ii) The benefits of locating and counseling any individual who the infected subject may have exposed to HIV and the availability of any services with respect to locating and counseling such individual.

(f) **Blinded HIV-related testing**.—Blinded HIV-related testing for purposes of research performed in a manner by which the identity of the test subject is not known and may not be retrieved by the researcher is prohibited, unless reviewed and approved by the institutional review board established by the department except for testing pursuant to research approved by an institutional review board prior to the effective date of this act. The department shall make a good faith effort to maintain records of the results of blinded HIV tests performed in this Commonwealth and shall, on a yearly basis, forward information concerning the results to the appropriate committees of the General Assembly.

(g) **Exceptions**.—

(1) The provisions of subsections (a), (b), (c), (d) and (e) shall not apply to the following:

(i) The performance of an HIV-related test on a cadaver by a health care provider which procures, processes, distributes or uses a human body or a human body part, tissue or semen for use in medical research, therapy or transplantation.

(ii) The performance of an HIV-related test for the purpose of medical research not prohibited by subsection (f) if the testing is performed in a manner by which the identity of the test subject is not known and may not be retrieved by the researcher.

(iii) The performance of an HIV-related test when the test result of a subject is required by an insurer for underwriting purposes. However, the insurer shall satisfy the requirements of subsection (h).

(2) The provisions of subsections (a), (b) and (c) shall not apply to the performance of an HIV-related test in a medical emergency when the subject of the test is unable to grant or withhold consent and the test result is medically necessary for diagnostic purposes to provide appropriate emergency care to the subject.

(3) The provisions of subsections (d) and (e) shall not apply when a negative HIV-related test result is secured by a subject who has taken the test solely to satisfy a requirement for donating a human body or human body part, tissue or semen for use in medical research, therapy, transfusion or transplantation. However, if the subject requests identification of a negative test result, the test result shall be provided to the subject in accordance with subsection (d).

(h) **Requirements applicable to insurers.**—

(1) No HIV-related test shall be performed without first obtaining the informed written consent of the subject. Any consent shall be preceded, in writing, by:

(i) A disclosure of the effects of the test result on the approval of the application, or the risk classification of the subject.

(ii) Information explaining AIDS, HIV and the HIV-related test.

(iii) A description of the insurer's confidentiality standards.

(iv) A statement that, because of the serious nature of HIV-related illnesses, the subject may desire to obtain counseling before undergoing the HIV-related test.

(v) Information concerning the availability of alternative HIV-related testing and counseling provided by the department and local health departments, and the telephone number of the department from which the subject may secure additional information on such testing and counseling.

(2) The insurer is required to disclose to the subject a negative test result on an HIV-related test only if the subject requests notification.

(3) The insurer shall not disclose to the subject of an HIV-related test a positive test result. On the form on which the insurer secures the subject's written consent to the HIV-related test, the subject shall be required to designate to whom a positive test result shall be disclosed. The subject shall have the choice of designating a physician, the department or a local health department, or a local community-based organization from a list of such organizations prepared by the department. The insurer shall notify the designee of a positive test result.

(4) A positive test result shall be disclosed to the subject, by the designee, in accordance with subsections (d) and (e). The department may elect to have its disclosure responsibilities satisfied by a local health department.

1990, Nov. 29, P.L. 585, No. 148, Sec. 5, effective in 90 days.

Sec. 7606. Certification of significant exposure and testing procedures

(a) **Physician's evaluation of significant exposure.**—

(1) Whenever an individual health care provider or first responder experiences an exposure to a patient's blood or bodily fluids during the course of rendering health care or occupational services, the individual may request an evaluation of the expo-

sure, by a physician, to determine if it is a significant exposure as defined in this act. No physician shall certify his own significant exposure or that of any of his employees. Such requests shall be made within 72 hours of the exposure.

(2) Within 72 hours of the request, the physician shall make written certification of the significance of the exposure.

(3) If the physician determines that the individual health care provider or first responder has experienced a significant exposure, the physician shall offer the exposed individual the opportunity to undergo testing, following the procedure outlined in section 5.[1]

(b) **Opportunity for source patient to consent**.—

(1) In the event that an exposed individual health care provider or first responder is certified to have experienced a significant exposure and has submitted to an HIV-related test, no testing shall be performed on a source patient's available blood unless the certifying physician provides a copy of the written certification of significant exposure to the source patient's physician or institutional health care provider in possession of the available blood and the source patient's physician or institutional health care provider has made a good faith effort to:

(i) Notify the source patient or substitute decisionmaker of the significant exposure.

(ii) Seek the source patient's voluntary informed consent to the HIV-related testing as specified in section 5(a).

(iii) Provide counseling as required under section 5(b).

(2) The source patient's physician or institutional health care provider that receives a certification of significant exposure shall begin to comply with the request within 24 hours. If the source patient's physician or institutional health care provider is unable to secure the source patient's consent because the source patient or the source patient's substitute decisionmaker refuses to grant informed consent or the source patient cannot be located, the source patient's physician or institutional health care provider shall arrange for an entry to be placed on the source patient's medical record to that effect. If these procedures are followed and the entry is made on the source patient's medical record, then HIV-related tests shall be performed on the source patient's available blood if requested by the exposed individual health care provider or first responder who has submitted to an HIV-related test.

(3) The physician ordering the HIV-related test on a source patient's available blood on behalf of the source patient's physi-

---

1. 35 P.S. Sec. 7605.

cian or institutional health care provider shall comply with section 5(c) through (e).

(4) The health care provider or first responder shall be notified of the results of the HIV-related test on the source patient's blood if the health care provider or first responder's baseline HIV-related test is negative. Further disclosure of the test results is prohibited unless authorized under section 7.[2]

1990, Nov. 29, P.L. 585, No. 148, Sec. 6, effective in 90 days.

Sec. 7607. Confidentiality of records

(a) **Limitations on disclosure**.—No person or employee, or agent of such person, who obtains confidential HIV-related information in the course of providing any health or social service or pursuant to a release of confidential HIV-related information under subsection (c) may disclose or be compelled to disclose the information, except to the following persons:

(1) The subject.

(2) The physician who ordered the test, or the physician's designee.

(3) Any person specifically designated in a written consent as provided for in subsection (c).

(4) An agent, employee or medical staff member of a health care provider, when the health care provider has received confidential HIV-related information during the course of the subject's diagnosis or treatment by the health care provider, provided that the agent, employee or medical staff member is involved in the medical care or treatment of the subject. Nothing in this paragraph shall be construed to require the segregation of confidential HIV-related information from a subject's medical record.

(5) A peer review organization or committee as defined in the act of July 20, 1974 (P.L. 564, No. 193), known as the Peer Review Protection Act,[1] a nationally recognized accrediting agency, or as otherwise provided by law, any Federal or State government agency with oversight responsibilities over health care providers.

(6) Individual health care providers involved in the care of the subject with an HIV-related condition or a positive test, when knowledge of the condition or test result is necessary to provide emergency care or treatment appropriate to the individual; or health care providers consulted to determine diagnosis and treatment of the individual.

2. 35 P.S. Sec. 7607.   **1.** 63 P.S. Sec. 425.1 et seq.

(7) An insurer, to the extent necessary to reimburse health care providers or to make any payment of a claim submitted pursuant to an insured's policy.

(8) The department and persons authorized to gather, transmit or receive vital statistics under the act of June 29, 1953 (P.L. 304, No. 66), known as the Vital Statistics Law of 1953.[2]

(9) The department and local boards and departments of health, as authorized by the act of April 23, 1956 (1955 P.L. 1510, No. 500), known as the Disease Prevention and Control Law of 1955.[3]

(10) A person allowed access to the information by a court order issued pursuant to section 8.[4]

(11) A funeral director responsible for the acceptance and preparation of the deceased subject.

(12) Employees of county mental health/mental retardation agencies, county children and youth agencies, county juvenile probation departments, county or State facilities for delinquent youth, and contracted residential providers of the above-named entities receiving or contemplating residential placement of the subject, who:

> (i) generally are authorized to receive medical information; and

> (ii) are responsible for ensuring that the subject receives appropriate health care; and

> (iii) have a need to know the HIV-related information in order to ensure such care is provided.

The above-named entities may release the information to a court in the course of a dispositional proceeding under 42 Pa.C.S. Secs. 6351 (relating to disposition of dependent child) and 6352 (relating to disposition of delinquent child) when it is determined that such information is necessary to meet the medical needs of the subject.

(b) **Subsequent disclosure prohibited**.—Notwithstanding the provisions of the Vital Statistics Law of 1953 or section 15 of the Disease Prevention and Control Law of 1955, no person to whom confidential HIV-related information has been disclosed under this act may disclose that information to another person, except as authorized by this act.

(c) **Required elements of written consent to disclosure**.—A written consent to disclosure of confidential HIV-related information shall include:

> (1) The specific name or general designation of the person permitted to make the disclosure.

---

2. 35 P.S. Sec. 450.101 et seq.   **4.** 35 P.S. Sec. 7608.

3. 35 P.S. Sec. 521.1 et seq.

(2) The name or title of the individual, or the name of the organization to which the disclosure is to be made.

(3) The name of the subject.

(4) The purpose of the disclosure.

(5) How much and what kind of information is to be disclosed.

(6) The signature of the subject.

(7) The date on which the consent is signed.

(8) A statement that the consent is subject to revocation at any time except to the extent that the person who is to make the disclosure has already acted in reliance on it.

(9) The date, event or condition upon which the consent will expire, if not earlier revoked.

(d) **Expired, deficient or false consent**.—A disclosure may not be made on the basis of a consent which:

(1) has expired;

(2) on its face substantially fails to conform to any of the requirements set forth in subsection (c);

(3) is known to have been revoked; or

(4) is known by the person holding the information to be materially false.

(e) **Notice to accompany disclosure**.—Each disclosure made with the subject's written consent must be accompanied by the following written statement:

This information has been disclosed to you from records protected by Pennsylvania law. Pennsylvania law prohibits you from making any further disclosure of this information unless further disclosure is expressly permitted by the written consent of the person to whom it pertains or is authorized by the Confidentiality of HIV–Related Information Act. A general authorization for the release of medical or other information is not sufficient for this purpose.

(f) **Duty to establish written procedures**.—An institutional health care provider that has access to or maintains individually identifying confidential HIV-related information shall establish written procedures for confidentiality and disclosure of the records which are in accordance with the provisions of this act within 60 days of the effective date of this act.

1990, Nov. 29, P.L. 585, No. 148, Sec. 7, effective in 90 days.

Sec. 7608. Court order

(a) **Order to disclose**.—No court may issue an order to allow access to confidential HIV-related information unless the court finds, upon application, that one of the following conditions exists:

(1) The person seeking the information has demonstrated a compelling need for that information which cannot be accommodated by other means.

(2) The person seeking to disclose the information has a compelling need to do so.

(b) **Order to test and disclose**.—No court may order the performance of an HIV-related test and allow access to the test result unless the court finds, upon application, that all of the following conditions exist:

(1) The individual whose test is sought was afforded informed consent and pretest counseling procedures required by section 5(a) and (b) and the subject refused to give consent or was not capable or providing consent.

(2) The applicant was exposed to a body fluid of the individual whose test is sought and that exposure presents a significant risk of exposure to HIV infection. A determination that the applicant has incurred a significant risk of exposure to HIV infection must be supported by medical and epidemiologic data regarding the transmission of HIV, including, if available, information about the HIV risk status of the source individual and the circumstances in which the alleged exposure took place.

(3) The applicant has a compelling need to ascertain the HIV test result of the source individual.

(c) **Compelling need**.—In assessing compelling need for subsections (a) and (b), the court shall weigh the need for disclosure against the privacy interest of the individual and the public interests which may be harmed by disclosure.

(d) **Pleadings**.—Pleadings under this section shall substitute a pseudonym for the true name of the individual whose test result is sought. Disclosure to the parties of the individual's true name shall be communicated confidentially in documents not filed with the court.

(e) **Notice**.—Before granting an order for testing or disclosure and as soon as practicable after the filing of a petition under this section, the court shall provide the individual whose test result is sought with notice and a reasonable opportunity to participate in the proceeding if the individual is not already a party.

(f) **In camera proceedings**.—Court proceedings under this section shall be conducted in camera, unless the individual agrees to a hearing in open court or unless the court determines that a public hearing is necessary to the public interest and the proper administration of justice.

(g) **Expedited proceeding**.—The court shall provide for an expedited proceeding if it is requested by the applicant and the application includes verified statements that:

(1) The applicant has been exposed to a body fluid that poses a risk of HIV infection from the individual whose test result is sought.

(2) The exposure occurred within six weeks of the filing of the application.

(3) The exposure involves:

(i) a percutaneous injury to the applicant's skin from a needle stick or other sharp object;

(ii) contact of the applicant's eyes, mouth or other mucous membrane;

(iii) prolonged contact of the applicant's skin.

An expedited proceeding on the application shall be held no later than five days after the court complies with subsection (e), pertaining to notice requirements.

(h) **Safeguards against disclosure.**—Upon the issuance of an order to disclose the information, the court shall impose appropriate safeguards against unauthorized disclosure which shall specify the following:

(1) The particular information which is essential to accommodate the need of the party seeking disclosure.

(2) The persons who may have access to the information.

(3) The purposes for which the information will be used.

(4) The appropriate prohibitions on future disclosure as provided for in section 7.

1990, Nov. 29, P.L. 585, No. 148, Sec. 8, effective in 90 days.

Sec. 7609. Civil immunity for certain physicians

(a) **Permissible disclosure.**—Notwithstanding the provisions of section 7,[1] a physician may disclose confidential HIV-related information if all of the following conditions are met:

(1) The disclosure is made to a known contact of the subject.

(2) The physician reasonably believes disclosure is medically appropriate, and there is a significant risk of future infection to the contact.

(3) The physician has counseled the subject regarding the need to notify the contact, and the physician reasonably believes the subject will not inform the contact or abstain from sexual or needle-sharing behavior which poses a significant risk of infection to the contact.

(4) The physician has informed the subject of his intent to make such disclosure.

---

1. 35 P.S. Sec. 7607.

(b) **Subject not to be identified**.—When making such disclosure to a contact, the physician shall not disclose the identity of the subject or any other contact. Disclosure shall be made in person except where circumstances reasonably prevent doing so.

(c) **Duties relating to contacts**.—A physician shall have no duty to identify, locate or notify any contact, and no cause of action shall arise for nondisclosure or for disclosure in conformity with this section.

(d) **Other immunity**.—The physician who certifies that a significant exposure has occurred as provided by section 6^2 shall not be subject to civil liability for the exposure evaluation if acting in the good faith and reasonable belief that the certification was appropriate and consistent with this act.

1990, Nov. 29, P.L. 585, No. 148, Sec. 9, effective in 90 days.

Sec. 7610. Civil cause of action

Any person aggrieved by a violation of this act shall have a cause of action against the person who committed such violation and may recover compensatory damages. In the event of a violation of section 6 by a source patient's physician or an employee thereof, an aggrieved person may recover reasonable attorney fees and costs.

1990, Nov. 29, P.L. 585, No. 148, Sec. 10, effective in 90 days.

Sec. 7611. Separate violations

Each disclosure of confidential HIV-related information in violation of this act or each HIV-related test conducted in contravention of this act is separate for purposes of civil liability.

1990, Nov. 29, P.L. 585, No. 148, Sec. 11, effective in 90 days.

Sec. 7612. Disease Prevention and Control Law

Insofar as the provisions of the act of April 23, 1956 (1955 P.L. 1510, No. 500), known as the Disease Prevention and Control Law of 1955, [1] are inconsistent with this act, this act shall apply.

1990, Nov. 29, P.L. 585, No. 148, Sec. 12, effective in 90 days.

2. 35 P.S. Sec. 7606.   **1.** 35 P.S. Sec. 521.1 et seq.

Index

References are to Pages